The Dumbarton Oaks Anthology
of Chinese Garden Literature

湖門由二里至湖八里
三里至蕉石鳴琴四里
回西湖

行宮
又自西湖
行宮四里經玉帶騎虹至
蘇堤森驛三里至花港
觀魚七里至留餘山居
五里至法雲寺五里至
虎跑泉十一里經水樂
洞至理安寺七里至龍
井十二里經雷峰西照
至南屏晚鐘二里至敷
文書院二里進鳳山門
四里經瑞石古洞至吳
山大觀四里至杭州府

行宮
又自杭州府
行宮四里出候潮門三里
至浙江秋濤四里至鳳
凰山十里至六和塔十
三里至雲樓寺二十七
里進鳳山門回至杭州
府

自杭州府
行宮起
一里至宗陽宮
九里至滿營教場
一里出錢塘門係杭州
府錢塘縣界
四里經保俶塔大佛寺
至斷橋殘雪
一里至平湖秋月
一里經吟香別業梅林
歸鶴至西湖

行宮
計程十七里
又自西湖

行宮
二里至曲院風荷三
里經黃山積翠至玉泉
魚躍三里至雙峯插雲
四里至雲林寺二里至
韜光六里經北高峯至
上天竺十二里回西湖

行宮
又自西湖

笇
至六里至柳浪聞鶯三里至
至小有天園一里至三

北高峯

韜光觀海

玉泉魚躍

黃山積翠

冷泉
猿嘯

雲林寺

雲插峯雙

蕉石鳴琴

花港觀魚

玉帶晴虹

湖山春社

曲院
荷風

聽春堤蘇曉

六一泉

三潭印月

心平湖
眺

行宮
西湖

吟香別業

平湖
秋月

斷橋
殘雪

梅林歸鶴

大佛寺

保俶塔

柳浪聞鶯

昭慶寺

水門

杭州府

錢塘門

嬌防汛

行宮

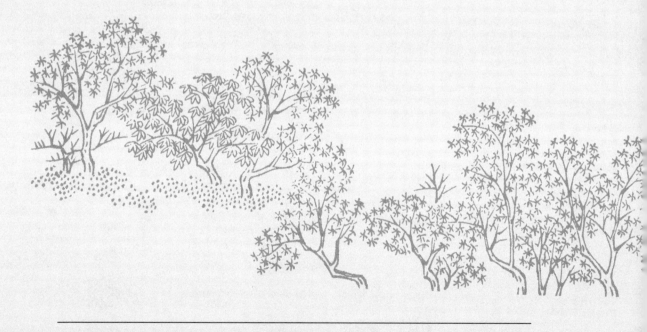

EX HORTO

DUMBARTON OAKS TEXTS IN GARDEN AND LANDSCAPE STUDIES

The Dumbarton Oaks Anthology of Chinese Garden Literature

ALISON HARDIE AND
DUNCAN M. CAMPBELL, Editors

DUMBARTON OAKS RESEARCH LIBRARY AND COLLECTION
WASHINGTON, D.C.

LIBRARY OF CONGRESS CATALOGING-IN-PUBLICATION DATA

Names: Campbell, Duncan (Duncan Murray), editor. | Hardie, Alison, editor.

Title: The Dumbarton Oaks anthology of Chinese garden literature / Alison Hardie and Duncan M. Campbell, editors.

Other titles: Ex horto: Dumbarton Oaks texts in garden and landscape studies.

Description: Washington, D.C. : Dumbarton Oaks Research Library and Collection, [2020] | Series: Ex horto: Dumbarton Oaks texts in garden and landscape studies | In English; with authors' names also in Chinese. | Summary: "The Dumbarton Oaks Anthology of Chinese Garden Literature is the first comprehensive collection in English of over two millennia of Chinese writing about gardens and landscape. Its contents range from early poems using plant imagery to represent virtue and vice, through works from many dynasties on both private and imperial gardens, to twentieth-century prose descriptions of the reconstruction of a historic Suzhou garden. Most passages have been translated for this publication, but a number of previously published translations are also included. The anthology is divided into nine chapters: five chronological, covering the pre-Qin period to the Qing dynasty; and four thematic, on rocks and flora, the evolution of a single site (Canglang Pavilion in Suzhou), gardens of the mind, and the interplay between garden and landscape as seen through Mount Tai and West Lake. An introductory essay positions Chinese gardens and garden literature in their cultural context. Care has been taken to translate plant names as accurately as possible (given the limitations of the sources), and the anthology includes a glossary showing translated names, Chinese names, and binomials"—Provided by publisher.

Identifiers: LCCN 2019031068 | ISBN 9780884024651 (hardcover)

Subjects: LCSH: Horticultural literature—China—Translations into English. | Chinese literature—Translations into English. | Gardens, Chinese—In literature. | Gardens in literature. | Landscapes in literature. | Plants in literature. | Gardens, Chinese—China—History. | Gardens—China—History. | Landscape gardening—China—History.

Classification: LCC SB318.34.C6 D86 2020 | DDC 635.0951—dc23

LC record available at https://lccn.loc.gov/2019031068

COVER, FRONTISPIECE, AND INTERIOR ILLUSTRATIONS: Gao Jin deng ji 高晉等輯, *Nan xun sheng dian: yi bai er shi juan* 南巡盛典: 一百二十卷 (Chaingning, 1771).

www.doaks.org/publications

CONTENTS

FOREWORD   *xvii*

PREFACE   *xix*

INTRODUCTION   *xxiii*

ACKNOWLEDGMENTS   *xxxix*

CHAPTER 1: EARLY GARDEN TRADITIONS   *1*

Book of Songs: "There are Peach-Trees in the Garden," translated by JAMES LEGGE; "In the South" and "Magic Tower," translated by ARTHUR WALEY   *3*

QU YUAN (attrib.), *Songs of the South*: "On Encountering Trouble" (extract) and "The Fisherman," translated by DAVID HAWKES   *6*

CONFUCIUS (attrib.), *Analects*: VI:21: The pleasure of the mountains and rivers; XIII:4: An old gardener; XVII:9: *Book of Songs*; and XVIII:6: Changju and Jieni, translated by JAMES LEGGE   *8*

ZHUANG ZHOU (attrib.), *Zhuangzi*: Chapter 1: "Free and Easy Wandering" (extract); Chapter 12: "Heaven and Earth" (extract); and Chapter 17: "Autumn Floods" (extracts), translated by BURTON WATSON   *9*

MENCIUS (attrib.), *Mencius*: IA:2: King Wen's park; IB:2: King Wen's park; IB:1: The king's love of music; IVA:8: Canglang water; and VIA:8: Ox mountain, translated by JAMES LEGGE   *11*

The Guideways through Mountains and Seas: The plateau garden of the supreme god, translated by RICHARD E. STRASSBERG   *14*

GE HONG (attrib.), *Miscellaneous Records of the Western Capital*: Palace of dazzling glory and Yuan Guanghan's garden, translated by DUNCAN M. CAMPBELL   *16*

ZHANG HENG, "Rhapsody on the Western Capital": Shanglin Park, translated by DAVID R. KNECHTGES   *17*

LIU YIQING, *A New Account of Tales of the World*: Chapter 2: "Speech and Conversation," item 61 and item 91, translated by RICHARD B. MATHER   *20*

PAN YUE, "Rhapsody on Living in Idleness" (extracts), translated by DAVID R. KNECHTGES   *21*

SHI CHONG, "Preface to the Golden Valley Poems," translated by RICHARD B. MATHER   *23*

History of the Jin Dynasty, "Biography of Shi Chong," translated by HELMUT WILHELM   *24*

WANG XIZHI, "Preface to the Orchid Pavilion Poems," translated by H. C. CHANG   *26*

TAO QIAN, "The Gentleman of the Five Willows" and "The Peach Blossom Spring," translated by J. R. HIGHTOWER; "Homeward Bound," translated by H. C. CHANG; and "Written While Drunk," translated by WILLIAM ACKER   *28*

ZONG BING, "Introduction to Painting Landscape," translated by SUSAN BUSH and HSIO-YEN SHIH   *32*

XIE LINGYUN, "Reading in My Study," translated by H. C. CHANG; and "Rhapsody on Dwelling in the Mountains" (extracts), translated by DAVID R. KNECHTGES   *34*

TAO HONGJING, "A Letter to Secretary Xie" (extract), translated by H. C. CHANG   *37*

YANG XUANZHI, *A Record of the Monasteries of Luoyang*: South of the city wall: Jingming Monastery and West of the city wall: Baoguang Monastery, translated by W. J. F. JENNER   *38*

CHAPTER 2: GARDENS OF THE TANG DYNASTY *45*

PART 1: GARDEN AS MOUNTAIN RETREAT

SHANGGUAN WAN'ER, "Twenty-Five Poems on a Visit to the Estate of Princess Changning" (extracts), translated by WILT IDEMA and BEATA GRANT; and "Visiting Princess Changning's Pool-for-Setting-Winecups-Afloat," translated by STEPHEN OWEN   *50*

WANG WEI, "A Letter to Scholar Pei Di," translated by PETER HARRIS   *52*

WANG WEI and PEI DI, "The Wang River Collection," translated by PETER HARRIS   *53*

DU FU, "Taking Down a Trellis" and "My Thatched Roof is Ruined by the Autumn Wind," translated by STEPHEN OWEN   *60*

BAI JUYI, "A Record of the Cottage," translated by RICHARD E. STRASSBERG   *62*

BAI JUYI, "Presented to the Landlord Mu the Thirty-Sixth after I Visited the Yunju Temple," translated by XIAOSHAN YANG   *66*

LIU ZONGYUAN, "Eastern Mound by Longxing Temple of Yongzhou," translated by H. C. CHANG   *66*

PART 2: URBAN GARDENS

BAI JUYI, "On the Waterside Pavilion of Attendant Censor Wang," translated by XIAOSHAN YANG   *68*

YUAN ZHEN, "Harmonizing with Letian's Poem on the Pavilion of the Wang Family," translated by XIAOSHAN YANG   *69*

BAI JUYI, "In Front of My Cottage I Recently Dug a Pond to Raise Fish and Plant Lotus, Providing the Delight of Seclusion Every Day," translated by XIAOSHAN YANG   *69*

BAI JUYI, "The Pavilion in My Prefectural Residence," translated by XIAOSHAN YANG   *70*

BAI JUYI, "On the Snow Pile Estate of the Xue Family at Pingquan," translated by XIAOSHAN YANG   *71*

BAI JUYI, "On My Garden Pond, with a Preface," translated by XIAOSHAN YANG   *71*

BAI JUYI, "Night Scene on the Pond," translated by XIAOSHAN YANG   *74*

BAI JUYI, "On My House in the Lüdao Ward" (one of three), translated by XIAOSHAN YANG   *74*

BAI JUYI, "Sailing on the Pond in Spring," translated by XIAOSHAN YANG   *75*

BAI JUYI, "Staying Over at the Waterside Pavilion of the Mansion of Governor Dou," translated by XIAOSHAN YANG   *76*

BAI JUYI, "Middling Hermit," "Inscribed on the Western Pavilion," and "Upon My Small Garden," translated by XIAOSHAN YANG   *76*

BAI JUYI, "Playfully Presented, on Behalf of My Garden," "Another Playful Reply," "On My Family Pond, Written in Leisure, Sent to the Daoist Adept Zhang of Mount Wangwu," and "Written on Mansions in Luoyang," translated by XIAOSHAN YANG   *78*

WU YUANHENG, "Playfully Presented to Wang Zhongzhou, upon Hearing That Peonies Were Blossoming at His Place," translated by XIAOSHAN YANG   *80*

LIU YUXI, "Strolling in the East of the City," translated by XIAOSHAN YANG; and "The Scholar's Humble Dwelling," translated by JAMES BLACK   *81*

ZHANG YAOTIAO, "Spring Thoughts (Two Poems)" (second poem), translated by JEANNE LARSEN   *82*

WEI ZHUANG, "Sent to the Owner of the Garden," translated by XIAOSHAN YANG   *83*

LIU ZONGYUAN, "Camel-Back the Gardener," translated by HERBERT GILES   *83*

PART 3: SOUTHERN LANDSCAPES IN NORTHERN CLIMES

YAO HE, "On Vice-Director Xue's Waterside Pavilion in Chang'an," translated by XIAOSHAN YANG   *85*

MENG JIAO, "Visiting Mr. Han's Estate in the South of the City," translated by XIAOSHAN YANG   *85*

XU NING, "Roaming on the Pond in the Residence of the Vice-Minister," translated by XIAOSHAN YANG   *86*

BAI JUYI, "A Question Posed to Cultivated Talent Cheng at a Casual Dinner on the Pond," translated by XIAOSHAN YANG   *87*

BAI JUYI, "A Newly Built Small Shoal," translated by XIAOSHAN YANG   87

BAI JUYI, "Three Quatrains on My Family Garden" (first quatrain), translated by XIAOSHAN YANG   88

BAI JUYI, "Observing the Picking of Lotus Flowers," translated by XIAOSHAN YANG   88

CHAPTER 3: ROCKS AND FLORA   93

PART 1: ROCKS

BAI JUYI, "A Pair of Rocks," translated by XIAOSHAN YANG   96

BAI JUYI, "An Account of Lake Tai Rocks," translated by XIAOSHAN YANG   98

LU GUIMENG, "The Lake Tai Rock," translated by XIAOSHAN YANG   100

NIU SENGRU, "Prefect Li of Suzhou Presented Me with Some Lake Tai Rocks, the Strange Shape of Which Was Matchless; Hence I Wrote Twenty Couplets, Which I Presented to Mengde and Letian," translated by XIAOSHAN YANG   101

PI RIXIU, "The Lake Tai Rocks: A Product from the Top of the Sea-Turtle Mountain," translated by XIAOSHAN YANG   103

SU SONG, "After Leaving the Ministry Early in the Morning, as I Passed with My Colleagues the Western Pavilion of Tan Wensi, I Sang of the Lake Tai Rock," translated by XIAOSHAN YANG   105

HU SU, "The Lake Tai Rock," translated by XIAOSHAN YANG   105

DU WAN, Stone Catalogue of Cloudy Forest: "Lingbi Rocks" and "Lake Tai Rocks," translated by JOHN HAY   106

SU SHI, "Matching Governor Liu's Poem on Rock Forest Pavilion. Originally Objects in the Tang Gardens, the Rocks Had Been Scattered among the Common People and Were Purchased and Obtained by Liu," translated by XIAOSHAN YANG   108

WEN TONG, "Two Poems Composed after Transcribing 'Record of Plants and Trees at Pingquan,'" translated by XIAOSHAN YANG   110

MEI YAOCHEN, "On the Ugly Rock in Liu Zhonggeng's Garden in Zezhou," translated by XIAOSHAN YANG   111

LIU KEZHUANG, "The Herb Islet" (quatrains two and three of four), translated by XIAOSHAN YANG   112

TOQTO'A, The History of the Song Dynasty: "The Biography of Mi Fu" (extract), translated by DUNCAN M. CAMPBELL   113

LIN YOULIN, The Stone Compendium of the Plain Garden: "Preface," translated by STEPHEN LITTLE   114

JI CHENG, The Craft of Gardens: "Selection of Rocks" (extracts), translated by ALISON HARDIE   115

ZHANG DAI, Taoan's Dream Memories: "Brook Pavilion of the Auspicious Plants," translated by DUNCAN M. CAMPBELL   117

ZHENG XIE, "Bamboo and Rock," translated by DUNCAN M. CAMPBELL   119

PU SONGLING, "The Ethereal Rock," translated by JUDITH ZEITLIN   120

PART 2: FLORA

ZUO FEN, "Rhapsody on Pine and Cypress," translated by WILT IDEMA and BEATA GRANT   123

DAI KAIZHI, "Treatise on the Bamboo" (extract), translated by MICHAEL J. HAGERTY   124

LIU YIQING, A New Account of Tales of the World: Chapter 23: "The Free and Unrestrained," item 46, translated by RICHARD B. MATHER   125

LADY HOU, "Looking at the Plum Tree," translated by WILT IDEMA and BEATA GRANT   126

EMPRESS WU ZETIAN, "Proclaiming an Imperial Visit to the Shanglin Park on the Eighth Day of the Twelfth Month," translated by HUI-SHU LEE   126

LI DEYU, "Record of the Plants and Trees of My Mountain Villa at Pingquan" and "Exhortation to My Children and Grandchildren about the Mountain Villa at Pingquan," translated by XIAOSHAN YANG   127

YE MENGDE, "Colophon to 'Record of the Plants and Trees of My Mountain Villa at Pingquan,'" translated by JOHN HAY   *131*

YU XUANJI, "Selling Wilted Peonies," translated by JENNIFER CARPENTER   *132*

LIN BU, "Small Flowering Plum in the Garden on the Hill" (first of two), translated by HANS H. FRANKEL   *133*

OUYANG XIU, "An Account of the Tree Peonies of Luoyang," translated by JAMES M. HARGETT   *133*

ZHOU DUNYI, "On the Love of the Lotus," translated by DUNCAN M. CAMPBELL   *144*

LI QINGZHAO, "On Smelling the Fragrance Emitted by the Fading Plum Blossoms beside My Pillow, to the Tune Pattern: 'Telling My Innermost Feelings,'" translated by EUGENE EOYANG   *145*

FAN CHENGDA, "Treatise on the Flowering Apricot" (extracts), translated by JAMES M. HARGETT   *146*

JIANG KUI, "To the Tune Patterns: 'Hidden Fragrance' and 'Sparse Shadows,'" translated by AN-YAN TANG   *150*

GUAN DAOSHENG, "Rhyme-Prose on Tall, Slender Bamboo," translated by JENNIFER PURTLE   *152*

ZHANG QIANDE, *A Treatise of Vase Flowers*: "Preface," "Picking Branches," and "Caring," translated by HUI-LIN LI   *154*

HU YINGLIN, "Connoisseurs of Flowers," translated by ALISON HARDIE   *155*

CHEN JIRU, "Colophon to *A History of the Flower*," translated by DUNCAN M. CAMPBELL   *157*

YUAN HONGDAO, *A History of the Vase*, translated by DUNCAN M. CAMPBELL   *158*

ZHANG DAI, *Taoan's Dream Memories*: "Flowering Apricot Bookroom," "Without Doubleness Studio," "Belvedere of the Mountaintop Flower," "The Sweet Tangerines of the Chen Clan of Fanjiang," and "Jin Rusheng's Flowers and Trees," translated by DUNCAN M. CAMPBELL   *168*

ZHANG DAI, "Letter to Jin Rusheng," translated by DUNCAN M. CAMPBELL   *172*

YE HONGXIANG, "To the Tune '*Qiu rui xiang*: Admiring Cassias in the North Garden,'" translated by KANG-I SUN CHANG and CHARLES KWONG   *173*

SHEN FU, *Six Records of a Floating Life*: "The Pleasures of Leisure" (extract), translated by LEONARD PRATT and CHIANG SU-HUI   *174*

JIN YI, "Peonies," translated by ANTHONY C. YU   *175*

GU TAIQING, "To the Tune '*Jiang cheng zi*: Fallen Flowers,'" translated by IRVING YUCHENG LO   *175*

QIU JIN, "Plum Blossoms" (nos. 3 and 10), translated by LI-LI CH'EN   *176*

CHAPTER 4: GARDENS OF THE SONG DYNASTY   *181*

PART 1: IMPERIAL GARDENS ───────────────

EMPEROR HUIZONG and ZHANG HAO, "Record of the Northeast Marchmount," translated by JAMES M. HARGETT   *184*

WANG YINGLIN, *Sea of Jades*: "Garden of the Jade Ford" (extract), translated by STEPHEN H. WEST   *192*

MENG YUANLAO, *Dreaming a Dream of Splendors Past in the Eastern Capital*: "Opening of the Reservoir of Metal's Luster and the Park of the Rosequartz Grove" and "Searching Out the Spring," translated by STEPHEN H. WEST   *195*

PART 2: PRIVATE GARDENS ───────────────

SIMA GUANG, "An Account of the Garden of Solitary Enjoyment" and "The Garden of Solitary Enjoyment: Seven Songs," translated by JAMES M. HARGETT; "In Response to a Poem by Vice-Minister Zhao on My Plot of Herbs" and "Two Quatrains in Reply to Anzhi Thanking Me for My Herb Transplants," translated by XIAOSHAN YANG   *204*

SIMA GUANG, "Harmonizing with Junkuang's Poem on the Eastern Estate of the Duke of Lu," translated by XIAOSHAN YANG   *210*

FAN ZHEN, "Harmonizing with Junshi's Poem on 'Purchasing the Estate at the Stream of Piled Rocks,'" translated by XIAOSHAN YANG   *211*

SU SHI, "Sima Junshi's Garden of Solitary Enjoyment," translated by XIAOSHAN YANG   *212*

SIMA GUANG, "Sitting Alone in the Flower Hut," translated by XIAOSHAN YANG   213

SHAO YONG, "Matching Junshi Duanming's 'Sitting Alone in the Flower Hut,'" translated by XIAOSHAN YANG   213

SHEN GUA, "My Account of Dream Stream," translated by RICHARD E. STRASSBERG   214

SU SHI, "Record of the Zhang Family Garden at Lingbi," translated by STEPHEN H. WEST   215

ZHU CHANGWEN, "Record of My Plot of Joy," translated by STEPHEN H. WEST   217

LI GEFEI, "Record of the Celebrated Gardens of Luoyang," translated by KENNETH J. HAMMOND   222

LI QINGZHAO, "Lyric to the Tune *Huan xi sha*" and "Lyric to the Tune *Xiao chong shan*," translated by EUGENE EOYANG   232

LU YOU, "Small Garden," translated by STEPHEN OWEN; and "Lyric to the Tune 'Phoenix Hairpin,'" translated by ALISON HARDIE and CATHARINE OTTON-GOULDER   233

CHAPTER 5: FOLLOWING THE FORTUNES OF A SINGLE SITE: CANGLANG PAVILION   239

SU SHUNQIN, "Record of Canglang Pavilion," translated by YINONG XU   245

SU SHUNQIN, "Passing by Suzhou," translated by YINONG XU   247

SU SHUNQIN, "Intoned in a Reflective Mood after a Siesta in the Summer Heat," translated by YINONG XU   247

SU SHUNQIN, "Canglang Pavilion," translated by YINONG XU   250

SU SHUNQIN, "Watching the Fish at Canglang Pavilion," translated by YINONG XU   250

SU SHUNQIN, "Visiting Canglang Pavilion as the Sky Clears Up," translated by YINONG XU   250

SU SHUNQIN, "Walking in Solitude Around Canglang Pavilion," translated by YINONG XU   250

SU SHUNQIN, "Intoned Quietly at Canglang Pavilion," translated by YINONG XU   251

SU SHUNQIN, "A Local Official Visited Me at Canglang Pavilion, Whereupon We Held a Grand Banquet, and I Thanked Him the Next Day with a Poem," translated by YINONG XU   251

SU SHUNQIN, "Thinking of Guanzhi at Canglang Pavilion," translated by YINONG XU   252

OUYANG XIU, "Canglang Pavilion," translated by YINONG XU   252

MEI YAOCHEN, "Sent to Be Inscribed on Su Zimei's Canglang Pavilion," translated by YINONG XU   254

ZHU CHANGWEN, *Supplementary Notes to the Illustrated Gazetteer of Wu Prefecture* (extract), translated by YINONG XU   256

YE MENGDE, *Shilin's Remarks on Poetry* (extract), translated by YINONG XU   257

GUI YOUGUANG, "Record of Canglang Pavilion," translated by YINONG XU   258

SONG LUO, "Record of the Restoration of Canglang Pavilion," translated by YINONG XU   259

YOU TONG, *A Brief Gazetteer of Canglang*: "Preface," translated by YINONG XU   262

SONG LUO, *Collected Works of Su Zimei*: "Preface," translated by YINONG XU   265

WU CUNLI, "Record of the Restoration of Canglang Pavilion," translated by YINONG XU   266

ZHAO YI, *Collection of Studies after Work in the Cultivated Field*: "Canglang Pavilion," translated by YINONG XU   269

LIANG ZHANGJU, "Record of the Restoration of Canglang Pavilion," translated by YINONG XU   271

ZHANG SHUSHENG, "Record of the Restoration of Canglang Pavilion," translated by YINONG XU   274

ANONYMOUS, "Record of a Tour of Canglang Pavilion," translated by YINONG XU   277

LI MINGWAN and FENG GUIFEN, *Suzhou Prefectural Gazetteer* (extract), translated by YINONG XU   288

YAN WENLIANG, "Record of the Restoration of Canglang Pavilion," translated by YINONG XU   292

JIANG HANCHENG, *A New Account of Canglang Pavilion*: "Preface," translated by YINONG XU   293

GAO GUANWU, "Record of the Restoration of Canglang Pavilion," translated by YINONG XU   295

JI YONG, "Notes on Gardens in Suzhou" (extract), translated by YINONG XU 297

CHEN CONGZHOU, "Suzhou's Canglang Pavilion," translated by YINONG XU 299

QIAN DINGYI, "A Record of the Restoration of Canglang Pavilion," translated by YINONG XU 302

CHAPTER 6: PRIVATE GARDENS OF THE MING DYNASTY 309

ZHU JING'AN, "Impromptu on a Trip," translated by MICHELLE YEH 313

CHEN DEYI, "Impromptu on a Summer Day," translated by MICHELLE YEH 314

WEN ZHENGMING, "A Descriptive Sketch of Wang's Garden of the Unsuccessful Politician,'" "The Bower Adjoining the Rock," and "Little Canglang Pavilion," translated by MO ZUNG CHUNG 314

QIAN YONG, "Inscription to 'A Descriptive Sketch of Wang's Garden of the Unsuccessful Politician,'" translated by MO ZUNG CHUNG 318

DUAN SHUQING, "Spring Night," translated by CHARLES H. EGAN 320

WANG SHIZHEN, "Record of the Yanshan Garden," translated by ALISON HARDIE 321

WANG SHIZHEN, "Poem Sequence on the Yanshan Garden," translated by ALISON HARDIE 346

QIAN SUYUE and ZHANG CAI, eds., Gazetteer of Taicang Subprefecture: "The Garden of the Deer Park Stream of the Wang Family," "The Yanzhou Garden," "The Langye Garden for Evading Thorns," and "Wang Jingmei's Plain Plot," translated by ALISON HARDIE 356

WANG SHIZHEN, "Record of the Garden for Seeking One's Own Aims," translated by ALISON HARDIE 361

WANG SHIZHEN, "Record of Wandering in the Famous Gardens of Jinling," translated by KENNETH J. HAMMOND 363

PAN YUNDUAN, "An Account of Pleasurable Garden," translated by RICHARD E. STRASSBERG 374

FANG YUEGONG, ed., Gazetteer of Songjiang Prefecture (extract), translated by ALISON HARDIE 379

QIAN YONG, Collected Talks from the Lü Garden: "Pleasurable Garden," translated by ALISON HARDIE 380

YUAN HUANG, "Record of the Hall Surrounded by Jade of Master Sitting-in-Reclusion," translated by ALISON HARDIE 381

CHEN JIRU, A History of Gardens: "Preface," translated by STANISLAUS FUNG 392

XU YUAN, "A Spring Day, Tending the Family Garden," translated by MARY ELLEN FRIENDS 393

LU QINGZI, "In the Manner of Tao Qian" and "Living the Quiet Life," translated by MAUREEN ROBERTSON 394

WANG SIREN, "On Mi Wanzhong's Ladle Garden," translated by PHILIP K. HU 395

SUN GUOMI, "Record of Sightseeing in Ladle Garden," translated by PHILIP K. HU 397

WEN ZHENHENG, Treatise on Superfluous Things: "Rooms and Retreats" (extracts) and "Water and Rocks" (extracts), translated by DUNCAN M. CAMPBELL 401

FANG WEIYI, "Spring Rain," translated by PAULA VARSANO 403

GU RUOPU, "Palace Songs" (no. 7), translated by MAUREEN ROBERTSON 404

QI BIAOJIA, "Footnotes to Allegory Mountain," translated by DUNCAN M. CAMPBELL 404

ZHANG DAI, "To Qi Biaojia," translated by DUNCAN M. CAMPBELL 435

DONG XUAN, "A Visit to Allegory Mountain," translated by ALISON HARDIE 436

LIU SHI, "Qi Youwen's Allegory Mountain Thatched Hall," translated by ALISON HARDIE 445

SHANG JINGLAN, "Allegory Garden," translated by DUNCAN M. CAMPBELL; and "On a Spring Day in Allegory Garden Gazing at the Plum Blossoms," translated by WILT IDEMA and BEATA GRANT 445

SHANG JINGLAN, "Rejoicing That My Second Son Studies in the Purple Fungus Studio" and "Visiting the Secret Garden," translated by ELLEN WIDMER 446

QIAN YONG, Collected Talks from the Lü Garden: "Allegory Garden," translated by ALISON HARDIE 447

ZHENG YUANXUN, "A Personal Record of My Garden of Reflections," translated by DUNCAN M. CAMPBELL *448*

ZHENG YUANXUN, *The Craft of Gardens*: "Foreword," translated by ALISON HARDIE *457*

RUAN DACHENG, "A Banquet in the Garden Pavilion of Secretary Wang Shiheng (no. 3 of 4)," "On Ji Cheng's Arranging of Rocks and On Reading His Poems," and "Miscellaneous Songs on Garden Living," translated by ALISON HARDIE *459*

LIU TONG and YU YIZHENG, *Brief Guide to the Sights and Features of the Imperial Capital*: "Haidian," translated by DUNCAN M. CAMPBELL *461*

CHAPTER 7: GARDENS OF THE MIND *467*

PART 1: THE THEORY OF GARDENS

CHEN SUOYUN, "The Biography of Mountain Man Zhang, the Recliner on Rocks," translated by ALISON HARDIE *472*

JI CHENG, *The Craft of Gardens*: "Author's Preface," translated by ALISON HARDIE *475*

WU WEIYE, "The Biography of Zhang Nanyuan," translated by ALISON HARDIE *477*

ZHANG CHAO, "Marginal Comment to 'The Biography of Zhang Nanyuan,'" translated by DUNCAN M. CAMPBELL *482*

QIAN YONG, *Collected Talks from the Lü Garden*: "On the Making of Gardens," translated by DUNCAN M. CAMPBELL *483*

PART 2: GARDENS OF THE IMAGINATION

TANG XIANZU, *The Peony Pavilion*: "Scene Ten: The Interrupted Dream," translated by CYRIL BIRCH *485*

CAO XUEQIN, *The Story of the Stone*: Chapter 17 (extract), translated by DAVID HAWKES *497*

LIU SHILONG, "Record of the Garden That Is Not Around," translated by STANISLAUS FUNG *515*

SUN CHENG'EN, "Record of the Pavilion of Borrowing Borrowing," translated by STANISLAUS FUNG *518*

HUANG ZHOUXING, "Record of the Make-Do Garden" (extracts), translated by STANISLAUS FUNG *519*

ZHANG DAI, *Taoan's Dream Memories*: "A Record of Langhuan Paradise," translated by DUNCAN M. CAMPBELL *521*

DAI MINGSHI, "A Record of the Garden of My Mind," translated by DUNCAN M. CAMPBELL *523*

CHAPTER 8: GARDENS OF THE QING DYNASTY *529*

PART 1: PRIVATE GARDENS

WU WEIYE, "Thoughts Stirred on Meeting the Gardener of the Royal Academy in Nanjing" (extract), translated by STEPHEN OWEN *533*

WANG SHIMIN, "Record of the Division of Property in Pleasure in the Suburbs," translated by ALISON HARDIE *534*

LI YU, *Random Ventures in Idleness*: "Housing" (extract), "Paths," "Height," and "The Selection of Scenery through Borrowing" (extract), translated by DUNCAN M. CAMPBELL *537*

XU QIANXUE, "A Record of the Garden That Borders upon Greenness," translated by DUNCAN M. CAMPBELL *545*

WANG HUI, "On a Summer Day, I Write about the Place Where We Are Staying," translated by MAUREEN ROBERTSON *548*

GU ZHENLI, "*Lang tao sha*: Remembering My Female Companions in Our Old Garden," translated by KATHRYN LOWRY *548*

HOU CHENG'EN, "To the Tune *Yu meiren*," translated by CAROL R. KAUFMANN *549*

YUAN MEI, "Six Records of My Garden of Accommodation," translated by DUNCAN M. CAMPBELL and STEPHEN MCDOWALL *549*

QIAN DAXIN, "A Record of the Garden of the Master of the Fishing Nets," translated by DUNCAN M. CAMPBELL 560

LI DOU, *The Pleasure-Boats of Yangzhou*: "Record of the Northern Suburbs (Middle Part): New Town" (extract), "Record of the West of the City" (extract), "Record of Rainbow Bridge: First Part" (extract), "Record of West of the Bridge" (extract), and "Record of West of the Ridge" (extract), translated by LUCIE OLIVOVÁ 566

LI DOU, *Aitang's Catalogue of Song Titles* (extract), translated by GINGER CHENG-CHI HSU 574

GAN LIROU, "Remembering the Past: Twelve Quatrains" (no. 5), translated by GRACE S. FONG 575

SHEN FU, *Six Records of a Floating Life*: "The Joys of the Wedding Chamber" (extract), "The Pleasures of Leisure" (extracts), and "The Delights of Roaming Afar" (extract), translated by LEONARD PRATT and CHIANG SU-HUI 576

CHEN QIQING, "A Record of the Garden of the Peaceful Waves," translated by DUNCAN M. CAMPBELL 580

LINQING, *Wild Swan on the Snow: An Illustrated Record of My Preordained Life*: "Owning Half-Acre Garden," translated by DUNCAN M. CAMPBELL 588

TANG QINGYUN, "Early Summer Night," translated by MAUREEN ROBERTSON 590

OSMOND TIFFANY JR., *The Canton Chinese; or, The American's Sojourn in the Celestial Empire*: "Chapter VIII: The Environs of Canton" (extracts) 591

ROBERT FORTUNE, *A Residence among the Chinese*: "Chapter X," Howqua's Garden 595

PART 2: IMPERIAL GARDENS

THE KANGXI EMPEROR, "Record of the Garden of Uninhibited Spring," translated by HUI ZOU 598

THE KANGXI EMPEROR, *Imperial Poems on the Mountain Estate for Escaping the Heat*: "A Lingzhi Path on an Embankment to the Clouds," translated by RICHARD E. STRASSBERG 602

THE YONGZHENG EMPEROR, "Record of the Garden of Perfect Brightness," translated by HUI ZOU 604

THE YONGZHENG EMPEROR, "Twelve Poems on Garden Scenes": "The Reading Hall Deep Inside Weeping Willows," "The Bamboo Cloister," and "The Peony Chamber," translated by WU HUNG 607

THE QIANLONG EMPEROR, "Latter Record of the Garden of Perfect Brightness," translated by HUI ZOU 608

THE QIANLONG EMPEROR, "Poem on the Garden of Eternal Spring, with Preface," translated by HUI ZOU 609

THE QIANLONG EMPEROR, "Record of the Garden of Clear Ripples on Longevity Hill," translated by HUI ZOU 611

ZHANG YUSHU, "Record of Touring the Rehe Rear Garden at Imperial Invitation," translated by STEPHEN H. WHITEMAN 612

BROTHER JEAN-DENIS ATTIRET, *A Particular Account of the Emperor of China's Gardens Near Pekin*, translated by SIR HARRY BEAUMONT 617

CHAPTER 9: LANDSCAPE INTO GARDEN, GARDEN INTO LANDSCAPE 633

PART 1: MOUNT TAI

The Book of Documents: "The Canon of Shun" (extract), translated by JAMES LEGGE 637

ANONYMOUS, *The Guideways through Mountains and Seas*: "Mount Great," translated by ANNE BIRRELL 638

SIMA QIAN, *Records of the Grand Historian*: "The Basic Annals of the First Emperor of Qin" (extract), translated by BURTON WATSON 638

MA DIBO, *A Record of the Feng and Shan Sacrifices*: The Supreme Mountain, translated by RICHARD E. STRASSBERG 640

CAO ZHI, "Mount Tai" (extract), translated by PAUL W. KROLL 644

LU JI, "A Chant of Mount Tai," translated by PAUL W. KROLL 644

XIE DAOYUN, "Ascending the Mountain," translated by PAUL W. KROLL 645

XIE LINGYUN, "A Chant of Mount Tai," translated by PAUL W. KROLL 646

DU FU, "Gazing Afar at the Marchmount," translated by PAUL W. KROLL 646

LI BAI, "Six Poems on a Journey to Mount Tai," translated by PAUL W. KROLL 647

DU RENJIE, "A Short Record of the Ascent of Mount Tai by Pacification Commissioner Zhang of Dongping," translated by ALISON HARDIE 650

WANG SHIZHEN, *Record of Visits to Taishan* (extracts), translated by PEI-YI WU 652

ZHANG DAI, "A Pilgrimage to Mount Tai" (extracts), translated by PEI-YI WU 654

ZHANG DAI, "An Inn in Tai'an," translated by RICHARD E. STRASSBERG 657

A SCHOLAR OF WESTERN ZHOU, *A Tale of Marriage Destinies That Will Bring Society to Its Senses*: A pilgrimage to Mount Tai, translated by GLEN DUDBRIDGE 658

THE KANGXI EMPEROR, "Mount Tai's Mountain Veins Originate in the Changbai Mountains," translated by BRIAN R. DOTT 664

ZHANG PENGHE, "Han Cypress," translated by BRIAN R. DOTT 665

XI PEILAN, "Traveling at Dawn to Watch the Sunrise," translated by IRVING YUCHENG LO 666

PART 2: WEST LAKE

BAI JUYI, "Spring Theme: Above the Lake" and "Walking in Spring by West Lake," translated by A. C. GRAHAM 668

SU SHI, "Drinking by the Lake: Clear Sky at First, Then Rain," translated by A. C. GRAHAM; "Boating at Night upon West Lake" (fourth of five quatrains), translated by DUNCAN M. CAMPBELL; and "Recalling West Lake, Sent to Fellow-Graduate Chao Meishu," translated by LIN YUTANG 668

ZHOU MI, *Recollections of Wulin*: "Roaming on West Lake," translated by STEPHEN H. WEST 670

GUAN HANQING, "Hangzhou Prospect," translated by STEPHEN H. WEST 671

ZHANG KEJIU, "Returning Late from the Lake," translated by STEPHEN H. WEST 672

YUAN HONGDAO, *Records of West Lake*, translated by STEPHEN MCDOWALL 674

ZHANG DAI, *Search for West Lake in My Dreams* (extracts) and *Taoan's Dream Memories* (extracts), translated by DUNCAN M. CAMPBELL 682

WANG RUQIAN, "A Record of My Untethered Garden," translated by DUNCAN M. CAMPBELL 706

LIU SHI, "Eight Quatrains on the West Lake of Hangzhou," translated by KANG-I SUN CHANG 708

ZHANG QIONGRU, "Dragon Well," translated by WILT IDEMA and BEATA GRANT 709

QIAN FENGLUN, "Meditation on the Past: In Jade Effusion Garden," translated by MAUREEN ROBERTSON 710

ZHAI HAO, *A Handy Guide to the Lake and Its Hills* (extract), translated by DUNCAN M. CAMPBELL 711

LINQING, *Wild Swan on the Snow: An Illustrated Record of My Preordained Life*: "Paying My Compliments to West Lake," translated by YANG TSUNG-HAN and JOHN MINFORD 713

XU ZIHUA, "Taking an Excursion at West Lake with Xuanqing, I Am Moved to Write," translated by GRACE S. FONG 714

CHINESE NAMING CONVENTIONS 717

SEXAGENARY DATING SYSTEM 719

LIST OF CHINESE DYNASTIES 720

CHRONOLOGICAL LIST OF AUTHORS 721

GLOSSARY 724

CREDITS 747

FOREWORD

In 2013, Dumbarton Oaks initiated a new series of translations, titled ex horto, of classic and rare texts on garden history and on the philosophy, art, and techniques of landscape architecture. To reach a large audience of both general readers and scholars, the institution is making available in English works in manuscript that have never been published and books that have long been out of print. The volumes so far cover a broad geographical and temporal range, from Qing dynasty China to modern Germany, and will eventually constitute a library of historical sources that have defined the core of the field. By making these works approachable, the series provides unprecedented access to the foundational literature of garden and landscape studies.

The present volume is the most ambitious publication in the series to date. It features a selection of Chinese texts on gardens, both prose and poetry, in various genres, from the Zhou dynasty (1045–256 BCE) through the Qing dynasty (1644–1911). China is home to several important related traditions of garden culture, which evolved in intense and perhaps unique relationships with the verbal and pictorial arts. Many Chinese poems, essays, and paintings take the garden as their subject matter; and it was often in those gardens that, particularly in the late imperial period, such writings and artworks were produced, presented, or both. This anthology gathers for readers an unprecedented and representative sampling of Chinese garden literature, with many of these texts appearing in English for the first time.

The project originated nearly two decades ago at Dumbarton Oaks and was orchestrated initially by Stanislaus Fung, then head of history and theory in the architecture program at the University of New South Wales in Sydney, now associate professor of architecture at the Chinese University of Hong Kong, in consultation with a diverse group of about twenty scholars working throughout the world, including in the United States, China, Britain, France, Australia, and New Zealand. All of these scholars, whatever their specific disciplinary affiliations or research foci, had also published on aspects of the garden in China; all of them, too, were insistent about the necessity to engage fully with the vast corpus of Chinese garden discourse, which spanned a period of some fifteen hundred years, very little of which was as yet available in translation. A series of three-day-long workshops was held for as many of the contributors as could attend (in 1999 at Dumbarton Oaks, with the support of Michel Conan, then director of Garden and Landscape Studies; in 2000 at Harvard University, under the aegis of Professor Peter K. Bol, Charles H. Carswell Professor of East Asian Languages and Civilizations; in 2002 at Dumbarton Oaks; and in 2003 at Harvard University), where the framework of the anthology was worked out, and, on some occasions, finished translations were discussed. Over time, the project generated a large volume of text (estimated at over eight hundred pages): translations of difficult texts accompanied by a wealth of scholarly exegesis, annotation, introductory essays for each proposed section of the anthology, general treatments of aspects of the design, architecture, and flora of the gardens of China, and so on.

The project then languished; it was revived in 2009 at the suggestion of Richard Strassberg, then a senior fellow in Garden and Landscape Studies at Dumbarton Oaks, with my full support and engagement, along with that of Jan Ziolkowski, director of Dumbarton Oaks. Duncan Campbell, as one of the original contributors, undertook the task of subjecting this body of material to rigorous editing that would form it into a publishable anthology, seeking to retain as much of the scholarly labor that had already been expended as possible. He edited the individual selections and created the basic organization of the book. On his appointment to a post that took up too much of his time to allow him to finish this task, Alison Hardie, another of the original contributors, stepped in to complete the editorial work; the chapter introductions and headnotes to individual selections are largely her work. It was also her idea to add a final chapter exploring the reciprocal relationships between the garden and the larger landscape.

In the development of the project, some aims proved to be elusive. The editors initially sought to be largely consistent in the references within the various writings to the flora, building types, and other features of the gardens represented. But since the volume includes both recent translations and some that are over one hundred years old, and since different generations of translators have followed different conventions, consistency has proved impractical. (For example, *prunus* is sometimes "plum" and sometimes "flowering apricot.") For the sake of readability, such differences are glossed over, but for those who are interested, the glossary highlights the extent to which the contributors to the volume have been concerned with attempting to be as precise as possible in translating the terminology of garden culture in China. With respect to illustrations, we had originally thought to have representative images for all the time periods and regions covered by the anthology. But this too proved impractical, since there is a great deal more surviving visual material from some periods than others, and greater and lesser amounts of this material in different eras revolve around images of gardens and landscapes. We have opted instead to feature throughout a suite of illustrations from a rare book in the Dumbarton Oaks Collection, *Nanxun shengdian* (*Magnificent Record of the Southern Tours*, 1771), a visual and written record of the Qianlong emperor's official travels through some of the most storied landscapes of China. Taken from a text much later than most in this volume and imperial in origin, these illustrations provide a visual essay that complements rather than parallels the translations, evoking the various characteristics and elements of Chinese gardens as they appeared in the eighteenth century.

Above all, this anthology is intended to foster a better-informed and more sophisticated general understanding of the garden in China, its variety and usage, and its intimately related literary discourse. Close study of texts is particularly important in the study of Chinese gardens, since few of the great gardens of China survived the vicissitudes of time; most exist only through and to the extent that they generated essays, poems, and pictures. As garden-building traditions of China show signs of revival, and as increasing numbers of Chinese gardens of various types are built around the world, we hope this anthology will illuminate both the past and the future of the Chinese landscape for scholars and students as well as for the general public.

JOHN BEARDSLEY
Director, Garden and Landscape Studies
Dumbarton Oaks

PREFACE

The *Dumbarton Oaks Anthology of Chinese Garden Literature*, long awaited, has now appeared, and it arrives at a most opportune moment for research on Chinese gardens. While Western interest in Chinese gardens began more than four centuries ago, the information available during most of this period was sporadically transmitted by amateurs and considerably filtered through their own cultural perceptions; it was also usually inaccurate. Despite some notable accomplishments in the recent past, it is only within the last few decades that the scholarly study of Chinese gardens in the West can be said to have begun to flourish. Important research has been carried out not only in such traditional disciplines as literature, art history, and architecture but also by utilizing the more recent interdisciplinary approaches of landscape and cultural studies. This is the first time an extensive collection of English translations of original Chinese sources has been gathered together. Covering more than two millennia, these texts reveal the multiple ways gardens in China have been experienced, represented, and remembered. Now, readers can vicariously travel to these significant places, most of which no longer exist. When observed through the eyes of the original owners and their privileged guests, these designed environments can be understood more authentically, as these writers articulate their aesthetic principles and record the social rituals that took place within the unique garden culture of traditional China.

It is widely recognized that language and writing have played a particularly important role in Chinese gardens as well as in many other gardens throughout East Asia that looked to them as models. Especially during the later imperial period, it was considered essential to append literary names and poetic couplets to structures, spaces, and objects in order to fully create the garden's identity. These names often constituted a portrait of the owner, reflecting his personal ideals, and they were also intended to serve as a guide for visitors as they formed their own perceptions. In addition, a considerable literature in prose and poetry was produced over the centuries celebrating these gardens. The genre of "garden records" (*yuanji*), in particular, often combined documentary details of a garden's design with a lyrical evocation of its imaginative ethos. Some of these pieces were widely disseminated and highly regarded for their literary qualities. They could confirm or raise the status of the more significant gardens of the time, locating them within an expanding cultural map of the empire for contemporaries and for posterity. Some of the more canonical pieces formed part of a hypertext of themes that others could reference in designing their own gardens. This world of gardens preserved in texts and images also enabled many readers to gain knowledge of these places from a distance without ever setting eyes on them. It is this literature, far more than the actual sites, that has survived through the centuries, outstanding examples having been selected for this anthology.

Research on Chinese gardens in the West may be said to have entered a new phase that began roughly during the 1980s. It is characterized by an expanded range of scholarly inquiry, the use of authentic sources, and a wider dissemination of knowledge through the activities of institutions and publications. No doubt this trend was greatly stimulated by the relaxation of travel restrictions on foreigners to and within China. Many more people have now been able to examine actual sites that have been preserved. The rich trove of materials in Chinese museums and libraries has also become more accessible to researchers, and this has led to a renewed appreciation of the materials held in similar institutions abroad. At the same time, important publications in Chinese about gardens appeared in greater numbers and became widely available. This included a valuable anthology of garden records, *Zhongguo lidai mingyuan ji xuanzhu* (An Annotated Anthology of Chinese Garden Records through the Ages, 1983), under the general editorship of the doyen of Chinese garden scholars Chen Congzhou (1918–2000). Such works contributed to a parallel increase in scholarly research in English that has resulted in a steady stream of dissertations, books, and articles. Among important contributions was the publication in 1988 of an English translation by Alison Hardie of a rare treatise on garden design, *Yuan Ye* (*The Craft of Gardens*) by the late Ming designer Ji Cheng (fl. late 16th–early 17th century). The growth of Chinese garden studies was subsequently recognized in 1999 by the influential journal *Studies in the History of Gardens and Designed Landscapes*, in two issues edited by Stanislaus Fung that were dedicated exclusively to articles about Chinese gardens. In the same year, the Garden and Landscape Studies program at Dumbarton Oaks decided to expand its focus to include Chinese gardens by initiating a project to compile this anthology. This was followed by the program's ongoing support for further research, the appointment of senior and visiting fellows, the organizing of symposia and lectures, and the inclusion of articles on Chinese gardens in its various publications. This volume, the second on Chinese gardens issued in the ex horto series, owes its achievement to the initial direction of Michel Conan, the subsequent unwavering support of Jan Ziolkowski and John Beardsley, and the three editors, Stanislaus Fung, Duncan Campbell, and Alison Hardie. It is surely destined to further expand existing knowledge and stimulate new directions in research.

It should be mentioned that the rapid growth in Chinese garden studies over the past few decades has also benefited from the construction of faithful replicas of Chinese gardens outside China, especially in the United States. These include the Astor Chinese Garden Court at the Metropolitan Museum of Art, New York (1981), the New York Chinese Scholar's Garden on Staten Island (1999), and the Lan Su Chinese Garden in Portland, Oregon (2000). Most notable is the twelve-acre Liu Fang Yuan, the Garden of Flowing Fragrance, at the Huntington Library, Art Collections, and Botanical Gardens in San Marino, California, which opened to the public in 2008. Modeled on the classic Suzhou gardens of the late Ming dynasty, it has been constructed with native Chinese materials by expert Chinese artisans who were brought over from Suzhou. Recently, the Center for the Study of the East Asian Garden has been established at the Huntington to further develop the garden's activities, which include an annual lecture series, symposia, art exhibitions, and regular music and opera performances. To date, several million people have visited this and similar gardens outside China. Just as Chinese garden literature informed the perceptions of connoisseurs in traditional China, so too the texts in this anthology can serve to enhance the experience of modern visitors.

Today, most of the gardens that were built and recorded in China can exist only in our imaginations as a result of reading these texts. Though we are removed from them in time, space, and culture, we can certainly share an attitude that many writers in traditional China expressed. For them, a significant garden was not just a valuable piece of property but, more importantly, an invention of the mind that depended on the skillful deployment of knowledge, taste, and the art of illusion. Reading these pieces may lead us to consider more fully the nature of our experience in such spaces. And it may even stimulate new conceptions, not only about how to create a garden but also about how to live in one.

RICHARD E. STRASSBERG
Professor Emeritus of Chinese
University of California, Los Angeles

INTRODUCTION

Gardens, and writings about gardens, have played an important role in the elite culture of China from early times to the end of the imperial period, and still do, in many ways (which are mentioned later), down to the present day. The importance of gardens to the elite has not always been related to the existence of actual, specific gardens or to the possession thereof; the representation of gardens in text and image has also been of major importance. The importance of representation, particularly textual representation, means that almost everything we know about gardens in premodern China comes to us through the mediation of the literate class; therefore, very little is known about non-elite gardening traditions.

For actual historical gardens, our evidence is thus largely dependent on texts (often written much later than the gardens to which they refer) and on images (which may be misleading in a whole variety of ways). Nevertheless, scholars in China and elsewhere have managed to construct a basic, generally accepted history of the development of gardens and their aesthetics in China, a history that is constantly being problematized, made more nuanced, amended, and added to as knowledge is advanced and new approaches are brought to bear.[1] That generally accepted history, as well as many of the ways it has been questioned, developed, or altered, is presented in the introductions to the chapters that follow, particularly the "chronological" chapters.[2] One of the main ways in which that history has been developed in recent years is by the acceptance that there is not one single, hegemonic tradition of "the Chinese garden," but that there are many varieties of gardens in China, according to time, place, ownership, and other factors. In particular, there has been a growing interest in different regional traditions and how garden aesthetics changed over time,

---

1   Two standard histories of gardens in Chinese are Zhou Weiquan, *Zhongguo gudian yuanlin shi* (Beijing: Qinghua daxue chubanshe, 1990), and Zhang Jiaji, *Zhongguo zaoyuan shi* (Taipei: Mingwen shuju, 1990). A more detailed study—both historical and aesthetic—of the gardens of Jiangnan is Yang Hongxun, *Jiangnan yuanlin lun* (Shanghai: Shanghai renmin chubanshe, 1994). Standard works on garden aesthetics are Zhang Jiaji, *Zhongguo zaoyuan lun* (Taiyuan: Shanxi renmin chubanshe, 1991), and Jin Xuezhi, *Zhongguo yuanlin meixue* (Nanjing: Jiangsu wenyi chubanshe, 1990), the latter taking a somewhat anachronistic Marxist/Kantian approach. Maggie Keswick, *The Chinese Garden: History, Art, and Architecture*, 3rd ed. (London: Frances Lincoln, 2003) is still the standard introduction in English.

2   Here we may briefly mention, as examples, Wang Yi, *Yuanlin yu Zhongguo wenhua* (Shanghai: Shanghai renmin chubanshe, 1990), an exhaustive study of the influence of Chinese culture, especially philosophy, on the evolution of gardens; Craig Clunas, *Fruitful Sites: Garden Culture in Ming Dynasty China* (London: Reaktion Books, 1996), a pathbreaking work on the social deployment of the garden in a particular historical period; and Xiaoshan Yang, *Metamorphosis of the Private Sphere: Gardens and Objects in Tang-Song Poetry* (Cambridge, Mass.: Harvard University Asia Center, 2003), a detailed study of changing attitudes to gardens, and especially rocks, as reflected in literature.

as well as a growing understanding of the importance of gardens in the lives of women and of the influence of women on gardens.[3] Some of these aspects appear in the selections in this anthology.

The study of Chinese garden history has been greatly influenced by how that study developed, initially in China itself, in the early part of the twentieth century. Unlike Europe and America, where the study of garden history was initiated largely by art historians, in China—where buildings have traditionally been very important features in gardens—this study was initiated by architects and architectural historians.[4] The focus initially was, therefore, on the layout of buildings and the aesthetics of the interrelationships between buildings and the other notable features of gardens: water, rocks, and plants. At first, there seems to have been an unspoken assumption that gardens had always been much as they were observed to be around the time of the transition from the imperial to the republican era, and it was only gradually that an understanding developed of stylistic changes over time, in both imperial and private gardens. Later still—and later in China than in Europe and North America—scholarly attention began to focus on the social aspects of gardens in China: on their use for self-representation and social networking as well as on the role of women within them.

At the same time, "the Chinese garden" became a symbol for the best of Chinese traditional culture. As China's influence in the world grew with the start of economic reforms in the late 1970s and the 1980s, the creation of "Chinese" gardens outside China, starting with the Astor Chinese Garden Court in the Metropolitan Museum of Art, became a way for the Chinese government to exert wider cultural influence.[5] Why did gardens, rather than any other form of cultural production, play this role? It could be argued that gardens, while varying widely across cultures, simply have a universal appeal at a very fundamental human level: an appeal to the senses of sight, hearing, smell, touch, and even taste, as well as to a human desire to be close to the processes of nature, the cycle of the seasons, and so on. It could also be that the plants, rocks, and buildings of a Chinese garden offered more familiarity to a Western audience than other art forms because of the time-honored acceptance of the chinoiserie aesthetic. But it is also arguable that, from a Chinese

---

3   Important studies of regional garden traditions are Mo Bozhi, "Guangzhou yangshang tingyuan," in *Mo Bozhi wenji* (Guangzhou: Guangdong keji chubanshe, 2003), 332–48; Mo Bozhi, Xia Changshi, and Zeng Zhaofen, *Lingnan tingyuan* (Beijing: Zhongguo jianzhu gongye chubanshe, 2008); and Jerome Silbergeld, "Beyond Suzhou: Region and Memory in the Gardens of Sichuan," *The Art Bulletin* 86 (2004):207–27. On women and gardens, and the garden as feminine space, see Wu Hung, "Beyond Stereotypes: The 'Twelve Beauties' in Qing Court Art and the 'Dream of the Red Chamber,'" in *Writing Women in Late Imperial China*, ed. Ellen Widmer and Kang-i Sun Chang (Stanford: Stanford University Press, 1997), 306–65; and Alison Hardie, "Washing the *Wutong* Tree: Garden Culture as an Expression of Women's Gentility in the Late Ming," in *The Quest for Gentility in China*, ed. Daria Berg and Chloe Starr (London: Routledge, 2007), 45–57.

4   For example, Liu Dunzhen, *Suzhou gudian yuanlin* (Beijing: Zhongguo jianzhu gongye chubanshe, 1979); Liu Dunzhen, *Chinese Classical Gardens of Suzhou*, trans. Joseph C. Wang (New York: McGraw-Hill, 1993); and Tong Jun, *Jiangnan yuanlin zhi*, 2nd ed. (Beijing: Zhongguo jianzhu gongye chubanshe, 1984; Beijing: Zhongguo gongye chubanshe, 1963). Because of the vicissitudes of Chinese history in the twentieth century, many works published after 1976 were actually based on research carried out much earlier in the century. By contrast, one of the first serious studies of Chinese gardens in English was by an art historian: Osvald Sirén, *Gardens of China* (New York: Ronald Press, 1949).

5   Alfreda Murck and Wen Fong, *A Chinese Garden Court: The Astor Court at the Metropolitan Museum of Art* (New York: The Metropolitan Museum of Art, 1980).

point of view, "the Chinese garden" held a privileged position among other forms of cultural production because of the way its study had originated. As noted above, it had taken shape as a branch of architectural history, and was, therefore, particularly associated with the development of a "scientific" approach to knowledge, at a time (the early twentieth century) when "science" (along with "democracy") was seen in China as the only way to revive the country's fortunes and to allow it to take its rightful place in the community of nations.

The representative or symbolic value of the garden in China thus remains important through the twentieth and into the twenty-first century, however much the cultural context has changed. Gardens in China, no less than elsewhere, are a great deal more than the sum of their parts. Within Chinese culture, over many centuries, gardens acquired layers of cultural references that affected how they were understood and how they could be used to represent a wide range of ideas and ideologies. The first chapter of this anthology introduces some of the early texts, philosophical, historical, and literary, that contributed to the development of garden culture. As the educated "scholar-official" class became the dominant governing class from the Song dynasty onward, this textual tradition became an inescapable part of elite garden culture, so that by the late imperial period it is impossible to imagine a garden—or a text about a garden or gardens—that did not allude in some way to such cultural icons as the philosopher Zhuangzi, the poet Tao Qian, or the calligrapher Wang Xizhi (see chapter 1).

Historians and scholars of Chinese gardens are, however, sometimes guilty of taking the gardens too seriously. We solemnly discuss aesthetic theories, design principles, developments in style and layout, forgetting that the gardens were primarily intended for enjoyment, as well as for the display of cultural and economic capital, self-representation, and other more ambitious purposes. Seventeenth-century garden theorist Ji Cheng instructs us that "If mountains are constructed among the women's apartments, they should be firm and tall, with sheer cliffs which cannot be climbed. The reason they should be solidly built is as a precaution in case children play on them"[6]—this should be a reminder that a Chinese garden could be fun for all the family. So what kinds of activities went on, and how were Chinese gardens enjoyed in practical ways?

Let us start with the more refined pleasures. Most private gardens—at least those we know about—belonged to members of the scholar-official elite: not always officials themselves, but members of literati or mandarin families who were usually expected to serve in government, but might avoid the official rat race in favor of living on their rents or by the products of their pen, or rather, brush. The four traditional pastimes of the elite were *qin qi shu hua*: playing the zither (*qin*), playing chess (actually "encirclement chess" or *weiqi*, usually known in English by the Japanese-derived name *gō*), writing calligraphy, and appreciating paintings.

From Yuan Huang's "Record of the Hall Surrounded by Jade of Master Sitting-in-Reclusion" (see chapter 6), we can see the importance of chess to some garden owners and users. The owner of this garden, Wang Tingna, Master Sitting-in-Reclusion himself, was a recognized champion at the game, as well as a playwright, publisher, and philanthropist. He commissioned Zhu Zhifan (d. 1624), the top metropolitan graduate of 1595 and a noted calligrapher, to write a sequence of

---

6   Ji Cheng, *The Craft of Gardens*, "Mountains in the Women's Apartments" (Shanghai: Better Link Press, 2012), 107.

quatrains on the features of his garden, although Zhu never actually saw the garden. One of the poems, "Chess-Board Rock," reads:

> It takes a thousand years to complete a single game:
> Victory and defeat are totally meaningless.
> I would like to ask if by means of this game
> Sacred and profane can perhaps communicate.[7]

Chess, which was highly regarded as a game of strategy, also gained significance in the context of the garden because of its association with the immortals or transcendents of Daoist belief. There was a legend that a woodcutter who had gone up into the mountains to cut wood came upon two people playing chess. He laid down his axe and stood watching them for what seemed a short time, but when the game came to an end and he went to pick up his axe, the wooden handle had rotted away, so many years had passed, and he realized he had been in the company of two immortals. This story is frequently alluded to in garden literature, and sometimes in the names of gardens and their features: the Allegory Mountain garden, described in chapter 6, had a building named Rotten Axe-Haft Mountain House.

Some people, however, such as the garden designer and cultural entrepreneur Li Yu (1610/11–1680; see chapter 8), did not take either chess or playing the *qin* too seriously: "playing chess is a way to pass one's leisure time, but it is not what you would call fun; playing the *qin* is certainly good for one's spiritual development, but it is hardly the way to have a good time."[8] A slightly less elevated, although still cultural, garden activity was watching performances of drama, which in premodern China always included music and singing as well as speech. Some wealthy families in late imperial China kept their own opera troupes to perform for them whenever they wanted.

Many owners enjoyed the process of creating a garden, deciding on the layout of buildings, rocks, and watercourses; others preferred what in the West would be thought of as "proper" gardening, with actual plants. On the one hand, they could be quite snobbish about this, and expect the gardeners to do all the dirty work: "One spends a whole year looking after plants for ten days of enjoyment when they flower.... As for cultivating orchids and planting chrysanthemums, their methods were known in the most ancient times; to use them from time to time in instructing one's gardeners and testing their professional knowledge is part of the duty of a recluse."[9] On the other hand, they could do the practical work themselves, as the noted plantsman Jin Rusheng (see chapter 3) did in seventeenth-century Zhejiang:

---

7   Zhu Zhifan, *110 Poems on Scenes from the Garden of Sitting in Reclusion* (*Ti Zuoyin yuanjing shi*), in *Zuoyin xiansheng dingpu*, Huancuitang edition, ed. Wang Tingna, ca. 1609, *paobu*.33a.

8   Li Yu, "Listening to the Qin and Watching Chess," in *Xianqing ouji* (Random notes on idle feelings) (Beijing: Zuojia chubanshe, 1995), 345.

9   Wen Zhenheng, *Zhangwu zhi tushuo*, ed. Hai Jun and Tian Jun (Jinan: Shandong huabao chubanshe, 2004), 35.

Rusheng is a frail man much prone to ill health, and yet dawn each day, before he has washed his face or combed his hair, finds him kneeling upon a rush mat out along the steps, trapping beetles and rooting out cutworms; once each day he examines, one by one, the thousand or more plants he grows, from the tips of their flowers to the base of their stems, even the underside of every leaf. . . . All this he insists on doing himself, heedless of the chilblains on his hands or the sunburn on his forehead.[10]

But in some people's opinion, even the greatest writers of the past behaved badly toward flowering plants in the course of enjoying gardens: the sixteenth-century literary critic Hu Yinglin berates the great eleventh-century literary figures Su Shi and Ouyang Xiu for their mistreatment of flowers as large-scale party decorations (see his "Connoisseurs of Flowers" in chapter 3).

Of course, not everyone could afford a large and lavish garden. Those who were less well off, such as the playwright Zhang Fengyi (1527–1613; see "Record of the Garden for Seeking One's Own Aims" in chapter 6), could console themselves with the thought that they themselves were closer to nature than those who went in for exotic species of plants or the most elegant and expensive kinds of rock. And there were quite a few impoverished scholars who thought it was much better not to have a real garden at all, which would require expenditure of money, time, and labor—far better to create a garden in one's imagination, as we can see from several examples in chapter 7.

Whether the garden was imaginary or real, feasting, drinking, and associated pastimes took place there. A game much enjoyed by the literati was to float wine-cups along a watercourse (natural or artificial); before the cup reached the next participant, he had to compose a couplet of poetry in sequence with that of the preceding player, and if he failed to do so successfully, he was obliged to drink the contents of the cup. The occasion that gave rise to this pastime was a celebrated literary gathering in 353 at the Orchid Pavilion near Shaoxing in Zhejiang, commemorated in a famous essay by the great calligrapher Wang Xizhi (see chapter 1).

Some games were less intellectually demanding. The genre of painting known as "beauties in a garden" includes representations of court ladies playing the Chinese form of golf.[11] Gardens both imperial and private were much used by women of upper-class families and their servants. In fact, gardens were often seen as feminine spaces, suitable for romantic encounters, as we see in the great sixteenth-century play *The Peony Pavilion* (see chapter 7).

Gardens could be the scene of even more sensual pleasures. Most notorious was the Golden Valley Garden of the wealthy third-century official Shi Chong, which became a byword for luxurious living (see chapter 1). The sixteenth-century novel *The Plum in the Golden Vase* uses the antihero's gardens as the setting for a variety of erotic adventures, as well as to satirize his social climbing and lack of taste.[12]

---

10   Zhang Dai, "Jin Rusheng's Flowers and Trees," from *Taoan's Dream Memories* (see chapter 3).

11   On this game, see Anthony Butler et al., *Chui Wan: An Ancient Chinese Golf-Like Game* (St Andrews: Partick Press, 2017).

12   See David Tod Roy, trans., *The Plum in the Golden Vase, or, Chin P'ing Mei* (Princeton: Princeton University Press, 1993).

We can see, therefore, that, although gardens have often been presented as idyllic spaces of reclusion, both by their owners or others writing at the time and by modern commentators, the reality more often than not was that they were intensively used for enjoyment and social activity, as well as for self-representation. Scholars have also shown that the focus of garden culture has changed over time, for example, from productivity to aesthetics.[13] This is, of course, a matter more of representation than of actuality. Moreover, the representation of gardens in both text and image changes over time, particularly with the expansion of print culture. It may well be the case that the increasing availability of printed texts and images led to a more standardized understanding of the garden, perhaps reducing regional variations as well as variations between the styles of gardens owned by members of different social classes, whether emperors and aristocrats, gentry, merchants, or prosperous artisans; however, this standardization, if such it was, is still little understood.

The rise of fictional gardens is linked, obviously, to the expansion of printing, but also to increasing competition for scarce resources such as urban space and real property, as we explain in the introductions to chapters 6 and 7. Social, economic, and cultural changes in the sixteenth and seventeenth centuries also gave rise to a demand for what has become known as "connoisseurship literature,"[14] including works such as Ji Cheng's *Yuanye* (*The Craft of Gardens*; see chapters 3 and 7), which began to express ideas of how gardens could be theorized. These changes also gave greater social prominence to the craftsmen responsible for the practicalities of bringing gardens into being, and thus we learn something of these men, who in earlier centuries had been anonymous (see chapter 7).

Some of the ways late imperial gardens could be used, could have their meanings change over time, and could have their existence continue in literature long after their physical disappearance can be shown in more depth by examples in the later chapters of this anthology. One such garden was in the city of Yangzhou, north of the Yangtze River in Jiangsu Province, another on the outskirts of Shaoxing in Zhejiang Province, a third simply in the mind of the owner. As we shall see, all three are linked by the particular historical circumstances of their creation and certain biographical connections. Most importantly, however, they are tied together by an intricate web of relations in their various verbal representations; in this, they are particularly representative of the literary resonances among gardens of different places and eras that this anthology seeks to reveal. (For further details on these texts and their authors, see the relevant sections in the anthology.)

In the spring of the thirteenth year (1640) of the reign of the Chongzhen emperor of the Ming dynasty (1368–1644), some three years after Zheng Yuanxun[15] finished his account of the garden he had built for himself just south of the city of Yangzhou, entitled "Yingyuan ziji" ("A Personal

---

13   Clunas, *Fruitful Sites*.

14   See Craig Clunas, *Superfluous Things: Material Culture and Social Status in Early Modern China* (Urbana: University of Illinois Press, 1991).

15   Zheng Yuanxun (*zi* Chaozong, *hao* Huidong, 1603–1644), originally from She County in Anhui Province but a long-term resident of River Capital (Jiangdu), present-day Yangzhou. For his biography, see Hang Shijun, "Ming zhifangsi zhushi Zheng Yuanxun zhuan" (*Daogutang wenji* 1776, 29: la-7b); thanks to Michael Radich for supplying a photocopy of this source.

Record of My Garden of Reflections"; see chapter 6), and some five years after the completion of the garden itself, he hosted there a famous gathering to view the flowering of a single yellow tree peony. In time-honored manner, the assembled luminaries celebrated the occasion (and, by association, the garden and its master) by composing poetry. A collection of more than one hundred of these poems was then sent off to be judged by Qian Qianyi (1582–1664),[16] the preeminent literary figure of the day, before being published under the title *Yingyuan yaohua ji* (*The Jasper Flower Collection from the Garden of Reflections*).[17]

By Zheng Yuanxun's own account, his garden was occasioned by failure. It was designed, he avers, to provide him with a site where he could disengage from society and devote himself in equal measure to the care of his elderly mother and to his books. To the extent that this claim is not disingenuous—and Zheng seems perhaps somewhat too keen on offering other justifications for his garden as well (his addiction to the mountains and to the rivers, to bamboo and to trees, his mother's dream, his own destiny)—occasions such as this immortal party appear to have conspired against his desire for anonymous reclusion.[18] Worldly success was soon to follow the social and cultural prestige thus generated by his garden; by 1643, he had finally achieved success in the Metropolitan Examinations.

Ironically, however, it was now to be the circumstances of a dynasty in the final stages of collapse that cast its shadow over the life of the Master of the Garden of Reflections. In 1644, when Yangzhou was approached by the army of Gao Jie (d. 1645),[19] a bandit chief turned self-proclaimed Ming loyalist, the populace of the city, fearing the violence of his out-of-control troops, barred the gates against him. It fell to Zheng Yuanxun to attempt to mediate the crisis. In his "Brief Account of the Defense of the City of Yangzhou in the Yiyou Year (1645) of the Reign of the Hongguang Emperor," the historian Dai Mingshi (1653–1713),[20] who came from the same region as Zheng's ancestors, provides the following—probably over-dramatized—account of the outcome of his attempt:

Zheng Yuanxun, an Advanced Scholar of River Capital [Jiangdu = Yangzhou], a proud and somewhat peevish man, ventured out to parley with the troops. Having entered Gao Jie's encampment, Zheng then proceeded to dine and discourse with him with great

---

16   For a short biography of this man, see Arthur W. Hummel, ed., *Eminent Chinese of the Ch'ing Period 1644– 1912* (Washington, D.C.: Government Printing Office, 1943), 148–50.

17   In his preface to the collection, dated to the sixth month of 1640 and entitled "Preface," *Yao's Yellow Collection* (*Yaohuang ji xu* 姚黄集序), Qian Qianyi discusses the extent to which the blooming of Zheng's peony could constitute either an "Auspicious Flower" (*huarui* 花瑞) or a "Flower Monstrosity" (*huayao* 花妖).

18   Dong Qichang (1555–1636), the man who had coined the name of Zheng's garden, as explained at the beginning of his account of it, once claimed that "actually, nine out of every ten who withdrew to the mountains were extravagant men who lived lavishly"; see Qian Zhongshu, *Limited Views: Essays on Ideas and Letters*, trans. Ronald Egan (Cambridge, Mass.: Harvard University Press, 1998), 86.

19   On Gao Jie, see the biography in Hummel, *Eminent Chinese of the Ch'ing Period*, 410–11; and for a brief account of Gao Jie's role in the complex circumstances of the times, see Lynn A. Struve, *The Southern Ming, 1644–1662* (New Haven: Yale University Press, 1984), 23–26.

20   On Dai Mingshi, see the biography in Hummel, *Eminent Chinese of the Ch'ing Period*, 701–2.

merriment, Gao for his part rewarding Zheng for his efforts with gifts of pearls and silk. Upon his return to the city, Zheng appeared even more proud of himself, and addressed the crowd in the following manner: "General Gao has been summoned here by imperial command. If when he entered Nanjing he was simply obeying orders, how much more so is this the case with Yangzhou?" Aroused to great anger by what they understood to be Zheng's betrayal of the city in order to boost his own reputation, the crowd slaughtered him on the spot and proceeded to eat up his flesh.[21]

Notice of Zheng's first official posting, as Secretary in the Bureau of Operations in the Ministry of War, arrived in Yangzhou three days later.

The bulk of Zheng Yuanxun's account of his garden provides readers with a tour of the various sites of the garden. Like the garden, this tour wraps back around itself; we begin our stroll at the outer gate and toward the end of the tour we see again, growing beyond a wall, the tree that is visible from this spot.

The tension that runs throughout Zheng's account of his garden and doubtless dominated the decade-long process of its design and construction was that between the constrictions of the site (both its overall size and its lack of a mountain) on the one hand, and the desire to achieve "understated elegance of the simple and the rustic" (*puye zhi zhi*) while avoiding any anxiety about the exhaustibility of the delights it contained as one moved through it on the other.[22] To this end, the design of the garden, undertaken by the well-known garden specialist Ji Cheng (b. 1582; see chapters 3, 6, and 7)[23] embodies many of the conceits of concealment and disclosure, surprise and anticipation that feature in Ji Cheng's monograph on garden design, *The Craft of Gardens* (*Yuanye*).[24] The extent to which the Garden of Reflections sought to borrow from beyond its own walls views of sites of scenic beauty and historical importance was also, in Ji Cheng's terms, a true measure of the craft.[25] Significantly, the aesthetic sensibilities of both the master of the garden

---

21 Dai Mingshi, "Hongguang yiyou Yangzhou chengshou ji lüe" (A brief account of the defense of the city of Yangzhou in the *yiyou* year [1645] of the reign of the Hongguang emperor), in *Dai Mingshi ji* (Beijing: Zhonghua shuju, 1986), 351. With reference to Zheng Yuanxun's biography in Hang Shijun's *Daogutang wenji,* Li Dou presents a far more nuanced and sympathetic account of Zheng as a man much involved in local activities such as famine relief, for which see Li Dou, *Yangzhou huafang lu,* 169–70.

22 Li Dou, in his account of the Garden of Reflections (*Yangzhou huafang lu,* 167–69), which is based on Zheng Yuanxun's own account, makes this dimension of the garden even more explicit when he tells us that the garden was sited on an "elongated islet" in the midst of South Lake.

23 For a short biography (by Lien-che Tu Fang) of this most famous of Chinese garden designers, see L. Carrington Goodrich and Chaoying Fang, eds., *Dictionary of Ming Biography, 1368–1644* (New York: Columbia University Press, 1976), 1:215–16.

24 Elsewhere in his *Yangzhou huafang lu,* Li Dou describes the effect of such conceits: "Touring this space one feels oneself to be like an ant crawling through the twisting eye of a pearl, or to have encountered a screen of tinted glass, for every new twist and turn leads one on to yet another splendor"; see *Yangzhou huafang lu,* 139.

25 In the relevant section of his work, Ji Cheng has this to say about the technique of "borrowing scenery": "Making use of the natural scenery is the most vital part of garden design. There are various aspects such as using scenery in the distance, near at hand, above you, and at certain times of the year. But the attraction of

and those of his friend, the master of the craft, derived quite explicitly from their study of the traditions of landscape painting. Sadly, the Garden of Reflections appears not to have survived much beyond the dynastic transition that so tragically entangled its master, although the family tradition of garden building seems to have been maintained by succeeding generations.[26] Writing sometime around 1691, for instance, Fang Xiangying notes the disappearance of Zheng Yuanxun's garden in his account of the restoration of a garden then in the possession of Zheng's grandnephew Zheng Maojia:

> The prosperous and picturesque suburbs of River Capital once boasted so many gardens, and yet ever since the time of Emperor Yang of the Sui such gardens as "Firefly Park," "Labyrinth Tower," and "The Songs and Pipes of Bamboo West" have all long disappeared without trace. This is so even of Master Zheng Yuanxun's "Garden of Reflections" which was once the splendor of the age. In those days, whenever the yellow tree peony burst into flower, all the most famous literary men from throughout the empire would gather in this garden to eat and drink and to compose poetry. . . . Now, in the twinkling of an eye, fifty years have gone by; the garden changed hands, its pavilions and gazebos fell into ruin and nobody any longer even knows where the garden had once been. This "Garden of Rest" once owned by Zheng Xiaru of the Ministry of Works alone has survived intact the ravages of war and calamity, proving once again that the vicissitudes of a garden are determined always by the fate of its owner.[27]

In the absence of the usual marker of cultural and social status—a pass in the Metropolitan Examinations—Zheng Yuanxun employed the leverage afforded him by ownership of a celebrated garden to engage with members of the elite that he sought to join. The text they produced as a function of a gathering hosted in the garden served to earn him his reputation, as his biography makes clear: "Yuanxun's name now resonated among the highest ministers of state to the extent that in the Capital, all the senior officials of the various ministries would insist on asking anyone who had

---

natural objects, both the form perceptible to the eye and the essence which touches the heart, must be fully imagined in your mind before you put pen to paper, and only then do you have a possibility of expressing it completely." See Ji Cheng, *The Craft of Gardens*, trans. Alison Hardie (New Haven: Yale University Press, 1988), 121.

26 All three of Zheng Yuanxun's brothers owned celebrated gardens. It is said that the garden is to be recreated in Yangzhou in the near future, to cater particularly for an increasing domestic tourist market, on the basis of Zheng Yuanxun's account of its design.

27 See Fang Xiangying, "Chongqi Xiuyuan ji" (A record of the restoration of the Garden of Rest), in *Zhongguo lidai mingyuanji xuanzhu*, ed. Chen Zhi and Zhang Gongchi (Hefei, Anhui: Anhui kexue jishu chubanshe, 1983), 315. Zheng Xiaru (*zi* Shijie, *hao* Si'an) was Zheng Yuanxun's youngest brother. Li Dou, however, writing sometime before 1795, tells us that after the passage of more than a century the ruins of the Garden of Reflections remained (*yizhi youcun*) and that just to the south of where the garden had once been stood the shrine dedicated to Zheng Yuanxun and his brother Zheng Yuanhua (*zi* Zanke), former master of the Garden of the Fine Trees (*Jiashu yuan*).

recently returned from Guangling [Yangzhou]: 'And did you get to meet the Cultivated Talent Zheng [Yuanxun]?'"[28]

The Garden of Reflections, far from providing Zheng with a site for retreat and reflection, served as both context and pretext for an intensified engagement with the official and elite world, while the prose records and poems it generated ensured also that his reputation and that of his garden would long outlive both master and garden. The beginning of Zheng's account shows how he used the planning of his garden as a means to enhance his social connections, as an aspirant literatus painter as well as an aspirant official, with the eminent art critic Dong Qichang,[29] who obliged him by naming the garden and writing that name for him in Dong's own much prized calligraphy.

Earlier we quoted the Qing dynasty (but, significantly, Ming loyalist) historian Dai Mingshi's account of the sad death of the master of this particular garden. Dai, like men of his and previous generations, spent much of his youth in the gardens attached to either the academy or the monastery at which he studied in preparation for the examinations. In Dai's case, however, either the political circumstances of his day or the economic circumstances of his family seem to have prevented him from ever building his own garden, except in his mind. His collected works contains a short prose record, "A Record of The Garden of My Mind" (Yiyuan ji; see chapter 7), in which he imagines himself and his garden as situated in an idealized distant past.[30]

Well might Dai Mingshi have sought—vainly, as it turned out—to find his place of refuge in the mists of distant antiquity, beyond the time and space of the Chinese empire; in his case, we are fortunate to have remaining to us even this account of his quest. In 1711, in one of the most infamous cases of literary persecution during the Qing dynasty and as a result of his interest in the history of the courts (collectively known as the Southern Ming) that survived the fall of the capital to the Manchus in 1644, Dai Mingshi and all his scholarly associates, along with their entire families, were condemned to execution: Dai, it seems, had persisted in his use of Ming dynasty reign titles to date his history, rather than adopting those of his new masters. In this case, fortunately, the emperor, the great Kangxi (1654–1722; r. 1661–1722), then entering the last troubled decade of his rule, relented; only Dai was eventually executed, while a long-dead associate was disinterred in order to be dismembered, and their sons and families banished to the northernmost reaches of the empire. The interdiction on his writings remained in force until the mid-nineteenth century, however, when they were finally published under a false name.

Dai Mingshi is also connected to the third garden we address in this introduction, one roughly contemporary with that of Zheng Yuanxun, Qi Biaojia's Allegory Mountain garden (Yushan yuan) in Shaoxing. Dai knew the sons of its owner, both of whom suffered for their loyalist activities. Dai's own collected works, when they were finally published in 1841, contained a biography of the

---

28   Hang Shijun, Daogutang wenji, 29:2b. "Cultivated Talent" (xiucai) was a title for men who had not yet achieved the status of Elevated Person (juren) or Provincial Graduate, the stage before the Metropolitan Examination.

29   For a short biography of Dong Qichang (by Fang Chaoying), see Hummel, Eminent Chinese of the Ch'ing Period, 787–89.

30   Dai Mingshi ji, 386.

man to whom was attributed part of the garden's design. He had also doubtless read Qi's account of the garden, which is included in chapter 6 ("Footnotes to Allegory Mountain").

In the late summer of the eighth year (1635) of the reign of the Chongzhen emperor, Qi Biaojia was granted leave to quit his post with the Censorate and return to his native place of Shanyin in Zhejiang Province, ostensibly to care for his elderly mother.[31] He was to remain in retirement for the next nine years. Family and friends had gathered to welcome him home, and in his diary for that year, entitled "A Joyous Account of My Return South," Qi Biaojia records the happiness of the occasion. His diary entry for the very next day, however, perhaps affords us a greater insight into his state of mind at the time:

> First day seventh month: I have been home less than two days and already I find myself forced to try to escape my various social obligations. With Zheng Jiuhua [his amanuensis] as my only companion, I went to the Great Hall to sort out my books. Zhou Rudeng's[32] grandson Zhou Xianzhi happened to pay a call and I entertained him with a hospitable meal. Once he had departed I returned to my books and in the evening met up with my brothers to drink and converse.[33]

Over the course of the succeeding weeks, in between a continuing round of family and social engagements, Qi Biaojia seems to have spent as much time as possible reestablishing his library and sorting through his late father's books and writings. It is from an entry in his diary for early in the next month that we can date the genesis of his conception of the garden that he begins to build:

> Sixth day eighth month: The day dawned bright and clear. In the afternoon I went to visit my uncle's garden with Ma Yuanchang, and my brothers Jichao and Xiangjia. Along with my cousin Zhixiang I went to Allegory Mountain, this being where the monk Trackless had established his hermitage. The desire to choose a site and build a garden arose powerfully within me. We left Axe-Haft Mountain by boat and it was evening by the time we returned home.[34]

On the twenty-first day of the tenth month, no longer able to restrain his desire to build a garden, Qi Biaojia visited the site with his brothers and friends to draw up the plans.[35] Construction began in earnest shortly thereafter and for the next seventeen months Qi Biaojia devoted much of his

---

31   For a biography of Qi Biaojia, see Hummel, *Eminent Chinese of the Ch'ing Period*, 126.

32   On this important Ming thinker, see Goodrich and Fang, *Dictionary of Ming Biography*, 1:271–74. Qi Biaojia's father had been a student of Zhou's, and Qi himself, in turn, had studied under Zhou's son. Throughout the construction of his garden, Qi Biaojia was reading Zhou Rudeng's philosophical writings.

33   "Gui nan kuailu," *Qi Biaojia wengao*, 2:1022.

34   "Gui nan kuailu," *Qi Biaojia wengao*, 2:1025.

35   "Gui nan kuailu," *Qi Biaojia wengao*, 2:1032. Allegory Mountain was the original name of the mountain, and although Qi Biaojia proved happy to accept the suggestions of various friends for names of sites in his garden, he "did not dare rename the mountain itself," for which see "Gui nan kuailu," *Qi Biaojia wengao*, 2:1035.

energy to the design and construction of his garden.[36] By the eighth month of the next year, enough progress had been made on the garden that Qi was able to spend the night in his newly completed Quietist's Studio.[37] When the two ponds that became a feature of the garden were created late in the first month of the year after, the scenery of the garden "began gradually to acquire its excellence."[38]

By his own account, Qi inherited both his passion for garden design and the financial where-withal to indulge it from his father Qi Chenghan. "My father had a lifetime's passion for gardens," he tells us in the entry on his father's Intimate Garden in his account of the various gardens of his district, "and he built this garden after he had resigned from office. . . . Later on, he used all his income on developing it."[39] Both the scale and the context of Qi's own indulgence of his obsession, however, differed greatly. All too soon, visitors began to crowd their way into his garden and it rang with the commotion of a busy marketplace.[40] "From Master Zhu's place I returned to Allegory Mountain and sat in my Rotten Axe-Haft Mountain House reading the *Lankavatara Sutra*," he tells us on one occasion, "but the incessant trample of the crowds of visitors proved such that I greatly regretted ever having built this garden."[41]

Events elsewhere, of course, forced their way into his garden. Regular reports reached him of the collapse of the Ming political order.[42] The recent death of his mother having finally released him from his filial obligations, Qi Biaojia took up office again in 1644, and after the fall of Beijing and the suicide of the Chongzhen emperor, news of which reached Qi as he made his way to the Southern Capital, he was appointed Governor of Suzhou.[43] Factional infighting in the court of the Prince of Lu soon enforced his retirement, however, and he returned to Shanyin. Under intense pressure to accept office under the new dynasty, Qi Biaojia came to believe that the only way he

---

36   On the social implications of Qi's garden-building, see the important article by Joanna F. Handlin Smith, "Gardens in Ch'i Piao-chia's Social World: Wealth and Values in Late-Ming Kiangnan," *Journal of Asian Studies* 51, no. 1 (February 1992):58–81. During his retirement, Qi Biaojia was also involved in various philanthropic activities, for which see Joanna F. Handlin Smith, "Opening and Closing a Dispensary in Shan-yin County: Some Thoughts about Charitable Associations, Organizations, and Institutions in Late Ming China," *Journal of the Economic and Social History of the Orient* 38, no. 3 (1995):371–92.

37   "Linju shibi" (Occasional jottings from my sojourn in the woods), *Qi Biaojia wengao*, 2:1058.

38   "Shanju zhuolu" (Clumsy record of my sojourn on the mountain), *Qi Biaojia wengao*, 2:1073.

39   "Yuezhong yuanting ji" (Record of the gardens and pavilions of Shanyin), *Qi Biaojia ji*, 211.

40   Qi Biaojia makes this observation a number of times in his diaries; see "Shanju zhuolu," *Qi Biaojia wengao*, 2:1072, 1076. On the question of access to gardens such as that of Qi Biaojia during this period, see Clunas, *Fruitful Sites*, 91–103.

41   "Shanju zhuolu," *Qi Biaojia wengao*, 2:1077.

42   On this most dramatic of dynastic transitions from Ming to Qing, see Lynn A. Struve, *The Southern Ming, 1644–1662* (New Haven: Yale University Press, 1984), and her similarly titled chapter in *The Cambridge History of China*, vol. 7, *The Ming Dynasty, 1368–1644*, ed. Frederick W. Mote and Denis Twitchett (Cambridge: Cambridge University Press, 1988), 641–725.

43   On the important role Qi Biaojia played in attempting to pacify the countryside around the Southern Capital, see Jerry Dennerline, "Hsü Tu and the Lesson of Nanking: Political Integration and the Local Defense in Chiang-nan, 1634–1645," in *From Ming to Ch'ing: Conquest, Region, and Continuity in Seventeenth-Century China*, ed. Jonathan D. Spence and John E. Wills Jr. (New Haven: Yale University Press, 1979), 89–132.

could secure his family's future was by ending his own life.[44] The official history of the period records his demise in the following manner:

> In the fifth month of the next year [1645] the Southern Capital was lost, and by the sixth month, Hangzhou too, in turn, had fallen. [Qi] Biaojia thereupon began his fast. On the fourth day of the succeeding intercalary month, having told his family that he was going to repair early to his bedchamber, he proceeded to his lake wherein he sat bolt upright and awaited his death. He was forty-four years old.[45]

There is a record of his last conversation with one of his sons. A relaxed smile on his lips, he turned to him and said: "Although your father did not fail in his family duties, I was, however, somewhat too addicted to the springs and the rocks. I was lavish in constructing my garden and this was my failing."[46] He was buried in his garden, in a coffin he had already prepared for himself. We can see from the remarks of Qian Yong (1759–1844; see chapter 6) that in later times the garden was more notable for its association with a Ming martyr than for its aesthetic qualities.

Qi Biaojia seems to have begun his account of his garden late in the ninth year of the reign of the Chongzhen emperor (1636).[47] His diaries show that he worked intensively on it during the fourth and fifth months of the next year, at the same time that he was reading both Wang Shizhen's (1526–1590) "Record of My Mount Yan Garden" (see chapter 6) and Li Daoyuan's (d. 527) *Footnotes to the Classic of the Waterways*,[48] finishing it on the twenty-first day of the fifth month.[49] Having circulated the manuscript among friends,[50] Qi made some changes before having it copied and sent for printing.[51] By this time, the text had acquired its present title. Construction of the garden continued, of course, and in his diaries Qi Biaojia speaks of having a friend put the finishing touches to a text (no longer extant) entitled "More Footnotes to Allegory Mountain."[52] We also have Dong Xuan's "A Visit to Allegory Mountain" (chapter 6), which provides some information on the garden not included in Qi Biaojia's own writing, as well as poems written after Qi's death by his widow, Shang Jinglan (some examples are in chapter 6), and a number of poems on the garden by other writers, thus providing us a rich body of work on this garden.

---

44 See the final pages of his diary: Qi Biaojia, *Qi Zhongmingong riji* (Shaoxing: Shaoxing xian xiuzhi weiyuanhui, 1937); and Qi Biaojia, *Qi Zhongmingong riji* (Hangzhou: Hangzhou gujiu shudian, 1982).

45 *Ming shi* (History of the Ming) (Beijing: Zhonghua shuju, 1974), 23:7054.

46 From the biography of Qi Biaojia written by Xie Jin, as cited in *Qi Biaojia ji*, 252.

47 "Linju shibi," *Qi Biaojia wengao*, 2:1062.

48 On this important geographical source, see William H. Nienhauser Jr., ed., *The Indiana Companion to Traditional Chinese Literature* (Bloomington: Indiana University Press, 1986), 710–12.

49 "Shanju zhuolu," *Qi Biaojia wengao*, 2:1085–87.

50 The collected works of Zhang Dai, who was related to Qi Biaojia by bonds of both marriage and friendship (on whom see Hummel, *Eminent Chinese of the Ch'ing Period*, 53–54) contains two colophons on the text, for which see *Langhuan wenji* (Changsha: Yuelu shushe, 1985), 210–11.

51 "Shanju zhuolu," *Qi Biaojia wengao*, 2:1095.

52 "Zijian lu" (Record of my self-admonition), *Qi Biaojia wengao*, 2:1127.

We hope these remarks have served in brief to suggest the complexity of the entanglements of three particular owners with their gardens, which, in turn, were entangled with political and literary history. We know more about these individuals and their gardens than about many others, but we can consider them typical of some of the ways, by means of garden ownership and connoisseurship, that the elite of late imperial China interacted with their peers, tried to cope with the problems of their times, and placed themselves in relation to the long cultural tradition they had inherited. Their actions and writings were incorporated, in turn, by later literati into that still vital tradition. Although that cultural heritage has now largely ceased to be a living entity, as the social structures that nurtured it have gone beyond recall, it nevertheless has a profound effect on how present-day Chinese culture is perceived and understood.

The history of gardens in China, however it is interpreted, cannot be separated from the literature that surrounds, informs, and describes them. That literature gives us a rich body of material through which to understand the aesthetic foundations, perception, reception, and use of these gardens. We hope, therefore, that this anthology will serve to generate a better-informed and more sophisticated general understanding of gardens in China, their changes over time and space, their variety and usage, and the intimately related literary discourse. At the same time, we hope the anthology might impel greater study of garden and landscape histories both in China and in comparative contexts. China's long tradition of engagement with gardens as physical and imaginative sites surely has much to teach us about the significance of designed landscapes in the fullness of cultural expression.

This anthology seeks to be comprehensive without being exhaustive. The corpus of Chinese verbal representations of gardens, in a variety of forms of prose and poetry, is vast. For present purposes, we have sought to do little more than present some of the more important and representative of these writings, both in terms of their content and their literary forms, setting them in literary and historical contexts that reveal, we hope, the extent to which the authors (and traditional readers) of these writings conceived of themselves as participating in and contributing to a continuous and echoing discourse on gardens and their uses. We have made a particular effort to include writing by women in order to remind readers of the importance of gardens for elite women (and indeed for other women such as courtesans) in the imperial period. We hope this will go some way to counteract the emphasis on male ownership of gardens in much scholarly literature. Although the time span covered stretches back to the earliest recorded times in China's history, the weight of the anthology falls in the late imperial period, during which the private garden flourished as never before or since, and for which we have the most literary and visual evidence. Yet the texts chosen demonstrate the deep continuities and resonances in the long history of Chinese garden literature, reaching far back from the late imperial period to some of the earliest surviving literary and historical texts.

We are, however, very aware of the impossibility of including everything relevant to gardens in China. Those familiar with the topic will undoubtedly miss favorite pieces. In the attempt to cover the broadest range possible and give a sense of the richness of the literary tradition related to gardens, we have structured some chapters chronologically and some thematically. Chapter 5 relates to a single garden in Suzhou, for which there is a particularly rich heritage of writing; the final chapter (chapter 9) focuses on two significant landscapes (Mount Tai in Shandong and

Hangzhou's West Lake) to suggest the ways these managed landscapes, despite their varying purposes, reflected attitudes toward gardens and, in turn, were reflected in gardens, both imperial and private; we hope readers will find this thought-provoking.

Above all, the anthology seeks to be readable. The traditional Chinese discourse on gardens was a literary rather than a professional one; owners wrote about their gardens in order to be admired and remembered as much for their skill with the brush as for the beauty or cleverness of the design of their garden. Through the medium of translation, we trust this anthology has managed nonetheless to retain something of the power and beauty of the poems, prefaces, essays, and other texts by some of China's greatest writers.

To make the anthology as readable as possible, especially for those with no knowledge of the Chinese language, we have kept Chinese characters in the main body of text to a minimum, showing only the titles of passages and the authors' names in Chinese; other Chinese vocabulary is in the glossary at the end. Where a title or subtitle has no Chinese, it is because that was not a named section in the Chinese original, but has been given a name by the translator or editors for ease of reference. For consistency, all transliteration is in Hanyu pinyin, including in preexisting translations that originally used Wade-Giles or other systems; we have also regularized some spelling and punctuation for clarity and internal consistency.

In previously published translations, all footnotes are the translators' unless indicated otherwise. Where the editors felt it useful to refer the reader to another part of the anthology, a reference is inserted in square brackets. In translations prepared for this anthology—which constitute the largest part—we have not distinguished between translators' and editors' notes.

The completion of this anthology has required many years and much work from a great number of scholars. It cannot, however, be final. We look forward to further work from other scholars that will help to make the riches of the Chinese garden tradition accessible to readers with little or no Chinese language, perhaps a critical study and collection of visual images (in the form of paintings, woodblock prints, and other media) of gardens in China. Research on gardens in non-elite, popular culture of the past would generate a significant addition to knowledge; historical evidence appears to be sparse, but to judge by the situation in recent times down to the present, gardens (if not their representations) have also long been important at the non-elite level, at least among those with some disposable income, if not among subsistence farmers. It is to be hoped that more knowledge of non-elite gardening traditions in premodern China can be recovered. There is still much to be explored.

ALISON HARDIE

DUNCAN M. CAMPBELL

ACKNOWLEDGMENTS

I should start with thanks to Dumbarton Oaks generally, to Jan Ziolkowski and John Beardsley in particular, to Richard Strassberg, who until 2010 served as senior fellow, and to all in that charmed community of scholarship who made my family and me so welcome there. Dumbarton Oaks was involved in the very inception of the project; I am extremely grateful for this remarkable institution's continuing commitment to the project during years when nothing much seemed to be happening with it, and for their confidence (not misplaced, I hope) that I could serve to bring it to a conclusion. I should also make note of the grace and generosity of the responses of the various contributors to the anthology as I attempted to pick up a project that I imagine many of them had considered moribund. I hope I have lived up to the responsibilities laid on me: to repay that trust on the part of both institution and contributors, and to prove also that an anthology of translations of Chinese writings on gardens is a worthwhile project.

DUNCAN M. CAMPBELL

I would like to thank the community at Dumbarton Oaks, in particular the director, Jan Ziolkowski; John Beardsley, director of Garden and Landscape Studies; Anatole Tchikine, assistant director of Garden and Landscape Studies; and Jane Padelford, administrator, for enabling me to spend four very happy and productive months there from October 2015 to early February 2016, as well as a further month in April–May 2016, working on bringing this anthology to completion. I owe thanks to the contributors who generously allowed me to make use of their original explanatory material in the chapter introductions; several of them additionally helped me with revisions or additions to their sections. I would also like to thank the two anonymous external readers of the draft manuscript, who made many supportive and helpful comments and suggestions, which I have tried to incorporate as much as possible into the final text. Thanks to Tong Shenxiao of Edinburgh University Library for his invaluable help. Finally, I would like to express warm thanks to Stan Fung, who originated this project and brought together such a congenial group of contributors, whose friendship and collegiality over the years have greatly enriched my life, and who have taught me to think about gardens in new and interesting ways.

ALISON HARDIE

南高峰

北高峯

御碑亭

Early Garden Traditions

T his first chapter presents a selection of texts from at least the seventh century BCE to the sixth century CE. They have generally been presented in the chronological order of the events to which they refer, rather than of their (actual or supposed) authors; for example, the extracts from the *Miscellaneous Records of the Western Capital* are placed according to the dates of the Former Han dynasty, their subject, rather than those of Ge Hong, the author to whom they are attributed. Most of these passages are texts to which later writers on gardens constantly referred; in some cases, they are intended as representative works of authors who played an important part in developing the tradition of garden literature.

These texts include a wide variety of forms: formally structured *shi* poems; short lyrics usually composed to match a preexisting tune or tune-pattern (*ci*); long passages of "rhapsodies" or "rhyme-prose" (*fu*) with grandiloquent vocabulary in lines of varying length; philosophical, narrative, or descriptive prose; letters; prefaces; and so on. They give a sense of the variety of literary forms to be found in the classical tradition, as well as the variety of content. The later chapters of this anthology make many references to these early texts. Once the Chinese education system, with its close links to the imperial civil service examinations, became institutionalized, as it increasingly was from the Tang dynasty onward, and particularly from the Song, there was a quite clearly defined body of knowledge shared among the elite; a substantial number of standard texts were known by heart by all educated men. Consequently, even a passing reference to an earlier classical text would be picked up immediately by a listener or reader, thus giving a wider frame of reference. It is, therefore, often difficult for the modern reader (whether Chinese or not) to fully understand much of premodern literature because of a lack of relevant cultural knowledge. The texts presented in this chapter should supply some of the basis for reading and appreciating the writings that appear in the following chapters.

Not all of these early texts are overtly about gardens. The poems collected in the *Book of Songs* and the *Songs of the South*, for example, seldom refer to gardens, but make extensive use of plant imagery to express moral values. The allegorical use of plants remained a feature of Chinese culture and played an important role in defining which plants were considered desirable in a garden, even though Chinese scholars in later times were probably just as uncertain as we are today about the exact identity of many of the plants mentioned in early poetry.

The classics of Confucian philosophy, particularly the *Analects* and the *Mencius*, were important sources for some views of garden culture. The *Analects* established that "the wise find pleasure in water; the virtuous find pleasure in hills"; this became a standard justification for the enjoyment of gardens, even those with only "a dipperful of water and a fist-sized rock," as the phrase went, to stand in for vast lakes and lofty mountains. The views expressed by Mencius on the importance of the ruler "sharing his pleasure with the multitude" also provided a moral basis for garden ownership and a justification for the ruling class indulging in garden construction, provided this could in some way be construed as benefiting others, for example by providing the spectacle of lantern displays at the Lantern Festival, or by growing medicinal herbs for charitable use: these are both examples from some of the gardens described in chapter 6.

Important as the Confucian textual tradition was, among early texts it was the Daoist classics that supplied the widest range of allusions employed by later writers on gardens. The lively anecdotes in the *Zhuangzi*, some of which are included in this chapter, provided many examples of recluses who rejected worldly ambition in favor of nourishing their internal life. Zhuang Zhou himself is said to have preferred to emulate the turtle "dragging his tail in the mud" rather than submitting to the pressures of officialdom, while the old gardener who lugs a pitcher to and from the well rather than using a well sweep to water his plants rejects the "machine heart" that results from the use of mechanical contrivances. Later chapters of this anthology show how frequent were allusions to these texts.

Once the "Warring States," with their competing philosophers and practitioners of statecraft, had been unified by the oppressive and short-lived Qin dynasty, the subsequent Han dynasty set the pattern for the succeeding two millennia of imperial rule. The political stability, economic prosperity, and military strength of the Han provided the conditions for the establishment of extensive imperial parks, modeled on the imagined splendors of the legendary sage kings' reigns, and even for wealthy commoners to own splendid gardens, such as that of Yuan Guanghan (see *Miscellaneous Records of the Western Capital* in this chapter).

After the fall of the Han dynasty in the early third century, the period of disunion that lasted until the empire was reunited by the Sui in the late sixth century proved important in the formation of the literati self-image in relation to garden culture as well as more generally. The dangers of political instability, with one short-lived kingdom succeeding another and much internecine struggle at every court, left many of the ruling class frustrated in their ambitions for an official career. To compensate, many turned to deliberate eccentricity of behavior, often intended to disguise their real feelings or intentions, or went into reclusion, developing a culture of eremitism based on Daoist or Buddhist beliefs or a combination of the two. Some of the best known of these eccentrics were the Seven Sages of the Bamboo Grove; many anecdotes about their unconventional behavior were compiled in *A New Account of Tales of the World* and other collections. Important writers from this period include Pan Yue, Xie Lingyun, and Tao Qian, whose poems and rhyme-prose on their gardens and their ideals of reclusion became a rich source of inspiration for later garden-owners, who modeled their own identities as recluses on the earlier writers' self-representations. Tao Qian, in particular, came to be regarded as the ideal of the garden-loving recluse, and it would be hard to find a later garden that did not in some way allude to his much-loved poems.

During this period of disunion, we also find the first surviving attempts to construct theories of painting; a number of short essays survive from people whose names we know as painters from later writers, although unsurprisingly none of their original works have survived to the present day. Here we have included, as a representative example, the painter Zong Bing's (4th–5th century) "Introduction to Painting Landscape." As landscape painting developed in later centuries—particularly after the Tang—into the dominant form of elite painting, the links between garden design and landscape painting grew ever closer, and literati commenters on gardens often looked back to such early texts on painting theory and the no-longer-extant works of early painters as a source of inspiration or justification for their own concepts of landscape design.[1]

Although we have very little solid evidence about gardens and parks in the pre-Qin period, and what we know about them from the Han through the period of disunion is often highly speculative, these early centuries of Chinese history were extremely important in establishing a garden tradition, a culture of reclusion in the garden, a canon of desirable and essential garden plants, and a lineage of writers on garden living that later garden-owners looked back on as forerunners. Despite the relative sparseness of writing explicitly about gardens—at least until the fourth century—many texts from this early period became an integral part of the culture and tradition of gardens in the Chinese world.

Book of Songs (*Shijing* 詩經)

"There are Peach-Trees in the Garden" (*Yuan you tao* 園有桃), "In the South" (*Jiumu* 樛木), and "Magic Tower" (*Lingtai* 靈臺)

The *Shijing* (*Classic of Poetry, Book of Odes*, or *Book of Songs*) is a collection of 305 poems apparently dating from the twelfth to the seventh century BCE (although the original dates are uncertain). It was traditionally believed to have been compiled by the great sage Confucius. Although this was almost certainly not the case, Confucius regarded the collection as very important, and it became one of the so-called Confucian classics. The contents range from orally composed folk songs to dynastic hymns. The examples here are folk songs, or at least take that form, characterized by repeated lines and phrases. In the Confucian exegetical tradition, what appear to the modern reader as simple, sometimes erotic love songs might be interpreted as representing the faithful

---

1   For an accessible introduction to the links between painting and garden design, see Hu Dongchu, *The Way of the Virtuous: The Influence of Art and Philosophy on Chinese Garden Design* (Beijing: New World Press, 1991), especially chapters 3–5. See also Maggie Keswick, *The Chinese Garden: History, Art, and Architecture*, 3rd ed. (London: Frances Lincoln, 2003), especially "The Painter's Eye," 102–27. For relevant texts on painting theory, see Susan Bush and Shih Hsio-yen, eds., *Early Chinese Texts on Painting* (Cambridge, Mass.: Harvard University Press, 1985).

relationship between sovereign and minister. The first poem given here, in a plain and literal translation by the Scots missionary and translator of all the Confucian classics James "Chinese" Legge (1815–1897), uses characteristic vegetal imagery to represent the utility of the loyal government official. The second poem is categorized by translator Arthur Waley (1889–1966) as an invocation of "blessings on gentlefolk"; the tree represents the lord and the creepers that surround it represent the common people dependent upon his support. The "Magic Tower" (probably more of an earthen platform than an architectural structure) was said to have been built by the semi-legendary King Wen of Zhou (11th century BCE?) in his royal park, the Magic (or Numinous) Park, with the wholehearted support of the common people. The Moated Mound, presumably also in the royal park, was where young men were trained in archery and other gentlemanly accomplishments.

"There are Peach-Trees in the Garden"
TRANSLATED BY JAMES LEGGE

Of the peach trees in the garden
The fruit may be used as food.
My heart is grieved,
And I play and sing.
Those who do not know me
Say I am a scholar venting his pride.

"Those men are right;
What do you mean by your words?"
My heart is grieved;
Who knows the cause of it?
Who knows the cause of it?
They know it not, because they will not think.

Of the jujube trees in the garden
The fruit may be used as food.
My heart is grieved,
And I think I must travel about through the State.
Those who do not know me
Say I am an officer going to the verge of license.
"Those men are right;
What do you mean by your words?"
My heart is grieved.
Who knows the cause of it?
Who knows the cause of it?
They do not know it, because they will not think.

"In the South"

TRANSLATED BY ARTHUR WALEY

In the south is a tree with drooping boughs;
The cloth-creeper binds it.
Oh, happy is our lord;
Blessings and boons secure him!

In the south is a tree with drooping boughs;
The cloth-creeper covers it.
Oh, happy is our lord;
Blessings and boons protect him!

In the south is a tree with drooping boughs;
The cloth-creeper encircles it.
Oh, happy is our lord;
Blessings and boons surround him!

"Magic Tower"

TRANSLATED BY ARTHUR WALEY

When he built the Magic Tower,
When he planned it and founded it,
All the people worked at it;
In less than a day they finished it.

When he built it, there was no goading;
Yet the people came in their throngs.
The king was in the Magic Park,
Where doe and stag lay hid.

Doe and stag at his coming leapt and bounded;
The white herons gleamed so sleek.
The king was by the Magic Pool,
Where the fish sprang so lithe.

On the upright posts and cross-beams with their spikes
Hang the big drums and gongs.
Oh, well-ranged are the drums and gongs,
And merry is the Moated Mound.

Oh, well-ranged are the drums and gongs!
And merry is the Moated Mound.
Bang, bang go the fish-skin drums;
The sightless and the eyeless[2] ply their skill.

Songs of the South (Chuci 楚辭)

"On Encountering Trouble" (Li sao 離騷; extract) and "The Fisherman" (Yufu 漁父)

ATTRIBUTED TO QU YUAN 屈原 (?340–278 BCE)
TRANSLATED BY DAVID HAWKES

After the *Classic of Poetry*, the *Songs of the South* (or *Songs of Chu*, a state in the Yangtze valley region, far to the south of the "cradle of Chinese civilization" in the Yellow River valley) is the second great collection of early poetry. Rich in natural imagery, it is believed to reflect a shamanistic culture very different from that of the Yellow River area. The collection was traditionally associated with the figure of Qu Yuan, supposedly a government minister who suffered slander and, alienated from his sovereign, drowned himself in the Miluo River (whose waters ultimately join the Yangtze). The narrator of the very long poem "On Encountering Trouble," or "Encountering Sorrow" (only a brief extract is given here), goes on a shamanistic spirit journey to find an ideal sovereign, represented as a fair lady (actually the Chinese term *meiren* does not specify gender, but the term is most often used of women). His own fine qualities and the dastardly qualities of his enemies are represented by beautiful flowers and noxious weeds. The second poem here, "The Fisherman," consists of a dialogue between the legendary figure Qu Yuan and an anonymous fisherman, who ends by reciting a jingle about the Canglang's waters that means the gentleman should adapt to circumstances (see the explanation given in the introduction to chapter 5). This rhyme, which also occurs in the *Mencius* (see below), became a standard allusion, frequently used by later writers.

"On Encountering Trouble" (extract)

The age is disordered in a tumult of changing:
How can I tarry much longer among them?
Orchid and iris have lost all their fragrance;
Flag and melilotus have changed into straw.
Why have all the fragrant flowers of days gone by
Now all transformed themselves into worthless mugwort?
What other reason can there be for this
But that they all have no more care for beauty?

---

2   Blind musicians.

I thought that orchid was one to be trusted,
But he proved a sham, bent only on pleasing his masters.
He overcame his goodness and conformed to evil counsels:
He no more deserves to rank with fragrant flowers.
Pepper is all wagging tongue and lives only for slander;
And even stinking dogwood seeks to fill a perfume bag.
Since they only seek advancement and labor for position,
What fragrance have they deserving our respect?

"The Fisherman"

After Qu Yuan was banished,
He wandered sometimes along the river banks, sometimes along the marsh's edge,
    singing as he went.
His expression was dejected and his features emaciated.
A fisherman caught sight of him.
"Are you not the Lord of the Three Wards?" said the fisherman.
"What has brought you to this pass?"
"Because all the world is muddy and I alone am clear," said Qu Yuan,
"And because all men are drunk and I alone am sober,
I have been sent into exile."
"The Wise Man is not chained to material circumstances," said
the fisherman, "but can move as the world moves.
If all the world is muddy, why not help them stir up the mud
and beat up the waves?
And if all men are drunk, why not sup their dregs and swill their
lees?
Why get yourself exiled because of your deep thoughts and your
fine aspirations?"
Qu Yuan replied, "I have heard it said:
'He who has just washed his hair should brush his hat; and he
who has just bathed should shake his clothes.'
How can I submit my spotless purity to the dirt of others?
I would rather cast myself into the waters of the river and be
buried in the bowels of fishes,
than hide my shining light in the dark and dust of the world."
The fisherman, with a faint smile, struck his paddle in the water
and made off.
And as he went he sang: "When the Canglang's waters are
clear, I can wash my hat-strings in them;
When the Canglang's waters are muddy, I can wash my feet in them."
With that he was gone, and did not speak again.

Analects (*Lunyu* 論語)

VI:21: The pleasure of the mountains and rivers; XIII:4: An old gardener; XVII:9: *Book of Songs*; and XVIII:6: Changju and Jieni

ATTRIBUTED TO CONFUCIUS (KONG QIU 孔丘, CA. 551–CA. 479 BCE)
TRANSLATED BY JAMES LEGGE

The *Analects* of Confucius is one of the foundational texts of the Confucian tradition. It was compiled, possibly around 400 BCE, by followers of Confucius, not by the philosopher himself. As it was learned by heart by every educated Chinese person, the Master's (Confucius's) pithy sayings were familiar to all. The idea of the wise finding pleasure in water and the virtuous (or benevolent) finding pleasure in hills or mountains is alluded to innumerable times in writings on gardens and landscapes. As in other pieces without Chinese titles, these extracts have been given English titles for convenience of reference; they are not titled in the original text.

VI:21: The pleasure of the mountains and rivers

The Master said, "The wise find pleasure in water; the virtuous find pleasure in hills. The wise are active; the virtuous are tranquil. The wise are joyful; the virtuous are long-lived."

XIII:4: An old gardener

Fan Chi requested to be taught husbandry. The Master said, "I am not so good for that as an old husbandman." He requested also to be taught gardening, and was answered, "I am not so good for that as an old gardener."

XVII:9: *Book of Songs*

The Master said, "My children, why do you not study the *Book of Poetry*? The *Odes* serve to stimulate the mind. They may be used for purposes of self-contemplation. They teach the art of sociability. They show how to regulate feelings of resentment. From them you learn the more immediate duty of serving one's father, and the remoter one of serving one's prince. From them we become largely acquainted with the names of birds, beasts, and plants."

XVIII:6: Changju and Jieni

Changju and Jieni were at work in the field together, when Confucius passed by them, and sent Zilu to inquire for the ford.

Changju said, "Who is he that holds the reins in the carriage there?" Zilu told him, "It is Kong Qiu." "Is it not Kong Qiu of Lu?" asked he. "Yes," was the reply, to which the other rejoined, "He knows the ford."

Zilu then inquired of Jieni, who said to him, "Who are you, Sir?" He answered, "I am Zhong You." "Are you not the disciple of Kong Qiu of Lu?" asked the other. "I am," replied he, and then Jieni said to him, "Disorder, like a swelling flood, spreads over the whole empire, and who is he that will change its state for you? Than follow one who merely withdraws from this one and that one, had you not better follow those who have withdrawn from the world altogether?" With this he fell to covering up the seed, and proceeded with his work, without stopping.

Zhuangzi 莊子

Chapter 1: "Free and Easy Wandering" (*Xiaoyao you* 逍遙遊; extract); Chapter 12: "Heaven and Earth" (*Tiandi* 天地; extract); and Chapter 17: "Autumn Floods" (*Qiushui* 秋水; extracts)

ATTRIBUTED TO ZHUANG ZHOU 莊周 (CA. 369–CA. 286 BCE)
TRANSLATED BY BURTON WATSON

The philosophical work known as the *Zhuangzi* (*Master Zhuang*) is associated with the Daoist philosopher Zhuang Zhou, but it was probably formed over a period of time from the work of various authors. Its value is literary as much as philosophical, much of it being of the highest literary merit. The use of fables to express philosophical ideas has provided Chinese culture with a treasury of memorable stories that are constantly referred to in later writings. The idea of the value of the useless, expressed in the first passage below, was used to justify withdrawal from the competitive world of officialdom and the cultivation of the apparently unproductive space of the garden. The debate on whether one can know whether fish are happy (see the third extract) became a topos in garden culture, and, together, the two stories of the happy fish and the tortoise (or turtle) that drags its tail in the mud provide the source of constant allusions to the rivers Hao and Pu, as represented in garden watercourses.

Chapter 1: "Free and Easy Wandering" (extract)

Huizi said to Zhuangzi, "I have a big tree of the kind men call *shu*. Its trunk is too gnarled and bumpy to apply a measuring line to, its branches too bent and twisty to match up to a compass or square. You could stand it by the road and no carpenter would look at it twice. Your words, too, are big and useless, and so everyone alike spurns them!" Zhuangzi said, "Maybe you've never seen a wildcat or a weasel. It crouches down and hides, watching for something to come along. It leaps and races east and west, not hesitating to go high or low—until it falls into the trap and dies in the net. Then again there's the yak, big as a cloud covering the sky. It certainly knows how to be big, though it doesn't know how to catch rats. Now you have this big tree and you're distressed because it's useless. Why don't you plant it in Not-Even-Anything Village, or the field of Broad-and-Boundless, relax and do nothing by its side, or lie down for a free and easy sleep under it? Axes will never shorten its life, nothing can ever harm it. If there's no use for it, how can it come to grief or pain?"

Chapter 12: "Heaven and Earth" (extract)

Zigong traveled south to Chu, and on his way back through Jin, as he passed along the south bank of the Han, he saw an old man preparing his fields for planting. He had hollowed out an opening by which he entered the well and from which he emerged, lugging a pitcher, which he carried out to water the fields. Grunting and puffing, he used up a great deal of energy and produced very little result.

"There is a machine for this sort of thing," said Zigong. "In one day it can water a hundred fields, demanding very little effort and producing excellent results. Wouldn't you like one?"

The gardener raised his head and looked at Zigong. "How does it work?"

"It's a contraption made by shaping a piece of wood. The back end is heavy and the front end light and it raises the water as though it were pouring it out, so fast that it seems to boil right over! It's called a well sweep."

The gardener flushed with anger and then said with a laugh, "I've heard my teacher say, where there are machines, there are bound to be machine worries; where there are machine worries, there are bound to be machine hearts. With a machine heart in your breast, you've spoiled what was pure and simple, and without the pure and simple, the life of the spirit knows no rest. Where the life of the spirit knows no rest, the Way will cease to buoy you up. It's not that I don't know about your machine—I would be ashamed to use it!"

Zigong blushed with chagrin, looked down, and made no reply. After a while, the gardener said, "Who are you, anyway?"

"A disciple of Kong Qiu [Confucius]."

"Oh,—then you must be one of those who broaden their learning in order to ape the sages, heaping absurd nonsense on the crowd, plucking the strings and singing sad songs all by yourself in hopes of buying fame in the world! You would do best to forget your spirit and breath, break up your body and limbs—then you might be able to get somewhere. You don't even know how to look after your own body—how do you have any time to think about looking after the world! On your way now! Don't interfere with my work!"

Chapter 17: "Autumn Floods" (extracts)

Once, when Zhuangzi was fishing in the Pu River, the king of Chu sent two officials to go and announce to him: "I would like to trouble you with the administration of my realm."

Zhuangzi held on to the fishing pole and, without turning his head, said, "I have heard that there is a sacred tortoise in Chu that has been dead for three thousand years. The king keeps it wrapped in cloth and boxed, and stores it in the ancestral temple. Now would this tortoise rather be dead and have its bones left behind and honored? Or would it rather be alive and dragging its tail in the mud?"

"It would rather be alive and dragging its tail in the mud," said the two officials.

Zhuangzi said, "Go away! I'll drag my tail in the mud!"

Zhuangzi and Huizi were strolling along the dam of the Hao River when Zhuangzi said, "See how the minnows come out and dart around where they please! That's what fish really enjoy!"

Huizi said, "You're not a fish—how do you know what fish enjoy?"

Zhuangzi said, "You're not I, so how do you know I don't know what fish enjoy?"

Huizi said, "I'm not you, so I certainly don't know what you know. On the other hand, you're certainly not a fish—so that still proves you don't know what fish enjoy!"

Zhuangzi said, "Let's go back to your original question, please. You asked me *how* I know what fish enjoy—so you already knew I knew it when you asked the question. I know it by standing here beside the Hao."

Mencius (*Mengzi* 孟子)

IA:2: King Wen's park; IB:2: King Wen's park; IB:1: The king's love of music; IVA:8: Canglang water; and VIA:8: Ox mountain

ATTRIBUTED TO MENCIUS (MENG KE 孟克, 372–289 BCE)
TRANSLATED BY JAMES LEGGE

After the pithy and often cryptic *Analects* of Confucius (see above), the *Mencius* (*Mengzi* or *Master Meng*) is the earliest surviving work of explicitly "Confucian" philosophy. As with the *Analects*, it was compiled by disciples of Mencius, not written by the Master himself. Unlike some of his contemporaries, Mencius believed in the fundamental goodness of human nature, and continued Confucius's doctrine of government by moral force (*de*) rather than by coercion. His insistence that rulers should not alienate land from the people and should "share their pleasure" in gardens and landscapes provided an ethical underpinning for later garden culture (for an alternative translation of the poem on King Wen's park from the *Book of Songs*, see "Magic Tower" above). His critique of the over-exploitation of Ox mountain has sometimes been cited in modern times as an early instance of environmentalism, though Mencius was in fact talking about moral cultivation.

IA:2: King Wen's park

Mencius, another day, saw King Hui of Liang. The king went and stood with him by a pond, and looking round at the large geese and deer, said, "Do wise and good princes also find pleasure in these things?" Mencius replied, "Being wise and good, they have pleasure in these things. If they are not wise and good, though they have these things, they do not feel pleasure. It is said in the *Book of Poetry*,

He measured out and commenced his marvelous tower;
He measured it out and planned it.
The people addressed themselves to it,
And in less than a day completed it.
When he measured and began it, he said to them—be not so earnest:
But the multitudes came as if they had been his children.
The king was in his marvelous park;
The does reposed about,
The does so sleek and fat:
And the white birds shone glistening.
The king was by his marvelous pond;
How full was it of fishes leaping about!

King Wen used the strength of the people to make his tower and his pond, and yet the people rejoiced to do the work, calling the tower 'the marvelous tower,' calling the pond 'the marvelous pond,' and rejoicing that he had his large deer, his fishes, and turtles. The ancients caused the people to have pleasure as well as themselves, and therefore they could enjoy it."

1B:2: King Wen's park

The King Xuan of Qi asked, "Was it so, that the park of King Wen contained seventy square *li*?" Mencius replied, "It is so in the records." "Was it so large as that?" exclaimed the king. "The people," said Mencius, "still looked on it as small." The king added, "My park contains only forty square *li*, and the people still look on it as large. How is this?" "The park of King Wen," was the reply, "contained seventy square *li*, but the grass-cutters and fuel gatherers had the privilege of entrance into it; so also had the catchers of pheasants and hares. He shared it with the people, and was it not with reason that they looked on it as small?"

1B:1: The king's love of music

Zhuang Bao, seeing Mencius, said to him, "I had an interview with the king. His Majesty told me that he loved music, and I was not prepared with anything to reply to him. What do you pronounce about that love of music?" Mencius replied, "If the king's love of music were very great, the kingdom of Qi would be near to a state of good government!"

Another day, Mencius, having an interview with the king, said, "Your Majesty, I have heard, told the officer Zhuang, that you love music;—was it so?" The king changed color, and said, "I am unable to love the music of the ancient sovereigns; I only love the music that suits the manners of the present age."

Mencius said, "If your Majesty's love of music were very great, Qi would be near to a state of good government! The music of the present day is just like the music of antiquity, as regards effecting that."

The king said, "May I hear from you the proof of that?" Mencius asked, "Which is more pleasant,—to enjoy music by yourself alone, or to enjoy it with others?" "To enjoy it with others," was the reply. "And which is the more pleasant,—to enjoy music with a few, or to enjoy it with many?" "To enjoy it with many."

Mencius proceeded, "Your servant begs to explain what I have said about music to your Majesty.

"Now, your Majesty is having music here.—The people hear the noise of your bells and drums, and the notes of your fifes and pipes, and they all, with aching heads, knit their brows, and say to one another, 'That's how our king likes his music! But why does he reduce us to this extremity of distress?—Fathers and sons cannot see one another. Elder brothers and younger brothers, wives and children, are separated and scattered abroad.' Now, your Majesty is hunting here.—The people hear the noise of your carriages and horses, and see the beauty of your plumes and streamers, and they all, with aching heads, knit their brows, and say to one another, 'That's how our king likes his hunting! But why does he reduce us to this extremity of distress?—Fathers and sons cannot see one another. Elder brothers and younger brothers, wives and children are separated and scattered abroad.' Their feeling thus is from no other reason but that you do not allow the people to have pleasure as well as yourself.

"Now, your Majesty is having music here. The people hear the noise of your bells and drums, and the notes of your fifes and pipes, and they all, delighted, and with joyful looks say to one another, 'That sounds as if our king were free from all sickness! If he were not, how could he enjoy this music?' Now, your Majesty is hunting here.—The people hear the noise of your carriages and horses, and see the beauty of your plumes and streamers, and they all, delighted, and with joyful looks, say to one another, 'That looks as if our king were free from all sickness! If he were not, how could he enjoy this hunting?' Their feeling thus is from no other reason but that you cause them to have their pleasure as you have yours.

"If your Majesty now will make pleasure a thing common to the people and yourself, the royal sway awaits you."

IVA:8: Canglang water

Mencius said, "How is it possible to speak with those princes who are not benevolent? Their perils they count safety, their calamities they count profitable, and they have pleasure in the things by which they perish. If it were possible to talk with them who so violate benevolence, how could we have such destruction of States and ruin of Families? There was a boy singing,

'When the water of the Canglang is clear,
  It does to wash the strings of my cap;
When the water of the Canglang is muddy,
  It does to wash my feet.'

Confucius said, 'Hear what he sings, my children. When clear, then he will wash his cap-strings; and when muddy, he will wash his feet with it. This different application is brought by the water on itself.' A man must first despise himself, and then others will despise him. A family must first destroy itself, and then others will destroy it. A State must first smite itself, and then others will smite it. This is illustrated in the passage in the Tai Jia, 'When Heaven sends down calamities, it is still possible to escape them. When we occasion the calamities ourselves, it is not possible any longer to live.'"

VIA:8: Ox mountain

Mencius said, "The trees of Ox mountain were once beautiful. Being situated, however, in the borders of a large State, they were hewn down with axes and bills;—and could they retain their beauty? Still through the activity of the vegetative life day and night, and the nourishing influence of the rain and dew, they were not without buds and sprouts springing forth, but then came the cattle and goats and browsed upon them. To these things is owing the bare and stripped appearance of the mountain, and when people now see it, they think it was never finely wooded. But is this the nature of the mountain?"

The Guideways through Mountains and Seas (*Shanhai jing* 山海經)

The plateau garden of the supreme god

ANONYMOUS (4TH–1ST CENTURY BCE)
TRANSLATED BY RICHARD E. STRASSBERG

The Guideways through Mountains and Seas was traditionally attributed to the culture-hero Yu, who regulated the waters. The present text was edited in the Han dynasty, but the earliest portions probably date from around 320 BCE. It takes the form of a mythical geography of the known or semi-known world, including much ancient mythology and folklore. It was later seen as an early instance of "recording the strange" (*zhiguai*) or the literature of the supernatural. As in the extract below, it could provide marvelous descriptions of legendary gardens, analogous to the Garden of the Hesperides or the Garden of Eden in other cultural traditions. Mount Kunlun, mentioned in this extract, was later identified with the Buddhist *axis mundi*, Mount Kailas or Mount Meru, and was often evoked in connection with garden rocks ("mountains").

The plateau garden of the supreme god

Three hundred twenty *li* farther west [along the third guideway through the Western Mountains] is Sophora River Mountain. The Qiushi River emanates from it, flows north into the You River, and contains many snails. On the mountain's heights is much green realgar, the finest quality of Langgan-Stone, yellow gold, and jade. On its southern slope are many grains of cinnabar, while on its northern slope are much glittering yellow gold and silver. This place is actually the location of the Supreme God's Plateau Garden. Yingshao is in charge of it. His form resembles the body of a horse with a human face, tiger's stripes, and bird's wings. Yingshao travels a circuit through the Four Seas and makes a sound like someone reciting texts. This mountain provides a view south toward Mount Kunlun, whose aura is fiery brilliant and whose energy is powerfully abundant. To the west is a view of the Grand Lake where Lord Millet is buried. In the middle of it is much jade, while along its southern banks are many giant Yao-Trees from whose tops grow many Ruo-Trees. To the north is a view of Mount Zhubi, where Lilun, the Sophora Tree Demon, resides. It is also the dwelling place of hawks and falcons. To the east is a view of the four levels of Constancy Mountain. The Exhausted Demons reside here, each group occupying a corner of the mountain. There is also the Overflowing River, whose water is clear and flows freely. There is a celestial god here whose form resembles an ox with eight feet, two heads, and a horse's tail. He makes a buzzing sound like a beetle. If seen by people, it is an omen of war in the town.

Four hundred *li* farther southwest is Mount Kunlun. It is actually the earthly capital of the Supreme God. The god Luwu administers it. His divine form resembles a tiger's body with nine tails, a human face, and tiger's claws. This god administers the nine regions of heaven as well as the cycle of four seasons in the Supreme God's garden. There is an animal here with the form of a goat but with four horns called the Tulou that devours men. There is a bird here with the form of a bee, as large as a mandarin duck called the Qinyuan. If it stings a bird or animal, it dies; if it stings a tree, it withers. There is a bird here called the Quail-Bird, which is in charge of the Supreme God's stored treasures. There is a tree here similar to the pear with yellow blossoms and red fruits with the taste of a plum but without pits called the Sand-Pear. It can protect against floods, and eating it can prevent drowning. There is a plant here called the Pin-Plant whose form resembles a sunflower but with the taste of a scallion. Eating it will alleviate fatigue. The Yellow River emanates from here and flows south, then east to Never-Reach River. The Red River emanates from here and flows southeast into the River That Floods Heaven. The Oceanic River emanates from here and flows southwest into the Ugly Mire River. The Black River emanates from here and flows west into the Dayu River. Here, there are many strange birds and animals.

Miscellaneous Records of the Western Capital (*Xijing zaji* 西京雜記)

Palace of dazzling glory and Yuan Guanghan's garden

ATTRIBUTED TO GE HONG 葛洪 (283–343)

TRANSLATED BY DUNCAN M. CAMPBELL

The *Miscellaneous Records of the Western Capital* forms a sort of history of the Former Han dynasty, when the capital was located at Chang'an (present-day Xi'an); this is idealized as a time of stability from the perspective of a later, more chaotic era. The content, however, is more varied than in a formal dynastic history, thus providing a rich resource for later anthologists. Although sometimes attributed to the philosopher and recluse Ge Hong, or to an earlier author of a manuscript owned by his family, it probably dates in its present form to around 500 CE. The description of the garden of Prince Xiao of Liang recalls Mencius's comments on the garden of King Hui of Liang (though Prince Xiao was a member of the Han imperial house, not a descendant of the Liang rulers). The garden of Yuan Guanghan suggests the rise of commercial wealth in the relatively stable economic and political conditions of the Former Han; his position can be compared with that of Shi Chong (see below) in the subsequent Jin dynasty.

Palace of dazzling glory

Prince Xiao of Liang was addicted to the pleasures of constructing palaces and chambers, parks, and gardens. He ordered built the Palace of Dazzling Glory; he had laid out Hare Garden. In the midst of the garden rose a hundred numinous mountains, upon which were to be found the Minute Rock, Falling Gibbons Craig, and the Cavern for Roosting Dragons. The garden contained also Wild Goose Pond, within which were found Crane Isle and Wild Duck Sandbank. His various palaces and monasteries stretched continuously for several dozen *li* and contained a complete inventory of all the most unusual fruits, rare trees, weird birds, and strange animals. Here, daily, the master would sit fishing, accompanied by his palace retainers and his guests.

Yuan Guanghan's garden

Yuan Guanghan, a rich man of Maoling, had accumulated wealth of inestimable proportions. His serving boys alone numbered eight to nine hundred. In the foothills of North Mang Mountain he built for himself a garden, four *li* from west to east, five *li* from north to south, and through which flowed a rapid stream. Rocks were shaped to form a mountain range more than ten *zhang* high and which extended for several *li*. In his garden he raised white cockatoos and purple mandarin ducks, black oxen and blue rhinoceros, and all sorts of strange animals and weird birds. Sand was piled up to form islands and the flowing stream was forced to billow waves. Into the garden he introduced river terns and sea cranes, pregnant hens and chirping fledglings, and the extensive forest and large pond was dense with rare trees and unusual plants. Numerous buildings abutted each other, and such were his tall towers and long galleries that one could not hope to explore them all before the shadows began to gather around one. Later on, Yuan Guanghan was sentenced to death for a crime. His garden was confiscated and became part of the imperial gardens, and all his birds and animals were taken to live in the Upper Forest Park, and his plants and trees, too, were transplanted there.

"Rhapsody on the Western Capital" (*Xijing fu* 西京賦)

Shanglin Park

ZHANG HENG 張衡 (78–139)
TRANSLATED BY DAVID R. KNECHTGES

The "rhapsody" or "rhyme-prose" (*fu*) is a characteristic literary genre of the Han dynasty. The meter is irregular, thus distinguishing the genre from poetry with the more widely used regular meter of four or five syllables (characters) to a line, while the use of rhyme distinguishes it from prose. The *fu*, which is at least partly a development of the *sao* (elegy) form employed in the *Songs of the South* (see above), is characterized by its length and by the extravagance of the language, with much use of obscure names of birds, beasts, and plants. *Fu* were often presented to the ruler as a way to honor him, and they might also have an admonitory function (for example, warning against extravagance). That appears to be one of the functions of the following work by Zhang Heng, which describes the luxurious life of the former capital city, Chang'an (present-day Xi'an); by Zhang Heng's time, the capital had been moved east to Luoyang, following the brief seizure of power by Wang Mang (r. 9–23) that divided the Former (Western) Han from the Later (Eastern) Han dynasty. Zhang Heng is here following the example of an earlier poet, Sima Xiangru (179–117 BCE), who wrote on the Shanglin Park at the height of the Western Han. The Shanglin Park was the imperial park, used particularly as a game reserve for imperial hunts; a description of the hunt follows the introductory section that appears here. Zhang Heng was a distinguished writer of *fu*, but is also known as a great mathematician and astronomer.

Shanglin Park

The forbidden Shanglin Park,
Straddling valleys, covering hills,
Ranging eastward to Tripod Lake,
Diagonally intersecting Delicate Willows,
Enclosed Tall Poplars, annexed Five Oaks,
Enfolded the Yellow Mountain, reached Ox Head.

The encircling walls stretched continuously,
Four hundred *li* and more.
Plants here did grow;
Animals here did rest.
Flocks of birds fluttered about,
Herds of beasts galloped and raced.
They scattered like startled waves,
Gathered like tall islands in the sea.
Bo Yi would have been unable to name them;
Li Shou would have been unable to count them.[3]
The riches of the groves and forests—
In what were they lacking?

As for trees, there were:
    Fir, juniper, windmill palm, *nanmu*,
    Catalpa, cudrania, elm, and liquidambar.
    Beautiful vegetation grew in thick clumps,
    As lush as Deng Grove.[4]
    Luxuriant and dense, verdant and bosky,
    They rose straight and tall, towering upward,
    Spewing blossoms, sending forth blooms,
    Spreading leaves, casting shadows.

As for plants, there were:
    Wood sorrel, nutgrass, eulalia, wool grass,
    Vetch, bracken, iris,
    Arthraxon, frittilary, carex,
    Hollyhock, and *huaiyang*.
    They grew in clusters, overgrown and rank,
    Covering the swamp margins, blanketing the ridges.
    Arrow bamboo and giant bamboo thickly spread,
    Forming fields and groves.
    Mountains and valleys, plains and bogs,
    Were boundless, without limit.

---

3   Bo Yi was a minister to the Emperor Shun. He accompanied the Great Yu to the Northern Sea and helped him identify the animals they encountered on the trip. See *Liezi* 5.54. The lost *Shi ben* (Genealogical Origins), a record of the great noble families and dignitaries of ancient China, says Li Shou made mathematical computations for the Yellow Lord. See *Shiji* 26.1256, n.2.

4   Deng Grove (*Deng lin*) was formed from the staff of the great Kuafu. Kuafu tried to race the sun. He became thirsty and drank the Yellow and Wei Rivers dry without quenching his thirst. He then went north to drink from the Great Marsh, but died of thirst before he arrived. His discarded staff turned into the thick forest known as Deng Grove. See *Shanhai jing* 8.2b.

Then, there was

    The divine pool of Kunming,

    With its Black Water and Dark Foot shrine.[5]

    It was surrounded by a "metal" dike,[6]

    Planted with weeping willow and purple osier.

    The precious Camphor Lodge[7]

    Thrusting itself upward, rose from the middle of the pond.

    The Oxherd stood on the left;

    The Weaving Maid occupied the right.[8]

    The sun and moon exited and entered here,

    Just like Fusang and the Murky Shore.[9]

Within it there were:

    Giant soft-shelled turtles, alligators, and the monstrous trionyx,

    Sturgeon, carp, whitefish, ide,

    Paddlefish, giant salamanders, golden catfish, gobies.

    With their long foreheads, short necks,

    Large mouths, cleft snouts,

    They were most amazing creatures, most unusual species.

---

5   The "Celestial Questions" of the *Chu ci* (*Songs of the South*) alludes to two mythical places called the Black Water (Hei shui) and Dark Isle (Xuan zhi). Wang Yi says that Dark Isle was the name of a mountain in the west. See *Chu ci buzhu* (Hong Kong: Zhonghua shuju, 1963), 3.9a. He identifies Black Water as a river that flowed out of the Kunlun Mountains. Hong Xingzu (*Chu ci buzhu* 3.9a) quotes Zheng Heng's line and says that the Kunming Pond had replicas of the Black Water and Dark Isle. The Dian Lake of the southwest had a Black Water Shrine (see *Han shu* 28A.1601) and presumably this was replicated at the Kunming Pond.

6   The metal dike (*Jin di*) was actually made of stone. See Xue Zong (*Wen xuan* 2.65). The term "metal" is metaphorical and indicates only that the dike was strong.

7   The Camphor Viewing Tower (Yuzhang guan), also known as the Kunming Viewing Tower, was built in the lake. The emperor used it for entertaining court guests and observing performances of various sorts that were staged in the lake. See *Sanfu huangtu* 4.69–71, 5.92.

8   There were stone replicas of the mythical lovers Oxherd (Qian niu) and Weaving Maid (Zhi nü). Oxherd was located on the eastern shore, and Weaving Maid on the western shore. This presumably was intended to represent the myth of the separation of the constellations, Oxherd (Altair) and Weaving Maid (Vega), that occupied opposite sides of the Han in the Clouds, the bright "Sky River" known in the West as the Milky Way. They were allowed to meet only once a year, on the seventh day of the seventh moon, when a flock of magpies formed a bridge for them to cross the river. See *Sanfu huangtu* 4.4a.

9   Fusang, also known as the Fu tree, is the name of a "solar tree" above the Dawn Valley (Yang gu) at the extreme eastern limits of the world. According to accounts preserved in the *Shanhai jing* (*Guideways to Mountains and Seas*), the ten suns bathed on the Fusang tree. Nine suns remained on the lower branches, while one rested on top (9.3a–b). As soon as one sun arrived on a branch, another left. Each sun carried a three-legged crow (l 4.5a–b). The Murky Shore (Meng si), also known as Murky Valley (Meng gu; see *Huainanzi* 3.10b), is the depression into which the sun sinks at the end of the day. See "Celestial Questions," *Chu ci buzhu* 3.10b.

As for birds, there were:
>
> Turquoise kingfishers, gray cranes, bustards,
> Wild geese and the great fowl.
> At the first of spring they came to visit;
> In late autumn they headed for warmer climes.
> South they flew to Hengyang;
> North they nested at Yanmen.
> The swift peregrines, the homing mallards,
> Flapped their wings with an uproarious din.
> Their various forms and diverse sounds
> Cannot be completely described.

A New Account of Tales of the World (*Shishuo xinyu* 世說新語)

Chapter 2: "Speech and Conversation" (*Yanyu* 言語; item 61 and item 91)

LIU YIQING 劉義慶 (403–444)
TRANSLATED BY RICHARD B. MATHER

A New Account of Tales of the World, compiled in ca. 430 under the patronage of Liu Yiqing, a prince of the Liu Song dynasty (420–479), is a collection of anecdotes about notable people who lived mostly in the Eastern Jin (317–420) during the period between the end of the Later (Eastern) Han (206–220) and the foundation of Liu Song. The tales are divided into categories such as "Virtuous Conduct," "Speech and Conversation" (as here), "Reclusion and Disengagement," and "The Free and Unrestrained." Emperor Jianwen of the Eastern Jin dynasty, whose personal name was Sima Yu (320–372), reigned briefly from 371 to his death in 372. Wang Xianzhi (344–386) was a son of the "Sage of Calligraphy" Wang Xizhi (303–361; see below) and was sometimes thought to surpass his father's skill in calligraphy.

Chapter 2: "Speech and Conversation," item 61

On entering the Flowery Grove Park Emperor Jianwen looked around and remarked to his attendants, "The spot which suits the mind isn't necessarily far away. By any shady grove or stream one may quite naturally have such thoughts as Zhuangzi had by the Rivers Hao and Pu, where unselfconsciously birds and animals, fowls and fish, come of their own accord to be intimate with men."

Chapter 2: "Speech and Conversation," item 91

Wang Xianzhi said, "Whenever I travel by the Shanyin road [in Kuaiji Commandery], the hills and streams naturally complement each other in such a way that I can't begin to describe them. And especially if it's at the turning point between autumn and winter, I find it all the harder to express what's in my heart."

"Rhapsody on Living in Idleness" (*Xianju fu* 閒居賦; extracts)

PAN YUE 潘岳 (PAN ANREN 潘安仁; 247–300)

TRANSLATED BY DAVID R. KNECHTGES

In the following rhapsody (*fu*), Pan Yue, an official of the Jin dynasty until he met his death by execution, recounts his disillusionment with official service and expresses delight at retirement to his country estate. Other sources suggest that Pan was, in fact, highly ambitious, and far from happy to withdraw to the countryside. Such claims of pleasure in retirement, which are often to be found in later writers, must always be regarded with some suspicion.

Pan begins with a long prose introduction that contains a detailed account of the various offices he held before he took up a brief retirement between 295 and 297. The rhapsody is one of the main sources from which we can now reconstruct important events in Pan Yue's life. In the rhymed portion of the piece, he first provides a description of the capital, Luoyang, including its ritual buildings, military headquarters, and educational institutions. He then follows with a delightful account of his villa in the Luoyang suburbs, with its orchards and vegetable garden. His concept of living a retired life in one's garden as "the way the inept person engages in government" or "the administration of the artless" became a topos of garden culture; it is alluded to, for example, in the name of one of the best-known "classical" gardens in China, the Artless Administrator's Garden in Suzhou, also known as the Humble Administrator's Garden or Garden of the Unsuccessful Politician (*Zhuozheng yuan*), although it can be seen from Pan Yue's words that these latter translations are not entirely appropriate.

"Rhapsody on Living in Idleness" (extracts)

From the time I took the youth cap until the age when I commenced "to understand fate,"[10] I changed positions eight times. I once advanced in rank, and twice resigned. I once had my name removed from the official roster, and I once was unable to accept a position. Three times was I transferred. Although my successes and failures have something to do with fate, I rather believe what happened to me is the result of my ineptitude....

... Thereupon, having seen the measure of knowing enough and knowing where to stop, I hope that my desires may become like drifting clouds. I have built a house and planted trees where I may roam and ramble in self-contentment. My ponds are sufficient for fishing, and the income from grain-husking can take the place of tilling the land. I water my garden, sell vegetables in order to supply food for my morning and evening meals. I raise sheep and sell dairy products in order to anticipate the expenses of the summer and winter offerings. Oh, to be filial above all else and to be amicable with one's brothers is the way the inept person engages in government. Thus I have now written this "Rhapsody on Living in Idleness" in order to sing of my situation and express my feelings. The piece goes:

---

10   This indicates the age of fifty, according to Confucius.

I

I have roamed the long orchards of the canons and scriptures,
Strolled the lofty courses of the ancient sages,
And thick skinned though I may be,
Within I blush before Ning and Qu.[11]
When the Way prevails I do not serve;
When the Way does not prevail, I do not feign stupidity.
How insufficient my shrewdness and guile!
What a surplus of ineptitude and misfortune!

IV

And now I have established my abode,
Built a house, and dug a pond.
Tall poplars reflect in the pools,
Fragrant spiny lime bushes are planted as a hedge.
Playful fish splash and leap,
Lotus blossoms unfold and spread.
Bamboo trees are lush and luxuriant,
There are wondrous fruits of assorted kinds:
The pears of Sir Zhang's Great Valley,
The varnish persimmons of the Marquis of Liang,
The soft-branch jujubes of King Wen of Zhou,
The plums of Zhu Zhong of Fangling,
All have been planted here.

The three *tao*[12] mark the difference between cherry and walnut;
The two sour apples glisten with hues of crimson and white.
Such rarities of pomegranate and grape,
Drooping heavily, spread out at their side.
Black plum, apricot, dwarf cherry,
Are dressed in profuse blooms and pretty patterns.
Flowers and fruit glisten so brightly
Words cannot completely describe them.

---

11 According to the *Analects* v.20, "The Master said, 'When good order prevailed in his country, Ning Wu acted the part of a wise man. When his country was in disorder, he acted the part of a stupid man'"; and in xv.6, "'A superior man indeed is Qu Boyu! When good government prevails in his state, he is to be found in office. When bad government prevails, he can roll his principles up and keep them in his breast.'" *The Chinese Classics*, vol. 1, *The Confucian Analects, The Great Learning, and the Doctrine of the Mean*, ed. and trans. James Legge (Oxford: Clarendon Press, 1893–1895), 180, 296 (transliteration altered).

12 Editor's note: the word *tao* on its own is usually translated as "peach," but it is also an element in the Chinese words for cherry (*yingtao*) and walnut (*hetao*).

Of vegetables there are onions, leeks, garlic, taro,
Green bamboo shoots, purple ginger,
Sweet flavors of water dropwort and shepherd's purse,
Pungent aroma of smartweed and cutchery,
Mioga ginger clinging to the shade,
Bean leaves in season facing the sun,
Green mallows laden with dew,
White scallions covered with frost.
And then, in chill autumn, when heat retreats,
And in mellow spring, when cold departs,
When gentle showers have newly lifted,
In the six directions all is clear and bright....

VI

In retirement I seek within to examine myself;
Truly my usefulness is slight and my talents poor.
I hold to Zhou Ren's fine words—
But dare I exert myself and join the ranks?[13]
Barely have I protected my humble self;
How could I emulate the sage and wise?
I look up to the "many wonders" and cut off profane thoughts,
Living carefree, nurturing my ineptness to the end of my days.

"Preface to the Golden Valley Poems" (*Jingu shiji xu* 金谷詩集序)

SHI CHONG 石崇 (249–300)

TRANSLATED BY RICHARD B. MATHER

Shi Chong was a noted man of letters of the Western Jin dynasty (265–316). He rose to high office but eventually fell foul of the factional conflict endemic to government at the time and was executed along with many members of his family. He had become extremely wealthy, allegedly by unsavory means, and the extravagance of his life became legendary. His garden, the Golden Valley, renowned for its luxury, was regarded as the ideal to which the most splendid gardens aspired; it is described in the following passage. Shi Chong's own description of his garden is followed by his biography from the official Jin history, which gives the standard account of his life, with a moralistic reflection on the vanity of riches.

---

13   In the *Analects*, Confucius tells an inquirer, "A saying of Zhou Ren goes, 'He who can exert himself may join the ranks [of officials]'" (*Lunyu* 16.1).

"Preface to the Golden Valley Poems"

In the sixth year of the Yuankang era [296], from the post of grand master of chariots, I set out from Luoyang as commissioner of military affairs in Qing and Xu Provinces [Shandong and northern Anhui and Jiangsu]. I own a villa on the outskirts of Henan Prefecture, by Golden Valley Creek [near Luoyang], with some high and some low ground. There are clear springs and verdant woods, fruit trees, bamboos, cypresses, and various kinds of medicinal herbs, all in great abundance. In addition, there are water mills, fish ponds, caves in the earth, and all things to please the eye and delight the heart.

The libationer and General Chastising the West, Wang Xu, was due to return to Chang'an, so I and the other worthies escorted him as far as the creek. Day and night we roamed about and feasted, each time moving to a different place, sometimes climbing to a height and looking down, sometimes sitting by the water's edge. At times seven- or twenty-five-stringed zithers, mouth organs, and bamboo zithers accompanied us in the carriages, and were played in concert along the road. When we stopped, I had each person perform in turn with the orchestra. Then each one composed a poem to express the sentiments in his heart. Whenever anyone could not do so, he had to pay a forfeit by drinking three dipperfuls of wine. Moved by the impermanence of our lives, and dreading the unappointed hour of falling leaves, I have duly recorded below the offices, names, and ages of those who were present. In addition, I have copied their poems and appended them after the names, in hopes some curiosity-seeker of later times may read them.

History of the Jin Dynasty (*Jinshu* 晉書)

"Biography of Shi Chong" (*Shi Chong zhuan* 石崇傳)

TRANSLATED BY HELMUT WILHELM

After several transfers of office, Shi became Chief of the Cavaliers at Disposal. Emperor Wu, on account of his being the son of a meritorious official and on account of his own great talents, had profound respect for his talents. . . .

While Shi Chong was in the south, he obtained a serpent-eagle and gave it as a present to the General of the Rear, Wang Kai. At that time it was against the rules to transport these birds across the river, and he was impeached by the Colonel Fu Di; but he was exculpated by Imperial mandate. The bird, however, was burned in the Public Market.

Shi Chong was a versatile man and had the spirit of a genius; he was bold and never exercised restraint. When he was at Jingzhou he captured envoys and merchants, and thus he became extremely rich. His resources were boundless. . . . He had a summer resort in Golden Valley north of the river; it was also called Catalpa Pond. Those who accompanied him on his farewell, practically the whole capital, were given a drinking party under specially raised canopies at this place.

When he arrived at his headquarters, he had a drinking bout with the prefect of Xuzhou, Gao Yan, and insulted him. The officer in charge memorialized about it, and Shi was cashiered. Later he was appointed Commander of the Imperial Guard. Together with Pan Yue, he cultivated the acquaintance of the powerful Jia Mi. He became very intimate with Jia, and was known as one of his circle of Twenty-Four Friends. Every time the Lord of Guangcheng [Jia Mi] went out, Shi Chong would descend from his carriage and stand at the left of the road, stare into the dust and do obeisance. This was the extent to which he would humble himself in his flattery.

His personal property was extensive. His mansion was vast and elegant and contained over a hundred women's apartments. All his women were richly clad in silk and embroidery, laden with ear ornaments of gold and jade. His musicians were the finest of their time, and his kitchen served every imaginable delicacy of water and land. With members of the consort clan, such as Wang Kai and Yang Xiu, he competed in the display of luxury. Wang Kai had his pots cleansed with syrup, Shi Chong had his stove fired with wax. Wang Kai produced a canopy made of scarlet silk, measuring forty *li*; Shi Chong produced a canopy of brocade measuring fifty *li*, in order to outdo him. Shi Chong polished his rooms with spices, Wang Kai used clay ointment. This was the way they tried to outdo each other in luxury. Emperor Wu always sided with Wang Kai.

Once the emperor presented Wang Kai with a coral tree over three feet high, luxuriantly branching, such as could hardly be matched in the world. Wang Kai showed it to Shi Chong, who struck it with an iron scepter and broke it with one stroke. Wang Kai was deeply distressed, believing Shi Chong had done it because he envied him his treasure. When Wang Kai raised his voice and showed anger in his face, Shi Chong said: "This is no cause for resentment. I shall presently make amends." Thereupon he ordered his servants to produce all his own coral trees. Among them there were six or seven which were three or four feet high, the span of whose branches surpassed the ordinary and whose luster competed with the sun. There were many to equal the one of Wang Kai. At this Wang Kai was dejected and had to concede defeat...

When it came to the execution of Jia Mi, Shi Chong was dismissed for being of his clique.

At that time the Prince of Zhao, Sima Lun, had usurped the power. Shi Chong's nephew, Ouyang Jian, had a rift with Sima Lun. Shi Chong owned a concubine named Green Pearl, who was of dazzling beauty and knew how to play the flute well. Sun Xiu sent somebody to fetch her away from him. Shi Chong was at the time at his resort in Golden Valley. He had just ascended the terrace to enjoy the landscape, and his women

were at his side. When the messenger had stated his request, Shi Chong had every
one of his slave girls and concubines, several tens of them, led out, and showed them
to the messenger. They were all of them scented with orchid and musk, and dressed
in the finest silk gauze. Shi Chong said to the messenger: "Pick any one of these!" But
the messenger replied: "This certainly is a great display of beauty. I have, however,
received express orders to bring Green Pearl. I would not know which one of these is
her." Whereupon Shi Chong changed his countenance and said: "It happens that I love
Green Pearl. She is not available." The messenger replied: "Your Excellency, you are
conversant with the affairs of past and present, you are equally discerning about affairs
remote and close at hand. I beg you to think this over." "No," insisted Shi Chong. The
messenger departed and returned again; but Shi Chong was adamant.

Sun Xiu, in his anger, induced Sima Lun to have both Shi Chong and Ouyang Jian
executed. But Shi and his nephew learned about their secret plans. Together with the
Imperial Secretary Pan Yue they secretly induced Sima Yun, Prince of Huainan, to
enter into a conspiracy against Sima Lun and Sun Xiu. Sun Xiu, however, got wind of
this and he forged an Imperial mandate to arrest the three of them. Shi Chong was just
having his evening meal in the upper story, when the armed guards arrived at the gate.
He said to Green Pearl: "Now I shall suffer punishment for you." She burst into tears
and said: "It is fitting that I should incur death in front of the officials." Thereupon she
threw herself down from the upper story and died. Shi Chong said: "I shall probably
just be banished to Jiaozhou or Guangzhou." But when the carriage reached the execution ground of the Eastern Market, Shi Chong said with a sigh: "The scoundrels merely
covet my family fortune." The guard answered: "You knew that your wealth would
bring you ruin; why did you not disperse it long ago?" Shi Chong had no reply.

Together with Shi Chong, his mother and older brother, his wife and children irrespec-
tive of their ages, were all put to death. Altogether fifteen people died. Shi Chong was
at that time in his fifty-second year.

"Preface to the Orchid Pavilion Poems" (*Lanting xu* 蘭亭序)

WANG XIZHI 王羲之 (309–CA. 365)
TRANSLATED BY H. C. CHANG

This preface by the great calligrapher Wang Xizhi is famous not just for its literary merit but more
particularly because of its status as one of China's greatest works of running-script (*xingshu*)
calligraphy. In fact, the calligraphy survives only in the form of copies from no earlier than the
Tang dynasty, the original having accompanied the Tang emperor Taizong to his tomb. Wang
Xizhi's family was originally from Shandong, but he settled in Shanyin, now Shaoxing in Zhejiang
Province, in China's prosperous cultural heartland. The "luxuriant woods and tall bamboos"
described by Wang became the sine qua non of any garden. Wang Xizhi's preface speaks not

only of socializing with one's contemporaries but also of diachronic communication and understanding between the literary men of different eras, a theme that provided much comfort to later writers who felt alienated from their own contemporaries—often for the practical reason that, as officials posted to distant parts of the empire, they were literally isolated from any kindred spirits. In connection with the festival of purification or lustration referred to in the text, a ritualized game was played: the participants sat beside a stream along which wine cups were floated; before a cup reached a participant, he had to improvise a poem (or poetic couplet), and if he failed to do so, he was "sconced" by drinking from the cup. This became a game much enjoyed by the elite; later gardens often included artificial meandering watercourses intended for reenactment of the Orchid Pavilion gathering.

"Preface to the Orchid Pavilion Poems"

In the ninth year of the Yonghe reign [353], which was a *guichou* year, early in the final month of spring, we gathered at the Orchid Pavilion in Shanyin in Guiji for the ceremony of purification. Young and old congregated, and there was a throng of men of distinction. Surrounding the pavilion were high hills with lofty peaks, luxuriant woods, and tall bamboos. There was, moreover, a swirling, splashing stream, wonderfully clear, which curved round it like a ribbon, and we seated ourselves along it in a drinking game, in which cups of wine were set afloat and drifted to those who sat downstream. The occasion was not heightened by the presence of musicians. Nevertheless, what with drinking and the composing of verses, we conversed in whole-hearted freedom, entering fully into one another's feelings. The day was fine, the air clear, and a gentle breeze regaled us, so that on looking up we responded to the vastness of the universe, and on bending down were struck by the manifold riches of the earth. And as our eyes wandered from object to object, so our hearts, too, rambled with them. Indeed, for the eye as well as the ear, it was pure delight! What perfect bliss!

For in men's association with one another in their journey through life, some draw upon their inner resources and find satisfaction in a closeted conversation with a friend, while others follow their inclinations and abandon themselves without constraint to diverse interests and pursuits, oblivious of their physical existence. Their choice may be infinitely varied, even as their temperament will range from the serene to the irascible. When absorbed by what they are engaged in, they are for the moment content, and in their content they forget that old age is at hand. But when eventually they tire of what had so engrossed them, their feelings will have altered with their circumstances, and, of a sudden, complacency gives way to regret. What previously had gratified them is now a thing of the past, which in itself is cause for lament. Besides, although the span of men's lives may be longer or shorter, all must end in death. And, as has been said by the ancients, birth and death are momentous events. What an agonizing thought!

In reading the compositions of earlier men, I have tried to trace the causes of their melancholy, which too often are the same as those that affect myself. And I have then confronted the book with a deep sigh, without, however, being able to reconcile myself to it all. But this much I do know: it is idle to pretend that life and death are equal states and foolish to claim that a youth cut off in his prime has led the protracted life of a centenarian. For men of a later age will look upon our time as we look upon earlier ages—a chastening reflection. And so I have listed those present on this occasion and transcribed their verses. Even when circumstances have changed and men inhabit a different world, it will still be the same causes that induce a mood of melancholy attendant on poetical composition. Perhaps some reader of the future will be moved by the sentiments expressed in this preface.

"The Gentleman of the Five Willows" (*Wuliu xiansheng zhuan* 五柳先生傳), "The Peach Blossom Spring" (*Taohua yuan ji* 桃花源記), "Homeward Bound" (*Guiqulai xi ci* 歸去來兮辭), and "Written While Drunk" (*Yinjiu shi* 飲酒詩)

TAO QIAN 陶潛 (365–427)

Tao Qian, also known as Tao Yuanming (his *zi* or social name), is one of the canonical figures of Chinese garden culture. Living in the turbulent Eastern Jin dynasty, he rejected life as a government official to withdraw into private life on his family estate. Although he presents himself as a simple recluse of limited means, subsisting on what he could himself produce by farming, he was in fact—like most officials of the time—a wealthy man with substantial inherited property, and it is unlikely that he ever so much as handled a farm implement. Nevertheless, with his fondness for wine and chrysanthemums, he is a much-loved figure thanks to the agreeable image of himself that he presents in his "autobiography," "The Gentleman of the Five Willows," and in his poems, particularly "Homeward Bound" and the short poems of his sequence "Written While Drunk." His prose narrative and poem recounting the fable of the fisherman who discovers the rural utopia of the Peach Blossom Spring (only the prose narrative is included here) reflect the desire felt by so many, officials and others, to escape from the vicissitudes of politics and lead the simple life. Later texts on gardens rarely omit an allusion to the Peach Blossom Spring, and innumerable works of art refer to it also.

"The Gentleman of the Five Willows"
TRANSLATED BY J. R. HIGHTOWER

I don't know where this gentleman was born and I am not sure of his name, but beside his house were five willow trees, from which he took his nickname. He was of a placid disposition and rarely spoke. He had no envy of fame or fortune. He was fond of reading, without puzzling greatly over difficult passages. When he came across something to his liking he would be so delighted he would forget his meals. By nature he liked wine, but being poor could not always come by it. Knowing the circumstances, his friends and relatives would invite him over when they had wine. He could not drink without emptying his cup, and always ended up drunk, after which he would retire, unconcerned about what might come. He lived alone in a bare hut, which gave no adequate shelter against rain and sun. His short coat was torn and patched, his cooking pots were frequently empty, but he was unperturbed. He used to write poems for his own amusement, and in them can be seen something of what he thought. He had no concern for worldly success, and so he ended his days.

"The Peach Blossom Spring"
TRANSLATED BY J. R. HIGHTOWER

During the Taiyuan period [376–396] of the Jin dynasty a fisherman of Wuling once rowed upstream, unmindful of the distance he had gone, when he suddenly came to a grove of peach trees in bloom. For several hundred paces on both banks of the stream there was no other kind of tree. The wild flowers growing under them were fresh and lovely, and fallen petals covered the ground—it made a great impression on the fisherman. He went on for a way with the idea of finding out how far the grove extended. It came to an end at the foot of a mountain whence issued the spring that supplied the stream. There was a small opening in the mountain, and it seemed as though light was coming through it. The fisherman left his boat and entered the cave, which at first was extremely narrow, barely admitting his body; after a few dozen steps it suddenly opened out onto a broad and level plain where well-built houses were surrounded by rich fields and pretty ponds. Mulberry, bamboos, and other trees and plants grew there, and criss-cross paths skirted the fields. The sounds of cocks crowing and dogs barking could be heard from one courtyard to the next. Men and women were coming and going about their work in the fields. The clothes they wore were like those of ordinary people. Old men and boys were carefree and happy.

When they caught sight of the fisherman, they asked in surprise how he had got there. The fisherman told the whole story, and was invited to go to their house, where he was served wine while they killed a chicken for a feast. When the other villagers heard about the fisherman's arrival they all came to pay him a visit. They told him that their ancestors had fled the disorders of Qin times and, having taken refuge here with wives and children and neighbors, had never ventured out again; consequently, they had lost all contact with the outside world. They asked what the present ruling dynasty was, for they had never heard of the Han, let alone the Wei and the Jin. They sighed unhappily as the fisherman enumerated the dynasties one by one and recounted the vicissitudes of each. The visitors all asked him to come to their houses in turn, and at every house he had wine and food. He stayed several days. As he was about to go away, the people said, "There's no need to mention our existence to outsiders."

After the fisherman had gone out and recovered his boat, he carefully marked the route. On reaching the city, he reported what he had found to the magistrate, who at once sent a man to follow him back to the place. They proceeded according to the marks he had made, but went astray and were unable to find the cave again.

A high-minded gentleman of Nanyang named Liu Ziji heard the story and happily made preparations to go there, but before he could leave he fell sick and died. Since then there has been no one interested in trying to find such a place.

"Homeward Bound"

TRANSLATED BY H. C. CHANG

Being poor, with insufficient land to support my family of numerous young children and no reserve of grain in store, I saw no means of gaining a livelihood. Relatives and friends encouraged me to take a post under a magistrate, and of this scheme I cherished some vain hopes. It was a time of turmoil and the regional commanders relied on personal patronage for loyal support, and my uncle, taking pity on my circumstances, obtained for me an actual magistracy over a small district. The realm not being at peace, I was reluctant to seek employment in a distant place; but Pengze was no more than a hundred *li* from my home. The holder of the office enjoyed, moreover, the privilege of the sole use of a measure of land, which I thought would yield a large quantity of millet for my brewing. I, therefore, accepted the appointment with alacrity.

But a short time after, I began to pine for home and to have thoughts of returning to my native village. What had brought this about? My disposition was so inclined to the carefree state, it would not comply with the rigorous demands of artificial routine. Though hunger and cold might indeed be pressing, I now suffered from the additional malady of fighting against my own nature. When engaged in the service of others, I but enslaved myself in order to appease my belly. With a rueful sigh I concluded that I had been false to my true aims. I looked forward, however, to the harvest, when I could gracefully retire after a full year's service. Then my sister died at Wuchang, and since I had to hurry to the funeral, I resigned forthwith from the magistracy. From mid autumn to winter, I was in office for eighty-odd days. In setting forth the events, I have but followed my own inclinations, for which reason I entitle the piece "Homeward Bound," which was written in the eleventh month of *yisi* year [405].

Homeward bound I am at last!
The fields and orchards are overgrown with weeds—why did I tarry?
I who have enlisted my soul in the service of my body
Am the sole cause of my regrets and unshared grief;
The past is irretrievable, now that I realize my folly,

But the future still is mine!
Nor is it far that I have strayed
When I know myself now to be right, though wrong only yesterday.
The boat rocks gently as it moves upstream
Against a wind which lifts my cloak and swells my sleeves.
I ask the way of a man on the shore
And under the faint light of dawn bend my steps toward home.

Once again I see the house and doorway
With joy in my heart and wings on my feet.
The servants come forward to greet me,
And my young son stands waiting demurely at the gate.
Grass has overgrown the paths
But the pines and chrysanthemums are still there.
Leading my boy by the hand, I enter the house
And find that luxury—a jar of wine—on the table.

I pour myself a cup of good cheer;
I am gladdened by the sight of each tree in the courtyard;
At the south window the view defines my aspirations;
These rooms, though tiny, offer more than mere comfort.
My garden grows more interesting with each day's visit;
My gate seldom creaks to welcome a visitor.
Supported by a bamboo staff, I would pause in my ramblings
And time and again lift my head to gaze afar
At some mysterious cloud hovering near the mountain peak
Or the birds, weary of wandering, returning to their nests.
In the fading twilight before darkness descends,
I would touch and linger by a lone pine tree.

Homeward bound I was, and at home I am!
And I ask, too, to break off all ties with the world!
For the world's way is not my way,
And I will not seek the right of admission to it again.
I delight in the homely sentiments of near ones and dear ones
And beguile the time with my books and my guitar.
The farmers tell me with glee that spring is at hand
And they will start the winter's toil in the western fields.
I would mount my chariot
Or set off in a canoe
To ferret out the secrets of some dark ravine
Or try the slope of some hillock.

The trees are running with sap,
The fountains are again trickling;
The myriad objects in the pageant of the seasons
Govern my alternate phases of action and of rest.

Alas, how much longer shall this my body inhabit the earth?
Why not be guided by my soul though I may too soon perish?
What was it I sought so busily and so restlessly?
Not wealth, not rank—these are not among my wishes,
And the sphere of the immortals is beyond my reach.
To walk alone with a sense of uplift on a fine morning
Or potter about in the fields, is all I desire,
To ascend the eastern eminence and whistle to the cosmic forces
Or compose verses to the sound of a rushing stream,
And so end my days in accordance with the cycle of growth and decay,
Rejoicing in heaven's will without doubt or suspicion.

"Written While Drunk"
TRANSLATED BY WILLIAM ACKER

I built my house near where others dwell,
And yet there is no clamor of carriages and horses.
You ask of me "How can this be so?"
"When the heart is far the place of itself is distant."
I pluck chrysanthemums under the eastern hedge,
And gaze afar toward the southern mountains.
The mountain air is fine at evening of the day
And flying birds return together homeward.
Within these things there is a hint of Truth,
But when I start to tell it, I cannot find the words.

"Introduction to Painting Landscape" (*Hua shanshui xu* 畫山水序)

ZONG BING 宗炳 (375–443)
TRANSLATED BY SUSAN BUSH AND HSIO-YEN SHIH

The Liu Song dynasty (420–479) painter Zong Bing, from central China, was a lay member of the Buddhist community on Mount Lu in Jiangxi founded by the patriarch Huiyuan (334–416), and was influenced by the "landscape Buddhism" that also features in the thinking of writers such as Xie Lingyun (see below). Zong Bing is possibly best known not so much for his essay "Introduction to Painting Landscape" as for his reputed invention of the concept of "recumbent wandering" or "roaming in the imagination" (*woyou*), described in his biography in the official *History of the [Liu] Song*: "When he was ill, he returned home to Jiangling, and said with a sigh, 'Old age and illness have both come upon me, and I am afraid I am unlikely to see all the famous mountains; all I can do is purify my thoughts and observe the Way, and wander among them from a recumbent position.' He drew all the places he had visited on the walls of his room, and told people, 'I hold my zither and strike it, to make the mountains all resound.'"[14]

"Introduction to Painting Landscape"

Sages, possessing the Dao, respond to things. The virtuous, purifying their thoughts, savor images. As for landscape, it has physical existence, yet tends toward the spiritual. Therefore, such recluses as the Yellow Emperor, Yao, Confucius, Guangcheng, Dakui, Xu You, and the brothers Boyi and Shuqi from Guzhu insisted on roaming in the mountains Kongtong, Juci, Miaogu, Ji, Shou, Tai, and Meng. These have also been praised as the pleasures of the humane and wise. Now, sages follow the Dao through their spirits, and the virtuous comprehend this. Landscapes display the beauty of the Dao through their forms, and humane men delight in this. Are these not similar?

When I was deeply attached to the Lu and Heng mountains, and roamed with abandon the peaks of Jing and Wu, I did not realize that old age was approaching. Ashamed of being unable to concentrate my vital breath and attune my body, I am afraid of limping among those who climb Stone Gate. Therefore, I paint images and spread colors, constructing cloudy peaks.

If truths that were abandoned before the period of middle antiquity may still be sought by the imagination a thousand years later, and if meaning that is subtler than the images of speech can be grasped by the mind in books and writings, what then of where one's body has strolled and one's eyes rested repeatedly when it is described form for form, color for color?

However, the Kunlun mountains are immense and the eyes' pupils small. If the former come within inches of the viewer, their total form will not be seen. If they are at a distance of several miles, then they can be encompassed by inch-small pupils. Truly, the farther off they are, the smaller they will appear. Now, if one spreads thin silk to capture the distant scene, the form of Kunlun's Lang peak can be encompassed in a

---

14   Liang Shenyue, ed., *Songshu* (Beijing: Zhonghua shuju, 1974), 4:2279 (*Liezhuan* 53).

single inch. A vertical stroke of three inches will equal a height of thousands of feet, and a horizontal stretch of several feet will form a distance of a hundred miles. That is why those who look at paintings are only troubled by awkwardness in the likeness and do not consider that diminution detracts from verisimilitude. This is a natural condition. In this way, the lofty elegance of the Song and Hua mountains as well as the soul of deep valleys can all be included in one picture.

If response by the eye and accord by the mind to nature is considered a universal law, when similitude is skillfully achieved, eyes will also respond completely and the mind be entirely in accord. This response and accord will affect the spirit and, as the spirit soars, the truth will be attained. Even though one should again futilely seek out remote cliffs, what more could be added? Furthermore, the spirit, which is essentially limitless, resides in forms and stimulates all kinds of life, and truth enters into reflections and traces. One who can truly describe things skillfully will also achieve this.

Thus, I live at leisure, regulating my vital breath, brandishing the wine-cup and sounding the lute. Unrolling paintings in solitude, I sit pondering the ends of the earth. Without resisting the multitude of natural promptings, alone I respond to uninhabited wilderness where grottoed peaks tower or high and cloudy forests mass in depth. The sages and virtuous men who have shone forth throughout the ages had myriad charms of nature fused into their spirits and thoughts. What then should I do? I rejoice in my spirit, and that is all. What could be placed above that which rejoices the spirit?

"Reading in My Study" (*Zhaizhong dushu* 齋中讀書) and "Rhapsody on Dwelling in the Mountains" (*Shanju fu* 山居賦; extracts)

XIE LINGYUN 謝靈運 (385–433)

Xie Lingyun, who bore the title Duke of Kangle, is one of the great poets of the Wei-Jin era, and one of the earliest exponents of landscape poetry with a Buddhist coloring. He was from a wealthy and influential family, but his official career was affected by the turbulence of his time, and at one point, over the period from 423 to 426, he withdrew to the family property in what is now Zhejiang Province. Here he developed what was evidently a landscaped estate rather than just a garden, and wrote the lengthy "Rhapsody on Dwelling in the Mountains," short extracts of which appear after his poem "Reading in My Study." Xie's original text includes a detailed commentary on each section of the rhapsody (*fu*), but it is omitted here except for his brief commentary on the last section quoted. Xie celebrates the rich natural resources of his estate but contrasts its tranquility, providing a refuge for Buddhist practitioners as well as for himself, with the extravagant luxury of earlier gardens such as Shi Chong's Golden Valley (see above).

"Reading in My Study"

TRANSLATED BY H. C. CHANG

Amid the magnificent splendor of the capital,
I still cherished the lonely hills and ravines;
Now I am back among the streams and mountains,
My solitary disposition approves the sequestered scene.

Unmolested by contentious litigants in my empty office,
So quiet, the courtyard hums with the singing of birds,
Often ailing or convalescing, I have abundant leisure,
Which I devote to the writing of prose or verse.

To give scope to my ambitions, I survey times past and present,
My prolonged reading being relieved by occasional jesting
At the expense of the ancient hermits toiling on the land
Or the slippery career of the soldier-scholar-courtier.

For carrying a halberd all day long fatigues the body and mind,
And tilling the soil is unqualified drudgery.
Each mode of living has some inherent defect:
The wise adapt their aims to the conditions of their lives.

"Rhapsody on Dwelling in the Mountains" (extracts)

TRANSLATED BY DAVID R. KNECHTGES

Section 6
As for the place where I made my dwelling:
To the left there is a lake, on the right is a river;
Wherever one goes there are islands, wherever one turns there are holms.
It faces mountains and backs onto small hills;
On the east it is obstructed, and on the west it slopes downward.
It enfolds that which "engorges and disgorges";
Vastly extended, the land twists and twines.
Stretching continuously, it bends and winds;
True and straight, it becomes flat and even.

Section 17
Trails between the fields run this way and that;
Raised pathways criss-cross.
We channel waterways to direct the flow;

Arteries spread out and conduits converge.
Thickly growing—lush millet,
Sweet-smelling—fragrant rice,
As summer ends, the early crop ears,
As autumn begins, the late crop ripens.
There are also mounded and level plots
To grow hemp and wheat, spiked millet and soybeans.
Awaiting the time, watching the seasons,
First we sow, then reap.
Being provided with grain to eat and beverages to drink,
I can refuse to be artisan or merchant, forester or pastor.
Why should livelihood depend on great riches,
For the order of things finds sufficiency in a full stomach.

Section 29
When I first designed a plan [for my estate],
Leaning on a walking stick, I traveled alone.
I entered streams, crossed rivers,
Climbed ranges and walked over mountains.
Upon traversing a peak, I did not rest;
Upon tracing a spring to its source, I did not stop.
I was combed by the wind, bathed by the rain;
Braving the dew, I used the stars for light.
I fully examined my shallow thoughts,
Exhausted all my defective ideas.
Using neither turtle shell nor milfoil,
I selected the good, chose the unusual.
Cutting through thick growth, I opened a trail;
I explored rocks, scoured cliffs.
Four mountains wound around me;
A pair of streams sinuously flowed.
Facing the southern peaks
I built a scripture terrace.
Against the northern hill
I constructed a lecture hall.
Beside a precipitous peak
I set a meditation chamber.
Overlooking a deep stream
I placed houses for monks.
By tall trees a hundred years old
One receives the sweet fragrance of a myriad ages.
I cherish springs that have flowed from antiquity;

I admire the purity and durability of their rich liquid.
I bade farewell to the pretty pagodas of the suburbs;
I withdrew from the world by city walls.
I am delighted to see simplicity and embrace the uncarved block;[15]
And I truly have found sweet dew in the place of the Way.[16]
Commentary: This is to say that when I first made a plan for my estate, I walked alone and suffered all manner of hardships. I exhausted my shallow and defective thoughts and did not avail myself of turtle shell or milfoil divination. He who is poor does not consider the merely pretty as beautiful. This is why I found contentment in a thatched hut. Thus, I bade farewell to the suburbs and withdrew from city walls. Truly pure emptiness and quiet solitude are the place one can obtain the Way.

"A Letter to Secretary Xie" (*Da Xie zhongshu shu* 答謝中書書; extract)

TAO HONGJING 陶弘景 (456–536)

TRANSLATED BY H. C. CHANG

Tao Hongjing was an important Daoist philosopher who became a leading figure in the Maoshan (Mount Mao) or Upper Clarity (*Shangqing*) sect of Daoism. He compiled *The Declarations of the Perfected* (*Zhen'gao*), a collection of revelations allegedly granted to Daoist adepts on Maoshan, which became part of the Daoist canon. Tao also wrote extensively on herbal medicine, a topic related to the Daoist search for immortality or extended life. He came from a family of officials, and as a young man he worked as a royal tutor, but later became a recluse. In the early sixth century, Emperor Wu of Liang frequently sent to ask his advice, but he refused to come to the court; as a result, he became known as "the Prime Minister in the mountains" (*shanzhong zaixiang*). The description in this letter, addressed to an official in charge of transmitting imperial orders, of lofty peaks and clear waters was later felt to reflect Tao's own exalted moral character. It is interesting that, as a Daoist, he cites the Buddhist Xie Lingyun (see above) as someone who shared his own appreciation of landscape.

"A Letter to Secretary Xie" (extract)

The beauty of hills and streams has been acknowledged from ancient times. Here, high peaks rise above the clouds; a rivulet, clear to its bottom, flows between rocky banks. Before me is a pageant of colors with the dark pine woods and the green bamboos flourishing in all seasons. As the mists lift at dawn, the monkeys and the birds cry in loud dissonance. And when the sun sets, the fish come out of hiding to chase one another.

---

15 The "uncarved block" is a Daoist term implying simplicity; it occurs in both the *Daode jing* and the *Zhuangzi*.

16 The "place of the Way" (*dao chang*) is a Chinese translation of *Bodhimandala*, literally "truth plot." Here it designates the place for attaining the Buddha truth. See William Edward Soothill and Lewis Hodous, *A Dictionary of Chinese Buddhist Terms* (1937; reprint, Kaohsiung: Buddhist Culture Service, n.d.), 416.

This indeed is paradise on earth. And yet since Xie Lingyun, there has been no one capable of entering wholeheartedly into the wonders of man's natural surroundings.

A Record of the Monasteries of Luoyang (*Luoyang qielan ji* 洛陽伽藍記)

South of the city wall: Jingming Monastery and
West of the city wall: Baoguang Monastery

YANG XUANZHI 楊衒之 (D. CA. 550)
TRANSLATED BY W. J. F. JENNER

A Record of the Monasteries of Luoyang is an account of the city (by no means just its monasteries) which formed the short-lived capital (493–534) of the Northern Wei dynasty. The author, Yang Xuanzhi, about whom little is known, had been an official there and evidently knew the city well before its abrupt decline; it was a visit to its ruins which inspired him to compile the *Record*. Yang includes descriptive and factual information, historical records, and urban legends, such as ghost stories, in a clear and readable style. His work contributed to the reputation of the Northern Wei as a brilliant cultural era which provided a basis for much of later elite literati culture.

South of the city wall: Jingming Monastery

The Jingming Monastery was founded by the Emperor Xuanwu during Jingming [500–503]—hence the name. It lay 1 *li* outside the Xuanyang Gate to the east of the imperial highway. The monastery extended for 500 paces from east to west and from north to south. It faced the Shaoshi hill of Mount Song, and behind it was the wall of the imperial city. The shade of its dark trees and the patterns of its green waters made it a refreshing and beautiful place and there were over 1,000 rooms in its towering buildings. The windows and gutters of many-storied halls and structures joined and faced each other; dark terraces and purple pavilions were connected by flying passages. No matter what the season outside, it was never freezing or torrid in here; beyond the eaves of the buildings were only hills and lakes. Pine, bamboo, orchid, and iris overhung the steps, holding the wind and gathering the dew as they spread their fragrance.

During Zhengguang [520–525] the Empress Dowager built a seven-storied pagoda here which rose to a great height; this was why Xing Zicai [Xing Shao, b. 496] said in the inscription he wrote for it:

> One looks down and hears the thunder
> While shooting stars flash past.

The splendor of the monastery's ornamentation rivaled the Yongning [Monastery]; its golden pole and precious bells gleamed beyond the clouds.

There were three ponds in the monastery where reeds, rushes, water-chestnuts, and lotuses grew. Yellow turtles and purple fish could be seen among the water-weeds; black ducks and white geese dived and swam in the green waters. There were edge-runner mills, rotary mills, pounders, and bolters all powered by water. This was regarded as the finest of all the monasteries.

In those days the Great Blessing was very popular. On the seventh day of the fourth month all the statues in the capital were brought to this monastery. According to the Department of Sacrifices of the Chancellery they numbered over 1,000. On the eighth the statues were taken in through the Xuanyang Gate to the front of the Changhe Palace where the emperor scattered flowers on them. The gold and the flowers dazzled in the sun, and the jeweled canopies floated like clouds; there were forests of banners and a fog of incense, and the Buddhist music of India shook heaven and earth. All kinds of entertainers and trick riders performed shoulder to shoulder. Virtuous hosts of famous monks came, carrying their staves; there were crowds of the Buddhist faithful, holding flowers; horsemen and carriages were packed beside each other in an endless mass. When a monk from the West saw all this he would proclaim that this was indeed a land of the Buddha.

West of the city wall: Baoguang Monastery

The Baoguang [Precious Light] Monastery was outside the Xiyang Gate and north of the imperial highway. It contained a three-storied pagoda on a stone base which seemed very old from the way it looked and was built. It was painted and carved.

The recluse Zhao Yi [3rd century] sighed when he saw it and said, "the Stone Pagoda Monastery of the Jin dynasty has now become the Precious Light Monastery." When asked why he said this he replied, "The forty-two temples of the Jin were all destroyed except this one. That was the bath-house," he said, pointing to a place in the garden. "There should be a well five paces in front of it." When the monks dug there they found a building and a well. Although the well had been blocked up, its brick top was as good as new. There were still several dozen flagstones below the bath-house. The garden was level and spacious, and all who saw its luxuriant fruit and vegetables sighed with admiration.

There was a pool in the garden, called Xian Pool,[17] whose banks were covered with reeds. The pool itself grew water-chestnuts and lotuses, and was surrounded with green pines and emerald bamboo. On fine mornings the gentlemen of the capital

---

17 Named after the place where the sun bathed.

would ask for bath leave and invite their friends to make a trip to this temple with them. Their carriages would pack in crossboard to crossboard, and their feathered canopies made a continuous shade. Sometimes they amused themselves by drinking wine among the trees and streams, writing poems about the flowers, breaking off lotus roots, and floating gourds.

At the end of Putai [532], Erzhu Tianguang [496–532], governor of Yong Province and Prince of Longxi, assembled horse and foot in this monastery. All the gates of the monastery collapsed for no cause, to Erzhu Tianguang's horror. The same year he was executed in the eastern market, after being defeated in battle.

断
橋

Gardens of the Tang Dynasty

The Tang dynasty[1] (618–907) is often regarded as the zenith of China's cultural glory. Until the An Lushan rebellion of the mid-eighth century that presaged dynastic collapse, the Tang held the greatest extent of territory under Chinese control before the Qing dynasty; the relative security of the Silk Road trade routes led to unprecedented economic prosperity as well as to a cosmopolitan culture that absorbed influences in music, the visual arts, and luxury consumption from Central Asia and beyond. This was probably helped by the fact that the imperial family, surnamed Li, was of mixed Han Chinese and Turkic origin and, therefore, itself a product of cultural intermingling. Merchants of many different ethnic origins settled in the capital, Chang'an (modern Xi'an), which was the largest city in the world at the time, with a population estimated at one million; trading ports on the south coast, such as Guangzhou (Canton) and Quanzhou (known to Arab merchants as Zaytoun), also attracted seafaring traders from the far shores of the Indian Ocean, making new, exotic objects and products available to the people of China's heartland. Buddhism, originally a religion of foreign origin, attained enormous cultural and economic as well as ideological influence during the Tang. Tang poetry—characterized by the development of "regulated verse" (*lüshi*) with strict rules of prosody—is justly famous in China and beyond. The period also saw the rise of prose narrative intended for entertainment as much as instruction, which became the precursor to later, self-consciously fictional narratives.

---

1   This introduction, and the headnotes to many of the poems, have drawn substantially from essays Xiaoshan Yang originally wrote for the projected earlier version of this anthology, and from his book *Metamorphosis of the Private Sphere: Gardens and Objects in Tang-Song Poetry* (Cambridge, Mass.: Harvard University Asia Center, 2003). This introduction has also benefited from the introduction originally written by Stephen H. West for the Song dynasty chapter.

The invention of printing—using both woodblocks and movable type—helped to spread familiarity with the classical texts used as the basis for the government examinations, as well as with religious scriptures and secular texts intended for either instruction or entertainment, though it was not until the Song dynasty that China truly became a "print culture."

Although the Tang dynasty marks the first flowering of the literati culture that would come to fruition in the Song, in the early part of the dynasty, much cultural activity centered on the court; under the rule of Empress Wu (Wu Zhao or Wu Zetian; see below) and the emperors controlled by her, court culture was dominated by powerful women such as the Taiping and Anle princesses, and the courtier poet Shangguan Wan'er (see below). The princesses used their power and wealth to develop splendid country estates that were celebrated in verse by Shangguan and other court poets. In them, we see both grandiloquent praise of the estates' splendor and specious claims of the owners' status as "hermits" or "untrammelled immortals." After the reinstatement of Confucian orthodoxy in place of Empress Wu's promotion of Buddhism, the power of court women was severely curtailed. Nevertheless, the model for women writing on gardens had been established.[2]

The reassertion of Confucianism contributed to the incipient formation of the literati or scholar-official class (although it did not become a significant social force until the Song, as discussed in the introduction to chapter 4); it also owed its origins to the institutionalization of the competitive government examination system under the short-lived Sui dynasty (581–618) that preceded the Tang. Examinations were first used to select officials much earlier, under the Han, but only a small minority of officials sat these examinations; most were selected through familial or other personal connections. The Sui's relatively systematic use of examinations marks the beginning of the transition from aristocratic government to the bureaucratic government that became such a notable feature of China's sociopolitical structure (and itself influenced the development of the civil service in European countries in the eighteenth and nineteenth centuries). Now it was intellectual ability rather than aristocratic birth that led to political position and social prestige.[3]

This new bureaucratic class of scholar-officials gradually developed a distinctive culture that differed significantly from the culture of the great aristocratic families. Aristocratic culture was predicated on great wealth arising from extensive landholding and kinship or marital connections with the imperial court. Scholar-official or literati culture was more influenced by the common heritage of classical and later literature that formed the basis of scholarly education; it made a virtue of simplicity, even if plain living was not actually practiced by the wealthier literati families. As a consequence of cultural change, this is the first era that witnessed a close aesthetic relationship between poetry and painting,[4] and also the first in which we can identify involvement of the

---

2 On Tang court women and their estates, see Rebecca Doran, *Transgressive Typologies: Constructions of Gender and Power in Early Tang China* (Cambridge, Mass.: Harvard University Asia Center, 2016).

3 See Peter K. Bol, *This Culture of Ours: Intellectual Transitions in T'ang and Sung China* (Stanford: Stanford University Press, 1992).

4 See, for instance, Tai Jianying, *Tang Song ti shuhua shi xuanxi* (Beijing: Changzheng chubanshe, 1991), 377–78.

educated class in the planning and execution of private gardens.[5] As a result, it is also the first time that the integration of the principles of painting and poetics into both the construction and appreciation of private gardens became a notable trend. For the first time on a large scale, architecture became a key feature in the construction of private landscapes, and the careful placement of pavilions, viewing terraces, and occasional buildings in the small space of the enclosed garden provided a vertical vantage point from which to view the metonymical cosmos of the garden and extend its horizon both literally and figuratively.

The growing disjunction between aristocratic and scholar-official culture in the Tang created a very different social situation from the overlap between the aristocratic and official classes during the Han dynasty and the period of disunion between the Han and Tang. Nevertheless, the beginnings of literati culture can be perceived in the Wei-Jin period (3rd–5th century), whose eccentric literary men (such as the Seven Sages of the Bamboo Grove) were regarded by later scholars as models for living the reclusive life.

The tradition of eremitism or reclusion, which first came to prominence in the Wei-Jin era as an escape from political and social instability, was very important in the garden culture of the Tang literati. In their case, however, the greater social power of this group meant that there was less of a tendency toward the "negativity and withdrawal" that had characterized intellectual life in the period between Han and Tang,[6] and reclusion functioned more as a relief from the pressure of official duties and the stresses and strains of factional conflict at court. We can also see in the Tang attitude to eremitism the influence of Buddhism with its rejection of worldly concerns. The fact that scholar-officials might combine an ideological commitment to Buddhism or to eremitism with the pursuit of a career in government may strike us as hypocritical, but they were certainly no more so than the Christian who unaccountably fails to love her neighbor or give generously to the poor.

Another innovation of gardens in the Tang dynasty lay in the secularization of Buddhist and Daoist monastery gardens. In the cities, they functioned as the first public gardens. Buddhism in particular, with its theoretical belief in and practical execution of the idea that "the Dharma law is equal and without hierarchy," turned its gardens into spaces of social intercourse and public activity, places that combined ritual function with social pleasures. They became an aestheticized extension of Buddhism's overall social policy, which included funeral rites for the unclaimed dead, soup kitchens, and pharmacies. One can imagine that the attention paid to maintaining gardens had an economic incentive as well, since Buddhism relied to a great extent on lay donations, bounty from the sleeves of those who found sanctuary there. In the countryside, spaces formerly given over to religious ritual activity became famous as scenic sites to be visited. The appreciation and popularity of such places is intimately related to the rise of travel and sightseeing.[7] If the private gardens of the Tang (and the Song) are celebrated in poetry, visits to Buddhist and Daoist gardens became a focal point of the writing of prose *ji* or "records" that often described them in lavish detail.

---

5   See Zhou Weiquan, *Zhongguo gudian yuanlin shi* (Beijing: Tsinghua University Press, 1999/2003), 168–72, "Wenren yuanlin de xingqi."

6   Ibid., 122.

7   Ibid., 175–77.

We can see in Tang writing on gardens the fusion of opposing impulses. Bai Juyi, taking up earlier adumbrations of the theme, wrote about different ranks of hermit: the petty hermit who goes into reclusion in the mountains, where he has no temptations to distract him; the middling hermit who finds his hermitage in the city, where he can combine some degree of reclusion with access to the conveniences of life; and the great hermit, who is able to maintain the detachment of a recluse even amid the glory and stress of life at the center of government. Bai concluded that the status of middling hermit (a term he first introduced in the title of a poem written in 829) was the most appropriate for functionaries such as himself to aspire to. This combination of "urban reclusion" with one's official duties was best achieved by means of an urban garden, which could mimic the solitude of the wilds without taking one away from the intellectual stimulus of like-minded friends and the practical advantages as well as the entertainments of urban life. Bai Juyi was probably the most significant garden-owner in formulating, articulating, and promoting the idea of the urban garden as possessing the best of both worlds. In the urban garden, we can discern a compromise, if not synthesis, between the opposing impulses in the Chinese eremitic tradition: the country was reconciled with the city, spiritual integrity with material comfort, and public responsibilities with private freedom. The preference for urban gardens is reflected in the greater number of compositions about them, compared to "mountain retreats," that we see in this chapter.

Bai Juyi—whose extensive oeuvre has allowed later readers to "know" him more intimately than almost any other Chinese poet—also found that, even if his own garden was much less grand than those of wealthier acquaintances, his personal ownership of it tipped the balance in its favor, at least as far as he was concerned.

New scenic features were added to gardens as the skills of garden designers and builders entered a new stage of sophistication. The placement of large stones (see the introduction to chapter 3), the construction of mounded earth "false mountains" (*jiashan*), the use of canals for water features, and particularly the transplantation and grafting of exotic plants made for a new form of garden that became the prototype for what was to follow. This creation of a private space unique to oneself, which we find reflected in the poems of Bai and others, foreshadows the much more prominent use of gardens, in the Song dynasty and later, as sites of self-representation for their owners.

The possession of a permanent home base, in or near either their hometown or the capital (or another major city), was obviously desirable for officials who might be posted anywhere in the empire for years at a time. It was not surprising, therefore, that the house and garden that formed this base should become the owner's "hermitage," his escape from the world of work. The movement of officials around the empire that made the possession of a retreat so desirable (but kept them away from it for long periods) also fed into garden culture in other ways, as we can see from many of the poems and passages of prose in this and the next chapter. It led to a familiarity with different parts of the empire, with their different climates, geographies, and horticultural conditions, which often stimulated officials to try to recreate distant landscapes in their home environments (as we can see in part 3 of this chapter, "Southern Landscapes in Northern Climes"). The movement of officials around the empire provided opportunities for the acquisition of exotic flora and fantastic rocks that would be transported back, often at considerable expense in money and labor, to one's garden at home; there are many examples of this in chapter 3, and more is said there about this phenomenon.

An official posting to the middle Yangtze River region centered on the Xiang River would arouse thoughts of the two goddesses of the river, wives of the legendary sage-king Shun; it would also prompt remembrance of the poet Qu Yuan, the supposed author of the *Songs of the South* (see chapter 1), the archetype of the venomously slandered and unjustly exiled official, who eventually drowned himself in the Miluo River, a tributary of the Xiang. When Tang poets evoked the image of the Xiang River in their descriptions of urban gardens, however, they usually stripped it of melancholy or exilic associations and configured it instead as an imaginary space of freedom, as is the case with Meng Jiao's poem "Visiting Mr. Han's Estate in the South of the City," included here. In northern gardens, associations with these distant landscapes could be made by the names applied to garden features as well as by the introduction of actual southern rocks or flora.

More than the upper and middle reaches of the Yangtze, it was the landscape of the lower Yangtze and the delta area, known as Jiangnan ("South of the River") that was most eagerly emulated in northern gardens. The Tang dynasty witnessed the first wholesale transplanting from the south of plants meant specifically for viewing pleasure.[8] Wang Fangqing's (d. 702) "Account of Flora in Gardens" (*Yuanting caomu shu*) and Li Deyu's "Record of the Plants and Trees of My Mountain Villa at Pingquan" (see chapter 3) list some seventy or more exotics transplanted from Jiangnan, and Li's protégé, Duan Chengshi (d. 863), lists nearly two hundred more, including a large number that he says originated from Persia or Asia Minor (*Fulin guo*) in sections of his *Youyang Miscellany* (*Youyang zazu*) given over to horticulture.[9]

Although the emulation of Jiangnan gardens could be achieved in the north by the introduction of "exotics" (like the rocks and white lotus flowers from Suzhou that Bai Juyi describes in his poem "Lotus Flowers and Rocks"), the cultivation of a southern-style garden was more than just a matter of introducing such items. It was also often informed by the idea of building a hermitage in the city (facilitating life as a "middling hermit"), as we can see in poems such as Bai Juyi's "A Newly Built Small Shoal," which incorporates an allusion to a famous first-century recluse. In another poem, one of Bai's "Three Quatrains on My Family Garden," the recreation of the Jiangnan waterscape in the northern garden is presented as a process not only of reduction in size but also of refinement in substance. We can see a similarly controlled experience in Bai's poem "Observing the Picking of Lotus Flowers," in which Bai's concubine reenacts on his garden pond the poetic topic of the traditional "Songs for Picking Lotuses," while the garden pond itself is represented as a milder and safer miniaturization of the Jiangnan waterscape.

Jiangnan was the usual location replicated in northern gardens, but the far south also made its contribution to Tang gardens. Along with a general interest in exotics, the Tang dynasty saw an upsurge in the number of books written about the far south of China, Lingnan ("South of the Mountain Range") or Nanyue (Nam-Viet, referring to an area mostly north of, but including part of modern Vietnam), which was being "civilized" and incorporated into the Tang empire. There was some officially sponsored publication of maps and gazetteers, but most of these government publications were concerned with the more economically and socially important region of the

---

8 Ibid., 123.

9 For Duan Chengshi's work, see Carrie E. Reed, *A Tang Miscellany: An Introduction to Youyang Zazu* (New York: Peter Lang, 2003).

Yangtze basin and Zhejiang. There are, however, a significant number of privately produced studies of the climate, landscape, natural history, and ethnology of the far south. These brought some knowledge of the area to inhabitants of the Chinese heartland, and an interest in the exotic south was added to an interest in the exotic "west" (Central Asia). Rare birds were seen as desirable denizens for Tang gardens and parks; the vogue for this led to similar complaints from moralists as for the collection of rocks, that resources were being wasted on frivolities and farmers being lured away from their proper, productive occupations by the prospect of enrichment through supplying such demands. There is already evidence of peacocks (the Burmese or Javan peacock, *Pavo muticus*, rather than the Indian peacock, *P. cristatus*) in aristocratic Chinese gardens in the third century, but in the eighth century, the Emperor Xuanzong had an almost equally impressive silver pheasant (*Lophura nycthemera*) brought to the imperial gardens in Chang'an.[10] Exotic flora and rocks are discussed in detail in chapter 3.

Imperial gardens reached a height during the Tang that had been unequaled since the Han. Huge garden complexes were constructed at the two capitals of Chang'an and Luoyang, and there were large "visiting imperial gardens" (*xinggong yuyuan*) and "separate imperial retreats" (*ligong yuyuan*) in scenic spots near the capitals, the most famous of which was, of course, the hot springs complex at Lishan, the celebrated Palace of Floriate Clarity (*Huaqing gong*).[11] These were enormous enclosed spaces, which for the first time demonstrated the conventional patterns of arrangement, architecture, and siting used to place the emperor in the center of a political and social performance of power in the garden.

In summary, for a variety of socioeconomic and cultural reasons, the Tang dynasty marks a decisive development and change in the creation and use of gardens, particularly private "literati" gardens, which form the basis on which Chinese gardens continued to evolve during the remainder of the imperial period.

PART 1

GARDEN AS MOUNTAIN RETREAT

"Twenty-Five Poems on a Visit to the Estate of Princess Changning" (*You Changning gongzhu liubei chi ershiwu shou* 遊長寧公主流杯池二十五首; extracts) and "Visiting Princess Changning's Pool-for-Setting-Winecups-Afloat" (*You Changning gongzhu liubei chi* 遊長寧公主流杯池)

SHANGGUAN WAN'ER 上官婉兒 (664–710)

Shangguan Wan'er was the granddaughter of an important official of the early Tang. After his fall and execution in 665, she (still a child) and her mother were taken into the palace as slaves. Her literary

---

10   On the Tang preoccupation with the exotic, see Edward H. Schafer, *The Golden Peaches of Samarkand: A Study of T'ang Exotics* (Berkeley: University of California Press, 1963), and *The Vermilion Bird: T'ang Images of the South* (Berkeley: University of California Press, 1967).

11   These gardens are covered thoroughly in Zhou Weiquan, *Zhongguo gudian yuanlin shi*, 124–52.

ability came to the notice of Empress Wu, to whom she became a sort of private secretary. She became highly influential at court, in both political and cultural affairs, and was made an imperial consort to Empress Wu's son, Emperor Zhongzong, presumably as a way of regularizing her position, since there is no indication of any sexual relationship with the emperor. She became dangerously embroiled in court politics, and was condemned to execution after the death of Zhongzong.

"Twenty-Five Poems on a Visit to the Estate of Princess Changning" (extracts)
TRANSLATED BY WILT IDEMA AND BEATA GRANT

III
Waving gently—bamboo shadows,
Tossed by winds the sighs of pines.
There's no need for song and music,
This suffices to please one's mind.

V
Twigs and branches thick and dense:
"Harmony of form and substance."
Trees and mountains serve as friends,
Pine and cassia are neighbors.

VII
Don't tell me about peaks well-rounded,
Don't speak about islands square:[12]
None can compare to this simple lodge,
A true meeting-place of the immortals!

XVI
The springs and rocks are rich in fairy-pleasures
As peaks and gullies etch the weirdest forms.
What is there here to please your ears?
Just listen to the lilting of the streams.

XVII
I climb steep cliffs to my heart's desire,
It clears out the eyes, delights the soul.
The wind-tossed bamboos serve as flutes,
The flowing streams as sounding zithers.

---

12 "Peaks well-rounded" and "islands square" are the abodes of the immortals.

XX

A waterfall: the clear sky brings us rain,
A bamboo grove: day has turned to night.
The mountains offer much one may enjoy,
Please tell that to those pampered princes!

XXI

Sitting by a pond I wield a while my brush,
Leaning on a rock I compose a poem.
At times I strum a tune of streams and hills:
Forever let me live a hermit's life!

"Visiting Princess Changning's Pool-for-Setting-Winecups-Afloat"
TRANSLATED BY STEPHEN OWEN

Propped on my staff, I looked over wispy peaks,
Then with hazardous pace descended frosty trails.
My goals grew serene the deeper I went in the hills,
I strayed on the path that bent with the mountain stream.
Slowly I sensed detachment in my soul,
And noticed at once how fogs were sinking low
Be not dismayed I wrote upon that tree—
It was because I cherished this hidden rest.

"A Letter to Scholar Pei Di" (*Yu Pei xiucai Di shu* 與裴秀才迪書)

WANG WEI 王維 (699–759)
TRANSLATED BY PETER HARRIS

Wang Wei has become known as the archetypal Tang dynasty poet of landscape, particularly for his sequence of poems (see below) on the sites of his estate, Wangchuan (Wang River, a different character from the poet's surname, or Wheel River, so called from the appearance of its swirling current) at Lantian, near the Tang capital Chang'an; these poems were matched by his close friend Pei Di, the addressee of the following letter. Wang Wei was also famous as a painter; none of his paintings survive, but some, including one of his Wangchuan estate, are known through early copies. He was a convinced Buddhist, and presents his estate as a site of transcendence into which no worldly concerns are allowed to intrude; his landscape poetry in some ways harks back to the poetry of Xie Lingyun (see chapter 1). The name of the "Deer Enclosure"—on which Wang wrote one of his best-known and best-loved poems (see below) —alludes to the Deer Park near Varanasi (Benares), in which the Buddha preached on the Four Noble Truths. Wang Wei's writing gives the impression of a simple country life, but it is clear that he came from a wealthy, upper-class background and lived on an extensive estate. He had a somewhat unstable official career, and became caught up in the An

Lushan rebellion (755–763); this led to charges of treason, which fortunately were dismissed. Wang Wei ended his days restored to office, but spending much time on his country estate. The landscape architecture of the Wangchuan estate can be credited with initiating the type of private garden, widespread in later times, whose layout is based on a collection of named scenic spots.

"A Letter to Scholar Pei Di"

With the lunar year drawing to a close and the weather pleasant and warm, it is just the time to visit our mountain haunts. But you are busy studying the classics, and I do not want to disturb you. So I have gone off into the hills on my own.

Before going I stopped at Ganpei temple and had a meal with the monks there. Then I went north across the dark Ba river, where a clear moon shone on the city walls. By night I climbed Huazi Ridge. The rippling waters of the Wang river rose and fell, and with them the light of the moon. In the cold mountains distant fires lit up the land beyond the forests and then were lost. A lone dog in a secluded alley howled with a sound like a mountain cat. The noise of villagers pounding grain into the night was interspersed with the slow chimes of a temple bell.

Now the servants have fallen silent and I am sitting on my own. I am thinking of times past, when we would compose poems walking hand in hand along narrow pathways and standing by clear-flowing streams. Spring will soon be here, with trees and plants putting out new leaves and shoots. The mountains in spring will be something to see— whitefish coming out of the water, gulls spreading their wings, dew glistening on green river marshes, pheasants crowing early in the wheatfields. All this is not far away. Could you come roaming the hills with me? If it weren't for your pure and unworldly nature I wouldn't think of inviting you on such an idle venture. That said, it would be deeply satisfying—do give it some thought.

People carrying wood for dye are setting off—I'll stop here and have them take this—

From your mountain dweller Wang Wei.

"The Wang River Collection" (*Wangchuan ji* 輞川集)

WANG WEI 王維 AND PEI DI 裴迪 (B. 716)
TRANSLATED BY PETER HARRIS

As noted above, Wang Wei's sequence of twenty poems on his Wang River estate were matched in a set by Pei Di; matching or "harmonizing" with poems by friends and acquaintances became an important part of elite social exchange in imperial China. After Wang Wei's preamble come his twenty poems, each of them four lines long and paired with his friend Pei Di's matching four-line poem. Not much is known of the life and career of Wang Wei's younger contemporary and friend Pei Di, and not many of his poems survive. They first met in ca. 740, when Wang was out of office and living in the Zhongnan mountains south of the capital. Pei seems to have been of a more practical temperament than Wang Wei, and to have persisted in pursuing an official career. In 760 (about the time of Wang Wei's death), Pei is known to have met Du Fu (see below) in Sichuan, and the two exchanged poems. Pei's date of death is unknown.

"The Wang River Collection"

My country home lies in the mountain valley of the Wang River. Among the places to wander in there are Meng Wall Hollow, Huaizi Ridge, Grainy Apricot Lodge, Fine Bamboo Mountain Range, Deer Enclosure, Magnolia Enclosure, Dogwood Bank, Pagoda Tree Footpath, Lakeside Pavilion, Southern Cottage, Lake Yi, Willow Waves, Luan Family Rapids, Gold Dust Spring, White Pebble Rapids, Northern Cottage, Bamboo District Lodge, Lily Magnolia Hollow, Lacquer Tree Grove, and Pepper Garden.

When we were relaxing there Pei Di and I composed four-line poems about these places.

Meng Wall Hollow
A new home by a gap in the Meng wall—
Of the old trees, a few gnarled willows are left.
Those who come in future, who will they be,
Grieving in vain for what others had before?

He has built his cottage under the old wall
And sometimes climbs to the top of the old wall too.
The old wall is not what it used to be—
Nowadays people come and go as they please.

Huazi Ridge
Birds fly away to the ends of the earth;
The mountains have an autumn look again.
Going up Huazi Ridge, and coming down,
I am moved by feelings of the utmost sorrow.

As the sun goes down the wind stirs in the pines;
On the way home there's a thin dew on the grass.
Piercing the clouds, the sun's rays fill our footprints
And the blue-green of the hillside touches our clothes.

Grainy Apricot Lodge

We cut grainy apricot wood for beams,
And bind sweet-smelling thatch for the eaves.
I do not know if the clouds among the rafters
Will go to make rain among men.

High, up high, Grainy Apricot Lodge—
We have climbed there many times each day.
The southern ranges and the northern lake—
We see them ahead and turning, behind us too.

Fine Bamboo Mountain Range

Sleek stems reflected in empty winding waters;
Dark green and emerald, floating on gentle ripples.
Secretly we take the Mount Shang track
Without the woodcutters knowing.

A bright running stream, winding then flowing straight,
Fine green bamboo, thick and growing deep—
Taking the path straight up through the mountains,
We sing as we go, our eyes on familiar peaks.

Deer Enclosure[13]

In the empty mountain no one to be seen,
Only the distant sound of people's voices.
The evening sun enters the deep wood,
Shining again on dark green moss.

In the dusk we see the cold mountains,
We who are travelers wandering alone,
Unaware of what happens in the pine forest
Except for the tracks left by the deer.

Magnolia Enclosure

The autumn hills hold back the last of the light;
Birds fly past, chasing companions up ahead.
Rich emerald greens, at times distinct and clear—
The evening mist has no place to settle.

---

13   Editor's note: with its enigmatic Chan (Zen) Buddhist atmosphere, this is perhaps Wang Wei's best-known
     and best-loved poem; innumerable attempts have been made to render it into English and other languages.

A misty haze with the setting sun, and birdsong
Mingling with the waters of the stream.
The path beside the stream winds back and away—
When will its fine seclusion come to an end?

Ailanthus Bank
They bear a fruit that's red and also green,
And then they bloom a second time, like flowers.
In the hills I entertain my guests
By setting out these cups of ailanthus.

Their drifting scent could be taken for pepper or cinnamon;
Their splayed leaves find space among sleek bamboo.
Though they still enjoy the light of the distant sun
Their dense dark growth stays naturally cold.

Pagoda Tree Footpath
The narrow path is shaded by pagoda trees,
Its dark shadows a mass of green moss.
The gatekeeper still sweeps it clean in welcome,
Worried in case a monk from the hills comes by.

Pagoda Tree Footpath to the south of the gate—
That is the track leading to Lake Yi.
As autumn comes with heavy rain in the hills
No one is there to sweep the fallen leaves.

Lakeside Pavilion
A light boat greets the arriving guest,
Coming over the lake from far away.
Across the gallery we raise our cups;
On every side the lotus is in bloom.

Across the gallery an expanse of moving water;
A solitary moon swaying to and fro.
Gibbons' cries from the mouth of the valley
Are brought by the wind through our open doors.

Southern Cottage

Toward the Southern Cottage the skiff goes;
The Northern Cottage is distant, hard to reach.
Over there on shore I make out people's homes—
Too far away for us to recognize each other.

Following the breeze the single boat comes to rest
On the lake shore near the Southern Cottage.
As the sun sets into Mount Yanzi
Clear waves spread supremely far and wide.

Lake Yi

Playing flutes we reach the distant shore;
At sunset I see you on your way.
Back on the lake, with a turn of the head I see
Dark mountain green unfurling white clouds.

A boundless expanse, the lake in all its breadth,
Its glittering blue shared with the hue of the sky.
We sail to the shore, then whistle loud and long
And conjure up a breeze from every side.

Willow Waves[14]

Row on row, unbroken, gossamer willows
Their images inverted into the clear ripples.
A study of those on the royal moat—yet not,
For there the spring winds bring the pain of parting.

Their colors match the reflections in the moat;
They blow in the wind like scattered threads of silk.
Their shadowy mass has found good ground to grow in—
Surely they'd hold their own with those of Tao Qian!

Luan Family Rapids

The wind howls in the autumn rain,
The water flows swiftly over the stones.
Jumping waves smack into one another;
White herons start up in fright, then drop down again.

---

14   Editor's note: twigs from the willow, the Chinese word for which sounds the same as the word for "stay,"
were offered by friends on parting. The fifth-century poet Tao Qian (see chapter 1) was renowned for the willows growing in his beloved garden.

By the far bank water clatters over stones;
We walk at the riverside to the southern ford.
Ducks and gulls go floating across the river,
Drifting close to the people from time to time.

Gold Dust Spring

Drink daily from Gold Dust Spring,
And have a thousand years or more of youth.
Blue phoenixes will whirl your dappled dragons upward;
In plumes and feathers you'll attend the Jade Emperor's court.

The waters lie immobile, undisturbed,
Glinting gold and jade, as if they were there to take.
Alone at the crack of dawn with its bright white light,
I go and draw the first spring water of the day.

White Pebble Rapids

Clear shallow water, White Pebble Rapids,
Green rushes sturdy enough to grasp.
Families live east and west of the water,
Wash their silk under the bright moon.

Dangling my feet I sit by the edge of the water,
Run my fingers indifferently through the waves.
As the sun goes down and cold comes over the river
The floating clouds look pale, bereft of color.

Northern Cottage

By the Northern Cottage to the north of the lakewater,
Trees intermingled dapple the red balustrades.
The Southern River's waters meander through,
Lit up, then lost, on the edges of the black forest.

Below the Northern Cottage in the southern mountains
I would make a home looking down on Lake Yi.
I would often want to go off cutting firewood,
Or take my skiff out to the lake and marshes.

Bamboo District Lodge
Sitting alone among secluded bamboos
I play the zither, whistle on and on;
Deep in the woods, unknown to the world,
A bright moon comes and shines on me.

When I visit Bamboo District Lodge,
Daily I grow closer to the Way.
Only the mountain birds come and go—
Dark and deep, no worldly presence here.

Lily Magnolia Hollow
On the tips of branches, hibiscus flowers
In the hills bear petals cased in red;
Down by the stream, by the deserted house,
They bloom in profusion, then fall to earth.

On the green bank where the spring grass gathers,
A young gentleman sits back and take his ease.
To add to his pleasure there are lily magnolia flowers,
Making a riot of color with the lotus blossom.

Lacquer Tree Grove[15]
That man of old was not a proud official:
He had had no experience of the world's affairs,
And so by chance took on a minor posting,
His charge an inanimate cluster of trees.

By nature I've always loved the life of leisure;
I promised it to myself and at last it's achieved.
Wandering round the Lacquer Tree Grove today
I'm back to sharing the pleasures of Old Man Zhuang.

---

15 Editor's note: the poet Guo Pu once called the Daoist philosopher Zhuangzi "proud" for serving as an
official in charge of a lacquer tree orchard.

Pepper Garden[16]

With cup of cinnamon I greet the son of god,
Pollia I give as a gift to the fair one;
Pepper libations I make to the jade mat—
Let my lord come down from among the clouds!

Their red thorns get entangled with people's clothes;
Passers-by linger to savor their fragrant scent.
You can use them to fine effect when cooking food—
So come, my lord, and stoop to pick some peppers.

"Taking Down a Trellis" (*Chu jia* 除架) and "My Thatched Roof is Ruined by the Autumn Wind" (*Maowu wei qiufeng suo po ge* 茅屋為秋風所破歌)

DU FU 杜甫 (712–770)
TRANSLATED BY STEPHEN OWEN

Du Fu is one of the greatest poets of the Tang dynasty; possibly the greatest, unless Li Bai (Li Po, 701–762) merits that title. Du Fu—as socially responsible as Li Bai was extravagantly romantic—always aimed for a career in government but never succeeded in passing the examinations, and then, in 755, was swept up in the disturbances of the An Lushan rebellion (755–763). He traveled around the country in considerable poverty and distress, and spent several years in Sichuan, where the court had fled when forced by the rebellion to leave the capital Chang'an. His years in Sichuan were relatively peaceful and happy, but his experience in the upheavals of civil war and his empathetic response to the suffering of others infused his poetry with profound human feeling; his response to nature is generally to see the natural world as a mirror of the human condition. After the suppression of the rebellion, Du Fu died on the journey back to the capital. "Taking Down a Trellis" is a rather rare admission in poetry of the practicalities of keeping a garden.

"Taking Down a Trellis"

These sticks, tied together, are falling apart,
the gourd leaves grow fewer and shriveled.

I enjoyed good luck that its white flowers formed,
it can hardly refuse to shed its green vines.

---

16 Editor's note: this poem briefly invokes the shamanistic culture of the *Songs of the South* (see chapter 1), with their invocations of the spirits and lists of herbs and aromatic plants. Pei Di's response humorously subverts this air of grandeur.

Autumn insects' voices do not leave it,
and what will the birds think at twilight?

But the cold is coming, all now grows bleak—
man's life, too, always begins well.

"My Thatched Roof is Ruined by the Autumn Wind"

In the high autumn skies of September
    the wind cried out in rage,
Tearing off in whirls from my rooftop
    three piles of thatch.
The thatch flew across the river,
    was strewn on the floodplain,
The high stalks tangled in tips
    of tall forest trees,
The low ones swirled in gusts across ground
    and sank into mud puddles.
The children from the village to the south
    made a fool of me, impotent with age,
Without compunction plundered what was mine
    before my very eyes,
Brazenly took armfuls of thatch,
    ran off into the bamboo,
And I screamed lips dry and throat raw,
    but no use.
Then I made my way home, leaning on a staff,
    sighing to myself.
A moment later the wind calmed down,
    clouds turned dark as ink,
The autumn sky rolling and overcast,
    blacker toward sunset,
And our cotton quilts were years old
    and cold as iron,
My little boy slept poorly,
    kicked rips in them.
Above the bed the roof leaked,
    no place was dry,
And the raindrops ran down like strings,
    without a break.
I have lived through upheavals and ruin
    and have seldom slept very well,

But have no idea how I shall pass
    this night of soaking.
Oh, to own a mighty mansion
    of a hundred thousand rooms,
A great roof for the poorest gentlemen
    of all this world,
        a place to make them smile.
A building unshaken by wind or rain,
    as solid as a mountain,
Oh, when shall I see before my eyes
    a towering roof such as this?
Then I'd accept the ruin of my own little hut
    and death by freezing.

"A Record of the Cottage" (*Caotang ji* 草堂記)

BAI JUYI 白居易 (772–846)

TRANSLATED BY RICHARD E. STRASSBERG

For centuries, Bai Juyi has been one of China's best-loved poets, not only in China itself but also in other parts of East Asia, particularly Japan. Part of the reason for this is his pursuit of simplicity and directness in diction; his poems are said to have been known at all levels of Chinese society. He worked with his close friend Yuan Zhen (see below) on developing and refining his literary style. Rather like Du Fu (see above), Bai often showed in his poems great empathy for the suffering of the ordinary people for whom he was responsible as a civil servant. Bai's formal name was Letian, literally meaning "delighting in fate" or "delighting in Heaven," suggesting his equable personality and willingness to take life as it came. Here we read a prose account of his dwelling on Lushan (Kuanglu Mountain), a mountain particularly associated with Buddhist reclusion; the year before he wrote this account, Bai had been charged with offenses in his personal life as well as his official conduct, and had been sent away from the capital to the post of vice-prefect of Jiangzhou, so it was under these adverse circumstances that he built his cottage in his place of exile. He was aware, too, that enjoyment of his cottage and its surroundings had to await leisure from his official and domestic obligations. In part 2 of this chapter, "Urban Gardens," we find a number of his poems, showing his delight in garden living. Although he is considered a poet of the mid-Tang, Bai lived at a time when the Tang dynasty (which officially ended in 907) was in decline, as the power of the military governors, who had been given free rein in order to suppress the An Lushan rebellion, was tearing the once centralized empire into fragments. Bai's quietism is an understandable response to his time, although he had a long and relatively successful official career after obtaining his presented scholar degree in 800; however, he also suffered periods of banishment for offending higher officials. He was fortunate to be posted to two of China's finest cities, Hangzhou (822–824) and Suzhou (825–826); while in Hangzhou, he directed irrigation work on the West Lake, adding to both its utility and its beauty.

"A Record of the Cottage"

The unique beauty of Kuanglu Mountain ranks foremost in the world. The peak on the north side is called "Censer," and the temple north of this peak is called "Cherished Virtue."[17] Between the peak and the temple, the scene is absolutely unsurpassed and ranks foremost on Mount Lu. In the autumn of the eleventh year of the Yuanhe reign period [816], I, Bai Letian of Taiyuan, saw it and fell in love with it. I was like a far-ranging traveler who passes through his hometown and who so yearns for it that he is unable to leave. So I built a cottage beside the temple facing the peak.

In the spring of the following year, the cottage was completed: three rooms divided by two columns forming two side-chambers with four windows. Its proportions and features agreed with my conception and means. When a window on the north side is opened, cool breezes enter to protect me from the intense summer heat. The high roof facing south absorbs the sunlight so I can withstand the extreme cold in winter. The wood was evenly hewn and left unpainted; the walls were plastered but not white-washed. For the steps, stone was used; for covering the windows, paper. Along with the bamboo shades and burlap curtains—all of this was in accord. In the central room are four wooden couches and two screens of white silk, a lacquered *qin* zither, and books on Confucianism, Daoism, and Buddhism, two or three volumes of each. Ever since I moved in to become the master of it all, I look up at the mountain, bend down to listen to the spring, and gaze at the bamboo, trees, clouds, and rocks beside me. This occupies me completely from dawn to dusk. Suddenly, something may attract my attention and captivate me. Then I feel at ease with my surroundings and inwardly in harmony. After one night, my body is at peace; after the next night, my mind is joyful, and after the third night, I feel thoroughly relaxed and carefree though unable to understand why.

I asked myself the reason for this and found the answer: in front of this dwelling is a flat ground about ten *zhang* in area. In the middle is a raised terrace covering half of it. To its south is a square pond about twice the size of the terrace. Mountain bamboo and wildflowers ring the pond, and in the midst of the pond are white lotus and white fish. Farther south, one reaches a rocky ravine. Lining the ravine are ancient pines and old firs, each about as large as a circle formed by ten men. I don't know how many hundreds of feet high they are. Their long limbs pat the clouds as their lower branches stroke the pond. They stand erect like banners or resemble open parasols, or seem like dragons and snakes slithering along. Below the pines is much dense brush and many creeping vines. Their leaves have intertwined to form a canopy which blocks the sun

---

17 Kuanglu 匡廬 (literally, "hermitages of the Kuangs") is popularly known as Lushan 廬山 or Mount Lu. It was named after the seven Kuang brothers who retired and built thatched hermitages here to cultivate the Dao during the Zhou dynasty. Censer Peak 香爐峰 is named after its shape, which resembles an incense burner. "Cherished Virtue" (*yiai* 遺愛) refers to the love that later generations feel for virtuous officials in the past.

and moon so that their light never reaches the ground. At the height of summer the air is like autumn during the eighth and ninth months. White stones have been spread out to form a path leading in and out. Five *bu* north of the cottage are layers of crags and piles of rocks like an ornamental inlay or anthills on top of which various kinds of trees and wild plants grow. Their verdant shade is copious and their red fruits are abundant. I don't know their names. They remain unchanged through the four seasons. And then, there is a cascade whose water I use to brew the tea leaves growing hereabout. When enthusiasts see this, they can spend days in endless enjoyment. To the east of the cottage is a waterfall three feet high that splashes down along the edges of the stairs into a stone channel. At dawn and at dusk, it resembles white silk. At night, it sounds like tinkling jade ornaments or like *qin* and *zhu* zithers. The western side of the cottage leans against a foothill on the right side of a crag to the north. I split some bamboo and built an aqueduct through the air to bring over water from the spring on the crag. Like a divided artery or a suspended line, it flows onto the roof and then drips down onto the stairs like a string of pearls while its mist is like rain drops and dew drops, dripping, spraying, sprinkling, scattering as the wind blows it far away. From every side of the cottage, one's eyes, ears, and feet can reach: in spring, the flowers of Embroidered Valley; in summer, the clouds of Stone Gate Ravine; in autumn, the moon over Tiger Stream;[18] in winter, the snow on Censer Peak. When overcast, these scenes are obscured, but in clear light, they become visible. At dusk, all things are swallowed up, then, at dawn, they are disgorged. There are a thousand transformations and ten thousand appearances—I could not possibly record all of them in detail. So I can only say that the scenery here ranks foremost on Mount Lu.

Ah! When a man builds a substantial home, embellishes it with fine furnishings, and dwells comfortably therein, he finds it difficult to avoid an attitude of proud satisfaction. Now I am the master of all these things. With these things before me, my understanding can grow, knowing that they represent excellent examples of their types. How could I not feel outwardly at ease and inwardly in harmony, with my body at peace and my mind joyful? In the past, eighteen men including Yong, Yuan, Zong, and Lei came to this mountain together and wished to remain here until their deaths.[19]

---

18   Tiger Stream (Huxi 虎溪) is in front of the Eastern Forest Monastery (Donglinsi 東林寺) and is known in legend as the border beyond which the eminent monk Huiyuan (334–416) would not cross, except on one occasion, when he was seeing off the poet Tao Qian (365–427) and the Daoist Lu Xiujing 陸修靜 (ca. 406– ca. 477). Absorbed in conversation, Huiyuan forgot his usual rule; he was reminded of it only when he heard the roar of a tiger, whereupon the three friends broke into laughter. This legend began to circulate in the Tang and is without historical foundation, for Lu Xiujing's dates place him much later than both Huiyuan and Tao.

19   Huiyong 惠永 was abbot of the Western Forest Monastery (Xilinsi 西林寺) and Huiyuan was abbot of the Eastern Forest Monastery (Donglinsi 東林寺). Zong Bing (375–443), a lay Buddhist and art critic, spent a period of retreat on Mount Lu. Lei Cizong 雷次宗 (386–448), another lay Buddhist, also dwelled in retirement on Mount Lu. These figures were among the "Eighteen Worthies of the White Lotus Society" (*Bailian shi baxian* 白蓮十八賢), the most outstanding members of a prominent lay Buddhist association. Of the four

Though they lived a thousand years before my time, I understand them, for they felt as I do. Moreover, I recall that throughout my life, whether dwelling in a humble house or behind the vermilion gates of an official residence, wherever I have stopped, even if for a day or two, I have always piled up a few baskets of earth to make a terrace, gathered small rocks to form a mountain, and built a ring around a few ladles of water to make a pond—such is my obsession with landscape!

Suddenly one day, my fortunes reversed and I came to serve here in Jiangzhou.[20] The prefect consoled me with his kindness, and Mount Lu has received me with the spiritual beauty of its scenery. Heaven has provided me with this opportunity and Earth has provided me with this place. I finally have been able to fulfill my desire, so why search for more? Yet, I am still constrained by this superfluous position and have not been able to conclude some lingering matters. I can only come and go and have not the leisure to dwell here in peace. I must await a future time when my brothers and sisters have all been married off, when my term as vice-prefect is completed, and when I can decide on my own whether to serve or retire. Then, with my left hand leading my wife and children and my right hand grasping a *qin* zither and books, I will certainly spend the rest of my days here and fulfill my life's ambition. The pure streams and white rocks will bear witness to these words.

On the twenty-seventh day of the third month [April 17, 817], I moved into this new cottage. On the ninth day of the fourth month [April 28], I served a vegetarian feast, tea, and fruits to entertain twenty-two people including Yuan Jixu of Henan, Zhang Yunzhong of Fanyang, Zhang Shenzhi of Nanyang, venerables of the Eastern and Western Forest Temples Cou, Lang, Man, Hui, and Jian[21] and on this occasion, I composed "A Record of the Cottage."

---

mentioned only Huiyong and Huiyuan remained on the mountain. Zong Bing fell ill and left, and Lei Cizong accepted an official appointment.

20 This refers to Bai's demotion to vice-prefect of Jiangzhou.

21 Yuan Jixu 元集虛 of Henan (from modern Luoyang, Henan) had served as chief musician and later retired to Mount Lu. Zhang Yunzhong 張允中 of Fanyang (modern Beijing) and Zhang Shenzhi 張深之 of Nanyang (modern Nanyang, Henan) remain unidentified. Cou is the monk Shencou 神湊; Man is the monk Zhiman 智滿; Jian is the monk Shijian 士堅, all from the Eastern Forest Monastery. Lang 朗 and Hui 晦 remain unidentified.

"Presented to the Landlord Mu the Thirty-Sixth after I Visited the Yunju Temple" (*You Yunju si zeng Mu sanshiliu dizhu* 遊雲居寺贈穆三十六地主)

BAI JUYI 白居易

TRANSLATED BY XIAOSHAN YANG

In poems by Bai Juyi and others in the next section, "Urban Gardens," we find many variations on the idea that true ownership of a garden depends on love for the garden scenery. In this poem, on the mountain site of a temple, no doubt with an associated garden, we find the extension of this idea to wilder scenery: although Mr. Mu is the "landlord" of this territory, the ending of the poem affirms Bai himself as the one to whom the mountain really belongs. His love of the mountain (and we recall that, according to Confucius, it is the humane person who loves mountains) supersedes the legal ownership of the land as a higher and more genuine form of possessing "spectacular sites."

"Presented to the Landlord Mu the Thirty-Sixth after I Visited the Yunju Temple"

In the depth of the tangled peaks lies the path to the Yunju Temple;
As we tread together among the flowers, I alone treasure the spring.
Spectacular sites originally have no established owners;
Mountains mostly belong to those who love mountains.

"Eastern Mound by Longxing Temple of Yongzhou" (*Yongzhou Longxing si dong qiu ji* 永州龍興寺東丘記)

LIU ZONGYUAN 柳宗元 (773–819)

TRANSLATED BY H. C. CHANG

Liu Zongyuan was distinguished as a master of lucid and readable prose; although some of his poems are well known, he was not one of the great Tang poets. He was a leader of a literary movement advocating a return to the austere prose style of the pre-Han classics, as opposed to the florid "parallel prose" style which had been adopted from the Han dynasty onward and had become a requirement for the government examinations. After rapid promotion in his official career, he got into trouble and was sent away from the court to posts in remote parts of the country. Yongzhou was one of these places, and Liu's records of his excursions around the town are some of the most significant early Chinese travel records; the genres of travel and garden records have considerable overlap. Liu's eight accounts of Yongzhou constantly view its natural surroundings through the lens of his experience of exile, particularly when he uses hitherto unappreciated landscapes as a metaphor for his own talent that was being wasted in a remote region, far away from the center of power. Liu is particularly famous for his allegorical writings such as "Camel-Back the Gardener" (see part 2 of this chapter); the Daoist influence that can be seen in this essay also pervades his other work. He died in office in his second place of exile in the far south.

"Eastern Mound by Longxing Temple of Yongzhou"

Those in quest of interesting scenery take delight chiefly in two types of view: the expanse and spaciousness of the open view, and the immediate impact and hidden mysteries of the confined view. Where the ground rises steeply over potential obstructions or breaks through thick vegetation to give an impression of vast space and distance, it is suited to the open view. Where a hillock or mound intrudes or shrubs and undergrowth lie in concealment to offer unexpected scenes at every turn, the spot is more suited to the confined view. Where an open view presents itself, one may enhance its attraction by building raised terraces and projecting pavilions, to enable the rambler to follow the revolving motions of the sun and the stars or to watch a storm in progress; and it would be idle to complain that the view is too sweeping. Where a confined view presents itself, one may also enhance its attraction by planting trees with a rich foliage or piling up rocks, to suggest the effect of a grotto or recess or arbor or clearing; and it would likewise be idle to complain that the view is too restricted.

That which I call Eastern Mound offers the confined view. To begin with, it was waste land outside the temple grounds. When I bought it, I joined it to the temple, to whose northeastern glade it formed an extension. Without disturbing its natural contours, which included hollows and cavities, swamps and islets, I had a thick screen of bamboos planted, and a bridge with many bends built across the swamps. And I also had nearly three hundred trees planted, including cinnamon, juniper, pine, fir, catalpa, and cedar. I then had ornamental plants and rocks laid out in criss-cross patterns all over the mound. The ground was now a carpet of green grass, and the trees provided shade and seclusion; and in this labyrinth wanderers often found that they no longer knew the route by which they had entered. The air was balmy without being oppressive, for there would usually be a cool breeze. A water pavilion and a hut further added to the interest of this example of the confined view.

And yet visitors have been heard to remark on its narrow and restricted views as a shortcoming. Shortcoming indeed! Longxing, so prominently situated, is, to be sure, a temple of which the district may well feel proud. From its towers one may salute the "Old Man" star;[22] a re-sited main gate has opened up the prospect of the river Xiang and its valley. In short, a pre-eminent example of the open view. But to accord the same treatment to this little mound and denude it by removing its trees and vegetation would cause it to lose its natural advantages. And this would be to reduce what I maintain to be the two types of view to a single one. For indeed—

> Eastern Mound is a secluded place,
>> Where the weary traveler may rest his feet;

---

22 Canopus

Eastern Mound is dark and mysterious,
    Yet there is much to delight the eye;
The foot of Eastern Mound
    Provides a retreat from the muggy heat;
At the top of Eastern Mound
    Joyfully the people congregate;
I will admit it, the view is confined—
    Will no one wander there with me?

Being without the awe-inspiring virtues of Duke Shao,[23] whose people kept his memory green after his death by jealously guarding his favorite tree, I do greatly fear the descent of shears and axes upon this my mound. And so I address this appeal to gentlemen of a future age who may hold opinions different from mine in regard to landscape views.

PART 2

URBAN GARDENS

"On the Waterside Pavilion of Attendant Censor Wang" (*Ti Wang shiyu chiting* 題王侍御池亭)

BAI JUYI 白居易 (772–846)
TRANSLATED BY XIAOSHAN YANG

In this poem, written in 815 in Chang'an, Bai plays with the idea of the true ownership of gardens attaching to those with the aesthetic sensitivity to appreciate the garden and the ability or opportunity to give full play to that sensitivity. Behind the idea of aesthetically possessing a garden without actually owning it was the phenomenon of absenteeism among garden owners in such metropolitan cities as Chang'an and Luoyang. Attendant Censor Wang Qi (760–847), in this poem, was not an absentee landlord in the usual sense of the phrase but, entangled in his official business, had little time to visit his own garden, thereby forfeiting his identity as its owner—an identity taken over by Bai Juyi as a frequent visitor. Bai reprises this idea in "Staying Over at the Waterside Pavilion of the Mansion of Governor Dou" (see below).

"On the Waterside Pavilion of Attendant Censor Wang"

Locked deep inside the vermilion gate, the spring pond is full;
Roses fall upon the bank and nutgrasses soak in water.
Who after all is the owner of the pond of this garden?—
Seldom comes the owner, often comes the guest.

---

23   Duke Shao was the founder of the ruling house of Yan in the Zhou dynasty.

"Harmonizing with Letian's Poem on the Pavilion of the Wang Family" (*He Letian ti Wang jia tingzi* 和樂天題王家亭子)

YUAN ZHEN 元稹 (779–831)
TRANSLATED BY XIAOSHAN YANG

Yuan Zhen, a close friend of Bai Juyi, was both a great poet and a distinguished statesman of the Tang dynasty. Yuan is said to have been a descendant of the royal family of the Tuoba Wei, the non-Chinese dynasty that ruled in the north from the late fourth to mid-sixth century. In 803, he and Bai Juyi passed a special imperial examination and were both appointed to posts in the imperial library; this was the start of a famous friendship and literary collaboration. Yuan was particularly influential in reviving the folk-song style of the old "Music Bureau" (*yuefu*) ballads, which he used to comment on current affairs; Bai also participated in this movement. Here Yuan responds, in the same meter and rhyme-scheme, to the quatrain above by his friend Bai Juyi, similarly contrasting the financial power of the wealthy to purchase land with their lack of leisure, if not disposition, to enjoy it.

"Harmonizing with Letian's Poem on the Pavilion of the Wang Family"

Blown by the wind, sheaths of bamboo shoots drift upon red steps;
Beaten by the rain, flowers of paulownia trees cover the green nutgrasses.
In the grand capital city, people with wealth have no days of leisure;
Many buy a pond, few sail upon it.

"In Front of My Cottage I Recently Dug a Pond to Raise Fish and Plant Lotus, Providing the Delight of Seclusion Every Day" (*Caotang qian xin kai yi chi yang yu zhong he ri you you qu* 草堂前新開一池養魚種荷日有幽趣)

BAI JUYI 白居易
TRANSLATED BY XIAOSHAN YANG

This poem was written in 817, when Bai was stationed in Zhongzhou, on the Yangtze River some distance downstream from its junction with the Jialing River. As in the later poem "Sailing on the Pond in Spring," which refers to his garden residence in Luoyang, Bai's preference for what is immediately at hand to the farther away (the Three Gorges were somewhat farther downstream) is predicated on the former being part of a possessed space. The claim to ownership here is further strengthened through the act of naming the new construction "Pond of the Bai Family."

"In Front of My Cottage I Recently Dug a Pond to Raise Fish and Plant Lotus,
Providing the Delight of Seclusion Every Day"

The waters of the Three Gorges bellow;
Effusive are their waves of the ten thousand acres.
Those cannot compare with the newly dug pond,
Where a breeze stirs some ripples.
Small duckweeds are added to the shallow water;
Newborn cattails are turning luxurious.
Red carps are two or three inches long;
White lotus flowers number eight or nine sprays.
Circumscribing the water, a path is about to be completed;
Protecting the bank, fences have been just stuck in.
Already by the traveler in the mountain,
It is called the Pond of the Bai Family.

"The Pavilion in My Prefectural Residence" (*Jun ting* 郡亭)

BAI JUYI 白居易

TRANSLATED BY XIAOSHAN YANG

Bai Juyi's representation of the urban garden as a hermitage in the city predated his ownership
of the Lüdao house and garden in Luoyang, where he was to develop this theme to the full (see
below). It seems to have first emerged in his Hangzhou years (822–824), especially in the poems
describing his prefectural residence, of which this one, written in 822, is representative. On both
the thematic and the lexical levels, the poem foreshadows "Middling Hermit" (see below).

"The Pavilion in My Prefectural Residence"

In early morning I get up to take charge of official business;
At noontime I lie down with my gate shut.
Except when I personally take care of my light duties,
Most of the time I am in front of my zither and books.
Besides, there is the Xubai Pavilion;
Sitting there, I can see Haimen Mountain.
When the tide comes, I lean on the rails;
When guests arrive, I set up a dinner party.
All day long, I face clouds and waters;
Sometimes, I listen to pipes and strings.

In this way I spend my days:
Neither busy, nor idle.
The woods in the mountains are too desolate;
The halls in the palaces are too noisy.
Only this pavilion in the prefectural residence
Gets to be between quiet and hustle.

"On the Snow Pile Estate of the Xue Family at Pingquan" (*Ti Pingquan Xue jia Xuedui zhuang* 題平泉薛家雪堆莊)

BAI JUYI 白居易
TRANSLATED BY XIAOSHAN YANG

This country estate was one Bai considered buying before eventually purchasing his garden residence in the more urban setting of the Lüdao ward of Luoyang, to which many later poems refer.

"On the Snow Pile Estate of the Xue Family at Pingquan"

A grotesque rock of a thousand years, it must have formed by itself;
A magical font with a belt of watercourse, by whom was it dug?
The rock twists into the curling neck of a blue snake;
The fount spurts out a shining pile of white snow.
Under the blazing sun and in dry spell, rain can be constantly seen;
In the gloomiest twelfth month, thunders can still be heard.
What I regretfully sigh over is that it is located so far away from the gate of the capital
That I wouldn't get to come here every day on a palanquin.

"On My Garden Pond, with a Preface" (*Chishang pian bing xu* 池上篇并序)

BAI JUYI 白居易
TRANSLATED BY XIAOSHAN YANG

Bai Juyi's private garden in the Lüdao ward of Luoyang provided the site for his life as a "middling hermit." Bai purchased the house in 824 from the Tian family; previously it had belonged to a member of the same family as Bai's wife, née Yang. In 825, after staying in Luoyang for ten months, Bai Juyi left to take up an appointment as governor of Suzhou. In 829, he returned to Luoyang and stayed there for the rest of his life. Of the components of the garden, the pond was the most important site. During the day, the pond provided a space for such pleasurable activities as drinking and boating; at night, it turned into a quiet place for reflection, as described in "Night Scene on the Pond" (see below).

"On My Garden Pond, with a Preface"

The best scenery of the capital city lies in the northeast corner; the best of the northeast corner lies in the Lüdao Ward; the best of the Lüdao Ward lies in the northwest corner. The first residence inside the gate of the north wall is where Old Man Bai Letian has retired in old age. It measures seventeen *mu*, with one-third occupied by the house, one-fifth by water, and one-ninth by bamboo, criss-crossed by islets, trees, bridges, and footpaths.

Earlier, when Letian first came into possession of the place, he was very pleased but thought: "Although I have a terrace and a pond, they cannot be kept for long if I do not have grain." Therefore he built a granary east of the pond. Then he thought: "Although I have children, they cannot be taught without books." Therefore he built a library north of the pond. Then again he thought: "Although I have guests and friends, they cannot be entertained without zither and wine." Therefore, he built a pavilion for playing the zither west of the pond and added stone wine cups there.

When Letian was relieved as the prefect of Hangzhou, he brought back with him a rock from Tianzhu Mountain and two cranes of Huating breed. At that time he began to build West Flat Bridge and constructed Pond Loop. When he was relieved as the prefect of Suzhou, he brought back with him rocks from Lake Tai, white lotuses, caltrops with twisted waists, and a boat of blue planks. Then he built Central High Bridge, which connected the paths of the three islets. When he was relieved as the vice-director of the Bureau of Punishments, he had a thousand *hu* of millet and a cart of books. In addition, he gathered ten servants that could sing as well as play pipes, chime-stones, and strings.

Earlier, Chen Xiaoshan of Yingchuan taught him a brewing method, which produced wine with excellent bouquet; Cui Huishu of Boling gave him a *qin* with clear resonance; Jiang Fashou, a guest from Shu, taught him the music tone "Autumn Thoughts," with sounds that were quite serene; Yang Zhenyi of Hongnong gave him three slates of dark blue rock in rectangular shape with level and smooth surfaces, on which one can either sit or lie. It was not until the summer of the third year of the Dahe reign [828] that Letian's request to be appointed advisor to the heir apparent was granted, so that he was assigned to a branch office of the court in Luoyang, where he retired to his garden pond. What he obtained during his three appointments and what the four gave him, plus his untalented self, now all became things of the pond.

When the wind blows upon the pond in spring, when the moon shines on the pond in autumn, when the lotuses blossom on the fragrant water at dawn, when the cranes cry over the clear dew at dusk,[24] he would rub Yang's rocks, raise the cup with Chen's wine, take hold of Cui's *qin*, and play Jiang's "Autumn Thoughts." Insouciant and self-contented, he became oblivious of everything else. After he was done with drinking and playing his *qin*, he directed his boy musicians to climb the Pavilion on the Middle Islet to play "Prelude to Rainbow Skirts."[25] As the sound drifted with the wind, it sometimes converged and sometimes dispersed, lingering for a long time among misty bamboo groves and moonlit waves. Before the music was done, Letian was already intoxicated and fell in drunken slumber on the rocks. As he got up, he chanted out, impromptu, what was neither Regulated Verse nor Rhapsody. Turtle[26] happened to be holding the writing brush, so he had the piece inscribed on the rocks. As it began to resemble roughly verse stanzas, it was given the title "On My Garden Pond":

In a house on ten *mu* of land,
With a garden of five *mu*,
There is a pond of water,
And ten thousand stalks of bamboo.
Don't say the land is too narrow;
Don't say the location is isolated.
Enough for me to stand on my own,
Enough for me to settle down.
There are halls and pavilions;
There are bridges and boats;
There are books and wine;
There are songs and strings.
There is an oldster in the midst of them,
With his white hair fluttering.
He appreciates his lot and knows when to be content,
Wanting nothing beyond what he has,
Like a bird choosing a tree to perch that
Only seeks a stable nest;
Like a frog staying in a dry well that
Does not know how wide the ocean is.

---

24 In the eighth month of the year, we are told in the *Record of the Wind and Earth* (*Fengtu ji* 風土記), when the white dew begins to fall, cranes voice high-pitched calls of warning to each other to move to a different place to avoid any forthcoming danger.

25 "Rainbow Skirts" (*Nishang* 霓裳) is the abbreviation of "Music of Rainbow Skirts and Coats of Feathers" (*Nishang yuyi qu* 霓裳羽衣曲). Originally from Liangzhou, this musical suite and dance were introduced to the Tang court during the Kaiyuan reign (713–741) and became particularly popular because of the deft performance by Emperor Xuanzong's prized consort Yang Guifei. By Bai Juyi's time, the dance form had been lost, but he managed to recover the music with the help of his friend Yuan Zhen. The "Prelude" (*Sanxu* 散序), the first part of the musical suite, was not accompanied by dance.

26 Turtle, A Gui 阿龜, was the son of Bai Juyi's brother Bai Xingjian (776–826).

Magical cranes and strange rocks,
Purple caltrops and white lotuses,—
Those are all what I love,
And they are all in front of me.
Drinking a cup occasionally,
Chanting a poem from time to time.
Wife and children are happy;
Roosters and dogs are at ease.
What leisure, what fun!
I shall spend the rest of my life in here.

"Night Scene on the Pond" (*Chishang yejing* 池上夜景)

BAI JUYI 白居易
TRANSLATED BY XIAOSHAN YANG

The thematic thrust of this poem lies in the last couplet, where the garden pond supersedes the Canglang river (see chapter 1) as the symbolic place for preserving integrity through reclusion.

"Night Scene on the Pond"

From the clear sky stars and the moon fall into the pond,
With pellucid freshness and spotless green, it shimmers from inside out.
Clear and crystal, dew on the mat embraces the anointment of night;
Rustling and flicking, wind on my robe precedes the coolness of autumn.
Wild birds descend where there is no disturbance of people;
Still grasses smell fragrant as I just wake up from sleep.
My only question is whether I can get rid of dust and dirt;
Why do I have to go to the Canglang Waters to wash my tassels?

"On My House in the Lüdao Ward" (*Lüdao ju san shou zhi yi* 履道居三首之一; one of three)

BAI JUYI 白居易
TRANSLATED BY XIAOSHAN YANG

Don't be disappointed that our ground is narrow and our pavilion small;
Don't regret that our family is poor and our means meager.
For the grand there are tall gates locking spacious mansions,
Yet their owners have never returned even in old age!

"Sailing on the Pond in Spring" (*Fan chunchi* 汎春池)

BAI JUYI 白居易

TRANSLATED BY XIAOSHAN YANG

This poem, written in 825, is thematically and stylistically typical of Bai's numerous poems on his Lüdao garden. The opening lines are a fine example of Bai's contrastive rhetoric, through which he highlights, and yet reconciles, the opposites within the garden. The first couplet seems to contain a nostalgic scene in his memory; instead of being an object of desire, however, images of faraway natural landscapes turn out to be foils for the superiority of the artificial, but possessed, spaces of the garden pond. Instead of a transition from visual to mental experience (the usual practice in Chinese poetry), Bai moves in the opposite direction, from the imagined to the actual, while negating what is absent and affirming what is present, expressing his contentment with the garden scenery that has "fallen into his hands" by the will of Heaven, which thus endorses his love for it.

"Sailing on the Pond in Spring"

White duckweed at the bends of the Xiang Isles,
Green bamboo at the mouth of the Shan Creek:
Each lies at one end of the earth—
Though truly lovely, they are not in my possession.
How can they compare with what is inside this yard,
Where water and bamboo crisscross left and right?
Hundreds and thousands of stalks of frosty bamboo;
Six or seven *mu* of misty waves.
The deep and clear water stirs on stairs and pavements;
Its light and pellucidity glint on doors and windows.
The snakeskin of the bamboo has fine patterns;
Its mirror surface is pure without a speck.
The owner comes over the bridge—
An old man supported by two servant boys.
Fearing to sully the clear and cool waves,
I first shake off my dusty ribbons.
On the waves, a single leaf of a boat,
In the boat, a large jug of wine.
The jug opened, the boat untied:
Off I go, wherever chance takes me.
Now I circle before Cattail Beach,
Then I moor behind Peach Isle:
Leaving alone flowers that fall into my cup,
Running into willows that brush low into my face.
Half tipsy I lose all sense of where I am,
Leaning on the oars, I dumbly turn my head.

I no longer know where this is—
Is it still the human realm or not?
Since this pond was originally dug, who knows
How many owners have passed it on to others?
The Yang family has been gone for a long time,
But the Tians were here not that long ago.
Heaven gave it to one who loves waters:
Finally it fell into my hands.

"Staying Over at the Waterside Pavilion of the Mansion of Governor Dou" (*Su Dou shijun zhuang shuiting* 宿竇使君莊水亭)

BAI JUYI 白居易
TRANSLATED BY XIAOSHAN YANG

In this poem, written in 828, Bai again plays with the idea of garden ownership: Bai himself, as a constant visitor, is a truer "owner" of Governor Dou's garden than the governor himself, who is absent on an official posting.

"Staying Over at the Waterside Pavilion of the Mansion of Governor Dou"

Where is the governor?—he is in Jiangdong.
The willows by the pond are turning yellow-green and the apricots pink.
Whenever I am in the mood I come over, and whenever coming over stay over—
Who can tell who the owner is?

"Middling Hermit" (*Zhong yin* 中隱), "Inscribed on the Western Pavilion" (*Ti Xi ting* 題西亭), and "Upon My Small Garden" (*Zi ti xiao yuan* 自題小園)

BAI JUYI 白居易
TRANSLATED BY XIAOSHAN YANG

This poem, written in 829, shortly after Bai's final retirement to Luoyang, appears to be the first instance of the use of the term "middling hermit." It takes up themes from earlier poems such as "The Pavilion in My Prefectural Residence" (see above) of 822; the line "Neither busy, nor idle" is repeated from there. There are, however, two new elements or motifs in Bai Juyi's poetry after his move to Luoyang: first, an emphasis on the ownership of a garden both as a guarantor and as an embodiment of the life of a middling hermit; and second, the importance of an urban location in providing practical comfort and convenience conducive to an untroubled life.

"Middling Hermit"

Great hermits reside in the capital;
Petty hermits go into the mountains.[27]
In the mountains it is too desolate;
In the capital it is too boisterous.
It would be better to be a middling hermit:
Hiding in the Regency in the Eastern Capital.
As if in office, as if in seclusion,
Neither busy, nor idle.
You don't exert your mind or body;
Yet you are spared hunger and cold.
There is no official business all year round,
Yet there is salary every single month.
If you are fond of climbing,
There is Autumn Mountain south of the city;
If you like wandering around,
There is Spring Park east of the city;
If you want to get drunk,
You can frequent banquets;
In Luoyang there are many gentlemen,
With whom you can chat freely;
If you want to sleep on thick pillows,
Just shut yourself deep inside the abode;
Then there will be no guests in carriages
Showing up at your front gate unexpectedly.
In this world there is only one life to live,
And it is difficult to have it both ways.
Humble, and you suffer from cold and hunger;
Noble, and you are full of worry and fear.
It is only this middling hermit
Who can live in both prosperity and peace.
Frustration and success, abundance and scarcity:
He lives right in between those four.

---

27 The first couplet here is a rewriting of its counterpart in Wang Kangju's 王康琚 "Against Summoning the Recluse" (*Fan zhaoyin shi* 反招隱詩) (4th century): "The petty hermits hide in the hills and marshes; / The great hermits hide in the court and marketplace."

"Inscribed on the Western Pavilion"

Much have I seen of the rich and noble of the vermilion gates;
Their bodies are gone before their gardens are finished.
Luckily, since I became the master of the Western Pavilion,
I have been visiting this pond for five years.

"Upon My Small Garden"

Not competing for the splendor of the mansion;
Not competing for the grandeur of the garden,
I only compete to be present as owner,
Which I have been for over ten years running.
I look around at this and that grand house,
Lining up inside the capital city;
With white walls flanking vermilion gates,
Splendidly they face each other across wide streets.
But where on earth are their owners?—
The wealthy and noble are gone and will not return.
The pond was opened up only for the fish;
The trees were planted only for the birds.
How can they compare with the owner of this small garden,
Who comes with a walking stick whenever he has leisure?
Now and then he meets with relatives and friends,
The whole night through they enjoy wine and zither.
With all this he may content himself—
There is no need to be envious of big ponds and terraces.

"Playfully Presented, on Behalf of My Garden" (*Dai linyuan xi zeng* 代林園戲贈),
"Another Playful Reply" (*Chong xi da* 重戲答), "On My Family Pond, Written in
Leisure, Sent to the Daoist Adept Zhang of Mount Wangwu" (*Xian ti jiating chi
ji Wangwu Zhang daoshi* 閑題家庭池寄王屋張道士), and "Written on Mansions
in Luoyang" (*Ti Luoyang zhaidi* 題洛陽宅第)

BAI JUYI 白居易
TRANSLATED BY XIAOSHAN YANG

The first poem was written on returning from a social gathering in the extensive garden of a
grand mansion owned by Pei Du (765–839), which was known as one of the finest gardens in
Luoyang. In this as well as other poems, however, Bai expresses greater satisfaction with his
own garden because in it he is host (or owner; the Chinese words are the same) rather than
guest, and the intimate relationship he has with his own garden is preferable to the grandeur

of others gardens. Moreover, in his relationship with his own garden, the length of duration compensates for small size.

"Playfully Presented, on Behalf of My Garden"

In the southern courtyard there have been few gatherings this fall;
In the western ward there have been frequent comings-and-goings recently.
Excellent as the pond and pavilion of the Grand Councilor are—
How can being a guest compare to being a host?

"Another Playful Reply"

Small pool, low pavilion, they are lovely to myself;
Big pond, tall terraces, they do not have anything to do with me.
Don't envy the excellence of the garden of the Pei family—
Would I be human if I should detest the old and love the new?

"On My Family Pond, Written in Leisure, Sent to the Daoist Adept Zhang of Mount Wangwu"

There are white rocks shining;
There is clear water murmuring;
There is an old man with a snow-white head,
Strolling and sauntering all around.
Neither advancing on the road to high positions,
Nor retreating to the deep mountains.
The deep mountains are too empty;
The road to high positions is too difficult.
Neither can compare with the pond on my family ground,
Where I am joyful and leisurely, without worry.
There is food to suit my palate;
There is wine to flush my cheeks.
In a trance I roam around in the land of intoxication;
Shutting down my hearing and seeing, I visit the gate to subtlety.
Enlightened by the book of five thousand words,[28]
I have lived in leisure for the past twelve years.[29]
To the rich I do not throw my glance;

---

28 A reference to the Daoist classic *Laozi* 老子, also known as the *Daode jing* 道德經.

29 Bai Juyi's poem was written in 840, twelve years after he retired to Luoyang in 829.

With the powerful I do not strain to associate.
Only with Master of the Temple of Heaven,
Do I exchange visits from time to time.

"Written on Mansions in Luoyang"

Whose mansions are those with woods and water?
Their gates are tall and their grounds wide.
Hanging fish pendants cling to the blue gables;
Running horse figures protect the vermilion fences.
Their arbors envelop the warmth of the mist in spring;
Their yards lock in the chill of the moonlight in autumn.
The pines are oozing pitch as if pasted with amber;
The bamboos are powdery, as if spread with pearl-like jade.
Who might be the owners of the ponds and terraces?
Most of them are generals and ministers.
Never having been here throughout their lives;
They can only roll open their estate maps to take a look.

"Playfully Presented to Wang Zhongzhou, upon Hearing That Peonies Were Blossoming at His Place" (*Wen Wang Zhongzhou suoju mudan hua fa yin xizeng* 聞王仲周所居牡丹花發因戲贈)

WU YUANHENG 武元衡 (758–815)
TRANSLATED BY XIAOSHAN YANG

Wu Yuanheng was a distant relative of Empress Wu Zetian, who ruled China as regent for her husband and son from 675 to 690 and then in her own name (the only woman ever to do so) from 690 to 705. Wu Yuanheng's lasting importance is as a statesman, not as a poet, although he was considered by one late-Tang critic to be the leading poet in a style described as "precious and beautiful" (*guiqi meili*). After a significant official career, in which he seems to have made as many enemies as allies, he was assassinated by associates of a warlord who believed Wu was the chief proponent of a military campaign against him. In this poem, as in those by Bai Juyi and Yuan Zhen above, we see Wu questioning the true ownership of the unvisited garden.

"Playfully Presented to Wang Zhongzhou, upon Hearing That Peonies Were Blossoming at His Place"

I hear that flowers are blossoming in your yard in late spring;
Chang'an's talents should be frequently watching them.
Flowers blossom, flowers fall, but no one sees them;
May I ask who the owner is?

"Strolling in the East of the City" (*Chengdong xianyou* 城東閒遊) and "The Scholar's Humble Dwelling" (*Loushi ming* 陋室銘)

LIU YUXI 劉禹錫 (772–842)

Liu Yuxi was a close friend of both Liu Zongyuan and Bai Juyi (see above), and is known as a writer of both prose and poetry. His family is said to have been of non-Chinese origin, and his own periods of political banishment to regions of south China inhabited by non-Chinese people also seem to have stimulated an interest in folk culture that led to his introduction into "high" poetry of folk-song motifs. He also wrote poems of political protest (that led to his banishment). Although his work has been generally underestimated by contrast with that of his contemporaries, his "Inscription for a Humble Dwelling" ("The Scholar's Humble Dwelling"), which can be understood either as a poem with lines of irregular length or as a short passage of parallel prose, is very well known. In "Strolling in the East of the City," Liu, like other poets, plays on the idea of absentee ownership, but his treatment has a hidden twist. The garden he describes lacks a permanent aesthetic owner. Even though "men of leisure" enjoy it "all day long," the dispersal of the guests at sunset signals the beginning of a long night's journey of the "spring scenery" into unappreciated oblivion. The poem begins with a question about the whereabouts of "the owner of the pond and pavilion" and ends with a picture of a scene devoid of human presence.

"Strolling in the East of the City"
TRANSLATED BY XIAOSHAN YANG

May I ask where the owner of the pond and pavilion is?
Most of the time he is positioned at the ford to high officialdom.
With thousands in gold he purchased such supreme scenery,
Only to let it belong to men of leisure all day long.
Zigzagging, they enter the bamboo paths;
Winding, they tour the flower bushes.
At sunset, the guests disperse,
With spring scenery pointlessly locked up in the garden.

"The Scholar's Humble Dwelling"
TRANSLATED BY JAMES BLACK

Who heeds the hill's bare height until
Some legend grows around the hill?
Who cares how deep the stream before
Its fame is writ in country lore?
And so this humble hut of mine
May shelter virtues half divine.
The moss may climb its ruined stair,
And grassy stains the curtain wear,

But scholars at their ease within,
For all but Ignorance enters in,
With simple lute the time beguile,
Or *Golden Classic*'s page a while.
No discords here their ears assail,
Nor cares of business to bewail.
This is the life the Sages led.
"How were they poor?" Confucius said.

"Spring Thoughts (Two Poems)" (*Chun si* 春思; second poem)

ZHANG YAOTIAO 張窈窕 (9TH CENTURY)
TRANSLATED BY JEANNE LARSEN

As is the case with many early women writers, little is known of Zhang Yaotiao beyond her name. She is believed to have lived in Chengdu, in Sichuan.

"Spring Thoughts (Two Poems)" (second poem)

II
This phoenix tree beside the well:
       I moved it here myself.
During the night, flowers
       opened up
              on the farthest
                     branch.
If I hadn't planted it
       deep in the compound,
              near the women's rooms,
Spring would pass
       the household gate
              and I—
                     how would I know?

"Sent to the Owner of the Garden" (*Ji yuanlin zhuren* 寄園林主人)

WEI ZHUANG 韋莊 (836–910)

TRANSLATED BY XIAOSHAN YANG

Wei Zhuang was a poet of the very late Tang. His intention to undertake a government career was disrupted by the instability of the period, particularly the rebellion of Huang Chao (d. 884). He is particularly noted for an unusually long and vivid narrative poem about the events of the rebellion, entitled "Lament of the Lady of Qin" (*Qin fu yin*). He was also an innovator in the lyric poem (*ci*) form, which reached its height in the Song dynasty. After the fall of the Tang, Wei Zhuang's last years were spent in the service of the short-lived Former Shu dynasty (907–925), which he served with distinction. In this poem, Wei achieves some variety, if not novelty, in the theme of the absentee owner (see poems by Bai Juyi, Yuan Zhen, and Liu Yuxi above) by refraining from laying claim to the garden as an aesthetic space. Nonetheless, he establishes a more enduring relationship to the garden at the end of the poem. At the moment when the garden, with the disappearance of the visitor, is about to fade into the emptiness of the night (as it does in Liu Yuxi's poem above), he promises to come back; just as the owner is "constantly absent," so Wei Zhuang's experience is constantly repeatable.

"Sent to the Owner of the Garden"

The owner is constantly absent;
For whom do things in spring blossom?
Just as the pink petals of charming peach trees are about to fall,
The snow-white flowers of luxuriant pear trees press forward.
At dawn the fish-hawks chirp in leisure;
At dusk the sightseeing guest leaves alone.
There are still flowers remaining here,
Those are still worth a trip back with wine.

"Camel-Back the Gardener" (*Zhongshu Guo Tuotuo zhuan* 種樹郭橐駝傳)

LIU ZONGYUAN 柳宗元 (773–819)

TRANSLATED BY HERBERT GILES

For Liu Zongyuan, see above.

"Camel-Back the Gardener"

I do not know what Camel-Back's real name was. Disease had hunched him up behind, and he walked with his head down, like a camel. Hence, people came to give him the nickname of Camel. "Capital!" cried he, when he first heard of his sobriquet; "the very name for me." And thereafter he entirely left off using his proper name, calling himself "Camel-Back."

He lived in the village of Peace-and-Plenty, near the capital, and followed the occupation of a nursery-gardener. All the grand people of the city used to go and see his show; while market-gardeners vied with each other in securing his services, since every tree he either planted or transplanted was sure to thrive and bear fruit, not only early in the season but in abundance. Others in the same line of business, although they closely watched his method, were quite unable to achieve the same success.

One day a customer asked him how this was so; to which he replied, "Old Camel-Back cannot make trees live or thrive. He can only let them follow their natural tendencies. Now in planting trees, be careful to set the root straight, to smooth the earth around them, to use good mold, and to ram it down well. Then, don't touch them; don't think about them; don't go and look at them; but leave them alone to take care of themselves, and nature will do the rest. I only avoid trying to make my trees grow. I have no special method of cultivation, no special means for securing luxuriance of growth. I only don't spoil the fruit. I have no way of getting it either early or in abundance. Other gardeners set with bent root, and neglect the mold. They heap up either too much earth or too little. Or if not this, then they become too fond of and too anxious about their trees, and are for ever running backward and forward to see how they are growing; sometimes scratching them to make sure they are still alive, or shaking them about to see if they are sufficiently firm in the ground: thus constantly interfering with the natural bias of the tree, and turning their affection and care into an absolute bane and a curse. I only don't do these things. That's all."

"Can these principles you have just now set forth be applied to government?" asked his listener. "Ah!" replied Camel-Back, "I only understand nursery-gardening: government is not my trade. Still, in the village where I live, the officials are for ever issuing all kinds of orders, as if greatly compassionating the people, though really to their utter injury. Morning and night the underlings come round and say, 'His Honor bids us urge on your plowing, hasten your planting, and superintend your harvest. Do not delay with your spinning and weaving. Take care of your children. Rear poultry and pigs. Come together when the drum beats. Be ready at the sound of the rattle.' Thus are we poor people badgered from morn till eve. We have not a moment to ourselves. How could anyone flourish and develop naturally under such conditions? It was this that brought about my illness. And so it is with those who carry on the gardening business."

"Thank you," said the listener. "I simply asked about the management of trees, and I have learnt about the management of men. I will make this known, as a warning to government officials."

PART 3

SOUTHERN LANDSCAPES IN NORTHERN CLIMES

"On Vice-Director Xue's Waterside Pavilion in Chang'an" (*Ti Chang'an Xue yuanwai shuige* 題長安薛員外水閣)

YAO HE 姚合 (781–846)

TRANSLATED BY XIAOSHAN YANG

Yao He, a native of what is now Henan Province in northern China (although his family originated from the southeast), was a minor poet and anthologist of the mid-to-late Tang. His exact dates are somewhat uncertain, but he received his presented scholar degree in 816; this achievement was followed by a rather distinguished official career (including a period as prefect of Hangzhou), although he never attained really high office until a posthumous award of the position of Minister of Rites. During his official career, he became acquainted with many famous officials and writers of the time, such as Li Deyu, Bai Juyi, and Liu Yuxi.

"On Vice-Director Xue's Waterside Pavilion in Chang'an"

> With the pavilion newly completed, tall and upright,
> The scene becomes all the more bright and clear.
> Rocks are all of the colors as found in Lake Tai;
> Waters are filled with sounds from the Xiang Isles.
> Emerald bamboo grows covered with powder;
> Bit by bit dew drops along lotus flowers.
> From time to time you lean against the window to gaze out;
> From among what lies hidden you seek out a footpath to walk.
> In the sparse woods the warbling birds can be seen;
> In the nearby pond the feelings of the fish can be appreciated.
> In your break from office you invited a guest in leisure;
> With wine you welcomed him and sent him off.

"Visiting Mr. Han's Estate in the South of the City" (*You chengnan Hanshi zhuang* 遊城南韓氏莊)

MENG JIAO 孟郊 (751–814)

TRANSLATED BY XIAOSHAN YANG

Meng Jiao, who came from present-day Zhejiang Province, was one of the writers who, around the year 800, promoted an archaizing movement, aiming to return to an ancient simplicity of diction in place of the excessively smooth and elaborate style current among his contemporaries. Meng's generally harsh and sometimes angry tone has made his poems rather unpopular, but in his occasional social poetry his style can be quite gracious. Here, Meng draws a parallel between a garden in Luoyang and the south-central landscape of the Xiang River, which flows into the middle reaches of the Yangtze; he imagines this as a territory of supernatural beings ("the immortals").

"Visiting Mr. Han's Estate in the South of the City"

At first I thought that the waters of the limpid Xiang River
Were locked up inside the vermilion gate.
Frequently the moon shows from the bottom of the water,
Shaking and waving with the wind on the pond.
Clear air moistens bamboo groves;
White light extends to the empty firmament.
Waves push up the birds dashing toward the expanse of heaven;
Fragrant are the bushes on the bank, golden and green.
Who would expect that within a few acres,
The zigzagging path would never end?
I wish to join the company of the immortals,
Floating freely to Great Infinity.

"Roaming on the Pond in the Residence of the Vice-Minister" (*Shilang zhai fan chi* 侍郎宅泛池)

XU NING 徐凝 (FL. 813)
TRANSLATED BY XIAOSHAN YANG

From present-day Zhejiang Province in southeast China, Xu Ning is a somewhat obscure Tang poet; he is said to have avoided an official career and to have spent his time traveling and visiting friends, with whom he exchanged poems. He ended his days as a recluse in his hometown. The "residence of the Vice-Minister," which is the subject of this poem, is Bai Juyi's garden residence in the Lüdao ward of Luoyang (see above).

"Roaming on the Pond in the Residence of the Vice-Minister"

Lotus flowers circled by the bamboo banks,
An orchid boat wobbling amid fox nut leaves,
Inside the vermilion gate in north Luoyang, who would have thought
It would be just like roving around on the green waters of Jiangnan?

"A Question Posed to Cultivated Talent Cheng at a Casual Dinner on the Pond" (*Chishang xiao yan wen Cheng xiucai* 池上小宴問程秀才)

BAI JUYI 白居易

TRANSLATED BY XIAOSHAN YANG

This and the following three poems refer to the development of Bai Juyi's Luoyang garden after his return from his brief period of office as governor of Suzhou (825–826). His experience of southern gardens and his acquisition of southern plants, such as the white lotuses mentioned in "Observing the Picking of Lotus Flowers," led him to adapt his northerly garden to a Jiangnan style. His success in doing so was recognized by others, if we can trust the evidence of Xu Ning in the poem immediately above.

"A Question Posed to Cultivated Talent Cheng at a Casual Dinner on the Pond"

> I myself surely appreciate the excellence of my garden in Luoyang,
> Where articles from Jiangnan have accompanied me secretly.
> Rinsed clean, red grains are cooked into fragrant rice;
> Cut thin, fish with purple scales are boiled with water-shield.
> Rain drops on the canopy of the Blue Sparrow Boat;
> Waves shake the reflection of the flowers in the White Lotus Pond.
> Putting down the cup, I asked the guest from Suzhou a question:
> "Isn't it here exactly like when you were on the Wusong River?"

"A Newly Built Small Shoal" (*Xin xiao tan* 新小灘)

BAI JUYI 白居易

TRANSLATED BY XIAOSHAN YANG

This poem is a fine example of using a southern-style garden to suggest the creation of a hermitage in the city. The shoal is constructed like a stage, with the fishing rod as its single prop. Unravelling its emblematic significance takes little more than rendering the implicit obvious. In duly expressing his homesickness at the sight of the shoal, the "guest from Jiangnan" already pays an expected compliment to the garden's owner for his dexterity in creating a Jiangnanesque landscape in a northern garden. He also takes the required further step to decipher the coded meaning of the fishing rod when he compares what he sees in the garden specifically to the spot where Yan Guang (1st century), one of the most admired recluses in the Chinese tradition, used to fish.

"A Newly Built Small Shoal"

Over the shallow rocks and level sand flows the chilly water;
By the waterside a slanting fishing rod is stuck on the ground.
Seeing it, the guest from Jiangnan turned homesick:
"This is just like Yanling's Fishing Spot on the Seven-Mile Shoals," he said.

"Three Quatrains on My Family Garden" (*Jiayuan san jue* 家園三絕; first quatrain)

BAI JUYI 白居易
TRANSLATED BY XIAOSHAN YANG

In this poem, the recreation of the Jiangnan waterscape in the northern garden is presented as a process not only of reduction in size but also refinement in substance. The essence of wild nature, drawn into the controlled space of the garden, is captured, but its uncontrolled forces are kept out. The garden as nature reconstructed and refined allows the garden owner to control his own and his visitors' experience.

"Three Quatrains on My Family Garden" (first quatrain)

The Canglang Gorge's waters and Ziling's shoals;
The road is far, the river is deep—to go there would be difficult.
How can they compare with this family pond winding through the small courtyard,
Where a fishing rod is stuck under the steps from my bedroom?

"Observing the Picking of Lotus Flowers" (*Kan cai lian* 看採蓮)

BAI JUYI 白居易
TRANSLATED BY XIAOSHAN YANG

This poem presents a controlled experience of the garden as nature reconstructed and refined. Devoted to the description of the beauty of southern girls picking lotus flowers, the mildly erotic "Songs for Picking Lotuses" formed a subgenre in Southern Dynasties "ballads" (*yuefu*) and remained extremely popular in the Tang. Here, a poetic topic was physically reenacted on Bai's garden pond as his concubine picked lotuses. The poem emphasizes smallness, the miniaturization of the scene. Jiangnan is evoked not only by the white lotus flowers that Bai had transplanted from Suzhou but also by the transformation of a member of the Bai household into an elusive, free-moving nymph as depicted in ballads. The garden pond is not just the Jiangnan waterscape in miniature, it is also a negation of Jiangnan's "terrible wind and waves." The element of danger is included for the purpose of stressing the superiority of the garden pond as a safer space than the real Jiangnan. Hence, the twist that while every detail in the poem purports to evoke Jiangnan,

Bai Juyi can smugly declare that his pond is "not like Jiangnan." The pseudo-Jiangnan has poetically triumphed over the authentic Jiangnan.

"Observing the Picking of Lotus Flowers"

In idleness Little Peach goes on a little lotus boat;
Half of what she picks are pink lotus flowers and half white.
This is not like Jiangnan with its terrible wind and waves;
The Lotus Pond is right in front of my couch.

平山堂

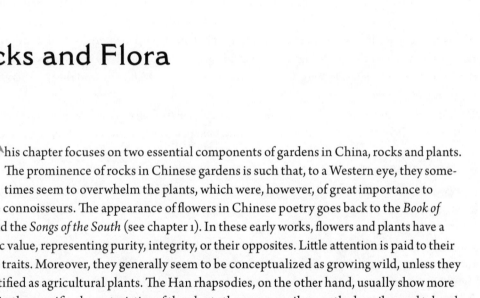

Rocks and Flora

This chapter focuses on two essential components of gardens in China, rocks and plants. The prominence of rocks in Chinese gardens is such that, to a Western eye, they sometimes seem to overwhelm the plants, which were, however, of great importance to Chinese connoisseurs. The appearance of flowers in Chinese poetry goes back to the *Book of Songs* and the *Songs of the South* (see chapter 1). In these early works, flowers and plants have a symbolic value, representing purity, integrity, or their opposites. Little attention is paid to their physical traits. Moreover, they generally seem to be conceptualized as growing wild, unless they are identified as agricultural plants. The Han rhapsodies, on the other hand, usually show more interest in the specific characteristics of the plants they so magniloquently describe, and take a less moralistic attitude toward them. Once we reach the period of disunion between Han and Tang, we start to find a more pragmatic interest in the nature and uses of plants, as in Dai Kaizhi's "Treatise on the Bamboo," excerpted in part 2 of this chapter. And as garden culture spreads more widely through the upper levels of society, particularly in the Tang period, we find a more possessive attitude to the flora cultivated in private gardens (for example, in Li Deyu's "Record of the Plants and Trees of My Mountain Villa at Pingquan") and an increasingly close attention to the subtleties of different species, types, colors, and forms of flowers and plants.

Mention of garden rocks in Chinese literature dates back to the Han rhapsodies (*fu*; see chapter 1), but rocks did not emerge as a regular poetic topic until the sixth century, as a byproduct of the new genre of "poetry on objects" (*yongwu shi*). Rocks in "poetry on objects" tend to be generic in nature, lacking physical specificity (as with early mentions of plants) and functioning primarily as easily understood symbols or objective correlatives of the poet's feelings and ideas. By the ninth century, we start to see the development of a rock aesthetic valorizing the ugly, the grotesque or strange, and the useless; Lake Tai rocks became particularly valued in this respect. At the same time, a distinctive relationship between rock-fancier and rock is formulated in terms of possession, obsession, and self-expression. This relationship continues, becoming even more prominent, into the late imperial period.

In the Chinese garden tradition, rocks are important for a number of reasons. First, in associative contrast with water, they represent the *yang* (masculine) principle to water's *yin* (feminine); as such, rocks and water represent the twin formative principles of the cosmos. At the same time, rocks represent the solidified form of water, namely clouds, whose shapes are seemingly random and mutable. Rocks also function as the bones in the structure of the garden, while water forms the veins or arteries.

On a different scale, rocks stand for mountains, or actually are mountains in miniature; this is the case whether the mountain is a single rock or a group of rocks formed into a rockery structure. Corresponding to rocks and water as *yang* and *yin*, rocks and water are also mountains and oceans or rivers, contained within the limited space of the garden. Mountains are the very opposite of the urban environment where many, if not most, gardens were located; they provide a remote haven where the urban hermit can withdraw into reclusion. They are also the habitation of the "immortals" of Daoist legend, and provide a space where the human and the supernatural can meet and make contact.

Finally, rocks had an aesthetic value in themselves. Especially in the late imperial period, they became valued for their qualities of *tou*, *lou*, and *shou*: penetration, foramination, and emaciation. We can see examples of this in the passages in this chapter, and also other paradoxically valued qualities such as "clumsiness" or "awkwardness" (*zhuo*).

As well as being the object of admiration, rocks could be a source of moral anxiety and could prompt moral judgment. The expense of acquiring a particularly valued rock could be regarded as improper extravagance, as could the expense of transporting a rock over a great distance to one's garden. The idea that the acquisition of rocks and their introduction to urban gardens required the "breaking down of city walls" and excessive toil on the part of laborers and draft animals (who should have been attending to the productive work of agriculture) became a commonplace in critiques of rock collecting. An awful warning was provided by the fate of the Song dynasty under Emperor Huizong, whose construction of the Northeast Marchmount (see chapter 4) and rapacious acquisition of fine rocks and flora from all over the empire was said to have led directly to the Jurchen invasion and the collapse of the Northern Song. The collecting of rocks was, thus, linked with a perpetual anxiety about official corruption and the collapse of public order.

Those literati who were disinclined to give up their habit of collecting found various ways of justifying themselves. They might claim rock collecting as their only vice, and vaunt their lack of interest in other worldly pursuits. They might point out that the Creator of Change (*zaohua*, roughly analogous to the European concept of a personified Nature) must have had a purpose in forming "strange rocks," and that an interest in them brought one in harmony with the cosmos. They might draw on the longstanding Daoist notion of the value of uselessness, expressed in Zhuangzi's parable of the gnarled tree (see chapter 1); the ability to affirm the useless signals an attitude, a withdrawal from the world of practicalities into the realm of spiritual freedom, where a private system of values could operate. Writers might see a parallel between the appreciation of rocks and the discernment of human talent, or use the relative ranking of different rocks as a symbol of the human sociopolitical order. The topos of the solitary rock provided a way for the writer to project a self-image as a pure-minded man standing aloof from the vulgar world.

As time went on, the idea of an "addiction" to or obsession (*pi*) with rock collecting changed from a sign of moral weakness to an indication of authenticity and exceptional personality. Great potential could be claimed for the apparently grotesque, ugly, and useless rock, which became a symbol of the actual or potential official who was neglected and unappreciated by his sovereign. The unchanging nature of rocks also became a symbol of constancy and, thus, of loyalty to a lost dynasty; this is one way we should read the early Qing writer Pu Songling's short story "The Ethereal Rock."

The changelessness of rocks is a contrast to the ever-changing nature of plants. Even those plants that are themselves symbols of constancy, such as evergreen pine trees, change slowly over time as they grow. The mutability of flowering plants was valuable, as it marked the cycle of the seasons. Plants had value both in situ, as component parts of the larger whole of the garden, as well as on their own, as either individual potted plants for display in an interior or exterior space or as cut flowers for interior decoration. Examples of these different uses appear in the passages in this chapter.

Of course, plants were valued not only for their visual beauty but also for other reasons. A rare plant or flower might bring a touch of the exotic to an otherwise ordinary garden. Both fragrance and sound were greatly appreciated. The fragrance of particular flowers was closely associated with the relevant season: the fragrance of wintersweet (*Chimonanthus praecox*) and flowering apricot (*Prunus mume*)[1] with late winter or early spring, that of the lotus with summer, and the osmanthus (sometimes called cassia) with autumn. The sound of rain pattering on banana leaves was felt to be particularly attractive, and the sound of pine trees blown by the wind evoked ocean waves. And, of course, in a culture in which haute cuisine is as highly valued as it is in China, the taste of fruit and other edible parts of plants was also highly valued, as we can see, for example, from Zhang Dai's praise of the sweet tangerines grown by the Chen clan.

Plants also had a variety of long-established symbolic meanings. Some are obvious and almost universal, like the association of evergreens with long life and constancy, or the rather blowsy herbaceous peony with wealth and prosperity. Others depend on a play on words, as in the case of bamboo as a symbol of integrity: the characteristic joints (*jie* in Chinese) of bamboo sound the same as the word for integrity (also *jie*). The hollow stalk of the banana (*Musa basjoo*) appealed to Buddhists as replicating the "empty heart," free from passion, to which the Buddhist believer aspires. Some flowers could have more than one significance: the orchid or cymbidium, with its subtle fragrance, often stands for the gentlemanly virtues of purity and modesty, but in a more erotic context, the form of the flower can suggest the female genitals. As in many cultures, flowers are often equated with female beauty and femininity; this is particularly the case for the flowering apricot, whose flowers are both beautiful and highly fragrant. There are legends in which supernatural women appear in the guise of a flowering apricot tree, and the Song dynasty recluse Lin Bu justified his solitary life by claiming that the flowering plum was his wife and the cranes his children.

The acquisition of rare plants raised some of the same moral problems as did rock collecting, laying the collector open to accusations of extravagance and possible corruption. Because plants

---

1   *Prunus mume* (Chinese *mei*) is, strictly speaking, a flowering apricot, but is often translated as plum or plum-blossom; both translations are used in this anthology according to the preference of individual translators.

are living things, closer in nature to humans or animals than to rocks, it was possible to accuse people of bad behavior or even cruelty toward them, as Hu Yinglin does in "Connoisseurs of Flowers," where he explicitly draws a parallel between flowers and beautiful women. Particularly in the late imperial period, at a time of social change and instability, the literati would make use of the appreciation or rejection of certain flowers as a marker of good taste that could distinguish their class from the upwardly mobile, purportedly vulgar merchant class. Thus, Wen Zhenheng, arbiter of taste and author of the *Treatise on Superfluous Things* (see chapter 6), shudders at the idea of growing roses on a trellis in a gentleman's garden (though he allows that this is acceptable in the ladies' quarters),[2] and in relation to flower arranging says firmly that "it is particularly important to have no more than one or two varieties [of flower in a vase], since too many gives the appearance of a wine shop."[3]

We can see, therefore, that rocks and plants were important in Chinese garden culture not just for their aesthetic contribution to the garden but also for their moral and symbolic value as well as for their significance as markers of the social and aesthetic standards of the garden's owner. The poems and passages of prose that follow give some idea of the different meanings that rocks and flora held for the literati who contributed to the Chinese garden tradition.[4]

PART 1

ROCKS

"A Pair of Rocks" (*Shuangshi* 雙石)

BAI JUYI 白居易 (772–846)

TRANSLATED BY XIAOSHAN YANG

For Bai Juyi, see chapter 2. Bai can be credited with the "discovery" of the Lake Tai rock as the privileged type of "scholar's rock." In 826, while prefect of Suzhou, he chanced upon a pair of rocks by Lake Tai. Immediately attracted to their bizarre looks, he had them carried to his official residence in the city. To commemorate this fortunate acquisition, he wrote this poem. In characterizing the rocks as "grotesque and ugly," Bai Juyi sets the basic parameter of the Chinese rock aesthetic; these qualities are often concretized, as here, by comparing the shape of rocks to sharp weapons or awesome creatures such as dragons and tigers. Mention is almost always made of the perforations and cavities as contributing factors to their grotesqueness. Bai's poem also broaches the theme that the ability to appreciate such qualities is a blessing of the privileged few; this aesthetic sensitivity, moreover, easily translates into moral acuity in perceiving hidden potential.

---

2 Wen Zhenheng, *Zhangwu zhi* 2.10.

3 Wen Zhenheng, *Zhangwu zhi* 10.6; translation from Craig Clunas, *Superfluous Things: Material Culture and Social Status in Early Modern China* (Honolulu: University of Hawai'i Press, 2004), 44.

4 For a wide survey of traditional botanical knowledge in China, see Georges Métailié, "Traditional Botany: An Ethnobotanical Approach," trans. Janet Lloyd, in *Science and Civilisation in China*, vol. 6, part 4 (Cambridge: Cambridge University Press, 1994).

"A Pair of Rocks"

Dark sallow, two shards of rock,
Their appearance grotesque and ugly.
Of vulgar use they are incapable;
People of the time detest and abandon them.
Molded into their current shapes from their primordial cast,
I got them at the mouth of Lake Dongting;
For ten thousand years they had been left at water's bank,
Then all of a sudden they fell into my hands.
I had them carried into the city;
Washing and scrubbing, I rid them of mud and dirt.
Their holes are black with deep imprints of smoke;
Their cavities are green with the color of thick moss.
Like the twisting feet of old dragons,
Like the piercing head of an ancient sword.
Suddenly I feel as if they had fallen from Heaven,
Unlike what exists in the human realm.
One of them can prop up my *qin*;
The other can hold my wine.
Their towering cliffs are a few feet high;
Their splashing concaves contain one liter of water.
Five strings lean on their left;
One jug is placed on their right.
Before the sunken cup is emptied,
I am already long drunk like a jade mountain that has collapsed.[5]
Each man has his own penchant;
All things seek their own companions.
I am beginning to feel that the world of youngsters
Would not accommodate a man with drooping white hair.
Turning my head around, I ask the pair of rocks:
"Can you keep company with an old man like myself?"
Though the rocks cannot speak,[6]
They promise that we will be three friends.

---

[5] The allusion here is to the tall and handsome Ji Kang, who, when drunk, was said to resemble a "jade mountain about to collapse."

[6] Editor's note: after a rock was heard talking in Weiyu in the state of Jin, we are told in the *Zuo Commentary* (Duke Zhao, 8th Year), Music-Master Kuang explained to the Marquis of Jin that, although rocks cannot talk, sometimes gods and spirits attach themselves to, and speak through, the rocks. See *The Chinese Classics*, vol. 5, *The Ch'un Ts'ew, with the Tso Chuan*, ed. and trans. James Legge (Oxford: Clarendon Press, 1893–1895), 622.

"An Account of Lake Tai Rocks" (*Taihu shi ji* 太湖石記)

BAI JUYI 白居易

TRANSLATED BY XIAOSHAN YANG

Bai Juyi's text provides some insight into the latent anxiety of petrophiles at this time and reveals some of their strategies to justify their obsession. The subject of Bai's essay is the "addiction" of his friend Niu Sengru ("Duke Qizhang"; see below) to rock collecting. It is not so much the rocks themselves as the process of collecting that generates much of the anxiety in Bai's discussion. Lake Tai rocks were difficult to harvest from their natural setting and even more difficult to transport from their place of origin to distant northern cities like Luoyang. While Bai tries to justify Niu's addiction to rocks on the grounds of his lack of interest in other mundane things, there is a hint of criticism of his subordinates who expend their efforts on presenting him with "the most splendid and fantastic specimens." Ultimately, Bai endeavors to invest Niu Sengru's aesthetic pursuit with moral and spiritual significance by resorting to the familiar parallelism between his appreciation of rocks and his ability, as a senior official, to discern and promote unrecognized human talent.

"An Account of Lake Tai Rocks"

All the wise men of ancient times had things to which they were addicted. Master Huangfu Mi [215–282] was addicted to books, Courtier Ji Kang [223–265] to the *qin*, Master Tao Qian to wine. In the present time, Duke Qizhang, Counselor-in-Chief, is addicted to rocks. Different from those three things, rocks have no patterns or sound or smell or taste. Why is it that His Lordship is addicted to them? Everybody feels it to be odd, but I alone understand it. In the past, my old friend Master Li Yue once said, "If a thing suits my mind, then its use is great." What he said is really true. It is nothing but a matter of suiting one's mind. From this one can understand Duke Qizhang's addiction.

In his capacity as Minister of Education, Duke Qizhang officiates as the Protector of Luoyang. For maintaining his household, he has no valuable property; for nourishing his body, he has no superfluous things, except for a house that he set up in the eastern part of the city and a villa that he built south of the city wall, where he carefully keeps his houses and prudently chooses his guests. He does not force himself to be friendly and lives constantly without socializing. When in leisure, he keeps company with the rocks. Rocks have separate genealogies. Those of Lake Tai are first rate, second to them are those of Luofu and Tianzhu. What His Lordship is addicted to are the first-rate rocks.

Earlier, many of the subordinates of His Lordship were in charge of regions with rivers and lakes; many of them knew that the heart of Duke Qizhang was set on nothing but rocks. Therefore they gathered rocks from the deep and the far away and presented him with the most splendid and fantastic specimens. In four or five years, piles of rocks arrived. For the sake of integrity, these were the only things that His Lordship would not decline. He arranged them in columns in his house east of the city and his villa south of the city.

So abundant are those rocks, and so varied are their shapes! Some twist in the body and protrude at the top, like bright clouds atop a numinous hill; some stand upright and dignified, like figures of immortals and transcendents. Some are daintily smooth and finely cut, like jade tablets and nephrite ladles; some are sharp and cutting, like swords and halberds. Then there are those that are like dragons and phoenixes: as if huddling, as if agitating; about to glide, about to jump; there are those that are like monsters and beasts: as if prowling, as if gathering; about to grab, about to fight. There are those whose holes open up at dusk against fierce wind and gloomy rain, as if they were sucking in clouds and spurting out thunders; as they stand tall, the sight of them inspires awe. There are those whose peaks appear like dark black ink at dawn when the mist has lifted and the scenery become bright, as if they were brushed by mountain wind and painted with black pigment; they appear so amiable that one can be intimate and play with them. From dawn to dusk, they look so different and the changes cannot be described. To sum it up, the Three Mountains and the Five Marchmounts, hundreds of caves and thousands of valleys are all twisted and contracted here.[7] What stands a hundred yards tall can be held in a fist; what expands for a thousand miles can be obtained in a moment. That is why they can be used to suit the mind of His Lordship.

Once His Lordship and I examined them closely and then, as we looked at each other in wonder, I said, "Aren't these things in which the Fashioner-of-Things revealed his intention? Or were they formed by chance as they naturally congealed into their current shapes from their primordial casts? Yet we don't know how many tens of thousands of years have passed since they took their immutable forms. Some of them have been located in the corners of the seas; others have fallen into the bottom of the lakes. The tall ones are only dozens of feet high; the heavy ones weigh almost a thousand pounds. Once they came without being whipped and arrived without legs,[8] they showed off their oddness and displayed their grotesqueness, all becoming things in the eyes of Your Lordship. Then Your Lordship received them as distinguished guests, regarded them as sages, treasured them as precious jade, and loved them as sons and grandsons. I wonder if they were summoned by your deliberate intention? Or were

7   The Three Mountains refer to the three legendary mountains in the ocean: Fangzhang 方丈, Penglai 蓬萊, and Yingzhou 瀛洲; they are the dwelling places of immortals. The Five Marchmounts are the five sacred mountains in China: Mount Song 嵩, Mount Tai 泰, Mount Hua 華, Mount Heng 恆, and Mount Heng 衡.

8   There are two allusions here. The first is to the legend that the First Emperor of Qin (r. 221–210 BCE) once built a stone bridge in order to cross the sea to see where the sun rose. Helping the emperor was a magician who could drive the stones into the sea. If the stones did not go fast enough, he would whip them so that they would bleed and turn red. The second allusion is to a passage in Kong Rong's (孔融, 153–208) "On Sheng Xiaozhang" ("*Lun Sheng Xiaozhang shu*" 論盛孝章書), *Wenxuan* 41.1874–75: "The reason why pearls and jade can arrive without legs is because people love them. Not to mention worthy people who do have legs!"

those superb creatures simply returning to their proper place? How could they have come for nothing? There must have been a purpose."

The size of the rocks varies. They are divided in four classes, graded as Class A, Class B, Class C, and Class D. Each class is further divided into Rank One, Rank Two, and Rank Three. The dark side of each rock is inscribed with its grading, such as "Niu's rock, Class A Rank One, Class C Rank Two, or Class B Rank Three."

Alas! After tens of thousands of years, these rocks are scattered all over the world, moving around unknown. Who would have known them? I want to make sure that latecomers who have the same relish as I do understand where His Lordship's addiction for rocks comes from as they look at those rocks and read what is written on them. Written on the *guichou* day of the fifth month of the third year of the Huichang era [843].

"The Lake Tai Rock" (*Taihu shi* 太湖石)

LU GUIMENG 陸龜蒙 (D. 881)
TRANSLATED BY XIAOSHAN YANG

Lu Guimeng, who took the cognomen "Master Who Follows Heaven," was a Tang poet from Suzhou who became something of a canonical figure in later garden culture for his life as a recluse. He lived in retirement in the Suzhou area, studying, collecting and editing books, and working on his farm and tea plantation; his home is said to have been on the site of the later Canglang Pavilion garden (see chapter 5). Although he was well versed in the Confucian classics, he appears to have been a convinced Daoist, and was particularly associated with the Daoist site of Maoshan, near Suzhou. Much of his poetry is concerned with the natural world, but he also wrote on agricultural tools and techniques, an unusual subject for elite writers of the time. By the time Lu wrote this poem, the appreciation of Lake Tai rocks had become more widespread. Lu, therefore, cannot be distinctive by speaking positively of the rock's grotesqueness and uselessness, but has to establish his individuality not through his appreciation of the useless but through his difference from "all under heaven" in their fetishization of the rock and his refusal or inability to set it up by his garden pond.

"The Lake Tai Rock"

Weren't there rocks in other mountains?
Their shapes were all commendable.
Once they met the skilled workmen,
Their natural essence was changed.
Some were planted as the foundation of tall buildings,
Boulders turning into a grand palace.
Some were cut into soft jade,
Brilliant light emanating from glossy gem.

Some were used for breaking the enemy:
Hundreds of cannon pellets joining in fierce fight.
Some were used as mirrors,
Into which one can look oneself even after ten thousand years.
Now this one from the Dongting Lake
Is chosen not for any of those purposes.
Jagged and notched, it really has no talent,
And yet its appearance is valued by all under heaven.
What is rare is its hollow concaves;
What is prized is its jutting peaks.
Deep caves are pierced on its flanks
Smooth bracelets are inlaid on its surface.
Finely cut, like the Window with Nine-Layered Jade;[9]
Delicate, like the Fan of Five-Fold Enlightenment.[10]
Now appearing as a bit of newly carved blue cloud;
Then breaking into a patch of autumnal sky.
As I am not able to set it up by my garden pond,
I can only look at it longingly as wind blows against it.

"Prefect Li of Suzhou Presented Me with Some Lake Tai Rocks, the Strange Shape of Which Was Matchless; Hence I Wrote Twenty Couplets, Which I Presented to Mengde and Letian" (*Li Suzhou yi Taihushi qizhuang juelun, yin ti ershi yun fengcheng Mengde Letian* 李蘇州遺太湖石奇裝絕倫因題二十韻奉呈夢得樂天)

NIU SENGRU 牛僧孺 (780–848)

TRANSLATED BY XIAOSHAN YANG

Niu Sengru rose to be a very senior official of the Tang dynasty, noted for his incorruptibility and firm principles. Because he had supported two other officials in an accusation against the father of Li Deyu (see below), he and Li became enemies, each leading a faction within the court. In the course of this feud, Niu Sengru was exiled to the far south of China, but on the accession of a new emperor he was pardoned, brought back to court, and given a sinecure that enabled him to enjoy his final years in the "eastern capital," Luoyang. He is not particularly renowned as a poet; however, as an educated scholar-official he was more than capable of producing occasional verse such as this, dedicated to his friends Liu Yuxi (Mengde) and Bai Juyi (Letian; for both see chapter 2). In 838, Li Daoshu, prefect of Suzhou, sent these rocks to Niu in Luoyang as a gift; Niu's poem is a celebration of this addition to his rock collection. The basic categories of images

---

9 In the Daoist celestial palace, there is a Hall of Nine-Layered Jade (*Jiulin zhi tang* 九琳之堂). The Window with Nine-Layered Jade is apparently meant to recall this supernatural edifice.

10 The term Fan of Five-Fold Enlightenment (*Wumingshan* 五明扇) has multiple meanings. In Daoist lore, it designates a ritual fan in the divine palace on the highest of the nine layers of heaven (*Shenxiao* 神宵).

in the poem (the comparison to awesome beasts and weapons, the pierced openings, and so on) are familiar; they recall Bai's earlier poem "A Pair of Rocks" (see above). In his adoring attitude to his "brother[s] ten years my senior" (the rocks), however, Niu seems to have less power over his rocks than Bai does.

> "Prefect Li of Suzhou Presented Me with Some Lake Tai Rocks, the Strange Shape of Which Was Matchless; Hence I Wrote Twenty Couplets, Which I Presented to Mengde and Letian"
>
> When were their rough casts first molded?—
> Now their hollow concaves are already formed.
> Rising and squatting, like dragons and tigers in fighting,
> Commanding demons, they startle ghosts and spirits.
> Some carry the still, fresh water of the rain;
> Others resound like jade breaking when lightly tapped.
> Some are jagged, like clusters of sharp swords;
> Others are like a net of strand, with slim fishing lines.
> Close to water, they stir up strange cool;
> By pine trees, they add to the pristine purity.
> Some have faint scales all over their bodies;
> Others possess lighted pierced openings as in a grotto heaven.
> Their ugly convexes are like protruding noses of the barbarians;
> Their deep concaves are shaped like beasts carved on cups.
> In thunder and wind, they seem to be transmuting;
> In gloomy darkness, they appear to be moving.
> In the teeth-twittering chill of the morning,
> A few twisting slates traverse the ground.
> The local deity is suffering from their suppression;
> The feet of gigantic turtles have difficulty supporting them.
> It was kind of the prefect of Gusu
> To appreciate my lazy and relaxed inclination.
> In order to search for the objects in the Lake
> He did not fear whales in the waves.
> Traveling assiduously over waters for more than a thousand miles,
> They made only a hundred stops across mountains and rivers.
> When they were first displayed by the pond,
> Gold and jade became trifling.
> My soul was still startled as I gazed at them from the flanks,
> Only after I looked at them from all around did my mind gradually ease.

As if meeting a friend with three virtues,[11]

As if facing a brother ten years my senior.

Exciting my mood, they augment their magical power

Dispelling my trouble, they break a nightlong drunkenness.

Compared to humans, they would be Qi the Hoary Head;

Evaluated for rank, they would be among lords and ministers.

I think about these treasures in my garden:

Finesse of appreciation is needed for them.

For poet-immortals there are Liu and Bai,

Whom I have received several times for your sake.

"The Lake Tai Rocks: A Product from the Top of the Sea-Turtle Mountain" (*Taihu shi chu Guishan tou* 太湖石出龜山頭)

PI RIXIU 皮日休 (CA. 834–CA. 883)

TRANSLATED BY XIAOSHAN YANG

Pi Rixiu is a minor but interesting literary figure of the late Tang dynasty. He was a close friend of Lu Guimeng (see above), whom he met in Suzhou (of which Lu was a native) when Pi was posted there; aspects of their poetic styles are considered similar. Pi's early poetry shows a concern for the living conditions of rural people. During and after his stay in Suzhou, he became interested in developing a formalistic and elaborate style, of which the following poem is an example. The moral anxiety about rock collecting that poets like Bai Juyi, in the early decades of the ninth century, had largely managed to suppress has now come to the surface in an overt criticism of petromania. This poem is unprecedented in offering a firsthand report of the sufferings inflicted on commoners by the craze in high society for Lake Tai rocks. The familiar imagery of the grotesque and ugly is now framed within a critique of the misappropriation not only of nature's wonders but also of human labor. The process of transporting the rocks correlates with the collapse of public order on a national scale near the end of the Tang dynasty. At the end of the poem, Pi Rixiu gives a poignant twist to the familiar motif of the correspondence between appreciating the value of the rocks and recognizing human talent: the fanatic zeal with which the Lake Tai rocks are gathered is juxtaposed with the neglect of those who were willing (and perhaps able) to rescue the Tang empire from its imminent demise.

In 880, Pi Rixiu was caught up in the rebellion led by Huang Chao and became an adviser to the rebel leader; the evidence suggests that Pi then offended Huang Chao in some way and was executed as a result.

---

11 According to Confucius (*Analects* XVI:4), there are three kinds of people with whom it is advantageous to make friends (*yizhe san you* 益者三友): "friendship with the upright; friendship with the sincere; and friendship with the man of much observation."

"The Lake Tai Rocks: A Product from the Top of the Sea-Turtle Mountain"

This mountain has a bank of rocks,
Beaten by the waves as if they were being slaughtered.
Tens of thousands of attacks by the snow-white battle formations,
Scraping the moss-covered cliff from top to bottom.
The rocks must be the crafty tricks of Heaven;
Truly they cannot be the ingenuity of humans.
For the able-bodied men to gather the rocks,
Is more difficult than to net the corals.
What do they look like?—
Even a painter with demonic skills could not picture them.
Some curve like reptiles;
Others squat like tigers.
Intertwining like interlocked hooks,
Overlapping like calyx attached to each other.
Some look like the bones of a giant;
Others look like the tallies[12] of the Supreme God.
Swelling, like bamboo shoots of the Yundang Mountain,
Tinkling, like beads of beautiful gem.
Where they break, the mouth of a spring is exposed;
As they are removed, they still carry beards of sand.
People young and old are mobilized to find them;
Boats big and small are deployed to carry them.
One look by the grand marquises,
And their value surpassed the pearl under the chin of the black dragon.[13]
With rich reward for these treasures,
They travel all the way to the distant capital.
To the earth mountains of the Five Marquises
You are wanted to add to cliffs and caves.
If they find what suits their mind in what they play with,
Ranks and salary are awarded on the spot.
Should there be noblemen coming to the emperor's rescue
Rising from the district of Lake Tai,
They would, laughingly toward the west, ask:
"Would we get to be treated the same as the rocks?"

---

12   Editor's note: tallies were objects of two matching halves used to authenticate official correspondence or orders; they could evidently be used in supernatural as well as human bureaucracies.

13   According to the *Zhuangzi*, the most precious pearl lies in the deepest water under the chin of a black dragon.

"After Leaving the Ministry Early in the Morning, as I Passed with My Colleagues the Western Pavilion of Tan Wensi, I Sang of the Lake Tai Rock" (*Shengzhong zao chu yu tongliao guo Tan Wensi Xixuan yong Taihu shi* 省中早出與同僚過譚文思西軒詠太湖石)

SU SONG 蘇頌 (1020–1101)

TRANSLATED BY XIAOSHAN YANG

Su Song was a remarkable man who combined a career as a senior official and ambassador of the Northern Song court with extensive research and writing on what would now be regarded as scientific subjects such as astronomy, cartography, and pharmacology.[14] His interests were similar to those of his contemporary Shen Gua (see chapter 4); both men made significant technological achievements. He was also a competent poet and a discerning collector of antiques. Su Song retired from his official career in 1097, in his late seventies, with a generous pension and the honorary title of Junior Preceptor of the Heir Apparent; he died a few years later. Unlike the poetry of the late Tang, this poem reveals no discomfort over the transportation of the rock across the great distance from Lake Tai to the capital city. Instead, at the sight of the rock, busy officials can fantasize about living near rivers and lakes. The conventional association between the sight of fantastic rocks and the evocation of a reclusive mood links the descriptive and reflective parts of the poem.

> "After Leaving the Ministry Early in the Morning, as I Passed with My Colleagues the Western Pavilion of Tan Wensi, I Sang of the Lake Tai Rock"
>
> Mount Dongting merges with the water of Zhenze;
> Precipitous, a grotesque rock comes out from beneath the waves.
> Who said it could not be had because it was too far away?
> With your passion for wonders, you got it here in no time.
> I love your small verandah, only a dozen feet long;
> Fresh flowers cover the ground, red mixing with purple.
> As I chance to lean on the rail and watch the fantastic peak,
> My thoughts of rivers and lakes in autumn arise.

"The Lake Tai Rock" (*Taihu shi* 太湖石)

HU SU 胡宿 (995–1067)

TRANSLATED BY XIAOSHAN YANG

Hu Su came from near Suzhou, and thus from near the source of Lake Tai rocks. A successful official career led to a post as governor of Hangzhou; he died in office before he could take up a promotion to Junior Tutor of the Heir Apparent. His collected works are lost, but some poems survive in various later collections. In this poem, Hu treats his obsession with the rock with lighthearted self-ridicule.

---

14   For more information on Su Song, see Colin A. Ronan and Joseph Needham, *The Shorter Science and Civilisation in China* (Cambridge: Cambridge University Press, 1994), 4:225–38.

"The Lake Tai Rock"

Lead, pine trees, and stones from Haidai would be obtained in vain,[15]
If the cold jade from the foot of the Dongting Mountain were missing.
Shaped by the gurgling water into a solitary cloud,
Exhausting the sound of white waves over a thousand years.
Who would expect to meet the Weaver Girl by her loom?
I felt as if I were seeing Chuping under the mountain cliffs.[16]
Over the years my appreciation of this object has turned into a disease,
Unaware how many times a day I walk around the green moss.

Stone Catalogue of Cloudy Forest (*Yunlin shipu* 雲林石譜)

"Lingbi Rocks" (*Lingbi shi* 靈璧石) and "Lake Tai Rocks" (*Taihu shi* 太湖石)

DU WAN 杜綰 (FL. 1120–1130)
TRANSLATED BY JOHN HAY

Very little is known about Du Wan other than what can be inferred from the *Stone Catalogue* itself, with its "Introduction" dated 1133 by Kong Chuan, although we are told he was a descendant of the Tang poet Du Fu (see chapter 2). The content of the *Stone Catalogue* implies familiarity with the Song imperial collection, and it has been suggested that Du Wan himself may have been employed in forming the collection.[17] Internal evidence shows that the catalogue was completed between 1126 and 1130. Although rocks with aesthetic value are prioritized by being placed at the beginning of the text, Du Wan also describes rocks or stones that have utilitarian value being used, for example, as whetstones, for masonry, or for making pigments. Du Wan's comments on particular types of rock were often repeated by later writers, for example, by the Ming garden theorist Ji Cheng (see below). In addition to the physical attributes and uses of rocks, Du Wan also mentions the arduous process of hauling Lake Tai rocks out of the water; we have already seen that the hardships involved in the production of the rocks had been a concern for petrophiles from the mid-Tang onward.

"Lingbi Rocks"

Lingbi rocks: Suzhou in Lingbi [County], the place is called Qing[shi] shan, "Sonorous Stone Mountain." The rocks are produced within the soil. When excavations have

---

15   These were among the tributes presented to the Great Yu from Qingzhou.

16   In the *Biographies of the Divine Immortals* (*Shenxian zhuan* 神仙傳), traditionally attributed to Ge Hong, we are told that at the age of fifteen, Huang Chuping 黃初平, a shepherd, met a Daoist priest who led him to a stone house in the mountain. Years later, Huang Chuping mastered the Daoist techniques, among which was his ability to turn white rocks into sheep.

17   Edward H. Schafer, *Tu Wan's Stone Catalogue of Cloudy Forest* (Berkeley: University of California Press, 1961), 16–18.

been going on for many years, the pits are many tens of feet deep. They are thickly encrusted with mud and only when the locals have scraped off two or three layers with iron knives is the rock revealed. After this, they are brushed clean and glossy, with brushes of Yellow Bud or bamboo, dipped in magnetite powder. When tapped, they have a hard, clear sound. Some of them have cemented earth at their base which cannot be removed, and this must be taken into account when positioning them for display. When still in the soil, they grow in various shapes according to their size. Some form animals, others mountain ranges with cliffs pierced by cavities. The best ones have twisting and turning configurations. Some shapes are more blockish, while others are flattish, with patterns forming clouds, sun and moonlight, and Buddhist images, even scenery of the four seasons. These have to be chiseled, ground and polished to complete their beauty. Mostly they have one or two such sides, sometimes three, but not one or two out of a hundred have four. . . . Recently, the Zhang family's Lan'gao Pavilion, in Lingbi, has had a large array of fine specimens, each between ten and twenty feet high. . . . There is another kind, with a surface wrinkled like a peach stone, rather black in color and larger specimens between two and three feet high. Small examples are about a foot, or even as small as a fist, with a sloping foot in the shape of a large mountain. Rare examples have high peaks and cavernous cliffs. Another kind is found in newly excavated pits in the yellow mud. It has mountain ranges, recessed and hollowed in an extremely intricate way. These also need to be well cleaned. They give a slight sound when tapped, but the material is pale grey, slightly friable and rather easily worked. They are not as good as the glossy and hard stones from Sonorous Stone Mountain. They must be kept out of the wind and sun. Otherwise, if left long in the sunlight, they will turn white and their resonance will disappear. These are the floating sonorous stones from the Si River, spoken of in the *Classic of History*.

"Lake Tai Rocks"

The rocks of Lake Tai in Pingjiang Prefecture are produced in the waters of Lake Dongting.[18] They are hard and glossy, with strange configurations of hollow "eyes" and twisting peaks. One kind is white, another is bluish black, while another is light blue. They have a net of raised patterns all over, their surfaces covered with small cavities, worn by the action of wind and waves. These are called "pellet nests." When these stones are tapped, they resound slightly. Those who harvest these stones dive for them, mallet and chisel in hand, a very toilsome business. When a fine specimen has been cut free, it is bound with huge ropes and then winched up into a large boat. Those that are slightly inferior in their characteristic hollows and crags are improved by more chiseling and then aged by re-submersion, so that the stone may be scoured by wind and rain and its patterns restored to a living appearance. The largest of these rocks are from thirty to fifty feet high and the best are not less than several tens of feet. There are some

---

18   Another name for "Grand Lake," Tai Hu.

no larger than a foot, which are suitable for standing by a balcony railing. This size may also be used in building artificial mountains which, when set among spacious groves, are a magnificent sight. There are also exquisite miniatures, which may be placed on stands for one's pleasure.

"Matching Governor Liu's Poem on Rock Forest Pavilion. Originally Objects in the Tang Gardens, the Rocks Had Been Scattered among the Common People and Were Purchased and Obtained by Liu" (*Ciyun Liu jingzhao Shilin ting zhi zuo shi ben Tangyuan zhong wu sanliu minjian Liu goude zhi* 次韻劉京兆石林亭之作石本唐苑中物散流民間劉購得之)

SU SHI 蘇軾 (1037–1101)

TRANSLATED BY XIAOSHAN YANG

Su Shi, also known by his studio name Su Dongpo (Su of the East Slope), was one of the great writers, calligraphers, and collectors of the Song dynasty, as well as a government official and leading figure in the factional conflicts of his time.[19] Although he was strongly influenced by the poetry of Tao Qian (see chapter 1), his own literary style is famous for its "heroic abandon" (*haofang*). He was influential in developing an interest in rock collecting among Song literati. His political vicissitudes caused him to travel all over the empire, sometimes succeeding in taking with him new acquisitions for his rock collection, sometimes regretfully forced to leave them behind.

In this poem on Liu Chang's (1019–1068) collection of rocks, Su's philosophical conviction of the importance of maintaining a proper detachment from things outside oneself is mingled with indirect moral criticism. In a poem titled "Newly Built Stone Forest Pavilion," Liu Chang had characterized the pavilion as a middle ground between the court and the mountains, where he could lead the life of a hermit-official. Instead of affirming Liu's moral complacency, Su reminds him of the example of Niu Sengru (Duke Qizhang; see above) to sound a warning against petromania as a dangerous passion. Su's lecture on the natural cycle of the dispersal and convergence of things is targeted at Liu as a rock collector, and the message is clear: all human accumulations are transitory, and an obsession with collecting is not only a philosophical folly but also a moral hazard. The reference to the fall of the Houses of Liu (the Han rulers) and Li (the Tang rulers) carries a particularly pungent sting, because at the time Liu Chang was stationed in Chang'an, the capital of both the Han and Tang dynasties.

---

19   For the life of Su Shi, see Ronald C. Egan, *Word, Image, and Deed in the Life of Su Shi* (Cambridge, Mass.: Council on East Asian Studies, Harvard University, 1994); for a more old-fashioned but still readable account, see Lin Yutang, *The Gay Genius: The Life and Times of Su Tungpo* (New York: J. Day Co., 1947).

"Matching Governor Liu's Poem on Rock Forest Pavilion. Originally Objects in the Tang Gardens, the Rocks Had Been Scattered among the Common People and Were Purchased and Obtained by Liu"

The old capital is wasted day by day;
Old times cannot be returned.
Only these rocks from the ancient gardens
Are still scattered in the human realm.
Only after your arrival were they bought and preserved,
Without worrying about the hardships in getting them all the way here.
Suddenly, from dust and dirt
They came to face your countenance of ice and snow.
Their thin bones jutting out in majesty,
Their blue roots washed by murmuring water.
In the Tang there was Duke Qizhang
Whose relish of rocks was unsurpassed since antiquity.
He wanted all of them to belong to the Niu family,
Carving and chiseling his name all over them.
Alas! How natural it is
For them to gather and scatter in cycles.
One man's loss is another man's gain,
As long as they do not disappear from the human realm.[20]
Witness the end of the Houses of Liu and Li,
When even the rivers and passes could not be protected.
The hundred rocks were to those
What a light feather is to the Tai Mountain.
One should just drink facing these rocks,
Treating myriad things as trifles.

---

20   The allusion in lines 15–18 is to the following story, found in the *Garden of Tales* (*Shuoyuan* 說苑): "King Gong of Chu went hunting and lost a bow. When his attendants asked permission to look for it, the King said: 'Leave it! A bow lost by a man of Chu will be found by another man of Chu. Why bother with looking for it?' Confucius heard about it and said: 'What a pity that he was not great enough. He could have said "A bow lost by one man will be found by another man" and nothing more. Why did it have to be another man of Chu?'"

"Two Poems Composed after Transcribing 'Record of Plants and Trees at Pingquan'" (*Shu Pingquan caomu ji ershou* 書平泉草木記二首)

WEN TONG 文同 (1018–1079)

TRANSLATED BY XIAOSHAN YANG

Wen Tong, who came from Sichuan in western China, was a cousin of Su Shi (see above). He is best known as a painter specializing in bamboo, but he was also an official and a poet. He is said to have inspired the expression "to have the complete bamboo in one's heart" (*xiong you cheng zhu*), meaning to have in mind a complete plan (especially for a painting, poem, or other artistic endeavor) before embarking on the work. He kept pet gibbons, and wrote a surviving elegy on the death of one of them.

In this pair of poems, Wen combines philosophical critique with a moral condemnation of Li Deyu (the Duke of Wei), the owner of the Pingquan (Level Spring) estate (see chapter 2). In the first poem, the completeness of Li's collection is contrasted with its disintegration "before his body turned cold." His seemingly supreme power offers no guarantee for the permanence of his possessions. The first couplet of the second poem becomes particularly poignant if we read it against Bai Juyi's reassuring generalization in "An Account of Lake Tai Rocks" (see above) that "all the wise men of ancient times had things to which they were addicted." Whereas with Bai, "addiction" was a spiritual asset, it becomes a moral and philosophical liability in Wen Tong's unequivocal diagnosis of selfishness as the root cause of Li Deyu's failure. Philosophically, the addiction turns an otherwise intelligent man into a maniac. Morally, it points to the extravagant collecting as a sign of official corruption. Wen minces no words in his verdict that those who helped to build up Li's collection were "no upright and pure gentlemen."

"Two Poems Composed after Transcribing 'Record of Plants and Trees at Pingquan'"

One
When the Duke of Wei was in charge of government,
His power equaled that of heaven and earth.
Cultivating trees and plants at Pingquan,
He grabbed spring scenery from all corners.
He had to have them all, from the Eastern Sea to the Tai Mountain,
Able to command even ghosts and spirits.
How laughable that before his body turned cold,
It was said that they already belonged to others.

Two
Not that His Lordship was not intelligent,
But that his addiction led him to this.
Had he not been enticed by his selfishness,
How could these things have got here?
Who were those that got them here?—

Surely they were no upright and pure gentlemen.
The trees and plants have certainly turned into dust,
But his infamy has not yet ended.

"On the Ugly Rock in Liu Zhonggeng's Garden in Zezhou" (*Yong Liu Zhonggeng Zezhou yuanzhong choushi* 詠劉仲更澤州園中醜石)

MEI YAOCHEN 梅堯臣 (1002–1060)

TRANSLATED BY XIAOSHAN YANG

Liu Yisou (formal name Zhonggeng; 1017–1060), the owner of the rock that is the subject of this poem, was one of the polymaths, like Hu Su (see above) and Shen Gua (see chapter 4), who flourished in the intellectually adventurous Song dynasty; he was a noted astronomer and mathematician, among other accomplishments. Mei Yaochen was a leading poet of his time. He was a close associate of the writer Ouyang Xiu (see below), who edited his collected poems. Almost none of Mei's prose work survives. Much of his early poetry addresses social problems such as the hardships suffered by the rural population or corruption in the civil service. His later poems employ an "even and bland" (*pingdan*) style, in contrast to the more elaborate style of the late Tang, and helped to usher in a more realistic and plainspoken style characteristic of the Northern Song. In this poem, Mei gives a detailed, realistic description of the rock in question, while showing some anxiety that indulgence in expensive aesthetic tastes will lead to moral confusion. Liu Yisou's transportation of huge rocks over a great distance is unfavorably contrasted with the admirable customs of the "ancients." Without a moral anchor, Liu's fascination with the "strange and unusual" Lake Tai rocks appears to lack spiritual substance. Aesthetic relativism with regard to the ugly and the fair portends a moral confusion in human affairs.

"On the Ugly Rock in Liu Zhonggeng's Garden in Zezhou"

The Lake Tai rock at your house—
How did you get it from Lake Tai?
Lake Tai is at the southeast of the world,
Mount Taihang is at the northwest.
The two are three thousand miles apart,
Why would one take the trouble even though one was able to?
The ancients did not bother with boats and carts;
This thing of crude essence has not wings of its own.
From its holes creeping figs come out,—
Creeping figs have been planted by it.
Like a snake in autumn emerging therein,
With its tongue spitting out a banded rainbow.
You once boasted to me
About how strange and unusual it was.

It has been disliked by the world for its ugliness;
Now you take its ugliness as a virtue.
Nothing is ugly or fair in itself;
What one values is not being befuddled between ugly and fair.

"The Herb Islet" (*Yaozhou* 葯洲; quatrains two and three of four)

LIU KEZHUANG 劉克莊 (1187–1269)
TRANSLATED BY XIAOSHAN YANG

Liu Kezhuang was a leading literary critic toward the end of the Southern Song dynasty. He was from Putian in what is now Fujian Province, rather far from the cultural and political centers of China. His surviving works include a wide variety of genres, and he was also active as a government official. Because of disapproval of his political activities (he was associated with a senior official thought to have been responsible for the collapse of the dynasty), his literary work has often been discounted. In these quatrains (a form typical of Liu), he reflects on the dangers posed by obsessive rock collecting and the negative history of strange rocks, alluding to the Song emperor Huizong's notorious "Northeast Marchmount" (*Genyue*; see chapter 4), constructed in the Xuanhe reign period, and to the Level Spring (*Pingquan*) Garden during the Tang dynasty (see below), which was dismantled after the death of its owner Li Deyu, Marquis of Zanhuang.

"The Herb Islet" (quatrains two and three of four)

Two
Once they made people toil like dogs and horses;
Then they surrendered as prisoners after the fall of the kingdom.
Of the rocks scattered in the lake,
Are there any from the Northeast Marchmount of the Xuanhe era?

Three
Those grotesque and strange rocks:
Who could tell whether they are ugly or fair?
Don't let the Marquis of Zanhuang see them,
He would certainly have them carted to Pingquan.

The History of the Song Dynasty (*Songshi* 宋史)

"The Biography of Mi Fu" (*Mi Fu zhuan* 米芾傳; extract)

TOQTO'A 脫脫 (1314–1356)

TRANSLATED BY DUNCAN M. CAMPBELL

This extract from the biography of Mi Fu in the official history of the Song dynasty, compiled during the Yuan dynasty under the supervision of Toqto'a (Chinese: Tuotuo), a senior Mongol official, focuses on the great calligrapher's eccentric personality. Mi Fu (whose name is sometimes incorrectly transcribed as Mi Fei) became a canonical figure in later garden culture as a result of his obeisance to the "strange rock" he honored as his elder brother. Mi Fu and his son Mi Youren (1086–1165) both became known as landscape painters with a distinctive style, but Youren never attained his father's level in calligraphy. Although born to a privileged life in the imperial household, where his mother was employed as wet-nurse to the future Emperor Shenzong (1048–1085; r. 1067–1085), Mi Fu's inability to submit to convention meant he never had a successful official career. He was a great collector and connoisseur, as well as a creator, of painting and calligraphy. He was also a close friend of Su Shi (see above).

"The Biography of Mi Fu" (extract)

Mi Fu's prose was both strange and risky, and never indulged in cliché. His calligraphy was particularly fine, first firm and then soaring, very much in the manner of Wang Xianzhi. He also painted landscapes and portraits, excelling at these as well. He was an expert at copying past masters, to the extent that his copies were indistinguishable from the originals. He was a connoisseur of some very considerable discrimination, and whenever he encountered antique vessels or fine paintings and calligraphy, he would make the greatest efforts to acquire them, resting content only once he had done so. The statesman Wang Anshi chose a few lines of his poetry to inscribe upon a fan; Su Shi, too, delighted in praising him. In his dress and cap, he imitated the men of the Tang dynasty, and his deportment was both relaxed and elegant, his speech clear and fluent. Wherever he was, people would gather around to observe him. He was fastidious about cleanliness, this habit becoming something of an obsession. He would never share the use of clothing or cups with others. His eccentricities were such that they occasion laughter. A large rock stood just within the Wuwei Prefectural seat, extraordinarily ugly of appearance. On catching sight of it, Mi Fu was delighted: "This rock is worthy of my obeisance." Thereupon, he immediately donned his official robe and cap and bowed before it, addressing it as his elder brother. He proved incapable of rubbing along with the times and so experienced various difficulties in his official career.

The Stone Compendium of the Plain Garden (*Suyuan shipu* 素園石譜)

"Preface" (*Zi xu* 序)

LIN YOULIN 林有麟 (1578–1647)
TRANSLATED BY STEPHEN LITTLE

Lin Youlin, a late-Ming rock collector who compiled *The Stone Compendium of the Plain Garden* in 1613, came from Huating in Jiangsu, close to the sources of many of the most prized rocks, including Taihu and Kunshan rocks. "Plain Garden" was the name of the Lin family's garden. Although Lin Youlin served for a time as an official, his family's wealth enabled him to live a leisured life replete with cultural activities such as collecting works of art and "strange rocks." His compendium, which is lavishly illustrated with woodblock prints, introduces both types of rock and individual stones, some with inscriptions by famous literary men and some without; apparently, the illustrations are based on Lin's own paintings.

"Preface"

Large stones, characterized by jagged ridges, are all found among the Five Sacred Peaks. The habitations of those who can effect transformations are among what the Daoist books call cavern-heavens, blessed realms, and numinous traces. In all these places can be found strange blue and green stones.

I am fond of traveling, and, every year, wearing a deerskin jacket and carrying a dragon-handled staff, I enter among the five lakes and mysterious clouds. Going west, I reach Stone Citadel, and in the furthest extent arrive at the realms of waterfalls, bridges, pools, and wild geese, where I stop—this is what is called "being moved by layered clouds." . . . I am like Zong Bing, who enjoyed looking at landscapes as he reclined.

In my home there were two stones, which had belonged to my ancestors; their names were Humble Hermitage Mountain and Mysterious Pond. These were located to the left of the Hall of Retirement. During my childhood, whenever I could, while playing the *qin* zither and chanting poetry, I would move and stand before them. Each time I would burn incense and quietly face them, and was in awe as their appearance changed. It was like being in the presence of a venerable Buddhist monk.

In the Plain Garden I have built the Mysterious Pond Hall in which to offer ritual worship to stones. In addition, I have recreated the stony vestiges of the ancient Wu kingdom, with walls, moats, peaks, caverns, more or less complete. When the rain is heavy, moss fills the hall; at autumn's peak in the tall grove, wind enters the beams. . . . There I arrange my hermit's desk. Content and silent, I am completely washed clean of the affairs of the human realms.

I have often said that calligraphy, famous paintings, old inscriptions, and ritual bronze vessels cause people to go beyond themselves. But stones are what really bring one close to Chan, and the pure masters nod their assent, like arrows flying unopposed.

Like Mi Fu and Su Shi, I say that with these one can travel like a god to the limit of the numinous realm. The writings of these crazy old men extend from antiquity—perhaps from this one can attain some degree of enlightenment. Beyond the Nine Provinces of the known world are another Nine Provinces, and the Five Sacred Peaks can be found in a single stone—like entering into a mustard seed. If one subscribes to this view, then everything is as peaceful as a child. . . . One can have the peaks such as Mount Song, Mount Hua, Mount Heng, and Mount Tai in miniature.

Thus I have examined old volumes, from the time of Emperor Huizong on, and later images and poems, and have classified and edited them. Now I have completed four volumes, and my friend, District Magistrate Huang, has seen and approved them. One could say that he is a friend of stones. The ancients said that to read ten thousand books was equivalent to a hundred wealthy cities of the south. Personally, I have gone beyond ten thousand books, and would take just one piece of azure Heaven—would it not surpass all the treasures of the ancients?

The Craft of Gardens (*Yuan ye* 園冶)

"Selection of Rocks" (*Xuan shi* 選石; extracts)

JI CHENG 計成 (1582–CA. 1642)
TRANSLATED BY ALISON HARDIE

Almost nothing is known of the life of Ji Cheng. He lived during the late sixteenth and early seventeenth centuries, during the last years of the Ming dynasty, at a time of great social and economic change and political upheaval. He seems to have been of humble origins, although probably from the literati rather than the artisan class; apart from his great work on garden design, *The Craft of Gardens*, lost in China for many centuries before being found in a Japanese library in the 1930s, nothing else he wrote remains extant. No garden known to have been designed by him still exists.

The Craft of Gardens, written between 1631 and 1634, is the first surviving—and possibly actually the first—general manual on landscape gardening in the Chinese tradition. Ji Cheng's method is revealing: rather than offering step-by-step instructions to the would-be garden designer, he instead emphasizes the importance of basing the design of the garden on the existing features of the landscape, and uses poetic descriptions to build up an atmosphere that might serve to inspire.

In this part of *The Craft of Gardens*, Ji Cheng discusses the selection and acquisition of rocks as an essential part of garden-making. He is both following earlier texts, such as Du Wan's *Stone Catalogue of Cloudy Forest* (see above), and drawing on his own practical experience as a designer of rockwork for gardens.

"Selection of Rocks"

In order to learn where rocks can be obtained, you must seek far and near through the mountains. No price need be paid to the mountains for the rocks; the only expense is the labor. You must climb up and search as far as the mountain-tops, winding hither and yon to the end of the road. It is most convenient if the rocks can be transported by water, and then it does not matter if they are a thousand miles distant; however, if it does not take too long to get them, they can be carried on shoulder poles. In picking out interesting rocks, do not limit yourself to elaborate ones resembling filigree; they must also be able to stand alone. In seeking out strong stones, you should also look for solid, hefty ones, which can be piled on top of each other. You should first select good quality rocks with no cracks, and then fit the jagged edges together. If there are too many cracks there is a danger of their breaking, though if they are concave they may be used to form an overhanging precipice. From ancient times, the rocks of Lake Tai have been most famous; other than these, amateurs of landscape only knew the name of the "patterned rocks." Nowadays people simply choose rocks from illustrations; what does the ignorant multitude know of the beauty of Yellow Mountain? Small-scale mountains should imitate the work of the Master of the Cloud Forest, Ni Zan, and large ones should honor the style of Huang Gongwang. The individual pieces of rock may look clumsy and awkward, but when piled up they will seem all the more awe-inspiring. This sort of rock is good for arranging together, and moreover can be collected anywhere in the mountains. Rocks are not like plants or trees; once gathered, they gain a new lease of life. People, too, not content with achieving nothing, are prepared to seek fame and fortune however far this takes them.

Rocks from Mount Kun: The rocks in the ground near Maanshan in Kunshan County are covered by red soil. Once they have been dug out of the ground, you have to spend an inordinate amount on having them picked free of soil and washed down. They are knobbly in shape and stretch up into the air, without the sloping shoulders of a more rounded mountain peak, and when you tap them they give out no sound. Their color is pure white. They can be set about with small trees, or have irises planted in their interstices, or else they can be set in troughs to make the focal point of a miniature landscape. They cannot be put to any major use.

The Patterned Rock Convoy: The patterned rocks from the Song dynasty appear all over the area of Henan which borders on Shandong. These were the rocks left behind during the transportation. Many of these rocks are extremely intriguing. Because the route overland is very difficult, collectors take just a few pieces to place in their gardens, but even so they add considerable interest.

Taoan's Dream Memories (*Taoan mengyi* 陶庵夢憶)

"Brook Pavilion of the Auspicious Plants" (*Ruicao xiting* 瑞草溪亭)

ZHANG DAI 張岱 (1597–CA. 1684)

TRANSLATED BY DUNCAN M. CAMPBELL

Zhang Dai is one of the great late-Ming prose writers, although it is only recently that the magnitude of his achievement as a historian of his dynasty has been recognized.[21] Zhang Dai began life as the playboy scion of a wealthy and cultured family of Shaoxing (in present-day Zhejiang Province) who lost most of their property after the fall of the Ming dynasty. Writing after this crisis, Zhang Dai nostalgically recalled the scenes, events, and people of his youth in *Taoan's Dream Memories* (Taoan or "Joyous Hermitage" was one of Zhang Dai's studio names) and *Seeking the West Lake in Dreams* (*Xihu mengxun*). As he said in his "Self-Wrought Tomb Inscription," he had enjoyed the best of "luxurious quarters, pretty maids, beautiful boys, fresh clothes, fine foods, fast horses, painted lanterns, fireworks, opera, music, antiques, and flowers and birds."[22] The lanterns, fireworks, and opera, at least, were enjoyed in the gardens of the Zhang family or of their numerous relatives and friends, and Zhang Dai himself took a great interest in garden design and cultivation (as we can see also from passages in the "Flora" section of this chapter, and from the letter in chapter 6).

"Brook Pavilion of the Auspicious Plants"

The Brook Pavilion of the Auspicious Plants was situated upon one of the branch foothills of Dragon Hill and stood no taller than the buildings that surrounded it. Declaring that fantastic rocks were sure to be found just beneath the surface here, my cousin Zhang E proceeded himself to wield the hoe and hump away basketfuls of earth, insisting on uncovering the rocks before his own stonemasons had time to do so. Earth was carted away and rocks broken up, down to a depth of more than three *zhang*, at which point the foundation was pounded flat and a building constructed. If today a building went up, tomorrow it would be dismantled, only to be reconstructed the day after, and then, the next day, dismantled yet again. This was done a full seventeen times before finally the Brook Pavilion was completed. In actual fact, however, there was no brook here, so the pavilion had then to be given a brook. When the brook was found to be somewhat inadequate, a pool was formed and a gully created, several hundred hands being assembled each day to complete this task. Then my cousin made the decision that he might as well have a pond excavated, that the pond might as well be widened by a *mu*, and that this pond needed to be given a depth of eight *chi*. But the site was without water, and so the pond was filled up bucketful after bucketful, and a table-like rock was left standing in the middle, around which the water eddied as if around a floating

---

21 On Zhang Dai's life and work, see Jonathan D. Spence, *Return to Dragon Mountain: Memories of a Late Ming Man* (New York: Viking, 2007).

22 Philip A. Kafalas, *In Limpid Dream: Nostalgia and Zhang Dai's Reminiscences of the Ming* (Norwalk, Conn.: EastBridge, 2007), p. 53.

mountain peak, and the whole garden began to acquire a most exquisite look. And then my cousin decided that the mountain rock, having been only recently exposed, lacked the requisite cast of age and hoariness, so he had it coated in horse dung and planted with moss and lichen. When the moss did not immediately grow, he summoned painters to color the rock with the blue and green pigments of azurite and malachite. On yet another day, having stood there looking all about him, my cousin suddenly declared that the rock table ought not to be without a Heaven's Eye pine or two coiled upon it and so at great expense he purchased five or six such pines and had holes bored in the rock for the trees to be planted. The rock, unable to withstand the impact of the metal rods, split apart; neither rock nor covered in trees, it was now no longer even a table. Enraged by this development, my cousin ordered men to continue work all night, in the attempt to shape it into the form of a mountain inkslab. But when work had been completed, the rock was missing a corner, so my cousin had another huge rock carted here to make up the deficiency. By nature impetuous, my cousin could not wait until the trees grew large but rather would have them replaced by larger trees, and when these transplanted trees died, he would search out even larger trees to replace them with. This would go on endlessly, with live trees replaced by ones that would die, these dead trees in turn replaced, and in this way his trees could not but die, but would never die immediately.

By now, the Brook Pavilion was a good four *zhang* lower than had been its original foundation and so my cousin had earth moved and a large hill built up to the east of it and had buildings of a full *mu* in area constructed, but these too were all prone to the vicissitudes of constant change. Once a building had been completed, he would sit looking at it for a long while, but by the next day it would in all probability have disappeared. In this way, although the Brook Pavilion was itself a tiny structure, the expenditure lavished upon it was truly enormous.

One day, my cousin happened to be reading a novel when he came across the following tale:

> On a dream tour of Hell one day, Yao Chong found himself in a huge workshop wherein a thousand forges blazed and several thousand evil ghosts labored, and where the molten metal flowed urgently. Upon inquiry, he was informed: "We are forging the Prince of Yan's ill-gotten gains." Later, he reached a place where the forges stood idle, attended only by one or two exhausted ghosts listlessly working the bellows. When Yao Chong asked where he was, their reply was: "This is the treasury of the Master." When Yao Chong awoke from his dream, he sighed to himself: "Even the wealth of a Prince of Yan is only held at the pleasure of Heaven."

Much taken with this story, my cousin decided to take the sobriquet "Guest of the Prince of Yan."

My second uncle had accumulated a fortune of some forty to fifty thousand taels, but all this flowed away rapidly through my cousin's hands. In the *jiashen* year [1644], when my uncle died in office in Huaian, my cousin hastened there to attend his funeral, returning with more than 20,000 taels worth of accumulated salary, along with the various baubles and bolts of silk that my uncle had saved and collected. Within three months, all this too had gone. Contemporaries likened him to Yu Hong and his "Four Exhaustions."[23] As to the living quarters attached to the Brook Pavilion, not a day would go by without these being erected, renovated, or sold in an endless tumult of activity. My friend Xia Erjin would while away his days cutting out cloth to make lanterns in the shapes of flowers, and everyone called him a "Bankrupt Emperor Yang of Sui." My cousin, for his part, they labeled an "Impoverished First Emperor of Qin." It is enough to bring a wry smile to one's lips.

"Bamboo and Rock" (*Zhushi* 竹石)

ZHENG XIE 鄭燮 (1693–1765)
TRANSLATED BY DUNCAN M. CAMPBELL

The poet, painter, and calligrapher Zheng Xie, better known by his sobriquet Zheng Banqiao, was born in Xinghua in Jiangsu Province. His artistic reputation as (in later parlance) one of the "Eight Eccentrics of Yangzhou" was earned during the decade he spent in that city eking out an existence by selling his paintings and calligraphy. Having passed the Metropolitan Examination in 1736, he served in office for a decade before retiring home in 1753, again to devote himself to his art. As a painter, he specialized particularly in depictions of orchids, rocks, and bamboo. The painting for which the colophon below was written was executed in the last year of Zheng Banqiao's life.

"Bamboo and Rock"

A thatched studio just ten foot wide; a single square Heaven's Well courtyard. A tall bamboo or two; a stone bamboo shoot several feet high. A spot not large; an expenditure not great. But here in the breeze or in the rain there is music to be heard; in sunlight or in moonlight, the shadows forever dance; when waxing lyrical or in one's cups, there is passion to be felt; and when idle or when depressed, there is always a companion to be found. It is not just a case of me loving the bamboo and the rocks, for they too, for their part, love me. Men there are who spend tens of thousands on building their gardens, only to find that, traveling here and there on official business, they die without

---

23 The biography of Yu Hong, in the *History of the Liang* (*Liang shu* 梁書), says that he would often tell people, "Any commandery that I take charge of can soon be said to suffer from the Four Exhaustions; the rivers become exhausted of their fish and turtles, the hills of their roebuck and deer, the fields of their rice and grain, and the villages of their populace. The hero born in this age is like the finest dust that settles upon the yielding grass, like the white colt glimpsed as it bolts past the crack in the wall. The joys and pleasures, wealth and honor afforded man—how long do they last?"

ever having been able to return home to enjoy its delights. For men such as myself who, by contrast, can only dream of visiting famous mountains and great rivers if at all then only very infrequently, what is better than a single room with a miniature vista, replete with emotion and with taste and which over the passage of time constantly renews itself? Facing this scene, crafting such a realm, is not at all difficult; and having done so, one may then either "roll it up and withdraw into it in order to hide away in mysteriousness," or "unroll it and thus extend oneself throughout all four quarters."

Fourth month of the *yiyou* year [1765] of the reign of the Qianlong emperor, painted by Zheng Xie (Banqiao).

"The Ethereal Rock" (*Shi Qingxu* 石清虛)

PU SONGLING 蒲松齡 (1640–1715)

TRANSLATED BY JUDITH ZEITLIN

Pu Songling's *Strange Tales from Make-Do Studio*, also known as *Strange Stories from a Chinese Studio* (*Liaozhai zhiyi*), from which this tale is taken, is one of the best loved of traditional Chinese story collections and still much read today. The collection is a mixture of fictional narratives and stories that purport to be true accounts of strange experiences reported to Pu by friends and acquaintances.

Pu Songling, from Shandong, was unsuccessful in his many attempts to pass the imperial examinations, and earned his living as a private tutor. It was his literary work that eventually brought him fame instead.

"The Ethereal Rock"

Xing Yunfei, a native of Shuntian [Beijing], was a lover of rocks. Whenever he saw a fine rock, he never begrudged a high price. He once happened to be fishing in the river when something caught in his net. As the net began to grow heavy, he drew it out, and there was a rock barely a foot high. All four sides were intricately hollowed, with layered peaks jutting up. He was as delighted as someone who has received a rare treasure. After he got home, he had a piece of dark sandalwood carved into a stand for the rock and placed it on his desk. Whenever it was going to rain, the rock would puff out clouds; from a distance it looked as though it were stuffed with new cotton wool.

A rich bully called at his door and asked to see the rock. As soon as he clapped eyes on it, he handed it over to his muscular servant, then whipped his horse, and galloped straight away. Xing was helpless: all he could do was stamp his foot in sorrow and rage. Meanwhile, the servant carried the rock until he reached the banks of a river. Tired, he was just resting his arms on the railing of the bridge when he suddenly lost his grip, and the rock toppled into the river. When the bully learned of this, he flew into a temper and whipped the servant; then he brought out gold to hire skilled swimmers, who then tried a hundred different ways to find it. But in the end the rock was not located, and the bully posted a reward notice and went away. From then on, seekers of the rock daily filled the river, but no one ever found it.

Some time later, Xing went to the spot where the rock had fallen in. Looking out at the current, he sighed deeply. All of a sudden he noticed that the river had turned transparent and that the rock was still lying in the water. Xing was overjoyed. Stripping off his clothes, he dove into the water and emerged cradling the rock in his arms. Once he got home, he didn't dare set the rock in the main hall, but instead cleansed his inner chamber to receive it.

One day, an old man knocked on his gate and asked permission to see the rock. Xing made the excuse that it had been lost long ago. The old man smiled and asked: "Can't I at least come in?" So Xing invited him into the house to prove that the rock wasn't there. But when they got inside, the rock was once again displayed on the desk. Xing was speechless with shock. The old man patted the rock and said: "This is an heirloom that belongs to my family. It's been lost for a long time, but now I see it's here after all. Since I've found it, please give it back to me." Xing was really hard-pressed and began to argue with him over who was the owner of the rock. The old man smiled and said: "What proof do you have that the rock belongs to you?" Xing could not reply. "Well, I definitely recognize him," said the old man. "He has 92 crannies altogether and in the largest crevice are seven characters that read: OFFERED IN WORSHIP: ETHEREAL, THE CELESTIAL ROCK."

Xing inspected it closely, and in the crevice were indeed tiny characters fine as grains of rice. Only by squinting as hard as possible could he make them out. He then counted the crannies, and they numbered exactly as the old man had said. Xing had no way of refuting him. Still, he held onto the rock without giving it up. The old man smiled and then addressed the rock: "It's up to you to decide whom you belong to." He joined his hands politely and went out. Xing escorted him beyond the gate. When he returned, the rock had disappeared.

Xing raced after the old man, who was strolling at a leisurely pace and had not gone far. Xing ran over and tugged at his sleeve, begging him to give back the rock. "Amazing!" said the old man. "How could a rock almost a foot high be hidden in my sleeve?" Xing realized he was a god, and tried to forcibly drag him back home. Then he prostrated himself before the old man and implored him. "Does the rock really belong to you or to me?" asked the old man.

"It really belongs to you, but I beg you to surrender what you love."

"In that case," said the man, "the rock is certainly there." Xing went into his chamber and found the rock already back in its former place. "The treasures of the world should belong to those who love them," said the old man. "I do indeed rejoice that this rock can choose his own master. But he was in a hurry to display himself and emerged too early so that his demonic power has not yet been eradicated. I was actually going to take him away and wait three more years before I presented him to you. If you wish to keep him, you must forfeit three years of your life; only then can he remain with you forever. Are you willing?"

"I am."

The old man then used two fingers to pinch together one of the rock's crannies, which was soft like clay and closed up with the touch of his hand. After closing three of the crannies, he stopped and said: "The number of crannies on this rock now equals the years of your life." The old man then said good-bye and prepared to leave. Xing desperately tried to detain him, but he was adamant. Xing then asked his name, but he refused to say and departed.

A little more than a year later, Xing had to go away from home on business. That night robbers broke into his house; nothing was stolen except for the rock. When Xing returned, he was stricken with grief over his loss and wanted to die. Though he made a thorough investigation and offered a reward, not the slightest clue turned up.

Several years later, he went by chance to the Baoguo temple. He noticed someone selling rocks and there discovered his old possession among the wares. He identified the rock as his, but the seller refused to acknowledge his claim, so the two of them took the rock to the local magistrate. "What evidence do you have that the rock is yours?" the magistrate asked the rock seller. The man was able to recite the number of crannies, but when Xing challenged him by asking if there was anything else, he was silent. Xing then mentioned the seven-character inscription in the crevice as well as the three fingermarks. He was thus proven to be the rock's true owner. The magistrate was going to flog the rock seller, but the merchant insisted that he had bought it in the market for twenty pieces of gold and so he was released.

When Xing got the rock home, he wrapped it in brocade cloth and hid it in a casket. He would only take it out from time to time to admire it, and even then he would burn rare incense beforehand.

There was a certain government minister who offered to buy the rock for 100 pieces of gold. "I wouldn't exchange it even for 10,000 pieces of gold," said Xing. Furious, the minister plotted to implicate him on a trumped-up charge. Xing was arrested and had to mortgage his land and property to cover his expenses. The minister sent someone to hint at what he desired to Xing's son, who then communicated it to his father. Xing said he would rather die and be buried along with the rock, but in secret, his wife and son contrived to present the rock to the minister. Only after he had been released from prison did Xing discover what they had done. He cursed his wife and beat his son and tried repeatedly to hang himself, but a member of the household always discovered him and saved him in time.

One night he dreamed that a man came to him and said: "I am Mr. Ethereal Stone." He cautioned Xing not to be sad, explaining: "I'll only be parted from you for about a year. Next year on the twentieth day of the eighth month, you may go to the Haidai gate just before daybreak and redeem me for two strings of cash." Xing was overjoyed at receiving this dream and carefully made a note of the date.

Meanwhile, since the rock had entered the official's household, it had ceased its miraculous puffing of clouds, and in due course the official no longer valued it very highly. The next year the official was discharged from his post on account of some wrongdoing and sentenced to death. Xing went to the Haidai gate on the appointed day. It turned out that a member of the official's household who had stolen the rock had come out to sell it, and so Xing bought it for two strings of cash and brought it home.

When Xing reached the age of 89, he prepared his coffin and funerary garments and also instructed his son that the rock must be buried along with him. After his death, his son respected his last wishes and interred the rock in his tomb.

About half a year later, grave robbers broke open his tomb and stole the rock. His son learned of this, but there was no one he could question. Several days later, he was on the road with his servant, when he suddenly saw two men run toward him, stumbling and dripping with sweat. Staring up at the sky, they threw themselves to the ground and pleaded: "Mr. Xing, don't hound us! We did take your rock, but we got only four ounces of silver for it!" Xing's son and his servant tied up the two men and hauled them off to the magistrate. The moment the two men were interrogated, they confessed. When asked what had happened to the rock, it turned out they had sold it to a family by the name of Gong. When the rock arrived in court, the magistrate found that he enjoyed toying with it. He conceived a desire for it and ordered it placed in his treasury. But as one of his clerks picked up the rock, it suddenly fell to the ground and smashed into a hundred pieces. Everyone present turned pale. The magistrate had the two grave robbers severely flogged and then sentenced them to death. Xing's son gathered up the shattered pieces and buried them again in his father's tomb.

The Historian of the Strange remarks: "Unearthly beauty in a thing makes it the site of calamity. In this man's desire to sacrifice his life for the rock, wasn't his folly extreme! But in the end, man and rock were together in death, so who can say the rock was unfeeling? There's an old saying 'a knight will die for a true friend.' This is no lie. If it is true even for a rock, can it be any less true for men?"

PART 2

FLORA

"Rhapsody on Pine and Cypress" (*Songbo fu* 松柏賦)

ZUO FEN 左芬 (D. CA. 276)

TRANSLATED BY WILT IDEMA AND BEATA GRANT

Zuo Fen is one of the sparse group of literate women in early imperial China whose names we know. She was the younger sister of the poet and official Zuo Si (ca. 255–ca. 306). As a result of her talent, she was introduced into the imperial palace with the rank of concubine (in name only) of the reigning emperor of the Jin dynasty (265–419); she is said to have been greatly respected at court. She is known to have written several rhapsodies (an important poetic form in the Han and beyond), but this is the only one that survives at any length.

"Rhapsody on Pine and Cypress"

How came about this profusion of extraordinary trees
Lodging on the rockiest reaches of the steepest peaks,
Covering the winding meanders of the darkest gullies,
And shading the shining waves of the clearest streams?

They elevate in mighty majesty their towering trunks,
And gather redolent fullness in their verdant needles.
They display their mossy coats of slender sprouts,
And spread the flourishing growth of long tendrils.
They arrange the clear pattern of their sparse cones—
Scenting their rich foliage in endless fragrance.
Their tangled abundance spreads far and wide,
Their air is refreshingly clear and cool.
They respond to the winds by shaking their boughs,
Which sound like the echoes of pipes and strings.
Being endowed with nature's firmness and fortitude,
They will not shed their needles in coldest winter.
Even through freezing frost assails their bark,
They flourish splendidly at the approach of spring.
They are like gentlemen in their response to the times,
And also like hermits in maintaining their fortitude.
Rambling below them Red Pine found the Way,
Eating their seeds the lover of texts extends his life.
The *Book of Odes* sings of their glorious profusion,
Equal to the Southern Mountain in eternal peace!

"Treatise on the Bamboo" (*Zhupu* 竹譜; extract)

DAI KAIZHI 戴凱之 (5TH CENTURY)
TRANSLATED BY MICHAEL J. HAGERTY

Very little is known about Dai Kaizhi, author of the fifth-century "Treatise on the Bamboo"; the book itself survives only in the form of quotations by a Song dynasty scholar. Dai was evidently a Daoist with a belief in the importance of investigating natural phenomena (such as plants) in order to understand one's own place in the universe; it is also thought that Dai's travels in southern China inspired in him an interest in the economy of the lower Yangtze region, in which bamboo played an important part as a material for construction and manufacturing as well as for food.

The book was written in tetrasyllabic verses and covers many different kinds of bamboo, with their ecology and uses.

"Treatise on the Bamboo" (extract)

Within the vegetable kingdom,
There is a thing called bamboo.
It is not hard or soft,
Neither is it plant or tree.

Slightly different in being hollow and solid,
But mostly alike in having sections.
Some flourish in sand and near water,
And others thrive on cliffs and uplands.

Of spreading foliage, they luxuriantly grow,
Into a turquoise forest beautiful.
Of such a substance that they thrive in winter,
But of a nature that dreads the extreme cold.
About the Nine Rivers they sparingly grow,
While around the Five Mountains they thickly flourish.

A New Account of Tales of the World (Shishuo xinyu 世說新語)

Chapter 23: "The Free and Unrestrained" (Rendan 任誕; item 46)

LIU YIQING 劉義慶 (403–444)

TRANSLATED BY RICHARD B. MATHER

For Liu Yiqing's *A New Account of Tales of the World*, see chapter 1. This anecdote about the calligrapher Wang Huizhi (d. 386 or 387), son of the "Sage of Calligraphy" Wang Xizhi (see chapter 1), is one of the best-known Chinese literary allusions. Bamboo is often referred to as "this gentleman" (*ci jun*), and pavilions set among bamboo may be named "This Gentleman Pavilion." Many centuries later, the scholar-official Su Shi (see above) remarked, "It is better to have no meat to one's meals than no bamboo in one's dwelling."

Chapter 23: "The Free and Unrestrained" (item 46)

Wang Huizhi was once temporarily lodging in another man's vacant house, and ordered bamboos planted. Someone asked, "Since you're only living here temporarily, why bother?" Wang whistled and chanted poems a good while; then abruptly pointing to the bamboos, replied, "How could I live a single day without these gentlemen?"

"Looking at the Plum Tree" (*Chunri kan mei* 春日看梅)

LADY HOU 侯夫人 (7TH CENTURY)
TRANSLATED BY WILT IDEMA AND BEATA GRANT

Lady Hou is supposed to have been a concubine of Emperor Yang of Sui (r. 604–618), the "wicked last emperor" whose degeneracy reputedly led to the downfall of the short-lived Sui dynasty, the predecessor of the Tang. The implication of the poem is that the virtuous Lady Hou is neglected by the emperor, who has turned from her to "common flowers." As so often in women's poems (and in poems about women by men), women are equated with beautiful but fragile and transient flowers.

"Looking at the Plum Tree"

I

The snow on the steps not yet melted away—
I roll up the curtain, my brows knit in a frown.
The plum tree in the courtyard shows her sympathy:
On a single branch an early touch of spring!

II

Her fragrance pure, her wintry splendor fine:
Who else appreciates this heavenly perfection?
Once the plum sheds its jade, warm weather comes,
Passing out an easy spring to all the common flowers.

"Proclaiming an Imperial Visit to the Shanglin Park on the Eighth Day of the Twelfth Month" (*Layue xuanzhao xing Shangyuan* 臘月宣詔幸上苑)

EMPRESS WU ZETIAN 武則天 (624/7–705)
TRANSLATED BY HUI-SHU LEE

Empress Wu formally took power in her own name in 690, after many years of ruling as regent for her ailing husband and then her son; the alleged event described in this poem and its preface took place the following year. Her rule was opposed by most senior officials, and in order to supplant their Confucian ideology, she was active in promoting Buddhism and indeed proclaimed herself to be a manifestation of Buddha. The eighth day of the twelfth month is a Buddhist festival. The preface to this poem emphasizes both the officials' hostility and the empress's own supernatural ability to affect the course of nature, which confirms her right to hold power. The sovereign's beneficent influence on the natural world, often supposedly shown in the blooming of flowers in unusual profusion or out of season, is a trope of writing on Chinese rulership. The imperial park was named the Shanglin Park in reference to the great hunting park of the Han dynasty rulers (see chapter 1).

"Proclaiming an Imperial Visit to the Shanglin Park on the Eighth Day of the Twelfth Month"

On the eighth day of the twelfth lunar month, the second year of the Tianshou reign [691], some officials intended to deceive me into visiting the Shanglin Park by announcing that flowers were already in bloom there. In fact, they were planning a conspiracy. I agreed to their invitation but soon after suspected their scheme. Thus, I dispatched a messenger to release this proclamation. The next morning the Shanglin Park was suddenly filled with the blossoming of well-known flowers. The officials all sighed over this unusual phenomenon.

Tomorrow morning I will make an outing to Shanglin Park,
With urgent haste I inform the spring:
Flowers must open their petals overnight,
Don't wait for the morning wind to blow!

"Record of the Plants and Trees of My Mountain Villa at Pingquan" (*Pingquan shanju caomu ji* 平泉山居草木記) and "Exhortation to My Children and Grandchildren about the Mountain Villa at Pingquan" (*Pingquan shanju jie zisun ji* 平泉山居戒子孫記)

LI DEYU 李德裕 (787–850)
TRANSLATED BY XIAOSHAN YANG

As noted above under Niu Sengru, Li Deyu was the leader of an important faction at the Tang court. He came from a long-standing scholar-official family. Early in his career, he came into conflict with the faction associated with Niu Sengru, and, possibly as a result, spent much of his early career not at court but in the provinces, where he is said to have been a highly effective administrator. Eventually, he was recalled to court and became chancellor in 833; he did not retain this position for long, however, and soon found himself back in the provinces. On a change of emperor in 840, Li returned to court as chancellor. He became embroiled in factional disputes over the conduct of military conflicts with tribes on the northern borders of the empire, which brought him into opposition with powerful, semi-independent military governors of the border regions. He was also instrumental in an anti-Buddhist campaign in 845 (an attempt to bring the economic resources of Buddhist establishments under state control). In 846, however, on the accession of yet another emperor, Li Deyu was demoted and had to leave the capital; he died in internal exile in the far south a few years later.

In the first essay, Li makes a virtue of his peregrinations in the provinces by listing the wide range of plants and rocks he acquired for his garden east of Luoyang. His "Exhortation to My Children and Grandchildren about the Mountain Villa at Pingquan" never to let the Level Spring (Pingquan) villa and garden out of the family's hands must surely reflect his personal knowledge of the vicissitudes of political life, in which one misstep could lead to the complete loss of status, property, and even life itself. In fact, all his sons died in internal exile, and only one grandson was left to inherit the garden. According to a writer in the early Song dynasty, traces of the garden could still be seen at that time, though all but two rocks had been removed—as Li feared—by the powerful.

"Record of the Plants and Trees of My Mountain Villa at Pingquan"

I once pondered why the book catalogue at the house of Duke Shiquan included *Explanations of Garden Plants and Trees*.[24] I understood thereby that there must have been a reason for what was treasured by ancient wise men. In the past twenty years, I served thrice in Wu and once in Huainan. Excellent trees and fine plants were what I liked by nature. Some of them were sent by colleagues; others were obtained from woodcutters. At first, there were only a few items; now, there are plenty. Mindful that those who study the *Book of Songs* learn much about the names of plants and trees and that those who work on "On Encountering Trouble" always thoroughly comprehend the beauty of fragrant iris, I decided to compose a record of their native mountains and streams so as to expand knowledge.

Among the extraordinary plants are golden pine and jade tree from Tiantai;[25] cherry apple, nutmeg yew, and juniper from Jishan; red cassia and big-leaf magnolia from Shanxi;[26] fragrant saltcedar and lily magnolia from Haiqiao [Lingnan]; green spirit and phoenix gathering from Tianmu;[27] laurel, green breeze, arbutus from Zhongshan;[28] mountain cassia and palace tree from Qu'e;[29] goldenrain, swamp honeysuckle, and azalea from Jinling; mountain peach, false cypress, and sea bilberry from Maoshan; weeping cypress,[30] red mung beans, and mountain cherry from Yichun; and chestnut, pear, and dragon juniper from Lantian.

---

24   Duke Shiquan was Wang Fangqing (d. 702), a bibliophile whose collection was said to match that of the palace library, and whom Li held in high regard as a stateman. Sadly, his *Explanations of Garden Plants and Trees* (*Yuanting caomu shu* 園庭草木疏) is no longer extant.

25   Golden pine is the umbrella pine (*Sciadopitys verticillata*), so called because its needles have a golden color—Li Deyu wrote a number of poems about this tree. The branches of jade tree hang down like those of the willow; its berries are bead-shaped and turn from green to dark green to red over the course of three years.

26   The red cassia has white flowers with red pistils and stamens, as Li notes in relation to a poem he wrote.

27   Green spirit and phoenix gathering are supposed to be magic trees, though it is not known what exactly they are.

28   Green breeze is otherwise unknown. The laurel of Zhongshan is distinct for the light yellow color of its flowers, as Li Deyu makes clear in a poem.

29   Qu'e here is probably a reference to Qufang, modern-day Danyang in Jiangsu Province. The mountain cassia, with purple flowers, is a special product of this town. Palace tree (also called Greenhouse Tree, *wenshishu* 溫室樹) is probably a generic name for trees planted inside the palace.

30   The leaves of the weeping cypress remain red throughout the year, in contrast to other cypresses whose leaves turn red temporarily when frosted.

Among the fine specimens of water plants are such lotus varieties as lotus with layered petals from Pingzhou and white lotus from the Furong Lake;[31] and fragrant iris from the East Stream of Maoshan.[32]

Then there are also rocks from Riguan, Zhenze, Fuling, Luofu, Guishui, Yantuan, Lufu, and Louze.

Those that can be found in other famous gardens along the Yi and Luo rivers are not recorded here. Isn't this like Pan Yue [247–300] who praised the splendor of his prune and plum in his rhapsody on "Living in Idleness" or Tao Qian who, upon his return home, was delighted that his pine and chrysanthemum were still there? Therefore, I listed all the elegant names and inscribed them on stone.

Late in the year *jiwei* [839], I got camellia from Panyu; purple lilac from Wanling; hundred-petaled hibiscus and hundred-petaled rambler rose from Guiji; purple laurel and trumpet flower from Yongjia; oceanside photinia from Tiantai;[33] oleander from Guilin; strange rocks from Tailing and Bagong; water stones from Wushan, Yantuan, and Langyatai, which are placed next to the clear fountain stream, while rocks with immortals' footprints and deer footprints are set in front of Buddha's bed.

In that year, I also got double-flowered hibiscus from Zhongling; genuine red cassia from Shanzhong;[34] four-season azalea, rosary pea, Tartarian aster root, red glorybower, mountain tea, double-flowered rambler rose, cottonwood hibiscus from Jishan; cassia, purple photinia from Dongyang; tree peony, prince's-feather, chestnut-leaved oak, date with yellow pith, red fir, and jujube from Jiuhuashan.

In the year *gengshen* [840], I obtained lily magnolia, nanmu, bamboo, golden bramble, red magnolia, pole butterflybush, and curving chestnut from Yichun, as well as mountain ginger and blue lily.

"Exhortation to My Children and Grandchildren about the Mountain Villa at Pingquan"

When I began to build the villa at Pingquan, I was carrying out a plan that I had made a long time before. I was away from home for fourteen years while waiting upon my late father, the grand preceptor ennobled as Loyal and Exemplary Duke. During those

---

31 Li Deyu wrote poems about both the lotus with layered petals and the white lotus.

32 Growing in shallow waters, the fragrant iris is also called stream iris, with purple flowers.

33 The photinia usually grows in warm climates and cannot endure cold weather. Li Deyu's specimen, however, was unique in that its dense branches and leaves could resist frost and snow, as we see from a poem he wrote about it.

34 For the genuine red cassia, see note 26.

years, we climbed Guiji Mountain, explored the Cave of Yu, traversed the rivers and lakes of Chu, ascended Wu Mountain, toured the Yuan and Xiang Rivers, and took in views of Heng and Qiao Mountains. Whenever my late father tied his boat to enjoy the clear prospect, his mood would be stirred; his melancholic thoughts would extend far away, and he would look in the direction of the Yi River. Once he wrote a poem:

> From the southern peak of Longmen spreads the Yi River plain;
> Its plants and trees, and people's homes exist in front of my eyes.
> As pears and jujubes ripen in the northern prefecture,
> In an autumn dream, my soul reaches a suburban garden there.

Moved by the poem, I made up my mind to retire to the Yi and Luo Rivers.

While serving as prefect of Jinling, I obtained the old residence of Recluse Qiao west of Longmen Mountain. At the end of the Tianbao reign [742–756], the recluse fled this place to roam afar. It was overgrown with trees and grasses. However, among the small peaks of Shouyang Mountain, there were vetches and ferns; along the path of Shanyang Mountain, there remained bamboos. Thereupon, wild brambles and shrubs were cut down; foxes and jackals were driven away. A house like that of Master Ban began to be built; the tract was gradually shaped like that of Oldster Ying. Then I obtained some precious plants and fantastic rocks from Jiangnan, which were set up in the courtyard. Thereby the lifelong desire of my heart was satisfied.

I once observed that one honors the Way in deciding whether to take up office or stay in reclusion; one honors the times in deciding whether to advance or to withdraw. Through the ages many worthies and wise men have had regrets. The Patriarch of the Mysterious Teaching [Laozi] hid himself as scribe under the column; Liu Hui cultivated his virtues while serving as chief judge; Bing Manrong of the Han would not take a post paying more than six hundred piculs of grain a year. All of them avoided humiliation or harm, but they lived so long ago, and I cannot reach them now. Fan Li of the Yue urged Wen Niu to avoid the lure of office; the Marquis of Liu bid farewell to the world and found sustenance in the doctrines of the Yellow Emperor and Laozi. Those men were of the next rank. Fan Chui was persuaded in a conversation with Cai Ze to retire from high office; seeing that vassals with merits usually ended in failure, Deng Yu stayed away from fame and power. They were of yet another lower rank.[35]

As to myself, if I were a mallow, I would not have the wisdom to protect my feet; if I were a goose trying to hide away, I would suffer the calamity of the one that could not cackle. Although I have rocks lying around the spring, the time for me to return is not

---

35 Editor's note: Li Deyu appeals to well-known historical precedents of people who were content with a humble position, or who gave up office completely.

remotely in sight. I will, therefore, leave this wooded villa to my descendants. Whoever sells the villa at Pingquan will be disowned by me. Whoever sells one piece of rock or a single plant will not be considered a good member of the family. If, after I pass away, the villa is to be forcefully taken away by the powerful and the noble, you should tell them tearfully about the charge of your ancestor. That is what I want you to do. In the *Book of Songs*, one reads:

> The mulberry and catalpa trees,
> We should respect and revere.

That was because the trees were planted by their parents. In ancient times, the people of Zhou longed for Earl Zhou and consequently loved the tree under which he had rested. In recent times, District Magistrate Xue would sob in tears whenever he saw the rock in the Secretariat upon which his late grandfather had sat. How can you not admire such behavior? Only when cliffs turn into deep valleys and valleys into ridges can you let go of the villa.

"Colophon to 'Record of Plants and Trees of My Mountain Villa at Pingquan'" (*Pingquan shanju caomu ji ba* 平泉山居草木記拔)

YE MENGDE 葉夢得 (1077–1148)
TRANSLATED BY JOHN HAY

Ye Mengde was considered a follower of Su Shi (see above) in his poetic style. He had a distinguished official career spanning the fall of the Northern Song to the Jurchen Jin dynasty and the transfer of the Southern Song capital to Hangzhou. His biography in the official *History of the Song Dynasty* makes much of his outspoken advice to the emperor, his concern for the common people under his administration, and his military and strategic abilities in combating the Jurchen invaders.

Although his family came from Suzhou, Ye purchased a property near Huzhou in northern Zhejiang, which he named "Stone Forest" (*Shilin*), evidently in reference to the collection of rocks that he refers to in this colophon to Li Deyu's "Record" (see above). We might expect him to comment more on the vanity of Li Deyu's hope for the permanence of his garden, or even to draw some parallel between the fall of the Tang as presaged in the destruction of Li's garden and the peril of his own dynasty, but instead he seems to align himself and his passion for his rocks with Li's pathological love of the Pingquan garden.

"Colophon to 'Record of Plants and Trees of My Mountain Villa at Pingquan'"

Ouyang Xiu [1007–1072] used to laugh at Li Deyu's remark that neither his sons nor grandsons would ever give away one tree or one plant of the Pingquan estate.... But the love of rocks is truly pathognomonic. All those instances of former and present literary gentlemen that one sees in poetry and song, are not necessarily of the true passion; those who have this passion are absolutely unable to find release. In the Shaoxing era [1094–1098], I obtained second-place in the spring examination and, on my way home to Suzhou my route passed through Lingbi, where are found the stones which people consider so rare in quality. At the time I was sick, in bed in the boat. I was finding the noises of travel irritating and heard the tea shops all trying to sell these stones. At that time buyers both public and private seemed not in need and aristocrats were not placing much value on them. I quickly bought one, about four feet in length. It should have cost about eight hundred in silver but all I could produce was seven hundred. So I borrowed the balance from someone sharing my accommodation. Unexpectedly, my illness suddenly disappeared, as I lay at night embracing the stone. So then I knew that my passion for stones was not simply a manner of speaking. When traveling through valleys from this point on, I excavated in cliffs and caves and obtained stones of ever rarer quality from within the soil. Now in my estate at Mount Bian, I have uncovered more than ten caves with such stones, and have them standing like a forest, innumerable on all sides. And this passion within my heart cannot be called anything other than pathognomonic.

"Selling Wilted Peonies" (*Mai can mudan* 賣殘牡丹)

YU XUANJI 魚玄機 (844–868)

TRANSLATED BY JENNIFER CARPENTER

Yu Xuanji is one of the earliest female poets whose work survives in any quantity (about fifty poems). What we know of her life seems to be largely legendary; she is supposed first to have been the concubine of an official, and then when he abandoned her, to have worked as a courtesan but also to have lived in a Daoist convent. She is said to have died young, possibly by execution. The writer clearly sees the wilting peonies as an objective correlative of her own situation, a beautiful but ephemeral "flower" available at such a high price that it deters the man ("my dear prince") she hopes will make the purchase.

"Selling Wilted Peonies"

I sigh into the wind at how often the flowers fall;
Their tender feelings melt away unseen: another spring gone by.
It must be because their price is so high that no one wants them,
And because their scent is so strong that butterflies won't love them.
These red blooms are fit to grow only within the palace:
How can their jade-green leaves bear to be sullied by the dust of the road?
When, at last, their roots are transplanted to the Imperial Park,
Then, my dear prince, you will regret that they are no longer for sale.

"Small Flowering Plum in the Garden on the Hill" (*Shanyuan xiaomei* 山園小梅; first of two)

LIN BU 林逋 (967–1028)

TRANSLATED BY HANS H. FRANKEL

Lin Bu was a native of Hangzhou who lived as a recluse on Solitary Hill (Gushan) on the West Lake. Although he came from a lineage of scholars, he never attempted an official career. Like Tao Qian (see chapter 1) many centuries before, he became a canonical figure in later garden culture; he claimed the flowering plum was his wife and the cranes his children, in preference to a conventional family. His biography in the official history of the Song dynasty states that for twenty years he never set foot in the city. He was a fine poet in both *shi* and *ci* poetic forms; most of his poems are concerned with his life as a recluse, and particularly, as here, with the beauty of the flowering plum.

"Small Flowering Plum in the Garden on the Hill" (first of two)

> When other fragrant plants have withered, it alone is lovely,
> It holds a monopoly on charm in the small garden.
> Its sparse shadows are horizontal and slanted—the water is clear and shallow;
> Its hidden fragrance wafts and moves—the moon is hazy and dim.
> A frosty bird, about to alight, first eyes the tree stealthily;
> A powdered butterfly, if it could know it, would be spellbound.
> Luckily I have a little song with which to approach it,
> No need for the beat of sandalwood clappers or shared drinks in golden cups.

"An Account of the Tree Peonies of Luoyang" (*Luoyang mudan ji* 洛陽牡丹記)

OUYANG XIU 歐陽修 (1007–1072)

TRANSLATED BY JAMES M. HARGETT

Ouyang Xiu was highly influential, both as a government official and as a literary man who produced a very diverse body of work. He is held to be one of the Eight Great Prose Masters of the Tang and Song. He acknowledged the influence of the Tang dynasty prose master Han Yu (768–824) on his own limpid, "ancient-style" prose, although his style is quite distinct from that of Han Yu. Ouyang Xiu, a member of the literary and political circle of Su Shi (see above), was highly regarded for his literary achievements even by political opponents such as Wang Anshi. As a young man, he lived a somewhat dissolute life, but claimed to have reached an understanding of the Way by the age of thirty; nevertheless, both his prose and his poetry retained a playful and humorous tone that sometimes misled readers into overlooking their more serious intent. A good example is one of his most famous pieces, "Record of the Old Drunkard's Pavilion" (*Zuiweng ting ji*), which recounts his enjoyment of a pavilion in the countryside near Chuzhou (in present-day Anhui Province) during his official posting there in 1049; ostensibly a record of his own self-indulgence and casual attitude to his official duties, the essay reflects his affection and concern for the ordinary people under his administration.[36]

The city of Luoyang, the secondary capital of the Song dynasty, was famous for its peonies, both herbaceous and tree peonies. Ouyang Xiu's categorization and environmental or geographical analysis of peonies may reflect the protoscientific attitudes and interests shown in the work of his contemporaries such as Su Song (see above) and Shen Gua (see chapter 4).

"An Account of the Tree Peonies of Luoyang"

Part I: Flower Classification and Ranking

Peonies are produced in Dan County and in Yan County; in the east they are produced in Qing County; in the south they are also produced in Yue County.[37] Yet those produced in Luoyang today are number one in the world. Luoyang's so-called Dan County Flowers, Yan County Reds, and Qing County Reds are all especially outstanding in their native areas. After coming to Luoyang, however, they were regarded merely as a variety of common flower. They never go beyond the rank of third grade and cannot independently rival the flowers of Luoyang. Since the flowers of Yue come from far away and are scarcely known, they are not even worth mentioning. Even natives of Yue would never dare to praise them and argue that they are superior to the flowers of Luoyang. And so it turns out that the flowers of Luoyang are number one in the world.

In Luoyang one also finds varieties of peony such as Yellow Shaoyao, Deep-Red Peaches, Lucky Lotus, Thousand-Petal Plums, and Red-Lush Plums, none of which are inferior to those produced elsewhere. And yet natives of Luoyang do not dote on them much at all, but instead refer to them as "fruit-flower" or call them "this particular flower" or "that particular flower." As for peonies, they are not called by name. They are simply called "flowers." The idea here is that when referring to the unique peony among the true flowers of the world, those who give names to them need not add the name "peony," and yet everyone will know what it is. Such is the fondness and admiration for the peony in Luoyang.

---

36   This much-loved essay has been frequently and variously translated; for example, "The Pavilion of the Old Drunkard," in *Inscribed Landscapes: Travel Writing from Imperial China,* ed. Richard E. Strassberg (Berkeley: University of California Press, 1994), 162–64; "A Record of the Pavilion of an Intoxicated Old Man," in *The Columbia Anthology of Traditional Chinese Literature,* ed. Victor H. Mair (New York: Columbia University Press, 1994), 590–91; "An Account of the Pavilion of the Drunken Old Man," in *An Anthology of Chinese Literature: Beginnings to 1911,* ed. Stephen Owen (New York: W. W. Norton, 1996), 613–14; and "The Old Toper's Pavilion," in *The Chinese Essay,* ed. David Pollard (New York: Columbia University Press, 2000), 50–51.

37   Dan County corresponds to modern Yichuan in Shaanxi Province. Yan County was in what is now Yan'an, also in Shaanxi. Qing County was in Shandong Province; the administrative center of Yue County corresponds to modern Shaoxing in Zhejiang Province. Peony cultivation during the Northern Song certainly extended beyond the areas mentioned here by Ouyang Xiu. For instance, beginning in the Tang dynasty, peonies thrived in Chang'an and also flourished in and around Chengdu, Sichuan Province, especially during the Song.

Many of those who discuss such matters speak of Luoyang's location within the Three Areas of the River[38] as a place of ancient virtue. Long ago the Duke of Zhou used graduated instruments to investigate where the sun rises and sets.[39] Through his measurements he came to know the cycles of cold and heat, wind and rain, and the perverse and favorable in this place. They also say it may well be that Luoyang is the center of heaven and earth, and that the abundance of plants and trees here that obtain "the harmony of central *qi*" are many.[40] For this reason, we are told they are uniquely different from the flora in other places. I strongly believe this is not the case.

Now, within the territory of the Zhou, Luoyang was the destination of tribute from the Four Quarters.[41] The distance to get there was about the same from anywhere in the empire. It was located at the center of the Nine Regions.[42] When considered within the vast embrace of Heaven and Earth and the Kunlun Mountains, Luoyang is not necessarily the center. What is more, even if it were so, the harmonizing *qi* of Heaven and Earth would properly spread to the Four Quarters above and below rather than be limited, for selfish reasons, to one central region.

Now, as for "centrality" and "harmony," they possess a constancy of *qi*. Since they express this constancy in things, it is also fitting that things have a constancy of form. As for the constancy of things, this means they are neither especially beautiful nor especially ugly. In situations where there is a deficiency in primal *qi*, beauty and ugliness separate and join, yet do not harmoniously mix together. Thus, things that are extremely beautiful or extremely ugly result from an imbalance of *qi*. The beauty of a flower and the ugliness of a knobby tree, twisted and gnarled, although

---

38   The expression "Three Areas of the River" refers to locations along the course of the Yellow River; specifically, the eastern, middle, and southern sections. These areas are significant because at one time or another they hosted capital cities in ancient China.

39   The Duke of Zhou was a descendant of one of the founding fathers of the Zhou dynasty (1046–256 BCE). He played a key role in the consolidation of Zhou rule, and in later dynasties was regarded as one of the great sages of antiquity. The stronghold the duke established at Chengzhou later became the city of Luoyang. About fifty miles southeast of Luoyang is a structure known as "The Duke of Zhou's Observatory for Measuring the Sun Shadows" (*Zhougong cejing tai* 周公測景臺); Ouyang Xiu's mention of "graduated instruments to investigate where the sun rises and sets" is a reference to this observatory. Astronomers in ancient China considered this place the center of the world.

40   That is, *qi* 氣 (vitality, life-force, pneuma) that derives from the central part of China (*zhong* 中). "Central," in this case, means the place in the upper Yellow River basin (modern Shanxi and Shaanxi) where Chinese civilization was traditionally thought to have begun. The Center, along with the four points on the compass (designating the four parts of China), defined the Chinese world.

41   Luoyang served as the capital of China during the Eastern Zhou dynasty (771–256 BCE). Hence, it received tribute from the Four Quarters (*Sifang* 四方) of the empire.

42   The reference here is to the traditional Nine Regions (*Jiuzhou* 九州) of China organized by the legendary emperor and controller of floods, Great Yu.

in grotesqueness and attractiveness they are different, yet the imbalance and deficiency derived from their allotted *qi* is equal.

The circumference of Luoyang's city walls is several tens of *li*, and yet none of the flowers in its various outlying townships match the quality of those in the city. If you leave the environs of the city, then flowers cannot be grown there. How is it, then, that those flowers with the beauty of unbalanced *qi* alone congregate within this space of several tens of *li*? This indeed is one of the great puzzles of Heaven and Earth that just cannot be solved.

In general, inconstant things that cause harm to man are called calamities; inconstant things that only bring wonder or amazement but do not bring harm are called anomalies. It is said in the *Zuo zhuan* that: "Heaven contravening the seasons makes calamities; Earth contravening things makes anomalies." The peony is an anomaly among plants and trees and a wonder among the ten thousand things. Compared to the knobby tree, twisted and gnarled, I venture to say that it is only weighted on the side of beauty and thus is regarded favorably by men.

During my stay in Luoyang I saw four springs. I first arrived in Luoyang in the ninth year of the Tiansheng reign period [1031], third month. Since I arrived late in the season, I saw only the late-blooming varieties of peonies. In the following year, together with my friend Mei Yaochen [1002–1060], I went sightseeing in the Shaoshi section of Mount Song, Goushi Ridge, Mount Shitang, and the Purple Cloud Grottoes.[43] By the time we got back it was too late to see peonies. Then in the following year I was in mourning and did not have the time to view the peonies.[44] In the following year, when my term of office as Judge in the Regent's Office[45] was over and I was released and left for the capital, I could see only the early varieties. So, I have never seen peonies at the height of their blooming season. However, the flowers that my eyes gazed upon were unsurpassed in their beauty.

When I was living in the prefecture I once paid a visit to Qian Sigong[46] at the Tower of the Twin Cassias, where I saw a single, small standing-screen behind a chair. Its surface

---

43 These are all well-known scenic sites in the general vicinity of Luoyang. Mount Song, one of China's "Five Sacred Marchmounts" (*Wuyue* 五嶽), is the most famous among them.

44 This is probably a reference to Ouyang Xiu's second wife, née Yang, who died in 1035, presumably in childbirth.

45 The main Regent's Office was in the Northern Song capital of Kaifeng, but auxiliary capitals like Luoyang (the *Xijing* 西京, or "Western Capital" of the Song) had branch offices. During his three years in Luoyang (1031–1034), Ouyang Xiu served as a judicial officer on the staff of the prefect, Qian Weiyan, for whom see below.

46 Qian Sigong is Qian Weiyan (962–1034), a Northern Song official who held many top government posts throughout his career. Ouyang Xiu's appointment in Luoyang was his first government post. Qian Weiyan was the governor (or "prefect") of Luoyang at the time. Mei Yaochen also served on Qian's staff.

was completely covered with tiny written characters. Sigong pointed to the screen and said: "If you desire to write something about the classifications of flowers, here are the names of more than ninety varieties of peonies." At the time I did not have the leisure to read through the names, but those I have seen myself and those referred to by most people today only amount to thirty-odd varieties. I have no idea where Sigong found so many of them. As for the others, though they have names, they are not well known and not necessarily beautiful. Thus, those that I record here only include the especially famous ones. I rank them as follows:

1. Yao Yellows
2. Wei Flowers
3. Shouan Fine Petals
4. Waistband Reds; also called Qing County Reds
5. Niu-Family Yellows
6. Wading Creek Deep Reds
7. Zuo Flowers
8. Tribute Reds
9. Petal-Base Purples
10. Crane-Neck Reds
11. Color-Enhanced Reds
12. Reverse-Halo Sandalwood Hearts
13. Cinnabar Reds
14. Nine-Stamen Pearls
15. Yan County Reds
16. Multi-Petal Purples
17. Shouan Coarse Petals
18. Dan County Reds
19. Lotus Flower Perianths
20. 105s
21. Onion Flowers[47]
22. Sweetgrass Yellows
23. One-Press-With-the-Finger Reds
24. Castanet Whites

Part II: Flower Explanation and Nomenclature

As for the names of peonies, in monographs some are organized by family name, some by county of origin, some by place of origin, some by color, and some that exemplify some distinguishing feature. Yao Yellows, Niu Yellows, Zuo Flowers, and Wei Flowers are known because of their association with a particular family name. Qing County,

---

47 *Lutai* 鹿胎 (literally, "deer womb") is an alternate name for the *cong* 蔥, or Chinese small onion. This variety of peony was red with a tinge of yellow, and had white spots that resembled onions.

Dan County, and Yan County Reds are known because of their association with a particular county; Shouan Fine and Coarse Petals, and Wading Creek Deep Reds are known because of their association with a particular place; One-Press-With-the-Finger Reds, Crane-Neck Reds, Cinnabar Reds, Castanet Whites, Multi-Petal Purples, and Sweetgrass Yellows are known because of their special colors; Tribute Reds, Color-Enhanced Reds, Nine-Stamen Pearls, Onion Flowers, Reverse-Halo Sandalwood Hearts, Lotus-Flower Perianths, 105s, and Petal-Base Purples all are organized in monographs by their distinguishing features.

Yao Yellows and Thousand-Petal Yellow Flowers originate in the Yao family household. The first appearance of these flowers took place within the last decade. The Yao Family lives at Adjutant Bai Yuyi's Slope. This area is part of Heyang,[48] yet the flowers were never transmitted to Heyang. They were instead transferred to Luoyang. There are not very many of them in Luoyang either. In a year's time they produce no more than just a few buds.

Niu Yellows are also thousand-petaled and originate with the Niu family. Compared to Yao Yellows, they are slightly smaller. Emperor Zhenzong [r. 997–1022] once performed sacrifices at Fenyin.[49] On his return to the capital he passed through Luoyang. He attended a parting banquet at the Clear Scene Pavilion, where Mr. Niu presented him with these flowers. Their name subsequently became well known.

As for the Sweetgrass Yellows, they are single-petaled and in color resemble sweetgrass. Natives of Luoyang are good at distinguishing flowers. When they see the tree a peony grows on they know what kind of flower it produces, or so it is said. Only the Yao Yellows are easy to recognize. If you chew on the petals, they do not taste foul.

As for the Wei Family Flowers, they are thousand-petaled with fleshy-red flowers. They originated in the home of Wei Renpu [911–969], the Prime Minister. Those gathered first were seen on the hills in Shouan,[50] which were hewn so they could be sold to Mr. Wei. Mr. Wei's pools and lodgings were very extensive. Tradition says that the first time these flowers appeared there were people who desired to examine them, so someone imposed a tax of ten-odd coppers. After paying they could then board a boat and be ferried across a pond to the flower site. Mr. Wei collected ten-odd strings of cash each day. Later he died broke and they sold off his garden. Today the original grounds of his garden are in the woods and pools behind the Universal Light Monastery. The monks of the monastery now cultivate the land there in order to grow mulberry and wheat.

---

48   Heyang corresponds roughly to modern Meng County in Henan Province.

49   Modern Baoding County, Shanxi Province.

50   Shouan Township (modern Yiyang County, Henan Province) was about twenty-five miles southwest of Luoyang.

The flowers passed down from common people's families are very numerous. There are even people who count the number of petals on various kinds of peonies. They say it can reach 700 petals in some cases. Qian Sigong once said: "People refer to peonies as the 'King of the Flowers.' These days Yao Yellows really can serve as 'king.' This being the case, then the Wei Flowers are the 'empress'."

As for the Waistband Reds, they are single-petaled with deep red flowers. They originate in Qing County, so they are also called Qing County Reds. Zhang Qixian, the Charioteer-Archer,[51] had a high official's residence in the Worthies and Ministers Ward of the Western Capital [Luoyang]. He used camels to transport the peonies from Qing County. They then became known in Luoyang. Their color varies. At the "waist" they wear a "waistband." Thus, they are referred to as "Waistband Reds."

As for the Tribute Reds, they are big, multi-petaled, and have light red flowers. After Charioteer-Archer Zhang left his ministerial post he lived in Luoyang. There was someone who presented these flowers to him. For this reason they are called Tribute Flowers.

Color-Enhanced Reds are multi-petaled. They are white when they first bloom, but after several days they gradually turn red. By the time they reached Luoyang there were already varieties of them available in deep red. This is a good example of the outstanding ingenuity of the Fashioner-Creator.[52]

As for the Crane-Neck Reds, the flowers are multi-petaled. They are white on the outside and yet fleshy-red on the inside—like the color of neck feathers on a crane.

The Delicate-Petal and Rough-Petal varieties from Shouan are both thousand-petaled with fleshy-red petals. They originate from Brocade Screen Mountain in Shouan Township. Those with slender petals are especially remarkable.

As for the Reverse-Halo Sandalwood Hearts, they have multi-petaled red flowers. As a rule, the color gets deeper as you move closer to the perianth. As you approach the ends, the color gradually lightens. From the outside, this flower has a deep color.

---

51 Zhang Qixian (943–1014) passed his Advanced Scholar examination in 977 and thereafter held a succession of government posts. During the reign of Emperor Zhenzong, he was appointed Minister of War, one of the highest posts in government (the title "Charioteer-Archer," though used during the Song to indicate the Vice-Director of the Department of State Affairs, may refer here to Zhang Qixian's post in the Ministry of War). He subsequently got into some political difficulties, and even spent some time in prison before finally retiring to Luoyang.

52 The term *zaohua* 造化 (or *zaohuazhe* 造化者), translated here as "Fashioner-Creator," refers to the universal force responsible for the creation of all things.

But as you move closer to the perianth it is pale white, while the spots in its heart are deep sandalwood color. This is especially adorable.

As for the One-Press-With-the-Finger Reds, they have multi-petaled light red flowers. The tips of the petals are deep red with a single spot—just as if someone used their finger to leave a spot there.

As for the Nine-Stamen Pearl Reds, they have thousand-petaled red flowers. On the petals there is a single white spot like a pearl. Moreover, the petals mass and contract their buds to form nine clusters.

As for the 105s, they have multi-petaled white flowers. In Luoyang, the Grain Rain is regarded as the blooming period for peonies.[53] However, these flowers often go 105 days before blooming, at the earliest.

As for the Dan County and Yan County flowers, both have thousand-petaled red flowers. I do not know the reasons for them coming to Luoyang.

As for the Lotus-Flower Perianths, they have multi-petaled red flowers. Their green pedicels are three-layered, like the perianth of a lotus flower.

As for the Zuo Flowers, they have thousand-petaled purple flowers. They originate in the family of some common people surnamed Zuo. The petals are dense and even like a cut-out pattern. They are also referred to as Flat-Headed Purples.

As for the Cinnabar Reds, they have multi-petaled red flowers. I do not know their place of origin. There was a member of the Min Clan who was skilled at grafting flowers and took it up to make a living. He bought land in front of the Worshipping Virtue Temple and managed a flower-garden, where he had these flowers. The powerful families in Luoyang still do not possess them. Thus, their name is not very well known. When the petals of its flowers are very fresh, if you turn them toward the sun they resemble the color of gibbon's blood.[54]

As for the Petal-Base Purples, they have thousand-petaled purple flowers. Their color resembles ink. They are also referred to as Ink-Purple Flowers. When arranged in clusters, one must grow a large branch beside them, and train its leaves to cover the flowers. Compared with other flowers, their blooming period can be extended for as long as ten days. Oh! The Fashioner-Creator indeed has been so kind! As for the origin

---

53   Grain Rain (*Guyu* 穀雨) is the rainy season in spring, just before the start of summer.

54   In the Tang dynasty, "gibbon's blood" (*xingxue* 猩血) was originally a term used to describe a scarlet dye seen in some imported Western textiles.

of these flowers, compared to the other flowers, it is the most obscure. Tradition has it that at the end of the Tang there was a eunuch who served as Inspector of the Armies, and these flowers originated in his home. They are thus also referred to as Inspector of the Armies Purples. Over time they have lost their family-name association.

As for the Castanet Whites, they have single-petaled white flowers. The petals are slender and long like castanets. Their color is like jade and yet deep like sandalwood heart. People in Luoyang do not have many of them. Once I went with Sigong to the Prosperous Majesty Monastery and saw some. I asked the monks there and thereby learned the name. I never saw any more after that.

As for the Wading Creek Crimsons, they have thousand-petaled crimson flowers. They originate in the Wading Creek Monastery. This monastery is behind Dragon Gate Mountain. Originally, this was the villa of the Tang minister Li Fan.[55] Today these flowers have already disappeared from the monastery, but there are still some people who have them. The flowers were originally purple. The crimson ones that appear suddenly in clusters have no more than one or two buds. If in the following year they are grafted onto a separate branch, natives of Luoyang refer to these as "Switching-the-Branch Flowers." Thus, such graft-heads are especially hard to come by.

As for Onion Flowers, they have multi-petaled purple flowers. They have white spots that resemble the patterns on an onion. The former home of Minister Su Yugui has them today.[56] As for Multi-Petaled Purples, I do not know where they come from. Earlier, before the appearance of the Yao Yellows, the Niu Yellows were number one; before the Niu Yellows, the Wei Flowers were number one; before the Wei Flowers, the Zuo Flowers were number one. Prior to the Zuo Flowers, there were only the Su Family Red, the He Family Red, and the Lin Family Red varieties. All of these are single-petaled flowers, and were number one in their time. After the appearance of the multi-petaled and thousand-petaled flowers, they were demoted. People today no longer give them weight.

At first, descriptions of peonies were not available in writing. Only herbal plants were recorded in the *Materia Medica*. However, among flowers the peony did not hold high rank. For the most part, the Danzhou and Yanzhou varieties were already growing in the West. When they extended to places along the Bao-Xie Road[57] they became especially numerous and indistinguishable from the southern wild jujube. Local residents

---

55   Li Fan (754–811) is a well-known Tang dynasty political figure. The Wading Creek Monastery, the reputed site of Li's villa, was in fact situated in a cave on the north side of Dragon Gate Mountain. Located just south of Luoyang, this is the site of the famous Dragon Gate (*Longmen* 龍門) Buddhist cave complex.

56   Su Yugui (895–956) was a major political figure active in the Five Dynasties period.

57   An ancient strategic artery that connected Shaanxi and Sichuan.

there gathered and used them [the trees] for firewood. The peonies of Luoyang began to flourish after the time of Wu Zetian in the Tang.[58] However, I have never heard of any famous literary works about peonies, such as those by writers in the class of Shen, Song, Yuan, and Bai,[59] all of whom sang about plants and grasses. I reckon that if peonies then were as extraordinary as they are today, those poets would have described them in verses, yet they are silent about peonies and such works have not been handed down. There is only Liu Mengde's poem "Singing of the Peonies at Yu Zhaoen's Residence," but he merely talks about "A single cluster—a thousand, ten-thousand buds" and says nothing about their beauty and uniqueness.[60] Xie Lingyun spoke of the many peonies among the streams and bamboo at Yongjia.[61] Today the flowers of Yue are not as distant from various points in the empire as those of Luoyang. For this reason, since ancient times the flowers of Luoyang have never flourished more than they do today.

Part III: An Account of Customs

As for the customs of Luoyang, just about everybody is fond of flowers. In springtime, people in the city, whether noble or commoner, all adorn themselves with flowers. Even burden-toting laborers follow this custom. When the flowers bloom, gentry and commoners vie in devising pleasure outings. Oftentimes, at an ancient monastery or abandoned house with pools and terraces, they make a market-place, erect tents and awnings, and the sounds of pipe-music and singing are heard everywhere. Most of the excitement takes place at the Crescent Moon Dike, Zhang Family Gardens, Crabapple-Plum Ward, and at the home of Director Guo on East Street near the Eternal Longevity Temple. When the flowers fall from their branches, then it is over. There are six post-stations between Luoyang and the Eastern Capital.[62] In the old days flowers were not presented to the emperor in Kaifeng. The presentation of flowers to the throne first dates from the time when Minister Li Di from Xuzhou became Regent.[63] Each year a yamen clerk

---

58 Empress Wu Zetian (612–705); tradition has it that she was fond of commanding flowers to bloom in the presence of her courtiers (see "Proclaiming an Imperial Visit to the Shanglin Park on the Eighth Day of the Twelfth Month" earlier in this section).

59 Tang dynasty poets Shen Quanqi (ca. 650–713), Song Zhiwen (d. 712), Yuan Zhen (779–831), and Bai Juyi (772–846)

60 Liu Mengde is Liu Yuxi (772–842), a leading writer of the Tang period perhaps best known for his political poems (see chapter 2). The particular verse mentioned here by Ouyang Xiu is not found among Liu Yuxi's extant poetry. He does, however, have an extant quatrain (apparently unknown to Ouyang Xiu) titled "Admiring the Peonies" (*Shang mudan* 賞牡丹).

61 Xie Lingyun (385–443) is considered the foremost landscape poet of the Six Dynasties (see chapter 1). For a time, he served in a government post in Yongjia (modern Wenzhou, Zhejiang Province).

62 Kaifeng, about two hundred miles to the west of Luoyang.

63 Probably a reference to Li Di (971–1047), who served in several government posts in the Northern Song. According to his biography in the *History of the Song Dynasty*, Li Di was promoted to the rank of Regent while the Emperor Zhenzong was visiting Bozhou (in present-day Anhui Province).

is dispatched who, riding post-station mounts, reaches the capital in a day and a night. That which is presented to the throne only amounts to three buds of the Yao Yellow and Wei Flower. The buds are packed solidly with vegetable leaves in a bamboo container covered with lotus roots; this to prevent shaking while traveling on the envoy's horse. Wax is used to seal the flower stems so the flowers will not fall off for several days.

Most families in Luoyang have flowers but few of these come from large trees. Presumably, if they are not grafted, then they are not elegant. In early spring people from Luoyang take small cuttings to sell in the city. These are referred to as "mountain combs." People arrange their land, make bordered plots, and plant the cuttings. In the fall they are grafted. A skilled and especially famous grafter of flowers is referred to as "Gate [*Men*] the Gardener." (Note: Presumably, his original surname was Eastgate, or perhaps it was Westgate, but it is customary to just call him Gate the Gardener. Also, following present-day custom, those called by the family name Huangfu are just called the Huang Family.[64]) Among the rich families there are none who do not employ Gate the Gardener.

One graft of a Yao Yellow is worth 5,000 cash. Contracts to purchase them are made in the fall. Payment is made after the flowers appear in spring. The people of Luoyang are very attached to these flowers, and do not wish them to spread elsewhere. When the powerful and rich seek a graft of a Yao Yellow, they will probably be given one that has been killed by dipping it in boiling water. When the Wei Flowers first made their appearance, grafts were still worth 5,000 cash, and even today they are still worth 1,000. Grafting must take place after the Altar sacrifices and before the Double Ninth festival.[65] Beyond this time is unsuitable. To make a graft, cut the stalk about five to seven inches from the ground, then insert the graft. Seal and wrap the graft with mud, pack it with soft earth, make a hood from rush leaves and cover it, not allowing exposure to wind and sun. But on the south-facing side leave a small opening in order to facilitate air-flow. When spring comes, remove the covering. This is the method for grafting flowers. (Comment: one may also use a tile [for the hood].)

To grow a tree peony from seed, one must select a good place, completely remove the old soil, take fine soil and mix it with one catty of dried powder from a *bailian*

---

64   This note presumably comes from the pen of Zhou Bida (1126–1204), who wrote a critical study of the variant readings in Ouyang Xiu's collected works.

65   During the Song dynasty, the *She* (or Altar) sacrifices (to earth) were conducted twice a year: once in spring, on the fifth day after the Beginning of Spring (*Lichun* 立春), which falls in early February in the Western calendar, and once in fall, on the fifth day after Beginning of Autumn (*Liqiu* 立秋; usually on the seventh or eighth day of the eighth month on a lunar calendar; roughly mid-August in the Western calendar). Presumably, Ouyang Xiu's reference is to the autumn sacrifices. The Double Ninth or Double Yang Festival took place on the ninth day of the ninth lunar month (roughly mid-October in the Western calendar).

vine.[66] Presumably because the roots of the peony are sweet, they attract many insects that feed on them. The *bailian* powder can kill the insects. This is the method of growing tree peonies from seed.

As for watering the flowers, naturally there are appropriate times: some people prefer before sunrise, others after the sun sinks in the west. In the ninth lunar month, water once every ten days; in the tenth and eleventh months, water once every two or three days; in the first month, water every other day; in the second month, water once a day. This is the method of watering flowers.

If a stalk produces several buds, select the smaller ones and remove them, leaving only one or two buds. This is referred to as "peeling off." The fear is that their veins will divide. As soon as a flower has fallen, its pedicel is then snipped off so as to prevent the forming of seeds. The fear is that the plant will age too readily. In early spring the cattail hood is removed. Then take several branches from the jujube and cover the flower bush. The *qi* of the jujube is warm; it can guard against frost and will not harm the flower-buds. The same precautions can be used with larger tree peonies as well. This is the method for nurturing flowers.

Those flowers that gradually become smaller have probably been harmed by boring-type insects. It is essential to find their dens and stuff them with sulfur powder. Next to the dens are smaller holes resembling the eye of a needle. This is where the insect larvae hide. Gardeners call these "*qi*-vents." They use the tip of a large needle dipped in sulfur powder to inject the *qi*-vents, and the insects then die. After the insects die the flowers flourish once again. This is the method of treating flowers for disease. If cuttlefish bone is used to inject the flower trees, as soon as it penetrates the bark, the flowers die without exception. This practice is a taboo when it comes to raising flowers.

"On the Love of the Lotus" (*Ai lian shuo* 愛蓮說)

ZHOU DUNYI 周敦頤 (1017–1073)
TRANSLATED BY DUNCAN M. CAMPBELL

Zhou Dunyi was one of the remarkable group of philosophers in the Song dynasty who developed the "Study of Principle" (*lixue*), or what we now know as neo-Confucianism. This philosophical development was, in part, a reaction to the influence in the Tang dynasty of Buddhism, which with its sophisticated cosmology posed a challenge to the pragmatic, this-worldly nature of Confucian ethics. Zhou's famous short eulogy of the lotus is interesting, therefore, in that its subject is the flower particularly associated with Buddhism. Zhou uses its association with purity ("rising unsullied from the mud") to claim his superiority to the "crowd" who value the showy and expensive

---

66 The *bailian*'s tuberous root is commonly used in Chinese medicine. Here, it is used as an insecticide.

tree peony; furthermore, he associates his own love of the lotus with the canonical garden poet Tao Qian's love of the relatively humble chrysanthemum.

"On the Love of the Lotus"

Many are the flowers and trees of land and of water that are worthy of our love. Of these, Tao Qian of the Jin dynasty loved only the chrysanthemum. From the Tang dynasty onward, it was the tree peony that became the focus of all the love of the men of the age. For my part, I reserve my love for the lotus alone, rising unsullied from the mud, bathing in the clear ripples but never with meretricious intent, wholesome within and straight without, neither spreading like a vine nor sprouting from a branch, its fragrance growing ever more pure as it spreads about, standing tall and erect, to be observed from afar but not dallied with up close. To my mind, then, the chrysanthemum is akin to the recluse, and the tree peony to the wealthy man of standing, whereas the lotus is the gentleman among the flowers. Alas, ever since Tao Qian's day, few have been those who love the chrysanthemum, and who but myself loves the lotus? It is the love of the tree peony that now suits the crowd.

"On Smelling the Fragrance Emitted by the Fading Plum Blossoms beside My Pillow, to the Tune Pattern: 'Telling My Innermost Feelings'" (*Su zhongqing: Zhenpan wen canmei pen xiang* 诉衷情：枕畔闻残梅喷香)

LI QINGZHAO 李清照 (1084–CA. 1151)
TRANSLATED BY EUGENE EOYANG

Li Qingzhao is China's most famous woman poet. She was born in northern China to a scholar-official family in the late Northern Song dynasty, and became known for her poetry at a young age. When the north fell to the Jurchens who established the Jin dynasty, she and her husband—believed to be the inspiration for her love poems—fled to the south with some of their art collection, although they lost much of their extensive library. Soon thereafter her husband died. She edited his collected works, and continued to write poetry and literary criticism, some of which survives. Most of her poems are in the *ci* (lyric) form, composed to a preexisting tune or metrical pattern, as is this one, which plays on the ability of the flowering plum's persistent fragrance to return her to the dream of her absent husband (the phrase "spring sleep" suggests an erotic dream).

"On Smelling the Fragrance Emitted by the Fading Plum Blossoms beside My Pillow, to the Tune Pattern: 'Telling My Innermost Feelings'"

Last night I was very drunk and careless in undressing,
Flowering-plum calyxes remained stuck in my hair.
As I awake, the stench of wine ruins my spring sleep,
The dream is receding, I can't get back to it.

People are still,
The moon is stationary,
The kingfisher curtain hangs.
I just crush the stamens,
Just to wring out a little more fragrance,
Just to prolong the time.

"Treatise on the Flowering Apricot" (*Fancun meipu* 范村梅譜; extracts)

FAN CHENGDA 范成大 (1126–1193)
TRANSLATED BY JAMES M. HARGETT

Fan Chengda, who came from Suzhou, was one of the outstanding poets of the Southern Song dynasty, as well as having a successful, though not stellar, official career. In later life, he called himself the Recluse (or Lay Buddhist) of Stone Lake (or Rocky Lake), after the location of his home near Suzhou. A sequence of sixty poems that he wrote on his life there, entitled "Miscellaneous Emotions on the Four Seasons in the Fields and Gardens,"[67] is regarded as his most characteristic poetic work ("fields and gardens" can be understood as referring to pastoral or rural life, and looks back to the poetry of Tao Qian), but he also wrote an important geographical treatise as well as other prose work, including accounts of travel and this "Treatise on the Flowering Apricot," which can also be related to his interest in topography.

"Treatise on the Flowering Apricot" (extracts)

Preface

The blossom of the flowering apricot is an extraordinary thing in the Underheaven. No matter whether one is wise and worthy or stupid and degenerate, none would dare to have a contrary opinion. Literati who study gardening must always first plant flowering apricot trees. Moreover, they never loathe having an abundance of them. As for other flowers, whether literati possess them or not, or whether they are numerous or few, is in no case connected to their worth. I had several hundred flowering apricot trees on Jade Snow Slope at Rocky Lake. In recent years I also bought from one Mr. Wang some rental cottages south of the retreat measuring seventy bays. I had them all torn down and turned the place into Fan Village. One-third of its land is devoted to flowering apricot trees. The flowering apricot trees cultivated around Wu are particularly abundant, and their varieties are all different. Only now have I acquired specimens of all of them, and accordingly have compiled this treatise on those specimens I have acquired so it might be passed on to my fellow connoisseurs.

---

67   See J. D. Schmidt, *Stone Lake: The Poetry of Fan Chengda, 1126–1193* (Cambridge: Cambridge University Press, 1992).

River Flowering Apricot

River Flowering Apricot are those with drupes and which can be grown from seed; found in the wild, they have not undergone cultivation or grafting. They also go by the name "Straight-Foot Flowering Apricot." Sometimes they are also referred to as "Wild Flowering Apricot." As a general rule, those flowers which have an aura of utmost purity and that grow in the mountains, by rivers, and in desolate winter are all from this tree. Its flowers are somewhat small, yet they are sparse[68] and frail, and carry a graceful bearing. Their fragrance is the purest of all. The fruit is small and hard.

Early Flowering Apricot

As for the Early Flowering Apricot tree, its blossoms are superior to those on the Straight-Foot variety. In Wu spring comes late, so common flowering apricot flowers do not glisten and gleam upon the branches until the second lunar month. Only this variety blossoms before the Winter Solstice. Hence, it has acquired the name "Early." There is another and similar variety along the lake at Qiantang [Hangzhou] that blossoms especially early. Once, on Double Ninth Day, I picked some myself, and then came up with the line "Horizontal branches of Early Flowering Apricot blossom across from the chrysanthemums."

Flower vendors in the Exile Metropolis[69] vie to be first to create a sensation: at the start of winter, Early Flowering Apricots are picked before they have blossomed, and the branches are placed in a bathhouse, where the buds are warmed open. The name "Early Flowering Apricot" is then forced upon them. In actual fact, however, such blossoms are petty and paltry, and lack fragrance.

I formerly served as Protector of Guilin. By the Start of Spring, the flowering apricot season had already passed. On Prime Night[70] I tasted some green fruit of the flowering apricot, but, being out of place, they did not taste right.

The Tang poet Du Fu's poem reads: "Stamens of the flowering apricot burst open before the twelfth month; / Their flowers abound once the year is over."[71] Only the transition period between winter and spring can properly be regarded as the "flowering apricot season," simple as that.[72]

---

68   "Sparse" (*shu* 疏) here means that the flowers grow individually rather than in clusters.

69   Hangzhou, the capital of the Southern Song dynasty, after the conquest of northern China by the Jurchen Jin dynasty.

70   The fifteenth day of the first lunar month.

71   These are the opening lines of Du Fu's poem "The River Flowering Apricot" (*Jiangmei* 江梅). Du Fu wrote this poem in Sichuan, where wild flowering apricots grew along the banks of the Yangtze River.

72   Fan Chengda here expresses an attitude that was common during the Song dynasty and appears often in his writings, namely that the transplantation of fruit trees to regions where they are not native always produces

Government-Compound Flowering Apricot

As for this variety of flowering apricot, around Wu gardeners take branches of Straight-Foot Flowering Apricot and graft them to other specimens that have full flowers and attractive fruit. The resulting blossoms are broad and plump. The fruit is also delightful, and can be added into simmering decoctions. The "Government Flowering Apricot" referred to by the men of the Tang are limited to those grown in the gardens of government administrative centers, and are not the same as the Government-Compound Flowering Apricot described here.[73]

Old Flowering Apricot

These are most abundant in Guiji [Shaoxing]. They are also found intermittently in Siming [Ningbo] and Wuxing [Huzhou], also both in Zhejiang Province. Their branches gnarl and twist downward into a myriad shapes. Dark-green lichens, scaly and cracked, completely seal up the flower's stem. There are also mossy whiskers that hang down among the branches, some of which are several *cun* in length. Whenever the wind blows, their green silky filaments flip and flutter in a most pleasing way. Earlier, it was thought these were referred to as "old trees" because they had experienced long-term exposure to wind and sun. But if one carefully investigates those Old Flowering Apricot trees produced in Guiji, even young trees bear mossy scars. These are presumably some other variety, and are not necessarily simply "old trees." I once transplanted ten Old Flowering Apricot trees from Guiji. After a year, although the flowers bloomed abundantly, the moss had almost completely peeled off. But those Old Flowering Apricot trees I have acquired from Wukang Township in Hu County in fact do not change when transplanted and retain their moss. This is because local conditions in Guiji are not compatible with those of Suzhou, as Guiji is separated from Suzhou by a river. Hu and Su counties on the other hand, share a border. Thus, the suitability of the local soil sometimes is a match and sometimes it is not. In general, the petals on Old Flowering Apricot trees with abundant moss are firmly sealed up by the lichen, and the flowers can only bloom through the

---

unsatisfactory results. Fan and his fellow literati expressed this understanding with the words "suitability of the local soil" (*tuyi* 土宜), the idea being that everything is unique to a particular place; its people, products, flora, and fauna, all develop as a result of response and adaptability to unique local conditions, specifically the soil. Thus, the flowering apricot blooms even before the start of the New Year (instead of after it). This, Fan informs readers, is confirmed in the Du Fu couplet he cites. For Fan, there was only one true season for the flowering apricot—the transition period between winter and spring, and any seasonal variation thereof produced odd, substandard flowers and fruit. The implication of this is that true connoisseurs of the flower could never admire and appreciate such aberrations.

73 Fan Chengda here seeks to distinguish clearly between "Government-Compound Flowering Apricots" and "Government Flowering Apricots," only the first of which constitutes a variety. The latter are mentioned often in Tang poetry, as in Du Fu's couplet "By the Eastern pavilion, government flowering apricot stir poetic moods; /Just as they did for He Xun in Yangzhou." He Xun (ca. 468–ca. 520), an official of the Liang dynasty, once held office in Yangzhou. The government compound where he lived supposedly contained a single Old Flowering Apricot, under which He Xun would sit alone and find inspiration to compose poems on the flowering apricot. After he had returned north, we are told, He Xun so missed this tree that he requested a second posting to Yangzhou.

cracks and fissures. Although the flowers are limited, because the pneuma is concentrated, they are nonetheless full and plump, exquisite and superlative. Those trees from which the moss has peeled off produce a lot of flowers, which are the same as the flowers of the Common (or River) Flowering Apricot.

Twenty *li* from Chengdu there are recumbent flowering apricot trees, which sprawl and spread over the ground for over ten *zhang*. Tradition has it that they are a product of the Tang dynasty. They are referred to as Flowering Apricot Dragon trees. Connoisseurs take along wine with them when they go on outings to observe them.

The wine houses in Qingjiang Township have flowering apricot trees as big as several bays of rooms, with adjacent branches hanging down all around, around which several tens of people can spread out mats and sit down. Ren Zhao, the Transport Commissioner, bought some of these trees and built the Riding-the-Wind Pavilion from which to look down upon them. Because of this he subsequently built a large garden, which he referred to as the Coiling Garden. Among the marvelous Old Flowering Apricot trees I have seen in my life, only in these two places are they exemplary. I have jotted this down to append to this entry on the Old Flowering Apricot.[74]

Epilogue

The excellence of the blossoms of the flowering apricot is judged by their bearing; their eminence is judged by their character. Thus, those with branches horizontal and slanted, sparse and frail,[75] and those on age-old branches that are marvelous and fantastic, are the most esteemed. Newly grafted young trees will have delicate twigs sprout straight up after a year, perhaps three or four *chi* in length and resembling the branches of the roseleaf raspberry and multiflora rose. Around Wu these are referred to as "lively branches." The value of these branches is based on the reality of people scheming for profit, and has nothing to do with bearing and character! There is another variety with strength and force gained from planting them in manured soil, which produces short, yellow twigs on their branches. In shape they resemble jujubes, and the flowers are densely mixed together. These are also not of the highest rank.

---

74 As far as I have been able to determine, this variety of "Old Flowering Apricot" is not described anywhere else in Chinese horticultural literature and has no Latin (or scientific) name. They do have an alternative name, however, not mentioned by Fan: "Mossy Flowering Apricot" (*taimei* 苔梅; also called *gu taimei* 古苔梅, "Ancient Mossy Flowering Apricot"). Furthermore, based on Fan's descriptions of this type of Flowering Apricot in Suzhou, Guiji, and Huzhou, there appears to have been more than one variety of the tree throughout Jiangnan during the Song dynasty.

75 The expression "horizontal and slanted, sparse and frail" (*hengxie shushou* 橫斜疏瘦) is no doubt inspired by the first line of Lin Bu's often-quoted and much-praised couplet, "Its sparse shadows are horizontal and slanted—the water is clear and shallow; / Its hidden fragrance wafts and moves—the moon is hazy and dim" (疏影橫斜水清淺; / 暗香浮動月黃昏) from "Small Flowering Plum in the Garden on the Hill," as given earlier in this chapter.

Only in modern times have people begun to paint ink flowering apricots. In Jiangxi there is one Yang Wujiu [1097–1169] who is especially famous for painting ink flowering apricots. Those among his followers who imitate Yang's style are truly numerous. But when you scrutinize Mr. Yang's paintings, you notice that for the most part they are all lively branches and nothing more. Although his brushwork is distinctive and incisive, his paintings are far removed from real flowering apricot blossoms. Only the work of Lian Xuanzhong has a somewhat distinguished demeanor, but people of recent generations rarely value him. I have thus appended these comments to the end of my treatise.

"To the Tune Patterns: 'Hidden Fragrance' and 'Sparse Shadows'" (*An xiang* 暗香; *Shu ying* 疏影)

JIANG KUI 姜夔 (CA. 1155–CA. 1221)
TRANSLATED BY AN-YAN TANG

Jiang Kui is one of the outstanding poets of the Southern Song, although he also gained renown as a literary critic and musician. He is best known for his *ci* (lyric) poetry, usually set to preexisting tune patterns, but also wrote *shi* poetry, with lines of regular length. It was characteristic of him to precede his *ci* poems with a short prose preface explaining the circumstances of their composition; this makes his poems much more personal and individual than is usual for this genre. This pair of poems was prompted by Jiang's friend Fan Chengda (see above), and rather than take the usual approach of setting the lyrics to preexisting tunes, Jiang also composed the music to which the lyrics were to be sung. Like many of his songs, these can be categorized as "songs on objects" (*yongwu ci*), in which a particular object—in this case the flowering plum/apricot—prompts an expression of the poet's feelings rather than a mere description of the object. Jiang's originality led Fan Chengda to compare him to the eccentric writers of the period between the Han and Tang dynasties. He had a powerful influence on later *ci* poetry.

"To the Tune Patterns: 'Hidden Fragrance' and 'Sparse Shadows'"

Preface
In the winter of the year *xinhai* [1191–1192] I went to visit "Stone Lake," Fan Chengda, traveling through snow. After I had stayed with him for a whole month, he gave me paper to write poems, and asked me to set them to music. When these two songs were finished, he held them and fondled them, unwilling to put them down; he ordered a musician and a singing-girl to practice them. They sounded harmonious and graceful. He then titled them "Hidden Fragrance" and "Sparse Shadows."

"Hidden Fragrance"
In the past, the moon's splendor—
How many times did it shine on me blowing the flute by the flowering plums?
I summoned the jadelike lady:

Without concern for the clear cold, she picked blossoms with me.
This He Xun[76] is now getting old,
Forgetting the use of the spring wind poet's brush,
But admiring the sparse blossoms beyond the bamboo,
Whose cold fragrance enters the splendid banquet hall.
The River Land just now is desolate.
I lament that the road is too far to send blossoms
And tonight the snow is beginning to pile up.
In front of the wine vessel of kingfisher hue, tears come easily.
The red calyxes do not speak, restless with longing memories.
I always remember the place where we held hands:
A thousand trees pressed on West Lake's cold blue-green.
And again petal after petal was blown away.
When shall we meet again?

"Sparse Shadows"
On mossy branches, rows of jade.
Blue-green birds, tiny, tiny,
Roost together on the branches.
As travelers we met
At the corner of the fence at dusk.
Without speaking she leans on a tall bamboo.
Zhaojun could not get used to the remote barbarian sands,[77]
But secretly longed for the Yangzi Valley.
I think it is her waist pendant returning in moonlit nights,
Transformed into these blossoms, hidden and lone.
I still recall what happened of old deep in the palace:
When that lady was asleep,
A blossom came flying close to her moth-antenna eyebrows that were painted dark
   green.[78]

---

76   Editor's note: He Xun (ca. 468–ca. 520) wrote a poem "On the Early Flowering Apricot" (*Yong zao mei* 詠早梅) that ends with the lines, "It must know that it will soon wither, / And so it hastens to appear in early spring," apparently foreshadowing his own early death.

77   Wang Qiang (Zhaojun) was a lady in the harem of the Han emperor Yuan. The emperor gave her as a bride to the king of the Xiongnu in 33 BCE. She is said to have lived and died unhappily in the steppe country of the Xiongnu. Jiang Kui must have had in mind a poem by Du Fu about her that contains the line, "In vain her soul comes back with tinkling pendants in the moonlit night."

78   The story is told in *Taiping yulan* 太平御覽 30.1b, crediting *Za wuxing shu* 雜五行書, as follows: "The Princess of Shouyang, daughter of Empress Wu of Song [r. 420–422], was reclining under the eaves of Hanzhang Palace on the Man Day [the seventh day of the first month] when a plum blossom dropped on her forehead, forming a five-petal floral pattern. She was unable to shake it off. [Her mother] the empress made her keep it, wanting to see how long it would last. After three days it finally fell off when washed. The palace ladies admired it and ended up imitating it. This is [the origin of] the present-day plum-blossom make-up pattern."

Don't be like the spring wind,
Don't neglect her delicate beauty,
Early prepare for her a golden chamber.[79]
If you let each petal float away on the waves
You'll suffer the pain of hearing Jade-Dragon's sad tune.[80]
Thereafter, when you want to find again her hidden fragrance,
She'll have entered through the little window into the horizontal scroll.

"Rhyme-Prose on Tall, Slender Bamboo" (*Xiuzhu fu* 修竹賦)

GUAN DAOSHENG 管道昇 (1262–1319)
TRANSLATED BY JENNIFER PURTLE

Guan Daosheng, the wife of the celebrated painter Zhao Mengfu (1254–1322), was herself a noted painter, especially of bamboo. Here, in a rhapsody or rhyme-prose (*fu*), the poetic form that flourished much earlier, in the Han dynasty, she celebrates the "gentlemanly" plant, describing its beauty, its characteristics, and its association with famous people of the past.

"Rhyme-Prose on Tall, Slender Bamboo"

Leafy, leafy, tall, slender bamboo,
Neither tangled nor creeping,
Neither grass nor tree.
Its virtue, exalted, rises above the world;
Its bearing, dignified, stands above vulgarity.
Leaves deep like kingfisher plumes,
A trunk dark like teal jade:
It alone grows on Mount Tai's side
And in the thousand acres of the Wei River's bends.
It brings a cool whirlwind from the distant peak,
And gladdens the beautiful woman in the empty valley.

One sees how it faces the bending balustrade,
Overlooks pure ripples.
Its beauty overtakes that of the Milky Way;

---

79 When Liu Che (156–87 BCE; r. 141–87 BCE as Emperor Wu of Han) was a child, he was fond of his cousin Ajiao and said, "If I could have Ajiao as my wife, I would have a golden chamber built to keep her in." This anecdote is told in *Han Wu gushi* 漢武故事, attributed to Ban Gu (32–92) but believed to have been written by Wang Jian (452–489).

80 *Yulong* ("Jade-Dragon") is sometimes used in literature as the name of a horizontal flute (*di* 笛). The "sad tune" is the *yuefu* tune *Meihua luo* 梅花落, "Plum Blossoms Fall," which was originally played on the horizontal flute; the falling of plum blossoms represents the decay of youth and beauty.

Its shadows flow in pliant waves.
Azure clouds gather over it in summer;
Verdant dew drops down from it at dawn.
Pattering, pattering rain washes it clean,
Swirling, curling breeze spreads it out.
A morning crane's long call,
The autumn cicada's solitary cry;
The intermittent sounding of *zhong* and *qing*[81]
And the mingled shrillness of *sheng* and *yu*.[82]

Then on fine moonlit nights
Or at winter's end when snow is piled high,
Shadows sweep the rocks' surface,
And snapping is heard from the midst of the grove.
Its meaning reaches that of Greatest Antiquity,
While sound sinks into an empty cave.
Ears and eyes are opened, washed clean by it;
Spirit and emotion are pleased by it.
For its match is the exquisite teal *wutong*,
And it finds a friend in the green pine.
Before it, rushes and willows are ashamed of their weakness;
Peach and pear trees, abased by their emptiness.

It makes the song of the fishing pole for the Maiden of Wei,
And intones the "River Bend Tune" in the "Airs of the States."[83]
Thus Ziyou chanted beneath it,
And Zhongxuan rested in its midst.[84]
The Seven Worthies acted in harmony [under it];[85]
The Six Idle Ones left their lofty imprint [upon it]—[86]
All with good cause.

---

81 Editor's note: percussion instruments.

82 Editor's note: wind instruments.

83 In the "Airs of the States" section of the *Book of Odes*, see the opening of poem 59—"Tapering are the bamboo rods, with them they angle in the Qi river; do I not think of you?" (spoken by a woman of Wei to her absent lover)—and poem 55—"Look at that cove of the Qi, the green bamboo is luxuriant" (Karlgren, *Book of Odes*, 41, 37; second translation modified).

84 Editor's note: Ziyou is Wang Huizhi (see above under *A New Account of Tales of the World*); Zhongxuan is Wang Can (177–217), a poet and official at the end of the Eastern Han dynasty.

85 The Seven Worthies of the Bamboo Grove.

86 The Six Idle Ones of the Tang, who met alongside Bamboo Creek and thus are associated with bamboo.

What's more—the voice of the phoenix at Xie valley,[87]
The transformation into a dragon at Gepo![88]

Its heart is empty,
Its joints substantial,
And its trunk and leaves unchanging throughout the four seasons:
From these I perceive a gentleman's virtue.

A Treatise of Vase Flowers (*Pinghua pu* 瓶花譜)

"Preface" (*Xu* 序), "Picking Branches" (*Zhe zhi* 折枝), and "Caring" (*Ziyang* 滋養)

ZHANG QIANDE 張謙德 (1577–1643)
TRANSLATED BY HUI-LIN LI

Zhang Qiande, about whom little is known other than that his home was in Kunshan (near Suzhou), wrote *A Treatise of Vase Flowers* (or *Treatise on Flower Arranging*) in 1595; he followed it the next year with a treatise on goldfish.

"Preface"

Among the things of refined living, flower arrangement is the most difficult. Not one in a million can explain it. In former times, Jin Ren wrote a literary treatise when he was only a young boy. I am also in my boyhood writing these lines. Whether they are right or wrong, and to be followed or not, the understanding readers will make their fair criticism. It is not necessary for me to add more words here.

"Picking Branches"

To cut flowers, it is best to go to the nearest garden, and in the early morning before the dew disappears. Choose half-opened ones for arrangement, and their color and fragrance will not diminish for several days. Flowers cut later in the day, after the dew has dried, not only do not have sufficient fragrance and brightness in color, but will also wilt in only one or two days.

In picking flowers, it is necessary to select first the stem. The stem may be luxuriant above and slender below. It may be taller on the left and shorter on the right, or vice

---

87 Xie Valley lies in the Kunlun Mountains, far to the west of China. The Yellow Emperor obtained bamboo from this place to establish the Chinese musical scale. According to a parallel story, the Yellow Emperor based the scale on the phoenix's call, hence the equivalence of phoenix and bamboo as sources of harmonious sound.

88 At Gepo in Henan during the Eastern Han dynasty, Fei Changfang transformed his bamboo staff into a dragon. See *Han shu*, "Fang shu lie zhuan," 82.2743–44.

versa. It may have two branches crisscrossing each other, gnarled and crooked in shape. It may have a stout vigorous stalk in the center, sparse atop and fence-like below, covering the mouth of the vase. Whether ascending or hanging, tall or low, sparse or dense, and oblique or upright, the branches that have a natural beauty must show the appealing features of cut flowers as depicted by the painter. Straight branches and windblown flowers are not suitable for refined arrangement.

Both herbaceous and woody stems can be used for arranging in vases. There are two ways of cutting them: use fingers for herbaceous plants and scissors for woody ones. One who considers himself a lover of flowers should take note of this.

It is easy to select and cut woody stems for their best features, while it is most difficult to select and cut herbaceous ones. It is hard to achieve exquisiteness except by intensive study of masterpieces of flower painting.

"Caring"

Flowers live by the nourishment of rain and dew. To use rain water in a vase is to let the flowers have the benefit of rain and dew. Some flowers need honey in the water while others need boiling water. It is up to the connoisseurs of flowers to devise ways according to the material.

It is often necessary to store quantities of rain water to have on hand for use as the first choice for nourishing flowers. If this cannot be had, use clear and clean water from lakes and rivers. Do not use water from wells, as it is often salty and, if used, the flowers will not grow well.

When water is used for flowers in a vase, it gradually accumulates harmful matter. Change the water every day and the flowers will keep fresh for a longer period. If it is not changed for two or three days, the flowers will often fade and drop.

Vase flowers should be placed in a sheltered place outside the room at night for exposure to the dew. This will prolong the life of the flowers for several days.

"Connoisseurs of Flowers" (*Biehua ren* 別花人)

HU YINGLIN 胡應麟 (1551–1602)
TRANSLATED BY ALISON HARDIE

Hu Yinglin, who came from what is now Zhejiang Province in southeast China, was an important proponent of the "archaic" style of literature during the late Ming dynasty. He was a protégé of Wang Shizhen (see chapter 6), who was also a garden enthusiast. Hu Yinglin failed the highest degree of the civil service examinations at least eight times between 1577 and 1598, and thus never had an official career; instead, he concentrated on writing and literary criticism. His essay "Connoisseurs of Flowers" relates both to the late-Ming vogue for short personal essays (*xiaopin*) and to a genre that has been called "connoisseurship literature," which seems to have arisen from a sensitivity among the old elite about the basis of their claim to be the guardians of culture as well as from a fear of the social threat from the rise of a wealthy merchant class.[89] Hu's comments on the "vulgarity" of picking and otherwise mistreating flowers align his essay with this type of writing. The interesting thing is that the people he specifically accuses of vulgar behavior are Su Shi and Ouyang Xiu (see above), two highly distinguished cultural figures of the Song, who are contrasted with the late Tang poet Bai Juyi and his great friend Yuan Zhen (see chapter 2); this may reflect Hu's opinion on the superiority of Tang to Song literature. His spoof "notice" to visitors plays on the traditional poetic assimilation of flowers with beautiful women, to humorous effect.

"Connoisseurs of Flowers"

People who love flowers are rare enough, but people who are connoisseurs of flowers are even rarer—not that anyone who is a connoisseur is not a lover of flowers. Nowadays, it is not just the case that vulgar people fail to cultivate flowers at home; even enthusiasts who do cultivate them are ignorant of their names. To regard them as ordinary plants, to treat them as invasive shrubs, is something that really ruins a good atmosphere. So it was that the men of old said that it is rare to find a connoisseur of flowers. People often plant crepe-myrtle and banksia roses, but it was Bai Juyi who really loved them. So one of his poems says: "Apart from Yuan Zhen who would love them at first sight, few are the connoisseurs of flowers in this world." And also: "Transplanted here, they must take pride of place; none but a connoisseur should gaze upon their face." Thus, one may say that Grand Mentor Bai was the master connoisseur of flowers, while Yuan Zhen was merely an ordinary connoisseur.

However, there were also literati of former times who did things which could really ruin the atmosphere. For example, breaking off flowers is the worst sort of vulgar behavior, but even Su Shi and Ouyang Xiu were guilty of this crime: Su Shi, when holding a large gathering of guests at the Southern Chan Zifu Temple in Dongwu [in Shandong Province], cut over seven thousand peony flowers and arranged them in vases for the delectation of the Buddha. When Ouyang Xiu held a party in Yangzhou, he collected one thousand lotus flowers, placed them in decorated bowls set around the banqueting area, and told the guests to pass them around and each to remove one petal; whoever was left with the petal-less stalk then had to drink a cup of wine. What cruel people! What had become of their love of flowers?

---

89   Craig Clunas, *Superfluous Things: Material Culture and Social Status in Early Modern China* (Urbana: University of Illinois Press, 1991).

Once when my own flowers were in bloom, I wrote a large notice and hung it among the flowers, saying:

> A fine flower is like a beautiful woman: it should be enjoyed but not abused, adored but not maltreated. Whoever plucks a single petal tears a beautiful woman's clothes; whoever leaves one mark on a flower bruises the beauty's skin; whoever twists off a stem, breaks the beauty's arm; whoever sprays alcohol on the flowers, spits in a beauty's face; whoever brings incense near the flowers, blows smoke in the beauty's eyes; whoever approaches the flowers in a state of undress and unpleasant disarray is chasing stark naked after the beauty. If you have to go up close and peer at them, you must be blind; if you have to bend over and sniff at them, your nose must be blocked. The saying goes: "It is better to encounter a savage beast than a ruined atmosphere." If you will not listen to reason, you will never be invited again.

Alas! Although these were jesting words, they came from a true love and regard for the fragrance and beauty of flowers. All persons in agreement with my views are requested to comply with the above.

"Colophon to *A History of the Flower*" (*Huashi ba* 花史拔)

CHEN JIRU 陳繼儒 (1558–1639)

TRANSLATED BY DUNCAN M. CAMPBELL

The writer and calligrapher Chen Jiru, from Huating in Jiangsu Province, became the preeminent cultural figure of his age, despite never having advanced far in the civil service examinations or holding office. Well connected (his friends included the art critic Dong Qichang, the leading literary critic Wang Shizhen, and the senior official Wang Xijue), Chen lived on the products of his fluent and prolific pen.[90]

A History of the Flower was written by Chen Jiru's friend Wang Lu (Zhongzun) in 1618. To have a short essay by the distinguished Chen Jiru appended to it would undoubtedly have added to the book's appeal to readers, as Wang Lu himself was not particularly well known. Books such as *A History of the Flower* belong to the connoisseurship literature of the late Ming, which might either assert the good taste of the literati class or give cultural advice to wealthy merchants and others who aspired to upward social mobility.

"Colophon to *A History of the Flower*"

To be rustic but not to understand the pleasure to be derived therefrom, this is the lot of the woodcutter and the shepherd; to have fruit and melons in the hand but never to

---

90   The most detailed study of Chen Jiru available in English is Jamie Greenbaum, *Chen Jiru (1558–1639): The Background to, Development and Subsequent Uses of Literary Personae* (Leiden: Brill, 2007).

taste their delights, this is the lot of the nurseryman and the peddler; to possess both flowers and trees but to be incapable of enjoying them, this is the lot of the prominent official and the wealthy man. Of all the many worthies of ancient times, Tao Qian alone lodged his passions always in the mulberry, the hemp, the pines and the chrysanthemum, in the fields of the wilds and beside the wattle hedge. Su Shi too had a passion for planting and could himself graft both flowers and trees. Such predilections derive from one's innate nature and can never be affected. Were someone to affect such sensibilities, even if I presented him with a copy of *A History of the Flower*, he would in all probability cast it aside with an angry frown upon his face. If, on the other hand, I were to do so to a man whose innate nature drew him toward such things and who was moreover passionate about them, then he would doubtless invite me to join him as he reclined amid the woods, to observe the flowers as they bloomed and then faded away, for the trajectories of the lives of the flowers are surely no different from the ruts along which progress the rise and fall of states, the waxing and waning of kingdoms. It may well be true, then, when I claim that this *History of the Flower* contains all that is to be found within the twenty-one official dynastic histories.

A History of the Vase (*Ping shi* 瓶史)

YUAN HONGDAO 袁宏道 (1568–1610)

TRANSLATED BY DUNCAN M. CAMPBELL

Late-Ming literature might have been very different without the influence of Yuan Hongdao and his brothers Zongdao (1560–1600) and Zhongdao (1570–1624), who with their close literary associates formed the Gongan School (named for their birthplace in present-day Hunan Province). Influenced by the ideas of the philosopher Wang Yangming (1472–1529) and particularly by his radical follower Li Zhi (1527–1602), the Yuan brothers promoted writing based on personal experience and authentic emotion rather than on imitation of classical authors; nevertheless, reading the classics was an important part of their personal experience, and they never wished to reject classical influences entirely. Their interest in personal experience and the conditions of daily life contributed to the development of late-Ming connoisseurship literature and other forms of belles lettres dealing with relatively trivial subjects such as *A History of the Vase* (a treatise on flowers and flower arranging).[91]

A History of the Vase

Introduction
Having eschewed the pleasures of both song and sex, it is to the mountains and the rivers, to flowers and to bamboo that the mind of the recluse of grace and learning turns

---

91   For other translations from Yuan Hongdao's work, see Jonathan Chaves, trans., *Pilgrim of the Clouds* (New York: Weatherhill, 1978; rev. ed., Buffalo: White Pine Press, 2005); on his work in general, see Chih-p'ing Chou, *Yüan Hung-tao and the Kung-an School* (Cambridge: Cambridge University Press, 1988/2006).

in pursuit of its divertissements. Mountains and rivers, flowers and bamboo invoke no questions of fame or reputation and lie quite beyond the reach of our impatient scrambling for fortune. The ordinary man, stuck as he is along the precipices of hubbub and within the swamps of profit, his eyes blinded by worldly dust and sand, his heart sorely taxed by his various schemes and calculations, finds himself without the time to enjoy the pleasures afforded him by such things, even were he of a mind to do so. The recluse of grace and learning, by contrast, seeks to avail himself of every opportunity to take possession of that which happens to come his way, if only for the duration of a single day. Dwelling as he does in a place of non-contestation, the recluse of grace and learning is defined by the fact that he relinquishes all things to other men under Heaven; only the mountains and the rivers, flowers and bamboo, these, even were he prepared to relinquish them to others, others would not necessarily be willing to accept. So it is that he lives therein in peace, his possession of these things incurring no calamity.

Alas, this is the stuff of the recluse, the conduct of a hero of considerable resolve, whereas all my life, although I have desired to be such a man, I have proven quite incapable of becoming one. Fortunately, however, it has been my lot to have oscillated between spells in office and periods of reclusion and if I cannot hope to obtain that which everybody else hastens toward and competes over, I do nonetheless wish to doff my bamboo hat on the heights and to wash my cap strings in the Canglang waters. In this pursuit I have been fettered by the minor official postings that have come my way and the only pleasures afforded me have been the cultivation of flowers and the planting of bamboos. Even in this respect, my official residences have proven small and mean and moreover I have constantly been transferred hither and thither, so I have had no alternative but to have recourse to gallbladder-shaped vases and cut flowers, changing their arrangements in accordance with the alternation of the seasons. In this way, all the most famous blossoms in the possession of the men of the capital have, all of a sudden, become objects of display upon my table. Without having to endure the ordeal of grafting and weeding, watering and bending my back, I have luxuriated in the joy of smell and sight afforded me by flowers, never needing to covet the flowers I pick or compete for those that I happen to encounter. All this, I can write about, and yet such things are but the momentary pleasures afforded one's mind, and to which one should never become habituated at the cost of forgetting that great joy inspired within one by the mountains and the rivers themselves. I, Master Stone, have made the following record therefore, listing below both the nomenclature and the rankings of the vase, to be shared with all men who happen to be as afflicted by the same craze as myself but whose circumstances are similarly impecunious.

One: Nomenclature

So bitterly cold is the climate of Yanjing[92] that most of the famous flowers of the south cannot survive here; those few that do grow are inevitably in the possession either of powerful eunuchs or large estate holders. Having no reason even to lift the curtain of such personages, the poor Confucian scholar can but pick up that which is close at hand and easily obtainable. In this respect, selecting flowers is akin to choosing friends. Although I may well desire to befriend those extraordinary and untrammelled scholars of the mountains and the forests, they for their part lose themselves amid the deer and the wild boar, hiding themselves away within the thick grasses, and I have had no opportunity to encounter them. For this reason, then, those men who live in important districts and large cities who have been identified as being scholars of outstanding abilities and who have commonly been accepted as such are the ones that I wish to befriend, choosing those among them those who are close at hand and easily met with.

So too it is that from among the various flowers I select only those that are close at hand and easily obtainable: as the winter gives way to spring, it is the flowering apricot and the crabapple that I pick; in spring, it is the tree peony, the white peony and the pomegranate; by autumn, it is the cassia, the lotus and the chrysanthemum; and during winter, it is the wintersweet. Within my single chamber, the fragrance of a Xun Yu alternates with the powder of a He Yan,[93] as these flowers each take their turn as my guest. Although I pick only those flowers that are close at hand, in the end I do not dare to be excessive in my choice and if I find myself without any flowers at all, I prefer to make an arrangement with a shoot or two of bamboo or a couple of branches of cypress to serve in their stead. In the words of the song: "Even if you have no old men ripe in judgment, / At least you have your statutes and laws,"[94] and so how could I allow the vulgar men of the wells and the marketplaces to besmirch the ranks of the worthy, thus earning for myself the undying ridicule of some latter-day Huangfu Mi for merely pretending to the reputation of a recluse?[95]

Two: Hierarchy

Of the three thousand concubines once found within the palaces of the Han dynasty, it was Zhao Feiyan alone who claimed pride of place; although Xing and Yin were both similarly favored by the emperor's attentions, they could but stand by and gaze at her, tears streaming down their cheeks. This serves to highlight the fact that when faced

---

92 The area around Beijing in northern China.

93 It was said of Xun Yu (163–212) that wherever he happened to sit would remain fragrant for three days afterward; in the "Appearance and Behavior" chapter of *A New Account of Tales of the World*, we are told that He Yan (ca. 190–249) was never without a powder-puff in hand.

94 This is a couplet from Poem 255 of the *Book of Songs*.

95 Huangfu Mi (215–282) was the author of the *Biographies of the High-Minded* (*Gaoshi zhuan* 高士傳).

with sublime beauty, lesser beauty is forced to bow its head in acknowledgment; rare and beautiful things tend always to transcend their own categories.

What a crime it would be, then, to have a woman of surpassing beauty ride in the same carriage as a crowd of lesser concubines or to ask a good and virtuous man to yoke himself to one of ordinary talents! Of the flowering apricots, it is the Double-Petal, the Green Calyx, the Jade Butterfly, the Hundred-Petal and the Light Yellow that constitute the highest varieties; with the crabapple, it is the Western Palace and the Purple Brocade varieties that are the best; the Yellow-Stemmed, the Green Butterfly, the Watermelon Stalk, Big Red, and the Dancing Green Lion varieties of the tree peony are pre-eminent; the Crowning Fragrance, Yellow Emperor's Robe, and Precious Adornment white peonies that are the most superior varieties; it is the Deep Red Double-Flower variety of the pomegranate that is most desired; with the lotus, it is the Azure Flower Brocade-Border variety; with the cassia it is the Ball and the Early Yellow varieties; as to the chrysanthemum, it is the Variegated Crane Feather, the Xi Shi, and the Cut Floss varieties; and finally, with the wintersweet, it is the Fragrance of the Mouth of the Musical Stone variety.

All these flowers are famous and by rights the studio of the impecunious scholar can never hope to display them all. I have made mention only of the above varieties simply so as to deliver judgment upon their multifarious fragrances in order that the extraordinary among the flower kingdom do not find themselves surrounded by the ordinary beauties of the boudoir. And yet, a single word of praise proves more glorious even than donning the splendid robes of office, and so, serving today as I do as the Donghu of Stamen Palace, fixing for all time the *Spring and Autumn Annals* of the Forest of Flowers, how can I not write with utmost seriousness and in all possible trepidation? As Confucius himself has said: "This principle, I will myself henceforth adopt."[96]

Three: Vessels

The vases used to hold one's flowers need to be fine and delicate; after all, one would not have the concubines Yang Guifei and Zhao Feiyan wait upon one in the privy, or invite poets such as Xi Kang, Ruan Ji, He Zhizhang or Li Bo to join one for a drink in a tavern.

I remember once having seen an old beaker in the collection of a man of Jiangnan, the bluish-green glaze of which seemed so deep as to enter the very bones of the pot, its mottled sandstone underglaze gathered in clumps. It was a veritable Golden Chamber for flowers. Somewhat inferior to this beaker are the products of the Imperial, the Elder

---

96 In the *Zuo zhuan* (Duke Xuan, 2nd Year), Donghu of the state of Jin is praised by Confucius himself as being the paragon of the fearless historian; see *The Chinese Classics*, vol. 5, *The Ch'un Ts'ew, with the Tso Chuan*, ed. and trans. James Legge (Oxford: Clarendon Press, 1893–1895), 290–91.

Brother, the Elephant and the Dingzhou kilns, all of which, with the delicate splendor of their sheen, constitute the meditation cells of the Flower Spirit.

In general terms, it is appropriate for the vases placed in one's studio to be small and squat, and both the copperware (whether of the flower beaker, copper goblet, ritual jar, rectangular-mouthed Han ewer, plain warming vessel, or flat ewer shape) and the porcelain vessels (of the paper-mallet, goose neck, herb sack, lower jar, lower purse, milfoil stalk, or reed-mallet shape) should all be diminutive in size of manufacture before they are fit playthings for the man of elegance. If not, how would they differ from the vessels used during ancestral rites in one's Clan Hall? Even were they to be ancient, they would nonetheless seem vulgar. Furthermore, although flowers vary in terms of their natural sizes, even the tree peony, the white peony, and the lotus, all of which are large of form, should not be exempted from this rule.

I have heard that flowers placed in copper vessels long buried underground and thus saturated by the breath of the soil, remain as brilliant of hue as they were while still on their branches, and if still in bud, they bloom quickly and prove slow to fade. If a vase is sturdy enough, then the same is true of pottery. This makes one aware of the fact that precious antique vases are not mere baubles. Impecunious and unimportant scholars, however, have not the wherewithal to possess such things, and even to get hold of a porcelain vase or two from such kilns as those of the Xuande [1426–1435] and Chenghua [1465–1487] reign periods makes one feel like a beggar who has suddenly come into a fortune. With winter flowers it is appropriate to use pewter flutes for, in the harsh cold of the north, even copperware is susceptible to cracking when it freezes over, this being true not just of porcelain. One can also throw a pinch or two of sulfur into the water.

Four: Water
Water from the Azure Cloud Temple of the Western Hills near the capital, from Torn Silk Lake or from Dragon King Hall may all be used, whereas water taken from beyond High Ridge Bridge is of a most inferior grade. All water used in vases should have weathered the effects of wind and sun. However sweet the taste of water from places such as Mulberry Garden, Full Well, Sandy Hole or Mother Wang's Well, flowers do not flourish when standing in it. On the other hand, bitter water is most especially tabooed for its taste proves brackish in the extreme and it is inferior even to water that has been used to preserve plums. The method for storing water is as follows: as it is being poured into the vats for the first time, throw in a burning lump of coal. If this is done, the water will last for years without going off; quite apart from being perfect for preserving flowers, such water may even be used for brewing tea.

Five: Consonances

When arranged in a vase, cut flowers should neither be too many nor too few. At most, only two or three varieties should be used, most exquisitely arranged only when their relative heights and densities are disposed in a painterly fashion. It is a taboo to place vases in pairs, to arrange them in a uniform manner or in rows, and it is also a taboo to bind the stems of the flowers with rope. What may be termed orderly in the case of flowers is in fact a matter of irregularity and asymmetry, of a naturalness of manner, somewhat akin to the willfully disjunctive flow of the prose of Su Shi of the Song dynasty, or the poems of the Tang poet Li Bai in their resistance to the rules of prosody. This constitutes true orderliness! If the leaves and stems are merely arranged symmetrically and the reds and whites simply balanced, the arrangement will resemble nothing so much as the trees that grow within the courtyards of provincial-level officials or the ornamental pillars that stand at the gateway of a tomb. How could this possibly constitute orderliness!

Six: Taste

The room should contain nothing more than a single unadorned table and a simple rattan bed. The table should be thick and wide, finely worked and glossy of finish. Tables with lacquered borders, golden-painted beds with mother-of-pearl inlays or vase stands decorated with flowers, all of which are much in evidence here in the capital, should be stored away out of sight.

Seven: Malignities

It is not appropriate to burn incense beside a vase of flowers for the same reason that it is inappropriate to add fruit to one's tea; if tea can be said to embody its own authentic flavor, not captured by the words "sweet" or "bitter," so too do flowers have their own authentic fragrances, not to be replicated by the smoke and flames of incense. It is the solecism of the philistine to act in a manner that detracts from that flavor as much as it is to destroy that fragrance. Cut flowers, when assailed by the poison of burning incense, immediately wither and dry up; incense is their keenest adversary. Both stick and blended incense are especially to be avoided for both contain secretions of the musk deer. Long ago, Han Xizai maintained that with cassia flowers it was appropriate to burn "Dragon's Brain" camphor, aloes-wood with the rose-leaf raspberry, "Four Perfections" incense with orchids, musk with the magnolia, and sandalwood with the gardenia. But this is no different from adding meat to a dish of bamboo shoots, the very sort of thing much in evidence in the kitchens of officials or to be had from street stalls, and not at all to the taste of the man of refinement! As to candle soot and coal smoke, these too serve to damage flowers, and should never be allowed to do so. To call all such things the taboos of the flowers is perhaps appropriate.

Eight: Bathing

The capital is prone to the occasional dust storm and when the wind begins to howl one quickly finds that an inch of dust has settled upon one's cleanest windowsills and most spotless side-tables. To the sovereign of the vase, such a circumstance proves most vexatious and constitutes the greatest possible disgrace. One's flowers, therefore, require a daily bathing. After all, even Nanwei and Qingqin, those two beauties of old, would not have earned their fame had they not made their toilet everyday with bandoline and powder, with brush and oil. Were I today to allow my few leaves and fading blooms to stand with their faces besmirched and their skins covered in filth, never undertaking the labor of their toilet and allowing the dust to cause them to wither and die, what then would I have left to view?

Just as flowers experience their own gamut of emotions, from that of happiness to that of anger, so too do they have their periods of wakefulness and of sleep, their own "dawns" and their own "dusks," and if the efforts of the flower-bathers are to serve as life-giving rain, they need to accord with the flowers' own schedules. Days on which a wan sun shows through the light clouds, or a fine moon rises at sunset, constitute the flowers' "dawn"; when the wind howls and the rain seems endless, or when flowers find themselves standing under a scorching sun or out in the bitter cold, such times constitute the flowers' "dusk." When their pale red lips bask in sunlight and their seductive bodies find protection from the buffeting wind, this is their happiness; when they seem drunk and confused or withdrawn of spirit, when their hues appear indistinct, this is their sorrow. When their stems droop to rest upon the balustrades, as if unable any longer to resist the breeze, this is when they are dreaming; when their captivating eyes glance around with distain and their radiance dazzles one's eyes, this is their time of wakefulness.

At "dawn," they should stand in an empty courtyard or within a large hall; at "dusk," within a tiny room or secluded chamber; during their times of sorrow, they should sit with bated breath and on the edge of their chairs, when happy, amid laughter and jollity, when in their dreams the blinds should be lowered and the curtains drawn, when waking, their toilet should be attended to. Only in this way can their true natures be given pleasure and their spells of activity and repose be properly regulated. It is best to bathe them during their "dawns," next best to do so during their sleep, and lastly, to do so when they are happy. To bathe them during their "dusks" or when they are sorrowful is to do little more than to mete out punishment upon them and is not something that I would ever do.

The method of bathing flowers is to sprinkle them lightly with the purest water which has been drawn from the sweetest spring, like a shower of gentle rain arousing somebody from his drunken stupor, like the pure dew that insinuates itself beneath one's skin. One's hands must never touch the flowers directly, nor should one ever use one's fingernails to pluck them. Their care should never be entrusted to an ordinary bondservant or a slovenly maid. The flowering plum is most appropriately bathed by a recluse, the crabapple by a guest of grace and refinement, both the white and the tree peonies by a glamorously adorned young girl, the pomegranate by a lascivious bond-maid, the cassia by a precocious son, the lotus by a seductive concubine, the chrysan-themum by an extraordinary man besotted with the ancients, and the wintersweet by an emaciated monk. Winter flowers, however, are by nature averse to bathing; they for their part should be protected from the elements by thin silk gauze. If these precepts are abided by, both the spirit and the color of the flower will manifest itself of its own accord and their lives will be prolonged. How then could I arrogate to myself this beneficence?

Nine: Subordinates

Flowers have their subordinates, just as those within the palace have their imperial concubines and ladies within their boudoirs have concubines and serving maids. Many are the beautiful and bewitching flowers and plants of the mountains, flirting and dallying; how could one ever be short of favorites?

The flowering apricot takes the yellow winter jasmine, the winter daphne, and the camellia as its bondmaids. For the crabapple, it is the phoenix-eye, the red crabapple, and the lilac; for the tree peony, it is the rugosa, the rambler, and the banksia rose; for the white peony, it is the opium poppy and the hollyhock; for the pomegranate, it is the crepe-myrtle, the big red tree peony, the thousand-petal pomegranate and the common hibiscus; for the lotus, it is the mountain alum and the hosta; for the cassia, it is the hibiscus; for the chrysanthemum, it is the yellow and the white camellia and the begonia; for the wintersweet, it is the narcissus. Each bondmaid has her own inimita-ble bearing and each reigns supreme throughout her own respective season.

With their contrast between the gaudy and the understated, the elegant and the vulgar, each of these bondmaids is ranked according to her own merits. Both the demeanor and the personality of the narcissus, for example, tend toward the ethereal, like Liang Yuqing, the maid who served the Weaver Girl. The camellia, by contrast, is nubile and beautiful, the winter daphne exceedingly perfumed, the rugosa rose graceful, the hibiscus bright and gaudy, like Shi Chong's bondmaid Xuanfeng or Jingwan of the Yang family. Both the red crabapple and the apple are seductive and approachable of disposi-tion, like Xiechou, Scholar Pan's concubine. The opium poppy and the hollyhock stand handsome beside the wattle fence, like Sikong Tu's favorite Luantai. The mountain alum is chaste and retiring with the air of a recluse, like Yu Xuanji's Luqiao. The grace of the yellow and the white camellias is superior even to their beauty, like Guo Guanjun's Chunfeng. The lilac is thin, the hosta aloof, the begonia charming but with a hint of pedantry about her, like the serving girls of Zheng Kangcheng and the Flourishing Talent Cui. I am unable to come up with appropriate analogies for each and every one of the others but the important thing to keep in mind is that they are all famous.

Soft and pliant, slender and artful, suffused with the air of jollity, how could they possibly prove inferior to the pomegranate of Su Shi or the spring grasses of Bai Juyi?

Ten: Connoisseurship

Xi Kang was partial to metalwork, Wang Ji to horses, Lu Yu to tea, Mi Fu to rocks and Ni Zan to cleanliness, and all these men invested these things with their own sense of grievance and their own unparalleled individuality. In my observation, in this world of ours, all those men whose conversation proves most unpleasant to the ear and whose appearance is most hateful to the eye are precisely those who are without obsessions. When one is truly obsessed with something, one drowns oneself in it and becomes completely besotted by it, pursuing it as if one's very life depended upon it. What time do such men have to spare for thoughts of money or of servants, of office or of trade?

As soon as one of the ancients afflicted by the obsession for flowers heard in conversation mention of a rare flower, he would seek to track it down in the deepest valleys and along the highest ridges, not shrinking from doing injury to his legs, heedless of either bitter cold or scorching sun, unconscious of the chafing to his hands or encrusted mud and dripping sweat. When a particular flower was about to burst from bud, he would have his pillow and his mattress moved and sleep beside it so that he could observe the flower as it grew from tiny to fully-blooming, observe it as it wilted and then dropped forgotten upon the ground, only then quitting its side. He would either gather around him a thousand plants and ten thousand varieties in order that he might gain an exhaustive understanding of the entire process of their transformation or he would restrict himself to a single branch and a couple of rooms so that he could experience to the fullest that particular flower's delight. A single sniff of a leaf was enough to tell him whether that plant's flower would be large or small; with a quick glance at the roots he would know if the flower was to be red or white. This may be called the true love of flowers, and this I call a true craze.

My own cultivation of flowers, by contrast, is merely a way for me to overcome the tedium and loneliness of my idle days, not at all what may be termed a true craze. Were I truly to be crazed by the flowers, I would already have become a man of the cave entrance to Peach Blossom Source, not a man still mired in the dust of the officialdom of this world of ours!

Eleven: Appreciation

Flowers are best appreciated with a cup of tea in hand, second best amid conversation, worst of all while drinking wine. As to wine from the Palace Winery and Zhejiangese tea, along with all kinds of lewd or vulgar conversation, these are the very things that the Flower Spirits most detest and revile. For my part I would far prefer then to sit like a rotten stump with my mouth tightly shut rather than incur the ire of the flowers. The appreciation of flowers is, I believe, a matter of both proper time and rightful place, and when the time is not right, it is boorish in the extreme to entertain guests casually.

The appropriate circumstances for the appreciation of winter flowers are after the first fall of snow, during a break in the snow, under a new moon, within a warm room. The appropriate circumstances for the appreciation of spring flowers are clear days, days that retain a slight nip in the air, within a lavish hall. Summer flowers are most appropriately appreciated after a shower of rain, in a bracing breeze, within the shade of a fine tree, beneath the bamboo, while standing in a riverside belvedere. For autumnal flowers, it is under a chill moon, at sunset, upon an empty flight of steps, along a mossy pathway, besides jagged rocks entwined by ancient vines that provide the most appropriate circumstances for their appreciation. To pay no heed to wind or sun, not to choose a fine spot, to seek to appreciate flowers when one's mind is wandering and not at all on the matter at hand, this is surely little different from viewing flowers in a brothel or in a tavern.

Twelve: Taboos
The Song dynasty scholar Zhang Zi's *Flowering Apricot Classifications from the Hall of Jade Radiance* is an exquisitely written work that I have long admired. Modeling myself on his example, therefore, I have come up with the following maxims, to be displayed within my Studio of the Vase.[97]

There are fourteen things that bring pleasure to the flowers: clear windows, spotless side tables, ancient tripods, Song dynasty inkstones, the soughing of the wind in the pines, the burbling of a brook, a host both susceptible to enthusiasms and with poetic sensibilities, a visiting monk conversant in the art of brewing tea, a gift of wine presented by a visitor from Jizhou, houseguests skilled in painting flowers, the arrival of a particularly rich and light-hearted friend, transcribing books on the cultivation of flowers, a brazier singing away in dead of night, and wives and concubines busy editing anecdotes about the flowers.

There are twenty-three things that serve to defile flowers: a host always too busy receiving guests, a philistine who makes an unannounced appearance, twisted branches, an uncouth monk discoursing about Chan, dogs fighting beneath the window, the singing boys of Lotus Seed Lane, the raucous tunes of Yiyang, an ugly woman wearing a cut flower in her hair, discussions about promotion and transfer, false declarations of love, owing somebody an as yet unwritten but socially obligated

---

97   In the preface to *Flowering Apricot Classifications from the Hall of Jade Radiance* (*Yuzhaotang meipin* 玉照堂梅品*), Zhang Zi 張鎡 (1153–after 1211) tells how he put on display in his hall his fifty-eight rules for the appreciation of the flowering apricot "as warning to all comers, for although the men of this age all know of the excellence of the flowering apricot, they are incapable of loving and respecting them."

poem, a rich man drumming one for the repayment of one's debts, having recourse to rhyming dictionaries when composing poetry, disorderly piles of tattered books, Fujianese brokers, forged Suzhou paintings, mouse droppings, the slime trails left behind by snails, haughty servants, the wine running out as soon as the drinking games have begun, living next door to a tavern, a desk piled high with poems full of expressions such as "yellowest gold" and "whitest snow" and "the auspicious clouds hanging above the Central Plains."

The philistines of the capital are especially prone to vying with each other to frolic in this manner and, whenever the flowers begin to bloom, they unfurl their crimson screens.[98] As I see it, many are those who defile the flowers, few there are who truly enjoy them. And if one is honest about the matter, one realizes that even among one's own set there are some who occasionally infringe these principles. It is for this reason that I have compiled this set of protocols, to serve as a constant reminder, to myself as much as to anyone else.

Taoan's Dream Memories (*Taoan mengyi* 陶庵夢憶)

"Flowering Apricot Bookroom" (*Meihua shuwu* 梅花書屋), "Without Doubleness Studio" (*Buer zhai* 不二齋), "Belvedere of the Mountaintop Flower" (*Yanhua ge* 巘花閣), "The Sweet Tangerines of the Chen Clan of Fanjiang" (*Fanjiang Chen shi ju* 樊江陳氏橘), and "Jin Rusheng's Flowers and Trees" (*Jin Rusheng caohua* 金乳生草花)

ZHANG DAI 張岱 (1597–?1684)
TRANSLATED BY DUNCAN M. CAMPBELL

For Zhang Dai, see above in the "Rocks" section of this chapter.

"Flowering Apricot Bookroom"

When the old buildings behind Calyx Ledge Tower fell into ruin, I had a four-*chi*-deep foundation rammed, and upon this I constructed a large one-roomed study. Off to the side of the study I extended an alcove that resembled a gauze screen, and there I placed my couch. The study was surrounded by open space and having built a platform along the base of the back wall, I proceeded to plant three large tree peonies in a bed of watermelon mulch. Soon the flowers grew higher than the wall and, within the space of a year, they had produced more than three hundred blooms. Two Western Palace crab-apple trees stood in front of the platform, and when in blossom they resembled a deep fall of fragrant snow. The four front walls were high, and opposite these I established a stone terrace upon which I placed a peak or two of Great Lake Rock. The gnarled trunk of the West Brook flowering apricot and one or two Yunnanese camellia trees stood

---

98 One of Zhang Zi's fourteen "Abominations" is "unfurling crimson screens in front of the flowers."

seductively beside the rocks. Beneath the flowering apricot, I planted a blue crown passion-flower and soon it had entwined itself around the trunks like tassels. The bamboo shed visible beyond my window was covered in rambling rose. Below the steps, kingfisher grass grew dense, in the midst of which, here and there, were dispersed a crabapple tree or two. Beyond the clear front and back windows, the rambling rose and the crabapple trees gradually began to cast their shadow. Here I would sit or lie, not allowing any but the most refined and honored of guests to join me. Out of admiration for Ni Zan the Eccentric's "Belvedere of Pure Intimacy," I named my study "Cloud Forest's Secret Belvedere."[99]

"Without Doubleness Studio"[100]

The tall paulownia trees of Without Doubleness Studio stretched three *zhang* into the sky, casting about them a tapestry of blue-green shade. To the west of the garden wall, where the ground opened out slightly, the shade was supplemented by that of the wintersweet, but it was nonetheless only on overcast days that the sun's rays did not penetrate here. The wall outside the back window was higher than the window-sill, and there several square bamboos soughed away in the breeze, calling to mind a horizontal scroll by the Yuan dynasty Master Sheng Mou [1310–1360] entitled: "The sounds of autumn ring in one's ears." The down-cast shafts of sunlight, when seen dancing within the gaps in the shade, glistened like glass or mica, and sitting there made one feel oneself transported to the Land of Purity. Books lined all four walls, overflowing the shelves and scattered upon the couches; tripods, vases, goblets, and jars were everywhere to hand. To the left I placed a stone couch and a bamboo side-table, screening the area off with a gauze curtain to keep the mosquitoes and the flies away. As the dark shade began to penetrate the gauze it would turn my face a brilliant jade-green.

During the long days of summer, the scent of the Fujianese orchids, the jasmine, and the fragrant grasses would insinuate itself within the folds of my gown. Around the time of the Double Ninth Festival, the chrysanthemums would be shifted to stand beneath the north window, the pots arranged in five rows of differing heights. So brilliant was the hue of the flowers in the crystal-clear rays of the sun that it was as if they had been immersed in an autumnal river. In winter, the paulownia trees lost their leaves and the wintersweet would burst into flower, a warm sun would bathe the windows and the warmth of the fire-red brazier would be supplemented by that provided by felt rugs; narcissi had been planted amid the white Mount Kun pebbles and arrayed at the foot of the steps. In spring, mountain orchids would cover the base

---

99 This is a reference to the painter Ni Zan (1301–1374), one of the "Four Great Masters" of the Yuan dynasty, whose studio name was "Cloud Forest" (Yunlin).

100 The phrase translated as "Without Doubleness" combines suggestions of "peerless" and "without distractions."

of the surrounding walls, and beyond the sill a half *mu* of white peonies would burst into blossom, many of them specimens of unusual varieties. There it was that I would doff my gown and stretch out my legs, never going out my door except on most pressing business as the seasons turned from hot to cold. Thinking back upon it now, it was as if the studio belonged to a different world.

"Belvedere of the Mountaintop Flower"

The Belvedere of the Mountaintop Flower[101] stood within the Pine Gully and below Mushroom Skin Pavilion, set among layered cliffs and ancient trees, poking up above the tips of the forest and surrounded, in autumn, by red leaves. In the eddy that formed as the gully stream forked beneath the slope, the rock foundation of the mountain was sharp and angular, as if set in opposition to the water. The belvedere was given neither door-sills nor lattice windows, nor was a tower or platform built there, the intention being to signal the fact that the conception of the belvedere was as yet not fully realized.

My great-uncle Zhang Wuxue returned from Guangling with a bellyful of ideas for gardens and pavilions and sought to try them out here by building terraces, pavilions, and galleries, by erecting a plank bridge, by having a tower placed directly opposite, by siting beside it halls and belvederes, by entwining the hill with an undulating line of flowering apricot trees. And yet, his efforts in this respect appeared altogether too stiff and solid and crowded, giving only a constricted expression of his original conception, like an ink slab placed within a stone grotto. Standing upon the other side of the river and gazing over at the hill, at the belvedere, at the rock foundation and at the pines that stood in Pine Gully, perversely, the "true face of Mount Lu" could only be obtained from beyond the hill itself.

My uncle requested that I supply him with a couplet. To capture the small details of the place, I came up with the following lines:

> Hidden within the folds of Mi Fu's Sleeve,
> At home in a fan painting of Wang Wei's Wangchuan estate.

---

101 In the "Gardens Within the Town Walls" section of his "Record of the Gardens and Pavilions of Shanyin," Zhang Dai's friend Qi Biaojia (1603–1645) provided the following note on this garden: "This garden is found behind Master Zhang Wuxue's mansion, that is, on the southern foothills of Dragon Hill. Here stone cliffs stand sheer, below which water has been gathered to form a small pond. Flying plank and zigzag bridges provide circuitous passage across the pond, and pavilions and terraces have been built, all appearing like a bouquet of flowers on layered embroidery. I think that even in its own day, Golden Valley could not have stood comparison with this garden."

"The Sweet Tangerines of the Chen Clan of Fanjiang"

The Chen clan of Fanjiang had established an orchard on a patch of land they had cleared, enclosing it with a fence of hardy orange tree. The staple grown here is the betel vine, the leaves of which are made into paste; the glutinous rice is used to ferment wine. This wine, fragrant in the extreme and a dull amber color, has won the praises of all serious drinkers. The fruit and the melons produced by the orchard are steeped in honey to make comfit. More than a hundred of Xie's tangerine trees have been planted here, the fruit of which is not picked when still green or when still sour. Only once the fruit has turned orange on the trees after the first falls of frost are they picked, and even then this is done by cutting them off the trees with their stems still attached. When such a procedure is followed, the skins of the tangerines prove thick and easy to peel, their color is deep orange, their flesh firm, their segments easily divided, their taste sweet and fresh. The tangerines produced at Fourth Gate, Tao's Embankment, Daoxu, even Tangxi, cannot stand comparison with them.

Each year I would insist on visiting this orchard, even if it was late in the season and the tangerines were expensive and few to be had. Once I had made my purchase, I would store the tangerines in earthenware vats upon a mat of rice straw from Champa or dried pine needles. Every ten days or so, whenever the straw had begun to molder, I would have it replaced, and in this way the tangerines could be made to last until toward the end of the third month, as sweet and crisp as when first picked. The Master of Hardy Orange Township earns himself a hundred bolts of silk a year from his hundred or so tangerine trees, these trees truly living up to their sobriquet "Wooden Slaves."

"Jin Rusheng's Flowers and Trees"

Jin Rusheng loves gardening.[102] A patch of fallow ground lay in front of his residence, bordered by a stream. On the banks of this stream, Rusheng constructed a small three-bay studio, extending its foundation to the north in a rectangular rather than a square shape, and erecting a bamboo fence encircling the land to the left of the structure. To the north, his garden abutted the street, and here he put up a wall of pounded earth, within which he raised a parterre to protect the foundations of the wall. In front of this again, he raised a stone parterre, more than a *zhang* long and elongated. In front of this parterre he piled up some Snail Mountain rocks to create a fold or two of artificial mountain, most painterly in its appearance.

---

102 Qi Biaojia's "Record of the Gardens and Pavilions of Shanyin" contains a short note on Jin Rusheng's garden: "Also a Garden (*Yeshi yuan* 也是園): The garden is found beside Dragon Gate Bridge, and its Master is Jin Rusheng. Here he raises several hundred flower specimens, most of them from unusual places and of the rarest variety, such that even experienced gardeners cannot identify them. As bright as brocade, the flowers bloom away throughout all four seasons of the year. Although the Master himself lives in the smallest of dipper-sized houses, the shoes of those who come to view his flowers are always piled high outside his door."

The hundreds of specimens he grows here are planted interspersed with each other, the bright beside the dull, the dense beside the spare, all in exquisite fashion. In spring, opium and Beauty of Yu poppies reign supreme over the garden, accompanied by mountain orchids, white jasmine and sicklepod. As spring draws toward its close, these are replaced by the white peonies, accompanied in their turn by the blue crown passion-flower, the local day-lily, the purple orchid and the mountain alum. In summer, it is the Sweet William and the Fujianese orchid that dominate, accompanied by the hollyhock, the Tibetan chrysanthemum, the coffee senna, the Arabian jasmine, the wild ginger and the pearl orchid. By autumn, these have been replaced by the chrysanthemum, as queen of the garden, accompanied by the pinks, the yellow mallow, the monkshood, the longevity lotus, the amaranth, the begonia, the tricolored amaranth and the dwarf cockscomb. Winter is the season of the narcissi, accompanied by the pot marigolds. As to trees and shrubs, such as the purple and the white lilacs, the green calyx and Jade Butterfly flowering apricots, the winter plum and Western Palace crabapple, the Yunnanese camellia, the sun cinnabar and the white pear, these have been planted at the end of the wall and in the corners of the studio, affording protection from the scorching sun.

Rusheng is a frail man much prone to ill health, and yet dawn each day, before he has washed his face or combed his hair, finds him kneeling upon a rush mat out along the steps, trapping beetles and rooting out cutworms; once each day he examines, one by one, the thousand or more plants he grows, from the tips of their flowers to the base of their stems, even the underside of every leaf. It is the fire ants that damage the flowers, the black centipedes that wither the stems, the earthworms and the millipedes that injure the roots, while it is the weevils and the hairy caterpillars that attack the leaves. To deal with the fire ants, Jin Rusheng places dried salt fish bones or turtle shells among the plants, eradicating them once they have been enticed out of their burrows. Wrapping hessian sacking over the head of his hoe, he scrapes off all the centipedes. In dead of night, with lantern in hand, he kills the millipedes. He rids the garden of earthworms by irrigating the parterres with a limestone and river water mixture, while he poisons the hairy caterpillars with nightsoil. He searches the weevil burrows with a ground iron wire. All this he insists on doing himself, heedless of the chilblains on his hands or the sunburn on his forehead. Delighted by his efforts, the Green Emperor has recently produced for him three auspicious fungi as a token of his favor.

"Letter to Jin Rusheng" (*Yu Jin Rusheng* 與金乳生)

ZHANG DAI 張岱 (1597–CA. 1684)

TRANSLATED BY DUNCAN M. CAMPBELL

I came calling upon you, my dear friend, unannounced, only to find that you had gone off elsewhere. What a very grave disappointment!

In previous years I have been fortunate enough to be rewarded with plants from your garden and although I have no right to expect such favor again, I do however beg for a pink and a yellow amaranth, one or other variety of Joseph's Coat, or a specimen or two of pot marigold in full bloom, so that I may bring a patch of autumnal color to the stepped gallery of my garden, with mingled red and resplendent gold. Such would exceed my fondest wishes, and I tremble in anticipation as I brush this note.

I, Zhang Dai, bow my head to you, my respected friend and fellow society member, Grand Scribe Jin Rusheng. If you do indeed happen to have spare some rare specimen or other, then surely there would be no harm in your sending one or two my way, for which I would be, naturally, eternally grateful.

"To the Tune '*Qiu rui xiang*: Admiring Cassias in the North Garden'" (*Qiu rui xiang: Beiyuan kan gui* 秋蕊香:北園看桂)

YE HONGXIANG 葉宏緗 (CA. 1636–1725)
TRANSLATED BY KANG-I SUN CHANG AND CHARLES KWONG

From Kunshan near Suzhou, Ye Hongxiang gained a reputation for moral as well as poetic excellence; widowed in her twenties, she followed the Confucian ethos of widow chastity, never remarrying though she lived into her eighties. Despite her personal virtue, her work was clearly influenced by the courtesan poet Liu Rushi (Liu Shi; see chapter 9).

"To the Tune '*Qiu rui xiang*: Admiring Cassias in the North Garden'"

Terrace trees, pavilion, pond, deep mansion;
Plums and bamboos, willows, paulownias—all verdant and fresh.
Autumn wind and sparkling dew work so many changes
That the world is now a Palace of Great Chill.[103]

Need there be heavenly fragrance sent down by the moon?
Leaning on the railing, I observe clumps of trees.
As sounds from the lute float in the silvery sky,
The autumn hills have half yellowed.

---

103   Editor's note: the Palace of Great Chill is in the moon.

Six Records of a Floating Life (*Fusheng liuji* 浮生六記)

"The Pleasures of Leisure" (*Xianqing jiqu* 閒情記趣; extract)

SHEN FU 沈復 (1763–CA. 1810)

TRANSLATED BY LEONARD PRATT AND CHIANG SU-HUI

Little more is known about the author of this remarkable autobiography than he cares to tell us in the pages of *Six Records of a Floating Life*, probably completed sometime around 1810 but first published only in 1877, by which time the final two records had been lost. Although Shen Fu failed at almost everything to which he turned his hand in life, his beautifully written autobiography has brought posthumous fame to him and his beloved wife Chen Yun. Shen Fu's family originated in Suzhou, but he spent much of his life "floating" around China. He had no success in the civil service examination system, became estranged from his family, and was a hopeless businessman; the most successful job he had was as a private secretary to a more prosperous friend. His autobiography is not arranged chronologically, but is divided into six sections (of which only four survive) dealing with his views on and experiences of different aspects of life; the surviving sections cover marriage, leisure pursuits, misfortune (of which Shen had ample experience), and travel. His account of his and Yun's leisure pursuits is particularly revealing on the importance of flowers and gardens to cultured Chinese people of this time.

"The Pleasures of Leisure" (extract)

When I was a little older I became obsessed with a love of flowers, and found much delight in pruning miniature potted trees to make them look like real ones. It was not until I met Zhang Lanbo, however, that I began to really learn how to prune branches and care for sprouts, and later to understand grafting and the creation of miniature rock formations in the pots. My favorite flower was the orchid, because of its elegant fragrance and charming appearance, though it is difficult to obtain ones that can be considered truly classic.

Shortly before Lanbo died he presented me with a pot of orchids that looked like lotus flowers. The centers were white and broad, and the edges of the petals were straight. They had thin stems, and the petals themselves were quite pale. This was a classic flower, and I treasured mine like a piece of old jade. When I was away from home Yun would water it herself, and its flowers and leaves grew luxuriantly. After I had had it for almost two years, however, it suddenly dried up and died. I dug it up and found the roots in good condition, white as jade with many new shoots. At first I could not understand it, and could only sigh at the thought that I was simply not lucky enough to raise so fine a flower. Only later did I learn that someone who had asked for a cutting and been refused had poured boiling water over it and killed it. I swore that from that time on I would never grow orchids again.

My next favorite flower was the azalea. Although it has no fragrance to speak of, its colors are long-lasting and it is easy to prune. But because Yun loved their branches and leaves, she could not stand seeing me prune them too much, so it was difficult to raise them properly. It was the same with all my other plants.

Every year chrysanthemums would grow east of the fence, blooming in the autumn. I preferred to pick them and put them in vases, rather than raise them in pots. It was not that I did not enjoy looking at them in pots, but because our house had no garden I could not grow them in pots myself, and had I bought them in the market and transplanted them, they would have looked all jumbled and wrong. I did not want that.

"Peonies" (*Mudan* 牡丹)

JIN YI 金逸 (1770–1794)
TRANSLATED BY ANTHONY C. YU

Jin Yi, from Suzhou, was a student of the celebrated writer Yuan Mei (1716–1797; see chapter 8), who included a large number of her poems in his anthology of work by his female students, and also composed her grave inscription. Her work is clearly influenced by her teacher. Jin Yi's poems show that she and her husband enjoyed composing poetry together.

"Peonies"

I see and care greatly for you
Who come twice in fresh fair weather,
Outdoing all other beauties—
The hundred gems of the tower.
Rain-soaked you vie with spring for glamour;
Wind-whipped you make piles of brocade.
Pity how those butterflies tire
From circling you a thousand times.

"To the Tune '*Jiang cheng zi*: Fallen Flowers'" (*Jiang chengzi: Luo hua* 江城子：落花)

GU TAIQING 顧太清 (1799–CA. 1876)
TRANSLATED BY IRVING YUCHENG LO

Gu Taiqing, a Manchu, was distantly related to the Qing imperial family, but raised by bond-servants, whose Chinese surname she adopted. She became the concubine of Prince Yihui (1799–1838), with whom she shared an interest in poetry. She bore him seven children, but on his early death she was forced to leave the household and to raise the children on her own. Despite the difficulties of her life, she was a very prolific poet, and a thousand of her poems survive.

"To the Tune 'Jiang cheng zi: Fallen Flowers'"

Flowers bloom, flowers fall, all in the same year.
I pity the faded reds
And blame the east wind,
They vex me so, these fallen petals aplenty;
Like snow flurries pelting at the curtained window.
To sit watching whirling blossoms—flower-gazing time is past.
Spring again is gone—
Far too hastily!
With whom can I share my grief in pitying the flowers?
Too lazy for my morning make-up,
So overpowering is my sorrow.
When the swallows return,
A crimson shower falling east of my painted chamber.
Lying everywhere, the spring grief cannot be pecked away;
So utterly thoughtless
Are the wandering honeybees.

"Plum Blossoms" (*Mei shizhang* 梅十章; nos. 3 and 10)

QIU JIN 秋瑾 (1875–1907)
TRANSLATED BY LI-LI CH'EN

Qiu Jin is famous as a feminist and revolutionary martyr: she was executed in her native Shaoxing in 1907 for her opposition to the Qing dynasty. She had a happy and active childhood, studying martial arts and horseback riding as well as literature. The breakdown of an unhappy marriage led her to move in 1904 to Japan, which was seen by Chinese progressives at the time as a model for how an Asian country might modernize itself. There she studied, wrote, edited a journal, and joined revolutionary societies agitating for the overthrow of the Qing. After returning to China in 1905, she supported herself as a teacher while continuing to work for the revolution. It is probable that, as she hoped, her martyrdom inspired others to bring the cause to fruition. In these two short poems (from a group of ten), the plum blossom that defies the cold clearly represents the poet's feelings of isolation and moral strength.

"Plum Blossoms" (nos. 3 and 10)

The whole world rushes to praise red and mauve.
Plum blossom's plain-white isn't *à la mode*.
Banished to the earth's ends—
    unappreciated—

Haggard—
    she loses her frost-defying, snow-challenging glow.

Her icy beauty defies the aggression of snow and frost.
Refusing to decorate jade palaces, she
    adorns an ancient peak.
Her sublimity lies in her independence.
Wealth and high position are powerless
     to alter
        her heart's
            pristine
                inclination.

Gardens of the Song Dynasty

The garden entered a new era in the late Tang and the Song. The Han Chinese world changed dramatically after the An Lushan rebellion in the mid-eighth century and although the Song continued many Tang traditions, these were radically altered by new social and cultural conditions and consequently by new aesthetic sensibilities. Gardens continued to be a major feature of the physical and mental landscape, but they also took on new meaning in their two primary forms: the imperial and the private garden. There was, to be sure, a third form of garden—gardens in Buddhist or Daoist monasteries—but during the Song, the design and function of the monastic garden was subsumed by that of the literati, surely the largest group of private garden owners.

The fall of the Tang and the intervening century of conflict between the ephemeral states known collectively as "The Five Dynasties" witnessed a serious diminution of Chinese power in east Asia. Years of conflict with the Khitan (and their sinicized state, the Liao), the Tangut (the state of Xixia), and then the Jurchen (the Jin) and the Mongols (who later established the Yuan dynasty) reduced the military and political reach of the Central Kingdom. The first emperor of the Song, noting that it was powerful regional commanders who finished off the late great dynasty, the Tang, stationed half of the army within a hundred miles of the capital at Bianliang (modern Kaifeng), and consequently the border areas were nearly always in a state of contestation.

As we saw in chapter 2, the Tang dynasty had produced many new phenomena in garden culture, including the development of a new self-confidence in literati culture, the integration of the principles of painting and poetry into the construction and appreciation of gardens, the transportation of southern rocks and flora to the gardens of the north, new skills in rockery and garden construction, and the secularization of Buddhist and Daoist temple gardens.

The further changes that took place in the Song began at the center of the empire. The capital itself was of an utterly different kind than earlier capitals (particularly Chang'an), which were administrative and ritual centers that were carefully planned and sited along cosmic terrestrial and astral axes and divided into walled wards, each small block subject to a curfew to restrict free movement within the city. Markets were also confined to wards given over to commercial interests. Tang Chang'an was certainly cosmopolitan, but there were clear hierarchical boundaries built into the physical layout of the city.

Song Bianliang (modern Kaifeng) shattered the ritual model of a capital. The change was wrought by several factors. By the end of the Tang, the area south of the Yangtze River had become the agricultural center of China: the abundance of water and warm weather combined to make the growing season in the south much longer than in the north, while the introduction of new strains of double-cropping rice greatly increased agricultural production. Bianliang, at the nexus of a canal network that reached into Jiangnan, Shandong, and the Shaanxi and Shanxi areas, soon became a commercial center that was home to itinerant and expatriate merchants. By the Latter Zhou dynasty (ca. 950), the smaller inner city had spilled outside its walls, forcing the last emperor of that dynasty to construct a new outer wall some seventeen miles in circumference. Driven by an enormous increase in population during the Song, urban areas generally became extremely crowded. Ward walls were replaced by shops that faced and encroached on the streets. Streets themselves were constantly narrowed, and instead of gates leading into each ward, street corners were marked by poles or trees.[1] The city was, moreover, arranged according to market function. Streets were given such names as "Wheat Stalk Alley," "Fruit Guild Street," "Yarn Street," and "Paper Alley," indicating that, like modern Chinese cities, the urban landscape of Bianliang was mapped by economic activity.

Urban commercialism powered a uniquely protocapitalist form of consumption, and it drew on a developing system of handicraft production to meet the material needs of the capital's citizens.[2] Economic advances were accompanied, however, by a social and political anxiety that resulted from intense factional strife at court and repeated conflicts along the northern and western borders. This seems to have bred a mild hedonism that, coupled with the material excesses of the capital, led to a form of frivolous and excessive lifestyle for both court and citizens. While this culminated in the reign of Huizong, the Northern Song capital clearly seems to have always been a site of excess. For instance, the preface to *Dreaming a Dream of Splendors Past in the Eastern Capital* (*Dongjing menghua lu*) displays a playland of spectacle and sensual enticements (see below).

Gardens were deeply implicated in pleasures that now extended from the aesthetic to the sensual to the sexual. The case was no different in the Southern Song capital of Hangzhou, where West Lake provided a vast pleasure garden (see chapter 9). Zhou Mi (1232–1298) wrote a description of

---

1   Heng Chye Kiang, *Cities of Aristocrats and Bureaucrats: The Development of the Medieval Chinese Cityscapes* (Singapore: Singapore University Press, 1999), gives a wonderfully detailed account of the transformation of the city in the Tang and Song eras.

2   Stephen H. West, "The Emperor Sets the Pace: Court and Consumption in the Northern Song," in *Selected Essays on Court Culture in Cross-Cultural Perspective*, ed. Lin Yaofu (Taipei: National Taiwan University Press, 2000), 25–50.

the West Lake with its pleasure-boats and sensual enjoyments, stating that the local epithet for the area as "a cauldron where money is smelted" is "in no way excessive."

PART 1

IMPERIAL GARDENS

There were three major types of gardens in Bianliang (modern Kaifeng), the capital of the Northern Song (960–1125): imperial parks, monastery and temple grounds, and private gardens. Numbered among these enclosures were four imperial parks, one at each of the cardinal gates. A fifth, the celebrated *Genyue* (the "Northeast Marchmount"), which was sited next to the Forbidden City (the "Grand Interior"), was constructed as a private miniature of the empire, a botanical and zoological collection of exotica from all parts of China, the rapacious collection of which drove the state into moral and financial bankruptcy. All the parks except the Genyue were opened for use by officials and the court at set times of the year or on unique occasions, and one major site, a complex on the western side of the capital, was opened for six weeks to the general populace. In a practical sense, imperial parks also served as productive gardens, stables, menageries, and for a variety of other purposes. At the same time, the general populace made use of gardens—imperial and other—for their own purposes.

It is clear that for the bureaucrat, the imperial park was primarily a place for ritual and practical use, and this is reflected in the formal historical materials gathered by encyclopedists. Such are the "Record of the Northeast Marchmount" and the passage on the Garden of the Jade Ford presented below. For everyone, the gardens of Bianliang—whether imperial gardens or those belonging to individuals or to temples—were an important social space: they were toured for flower viewing, served as sites of banquets and drinking parties, and provided the necessary context and stimulus for the creation of poetry and prose that celebrated the passage of the seasons and the fellowship of humans amid change. But for ordinary people, it was the opening of the parks to all and the concurrent staging of imperial spectacle that figured most significantly in their lives. For common folk of the capital, festivals set in gardens ranked with religious or imperial rituals in terms of their importance, and people were inclined to treat all these occasions alike: not as sacred events or humbling moments of awe before imperial majesty, but as nodal points of the urban year that were thickened by sensuous and material pleasures: entertainment, food, gambling, and prostitution. Parks were productive sites in this way, too, creating sets of social relations that were capable of emptying out imperial displays of power because the very audience meant to be cowed by that display created an alternative signification for such occasions. In the popular mind, imperial spectacles were subverted by sensation and material pleasure; their staging incidentally created a space where the hierarchies of privilege that were meant to mark the royal family and a noble meritocracy were canceled out by desire and leveled by the power of consumption.

"Record of the Northeast Marchmount" (*Genyue ji* 艮嶽記)

EMPEROR HUIZONG 宋徽宗 (1082–1135; R. 1101–1125)
AND ZHANG HAO 張淏 (CA. 1180–1250)
TRANSLATED BY JAMES M. HARGETT

The *Genyue* or Northeast Marchmount formed the centerpiece of a manmade imperial pleasure park constructed within the walled confines of the Eastern Capital of the Song at Bianliang (Kaifeng), in its northeastern section. The park came to be known by the name of its most conspicuous feature. The graph *gen* is the seventh of the Eight Diagrams (*bagua*) of the *Yijing* (*Classic of Changes*). *Gen* represents not only mountains and the northeast compass point but also sons, and thus male fertility. The motivation for building the "mountain" was to ensure a good supply of heirs for the Emperor Huizong, and indeed he did father thirty-one sons (and thirty-four daughters) by nineteen wives. Moreover, by imitation and miniaturization, many of the most admired landscapes in the empire were rendered accessible to the emperor at his seat in the capital.

The park later became closely associated with the downfall of the Northern Song dynasty. Construction depended on the notorious "Flower and Rock Network" based on a "Response and Service Bureau" (or "Provision Bureau") set up in Suzhou in 1105 (well before the start of construction of the Genyue itself). Rocks and rare plants and animals were transported to the capital from all over the empire by means of the "Flower and Rock Network," with huge corruption, waste, and oppression of the populace, and equally huge profits to those imperial servants who ran the network. At the same time, the emperor's interest in these projects was believed to have distracted his attention from such pressing matters as the military situation on the northern borders, where the Jurchen people were threatening the territorial integrity of the Song empire.

Construction of the Genyue probably began in early 1118; its completion was announced in 1122. By 1126, the city of Kaifeng was under siege by the Jurchens who formed the Jin dynasty, and the park and its mountain were utterly destroyed—the rocks used as missiles, the trees cut down for firewood, and the animals slaughtered to feed the army.[3]

There are several literary descriptions of the Northeast Marchmount. The authors included here are Zhang Hao, an official about whom little is known; Zuxiu, a Buddhist monk from the Sichuan region who is known to have visited the park on at least two occasions; and Zhao Ji, the Emperor Huizong himself.

"Record of the Northeast Marchmount"

When Huizong first ascended to culmination,[4] His august heritors were not yet extensive in number. There was a formulae gentleman[5] who said that the earth at the northeastern corner of the Capital City is in harmony with the Canopy of Heaven

---

3 For a more detailed history and a description of the Genyue, see James M. Hargett, "Huizong's Magic Marchmount: The Genyue Pleasure Park of Kaifeng," *Monumenta Serica* 38 (1988–1989):1–48.

4 Zhao Ji inherited the throne in 1100, though 1101 is technically the first year of his reign.

5 Editor's note: a geomancer or expert in divination.

and the Chassis of Earth. Only its contours and conformations are somewhat low. If they were raised and heightened a little, the august heritors would then be abundant and ample. His Highness consequently mandated that earth be used to bank up its hillocks and mounds, making them somewhat larger than they had been formerly. And, as predicted, there was a response [in the form] of numerous sons. From this time forward, there was regular security within the seas and lack of incident at the imperial court, and His Highness devoted quite a bit of attention to parks and preserves. During the Zhenghe period [1111–1118], he proceeded to visit its site. Afterward there was a great mobilization of craftsmen and laborers who built a mountain designated Longevity Mountain, the Northeast Marchmount. It was mandated that the eunuch Liang Shicheng would be solely responsible for directing the project. At the time there was one Zhu Mian who gathered rare and odd flowers, trees, bamboos, and rocks in Zhe in order to advance them to the capital. This was designated the Flower and Rock Network. A Response and Service Bureau was specifically set up in Pingjiang [Suzhou]. As for the expenses involved in shipping specimens to the capital, they are easily reckoned to be almost infinite. Common people were dispatched to search around cliffs and sift through swamps. Shrouded and secret locales were not disregarded. Each flower and each tree selected for later confiscation was wrapped with a yellow imperial seal. If someone was even slightly inattentive in guarding and watching over them, he was then charged with a crime. Mountains were hacked to pieces and rocks were carted away. Despite the unfathomable gulfs in the lakes and rivers, to which human efforts could not reach, every possible scheme was used in order to get the rocks out and to their destination. This system was called Divine Conveyance. The boats continued, one after another, day and night, without a break. Four commands from Guangji were depleted in order to provide hauling officers. Still, they did not supply enough. At that time, there was response and service from most of the Overseer-Inspectors and Commandery Guardians in the Southeast, and the Trade Argosy Inspectors in Guangdong and Guangxi. There were also those who, without waiting for an imperial order, sent objects to the planning and calculating eunuchs in the capital. That which they proffered as tribute as a rule included such items as rocks from Lingbi and Lake Tai, marvelous bamboos and odd flowers from the two circuits of Zhejiang, veined rocks from Deng and Lai, striped bamboos from Hu and Xiang, and wonderful fruits and odd trees from Sichuan, all of which reached their destination by traversing the seas, by being ferried across the Yangtze River, and by having openings chiseled for them through ramparts and barbicans. Later, His Highness also became aware of the troubles this was causing, and thus increased the prohibitions and restrictions somewhat, allowing only Zhu Mian and Cai You [1077–1126] to send in tribute. The stores and stockpiles of the depositories and repositories were drained; the adepts and artists in the Underheaven were gathered. In all, it took six years before the project was completed. It was also hailed as Myriad Years Mountain. Of the marvelous flowers and beautiful trees, rare birds and odd beasts, there were none that were not assembled and accumulated. Soaring lofts and outstanding belvederes, imposing and magnificent, extraordinary and elegant, reached perfection here. Ten years later, when the men of Jin attacked the capital, a great snowstorm left over a foot of snow on the ground. An imperial rescript commanded that the common people be allowed to chop and cut for firewood as they pleased. On this day the hundred surnames were running around in a panic, about 100,000 of them. The terraces and arbors, palaces and chambers, were all destroyed and demolished, and officials could do nothing to stop them. I recently read through the national histories, as well as through various chronicles, and learned about Genyue's essentials and peripherals as they are here described. In each case, I regretted that I was unable to acquire more specific information about related matters. Later, I acquired and read the text of Huizong's imperially-authored record, as well as the "Record of the Florescent Solarity Palace" written by Zuxiu, a monk from Shu. The so-called Longevity Mountain, the Northeast Marchmount, then rose majestically before my eyes. Because of this, from each I have gleaned a summary in order to provide information on what has been lost and forgotten.

The imperially-authored "Record of the Northeast Marchmount"[6] in summary reads:

Thus, the site was measured out according to plan. Corvée labor was provided; craftsmen were supplied; earth was piled up; the rocks were amassed. Deep gulfs like those of Dongting, Hukou, Sixi and Chouchi were set in place, together with the various mountains of Sibin, Liulü, Lingbi, and Furong. The most extraordinary, marvelous, prominent, odd, and gem-like stones were then gathered. They proceeded to the lands of Gusu, Wulin, Ming and Yue, and to the countrysides of Jing, Chu, Jiang, Xiang, and Southern Yue, whence they transmitted loquat, orange, pomelo, sourpeel tangerine, sweetpeel tangerine, betel-nut palm, Chinese juniper, and lichee trees, as well as gold moth, jade bashfulness, tiger ear, phoenix tail, jasmine, oleander, Indian jasmine, and magnolia plants. Ignoring variations in geography and differences in climate, all the trees and plants generated and grew, and matured and mellowed, by carved railings and winding balustrades. And rocks were bored and fissures exposed; hillocks were linked and mounds joined. East and west face one another; front and rear connect with one another. On the left are mountains and on the rights are streams. On the flanks are creeks and on the sides are rises, linked and lined and bountiful and brimming, swallowing up mountains, embosoming dales. To its east, then, is a lofty peak standing erect. Below it are planted flowering apricot trees in myriad numbers. Their green perianths are supported by pedicels, fragrant and redolent, aromatic and rich, which join to form the mountain's base. This is designated the Hall of Flowers with Green Perianths. Next, off to the side, are the Receiving Mists and Kunlun Clouds Kiosks. There is a building that is square on the inside and round on the outside, like a half-moon. This is known as the Documents Lodge. Next there is the Eight Immortals Lodge, the structure of which is round like a disk. Next are the Cliff of Purple Rocks,

---

6   Written by Zhao Ji, the Emperor Huizong. The imperial record was inscribed and installed in the park.

the Ledge of Propitiating the Realized Ones, the Pavilion of Grasping Loveliness, and the Hall of Dragon's Song. To its south, then, is the jagged and cragged Longevity Mountain. Its two peaks are erect side-by-side; its aligned cliffwalls are like screens. A waterfall descends into the Wild Goose Pool. The pool water is clear and fresh, wavy and ripply. Wild ducks and wild geese float and dive on the surface of the water. Those roosting and resting among the rocks are beyond reckoning in number. The kiosk atop the mountain is called Honk-Honk. Directly to the north is the Scarlet Empyrean Loft, where peaks and ridges rise prominently in thousands of folds and in myriad layers, for who knows how many tens of *li*. And in square area they encompass several tens of *li*. To the west, then, is grown ginseng, hill-thistle, boxthorn, chrysanthemum, yellow-germ and hemlock-parsley, which blanket the mountains and pervade the embankments. The center of this area is designated the Herb Shanty. Moreover, standing grain, hemp, pulse, wheat, millet, beans, rice, and sorghum are grown there. The homes constructed in this area resemble farmhouses; thus it is known as West Village. Above [on a nearby mountain?] there is a kiosk called Nesting-in-the-Clouds. From its heights emerge peaks and tors, whence one can scan the multitudes of precipices below, which seem to be in the palm of your hand. Advancing north from the south, you move along the ridge of a hillock between two rocks. Stretching and sweeping for several *li*, the ridge faces the mountains in the east. Water emerges from openings in the rocks, spurting and gushing, soaring and streaming downward, making the rocks look like fright masks. These are known as White Dragon Strand, Sleek Dragon Gorge, the Coiling Loveliness, Shimmering Brightness, and Bestriding Clouds Kiosks, and the Arhat Cliff. Next, halfway up the mountain in the west, there is a loft called Nestling-Against-Halcyon. Verdant pines, dark and dense, are spread out in front and in back of it. This area is designated Myriad Pines Precipice. Two mountain passes have been put in place above and below it. Emerging from the passes, you descend to a level area where there is a large, square mere. In it are two islets. The east islet forms the Reed Holm; the kiosk there is called Floating Solarity. The west islet forms the Flowering Apricot Holm; the kiosk there is called Cloudy Billow. The mere water flows westward to form the Phoenix Pond, and goes out eastward to form the Palette Pond. The area between them is apportioned by two lodges. The one to the east is called Flowing Cyan; the one to the west is called Ringing the Mountain. The lodges have a gallery called Nesting Phoenix, and a hall called Three Lovelies, which was presented with a sacred image of Consort An, the Jade Realized One of the Nine Flower Mountain. Behind the pool to the east, a structure has been built below a mountain called the Scattered Clouds Auditorium. Again, if one holds onto the rocks and ascends the ledgeway, which coils and moves, reels and winds, eventually the mountain cuts you off and the road divides. From there you continue onward by means of a wooden catwalk. Supported by rocks stacked in the air, it circles and rings, winds and bends, as hard as the road to Shu. You then clamber and scramble up it until reaching the Medial Kiosk. Here, in front of the tallest of the various mountains, giant rocks have been aligned, which are generally about three *zhang* in height. This is designated the Arrayed Rows. Artful and fantastic are the crags and cliffs. Liana and lichen spread and sprawl like dragons, like phoenixes. They cannot be followed to the end. The Foothill Clouds and Mid-Mount Kiosks are positioned to the right; the Culminate Vision and Leafy Forest Kiosks are positioned to the left. To the north one looks down into the Luminous Dragon River, the long waves and distant banks of which extend for ten-some *li*. Its upper reaches pour into the mountains. Rushing and gushing as it moves westward, it forms the Rinsing with Jade Pavilion. Next, it moves into the rocks to form the Refining Cinnabar Kiosk, and the Concentrated Observation and Picture Mountain Kiosks. Below, one scans the boundary of a stream, and sees the Toper's Wineshop and Qingsi Gallery. Along the northern shore of the River are myriad bamboos of dark-green halcyon, dense and luxuriant. If you look upward, you cannot see the sky. Here we find the Surpassing Cloud Retreat, Treading Clouds Terrace, Passing-Away-Idleness Lodge and Soaring Pinnacle Kiosk. There are no assorted flowers or odd trees here. Bamboos are found on all four sides. Next, a tributary stream of the River forms Mountain Village, and forms Veer Creek. From the mountain paths and rocky fissures one grabs hold of branches and descends to a tract of level land. If you stand at its center and look all about, then cliffs, gorges, grottoes, caves, kiosks, galleries, lofts, and belvederes, towering trees and rich herbage, some high up and some down low, some distant and some nearby, one protruding and the other receding, one blooming and the other fading, completely surround you on all four sides. If you dilly-dally around and look about, it seems as if you are in the folds of hills and great straths, at the bottom of deep vales and secluded cliffs, unaware that the capital district of Kaifeng is limitless and boundless, extensive and expansive, and level and even. Moreover, you are unaware that within the outer walls and barbicans, domains and assemblages, it is bustling and crowded and congested and jammed. Truly this is something fashioned in Heaven and put in place on earth, something the spirits have devised and the Mutator has labored at, and something that could not have been made by man. Here I offer up a summary and a sketch of it.

Zuxiu's "Record of the Florescent Solarity Palace" reads:

At the beginning of the Zhenghe period [1111–1118] the Son of Heaven mandated that Longevity Mountain, the Northeast Marchmount, be built in the eastern nook of the Forbidden City, and decreed that eunuchs would be responsible for its construction. Boats were used to convey the rock; carriages were used to cart the earth. They mobilized myriad numbers of irregular troops to construct hillocks and mounds, more than ten *ren* in height, to which rocks were added from Lake Tai and Lingbi. Imposing and upthrust, jagged and erect, in achievement they surpass heavenly creations. All of the rocks are furious and angry, pushing and shoving, as if they are kicking and biting one another. Teeth, horns, mouths, noses, heads, tails, claws, and spurs—a thousand postures, ten-thousand shapes, thoroughly marvelous and completely fantastic. Supported by twisting trees and swollen liana, they are interspersed with boxwood trees and parallel-azure bamboos, which shade their tops. Next, along the conformation of the boulders' circuit and orbit, rocks have been split and trails have been opened. Where there are precipitous dangers, ledgeways have been put in place; where there is soaring emptiness, catwalk-galleries have been erected. Then one continues on to the summit's crest, where lofty trees have been added to cap it off. They searched the distant quarters for rare materials, exhausted the Underheaven to draft craftsmen of superlative talent, and then planned and commenced work on the park. To the tops and bases of the mountains were conveyed the rare birds and marvelous beasts from the four quarters, which were easily reckoned to be almost infinite in number. Yet these were regarded as insufficient. Ponds were sunk, making creeks and torrents; rocks were layered, making barriers and obstacles. They preserved the fantastic quality of the rocks, and did not try to enhance them by chopping and chiseling. Subsequently, surplus earth was amassed and made into mountains. The bones of the mountains lay exposed and revealed; the angles of the peaks seem to be honed. The one that floats on air and possesses cloud-like contours and crane-like postures is called Approaching-in-Flight Peak. The one that is loftier than a crenellated parapet, which rolls along like a long whale, whose girth measures 100 *chi*, and where flowering apricot trees are planted in myriad numbers, is called Flowering Apricot Precipice. The one that connects with the remaining hillocks, and where vermilion apricot and duck-feet[7] trees are grown, is called Apricot Tor. Next, the one where earth has been added and rocks have been layered, among which cracks and caves have been left in order to plant boxwood trees, is called Boxwood Stack. The one where hillocks have been constructed and built in order to plant lilac, among which rocks have been amassed, and along which dangerous heights have been put into place, is called Lilac Cliffwall. Next, the one where fiery-red rocks have been procured, kept in their natural state, and added up to form a mountain, and where fagara and orchids have been randomly planted below it, is called Fagara Steep. The one on the periphery of the joining waters, where earth has been added to make a great slope, and along its south-eastern flank cypress branches and trunks are pliable and thick, bent down over it to no end, with leaf upon leaf forming the shape of carriage-screens, canopies, simurghs, cranes, krakens, and dragons, easily myriad in number, is called Draconic Cypress Slope. Running westward along Longevity Mountain, transplanted bamboos form a forest. Also, a small trail has been opened up that extends for a hundred and some double-paces. Among the bamboos are those of similar root but of different trunk. One could not chronicle them to the limit. All are precious tribute from the four quarters. Moreover, they are intermixed with parallel-azure bamboos, with a ratio of eight or nine to ten. This area is called Mottled Bamboo Foothill. Next, they acquired purple rocks, sleek and clean and seemingly pared, with a surface diameter of several *ren*. Because of this, a mountain was made out of the rocks. The mountain is secured [by the purple rocks?], and stands prominently. On the shady side of the mountain wooden buckets have been put into place; on the

---

7   Editor's note: duck-feet trees are ginkgos, from the shape of the leaves.

summit's crest a deep pool has been built. When the imperial carriage and cortege approach to grace the mountain, water-workers are mobilized to climb to the crest of the mountain where, upon opening the sluice gate, water pours down to form a cascade. This is called Purple Rock Wall. It is also known as Cascade Screen. From the foot of the Northeast Marchmount, they have cut into the rocks to make steps. All of the rocks are gentle and smooth, clean and sleek. This called Paying Court to the Realized Ones Ledge. Next, upon islets are planted fragrant trees, which are dominated by flowering crabapple trees. This is called Flowering Crabapple Stream. West of Longevity Mountain is a separately built garden-preserve. This is called Herb Shanty. Of the park's palaces, chambers, terraces, and arbors, those commanding prominent reputation are called Rose-Gem Ford Basilica, Scarlet Empyrean Loft, and Hall of Flowers With Green Perianths. From terraces constructed at heights of one thousand *ren* one looks around at the Metropolis City of Kaifeng, which seems but an instant away. They have fashioned the Cyan Vacuity Grotto-Heavens. Myriad mountains ring them. Three Grottoes have been opened to form the *Pin*-Graph Gate,[8] which is used to give passage to the parks in front and in back. An octagonal kiosk has been erected in its very center, the rafters, beams, windows, and pillars of which are all inlaid with carnelian agate. Its site has been composed to form a dragon-shaped foundation. The Luminous Dragon River is conducted to run eastward and then exit at the Anyuan Gate, in order to be prepared for when the Dragon Boat travels to grace the two gardens of East and West Gathering Luminescence. To the west, then, the Dragon Boat progresses upstream to the Luminous Dragon Gate, in order to grace the Winding River Pool Kiosk. Also, when the sluice gate is opened at the Xiao-Xiang River Kiosk, He gains passage to the Celestial Waves Gate. To the north, He graces the Gathering Fragrance Park. Beyond its barriers a buttress has been constructed to guard it. By shoreline waters are planted scarlet-colored peach, flowering crabapple, lotus, and weeping willow trees. Not the slightest crack of space is left unused. Next, on a former site is built the Rustic Inn Foothill and the Managing Agriculture Orchard. In the east and west two passes have been opened up, on each side of which are suspended cliffs. The ledgeways there are narrow and intimidating; the rocks are numerous; the peaks are angular. Visitors tremble with fear and shudder with fright. In general, those people who ascend the multitudes of peaks in the park exit and enter the Genyue through these two passes and no other. Next, they have made six or seven surpassing places for sauntering called Frolicking Dragon Torrent, Overflowing Spring Slope, Peach Blossom Sluice Gate, Wild Goose Pond, and Delusive Realization Grotto. As for the other surpassing landmarks, they cannot be thoroughly chronicled here. When work on the project was completed, His Highness named it "Florescent Solarity Palace." However, the area known as Florescent Solarity for the most part constitutes masses of mountains aligned in a ring. In its center one finds several tens of *qing* of

---

8   Editor's note: this gate was presumably in the shape of the character *pin*, 品, which looks like three openings, or "grottoes."

level, uncultivated land. In order to manage the gardens and orchards, and in order to give access to the palace gate in the west, a trail has been opened up that is broader than the Speedway.[9] All the great rocks on its left and right stand as thick as a forest. Yet there are merely a hundred-some of them. The more prominent of the boulders are named Divine Conveyance, Radiant Merit, Diffuse Felicity, and Myriad Longevity Peaks. Only Divine Conveyance Peak measures a hundred spans in breadth, and six *ren* in height. It has had bestowed on it the rank Marklord of Pangu, and has been positioned in the center of the way. Rocks have been packed up and made into a kiosk in order to shelter it. The kiosk is 50 *chi* in height. The text of the imperially-authored record was written out personally by Huizong. A stele three *zhang* high has been erected near the south-eastern nook of the Divine Conveyance Peak. As for the other rocks, some resemble companies of ministers passing into a command tent to attend upon the emperor, their countenances composed in a serious manner, as if they could not commit a transgression. Some are shuddering with fright as if paying reverence to the awesomeness of Heaven. Some are aroused to action and moving in haste. Moreover, they seem to be hunched and humped over as they hasten forward. As for their fantastic shapes and abundant postures—how numerous are those people to whom they give pleasure! Since His Highness takes delight in them, all have been conferred and bestowed titles. Guardian clerks take royal compositions and paintings and array them on the sunny side of the rocks. Each of the other pavilions, arbors, courtyards, and trails has a giant rock. Deployed and arrayed in a starry arrangement, each has been conferred and bestowed with a name. Only the giant rock before Divine Conveyance Peak is adorned with graphs of gold appliqué. All of the remaining rocks are adorned with graphs of bluish kohl and that is all. This is the means used to grade those rocks that are primary and those that are secondary. Thereupon, names were mandated for the multitude of peaks. In summary they are called: Ascendant Dragon of the Dawning Sun, Seated Dragon Gazing-at-Clouds, Jade Dragon With Raised Head, Venerable Pine of Myriad Longevities, Perched-in-Roseate-Clouds and Stroking the Triaster Stars, Embouching the Sun and Spewing the Moon, Arrayed-in-the-Clouds and Reaching-to-the-Dipper, Thunder Gate and Lunar Den, Squatting Leviathan and Sitting Lion, Heaped Azure and Concentrated Cyan, Golden Sea Turtle and Jade Tortoise, Layered Halcyon and Unique Loveliness, Perched-in-Mists and Hidden-in-Clouds, Windy Gate and Thunder Cave, Jade Loveliness, Jade Cavity, Pointed Clouds and Nesting Phoenix, Engraved and Cut, Whole and Complete, Rising Mound of Sunny Prospect, Penglai, Yingzhou, Sumeru, Longevity Star for Venerable Men, Propitious Clouds and Auspicious Vapors, Smooth Jade, Spurting Jade, Bouquet of Jade, Cut Jade, Amassed Jade, Layered Jade, and Clustered Loveliness. And the one situated on the holm is called Hovering-Over-the-Fishes. The one standing on the riverbank is called Dancing Sylph. The one crouched alone in the middle of the islet is called Jade Unicorn. The one capping Longevity Mountain is called Little Peak on the

---

9 The main north-south avenue in Kaifeng, which had one lane reserved for the emperor's use.

Southern Screen. And those near the sides of the pools are called Cowering Rhinoceros, Raging Beast, Ceremonial Phoenix, and Raven-Black Dragon. Those that stand at the descending springs are called Tarrying Cloud and Nocturnal Fog. Moreover, they have made the Storing Mists Vale, Dripping Halcyon Cliff, Seizing Clouds Screen, and Amassed Snow Precipice. The one among them where yellow rocks have fallen by the boundary of a kiosk is called Embracing Calves Heavenly Gate. Next, there are two large rocks that complement the Divine Conveyance Peak. They are specially positioned so as to dominate the masses of rocks. A kiosk has been built to shelter them. The one laid out at the Encompassing Spring Hall is called Cliff of Unique Loveliness and Grand Tranquillity in the Jade Capital. The one laid out at the Hall of Flowers With Green Perianths is called Marvelous Peak of Propitious Clouds and Myriad Postures. The beauties embraced in the Underheaven, and the surpassing sights preserved from past and present, are here fulfilled. In the intercalary eleventh month in the prime year of the Jingkang period [1126–1127], Kaifeng was attacked. The people of the metropolis and I arrayed ourselves by the walls, and hid from the caitiffs on the summit of Longevity Mountain, the Northeast Marchmount. At that time, the sky had just cleared after a great snowfall. The hillocks, straths, forests, and dammed-ponds stood out like an album of paintings. In general, the beauties of the Underheaven, and the surpassing sights of past and present, are situated herein. I, Zuxiu, looked around the park for several days. Oh! How surprising and startling! I believe it to be the outstanding sight in the Underheaven, and that heavenly creations are in some ways incomplete when compared with it. In the spring of the following year [1127], I again sauntered to the Florescent Solarity Palace, but by then the common people had laid it to waste.

Sea of Jades (Yuhai 玉海)

"Garden of the Jade Ford" (Yujin yuan 玉津園; extract)

WANG YINGLIN 王應麟 (1223–1296)
TRANSLATED BY STEPHEN H. WEST

Wang Yinglin was a classical scholar and philologist as well as an official at the end of the Southern Song dynasty. He obtained his presented scholar degree at an early age and went on to become a high official. After the final collapse of the Song, he lived in retirement for twenty years. The *Sea of Jades* is an encyclopedia he compiled while studying for an advanced degree.

"Garden of the Jade Ford" (extract)

In the fourth month of the fourth year of Jianlong reign [963], [Emperor Taizu] visited the Garden of the Jade Ford where he reviewed the riding and archery of the various troops of his personal guard. On the eighteenth day he gave a feast for officials in his retinue. One text says that [Emperor Taizu] visited the Garden of the Jade Ford on the day *yiyou*, the sixteenth day of the fourth month, in the summer, of the first year of Jianlong [960]. In the second month of the fourth year of the Qiande reign [966] he visited the Garden of the Jade Ford to review riding and archery of the guards. In the ninth month he observed the scything of the wheat. In the third month of the fifth year of Yuanyou [1090], [Emperor Zhezong] gave a feast at the Garden of the Jade Ford to send off the Grand Tutor Wen Yanbo.

The park is located outside of the Gate of Southern Infusion, where it is split into two gardens that line the road. The waters of the Min River are fed into the parks where they are further split to flow through the gardens. The park was created during the Xiande reign period of the Latter Zhou [955–960] and our dynasty has perpetuated it. The Bureau of Lesser Military Assignments and the Directorate of the Palace Domestic Service were in charge of the soldiers attached to the park and the civil managers, respectively, to the number of 266 men. The seasonal items from the park were all dispatched to supply the Grand Interior. In the second month of summer the Son of Heaven visited to observe the gathering of the wheat (half of the Garden of the Jade Ford was planted in wheat). He also feasted his retinue of officials here at this time and bestowed gifts on the park officials and the gardeners according to their rank. Moreover, five hundred sheaves of wheat stalks were advanced, together with ten *hu* of wheat grain,[10] and one hundred sacks of flour, and he ordered that these be evenly distributed to parties both inside and outside of the court. Generally, when the Khitan envoys assigned to pay court or bring tribute came to the capital they were all brought to the garden for a feast and for archery contests. Generally, those members of the Bureau of the Imperial City who were commissioned as officials of parks and reservoirs all belonged to this.

Yang Kan's "Rhapsody on the Imperial Domain" reads:
    Images of the prospect a transcendents' isle,
    The garden's name is Jade Ford.
    Precious fruits are offered in summer,
    Rare flowers advanced in the spring,
    Hundreds of pavilions, thousands of trees.
    Amid the forest and along the banks of the rivers
    Were
    Qilin, revealing benevolence,
    Zouyu, making propriety known,
    The auspicious sign of the sacred sheep of one horn,
    The favorable portent of the miraculous rhinoceros of tri-cloven hooves,
    Bengal tigers imported from India,
    Tamed elephants presented by Jiaozhi.

---

10   Ten *hu* is about 33,500 liters.

. . . Peacocks, kingfishers,
Silver pheasants, white pheasants,
Twisting and turning, rills and fields,
High and low, rice paddies and vegetable plots,
Workers from Yue wield dibble sticks,
Buffalo from Wu tread the mud.

When the frost is early they scythe quickly.
When spring is late, they plant later.
How the rural scenery of Jiangnan
Has appeared beneath the hub of the chariot—as though transplanted!
Snow encloses winter sprouts,
Rain moistens summer awns,
Just when the new wheat is timely offered,
So the path is cleared and He arrives Himself—
At the royal chariot a thousand officers are put in retinue
In the faubourgs a myriad horse are put in formation.
Once He has witnessed the harvesting, then it is called "over,"
And as soon as they have feasted and been rewarded, then it is done.

From the sixteenth day of the fourth month of the first year of Jianlong [960] to the
fourteenth day of the fifth month of the ninth year of Kaibao [976] Emperor Taizu
visited the park a total of thirteen times.

On the twenty-seventh day, *yiwei*, of the twelfth month of the first year of the Taiping
xingguo reign period [977] and the thirteenth day of the eleventh month of the fourth
year [979], Emperor Taizong visited the park twice.

From the seventh day of the fourth month of the fifth year of the Xianping reign period
[1002], when he "observed the wheat," to the seventh day of the fifth month of the
fourth year of the Tianxi reign period [1020], Emperor Zhenzong visited the park ten
times. From the twelfth day of the fifth month of the third year of Tiansheng reign
[1025] to the eleventh day of the fifth month of the Qingli reign period [1044], Emperor
Renzong visited the park three times.

Dreaming a Dream of Splendors Past in the Eastern Capital (*Dongjing menghua lu* 東京夢華錄)

"Opening of the Reservoir of Metal's Luster and the Park of the Rosequartz Grove" (*Kai Jinming chi Qionglin yuan* 開金明池瓊林苑) and "Searching Out the Spring" (*Tan chun* 探春)

MENG YUANLAO 孟元老 (FL. 1126–1147)
TRANSLATED BY STEPHEN H. WEST

Dreaming a Dream of Splendors Past in the Eastern Capital describes life in the Northern Song capital Bianliang (present-day Kaifeng) between 1117 and 1125. The first five of ten chapters are a synchronic description of major areas of plebeian and royal activity within the capital. The second half provides a calendar of the major festivals and events that were performed on this urban stage. From this second section comes the description of the annual celebration known as "Searching Out the Spring."

The preface by Meng Yuanlao dates the work's composition to 1148, two decades after the destruction of the capital in the Jin conquest of North China; it was first published several decades later, in 1187, by which time the author was probably no longer alive. We know little about him other than what he himself tells us in the preface, and his dates are uncertain. It has been speculated that he was related to, or actually was, Meng Kui, who supervised the construction of the Northeast Marchmount, and that this is the reason the park and its mountain are not mentioned in *Dreaming a Dream of Splendors Past in the Eastern Capital*, because of the reputation the park had acquired for causing the downfall of the Northern Song. The text is full of fascinating everyday details of life in the old capital, and is written in a lively, colloquial (some have said vulgar) style that Meng tells us he intended to be comprehensible to educated and uneducated readers alike.[11]

The function of the imperial gardens in the lives of commoners, sometimes identified as "people of the capital" (*duren*) becomes a clear focus of interest in *Dongjing menghua lu*. This is a group that is largely silent in historical and bureaucratic materials, which suggests that we are witness here to the creation of an alternate historicity created by a special class of city-dweller.

The text shows us that the imperial gardens had multiple functions: they were a site for annual reviews of the imperial guard; a place to give feasts of appreciation for officials; a site for agricultural rituals; a menagerie, including stables for the elephants used in imperial parades; a productive garden that provided vegetables, fruit, and grain to the forbidden city; a venue for holding feasts for visiting envoys from the northern state of Liao, governed by the Khitan; and a location for giving intimate banquets for favored members of the bureaucracy. The Reservoir of Metal's Luster was originally excavated so naval units of the military could practice their skills, although these exercises later devolved into simple entertainments. Gradually, the park complex west of the city began to take over nearly all the imperial activities, and from the middle of the eleventh century onward, it became the primary site of pleasure. It captured all the yearly ritual and social duties of the emperor, and on one special occasion the complex became one of a handful of sites within the capital precincts where the emperor presented himself to public view.

---

11   For a detailed analysis of the text, see Stephen H. West, "The Interpretation of a Dream: The Sources, Evaluation, and Influence of the *Dongjing Menghua Lu*," *T'oung Pao* 71, no. 1 (1985):63–108.

Official representations of these events strove to maintain a top-down hierarchy of distinctions between social classes (based on a complicated social calculus of education and ethics). But spectacle, employed in service of foregrounding the power of the emperor and invoking awe in his subjects, was easily subverted in the eyes of ordinary city dwellers to become either a display of the sensuous or a marker of consumer power. The New Year celebrations and the opening of the imperial Reservoir of Metal's Luster provided occasions when social classes that might normally be separated in life rubbed elbows in the pursuit of pleasure.

The *Dongjing menghua lu* makes its distinctions inversely: only after it discusses the pleasures of the ordinary—gambling, food, sex, and performance—does it turn to a class it identifies as *gui*, a word that can mean "valued" or "noble" when applied ethically from the top down, but means simply "rich" or "high-class" when applied from the bottom up. The court, its meritocracy, and even rich merchants are all conjoined in an indistinguishable group identified simply as the privileged.

For the author, the opening of the garden was a way to create a secular, democratic space linked to pleasure and consumption, where hierarchies were levelled by desire and pleasure. This may have hollowed out the ritual significance of the occasion, in which the emperor's actions invoked the special relationship that existed between rulership, the seasons, the flow of *yin* and *yang*, and the nodal points of agricultural life. It nevertheless strengthened the bond between urban dwellers and the emperor. They regularly turned out for imperial ritual, forming, as the text says, "walls of onlookers" at every event, or to watch the emperor's transit through the city. Spectacle lay at the center of each interpretation—secular and ritual—because performance lies at the center of both, as urban theater or imperial ceremony. For the author, it was certainly theater, and the emperor was the lead actor. Paradoxically, the seasonal regularity of leisure and performance that imperial displays provided had the desired effect of confirming stability and power in the mind of the ordinary city dweller. They loved this emperor because he provided a stable set of leisure activities, and as these occasions turned ritual into holidays, imperial gestures originally meant to signal power and authority were subverted in the popular mind into a good time.

"Opening of the Reservoir of Metal's Luster and the Park of the Rosequartz Grove"

On the first day of the third lunar month, the Reservoir of Metal's Luster and the Park of the Rosequartz Grove are opened just outside the Gate of Compliance to Heaven. The rituals and activities of the emperor's visit to the Reservoir are rehearsed. Although attendants of the Forbidden City, officials, and commoners are allowed to enjoy the sights, the Censorate makes a public announcement that they cannot investigate public behavior at this time. The Reservoir is located north of the road that exits the Gate of Compliance to Heaven, and it is approximately nine *li* and thirty double-paces in circumference. The diameter is something over seven *li*. After one enters the Reservoir gate, about a hundred double-paces west along the southern bank is the Hall Overlooking the Water, which faces north. The emperor holds a feast here when he visits to observe the races to capture the flag. In days past it was put up on the spot using multicolored tents, but during the Zhenghe reign [1111–1118] a permanent hall was constructed of earth and wood. Some hundred paces farther to the west is the

Immortal's Bridge, a triple-span arched bridge running several hundred paces north and south, that has red lacquered balustrades, "geese posts" in line underneath, and has a pronounced hump right in the center. It is called Camelhump Arch and it is shaped like an arching rainbow. Where the bridge ends there are five halls right in the center of the Reservoir on an island of rockwork. In the hall that faces north an imperial awning is erected, enclosing a dragon couch of red lacquer with gold appliqué, and a windscreen decorated with dragons disporting amid the clouds and waters of rivers.

Roamers are not prohibited here, and in the winding corridors of the halls, those both above and below, there is wagering for money and goods or food and drink, entertainers who perform, and stages erected on all sides. On the edges of the bridge itself are tile basins that are used for coin tossers to wager for money, and parasols everywhere you look. At the south side of the bridge a lattice gate has been erected and just inside the gate, facing each other, are bunted lofts—every time there is a race for the flag music is played and singsong girls are lined up atop the lofts. Now, just across from the lattice gate, on the south side of the road, there is a very tall raised brickwork dais, with a multistoried prospect tower on top. It is more than a hundred *zhang* in width and is called Tower of the Ford of Jewels. From the front of this dais to the gate to the Reservoir is an open strip of about a hundred *zhang*. The Tower overlooks the Immortal's Bridge and the water halls below, and the Son of Heaven comes to this place to view the mounted archers and the hundred entertainments.

On the eastern side of the Reservoir weeping willows are next to the wall and also to the water. On both sides of the avenue delineated by these lines of willows are bunted canopies and boxes that overlook the water and can be rented to observe the race for the flag. On the eastern side of the road are wineshops and foodstands, gambling arenas, stages for entertainment, and pawnshops (if items are not redeemed within a few days, they are released for sale right after the Reservoir closes).

Going north from here one comes straight to the rear gate of the Reservoir, which is also the West Watergate for the Bian River. The western slope of the reservoir is devoid of any buildings, there are just weeping willows dipping into the water and wispy grasses spreading along the dike. Roamers are few here, and are mostly fishermen, who must first purchase a license at the Reservoir Office before being allowed to fish. Roamers get these fish—without quibbling about price—and draw near the water to slice them into a mince as an accompaniment to a fragrant flagon of wine. This is indeed the most wonderful taste of the whole season. When all of the water exercises are finished, the smaller dragon boats are tied up here. On the north side of the reservoir, directly opposite the five halls of the water palace, a huge boathouse is erected, where they moor the large dragon boat. This is called the Cavernous Building.

The Son of Heaven normally picks the twentieth day to make his visit. All of the companies and squadrons of the Imperial Guard put branches of flowers into their hairwraps, and throw on dragon robes fretted with golden threads and cinches that are either golden belts or silken waistwraps—they vie with each other to be the freshest and most original. From the imperial warehouses they issue golden spears, bows, and swords sheathed in jewels, pennants embroidered with dragon and phoenix, damask woven bridles with scarlet tassels. Their myriad horses race with each other, the sounds of their harness bells shaking the earth.

THE SON OF HEAVEN VISITS THE HALL THAT OVERLOOKS THE WATER TO GIVE A FEAST AND OBSERVE THE RACE FOR THE FLAG

The Son of Heaven visits the Hall that Overlooks the Water to feast his various ministers. From the front of the hall, a covered pier is extended into the water, on which a ceremonial guard is stationed. Four multihued craft are arranged in a row in the water near the hall, and the hundred entertainments of the various troops are presented on board. These include flag twirling, lion and panther dances, the knife toss, the barbarian shield, and skits on ghosts and spirits. Two other boats are lined up, which are for the orchestra. There is one other small craft, with a small bunted loft lashed together on top, at the base of which are three small doors, just like the openings of a puppet stage, which open directly into the water. On the orchestra boat, the Adjutant intones the Felicitation, and music is played. The center door of the bunted loft opens up and small wooden puppets come out: a small boat is rowed by a small boy while a white-robed person fishes. They slowly row around in a circle, speaking to each other until music is played again and the little boat goes back into the tent. This is followed by wooden puppets who play football, dance and whirl, and the like. Each of these sessions also intones a Felicitation, and sings a duet of alternating lines. More music is played and it comes to an end. This is called "water puppetry."

There are also two painted boats on which swings are erected; on their sterns the acrobats climb up a pole. The Overseer of the Left and Right Troops leads the activities, and the drums and flutes match with their sounds. Then someone climbs up on the swing, and when he is nearly level with the frame of the swing, he does a tumble and somersaults into the water. This is called Water Swing.

After the water skits are finished, the musicians' boats of the "hundred entertainments" line up and sound their gongs and drum, playing music and twirling their flags in time. Together with the puppet boat they form two phalanxes and retire from the area. Some twenty small dragon craft, each carrying scarlet-robed soldiers, fifty or more to a boat, set up flags, drums, and gongs. On the prows of the boats military officers twirl flags and beckon the craft forward—those officers are all Commanders in the Tiger-Winged Navy.

Then there are ten tiger-headed craft, with a person standing on each prow, dressed in polychrome damask and holding a small flag. Everyone else is dressed in short blue robes, with peaked headscarves. They make their oars dance in unison—these are men who have dropped out of their regular profession.

Two flying-fish boats, colorfully decorated with splashes of gold, are the most artful of the lot, and there are some fifty people on board, dressed in theater garb of various hues, and scattered among them at intervals are small flags of various colors and scarlet parasols. They beckon and dance to the left and right, ring small gongs, and rattle drums. There are also two loach craft, which can only hold one person who paddles by hand—these are made of a single log. They all present to the emperor rare flowers and stones that were presented by Zhu Mian.

The various smaller craft all race to the "Cavernous Building," to pull out the grand dragon boat to go to the Water Hall. The smaller dragon craft race with each other to be first to circle and glide around, to lead it on its way forward. The tiger-headed boats pull out the dragon boat with ropes. This great dragon boat is about thirty or forty *zhang* long and about three or four *zhang* wide. Its head and tail have gills and scales, all of which are carved and gilded with gold. The planking on the hull is a neutral color, and there are ten or more compartments on either side: these are provided for the various groups of consorts to rest upon. In the center the imperial throne is set up, behind a windscreen of dragons sporting in the water. The hull itself is several feet deep, and on the very bottom are closely placed large pieces of cast iron in a shape that mimicks large silver coins, but as large as tabletops, to weigh it down, and to keep it from yawing and rolling. There are storied towers on top of the deck, platforms and observatories, and a railing, inside of which the imperial seat is securely placed. One person stands on the dragon's head, twirling flags, and under the awnings on the left and the right are arranged six oars that undulate as though flying through the air. The ship goes to one side of the Water Hall, where it is anchored.

From the front of the Water Hall to the Immortal's Bridge, they have previously stuck red flags in the water to mark off the distances. The so-called little dragon craft line up in front of the Water Hall, facing each other on the east and west, and the tiger-headed, flying-fish, and other boats spread out behind them, as though making two formations. In a little while a military officer at the awning in front of the Water Hall beckons them with a red flag and the dragon boats all come out of formation while beating gongs and drums. They row around, making a round formation called "Circling," and the two formations of boats race through each other's lines; this is called "Crossing Heads." A second flag and they all line up east of the five halls, where they form ranks and rows and face the Water Hall. Then a military officer on a small skiff carries out a long pole that is strung with items like damask, bunted cloth, and silver bowls. This is called "the target pole." It is stuck into the water close to the Water Hall. Once again they are summoned by the flag and two rows of boats come forward together to the sound of drumbeats. The fastest captures the flag, then they shout out "ten thousand years!" and make an obeisance. Together with all of the boats, like the tiger-headed craft, they line up together and each races three times for the flag before it is all over. Then the smaller craft again lead the great dragon boat back into the Cavernous Building.

INSIDE THE RESERVOIR AND PARK PEOPLE ARE ALLOWED TO WAGER ON GOODS AND PLAY GAMES

Inside the reservoir, in addition to the areas occupied by wine houses and entertainers, there are many small booths set up that are made out of knotted multicolored hangings, where items are displayed that are to be won by wagering: jewels, curiosities, and geegaws, bolts of cloth, tools, and vessels for tea and wine. There are those who have wagered and won 450 taels of silver from a bet of only 50 taels, even to the point that carts and horses, property and houses, singing beauties and dancing girls have all been wagered and won for an agreed-upon price. In addition to well-known games like "try the big head" and "happy at three," there are others too numerous to mention.

The fish, lotus, and fruits presented by the Office of the Reservoir and Park are rewarded at imperial pleasure according to their quality. The miniature dragon boats built by the Construction Bureau of the River Palace, carved from ivory and inlaid with jade, are the acme of artistry. Among those entertainers who accompanied the Son of Heaven to perform at the reservoir during the Xuanhe [1119–1125] and Zhenghe [1111–1118] reigns were: Multitalented Zhang, Mr. Eyes-All-Over, Whiff-of-Immortality Song, and Yin Shi'an, all of whom performed on strings, as well as Unflappable Li, who operated water puppets. The others are too numerous to count.

Food at the reservoir: rice gruel, chilled sweet green pea soup, snails, plum wine, dried haw fruit, dried apricots, flowering apricot, crisp plums in fragrant herbs, freshly cut fish mince, black carp, salted duck eggs, and various kinds of spicy pickled vegetables. After the water exercises are finished, on flat black-lacquered boats pulled by two hawsers, noble families set up their own household music and float about the reservoir. During the Xuanhe and Zhenghe reigns there were also large and small boats for rent, and commoners were allowed use of the boats for pleasure. Their prices varied.

"Searching Out the Spring"

After the lamps have been brought in, people of the capital strive to be the first to go out of the city walls to "search out the spring."

South of the City: the Garden of the Jade Ford, which imitated the rectangular pond, the pavilions, and kiosks of other places, and the Belvedere of the Jade Transcendent.

Going westward from Twisting Dragon Bend are the Ten Foot Buddha's Garden, the Garden of Grand Marshal Wang, and Meng Jingchu's Garden, which is located in front of the Revered Sage Temple, the Ridge for "Looking at the Reclining Ox," and the Shrine to the Knight Errant of the Sword. Eastward from Twisting Dragon Bend there are even more gardens outside of Chen Prefecture Gate.

Outside of the Song Prefecture Gate on the east of the City are the Grove of Delight, Water Chestnut Reservoir, the Ridge of Solitary Pleasures, Inkstone Terrace, Spider Loft, and the Mai Family Garden. At Rainbow Bridge is the Wang Family Garden. Between Cao Prefecture Gate and the Song Gate is the Eastern Imperial Garden, and the Qianming Exalting Xia Nunnery.

North of the City is the Garden of Prince Consort Li.

West of the City the grand avenue of the New Zheng Prefecture Gate goes directly past the Reservoir of Metal's Luster: westward from there is a Daoist Cloister, in front of which are nothing but brothels. Farther westward is the Loft for Feasting Guests. Here are pavilions and kiosks, twisting and turning ponds and dikes, swings and painted boats. Drinkers can rent small craft on which to hold their feasts and float around to sightsee. It is just opposite the Belvedere of Auspicious Fortune and runs all the way to Plankbridge, where there are the Loft of Gathered Worthies and the Loft of Lotus Blossoms—both of which are "parting restaurants" for those going on official duties along the five highways that lead to Hedong and Shaanxi. This is where banquets are normally held to send people off. Past Plankbridge are Lower Pine Garden, Grand Minister Wang's Garden, and Apricot Blossom Ridge.

Southward, along the Alley of the Winged Tigers of the Water that runs from the corner of the Reservoir of Metal's Luster, downstream from the watermill is the Garden of Grand Preceptor Cai. South of that are the Nunnery of the Garland Sutra and Little Missy Wang's Wineshop in an alley just west of Horse-Washing Bridge. Northward, along the Golden Water River is the Nunnery of the Two Zhes, the Baluo Monastery, and the Seed Raising Garden—here the flowers and trees of all four seasons are in the thickest profusion to behold. Southward are the Liang Medicinal Herb Garden and the Garden of Grand Preceptor Tong. Further southward are the Monastery of the Iron Buddha, the Monastery of Great Fortune, and the Eastern and Western Villages of Cypress and Elm.

North of the City: Pattern-on-Heaven Slope, Cornerbridge, all the way to King Cang Jie's Shrine, the Nunnery of the Eighteen Longlife Sages, and Codger Meng the Fourth's Wineshop. Northwest of the City were originally Commoner's Garden,

Cang Jie's Terrace, and several "cup-floating" pavilions and kiosks where people were allowed in to enjoy the spring.

Generally, the environs of the capital were replete with gardens and orchards, and there is no empty space within a hundred *li*. One after the other, fallow lands fill out with the face of spring, the pitchpipes of spring loudly proclaim clear weather, thousands and thousands of flowers strive with each other to blossom. Lithe willows lean to embrace whitewashed walls; on interlaced paths sandalwood wheels turn in the warmth, fragrant grasses are like a carpet; proud mounts neigh with head held high, apricot blossoms are like an embroidery; orioles twitter in the fragrant trees, swallows dance in the clear void. Red make-up sets tunes to music in the jeweled kiosks and storied towers, white faces sing as they walk, drawing near painted bridges and flowing waters. Raise the eyes and there are coy laughs swinging on swings, come upon any place and there is wild abandon kicking the ball. Pick the best place to search out the fragrance, and flowers and catkins drop into golden goblets; snap off kingfisher green, stick red into the hair, and bees and butterflies secretly follow homeward-bound mounts. This is then all continued by the Festival of Clear and Bright.

PART 2

PRIVATE GARDENS

It was in the Song dynasty that the Chinese social structure shifted decisively from aristocratic government to bureaucratic government.[12] The qualification for office changed from pedigree to education. The scholar-official ("mandarin") class became the dominant class in society; even those members who were unable to attain office formed the elite in their locality and expected to play a prominent role in local affairs. The intellectual and cultural interests of the scholar-official class started to set standards for society as a whole. We see, for example, significant changes in literature and the visual arts in this period, as well as, more noticeably, in philosophy. What is now called neo-Confucianism (in Chinese, *daoxue*, the study of the Way, or *lixue*, the study of principle) developed partly as a reaction against the dominance of Buddhism in the Tang dynasty. Buddhism had appealed to both the court and the common people; neo-Confucianism was an ideology specific to the scholar-official class (although its emphasis on ritual and loyalty within a hierarchical system was also very advantageous to the imperial court).

---

12   On this shift and its intellectual underpinnings, see Peter K. Bol, *"This Culture of Ours": Intellectual Transitions in T'ang and Sung China* (Stanford: Stanford University Press, 1992).

It is no coincidence that private gardens belonging to individuals who might or might not be wealthy first became widespread during the Song dynasty. In the Tang dynasty, the gardens for which information has survived were mostly those belonging to members of the imperial family or to the great landowning aristocratic families. In the Song, we start to hear of many more gardens belonging to senior government officials, who in many cases—because of the association between literary ability and government office brought about by the imperial examination system—were also distinguished literary men. These men wrote prolifically in both prose and verse about their gardens and those of their friends and associates; many examples appear in this section. They might use the garden to affirm their place in Confucian tradition, as Sima Guang does by the naming of features in his Garden of Solitary Enjoyment, or as a manifestation of a correct ideological orientation, as Su Shi does in his "Record of the Zhang Family Garden at Lingbi." Alternatively, the garden might be presented as a place of quiet retreat (as in Shen Gua's Dream Stream) or of withdrawal from the scholar-official's duty to govern for the good of society, as some of Sima Guang's friends suggest by way of urging him to return to official activity. It is clear that while gardens in the Tang were primarily sites in which to demonstrate wealth and celebrate social connections, private gardens in the Song—while also fulfilling these functions— had a much more prominent ideological content, which served to advance the self-image of the scholar-official class.

The previous section of this chapter demonstrates that ordinary people made use of imperial gardens in their own ways, and this appears to have been the case also for well-known private gardens, which might be opened to the public at certain times of the year. We know, for example, that Sima Guang's garden in Luoyang was visited by the public during the New Year festivities, on payment of a fee to the head gardener (one thinks of Elizabeth Bennet and her relatives visiting Mr. Darcy's Pemberley estate in Jane Austen's *Pride and Prejudice*). As far as we know, private gardens in previous dynasties were closed to outsiders and did not play this public role. The relative openness of Song private gardens, compared to Tang, was part of the scholar-official class's move to assert their standing in local society.

As neo-Confucian thought placed a growing emphasis on individual sensibility—an intellectual trend that would come to fruition in the mid-to-late Ming—the private garden also became the locus for romance, as in the story of Lu You's meeting with his former wife (see the final poem in this section). This is a contrast to the cautionary tales of sexual excess associated with grand gardens in earlier dynasties (such as the stories about the wicked king Zhou, the last ruler of the Shang dynasty, and his concubine Daji, or Shi Chong's Golden Valley Garden; see chapter 1). By comparison with earlier gardens, the private garden in the Song dynasty has become a domestic space.

"An Account of the Garden of Solitary Enjoyment" (*Duleyuan ji* 獨樂園記),
"The Garden of Solitary Enjoyment: Seven Songs" (*Dule yuan qi yong* 獨樂園七詠),
"In Response to a Poem by Vice-Minister Zhao on My Plot of Herbs" (*Chou Zhao shaoqing Yaoyuan jian zeng* 酬趙少卿藥園見贈), and "Two Quatrains in Reply to Anzhi Thanking Me for My Herb Transplants" (*Chou Anzhi xie yaozai er zhang* 酬安之謝藥栽二章)

SIMA GUANG 司馬光 (1019–1086)

Sima Guang (formal name Junshi) was an official who was actively involved in the political controversies of the eleventh century, opposing the financial reforms introduced by Wang Anshi (1021–1086). He was also a notable historian, writing *A Comprehensive Mirror for the Aid of Government*, a monumental history from the Warring States (475–221 BCE) down to the end of the Five Dynasties (907–960 CE), which was modeled on the great Han dynasty historian Sima Qian's (ca. 145–ca. 85 BCE) *Records of the Grand Historian* (*Shiji*). The *Comprehensive Mirror for the Aid of Government* was written during one of Sima Guang's periods out of office, when he was in disagreement with the government officials in power. He adopted the self-deprecatory name "Old Pedant"; the word translated as "pedant" also suggests the idea of contrariness or "someone who runs against the grain." This is how he refers to himself in "An Account of the Garden of Solitary Enjoyment," which was also written during the period when Sima Guang was resident in Luoyang, at a distance from the capital Bianliang (modern Kaifeng). Luoyang was a city with a long history as a center of imperial power, which in the Song became a locus for the emergence of voices of literati autonomy from court control. The tone of this text is slightly defensive, as though Sima Guang is responding to actual or potential criticism for his self-indulgence in making and enjoying his garden. The essay gives what seems mainly to be a factual description of the garden, while the related poem sequence goes into more detail on the allusions behind the names of the features in his garden, relating his own feelings and experiences to those of earlier writers or historical figures.[13]

"An Account of the Garden of Solitary Enjoyment"

TRANSLATED BY JAMES M. HARGETT

Mencius once said: "Enjoying music in solitude is not as enjoyable as enjoying music with others; enjoying music with the few is not as enjoyable as enjoying music with the many."[14] He was speaking of the enjoyment of kings, nobles, and great men, and this is not something that the poor and humble can attain. Confucius once said: "Eating coarse rice, drinking water, and pillowing on a bent arm—there is enjoyment in these things as well."[15] Yanzi took his meals from a single bamboo container, drank from a

---

13 For a detailed discussion of these names, see Robert E. Harrist Jr., "Site Names and Their Meanings in the Garden of Solitary Enjoyment," *The Journal of Garden History* 13, no. 4 (1993):199–212.

14 *Mencius* 2A:9

15 *Analects* VII:26

single gourd, but it never diminished his enjoyment.[16] This is the enjoyment of sages and worthies, and not something that fools can attain. Now, for the wren that nests in the forest, needing nothing more than a single branch, or the mole that drinks at the river, wanting nothing more than a full stomach, each fulfills its allotment and is content with it. This is precisely what the Old Pedant enjoys.

In the fourth year of the Serene Peace reign [1071], the Old Pedant began his residence in Luoyang. In the sixth year [1073], he bought twenty *mu* of farmland in order to construct a garden in the Revering the Worthies Ward of the northern section of the city. Inside it he built a hall and stocked it with books from home numbering 5,000 volumes. This he named the Reading Hall. South of the hall there is a group of buildings. A stream led to flow northward passes below their eaves. A pool was made in the center, three *chi* square and deep. The stream separates into five parts; the branches pour into the pool like a tiger's claw. From north of the pool the branches flow underground and emerge at the north steps. It then cascades and pours down into the courtyard like an elephant's trunk. From here it divides into two channels, which ring the four corners of the courtyard. They rejoin in the northwest and exit the garden. This he named the Dallying with Water Gallery.

North of the hall another pool was made. In its center is an islet. Bamboo is planted on the islet. The islet is round like a jade ring. It measures three *zhang* in circumference. The tips of the bamboo there are fastened and tied together like those on a fisherman's cottage. This he named the Fishing Hut.

North of the pool there is a horizontal structure with six bays. The Old Pedant thickened its clay walls and thatched roof so as to counter the intense heat of the sun. Its door opens out to the east. Arrayed from north to south are lattice windows so as to invite cool breezes. In front and back are planted numerous attractive bamboos, making this a place that dispels the summer heat. This he named the Planting Bamboo Studio.

East of the pond he arranged the land into 120 plots, with an assortment of dill, plants, and medicinal herbs arranged according to their names. North of the plots he planted bamboo, in squares like those on a chessboard, measuring one *zhang* across. He bent their tips and joined them together into a canopy in order to make a structure. The bamboos in front of it line the path so that it resembles a strolling veranda, with creepers and herbal plants covering it everywhere. On each of the four sides he planted woody herbal plants to make a protective hedge. This he named the Gathering Herbs Patch.

---

16   *Analects* VI:22

South of the patch he made six pens. Herbaceous peonies, tree peonies, and assorted flowers occupy two pens each. Each variety planted is limited to two samples, simply for the purpose of recognizing their name and appearance, not to aim at having many. North of the pens he made a pavilion. This he named the Watering Flowers Pavilion. Luoyang City is not far from the mountains, yet its forests and brush are thick and dense. Often it seems the mountains are not visible from there. And so in the garden he constructed a terrace with a transverse structure on top of it in order to gaze upon Wan'an and Huanyuan and even to Taishi.[17] This he named the Viewing Mountains Terrace.

On most days the Old Pedant can be found in the hall reading. On the highest level he chooses his teachers from among the sages; on the secondary level he chooses his friends from among the assembled worthies. He pries into the origins of humanity and righteousness; searches out the sources of ceremony and music. The timeless principles of all things that existed before matter took form and that exist beyond infinity of the four directions—these arise and gather before his eyes. His only shortcoming is that his study of these principles has not yet reached perfection. So why, then, seek this knowledge from others? Indeed, why wait for it to come from the outside? When his resolve is weary and his body is tired, he casts his rod to catch a fish, holds up his gown and gathers herbs, dredges ditches and waters flowers, wields an axe and splits bamboo, and pours out hot water to cleanse his hands. From heights his eyes scan at will. Footloose and fancy-free, he lingers about, pursuing only what interests him. When bright moonlight arrives or when clear breezes come of their own accord, nothing holds back his movements, nothing blocks his way. He has complete control over what he sees, what he hears, what he inhales, and what he exhales. He walks alone here! He is boundless here! And he is unaware of any other place between heaven and earth so joyous that it could replace this spot. He thus combined these qualities and named it: Garden of Solitary Enjoyment.

Someone faulted the Old Pedant, saying: "I've heard that whatever delights the Superior Man must be shared with others. Now you, Sir, alone have gotten enough for yourself, but you do not extend it to others. Is this acceptable?" The Old Pedant offered apologies, saying: "How can an old fool be compared to a Superior Man? My only fear is not having done enough to enjoy myself. How, then, could my enjoyment be extended to others? Moreover, what delights this old man is trivial and common, humble and rustic, all of which have been rejected by the world. Although you recommend I extend these delights to others, they will just reject them. How, then, can I force them? It is certain that if there were people willing to share these joys I would then twice bow down and make them offerings. How could I dare to monopolize them myself?

---

17 Wan'an, Huanyuan, and Taishi are names of mountains in the general vicinity of Luoyang. The last of these, Taishi, refers to Mount Song (*Songshan* 嵩山), one of China's Five Sacred Marchmounts (*Wuyue* 五嶽).

GARDENS OF THE SONG DYNASTY

"The Garden of Solitary Enjoyment: Seven Songs"

TRANSLATED BY JAMES M. HARGETT

One: "The Reading Hall"
How I admire Dong Zhongshu!
He probed the classics while guarding seclusion and privacy.
Though where he lived there was a garden,
For three years his eyes never wandered there.
Depraved doctrines—far and distant from his ears;
Sagely words—filled and satisfied his belly.
When he sent forth slips and ascended the Han Court,
The Hundred Schools began to fade and submit.[18]

Two: "The Fishing Hut"
How I admire Yan Guang!
In wooly furs he fished in rocky rapids.
Although the emperor was an old friend,
He searched high and low, but Guang could never be found.
A ducal minister post—how could this not bring him great honor?
Yet high office was not enough to compromise Guang's integrity.
What need did he have to be a boaster and flatterer,
Who, for a meager official salary, would feign a hundred demeanors?[19]

Three: "Gathering Herbs Patch"
How I admire Han Kang!
He gathered herbs and sold them in the capital market.
Kang had a conscience, so how could he cheat anyone?
For this reason he never sold his goods at two prices.

---

18   Lines 3–4: Before entering government service, Dong Zhongshu was a model scholar. One account says that he was so diligent in his reading that at one point he closed the window blinds in his house and for three years never once looked out into his garden. Lines 7–8: Some of the ideas that Dong Zhongshu suggested to Emperor Wu of the Han (r. 141–87 BCE) were responsible for establishing the thought of Confucius as the official state ideology of the Han dynasty. As a result, various contending ideas from the "Hundred Schools of Thought" began to "fade and submit." The expression "send forth slips" (*face* 發策) usually means "set out the topics for the imperial examinations," though here it might also refer to Dong Zhongshu's replies to policy questions from the emperor, which (presumably) were written on bamboo or wooden slips (*ce* 策).

19   Yan Guang was a boyhood friend of Liu Xiu, who later became Emperor Guangwu of the Han (r. 25–57). Although summoned to public office by the emperor, Yan Guang steadfastly refused and instead lived as a recluse in the mountains of central Zhejiang. He often fished at a place that later became known as the Yan Ling Rapids (*Yan Ling lai* 嚴陵瀨). Line 2: Yan Guang was once spotted wearing a "wooly fur coat" (*yangqiu* 羊裘) while fishing. Lines 5–6: These lines are inspired by a passage in the *Mencius* (13A:105): "Hui of Liuxia would never have compromised his integrity for the sake of a ducal minister post." "Ducal minister" (*sangong* 三公) is a collective reference to the top three ministerial posts of the Han government.

But what was he to do about the girl
Who figured out who he was?
So he ran off scared, to the farthest ends of the mountains,
Where, deep in fear, he was encumbered by fame.[20]

Four: "Viewing Mountains Terrace"
How I admire Tao Qian!
Shaking the dust from his clothes, he left office forever.
Waving his hand to decline the Liang ruler's command;
Like a sacrificial bull, he dreaded the gilded yoke.
He revered his prince—how could his heart ever forget that?
Yet when living in mountains one's spirit can be nurtured.
It's been a thousand years since his "rash deed,"
Yet today I still admire his lofty spirit.[21]

Five: "Dallying With Water Gallery"
How I admire Du Mu!
In nature and temper he was always lofty and free.
Completing his pavilion by the edge of a stream,
He rambled and frolicked, passing away the long days.
He washed his ink stone so he could copy out his poems;
When floating wine cups found it fitting to draw in his knees.
Do not choose to wash the tassel of the cap,
For red dust pollutes the pure and upright.[22]

---

20   Line 1: According to one well-known account, Han Kang (fl. ca. 147–167) often picked herbs on famous mountains, and then sold them in the markets at Chang'an, always at the same price (as common herbs). He did this for more than thirty years until one day, while selling herbs at market, he refused to give a cheaper price to a young girl, who then became angry. The girl subsequently realized that this man must be none other than Han Kang (because he would only sell at one price). Frightened because he wished to maintain his anonymity (and thereby preserve his integrity), Han Kang supposedly ran off to live in the mountains.

21   Title: The name of Sima Guang's terrace is drawn from a couplet in the fifth of Tao Qian's twenty famous "Drinking Wine" poems, as found in chapter 1: "I pick chrysanthemums under the eastern hedge, / I gaze off at South Mountain." Line 2: *Fuyi* 拂衣 ("shake the dust from one's clothes") is a trope meaning "leave government service and retire to the mountains or countryside." Line 7: There is wordplay in this line; specifically, Sima Guang's use of the expression *qingju* 輕舉 (literally, "lightly/gently arise"). This term is often used in the sense of "to act rashly or blindly." Another common gloss is *yindun* 隱遁 (to hide; to escape; run off). And finally, *qingju* can also mean *dengxian* 登仙, or "ascend and become an immortal." Now, in the context of this verse, all three meanings of *qingju* seem to be working at the same time: (1) Tao Qian acted rashly or blindly by resigning from his official post; (2) Tao Qian left his government job to run off or escape to the countryside in order to nurture his spirit and be free of the shackles or yoke of government service; and (3) Tao Qian's lofty integrity has resulted in his becoming an immortal (in the figurative sense). The decision to follow the first of these glosses in the translation is arbitrary.

22   Du Mu (803–853) is a well-known poet and essay writer of the Tang dynasty. While serving as prefect of Chizhou, he erected a building there named the Dallying with Water Pavilion (*Nongshui ting* 弄水亭). There

Six: "Planting Bamboo Studio"
How I admire Wang Huizhi!
Even at a rented house he planted bamboo!
He couldn't live a day without them;
Felt relaxed and at ease when they were constantly in sight.
Snow and frost only come from evanescent whiteness,
But bamboo stalks and leaves never lose their green.
Wang Huizhi's fate was far superior to that of Shi Chong,
Whose coral treasures filled the Golden Valley.[23]

Seven: "Watering Flowers Kiosk"
How I admire Bai Juyi!
After retiring he made his home on Walkway Lane.
He brewed wine, and when the wine was ripe,
He watered his flowers, and the flowers were perfect.
He composed poems and sent invitations to guests and friends;
Beside railings he was forever falling down drunk.
His painting has been handed down until today:
Those revelers are known as the Nine Elders.[24]

"In Response to a Poem by Vice-Minister Zhao on My Plot of Herbs"

TRANSLATED BY XIAOSHAN YANG

My humble disposition is stubbornly impractical and eccentric;
My garden I named "Solitary Enjoyment."
The whole city vies to grow flowers;

---

was a stream in front of the pavilion where he would sometimes wash his ink stone. Line 6: "Floating wine cups" (*fanshang* 泛觞) refers to the ancient custom of placing a wine cup on a large lotus leaf and then delivering it to guests downstream, either by a favorable current or with a skillful push. The expression "draw in his knees" (*cuxi* 促膝) means to sit in very close proximity to someone else, especially while chatting or drinking. Sima Guang seems to be referring here to Du Mu's intimate social gatherings with friends. Lines 7–8: On "Wash the cap tassel" (*zhuo guanying* 濯冠缨) see *Mencius* IVA.8, as given in chapter 1. "Red dust" (*hongchen* 紅塵) is a Buddhist term that refers to the mundane world. The last two lines of Sima Guang's poem might be paraphrased something like this: "Don't make preparations to take up a government position, for the 'red dust' of the human world will only pollute your pure and upright character."

23 Wang Huizhi (d. 388) was the fifth son of the famous calligrapher Wang Xizhi. Wang Huizhi is perhaps best known for his undisciplined and eccentric personality and his obsession with bamboo (see chapter 1). Lines 7 and 8: On Shi Chong (249–300), see both his own "Preface to Golden Valley Poems" and the biography of him in chapter 1.

24 Line 1: "Walkway Lane" refers to the Lüdao Ward, where Bai Juyi's garden was (see chapter 2). Lines 7 and 8: Bai Juyi had a circle of friends in Luoyang known as the "Nine Elders" (*Jiulao* 九老). In 845, they assembled at his garden, and Bai painted a portrait of the group. His painting is no longer extant.

To cultivate my land, I only grow herbs.
Personally shouldering a hoe, I transplant them;
Frequently emptying my money bag, I purchase them.
With over a hundred plots crisscrossing;
I regret my knowledge is not vast.
When I cannot yet cure the diseases of my own body,
How can I talk about remedying the ailment of the people?

"Two Quatrains in Reply to Anzhi[25] Thanking Me for My Herb Transplants"
TRANSLATED BY XIAOSHAN YANG

No. 1
The residents of Luoyang plant flowers, not herbs;
How idiosyncratic is the partiality of men of our type.
Although taking herbs can stop hundreds of illnesses,
Not to be cured is the disease of our love of leisure.

No. 2
With earth protecting their roots, I personally moved them;
Carrying a hoe and channeling the spring water, you personally planted them.
To please the eye, we should eradicate the evil weeds;
Supporting the endangered, we treasure them more than refined gold.

"Harmonizing with Junkuang's Poem on the Eastern Estate of the Duke of Lu" (*He Junkuang Lu gong Dongzhuang* 和君貺潞公東莊)

SIMA GUANG 司馬光
TRANSLATED BY XIAOSHAN YANG

The surname and identity of "Junkuang," to whose poem Sima Guang is responding, appear to be unknown, and the poem is not known to survive. Duke of Lu was the title of Wen Yanbo (1006–1097), a noted chancellor who served under four Song emperors. This poem, ostensibly about a garden estate, carries an implicit criticism of the political situation at the time.

"Harmonizing with Junkuang's Poem on the Eastern Estate of the Duke of Lu"

High peaks in the distance overlap with a thousand miles of snow;
A patch of sky lowers down to the bank of the Yi River.
A hundred acres of level field extending from your villa,

---

25   Editor's note: Wang Anzhi (not to be confused with Sima Guang's political opponent Wang Anshi) was a poet of the Song dynasty.

Two lines of sparse willow trees brushing the clear spring.
The country wants a rock pillar to prop its colossal structure;
The people need a towering ship to cross a grand river.[26]
You, like Prime Minister Xiao, the right hand of the emperor,[27]
Settled on the idle land in a desolate and remote spot.

"Harmonizing with Junshi's Poem on 'Purchasing the Estate at the Stream of Piled Rocks'" (*He Junshi xin mai Dieshi xi zhuang* 和君實新買疊石溪莊)

FAN ZHEN 范鎮 (1008–1089)

TRANSLATED BY XIAOSHAN YANG

Sima Guang's friend Fan Zhen achieved first place in the Palace Examination of 1038, and subsequently became known as an official who did not hesitate to speak his mind on matters of state. In the policy disputes of the eleventh century, he opposed Wang Anshi and supported Sima Guang. In the following poem, he urges Sima Guang (Junshi) to come out of retirement and participate in government. Fan was a convinced Confucian, with no time for Daoism or Buddhism. Like his friend, he was a noted historian and literary man; his tomb inscription was composed by the great writer Su Shi (see below and chapter 3).

"Harmonizing with Junshi's Poem on 'Purchasing the Estate at the Stream of Piled Rocks'"

Only when painted will the foot of a snake be known as superfluous;
Through the hole of a pipe how can the spots of a leopard be fully recognized?
Those who possess the Way should always help the world;
I do not understand why you live in the mountains at the time of peace.
With your profound learning and widespread fame, it is difficult for you to hide;
Only a man like myself, with eyes dizzy and heart pumping, can get to be idle.
I figure that you, facing the scenery by the stream of Piled Mountain,
Would not be able to idle away the days of your life.

---

26   Editor's note: this couplet contains two classical allusions to the role of loyal ministers of state.

27   Editor's note: Xiao He (d. 193 BCE), the right-hand man of Liu Bang, founder of the Han dynasty, was eventually obliged by the emperor's jealousy to retire to a simple house in a remote location. Sima Guang implies that the political situation of Wen Yanbo is similar.

"Sima Junshi's Garden of Solitary Enjoyment" (*Sima Junshi Dule yuan* 司馬君實獨樂園)

SU SHI 蘇軾 (1037–1101)

TRANSLATED BY XIAOSHAN YANG

For Su Shi, see chapter 3. In this poem, Su Shi is responding to Sima Guang (Junshi), who has sent him a copy of "An Account of the Garden of Solitary Enjoyment." Like Fan Zhen, Su Shi implicitly urges Sima Guang to come out of retirement and take his proper part in government.

"Sima Junshi's Garden of Solitary Enjoyment"

Above your house there are green mountains;
Below your house there are flowing rivers.
Inside there is a garden of five *mu*,
Where flowers and bamboo are both elegant and wild.
The fragrance of the flower assails your cane and shoes;
The color of the bamboo invades your cup and flagon.
With goblets of wine you enjoy the late spring;
With chess games you spend the long summer.
Luoyang has seen many gentlemen since ancient times;
Its customs remain lofty today.
You, Sir, lie at home and do not go out,
Yet you attract everybody from the clubs of Luoyang.
Although you share your joy with everybody else,
There is something in which you take joy in solitude.
Your talent is perfect, but your virtues are not shown outside;
You take pride in your being known by few.
Why are you, Sir, talking about being solitary?—
The four seas look to you for edification.
Children sing of Junshi;
Footmen know about Sima.
Where would you turn with all this?
The Fashioner-of-Things wouldn't let you go.
Fame chases the likes of us—
Such is the penalty inflicted by Heaven.
Clapping my hands, I laugh at you, Sir,
For imitating the deaf and the mute for years.

"Sitting Alone in the Flower Hut" (*Huaan du zuo* 花庵獨坐)

SIMA GUANG 司馬光

TRANSLATED BY XIAOSHAN YANG

A desolate garden, on a mere *mu* of land:
With my mind content, I still consider it too much.
Although not living in hills and valleys,
I constantly feel I am hiding among fig-leaves and rabbit-floss.
As I have forgotten about machinations, birds come down from the woods;
When I look into the distance, wild geese fly by toward the frontier.
To the guest from court and market, I ask,
How thick is the red dust out there?

"Matching Junshi Duanming's 'Sitting Alone in the Flower Hut'" (*He Junshi Duanming Huaan du zuo* 和君實端明花庵獨坐)

SHAO YONG 邵雍 (1011–1077)

TRANSLATED BY XIAOSHAN YANG

This poem is a response by Shao Yong to the preceding poem by Sima Guang (named here as Junshi Duanming) on the Flower Hut in a small garden beside his official residence in Luoyang; this was before the construction of the Garden of Solitary Enjoyment. Shao Yong was a noted philosopher who made a living by teaching and avoided official service; he was closely associated with such eminent neo-Confucians as the Cheng brothers, Zhou Dunyi, and Zhang Zai.

"Matching Junshi Duanming's 'Sitting Alone in the Flower Hut'"

Sitting quietly, you nourish your innate harmony,
From whence much is attained.
Deep and cavernous, like a grand edifice,
Dense are the wisterias it draws.
Forgetting about the manners of a noble minister,
You can accommodate a rustic guest passing by.
Heavy are the weal and woe of the time tied up with you,
And yet you would never talk about how you feel.

"My Account of Dream Stream" (*Mengxi zi ji* 夢溪自記)

SHEN GUA 沈括 (CA. 1031–1095)

TRANSLATED BY RICHARD E. STRASSBERG

The official and polymath Shen Gua (sometimes transcribed as Shen Kuo) was an adherent of Wang Anshi's faction, and thus a political opponent of Sima Guang and his associates. Nevertheless, it is clear that despite policy differences, there was a strong shared culture among the scholar-official class in the Song dynasty. Among other accomplishments, Shen was an astronomer who developed the use of the magnetic needle compass and the concept of true north. Shen's Dream Stream Garden, described below, was an estate on the outskirts of Zhenjiang (in present-day Jiangxi Province) to which he retired after being removed from office in the 1080s, following a military disaster for which he was not in fact responsible, until his death in 1095. Under the title *Dream Stream Brush Talks*, he compiled notes on a wide variety of topics reflecting his lifelong interest in the natural world and technology in addition to literature.

"My Account of Dream Stream"

I was but a few years past thirty when I dreamt that I had arrived at a place where I climbed a hill that was covered by a tapestry of flowers and trees. There was a stream at the foot of the hill, crystal clear as far down as the eyes could see, while tall trees formed a shady canopy above. In this dream of mine, I was delighted with the place and planned on dwelling here. Ever since that year, I dreamt about going to this place not once or twice, but three or four times, so that I felt that it was as familiar as if I had visited it in the course of my life. More than ten years later, I was demoted and exiled to serve as magistrate of Xuancheng. There was a monk named "Nothing-Beyond" who told me about the scenic beauty of Jingkou and, further, that there was a man of the town who had a vegetable plot for sale. He took this opportunity to persuade me to buy it for three hundred thousand in cash,[28] though I did not know where exactly it was located. After another six years had passed, I was further demoted due to the controversies at court over border defenses, so I made my home at Flatiron Cave in Xunyang and traveled to Hermitage Mountain, where I planned to spend the rest of my life.

In the first year of the Yuanyou reign period [1086], I went to Jingkou and visited the garden that the monk had established. Suddenly, I realized this was the very place I had dreamt about. I sighed and said, "This is where my destiny lies." Therefore, I abandoned my home in Xunyang and established a residence at the edge of Jingkou. The immense trees form a luxurious cover and a stream emerges from a canyon. This meanders, winding its way around the property on one side. I looked at it and said, "Dream Stream." The land along the stream rises straight upward to form a hill that a thousand

---

28   The figure of three hundred thousand cash appears to be out of keeping with what we know of both official salaries and prices for gardens at this time and is probably a textual error.

flowering plants cling to. This is the Pile of a Hundred Flowers. Midway up the pile, I built a house which was to be my perch. To the west, hidden among the flowers and bamboo, is the Nutshell Studio where I relax. The view from the studio takes in a pavilion crouching among the paths, dominated by giant trees rising a hundred *xun* above it. This is the Pavilion Among the Pile of Flowers. A retreat built of grasses propped against the summit of the pile is the Proud in Old Age Hall. With its back toward the hall and overlooking the face of Dream Stream is the Viridian Canyon Pavilion. West of the Pavilion Among the Pile of Flowers grow a myriad stalks of bamboo that form an encirclement and stir up ripples in the stream. This is the Bamboo Harbor. Southward past the bamboo, a narrow path along the stream becomes even tighter as it runs beside a wall—this is Apricot-Mouth. A place among the bamboo where banquets can be held is the Rustling Wind Hall. South of the shady bamboo, the pavilion by the waterside is Remote Studio. Located on top of rocks piled up to provide a panoramic scene is the Distant-View Pavilion.

I dwell within the city in a place where deer and pigs live among dense overgrowth and ancient trees. Some guests who visit depart with frowns on their faces, but I myself take delight in this place. I fish in the spring, go boating in the deep water, gaze upward and peer downward amid the flourishing trees and beautiful shade. The ancients I admire are Tao Qian, Bai Juyi, and Li Yue whom I call the "Three Contented Ones." Here I share a drink with them, along with those things in which I lodge my mind and my eyes: *qin*, chess, meditation, ink, cinnabar, tea, poetry, conversation, and wine, whom I call the "Nine Guests." I had been living here for four years when illness befell me. In the course of a year, my condition has deteriorated, and I have become like a withered tree. Am I not destined to take leave of this life here?

"Record of the Zhang Family Garden at Lingbi" (*Lingbi Zhang shi yuanting ji* 靈璧張氏園亭記)

SU SHI 蘇軾
TRANSLATED BY STEPHEN H. WEST

For Su Shi, see chapter 3.

"Record of the Zhang Family Garden at Lingbi"

The road east from the capital is traveled on by floating along the turbid flow of the canal or treading the yellow dust of the road. The fields and paddies stretch endlessly on, and in the end the traveler grows weary and loses interest in the scenery. After about eight hundred *li*, you finally reach the garden of Mr. Zhang at Lingbi, on the northern banks of the Bian Canal. From the outside the long bamboos are luxuriant and reach high into the sky, and the great trees are lush and deep. Inside, they have relied on seepage from the Bian to make ponds and pools, and have taken marvelous rocks from the mountains in order to make cliffs and mountains. In the calamus, reeds, lotus, and caltrops there one experiences the feeling of rivers and lakes. With the wonder tree, the plane tree, Chinese junipers, and cypress trees, it holds the aura of mountain forests. Rare flowers and beautiful grasses give it the manner of the capital, Kaifeng, and Luoyang regions. The painted halls and large buildings possess the cleverness of the regions of Wu and Shu. In its depths one can retreat away, in its richness one can be nurtured. The fruits and vegetables can give the neighbors their fill, and its fish, soft-shell turtles, bamboo shoots, and tubers can provide food for guests and travelers from the four directions.

I boarded the boat in Song Prefecture when I moved from Pengcheng to serve as magistrate in Wuxing, and reached here after three days' travel. I went by palanquin to knock at their gate, and I saw one of the sons of the Zhang family, Shi. Shi asked me for some writing to make a record of this.

Now the Zhang family has had eminent men for generations. They first came to reside in Lingbi in the time of his paternal elder uncle, the Palace Administrator, and his father, Grand Counselor of the Prefect, constructed this garden here, building the Pavilion of the Orchid Marsh in order to nurture their kin. When his posterity went out from here to serve as officials of the court, their names were renowned in their own time; he spent his remaining energies to augment and repair the garden—and this has been a period now of more than fifty years. Now the trees are all ten arm-spans in circumference and the banks and valleys are consequently hidden away. Every single one of the hundred things in the garden delights a person—these verify the amount of energy and time spent.

Ancient men of worth did not have to enter into public service, nor did they have to not enter public service. If they had to enter service, then they "forgot about their own bodies"; if they considered it necessary not to enter service, they "forgot about their lord." This can be compared to food and drink: always find the proper balance between hunger and satiety. This being the case, a man of learning seldom is able to tread the path of righteousness, or sacrifice himself to maintain his integrity. Those who stay in the private sphere find secure happiness in customary habit and are troubled by going out; those who do go out are seduced by self-benefit and forget to return. At this point one is subject to the criticism of thinking that one "surpasses" the customs of the times and of turning one's back on the support of one's parents; or one has the faults of coveting a salary and doing whatever is necessary to stay secure.

So, Mr. Zhang's father made farsighted and complete plans for his offspring, and for this reason built dwellings and planted a garden between the Bian and Si Rivers, a place where boats and carts of commerce and official caps and parasols converge.

The sustenance of every day, the pleasures of feasting and roaming are here in ready plenitude. He made it so that if his offspring opened the gates to go out to serve, they could make their way through the public world; if they closed their gates and retired to secluded tranquility, then they could live their life without shame at the foot of forested hills. Whether in terms of nurturing the self and governing one's nature in retirement, or in practicing righteousness or seeking one's ambitions, there was nothing that was not perfectly suitable. Therefore, those of his offspring who went into service were all acclaimed as superior officers and able talents; those who lived in retirement all possessed the practices of men of integrity and incorruptible recluses. This is the fecundity left by his father.

I was magistrate in Pengcheng for two years and came to love the customs of its land. I could not bear leaving as the day approached, and the elders of Pengcheng also did not have their fill of me yet. I will in the future buy land on the Si River and grow old there. To the south I could gaze upon Lingbi, and hear there, far off, the sounds of its chickens and dogs. In my cloth cap and sandals and with a cane, I could come and go in all seasons of the year in Mr. Zhang's garden, there to roam with his sons and grandsons— that day will surely come. Written on the twenty-seventh day of the third month of the second year of Yuanfeng [1079].

"Record of My Plot of Joy" (*Lepu ji* 樂圃記)

ZHU CHANGWEN 朱長文 (1039–1098)
TRANSLATED BY STEPHEN H. WEST

Although Zhu Changwen (*zi* Boyuan) obtained his presented scholar degree in 1057, he did not take office, having been lamed in a riding accident, but instead lived in retirement in his native city of Suzhou, where his "Plot of Joy" was. Later, on the recommendation of Su Shi (see chapter 3 and elsewhere in this chapter), he was appointed to educational and literary positions, but subsequently went into retirement again. He is best known as a calligrapher.

"Record of My Plot of Joy"

When a great man is used by his age, then he makes a Sage King Yao of his ruler and treats his subjects like the Sage King Shun; the richness of his grace reaches to his posterity. He stands equal in fame to Ji and Xie[29] and is the match of the Duke of Zhou

---

29 These are the legendary founders of the house of Zhou and Yin. Houji's mother was impregnated when she stepped in the footprint of the Deified Ancestor. At first, his mother wanted to abandon him, but he grew up to become the Grand Agriculturalist for the Sage King Yao. He was later enfeoffed and given a new surname, Ji, which became the royal name of the Zhou house. Xie was the Minister of Ethical Studies during Yao's reign. He was enfeoffed at Shang, where he founded the Shang (or Yin) Dynasty.

and the Duke of Shao.[30] If he is not used by his age then perhaps he fishes,[31] or works on constructing walls,[32] farms, or gardens. He labors his form and gives ease to his mind, befriending Ju and Ni,[33] standing shoulder to shoulder with Huang and Qi,[34] pursuing Yan and Zheng,[35] and tracing the spoor of Tao and Bai. Their successes and failures took different turns, but their joy in life was the same. So, such people do not let loose their personal desires because of high position, nor do they give up the integrity of their existence by residing in mountain forests. Confucius once said, "I find joy in Heaven and understand my fate, therefore I am without anxiety,"[36] and he said of his disciple Yan Hui, "He lived in narrow alleys . . . yet it never spoiled his joy."[37] And this, joy found under the meanest circumstances, can be called the highest virtue. Does having named my plot "Joy" not refer to this?

In the beginning, at the time of the Qian clan, when Qian Yuanliao, then the Prince of Guangling, began in fact to serve as Protector of Gusu, he was fond of putting groves and arbors in order. His various younger siblings and cousins followed his lead and each established gardens in any available vacant space, where they made terraces and ponds. Many of these abandoned sites still exist in the city today and my garden is one of them. When the Qian clan left their state[38] the garden became a dwelling place for citizens, and it passed through the hands of many families. During the Qingli era [1041–1048] my grandmother, Madam Wu, first obtained it through a purchase. My

---

30 Dan, the Duke of Zhou, and Shi, the Duke of Shao, were two regents who governed until King Cheng of Zhou reached a suitable age to rule.

31 This refers to Lü Shang, also known as Taigong Wang, a name that literally means "the one my father yearned for." He was a virtuous and aged man who lived in retirement, fishing. King Wen of Zhou met him while hunting, and they fell into a conversation "of complete accord." King Wen took him back to the seat of government and made him a teacher. Later, Lü Shang helped King Wu defeat Yin.

32 Referring to Fu Yue, who became the chief minister to the King of Yin. The king dreamed that he would find a man to aid him at Fuyan. Fu Yue was working there, building rammed earth walls, and after the king confirmed Fu's worthiness, he raised him to the rank of high minister.

33 Two hermits of the state of Chu, Chang Ju and Jie Ni, who posed a question to Confucius's disciple (and via him to Confucius himself) about the merits of eremitism versus that of service when the plowing was interrupted [see chapter 1]. They were yoked together to pull the plow.

34 Xia Huanggong and Qili Ji, two of the "Four Hoary-Headed Ones," who avoided the political disorder and chaos of the end of the Qin by becoming hermits on Mount Shang, where they picked mushrooms. They were all over eighty and had white hair and eyebrows, hence the name given them.

35 Yan Guang, better known as Yan Ziling, was a friend of the Guangwu emperor of the Eastern or Later Han dynasty. When Guangwu ascended the throne in 25, he summoned Yan to court, but Yan preferred his life of reclusion on Fuchun Mountain, where he hobnobbed with "fishermen and woodcutters." Zheng Zizhen was a recluse who refused a post in the Western or Former Han dynasty and took up farming instead.

36 A quotation from the "Appended Words" to the *Book of Changes*.

37 A quotation from the *Analects* VI:11.

38 In 978, after they submitted to the Song dynasty and the royal family moved to Bianliang (modern Kaifeng).

grandfather and father sometimes roamed for pleasure here or sometimes studied here, and every time there was a season of beautiful sights then they would welcome their parents here to see the scenery.[39]

Later on they slightly expanded the fallow land on the west in order to extend its footprint, and wound up with a square footage that exceeded thirty hectares. I made a request to them to work on the garden in order to make a place where my father might retire in old age. At the end of the Xining era [1068–1077] I built new outer walls and completely topped them with tiles. I was just about to construct the buildings, but the years of my father did not wait for me, and once I was orphaned I returned to this place and made my own residence there. Monthly I repaired things, yearly I added something new; and now that several years have passed, and although the broken-down buildings are completely unadorned and the overgrown courtyard is unbricked, still the essential interest of the scenery is basic and wild, as though one were in the cliffs and valleys—and this is something to be admired.

In the center of the garden there is a hall complex of three bays, along the edges of which are apartments, and this is for housing my relatives and clan. South of the hall complex there is another hall complex of three bays, and I have named it Hall of Mastering the Classics; this is for lecturing and discussing the Six Arts.[40] West of Hall of Mastering the Classics is a granary for rice, and this is for accommodating annual storage. There is a crane house, which is for raising cranes. There is the Youth's Study, and this is for instructing lessons for children.

Northwest of Hall of Mastering the Classics is a high ridge and I have named it Mountain View. On the ridge is the Qin Terrace, and at the western corner of that there is the Study for Chanting—these are where I have always played the *qin* or composed poetry, so I have named them from the activities there.

Below Mountain View is a pond, the water for which enters from the northwest, and I have constructed a gate over the waterway. The water winds away from the gate, twisting and turning until it is led to the side of the Ridge; then it is led to the east as a stream and runs close to the southeastern corner. There is a pavilion in the pond, called Ink Pond, and I have previously collected the marvelous calligraphic traces of the hundred artisans here and set them out for display. There is a pavilion on the bank of the pond, called Pen Creek, and the clarity of the water can be used to wash out pens. Beside the

---

39 Zhu Changwen's grandfather was Zhu Yi; his father was Zhu Gongchuo, who had passed the Advanced Scholar Examination in 1030, had been an official in the Song, and had risen to bear the honorary rank of Grand Master of Splendid Prosperity (rank five in the nine grades of the civil service).

40 A general term for the classics; more specifically, the *Book of Changes*, *Record of the Rites*, *Book of Music*, *Book of Songs*, *Book of Documents*, and *Spring and Autumn Annals*.

stream is the Fishing Spit, and its peacefulness can be taken advantage of to drop a silk line. Fishing Spit is directly across from Hall of Mastering the Classics. There are three bridges. The one crossing directly south across the stream is called Summoning the Recluse, the one that cuts across the pond to reach to Ink Pond Pavilion is called Secluded Wonders, and when one goes north along the side of the Ridge and then crosses over the waters in the western garden there is one called West Rill.

In the western garden is a grass hut, and behind the grass hut there is a Convent of the Garland Sutra. Southwest of the grass hut is a high mound, called Western Hill. The trees there are pines and Chinese junipers, the plane tree, and cypress trees, holly, little-leaf boxwood, wonder tree, and five-stamen tamarisk. Their leaves and branches twist and turn and are set aflutter by the wind; some are tall enough to reach the clouds, thick enough for a full embrace; some straight as a line, some crooked as a hook, some tendril out as though to attach to another plant, some bend over as though resistant, some tripartite like the legs of a tripod, some side by side like the halves of a hairpin; some round as umbrellas, some deep as tents, some dormant as exuviae, some like frightened snakes gliding away—their names cannot all be remembered, their shapes cannot all be put in writing.

Even though bent by snow and frost, struck and shaken by oppressive peals of thunder, though stubs and teeth, snapped and broken—their atmosphere never deteriorates. Flowers and grass reproduce in the spring and become orphaned in the fall, bask in the sun in the winter and flourish in the summer. Precious vines and covered-over flowers shine against each other from above and below, thoroughwort and chrysanthemum meander on and on, "rushes and reeds are deep and lush," green moss covers the banks, "compassionate bamboo"[41] lines the stone steps—I have collected many plants listed in the pharmacopoeia and in elegant writing.

Mulberry and paper mulberry mean one can raise silkworms, with hemp and ramie it is possible to weave; fruits of each season divide the paths, wonderful vegetables fill the paddies, ripened flowering apricot and plums sunk in water,[42] peeled cucumbers and cloven gourds—by this I delight my friends, by this I keep covenant with my kin. This is everything it possesses.

In this garden in the morning I recite the *Book of Changes* of Fu Xi and King Wen and the *Springs and Autumns* of Confucius. I seek for the essence and nuance within the *Book of Documents* and clarify the measures and cadences in the *Rites* and the "Record

---

41   That is, it does not propagate by spreading through the root system, and therefore it is suitable for planting next to buildings, stairs, etc. It is "compassionate" because it does not demand having its roots contained, nor is it invasive.

42   To cool them in summer.

of Music." In the evening I browse widely through the various histories, look over the hundred philosophers in sequence, investigate the rights and wrongs of the ancients, and rectify the successes and the failures of the histories of previous dynasties.

And when idle, I trail my cane to roam through the garden, ascend to heights and overlook the depths; flying feathers are not startled, white-headed cranes lead me on in front. I soak my hems or gather them up, depending on the depth of the stream's flow, dilly-dally on the flat plains. I plant trees and irrigate my garden; in the winter I plow and in the summer I weed.

Even a position among the three highest in government or an emolument of ten thousand catties would not be enough to exchange for this delight. Be it so, but I have observed that there is not one thing, among all activities and things, which is not completely empty, so what is the purpose of being so constrained by this as to make it a self-encumbrance? On another day, when the affliction of Zichun is healed[43] and when the encumbrance of Shang Ping is dispelled,[44] I will roam in my skiff across the seas and rivers, floating out to roam amid the mountains and peaks—no one knowing where the trip will finally end. Yet even so, this garden is the legacy of my father the Grand Master of Splendid Prosperity and is something over which I have labored for a long time. How can I forget the emotional connection to it?

Now, my younger siblings, you sons and grandsons, you protect this over the generations; do not let its dwelling become decrepit, do not harvest its trees. Study here. Find your sustenance here. This is enough to create happiness. Can just I, alone, find happiness here? Now Dai Yong chose to live here[45] and Luwang retired in solitude here;[46] their traces are still to be found. So a thousand years from now people of Wu will still be able to point to this place and say, "This is the old garden of the Zhu family."

First day of the twelfth month of the third year of Yuanfeng [1080]. Recorded by Zhu Boyuan of Wu.

---

43   According to the *Record of the Rites*, Zichun, one of Confucius's disciples and a music master, injured his foot when descending from a sacrificial hall. He became despondent because he was aware that one's body must be returned whole to one's parents, and that with "each step one must always remember one's parents."

44   Shang Ping, once he married, never asked again about family affairs. Since daughters-in-law carried on family sacrifices for the husband, his absence from home did not interfere with his filial duties. After he married (we are told in the *History of the Later Han Dynasty*), he left the affairs to his wife and "roamed through famous mountains and hills, and his place of demise is unknown."

45   A former worthy of Wu for whom a mansion was built; according to Zhu Changwen's *Supplementary Notes to the Illustrated Gazetteer of Wu Prefecture*, the Northern Chan Monastery was built on his old grounds.

46   The poet Lu Guimeng, who retired just south of the city. His residence later became the White Lotus Monastery (*Bailian si* 白蓮寺), as Zhu Changwen also notes in his *Supplementary Notes to the Illustrated Gazetteer of Wu Prefecture*.

"Record of the Celebrated Gardens of Luoyang" (*Luoyang mingyuan ji* 洛陽名園記)

LI GEFEI 李革非 (1045–1106)

TRANSLATED BY KENNETH J. HAMMOND

Li Gefei, a literary associate of Su Shi (see above and chapter 3) and an opponent of Wang Anshi's economic reforms (see under Sima Guang), is a rather obscure figure compared with his much more famous daughter, Li Qingzhao (1084–ca. 1151), who is considered China's greatest female poet (see chapter 3 and later in this chapter). He seems to have been a person of serious demeanor: his biography in the official history of the Song dynasty indicates that, at a time when literary creativity was an important criterion in the selection of government officials, Li focused his studies on exegesis of the Confucian classics. Service as an official in northern China was followed by an appointment in the Imperial University. Li made his mark as a writer and literary critic; his admiration for Tao Qian's style may have helped to prompt his interest in gardens. Also, although he does not say so, he may have been influenced by Yang Xuanzhi's *Record of the Monasteries of Luoyang* (*Luoyang qielan ji*; see chapter 1). The "Record of the Celebrated Gardens of Luoyang", written in 1096, is Li's best-known prose work. It records many gardens in the city that were already lost when Li was writing. In the final "Commentary" section, Li draws a famous parallel between the rise and fall of dynasties and the flourishing and decline of gardens. The "Record" influenced many later writers such as Wang Shizhen (1526–1590), whose "Record of Wandering in the Famous Gardens of Jinling" appears in chapter 6, and Qi Biaojia (1603–1645; see chapter 6), who composed a short "Record of the Gardens of Central Yue," Central Yue being the area of present-day Shaoxing.

"Record of the Celebrated Gardens of Luoyang"

The Garden of Fu Bi, Duke of Zheng[47]

The gardens and ponds of Luoyang for the most part date from the Sui and Tang; only the garden of Duke Fu of Zheng is most recent, and its scenery is also most excellent. The visitor goes out from the residence to the east, to the Spring Excursion Pavilion, then ascends to the Four Sceneries Hall, from which the superior vistas of this garden can be overseen. One goes south across the Bridge Across the Ford, then to the top of the Flowing Stream Pavilion, looking out over the Purple Bamboo Hall, and then returning. Going to the right through a tangle of flowers and trees, and along for more than a hundred paces, one passes the Shade Pavilion, the Terrace for Admiring Serenity, and ends at the Veranda of Rolling Waves. To the north is the Earth and Bamboo Grotto, through which one enters a large bamboo grove. It is called a grotto, but is really chopped out of the bamboo, with a stream led through it and a path going along above. Crosswise there is one passageway called the Earthen Bamboo, and lengthwise there are three passages, one called Water Bamboo, one called Stone

---

47   Editor's note: Fu Bi held the office of Grand Councillor (*zaixiang*) in the 1060s, but resigned because of his opposition to the policies of Wang Anshi; he was, therefore, a political associate of Sima Guang. He was successively ennobled as Duke of Han and Duke of Zheng, and died in 1083 at the age of eighty.

Bamboo, and one called Bamboo Pavilion. North of these five pavilions are arranged among the bamboos, called Clustered Jade, Rain Cloak, Hazy Wavelets, Among the Stalks, and Double Mountain. A little south is the Flowering Apricot Terrace, and a bit farther south than this is the Terrace of Bright Heaven, rising above the tips of the trees and bamboo. Following along to the south of the "grottoes" and turning back east is the Hall of Reclining Clouds, paired with the Four Sceneries Hall. North and south, left and right, are two mountains, with a stream running down between them. To sit here is the greatest pleasure in this garden. When the Duke of Zheng retired from government and retreated here, he declined to receive guests, and lived at ease in this garden for twenty years. The pavilions and terraces, flowers and trees, all were created and planted according to his views and designs, and so its intricate arrangements all are quite profound.

Mr. Dong's Western Garden[48]

In Mr. Dong's Western Garden the pavilions and terraces, flowers and trees are not arranged in regular ranks, but are scattered about. The scenery flourishes from year to year, and repairs are kept up regularly. Entering from the south gate, there are three halls facing one another. One hall slightly to the west sits beside a pond. Crossing over a bridge, one comes to a high terrace. Another hall farther west is encircled by bamboos, and within it is a stone lotus flower fountain, out of which water spouts. Windows open on all four sides, making it feel quite roomy, so that in the heat of summer one need not fear the sun. Pure breezes come, and one remains, not wishing to depart, amid the quiet calling of birds, each boasting its own calls. This is the pleasure of mountains and forests found within the walls of Luoyang. A small path leads to a pond, and south of the pond is a hall with a high pavilion. Although the hall is not of imposing size, it is complexly convoluted, so that the visitor arriving here invariably becomes lost; doesn't this resemble the Maze Tower of the past?[49] In the Yuanyou period [1086–1094] the Regent enjoyed giving banquets here.

Mr. Dong's Eastern Garden

Mr. Dong was wealthy and powerful in Luoyang, but in the Yuanfeng era [1078–1086][50] he fell behind in his taxes, and thus was forced to return to his home and fields. Though his two gardens in the city are overrun with weeds and in ruins, still their grand scale can be admired. The Eastern Garden faces north. Entering the gate

---

48   Editor's note: Mr. Dong was Dong Yan, a senior official in the Ministry of Works, who was dismissed for corruption and died in 1008.

49   Editor's note: the Maze Tower was a palace built in Yangzhou in the early seventh century by the notorious Emperor Yang of Sui to house his many concubines; its layout was so complex that it was supposed to be almost impossible to find the way out.

50   Editor's note: The Yuanfeng-era date cannot be correct, as it is seventy to eighty years after Dong Yan's death.

there is a juniper of some ten arm spans in circumference. The seeds are smaller than pine seeds, but their sweetness and scent are better. There is a hall one could live in, and during Mr. Dong's better times singing and dancing went on there, and when he was too drunk to go home he would stay there for ten days or more. To the south are mostly ruins; only the two pavilions Flowing Cups and Tiny Jade remain intact. To the west is a large pond, with a hall in the middle, on which a placard reads: "Jade Held in the Mouth." Water spouts on all four sides of the pond, its source concealed, so that night and day it seems like a waterfall, yet the pond never overflows. People in Luoyang who have gotten drunk here then climbed this hall and sobered up, and so they have a custom of calling this the Pond for Waking from Drunkenness.

Encircling Stream

Encircling Stream is the residential garden of Commander Wang.[51] Its Pavilion for Rinsing Flowers faces south upon a pond, which divides into two streams flowing north, which then pass by the Cool Veranda and reunite in another large pond. Because they wrap around this way, the garden derives its name. South of the veranda is the Tower of Many Vistas, facing south, from which one can see lofty Mount Gao and its eastern peak, Little Hall, and on to Dragon Gate, Great Valley, and many layered peaks, kingfisher green, like strange flowers spread out before one. North of the veranda is the Wind and Moon Terrace, facing north, from which one can see the old Sui and Tang dynasty gates and halls, the thousand doors of a myriad households, lofty peaks in the bright sun, extending more than ten *li*. This is what Zuo Si [235–307] spent ten years writing his rhapsody about. Here one can reach it in a single glance. Farther west is the Brocade Hall and the Terrace of Rustic Elegance. Within the garden are pines and junipers, flowers and trees of many varieties. Near the middle is a small island with a low wall, where one can pitch a tent and remain for a while to take in the fullness of the place. The Cool Veranda and the Brocade Hall can seat a hundred people, they are spacious and beautiful, and in Luoyang there are no others which can compare.

Mr. Liu's Garden

The Garden of Supervising Secretary Liu[52] has cool halls high and low, with an arrangement of a fitting human scale. Anyone familiar with the *Classic of Wood*[53] upon seeing this garden will say, "The buildings of the present age are generally overdone and

---

51   Editor's note: Wang Gongchen (1012–1085), the principal graduate (top metropolitan graduate) of 1030. Li Gefei was married to his granddaughter.

52   Editor's note: this may be Liu Yuanyu, who held this title and has a biography in the official history of the Song dynasty. He had a stormy political career, caught up in factional conflict, and acquired a reputation for rapacity and corruption.

53   Editor's note: from contemporary references, this appears to have been a construction or carpentry manual, which was already falling out of use in the Northern Song period. The content may have been similar to the surviving *Classic of Lu Ban*; see Klaas Ruitenbeek, *Carpentry and Building in Late Imperial China: A Study of the Fifteenth-Century Carpenter's Manual* Lu Ban jing (Leiden: Brill, 1996).

gaudy, so that one does not wish to remain long in them; only these halls are in accord with proper harmony." In the southwest is a terrace, about ten *zhang* on a side, with a tower across from a hall, and covered corridors winding about, with a railing encircling all. The decor is of trees and flowers, and there is nothing which is not beautiful and sedate. Luoyang people call it the Small World of Mr. Liu. Today it has been divided in two, and cannot compete with other gardens.

The Garden of Successive Springs

Recently the Chancellery Vice-Director Master An[54] bought this lonely grove of lofty trees from Mister Yin. Paulownia, catalpa, juniper, and cypress all are arrayed in ranks. There is a large pavilion called Successive Springs, and a taller one called Before Spring. The Successive Springs pavilion is covered with vines and weeds, and from atop it one can see north to the Luo River. As the waters flow turbulently to the east, passing under piled up stones of Heaven's Ford Bridge, they expend their rage and lodge beneath the embankment, which is now a jumble of boulders, with the water gushing over them and freezing into ice, the roar being audible for more than ten *li*. I once visited on the evening of the Lunar New Year and climbed this tower, listening to the water's sound. Staying awhile, the pure cold seeped into my bones, and I could not remain, and so departed.

The Flower Garden in the Compound of the King of Heaven

There are many kinds of flowers in Luoyang, but when one just says "flower" one speaks only of the tree peony. Many gardens have peonies planted in them, but only this one is called "Flower Garden." It has no other ponds or pavilions, only a hundred thousand stalks of peonies. Those in the city who depend on flowers for their living all find their home here. When it is blossom time, they unfold screens and tents, set up shops and stalls, and musical troupes perform. The gentlemen and ladies of the city set off fireworks, and wander about amid the blooms. When blossom time is past it returns to mounds and ruins; broken walls and bits of refuse can be seen scattered about. Every year peonies become more valuable, with Yaohuang and Weihua costing a thousand *qian*. Now no one even has Yaohuang to sell.

Returning to Benevolence Garden

Returning to Benevolence is the name of the street where the garden is located. The garden is at the end of the lane, and is about one *li* around the perimeter. On the north are a thousand stalks of both tree and herbaceous peonies; in the middle is a thousand *mu* of bamboo; and on the south are a facing rank of peaches and plums. This was the garden of the Tang Chief Minister Niu Sengru,[55] with seven *li* of junipers, and these

---

54   Editor's note: An Tao was a government official in the 1090s.

55   Editor's note: see chapter 3.

ancient trees remain. Recently the deputy secretary Li[56] built a pavilion among them. The wall of Luoyang is some fifty *li* square, and within are many large gardens, but this one is the most extensive.

Commander in Chief Miao's Garden

Marquis Miao[57] became wealthy and prominent, and wanted to live in the most beautiful place in the empire, and so chose Luoyang. He wanted to acquire the best garden and residence, and so he got the garden of the Chief Minister of the Kaibao era [968–976] Wang Pu,[58] and built there. The garden is quite ancient, and the scenery is all old; wishing to restore it and laboring to embellish it, he therefore drew on ideas from other famous gardens. From of old the garden has two sal trees facing one another, over one hundred *chi* in height. In spring and summer they look like mountains. Today a hall has been built north of them. Ten thousand stalks of bamboo are planted in two or three enclosures, with coarse skin like reddish jade, and appearing above like green jade rafters. Today a pavilion has been built south of them. On the east is a stream flowing in from the Yi River, wide enough to float ten stone boats. Today a pavilion has been built next to its course. There are ten large pines, with the waters led coiling around them. There is a pond suited for medicinal lotus, which today has a watercourse with a footboard above it. Facing this is a bridge and pavilion, grand and extravagant in form, yet this still does not attain the qualities of Chief Minister Wang's old garden. The land to the east of the river was acquired by Mr. Zhao of the Dragon Diagram Hall,[59] and there was also a grand residential garden built there. A bit to the north is Jiaru Street, named for the Zhou Eastern Capital, where there are the homes of seven Chief Ministers. Duke Wen of Lu and Chief Minister Cheng's residences are beside a pond and pavilion, but only the garden of Prince Zhao of Han can compare with the famous gardens.

The Garden of Prince Zhao of Han

The residence and garden of Prince Zhao of Han[60] were built at the beginning of our dynasty under imperial auspices and direction, and so almost equal the imperial palace

---

56   Editor's note: Li Qingchen, an official who obtained this title in 1094. His precocious literary talent had won the admiration of Ouyang Xiu, among others, and he served as a court archivist and historian as well as having a long career in government.

57   Editor's note: Miao Shou (1029–1095) was a highly effective senior military commander under Emperors Shenzong (r. 1067–1085) and Zhezong (r. 1085–1100).

58   Editor's note: Wang Pu had been premier under the Later Zhou dynasty, which preceded the Song, and remained premier into the early years of the Song dynasty. He retired in 964, during the Qiande reign-period (963–968) which preceded the Kaibao period, so Li Gefei is mistaken in his dates.

59   Editor's note: Zhao Shimin, a renowned scholar who became an academician of the Dragon Diagram Hall (*Longtu ge*) during the reign of Emperor Renzong (r. 1022–1063).

60   Editor's note: Zhao Pu (922–992) was a senior official in the early years of the Song dynasty, who served three times as Grand Councillor. On retirement in 992, he was given the honorary title of Grand Preceptor and was ennobled as Duke of Wei. He died later that year. In 998, he was posthumously enfeoffed as Prince of Han.

in design and decoration. The Prince of Han retired here after being Grand Preceptor, and after just a hundred days he died. His sons and grandsons have lived at the capital, rarely visiting here, and so it has mostly remained behind bolted doors. The high pavilions and great halls have become the haunts of birds and mice. Through the year a lonely fellow goes about with broom and dustpan or spade within. Whether in time of feasting and leisure or in more straitened circumstances the place remains fitting for its reputation.

The Great Benevolence Garden of Mr. Li

The "Record of the Plants and Trees of My Mountain Villa at Pingquan" by Li Deyu, Duke Li of Wei,[61] records more than a hundred varieties of plants. Nowadays the skilled craftsmen of Luoyang criticize red and repudiate white, and seek out odd woods, competing to create wonderful effects, so that every year rarities increase. Peach, plum, flowering apricot, apricot, lotus, chrysanthemum, each of some ten varieties, tree and herbaceous peonies of some hundred kinds, and plants and grasses from far way like orchids, jasmine, hortensia, or camellia, though known as difficult to transplant, only are cultivated in Luoyang, despite differing soil conditions. Therefore in the gardens of Luoyang trees and flowers of a thousand kinds can be seen. To the east of the Sweet Dew Garden is Mr. Li's Garden, maintained with great effort, and of the many varieties in Luoyang there are none which are not here. Within are five pavilions: Four Companions, Welcoming Kingfisher, Washing Tassels, Regarding Virtue, and Holding Aloof.

Pine Island

Pine, cypress, fir, Chinese fir, Chinese juniper, and common juniper all are fine trees. But in Luoyang we only love the juniper and honor the pine. Pine Island contains several hundred pine trees. In the southeast corner are some very rare specimens. In the Tang this was the garden of Yuan Xiangxian.[62] In our dynasty it was acquired by Chief Minister Lord Li of Wending,[63] and now is the garden of Mister Wu,[64] whose

---

61   Editor's note: see chapter 3. Li Gefei seems to mean the reader to understand that this garden originally belonged to Li Deyu, and perhaps that it is still owned by his descendants.

62   Editor's note: Yuan Xiangxian was a nephew of Zhu Wen, Emperor Taizu of the Later Liang dynasty (907–923). After Zhu Wen's son killed him and seized the throne in 912, Yuan assassinated the son and was rewarded by promotion to several military commands as well as the governorship of Kaifeng city. When Later Tang (923–936) conquered Later Liang, Yuan remained in power as a military commander, but died not long after, in 924.

63   Editor's note: Li Di was a Grand Councillor under both Zhenzong (r. 997–1022) and Renzong (r. 1022–1063). Between these appointments, he served as governor of Luoyang. On his death in 1047, he was given the posthumous title Wending. His son and grandson inherited the garden and continued to live in Luoyang.

64   Editor's note: Mr. Wu is unknown. The fact that he is referred to without an official title suggests that he was not a member of the scholar-official class. Sima Guang has a poem referring to a visit to "Mr. Wu's garden" in which he speaks of gardens changing hands with great rapidity.

family has passed it along for three generations. He has made considerable repairs to the pavilions, reservoirs and ponds, and has planted bamboo and trees. In the south he has built a terrace, and to the north a hall. In the northeast is the Compound of the Way, farther to the east of which is a pond, with a pavilion overlooking it in front. From the east an aqueduct brings water into the garden from a pure spring thinly trickling, slowly flowing along and reaching throughout the garden. Elsewhere there is nothing quite like this, and in Luoyang it is singled out for the name Pine Island.

East Garden
Wen Duke of Lu's[65] East Garden is a source of medicinal herbs. It is near the city's east wall, with a vast expanse of water and a broad aspect. Small boats float about here as if upon rivers and lakes. Two halls, called Deep Mirror and Dark River, stand gracefully amid the ponds, while two others, called Speckled Bamboo and Herb Garden, are built on rocks rising from the water. Coming out from his home about a *li* away one can sometimes see Grand Preceptor Lu, now ninety years old, strolling about with his walking stick.

Mr. Zhang's Purple Gold Terrace Garden
Following along the wall from the East Garden to the north, the garden of Mr. Zhang[66] also has winding waters and rich bamboos, with four pavilions. The *Account of the River Diagram*[67] says, "The Yellow Emperor reclined on the Terrace of Boundless Profundity," to which Guo Pu's commentary adds, "At the confluence of the Luo." Some maintain that this is the place referred to.

Mr. Hu's Garden North of the River
The two gardens of Mr. Hu[68] north of the river face each other and are a mere ten paces apart. They are at the foot of Mang Mountain, and wind along beside the Dark River. The riverbank is penetrated by two earthen galleries, over a hundred *chi* in length, with solid walls like a dike, and windows cut through in the front to overlook the water. The clear water is shallow by these cavelike rooms, but waterfalls rush along outside, and the overall effect is quite good. There are pavilions, trees and flowers arranged east of these two halls. One can ascend atop them and wander along, overlooking from the highest point what Heaven has bestowed and Earth established. As for lavishing

---

65   Editor's note: Wen Yanbo, twice a Grand Councillor under Renzong, was ennobled as Duke of Lu. He spent at least two periods of office in Luoyang, and lived in retirement there between 1083 and his death in 1097 (at the age of 92). Evidently he was still alive when Li Gefei was writing.

66   Editor's note: unidentified.

67   Editor's note: the "[Yellow] River Diagram" (*he tu*) and the "Luo [River] Writing" (*luo shu*), borne on the backs of a dragon and a turtle respectively, were mystical diagrams traditionally believed to be the origin of the *Classic of Changes* (*Yijing*).

68   Editor's note: unidentified.

human efforts and skills on it, in Luoyang there is only this garden which excels. But the names of pavilions and terraces in this garden are not suitable. As recorded they seem confused. For example, one terrace provides views on all four sides extending some hundred *li*, the Yi and Luo Rivers can be seen winding around, and forests extending luxuriantly, with haze and clouds setting off lofty towers and winding verandas which can sometimes be glimpsed and sometimes are concealed. It is the kind of scene a master painter would wish to record, yet it is named Enjoying the Moon Terrace. There is a small studio set amid pines and junipers, vines and bushes, with windows on its sides; everything which can be seen from the terrace is laid out before one, and the trees and shrubbery naturally greet one's eyes. Yet this place is called Studio for Studying Antiquity. There is this manner of error throughout.

The Garden of the Big Character Monastery

The Garden of the Big Character Monastery was the garden of Bai Juyi[69] in the Tang. Bai Juyi wrote "I Have a Residence in Lüdao Ward":

> In a house on ten *mu* of land,
> With a garden of five *mu*,
> There is a pond of water,
> And ten thousand stalks of bamboo.

Nowadays Mr. Zhang[70] has acquired half of it and made his Gathering in the Shade Garden. The waters and bamboo are among the best in Luoyang. But if one looks at the image of the garden as it was in the Tang, as for the various halls and streams, pavilions and trees, of what exists today that is called hall or pavilion, there is nothing which remains the same. Isn't it true that natural things last long, while things produced by human action cannot be relied on? Within the monastery stone inscriptions by Bai Juyi are numerous.

The Garden of Solitary Delight

When Sima Guang was in Luoyang he called himself the Old Pedant, and called his garden Solitary Delight. This garden is rather small, and can't compare in extent with others. The Reading Hall is of ten beams. The Watering Flowers Pavilion is also small, and the little structures called Dallying with Water Gallery and Planting Bamboo Studio are even smaller. The Viewing Mountains Terrace is only about eight *chi* in height. The Fishing Hut and the Gathering Herbs Patch are notable for their luxuriant growths of bamboo and grasses. Sima Guang composed prefaces and poems about

---

69   Editor's note: see chapter 2. This quotation is from Bai's "On My Garden Pond."

70   Editor's note: Zhang Qingchen. "A Record of the Gathering in the Shade Garden of Mr. Zhang" survives, written by one Yin Zhu.

these pavilions and terraces to leave to the ages. But what will be admired by men is not in this garden.

Lake Garden

Luoyang people say that in gardens it is difficult to unite six things: grandness of scale with deep quiet; lavish human effort with refined antiquity; abundance of streams and springs with gazing afar. The only garden which manages to combine all six of these things is the Lake Garden. I once had a chance to wander in this garden, and I can confirm this. In the Tang this was the garden of Pei, Duke of Jin.[71] In the middle of the garden is a lake, and in the middle of the lake is a hall called Hundred Flower Island. The name is old but the hall is new. North of the lake is a large hall called Four Harmonies. But this name is not adequate to express how wonderful this hall is. Of the four places one can reach, by an east-west footpath one comes to Cassia Hall. Rising abruptly from the lake is Welcoming the Sun Pavilion. Crossing a lateral pond and cutting through dense growth, then following a winding path one finally comes to the Flowering Apricot Terrace and the Studio for Knowing When One Has Attained It. Along a path one sees as if standing aloof, but then suddenly ascends to the Pavilion Encircled in Green. A vast and deep expanse of flowers and grasses spreads before a pond, where the finest of the pavilions, called Green Shade, stands. This is the general plan of things. But one cannot fully record the joys of hundreds of blossoms or the dazzling light of day, the movements of green and shade, the gurgling of water or splashing of fishes, gathering trees and peaks emerging, the differences of the four seasons, and all the delights of scenery.

Lü Wenmu's Garden

The Yi and Luo Rivers separately flow in to Luoyang from the southeast. The waters of the Yi are clearer, and it is better if one's garden pavilions can be built over these. Through the spring and summer months there is no problem with them running dry. Lü Wenmu's[72] Garden is located on the upper flow of the Yi, and the trees and bamboo are luxuriant. There are three pavilions; one in the middle of a pond and two beside it. A bridge straddles the water's flow, facing these pavilions.

---

71 Editor's note: Pei Du, a Grand Councillor in 815, was ennobled as Duke of Jin in 817. He served four successive emperors, twice acting as Regent of Luoyang. In addition to the Lake Garden, he owned another garden property in Luoyang at Meridian Bridge, known as the Hall of the Green Wilds (*Luye tang*), where in retirement he socialized with literary men such as Bai Juyi and Liu Yuxi (see chapter 2). He died in 838.

72 Editor's note: Lü Mengzheng (946–1011; posthumous name Wenmu) twice served Emperor Taizong (r. 976–997) as a Grand Councillor, and also served Emperor Zhenzong (r. 997–1022) in this capacity, but spent periods of retirement in Luoyang. After his final retirement in 1005, the official Song history tells us he spent his time joyfully and contentedly in his Luoyang garden, feasting every day with friends and family, and surrounded by his sons and grandsons; he was even visited there by the emperor himself. Lü died in 1011 and was given the posthumous title Wenmu.

There are to be found in the gardens of Luoyang some features worthy of being called truly special. For example the flowering apricots of Great Hidden Village, the Floating Cups in Supervising Secretary Yang's garden,[73] and the lion from the Lion Garden. This kind of flowering apricot blooms quite early, with a strong and powerful scent. People say this is because it was transplanted from Dayu Peak in Guangdong. As for Floating Cups, the water flows quite rapidly, yet strangely things do not bump into one another. The lion is not a stone lion at all, but extends some ten *zhang* (some say *chi*) underground. If this is examined it appears to be the worn down remnants of Empress Wu's Pole Star Column.[74] Beyond these there are also the four gardens called Finely Planned, Joined Together, Respectful and Tranquil, and the Stream Garden. These are all Sui and Tang palace gardens. Though they have long been plowed under as good fields, or planted as mulberry or hemp groves, where once were palace halls and lakes assembled, today from the ruins of these we can recognize their rise and fall, and wandering among them remember that the ten thousand things are not eternal, and that through time everything which arises will just as swiftly disappear.

Commentary

Luoyang is located at the very center of the world, in the defile between Mount Yao and the Mian River. It is an important strategic center for the Qin and Long regions,[75] where anyone seeking to unite the four quarters must necessarily contend. When the world is at peace, so too is it here; when there are troubles in the world, Luoyang is the first to suffer from the depredations of war. This is why I say, the waxing and waning of the realm follows the flourishing or decline of Luoyang. From the Zhenguan [627–649] and Kaiyuan [713–741] reign periods of the Tang dynasty, nobles and imperial in-laws began to build their mansions and palaces in the Eastern Capital, so that there came to be more than a thousand of them. But when the times of chaos and collapse began, and continuing through the cruel extremities of the Five Dynasties [907–960], their ponds and terraces, bamboos and trees were all trampled underfoot and reduced to mounds and wasteland by the armies. Lofty towers and great halls were reduced to ashes or left as smoldering ruins, sharing in the extinction of the Tang itself, so that now no place survives. This is why I say the thriving and declining of Luoyang follows the decline or flourishing of its gardens. Because the order or chaos of the realm follows the fortunes of Luoyang, and the fortunes of Luoyang follow the flourishing or decline

---

73   Editor's note: the owner of Great Hidden Village was Zhang Jingyu, who is referred to in some of Sima Guang's poems. Yang Wei was an official who lived in Luoyang after demotion from high office; he was much disliked in government circles for his tendency to switch sides according to which faction held the upper hand at the time.

74   Editor's note: Empress Wu (see chapter 2) made Luoyang her "divine capital," and in 695 ordered the casting of a bronze and iron column 105 *chi* (Chinese feet) high to symbolize her role as the link between the celestial and terrestrial realms. Known as the Axis of Heaven or Pole Star Column, it was set up in front of the palace gates.

75   Editor's note: equivalent to present-day Shaanxi and Gansu Provinces.

of its gardens, I wrote this "Record of the Celebrated Gardens of Luoyang"; is this not a vain effort? Alas! Nobles and worthies, once they have achieved positions at Court, give in to private indulgence, and this leads to the loss of proper order in the realm. They may retire to seek pleasure in their pavilions, but can they obtain it? This was the end of the Way for the Tang.

"Lyric to the Tune *Huan xi sha*" (*Huan xi sha* 浣溪沙) and "Lyric to the Tune *Xiao chong shan*" (*Xiao chong shan* 小重山)

LI QINGZHAO 李清照 (1084–CA.1151)

TRANSLATED BY EUGENE EOYANG

For Li Qingzhao, see chapter 3. These two lyrics present the garden as a setting both for daily life and for the poet's inner emotional life.

"Lyric to the Tune *Huan xi sha*"

I
In the little courtyard, by the vacant window,
    Spring's colors deepen,
With the doubled blinds unfurled
    The gloom thickens.
Upstairs, wordless,
    The strumming of a jasper lute.

Far-off hills, jutting peaks
    Hasten the thinnning of the dusk,
Gentle wind, blowing rain
    Play with light shade.
Pear blossoms are about to fall
    But there's no helping that.

"Lyric to the Tune *Xiao chong shan*"

Spring has come to the gate—spring's grasses green;
Some red blossoms on the plum tree burst open,
Others have yet to bloom.
From the "azure cloud" jar we grind "jade" tea cakes into dust.
Let's keep this morning's dream:
Break open a jug of spring!

Flowers' shadows press at the gate;
Translucent curtains spread over pale moonlight.
It's a lovely evening!
Over two years—three times—you've missed the spring.
Come back!
Let's enjoy this one to the full!

"Small Garden" (*Xiao yuan* 小園) and "Lyric to the Tune 'Phoenix Hairpin'" (*Chaitou feng* 釵頭鳳)

LU YOU 陸游 (1125–1210)

Lu You is one of the great poets of the Southern Song, perhaps the greatest. His gift, as Stephen Owen puts it, is to write "modest and diminutive celebrations of the moment."[76] His quatrain "Small Garden" is a good example of this: the poet has been reading the work of the earlier poet Tao Qian (see chapter 1) but turns from a secondhand garden experience to the reality (or imagination?) of tending his own garden. The second poem is one of the best known of all Song dynasty lyrics, and has attached to it the romantic story of Lu You and his first wife being forced by his mother to divorce; then later, after both had remarried, Lu You caught a glimpse of his first love visiting a garden in their native Shaoxing. Stricken with longing for the past, he wrote this lyric on a wall in the garden; when his former wife visited the garden again, she read it and wrote a matching lyric to the same tune. There may be no truth at all to the story, but it has captured the imagination of readers through the centuries. The garden is said to have been what is now known as the Shen Garden in Shaoxing; excavations have at least shown traces of a Song dynasty garden on the site.

"Small Garden"

TRANSLATED BY STEPHEN OWEN

Misty plants of my small garden
     reach to my neighbor's home,
and through the shade of mulberries
     a single path slants.
I lay here reading Tao Qian's poems,
     but before I finished the book,
I took advantage of gentle rain
     to go and weed my melons.

---

76   Stephen Owen, *Traditional Chinese Poetry and Poetics: Omen of the World* (Madison: University of Wisconsin Press, 1985), 243.

"Lyric to the Tune 'Phoenix Hairpin'"

TRANSLATED BY ALISON HARDIE AND CATHARINE OTTON-GOULDER

In soft pink hands, flask tied with yellow twine;
Outside the palace walls spring willows stand in line.
Cruel east wind, joy turned to bitter tears;
Hearts tied in knots, parted so many years:
    Woe, woe, woe!
Spring comes each year, while, weakened, we decline.
Threads of the shagreen gauze with blood-stained tears combine.
Peach flowers fall: pavilions, mute and bare;
Though vows may last, words we can never share:
    No, no, no!

座落

呂門

Following the Fortunes of a Single Site
CANGLANG PAVILION

Introduction and translations by Yinong Xu

Unlike other chapters of this volume, this chapter is devoted to a series of thirty texts on one specific site, known as Canglang Ting (or Canglang Pavilion), in the south of the time-honored city of Suzhou.[1] Here, I analyze some of the key texts among them that reveal the development over a millennium of the conception and perception of the site, and examine the site-text relationship.

Canglang Ting has commonly been translated as "Surging Waves Pavilion," wherein the word "pavilion" stands for *ting*. This translation, however, is very inaccurate, because the two characters *canglang* jointly denote "the bluish-green color [of water]," and *lang*, pronounced in the second tone in this particular two-character term, does not carry the usual meaning of "waves."[2] It is also sometimes known as "Azure Waves Pavilion," which is still not entirely accurate. In order to avoid inaccurate or clumsy translation, I use the Chinese modifier *canglang* throughout the chapter. In fact, the UNESCO listing of "Classical Gardens of Suzhou" under the World Heritage Sites uses the rendering "Canglang Pavilion."

The conventional rendering of the character *ting* as "pavilion" is seemingly less problematic than that of *canglang*, but the latent problems of its implications are more subtle and, thus, more easily overlooked. This interpretative problem arises from the assumption that what is signified by

---

1   The writing of this introduction benefited from comments by F. W. Mote, Michel Conan, and Peter K. Bol on my translation of the series of texts on Canglang Ting. For whatever errors may occur, I alone am responsible.

2   See Li Shan's (d. 689) commentary on Lu Ji, "Tang shang xing," in *Wenxuan* (Beijing: Zhonghua shuju, 1977), 28.15; and Lu Ji, *Ciyuan* (Beijing: Shangwu yinshuguan, 1988), 1008.

the term *ting* in the poem is a kind of simple, open structure that we usually encounter nowadays; the pavilion standing on top of the hill in the present garden of Canglang Ting is a perfect example. A *ting* in the eleventh century, however, could be quite different from one in the Ming and Qing periods. One of the most obvious differences is that a *ting* in Song times might have doors and windows on all four sides, with curtains installed, as revealed in a number of poems by Su Shunqin on the pavilions he visited and on Canglang Pavilion itself.[3] Thus, the pavilion can be either closed off from or opened up to the outside. It seems also possible that the interior space of the *ting* might sometimes be compartmentalized with screens, so that the four outer parts of the interior space could be differentiated from the central part.

The history of Canglang Pavilion goes back to the eleventh century, when the Northern Song scholar Su Shunqin (1008–1048, formal name Zimei), after being deprived of his official status on trumped-up charges, built a pavilion on the site of a deserted garden, gave it its present name, and wrote an essay entitled "Record of Canglang Pavilion" or *Canglang ting ji*.

The date of Su's construction of Canglang Pavilion is not clear. It has commonly been assumed by modern scholars that this occurred in the late summer or early autumn of 1045, shortly after his arrival in Suzhou, and that he composed the "Record of Canglang Pavilion" almost immediately thereafter.[4] However, we are informed by his poem "Changing Dwelling Places" that he changed his accommodation at least three times within a few months after his arrival in Suzhou.[5] It is, therefore, more plausible that Su Shunqin built Canglang Pavilion and wrote the "Record of Canglang Pavilion" in late 1046 or by the middle of 1047, and that from then on he gradually composed a number of poems associated with the site. Explicit statements that Su Shunqin actually *lived* at Canglang Pavilion did not occur until the twelfth and thirteenth centuries, and it is unlikely that he did, since he himself tells us he traveled by boat between Canglang Pavilion and his residence at Gao Bridge, which was some distance away.

There is no evidence that Su Shunqin either did or did not build any other structures than a single pavilion on the site. We should remember, however, that out of many types of buildings, such as *lou*, *ge*, and *tang*, the *ting* was the simplest. For Su Shunqin, to construct a *ting* was economical, non-extravagant, and yet sufficient for purposes of signification.

The purpose of Su Shunqin's self-identification and self-expression in the building of Canglang Ting was put into effect through literature. Su Shunqin cultivates and then expresses himself by addressing a set of fundamental relationships that always exist in the life of any literary man. These are the relationships of the self with heaven-and-earth and the myriad things *(tiandi wanwu)*, with the past of human events, and with the society of the time. The possibility of a relationship existing

---

3   See, for example, *Su Shunqin ji biannian jiaozhu* 3.238, 4.258, 4.284, 4.293, 4.313. It is interesting to note that in his poem "Sent to Be Inscribed on the Pavilion of Good Harvests and Joy" (4.244), Su Shunqin, having never seen the pavilion Ouyang Xiu built in 1046, nevertheless writes that "windows are opened on four sides."

4   See, for instance, Chen Zhi and Zhang Gongchi, eds., *Zhongguo li dai ming yuan ji xuanzhu* (Hefei: Anhui kexue jishu chubanshe, 1983), 17; Liu Shujie, "Suzhou ming yuan," in *Zhongguo dabaike quanshu bianjibu, Zhongguo dabaike quanshu: Jianzhu, yuanlin, chengshi guihua* (Beijing: Zhongguo dabaike quanshu chubanshe, 1988), 405; Fu Pingxiang and Hu Wentao's annotation in *Su Shunqin ji biannian jiaozhu*, 627; and Liu Xuejun, *Zhongguo gu jianzhu wenxue yijing shenmei* (Beijing: Zhongguo huanjing kexue chubanshe, 1998), 230.

5   "Qian ju," in *Su Shunqin ji biannian jiaozhu* 3.216 or *Su Shunqin ji* 3.40.

between "self" and "other" depends on the self, as a sentient being, having an affective, desirous, or emotional response with regard to the things, and consequently the objects of emotional response themselves come to function as outward projections of man's otherwise inchoate affects, desires, and emotions. Thus, the narration of these relationships in prose and poetry is a working out of the problems of self. These relationships are intertwined, and centered here on the problem of freedom from attachments.

It is a problem that Su Shunqin has to tackle at this moment of crisis in his life, and he brings it up directly in "Record of Canglang Pavilion," which begins with an explanation of his desire to build a pavilion of his own, in which to "give full vent to his feelings." One day, we are told, he found a suitable place and procured it at the cost of forty thousand cash. It was a deserted garden site owned around three quarters of a century earlier by a man named Sun Chengyou (936–985), who rose to high military office under the last ruler of the Wu-Yue kingdom (907–978), which preceded the Song. Since Su Shunqin does not tell us who owned the deserted garden after Sun Chengyou, nor the name of the person from whom he himself purchased it, the contrast of the different persons of Su Shunqin and Sun Chengyou is set forth, and is to be highlighted in later scholars' writings in association with Canglang Pavilion.

Su Shunqin then offers an account of what he did with the site and its immediate effect on him: as his mind became untroubled and the Way became luminous, he realized how despicable it was for him to have clashed with others over trifling interests in the turbulent arena of glory and dishonor, thereby blocking himself away from the true delight he found at the site of Canglang Ting. But his thinking does not stop here, as he reveals his frame of mind in the last section of the "Record of Canglang Pavilion." He makes clear that although his dismissal from office was both disastrous and humiliating, he was not disillusioned with the prospect of officialdom, nor was he prepared to give up his political aspirations. He may not have been optimistic about the immediate future of his official career, but his attitude toward it was positive. This frame of mind is most clearly expressed in Su's naming of the pavilion he built by the water. The term *canglang* comes from the well-known metaphorical lines in one of the Confucian classics, the *Mencius* (see chapter 1):

> When the Canglang waters are clear,
> I can wash my cap-strings in them;
> When the Canglang waters are muddy,
> I can wash my feet in them.[6]

To Su Shunqin, although the political situation of the 1040s was "muddy," it might not necessarily remain so; someday, government could once more be "clear" and upright.

---

6   In order to convey the meaning intended by Su Shunqin, we use here an adaptation of David Hawkes's translation of this rhyme from the *Songs of the South*, rather than Legge's translation from the *Mencius* (for both, see chapter 1).

The reason he felt so distressed over his misfortune, he argues, lay in his desire for fame and wealth, the addicted attachment he now deplores.[7] This is what he meant by the term "overcoming self" (*zi sheng*), which appears in "Record of Canglang Pavilion," alluding to a sentence in the Daoist classic *Daode jing*: "He who overcomes others has force; / He who overcomes himself is strong."[8]

Su Shunqin's working out of the problems of the self is set forth in the context of his relationships with both the past and the present. On the one hand, he sighs at those men of the past who failed to free themselves from such attachments; yet at the same time, he uses some specific terms, *canglang* and *zi sheng* ("overcoming self"), to explicate what attitude and action one should wisely take in either favorable or unfavorable times, alluding to men of the past who succeeded in doing so. On the other hand, he despises his competing with the contemporary "crowd" in the pursuit of fame and wealth, which now for him are only trifling interests. His use of the word "crowd" implies a feeling of conscious loneliness in his understanding of the problems; yet he actively seeks appreciation of it by his fellow literary men. The self-expression he achieved through erecting and naming the pavilion met with a sympathetic response from some of his noted contemporaries who shared his understanding, values, and aspirations.

By erecting and naming his pavilion and by writing about it, Su Shunqin transformed the meaning of the old garden. Garden construction is like literary composition in articulating the builder's or owner's thinking, expressing his values and aspirations, and inviting others to write about it. Similarly, garden reconstruction recomposes what has been written, thus adding to it new ideas, altering its value, and enriching its meaning. What Su Shunqin had done with the site by the time he wrote the "Record of Canglang Pavilion" was no more than erecting a pavilion, but by adding this single structure to the existing garden site and naming it, he recomposed an act of creation so that it now conveyed important messages that its predecessor had not.

The site, therefore, becomes simultaneously the setting for literary composition and the subject of it. A two-way working is in process here, simply because the site of the old garden lends itself to referencing all categories—nature, history, and society. It is there so that Su Shunqin can appropriate heaven-and-earth, the past of human events, and the society of his time all at once.

After Su Shunqin's death, the ownership of Canglang Pavilion changed quite a few times. It was possessed by the Chief Councillor Zhang Dun (1035–1106) in the second half of the eleventh century, and then became the garden-estate of Han Shizhong (1089–1151), a very famous general of the early Southern Song (1127–1279). The site was expanded and grand buildings were added to it in these periods. But around the turn of the fourteenth century, the site became occupied by Buddhist monasteries, and by then Su Shunqin's pavilion had long ceased to exist.

Two and half centuries later, in 1546, a monk named Wenying, while repairing the dilapidated Dayun monastery, erected a new pavilion by the side of the monastery, and named it Canglang. He then asked Gui Youguang (1506–1571), the well-known Ming scholar from Kunshan, to write

---

7   Su Shunqin wrote many poems revealing his acknowledgment of his desire for worldly success before he was expelled from office. See, for example, *Su Shunqin ji biannian jiaozhu* 2.116, 2.117, 2.131–132, 2.143, 2.156–157.

8   The phrase also appears in the *Lü shi chun qiu*, a text of the third century BCE: "He who intends to overcome others must first overcome himself; he who intends to make remarks about others must first remark upon his own [behavior]."

a "Record of Canglang Pavilion" noting this event, which Gui did in the form of a "conversation" with Wenying.

What Wenying says, as Gui Youguang records it, is that he erected a pavilion in the place where Su Shunqin's pavilion had once stood. Wenying was inspired by the story of Su, to be sure, but his pavilion is a different one, and he asked Gui Youguang to record *his* reason for this act. In other words, Wenying erected a pavilion in its own right and he did so by alluding to Su Shunqin's pavilion. Yet Gui Youguang turns the allusion into an attribution, insisting that Wenying merely "restored" what was once there and Wenying's pavilion not only owes its existence to that of Su Shunqin but is really a continuation of it; hence, Gui refers to "the process of Dayun monastery [once again] becoming Canglang Pavilion." This idea of the "restoration" of the pavilion is suggested by the name of the new pavilion, but also becomes plausible due to the designation of the whole place as Canglang Pavilion, a prerequisite that Gui Youguang has emphasized at the outset of his essay. Although the site was previously that of the garden estate of Sun Chengyou, its "real" history, Gui Youguang insists, starts from Su Shunqin, who originally constructed the pavilion and gave it its name. Eventually, it became the site of the monastery, but in the end Canglang Pavilion was reconstructed, which somehow transformed the monastery back into the site of its original significance. By emphasizing Wenying's association with the literary circle of Gui Youguang, a chain of identifications is established in which Gui Youguang himself is included in the history of the site. This history is basically a literary one. The name of Su Shunqin can last forever because he is a literary man, and because there are epigones who share his values and aspirations. Canglang Pavilion, thus, becomes a monument that "survives," albeit through reconstruction and renovation, both because of and for the memory of Su Shunqin and his values and aspirations carried by the name of the pavilion.

If the whole history of Canglang Pavilion were to be seen as a chain of episodes, Wenying's construction of a pavilion served merely as a prelude to the major event of the conversion of the site back to a garden in 1695 by the provincial governor of Jiangsu, Song Luo (1634–1713), who tells us that, on finding Canglang Pavilion in a dilapidated condition, he "immediately sought to have it repaired and restored," and his restoration work, he believes, brought Canglang Pavilion back to its former look. This line of thinking and action was followed in 1827 by Liang Zhangju (1775–1849), in 1873 by Zhang Shusheng (1824–1884), in 1928 by Yan Wenliang (1893–1983), and in 1940 by Gao Guanwu (1892–1953), although the specific intention of each of these men to pursue such a task came from both his personal experience and the historical conditions of his time.

But the question still arises: what had Song Luo restored? I have argued elsewhere[9] that Song Luo's sense of the continuity of the site does not dwell on the plane of its physical appearance; that Su Shunqin's Canglang Pavilion was to those rebuilders less a historical fact than a timeless image associated with Su's deeds and aspirations; and that what had been restored were the values signified by the name of the pavilion, values shared by Su Shunqin and the rebuilders of Canglang Pavilion.

---

9   Yinong Xu, "Interplay of Image and Fact: The Pavilion of Surging Waves," *Studies in the History of Gardens and Designed Landscapes* 19, no. 3–4 (July–December 1999):288–301.

Why, then, did Su Shunqin win the special remembrance of Song Luo and other later scholar-officials? I believe that it is precisely in the notable incongruity of his limited poetic works with Ouyang Xiu's high regard for his poetry, and in his failure to attain to official prominence in contrast to the success of many of his contemporaries, that the reason for his special remembrance lies. Su Shunqin's life is a classic example of the recurrent tragedy—"a worthy person does not meet his time" (*bu yu shi*).

It was this sense of regret for unfulfillment that, I believe, bore upon Song Luo's acts of reconstructing Canglang Pavilion and writing about it. Since Su Shunqin's adversity was not peculiar to Su himself—no scholar-official who aspired to long-lasting fame in literature and government service was immune to it—Song Luo had more than just an understanding of Su's feelings: he shared them. In his "Record of the Restoration of Canglang Pavilion," Song Luo's description of the garden's features and their effect on him not only is strikingly similar in style to Su Shunqin's "Record of Canglang Pavilion," but also deliberately repeats some of the features mentioned in the latter. This, prima facie, makes Song Luo's essay a simple pastiche. What Song Luo did, if only subconsciously, was to rewrite the story, because something in the earlier version both attracted and disturbed him. By additions, deletions, and alterations, he redirected the story and amended the sources of his anxiety.[10] He reproduced a scenario that would hopefully make things as they should be and should have been. In other words, the acts of Song Luo were not simple repetition, but rectification.

Su Shunqin's "writing" happens to both site and text, as does Song Luo's "rewriting." In mainstream Chinese literary thought, the true purpose of reading is not to seek a unique mode of experience for its own sake, but rather to attempt an understanding of the writer and his age, because the relation between reader and writer is a social one. This "knowing the person" (*zhi qi ren*) is also the principal purpose of visiting a site. For this reason, text potentially collaborates with site, and the two areas function correlatively, each requiring the other as a condition for its own meaningful existence.

Song Luo understood very well the important role the site plays in this process of remembrance. In the "Preface to *Su Zimei wenji*" that he compiled in 1698, he describes his discovery and repair of the site, which he found was enjoyed both by the Suzhou population at large and by his literati peers. For the site to take on the famous splendor of the region, the multitude, "the crowd," have to be relied on. But it is "my kind of people" in the past, present, and future who could recreate in their minds what it was like during Su's lifetime, and who could really understand its true significance, share the aspirations and values embedded in it, feel the uneasiness about the kind of adversity it implies, and seek to perpetuate it.

Song Luo surely read Su Shunqin's works prior to his construction project. But in order to understand better what kind of person Su Shunqin was and what his life was like, Song Luo has to take a series of actions: to "restore" what physically existed, to revisit the site, to ponder over the person of Su Shunqin, and to collect Su's literary works. This sequential order for a better understanding is important, in the sense that, although literary works function as a final touch in this process of knowing and remembering, the physical structure actually triggers the whole chain of actions.

---

10   Some of the phrases here are borrowed from Stephen Owen, *Remembrances: The Experience of the Past in Classical Chinese Literature* (Cambridge, Mass.: Harvard University Press, 1986), 37.

On the other hand, the site itself is like text, which can be revisited, restored, and rewritten. And such revisiting, restoring, and rewriting help bring the memory of the past back to life. This is reflected in a very graphic way by You Tong (1618–1704), the famous early Qing scholar from Changzhou, in his "Preface" to the *Brief Gazetteer of Canglang* compiled by Song Luo in 1696, in which he imagines Su's gratitude to Song for "retrieving what had been lost." The site, on which old structures were reconstructed and new structures were added, renders the act of remembrance more vivid.

"Record of Canglang Pavilion" (*Canglang ting ji* 滄浪亭記)

SU SHUNQIN 蘇舜欽 (1008–1048)

Su Shunqin came from a very successful official family that originated from Sichuan but had lived in the Northern Song capital Kaifeng for three generations. In 1034, Su Shunqin passed the imperial examinations for the esteemed presented scholar (*jinshi*) degree, and started his official career.

Politically, Su Shunqin was sympathetic toward Fan Zhongyan's (989–1052) cause, and subsequently became a supporter of the Minor Reform (or Qingli Reform) of 1043–1045, the precursor to Wang Anshi's later reforms. But this seemingly bright start to a promising career soon turned to disaster. As a result of a scandal connected with alleged misappropriation of official funds, Su Shunqin and one of his associates were not only forced out of office but also deprived of their official status and of all the privileges that came along with it, while all other participants were either demoted or banished from the capital.[11]

In the early spring of 1045, unable either to put up with the political atmosphere or to afford living in the capital, Su Shunqin traveled south and arrived in Suzhou in the fourth month of that year.[12] His "Record of Canglang Pavilion" takes up the story from there. Su Shunqin was subsequently restored to office in a fairly minor post, but his revived career was cut short by his early death in 1048.

"Record of Canglang Pavilion"

Removed from office because of an offence, I found myself without a home place to return to. Traveling by small boat to the South, I sojourned in Suzhou. Not until then did I settle myself in a rented house. That happened to be the season when the steamy

---

11   For modern but brief accounts of this incident, see James T. C. Liu, *Ou-yang Hsiu* (Stanford: Stanford University Press, 1967), 49–50; Jonathan Chaves, *Mei Yao-ch'en and the Development of Early Sung Poetry* (New York: Columbia University Press, 1976), 27; and Zhu Dongrun, *Mei Yaochen zhuan* (Beijing: Zhonghua shuju, 1979), 99–103.

12   Su Shunqin explained his feelings in a letter to a friend of his, Han Wei (1017–1098), who had reproached him for leaving the capital. See "Da Han Chiguo shu," in *Su Shunqin ji biannian jiaozhu*, ed. Fu Pingxiang and Hu Wentao (Chengdu: Bashu shushe, 1991), 615–18. This letter is incorporated in Su's biography in the *Song shi* (Beijing: Zhonghua shuju, 1977), 442.13079–81. For his arrival in Suzhou, see Su Shunqin, "Dongtingshan Shuiyue Chanyuan ji," in *Su Shunqin ji biannian jiaozhu* 9.686 or *Su Shunqin ji* 13.185.

mid-summer heat of the narrow, cramped ordinary local houses made it difficult even to breathe. I longed for a high and spacious place with crisp air, in order to give full vent to my feelings. But none such was available.

One day, passing by the prefectural school, I saw to its east lush trees and grasses, and high hillocks and broad waters, seeming not at all like a place within the walls of a city. Running alongside a stream there was a faint path amid many kinds of flowers and slender bamboos. Following this path a few hundred paces eastward, I came across a deserted plot of land, measuring some fifty to sixty *xun* in both length and width, and surrounded on three sides entirely by water. The land to the south of the wooden footbridge was even vaster, having no houses nearby but comprising just groves of trees screening each other on both sides. I consulted some old folk, and they said that during the years of the Qian family's Kingdom of Wu-Yue, this was the site of the garden estate of their close kinsman Sun Chengyou. The splendid configuration of the ponds and hills of the site suggested a lingering trace of the conception of that earlier garden. I was so taken with it that I paced back and forth around it. Then I procured it for forty thousand cash, and built a pavilion on the winding south bank of the stream, naming it "Canglang."

In front are bamboos, and behind is the water; over on the north bank again are endless bamboos. The reflected light of the limpid streams and the shadows of the emerald-green stems converge between the eaves and doors of the pavilion, particularly in harmony with the breezes and moonlight. My hair tied up with a piece of silk, I often row a small boat to go to the pavilion. Having arrived at the pavilion, so unrestrained do I become that thoughts of returning to my rented home in Suzhou disappear completely. When drinking from my wine cup, I sing aloud; when sitting with my legs stretched out, I throw my head back and whistle. Even old country folk do not come to this place; only the birds and fish share my joy. My body at ease, my mind thus becomes untroubled; nothing perverse seen or heard, the Way thus becomes luminous. Thinking back to that turbulent arena of glory and dishonor—the daily clashing with each other over petty interests, the separation from this true delight—is that not despicable!

Alas! Man is innately a sentient being. The affections can so teem within one that one's true nature lies concealed; this true nature only finds its expression when the affections are lodged in things external to oneself. But if one's affections remain lodged there too long, one can become obsessed with that external object, and that lodgement becomes second nature. Unless one overcomes this circumstance and changes it, one is bound to sink into melancholy, and such melancholy is not to be dispelled. It is the official career that has obsessed men most powerfully. Among talented thinkers and morally superior men in ancient times, many are those who suffered misfortune just once in their official careers and in consequence lost their lives. This was because they had not understood the way of "overcoming the self." My loss of office led to my gaining this place and this frame of mind; being content with living tranquilly and open-mindedly, I no longer compete with others. That is why I can again distinguish the essential from the extraneous, why I am now better aware whence flow our losses and our gains. Having achieved this abundant level of understanding, I can now laugh derisively at all the human vanity through unnumbered ages. And neither can I as yet forget that it is in Canglang Pavilion wherein my affections now lodge, for it is naturally this that enables me to overcome myself.

"Passing by Suzhou" (*Guo Suzhou* 過蘇州)

SU SHUNQIN 蘇舜欽

Coming eastward out of Pan Gate, I rub my eyes and gaze anew,
The patter of fine drizzle comes and goes, alternating clouds and sun.
Both green poplars and white egrets are self-content;
All the nearby rivers and the distant hills have their affective nature.[13]
In the waxing and waning of the myriad things lies Heaven's intent;
This solitary, involuntary traveler's bitterness brings only scorn from passers-by.
Fine scenery here is boundless but it is not my lot to stay.
Plying my oars I must press on even as the dusk descends.

"Intoned in a Reflective Mood after a Siesta in the Summer Heat" (*Xiare zhouqin ganyong* 夏熱畫寢感詠)

SU SHUNQIN 蘇舜欽

As the unendurable days of high summer threatened to last forever,
With girdle untied, I sat in the small gallery.
Facing the low table I could not eat;
I wiped away my sweat that fell like rain.
Rattling slowly over the mid-day point went the wheel of the sun,
And the elapse of time seemed unable to bring on the dusk.
Lying supine on a couch,
Soon I felt I had returned to my dreams,
Unruffled as all worldly worries subsided,
Disturbed only by the occasional buzz of flies.
The delight of sleep surpasses that of becoming an immortal and quitting the world,
A vague experience that is hard to express in full.
What happened this morning now appears as if it were yesterday,

---

13 In the 1820s, this sentence, together with one from Ouyang Xiu's "Canglang Pavilion" ("Fresh breezes and the bright moon are themselves priceless"), was borrowed by Liang Zhangju to form a couplet carved on the pillars of the pavilion that shares its name—Canglang Pavilion—with the whole garden site.

Recollections of it are half mixed with words from my dreams.
In a man's life health and strength are treasured,
So that he can pursue glory and honor while he may.
Even Great Yu of Xia valued every bit of time,
Thoroughly to regulate the ten thousand watercourses;
Combed by the wind, washed by the rain,
Though his son was crying, he would not even enter his own front door;
Let alone so ordinary a man as I,
—How could I not go out and rush about with great effort?
Why, then, do I indulge in slumbering by day,
Lazily clinging to these crumbling walls of my rented house?
Thinking back to a time in my youth,
Exerting myself with vigor and energy, I expected quickly to reach eminence.
With my writing brush I rode the air of antiquity,
In pursuit of just what the sages had bequeathed.
Should a winged steed that competes with thunder and lightning
Be willingly harnessed to short carriage-shafts?
As I was about to direct the water of the Bohai sea,
And stretch my hand out to wash Heaven and Earth,
My literary works unexpectedly brought adversity down upon myself,
Yet who had ever comprehended my statecraft views?
Seized by the head, I was put in prison,
Where I breathed feebly like an abandoned piglet.
My name struck from the service lists by the law-enforcing officer,
For the fault of merely hosting an evening meal.
My fellows and guests, dismissed and exiled in all directions,
Scurrying away like frightened rats to remote places.
The Nine Tigers, whose maws and teeth are vicious,
Intended to take this opportunity to grease their paws.
Thanks to the wisdom of the Son of Heaven on high,
I was punished neither with the iron cangue nor a shaving of the head.
My corporeal self now forced to wander around,
How could I bring succor to the multitude?
In the whole realm having no home to return to,
A boat has brought me to this riverside village.
In the spring rain I watch the transplanting of rice seedlings,
And at sundown I water the garden myself.
In the paucity of like fellows and friends in this strange land,
Who can distinguish between stone and jade?
I have rolled up and put away my books on beneficent statecraft,
And force myself to make conversation with the uncultivated.
Despite this idleness and privation, there is still something worth awaiting,

Thus I cannot bear the thought of drowning myself in the River Xiang.[14]
In the intense heat of summer, throughout the day I close the chamber's opening
To a small path outside, engulfed by noxious weeds.
And going out, I resent the noisy chirping of the birds;
Walking around, I see the wriggling of snakes.
Nothing but worm-eaten books now fills my trunk,
And nothing but turbid wine fills my cup,
For who now will talk and laugh with me,
And who can hold me to my moral principles?
All day long I face only my young children;
I am a thousand *li* distant from my brother.
Since this heart of mine is no longer of use,
When I am sleepless I can only stir and fret;
Besides, the sunlight of the day drags on so very long,
I just loathe the warmth of sleeping-mats and bamboo pillows.
There is not the faintest breeze from the north window,
Only the reflected gleam of the scorching sun.
How brilliant and dazzling is the radiant light,
That illumines all but the inside of the inverted tub.
There should be a time when the miasma will break up
And when, with bleeding mouth, I will call again at the palace gate.
Gloriously the state laws and regulations will then be properly restored,
And all kinds of injustice will be washed away.
Treachery and calumny will be thrown into the nether world,
And held down by Mount Kunlun's nine layers.
The path for pursuit of worthy careers will naturally become clear and bright,
The court and government will no longer be turbid,
And all the myriad things in the universe
Will share the grace of a benign and balmy ambience.

---

14   This is a reference to Qu Yuan (ca. 339–ca. 278 BCE), a minister of the state of Chu, who was slandered and banished, and who eventually committed suicide in despair by throwing himself into the River Miluo, a tributary of the Xiang (see chapter 1). Qu Yuan is alluded to also in Su's "Intoned Quietly at Canglang Pavilion," where he is referred to by his title Administrator of the Three Wards, as well as in some other poems by Su not included in this anthology.

"Canglang Pavilion" (*Canglang ting* 滄浪亭)[15]

SU SHUNQIN 蘇舜欽

A small path encircles the secluded hill,
Unexpectedly found in the midst of the city.
The lofty gallery faces the winding river,
And slender bamboos console my worried mien.
While my tracks are far away from the jackals and wolves,
My heart accompanies the carefree fish and birds.
I am willing to spend the rest of my life in this place,
Where I will have no spare time to attend to intrigue and artifice.

"Watching the Fish at Canglang Pavilion" (*Canglang guan yu* 滄浪觀魚)

SU SHUNQIN 蘇舜欽

Under dark green and yet limpid waves the playful fish swim into sight,
Now floating up, now diving down, chasing each other with delightful intimacy.
I lament that I cannot be as happy as this swarm of fish,
And have spent half my life vainly in this world of man.

"Visiting Canglang Pavilion as the Sky Clears Up" (*Chuqing you Canglang ting* 初晴遊滄浪亭)

SU SHUNQIN 蘇舜欽

Nighttime rain falls till dawn, and springtime's waters rise;
The tender clouds, thick and warm, playfully render it overcast and clear in turn.
The curtains are thin, the sun hazy, the flowers and bamboos quiet;
Now and then the young turtledoves coo to one another.

"Walking in Solitude Around Canglang Pavilion" (*Dubu you Canglang ting* 獨步遊滄浪亭)

SU SHUNQIN 蘇舜欽

A place of flowery branches inclining low and grass neat in view,
Cannot be entered on horseback; the best way is by walking without haste.

---

15   It is very difficult to accurately date this and the following six poems by Su Shunqin, all of which are associated with Canglang Pavilion. The present sequential order is established, tentatively, on the basis of internal evidence.

Time and again I carry wine and go there all alone;
Whenever I fall down drunk, only the spring breezes know.

"Intoned Quietly at Canglang Pavilion" (*Canglang jing yin* 滄浪靜吟)

SU SHUNQIN 蘇舜欽

Walking alone round the empty pavilion, treading along the stony path,
The emotional quality of such quietude is matchless in the world.
Chirping mountain cicadas buzz their way through the flimsy door;
Wild dark green creepers twist themselves into the broken windows.
The two sons of Lord Gu Zhu had met their time, but still died of starvation,
Soon after being banished, the Administrator of the Three Wards drowned himself in
    the river;[16]
I for my part, as well as eating my fill and sleeping in peace,
Now regret only that strong wine does not overflow my vats.

"A Local Official Visited Me at Canglang Pavilion, Whereupon We Held a Grand Banquet, and I Thanked Him the Next Day with a Poem" (*Junhou fang yu yu Canglang ting yin er gaohui yiri yi yi zhang xie zhi* 郡侯訪予于滄浪亭因而高會翌日以一章謝之)

SU SHUNQIN 蘇舜欽

This deserted pavilion is seldom visited by the ordinary man,
But I, a sojourner, have had my heart in it myself.
I planted the *wutong* trees and bamboos around the pavilion,[17]
In private also looking forward to what is yet to be.
Ten outriders came yesterday,
And one after another they galloped and swarmed outside the grove.
Waterfowl were startled by the reed flutes and drums;
Old country folk stared up at the canopy of the carriage.
Fond of quiet places in spare time after office,
You arrived as my guest, and thereupon a grand banquet was held.
Stepping on the rocky path, the servants carried the prepared food;
Overlooking the stream, you took your place and casually loosened your girdle.

---

16   The two sons of Lord Gu Zhu were the famous recluses Bo Yi and Shu Qi who, at the time of the Zhou conquest of the Shang, too ashamed to become subjects of the Zhou and therefore refusing to eat the grain of Zhou, retired to Mount Shouyang, where they subsisted on ferns, and eventually starved to death. The Administrator of the Three Wards is the poet Qu Yuan (see chapter 1).

17   The *wutong* trees and bamboos of this stanza allude to their early use in the *Zhuangzi*, where the fantastic bird would not stop at any tree but a *wutong*, and would not eat anything but bamboo seeds.

Your delight in blithely strolling around I fondly share;

Unstrained and unconcerned, we thus dropped even the least of etiquette.

The wine was so mellow that, once served, it was quickly drunk;

The roast meat was so delicious that, once tasted, it was gulped down.

Wantonly, a thousand chicken feet were eaten;

Clasped by its pincers, a crab was grabbed every now and then.

As beams of joy alternated with clever chaff,

Pricking up my ears I heard wise words.

When the dusk ended and the night began, the untiring gaiety went on,

Lingering on there, we intended to do this again.

Having become so befuddled as the night drew on,

You got yourself mounted in the saddle, but facing backward.

This following day, I suffer still the hangover,

And thus will not hasten to deliver my respects to you in person.

"Thinking of Guanzhi at Canglang Pavilion" (*Canglang ting huai Guanzhi* 滄浪亭懷貫之)[18]

SU SHUNQIN 蘇舜欽

Walking about in solitude at Canglang Pavilion but still finding no joy,

I idly climb up to the high terrace to gaze all about me.

Autumn has entered the grove, turning it somber red;

But sunlight passing through the bamboos makes them delicately emerald-green.

My drinking companions have scattered in dire straits, like swallows flying into a
    headwind;

The poets' society is in shambles, like the *wutong* tree after a frost.

And again you paid a visit here, but then quickly went away as before:

Who will keep this old and feeble man company the next time, in my cups, poems are
    chanted?

"Canglang Pavilion" (*Canglang ting* 滄浪亭)

OUYANG XIU 歐陽修 (1007–1072)

For Ouyang Xiu, see chapter 3.

The authors of the following two poems, Ouyang Xiu and Mei Yaochen, were not only friends of
Su Shunqin but two of the greatest writers of the Song dynasty. As had become the custom among

---

18   Guanzhi is the courtesy name of Fan Shidao (1005–1063), a native of Suzhou and a nephew of Fan
Zhongyan, with whom Su Shunqin had been associated at court early in his career.

literary men, these poems formed part of an exchange of poetry and prose associated with buildings they had constructed in their gardens or in the landscape.

By the eleventh century, the exchange of literary works among scholars had long been a wellestablished practice. What became particularly notable in this period were the considerable amounts of exchanged writings associated with events related to the construction of architectonic structures. These structures were often solitary buildings—and predominantly pavilions—constructed not primarily for pragmatic use, nor merely to provide a setting for the pursuit of elegant pastimes, but like the gardens of scholars of that time, principally for the purpose of self-identification and self-expression of their owners or builders; in other words, a structure of this kind functioned either as an extension of the identity of its owner or as a vehicle for expressing its owner's reflection on larger sociopolitical issues.[19] Su Shunqin's erecting the pavilion, naming it Canglang, and then writing about it should be seen as constituting a sequence of acts for just such a purpose. He sent his "Record of Canglang Pavilion," perhaps together with a few poems in association with the site or his visits to it, to his friends, including Ouyang Xiu, Mei Yaochen, Hu Su (996–1067), and Han Wei (1017–1098), who then responded to Su's invitation to write in association with Canglang Ting.

"Canglang Pavilion"

Zimei [Su Shunqin] sent me his Canglang prose and poems,
Inviting me to join him in composing Canglang pieces.
The Canglang place has its scenic features but I cannot be there,
Which makes me gaze eastward with longings in my heart.
The deserted river bend and its wild water are scenes of antiquity;
Where lofty groves and the emerald-green hillocks wind around each other.
New bamboos put forth shoots, adding signs of summer;
Old stumps sprout branches randomly, competing for the beauty of spring.
Waterfowl leisurely engage themselves in quacking,
Mountain warblers twitter to each other at sundown.
Who knows how many turns of rise and fall this place has seen,
Looking upward over the tall trees, all one sees is dark mist.
I should sigh that, not far from the reach of human traces,
And despite the paths leading here, surprisingly this place had not met its person.
Who can match your most extraordinary and wondrous discovery,
That led you to search out this remote abode of the immortals?
At first you found a small path leading into the dense grove,
Then the field of vision was widened as you reached a different and boundless realm.
Where winds are high, and the moon is bright, making the night most charming,

---

19   See Robert E. Harrist Jr., "Art and Identity in the Northern Sung Dynasty: Evidence from Gardens," in *Arts of the Sung and Yüan*, ed. Maxwell K. Hearn and Judith G. Smith (New York: The Metropolitan Museum of Art, 1996), 147–59.

An expanse of glistening light spreads over the jade-colored fields.
In such pure light one cannot distinguish between the water and the moon,
But only see ripples embraced by a blue vastness.
Fresh breezes and the bright moon are in themselves priceless;
How are they to be treasured if sold for merely forty thousand cash!
I nevertheless suspect that this realm was bestowed by Nature,
For Nature should show pity on a good man beset by cares.
In ancient times Chiyi departed, all alone,[20]
To the rivers and lakes where billows were boundless, with raging momentum;
He intended to escape from the rugged paths of the human world,
But only did so by testing himself in the deep pool of the *jiao* dragon.[21]
How can this stand comparison with drifting along freely in a little skiff,
Becoming inebriated and dozing off, rocking gently among the red lotus flowers and
    green waves?
How can a man just give it all up if he is still alive?
Composing new poems and drinking good wine may for the moment while away
    the time.
Even though you would not have vulgar guests arrive at your place,
You should not begrudge beautiful poetic lines spreading throughout the world
    of man.

"Sent to Be Inscribed on Su Zimei's Canglang Pavilion" (*Ji ti Su Zimei Canglang ting* 寄題蘇子美滄浪亭)

MEI YAOCHEN 梅堯臣 (1002–1060)

For Mei Yaochen, see chapter 3 and the note to Ouyang Xiu's poem above.

"Sent to Be Inscribed on Su Zimei's Canglang Pavilion"

I heard that you purchased the Canglang waters,
And have thereby become a Canglang man.
You erected a pavilion above the Canglang,
Everyday holding dear your Canglang.
You should be called the Old Man of Canglang,

---

20   There are two possible interpretations of the term *chiyi* (literally, "leather bag") in this line. It may refer to Wu Zixu (d. 484 BCE), who was the chief minister of the successive rulers of the state of Wu, Helü (r. 514–496 BCE) and Fuchai (r. 495–473 BCE). Tradition has it that Wu Zixu was killed for his forceful remonstration with King Fuchai and that his body was put in a leather bag to be left floating in the river. The second possible reference is to Fan Li, the chief minister of the ruler of Yue, Goujian (r. 497–465 BCE). After helping Goujian destroy Wu, Fan Li fled in a small boat and drifted upon the rivers and lakes, calling himself "Chiyi's leather."

21   The *jiao* dragon is a fantastic creature that lives in the abyss and is capable of causing floods.

Who in the end would retire to the bank of the Canglang.
Where is this Canglang?
—Lake Dongting is nearby.
The bamboos and trees planted earlier have grown dense;
Fish and crabs every now and then are suitable for angling.
The spring soup is mixed with the white *song* cabbage,
In summertime pots, purple water-shields are boiled,
Yellow mandarin oranges are picked late in the frosty season,
Fragrant rice is cooked at the time of the early jade snow.
Wandering about, you recite the poems "Summons to Reclusion,"[22]
When drinking, not bothering to tie up your hair in a kerchief.
As both worries and concerns are forgotten,
With whom do you share your comings and goings?
Yesterday I received a letter from Ouyang Xiu,
Relating quite vividly what has happened around him.
Previously when you first left the capital,
I advised you not to lose your way.
To all the four quarters you should not go,
For everything in the Central Region is refined.
Now you have settled yourself on what pleases you,
—Does not this take you far away from the world of dust?
With your hair hanging down loosely, you differ yet from Taibo;[23]
Associating with guests, you do not become Lord Chunshen.[24]
Do not indulge in what is esteemed by Wu custom,
For it is a Wu custom often to have one's body tattooed
—With [the pattern of] the *jiao* dragon, the thighs being pricked,

---

22   The term *zhao yin* has two related but opposite meanings: "to summon the recluse to governmental services" and "to summon to reclusion." The former finds its earliest use in the "Summons for a Recluse," a poem produced in the second century BCE and included in the *Songs of the South* anthology, whereas the latter first appeared in the poems of Zuo Si (ca. 250–305) and Lu Ji (261–303) in *Wen xuan*, which bear the same title, "Zhao yin."

23   Taibo, an early immigrant from Central China, has been regarded as the founder of the state of Wu. According to Sima Qian's *Records of the Great Historian*, the head of the Zhou tribe, Danfu, raised three sons: the eldest Taibo, the second Zhongyong, and the youngest Jili. Danfu intended to pass on his position to Jili, whose son Chang, later King Wen, was born with cosmically auspicious signs (*sheng rui* 生瑞). Taibo, therefore, came with Zhongyong to the area around what was known later as Suzhou and Wuxi: "Once Taibo came to Jingman, he entitled his own tribe Gou Wu. The aborigines appreciated Taibo's righteousness, and over one thousand households followed him and came under his rule, having him assume the title of Taibo of Wu."

24   Lord Chunshen (d. 238 BCE), a native of Chu whose name was Huang Xie, received this title in the first year of the rule of King Kaolie (r. 262–238 BCE) of Chu, and the area of Wu (around Suzhou) was conferred upon him in 241 BCE, thence becoming one of the famous four lords of the time, who attracted and took in large numbers of educated retainers.

The men of today in that land have not changed.[25]
At its root, reading books is to seek the Way,
Without regard for being lowly and poor.
One should transform his local community,
Wishing for ritual and righteousness to be perfected.

Supplementary Notes to the Illustrated Gazetteer of Wu Prefecture (*Wujun tujing xuji* 吳郡圖經續記; extract)

ZHU CHANGWEN 朱長文 (1039–1098)

For Zhu Changwen, see chapter 4.

Supplementary Notes to the Illustrated Gazetteer of Wu Prefecture (extract)

Su Zimei [Su Shunqin]'s Canglang Pavilion is situated east of the prefectural school. Once Zimei was dismissed from office, he traveled south to Suzhou. One day, passing by the prefectural school, he saw to its east lush trees and grasses, and high hillocks and broad waters. By a stream there was a small path among varied flowers and tall slender bamboo. Walking several hundred paces eastward along this path, he discovered a deserted plot of land, once the site of the garden and buildings of the military commander of the Zhong-Wu region, Sun Chengyou. An older conception of a garden lingered still in the splendid configurations of the low ponds and high hills. Zimei purchased the land and built a pavilion on it, named Canglang. In front were bamboos, and behind was the water; over on the north bank again were endless bamboos. Many of his respected contemporaries wrote poems on the place.

Zimei once claimed that both the tea of Suzhou picked beside the river, and the wine of the surrounding countryside, would suffice to allay all one's worries, while the water-shield and perch and the paddy-field crabs to be had here would suffice to please one's taste. He claimed further that in this region lived many eminent Buddhist monks and reclusive men of noble character, the monasteries were particularly splendid, and local families kept gardens, in which the rare flowers, fantastic rocks, winding ponds, and lofty terraces were such that each day the sun would set before the fish and the birds, lingering on in the gardens, knew it. Thus to the end of his life he did not leave this place.

---

25 By the early Han dynasty (206 BCE–220 CE), the people south of the River Yangtze were regarded by those of the Central Plain as progenies of the snake. This designation seems to have derived from the application of the snake to the general tattoo pattern in these areas—since the people in the south frequently conducted their livelihood activities in the water, growing rice or fishing, they were commonly tattooed with such patterns as small dragons (*longzi* 龍子) or snakelike creatures with scales, so as to avoid harm from aquatic beings including water snakes or sea snakes.

Shilin's Remarks on Poetry (*Shilin shihua* 石林詩話; extract)

YE MENGDE 葉夢得 (1077–1148)

For Ye Mengde, see chapter 3.

Shilin's Remarks on Poetry (extract)

To the south of the prefectural school lie several *qing* of accumulated waters.[26] To one side of the water stands a small hillock, winding and twisting as seen from either above or below. Perhaps this was created at the time of the Qian family by the Prince of Guangling, Qian Yuanliao. Since the earthen hill had been heaped up, water accumulated on this plot of land. The Ruiguang Monastery of the present day was once the site of his residence, whereas this plot of land was the site of his villa garden. During the Qingli reign period [1041–1048], after his dismissal from office and taking up of exile, Su Zimei procured it for forty thousand cash and settled here.[27] He built a pavilion by the water, naming it Canglang. This circumstance is what Ouyang Xiu referred to in the stanza of his poem that goes: "Fresh breezes and the bright moon are in themselves priceless; / How are they to be treasured if sold for merely forty thousand cash!" After Zimei's death, his descendants were unable to keep hold of it. Subsequently, its ownership changed time and again. It is now owned by the family of Chief Councillor Zhang Dun. They had its former site extended and a great belvedere built. They also built a hall on the hill. To the north of the pavilion across the water there is another artificial hillock called Cave Hill; this too, the Zhang family acquired. Once they had tidied up the ground, they excavated underneath and found it full of huge cleft rocks pierced throughout with holes, numbering over one thousand, all of which had been stored there in the time of the Prince of Guangling. The Zhang family proceeded to pile up these rocks to make up for the gaps in the hill. The two hills thus came face to face with each other. As a result, for a period of time the garden became an imposing sight. This story shows that perhaps any piece of land has its own course of events to follow.

---

26   Canglang Pavilion, from the time Su Shunqin built it, was east of the prefectural school, not south of it. There were at least two garden sites by the end of the Wu-Yue kingdom period (907–978). One was Nan Yuan (Southern Garden) in the southwest of the city, built by Qian Yuanliao. In 1035, Fan Zhongyan established the prefectural school in the southeast corner of Nan Yuan. The other garden, owned by Sun Chengyou, was to the east of Nan Yuan. The site of this Sun family garden was the one Su Shunqin acquired ten years after the establishment of the prefectural school. The second half of this account is in agreement with the story told in Su Shunqin's "Record of Canglang Pavilion." "To the south of the prefectural school" could well be a slip of the pen. This possible error is followed by Fan Chengda (1126–1193) in the entry on Canglang Pavilion in his *Wujun zhi* (*Gazetteer of Wu Commandery*), which, in turn, is followed by most of the Suzhou gazetteers of subsequent dynasties.

27   This is the earliest assertion that Su Shunqin actually resided at Canglang Pavilion. It is unlikely, however, that the site was ever Su Shunqin's abode.

"Record of Canglang Pavilion" (*Canglang ting ji* 滄浪亭記)

GUI YOUGUANG 歸有光 (1506–1571)

The Ming scholar Gui Youguang came from Kunshan, which is now effectively a suburb of Suzhou. Despite early signs of intellectual brilliance, it took him until the age of sixty to pass the highest level of the imperial civil service examinations, so his official career was a short one. He is chiefly remembered not for his official activities but for his distinction as a writer of classical prose; some of his short essays, such as his memoir of his mother, who died when he was a small boy, are still greatly loved today. The essay that follows, with its blend of the personal and the philosophical, is typical of his style.

"Record of Canglang Pavilion"

The monk Wenying resides at Grand Cloud Monastery. Surrounded by water, this was the place of Su Zimei [Su Shunqin]'s Canglang Pavilion.

Wenying has repeatedly asked me to write a "Record of Canglang Pavilion," saying: "In the past Zimei composed a 'Record' in which he recorded the splendor of his pavilion. I would like to ask you to record the reason why I too have built a pavilion." In response, I said:

> In the past, at the time of the Kingdom of Wu-Yue, when the Prince of Guangling governed Suzhou, he built the Southern Garden to the southwest of the inner city wall. His maternal kinsman, Sun Chengyou, also built a garden there beside it. Sun's garden did not fall into disuse until the Huaihai region surrendered to the Northern Song. Thereafter Su Zimei constructed his Canglang Pavilion, which marks its beginning. Eventually, Buddhist monks took it over for residence, and this is how Canglang Pavilion became Grand Cloud Monastery. It has been two hundred years now since the monastery came into being. Having searched back into the events of the remote past, Wenying had Zimei's structure restored amid what was left from the processes of desolation and dilapidation, and of submergence and extinction. In this way, Grand Cloud Monastery has once again become Canglang Pavilion.

> Changes from ancient times to the present are exemplified by alterations and changes of imperial court to marketplace. Once I ascended Gusu Platform[28] and gazed out over the vast misty expanse of the Five Lakes, the dense dark green of the encircling mountains. All that which had been built by Taibo and Yuzhong, all

---

28 Gusu Platform is said to have been built on Mount Gusu (or Guxu) to the west of the city of Suzhou by the rulers of the state of Wu around the turn of the sixth century BCE, and to have been burnt down by the invading Yue army in 481 BCE.

that which had been fought over by Helü and Fuchai, and all that which had been administered by Wu Zixu, Wen Zhong, and Fan Li,[29] all this had by now ceased to exist. From this perspective, what do this monastery and this pavilion amount to?

Things change indeed and do not last, but let us see it this way. Qian Liu was able to take advantage of the turmoil and usurp power, thus securing the Kingdom of Wu-Yue. His kingdom grew rich and his armies powerful, and his regime was to last for four generations. The sons and relatives of the Qian family took this opportunity to lead luxurious and extravagant lives. Their palaces, their villas, their gardens and parks, were the most splendid of their age. And yet, it was Zimei's pavilion alone that was admired and revered by you, a follower of the Buddha. From this respect we can see that there have been among men of learning those who wish to have their names passed on for more than a thousand years rather than letting their names seep away and eventually disappear completely along with the constructions associated with them.

Wenying reads books and likes poetry. He associates with my circle, and we all call him the Canglang monk.

"Record of the Restoration of Canglang Pavilion" (*Chongxiu Canglang ting ji* 重修滄浪亭記)

SONG LUO 宋犖 (1634–1713)

Song Luo (1634–1713) was a scholar-official from Shangqiu in present-day Henan Province—a long way from the prosperous Jiangnan region—and a major poet of the early Qing. In his capacity as the incumbent provincial governor of Jiangsu, he built a pavilion on top of the hill and retained for it the name Canglang Pavilion (Canglang Ting). Then in 1696, he wrote the "Record of the Restoration of Canglang Pavilion" before compiling his *Brief Gazetteer of Canglang* (*Canglang xiao zhi*). Two years later, he compiled the *Su Zimei wenji*, the *Collected Works of Su Zimei* (Su Shunqin), and wrote a preface to it.

"Record of the Restoration of Canglang Pavilion"

It has been nearly four years since I came to govern Jiangsu. I have sought to work and live in peace with the local government clerks and the populace, and the local government clerks and the populace likewise have forgiven me my lack of sophistication and my clumsiness. In this way, problems gradually became fewer, and although I continue to deal with strenuous matters, I am not at all vexed.

---

29 Wen Zhong was another prominent minister of the state of Yue in King Goujian's time.

Browsing through the maps and gazetteers of Suzhou on a day of leisure, I found the site of Canglang Pavilion established by Su Zimei [Su Shunqin] of the Song to the east of the prefectural school, only one *li* away from the provincial office. Passing by the site when I had a few moments to spare, I found that wild waters swirled around, and the huge rocks had fallen over. The small hills were enveloped by bleak mists and sprawling weeds; few human traces were to be seen. I therefore immediately sought to have it repaired and restored.

Having constructed a pavilion on top of the hill, I acquired the three words Canglang Pavilion [*cang lang ting*] written in clerical script by Wen Zhengming,[30] and then had them installed on the lintel of the pavilion, so as to bring it back to its former look. The pavilion, open and spacious, stands high, overlooking the surroundings. The lush greenness of the peaks of the southwestern hills outside the city walls lingers around its eaves. By the pavilion are a number of old trees, standing side by side but seemingly rearing up and wrestling with each other; they may have been here for over a hundred years.

Following the northern foot of the hill and turning slightly eastward, I built a small kiosk and named it "Overcoming Self," borrowing the term from Zimei's "Record." Going westward over ten paces down the slope the ground levels out; here I constructed a three-bay building. In front, this building abutted the ridge of the hill; behind, it was surrounded by the limpid stream. The building's plaque reads "Place for Watching the Fish," being thus named because of one of Zimei's poems. Across the stream I had placed a simple single-plank bridge so as to open the site to visitors. Beyond the stream were vegetable plots and houses, woven among each other like a piece of embroidery. To the south of the pavilion were meandering flights of stone steps flanked by zigzag wooden railings. To shelter these paths, I built a long veranda, its plaque reading "Walking Along the Winding Bank." Leaving the veranda by way of the door, one comes to a hall; the upturned corners of its roof resemble the wings of a flying bird. Zimei's tablet has been enshrined in this hall, and the plaque over the hall's entrance door reads "Memorial Shrine of the Honorable Su."[31] I have therefore retained this old building but had it renovated.

Whenever I had a moment's leisure I would repair here and stroll around. Walking along by myself with a cane in hand, I would be well received by the old country folk; the gulls and birds would not be startled by my presence. My mind would become vastly broadened and made magnanimous by this place, as if I were wandering beyond the mundane world.

---

30 Wen Zhengming (1470–1559) was a celebrated calligrapher, painter, and literary man of Suzhou (see chapter 6).

31 This temple was built in the early years of the Kangxi reign (1662–1722) by the provincial governor Wang Xinming.

Some may suspect that roaming about and sightseeing effectively leads to the neglect of one's official duties. I do not think so. Living every day in the midst of worldly affairs and being tied up with account books and official documents, my spirit is dampened and my thinking becomes bogged down. Dazed by the various matters that are placed before me one after another in no real order, I cannot distinguish them properly. Once I have stepped away from such matters and rested a while in a place of cool fresh air and vast openness, my faculties of sight and hearing seem to become more open and clear, and my aspirations and vigor more refreshed. Only then am I able to cope with matters that arise, and to remain unperturbed by things that emerge unexpectedly. I often recite a poem of Master Wang Yangming,[32] a stanza of which runs: "The Imperial Inspector knows not how to settle official matters, / But rather to view mountains everywhere and then to seek temples." How could the Master not have settled official matters? He viewed mountains and sought temples so as to relax his spirit and not to let his mind be fatigued by repeated worries. For this reason, he was able to resolve great difficulties and to decide on significant issues, yet in a calm and leisurely manner as if they were not serious matters. But, with my incompetence and clumsiness, how could I dare to claim that I had a tad of the Master's intelligence and ability? Yet I humbly wish to imitate it. Such being my thinking, how could this pavilion be considered useful merely for visiting and sightseeing?

The pavilion had been disused for nearly one hundred years. From the day it was restored, a Buddhist monk has been charged with its maintenance, and an arable field established as demesne. In this way, the pavilion will last for decades without falling into disrepair. So be it! Make it a government-owned resting place for travelers. Some day I will be leaving here, but this pavilion will remain intact once I have gone. Of those who come after me and ascend this pavilion, how could there not be one who shares this joy with me and who will then also seek a way to keep it perpetual?

Zimei's story is given in detail in the *History of the Song Dynasty*. As for the repeated ruin and rebuilding of this pavilion, there should be other sources that record it, and thus it is not related here. The present reconstruction was commenced in the eighth month of the year *yihai* [1695], and completed in the second month of the following year. An arable field of slightly over seventy *mu* was bought, and this account of mine was recorded and inscribed on the obverse of the stele, for the reference of those who are to come.

---

32 Wang Shouren (1472–1529), known as Wang Yangming, was a successful official and the most influential philosopher of the Ming dynasty.

A Brief Gazetteer of Canglang (*Canglang xiao zhi* 滄浪小志)

"Preface" (*Xu* 序)

YOU TONG 尤同 (1618–1704)

You Tong, who was himself from Suzhou, had a distinguished literary career at the Qing court, being one of the compilers of the official *Ming History*, before retiring home to Suzhou in 1682. He was one of the local notables who attended the Kangxi emperor on his visits to Suzhou during two of his southern progresses. In the essay below, he takes the opportunity of Song Luo's "reconstruction" of Canglang Pavilion and composition of *A Brief Gazetteer of Canglang* to highlight the literary and historical interest of his own home region.

"Preface"

The Grand Imperial Inspector, His Honor Song Luo of Shangqiu, has governed the Wu region for three years. During these three years, he has enhanced the administrative function of the local government and brought order among the people; every matter, great or small, has been dealt with. Having finished work each day, he possesses an air of tranquility as if free of any trouble. On his occasional days of leisure, he takes delight in strolling among the hills and waters.

By chance, he came across, to the east of the provincial government office, amid the unused land in the south of the city, the old site of Canglang Pavilion established by Su Zimei [Su Shunqin] of the Song. Only a handful of the old garden features remained, and few people ever chanced by or paid any attention to it. His Honor, meditating with a profound feeling on the past, had the pavilion tidied up and swept clean. Having repaired the hall and side rooms that contain the shrine [dedicated to Su Shunqin's memory], he proceeded to build a pavilion on the hill, and waterside pavilions and studios at lower points, all of which are encircled by winding verandas, towered over by lofty galleries, and joined together by crooked ponds. Trees and rocks interlock, and the scene has taken on an entirely new look.

Having had all this done, he then searched out all the relevant biographies and records about the site, collected all the poems associated with it, and compiled a *Brief Anthology of Canglang*. Since I am a man of the Canglang neighborhood, he asked me to write a preface. In private, I tend to sigh at those morally superior men of learning who follow differing paths of advance or retreat and lead different lives of prominence or destitution. Those on high are the Son of Heaven's exalted ministers, bathed in light as if they stood beside the sun and the moon. Abroad, they carry with them the standards and scepters of office, issuing orders that are passed with the urgency of a storm. Excessive are their power and ostentation indeed. Those men beneath, idle and uncalled-for as they seem to be, drift along with the tide of the times. When banished, they cannot but take to the wilds, upon remote mountains or the distant banks of rivers and lakes. Excessive too is their predicament. These two categories of men—those either having fulfilled their ambitions or those not having been able to do so—can be compared to water finding its way to the damp lowlands or fire accommodating itself to dryness, each following the dictates of its own kind. This should occasion no surprise. If the princes, and dukes, and dignitaries of today were caused to encounter those who have been banished from other places, they would see such men as dried fish and caged birds, to be cast away and never to be mentioned again.

Now, as a person of outstanding talent from a central prefecture, His Honor came to govern the Jiangnan region. Dealing with state affairs, he has been much too busy with various endless military tallies, civil law suits, and official documents. Yet he has gathered widely information about the deserted and the missing, and he has roved over the vast, open countryside, offering sacrifices to and grieving for those men who encountered misfortunes or were deprived of their careers. How distant, then, his attitude is from that of other dignitaries and how deep the consonance between him and the men of misfortune of the past! Alas! Whether the men of past and present can be considered the equal of each other or not, depends not on the traces they leave behind them but on their minds and hearts. Such men are unmoved by prestige and power but rely on each other in spirit. Perhaps there is a Way of literary composition that generates not estrangement between men, but mutual trust—the so-called harmony made by Heaven?

When Zimei sojourned in Suzhou, vast and empty seemed to him the unfamiliar place, where he found no one but his own shadow. In proximity, he exchanged visits only with local officials; at a distance, inebriated old men echoed songs with him. A poem of his, entitled "A Local Official Visited Me at Canglang Pavilion, Whereupon We Held a Grand Banquet, and I Thanked Him the Next Day with a Poem," which is contained in his collected works, decidedly does not record the official's name. The lines in it that go: "Wantonly, a thousand chicken feet were eaten; / Clasped by its pincers, a crab was grabbed every now and then" also tell of nothing more than a boisterous occasion of food and wine, while the poem as a whole never mentions any act of literary exchange. How was he to know that after the passage of a thousand years he would reap such an elegant reward? His response would be: "Song Luo, this noble man, has repaired my walls and buildings and wiped clean my clothes and caps. With writing brush and fine ink, he has retrieved that which had been lost and continued that which had been severed, hence making that 'piece of silk' and the small skiff appear still as they did in those years, so vivid that it is as if they could be summoned from the text when needed." One is forced to believe that literary composition has its spirit, and relations of friendship among men too have their Way. For having found just this one man who truly understands him, we can congratulate Su Zimei, even though he has long dwelt in the nether regions.

Furthermore, the waters of Canglang have never been Mr. Su's exclusively; if the time before his acquisition of the site is disregarded for the moment, then certainly after Su came Zhang and after Zhang came Han. Zhang Dun, the Duke of Shenguo,[33] in his capacity as Chief Councillor, had the garden further expanded to include large halls and cavernous hills, so grand that it became an imposing sight at the time. And then Han Shizhong, the Prince of Qi,[34] erected the Flying Rainbow Bridge, raised the Cool Breeze Terrace, and constructed the Hall of Cold Radiance. In terms of scale, building standards, vastness, and beauty, the garden now surpassed that of Canglang at least a hundredfold. However, in the blink of an eye, both the magnitude and spirit of the gardens of both Zhang and Han vanished completely. Even the joss sticks and candles placed before the Prince of Qi's shrine come and go from sight in the cold mist and the withered grass. When travelers pass by the site, local farmers and old country folk point it out to them, saying: "This is Su Zimei's Canglang Pavilion." From now on, Zimei's spirit tablet will be reinstalled and prayers will be offered to him; songs and poems will be composed and intoned for him. Once again people will say: "This is the shrine of the Honorable Su." In light of this, then, it is clear that in spite of a lack of virtue, high repute may be won through wealth and rank, but that a time will come when even meritorious and successful service end—unlike literary composition which is immortal. Although Su met with adversity in his own time, with His Honor Song Luo's undertaking, his fame becomes ever more illustrious; although Su's verse and prose are beautiful, with this *Brief Gazetteer of Canglang* compiled by His Honor, they will now be handed down for a longer time. This is why even the Grand Historian Sima Qian gave vent to his thoughts and feelings for those men whose ambitions were as immense and lofty as the blue-green clouds. How much more is this true of one such as I—how can I possibly not linger over Su's literary achievement and sigh repeatedly with admiration?

As for the scenery of the pavilion and the construction on the site, his Honor himself has an essay recording it, so I need not repeat his words here.

This preface respectfully written, three days after Shangyuan [eighteenth day of the first month] of the year *bingzi* [1696] of the reign of the Kangxi emperor, by You Tong, the Old Man of the West Hall, from Changzhou County.

---

33   The title Duke of Shenguo was conferred on Zhang Dun (1035–1106) around 1100.

34   The title Prince of Qi was posthumously conferred on Han Shizhong (1089–1151) sometime between 1162 and 1188.

Collected Works of Su Zimei (*Su Zimei wenji* 蘇子美文集)

"Preface" (*Xu* 序)

SONG LUO 宋犖

Sojourning in Suzhou to take up my official duties as Provincial Governor of Jiangsu, I found the site left behind by Su Zimei of the Song amid bleak mist and sprawling weeds. In a modest way, I restored what had been disused and abandoned, and repaired the walls and halls. It has been a number of years since then, and the Pavilion's vegetation and rockery have grown older with the passing of the years, while the fine blossoms and famous flowers have become more charming and graceful with the passage of the months. Moreover, the people of the Suzhou region, elegantly fond of anecdotes of the past, come on fine spring or autumn days in their walking shoes and gather here in crowds. The site has thus come to be one of the famed scenic sites of the prefecture. When people of my kind and I visit it, we ponder over the traces of what used to be. We pace around the place and then we begin to think about its person; thinking about its person, we surely contemplate and sigh over his life, and seek out his prose and verse. In this way, we come to some faint inkling of what it was like during his life. Perhaps this is the way of what Mencius called "to ascend and make friends of the men of antiquity."[35]

From early times there has been a volume of *Collected Works of Zimei* in several fascicles, this having long circulated throughout the world. Unfortunately, the printing blocks of this edition have been destroyed, so nowadays those who get to see his *Collected Works* are few. I have fortunately got hold of this volume and have been chanting my way through it. Zimei's verse is open and upright, with an air of self-contentedness about it; his prose is grand and vigorous and has extraordinary force. His writings are very much in keeping with the manner in which he conducted himself, and should they be matched against those of Chao Buzhi [1053–1110] and Zhang Lei [1054–1114], there certainly would not be a tinge of embarrassment for anyone. Yet Chao and Zhang emerged only later, in the days of a great flourishing of the study of ancient-style prose, whereas Zimei was a lonely figure advocating the return to ancient prose models when everyone else in the whole world shunned it. His talent and insight did have their forte that especially excelled, such that he sought to stem the decadent tide of Yang Yi [974–1020] and Liu Yun [971–1031], and pave the way for future leading figures of literature such as Ouyang Xiu [1007–1072] and Su Shi [1037–1101]. When men of learning talk about ancient-style prose in the early years of the Song, they often praise Zimei in the same breath as Mu Xiu [979–1032], but Mu Xiu is actually inferior to him.

---

35   In the *Mencius*, we read that "When a scholar feels that his friendship with all the virtuous scholars of the kingdom is not sufficient to satisfy him, he proceeds to ascend to consider the men of antiquity. He repeats their poems, and reads their books, and as he does not know what they were as men, to ascertain this, he considers their history. This is to ascend and make friends of the men of antiquity," for which, see *The Chinese Classics*, vol. 2, *The Works of Mencius*, ed. and trans. James Legge (Oxford: Clarendon Press, 1893–1895), 392.

Xu Dunfu from Suzhou is young in age but fond of antiquity. In collaboration with his elder brother, Nianxiu, he wished to have the printing blocks recut for Zimei's *Collected Works*, hoping that its circulation, along with that of my *Brief Gazetteer of Canglang*, could thereby be expanded. Delighted at this, I immediately pulled out my copy of the earlier edition and entrusted it to him. When the complete set of blocks for printing the book was ready, he asked me to write a preface. I responded, "In the past Ouyang Xiu said all that needs saying. His preface to the *Collected Works of Su Zimei* reads: 'Zimei was younger in age than I, but I took up my study of ancient-style prose rather later than he did.' And elsewhere, 'These literary works are like gold or jade. Even if cast aside and buried under dung and filth, they could not be eroded, and although they might be ignored for a while, there will surely come a time in later ages when they will again be collected and valued.' Ah! Do Zimei's writings not possess qualities that have been waiting for just this day?"

This preface written on the first day of the eighth month of the year *maoyin* [1698] of the reign of the Kangxi emperor, by the Canglang Sojourner Song Luo.

"Record of the Restoration of Canglang Pavilion" (*Chongxiu Canglang ting ji* 重修滄浪亭記)

WU CUNLI 吳存禮 (FL. 17TH–18TH CENTURIES)

Wu Cunli acted as provincial governor of Jiangsu from 1715 to 1723, and it was during this period that he became interested in the vicissitudes of Canglang Pavilion. He himself originated from Shaanxi Province, in the northwest of China, and before his appointment to Jiangsu he had been an official in Guangdong in the far south, where he was admired by the local population for his interest in local history and local education.

"Record of the Restoration of Canglang Pavilion"

I received my appointment as provincial governor in Jiangsu Province in the winter of the year *yiwei* [1715]. No sooner had I dismounted from my carriage than I immediately proceeded to the prefectural school. There, I paid my respects to Confucius, the First Teacher, and performed the appropriate ritual offering. Then I had assembled the scholars and ordinary people, and pronounced, item by item, the moral principles and legal codes. Once these acts had been completed, I stepped out of the gate of the prefectural school and gazed eastward. What I saw there was a pavilion set within a luxuriant grove, the upturned corners of its roof akin to the wings of a flying bird, hovering above the tips of the trees. Upon enquiry I was told that this was the former site of Canglang Pavilion of Su Zimei [Su Shunqin], once a subordinate prefectural official of Huzhou during the Song dynasty; it was also the one that Song Luo from Shangqiu had sought out some years previously and had restored, sometime after he had assumed his office as provincial governor.

At the time I was just beginning to handle local government affairs. Official documents and correspondence had accumulated to such an extent that I perused them from morning to night without a single moment of ease, and therefore had no leisure to pay a visit to the place. A whole year has passed since then. The local government clerks and the populace have been content with my easy-going and unaffected ways, and we get along with each other amicably. I have often thought about this so-called Canglang Pavilion. Tidings of the surviving traces of this former worthy [i.e., Su Shunqin] have been transmitted through song and poem, and have been recorded in gazetteers and annals. The pavilion must afford a high place from which one can gaze out into the distance. I had hoped to make a leisurely excursion to it, but an opportunity to do so has not presented itself.

In the summer of the year *jihai* [1719], I was especially favored by the Kangxi emperor when he bestowed upon me a copy of a poem that His Majesty himself had composed.[36] In the poem, the emperor holds the destitute people of the region very much at the forefront of his mind and urges officials such as myself to fulfill our duties. The whole realm now has gone through many decades of recuperation and the population has increased, so that the people now live in a state of peace and contentment amid conditions of ease and abundance. Even so, the emperor's sincere concern for Jiangnan still persists. As for both the affective capacities of literary practice and the outstanding talents of the scholars of the region, they too claimed the emperor's special attention as he bestowed his celestial words of praise and commendation. Since I dare not to keep the imperial poem to myself, I wish to have its text carved on stone so as to make as widely known as possible the emperor's gracious intent, in acknowledgement of the honor and favor shown to the literati of the Suzhou region. To this purpose, I consulted other officials and local elders. They all said, "Canglang Pavilion is in the southeast of the prefectural city.[37] It consists of several *qing* of accumulated water and refreshingly

---

36   On his visit to Suzhou during the last of his Southern Tours, in 1707, the Kangxi emperor composed the following poem: "I once noted, upon arrival here in Suzhou twelve years ago, / That both its literary practice and its talents are worthy of broadcast. / But as it is the thought of the hardship borne by the destitute people that I must keep in mind, / I have to strive regularly to exhort the officials to be virtuous." Apart from this poem, the Kangxi emperor also bestowed on Wu Cunli a couplet that read: "When rain, precious as oil, becomes ample, farming households are filled with bliss; / Where flowers, grown in the county, remain bright, local officials are honest and upright." The second half of the Kangxi emperor's couplet alludes to the story told about Pan Yue (247–300), a well-known scholar-official in the Western Jin dynasty (265–316). During his tenure as county magistrate of Heyang (in present-day Henan Province), he planted many peach and flowering apricot trees to signify his honest and upright administration.

37   In fact, geographically, Canglang Pavilion was (and remains) in the southwest of the city of Suzhou. But in 1719, when Wu Cunli wrote this essay, the city was still jurisdictionally divided into two parts (instead of the three from 1724) by the major north-south street called Wolong, Reclining Dragon (but later to be called

beautiful bamboos and trees. From the lie of the nearer hills and distant mountain peaks beyond the city walls, it appears as if they encircle and protect it. In terms of fame and splendor, it is the finest site in Suzhou prefecture. For the construction of a pavilion and the erection of a stele in the pavilion, only this place is appropriate." With this advice, I then proceeded to inspect and survey the place in person for the first time. As soon as I had climbed up to the pavilion, its elevated position and its command of a vast prospect, combined with the high ceiling of the pavilion itself and its openness on all four sides, put my mind at ease and broadened my field of vision. The blue peaks of the distant mountains floated above the clouds; the green water of the winding ponds rushed down into lower streams. Here and there in the garden, a few old trees, unevenly planted, set each other off, remaining verdant all the year round, never withering. Within the Wu region, this is truly a place with an extraordinary and numinous aura, and which has been neglected now for hundreds of years as if it has been awaiting the emperor's poem.

Therefore I organized the craftsmen and collected the building materials to construct in the garden a pavilion to house the stele on which the Imperial Rescript was to be carved.[38] At the same time, I also ordered that its nearby buildings be enlarged or repaired, so as to enhance the majesty and beauty of the pavilion. Since the scale of the Place for Watching the Fish that had previously been built was quite small, this in particular I had enlarged, its plaque now announcing "Gazing from the Bank of the River Hao." I further had constructed a boat-like studio to the left of Gazing from the Bank of the River Hao, its plaque announcing "Roving in the Mirror." The site is completely surrounded by water on its three sides, and bamboo has been planted around; hopefully this is the scene that Zimei described in his "Record" as "the reflected light of the limpid streams and the shadows of the emerald-green stems converge between the eaves and doors of the pavilion." To achieve this effect, all the buildings have been constructed in such a way as to look out over the streams, so that the site embraces the scenic features of the water. To the front of Roving in the Mirror is the Pavilion for Caressing the Clouds. To the west of this pavilion is the Walking along the Winding Bank Veranda; the open galleries stretch out bending and turning, inscriptions on stone by men of old displayed on their every wall. A small house was built too, its plaque announcing "Free and Unfettered," to be used as a place of rest. On the basis of the design of Song Luo's former site, what had still collapsed was renovated and repainted. Here a structure was enlarged, there a building was added. The configurational propensity of the garden was altered so that

---

Hulong, Protective Dragon), with the western part administered by Wu County and the eastern part by Changzhou County. This street, separating the prefectural school on its west side from Canglang Pavilion on its east side, was then taken as a reference point in designating the location of many urban structures. For this reason, Wu Cunli and his contemporaries all considered Canglang Pavilion to be in the southeast of the city.

38 A small pavilion, housing the stela, presently stands at the western foot of the hillock.

its multitudinous features now all line up in an encircling form, facing inward, like a myriad stars surrounding the polestar and a hundred rivers converging on the sea. Lofty and grand, bright and luminous, the place has now acquired the majestic look of ten thousand years.

As for the work on this project, I initiated it and the Salt Commissioner, the respected Liu Zhiying, assisted with it. In total, it took three months for the work to be completed. Thereupon I composed this "Record," describing the significance of this reconstruction. My account will allow those who visit the site in the future to know that, in this universe, a place with an extraordinary and numinous aura surely exists in expectation of an imperial composition. Such places are like the magnificent sun and moon in the sky, and the display of their brilliance continues for all time, never to be overshadowed. This place, from the time of the Kingdom of Wu-Yue through the Song, Yuan, and Ming dynasties, has been taken successively either by relatives of the ruling family or by powerful officials as their garden or park. The vicissitudes it has endured, its waxing and waning, are really not worth enumerating. Even when we take into account all those gifted men and outstanding scholars whose heroic character and lofty spirit served to dominate their own times, and whose names to be sure have not totally vanished, nevertheless one can scarcely reckon on the extent to which their former traces have become lost amid the bleak mists and overgrown plants. In this sense, how could it not be true that the splendor of Canglang Pavilion has been lent a much greater magnificence by the presence in it of the Imperial Rescript, on which the immortality of the pavilion's fame relies? As for the display that appears before one's eyes of all the ten thousand manifestations of nature when one ascends the pavilion to take in the view, looking upward and gazing far into the distance, I am incapable of describing this in detail; only the visitor himself will be able to comprehend it.

Collection of Studies after Work in the Cultivated Field (*Gaiyu congkao* 陔餘叢考)

"Canglang Pavilion" (*Canglang ting* 滄浪亭)

ZHAO YI 趙翼 (1727–1814)

Zhao Yi, reputedly a descendant of the Song imperial family, came from what is now Changzhou, not far from Suzhou. His childhood and youth were impoverished, but once he embarked on an official career he was very successful, especially in military affairs. Eventually his opposition to corrupt practices got him into trouble; after resigning from his official career, he taught at the Anding Academy in Taizhou, Jiangsu, which could trace its history back to the thirteenth century. In the final decades of his life, his literary and historical writing was highly valued by his contemporaries.

"Canglang Pavilion"

The world only knows that Canglang Pavilion in Gusu is the site left behind by Su Zimei [Su Shunqin], but not that, both before and after Zimei, the ownership of this garden changed several times. Note that the record made by Zimei himself states that he consulted some old folk who told him that at the time of the Qian family's kingdom, this was the site of the garden estate of their close kinsman Sun Chengyou.

Ye Mengde, however, in his *Shilin's Remarks on Poetry*, claims that this earlier garden was in fact built by Qian Yuanliao, the Prince of Guangling. During the Qingli reign period [1041–1048], Su Zimei, then living in exile after his dismissal from office, procured it for forty thousand cash. He built a pavilion beside the water and named it Canglang. This is the circumstance referred to by Ouyang Xiu in the stanza, "Fresh breezes and the bright moon are in themselves priceless; / How are they to be treasured if sold for merely forty thousand cash!" After Zimei's death, the garden came into the possession of the Chief Councillor Zhang Dun, who had it extended and some additional belvederes and halls built. To the north of the pavilion, across the water, there is another hillock called Cave Hill, which Zhang acquired as well. After this hill had been excavated, it was found to be full of large rocks, all of which were recessed and hollowed, numbering over a thousand in total, previously the possessions of the Prince of Guangling. These rocks were then piled up, adding height to the hill. Consequently, the garden became, for a period of time, unsurpassed in its imposing bearing. We can see from this that after Zimei, the site had then belonged to Chief Councillor Zhang.

Ye Mengde also writes that when Wang Yucheng [954–1001] was magistrate of Changzhou county, not a single day would pass by during which he would not bring guests up to Canglang Pavilion to take a drink there. He wrote a poem that gives the couplet: "Should I some day be successful in my career, / I will try to acquire the Southern Garden as refuge for the inebriated." At the end of the Daguan reign period [1107–1110], Cai Jing [1047–1126], the Duke of Lu, was dismissed from his post of Chief Councillor, and as he intended to return to his home place in the East, this garden was bestowed on him by imperial edict. The Duke has a poem, which runs: "To what end have I been the emperor's confidant for eight years? / Yet His Majesty has granted me Southern Garden as a reward, doting on me even though I was leaving his service. / One may laugh at Academician Wang in those early years, / Who chanted the poem about seeking to acquire the Southern Garden even before winning a decent official rank and scholarly fame." Thus, after Zhang Dun, the site then belonged to Cai Jing.

Moreover, Hong Mai [1123–1202], in his *Duiyu bian*, indicates that when Zimei bought the site, he spent only forty thousand cash; but that when owned later by the Han family, its value had reached several million. Thus, after Cai Jing, the site then belonged to the descendants of Han, the Prince of Qi.

All this being the case, to this date, those who have talked about Canglang Pavilion only know about Su Zimei; as for the three family names of Zhang, Cai, and Han, no one has written a record of their associations with it. How could it not be the case that the power of wealth and rank cannot be counted upon, whereas the talents and refinements of the literary men and the elegance of their styles can endure forever?

Interlinear note: Gui Youguang, in his "Record of Canglang Pavilion," states that after Zimei, Buddhist monks took over the site of Canglang Pavilion as their place of abode, thus converting it into the Grand Cloud Monastery; and that two hundred years later, Monk Wenying from the monastery searched back into the events of the remote past and restored Zimei's old structure, converting Grand Cloud Monastery back into Canglang Pavilion. It seems, though, that in this version of the story, the repeated change of ownership of Canglang Pavilion to Zhang, Cai, and Han has not been fully investigated. Nevertheless, from the end of the Song or the end of the Yuan, Canglang Pavilion was disused and became the site of the Buddhist monastery. Yet the monastery once again was converted back to today's Canglang Pavilion. From this circumstance, the pattern of its rise and fall can once again be seen.

"Record of the Restoration of Canglang Pavilion" (*Chongxiu Canglang ting ji* 重修滄浪亭記)

LIANG ZHANGJU 梁章鉅 (1775–1849)

Liang Zhangju, originally from Fujian, became a presented scholar at a relatively early age and had a stellar official career. In the early 1820s, he was posted to Jiangsu as surveillance commissioner; and after a brief posting to Shandong, he returned to Jiangsu as provincial administration commissioner, in which capacity he served with great success for eight years. In 1836, he was posted to south China, where he became involved in opposition to the opium trade. During the first Opium War, he led resistance to British attacks both in the south and in the Shanghai area after a posting back to Jiangsu, this time as provincial governor.

"Record of the Restoration of Canglang Pavilion"

Some years ago, when serving as the Commissioner of the Huaihai Circuit, I twice held the Acting Judicial Commissionership of Jiangsu. Passing by Canglang Pavilion, I deplored its state of dilapidation, and the thought of restoring it occurred to me. As I had to quit the region when each of my terms of service came to an end, my plans were never brought to fruition.

In the spring of the year *dinghai* [1827], I came to govern this region. Once slightly freed from reading official documents, I consulted about the restoration of Canglang

Pavilion with the Grand Imperial Censor, Tao Shu [1778–1839] from Anhua, and with the Prefects, Chen Luan from Jiangxia, and Li Tingyou from Zouping, among others. They all concurred with my proposal with alacrity. Building materials were then collected and craftsmen assembled. That which had fallen down was straightened up; that which had rotted away was replaced. After six months of work, the pavilion was all at once brought back to its former look. It would be appropriate to have a record of this project.

Investigation reveals that the site of the pavilion goes back to the Qian family of the Kingdom of Wu-Yue. Having acquired the site, Su Zimei of the Song initiated the building and naming of the pavilion. Thereafter, the site belonged to Zhang Dun, and then to Han Shizhong, the Prince of Qi. After the passage of several more centuries, it had very much fallen into ruin.

This situation continued until our present dynasty, when Song Luo from Shangqiu governed the Wu region and had the pavilion constructed anew. Here he still inscribed the attribution to Zimei—this is to follow the origin of the pavilion. And yet, although this was an appropriate attribution, whether something is passed on in this world and made known to later generations has little if anything to do with fame and rank, wealth and power. Take the examples of Pei Du and Li Deyu of the Tang dynasty; brilliant as their meritorious service and outstanding achievement were, not a single vestige can now be traced of the villas they built, Wuqiao and Pingquan respectively. By contrast, both the Lixia Pavilion on Beizhu[39] and the Crane Releasing Pavilion at Gushan[40] remain standing to this day, still fully capable of calling upon men of extraordinary talent to whistle and sing out their feelings, intensifying the sorrow that overwhelms us when we visit the sites of the past. That Song Luo tied the place to the poet Su Shunqin rather than to the officials Zhang Dun and Han Shizhong reveals an aspiration of this same kind.

Moreover, ever since Song Luo reconstructed the pavilion for the first time, there has been no lack of those who followed in his footsteps. Yet it is only Song Luo that scholar-officials seem to laud for the import of his efforts. Is it the case, then, that among usual construction works there exists a pattern of fortune and misfortune in terms of which is praised and remembered, and which is not? Or is it more the case that the people of Suzhou cherish the memory of Song Luo for reasons besides his reconstruction of the

---

39 The Lixia Pavilion was on a small island in Lake Daming in Ji'nan, Shandong. Initially built in the Northern Wei (386–534), the pavilion became famous because it was later associated with the Tang poet Du Fu (712–770) and other early literary figures. The name of the pavilion refers to a mountain of the same name, visible across the lake.

40 The Pavilion for Releasing Cranes, initially built during the Yuan or Ming dynasties to commemorate the reclusive Song poet Lin Bu (967–1028), was at the foot of Solitary Hill (Gushan) in Hangzhou. Its name refers to Lin Bu's fondness for these birds.

pavilion? Should this latter be the case, the circumstances of the people in later days can then be seen from the repair of a single pavilion. How could others dare not to exert themselves?

I undertook this project, however, emphatically not for enhancing the beauty of the pavilion's look, nor for indulging myself in pleasurable strolls around it—these are not what I am willing to do. It was just that I regarded myself as being fond of the remote past, and was trying to revive and promote literary elegance and dignity. In this regard, as something of a latecomer, I was enlightened by, and at the same time, cast reflection back on to, Song Luo as my forerunner, as yet without living up to his example in terms of the discharge of administrative affairs and protection of the people.

I would humbly say that it was the duty of the local official to promote that which had been neglected and to make up for that which was lacking, while at the same time constantly guarding against simply continuing along the same rut left by his prede-cessors. Previously, I had the Garden of Suitability repaired so that the lecture rooms could be restored;[41] the Temple of Famous Officials was renovated so that the ritual ceremonies and codes could be respected. Most recently, there was also the project to dredge the Rivers Wu and Song, and the pavilion was completed right at the time of these projects. This pavilion was visited by the Qianlong emperor [r. 1736–1795] in the course of his imperial stay in Suzhou. The writings of the Son of Heaven cast shining radiance upon Canglang Pavilion, so bright that it serves to illuminate the rivers and the valleys.[42] Were the opportune moment to have been missed and the pavilion not repaired, it would have been left in a more adverse state after long years of neglect and disuse, and then what would have served to promulgate the grace of the emperor? Besides, on bended knee I myself witnessed the emperor writing in his own hand the words "To wash the cap-strings" in order to emphasize the significance of the refer-ence. And the emperor earnestly gave instructions on affairs of state and the moral conduct of officials, and on exerting ourselves in concrete actions that always accord with the titles that we carry. These are words that I, in particular, as a petty official, must solemnly recite over and over again; and day and night I must seek to repay the

---

41 The Garden of Suitability is opposite Canglang Pavilion, directly across the stream. Previously a corner of the piece of land that is regarded as the site of the garden of Canglang Pavilion, it became separated from the garden site in 1767 when the Governor of Jiangsu, Shen Deqian (1673–1769), acquired it and constructed the Garden of Suitability, then called variously The Forest Close to the Mountain (*Jinshanlin* 近山林) and the Garden of Joy (*Le yuan* 樂園) as part of a tripartite structure, the other two parts being Academy of the Orthodox (*Zhengyi shuyuan* 正誼書院) to the east and the ancestral temple of the Shen family in the west. Already closely related therefore to an institution for classical education, it was turned into a "school garden" in 1827 by Liang Zhangju.

42 Among the many things the Qianlong emperor wrote in association with Canglang Pavilion, two inde-pendent sentences, written in the emperor's calligraphy, are most relevant to the points Liang Zhangju makes here: "I know not who are the 'washing the cap-strings' men" and "Send word to those who visit this pavilion: exert yourselves so that you are judged a man whose actions accord with his title."

imperial favor I have been shown with efforts that match the emperor's expectations, not with actions that are unworthy of them.

To the left of the pavilion there had been a shrine to Zimei, as well as two shrines, one to Han Shizhong, the Prince of Qi, and one to Song Luo; these too have been renovated and newly decorated. And to the east of the road prepared for the emperor, a vacant plot of land was adequately acquired to serve as a place where colleagues may drink wine and chant poems. The origins and vicissitudes of all these structures were briefly recorded and carved on stone. As for the respected Liang Hong, a distant member of my own clan, he must be accounted the most outstanding of all sojourners in Suzhou. With his noble character and graceful disposition, he was reverently looked up to by men of all ages. Thus, a multi-storied hall has been built by the side of the pavilion, where sacrifices can be offered to him, so that when the pavilion is repaired some day in the future, this shrine too can have the benefit of being repaired concurrently. In this way, it is to be hoped that the shrine will never be neglected. The deeds of Liang Hong should be recorded separately; I will not give note of them here.

"Record of the Restoration of Canglang Pavilion" (*Chongxiu Canglang ting ji* 重修滄浪亭記)

ZHANG SHUSHENG 張樹聲 (1824–1884)

As a young man in his native Anhui region, Zhang Shusheng was involved in resistance to the Taiping (1850–1864) and Nian (1853–1868) rebellions, and so came to the attention of senior officials including Zeng Guofan (1811–1872). He embarked on an official career and eventually became provincial governor of Jiangsu in 1872. At the end of the year, he was promoted to governor general of Jiangsu, Jiangxi, and Anhui, but then had to take mourning leave for the death of his mother. After the mourning period was over, he resumed his distinguished official career, and was involved in military resistance to Japanese aggression in Korea and the northeast as well as to French imperialism in Indochina. He died in office in Guangzhou.

"Record of the Restoration of Canglang Pavilion"

Over the course of the years, from the Song dynasty to the end of the Ming, Su Zimei's Canglang Pavilion has undergone frequent vicissitudes. During the reign of the Kangxi emperor of this present dynasty, the Imperial Inspector Song Luo repaired and restored the pavilion, turning it into a place for drinking wine and chanting poems. At that time, the refinement and taste of the literary talents of those men then associated with the new pavilion earned it great repute. When the governor of Jiangsu, Wu Cunli, was honored with a poem and an imperial inscription bestowed by the Kangxi emperor, he had them engraved on a stele and erected a pavilion to house the stele on the site. During the course of one of his Southern Inspection Tours, the Qianlong emperor stayed in Suzhou and commented on Canglang Pavilion, borrowing the original meaning of the word *canglang*—self-determination—in order repeatedly to admonish, instruct, and exhort the people of Suzhou, from official to craftsman to merchant. Consequently, officials and scholars, old country folk and children in the street, as well as sojourners, travelers, and guests from afar, all without exception took to looking up respectfully at the pavilion, gazing into the distance from it, sighing at the stories about it, and chanting the prose and verse associated with it, holding this pavilion in high esteem. But the local officials who administer this part of the land should fulfil their governmental duties and set worthy examples to ordinary people, and for them in particular, not a moment goes by that they dare ignore the emperor's words.

In the year *dinghai* [1827] of the reign of the Daoguang emperor, the imperial commissioner to Jiangsu, Liang Zhangju, had the pavilion reconstructed; at the same time, the governor, Tao Shu [1778–1839], recovered the portraits of more than five hundred famous and virtuous men of Suzhou Prefecture. These portraits he had copied and carved in stone, and built the Shrine to the Famous and Virtuous on a small, hitherto unoccupied, piece of land in the garden. Every year, sacrifices are offered here according to the seasons, but perhaps because the functions of the Shrine and of the Pavilion have been unrelated to each other for a long period of time, those who point out the place to others continue to say, "This is Canglang Pavilion."

In the year *guihai* [1863] of the reign of the Tongzhi emperor, I led the Huaihai army to Suzhou. At the time, all property, both public and private, had been swept away completely in course of the Taiping Rebellion. When I sought for what was called "the pavilion," it could no longer be pointed out to me, nor was it recognizable. In the eighth month of the year *renshen* [1872], I was appointed acting governor of this region. Thereupon, altars and temples, government offices and examination quarters—all the structures that the government and responsible officials should deal with—were one by one repaired or reconstructed in proper order. And the pavilion also began to be rebuilt. When I returned to the site a year later, the construction work had been completed. A ceremony of sacrifice was planned for the Shrine to the Famous and Virtuous. Prior to this event, I went to the site to take a look around. Seeing "the nearby rivers and distant hills," and "the convergence of the light and shadows," I applauded all the more the skills of that man of the past at the art of description. On top of the piled rocks stood a pavilion, the upturned corners of its roof looking like the wings of a flying bird. One can climb up to the pavilion and from there gaze out into the distance. This is Canglang Pavilion. Behind the pavilion was a south-facing, three-bay hall, its site being the most elevated and least damp to be found in the garden, with the crispest air. Picking up on the import of the sentence "nothing perverse is seen or heard, the Way thus becomes luminous" from Zimei's "Record," the hall was named Hall of the Luminous Way. To the right of the hall but slightly to its north was the Shrine of Su Zimei. All the other structures either followed the old inscriptions on the plaques installed in them or were adapted appropriately to present circumstances. But that structure that faces a bridge and borders on the stream, with its gate opening to the north and its plaque announcing Shrine of the Famous and Virtuous, though nominally under the category of "shrine," is in fact the gate through which the pavilion can be entered. At the southwest end of the garden there is a Buddhist monastery, named the Old Grand Cloud Monastery. The monastery has a separate, south-facing gate, giving on to the streets and alleys. The monastery is subordinate to the pavilion, with the resident monks responsible for all administrative matters. On the whole, among the structures built at this time, only the pavilion remains on top of the hill, a placement that remains the same as that established by the Imperial Inspector Song Luo. All the other structures have been arranged at will, and differ somewhat from the former look of Zimei's place. Yet the sights and scenes of hill and valley, and the splendor of its buildings, are said by all to be by no means inferior to those of past years.

Alas, among the great cities in the Southeast, Suzhou was reputed to be the most prosperous. Its famous gardens and old villas, its Buddhist monasteries and Daoist temples, were in many cases the legacy of preceding dynasties, and had not fallen into disuse over the centuries. It was only during the chaos caused by the Taiping rebels in their rout after four long years during which the city was taken as their bandits' lair, that all this was entirely reduced to ashes.

Canglang Pavilion, having been handed down for a thousand years, is where the intelligent and the elegant converge. The dazzling brilliance of the Imperial Rescript and other writings bestowed on the pavilion shines through. Even the Shrine of the Famous and Virtuous, from its first establishment, also became something upon which the locals fixed their eyes and turned their ears. Thus it seems appropriate that the proper planning and restoration of it did not have to wait until now. However, from the time when the disorder was brought to an end, it has taken us a long period of ten years to search for what was missing and make up for what had been lost. Only then was my plan realized. This was not because of the difficulties in mustering material resources and manpower, but rather due to the fact that the rise and fall of everything surely has its appointed hour.

For this reconstruction project, the Imperial Commissioner, En Xi, actually first initiated the proposal at the time when he was the acting governor, and the funds were raised by the former Acting Imperial Commissioner and the present Imperial Inspector, Ying Baoshi, whereas the construction work was supervised by the Expectants for Prefectural Appointment, Qian Baochuan and Liu Wenqi, and by the sub-prefect of a directly administered sub-prefecture, Ze Changwu. The total manpower used was over 61,500 man-days; the quantity of building materials that were used, such as good timber, hard bricks, iron and other materials, and pigments and lacquer, roughly corresponded to the amount of manpower used. On the day of its completion, people from both the city and the countryside came to have a look. All happy to see that the site had regained something of what it had been in previous times of peace, they then disregarded the great amount of labor and cost spent on it. Perhaps the intention of every man involved in the project was to work as cautiously and as conscientiously as possible, for fear that any non-beneficial measure could blight the beneficial scheme. Consequently, assessment of every craftsman's work was made according to its result while diligence was encouraged, and the expenses on the restoration were made sparingly while its scale was rendered grand. Such was their effort to satisfy people's hearts.

As for myself, I desire to visit this pavilion, because its reconstruction was no easy task; it is also because I consider all the more that the renown and virtue of the men of the past will surely never die out. Striving to accomplish real tasks while avoiding empty rhetoric, and reverently receiving constant admonishment from the emperors, both ordinary people and literati all look up to the great worthies of the past and are thereby encouraged to act. The hearts of a hundred generations are in accord, as right principles govern the state and good morals and manners flourish, responding to the cosmic harmony on high. With good harvests and a prosperous populace, and with all neglected tasks being now undertaken, this region will eventually regain the prosperity of a hundred years ago. In this sense, the successful reconstruction of the Pavilion is an excellent omen. May it be that this is an extravagant hope? For this hope, in particular, should we not make efforts all together?

"Record of a Tour of Canglang Pavilion" (*You Canglang ting ji* 遊滄浪亭記)

ANONYMOUS

Canglang Pavilion in Gusu is the site bequeathed to us by Su Shunqin of the Song. It was burnt down in the year *gengshen* [1860] by the Taiping rebels. Recently, the man who held the reins of local government,[43] seeing that the place, located east of the prefectural school, was eminently close to the Confucian Temple and thus had a bearing on the teaching of culture in the region, considered the dereliction and neglect of the place unsuitable to it; he therefore had it restored and at the same time had it further developed in both scale and structure. None of its features—its temples, halls, platforms, and waterside pavilions, its water, rocks, flowers, and trees—was arranged without having expended extraordinary thought. He undertook this project in this manner in order to regenerate that which had been neglected and to continue that which had been severed, an enterprise that should be seen as part of the task of nourishing the people and nurturing talent. This man's intentions were both good and profound indeed.

---

43   In all probability, the man referred to here is Zhang Shusheng, the author of the previous text.

In the spring of the year *yihai* [1875], when all the craftsmen had completed their work, I roamed around the place together with a few friends. Upon our arrival, we observed crowds of visitors there as if it were a marketplace; it was truly a scene that betokened an age of peace and plenty.

That which has been called Canglang is a pond of about half a *li* long and roughly from over ten paces to twenty or thirty paces wide. Along both banks of the pond are piled Yellow Mountain rocks of all shapes and sizes, some tall, some low, some jutting out and some curving in, forming range upon range of precipitous and perilous mountain ridges, all of which look quite fearsome. In the pond, numerous water lilies have been planted; their new blossoms dot the surface of the water. Over the pond is a zigzag bridge. The area to the north of this bridge is protected by a span of wall that is regularly pierced by flower windows.[44] Two or three paces south of the bridge stands the main gate, with the words "Shrine of the Five Hundred Famous and Virtuous" inscribed on top of it.

We then crossed the bridge and entered the Shrine. There immediately a rocky hill stood in our way. Along a small path on the hill one could twist and turn one's way up. Instead of taking this path, we entered a cavern, only to be delighted by its hidden depths and complex configuration. This cavern may well be connected to an opposite end, but, cut off in the middle by a rock, it is not open all the way through, and to get to that opposite end one has to make a long detour—not even Ni Zan's Lion Grove can lay claim to a uniqueness and supremacy of design like this.[45] There is an ancient well in the cavern; from a stele embedded in one of its stones we learned that the well was sunk during the Daoguang reign period [1821–1850] by the Imperial Inspector Chen Luan [1786–1839], in order to provide easy access to water for the monks. As the well was being dug, once the bottom had been reached, several bushels of ashes—signs of previous disasters in this place—were unearthed. Also found there were a few bricks dating back to the Han dynasty, these latter promptly having been fashioned into ink-stones.

Beneath the hill there is a small pond, the water of which is so pellucid that one can count the swimming fish. At the foot of the hill is a stone bridge; one of my companions said, "Every time after the rain, the water from the hill gushes out from right beneath the stone bridge, and then pours down into the pond. A rather extraordinary sight." After walking across the bridge and turning north for a few paces we entered

---

44   This kind of wall is called *huaqiang* (flower wall)—that is, a wall pierced regularly by "flower windows" (*huachuang*). The "flower windows" are of two kinds—openwork and tracery—of various outline shapes. They are most often set in freestanding walls or in a wall standing in the middle of a veranda to form a double veranda, serving both to divide and to link up garden spaces into ones of different character.

45   The garden of Lion Grove in Suzhou is known for its curiously-shaped rocks. It became particularly famed for its association with Ni Zan (1301–1374), self-styled "Ni the Foolish," an outstanding Yuan dynasty artist and poet and one of the great figures of Suzhou history.

a short veranda, then finding ourselves in a small south-facing waterside pavilion of three bays, encircled to its front by a wall pierced by flower windows. A round doorway stands to the western end of the wall, its inscription announcing: "Round Opening to a Mountain Path." Opposite, on the other side of the front wall, stands a bell tower, so high that it seems to stretch all the way over the clouds above; the bell is tolled at fixed times throughout night and day. At the foot of the wall stones of all shapes and sizes are piled to form a flower terrace, with an exuberant display of herbaceous peonies. Sadly, these flowers had passed their best when we visited the garden. An inscription found within the waterside pavilion reads: "Waterside Pavilion of Lotus Scent."[46] A couplet runs: "A little boat, with fish swimming around it, is poled away under the moon; / The small pavilion, looking out on the water, opens up for the flowers." The back wall is studded with a number of windows in the *hehe* style,[47] bordering right on the Canglang pond. Leaning on a windowsill here and gazing down at the pond, the bluish-green lotus leaves and clear blue water could be quite refreshing, but since we were caught up in the excitement of our tour of the garden at the time, we had not a moment to pause at this spot.

Coming out of the small waterside pavilion and walking southward, we entered a stretch of winding veranda. Set within this veranda and standing against the wall is a pavilion; in the pavilion an imperial stele has been respectfully erected, on which is inscribed the poem from the imperial brush of Kangxi bestowed upon Provincial Governor Wu Cunli. Also installed in the pavilion is a couplet composed by the emperor that reads: "When rain, precious as oil, becomes ample, farming households are filled with bliss; / Where flowers, grown in the county, remain bright, local officials are honest and upright."

Beyond the pavilion the veranda continues to zigzag southward, before turning eastward, and it rises up here and slopes down there, rather uneven along its way. The southern section of the veranda is perhaps its highest point, with a plaque reading "Walking Along the Winding Bank"—it faces the front hillock, with a pond separating the two. There is a small door opening to the south at Walking Along the Winding Bank. Entering the doorway, we were confronted with a number of small galleries, set in a transverse position and seemingly in the form of a boat. The western part of this complex is called "Clearness of the Western Hills," the east part is called "Eastern Field," and the inscribed plaque for the central part reads "Guesthouse of Refreshing Fragrance." In the small courts here, to either side, are planted small-leafed, flowering vines, as well as many other kinds of trailing plants, such as climbing figs, angelica, and wisteria.

---

46   All other sources give "Waterside Pavilion of Lotus Flowers."

47   The *hehe* (alternatively called *zhizhai* in northern China) window is characterized by a vertically tripartite framework in between two pillars of a building, in which the upper part is fixed to the structure, the middle part can be turned open outward on a horizontal pivot at the top, and the lower part is removable.

Slightly to the south of Clearness of the Western Hills there is a hall of three bays, facing southward. In all of the inner surface of the walls of the hall are imbedded carved stone figurines, these being the five hundred famous and virtuous men. The first of these figures commemorated is Taibo, the last being virtuous men of our present dynasty, such as Tang Bin [1627–1687] and Lu Longqi [1630–1693], who once held office here. The rest are men of fame and virtue from throughout the Jiangnan region. The plaque here reads: "Making Teachers for the People."[48] The central couplet reads: "The music is perfected, the rituals are clarified—this is the enterprise of the virtuous and the sage; / The rivers flow, the mountains remain still—this is the heart of the wise and the benevolent." To the left and right, another couplet reads: "The famous throughout thousands of years are gathered in this hall, in the fragrance of the ritual tables and vessels, their karmas having not followed the route of practice to Arhatship; / The former worthies told of in the official histories, collectively recording their achievements in literary compositions, their illustrious spirit having been inaugurated by Taibo's relinquishing of his claim to the throne." One further couplet on the outer front pillars reads: "The official caps and gowns of the worthy of a hundred generations have been assembled, the men who illumined antiquity and enlighten the present, their accomplishments all within the scope of Confucian morality and teaching; / The ritual tables and vessels throughout the San-Wu region are given pride of place, sustaining common practices and encouraging good customs, and not merely in matters of imperial examinations and literary composition."

In front of the shrine there is a clump of bamboos, encircled by a low railing. Deep within the bamboos a small building is faintly to be seen. There is also a short veranda to the west of the shrine, where a half-fronted pavilion has been built. Within this pavilion stands a stele; on its lower half is carved a portrait of Wen Zhengming, while the upper half carries an inscription in the hand of the Qianlong emperor. The plaque on the front of the pavilion reads: "Pavilion for Looking Up to the High Hill."[49] As we were pacing up and down, and looking all around us, we suddenly heard the beat of a wooden fish and Buddhist monks' chanting of the sutras, coming to us from the Monastery of White Clouds situated to the west,[50] with a small door by the side of the Pavilion for Looking Up to the High Hill opening onto it.

Entering this small door, we found ourselves inside the monastery. The first main hall enshrines Avalokitêśvara, the giver of sons. The plaque here announces:

---

48   This locution (*Zuo zhi shi* 作之師) comes from the *Book of Documents*.

49   The name of this pavilion alludes to an ode (Mao #218) in the *Book of Songs*, a couplet of which reads: "The high hill is looked up to; / The great road is easy to be traveled on"; see *The Chinese Classics*, vol. 4, *The She King or The Book of Poetry*, ed. and trans. James Legge (Oxford: Clarendon Press, 1893–1895), 393.

50   This may have been the remainder of Grand Cloud Monastery that Gui Youguang mentions in his "Record of Canglang Pavilion."

"Auspiciousness Leading to the Vermilion Ceremonial Robe." The principal couplet reads: "The winding water linked with the place of the immortals, the red color nicely setting apart a thousand lotus flowers, looking at the crenellations curving and encircling, one knows that there must be clouds of compassion hovering over the northern city wall; / The mundane world opening to the land of the Buddha, the emerald-green color enwrapping the cypresses' shadows, wishing the treasured son to be born and reared, one hears the repeated sutra chants with echoes of Southern Chan." One further couplet placed to either side of the principal one reads: "This splendid place adjoins the famed Shrine, and with the bright moon and clear streams, one may ask who, right at this place and moment, will point out the way; / The all-encompassing Dharma gives us its teaching in images, and though rooted in the Buddha-mind to bear good fruit, it all must make its start in the human heart." The inscribed plaque for the meditation hall at the back announces: "The Clouds of Compassion illuminate all," and its couplet reads: "The Buddhist monastery is immersed in fresh fragrances—surrounding the city walls, flowers are opening in their tender red grace; / The meditation hall is touched by distant sounds—on the other side of the wall, bamboos are tapping each other in their emerald-green delicacy."

As we were intoning the couplets, an old monk, Yuetan, appeared. He said to me: "I once composed some couplets in Jinling for laypeople to intone. The couplet for the Monastery of the Subtle Fragrance runs: 'The four hundred and eighty Buddhist monasteries were prosperous and splendid, but they all surrendered to the boundless misty rain;[51] / The thirty-six Cavern Heavens are remote and faint, so let us arrange for the moment a small gathering among these groves and springs.' And the couplet for the old pavilion at the Monastery of Manifesting Loyalty in Jinling runs: 'Ten thousand calamities would not wear away a slice of stone; / The solitary pavilion once again beholds the hills of the Six Dynasties.'" Over a cup of tea we chatted away together for quite a while, and this chance meeting can be called compatibility of the time. Off the top of my head I drafted a couplet at the meditation hall, which reads: "Within the shadow of the White Clouds is the place where monks stay; / Amid the fragrance of red lotuses is the place for Buddhist practice." But this was no more than to spice up our interest in the tour.

Leaving the Monastery of White Clouds, we continued to follow the previous route and returned to the front of the Shrine of the Famous and Virtuous. As we set foot in the depths of the bamboo grove opposite, we found a small building of several bays, having windows opening on its four sides, with a plaque reading: "Bamboos

---

51   The Tang poet Du Mu's (803–852) poem "A Quatrain on Spring in Jiangnan" (*Jiangnan chun jueju* 江南春絕句) gives the lines: "Of the four hundred and eighty Buddhist monasteries of the Southern Dynasties capital Jinling, / How many towers and terraces loom in the misty rain?"

of Exquisite Delicacy."[52] Here the tables, chairs, tea tables, and couches are all made of bamboo; teapots and teacups are provided in fair sufficiency, possibly because this is a place for visitors to tarry for a little while. We once again spent a few moments sitting there and sipping our tea; gazing around us at the emerald-green bamboos, in the thin sunlight filtered through the stems that were gently swayed by fresh breezes, all our vexations were dispelled.

Passing through the Bamboos of Exquisite Delicacy and turning slightly eastward, we then found yet another small building of a few bays, which looked rather complex and yet orderly in layout. Although this building is physically connected to the stone house in the south, to reach the stone house, however, one has to go quite a long way around. A few wutong trees had been planted in the courtyard east of the building, whereas to its southwest it was all bamboos. Since there were as yet no inscriptions for this place, one of my companions suggested, "Would it not be better if we simply called it 'Mountain Hut of Azure-Green Wutong Trees and Emerald Bamboos'?" To this suggestion, another of my companions responded, "Accurate it is indeed, but rather too explicit." I then interposed: "'Mountain Estate for Washing the Azure-Green' seems to be a bit more suitable," and further proposed a couplet: "After the rain, the place where the guests linger becomes greener, / In the chilly night, the coming autumn is heralded by the fallen leaves."

Passing through the Mountain Estate of Washing the Azure-Green and turning eastward, we reached the Hall of the Luminous Way. There is a stage opposite to the hall, as well as side halls on both its left and right; the scale of the hall is quite grandiose. Walking southward along the side hall to the west, we reached a small doorway opening westward; inside the doorway is the stone house. The inscription on a stone in front of the house reads: "Under the Skies Buddhist Followers Spreading Dharma."[53] Inside the stone house and on its lintel is the imperial inscription bestowed by the Daoguang emperor [r. 1821–1850], reading: "Studio for Imprinting on the Mind."[54] There are stone

---

52   In all other sources, the name of this building is given as "Emerald-Green Delicacy."

53   This inscription was written by Lin Zexu (1785–1850) when he was the Governor of Jiangsu. There exists in the folklore another interpretation of the term *zhengmeng* in this particular context, involving the story of a couple of flower-growing lovers who often used the stone room as their place of assignation, but who later were separated forcefully by a local bully. In this context, the phrase could be translated as "Heaven testifies to the pledge."

54   All other sources indicate that the inscription reads "Stone Cabin for Imprinting on the Mind" (*Yinxin shiwu*). Interpretations of this inscription are tentative. The term *yinxin* in Chan Buddhism signifies "having the Buddhist teachings imprinted on and verified in the mind, leading to sudden realization and awakening," which appears to be in line with the inscription as found here. Another, simpler, interpretation would be one that corresponds with the folktale about the two lovers: "imprint on the hearts." Still another possibility is said to have come from the personal experience of Tao Shu (1778–1839). When Tao was received in audience by the Daoguang emperor in 1835, he told the emperor that he studied at Shuiyue monastery in his home place, Anhua in Hunan Province; and in front of the monastery was the Shimen Pond, in the heart of which stood

tables and stools in the middle of the house, rendering it quite secluded and intriguing. Sitting upon a stool, I felt a stream of cold air blowing in through the stone window, sending shivers down my spine.

Coming out of the stone house and glancing upward, we saw that a tall, two-storied hall had been built on top of the stone house, its plaque reading: "Gazebo for Viewing the Mountains." Once we had mounted the stone stairs up on to the first floor, the scenery of the entire garden came into view. At this point, I said, "I have weak feet; no need to climb farther up." But one of my companions responded, "'If you wish to exhaust the distant view of one thousand *li*, / Then climb up one farther story of the tower.'"[55] We thus climbed up together to the top floor; the dwellings of the one hundred thousand households, along with Lake Tai and its surrounding hills of eight hundred *li*, thereupon were all brought within our field of vision.

Descending from the Gazebo, we resumed the route we had previously taken, and arrived at the Hall of the Luminous Way. Lofty, spacious, and grandly broad, it truly claims its place as the main building of the whole garden; the large characters on its name plaque, dignified and imposing, likewise prove equal to the hall's circumstances. The principal couplet here runs: "Once the tale of the man of fame and virtue is carved on the white and clean rock, accompanying the mist and water of Lake Juqu, and the clouds and hills of the Linwu cavern-heaven, it leaves its splendor to be appreciated only in this world; / When the perusing of official documents met with days of leisure, he would then loosen the belt to watch the weeding of the field, and stop the carriage to ask about the local customs, his interest never being merely in wine-drinking and poem-reciting, nor in idle strolling."[56] Another couplet runs: "In the grand picture of scenes perceptible to all six senses, this place still takes the share of the illumination of the present moon; / Ten years after the flames of war, the famous hill once again relies on great and enduring fame."[57]

---

an upright and foursquare rock, resembling a seal in shape and thus called "Seal Rock in the Heart" (*Yinxin shi*). After hearing of this, the Daoguang emperor wrote out the four characters *Yinxin shiwu* (Cabin of the Seal Rock in the Heart) and bestowed it on Tao Shu. Tao Shu then had the emperor's calligraphy carved on stone in his home place as well as over ten other places, including at Mount Lu, the Tower of Yueyang, Qingliang Hill in Nanjing, Golden Hill in Zhenjiang, and Canglang Pavilion in Suzhou.

55 Quoting a couplet from the Tang poet Wang Zhihuan's (688–742) poem "Climbing up the Guan Que Tower."

56 The first half of this couplet refers to Su Shunqin. "The white and clean rock" may allude to the second "Song of Herding the Cattle": "In the Canglang water and above the white and clean rocks, / There is a carp half a foot in length. / In a shabby, unlined garment cut at the shin, / I herd the cattle from early morning to midnight. / The yellow calves walk up to the slope of the hill to have a moment of rest, / —But I intend to give you up and go into service in the state of Qi." The second half of the couplet refers to Song Luo.

57 "The six senses" derives from Buddhist terminology, referring to sight, hearing, smell, taste, touch, and longing, which are generated from the "six roots" of all evil deeds: the eye, ear, nose, tongue, body, and mind. The sentence alludes to the Tang poet Li Bai's (701–762) *Ba jiu wen yue*: "The men of today cannot be in view of

The couplet on the pillars that are positioned on the left and right sides of the central front pillars runs: "The mist and water of the Pond of a Hundred Flowers are as pellucid as those of this place, which, like a painting, was re-traced last year—the predestined relationship made through the burning of joss sticks and candles suitably exists between Du Fu and Su Shunqin; / The wind and the waves of the ten-thousand *li* streams are most perilous, whereas at this place black dust can be washed off—the groves and streams make one feel at ease, whereby one understands that being invited to this place as a recluse is equivalent to the roaming of immortals."[58] One further couplet runs: "At this place, the fisherman's flute can be listened to in company, and I envy you gentlemen who, in your spare time after dealing with official documents, in refined mood, follow the example of Yu Liang [289–340] on the Southern Tower; / For the moment, the worldly cap strings may be washed a little, and I intend to pole a boat tomorrow and leave straightway, to the dark-blue sea where my sentiment agrees with that of the distant Cheng Lian."[59]

Moreover, in the middle of the Hall of the Luminous Way hangs a painting entitled "Scenes of Canglang Pavilion."[60] All the various scenic features in the garden, each patch of water or single stone, each twist and turn, have been fully depicted in this picture, without the slightest error. Also portrayed are the distant hills and the nearby city walls—views that fall outside the garden, looking as if they are now appearing and

---

the moon in the remote past, / The moon of today once shone upon the men of the remote past." "The flames of war" refers to the fall of the city of Suzhou to the Taiping rebels in 1860 and the destruction of Canglang Pavilion, along with many other structures in and around the city.

58   The Pond of a Hundred Flowers, about seven *li* west of the city of Chengdu, was the place where the great Tang poet Du Fu (712–770) built his Thatched Hut. The character for "pellucid" in this couplet has been replaced by a homophone meaning "affection" on the plaque that hangs presently in the hall, hence giving a sentence that reads: "The mist and water of the Pond of a Hundred Flowers share the affections with those of this place." The suggested association between Su Shunqin and Du Fu in this sentence apparently is based on more than the fact that Su shared his literary name, Zimei, with Du Fu, but such was Su's adoration for Du Fu that he took the *zi* or literary name of the latter as his own, and a number of Su's contemporaries seem to have regarded him as a follower of Du Fu. In the plaque that hangs in the hall presently, the character for "is equivalent to" in this couplet has been replaced by a word meaning "surpasses." The couplet was composed in 1874 by Xue Shiyu (1818–1885), a native of Quanjiao (in present-day Anhui) and 1853 *jinshi* degree holder.

59   The Southern Tower, also known as Tower for Playing with the Moon, alludes to the one south of Echeng County in Hubei Province. According to Liu Yiqing's *New Account of Tales of the World*, when Yu Liang, a brother-in-law of Emperor Ming (r. 323–325) of the Eastern Jin dynasty (317–420), was stationed at Wuchang, "on autumn nights when the air was fine and the views were clear, he would ask his subordinates such as Yin Hao and Wang Huzhi to climb up the Southern Tower and recite poems." Cheng Lian is believed to have been a master *qin* player in the Spring and Autumn period (770–476 or 722–479 BCE). Legend has it that Bo Ya, later famed for his skill at playing the *qin*, followed Cheng Lian and studied his art for three years, but still failed to reach its consummation. Cheng Lian then took Bo Ya to the Island of Penglai in the East Sea, where he made Bo Ya listen to the roar of the surging waves and the sad cries of the forest birds. Drawing his inspiration from these sounds, Bo Ya eventually became the most skilled of all *qin* players.

60   In all likelihood, this is a reference to "The Complete Depiction of All the Scenery of Canglang Pavilion" (*Canglang ting quanjing tu* 滄浪亭全景圖), drawn in 1883 by the Buddhist monk Jihang.

then disappearing among the barely discernible mist and clouds. To depict a scene of a thousand *li* on a one-foot scroll, this truly requires a miraculous brush, and the painting must be accounted a supreme example of the art.

After a while we came out of the hall and walked around behind it, where once again a sizable hillock blocked our way. This is the main hill of the garden, named Northern Slope. The hill stretches from here westward and joins the range situated just inside the entrance of the garden. On the hill stands a square stone pavilion, on which the three characters "Canglang Pavilion" [*cang lang ting*] have been inscribed. The couplet on the pillars reads: "Fresh breezes and the bright moon are themselves priceless; / All the nearby rivers and distant hills have their affective nature."[61] The pavilion is surrounded by quite a few extraordinary peaks, all of which defy description. Here there is also the stump of a huge withered tree, perhaps left over from the conflagration of the Taiping rebellion. Flowering apricots are planted everywhere, both on the hill and at its foot, as well as on the nearby level ground.

Walking eastward from the back veranda of the Hall of the Luminous Way, and then turning north, we found there a small, west-facing building, named the Realm of the Jasper Flower. Attached to the rear of the building is a south-facing gallery of three bays. Flowering apricots have been planted in the courtyard here as well, and the plaque for the gallery reads: Study for Revealing the Heart, perhaps picking up on the import of the line "A few touches of flowering apricot reveal the heart of Heaven and Earth."[62] Opening the screen door of the Study for Revealing the Heart and proceeding north, one comes across another and reverential pavilion that has been erected in the veranda. The stele that stands in this pavilion is inscribed, in Qianlong's imperial hand, with the words "The Pavilion for Sighing in Self-Reproach about the Tidal Floods."[63]

Passing through the pavilion and moving on north before turning west, we came to a very long stretch of veranda designed for strolling, closely bordering on the Canglang pond. The veranda is partitioned down the middle by a wall that is pierced by flower windows; one can walk on either side of the wall. The twists and turns to left and right and the undulations up and down of the veranda are incredible. At the eastern end of

---

61 This couplet is composed by Liang Zhangju, using one sentence from Ouyang Xiu's poem entitled *Canglang ting* and one from Su Shunqin's "Passing by Suzhou."

62 From Weng Sen's (fl. late thirteenth century) poem, "Joy in Reading Throughout the Four Seasons—Winter": "Where to find joy in reading? / —A few touches of flowering apricot blossoms reveal the heart of Heaven and Earth."

63 In 1747, the coastal area of Jiangnan was hit by hurricanes and subsequently was at the mercy of severe tidal flooding. The Qianlong emperor composed a set of seven poems, entitled "Sighing at the Disasters of the Tidal Floods in Jiangnan," expressing his concerns about the suffering people and his self-reproach, which were carved in stone and erected the following year by the incumbent Governor of Jiangsu, An Ning, at the eastern foot of the hill in Canglang Pavilion.

the veranda, a pavilion that is connected to the veranda stands above the purling water. Opposite the pavilion, on the north bank, a patch of weeping willows grows at the foot of the flower-windowed wall, encircled by red railings. The surface of the pond at this place is broadest, and it is here that the water caltrops and lotuses are most exuberant. Farther east as the pond becomes deeper, a few pleasure boats that are moored take the place of the lotus leaves. To the east of the pavilion a short wall demarcates the boundary of the garden; cultivated fields of dozens of *mu*, which do not belong to the garden, lie beyond this wall. But this pavilion offers a sight of splendor that in fact ranks first in the whole garden. Within the pavilion there is a small plaque reading: "Listening to the Chanting." Su Shunqin's "Record of Canglang Pavilion" is engraved on the screen here. I once again composed a couplet for the scene that goes: "A thousand red lotus float on the surface of three-foot-deep water; / One bend in the stream reflects the new moon, and half the pavilion is filled by the breeze." After standing in the pavilion for just a little while, I began to feel as if I were floating in the air, on the point of becoming an immortal.

Stepping out of the pavilion and walking westward around the veranda to its very end, we came across one more building of three bays, enveloped by galleries. It has windows on all four sides: those on the south open on the hillock, at the foot of which tree peonies are planted evenly; those on the north overlook the water; and those on the west join the main entrance of the garden. At this point, having come all this way from the west of the garden, one seems to have toured its entirety. The plaque here reads: "Kiosk Facing the Water." The couplet runs: "Wash the cap strings when it is clear, wash the feet when it is muddy; / The wise take joy in the waters, the humane take joy in the mountains." One more couplet on the outer front pillars runs: "The great virtue is called the generation of life; / The humane heart is its essential quality."[64] Reading a colophon to this couplet, we learnt that it had been written for a ceremony for releasing captive fish and animals.

Just as we intended to take our leave of the garden, having sat together in the kiosk for a while, one of my companions suddenly said, "There is one more quiet and secluded spot in this garden, to which I should direct you gentlemen." Everyone was surprised—since our tour had already reached all parts of the garden, what quiet and secluded place could there still be? Then, with my fellow visitor leading the way, we walked through the winding paths and rounded the curving verandas, once again arriving at the Monastery of White Clouds. After some negotiation with the old monk on the part of our guide, the monk led us into the monastery kitchen. Opening a small door and passing through it, we saw over a hundred peach trees, covering the whole

---

64   The colophon, written by Wu Changshuo (1844–1927), indicates that the couplet was composed in 1828 by a certain Cai Lin to commemorate the Buddhist practice of setting free captive fish and animals, performed at Canglang Pavilion in the summer of that same year.

area. Another of my companions objected: "This spot can't really be called 'quiet and secluded.'" "Not as yet," replied the companion who had made the original claim. On entering the peach grove, the old monk said, "These nectar peaches come from Shanghai, and were transplanted here by a senior official of the local government. Right now they are bearing fruit, and for this reason visitors are not permitted here. Behind the theater stage that is situated in front of the Hall of the Luminous Way, there is a door originally opening onto this place; now it is kept closed on purpose." I remarked, "Does not the poem 'Sweet Pear-Tree' from the *Book of Poetry* fit in with this circumstance?"[65] On hearing my comment, the old monk chanted "May the Buddha bless you all" several times before taking his leave.

As my companions and I came out of the peach grove, we saw a patch of farmland, its southeast end bounded by a bamboo fence. Looking out over the fence, the emerald peaks of the distant hills were like a painting; nearby were the rounded, embracing city walls, whereas slightly to the west stood Pan Gate and the old pagoda.[66] As we were gazing into the distance, the sound of a bell tolling came from the adjacent courtyard—perhaps the monks of the monastery were starting their evening vespers. Within the bamboo fence lie a few *mu* of cultivated fields. The second cropping of wheat had ripened and had now been reaped and taken to the threshing ground; the field was about to be re-ploughed for growing rice. There was also oilseed rape, the profuse seedpods of which were bursting open, but which had not yet been harvested. Mulberries and flax were planted on all the remaining plots of land, while chickens, ducks, and the like were present everywhere.

Into a plot of land there, a stream of cool spring water diverted from afar has been made to flow to form a pond; over the pond a small arched bridge of stone has been built. Along the edge of the pond peach and willow trees have been planted, encircling the pond; when fair breezes blow, the green shade cast by these trees seems about to drip. Bordering on the pond and facing west is a thatched cottage of a few bays, the reeds that cover the roof looking quite neat and clean. Beyond the eaves of the thatched roof there stand a shed-like frame for bean vines and a trellis for other climbing plants. A few old vines have spiraled their way up the trellis, while hyacinth beans and many other kinds of melons and vegetables are particularly abundant around the shed. Under the eaves of the cottage a well sweep, with its accessories, is set in place, and so is a complete set of farming implements. The bamboo tea tables and wooden couches

---

65   This poem, Mao #16, goes, in James Legge's translation: "This umbrageous sweet pear-tree; / Clip it not, hew it not down. / Under it the chief of Shao lodged. / This umbrageous sweet pear-tree; / Clip it not, break not a twig of it. / Under it the chief of Shao rested. / This umbrageous sweet pear-tree; / Clip it not, bend not a twig of it. / Under it the chief of Shao halted." See *The Chinese Classics*, vol. 4, *The She King or The Book of Poetry*, ed. and trans. James Legge (Oxford: Clarendon Press, 1893–1895), 26.

66   This is a reference to the Pagoda of Auspicious Light (*Ruiguangta* 瑞光塔) in the southwest corner of the city, built initially in 247 but thereafter undergoing many reconstructions.

inside the cottage rooms, as well as all kinds of furnishings, are plain and unadorned; paint has not been applied to them. There are windows on all four sides, through which one may look into the distance. The plaque for the room reads: "Gallery of Occasional Joy." The couplet here runs: "This structure derives from the nearby waters and distant hills; / An appreciation of it comes from somewhere between the poem's mood and the painting's intent." Sitting in the cottage room, the sweet fragrance of the vegetables and the wheat wafts in on the breeze, dispelling the slightest suggestion of extravagance and ostentation. I remarked, "Now this, indeed, can be called quiet and secluded. 'Mountains in layers, streams doubling back, perhaps there is no path out of here? / Willows darkening, flowers turning bright, and yet another village lies ahead' can serve to give a depiction of this place."[67]

We stepped out of the thatched cottage and walked south a few paces. After crossing the stone bridge and then turning slightly to the west, we arrived at yet another structure—a thatched pavilion. All around the pavilion is a vast openness, with only a few rocks piled here and there. Standing in the pavilion, we suddenly noticed that the sun was setting behind the hills, the flying birds were returning to their trees, and the smoke from evening meals being cooked was rising everywhere; thereupon we quit the garden together.

After returning home, all of the scenic features of the garden were still one by one present before my eyes. Turning up the wick of an oil lamp and dipping my brush in ink, I set myself the task of writing this record of our day.

Suzhou Prefectural Gazetteer (*Suzhou fuzhi* 蘇州府志; extract)

LI MINGWAN 李銘皖 AND FENG GUIFEN 馮桂芬 (1809–1874)

Li Mingwan, whose dates are unknown, was the son of a senior official. He himself gained his Elevated Person (*juren*) degree in 1835, and in 1840 he was awarded a special higher degree by "imperial favor"; that year happened to be the sixtieth anniversary of his father's gaining the presented scholar degree, and this was regarded as highly auspicious. Li Mingwan's first senior provincial posting was as prefectural governor of Songjiang in 1862, where he had to take measures for the relief of refugees from the Taiping rebellion. Shortly thereafter he was posted to Suzhou as prefectural governor, and it was in this post that he undertook the editing of the *Suzhou Prefectural Gazetteer*. Feng Guifen was a native of Suzhou who was known as an educator and writer. He was a student of Lin Zexu (1785–1850), the official charged with suppressing the opium trade in Guangdong. Like Li Mingwan, he gained his highest degree in 1840 (in Feng's case, he was the second-top metropolitan graduate). After a short official career, he joined the staff of the great reformist official Li Hongzhang (1823–1901). Feng was an early advocate of using Western scientific

---

67 The couplet comes from a poem by the Song poet Lu You.

and technical knowledge to benefit China. He lectured in various academies in his home region, and it is not surprising that Li Mingwan would appoint Feng, with his local knowledge and experience, as coeditor of the *Suzhou Prefectural Gazetteer*, which was eventually published in 1883, after Feng's death.

This extract contains several interlinear notes, which are a feature of premodern printed Chinese texts. The notes are printed in smaller characters than the main text (usually two vertical lines of notes to one vertical line of the main text). In this case, the editors of the gazetteer appear to be reproducing a preexisting text on the Canglang Pavilion, and adding notes with supplementary information or pointers to alternative sources or other relevant sections of the gazetteer.

Suzhou Prefectural Gazetteer (extract)

Canglang Pavilion is located to the south of the prefectural school.

> Interlinear note: Both the *Supplementary Notes on the Illustrated Gazetteer of Wu Prefecture* and the first of the Qianlong gazetteers indicate that it is located east of the prefectural school.

The garden consists of a few dozen *mu* of accumulated waters. There is a small hillock by its side, the configuration of which, from top to bottom, is tortuous and intertwines with the waters. *Shilin's Remarks on Poetry* considers it to have been the site of the Prince of Guangling's garden estate at the time of the rule of the Qian family; or it is said, by other sources, to have been built by the Qian family's close kinsman, the military commander of the Suzhou region, Sun Chengyou. During the Qingli reign period [1041–1048], Su Shunqin, *zi* Zimei, procured it and built a pavilion by the water, naming it Canglang. Ouyang Xiu composed a poem, one stanza from which reads: "Fresh breezes and the bright moon are in themselves priceless; / How are they to be treasured if sold for merely forty thousand cash!" The fame of Canglang became celebrated from this time onward. After Zimei's death, the garden's ownership changed time and again. Much later it was possessed by the family of Zhang, Duke of Shen. They had its former site extended and built a great belvedere. They also built a hall on the hill. To the north of the pavilion across the water there was what had been called Cave Hill; this too, the Zhang family acquired. Once they had tidied up the ground, they excavated underneath it and found it full of huge cleft rocks pierced throughout with holes, which were thought by some to have been stored there at the time of the Prince of Guangling. They further piled up these rocks to make up for the hill's deficiencies. The two hills faced each other. As a result, the garden became for a period of time an imposing sight. After the Jianyan reign period (1127–1130) calamity caused by the invasion of the Jurchen barbarians, the garden belonged to the family of Han, the Prince of Qi.

> Interlinear note: According to the *Gazetteer of Wu Prefecture*.

The Han family built a bridge on the two hills to link them up, named Flying Rainbow. Zhang Xiaoxiang [1132–1170] wrote the calligraphic inscription for the plaque. On one of the hills there were two trees with branches interlocked—they were still there during the Qingyuan reign period [1195–1200]. Today, the hall on the hill is called Cold Light. By its side there is a platform called the Pavilion of Chilly Breezes. There is also the Hall of Assisting with Destiny of the World; Geng Yuanding wrote a record of this hall. By the side of the pond is what is called the Pavilion for Washing the Cap Strings. The pavilion accompanied by flowering apricot trees is called the Realm of the Jasper Flower; the pavilion in the midst of bamboos is called Emerald-Green Exquisite Delicacy; and the pavilion beside the sweet cassia trees is called the Guesthouse of Refreshing Scent. However, the most splendid building here is Canglang Pavilion.

Interlinear note: From Lu Xiong's [1331–1380] *Gazetteer of Suzhou Prefecture*.

Throughout the Yuan and Ming dynasties, Canglang Pavilion was disused as a garden and became the place of Buddhist monasteries. During the Jiajing reign period [1522–1566], Prefect Hu Zuanzong [1480–1560] made use of Miaoyin Monastery on the site of Canglang Pavilion garden to establish the Shrine of Han, the Prince of Qi.

Interlinear note: See the section on "Shrines."

The monk Wenying reconstructed Canglang Pavilion by the side of Grand Cloud Monastery.

During the Kangxi reign period [1662–1722] of our present dynasty, the imperial commissioner, Governor Wang Xinming, constructed the Shrine of the Honorable Su.

Interlinear note: See the section on "Shrines."

Later, Director of the Board of Civil Office, Song Luo from Shangqiu, while governing the Wu region, sought out the traces of what survived and then reconstructed the pavilion on top of the hill. After acquiring the three characters *canglang ting* written in clerical script by Wen Zhengming, he had them installed on the lintel of the pavilion. Along the northern foot of the hill and around to the east, he built a small kiosk called Overcoming Self.

Interlinear note: Using the phrase as found in Su's "Record."

Over ten paces down the slope to the west, he built a three-bay building called the Place for Watching the Fish.

Interlinear note: So named by quoting one of Su's poems.

A long veranda was built to protect the pavilion on its south side, which is called Walking Along the Winding Bank. Coming out of the door of the veranda, there was a lofty hall; it was the Shrine of Zimei.

> Interlinear note: This information is derived from the gazetteers produced in both the Qianlong and Daoguang reigns, all of which agree with each other on this point.

In the seventh year of the Daoguang reign [1827], the Governor, Liang Zhangju, reconstructed Canglang Pavilion and wrote a record of the event. In the year *gengshen* [1860] of the Xianfeng reign, the city fell to the Taiping rebels and Canglang Pavilion was razed to the ground. In the twelfth year of the Tongzhi reign [1873], the Governor, Zhang Shusheng, reconstructed the pavilion and wrote a record of the event. The pavilion was rebuilt on the same spot as that built by Song Luo. To its south was the Hall of the Luminous Way; behind the hall were both the Eastern Field and the Clearness of Western Hills. Turning westward from that point there was the Shrine of the Five Hundred Famous and Virtuous. To the south of the Shrine was Emerald-Green Exquisite Delicacy; to the north of the pavilion were the Kiosk Facing the Water, the Pavilion for Reciting Poems in Quietude, and the Waterside Pavilion of Lotus Flowers—all these structures looked out over the water. As for the rest, such as the Guesthouse of Refreshing Scent, the Room for Smelling the Subtle Fragrance, the Realm of the Jasper Flower, the Study for Revealing the Heart, Walking Along the Winding Bank, the Stone Room for Imprinting on the Mind, and the Gazebo for Viewing the Mountains, more than half of them were reconstructed in accord with the conditions of the place, whereas their plaque inscriptions still refer to the old ones. The stone inscriptions inside Canglang Pavilion were all repaired and chiseled, so that they were brought back to their former look. These stone inscriptions included, for instance, the imperial poem and couplet bestowed on Governor Wu Cunli in the Kangxi reign; the imperial phrase, "Sighing at the Disasters of the Tidal Floods in Jiangnan," in the calligraphy of the Qianlong emperor and done in the twelfth year of his reign [1747]; the imperial poem inscribed on the small stone-engraved portrait of Wen Zhengming; the parting poem written by Su Shunqin of the Song for Wang Shu [997–1057] when taking leave of him; Tao Shu's [1778–1839] poem inscribed on the "Portrait of the Five Canglang Pavilion Elders";[68] Zhu Jian's [1769–1850] "Record of the Portrait of the Seven Friends";[69] Yang Zhu's inscription of a poem on the Picture of Discussing Poetry; the portraits of the five hundred famous and virtuous; the anonymous calligraphic inscription of the poem by Ouyang Xiu; Gui Youguang's "Record of

---

68   The Five Canglang Pavilion Elders were Pan Yijuan (1740–1830), Han Feng (1758–1834), Shi Yunyu (1756–1837), Wu Yun (1747–1837), and Tao Shu.

69   The Seven Friends were Tao Jian, Zhuo Bingtian (1782–1855), Zhu Shiyan (1771–1838), Liang Zhangju (1775–1849), Wu Tingchen, Gu Chun (1765–1832), and Zhu Jian.

Canglang Pavilion"; and all the records of reconstruction written after the Kangxi reign. Every spring and autumn now, visitors to Canglang Pavilion come and go endlessly like the shuttles of a loom.

"Record of the Restoration of Canglang Pavilion" (*Chongxiu Canglang ting ji* 重修滄浪亭記)

YAN WENLIANG 颜文樑 (1893–1988)

Yan Wenliang was a native of Suzhou who became well known as an oil painter and art educator. Like many other progressive artists and illustrators of the time, his early formal training in Western-style art came through apprenticeship at the Commercial Press in Shanghai. In 1922, he was instrumental in setting up one of China's earliest art colleges in Suzhou. The college initially rented space in a secondary school. Its finances were precarious, and in 1927 Yan was employed by a charitable organization in Suzhou as curator of the Canglang Pavilion garden, which was at this time somewhat dilapidated; his mission was to establish an art gallery there. He took this opportunity to have some of the buildings repaired for use by the art college, thereby establishing it on a firmer basis. After studying in France from 1928 to 1931, he returned to Suzhou to become principal of the college. After the establishment of the People's Republic of China in 1949, he continued his work as an art educator.

It is important to note that this was the time not long after the May Fourth Movement, when the values of Western modernity and Chinese tradition, perceived as a dichotomy, were vehemently debated. At the same time, the abolition of the imperial examination system in 1905 paved the way for further nationwide burgeoning of educational institutes for the "new culture," and in the world of fine art, Yan Wenliang's college was one of the earliest of such institutes. In this sense, Canglang Pavilion became a physical point where modern Western culture was placed in the face of traditional Chinese culture, as epitomized by the construction in 1931 of a new building with a Roman-style colonnade for the college, just adjacent to Canglang Pavilion.

The confrontation of the two cultural values in Yan Wenliang himself can be sensed in his deemphasizing the traditional cultural and literary import of the site, and in highlighting his nostalgic idealization of the Qing period in respect of its government policies and functions, which for him made it a more desirable alternative to the present time. In other words, the traditional interpretation of the site in cultural and literary terms is shifted by Yan to one of governance. This shift then leads to the issue of the public (*gong*) versus the private (*si*)—a new issue of social interest in modern China—as reflected in Yan's praise of the restoration work on this "public" site of splendor and fame rather than of cultural and literary history, seen as more important than numerous construction works on private villas and mansions, regardless of their cultural or literary import.

"Record of the Restoration of Canglang Pavilion"

There is this Canglang Pavilion in Wu Prefecture, which underwent a pattern of repeated rise and fall from the Song dynasty down through to the Ming. Not until the

Kangxi, Daoguang, and Tongzhi [r. 1862–1874] reigns of the former Qing dynasty, when Song Luo, Wu Cunli, Liang Zhangju, and Zhang Shusheng governed the Wu region, did they, in succession, engage themselves in the renovation of the place. During those years, justice, honesty, and austerity prevailed in the administration of government affairs; thus these men were able to execute their duties in an unhurried, peaceable and easy manner. They did not regard their local office as a post station, while the local men of virtue certainly have possessed attributes that enabled them to continue the commendable efforts of their predecessors. All this happened seventy or eighty years ago. The giant rocks have now shattered and collapsed; the site is laid waste and overgrown with weeds that have buried the small paths. As for the belvederes and waterside pavilions, their beams have cracked and their walls caved in.

When I took the post of Keeper of Canglang Pavilion from May last year [1927], I proposed that funds be raised for the pavilion to be repaired. But this proposal did not have any result. Wu Zishen [1894–1972] was heartily concerned about this circumstance. After having established the Fine Arts Training School in the garden, he took charge of the enterprise of repairing Canglang Pavilion, donating four thousand *yuan* of his own to be used for assembling building materials and gathering craftsmen. The reconstruction work lasted the whole year long. Thereupon, the Gazebo for Viewing the Mountains, Emerald-Green of Exquisite Delicacy, the Kiosk Facing the Water, the Hall of the Luminous Way, the Room for Smelling the Subtle Fragrance, the Study for Revealing the Heart, the Guesthouse of the Refreshing Scent, the Waterside Pavilion for Washing the Flowers—all of the many structures that previously had fallen into dilapidation—were now restored. It would not be an exaggeration to say that the garden has gradually been returned to the former look it had in Zimei's time. Among the gentlemen of our day who built their villas and constructed their mansions, I wonder how many there are who, like Wu Zishen, take on responsibility for the restoration of places of splendor and fame? For this reason, this event cannot but be recorded.

A New Account of Canglang Pavilion (*Canglang ting xinzhi* 滄浪亭新志)

"Preface" (*Xu* 序)

JIANG HANCHENG 蔣瀚澄 (1896/7–1981)

Jiang Hancheng (also known as Jiang Yinqiu) was a native of Suzhou who spent most of his career in the Suzhou area. He was on the faculty of a number of teachers' training colleges, and also taught librarianship; in 1935, he became director of the Suzhou Library. Jiang won considerable renown as a calligrapher in a range of styles, and was a significant figure in the Suzhou art world. In 1937, he was on the selection committee for the second National Art Exhibition organized by the Ministry of Education; a series of annual art exhibitions in Suzhou organized by Yan Wenliang (see above) had been the precursor to these events.

"Preface"

Canglang Pavilion, built by Su Zimei of the Song, is especially prominent. It is a place of fame and splendor in the Suzhou region. During the reign of the Kangxi emperor of the Qing dynasty, the Imperial Inspector Song Luo, following the examples of Zhang Dun and Han Shizhong, had the pavilion repaired and restored. He also compiled *A Brief Record of Canglang Pavilion*, in two chapters. One can enumerate those who later continued to repair Canglang Pavilion: Wu Cunli, the Imperial Inspector; Liang Zhangju, who at the time was serving as Governor of Jiangsu Province; and Zhang Shusheng, the Imperial Inspector immediately after the *Gengshen* [1860] upheaval and in the late years of the Tongzhi reign [1862–1874], now sixty years ago. The site had fallen into disrepair and desolation with each passing day. My fellow Suzhou native, Wu Zishen [1894–1972], was a scholar of cultural refinement and superior attainments. Grieved by the imminent ruin of the pavilion, he himself contributed a huge sum of money to repair and renovate it. All of its structures were brought back to their former outlook. I live in the vicinity of Canglang Pavilion. It was the place where, in my child-hood, I learned to play musical instruments and chant poems. All my places of work in recent years, in addition, have been very close to Canglang Pavilion. More than ten years have passed and my emotional bond with Canglang Pavilion has thus become ever tighter over the course of the past ten or so years. I often wished to continue the enterprise set out by Song Luo's *A Brief Record of Canglang Pavilion* by searching every-where and supplementing its account with all the records, descriptions, inscriptions, and poems that have been written since his time, as well as those earlier sources that he overlooked and did not include in his work. Having been much pressed for time, however, I was not able to concentrate my efforts to accomplish this task. Fortunately, Canglang Pavilion has now been renovated once again, inspiring me to complete my draft of an eight-chapter *A New Account of Canglang Pavilion* as a supplement to Song Luo's book. Ashamed by my own ineptitude and ignorance, I have relied on the guid-ance and assistance of such senior scholars as Jin Hegeng and Shen Zaihua. After the copying and proofreading had been completed, I wrote this preface to be attached to the volume, recording my reflections.

This preface is written in the seventh month of the seventeenth year of the Republic of China [1928], by Yinqiu, Jiang Hancheng, at the Garden of Suitability (Keyuan), Canglang.

"Record of the Restoration of Canglang Pavilion" (*Chongxiu Canglang ting ji* 重修滄浪亭記)

GAO GUANWU 高冠吾 (1892–1953)

Gao Guanwu, who was born in Jiangsu Province, had a military education, graduating from the Baoding Army Officers' College, but then worked in Shanghai, first as a journalist and then as a schoolteacher. After Sun Yat-sen established his Nationalist government in Canton in the early 1920s, Gao traveled south to join the Nationalists and embarked on a military career in the southern provinces of Guangdong and Guizhou. He participated in the Northern Expedition under Chiang Kai-shek in 1926–1927, but clashed with Chiang over the treatment of his commanding officer, and left the army, resuming his writing and teaching career in Shanghai. To make a living, he also undertook a number of other jobs, including running a restaurant on Fuzhou Road, Shanghai's notorious "Blood Alley" but also the location of many bookshops. In 1938, after the Japanese invasion of China, he joined a puppet government set up by the Japanese in Nanjing, becoming mayor of the city. To his credit, he organized the burial in a common tomb of over three thousand unburied victims of the Nanjing Massacre of December 1937, and had a memorial to them set up. When the puppet government in Nanjing amalgamated with the "Nationalist" government of the collaborationist leader Wang Jingwei, Gao Guanwu held a series of high official positions. His essay on Canglang Pavilion was written in or shortly after 1940–1941, when he was resident in Suzhou as a senior figure in the collaborationist Jiangsu provincial government. After the defeat of the Japanese, he lived in obscurity before dying of illness in 1953.

In the context of Gao's career, particularly noteworthy is his reference to Han Shizhong, a well-known Southern Song general. Without specifying in the text the enemies of Han Shizhong's campaigns, this passage may, on the surface, give an impression of Gao Guanwu's aspirations in relation to his own military background, but Han Shizhong was and is famed for his firm anti-Jurchen stance, and for helping restore the Chinese Song rule in Central China, whereas drinking, chanting of poems, roaming, and angling have never been part of the traditionally received story about him; they do, however, seem to relate to Gao's own enjoyment of the site. The implication is that such action—or inaction—is taken only because resistance to the invaders (Jurchen or Japanese) cannot currently be successful. Thus, it is not unreasonable to argue that by implicitly citing Han Shizhong's endeavors as a historical analogy, Gao silently expresses the idea, hidden in the other cases he has cited and under the cloak of his proclaimed aim of "promulgation of the Confucian moral code," of resisting the Japanese occupation and restoring China's lost territories and sovereignty.

"Record of the Restoration of Canglang Pavilion"

What is known as Canglang Pavilion was originally the garden estate of the son of Qian Liu [852–932], Prince Wusu, Yuanliao [887–942]. When Su Shunqin sojourned in banishment in Suzhou, he procured it for forty thousand cash from a close kinsman of the Qian family, the military governor Sun Chengyou. After his time, the site belonged to the family of Zhang Dun, the Duke of Shen, and then became a villa owned by Han

Shizhong, the Prince of Qi. The area encompassed by the garden was much extended; the elevated terraces and belvederes became much more splendid. Throughout the Yuan and Ming periods it was taken for Buddhist monasteries. The monk Wenying once resided there.

Since the beginning of the Qing dynasty, the garden was resurrected for the first time by Song Luo, then repaired for the second time by Liang Zhangju, and restored for the third time by Zhang Shusheng. Tao Zhu [1778–1839] from Anhua furthermore established a shrine to house the stone-engraved portraits of over five hundred famous and virtuous men. Well-known ministers, able generals, great Confucian scholars, upright officials, men of loyalty and moral integrity, exemplars of filial piety and fraternal love, and even figures in art and literature, as well as recluses—figures who have been referred to in Suzhou's historiographical works and whose deeds sufficiently enabled each of them to be a paragon for a hundred generations—are all gathered here. But the people of the Wu region maintain the former name given to the place by Zimei [Su Shunqin], Canglang Pavilion. Perhaps the shrine owes its existence to the pavilion, whereas the pavilion owes the spread of its fame to the shrine.

In the year *dingchou* [1937], with the full-scale invasion of China by Japan, the garden buildings tumbled down. In the year *gengchen* [1940], I came to govern this region. Cherishing the memory of the past, I read Zimei's text and took "Overcoming the Self" for joy. My mind went back to the time of Han Shizhong, the Prince of Qi, who started military operations from Suzhou; leading an army of several thousand men and sweeping over the Yangtze region, he became a famous general in the period of the Restoration.[70] This became the place for his drinking, chanting of poems, roaming, and angling. I further considered Tao Zhu's creation of the Shrine of the Five Hundred Famous and Virtuous; to venerate former thinkers and pass down these models for later generations—these intentions are profound and enduring. This place therefore appertains to the promulgation of the Confucian moral code. If by any chance it were to fall into disuse and lie waste, later generations would not have a source of inspiration for conducting themselves with integrity and honesty, and for giving expression of their sincere admiration for the noble characters. I therefore humbly resolved myself to continue the aspirations of Song Luo and Liang Zhangju, and to have the pavilion and the shrine brought back to the former state they had been in after the Imperial Inspector Zhang Shusheng rebuilt it seventy years ago.

---

70   Han Shizhong, the Song general who advocated resistance against the invading Jurchens, rather than accommodation with them, for forty-eight days in 1130 led an army of eight thousand against the overwhelming Jurchen force of one hundred thousand men. In this context, "Restoration" (*zhongxing* 中興) is a euphemism for the rule of the Song court over only part of its former realm.

In the spring of the following year, funds were raised and the repair work was discussed. The craftsmen were gathered; building materials were assembled. The work lasted for two months and cost over thirty-five thousand yuan. On the day of completion, prominent local figures and I proposed toasts to each other in accordance with ceremonial propriety. I once learned of the way of changes that once the trigram that connotes "Denudation" or "Erosion" has reached its limit, it becomes the trigram "Return."[71] The fall in the fortunes of the pavilion indicates the erosion of things at work; its rise, the impending return of times of prosperity. On days of leisure in spring and autumn, the people of the Wu region stroll around the pavilion, viewing the clearness of its waters and the luxuriance of its plants; they pay homage at the shrine, feeling enlightened in their minds and moved in their hearts. Scholars devote themselves to their books, as do the farmers in their fields, craftsmen in their workshops, and merchants in the marketplaces. Their customs become attuned to those of honesty and sincerity; their moral principles and conduct are tempered. Consequently, the desired accomplishment of peace and order throughout the realm will not be difficult to achieve. From this, we know that the age of prosperity is to return. And, given that this is the case, the rise and fall of one pavilion pertains to the waxing and waning of the circumstances of the age. As the Ode says, "Forever you may be linked to Heaven's charge / And bring to yourselves many blessings."[72] How could the people of the Wu region not exert themselves?

"Notes on Gardens in Suzhou" (*Ji Suzhou de yuanlin* 記蘇州的園林; extract)

JI YONG 紀庸 (1909–1965)

Ji Yong was a scholar of Chinese history and literature, as well as a prolific author on a wide variety of topics between the 1930s and the 1950s. Originally from northern China, he moved south during the Second Sino-Japanese War, and, like Gao Guanwu (see above), he joined the collaborationist "Nationalist" government of Wang Jingwei. During the Civil War, he was on the faculty of the National Social Education College, which was in the Artless Administrator's Garden (Zhuozheng Yuan) in Suzhou. In the early period of the People's Republic, he was director of the office for research on Chinese history at Jiangsu Normal College (now Suzhou University). "Notes on Gardens in Suzhou" was published in 1957.

"Notes on Gardens in Suzhou" (extract)

Canglang Pavilion
None of the gardens within the city is older than this one. Going there to have a look today, one would find its structures fairly mottled, emanating an aura of its antiquity.

---

71 This sentence comes from the *Book of Changes*.

72 *Shi jing* (Mao #235, "King Wen"). Arthur Waley, trans., *The Book of Songs* (New York: Grove Press, 1996), 228.

It is unlike the Lingering Garden, with its air of wealth and nobility, or the Garden of Affability that displays the manner of the nouveau riche. Although the buildings of Canglang Pavilion do not have either the look of splendor in green and gold or carved beams and painted rafters, there is nevertheless a touch of simplicity and dignity, one that well suits the character of Su Zimei [Su Shunqin] as a poet who retired from public life. Zimei's construction of Canglang Pavilion must have happened in the middle of the eleventh century; that was fully eight hundred years ago. This poet gave a dinner party with the money that came from the selling of scraps of paper from the office, thereby committing in elegant style a minor crime of embezzlement. He thereupon lost his official employment, and came to settle in Suzhou. A government official could always get a bit of petty cash, and thus he eventually managed to build this pavilion-garden. We can still see the carved stone bearing the poet's handwriting, which is inlaid into a wall near the Place for Watching the Fish; that flying cursive hand is truly "gorgeous." We do not know, however, if taking the *History of the Han Dynasty* as something to go with his wine is a story that happened while he was living here;[73] perhaps this honorable fellow was full of discontent in his heart, and as a result took this kind of thing as a dish for wine-drinking.

The author of *Six Records of a Floating Life*, Shen Fu [1763–ca. 1810], was a figure of simple and honest disposition. From my point of view, this poverty-stricken scholar in feudal society had suffered enough from his extended family's oppression and was treated with disdain by society. His work is full of flesh and blood, and he may be counted as a classical realist. His old dwelling was by the side of Canglang Pavilion, where he once enjoyed a beautiful full moon in early autumn with Yun, his beloved wife who also was his deeply understanding friend; that experience became an everlasting memory throughout his life. Yun was an interesting figure indeed; she longed to row a boat on moonlit nights on the river outside the pavilion garden. Coming to this place today, how could we possibly not feel like doing the same? Regrettably, there is no boat to row now. I think that such an expanse of flowing water outside Canglang Pavilion is really unsurpassed by other gardens: it flows so naturally, so delightfully, and with such transparent clarity, unlike those cases of "drifting wine cups on the meandering water" that have been deliberately mystified by some people and which tend only to make one feel awkward. Coming many a time across motionless anglers naturally increases my endless envy. The ancients said that when the Canglang waters were clear, cap strings could be washed in them; when muddy, one's feet could be washed instead. Nevertheless, I think that, no matter whether it is clear or muddy, washing one's feet in this stream of water would always be a delightful experience. Precisely for this reason, I find the small pavilion "Watching the Fish" all the more gratifying.

---

73   The author appears either to be unfamiliar with, or to have extracted from its original context, this amusing anecdote said to have taken place in Su Shunqin's father-in-law's house some time before he came to live in Suzhou.

Canglang Pavilion is famed for its engraved stone plaques; so is the Shrine of the Five Hundred Famous and Virtuous in particular. In order to gather engraved stones together, a rubbing of each of the three treasures in Suzhou's stone carvings—the Astronomical Chart, the Geographical Map, and the Map of the city of Pingjiang preserved in the Confucian Temple—is also hung in the "Hall of the Luminous Way." These days, particularly now that the opera *Fifteen Strings of Cash* is popular,[74] would you not wish to take a reverent look at "Clear as the Heavens Kuang"?[75] Please search carefully in the shrine and you will surely find him there, right alongside Zhou Chen [1381–1453], the provincial governor who always dealt with various matters in a bureaucratic way.

The Qianlong emperor was an utterly abominable man: he scribbled everywhere. On the east wall outside the Temple of the Five Hundred Famous and Virtuous there is an engraved portrait of Wen Zhengming, which, laconic and archaic in style, is full of spirit. Yet, perversely, the Qianlong emperor insisted on inscribing a poem on it and then went so far as to believe that, with his poem, Wen Zhengming "would rejoice at this unexpected meeting, not vouchsafed to any of his predecessors." This truly is somewhat akin to smearing the Buddha's head with dung—what ill luck for a literary man of such refined talents. On the adjacent walls there are also the "Portrait of the Five Canglang Elders" engraved by Tao Zhu, and the "Portrait of the Seven Friends" by Liang Zhangju's offspring, both worth viewing as well. Tao Zhu was once Governor of Jiangsu, stationed in Suzhou; later he became Dean of Youyi Art Academy,[76] the academy being located at the Garden of Suitability, just opposite to Canglang Pavilion. This great mandarin had a fine son-in-law; that is, the famous Lin Zexu [1785–1850].

About the pavilion itself, I am not willing to say much, because it is merely an ordinary pavilion on a hill of rocks, and that is all there is to it.

"Suzhou's Canglang Pavilion" (*Suzhou Canglang ting* 蘇州滄浪亭)

CHEN CONGZHOU 陳從周 (1918–2000)

Chen Congzhou was one of the great twentieth-century scholars of Chinese gardens. His family originated from the ancient city of Shaoxing in Zhejiang, a historic cultural center. After graduating in 1942 from university in Hangzhou, he worked in various higher education institutions, including St. John's University in Shanghai, before moving in the early 1950s to Tongji University

---

74   This Kunqu opera, written by an early Qing dramatist and based on a Ming dynasty vernacular story, has retained its popularity and was revived in 1956.

75   Kuang Zhong (1383–1443), a historical figure and once the prefect of Suzhou, was known as an upright official and champion of justice.

76   Perhaps a mistaken reference to the Zhengyi Shuyuan.

(Shanghai), where he spent the remainder of his career as a professor of architecture. One of his teachers in architectural history was the architectural historian and educator Liu Dunzhen, a pioneer in the modern study of Chinese garden history. Chen himself went on to teach and inspire many younger scholars and practicing architects. Chen's first book on gardens was *Gardens of Suzhou (Suzhou yuanlin)* of 1956; this was partly the outcome of personal visits to the gardens while teaching part-time in Suzhou. His five essays collected as *On Chinese Gardens (Shuo yuan)* and published in Chinese and English in 1984 have been influential in the interpretation of Chinese garden aesthetics.

"Suzhou's Canglang Pavilion"

Whenever the gardens of Suzhou are mentioned, people always feel that they are all enclosed within high walls, deeply secluded and tightly sealed off, thus being somewhat deficient in terms of openness. This, of course, was determined by historical conditions that engendered certain limitations to the garden. The ancient masters of crafts, however, were able to create in this small space a garden as an integral part of the house, having a style of its own, and setting apart the space of mountains and groves from the urban space. Should the walls of the garden be dismantled, the appearance of the garden would be changed immediately and would become worthless. Yet there is in Suzhou still another garden, Canglang Pavilion, a famous garden with which everyone is familiar as well. The outward appearance of this garden is not that of the enclosed type. The water of the Fengxi River swirls and meanders its way here from Southern Garden, passing by Grass Knot Monastery (where today stands Suzhou's largest lace-bark pine), its dimpled waves forming an expanse of bluish-green, encircling the garden all the way from the Terrace for Angling to the area around the Waterside Pavilion of Lotus Flowers. The ancient terrace and fine waterside pavilion, tall trees and long verandas, greet the visitor from the other side of the water even before he enters the garden; at this point, the visitor, already rapt in anticipation, is lost in reverie over it.

Canglang Pavilion is a garden that faces the water, but within the garden the hill dominates, and thus the hill and water are diametrically separated from each other. As the saying goes: "Water lends one a sense of vastness, rocks give one a sense of seclusion"—as the visitor crosses the level bridge and enters the gate of the garden, with the austerity of the hill and grove, the atmosphere under his very surprised eyes becomes that of deep silence and stillness; in the twinkling of an eye, the visitor's feeling changes because of it. The garden is surrounded by double verandas, that is, a veranda that is partitioned down the middle by a wall that is pierced by flower windows; one can walk on either side of it. The views from outside the garden cast themselves in through these openwork windows, most tempting to the visitor. The inside and outside of the garden look as if they are separated from each other but they are actually not; the precipice of the hill and the border of the water tend to be severed from each other but are still connected. This was the focus of attention in the garden concept of Canglang

Pavilion. If there had not been this encircling body of water, this single hill and solitary gully in the garden would have seemed prosaic and unworthy of a glance in the first place, and the garden as a whole would not have been able to compete with other gardens. With this one touch outside the garden, its distinctive character was ingeniously brought about; the employment of contrast here has the effect that "Without a single word, refinement and tastefulness are fully achieved."

The extent to which a garden looks hoary and ancient is determined by its trees that are old, and its rocks that appear to be simple and unwieldy; this garden is most prominent in this respect. At the same time, the halls and galleries have no embellishment, while the paths that are stone-paved and verandas that stretch obliquely all wind in and out of groves of bamboos and the shade of broadleaf plants, revealing a lofty and unsullied character without the slightest tinge of any ostentatious or effeminate manner. The Hall of the Luminous Way, spacious and well disposed and enclosed on all four sides, is the main hall of the garden. To its north the ridges and peaks of the hill look like screens; the one that towers up over the tall trees is that called Canglang Pavilion. There the visitor can have a visual command over the whole garden, whereas by the side of the hill the zigzag veranda, where one can lean on the railing and gaze out or have a rest, adapts itself to the contours of the slopes. Its western part has a few windows and forms some courtyards of its own; the openings of its doorways are all differently shaped. But this is not all; its openwork windows, taken as a category, rank first in terms of the variety of their types among those of the gardens in Suzhou.

The Gazebo for Viewing the Mountains is situated in the southwest corner of the garden, and is built on top of a cave that is both tortuous and concealed. At close range, one can look down from it at the former Southern Garden, a scene of level fields and village houses (which now all have been replaced by other buildings); far into the distance, one can gaze at the peaks of Mount Lengjia, Mount Qizi, and other mountains, a vision indistinctly present in front of the balustrade. In front, the garden is flanked by water; outside, the garden borrows the distant view of the mountains—both advantages have been utilized by this garden.

The garden is full of tall trees and slender bamboos; ten thousand stalks sway in the empty sky. The dripping emerald-green and the neat cerulean seep into the visitor's heart; the fragrance of orchids in the small courtyard fills the visitor's sleeves every now and then; the whitewashed walls and the shadows cast by the bamboo form an album of paintings made by Nature itself. They are suitable for viewing in stillness, for elegant rambling, for painting pictures, and for chanting poems. From Su Shunqin, Ouyang Xiu, and Mei Yaochen of the Song dynasty, right down to the famous painter Wu Changshuo [1844–1927] of modern times, well-known writings inspired by this place are so many that they would fill volumes and be so beautiful that one can hardly absorb them all. The quatrain by the earliest owner of Canglang Pavilion, Su Shunqin, in particular, best conveys the tranquil charm in these garden features:

> Night-time rain falls till dawn, and spring-time's waters rise;
> The tender clouds, thick and warm, playfully render it overcast and clear in turn.
> The curtains are thin, the sun hazy, the flowers and bamboos quiet;
> Now and then the young turtledoves coo to one another.

Canglang Pavilion is the oldest existing garden in Suzhou. At the time of the Qian family in the Five Dynasties period it was the garden estate of the Prince of Guangling, Qian Yuanliao; or it is said to have been built by their close kinsman, military commander of the Suzhou region, Sun Chengyou. In the Qingli reign of the Song, Su Shunqin (*zi* Zimei) purchased the piece of land and constructed a pavilion, naming it "Canglang." Later on it was owned by the family of Zhang, Duke of Shen. Destroyed during the Jianyan reign period [1127–1130], it then belonged to Han Shizhong. Throughout the Yuan and Ming, it became occupied by Buddhist monasteries. Miaoyin Monastery and the Shrine of Han, the Prince of Qi, were built during the Jiajing reign [1522–1566] of the Ming. The Buddhist monk Wenying restored Zimei's enterprise in the aftermath of desolation and disrepair. During the Kangxi reign of the Qing, Song Luo, while governing the Wu region, reconstructed Canglang Pavilion, added to it the Shrine of the Honorable Su as well as the Shrine of the Five Hundred Famous and Virtuous (today located to the west of the Hall of the Luminous Way), and built some other pavilions. Canglang Pavilion was repaired in the seventh year of the Daoguang reign [1827] and again in the twelfth year of the Tongzhi reign [1873], thereupon taking on its present configuration. Right inside the entrance there is a stone-engraved map, the most valuable pictorial and textual material on the history of the garden. This garden was different in nature from other gardens; that is, for a long period of time it functioned somewhat as a garden of a public character. The banquets of the "local gentry and officials" and the "elegant gatherings" of scholars all took place here, a circumstance suitable to the design and disposition of the garden, and having a style of its own.

"A Record of the Restoration of Canglang Pavilion" (*Chongxiu Canglang ting ji* 重修滄浪亭記)

QIAN DINGYI 錢定一 (1915–2010)

Qian Dingyi, a native of Changshu, near Suzhou, was a graduate of the Suzhou art college founded and directed by Yan Wenliang (see above), where he also taught in the Chinese painting department. After the establishment of the People's Republic of China, he worked as an interior and graphic designer, winning a number of awards.

"A Record of the Restoration of Canglang Pavilion"

The gardens of Suzhou are all enclosed by high walls, and their scenery does not escape beyond these walls. Canglang Pavilion alone is an exception: the garden is surrounded by water on three sides[77] and can be reached by a bridge; there is no separation between the inside and the outside by fence or wall. Growing beside the surrounding water there are many old trees, with remarkable branches that shade the water below and caress the clouds above. Once inside the garden, what the visitor sees are small hills, bamboos, and trees, while flowers and plants are so luxuriant that they block the visitor's view. Looking up, the brightness of the skies and the green of the trees strike against the front and sleeves of one's coat. Meandering along the double verandas, one can reach every part of the garden in a circuitous manner. The openwork windows, exquisite and delicate, in the walls standing between one side of the verandas and the other, not one exactly like any other, render the garden scenery rich in its variations, and endow it with the ingenuity of having the views obstructed and yet unobstructed. During each of the four seasons, the garden landscape presents its unique melody: on a late spring afternoon, one may sit in the Guesthouse of Emerald-Green Delicacy, feasting one's eyes on the graceful slenderness of tall bamboos; in the summer rain, one may recline in the Waterside Pavilion of Lotus Flowers, listening to the scattering of pearls from ten thousand lotus leaves; on a fine autumn day, one may stay in the Guesthouse of Refreshing Scent, smelling the wafted scent of sweet cassia flowers; in the winter snow, one may come to the Chamber for Smelling the Subtle Fragrance, searching for the fragrant message from flowering apricot trees blooming in the cold. Such are the kinds of elegant and pleasing activities that can at present still be sought, one by one.

In the past when Su Zimei resided here, with his refined fondness for the serenity of water and bamboo, he once wrote: "In front are bamboos, and behind is the water; over on the north bank again are endless bamboos. The reflected light of the limpid streams and the shadows of the emerald-green stems converge between the eaves and doors of the pavilion, particularly in harmony with the breezes and moonlight." In this respect, the garden scenery today is slightly inferior to that of Zimei's time.

The garden has the shrine of the Five Hundred Famous and Virtuous; five hundred and ninety-four portraits of men, Jizha of Wu[78] being the earliest, are engraved on stone and displayed around in its plain walls, significantly enhancing the character of this garden.

---

77   By the time Qian Dingyi wrote this essay, the garden had long been bordered by water on only one and a half sides, rather than "surrounded by water on three sides," as it may have been in Song times.

78   Jizha was the fourth son of King Shoumeng (r. 585–561 BCE) of the state of Wu. He has long been noted for his erudition and his principled declining of offers to succeed to the throne.

Tracing its history, the garden was first built by the Prince of Guangling, Qian Yuanliao, of the Kingdom of Wu-Yue, or, as also has been said, it was the garden estate of the Qian family's maternal kinsman, Sun Chengyou. In the middle of the Qingli reign period [1041–1048] of the Song, Su Zimei acquired this old garden, at a time when it was no more than bleak mists and trailing plants. He thereupon had a pavilion constructed by the water, and was the first to bestow on it the name Canglang. The site thereafter acquired its fame in the realm, this fame now having lasted over nine hundred years. For a time, Zhang Dun and Han Shizhong, both of the Song, successively resided in this garden; because associations with certain personalities lend weight to a place, the fame of this grove and stream became thereby even more prominent. Throughout the Yuan and Ming, it fell into disuse as a garden and became occupied by Buddhist monasteries. With the coming of the Qing period, Song Luo renovated it first, while Wu Cunli, Jueluo Yaerhashan [d. 1759],[79] and Liang Zhangju repaired it at later points. But as time had long passed since then, the garden was again gradually submerged in wild and overgrown thickets. In the sixteenth year of the Republic [1927], the Suzhou Fine Arts Training School, established by Yan Wenliang, took over the garden buildings to serve as its schoolrooms. In order to protect this splendid site, a native of Suzhou, Wu Zishen, generously contributed a huge sum of money to renovate the garden, so that it was brought back to its former appearance. In the twenty-sixth year of the Republic [1937],[80] the Japanese invaded Suzhou, and again almost nothing was left of the garden. After the founding of the People's Republic, the garden was completely renovated. In 1963, it was publicly listed as a historical and cultural site under the protection of Jiangsu Province. After going through the ten chaotic years of the Cultural Revolution, the garden was once more reconditioned and repaired. In 1986, the memorial gateway, "Splendors of Canglang," was moved back to its former location. No visitor to Suzhou will fail to take pleasure in looking at the new appearance of the garden.

The person who had been in charge of the renovation asked me to write a record of the process. In my childhood I studied at this place and later in turn taught here, having thus lived in this garden for over ten years from beginning to end. In the twinkling of an eye, it has been nearly forty years since I left the garden, but the feeling of regret at parting from it that I had in the past still lingers in my heart. Does not the reason why I could never forget it, even for a moment, lie in Zimei's noble aspiration and gracious disposition? It is due to all these reasons that I write this record, the date being the summer months of the year *wuchen* [1988].

---

79 Yaerhashan, a Manchu official, was appointed Prefect of Suzhou in 1741–1744, during which period he gained some fame through his work. He was executed in 1759 by the Qianlong emperor, and probably for that reason his name was omitted from the history of Canglang Pavilion in all the official local gazetteers compiled after that year.

80 In what may well be a printer's error, the date of the event is given erroneously in the original text as "the thirty-sixth year of the Republican period."

6

Private Gardens of the Ming Dynasty

W hile the Song dynasty saw the rise of the scholar-official class to dominance in government, the Yuan dynasty that followed initially saw the virtual exclusion of Chinese literati from government. This was partly because of distrust on the part of the Mongol rulers, who preferred to delegate power to officials of non-Han ethnicity, and partly because many Chinese people were unwilling to serve their Mongol overlords. This change in the social role of what had been the scholar-official class led to significant cultural change: educated men who would otherwise have been employed in government turned to professions such as medicine, thus raising the social status of doctors; painting became less representational and more a vehicle for the artist's self-expression; many literati became interested in vernacular art forms such as theater and developed the literary potential of drama. It is reasonable to assume that equally significant changes took place in the social and cultural aspects of gardens, but very little research has been done on gardens in the Yuan dynasty, so this is an area that remains to be studied (and it may explain why there is no chapter for the Yuan dynasty in this volume).

The Yuan dynasty lasted just under one hundred years (1271–1368) and was replaced by the Ming (1368–1644), a return to rule by an ethnically Han Chinese imperial family. Although the first Ming emperor, who was from a very humble background, was rather distrustful of educated officials, he recognized that they were essential to the running of the Ming empire, and the literati class reestablished their dominance of both government and culture. However, the Ming polity and society were very different from the Song. The restoration of peace and stability after the end of the Yuan, and later (from the sixteenth century) the rise of global trade with the influx of new silver from the mines of South America, led to considerable economic growth, which enlarged the literati class and the pool of aspirant scholar-officials (since more families could afford to educate their sons for the government examinations); it also increased the number of wealthy merchants. These economic and social changes had a great effect on garden culture in the Ming. Although the population grew significantly, there was no corresponding increase in the number of administrative positions, so the expansion of the literati class, bringing more intense competition for government appointments, meant that there was a greater number of unemployed would-be officials—a leisured class who created a demand for entertainment and amusement, which could be partially satisfied by the creation and enjoyment of gardens.

For the first half-century of the dynasty, the Ming capital was Nanjing, but the usurping Prince of Yan, who ruled as the Yongle emperor (r. 1402–1424), moved the capital north to Shuntian Prefecture in the region of his own power base, renaming it "Northern Capital" (Beijing). A shadow of the governmental structure remained in what was now the secondary capital, Nanjing (Southern Capital), providing relatively undemanding official positions to bureaucrats who did not make it to the central government in Beijing.

This concentration of well-off officials in the Jiangnan area (the lower Yangtze region), together with the region's milder climate, water resources, and lush vegetation, made Jiangnan an attractive residential area and a center of garden creation. Gardens also flourished in Beijing, despite its much harsher and drier climate, because of demand from officials, and also because of the extensive imperial parks. Another area with a distinctive garden culture was Huizhou (in what is now southern Anhui Province), on the very margins of the Jiangnan cultural heartland. This was an area that sent out merchants to other parts of China, many of whom became very wealthy and built lavish gardens in emulation of literati culture.[1] Other regions, such as Sichuan in the west and Guangdong in the south, must have had their own garden traditions, but little evidence of these survives from the Ming period.

One aspect of social change in the Ming dynasty that had a notable effect on garden culture was the rise of a better-educated artisan class, as a result of social mobility associated with economic change, and the growth in demand for specialists who could supply the accoutrements of the leisured life led by wealthy literati. One type of such artisans was the professional garden designer: in the mid- to late Ming, we first hear of individual and named garden craftsmen. A number of biographies or descriptions of such men, written by their educated patrons, survive; some are included in the next chapter, including that of one of the most influential, Zhang Lian (also known as Zhang Nanyuan, b. 1587). We also have other sources of written information on garden designers, for example, poems extolling their work, such as the poems Ruan Dacheng wrote for Ji Cheng; Ruan also wrote poems for another rockery creator, Zhang Kungang, who is otherwise unknown, while Wu Weiye addressed at least one poem to Zhang Lian (unfortunately too full of double entendres to be translated).[2]

The fact that such relatively minor works of literature as prose essays on garden designers or poems addressed to them have survived is an outcome of the enormous growth in the publishing

---

1   On the garden of one of these merchants, Wang Tingna, see Alison Hardie, "Think Globally, Build Locally: Syncretism and Symbolism in the Garden of Sitting in Reclusion," *Studies in the History of Gardens and Designed Landscapes* 26, no. 4 (October–December 2006):295–308.

2   For the poems addressed to Zhang Kungang, see Ruan Dacheng, *Yonghuaitang shiji*, ed. Hu Jinwang and Wang Changlin (Hefei: Huangshan shushe, 2006), 379, 445; for Wu Weiye's poem to Zhang Lian, see Wu Weiye, *Wu Meicun quanji*, ed. Li Xueying (Shanghai: Shanghai guji chubanshe, 1990), 129.

industry during the Ming dynasty—again, an effect of economic growth and the expansion of the leisured class, as well as a rise in literacy among the urban "middle class" (small-scale merchants and prosperous artisans) and especially women. The widespread demand for reading material of all kinds—a far greater demand than existed in the Song dynasty, when literacy was largely confined to the upper class, and female literacy, although not unknown, was still uncommon— prompted the development of new genres of writing, as well as the expansion and popularization of existing genres. Thus in the mid- to late Ming, we see the rise of what is known in Chinese as *xiaopin* (perhaps translatable as "minor categories"), a capacious genre that incorporates such things as short essays on notable events, customs, or objects; informal biographies of remarkable people; accounts of travel or experiences in distant places; and descriptions of gardens and the process of their creation. Many of these subgenres existed in the Song dynasty, but now become much more prominent and frequently published.

We find in the Ming a tremendous expansion of the "garden record" genre (*yuanji*), which we have already encountered in the Song dynasty with Sima Guang's "An Account of the Garden of Solitary Enjoyment," Su Shunqin's "Record of Canglang Pavilion," and other such descriptions of private (as opposed to imperial) gardens written by distinguished literati, including the multiple garden record in Li Gefei's "Record of the Celebrated Gardens of Luoyang." This was a genre that existed only in embryonic form in the Tang dynasty, one example being Li Deyu's "Record of the Plants and Trees of My Mountain Villa at Pingquan" (see chapter 3). In the Ming, however, almost all published collections of an individual writer's work seem to contain at least a few and sometimes many garden records, either of their own or of other people's gardens. The travel records (*youji*) genre may also contain accounts of gardens, and indeed there is considerable overlap between the two genres. Local gazetteers—officially or semi-officially published accounts of particular localities, often either prefectures or counties, with information on population data, economic production, history, notable individuals (either natives or sojourners), historic sites, etc.—very often contain short accounts of local gardens, both historical and contemporarily extant. Sometimes these merely quote from garden records by well-known literary men, sometimes an anonymous writer provides information on gardens that would otherwise be quite unknown.

In this period, we also have a much larger quantity than in previous dynasties of writing— especially poetry—by women. Although women rarely wrote in the more "public-facing" garden record genre, they wrote many poems about or inspired by gardens. Sometimes such poems are indistinguishable from those written by their male contemporaries, sometimes they seem to embody a distinctively female sensibility. We have endeavored to include a range of writing by women in this anthology, but there is no doubt that the proportion increases significantly in the chapters devoted to the Ming and Qing dynasties, and indeed we start this chapter with two examples.

A genre of writing that belongs particularly to the Ming is what has been called connoisseurship literature—that is, books about how to appreciate and participate in cultural objects and activities.[3] Although such books had earlier existed in some forms, such as Du Wan's *Stone Catalogue of Cloudy Forest* or Fan Chengda's "Treatise on the Flowering Apricot" (both in

---

3   See Craig Clunas, *Superfluous Things: Material Culture and Social Status in Early Modern China* (Urbana: University of Illinois Press, 1991).

chapter 3), new in the Ming is the sense that such texts are not only directed at a highly educated readership who could be assumed to be already familiar with the subject matter but also (or primarily) at those who really needed such information on cultural matters in order to be able to function socially in an environment where they might otherwise feel out of place. We know from much textual evidence that Ming literati were greatly exercised about the "problem" of newly wealthy merchants laying claim to the cultural heritage that the literati felt was theirs alone, for example, by collecting antiques or paintings, by creating gardens, and so on. Taste became a marker the literati could use to distinguish "people like us" from the sort of nouveaux riches who would make terrible social and cultural faux pas (the use of French terms to describe such delicate situations in English is a reminder of how similar social changes were negotiated in eighteenth- and nineteenth-century Europe). Connoisseurship literature could be employed either to consolidate the sense of belonging to the cultured upper class or (more generously) to enable the less cultured to find their way around at a new social level. Much of what survives of connoisseurship literature clearly has one or the other of these functions: for example, the *Treatise on Superfluous Things* (extracts from which are included in this chapter), by Wen Zhenheng, scion of a great Suzhou family, makes ex cathedra pronouncements on what is or is not vulgar, while *The Craft of Gardens* (see chapters 3 and 7), by the relatively lowly Ji Cheng, appears to be more of a how-to manual for the aspiring but not yet established man of culture.

Another aspect of growth in the publishing industry is the increase in illustrated publications. The reign of the Wanli emperor in the late sixteenth to early seventeenth century is conventionally regarded as the zenith of woodblock-printed illustration, and the quality of some of the work produced at this time is breathtaking. Woodblock printing made it possible for ordinary readers to become familiar with reproductions of works of art that would previously have been accessible only to the highly cultured and well connected. Woodblock-printed illustrations also popularized images of subjects, including gardens, in such a way that a shared cultural understanding seems to have developed across a much wider social range than before; in other words, both upper- and middle-class individuals would have a similar expectation of how a garden should look, whereas in earlier times they might have had very different ideas.

There is always a problem of how far paintings and illustrations can be taken as valid evidence for the actual appearance of contemporaneous gardens, but it seems reasonable to assume that they are at least evidence of what people at the time thought the ideal garden should look like. Where both written descriptions and painted or woodblock-printed images of the same garden survive, there is enough consistency to conclude that, at least within the topographical school of painting associated with the Suzhou region, images of gardens can be taken as broadly representative of their actual appearance. This is helpful in giving us a clearer idea of how garden style developed over time.

The late Ming dynasty was a time when garden style in the Jiangnan region, and subsequently elsewhere in China, underwent significant change, and it is more than likely that Zhang Lian (whose biography is included in chapter 7) was largely responsible for this change. Up to the beginning of the seventeenth century, the preference was for a rather ponderous and monumental style, with substantial buildings, fairly open spaces, massed plantings of a single type of shrub, tree, or bamboo, and substantial rock structures that aimed to represent real or mythical mountains such as the legendary abodes of the immortals or Kunlun in the far west, and were probably inspired by the monumental landscape paintings of the Song dynasty. In the first couple of decades of the seventeenth century, there is evidence for a marked change to a simpler, lighter style, with more delicate buildings, more mixed planting, and less imposing artificial mountains that aimed to suggest the existence of larger mountains nearby rather than to scale them down for inclusion inside the garden. This change can be linked to a change in aesthetic preference from the monumental Song paintings to the sparser, more monochrome landscapes of the great Yuan dynasty masters, such as Huang Gongwang and Wu Zhen, which tended to represent the gentler landscape of Jiangnan, rather than the mountain peaks of China's interior. This aesthetic change is particularly associated with the name of the art critic Dong Qichang (1555–1636). Wu Weiye's biography of Zhang Lian records that Dong and his friend and supporter Chen Jiru (1558–1639) spoke highly of Zhang's style. The writer and painter Wang Shimin (1592–1680), for whom Zhang Lian and his son Zhang Ran designed or renovated several gardens, including the garden called Pleasure in the Suburbs mentioned by Wu Weiye, and whose "Record of the Division of Property in Pleasure in the Suburbs" can be found in chapter 8, was a student of Dong Qichang. The "axe-cut" (*cun*) strokes in Zhang's work that Wu Weiye mentions can also refer to a type of brushstroke in ink painting. It seems reasonable, therefore, to conclude that Zhang's garden style was consciously modeled on the Yuan landscape painting style preferred by the more consciously progressive artists and critics of the time, and that his influence and that of his successors helped to establish this as the generally accepted garden style in the late seventeenth and early eighteenth centuries.[4]

The Ming dynasty is often regarded as the high point in the development of "classical" private gardens or so-called scholar gardens. The selections in this chapter are intended to give a sense not only of how gardens were perceived by people at the time but also of the variety of types of text in which they were celebrated; for some insights into the life and work of outstanding garden craftsmen of the time, see chapter 7. We have also included a few comments by later (Qing dynasty) writers that give an insight into the "afterlife" of some notable Ming gardens.

"Impromptu on a Trip" (*Kezhong jishi* 客中即事)

ZHU JING'AN 朱靜庵 (FL. 1450)

TRANSLATED BY MICHELLE YEH

Zhu Zhongxian, who is usually known by her studio name Jing'an, came from Zhejiang. Well educated but unhappily married, she was noted for a style influenced by ancient writers, avoiding conventionally feminine expression.

---

4   On this change in style, see Alison Hardie, "The Transition in Garden Style in Late Ming China/*Mingdai wanqi Zhongguo yuanlin sheji de zhuanxing*," *Landscape Architecture (Fengjing yuanlin)* 5 (2010), revised and expanded version (Chinese only) in Wu Xin, ed., *Shanshui zhi jing: Zhongguo wenhua zhong de fengjing yuanlin* (Beijing: Joint Publishing, 2015), 214–24.

"Impromptu on a Trip"

The splendid mansion is quiet, young swallows fly.
In the deep shade of green poplars, orioles sing.
The breeze is gone, the light curtain still,
I sit and watch flower shadows shift in the garden.

"Impromptu on a Summer Day" (*Xiari oucheng* 夏日偶成)

CHEN DEYI 陳德懿 (FL. 1476)
TRANSLATED BY MICHELLE YEH

Like her friend Zhu Jing'an (see above), Chen Deyi came from Zhejiang, and also seems to have had an unhappy life. At a young age, she achieved a reputation as a poet of landscape.

"Impromptu on a Summer Day"

Bamboo in the garden, layers of green,
Sheer windows covered with emerald gauze screen.
In a bowl, gold-thread grass is planted;
On the terrace, jade-hairpin flowers grow.
After the rain, the setting sun lingers,
But returning clouds take the sunset away.
In the remaining summer heat,
I stroll at ease listening to frogs in the pond.

"A Descriptive Sketch of Wang's Garden of the Unsuccessful Politician" (*Wangshi Zhuozheng yuan ji* 王氏拙政園記), "The Bower Adjoining the Rock" (*Yiyu xuan* 倚玉軒), and "Little Canglang Pavilion" (*Xiao Canglang ting* 小滄浪亭)

WEN ZHENGMING 文徵明 (1470–1559)
TRANSLATED BY MO ZUNG CHUNG

Poet, calligrapher, and painter Wen Zhengming, from Suzhou, was the preeminent artist of his age and a student of both Wu Kuan (1436–1504) and Shen Zhou (1427–1509), the major artistic figures of an earlier generation. After a short career at the capital between 1523 and 1527, Wen retired to his Jade Chime Mountain Hut in his hometown and embarked on a long-term and intense engagement with the cultural and literary traditions of the Wu region.

Wen's album "The Garden of the Unsuccessful Politician," painted in celebration of the garden of his friend Wang Xianchen in 1533, is justly famous and has been much studied. It contains a lengthy account of the garden, as given below in the 1920s translation of Mo Zung Chung, and paintings of thirty-one scenes from the garden with accompanying poems (two of which are also included here) written in three different types of calligraphy (a 1551 supplement offers further views of eight of the same scenes), and was in all likelihood intended as a gift to his friend. It is surely the most perfect example of the intense collaboration of the arts of prose, poetry, calligraphy, painting, and garden design that characterizes the garden culture of China, particularly during the Ming dynasty. The original 1533 album, which seems to have been in a private collection in Suzhou when this translation was first published, is now lost, though there are recurrent rumors that it still exists. The 1551 album, which uses the same poems as the earlier one (with slight differences), is in the Metropolitan Museum of Art in New York; the painting styles of the two albums are quite distinct.

The garden itself, known also in English as the Garden of the Humble or Artless Administrator, remains the most celebrated garden of the city that, increasingly over the course of the twentieth century, came to be regarded as China's "Garden City," Suzhou. Situated in the northeastern corner of the city (and next door now to the Suzhou Museum), the garden is one of Suzhou's largest. The site had once been the residence of the Tang dynasty poet Lu Guimeng (d. ca. 881; see chapter 3) but had become a temple by the Yuan dynasty. This temple had been abandoned by the time the censor Wang Xianchen returned to his hometown in 1509, dismissed from his post in the capital. Work on the garden was completed by around 1514. The earliest date of the use of the present name of the garden, derived from a line in the "Rhapsody on Living in Idleness" of the Jin dynasty poet Pan Yue (247–300; see chapter 1), "To spend one's days watering one's garden and selling vegetables, in order to provide for the necessities of day and night, such too may be considered the administration of the artless," is 1517.

The subsequent history of the garden, lost one night at the gambling table by Wang Xianchen's son sometime after his father's death, is a troubled one, characterized by long periods of neglect and many changes of ownership. Over the five-hundred-year life of the garden, almost every aspect of its original design and planting has changed. As it stands at present, the garden is largely the renovated version of a major restoration undertaken during the early 1870s.

"A Descriptive Sketch of Wang's Garden of the Unsuccessful Politician"

My friend Wang Huaiyu, also known as Wang Jingzhi, lives in the northeastern part of the city of Suzhou. His residence lies between the Lou and Qi Gates and consists of a large tract of waste land with a pond in the center. At considerable pains my friend undertook to beautify this piece of land by dredging and draining the swamps and by planting a large number of trees.

On the southern side of the pond he built a storied house which he named Dreamy Tower; on the northern side is a Rustic Villa with the Bower of Fragrance in front, and the Bower Adjoining the Rock in the rear, the latter being joined to Dreamy Tower on the north.

Spanning the pond is a small bridge known as the Little Flying Rainbow Bridge. Going across the bridge to the northern shore and turning westward along the bank, you come to the Lotus Cove surrounded with hibiscus bushes.

On the west, standing midway along the bank, is Little Canglang Pavilion, a bower which is shaded by a bamboo grove on the south. Beyond it to the west and jutting out into the water is a rock on which you may sit and bathe your feet in the placid water below. This is called the Place of Clear Meditation. Here the bank turns toward the north. There is a remarkably splendid view of the pond from this angle, with all the voluminousness of a true lake. On the opposite shore are a large number of fine trees. A group of willows stand farther toward the west; this is the Willow Cove.

On the eastern bank rises an earthen mound, called Terrace of Distant Thoughts. At its base is a flat piece of rock, the Fishing Rock, where you may beguile your leisure hours with fishing. From here northward the estate grows more and more secluded; the groves become denser and the water clearer. At this farther end, a small pond is dug and connected with the main body of water. In this smaller pond, called Splashy Pond, are planted many lotus. Encircling the shores are a thousand beautiful bamboos whose cool shade is especially inviting during the summer. Beneath their shade is a bower which is known as the Clean Retreated Bower. Farther on to the east is a group of orange trees. This is known as the Bower for Awaiting the Frost. Still farther east at the back of Dreamy Tower are many fine trees and the place is known as the Place for Listening to the Sighing Pines. Turning from this point to the front of Dreamy Tower you come to a group of ancient trees whose overhanging boughs and closely grown leaves cast a cool shade on the spot below, making it an ideal place for rest; this is the Place of Smiles.

Farther along the bank on the east is a stretch of fruit trees which serve as a welcome home to birds, hence the place is named the Bird's Paradise. At the far end of this grove are four locust trees which form a sort of tent; this is the Bower of Nature. Behind it is the Plum Slope; in the front is the Rosy Way, and still farther on is the Rosy Walk. Here the bank turns southward.

On the opposite shore is seen a large number of peach trees; this is the Peach-Tree Banks. On its south is the Bamboo Grove. Farther south is an old locust tree which casts an extensive shade; this is the Locust Tent. Below this runs a small brook spanned by a footbridge. From here on eastward you pass through a cool and shady bamboo grove with a few elms and locusts scattered about to fill the gaps. Beyond this, on the west, and bordering on the water, is the beautiful Owner's Favorite Bower. Behind is the Let Go Bower. On the left is the Plantain Balustrade.

All the bowers, buildings, and edifices are built with the front facing the water. From the Peach-Tree Banks southward the water flows in narrow streams until finally it runs under cover, reappearing at a distance of a hundred yards beyond, among the bamboos; this is the Mountain Stream Among Bamboos.

On the east of this is an orchard of flowering apricot trees which at blossom time presents a brilliant view of Fragrant Snow and makes one think of the happy land of the fairies. This place is known as the Garden of Gems. In this orchard is a bower named the Bower of Delicious Fruits and a spring named the Crystal Spring.

Among the subjects chosen by the artist for reproduction in this album are: one reception room, one storied house, six bowers, balustrades, ponds, coves, brooks, etc., making a total of thirty-one different views. The name given to the whole garden is Zhuo Zheng Yuan 拙政園, the Garden of the Unsuccessful Politician. The proprietor gave the reason for selecting this name in the following manner. He said: "In history, you remember, that Pan Yue, being dissatisfied with his own political career, retired and devoted his remaining years to building, tree-planting, gardening, and marketing of the greens. In his own words, 'This is also one form of administration except that it is undertaken by the less skilled class of politicians.'"

"My case is not unlike Pan Yue's. I have spent the better part of the last forty years in politics but with meager success. Many of my acquaintances have risen to high and responsible public posts, while I had to be content with the office of a City Magistrate, the highest post I ever held, and even from this I have recently retired. I therefore consider myself even more unsuccessful in public life than Pan Yue. I have built this garden as a memorial of my failure in politics."

According to my estimate, however, the case of my friend Wang is entirely different from that of Pan Yue. Wang is a scholar of recognized standing. In public life, he once served as a judicial officer. He possesses an enviable reputation for uprightness and integrity and for this very reason he had a bitter experience in politics, rising and falling, until finally he was thrown out of office. He is therefore not one who is willing to be content with the foul practices of the age, nor is he willing to drift along with the times. Quite dissimilar to this was the career of Pan Yue, who in actual practice was a shameless flatterer of the authorities of his age, bowing and stooping to their wishes only to bring misfortune upon himself at last. Though he is the author of this beautiful sentiment about the joys of a leisurely life he was never out of politics during the whole of his life and never was he able to enjoy the sweetness of leisure.

And there are almost any number of celebrities, in the past, who like Pan Yue were unable to gratify their heart's desire either because they were unable to free themselves from the bonds of politics or because they preferred to rise and fall with the times. My friend, however, withdrew from public life in the prime of his political career in order to enjoy the peace and happiness of a home life. For the past twenty years he has been busily engaged in building, tree planting, gardening, and marketing the greens, enjoying himself as many of the ancient celebrities could not, not to mention Pan Yue specifically. He compared himself to Pan Yue, perhaps, for the purpose of giving vent to the disappointment resulting from his failure in politics. There is no doubt that he enjoys this life more than he did politics. The average person sets his heart upon high office and wealth but he seldom understands that likely as not there are grave dangers hidden beneath, as if prearranged by Providence. Had my friend been successful in politics, the chances are that he would have suffered misfortune, but fortunately enough he has wisely chosen the leisurely life, and is now able to look down upon the vainglory of the world.

Happily enough, I am also retiring from public life. The course I took was not similar to that of my friend. I quite agree with him in his notion about worldly desires. Yet I haven't got a single *mu* of land wherein to express my heart's desire and I cannot help envying my friend's good fortune. I have therefore written this description of the garden in addition to a number of little verses on the various views in it.

The fifteenth day of the fifth moon of the twelfth year in the reign of Jiajing [1533]

"The Bower Adjoining the Rock"

Beside the bower is the verdure of a thousand bamboos,
And a moss-grown rock hewn from the renowned Mount Kun.
If you go up to the owner's hall to take a survey,
You'll find the breath of Spring everywhere.

"Little Canglang Pavilion"

On the bank of the Little Canglang Pond is built a small bower,
With green water surrounding its balustrades.
There still linger the breeze and the moon to cheer the fishermen,
And the country boy singing "Wash your hat-strings here."
In these rivers and lakes I mean to lodge my interest,
Though after the lapse of ages the fish and the birds know little about the past.
The poets Su Shunqin and Du Fu both died long, long ago,
And there remains none with whom I can vie in excellence as a hermit.

"Inscription to 'A Descriptive Sketch of Wang's Garden of the Unsuccessful Politician'" (*Wangshi Zhuozheng yuan ji ba* 王氏拙政園記拔)

QIAN YONG 錢泳 (1759–1844)
TRANSLATED BY MO ZUNG CHUNG

The description of the garden that follows is also from Kate Kerby and Mo Zung Chung's edition of Wen Zhengming's paintings and writings on the garden. Qian Yong, from the vicinity of Wuxi, near Suzhou, was a distinguished calligrapher, epigraphist, and literary man of the Qing dynasty, and the author of a collection of "note-form literature" (*biji wenxue*), *Collected Talks from the Lü Garden*, which includes a chapter on gardens (see chapter 7). This short "inscription" or colophon was appended to the Wen Zhengming album recorded by Kerby and Mo; a shorter version also appears in the gardens chapter of *Collected Talks from the Lü Garden*.

"Inscription to 'A Descriptive Sketch of Wang's Garden of the Unsuccessful Politician'"

On the seventh day after the Mid-Autumn Festival in the thirteenth year of Daoguang [1833], I passed Haichang on my way home from Lin'an. Under a rainstorm I paid a visit to my friend Zhongqing at Changan Village. It was then that he good-naturedly showed me this album of Wen Zhengming's Zhuo Zheng Yuan pictures, consisting of thirty-one paintings, with little verses accompanying each picture, written by the artist himself in neat calligraphs (in the "formal" and "clerkly" styles). This is undoubtedly the greatest masterpiece of the artist Wen Zhengming.

According to the *Suzhou Prefectural Gazetteer*, the Garden of the Unsuccessful Politician is located on North Street inside of Qinü Gate. It was first built by Wang Xianchen (Huaiyu), an Administrative Censor in the middle part of the reign of Jiajing [1522–1566]. After his death, his son, who had a propensity to gamble, lost the title to the whole garden in one night's game. The property was thus transferred to one named Xu, and thereafter, at the beginning of this dynasty it passed into the hands of Chen Zhilin, who was once a Prime Minister. Not long afterward, when a garrison was stationed in Suzhou, the garden was converted into the general's headquarters. There is in the garden a twin "gem-pearl" tea tree which is immortalized by the poet Wu Weiye (1609–1671) in a beautiful poem which may be found in his works. After the garrison left, the place was again made the official residence of the Defense Commissioner.

Shortly afterward, it was occupied by one Wang Yongning,[5] son-in-law of Wu Sangui, the famous leader of the Revolution against the Ming dynasty. Upon the defeat of Wu Sangui, the property was confiscated, until by the eighteenth year of the Kangxi era [1679] it was once more made the new official residence of the Defense Commissioner for Suzhou, Songjiang, and Changzhou. Thereafter it passed into the hands of the common people until it came into the possession of Jiang Qi, once a [Prefectural Governor]. The garden was named by him the Garden of Return, which became a favorite resort of famous scholars who gathered there in the spring and autumn to drink and to compose poems. The scene was commemorated in a picture entitled "A Happy Gathering at the Garden of Return." In the fifty years following, the ponds fell into a dilapidated condition, and the paths and walks were overgrown with moss and weeds; the garden lost all its glory of former days.

---

5   Editor's note: some sources give the name as Wang Yongkang.

Toward the middle part of the reign of Jiaqing it was bought by Zha Shitan, a scholar, who spent more than a year in eradicating the weeds, draining the ponds, watering the flowers and planting bamboos and the place was restored to its former beauty. Recently the garden was again mortgaged to Premier Wu Jing.

I am often of the opinion that the fortune of a garden is closely connected with that of its owner. If its owner enjoys a lasting fame, his garden will stand through the ages even though it may occasionally fall into decay; if the contrary is the case, the garden will eventually be left in ruins even though it may prosper for a time. Only I am of the opinion that literary compositions are more lasting than gardens and bowers, as the former have in them the quality of non-destructibility. This statement is fully borne out by the pictures and sketches and poems written by Wen Zhengming which vividly portray the original beauty and glory of the bowers, flowers, and trees. The reader may see clearly how through these three hundred years the garden prospered and fell into ruins, how it disintegrated like the dispersing cloud, and how it passed from hand to hand like the blowing wind. This is a subject that ought to arouse much melancholy thought on the part of any reader.

The extent to which my friend Zhongqing prizes this album, the long hours which he spent in its study, and the amount of new pleasure which he derives from it every time he turns over its leaves convincingly prove the truth of the foregoing statement that literary compositions last longer than bowers and gardens, in spite of the fact that the latter require much labor and planning in their composition.

As my boat happens to anchor for the night at Hangzhou on account of a high tide, I have undertaken to write the foregoing sketch in a rather random way under the lamplight.
Qian Yong, aged seventy-five.

"Spring Night" (*Chunye* 春夜)

DUAN SHUQING 端淑卿 (CA. 1510–CA. 1600)
TRANSLATED BY CHARLES H. EGAN

Duan Shuqing, from a leading scholar-official family of Dangtu (in present-day Anhui Province), was a writer of both *shi* (as here) and *ci* poetry in the mid-sixteenth century. She was taught by her father, a Confucian schoolmaster. She is said to have lived beyond the age of ninety.

"Spring Night"

In the remains of night a sliver moon rises above the tranquil garden.
Silently taking in the clear light, I'm not sound in my sleep.

The cuckoo's cry despairing—breaking a butterfly dream;
Mandarin ducks' water warm—protecting the sandy islet.
Groundless spring regrets lengthen with the season;
Limitless indolent sadness waits for wine to awaken.
Morning comes: I casually stroke an old pine and watch—
Enduring the sight of garden forms all green.

"Record of the Yanshan Garden" (*Yanshan yuan ji* 弇山園記)

WANG SHIZHEN 王世貞 (1526–1590)
TRANSLATED BY ALISON HARDIE

Wang Shizhen, sometime official and outstanding man of letters, a native of Taicang (today in Jiangsu Province, but then in the Southern Metropolitan Region), was one of the most important political and cultural figures of his age. From a wealthy and influential family, Wang Shizhen proved both precocious and immensely prolific, but much of his life was lived in the shadow of his father's execution, in 1560, largely as the result of vicious infighting at the court in Beijing. Although his father was posthumously rehabilitated in 1567, Wang's subsequent official career seems to have remained somewhat problematic, and in any case his commitment to pursuing high office seems to have dissipated.

He spent the 1560s to 1580s building three gardens in his hometown. The first of these was called the Garden for Evading Thorns (the thorns refer to political opponents); the second, the Lesser Jetavana. This second garden, named for the park where the Buddha gave some of his teachings, was later incorporated into Wang's largest and most elaborate garden, the Yanzhou Garden.

In this chapter, we include a series of nineteen poems on the last of these gardens, written by Wang Shizhen, along with his long eight-part record of the garden. This is followed by an extract from the Kangxi-era gazetteer of Taicang Subprefecture that deals with the various gardens owned by members of the Wang family. This is followed, in turn, by two other pieces by Wang Shizhen; his account of the garden of a Suzhou friend, and his collective account of the gardens of the Southern Capital, Nanjing.

"Record of the Yanshan Garden"

I

Slightly south from the Great Bridge is all a commercial area, which stops short after half a *li*; to the west a pathway suddenly appears, called "Iron Cat Alley," which is rather low-class. Follow the alley to the west for about 300 paces, and where the alley comes to an end, turn slightly south and then west again; less than half-way along the alley stands the Temple of Abundant Blessing. Before this is a rectangular pond twenty *mu* in area, with a disused vegetable-garden enclosing it to left and right; the pond is hazy and attracts the mist and moon, giving people a sense of being among the rivers Tiao and Sha.[6] To the right of the temple is my Yanshan Garden, which is also known as Yanzhou Garden.[7] Transversely before it lies a clear stream which is very narrow, with both banks planted with weeping willows, their shady branches entwined together so that they seem like a single tree. South of the stream are several *mu* of fertile fields belonging to the Zhang family; as the grain ripens, this becomes a yellow cloud spread across the landscape, and frequent wafts of the smell of baking make one think about "cooking the food of Yicheng."[8] West of the garden is the graveyard of the Zong family, with more than ten ancient pines and cypresses; farther west still is the temple of the Neighborhood Marquis of Hanshou,[9] with its azure tiles and carved roof-ornaments towering up into the clouds. All these sights add to the splendor of my garden.

Within the garden are three hills, one ridge, two Buddha chambers, five storied buildings, three halls, four studies, one gallery, ten pavilions, one decorated walkway, two stone bridges, six wooden bridges, five stone causeways, four each of caves, rapids and shallows, and two wine-cup meanders;[10] as for cliffs, stone stairways, streams and gullies, they are innumerable, and it is impossible to total up the area covered by bamboos, trees, flowers, plants, kitchen and medicinal herbs, and so on. This is what my garden contains.

The garden has an area of more than seventy *mu*, of which four-tenths consists of earth and rocks, three-tenths of water, two-tenths of buildings, and one-tenth of bamboos and trees. This is a summary of my garden.

It suits flowers: flowers adorn it from top to bottom as if embroidered all over it, and when visitors pass among them, the fragrance and color entrance their eyes and noses so that they cannot bear to leave. It suits the moon: you can move about in a boat or on foot, and where the moonlight touches them, the rocks seem even more ancient, the water even more lovely, as brilliant as though you were reposing in the Palace of Broad Chill and Pure Emptiness in the moon. It suits the snow: if you climb to a high point and look around, the myriads of battlements on the city wall and roof-ridges, with the peaks and trees of the garden, high and low, dipping or protruding, are a mass of jade-white, making one's eyes more alert. It suits the rain: drizzling or pouring, heavy

---

6   These were rivers near Huzhou, in northern Zhejiang, adjoining the south of Jiangsu.

7   Yanshan (Yan Mountain) and Yanzhou (Yan Prefecture) refer to the same mythical location.

8   Probably a reference to a wine named *Yichengchun* 宜城春 (spring in Yicheng).

9   The great general Guan Yu (d. 219), who was enfeoffed as Neighborhood Marquis of Hanshou, became apotheosized as the god of war. He is usually referred to as Guan Di or Guan Gong (Lord Guan), and remains the patron saint of both the police and the secret societies. His cult was popular among the literati at this period. Wang Shizhen seems to have had a fairly close association with this temple, for which he wrote an inscription, recording its rebuilding after 1580.

10 These statistics do not entirely tally with Wang Shizhen's own account in "Record of the Yanshan Garden."

or light, dense or fine, all is as perfect as it could be, the rippling waves form a pattern, and the minnows leap. It suits the wind: the jade-green dwarf-bamboo and the white poplars rustle harmoniously, making one forget one's weariness. It suits the summer heat: shrubs enclose the lofty gallery, so that the fierce sun is hidden; a light freshness surrounds one, so that one lingers, reluctant to leave. These are the splendors of my garden.

Since I retired from Yunyang,[11] I have taken up my lodging here. When I get up in the morning, I get the benefit of the sunrise and listen to the birds' dawn chorus. When I go to bed at night, I enjoy the sunset and listen to the birds' weary chirping. Either I put on my flat clogs or I summon a small skiff; if acquaintances come to call, I don't stand on ceremony. When the clear wine is brought in, I angle in the stream for fat fish to accompany it; when the yellow millet is just about cooked, I pick wild herbs as a condiment. A simply-coiffed servant follows me with pillow and mat; if I get drunk and want to sleep, my guests can make themselves scarce. These are the pleasures of garden living.

Prime ministers and high officials must be accompanied by an armed retinue, and their power is such that I cannot turn them away. I have to put on court dress and follow them around, and with the cries of "Make way!" the atmosphere is ruined. By nature I dislike haute cuisine and showy banquets that go on endlessly all evening. These are the misfortunes of living in my garden.

How did the garden come to be called Yanshan, or alternatively Yanzhou? When I was reading *The True Classic of the Flowery South*,[12] I came across the reference to "west of the great wilderness, north of Yanzhou;" it attracted my fancy, but I never found out where it was. Then I looked up the *Classic of Mountains and Seas of the West*,[13] which says: "In the mountains of Yanzhou is a five-colored bird which looks up to heaven and is called the Calling Bird. Therefore there is the custom of various music, song and dance, and there is a garden of the lofty axle-tree; lodging to the south is auspicious, and even the short-lived live to eight-hundred." Before I knew it, my spirit took flight with inspiration, soaring and gliding, in fits and starts; I said to myself "How could I hope for this?" Thereupon I used the name both for my garden and for my collected

---

11   Wang Shizhen was governor of Yunyang, in Hubei, between 1574 and 1576.

12   The text here refers to the *Zhuangzi* by means of an alternative title, but actually the quotation is from *Liezi*, where there is a description of the unreachably distant "land of Master Huaxu" being to the west of Yanzhou and north of Taizhou; Wang Shizhen seems to be quoting, rather inaccurately, from memory.

13   This refers to a chapter in the *Classic of Mountains and Seas*. With a substantial element of fantasy, this work was popular escapist reading among late Ming literati.

works,[14] simply to express my longing. For I cannot expect to be the companion of immortals; I am confined to my home, lodging beneath a roof of thatch. Once I happened to open *The Biography of Emperor Mu*, where it describes how: "The emperor drank to the Queen Mother of the West beside the Jasper Pond; the emperor then ascended Yanshan, and left the marks of his feet on the rocks of Yanshan, where he planted a scholar tree, on which was a sign saying 'Mountain of the Queen Mother of the West'"; this Yanshan, then, is the paradise of the Yellow Emperor and his consort the Queen Mother of the West, and is the jade-tablet archive of the immortals, but Master Jingchun[15] merely refers to "Yanzi, where the sun enters the earth." Now Yanzi is 360 *li* to the southwest of Bird-Rat Mountain, and there are many solid whetstones there that can be used for cutting; it is not far from Longshou. Both these accounts are from the pen of Guo Pu; perhaps he forgot what he had written before? The name I gave to my garden and my collected works, although I am afraid I have been over-arrogant in doing so, gives me pleasure by its resonance with these ancient texts.

Since my garden became known for its large size and beauty, everyone neighboring on the garden visits it on a daily basis, and other friends and strangers visit it every ten days or so, whereas I myself only set foot in it five or six times a year. Now that I have left and am living away from home, I feel I have even less right to the name Yanshan, and now I have added to it with this "Record," I seem still to have some attachment to gain and loss. Those who put their faith in the Great Vehicle[16] do not lust for the palatial residence of Indra; even if I followed Emperor Mu Man up to the summit of Yanshan, I should merely cast an eye on it and pass on; how much the more so with a residence of a mere few dozen *mu*? In the past, even a hundred joys would not have cancelled out my one grief;[17] now, if I am lucky enough to be able to gather all so-called joys and griefs together and consign them to oblivion, what further attachment could I have? For mountains, rivers, and the great physical world are all illusion; I am doing no more than merely recording my illusions in illusory words.

---

14   The collected works of Wang Shizhen, published in his lifetime, are known as *Documents of the Hermit of Yanzhou in Four Categories* (*Yanzhou shanren sibugao* 弇州山人四部稿); the continuation, published after his death by his sons, is *Documents of the Hermit of Yanzhou Continued* (*Yanzhou shanren xugao* 弇州山人續稿).

15   Guo Pu (276–324), a writer, scholar, and mystic, annotated both the *Classic of Mountains and Seas* and the *Biography of Emperor Mu*.

16   Mahayana Buddhism. Wang Shizhen was a devout Buddhist, and also a follower of the syncretic teaching of his neighbor Wang Daozhen's (1558–1580) daughter, the young female mystic who took the religious name Tanyangzi.

17   Wang Shizhen's father, Wang Yu, offended the powerful official Yan Song (1480–1567) and was executed in 1559. Wang Shizhen himself was unable to hold office until after he finally obtained his father's rehabilitation, following the impeachment of Yan Song for corruption in 1562.

II

Going west from the Temple of Abundant Blessing, there is a small stream of hazy appearance, with weeping willows linking their shade above; my garden in fact nestles against it. The board over the entrance gate reads "Yanzhou"; see the explanation in the previous section. Inside the gate, bamboo has been woven together to make a high fence, with trailing plants growing alongside it such as red and white roses, roseleaf raspberry, China rose, and lilac. When they are in flower, the eyes are overwhelmed as if with carving and embroidery; they spring up in clumps to the left and right, and even without a breeze the fragrance is apparent. Taking a quotation from Cen Shen of Jiazhou, I called this Path Imbued with Fragrance.[18] The path runs west and then stops, and one comes upon a low bridge, called Knowing the Ford;[19] this is the way to the Yanshan Hall. The space to the left of the high fence, a matter of six or ten paces in measurement, is planted with a mixture of elms, willows, and loquats, and fenced in as a home for my cranes. I was given a present of these birds, six of them in succession, and when they called in chorus, the sound pierced the heavens; but because of a lack of food I reduced their numbers to two. I named the place Clear Voice Palisade, referring to what one might occasionally hear on a quiet night. The space on the right I cleared to make a small orchard of a few square feet, which was entirely planted with orange trees, although the soil was not comparable to Dongting;[20] I named this Ode of Chu, referring to the words of Su Shi.[21] On the sunny north side of the path is a wall forming a boundary, with a gate through the middle and a sign over it reading "Lesser Jetavana."[22] When I first cleared this piece of land, I built a two-story belvedere in which to revere the Buddhist scriptures, and that is why it was called Lesser Jetavana. Later I supplemented it with the Daoist scriptures, and added islands, water-pavilions, terraces, lodges and so on; my ideas got more and more extravagant and the scenes grew more extensive day by day, so it is very different from its name. The name-board reflects the original concept.

---

18 The Tang poet Cen Shen (ca. 714–770) wrote a poem addressed to his fellow poet Du Fu (712–770) about their similar jobs in the bureaucracy; it includes the couplet, "At dawn we enter following the celestial scepter; / At dusk we return, imbued with imperial fragrance." The poem ends by observing that under the emperor's enlightened rule, censorial officials such as Cen Shen and Du Fu have little to do; by referring to this poem, Wang Shizhen is expressing gratitude to the emperor for his father's rehabilitation.

19 "Knowing the ford" means understanding the Way and is an allusion to a story in the *Analects*.

20 East and West Dongting are islands in Lake Tai, close to Suzhou, which were famous for their orange groves.

21 The Song poet Su Shi (1037–1101) wrote a calligraphic inscription about his fondness for growing oranges and his intention to build a pavilion named "Ode of Chu"; this in itself is an allusion to the "Ode on the Orange-Tree" in the *Songs of the South* attributed to Qu Yuan, where the orange tree functions as a parable for human conduct.

22 The original Jetavana Garden (or Park) was the site where Sakyamuni preached the sermon recorded in the *Surangama Sutra* (*Shoulengyan jing* or *Lengyan jing*), a sutra that had enormous popularity among late Ming literati.

On entering the gate there is a pavilion, its eaves upturned, with fine bamboo set in a row before it and surrounding it to the left and right and at the back. Counting up the names, there are ten different varieties. The decoration of the pavilion is all blue-green to match the reflections cast by the bamboo, and it is named This Gentleman, quoting from Wang Huizhi of our clan. To the pavilion's left, a path has been cleared through the bamboo; when visitors get this far, they can rest if they are tired; this is one of the places of which I have said that "the fierce sun is hidden in summer, and a light freshness surrounds one, so that one lingers, reluctant to leave." As one turns round, forming a backdrop to the bamboo is a tall rock-peak standing alone, with its head bent as though listening; as it faces toward the sutra chamber, I named it Nodding Rock, alluding to the story of Master Daosheng.[23] Ten *wu* from the peak, one comes upon a stone bridge, broad and flat, on which ten mats could be spread; previously I often awaited the moon here, but now other sites are better for that, so it could not go on being used; I named it Mantra Chanting, alluding to Sakyamuni expounding the dharma in the Heaven of the Thirty-Three Devas and then returning to the palace.

At this point one's field of view suddenly seems to open up; tall elms and ancient pines rival the sutra chamber in beauty, and the beautiful shade is no less than among the bamboo, although without the feeling of secluded depths. My friend Wen Peng[24] came here and was delighted with it; he wrote in large clerical script "Realm of Pure Coolness" in extraordinarily impressive characters, which I had carved in stone and set up on the sunny north side of the bridge,[25] to the right. If you go over the bridge and go straight up for several yards, you reach the sutra chamber; the rooms to either side of it hold the Buddhist and Daoist scriptures, of which the left-hand one carries the name-board "Treasures of the Dharma" and the right-hand one "Pearls of Mystery."[26] If I am alarmed by excessive numbers of visitors, I can scurry in here, merely to rest and refresh myself; I could not possibly read them all. If you open the window to the north, then Middle Island and West Hill, with their mountainous appearance, arise side by side, seeming to rear up and wrestle; the furthest parts of them seem to be as far away as the eye can see, while the nearest parts touch your eyebrows. The lower story of the sutra chamber is also very spacious; I commissioned Maestro You to paint the

---

23 Master Daosheng was a monk at the Tiger Hill monastery outside Suzhou in the Jin dynasty (3rd–4th century), who preached so eloquently on the *Nirvana Sutra* that even the rocks nodded in agreement.

24 Wen Peng (1498–1573), a son of the famous Suzhou literatus Wen Zhengming, was himself a well-known painter and calligrapher.

25 It is common in Chinese to use *yin* (shaded) and *yang* (sunny) as directional terms. In the case of a hill, the sunny side is the south and the shaded side the north, but in the case of a river or valley, the sunny side is the north and the shaded side the south. Presumably a bridge, especially a level rather than an arched one, can be considered in the same way as the watercourse it crosses, therefore the sunny side here should be the north side.

26 "Treasures of the Dharma" would contain the Buddhist scriptures and "Pearls of Mystery" the equivalent Daoist texts.

four walls with scenes from Buddhist mythology in dilute ink,[27] and set out a day-bed where I could lie down and rest whenever I felt like it. Behind the building I planted several azure parasol trees. Going north from here, the path is cut short where a body of water lies. To the left of the sutra chamber, facing south, is a declivity, facing Middle Island; here I had constructed a fancy building of three bays, extending over the water, where I could await visitors. Anyone who arrived could be seen clearly as though in a mirror, while flowers, trees, birds and fish came of their own accord to be close to men; I named it Meeting of Minds.[28] In front of it I planted several dozen pear, chestnut, and apple trees. To the right of the sutra chamber is the deer-house where I keep three deer; the gardeners also share it.[29] This is one of the scenic areas in my garden.

III

Knowing the Ford Bridge crosses Lesser Yanhua Stream; the stream, continuing north for a couple of hundred yards, comes to an end and the foothills of the two Western and Central mountains start to appear. As you walk along it, everything comes within your view; I gave it the name because it is like the Yanhua Stream in Wuxing, but smaller. To the west, a building of five bays overlooks the water, with a door in the middle, with a signboard written by Deputy Censor-in-Chief Zhang Jiayin reading "An Urban Forest."[30] In front is a wall to screen it. Turning slightly south, and then west, a wide open space has been cleared, where I intended to set up five Dongting or Lake Tai rocks to serve as the Five Elders Peaks of Lushan,[31] but I have not managed this yet. Meanwhile I have fenced it in and planted cherry-trees; once the cherries are mature, I can satisfy my greed at harvest time, as well as feasting my eyes on the flowers. The space to the left is similarly planted, and together they are called Cherry Bank. The hall of five bays, lofty and expansive, is called Yanshan Hall; the name is explained in the earlier section of the "Record." In the extensive space on its sunny or south side I made a flat terrace, from which one can obtain a complete view of the moon, and five magnolia trees are planted on each side, right and left; when in flower they reflect each

---

27   You Qiu (fl. ca.1540–1590) was a well-known professional painter in Suzhou. Buddhist figures, especially mural paintings, were the kind of subject that would be handled by a professional (artisan) painter rather than a literatus amateur. He was the son-in-law of the painter Qiu Ying (1494–1552).

28   This refers to an anecdote in the *New Account of Tales of the World* recounting Emperor Jianwen's reaction to Flowery Grove Park, as found in chapter 1 of this anthology.

29   Deer were valued for their association with Daoist recluses and immortals. Various parts of their anatomy could also be used for medicinal purposes. It is not clear whether the gardeners actually had to live with the deer, or just used the deer-house as a sort of potting shed.

30   Zhang Jiayin (1527–1588). Slightly later in the Ming dynasty, the phrase "An Urban Forest" was criticized by the writer Xie Zhaozhe (1567–1624) as a typical cliché of garden nomenclature.

31   Lushan or Mount Lu in Jiangxi was particularly associated with literary recluses of the Tang and Song dynasties such as Bai Juyi and Su Shi. It was also a Buddhist site. It had a number of notable peaks, including the "Five Elders."

other's brilliance like Snowy Mountain and Onyx Island.[32] If you pick the petals and fry them, they taste fragrant and crisp and stimulate the appetite. To the north of the hall there are two each of flowering apple and birchleaf pear trees; they are more than two spans in diameter, and the profuse blossom is a glorious sight as each shows off their varying attractions. Farther north we come to the edge of a lotus pond, about forty feet long from east to west, and half that from north to south. Every spring, sitting under the apple and the pear, I grow intoxicated even without wine; but at the height of summer, if I come to the pond when I am intoxicated, then I sober up even without tea. Whenever visitors stopped here on their way past, they would say to me in surprise: "This is by no means inferior to General Wang's Hibiscus Pond!"[33] I declined such an honor, but by coincidence I acquired a rock from an abandoned garden in my native village which was carved with the words "Hibiscus Islet" in ancient clerical script of the Kaiyuan period [713–741]—some said it was an heirloom of Fan Chengda's family— so I set it up to the right of the pond.[34] Following to the south of the pond one comes to a small gully which winds around to join up with the stream behind you and is surrounded on all sides by red and white standard hibiscus: another happy coincidence. Going east from the left side of the hall, along the bank of Lesser Yanhua Stream, there is a stone gateway blocking the path, with a signboard reading "The Bare Minimum,"[35] while the gateway to the right has one reading "Although Provided." The one called "Although Provided" is so named because it closes off the water.[36] Going through the gate named The Bare Minimum, one finds a stream on one's left and a pond on one's right. Going south along the pond, the shady side of it is covered with bamboo, which forms a fence round an area named Onyx and Jasper Bank. In this bank are planted one hundred red and white "bright" flowering apricots and four-colored peach trees, and also plums in the ratio of one to twenty; "Onyx" refers to the red and "Jasper" to the white. Farther west, there is a small, low bridge named "Minimal Possession," which gives another access to the mountain. From here you turn north once again; the gully twists every ten paces and is faced with Yellow Rocks,[37] through which winds a clear

---

32 These are habitations of the immortals.

33 "General Wang" is the great calligrapher Wang Xizhi (321–379), who held the title of General of the Right.

34 Fan Chengda (1125–1193), the Song dynasty poet and scholar-official, was one of the key figures in Suzhou garden culture. For extracts from his "Treatise on the Flowering Apricot," see chapter 3.

35 "The Bare Minimum" and "Minimal Possession" (see below) are phrases taken from the *Analects*.

36 Referring to a line in "Homeward Bound" by Tao Qian, one of the key texts of garden culture: "Although my dwelling is provided with a gate, it is usually closed," or in H. C. Chang's translation (see chapter 1): "My gate seldom creaks to welcome a visitor."

37 The name *huang shi* 黃石 literally means yellow rocks, and they are indeed of a yellowish color, but they are sometimes said to be so called because they originate from Yellow Mountain (*Huangshan* 黃山) in Anhui. They are not ornamental in the way that Lake Tai rocks are, and therefore are not individually valued, but are one of the most widely used types of garden rock. As we see later in this chapter, the Pleasurable Garden (*Yuyuan* 豫園) in Shanghai has a large rockery construction of *huang* rocks that is said to have been designed by Zhang Nanyang, who was also responsible for the design of much of Wang Shizhen's garden.

rivulet like a mirror; it is named Stone-Chime Bend Gully.[38] Along the gully it is all planted with standard hibiscus; this is in fact the place where the stone named Hibiscus Islet has been set up. To the left of the path is a bank of flowering apricot, which cannot be confined by the fence of bamboo but has burst out over the path. Where the path grows somewhat more open, the flowering apricot is even more luxuriant; it is named Fragrant Snow Path.[39] Where it opens out farther, a pavilion has been built, which blocks off the water of the stream in front of it; this stream converges with Stone-Chime Bend Gully. On the farther bank Western Yanshan begins, with strange rocks and singular trees, rising and falling, high and low, as if sitting, as if standing, as if dancing, as if rearing; you could sit all day in this pavilion drinking it all in, but visitors often pass it by without even noticing it. The pavilion is therefore called Replete with Mountains. If you turn again and go east for several dozen yards, then everything related to this path comes to an end, and you reach Assembled Splendors Bridge.

IV

Assembled Splendors Bridge crouches at the entrance to the mountains; I intended to erect an archway on the sunny or south side of it, with a sign-board saying "The Three Mountains of the Immortals in the Ocean,"[40] but I have not managed to do so yet. The bridge is made of stone, quite magnificent, and below it the waters of the various streams all converge. From on top of it, one can see all of Western Yanshan to the north, all of Middle Island to the northeast, and part of the blossom and bamboos around the Buddha chamber to the southeast, and through a declivity one can see the best view of Patterned Ripples Hall; the only thing one cannot see is the Eastern Mountain. This is why I named it Assembled Splendors. Only after crossing the bridge does one reach the start of the mountain path. A rock reclines by the path like a tiger, and there are northerly and southerly mountain ridges, the southerly lower and the northerly more precipitous. On the southeast face of the northern ridge stands a peak in solitary splendor, thrusting up into the clouds, which I named Hatpin of the Clouds. The summit of it is shaped like a lion, crouching slightly forward, so it is also known as the Lion in Ambush. Another peak to the right is slightly lower and seems to be attending on it; it is called the Attendant. Farther to the right again is an even more impressive peak, with a hole through the middle of it like a shooting mark, so it is called the Archery Target. All the peaks of the south ridge face forward, so from here one sees only their backs. Looking at them from the Pavilion Replete with Mountains, one can

---

38   Stone chimes have a right-angled shape.

39   "Fragrant snow" is a common literary term for flowering apricot blossom.

40   Gardens were often conceived as miniature versions of the three mountainous islands inhabited by immortals in the Eastern Ocean (sometimes equated with Japan), and might actually include three islands in a lake, three rocks in a pond, or, as in this case, three "mountains."

count them one by one. One looks like an ancient stele inscription and is called Great Yu's Seal Script;[41] the others I will not record.

Where the path turns north, one comes to a stretch of rapids, with a group of rocks rearing up from the water, very impressive and strange, lions, hornless dragons, sleeping oxen, rams pawing the ground, more than can be counted; as a group they are called Emerging Stars Shallows.[42] To the right of the rapids is a mountain ridge, and the rocks that form a sort of path along the ridge are known as Perilous Peak and Slender Waist of Chu, because of their shape.[43] There is a stone screen, the color of jade, and pleasantly smooth and low, called White Cloud Screen. The source of the rapids is Coiling Stream, which makes several dozen twists and turns before falling into Celestial Mirror Pool. One branch of it crosses below Hazy Tower to enter Submerged Dragon Cave, which connects to the pool and contains many remarkable rocks worth recording. As a whole, it embraces Hazy Tower to the front, and reclines on the mountains to the rear, following all their sinuous windings, which it is why it is called Coiling Stream. No distance at all from White Cloud Screen, the path is suddenly cut off by two rocks about a foot or so apart; below this the water of the stream bubbles out, and connects with Lesser Dragon Waterfall. The summit of Lesser Dragon Waterfall is a snail-shell shape like a covered food tripod, surrounded by singular rocks on its three sides, linked together as the slope descends to where the water collects in a deep pool; visitors who come here are startled into saying that there seems to be something in the depths, and this is what gives it its name. To the southwest of the waterfall a narrow path clambers upward, by which one can cut through to Lesser Snowy Ridge. I once visited Wind Alley on Stone Lord Hill on Western Dongting Island in Lake Tai; this rather resembles it, so I named the place Stone Lord Alley. About ten *wu* farther on, one comes to a cliff-face with a large flat rock set at the center of the foot; one can rest here if tired, and it is called Rest Cliff. Of the peaks which overhang the path here, the clumsy one is called Apparently Arrogant, the delicate ones Remaining Petals and Patchwork Habit,[44] a large clumsy one Extreme Simplicity, and one which forms a stone screen resembling white clouds, but slightly darkened, Dark Jade. Almost at the end one reaches a set of ten stone steps up which one can climb, which I jokingly

---

41 Great Yu was a mythical Chinese culture hero who was associated with flood control; a mysterious inscription, resembling the style of calligraphy known as seal script, was said to have been set up by him to record his activities.

42 The animal-shaped rocks are evidently conceived as representing constellations. The identification of features on the ground with celestial bodies was an important aspect of geomancy (*fengshui* 風水).

43 Perilous Peak is a hill near Suzhou. Slender Waist of Chu is a reference to a line in a poem by the late Tang poet Du Mu (803–852): "Slim waists of Chu broke my heart, light bodies danced into my palm," which itself alludes to the predilection of an early king of Chu for women with slender waists; plump women were usually preferred. *Poems of the Late Tang*, trans. A. C. Graham (Harmondsworth: Penguin Books, 1965), 123.

44 The cassocks of senior Buddhist monks are often made of a formalized patchwork of squares, as a sign of poverty.

named Stair of Mistaken Wandering. The reason I called it this is that the slope is an extension of the northwest bank of Hibiscus Pond, across the Bridge of Minimal Possession, and forming an elevated ridge like the backbone of a horse, entirely planted with cassia, about a hundred altogether, and called Golden Grains Ridge;[45] from here it levels out again and follows the course of Stone-Chime Bend Gully; where the gully comes to an end, there are ten stone steps to climb up, and then there is a single pavilion from which one can watch the harvest in the fields and which is called Overseeing the Harvest. There is a further level ascent of about ten paces to where a thatched pavilion is situated; the late and learned Wen Peng wrote me the title in ancient clerical script: "Single Thatched Pavilion Between Heaven and Earth." The linking of the strokes was very fine, so I had it carved into a plaque. When one reaches this point one gets a complete view of the rural landscape of the open ground to the west. On the shady north side of the pavilion is the summit of Lesser Dragon Waterfall; if you cross it and go west a bit and then turn north, there are several peaks of white rock, so I named it Lesser Snowy Ridge. If you follow it you reach the Stair of Mistaken Wandering, where the peaks such as Apparently Arrogant and Extreme Simplicity are right beside the path. If a visitor follows the stream and then ascends the steps when he reaches them, he emerges by a circuitous route before he has realized it at the old route by Minimal Possession Bridge; this is the mistake made in ascending by people who have lost their sense of direction in the first place.

If you go west again from the Stair of Mistaken Wandering, there are rocks overhanging the stream known as Black Cloud Pile and Thousand Year Fungus,[46] named from their extremely singular appearance. There are plenty of other rock peaks that could be named, but it is too tiring to write them all down. A bit farther on you find a cave, which is level going in but precipitous coming out; the rocks in the cave slant and tumble as though butting each other and are called Horns and Teeth, a quotation from the "Rhapsody on the Gaotang Shrine."[47] If you scramble up to the southeast, you reach a flat terrace which is the roof of the cave. Beside it are planted trees such as catalpa, magnolia, and walnut. One peak that faces south is named the Dilettante. A few *wu* to the southeast, there is a peak called Signpost through the Labyrinth; from here a great green slab of rock forms a bridge across space, an extremely splendid sight; it is called Green Rainbow. Following Green Rainbow farther west and then descending, you enter a cave with a building above it; this is Hazy Tower. The southern face of it is formed of delicate rocks stacked up on top of each other, extremely like the Flew-Here Peak in Hangzhou. Below it is a small precipice, into which I set a stone carving which

---

45 "Golden grains" refers to the small, yellowish, and extremely fragrant flowers of the cassia (*gui* 桂, more correctly osmanthus), which flowers in autumn.

46 The Ganoderma fungus was believed to be an elixir of long life.

47 Wang Shizhen here uses a variant reading of a line he quotes from Song Yu's (?332–?284 BCE) "Rhapsody on the Gaotang Shrine" (*Gaotang fu* 高唐賦).

I happened to obtain of Mi Fu's inscription on a portrait of the Cloth-Sack Monk; I named it Qici Cliff, Qici being the monk's name.[48] To the north I placed a pair of couches, half extending out from below the eaves, from which one could enjoy all the sights of the southerly mountain-ridge. Every time I sit here at the end of spring, the north wind blows the flowers down to cover my head-kerchief, and still I can't bear to tear myself away. If you turn right and climb up a wooden stairway, the vista suddenly expands because there is a wide open space in front of Hazy Tower, and there are all the three peaks including Hatpin of the Clouds which you saw as you came into the mountain earlier on. To the left a peak of Jinchuan rock stands out in splendor; it is real Jinchuan rock from Sichuan, and I named it Washing Flowers.[49] From here you then ascend Hazy Tower, which refers to Du Fu's couplet: "Atop the city-wall, beside the path, / A soaring tower stands all alone."[50] It also takes its name from the western ridge of Dongting, although this grandiose name is rather a case of the quail fluttering about unaware that it has not actually traveled 90,000 miles.[51] This tower is the highest point in the three Yanshan mountains; not only does it command a view of the entire garden as if in a mirror, but if you look out of the east doorway, then you see a myriad courtyards overlapping like fish-scales, azure roof-tiles and carved roof-ornaments, all linked together without intermission, and if you go out of the west doorway and ascend three steps you reach a terrace made of stone laid over wood and surrounded by a crimson balustrade, and if you gaze west you can see the Lou River like a strip of gauze, and Horse Saddle Mountain thirty *li* in the distance reveals itself when the leaves have fallen; gazing north, Mount Yu seems near although it is a hundred *li* away, and on fine clear days it is covered with a thick wash of azure. This place is named Grand Prospect Terrace; it is also called Pavilion for Gazing at Mount Yu, meaning that since one does not gaze at Horse Saddle Mountain, which is nearer, one's ambitions are far-reaching. I will omit its other beauties.

From the upper story of the tower, descending to the left, one reaches a rectangular terrace, smooth and flat above a precipice which extends several dozen feet down to Celestial Mirror Pool. This is the best place to appreciate the sights of the Western Mountain, and it is the first place that gets the moonlight. Sitting here makes one's thoughts naturally distant, and it is named Transcendence Terrace. A peak which

48 Mi Fu (1051–1107) was one of the outstanding painters and calligraphers of the Song dynasty. The Cloth-Sack Monk (*Budai heshang* 布袋和尚) was a monk in the later Liang dynasty (10th century) who collected alms in a sack.

49 Jinchuan rocks were a highly prized ornamental type, obtainable from various locations in China. The Jinjiang (Brocade River) in Sichuan is also known as Washing Flowers Stream.

50 A reference to the poem entitled "The highest tower in Baidi city" (*Baidicheng zui gao lou* 白帝城最高樓). The lines referred to actually read, "On the city-wall, by crooked paths, the army banners despair; / A soaring tower stands alone and hazy." Wang Shizhen is evidently quoting, none too accurately, from memory.

51 In the *Zhuangzi*, the quail that flutters about among the undergrowth is contrasted with the mighty roc that can fly for 90,000 miles.

reaches up to heaven in many places but does not pierce it is named Flirting with the Clouds; another which is just like a sagging belt for court dress is called Gentleman in Waiting; a rock which looks like someone wearing a topknot is called Wizard's Topknot; these all adorn the terrace. To the south of the tower, and slightly to the east, you reach a set of ten stone steps by which you can go down to White Cloud Gate, and if you go down a further set of ten steps to the northeast, there is a gate called Separation from the Mundane. This is the prime cave-heaven in my three Yanshan mountains. The air is fine and pure, sometimes bright, sometimes dim, the stalactites are moist and dripping, the precipitous cliff walls slant upward as if snapping their jaws or struggling. The water in it connects up to the left with the Celestial Mirror Pool, but the watercourse is entirely covered over with strange rocks; it draws in the Coiling Stream from the north, which enters it in an obscure way. If you bend over it and gaze down you get a glimpse of light like a star; because it is so obscure and difficult to fathom, it is called Submerged Dragon Pool. It also so happens that my late teacher Tanyangzi kept a magic snake in a cage here; in no time it escaped, and ten days later it reappeared at the Xu tomb, so the name is appropriate in this sense too.[52] The stone steps in the cave often break off, and visitors coming through here have to walk in single file, hand in hand, and even so they tend to stumble. When one emerges from the cave the scene is again bright and spacious. Slightly to the south, there is the Beach Pillowed on the Current, so named because when the water rises it is submerged. Beside it there are a number of fine rocks, one named Pecked by Eagles, and another Little Filigree. Farther to the north you come upon a small stone slab bridge, set exactly below Green Rainbow like its reflection, and named Female Rainbow. You then re-enter Horns and Teeth Cave, turn, and ascend to the previous terrace; slightly to the west is a pavilion surrounded by cassia trees and called Cassia Grove. Going back a little way you reach a terrace which starts you on the path to Central Yanshan. Although the terrace itself is insignificant, it is sited at the focal point of the three Yanshan mountains, and is named Node of Singularity. Descending from Node of Singularity, after several steps, the foothills of the different mountain peaks meet together and there are some rocks at the side, emerging from the water, from which one can fish; this is called Forgetting the Fish Jetty, referring to the idea expressed by Wang Hongzhi.[53] Beside the jetty is a rock sticking out like a beast's head, called Turtle Head. Then one turns and ascends again; there are rock peaks on all sides with red and white flowering apricot planted in the gaps between them, of which eight-tenths are white; there is also a pavilion set there named Surrounded by Jade. Beside it there are two peaks of Jinchuan and

52 The mystic Tanyangzi (Wang Daozhen) embarked on her religious career after the death of her fiancé, whose surname was Xu. Her own early death, and apparently also that of her companion snake, took place in the vicinity of Xu's tomb.

53 Wang Hongzhi was an official of the Jin dynasty. Once while fishing, he was mistaken for a fisherman and asked if he would sell his fish; he replied that he was not necessarily trying to catch fish.

axe-cut[54] rock; the axe-cut peak cuts through above the clouds, and is named Solitary Splendor. Turning slightly one arrives at Moonlit Waves Bridge, and that is the end of Western Yanshan.

V

Where Western Yanshan comes to an end, there is a body of water separating it by some distance from Central Yanshan; a bridge was built here to direct the water, and the two mountains hem it in on either side, so that if there is the slightest breeze it breaks into waves. If you come here on a moonlit night, the broken light on the ripples is very attractive. Someone gave me a copy of Cai Xiang's "Record of the Wan'an Bridge," in which the characters "moonlit waves" were particularly grand, so I copied them to make a plaque for the archway of the bridge.[55] Across the bridge, a single peak stands in the way, just like something painted by Lu Zhi, and I named it Ancient and Upright.[56] Farther on from this is Master Gourd's Tower;[57] to the right of its west wall there is a profusion of rock-peaks and so on; if you turn to the southwest, they overhang the water, their mighty, tortuous forms protruding into the void, all displaying their different forms to delight people in passing boats. Sticking up slightly from the water there are some particularly strange rocks, one like someone with both arms upraised, called Screened by Sleeves, and one as if drinking with head thrown back, called the Thirsty Lion, and a smaller one at its tail called the Lion Cub; there is one which appears to be floating upward called Crest of the Wave; one which looks miserable and about to sink into the water called Grieving by the River Xiang;[58] I will not refer to them all. A few *wu* farther on is Shuairan Cave, which is level both above and below, but has a mass of bony rocks on either side and suddenly widens and then narrows, as though a *shuairan* serpent had burrowed through the rock; hence the name. Where the cave is about to come to an end, two rocks stand on either side, just like two gate-keepers; the one on the left is tall and thin and the one on the right low and venerable; their combined name is the Stone Sentinels. If you turn and descend to the southwest, there is a large flat rock by the side of the water, which forms another angling jetty; as it is quite near the sutra chamber, it is a place where one can call a boat

54 This refers to a type of brushstroke used in Chinese painting.

55 Cai Xiang (1012–1067) was a famous calligrapher and scholar-official of the Song dynasty.

56 Lu Zhi (1496–1576) was a Suzhou landscape artist. His rocks tend to be massive rather than intricate. It is interesting that Wang Shizhen compares this rock to the work of a contemporary artist rather than one of the great landscape artists of the past.

57 Different authorities give different identities for Master Gourd or Master Flask, but the general story is that he was an immortal disguised as an itinerant medicine seller who hung up a flask in the market. A market official saw him disappear into it one night, followed him, and found that the flask contained an entire world.

58 When the mythical Emperor Shun died, his wives wept by the River Xiang; their tears marked the bamboo stalks, and this type of spotted bamboo is known as Xiang bamboo.

to ferry one across there, so it is called Return to the Western Paradise Ford.[59] If you turn back to the east by way of the cave mouth, and cross Clear Waves Causeway and traverse the mouth of Pearl-Rinsing Stream below it, of the rock-peaks which overhang the water from here on, some resemble lumps of white jade, others dark jade rings; all are venerable with many foraminations through them; one dark one which is particularly strange is named Celestial Bones, and a white one is named Carving of Chu. If you take a slight turn to the south, the two rock walls rise up with a very narrow space at the top, over which another rock has been laid, and this is called Lesser Cloud Gate; here you turn and enter a ravine. On either side of the ravine are strange rocks, making it remote and dank; looking up you cannot see the sun; the ravine walls wind along the stream as it twists and swirls, and together they make a splendid sight. I have remarked that although the ravine is no more than about three *xun* high, it has the appearance of Min'e Mountain in Kui Prefecture of Sichuan. There is no more than a few feet of space beside the stream along which to pass; if you were to make Elder Lingwei explore it, even he would come to a stop and not be able to proceed further.[60] This is the prime area in Central Yanshan. Where the ravine is about to end, one reaches a rock that if struck emits a clear ringing sound like a stone-chime; my brother[61] was delighted with it when he visited and named the ravine Chiming Jade, while I named the stream Pearl-Rinsing; my only regret is that I could not adequately bring out the beauty of the place.

From Chiming Jade Ravine one turns again and climbs about fifteen steps to reach an expansive stone balustrade; if you enter by the gate on the left, you come to the central two-story building of three bays. There is a rock screen in front of it, dark shading to black in color and very venerable, like Yingzhou or Lingbi rock, towering and writhing, replete with all kinds of different attitudes, showing no trace of having been constructed artificially; a couple of places in Ziyang Hermitage in Qiantang [Hangzhou] seem to resemble it, so I named it Ziyang Wall. A visitor said to me: "Most people when they set eyes on the intricate beauty of a real mountain say 'It could almost be artificial,' while when they see an artificial mountain which has been cobbled together they say 'It could almost be real'; I wonder how they would regard this rock-wall?" The summit of the rock-wall is planted with junipers, less than six feet in height but with trunks of about a hand's breadth; the grey-green of the foliage and the dark-red of the berries is particularly beautiful. The north window opens on a vast expanse, like suddenly seeing a whole new world. The rippling water spreads far and wide, reflecting the sky above it; red beams are thickset, lattice windows and decorated buildings stretch as far as the eye can see. Eastern Yanshan and Western Yanshan compete in morning and evening splendor. The building bears a sign-board: "Master Gourd's Tower," referring to the

---

59 The Buddhist paradise is in the west; returning to the west refers to death.

60 Elder Lingwei was a legendary figure sent by the King of Wu to explore caves.

61 Wang Shimao (1536–1588).

fact that you go into a narrow space but gain a broad vista. The left wing of the building is directly opposite the little ridge of Eastern Yanshan, which is covered with pink peach-blossom, with one tree of white blossom outstanding among them; I happened to visit here with my brother Shimao at the end of spring, when they were still dazzlingly colorful, so I called the place Borrowed Fragrance. The right-hand wing of the building gets a very pleasing view of the distant snow-scene around Hazy Tower in the winter, so I called it Immanent Snow. The view to front and rear from the ground floor of the building is the same as from the upper floor. Slightly to the east, Ganoderma fungus grows where it gets the rain running down from the eaves; it has now been growing for three years, and whenever it appears, the ground there is moist even when it has not rained, and purple ether hangs over it; it gleams like crystal in the sunlight, so I called the spot Splendid Fungus Place. Going on from in front of Immanent Snow, you follow a covered walkway up about three stages, and then turn south, where there is a building with a solemn statue of the Buddha seated on a lotus; this is called Chamber of Brahma's Voice, taking its name from the wind in the juniper trees on top of Ziyang Rock-Wall. Coming out of the chamber, one winds up three steps to the right, and then reaches the topmost summit, named Red Twist Peak, or alternatively Jade Filigree. It stretches up into the mists and is the finest of Lake Tai rocks. A slightly lower peak on its left is called Peak Through Which the Moon Penetrates, and the next lower one is called Spiral Peak; to the right the lower rock is a Jinchuan rock called Patchwork Sunset-Clouds Peak. Winding down again to the left, one keeps coming across fine rocks, with a single Jinchuan peak which is particularly choice, the finest of Sichuan rocks; it is named Dark Jade Bamboo-Shoot. From here you cross a stone slab bridge over Chiming Jade Ravine, which is called Turtle's Back. On the other side of Turtle's Back there is a pavilion directly ahead of you. There is nothing special in the pavilion except that the blossom from the sides of the ravine with the stream in it often reaches in at the sides; it is only a matter of yards from Master Gourd's Tower, and visitors can rest here while they wait for it to be unlocked; it is named Pausing on the Journey. Turning south from Pausing on the Journey Pavilion, you go down several steps and reach Dongling Bridge, and that is the end of Central Yanshan. When first my plans went awry and I became the Foolish Old Man,[62] this was the very first of the Yanshan mountains that I started with; where I moved it from was our old property by Mijing River, which was very well endowed with fine rocks, all with a provenance of several hundred years.[63] Even the base of the mountain was made with fine rocks suitable for

---

62   The Foolish Old Man is the proverbial figure who moved a mountain by working away at it over generations; this obviously refers to Wang Shizhen's garden construction, which he took up when out of government office as a result of his father's trial and execution.

63   A brief description of the Wang family's garden at Mijing 麋涇, or Michang jing 麋場涇, survives in a gazetteer of Taicang dating from the late Ming and revised in the early Qing (see below).

peaks. I did not just move rocks, but trees too: mountain alum[64] and dwarf pine-trees, with nine knots for every foot of branch, twisting and contorted; also peach-trees, flowering apricot, flowering apple, junipers and so on, which seemed to be deliberately rivaling the pines in their strange appearance. The ravines and streams pressed on the available space, the leafy branches intertwined, so that when visitors walked through their hats were knocked off and their sleeves caught up as they walked in close file, but this only made them enjoy themselves the more. But still I was not satisfied, so Eastern and Western Yanshan then followed; that is why I call myself the Foolish Old Man.

VI

Crossing Dongling Bridge, there is a peak blocking the way, called Elegant Peak. Going south from here, there are two peaks, and one tall parasol tree and a number of peach-trees which are very flourishing, and farther south is the Boat House, but these are not on the way to Eastern Yanshan. Turning north, there is a peak with "axe-cut" marks, called Dark Point, and another peak called Old Clumsy.[65] When you turn east, the path is all winding, and meanders upward for several dozen *wu*; there is a peak with sunken sockets like the cheek-bones of a poor old woman, called Azure Wrinkles. After that you reach a pavilion which faces north. On its left, there is a deep stream among leafy trees, delightfully secluded. It is only when you reach this pavilion that the splendors of Eastern Yanshan are revealed. From this point you can go through it and out by two different routes, so I named it Divided Splendor Pavilion.

The "sunny" route goes due north through a small stone gateway, and then opens out slightly, with a tall peak on the right with a pattern of stroke-marks as though it were cracked, which is named the Hundred-Piece Monk's Cassock. The lower one next to it is similar and is called the Lesser Hundred-Piece Monk's Cassock. They look like a monk and his acolyte having a casual chat. A peak slightly to the west is the most prominent, with two points inclined toward each other; the Mountain Master[66] named it the Crab's Pincer. Someone, feeling this was too vulgar, asked to give it a different name, but I said that this was a quotation from Minister of Personnel Bi Zhuo of the Jin dynasty; if I ever had an endless supply of Junshan wine, what could be so pleasant as having something like this to help it down? So I did not change it.[67] You ascend three

---

64   An evergreen shrub with fragrant white flowers, *Symplocos caudata* or *S. sumuntia*. It has no English name; "mountain alum" is a literal translation of the Chinese name.

65   Clumsiness or awkwardness (*zhuo* 拙) was a quality valued in elite art, since it marked its practitioners as free from the skill of the artisan.

66   This "Mountain Master" may have been the rockery designer Zhang Nanyang, who worked on Wang Shizhen's garden (see Wang's remarks at the end of this section). A biography of Zhang, by Chen Suoyun, can be found in chapter 7.

67   Toward the end of the sixteenth century, the literati were becoming particularly sensitive to suggestions of "vulgarity" in garden nomenclature. Wang Shizhen makes fun of his oversensitive acquaintance by claiming

steps slanting toward the northeast, and reach a broad terrace which has a wine-cup meander. On the terrace there is a Hibiscus Screen of carved stone. The stone faces west and is something over five feet high and twice that in breadth. It is called Cloud Root Cliff. When there is water in the meander then the wine-cups come bobbing down from an opening below the cliff, and as they pass through Hibiscus Narrows, the guests compete to seize them, not even caring when they soak their clothes and shoes. The water from the Stone Hibiscus channel pours over a rock to the east, and empties down into the pool, from which the spray splashes forcefully upward; it is just like a little Sage's Lodging,[68] and I called it Flying Gauze Ravine. Xu Ning's poem may be a bad one,[69] but there is nothing wrong with these two words "Flying Gauze"! But the two sights of Flying Gauze and the Crab's Pincer can only be appreciated from a boat and not otherwise. Descending ten or more steps from the place for floating wine-cups, one then comes to a large beach; as you look back you see a single peak facing north, as though nodding its head in approval of the beach view; it is called Reverencing Purity Peak. The beach slopes sharply downward, and you cannot always stop yourself sliding down it. It then becomes very extensive; there are four rows of ferocious rocks, and weeping willows, flowering apricot, and Sichuan flowering apples blending their shade together. If you pause here, then the delights of the pond, the south-facing eaves of Patterned Ripples Hall with their painted beams, the hills and glens of the two Yan mountains at dusk and dawn, in dim and bright light, all reach this place. If you read Xie Lingyun, Duke of Kangle's line "The radiant sunlight filled me with such joy," you really could forget to depart, so I entitled it Joyful Radiance Beach.[70] To the left you can see a very beautiful rock, named Brocade Cloud Screen. After that, you find your way southeast along a path in a gully, climbing up narrow steps on which you have to place your feet sideways; this is the other, rear side of Cloud Root Cliff. There is a pair of cisterns here, standing side by side, with a windlass; this is where the water is pumped up for the wine-cup meander. If you bend over and look down into the cisterns they look very deep, like the Sword Pool at Tiger Hill in Suzhou. Then you go down by a few steps to the east and reach an old hackberry tree, which is about two arm-spans in

---

that an obscure classical allusion, from *A New Account of Tales of the World*, underlies the purely descriptive name given to the rock by the (presumably uneducated) Mountain Master.

68   This was a waterfall on Hermitage Mountain (*Lushan* 廬山), the mountain particularly associated with reclusion.

69   The Tang poet Xu Ning (early 9th century) wrote a poem on the Hermitage Mountain waterfall, from which the description of the waterfall as "Flying Gauze" comes; the poem was later criticized by the Song dynasty poet and scholar Su Shi.

70   The lines come from Xie Lingyun's (385–433) poem "Written on the Lake on My Way Back to the Retreat at Stone Cliff" (*Shibi jingshe huan hu zhong zuo* 石壁精舍還湖中作): "Between dusk and dawn the weather is constantly changing, / Bathing mountain and lake alike in radiant sunlight. / This radiant sunlight filled me with such joy / That lost in delight I quite forgot to go home." See J. D. Frodsham, trans., *The Murmuring Stream: The Life and Works of the Chinese Nature Poet Hsieh Ling-yün (385–433), Duke of K'ang-Lo* (Kuala Lumpur: University of Malaya Press, 1967), 138.

circumference and casts a shade all around it for almost half a *mu*; there are peaches, flowering apricots and so on beside it to set it off. Originally, when the monks were about to sell me the land, they threatened to cut down this tree in order to get more out of me. I figured that mountains, waters, terraces, and pavilions were all easily constructed by human effort, but a tree could not easily be made to become ancient, and the price went up to twenty strings of a thousand cash before we settled; I built a pavilion from which to enjoy the sight of it, and called it Fine Tree Pavilion. Hackberry is an inferior tree;[71] that it should arrogate to itself the title of "fine" was merely fortuitous. The pavilion borders on the pond to the north and overlooks a stream on the south, and also benefits from the shade of the tree; although small, it is completely delightful. Beside the pavilion is a rock-peak, which looks from a distance like a lotus-blossom, though not so much so from close up, so I named it Resembling a Lotus. Turning away from Fine Tree Pavilion and going east there is a stone slab bridge which is of a true viridian color, called Jade Viridian Beam. You ascend three steps to the east, and then turn northwest and go up by a circuitous route until you reach a mountain-ridge resembling a long, narrow table; somewhat to the north, there is a mountain-ridge resembling the hump of a camel, with nine juniper trees enclosing it to front and rear that are very luxuriant. Their delicate filigree gleams darkly as though bathed in oil whenever the sun comes up; they always brush against one's face and the cones have a delicious fragrance; this is called Nine Dragon Ridge. Almost no distance away, you arrive at Three Paces Beam stone slab bridge, which is no more than three paces long, and dangerous. From here you turn and go downhill, and then twist and turn and again penetrate upward to a path lined by fine bamboo, and stop when you reach Clacking Clogs Walkway.[72] This is what is known as the "sunny" route.

The "shady" route is formed entirely by secluded paths. From where you look down on the stream you turn northward, and then go down some stone steps somewhat to the east, then turn again to go south, and only after several more turns do you come to the Temple of the Mountain Spirit. Beside the temple is a tree which grows at a slant through the wall to the south, so that not only does it cast its shade over the monks' pond, it then turns back and casts its shade over us as well. To its right is another tree, larger but similar; I had to pay a substantial sum to buy both of them from the monks, though the timber would not be worth one-fifth of what I paid. A path exits from the west side of the temple, and passes below Jade Viridian Beam; from here you can look down and catch a glimpse of the beauties of Retaining Fish Stream. Retaining Fish Stream starts from the Divided Splendor Pavilion and ends up at Broad Heart Pond. It is very long and winding,

71 Confucius said that a gentleman would not sit in the shade of the hackberry (*Celtis sinensis*).

72 In his description of this walkway, Wang Shizhen implies that the sound of footsteps comes in the form of the clacking of wooden clogs on the wooden floor; however, in the original story to which the name alludes, Emperor Ai of Han recognized the approach of his minister Zheng Chong by the sound of his shuffling leather sandals, so it sometimes seems more appropriate to translate the phrase as "shuffling sandals."

and passes through virtually seven-tenths of Eastern Yanshan. On either side are precipitous cliffs several fathoms high; it winds along with almost a hundred twists and turns, and even fish which swim into it get lost and cannot find their way out, which is why it is called Retaining Fish Stream. At blossom time the fallen petals also accumulate in it and cannot get out, so it has another name: Retaining Blossoms. Generally speaking, visitors who go around by the sunny route get the benefit of the splendors of pool and stream about equally; those who go by the shady route only encroach on the stream, and the path is not built up with stone steps; whether going up or down, it is extremely steep and slippery, unexpectedly rising and falling. If the visitors are going up, they have to hold on to each other's sleeves, and anyone who lets go for a moment takes a tumble; when going down, they are right on each other's heels, but if they get too close they trip each other up. So some visitors think it is too much trouble, but gentlemen who go in for the weird and wonderful are all the more delighted and say what fun it is. Where the stream comes to an end, the shady route emerges on the pond, but the path is blocked in two places; between the places there is a level slope, but then it is blocked again,[73] and in the middle a rock has been set up again to enable one to cross. Anyone who wants to cross must kilt up his robe and jump in order to make it, so it is called Kilted Robe Crossing. When women visitors reach here,[74] they are usually frightened into turning back, so it is also called Ford Which Repels Women. Having crossed here, you circle round behind Mingled Sunset-Clouds Pavilion, and then turn into the pavilion. Mingled Sunset-Clouds Pavilion faces Early Moonlight Pavilion at a distance; the last rays of sunlight over Western Yanshan fall here, hence the name; this is also a quotation from Xie Lingyun, Duke of Kangle.[75] From this point one links up with the sunny route's exit from the mountain, where Clacking Clogs Walkway is situated. Generally speaking, Central Yanshan is distinguished for its rocks, while Eastern Yanshan is distinguished for its vistas. The rocks in Eastern Yanshan do not amount to two-tenths of those in Central Yanshan, but it has five times as many vistas. Central Yanshan is the culmination of human ingenuity, while in Eastern Yanshan a natural attractiveness can at times be perceived. Human ingenuity is always introverted, while natural attractiveness is usually extroverted.[76] At the time there were two mountain experts, Mr. Zhang Nanyang being responsible for Central and Western Yanshan, and Mr. Wu[77] being responsible for

---

73   The passage as it stands is incomprehensible; the text seems to be corrupt.

74   Note that the Yanshan Garden is visited by women who are apparently not members of Wang Shizhen's family, indicating both that private gardens could be open to visitors unacquainted with the owner and that women at this time had more freedom of movement than is often thought.

75   The quotation comes from the same poem as that quoted earlier; in Frodsham's translation, "Forest and gorge were veiled in somber colors, / The sunset clouds mingled with evening haze."

76   The words translated "introverted" (zhongye 中擪) and "extroverted" (waita 外拓) are technical terms describing strokes in calligraphy.

77   A certain amount of information about Zhang Nanyang ("Mountain Man Zhang") has survived (see the biography of him in chapter 7), but Mr. Wu is otherwise completely unknown.

Eastern Yanshan. I jokingly observed that the superiority or inferiority of each Yanshan would show the superiority or inferiority of the two masters, but in fact each exerted his skill in such a way that one could make no distinction between them.

VII

Going east from Western Yanshan, when you reach the Pavilion Encircled by Jade, that is the end of the western mountain. Turning north you come to a stone gateway, with a signboard reading "Parting Regrets Peak." There are three or four other sights here, which means that things do not completely come to an end. From here on it is all earth mountains up which one ascends by a serpentine route, planted with a mixture of fine bamboo fenced in by a dry-stone dyke. On the right there is a lot of extra space that I plan to shade with fine trees, but they do not yet cover the whole area. Then you wind down again, and Broad Heart Pond is on the left-hand side. There is a thatched pavilion at the foot. When the moon comes up from the eastern mountain-ridge at night, and the golden waves ripple, reflecting the moon in a myriad points of light, this is the first place that the moonlight reaches, so it is called Early Moonlight Pavilion. Going north by the pavilion, you come to another set of stone steps, with several dozen large and small rocks piled up at varying heights on either side of the path, as if escorting one on the path out of the mountain. The water of a stream blocks the way, but there is a bridge over it called Knowing the Way Home, a quotation from Tao Qian, magistrate of Pengze.[78] After that there is another bridge, and somewhat to the east, the Patterned Ripples Hall. The hall overlooks the clear current; it has speckled-bamboo awnings and crimson railings, and it is charmingly reflected in the water; with the gentle blowing of a faint breeze, the ripples form like silk crinkling under a hot iron. It is the counterpart to Master Gourd's Tower in the Central Island. At night, the lights of lanterns twinkle across the water, and even the sound of quiet talking can be heard from one to the other, never mind music. I wonder how it compares to the scenery of the West Lake? I suppose the West Lake is superior for its greater extent. I selected some rather splendid lines of poetry from the *Selection of Literature* and requested Zhou Tianqiu[79] to write them in large characters on one of the three walls of the hall; this is some of the best calligraphy he has ever done in his life. The level lake scene on the left-hand wall, and the snow-
covered mountain-ridge on the right-hand wall, were both done by Qian Gu;[80] the snow scene is particularly impressive. As you come out of the Patterned Ripples Hall you turn

---

78 The name of the bridge alludes to Tao Qian's poem "Homeward Bound," which contains the line, "The birds, tired with flying, know their way home"; in H. C. Chang's translation (see chapter 1): "the birds, weary of wandering, returning to their nests."

79 Zhou Tianqiu (1514–1595) was a distinguished Suzhou calligrapher. The *Selection of Literature* (*Wenxuan* 文選) compiled by Xiao Tong (501–531), a prince of the Liang dynasty, was the standard anthology used in classical education.

80 The Suzhou artist Qian Gu (1508–ca. 1578), who painted an album that includes a view of the Yanshan Garden in 1574.

left and go into the approach to a gateway over which is written "Avoiding Society,"[81] and then it suddenly opens out into a valley with the wind blowing through it, forming an extensive open space. A hall of three bays encroaches upon it; this is particularly high and airy, with all four walls open to the outside, so that it catches the breeze from any direction; planted at intervals around it are a number of viridian parasol trees to keep off the summer sun; it is called Cool Breeze Hall. Once the parasol trees are mature, I should use the quotation from Cui Bao of Jinan and call it Phoenix Frond Lodge.[82] Several *wu* west from the hall is Literary Elegance Tower, also known as Nine Friends Tower. The reason it is called Nine Friends is that I have always loved reading books and viewing things like ancient rubbings and the work of famous calligraphers, next to that paintings, and next again ancient vessels, incense burners, tripods, and wine vessels. All the books in my collection are Song editions, of which the finest is Ban Gu's *History of the Han*; the finest of my calligraphy collection are Chu Suiliang, Duke of Henan's "Mourning Document," Yu Shinan, Count of Yongxing's "Epitaph for Princess Runan," and Grand Preceptor Zhong You's "Memorial Recommending Ji Zhi;"[83] my finest paintings are Zhou Fang's "Listening to the Qin" and Wang Jinqing's "Misty River and Towering Crags;"[84] my finest wine vessel is a cup from the Chai family kiln; my finest rubbings of ancient inscriptions are the Dingwu "Orchid Pavilion" and the Supreme Purity Tower collection:[85] this makes five friends altogether. In addition to these, I would include the *Treasuries* of the two religions,[86] the mountains and the rivers, and my own *Collected Works*,[87] making a total of nine. When I was in Yunyang[88] and homesick, I made a melancholy song to express my feelings, and not long afterward my resignation was accepted, so that finally I was able to spend morning and evening with the nine friends lodged in my house. In front of the belvedere, Literary Elegance Tower, one looks down on to a rectangular pond that is stocked with several hundred goldfish

---

81   Another reference to Tao Qian: "May my friendships be broken off and my wanderings come to an end."

82   Cui Bao (late 3rd–early 4th century) once described the branches of the parasol (*wutong* 梧桐) trees in his garden as "phoenix fronds."

83   Famous pieces of calligraphy thought to date from the Tang and Wei dynasties.

84   Zhou Fang was a painter from the Tang dynasty and Wang Jinqing from the Song; it is unlikely that these paintings were originals.

85   The Dingwu "Orchid Pavilion" refers to a Tang dynasty stone carving of Wang Xizhi's "Preface to the Orchid Pavilion Poems," one of the most famous pieces of calligraphy of all time. The Dingwu version (so called because the stone stela ended up in a place called Dingwu) was supposed to be the closest to Wang's original, buried with the Tang emperor Taizong (r. 627–649). The Song emperor Huizong (r. 1101–1125), a great lover of the arts, had a collection of early calligraphy carved on stone stelae that were placed in the Supreme Purity Tower in the imperial palace.

86   The Buddhist and Daoist canons.

87   It is not clear whether the Buddhist and Daoist canons are to be counted together as one "friend" and the mountains and waters as two, or the canons separately as two and the landscape as one, in order to arrive at the total of nine.

88   Where Wang Shizhen was governor from 1574 to 1576.

that swarm together in shoals when you feed them. I happened to acquire two large characters "Ink Pond" written by Mi Fu and had them carved on a stone which I set up on the sunny side of the pond. In fact the boys do often wash inkstones in it, so it is an accurate description. To the west of the building you go through an opening, wind about a bit, and then reach another building of three bays; in the central room one can honor statues of the founders of the three doctrines,[89] and it is named Participating in Unity. The room on the left has most of my Song editions, and is named New Wanwei Mountain;[90] the one on the right is a hothouse in which fires are burnt to ward off the cold, and it is known as Nest of Cocoon Clouds.[91] In the central courtyard are some fist-sized rocks concealing a small cave; the water outside the wall is channeled in to flow around the steps, forming a meander for floating wine cups. It passes through the darkroom to the west and pours out from a gargoyle spout into the Ink Pond with a delightful gurgling sound. Late in the twelfth month I take up my abode in Cocoon Clouds, and at the height of summer I repose in Cool Breeze Hall; at other times of the year I sit, morning and evening, in Literary Elegance Tower, picking up this or that volume at random to read, or I unroll a scroll or unfold an album to get a feeling of appropriateness to the season or my mood. Brush and ink is something with which heaven has endowed me in plenty and they just keep rolling along; wine is something that heaven sends as a reward for wielding brush and ink, and I don't feel the worse for wear even after several full cups; this is enough to see me through old age. But yet I can cast them aside at any time in the service of the King of the Void, the Buddha, and make do with a dipper of water, a homespun robe and a straw hut to shelter my body; after all, the so-called Literary Elegance Tower is only a matter of four walls. If my nine friends leave me I will never ask who their new host is. When you go out of Avoiding Society Gate, there is a kitchen, food-store, and a wine-cellar. Farther east, there is a two-story building of five bays that was used to store 30,000 fascicles of books; it has a sign-board reading "Lesser Youyang"; at present I have already passed it on to the younger generation, so the name is meaningless.[92] In front of the building is a high wall, and against it an extended walkway several hundred feet long going along the side of the Broad Heart Pond. This is in fact the back way from Patterned Ripples Hall out to the Langye Villa. People who enter here from the Yanshan Garden cannot bear to tear themselves away once they get to this point, whereas those who are coming out of the villa suddenly see their vista expand into a new world; either way, everyone thinks of the sound of clacking clogs here, so it is called Clacking Clogs Walkway. Originally, I asked You Qiu to depict the Peach Blossom Spring of Wuling on the wall, and then Yu Yunwen wrote the

---

89 Confucianism, Daoism, and Buddhism.

90 Wanwei Mountain was the source of Great Yu's mystic inscription, so it is associated with literature.

91 "Cocoon clouds" could simply be descriptive of billowing smoke, but it is likely that this "hothouse" was used by the women of the household for the cultivation of silkworms and actually housed their cloud-like cocoons.

92 Youyang was the name of a mythical mountain whose caves housed a library belonging to the immortals. The name of the building became meaningless when it ceased to be used as a library.

"Record of the Peach Blossom Spring" and the "Poem" in cursive script; these could be considered three outstanding works of art.[93] One evening there was a great rainstorm, and the whole thing collapsed leaving no trace, so I cut down the buildings on either side which were too high, and built a two-story building of three bays in the center; I did not get rid of the walkway below it, but you can look out from the upper story of the building; if you roll up the blinds you can see almost seven-tenths of the scenes in the garden; dimly and hazily they all appear before your eyes. So this constituted one of the splendors of the garden and visitors were delighted with it, therefore I no longer regretted the loss of my mural. Where the walkway comes to an end there is a gateway called Sharing with the Multitude.[94] Turning north, there is another gateway just beside the stream which flows right through the garden, with a signboard reading Langye Villa. Somewhat farther east, you cross a bridge and then go east again, and there is the retreat which I have made for my three sons to live in.[95]

VIII

For a mountain to be surrounded by water is a great wonder, and for water to have the benefit of a mountain is another great wonder. The origin of my garden was simply a piece of agricultural land beside an *Aranya;*[96] in piling up rocks and constructing buildings, the natural lie of the land gave me no advantages. The earth had to be excavated and then the holes filled with water to make ponds; the mountains grew taller day by day, while the ponds grew more lush and expansive, until the splendor of the water features could rival that of the mountains. The water source originates south of Knowing the Ford Bridge; there is a sluice-gate which connects it with the tidal river outside and which can be shut on occasion. Somewhat to the north is the sutra chamber; its ground plan is the shape of a carpenter's square, while water surrounds it on all four sides in the long rectangular shape of a jade tablet. Somewhat farther forward on the left-hand side, a stone building of three room-spaces has been built straddling the water, where my boats are moored. One of my boats has railings along its sides and dark oilcloth awnings, and can seat ten passengers. The other boat is too narrow to provide proper seating, and is only used for fetching wine and netting fresh fish. When the boat passes in front of the sutra chamber, it cannot get past the low bridge; both banks are thickly planted with

---

93   You Qiu was a professional painter in Suzhou, whereas Yu Yunwen (1512–1579) was a literatus calligrapher. The subjects of their collaborative work were the "Record of the Peach Blossom Spring" and the associated poem by Tao Qian, one of the key texts of eremitism and garden culture, a translation of which is in chapter 1 of this anthology.

94   This appears to be a reference to Sima Guang's (1019–1086) "Record of the Garden of Solitary Enjoyment" (see chapter 4), in which Sima Guang remarks that he has been criticized for not "sharing his enjoyments with the people," as recommended by Mencius.

95   Wang Shizhen's three sons were Wang Shiqi (b. 1554), Shisu (1556–1601), and Shijun (1569–1597). Wang Shiqi shared his father's enthusiasm for gardens, though he seems to have preferred a less elaborate style.

96   The Sanskrit word *aranya*, meaning a hermitage, is transliterated in Chinese as *lanruo* 蘭若. Wang Shizhen is presumably referring to the nearby Temple of Abundant Blessing.

pine, bamboo, peach, flowering apricot, flowering apple, and cassia, and on the ground are many fragrant plants to rejoice the sense of smell. A few dozen feet due north is Dongling Bridge in Central Yanshan. The banks below the bridge consist of sheer rockwalls with spiky points rising up, overgrown with ancient creepers, so that they seldom see the sun. Plants such as crepe-myrtle, jasmine, and banana shrub frequently impede the punting pole; this place is called Scattered Flowers Ravine. If you follow it to the east, the first thing you see is the so-called Crab's Pincer Peak, with the outflow of the wine-cup meander; as you watch the splendid sight of the waterfall, the spray sprinkles your face. Following somewhat farther to the east, beside Joyful Radiance Beach, is the very best place to moor. Farther east again, you reach Fine Tree Pavilion, then turning north you come to Mingled Sunset-Clouds Pavilion, then going along beside Clacking Clogs Walkway, you moor at Patterned Ripples Hall, where wine and refreshments can be summoned before taking a turn around Lesser Floating Jade island. Lesser Floating Jade rises less than a foot above the surface of the water, and is about ten feet in diameter, its size depending on the height of the water, and it is so called because of its resemblance to Floating Jade Island in Lake Bilang at Wuxing [Huzhou]. To the south of the island, you can sail past Master Gourd's Tower, picking red flowering apricot and double peach blossom; on your west side is Early Moonlight Pavilion, then if you go south, skirting the earthen mountain, you come out at Moonlit Waves Bridge, where you seem to have reached quite another world. The clear pool is as bright as a polished mirror, with Western and Central Yanshan on either side of it. There are soaring peaks both near and far: the nearer ones seem to entice you, the farther ones seem to gaze at you. In Central Yanshan, all the subordinate peaks around the Chamber of Brahma's Voice emerge; in Western Yanshan, the scenery of Submerged Dragon Cave and Xiling Beach is within your grasp. If you turn south, and then go somewhat east, you come to the mountain face [the front] of Central Yanshan; if you go somewhat to the west, you go under Assembled Splendors Bridge, and then reach the mountain face of Western Yanshan. These are all the finest parts of the entire Yanshan Garden, which can all be obtained in one turn of the rudder. The pond is called Celestial Mirror Pool, quoting the Green Lotus Hermit's line "the moon descends like a mirror floating in the sky."[97] Due south of it, you enter Yanhua Stream, and when you reach Knowing the Ford Bridge, you come to the end of the water route. I have drifted about in the boat on spring days, with wonderful flowers everywhere around me, whose colors and fragrance enraptured my eyes and nose; when they were about to take their leave, they cast their fate upon the light breeze, and whenever I passed, my wine cup and the lapels of my clothes were covered in petals. Once the blossom is nearly finished, the thick green foliage takes over, and I often stop the boat under the shade of willows or by a clump of bamboo, to enjoy the refreshing coolness, and listen to the delightful twittering of the golden orioles. As darkness starts to fall, the peaks and trees take on a purplish-blue glow. In a little while the moon comes up, and

---

97   The Green Lotus Hermit was a cognomen of the Tang poet Li Bai (701–762); the reference is to his poem "Farewell on the Ferry at Jingmen" (*Du Jingmen song bie* 渡荊門送別).

suddenly everything is changed; the peaks like jade filigree pierce the sky, now hidden, now revealed in a myriad postures, their reflection cutting through the waves, above and below rivaling each other in beauty; where the rocks do not cast a shadow, the water glitters like molten metal and a myriad sparkles dazzle the eye, and as the punt-pole is plied on the return journey, the water scatters into shining pieces. Startled fish leap from the water, and sometimes jump right into the boat. When the singers strike up, a rowing song arises over the water and the hills echo the sound; the sound of wind and percussion comes from the hillside and stirs up the water. On nights when the moon is full, the cocks crow in mistake for daybreak, and even at midnight one has no feeling of tiredness; even though the light of the sun is faintly appearing on the horizon, one's guests still cannot bring themselves to say they are leaving; instead they say: "I'm not worried about dawn coming; why can't we go on from dawn to the next dusk?" Really the wonder of the Yanshan Garden lies in its water, and that of the water in the moonlight, so I have described the water last, and I finish with a description of the moonlight.

"Poem Sequence on the Yanshan Garden" (*Yanshan yuan shi* 弇山園詩)

WANG SHIZHEN 王世貞

TRANSLATED BY ALISON HARDIE

"Entering Yanzhou Garden, to the North One Reaches Lesser Jetavana; to the West One Reaches Knowing the Ford Bridge and Comes to a Stop"[98]

To the east there is an abandoned temple;[99]
The surface of its clear pool is like a mirror.
A few paces away, after some twists and turns,
The scent of forests excites a feeling of seclusion.
Roseleaf raspberry is twined into a screen to be enjoyed in spring;
Oranges and pomelos decorate fruit-baskets in autumn.
The trees in Jetavana are easy to grasp;
The immortals' Spring can perhaps be descried.[100]

---

98 Each of the poems in the sequence is given a title describing a portion of the route around the garden. This can be compared with the description in Wang Shizhen's "Record of the Yanshan Garden"; the route followed in the poem sequence is equivalent to part of the route described in the "Record of the Yanshan Garden."

99 The Temple of Abundant Blessing.

100 Lesser Jetavana Garden was the original name of the central portion of the Yanshan Garden. It refers to a park in which the Buddha preached the sermon recorded in the *Surangama Sutra*. The immortals' spring refers to the Peach Blossom Spring in the famous story and poem by Tao Qian (365–427). Thus this couplet includes both a Buddhist and a Daoist reference.

Baby birds stretch out their gaping beaks,[101]
The voices of a myriad trees respond to each other.
Visitors' footsteps gather in flocks;
There is no need to open up Mr. Jiang's paths.[102]

"Entering the Gate of Lesser Jetavana, You Come to This Gentleman Gallery, Go Along the Bamboo Path, Cross Mantra Chanting Bridge in the Realm of Pure Coolness, and Reach the Chamber for Storing the Sutras"

My humble gateway is pillowed on a wandering path;
Generally the gate is firmly locked.
Within it, not since the beginning of the year
Have I spoken with secular visitors.
A secluded pavilion is embraced by flourishing dwarf-bamboo,[103]
With emerald and jade around three edges.
The fading sunlight brushes the tops of the trees;
The last rays are scattered in profusion.
In the gold which the superior sun spreads,
The dark moss brightens and then disappears.
Where the path comes to an end the splendid view appears of its own accord;
As the earth turns the heavens also open up.
White elms shade the silver river;
One might also think they had been set there by Brahma.
A pointed chamber for storing the sutras rises over the tops of the trees;
The two canons are each ranged in order.[104]
The Lord of the Void is not really vacant;
The Realm of Suffering contains true pleasure.[105]
I am in point of fact a bookworm:
How can I fail to keep myself busy?

---

101   This probably refers to the cranes that Wang Shizhen's "Record of the Yanshan Garden" tells us he kept in this part of the garden.

102   Jiang Xu (1st century BCE) constructed a retreat with three paths, where only two close friends ever visited him. "Three paths" came to be a conventional designation for a hermitage or retreat.

103   It is this bamboo from which This Gentleman Gallery (*Cijun ting* 此君亭) takes its name, in allusion to the words of Wang Huizhi (d. 388) about bamboo, "How could I live a single day without these gentlemen?" (see chapter 3).

104   This refers to the canons of Buddhism and Daoism, which were stored in the library wings of the building.

105   The Lord of the Void is a title given to the Buddha; the Realm of Suffering is this world.

"Crossing Assembled Splendors Bridge You Enter the Mountain; Going Along Stream and Ridge You Come to Hazy Tower"

This bridge forms the node of all the streams,
And slices the three mountains in half.
As you raise your head a single peak stands proud,
With pieces like hatpins at either side.
Below it is Emerging Stars Rapids,
With its weird rocks like birds and beasts in conflict.
If you walk there at night the sight of them may alarm you,
But sitting in meditation a profound enjoyment emerges.
The secret path still goes through;
As it winds along its direction is cut off in the middle.
White rocks meander around the clear stream;
You can lie on them and wash to your heart's content.[106]
Slightly farther south there is a cave at the back,
And you suddenly gain a prospect of the universe;
But if you look back, the mountains which you have entered,
Can all come to cling alongside your desk.
Thinking about this intricate contrivance,
I burst out laughing in delight.

"Going Down from the Summit of Hazy Tower, You Traverse Eastward through Submerged Dragon Cave"

The tall tower allows one to delight in the wide prospect;
As you extend your gaze around, your thoughts reach an end.
Bending down you encroach on the birds' flight-path;
With feet placed sideways you explore the serpent's lair.
A returning sunbeam travels through a crack,
And all the crystals sparkle like filigree.
Below is gathered a profoundly pure stream,
With a mighty rock set in its center.
You take three bird-hops to cross it,
And ahead, you are still afraid of the obscurity.
To the southwest is a hollow cave-mouth,
Cavernous and glistening;
It reaches in the distance to Emerging Stars Rapids,

---

106 This alludes to the folk song quoted by Mencius: "When the water of the Canglang is clear, / It does to wash the strings of my cap."

And near at hand connects to Celestial Mirror Pool.
The secluded emptiness cannot be lingered in for long;
I am about to float away in vacant vastness.

"From the Western Mountain You Climb Up Separate Steps to A Single Thatched
Pavilion between Heaven and Earth; to the Northwest You Can See the City Walls;
to the Southwest You Can See the Temple of the Martial Pacifying Prince"[107]

Going upstream beside the stony rapids,
After mounting ten steps you are suddenly on flat ground.
Originally you reckoned that you had gone deep into the mountains;
You would never have known that getting out of the mountains was so easy.
A coiled snail-shell topknot finishes off the summit of the cave,
And after a few paces there is a single thatched pavilion.
Looking down you can see the field divisions beyond the wall,
Fragrant among the clouds of yellow ripened grain.
The light of the setting sun floods the fine lookout tower;
The dusty battlements are like a screen.
A remote drum sounds from the cluster of shrines;
Wildfires spring up amid the withered cypresses.
When your exhilaration is over you intend to come down;
On the serpentine stream the remaining light is playing.
Suddenly as you cross Golden Grains Ridge,
The celestial fragrance drifts around your clothing.[108]

"Going Through the Back of the Western Mountain, You Pass Through the Pavilion
Encircled by Jade, Come Out at Parting Regrets Gate, and Take the Route Back"

Green Rainbow rock bridge straddles the high ridge;
The Female Rainbow rock bridge is concealed below it.
Going through beside it one crosses the obscurity;
Suddenly ascending one obtains expansiveness.
The Angling Jetty is so named because one is oblivious of fish,
And in any case there is no angler.
Ten thousand jades display their pure adornment;
Faint red emits its beauty.[109]

---

107 The Martial Pacifying Prince is one of the titles of the semi-legendary military hero Guan Yu. This temple to Guan Yu is mentioned also in the "Record of the Yanshan Garden."

108 The celestial fragrance is that of the cassia or osmanthus, whose small yellow flowers are referred to as Golden Grains.

109 "Ten thousand jades" refers to stalks of bamboo; the "faint red" is that of flowers.

Suddenly here is the route out of the mountains,
Which makes me regret the limitations of my eyes and legs.
At every step I turn my head back;
Who can at once give up this fine scenery?

"Going East from Moonlit Waves Bridge You Can See the Chamber of Brahma's Voice"

The soaring bridge is suspended from the western ridge;
In the distance it connects with Central Yanshan.
The bright moon arranges the patterned waves;
A myriad points of light pierce the mermen's palace.
The total of rock-peaks is twelve,
Which present their intricate beauty and compete to be the champion.
They jostle shoulders like ravening monsters,
Or lower their heads like thirsty rainbow-dragons.
One is miserable and wants to sink into the River Xiang;[110]
One is floating and reaches up alone into the wind.
Looking up you gaze at the forms among the clouds;
The voice of Brahma traverses the green and red.[111]
One pillar of brocade rears up abruptly;
A solitary peak is like jade filigree.
Although Wang Xianzhi would be exhausted trying to take it all in,
You do not need to lament that Ruan Ji's path has run its course.[112]

"Passing Through Shuairan Cave and Entering Little Cloud Gate You Can See the Summit of the Mountain, Which Although Separated by Water from the Back of the Chamber for Storing the Sutras Is Still Within Earshot of It"

A winding cave deep in the mountains;
Mighty rocks that cannot support a step.
If you want to check the sayings in the canon,
You can shout across from here.[113]

---

110   The wives of the mythical Emperor Shun grieved after his death by the banks of the Xiang.

111   This line is incomprehensible unless one has read Wang Shizhen's "Record of the Yanshan Garden," from which it is clear that the "green and red" here refers to the leaves and berries of juniper or yew trees, while the "voice of Brahma" is the sound of the wind soughing through them.

112   Ruan Ji (210–263), one of the "Seven Sages of the Bamboo Grove," lived in a time of political turbulence. To stay out of trouble, he avoided holding office and spent most of his time drinking. He was said to have wept whenever he came to the end of a path or road; this reminded him of how his own career was blocked by the times in which he lived.

113   The Chamber for Storing the Sutras, in which the texts of the Buddhist canon were kept, was just across the water.

The reflection of the chamber extends outstandingly;
All the peaks take on its elaborate decoration.
Turning your steps back you can investigate the brushwood gate,
And see stretching straight out the route through the clouds.
The south-facing cliff receives the patterned light;
The north-facing glen contains frozen ice.
Sweeping branches weave a canopy;
You can cross the stream by the ancient creepers.
Striking a stone chime, how clear is the sound:
Pure and expansive, like the Shaohu music.[114]

"The Back of Master Gourd's Tower Faces Little Floating Jade on Broad Heart Pond"

Central Yanshan is indeed replete with wonders;
Its sunny south-facing side is quite cramped.
Before you have gazed your fill on the scenery,
You have already exhausted the strength of your feet.
When this tower is opened to the north,
It is as though the whole universe was expanding.
Streams and peaks summon up their splendors;
Light and dark alternate from dawn to nightfall.
When you examine Little Floating Jade,
Its winding outline forms a scene all of its own.
Calling for wine you pour a libation to it;
You and I are host and guest.
You have to laugh that Master Gourd's flask
Has become something so appropriate despite being a bogus illusion.[115]

"Sailing on Broad Heart Pond, You Go Through Scattered Flowers Ravine to
Dongling Bridge"

Some water left behind after rain is sufficient to provide surging waves;
A vast expanse of water is also as small as rainwater collected in a hoof-print.[116]
And moreover in this realm of fish and birds,[117]
As you look up and down you perceive profound vastness.

---

114   The Shaohu music of the semi-legendary Shang dynasty was believed to have been particularly fine, although it did not survive.

115   The magic flask of legend held a whole world that could be entered through the mouth of the flask or gourd. The Chinese garden is felt similarly to enclose a whole world within a small compass.

116   Rainwater collected in a hoof-print was an image of something very small.

117   The "realm of fish and birds" refers to a hermitage or dream world.

There is plenty of room to pole a punt,
But it will scarcely take a sailing boat.
On the angled table are set out snacks and drinks;
The viridian of the hills is sometimes seen to encroach.
One wanders about Joyful Radiance Crossing,
And lingers around the Grove of Fine Trees.
The soaring waterfall comes right into one's face,
With a force as though plunging a thousand fathoms.
The whirling eddies collect in the eastern ravine;
The high banks emerge from the dark forest.
A light breeze scatters the red petals;
Those upon whom they alight keep on pouring their wine.
Even if a visitor was a really a pedant,
How could he not unfasten his shirt-collar?

"Crossing Dongling Bridge and Crab's Pincer Peak You Go Down to Joyful Radiance Beach"

The craggy summit was lacking in magnificence;
The flowers and bamboo were verging on the relaxed.
But when it was adorned with one or two rock-peaks,
This made it an extension of the near and distant mountains.
Drunk, I raise Mr. Bi's crab-claw;[118]
Suddenly I am soaring toward the clouds,
Floating cups by a stone hibiscus,
Sinking a well in a ring of green lotuses.
As the path turns the view is suddenly opened up;
How can you make the excuse that your feet are stumbling?
You can make use of the steps to sit among the greenery;
Approaching the islet, you can play with the rippling water.
In my incompetent way, I compose a song about forgetting to leave:
The romantic mood is really palpable.

"From the Back of Cloud Root Cliff You Pass Twin Wells and Turn Toward Fine Tree Pavilion"

Picking your steps you pass through Cloud Root,
And seem to see twinned shining stars.
Below is a spring a hundred feet deep,
With a windlass to plumb its glassy depths.

---

118   For a description of this feature of Wang's garden, see section VI of the prose account of his garden above.

People's hats appear and disappear along the stream;
The pavilion overlooks a rill at both front and back.
In what year was the old tree planted?
It has grown into the shape of a coiling dragon.
Played about by clouds and embraced by taro it sleeps;
It wards off the sun and creates profound shade.
The broad pond is untroubled by the summer heat;
The angular enclosure enjoys pure coolness.
Who needs the rock from Level Spring?
Just resting here will sober you up from wine.[119]

"From Divided Splendors Pavilion You Go Along Retaining Fish Stream and Cross Jade Viridian Beam"

The solitary pavilion borders on the edge of the wood;
Half-hidden, half-apparent, it crowns a strange peak.
Tall trees reach up to the zenith of the firmament;
A myriad shoots put out lush growth.
The abruptly stopping stream is like a lustrous snake,
Twisting and writhing.
A slight breeze ruffles the clear waves;
Fish-scales and turtle-shells suddenly rise and fall.
The roaming fish have lost their original route;
The fallen blossoms are attached to the revolving eddies.[120]
Over the steep ravine is propped a soaring beam,
By which you can explore the mountain's greenery.
The place you reach is available for investigating with your eyes;
You don't even notice that the strength of your feet is exhausted.

"Crossing the Dangerous Ravine by Jade Viridian Beam, You Reach Nine Dragons Ridge"

Where the stream forms a boundary the path is about to peter out,
When suddenly this beam appears athwart it.
Below it there must be a glen for casting oneself into;
Above, there is a route on which you can go across by placing your feet sideways.
Although you may be tottering on the brink of falling,

---

119 The Tang scholar-official Li Deyu had a rock in his Pingquan estate named the Sobering Stone; he claimed that he could sober up by resting against it.

120 According to Wang Shizhen's "Record of the Yanshan Garden," Retaining Fish Stream was also known as Retaining Flowers Stream.

You obtain a fantastic view.
Nine stout juniper trees are upstanding here,
Looking at each other with easy vigor.
They are anointed and bathed by the morning dew;
In the evening breeze their utterance is clearly audible.
During their lives they have no wish to be ennobled by the Qin;[121]
They only want not to go against their nature.

"Beside Broad Heart Pond is Mingled Sunset-Clouds Pavilion Which Lies Opposite Clacking Clogs Walkway"

There is nothing in the evening scene that is not lovely,
But this pavilion has superabundant attractiveness.
Purple and emerald lie on all the peaks;
The circling light plays on the dimpling ripples.
The tired birds are about to take to their roosts,
But they are still mindful of hunger and thirst.
The minnows are startled by a streak of light,
And they leap in shoals without restraint.
Although it is nearly dusk,
I call for wine to amuse myself.
As we enjoy ourselves the evening has come,
But who can I explain this thought to?[122]

"Ascending Arriving Jade Belvedere One Looks Down on Broad Heart Pond Which Lies Opposite the Western Mountain; Below It Is Clacking Clogs Walkway"

In the past I lodged in this belvedere;[123]
This belvedere overlooks Broad Pond.
The clear moonlight stirs the patterned waves;
The rippling light breaks through the curtains and blinds.
Hitching up my robe I rise and wander about,
As though I could see three sides at once.
The shining mirror hangs in the center of the heavens;
A myriad jades are twinkling.

---

121   An allusion to the pine tree on Mount Tai ennobled as Esquire of the Fifth Rank by the First Emperor of Qin, who took shelter under it in a rainstorm while on pilgrimage to the mountain (see chapter 9). Later scholars regarded this as an insult to an already noble tree.

122   The coming of evening suggests the arrival of old age.

123   It appears that the position of this building was in or near the Langye Villa or Garden for Evading Thorns, where Wang Shizhen lived before the construction of the Yanshan Garden.

From below comes the sound of clacking clogs:
An old friend is coming through the valley.
How sharp is the sound of his clogs,
But how gentle and pleasant his talk and laughter.
Naming the belvedere Arriving Jade for me,
Comparing in virtue it does not fall short at all.[124]

"Patterned Ripples Hall Overlooks Broad Pond and In Front of It Is Little Floating Jade"

The lofty gallery overlooks crimson balustrades;
The elegant walkway rises from among layers of scenery.
Patterned ripples arise in response to the breeze;
Minnows splash around from time to time.
There is an island nearby like an overturned cauldron,
And a distant crag like a shelved side-table.
I walk hand in hand with two or three of my sons,
Enjoying all this together.[125]
The blue mountains enter my room;
Light twinkles on the white walls.
I write a lyric to delight my heart,
But after reciting the words I still sigh three times.[126]

"Traversing Bamboo Path You Cross Knowing the Way Home Bridge and Enter Patterned Ripples Hall"

The distant ridge is embroidered with clumps of greenery,
And leads me to pass through a screen.
Even birds know to go home when they are tired,
And so much the more the feet of wandering men.
Through the seclusion, one reaches a level bridge,
And lingers to spread out pale-yellow straw mats.
The eyes which I have been feasting are already replete;

---

124 A reference to the *Book of Rites* (*Li ji* 禮記): "All wore the jade-stone pendant at the girdle. . . . A man of rank was never without this pendant, excepting for some sufficient reason; he regarded the pieces of jade as emblematic of the virtues [which he should cultivate]." See *The Sacred Books of China: The Texts of Confucianism*, vol.4, *The Li Ki*, trans. James Legge (Oxford: Clarendon Press, 1885), 19.

125 Wang Shizhen did have three sons, but this is primarily a reference to the *Analects*: "In late spring, after the spring clothes have been newly made, I should like, together with five or six adults and six or seven boys, to go bathing in the River Yi and enjoy the breeze on the Rain Altar, and then to go home chanting poetry." (D. C. Lau, trans., *The Analects*, 111).

126 Sighing three times is indicative of deep grief; Wang Shizhen is referring to the unjust execution of his father Wang Yu in 1559.

My feet which are exhausted can now rest.
If there is wine, I will call for it;
If there is no wine, tea will suffice.

"Early Moonlight Pavilion Is Encircled by Bamboo at the Back and at the Front It Overlooks Broad Heart Pool"

The new-risen sun is certainly splendid,
But it is no match for the early moonlight.
When all the ridges are still shrouded in darkness,
This pavilion catches the moonlight the earliest.
A faint glow appears on the brows of the building;
An obscure glimmer can be spied through the cracks.
The clumps of bamboo sound like shivering jade;
The bright waves look like molten gold.
I call for a wine-cup and drink it all in,
The crystalline glitter like pearls and amber.
It makes me feel in my chest
As expansive as the Mansion of Broad Chill.[127]

Gazetteer of Taicang Subprefecture (*Taicang zhouzhi* 太倉州志, 1642, revised 1678)

"The Garden of the Deer Park Stream of the Wang Family" (*Wangshi Michangjing yuan* 王氏麋場涇園), "The Yanzhou Garden" (*Yanzhou yuan* 弇州園), "The Langye Garden for Evading Thorns" (*Langye lici yuan* 琅琊離薋園), and "Wang Jingmei's Plain Plot" (*Wang Jingmei Danpu* 澹圃)

QIAN SUYUE 錢肅樂 (1606–1648) AND ZHANG CAI 張采 (1596–1648), EDS.
TRANSLATED BY ALISON HARDIE

"The Garden of the Deer Park Stream of the Wang Family"

Wang Shizhen's uncle Quiet Hermitage[128] says in his "Record of the Construction of the Yanzhoushan Gardens": "Going west along Cypress Screen, there is a pavilion overlooking a cliff; slightly to the west is the Quiet Hermitage. Coming out of the Hermitage and turning west for several dozen *wu*, there is the mountain hall. On the sunny south side of the hall there is a terrace on which are arranged strange rocks

---

127 The Mansion of Broad Chill is the abode of supernatural beings in the moon.

128 Wang Shizhen's father's elder brother was named Wang Yin, and took the studio name Master Quiet Hermitage (Jing'an xiansheng 靜庵先生) from the name of his garden. His "Record of the Yanshan Garden" mentioned here does not appear to have survived elsewhere.

and renowned plants. To the east and west, flourishing bamboo extends for several hundred *wu*. If you open the shutters of the hall to the north, you come upon a large rectangular pond, which is clustered with lotuses and water chestnuts.[129] Entering by stone gates to the left and right, there is a division into two bridges, each with a pavilion. To the left of the water, one can go deep into a rocky cave, and then cross a stone-slab bridge to reach a cliff. Where the cliff comes to an end there is another deep ravine. Above there is a transverse rock by which you make your way westward to reach a hill made of alum rocks.[130] It is clad in white flowers and named Snowy Mountain. The mountains are buttressed with earthen hillocks, which curve around Deer Park Stream like the spine of a serpent.[131] A myriad pine trees form a bristly carapace. When the garden was first completed, its scenery was the finest in the region of Wu. Later, once my brother had been executed, it fell into ruin;[132] all the rocks on the peak were moved to be used in Yanzhou Garden."

> Note: The section above records only the Garden of the Deer Park Stream from a short account of all the gardens of Yanzhou. This garden has now been hoed into flat agricultural land, and one can no longer gain any sense of how it once appeared. Whatever has remained of the original garden has in any case been redecorated. How dependent hills and trees are on written records!

"The Yanzhou Garden"

Popularly known as Wang Family Mountain, it is to the west of the Temple of Abundant Blessing and looks out to the front over a small stream.[133] The garden is over seventy *mu* in area. Close beside it on the left a shrine has been built to venerate the Master of Yanzhou, Wang Shizhen. Behind the shrine is the former site of the Lesser Jetavana Pavilion for Storing the Sutras. The pavilion itself has collapsed, but the stone bridge named Mantra Chanting survives. On the right one finds a wooden gate, and crosses Knowing the Ford Bridge to make one's way to Yanshan Hall. Turning northward from the east of the hall, there is a long stream, with water running into it from the west. It is bestridden by a stone bridge called Assembled

---

129 Water chestnuts are edible; they do not seem to have been regarded as a decorative plant. This suggests that the lotuses also were being grown in this pond for culinary purposes. Rectangular ponds, often used for growing lotuses and rearing fish, were much more common in the late Ming than one would assume on the basis of contemporary "classical" Chinese gardens.

130 These rocks were not necessarily made of alum, but will have resembled the "alum lumps" characteristic of the style of some earlier landscape painters.

131 The serpent referred to here, the *shuairan* 率然 ("all of a sudden"), was a mythical one. Wang Shizhen also describes a cave or tunnel in the Yanshan Garden as looking like the burrow of this serpent.

132 Wang Yin's younger brother, Wang Yu, the father of Wang Shizhen and Wang Shimao, came into conflict with the powerful minister Yan Song (1480–1567) and was tried and executed in 1559.

133 This description given here of the Yanshan Garden is as it was some time after its owner's death.

Splendors which crouches at the mouth of the three mountains. These three mountains are known as Western Yan, Central Yan, and Eastern Yan. The western one is popularly known as the dry mountain and the central and eastern ones as the water mountains. Across the bridge is Western Yan. Following the ridge to the north, one reaches the shallows called Emerging Stars. To the right are two peaks, which abut the ridge and overlook the path. After several *wu* the path stops; there are two rocks about a foot apart, from which the water of a stream flows downward through Lesser Dragon Waterfall. To the southwest of the waterfall is a thread-like path, to be climbed with bent back, called Stone Lord Alley. A few *wu* farther on, there is a cliff in which there is a massive flat rock, called Rest Cliff. Where the path ends there is a stone stairway called Stairway of Mistaken Wandering, by which one can find a cave called Horns and Teeth. Transversely above it is a great stone beam called Green Rainbow; following it down to the west, you enter a cave house. Above the cave is built an upper story called Hazy Tower. This is the highest point in the three Yan mountains. Looking to the west, the Lou River is like a strip of gauze; Horse Saddle Mountain is thirty *li* in the distance. Looking northward, Mount Yu, a hundred *li* away, seems near. This is called Grand Prospect Terrace. To the south of the tower and slightly east, one reaches a stone stairway; one descends ten steps to the northeast. The gate is called Separation from the Mundane. This is the prime cave-heaven in the three Yan mountains. To the left the water here mingles with Celestial Mirror Pool, the pool in turn surrounded by strange rocks. To the north it takes in Coiling Stream. Looking down, it seems like a single star. It is called Submerged Dragon Pool. Coming out of the cave, slightly to the south is the Beach Pillowed on the Current. Farther north you come upon a small stone-slab bridge directly below Green Rainbow, and named Female Rainbow. Entering Horns and Teeth again, you turn and climb up to Transcendence Terrace. Slightly to the west is Cassia Grove Pavilion. Following this you come to Node of Singularity Terrace. Down a few steps there is a rock beside which water emerges, where one can fish; it is called Forgetting the Fish Jetty. Turning slightly, one comes to Moonlit Waves Bridge and reaches Central Yanshan. Central Yanshan is in the midst of the water. To the south of Moonlit Waves, and turning slightly to the east, are arranged towering peaks. Just a few *wu* farther on, one reaches a cave called The Serpent. Passing through the cave, you turn to the southwest and descend; there is a rock lying by the water like a fishing jetty. Before the old Tower for Storing the Sutras collapsed, it lay right opposite on the south bank, and this was the place where one summoned the ferry. It is called Return to the Western Paradise Ford. Following the cave and turning east, one crosses Clear Waves Causeway; taking a slight turn to the south, there is a single rock lying athwart above two walls, called Lesser Cloud Gate. Turning, one enters Chiming Jade Ravine. The rocks of the ravine make a sound like stone chimes, hence the name. Turning and going up about fifteen steps, one finds a stone balustrade; this is Master Gourd's Tower. Descending on the left, one passes over a stone-slab bridge, called Turtle's Back. Over the bridge there is a pavilion called Pausing on the Journey. Turning south one descends several steps to reach Dongling Bridge. This is the end of Central Yanshan. The bridge was the way to Eastern Yanshan. Now the bridge has collapsed, so to reach Eastern Yanshan one must cross in a small boat. To the south of Divided Splendor Pavilion is all bamboo and trees. There are no longer any peaks or cliff-walls. To the north east of the pavilion there is a slope upward with three steps leading to Broad Terrace. The terrace has a rock carved to form the Hibiscus Screen. The western face of the rock is over five feet high and twice as wide. It is called Cloud Root Cliff. A channel below the cliff winds around and passes through to Hibiscus Screen; it is called Place for Floating Goblets. Going down a further dozen steps, there is a large beach sloping straight downward so that you can hardly keep your footing. This is called Joyful Radiance Beach. At the back of the cliff is a double well.[134] Looking down into it, it is like the Sword Pool at Tiger Hill. Slightly to the east is a pavilion called Fine Tree Pavilion. A small boat takes you over to the north; you ascend the bank and follow a walkway to the west; this is Patterned Ripples Hall, from which one can look down on a rectangular pond several *mu* in area. The hall is of three bays, and is opposite to Master Gourd's Tower. It takes in all the scenery of Central and Eastern Yanshan. Turning to the left of the hall and going in, one comes to an extensive porch of three bays. This is called Cool Breeze. Passing through Cool Breeze, going slightly east and facing north, there is a gate adjacent to the stream which runs through; a signboard says "Langye Villa." Elsewhere are recorded various places such as Literary Elegance Tower, Lesser Youyang Tower, and Clacking Clogs Walkway. Now they are all private houses and can no longer be visited.

> Note: The Master's own records of the Yan Garden were eight in number. Over the years up to now the garden has been sold off piecemeal to other people, and its former scenic splendors no longer exist. However, this garden was famous throughout the empire, unlike ordinary villas, so we have abridged the eight records and given a detailed account of what survives. This arouses feelings of immense regret.

"The Langye Garden for Evading Thorns"

To the east of Parrot Bridge, not five paces from the left gate of the mansion, there is a channel. A bridge crosses it. There is a gate looking on to the bridge, with a signboard saying "Garden for Evading Thorns." It cannot be more than ten *zhang* from east to west, and three times that from south to north. As you enter the gate there are two contorted pine trees and more than ten stems of square-sectioned bamboo. To the extreme south there is a pavilion called Bottle Hermitage. On three sides it is completely enclosed by about twenty flowering apricot trees. In front of it, rocks have been piled up to form a mountain, looking down on a container pond in which goldfish are kept. The diameter of the mountain can be measured in *zhang*. Within the mountain

---

134   According to Wang Shizhen's own "Record of the Yanshan Garden," this double well or cistern provided the water supply for the Place for Floating Goblets.

are to be found a mountain torrent, a cave, a ridge, and a stone-slab bridge. To the right side are two studies; to the left is planted bamboo. Among the bamboo are pavilions named Hair-Drying Pavilion and Bottle Hermitage. Behind it one comes to two small orchards with railings of bamboo, planted with a mixture of peaches, apricots, tree peonies and so on. Where the orchards end, one comes to a path. There is a wide terrace set with solitary peaks and piled with Dongting rocks. To the right and left are "Jade Butterfly" and "Green Calyx" flowering apricot trees, one of each, large enough to shade the terrace. Overlooking the terrace is a building of five bays, called Gallery of the Quail at Ease. The left-hand wing, because it benefits from the bamboo, is called Emerald Waves; the right-hand wing, which functions as a guest-room, is called Short Rest. The pond to the rear is called Lotus Marsh. Beyond the pond it is only a matter of feet from the wall. It is overhung by a contorted willow. Passing through Short Rest and turning northwest, there is a two-storied building of three bays to one side; in front of it is the kitchen and the bath-house. Wang Shizhen himself wrote a record of this place. Now it is locked up from one year's end to the next, and we have been unable to investigate its present condition.

> Note: Where Wang Shizhen lived was known as the New Manor. His son Shiqi opened up the land behind the residence and called it Frugality Garden. Wang Shizhen wrote a record of this place as well. Now it has been divided up among new owners so we do not describe it.

"Wang Jingmei's Plain Plot"[135]

This garden is in the southwest corner of the city, half a *li* distant from Yanshan. A semicircular pond was excavated at the side of the front gate. To the right was dug a long channel, about four hundred feet long. Beyond it were planted tall elms, interspersed with clumps of bamboo. Entering the gate, a broad expanse opens up to form a threshing-floor. There is a gallery called Studying Crop-Growing. Opening the door of the side-building on the left and going in, there are in all four successive courtyards of an elegant retreat. Each building is of five bays. Adjoining them is a tertiary building, as well as granaries and kitchens. The right-hand side building is the same as the left. When you open the gate there is an expansive space. In front of a level terrace there is a small pond. On piled rocks are cultivated tree peonies. In the center is a hall of three bays, called Clear Intentions. To the rear it overlies a large pond, and faces across to the Gallery for Studying Crop-Growing. Turning southward to the right of the hall, there is a study. Crossing over a small level bridge to the north, you enter a gate and go along the left-hand walkway; turning northward there is a small gallery. In the center of the steps are piled several peaks, which are all Lingbi or Ying rocks. Again, turning eastward, you pass through a water belvedere: surrounding three sides is a pond, planted

---

135 Wang Jingmei (Shimao; 1536–1588) was Wang Shizhen's younger brother.

with many lotuses. Going north from the water belvedere, and then slightly west, there is another gallery. Turning westward you reach two heated buildings, an ice-house, and a bath-house. Then to the east, you open a gate in a low wall, and going out you reach a double walkway, edged with luxuriant bamboo. Stretching to the north, it lies all alongside a pond. A bridge crosses the middle of the pond, leading, in the east, to the fruit orchard. The bridge is about seventy feet long and one-fifth as wide. The fruit orchard is very spacious. It is planted with oranges and mandarins grown for the table. In an open space vegetables are cultivated. By the bridge you return to a bamboo path, then turning northward, you cross another bridge, and slightly to the east you reach a raised terrace, planted with a mixture of all different types of flowers. Wang Shizhen wrote a record of this garden. Now it is rented out and occupied by various different families.

"Record of the Garden for Seeking One's Own Aims" (*Qiuzhi yuan ji* 求志園記)

WANG SHIZHEN 王世貞

TRANSLATED BY ALISON HARDIE

The garden written about in the following account by Wang Shizhen is that of his friend Zhang Fengyi (1527–1613), a Suzhou poet, playwright, and calligrapher.[136] Zhang Fengyi and his two younger brothers, Zhang Xianyi and Zhang Yanyi (whose exact dates are unknown), were all distinguished literary men. Having failed to progress far up the civil service examination ladder, Zhang Fengyi gave up the thought of an official career, consoling himself with his garden and his *qin* zither and living on the various proceeds of his fluent pen, in the form of both plays and calligraphy. Several of his plays survive.

"Record of the Garden for Seeking One's Own Aims"

The garden of my friend Zhang Fengyi is in the northeast corner of Suzhou. The garden is to the rear of his residence and is reached by a raised walkway. As soon as you enter the gate there is a sudden fragrance from a screen of mixed roseleaf raspberry[137] and roses. This path is named Collecting Fragrance, referring to the old traditions of Wu.[138] After the path has wound along for several dozen *wu*, there is a courtyard nearby like a covered walkway. This gallery is named Pleasant Spaces, indicating that one can let one's eyes roam through a wide vista. To the right, as one faces it, of the gallery there is a building of three bays in which to perform the rites to the statue of Mr. Zhang's

---

136　This Zhang Fengyi is not to be confused with two other men named Zhang Fengyi who were his near contemporaries (one died in 1636 and the other in 1643).

137　*Rubus rosifolius*, a kind of ornamental bramble (in Chinese, *tumi* 酴醾).

138　A reference to "Collecting Fragrance Path," a place to the southwest of Suzhou, where a king of Wu (the ancient state whose capital was Suzhou) had fragrant plants cultivated for his concubines to pick.

late father, named Hall of Trees in the Wind, to indicate the emotion he feels.[139] Although the hall is not half the size of the gallery, he would not venture to name the hall Pleasant Spaces as this would not have been respectful. On the right of the gallery, facing south, is a study in which to lodge his paintings and books of history; he named it Enjoying Friendship, to express his friendship with the ancients. Behind the study there is a lodge. This overlooks a large pond, in which there are many gold and silver carp, turtles and various small fish; this is named Pond of Decorated Fish, referring to what it is stocked with. Running across the pond is a bridge; following the bridge and going slightly southwest, there are more than ten old flowering apricot trees. The walkway there is named Fragrant Snow, referring to the virtue of the flowering apricots.

In Fengyi's own words: "Our Wu region is known within the empire as the champion for an abundance of pleasures. In our own city, King Fuchai's capital,[140] splendid mansions and renowned gardens can without doubt be numbered in the dozens; even if such gardens were to be enumerated on the fingers of many hands, however, my own garden would not come into the reckoning. Building materials selected from Sichuan and Hunan,[141] rocks selected from Dongting [Lake Tai], Wukang, Yingzhou and Lingbi,[142] plants selected from Guangdong, Indochina and Annam, birds selected from Gansu or Guangdong and Fujian:[143] my garden has absolutely none of these. But as for the rising sun in the morning, the moon at night, breezes in spring and snow in winter, these are things over which splendid mansions and renowned gardens have no monopoly, nor can they keep them for themselves; at least I can benefit from what is superfluous to them. I seek nothing else but to fulfill my ambitions. You must have noticed the generals, ministers, nobles, and great men who are active in the east of Chang'an;[144] it seems as though they have achieved everything they could possibly want, but yet other people always take the opportunity to thwart their aims. If one expands oneself

---

139 The name alludes to a story about an exemplar of filial piety found in *Han Ying's Illustrations of the Didactic Application of the Classic of Songs* (*Han shi wai zhuan* 韓詩外傳): "'The tree would be still, but the wind will not stop, the son wishes to look after them, but his parents will not tarry.' When they are past there is no [overtaking them—such are the years of our lives]; when they are gone there is no recalling them—such are our parents." See James Robert Hightower, trans., *Han Shih Wai Chuan: Han Ying's Illustrations of the Didactic Application of the Classic of Songs* (Cambridge, Mass.: Harvard University Press, 1952), 292.

140 Fuchai, who reigned from 495 BCE to his death in 473 BCE, is the best-known king of the ancient state of Wu.

141 Sichuan and Hunan, being relatively remote and mountainous, were sources of superior timber for construction.

142 These were some of the most desirable types of ornamental rock, and are mentioned in most catalogues of rocks, such as Du Wan's twelfth-century *Stone Catalogue of Cloudy Forest*. With the exception of Wukang rocks, they also occur in Ji Cheng's (b. 1582) *The Craft of Gardens*.

143 Plants or birds from these distant locations would be regarded as exotic and valuable.

144 Chang'an (present-day Xi'an) was the capital of China in the Tang dynasty and was often used by metonymy for the capital in later times; for most of the Ming dynasty, this was Beijing.

outwardly but is much thwarted inwardly, or is successful in what is of secondary importance but sighs gloomily about whatever one comes across, then a beautiful, fertile and central piece of land is equivalent to a stretch of thorny scrub inhabited only by sparrows; singing sounds like weeping and happiness looks like sorrow, yet one does not realize why this is. I do not harbor any ambition to extend myself outward, yet my aims seem to await me from hundreds of years ago, they seem to respond to me even at the edge of the wilderness, they seem to come together for me like a tally[145] even from hundreds of years in the future. How can one speak about such things with the rich and famous?"

When Master Wang heard this he sighed and said: "How fine is that which you seek, sir! Will you permit me to hear what exactly your aims are?" Fengyi smiled without replying. Master Wang said, after an interval, "There's the name for the garden!"[146]

"Record of Wandering in the Famous Gardens of Jinling" (*You Jinling zhuyuan ji* 遊金陵諸園記)

WANG SHIZHEN 王世貞

TRANSLATED BY KENNETH J. HAMMOND

In explicit imitation of Li Gefei's celebrated collective record of the gardens of Luoyang (see chapter 4), here Wang Shizhen provides a collective account of fifteen of the most celebrated gardens of Nanjing (formerly Jinling), which until 1420 was the capital of the Ming dynasty. After suffering an initial period of decline when the capital was removed to Beijing by the third emperor of the dynasty, Nanjing (a city with some history of serving as a capital) revived rapidly, in large part the result of its proximity to the wealthy and sophisticated Jiangnan region. The city was home to a government structure that paralleled that of the central government in Beijing, although it was of lesser importance. As the historian Frederick Mote has noted, "Nanjing, as opposed to Beijing, came to represent an attractive alternative course where previously there had existed only a single acceptable course for men of talent and ambition. The rich life of the great city came close to being politically subversive as well as morally scandalous in the late sixteenth and seventeenth centuries."

What is noteworthy about this account, particularly in contrast to that of Li Gefei, is that the majority of the gardens noted by Wang belonged not to literati such as himself, but rather to various members of a single aristocratic family, the Xu family, descendants of Xu Da (1332–1385), a military commander who was a close comrade in arms of the founder of the Ming dynasty, Zhu Yuanzhang (1328–1398; r. 1368–1398). Wang's discussion of the gardens of members of the nobility does not cede cultural territory to the aristocracy, but rather incorporates these spaces into literati

145 A tally, often used for identification, especially in a military context, consisted of two matching halves.

146 It was, of course, commonplace for a formal garden description (*yuanji*) to give an explanation for the name of the garden. Wang Shizhen has here contrived a clever variation on this commonplace by implying that the name Seeking One's Own Aims has come into existence by serendipity rather than cogitation.

discourse. Nanjing's proximity to other Jiangnan cities, where literati gardens were becoming so widespread, facilitated this sense of integration.

"Record of Wandering in the Famous Gardens of Jinling"

Li Gefei recorded nineteen gardens in Luoyang. Although Luoyang was known as the Ancient Capital, in the aftermath of the disorders of the Five Dynasties period it never fully regained its former glory. As for the officials who were living there, they were either posted there as magistrates or to other positions, or sought a retreat from the weariness of service. Their homes were mingled with those of scholars resting in exile from the capital. If one looked about carefully at what were called gardens and ponds, they provided the utmost of lovely views.

Now it has been some sixty years since our August Emperor set up the tripods at Jinling,[147] from where two sages led the universe.[148] The form of the city, within and without, comes down from antiquity. As for the officials and servitors of the imperial capital, where half the imperial bureaucracy is established, with mountains and streams of great beauty and the finest of human talents, how can it not be spoken of as like the ancient capital of the Song?

Could it be only the gardens and ponds which cannot be said to be like those described by Li Gefei? Does it not in fact excel that age? Now, literati gentlemen do not like to live away from the home districts, so there are few retired gentlemen's residences in Nanjing.[149] But if one goes but a little way around the city, everywhere are the marvels of nature, and Buddhist monasteries scattered all about. If one has just a bit more energy, how can one not encounter gardens and ponds equal to those of old?

I had been appointed to a position in the auxiliary capital, my official duties were relatively few, and I could thoroughly explore the scenes of Qixia Mountain, Xianhua Grotto, the rock cliffs at Yanji, and the Linggu Temple.[150] Later I went about to the

---

147   Setting up the tripods represents the founding of a dynasty. The term derives from the early Zhou, when the founding kings supposedly possessed a set of ritual bronzes that legitimized their rule. Jinling is an ancient name for present-day Nanjing, dating to at least the fourth century BCE under the state of Chu.

148   The two sages refer to the Hongwu and Yongle emperors. Wang does not include the second Ming ruler, the Jianwen emperor, though by the time of the composition of this essay the legitimacy of the Jianwen reign was being reestablished.

149   This contrasts with the large number of retired officials settled in Luoyang during the Northern Song, as described by Li Gefei.

150   Wang served in Nanjing in 1588–1589, culminating his career with his appointment as President of the Board of Punishments in July 1589.

famous gardens, such as those of the Prince of Zhongshan.[151] Altogether I visited ten, large and small. The most expansive was the East Garden of the sixth Embroidered Uniform Guard commander. The one with the most extensive purity was the West Garden of the fourth Embroidered Uniform Guard commander. Next in size, but grander in wonder, is the East Garden of the attached residence of the fourth Embroidered Uniform Guard commander. The one with the best ordered flowers is the West Garden of the attached residence of the Duke of Wei. Next smallest, but with the best ornamentation, are the South Garden of the Duke of Wei and the North Garden of the third Embroidered Uniform Guard commander. All of these are greater in extent than the gardens in Li Gefei's description of Luoyang. Although the gardens of Luoyang had water, bamboo, flowers, and trees, they lacked rockeries. In Li's description there are no accounts of rocks piled up into peaks and ridges. The gardens of Luoyang have long ago burned down and disappeared, and no traces can be found. We are lucky to have Li Gefei's "Record" to preserve them in men's eyes. But the gardens of Jinling have had no such record, so just as they were lucky to encounter me, so too have I been lucky enough to have the chance to visit them. How, then, could I not undertake to record them? Aside from the gardens of the Prince of Zhongshan's residences, only the Garden Harmonizing with Spring can be called a "petty state," and the bamboo garden of the Marquis of Wuding excels the Ten Thousand Bamboos Garden, so I have also recorded my visit there.

East Garden

The East Garden, also known as the Grand Mentor's Garden,[152] was bestowed by the emperor. It is located near the Gate of Accumulated Treasures.[153] The late Fifth Duke of Weiguo, Xu Fu, loved best his youngest son, the Embroidered Uniform Guard Commander Xu Tianci, and left to him all his worldly goods. At that time Xu Fu's grandson, Pengju, having only recently inherited the hereditary rank, was still in a weak position. Tianci therefore took over management of this garden on his behalf, and greatly enhanced its arrangement, making it first among the gardens in magnificence and in beauty. The Embroidered Uniform Guard Commander himself gave the garden

---

151   The Prince of Zhongshan was Xu Da, a military commander under Zhu Yuanzhang, enfeoffed in 1370 and also made Duke of Wei, a hereditary title that was passed down through the course of the dynasty. Many of the gardens described here" belonged to members of the Xu family. Beginning with Xu Da, the title Duke of Wei passed to Xu Huizu in 1388; Xu Qin in 1406; Xu Xianzong in 1424; Xu Fu in 1465; Xu Pengju in 1518; Xu Bangrui in 1572; and Xu Weizhi in 1589. Beginning with Xu Fu, these men were all Grand Commandants of the Nanjing garrison, a largely ceremonial title. Several members of the Xu family not in line to be Duke of Wei were appointed as officers of the Embroidered Uniform Guard, also largely ceremonial positions. These included Xu Tianci, younger son of the fifth Duke Xu, Xu Fu, and Tianci's sons, three of whom are mentioned in the text. One, the third Embroidered Uniform Guard Commander, is not named; the other two were Xu Jixun and Xu Zuanxun, listed as the fourth and sixth Embroidered Uniform Guard Commanders.

152   Xu Fu was granted the title Grand Mentor upon his death in 1517.

153   This was the main gate in the southern wall of the city. Many of the Xu family gardens were in this part of Nanjing.

its name East Garden, thus making clear his intention not to return it to Pengju. He later passed it on to his own son, the Embroidered Uniform Guard Commander Xu Zuanxun.

Entering the gate, one sees that a number of elms and willows have been planted here and there, with grasses and weeds growing out of control. If one goes along for about 200 paces there is another gate. Entering there and turning right there is a flower pavilion of three bays, rather spacious and bright, though not very tall. A signboard reads, "Distant Heart." In front there is a moon terrace of several peaks, with ancient trees capping them. Behind the hall is a small pond, with a "Little Penglai" on the opposite side, a mountain sunken in the pond, with ridges and peaks, caves and gullies, and several pavilions, all finely shaped. Two cypresses stand with their branches strangely intertwined, so that one can pass beneath them, entering and departing. This is called the Cypress Gate. There are high, luxuriant bamboos, providing pleasant shade; I have seen none more wonderful.

I went along by a vermilion plank wall to the left, and came to another hall, this one of five bays, with a placard reading, "One Glance." In front there was a large pond. In the central three bays one could spread ten mats. The other two bays are for the master's retainers to take rest in. Going out from the left bay one comes to a red bridge, with five or six zigzags, quite level, so that it is suitable for having a little drink. At the end of the bridge is a winged gazebo, quite large, gracefully reflected in the winding water, directly across from the One Glance Hall. Behind this hall, across a small stream, is a flat field of old trees, beyond which parapets and crenellations in the wall appear. On the right, where the water ends, there is a brick tower dimly discernable in the misty sky, which has been newly built by Zuanxun. A painted boat bears wine; on the left the water ends where one reaches the Balance Dyke.[154] The garden is roughly half a *li* from north to south. It is a steady source of excellent wood. Elders say that when the Zhengde emperor visited Nanjing[155] he came to fish in this garden, and was so delighted with it that he did not want to leave, remaining for several days in a pavilion here. It is said that it was in fact the Distant Heart Hall that had so entranced him. This hall has been weakened by wood rot from the water, and now cannot be used. The brick tower, too, has its door bolted, and one cannot ascend.

West Garden

The West Garden is also known as the Phoenix Terrace Garden. This is probably because in the next lane is the Phoenix Terrace.[156] This was formerly restored by Xu Tianci, who divided it to pass on to his two sons, so this part has come to be called the West Garden.

---

154   A Three Kingdoms site just south of Nanjing, on the Qinhuai River.

155   The emperor spent the period from mid-January through mid-September 1520 in Nanjing.

156   Phoenix Terrace dates back at least to the Tang, when Li Bai wrote a poem about it.

The garden is located outside the city wall, a bit to the south, outside the Gate of Accumulated Treasures by about two *li*. One enters the garden via a winding path, passing through three gates, and first comes to the Wandering Phoenix Hall. This differs a bit from the Distant Heart Hall of the East Garden, but is about twice as large. In front there is a moon terrace, with strange peaks and ancient trees; on the right a juniper three *zhang* tall, with a diameter a tenth of that. It is said that this tree was planted by Emperor Renzong of the Song himself, to honor the Daoist master Tao, more than 400 years ago. Its interwoven branches form a lovely screen. Beneath lie two ancient stones. The first, called Purple Smoke, is the tallest; nearly three *ren*, pale gray in color. Great Steward Qiao recognized it as being a supreme example of the rocks that once were part of Li Deyu's Pingquan estate. Another is called "Coxcomb." Mei Zhi of the Song and some of his worthy associates had various poems carved on this rock, so we know that already in his time this was a famous treasure. The last is known as "Engraved Rock." This bears a carving by the Regent of Jiankang Ma Guangzu. These last two stones are both inferior to Purple Smoke, their color and pattern not being at all praiseworthy.

Behind the hall several thousand bamboo are planted, with the Pavilion of Arriving Cranes squatting among them. To the left of the Wandering Phoenix Hall there is another screen of trees, with peach, clustered cassia, flowering crabapple, plum, and apricot, numbering several hundreds. Farther to the left is the Tower of Substantial Grace, which is especially beautiful. Before the tower is an old elm, large enough to reach one's arms all around, but not very tall. Its branches hang down to conceal the Lotus Pond, which has the appearance of a hidden dragon and thirsty lion. The pond is about ten *zhang* from north to south, and the water is so clear and lustrous it is like a mirror for arranging one's hair. On the north side of the pond rocks from Dongting, Xuanzhou, Jinchuan, and Wukang are piled up to form mountains, peaks and ridges, and caverns, with a pavilion topping all, smaller, though taller, than the one in the East Garden. These stones enclose a Little Canglang covering more than ten *mu*, circled round by drooping poplars, and clothed in duckweed, with fish leisurely leaping in the waves and swans playing, all making a lovely scene. On the south bank there is a terrace, from which one can see afar. It is framed by tall trees, so that the horizon cannot be seen. The northern bank is covered with bamboo which meander about, undulating and rising. At the end of the Little Canglang one comes to a smooth outcropping, with water on four sides, and a flower shed of three bays.

In his poem, Li Bai of the Tang said that the Phoenix Terrace had "three mountains" and "two streams." Their traces cannot now be seen. Xu Tianci, because of his proximity to this ancient site, and because of his own embellishments here, honored this place by naming it for the Phoenix Terrace; he dug a sweet water well and called it the Phoenix Spring, and called a nearby hillock the Foot of the Phoenix Hill.

South Garden

The South Garden of Duke Wei is across the road from his residence, a bit to the south-west. It is rather narrow running north to south, but is quite deep east to west. Entering the gate there is a vermilion wall, with mixed grasses growing on it. Going on ahead through another gate one comes to a sturdy hall of five bays. Before it rises a moon terrace, with rocks and grasses covering it. Going farther on there is yet another gate, and about ten paces past this is a hall of three bays, with verandas on all four sides, and behind this a multi-storied building, rather flimsy in appearance, but with quite lovely adornments up high, with vermilion rafters and painted ridgepole, ornately decorated windows and doors. On the *yang* side of the hall are some steps, with a pond in front of them. The pond is enclosed on three sides by piled up rocks, and goldfish are raised in it, some of them as long as two *chi*.

If one goes to the right along a path twisting some ten times as it ascends, one comes to a pavilion and tower, while if one descends to the left one reaches the Hall Number One,[157] the Pavilion of Cultivation, the Tower of Return, and the Pavilion of Accumulation, with strange rocks and wonderful trees, their branches woven together like teeth. Descending farther to the left, Mr. Jiang's place is on the west, with a small hall of three bays, extremely beautiful, with water spreading out on the western and southern sides, all with mountains and ridges round about.

The Duke of Wei's Western Plot

Going out from the central gate of the Duke's residence and passing through two gates on the west, then going south to another gate and entering, there is a hall with side "wings," then again a hall, and behind this another gate; then one sees the garden. Turning to the right one ascends a winding, rather dangerous, path up a low, steep hill, with old trees and odd grasses, causing one to step carefully and to glance about cautiously. Below one there is a deep natural gully, so narrow as to impede the flow of water, so that it cannot rise above the stones. The Embroidered Uniform commander says, "When this residence was bestowed on my ancestor the Prince of Zhongshan, a weaving shed and a stable stood here, but as the buildings were never repaired, the place became a rubble heap. His honor the Crown Prince's guardian, Xu Tianci, began the task of having it all removed."

There is a very beautiful area behind the hall, and in front stands a mountain of piled up rock, high enough that one can look out from here over the assembled mountains. There is a gazebo on top, quite lovely, with a plaque that reads: "Built by the present heir."[158]

---

157   The term Hall Number One was used during the Han dynasty to designate the principal residence in a compound. As this structure was usually the most beautiful, in time the term became a generic reference to a beautiful hall.

158   Xu Weizhi, who became Duke of Wei in 1589.

The East Garden of the Fourth Embroidered Uniform Guard Commander
Xu Jixun

At the eastern end of Grand Merit Ward is the residence of Xu Jixun, the third son of
the Master of the East Garden, a man known these days as the Fourth Embroidered
Uniform Guard Commander. It is his private residence, while he holds the seal of the
Embroidered Uniform Guard post here. As the home of the favored son of the Master
of the East Garden, the West Garden was the finest of the family's gardens, but it was
rather far away, and there was little time to go there. Adjacent to his residence was
some suitable open land for a garden, so he emptied his treasury, and over ten years the
garden was completed. As he then suffered from a foot ailment, for the most part he
stopped receiving guests, so no one got to wander through this garden. In the spring
of 1589, unexpectedly, I had an opportunity to do so.

Going in the gate and turning off to the southeast one comes to a very lovely hall, with
a moon pavilion in front of it. Behind the hall is a building, hung with vermilion curtains, with small courts on the left and right, and "ear" rooms flanking them. Turning
to the west one reaches a gate, where one descends broad stairs to a moon pavilion
where several rock peaks stand, in the midst of which is the Rock of the Accomplished
Gentleman.[159] My host said, "This rock was once an artifact of your home district of
Suzhou. At a former time the people of Suzhou were enduring a famine, but we had
surplus rice, so the the rock was acquired. There is no way to estimate how much it cost
to have it hauled here." To the north is a tall tower, with a base of more than three *chi*;
more than twenty steps lead up. From lofty windows at the front you can see as far as
the pagoda of the Baoen Monastery. It is ringed about on the north side by peaks and
ridges of a rockery.

Descending from the tower and going in to the rest of the garden there is a flower
veranda of three bays, facing north for a view of the mountains. Going up some stone
steps one reaches several pavilions with verandas, all quite pretty and neat. They seem
to be suited to the arch of a bridge.

The most amazing feature of the garden is a stone cavern, twisting about three times,
quite secluded, dark, and deep, so that one can not see inside, and even in the daytime lanterns must be hung to guide one's steps. Light does in fact shine through tiny
cracks, sparkling and looking like points of bright starlight. The cave water flows clear
and cold. It emerges and encircles a pavilion, lustrous and clear, so that one can see the
bottom. This mountain is really no more than fifty *zhang* in circumference, but walking
along all the intricate paths adds up to nearly a *li* the distance covered.

---

159 Dao Gai (d. ca. 549). Emperor Wu of the Liang dynasty once much admired the rock, which Dao Gai
proceeded to present to him.

The Garden of Ten Thousand Bamboo

The Garden of Ten Thousand Bamboo is adjacent to the Tile Palace Monastery, only about a hundred paces away. It, too, belongs to the family of the Dukes of Wei. It is occupied by the son of Master Bangning's concubine.[160]

The garden has a hall of three bays, with a terrace in front. The terrace has several rockery peaks, and is surrounded by a wall of several *ren* in height. There is a vermilion tower but this was tightly sealed. On the left the hall has a wing of three bays, also good for unrolling a mat. Beyond here, several tens of thousands of ornamental green-skinned, golden-veined bamboos stood erect, covering an area some two or three *qing* square. Sadly, the whole place seemed somewhat waterlogged and dilapidated. Although the master is certainly wealthy enough to do so, he has not sought to have water channels dug in order to divert the water into some ponds, thus also serving to attract the birds and the fishes.

The Family Garden of the Third Embroidered Uniform Guard Commander

The Third Embroidered Uniform Guard Commander is the second son of the Master of the East Garden, Xu Tianci, and the master himself of the Phoenix Terrace. When I went to visit the Phoenix Terrace, the host's home being not far away, he asked me to stop by here as well for a visit.

Going in through the central hall, then through two sets of inner chambers, one begins to reach the back gate. The gate opens, and one turns to the east, to a side hall of five bays, with broad steps, well suited, and finally to a moon pavilion with flowers and rocks. Turning again to the east there is an opening in the wall, and this brings one to a veritable fairyland, beginning with a set of mountain steps which one climbs, twisting through several tens of paces, until at the highest point there is a tower, and to the northeast rises Zhongshan, purple and green before one's eyes. East from here a narrow path leads up and down, with pavilions and little palaces scattered about, and beneath a stream flowing along, with two beautiful stone bridges spanning it, twisting through two grottoes, snaking about deep and quiet. At the furthest east the mountains end and a water pavilion of three bays rises. The pavilion has water on the north and south, and is open to views on three sides, which can be taken in in a single glance. Probably it is inferior in beauty to the South Garden at the home of the Duke of Wei, but it exceeds it in breadth. The garden's breadth, on the other hand, does not equal that of the East or West Gardens, but its mountains excel theirs in beauty.

---

160   This would be a grandson of the seventh Duke of Wei, Xu Pengju, and the nephew of the eighth Duke Xu Bangrui. Xu Bangning was Bangrui's younger brother.

The Golden Bowl Garden of General Li[161]

Aside from the two gardens of Mister Xu known as West Garden, there is yet another West Garden, which is the Golden Bowl Garden of General Li, the alternate residence of Xu Bangqing, son of the fifth Duke of Wei, Xu Fu.

Going out the Right City Gate about a *li* one comes to the place. A gate overlooks the main street. There is a hall of three bays, a bit low and shallow, and behind that a terrace. Going along the terrace and turning to the northwest, after about thirty paces one becomes enfolded by elms and tall poplars interwoven, creating a lovely green shade. After another thirty paces there is a hall of three bays, with a terrace to the south, four or five lake rocks, and tree peonies planted below. To the *yang* side of the hall rocks have been piled up to form a mountain, whose height I did not measure. Around it small channels are dug out, winding all about, on which wine cups can be floated. I don't know what the water source is. At the foot of the mountain is a pavilion, and beneath it a grotto, not more than five or six *chi* high; one must lean on the wall to enter the opening. It is said that on the other side of the wall is another mountain, with another pond, and that is the source of the water coming through. Standing here, one can see various tiers of hall and pavilion in the distance, so clearly that one can count them, but one cannot make one's way to them. On the left and right grow eight old junipers, the largest so thick of girth that you can barely get your arms around them. From here a path winds to the southwest; there is a range of rooms, some ten in number, clad with bricks and tiles, and, in front, a whitewashed wall. Outside the western wall stand ten thousand bamboo and ten tall elms, bright and fresh in the glow of the setting sun. To the northwest is a high mound, topped with a pavilion called Azure Clouds Over Deep Recesses. To the east one can see the Chaotian Palace, to the north one looks over the Bracing Mountain temple, the Tile Palace Temple, and the Nunnery of Numinous Response of Black Dragon Pool completes the view. There are other worthy places as well.

Of all the gardens of the Duke of Wei this is the most extensive, but it cannot be said to measure up to the lost ideals of Luoyang. "Golden Bowl Li" refers to a certain General Li from former times, but the story of how he came to be called "Golden Bowl" is so ridiculous that it cannot be believed.

The Garden of Xu Jiu's Residence

Xu Jiu is the uncle of the Duke of Wei, and his home is opposite the Duke's mansion.

One enters the gate and there is a rather sturdy reception hall, with a northern exposure. Turning off to the right of the gate, a bit southwest, or facing south from the

---

161   As noted at the end of this passage, the garden is named after a certain General Li, but how or why the term "Golden Bowl" became linked with him, or who he was, remains unknown.

courtroom, all is suitably laid out. In front there is a terrace, with rockeries and individual stones from Jinchuan and Wukang. Opening a gate to the right one finds another courtroom of equal sturdiness, but more beautiful. In front is a broad courtyard, with a vermilion balustrade along the south side, overlooking a pool. At three corners of the pool are strange rocks, while in the middle rise ridges and peaks, topped with pine, juniper, peach, and flowering apricot trees. Pavilions and halls, grottoes and ravines are to be found here, all entangled and plastered in red, and to the right and left are painted towers that face each other, and a single lofty stone, making a stone tower three stories high. The master of the garden turned to me to say, "The garden to the right of the residence is especially beautiful but is soon to be sold to the Duke of Wei to become part of his South Garden."

The Lake of Lightheartedness Garden[162]

The Lake of Lightheartedness Garden also belongs to Xu Jiu. One reaches it by going out the Three Mountain Gate and walking not quite a hundred paces. To the left of the garden stand towers and terraces, water pavilions, and flower pavilions, but all have been damaged and ruined by flooding. Although the master of the garden has no time to make the necessary repairs to the garden, nonetheless its scenery must be accounted the most beautiful, perhaps by virtue of the fact that to the *yin* side of the garden is the Lake of Lightheartedness, not quite half a *li* across, but perhaps ten times that in length. Only vaguely glimpsed on the other side of the lake, the land slopes away in an exquisitely serpentine manner.

The Garden for Sharing Spring

The Garden for Sharing Spring was built by the grandson, by a concubine, of Prince Qi.[163] It is located in the southwest of the city, just a few paces from the gentleman's residence. One enters by a gate wide enough to drive two carriages through abreast of each other. Turning to the right space suddenly opens out, with a grand moon terrace, rockeries and trees setting one another off, with the Hall of Auspiciousness as the focal point. Going from here through another gate there is a hall called Green Shade. The hall faces north, and behind it stretches out a pond with a tower, called Hall of Elegant Reflections. This hall faces south, and beside it stands the Scouring Jade Pavilion.[164] Earth and rock have been piled up here to form a mountain, upon which have been sited pavilions and terraces, studios and belvederes, around which grow peonies of both the tree and the herbaceous variety. The master of the garden passed away recently and so the gates of the garden are nowadays not always barred. Various gentlemen often now visit the garden, and say of it that it is as good as the East or West Gardens. In truth, it is not their equal.

---

162   The Lake of Lightheartedness (*Mochou hu*) lies outside the western wall of Nanjing. Its name is associated with singing girls in the local traditions of Luoyang and Shicheng, in Hubei, as well as Nanjing.

163   Zhu Chengcai, a commoner descendant of the seventh son of the founding Emperor Zhu Yuanzhang.

164   The term "scouring jade" refers to the sound of water flowing over rocks.

The Marquis of Wuding's Garden

Here, an earthen wall encloses a space of several *li*, planted entirely in bamboo, with an entrance to the north. This is the former garden of the Marquis of Wuding. One first encounters an east-facing studio, and once one has gone through this studio, one finds another one, also east facing. After another ten or so paces on, one comes across a waterside pavilion of three bays, overlooking a pond to its south. Another ten or so paces on brings one to yet another pond, surrounded by green bamboo, the largest the size of a bowl in circumference. The land here, for a full thirty *zhang*, has been cleared, and north to south for almost fifty *zhang* the bamboo stretches out, to the east in particular appearing like an endless expanse of green. When the tips of the soaring bamboos dance in the firmament, the summer sun seems never to set, and when the cool autumn breezes gently blow, the bamboos resound like jade being tapped or metal struck. The marquis's family lives in Yan. Each year men are sent to harvest the bamboo here, yielding perhaps a hundred pieces of gold.

The Garden for Taking Refuge in the City

The Garden for Taking Refuge in the City was the garden of the late Yao Zhe, of the Court of State Ceremonial. Entering the studio behind the hall, one finds a small but beautifully appointed studio, its courtyard backed by trees truly both strange and ancient. Another turn, this time to the east, takes one to a further studio, but this one proving rather more spacious than the last. Going out a gate here and passing along a winding alleyway one comes, after a little more than a hundred paces, to the garden itself. Knocking on the north gate, then going in, there is a thatched south-facing pavilion, its hunchbacked roof set so low one must bend forward to enter, lest one lose one's cap. To the left is a small mountain which, as it is hedged in bamboo, one cannot climb. In front of the mountain is a large pond, about seven or eight *mu* in area. A flat bridge stands to the right, so narrow that crossing it one must put one foot in front of the other and creep across. At the bridge's end there is a low hall of five bays, the middle three of which are called the Hall Amid the Forest. Behind the hall a studio is pillowed up against the pond, called Flock of Swans Pavilion. This last is now in a state of some considerable disrepair.

Mr. Wu's Garden

Mr. Wu's Garden was built by the younger brother of Wu Xianfu, an official in the Directorate of Education. From the Tiled Palace Monastery one goes southwest about one *li* to reach it. The garden contains a studio, open on all four sides, so there is no place to avoid the sun. To the *yang* side there is a square pond, with a flat bridge, upon the span of which I estimate one could spread out ten mats. At the end of the bridge there is a terrace of several *zhang*, with ancient trees and lofty peaks, protected by green bamboo. The pond can't be more than a few tens of *chi* in area. The water is blue and without dust. One hears the occasional gurgle of flowing water, this coming from where the water of the Blue Stream had been diverted to supply the pond. To the right stands a meditation cell with winged eaves. To the west stands a tower which, being most sumptuously appointed and inside which there is a shrine to the immortals, seems all very inappropriately matched.

The Purple Willow Garden

Metropolitan Graduate Wang's Purple Willow Garden is about half a *li* to the west of the Gate of Accumulated Treasures. Along a somewhat out-of-the-way lane one turns into the place, its large gate facing the river, across the river to the north from the imperial city itself. Once inside the gate, one encounters a hall of three bays. Facing south at this point, one looks out over several tens of hundreds of tree peony specimens, along with a single hydrangea with more than a thousand blossoms. Farther to the west an open space has been turned into an herbaceous peony plot containing three times as many plants as of tree peony. A pond stands to the side of the plot, said to contain a rare variety of gold-rimmed white lotus. When I visited the garden, however, the flowers were not yet the size of coins. This garden is like the flower garden at the Flower Garden in the Compound of the King of Heaven in Luoyang, only in miniature.

"An Account of Pleasurable Garden" (*Yuyuan ji* 豫園記)

PAN YUNDUAN 潘允端 (1526–1601)

TRANSLATED BY RICHARD E. STRASSBERG

Pan Yunduan, from Shanghai, was the second son of the highly regarded Ming official, Censor-in-Chief on the Left, Pan En (1496–1582). Yunduan became a metropolitan graduate in 1562 and served in several posts, retiring in 1577 from the position of Provincial Administration Commissioner on the Right in Sichuan.

From 1559 onward, Pan Yunduan began to construct a garden close to his father's residence in Shanghai, in order, he tells us, to provide a pleasant retreat for Pan En in his old age, hence the name Pleasurable Garden. Shanghai was then just a secondary port city that had only recently begun to recover from decades of predation by Japanese pirates. Sadly, Pan En did not live to see the garden completed, and after Yunduan's retirement in 1577, it became his own residence.

Over the course of some two decades, Pan more than doubled the original size of the garden, employing for the task the well-known garden designer Zhang Nanyang (1517–1596). In his garden, Yunduan pursued his interests as a bibliophile, art collector, poet, and patron of the theater. His renowned opera troupe performed Kunqu and other styles of opera under his direction.

Today only a small portion of the original garden still exists, and only a few of its structures bear the names mentioned in Pan Yunduan's account. Over the years, it has served as a school, as the headquarters for the British forces during the Opium War and, later, for the local Taiping rebels, as offices for the Qing dynasty government and for merchant guilds, as a garden adjacent to the Temple of the City God, and as a marketplace. The Pleasurable Garden, now covering about five acres, has undergone restoration and reconstruction many times; the most recent major reconstruction took place in the late 1950s. The adjacent Inner Garden, dating from 1709, has been incorporated into it. Opened to the public in 1961, the garden became a national heritage site in 1982 and is today a major tourist attraction. A few elements from the late Ming are still preserved, including several outstanding rocks.

"An Account of Pleasurable Garden"

Originally, off to the west of my family's residence, lay a few fields that were worked as a vegetable plot. In the *jiwei* year of the reign of the Jiajing emperor [1559], after I failed the examination for the metropolitan graduate degree, I collected a few rocks, had a pond dug, erected pavilions, and planted bamboo there. Some twenty years passed during which I abandoned and recommenced my efforts many times without bringing the garden to completion. In the *dingchou* year of the reign of the Wanli emperor (1577), after I had retired as a treasury official in Sichuan, I decided to fulfill my intention, adding fifteen more laborers to the task of shaping the land, and seventeen more to digging the pond. Work on the garden progressed year by year, exhausting my available funds. In time, I was able to present it to my aged father so that he might derive pleasure here from drinking with companions and chanting poems. Gradually, my garden has acquired fame as a scenic place.

Several pavilions were built on the eastern side of the garden to block off the noise of the city outside. In the center, a gate three bays wide with a placard above inscribed with the words "Pleasurable Garden" indicates that it is intended to please my aged father. After entering and proceeding several *wu* along to the west, one comes across another gate that states "Gradually Becoming More Beautiful." Westward again and just another twenty-odd *wu* farther on, a turn to the north brings one to an archway with the plaque: "A Bit of Paradise in the Human World." Passing under the arch, one finds a stone bridge arching across the water. On the other side of the bridge, one faces a tall wall where embedded in the middle is a stone plaque with the words "Joy Throughout the Empire," written in ancient script. Following along the wall eastward, to the west one comes across a hall called "Jade Blossoms" that stands facing some extraordinary rocks, including one named "Exquisite Jade." This belongs to the first rank among rocks and is said to have escaped the clutches of the emperor's Flower and Rock Network of the Xuanhe reign period [1119–1125]. The hall is named after one of these rocks.[165]

Behind this hall is a studio with a vermilion balustrade, standing beside a stream. The fish below are regularly fed from here, so the spot is called "The Joy of Fish." West of the studio, one finds a covered walkway extending more than ten *wu* before turning to the north where there is a pavilion with eaves like unfurled wings. The pavilion is

---

165   Pan's garden once contained five outstanding rocks, "Jade Blossoms" being one of them, hence the name given the hall. Today, three major rocks remain, including "Exquisite Jade."

built over the water and is called "Containing Green." Walking here feels akin to being on a cantilevered path upon a mountain, but the walker is unaware that he is crossing over water. Turning west after the pavilion, another walkway leads some thirty or so *wu* to yet another gate, "Pacing Auspiciously," where giant rocks rise on each side like a mountain pass. Hidden here is a broad courtyard a few *ren* deep and twice as wide, paved with stone as smooth as whetstones. Rocks with extraordinary shapes have been placed to left and right, protruding and receding like cliffs, slopes, and valleys. Planted in uneven arrangement among the rocks are specimens of famous flowers and rare trees. Set apart from these in front lies a large pond edged with stone balustrades.

There is a hall five bays in size that majestically faces the pond. It is named "The Hall of Happy Longevity," and the woodwork displays a considerable amount of painted and carved decoration. The chamber on the left is called the "Studio for Fulfilling the Four Beginnings," derived from one of my artistic names. It is like a symbolic accoutrement worn from the belt as a cautionary reminder.[166] The chamber on the right is called the "Studio of the Five Possibilities." This derived from what I wrote in a letter to my father when, as an official, I was obliged to endure traveling to the Huai River area: "Your unworthy son maintains that he has parents whom he could be serving, sons whom he could be instructing, and fields that he could be tending. Why do I still cling to a position that brings so little benefit?"[167] Then, in the beginning of the *dingchou* year [1577], I dreamt that a divinity presented me with a Daoist text that contained the words, "There are mountains where you could be gathering firewood and lakes where you could be fishing." The next day, I received permission to retire. Therefore, I combined these five possibilities into the name of the studio. Alas! The construction of The Hall of Happy Longevity was originally intended to delight my aged father. I will never cease regretting that my puny efforts and unwarranted procrastination prevented his seeing this hall completed during his lifetime.[168]

Stretching across the center of the pond is a prominent island with a pavilion named "Where Ducks Relax." On the southern side of the island rocky peaks are piled up shaded by bamboo and trees—it is another "South Mountain."[169] Proceeding west from the Studio of the Five Possibilities, one comes across the Border Pavilion to the

---

166 "Fulfilling the Four Beginnings" alludes to one of Pan Yunduan's artistic names, "Studio of Fulfillment" (Chongzhai 充齋). The "four beginnings" (*sishi* 四始) refer to the foundations of moral self-cultivation: humaneness, one's innate nature, sincerity, and study. According to the philosophical text *Master Hanfei* (*Hanfeizi* 韓非子), dilatory people should wear a bowstring from their belts to remind them of the need to act promptly while hasty people should wear a leather strap signifying restraint.

167 Pan Yunduan served as a vice-commissioner in the provincial administration commission for Yingtianfu (present-day Nanjing) and was required to travel north to the Huai River area to inspect grain shipments.

168 Pan En died in 1582, about midway through the construction of the Hall of Happy Longevity.

169 South Mountain alludes to the poet Tao Qian's famous lines, "I pluck chrysanthemums under the eastern hedge, / I gaze off at South Mountain in the distance."

south and the Tower for Moonlight Drinking on the right. Below, a covered walkway meanders away for some hundred or so *wu*. From the south, turning west and then walking northward, one finds a hall three bays in size called "Zhengyang." The ground floor here is a library with books arranged to the left and right, a most suitable place for quiet study. In front of this building, rocks from Wukang[170] have been piled up to form a mountain. Its layers rise high with a refined and lustrous appearance quite worth viewing and appreciating. If one ascends this hall, one finds a walkway that leads west to a three-story tower called the "Chunyang Pavilion." The top story is a shrine for offerings to the Daoist transcendent Lü Dongbin. Since I share the same birthday with Lü, my father gave me the personal name "Zhengyang."[171] The middle story contains a shrine to the local god of Qiyang. This is because while my father was administering Qiyang, he dreamt that a god holding two sprigs of cassia turned up, accompanied by two youths.[172] He said, "The Supreme God grants you these two sons because of your widespread benevolence." Not long afterward, my elder brother and I were born. Our father's command to us to sacrifice to this god is set forth in the "Record of the Shrine."

After descending from this pavilion, there is the "Cave of Lingering Spring" south of which stands a trellis with grape vines. Following west along the trellis and crossing a short bridge leads past a hill with bamboo to where a hundred flowering apricot trees conceal a hall named "Carpeted by Jade." East of Carpeted by Jade is the Shrine to Marquis Guan.[173] Exiting the shrine and proceeding east on a winding path takes one up and down past ridges, hills, ravines, caves, valleys, over bridges, and along banks. It is impossible to describe them all but each one is extremely delightful. Halfway up this mountain is the "Shrine to the Mountain God" and east of this, a pavilion facing north named "Drawing Forth Beauty." Drawing Forth Beauty stands in a glen formed by a group of peaks, and it faces a large pond. It and the Hall of Happy Longevity gaze across at each other. After arriving here by the mountainous path, one can rest for a while at the pavilion.

---

170   Mt. Wukang in Huzhou, Jiangsu, produces rocks prized by collectors: they are blue-green or yellow, very firm, and contain many holes.

171   Lü Dongbin is one of the Eight Transcendents (*Baxian* 八仙) of popular Daoism, believed to have been born in the Tang dynasty on the fourteenth day of the fourth lunar month in the fourteenth year of the Zhenyuan reign period (798). He was also known as Chunyangzi 純陽子 (Master of the Pure Yang-Force). Pan's name, Zhengyang, can mean "following the path of Lü Dongbin."

172   Qiyang refers here to the sub-prefecture of Qizhou in modern day Hebei Province, where Pan En had served as magistrate in 1523.

173   Guan Yu (d. 220) was a famous general who supported the Shu-Han state during the Three Kingdoms period. He later became a popular god and was canonized as a marquis.

East of the pavilion one comes across a large stone grotto. It is deep, dark, and secluded, comparable to Lord Zhang's and Shanjuan's Caverns.[174] Gazing upward from inside the cave, one can see the Mahâsattva Retreat, on the eastern side of which are Buddhist monastic quarters measuring five bays. Eminent monks who arrive here can obtain respite from their wanderings. As one exits from the retreat, extraordinary peaks stand erect like ascending dragons or horses at play. Their height blocks the clouds and obscures the moon for it is the highest point on this South Mountain. One looks out over the streams, mountains, and pavilions as if soaring on the wind or riding on air and peering at the mortal world down below—it is truly another realm up here. Descending northeast by the mountain path takes one by the Pavilion of Lingering Shadows. Then, the path meanders among the scattered rocks, turning north where one encounters a hall measuring three bays called the "Hall of Converging Scenes," connected with Snow Cave on the right and Waterside Studio on the left. Exiting Converging Scenes and traversing a zigzag bridge for about forty steps to its end brings one to what is called the Great Courtyard. This completes a tour of the sights south of Happy Longevity.

West of the Hall of Happy Longevity, a shrine has been built, three bays in size. It contains the memorial tablets of my ancestors, down to my great-great-grandfather, so that I can make offerings to them. A square pond was constructed behind here, where lotuses have been planted. Surrounding this site is a wall behind which stand innumerable tall bamboo. Beyond the bamboo is a long canal that leads both eastward and westward to the large pond in front so that one can travel in a circle by boat. East of the Hall of Happy Longevity is another chamber three bays in size called "Carefree" where a *qin*, books, and bronze vessels are displayed. Farther beyond is a tall building called the "Tower for Nurturing the Twilight Years" beside which is a kitchen and bath with all the proper facilities: this is where I reside. East of Carefree Hall is another residence where my youngest son Yunxian resides, making it convenient for him to visit me. Its main hall is called "Loving the Sun" to express the idea of caring for one's parents.

In all, I would not claim this garden to be the equal of the Wangchuan estate of Wang Wei or the Pingquan estate of Li Deyu. And yet, the way its plants and rocks lend themselves to viewing, the manner in which its halls and chambers provide comfort, and the extent to which I can tour through the garden by boat are sufficient to provide me with some passing scenery and bring happiness to my later years. It is just that the enormous expense has emptied the family coffers. Though I have no regrets that this

---

174   Lord Zhang may refer to Zhang Daoling (d. 156), one of the early leaders of religious Daoism or to Zhang Guolao (trad. fl. 7th–mid-8th century), later canonized as one of the Eight Transcendents. Shanjuan was recorded as a hermit during the time of the legendary thearchs Yao and Shun; he refused to accept an offer of the throne. Both caverns are well-known tourist sites in modern Yixing, Jiangsu Province.

passion of mine became an obsession, truly, this should serve as a warning to other gentlemen. If my sons and grandsons can forever refrain from following my ways and never pile up a mound of earth or plant even a single tree, then this would be an excellent thing indeed!

Gazetteer of Songjiang Prefecture (*Songjiang fuzhi* 松江府志; extract)

FANG YUEGONG 方岳貢, ED.

TRANSLATED BY ALISON HARDIE

In a record of the Pleasurable Garden found in a gazetteer of Songjiang Prefecture dated 1630, Wang Shizhen (see above) provides a somewhat more jaundiced view of Pan Yunduan's garden.

Gazetteer of Songjiang Prefecture (extract)

Wang Shizhen's "Record" reads as follows: "The Pans' Pleasurable Garden was built by Pan Yunduan and was completed only about five years ago. To its east is an open space of more than ten *mu*, with a lot of rubble collected there. There is an expansive gate overlooking it to the side, with a plaque reading 'Pleasurable Gateway.' When you turn toward the southwest on entering the gateway, a courtyard has been constructed, standing out on its own, with a plaque reading 'Courtyard of Moderation.' There is a stone bridge; across the bridge, slightly to the west, there is a hall called Jade Blossoms Hall. In front is an arrangement of rock-peaks called Five Elders. One peak is known as Exquisite Jade; it was transported here from Minister Zhu's garden in Black Mud Gully. It is elegant, glossy, foraminated and perforated, a wonder of nature's craft. It is similar to the Dragon Head Rock from Kunshan, but taller. These are all pieces from the time of the Sui and Tang dynasties; one wonders how they escaped the imperial requisition of the Xuanhe era. Forty-odd *wu* farther on, you come to a gaping gateway. It opens into a lofty hall of five bays, known as the Hall of Happy Longevity. It is tall enough to touch the clouds, with vermillion tiles and painted beams, dazzling in gold and azure. Two bays to the left and right are the commissioner's study, and this is particularly splendid and bright. In front of it is an open space of about ten *mu*, overlooking the large pond. On the left there is a building with a high gable, firmly secured with a strong door, where the Provincial Administration Commissioner and his concubines actually live. As you turn to the right there is a tall building; it is not a very fine building, and in the central courtyard there is a small 'mountain' constructed entirely from Wukang rocks. The commissioner had a great time organizing this. As you come out and follow the right bank of the pond, you then come to a not very ornate path which takes you into the 'mountain.' Following a serpentine route upward, you find yourself pillowed directly above the main pond, and directly opposite the Hall of Happy Longevity. Within the rockery there are peaks, crests, streams, gullies, pavilions, lodges and that sort of thing, but it is not very interesting. The bamboos are thin and sparse, the trees ordinary and contrived, and the same goes for the rocks; presumably the commissioner's capabilities just were not up to his grand ideas. The fact that there are many more buildings than streams and rocks is indicative of this."

Collected Talks from the Lü Garden (*Lüyuan conghua* 履園叢話)

"Pleasurable Garden" (*Yuyuan* 豫園)

QIAN YONG 錢泳
TRANSLATED BY ALISON HARDIE

For Qian Yong, see above. This brief account shows what later visitors found notable about the garden, and also indicates how much its atmosphere had changed by the early nineteenth century.

"Pleasurable Garden"

The Pleasurable Garden is within the walled city of Shanghai; it was constructed by Administration Commissioner Pan Yunduan, the son of Pan En, the Respectful and Decisive Lord,[175] in the Ming dynasty, and the Administration Commissioner himself wrote a record of it. Its site is very expansive; the garden contains a Hall of Happy Longevity, for which Dong Qichang wrote a "Song of the Hall of Happy Longevity," which was inscribed on a screen in letters three or four inches across. His original calligraphy still survives; I have seen it on the desk of Mr. Zhang Jiehang. In front of the hall there is a "Thousand-Man Seat,"[176] one of the finest of pond terraces, and beside the pond are some very remarkable Lake Tai rocks, known as the Peaks of the Five Elders, including those named Jade Filigree, Flying Stallion, and Jade Blossoms, which are said to have been left behind during the Xuanhe period.[177] Now the City God's Temple has been constructed within the garden, and it is occupied by merchants and has become a place of public assembly. There is a miscellaneous crowd of sightseers, and a constellation of women, not to mention the full gamut of quacks, geomancers, astrologers, and palm-readers, such that it surpasses even the Great Xiangguo Temple in the Eastern Capital [Kaifeng].

---

175   Posthumous appellations of this type were bestowed on distinguished officials.

176   Alluding to the "Thousand-Man Seat" at Tiger Hill in Suzhou, an extensive rock platform.

177   That is, they were requisitioned for the Song emperor Huizong's "Northeast Marchmount," but not transported to the capital.

"Record of the Hall Surrounded by Jade of Master Sitting-in-Reclusion" (*Zuoyin xiansheng Huancui tang ji* 坐隱先生環翠堂記)

YUAN HUANG 袁黃 (1533–1606)

TRANSLATED BY ALISON HARDIE

Yuan Huang was a scholar and official from Suzhou. Having made slow progression up the civil service examination ladder, his first official appointment, as county magistrate, occurred only in 1588, when Yuan was already in his fifties. In the early 1590s, Yuan, then serving in the Ministry of War, was implicated in military failures in Korea, forcing his resignation.

Despite (or as a result of) his somewhat lackluster official career, Yuan Huang was a critical figure in the late imperial intellectual trend toward the syncretism of Confucianism, Buddhism, and Daoism. His own particular interests seem to have been in aspects of religious Daoism, and he helped inspire a renewed engagement on the part of the Chinese scholarly elite with the "Ledgers of Merit and Demerit," whereby one recorded, day by day, an accounting of one's good and bad actions.

Wang Tingna (ca. 1569–after 1609), the son of a wealthy Huizhou (Anhui Province) merchant, was a poet, dramatist, chess player, collector, and publisher (of beautifully illustrated fine editions) who spent much of his life seeking to enter the world of the literati. Eventually, he was granted an official title, but no accompanying office, and his involvement in the civil service examinations was curtailed by the death of his father. Both his garden itself in Huizhou, the Garden of Sitting in Reclusion, and Yuan Huang's record of it testify to his success in finding acceptance in the literary and artistic circles of his age, and among his friends he claimed both the playwright Tang Xianzu (1550–1616) and the Italian Jesuit Matteo Ricci (1552–1610).

The name of the garden involves an allusion to the game of Chinese chess, better known in English by its Japanese-derived name *gō*, by way of an anecdote found in the *New Account of Tales of the World*: "Wang Tanzhi considered the game of encirclement chess a kind of 'sedentary retirement' [or 'sitting in reclusion'], while the monk Zhi Dun considered it 'manual conversation'."[178]

Throughout his record, Yuan Huang presents Wang Tingna's largely commercial publishing activities as being motivated solely by educational, and therefore socially responsible, aims.

"Record of the Hall Surrounded by Jade of Master Sitting-in-Reclusion"

I have twice visited the White Peak, where I rested my horse on the outskirts of Haiyang.[179] Dismounting, I laid aside my whip, and gazed around at the myriad encircling mountains, the lofty ones upraised, the low prostrate, the approaching

---

178   Liu I-ch'ing [Liu Yiqing], *Shih-shuo Hsin-yü: A New Account of Tales of the World*, trans. Richard B. Mather (Minneapolis: University of Minnesota Press, 1976), 367.

179   Haiyang is an old name for the eastern part of Xiuning county in Huizhou prefecture (in present-day Anhui Province), where Wang Tingna's Garden of Sitting in Reclusion was. Some scholars have suggested that the Hall Surrounded by Jade (which Wang Tingna used as the name of his publishing house) was in Nanjing, but Yuan Huang's text confirms that the garden was in Xiuning.

rushing onward, the static squatting, the active dancing, the still reclining, the linked like an enclosure, the disjoint like an incomplete jade circle. Layer upon layer of mountain-tops presented their emerald beauty, the forests reached out with green vegetation, the jade-green color was edible. What a splendid sight it was.

Mr. Wang Tingna was born here and his clan is assembled here; consequently he has built a retreat here. He entitled the garden "Sitting in Reclusion" and the main hall "Surrounded by Jade" and commanded me to write a record of them. Now a mass of peaks surround the gate, and luxuriant scenery enfolds it: there is jade entirely surrounding the retreat, and it is not just a name thought up by the owner for his hall. The owner dwells in the immediate environment but has a far-reaching heart; he has constructed a single dwelling but his wish is to provide a broad shelter. As the myriad things emerge, then the cosmos absorbs them and the people receive them. Amid this luxuriance, he extends himself widely in all directions. As he dwells within, his breast is entirely filled with jade and he need not feel ashamed of his four walls. His intention is truly far-reaching.

Behind the hall he built the Courtyard of Fine Trees,[180] and before it he piled up rocks to form five peaks, which he named the Five Ancients;[181] they look just like immortals making obeisance. Below these peaks is the Bridge of Transformation into an Immortal Feathered Being, giving access to those coming and going. To the right of the peaks is the Crane's Nest; water has been led in among the pillars to form a nine-fold meander for floating wine-cups, and a platform has been constructed for growing orchids, which produce a palpable fragrance. In keeping cranes he resembles Lin Bu but without benefiting from the scenery of Solitary Hill; his orchid pavilion makes him resemble Wang Xizhi, the General of the Right, although the timing is not confined to the third day of the third month. In his ascending the terrace and intoxicating his guests he resembles Du Fu of the Ministry of Works, but he has not had to pawn his spring clothes.[182] The master can be at his ease.

Going left from the hall one comes to the Gate of White Clouds; mounting into vacancy and gazing afar, one can obtain a distant view in all eight directions from a

---

180   The allusion in "Fine Trees" is to an incident in the *Zuo Commentary*, 2nd year of Duke Zhao; the "fine tree" is emblematic of mutual regard between kindred spirits, particularly brothers. Wang Tingna had at least one brother, with whom he had a close relationship; they organized a poetry society together.

181   The "Five Ancients" were peaks on Mount Lu, in Jiangxi, the mountain particularly associated with reclusion. However, there were also peaks known as the Five Ancients on Level with the Clouds Mountain (Qiyunshan), which was close to Xiuning, so the name bears both a local and a national resonance.

182   A reference to a poem by Du Fu (712–770), in which he speaks of pawning his spring clothes to buy wine.

single doorway, so the main gallery is named Unbordered Vastness.[183] Behind the gallery is Suspended Pearls Spring, and to the left is Dispelling Mockery Pavilion.[184] With the free and easy wandering of the Keeper of the Lacquer Plantation, when rambling in vastness, one can attain a boundless distance; without the constraint of the official who served Wang Mang one can both mock oneself and release oneself, forgetting both mind and surroundings. Another of the master's cognomina is "Mister Pine and Crane," so he made a Pine Courtyard in front of the gallery, with an ancient pine tree planted on the left, and a sculptured stone crane on the right. He has the loftiness of Tao Qian, and so he has a solitary pine at which to linger; he has no interest in becoming the wealthy governor of Yangzhou, and so the stone crane need not take flight.[185] How subtle is the significance he has implied in this. The master is fond of literary composition and is very well endowed in woodblock carving, so farther in there is a Place for Storage of Woodblocks, and beside it is a Printing House. I have heard it said that "Oral teaching reaches the present generation, but it takes books to reach a hundred generations." Wishing to increase the depth of his knowledge, he has an extensive store here.

Going along by the Printing House and walking up an ascending stairway, one reaches the Belvedere Which Leans on Mount Songluo; this faces Songluo but surpasses it in height. If one leans over the balustrade and looks down, there is the Gentleman's Grove, with new bamboo in all its glory. This gives one a sense of the master's pure style and lofty integrity. To the west of the belvedere is a mountain which matches it; the gallery here is entitled Crisp Air of the Western Mountains, and it seems to summon the dripping verdure of Benevolence and Longevity Hill and enclose it within its eaves.[186] Inside is Vessel and Tripod Corner, where calligraphy and precious antiques are stored, demonstrating his connoisseurship. Going right from the hall one comes to the Non-Resemblance Study; through a gate one enters a lane, named Storehouse of Writhing Vapors. From the lane one enters Rinsing with Jade Lodge, where the study is. Non-being is defined as the

---

183   This is a phrase taken from the *Zhuangzi*. The Keeper of the Lacquer Plantation (see below) was an official title attributed to Zhuangzi.

184   An allusion to the writer and philosopher Yang Xiong (53 BCE–18 CE), who, having been a Han official, also served the usurping ruler Wang Mang (r. 9–23 CE) and was the author of a rhapsody entitled "Dispelling Mockery."

185   A "Yangzhou crane" means having all one's wishes fulfilled; the reference is to a story about a group of people who were talking about what they would like most: one, to become governor of Yangzhou; another to be wealthy; another to ride on a crane (like an immortal); a fourth said he would like to ride to Yangzhou by crane with a pocketful of money, thus achieving all these desires at once.

186   The name given this gallery, "Crisp Air of the Western Mountains," suggests an indifference to worldly success, and derives, perhaps, from an anecdote about Wang Huizhi in *New Account of Tales of the World*: "While Wang Huizhi was serving as Huan Zhong's aide, Huan said to him, 'You've been in my headquarters a long time now. It's time we got together and put your affairs in order.' Wang at first made no answer, but merely looked high in the air and pressed his hand-board [*shouban*] against his cheek. Finally he said, 'Ever since morning the Western Hills certainly have had a lively air about them!'" See Liu I-ch'ing, *Shih-shuo Hsin-yü*, 428, transliteration altered.

removal of being, resemblance has the meaning of constancy. The master takes his cognomen Master Non-Resemblance from this, and has applied the same cognomen to his study retreat. So in the writings which he pores over and explicates, he wishes to apply vacuity to what exists and restore its original simple form.

To the right of the Lodge is Infinity Gate, so-called because from here on the beauty of the garden is infinite. On entering the gate one immediately ascends Myriad Rock Mountain, which is formed of piled up rocks. On the summit are Nine Immortals Peak, Chess-Board Rock, Brilliant Enlightenment Terrace, and Cassia Fragrance Pavilion. Once upon a time, the scholar of the decayed axe-haft encountered immortals playing chess and found a day turn into years, the Hermit of the Mountain Valley smelled the fragrance of cassia flowers and attained enlightenment: the scenes of all these events can be imagined here.[187] Below this are Sword Gate, Facing the Wall Cliff, and Slanting Valley.[188] From the cliff one crosses Mystic Ford Bridge. Above the bridge is Great Compassion House, and beside it Purple Bamboo Grove; these are for the worship of the Great Bodhisattva.[189] With Bodhidharma's nine years of determination, Sword Gate increases in steepness, and Slanting Valley increases in strangeness. With Guanyin's compassion to save all beings, the Mystic Ford increases in depth, and the Bamboo Grove increases in verdure.

Going north by the grove, one gradually climbs higher and then reaches the highest point of the garden. On the highest point is the Plain Pavilion, roofed with thatch, and comparable to an orchestra with sounding brass and jade tinkling in all directions around but with a stringless plain *qin* sited in the center, or like guests with formal hats and jade belt-ornaments politely ceding precedence to each other, while an old man in hempen clothes, leaning at his ease on a staff, stands alone and aloof; this is even more worthy of celebration in literature.[190]

---

187   The decayed axe-haft is a reference to the Rip Van Winkle legend of a woodcutter who came upon immortals playing chess and stopped to watch them; when the game ended, so many years had passed that his axe-haft had rotted away. The chess-playing element in this story is particularly appropriate for the chess champion Wang Tingna. The Hermit of the Mountain Valley is the Song poet Huang Tingjian (1045–1105).

188   Sword Gate was an extremely steep mountain pass, of great military importance, between Shaanxi and Sichuan. Facing the Wall is an allusion to the Zen patriarch Bodhidharma, who meditated facing the wall of a cave for so many years that his shadow became imprinted on the rock. Slanting Valley is probably a reference to the poet Tao Qian, who recorded in a poem an outing to "Slanting Brook" in 421.

189   Compassion is the quality particularly associated with Avalokitêśvara, the "Bodhisattva who hears the cry of the world" (*Guanshiyin Pusa*), usually referred to in Chinese as Guanyin.

190   Qualities such as plainness (*su* 素), blandness (*dan* 淡), and awkwardness (*zhuo* 拙) were important values in elite aesthetics at this time, as a way for the elite to distinguish themselves from the nouveaux riches, who lacked "taste." Wang Tingna, from a nouveau riche family himself, must have been particularly anxious to be associated with elite values.

Descending, one reaches level ground, where more bamboo is planted. Under the bamboo is placed a rock, forming the Stone Table in the Well-Grown Grove. To the left of the grove is the Cave for Perceiving Vacancy; without beams, without rafters, without purlins, without upturned eaves, it is built entirely of bricks, and its height reaches the clouds; one can escape the heat in it. At the mouth of the cave is the Pond for Cleansing the Heart, and beside it the Myriad Flowers Clump. Turning right from the pond one ascends White Harvest Ridge. On top of the ridge is the Terrace for Observing the Moon-Toad, where one can invite the moon from over the eastern hills and drink to it in the grove of myriad greenery; this is another scenic area.[191] Going down from the ridge, one reaches the Peony Grove and the Half-hymn Hermitage; this has both images and scriptures, providing everything necessary for Buddhist observance.[192] In front of the throne is a spring, the Green Lotus Cavity; the morning and evening rituals and recitations always take place here. To the left of the hermitage is a building whose plaque reads "Brightness of Dawn."[193] The master is always clearly aware that he should be like the beginning of the early daybreak. There is also a deep lane called Pure Ethereal Realm; from this realm one enters the Dwelling of Negative Nothingness. Not only is being removed, the negativity is actually doubled. So advanced is the master's learning.

Within the dwelling is the Shrine of Total Unity. When he has leisure he sits here in meditation, achieving the elimination of the myriad things. What more could one desire? Ahead, one overlooks Beating Pinions Pond; although one may beat one's wings for 90,000 miles one does not emerge from among the sapanwoods and elms.[194] Pine, bamboo, and flowering apricot each occupy one of the Three Islands in the pond; together with the master they make up four companions.[195] There is an Angling Jetty, a Winding Bridge, a Slope for Washing Ink-Stones, a Gourd Valley, and a Dragon Gate. Beside the pond is Crystallized Emerald Gallery. From the gallery one turns back

---

191   By legend, the moon is inhabited by a three-legged toad. White Harvest refers to autumn (in the Five Elements system, white is the color of autumn and of the west), and the moon is particularly associated with autumn, when the Moon Festival takes place. The concept of inviting the moon and drinking to or with it comes from a famous poem by Li Bai (701–762), "Drinking Alone Beneath the Moon."

192   The word translated here as "hymn" is the Chinese phonetic equivalent for the Sanskrit *gâthâ*. Interestingly, Wang Zhideng (1535–1612), who provided the calligraphy for Yuan Huang's "Record of the Hall Surrounded by Jade of Master Sitting-in-Reclusion," also had a studio named Half-Hymn Hermitage.

193   This is a quotation from *Zhuangzi*, indicating enlightenment.

194   In the *Zhuangzi*, the mighty roc which beats its wings and flies ninety thousand miles is contrasted with the small birds which flutter about among the sapanwoods and elms.

195   Pine, bamboo, and flowering apricot are known as the Three Friends in Winter, because of their ability to remain green or to blossom despite the cold. Three islands in a pond represent the three Islands of the Immortals in the eastern ocean. Such groups of islands were a regular feature of early Chinese gardens, although by Wang Tingna's time such obvious symbolism was coming to be seen as old fashioned.

across the Winding Bridge, and comes to Suspended Daybed Studio.[196] The master is by nature solitary and lofty; he is selective of those with whom he consorts. There is also the Eastern Wall, where paintings and books are stored.[197]

Going along here, one ascends a stone terrace named Achieved Life.[198] By rejecting the body, the body is preserved; this is the directive for achieving life. On the summit of the terrace is Hundred Cranes Tower, where there is an image of Chunyang which is reverently worshipped.[199] This is not a search for eternal life but for the achieved life. Below the tower is the Great Treasure Pass, and within it the Jasper Stamens Room,[200] where various cinnabar drugs are cultivated in order to benefit all the living, because he regards the sickness of all creatures as his own sickness. Deeper in is the Emerald Forest Residence, most quiet, and most deserted, where the drifting dust does not reach. In the midst a streak of sky appears, and this is named Heaven in Miniature. For as the space of a needle's eye and the space of outer space are basically the same space, so the sky which gives us light and the entire cosmos are basically the same heaven.

After this one goes out through the pass and crosses the terrace. To the west of the terrace is Flowers of the Void Lane. From the lane one can see the Secret Belvedere, which wind and rain cannot penetrate, nor the force of cold reach, and where even in the winter months no stove is needed.[201] In front of the belvedere is a fountain which spurts up several feet from the ground; this is what is known as the Spring Gushing to Heaven.[202] If one enters the Clump of Myriad Flowers, and wanders through the Grove of Peonies,

---

196 There is a story in the *Later Han History* (*Hou Hanshu* 後漢書) of someone who was very selective of his friends; when one particular friend visited him, he would provide him with a daybed to lie on, but at other times the daybed was hung up out of the way.

197 The constellation known as the Eastern Wall (so-called because it was to the east of Heaven's Gate) was believed to govern literature. The Eastern Wall, thus, came to be used as a name for the imperial library, and for libraries in general.

198 "Achieved Life" or "Mastering Life" is the title of a chapter of the *Zhuangzi*.

199 Cranes are associated with Daoist immortals. Chunyang is Lü Dongbin, one of the Eight Immortals, who was particularly revered by intellectuals. An essay by the famous dramatist Tang Xianzu (1550–1616) reveals that Wang Tingna acted as a medium for communications from Lü Dongbin. In Mi Wanzhong's Ladle Garden (see Philip Hu's translation later in this chapter), there was an inscription "in the spirit writing of Lü Dongbin." Mi and Wang Tingna may have known each other; they certainly had friends in common. This inscription may, then, have been acquired by Mi, directly or indirectly, from Wang.

200 These names have associations with Daoism and alchemy.

201 The name "Secret Belvedere" is associated with the imperial library, but Yuan Huang does not specify that this building was used as a library.

202 Yuan Huang's casual comment suggests an entirely natural spring, but the woodblock illustration shows an elaborate fish-shaped fountain with a vertical jet of water. It is tempting to see in this the influence of European hydraulic technology (Wang Tingna claimed to be acquainted with the Jesuit Matteo Ricci) but it is more likely that it derived from the pumps used in the brine-wells of Sichuan; one of the many hats worn by Wang Tingna was that of an official of the Salt Distribution Commission.

then the glorious red and purple can return even without spring's burgeoning.[203] Seated in the Cave for Perceiving Vacancy, facing the Pond for Cleansing the Heart, one is overwhelmed by pure coolness, and can forget the heat of summer. Climbing the Ridge of White Harvest, walking on the Terrace for Observing the Moon-Toad, one can listen to the sounds and enjoy the shadows which assist the arrival of the pure mood of autumn. Entering Flowers of the Void Lane and ascending Secret Belvedere, one can play the pitch-pipe to bring back the sunshine;[204] snow and frost fail to blast, and one can avoid the depths of winter. With the Slope for Washing Ink-Stones to provide for pen and tablets, with the Shrine of Total Unity to nourish one's true nature, with the paintings and books in the Eastern Wall to promote pure appreciation, the great conspectus of Confucianism is provided here. With the Terrace of Achieved Life, with the Tower of a Hundred Cranes, with the Pass of Great Treasure, the great conspectus of the gateway to the Way is brought together here. With the Cliff for Facing the Wall, with the House of Great Compassion, with Half-Hymn Hermitage, the great conspectus of Buddhism is provided here.[205] When there is something suitable for any time throughout the four seasons, and the three doctrines are unified without any omission, is what he possesses not great? Yet this is not all.

Outside the Hall of Pure Speech is the Mountain Retreat; to the right of the retreat there is the pool of a spring, pure and sweet, which is entitled Standing Alone. The entire world is defiled, and I alone am pure: is it not outstandingly unique? There is also the Water Moon Walkway; the water has no mind to attract the moon, while the moon has no intention of entering the water, yet the two purities are intermingled, coming together without pre-arrangement. So the right wing of the retreat is called Cloudy Region, and the left Misty Passage. The soaring of the clouds, the drifting of the mist seem constantly to reflect the moon in the water. Winding southward from Misty Passage, one reaches the main gate; in front of it is Central Street, where propriety and righteousness are the model, and the bent and twisted are eliminated; is this not what is referred to as reduplication of the solitary one?

Beside the street is Lofty Sunshine Lodge, which is not provided for the benefit of topers.[206] As the sun with its fine warmth, rises, the way of the gentleman is extended.

---

203 In other words, the brilliant flowers and colors of spring endure eternally.

204 The note produced by the pitch pipe is a *yang* sound and, therefore, can be used to summon up sunshine and warmth.

205 Whether or not this was entirely Wang Tingna's own intention, Yuan Huang stresses that the garden embodies aspects of all three of the major doctrines (Confucianism, Daoism, and Buddhism). Yuan himself was a philosopher who was very concerned with the syncretism of the Three Doctrines.

206 Someone who enjoys drinking and behaves in an unrestrained manner can be called a "toper from Gaoyang," in allusion to a story in the *Records of the Grand Historian*. The place-name Gaoyang literally means "lofty sunshine" or "lofty and sunny."

There is also Mystic Manor, where the farmers congregate, which reaches the ultimate in the wanderings of a pleasurable excursion, without forgetting the hardships of the agricultural life. How can one penetrate this with ordinary feelings? At the far end of the street is a pavilion which the local gentry have named Neighborhood of the Lofty Gentleman, to show their respect for his virtuous reputation. Beyond the Gate of Pure Speech there is also a lake several *qing* in area. The master's formal name is Changzhao, and so the lake is named Master Chang's Lake. Apparently he would like his own name and the beauty of the lake to endure equally imperishably. There are two boats on the lake, the larger called Floating Home and the smaller Single Leaf. Drifting eastward on board a boat, one passes first by Jade Forest Homestead, where the pure shade is palpable, then goes past Elegant Screen Rock, which presents to the sight the verdant green of embroidery. To the north one reaches River Islet Delight, where it seems as though the splendor of Penglai were before one's eyes.[207] Farther north one comes to Six Bridges, and below this it is just like the fine scenery of West Lake.[208] Crossing the bridge and turning to the west, there is the Turtle-Fishing Terrace; casting a line into the rivers and lakes is as weighty a matter as were the nine tripods to the royal house of Han, though whether or not one catches a turtle is immaterial.[209]

On the banks of the lake there is the Thatched Cottage with a Bamboo Fence; yellow butterflies flutter round the fence, and wild vegetables can be gathered: suddenly one seems very far away. Gradually one proceeds to Heaven-Released Pavilion, where bulrushes cast their shadows on the eaves and green waves lap around the steps, and one can be at one's ease. Boarding the boat again, one travels south to Lurking Fish-Scales Pond, which is the deepest part of the lake. Farther south one passes the Dragon Lord's Temple and the Spirit Vulture Island. The Dragon Lord is the senior of the water spirits, and this temple has been set up for his worship in order to pray for mild weather. Spirit Vulture is the most splendid mountain-peak in India; this island has been made to resemble it, so that one may dwell on eastern ground but have the west in sight; the soiled and the pure are thus combined.[210]

Going eastward again, one reaches Swirling Waves Jetty; passing the jetty one comes to Whetstone Pillar Rock;[211] the current of the stream winds like a ribbon while the

---

207   A "river islet" is a phrase often used to suggest a hermit's dwelling; Penglai is one of the Islands of the Immortals.

208   Six bridges could also mean a six-arched bridge. There were six bridges associated with the West Lake in Hangzhou.

209   The ideal fisherman is indifferent to whether or not he catches anything. Bronze tripods were signs of status in ancient China, and the nine tripods were the insignia of the Han dynasty.

210   Spirit Vulture Peak (in Sanskrit, Gṛdhrakūṭa) was where the Buddha preached the Lotus Sutra. Note that Yuan presents China as the "east" and impure, while India, the "west," is the pure source of Buddhism.

211   A rock in the Yellow River, symbolizing constancy under stress.

rock stands in the midst of the water; it is as though it had been formed as a pillar to withstand the wild waves. In the middle of the lake is Lake Heart Pavilion;[212] looking around there is nothing but water in all directions, as though it were right in the center. One can imagine the unsullied style of the lofty man. Neighboring on the pavilion is Myriad Brocade Embankment; the embankment lies across the lake, dividing the lake into two sections, and flowers and bamboo are planted at random on it. Walking along and enjoying them is like being on Shanyin road; their freshness links shade to shade, so that one does not have time to take it all in.[213]

Abandoning the boat and going on shore, one finds there the Chrysanthemum Path, the Peach-Blossom Bank, the Cassia Ridge, the Banana Grove, the Tea Mound, the Fruit Orchard, and the Herb Nursery.[214] One is not willing to lag behind it because of the late-blooming fragrance of the chrysanthemum, one does not strive to put oneself in front of it because of the early blossom of the peach, one does not alter one's manner of elegant simplicity because of the rich aroma of the cassia, one does not abandon one's cultivation of contentment because of the pure bitterness of tea, one does not forget the attempt to fill one's belly because of the hollow center of the banana palm. His body being amid the scenery, but his heart traveling beyond it, the master is surely able to embody objects without being made an object by objects. Moreover, the fruit has its orchard and the herbs their nursery; they can be used to entertain guests, to provide sacrifices to the ancestors, and to cure the people; truly they are of great benefit.[215]

Going along the bank past a mountain stream one reaches Red Cliff; not only does it resemble the scenery of the original Red Cliff in Wuchang, but Young Zhou's victory and Lord Cao's defeat seem to be vaguely visible to one's view.[216] Above Red Cliff are Nobleman's Rock and Mocking Dust Cliff: nobility and eminence are illusory, worldly dust is to be sneered at; one can distinguish between trivial and weighty.

---

212   This pavilion shares its name with the very famous Lake Heart Pavilion in the West Lake.

213   The "Shanyin road" refers to yet another anecdote in *A New Account of Tales of the World* [see chapter 1]: "Wang Xianzhi said, 'Whenever I travel by the Shanyin road (in Guiji Commandery), the hills and the streams naturally complement each other in such a way that I can't begin to describe them. And especially if it's at the turning point between autumn and winter, I find it all the harder to express what's in my heart.'" See Liu I-ch'ing, *Shih-shuo Hsin-yü*, 75, transliteration altered.

214   These features seem to form part of a productive estate beyond the boundary of the more ornamental garden itself.

215   The concept of fruit being used for presentation to guests comes from the *Record of Ritual* (*Li ji* 禮記). Yuan Huang, thus, stresses both the social responsibility of the owner and the practical value of the estate's produce.

216   The Red Cliff near Wuchang on the Yangtze River was the site of a crucial battle between the combined forces of Sun Quan and Liu Bei, under the command of the youthful Zhou Yu (175–210), and those of Cao Cao (155–220), in the Three Kingdoms period. The site was further immortalized in two rhapsodies by the great Song poet Su Shi (1036–1101).

To the west of the cliff is Flying Rainbow Ridge; after crossing the ridge one climbs again up Benevolence and Longevity Hill; looking at it is the same as being there. To the right of the hill is Calling Birds Lodge,²¹⁷ where men of outstanding brilliance from all directions can be assembled to hold seminars, in order to obtain solid benefit from their companionship. There are also Good Fortune Hermitage and Courtyard Communicating with the Mysteries; the images ranged in them are extremely different, but the worship paid to them is the same.²¹⁸ Before them is a river like a ribbon of jade encircling them. The rivers' and mountains' rivalry in singularity, the universe's production of luxuriance, are certainly not accidental. Crossing the river, one passes again by the various scenic spots and reaches Cave Spirit Temple; its Earth God is extremely responsive and brings blessings to this land; everyone competes to pray to him. Behind the temple is Celestial Flowers Altar, and also Illuminate Truth Hermitage; bhiksunis practice cultivation in it, and the sound of Sanskrit chants and the sound of the woods harmonize with each other.²¹⁹ To the east of the hermitage is Guangmo Mountain, encircling the back of the hall, so that the hall seems to be enlarged by its dependence upon it. How rich is the assemblage in the Garden of Sitting in Reclusion Surrounded by Jade.

In the *renyin* year of the reign of the Wanli emperor [1602], the garden was first completed, and the master composed poetry about it; his poems are very numerous. However hard I try I can never be as imposing as the master; because of this I feel very regretful. From of old, how many distinguished persons and men of chivalry have built terraces on mountains, led in water to make pools, developed gardens and built halls, spreading word of their splendors both far and near? And have any of them survived until now? Not to speak of the gardens of gentlemen and commoners, do even the Epang Palace of Qin, the Hanyuan Palace of Han, the Changle Palace of Tang, all of which exhausted the workmanship of construction and had the ultimate in elaborate decoration, still survive to this day?²²⁰ For splendor to turn completely to shards and rubble, and palaces to be transformed to ploughed fields, has been a commonplace throughout the ages. The reason that I particularly admire the Hall Surrounded by Jade is not merely because of its remarkable design or its splendid landscape. As the quotation goes: "The fame of mountains comes not from their height, but from the dryads that in them

---

217   An allusion to a poem in the *Book of Songs*, indicating a search for companionship.

218   The names indicate that Good Fortune Hermitage is Buddhist, while Courtyard Communicating with the Mysteries is Daoist.

219   Celestial Flowers Altar and Illuminate Truth Hermitage are both Buddhist establishments. Bhiksunis (Yuan uses the Chinese phonetic rendering of the Sanskrit word) are Buddhist nuns.

220   The ephemeral nature of garden constructions is a commonplace in garden literature. The Epang Palace was built by the First Emperor of Qin (r. 221–210 BCE); the Changle Palace was the residence of the Empress Dowager in the Han (not Tang) dynasty; the Hanyuan Palace was built in the Tang (not Han) dynasty, in 649–650.

delight."²²¹ Wang Tingna is erudite and a follower of the Way; he stands out like a crane from the common flock. The construction of this hall has a deep significance both in its purpose and in its naming. What meets the eyes alerts the heart, like the bowls, platters, doors, and window-shutters of the ancients, which all had admonitory inscriptions to alert and improve the viewer, and were not simply objects for refined aesthetic appreciation. I established my own retreat at Zhaotian,²²² which is quite well endowed with pines, bamboo, springs, and rocks; my purpose was not to search out the remarkable but to cultivate my virtue. I wish to join with Mr. Wang in bending my mind to the goal of negative nothingness, aiming for the mystery of perceiving vacancy, and probing the secret of the half-hymn, and so by self-reflection and concentrating our spirits, we briskly stimulate ourselves to even greater effort. So this hall indeed should have as imperishable fame as Zhuge Liang's retreat in Nanyang or Yang Xiong's pavilion in Western Shu.²²³

Twenty-first day of the intercalary second month of the thirtieth (*renyin*) year of the reign of the Wanli emperor of the Imperial Ming dynasty [1602]

Presented scholar by bestowal in origin, formerly by
Imperial order assisting in the administration of Jizhou, Liaoning, Baoding,
Shandong, etc., concurrently Commander of the Military Mission to Korea,
promoted to fourth rank, serving as Secretary of the Bureau of Operations of the
Ministry of War, Wang Tingna's kinsman, Attendant
Yuan Huang presents this "Record" with a respectful bow.²²⁴

Calligraphy by Wang Zhideng of Taiyuan.²²⁵

---

221   The quotation is from "The Scholar's Humble Dwelling" or "Inscription for a Humble Cottage" (*Loushi ming* 陋室銘) attributed to the Tang scholar and poet Liu Yuxi (772–842). Editor's note: in the translation given in chapter 2, these lines appear as "Who heeds the hill's bare height until / Some legend grows around the hill?"

222   Yuan Huang's cognomen was Zhaotian yinong, Leisured Farmer of Zhaotian.

223   The strategist Zhuge Liang (181–234) went into retreat and emerged to take office only after three visits to his cottage by Liu Bei. The Battle of Red Cliff took place the following year. Yang Xiong was born in Chengdu, in the region of Shu, now Sichuan, and did not go to the capital, Chang'an, until he was over forty.

224   Yuan Huang gives a formal list of all his titles, starting with the presented scholar (*jinshi*) degree that he obtained in 1586, and including a reference to his service in Korea, which was distinctly unsuccessful. The layout, in short lines, ensures that the reference to the emperor ("by Imperial order") comes at the beginning (top) of a line, as was required by convention. It is rather unusual for the author of a garden record to "sign off" in such a formal way; garden culture is after all supposed to be about the avoidance of officialdom. This underlines the fact that Wang Tingna's purpose in publishing this record by such a distinguished man had more to do with laying a claim to social status than with eremitism.

225   Wang Zhideng (1535–1612), from Suzhou, whose clan originated from Taiyuan in Shanxi, was noted as a calligrapher and poet. He did not undertake an official career, but knew everyone who was anyone in the scholar-official world of his time. As noted above, his studio shared its unusual name with one of the features in Wang Tingna's garden.

Many of the verses composed by the distinguished gentlemen in this anthology make use of the names of features in my humble garden based on those mentioned in the poems and record by Academician Zhu Zhifan[226] and Secretary Yuan Huang. Concerned that connoisseurs who cast their eyes on them might think the names were picked at random, I have respectfully appended the compositions of the two gentlemen for the perusal of distinguished readers.

Colophon by Wang Tingna, Master Non-Resemblance.[227]

A History of Gardens (*Yuanshi* 園史)

"Preface" (*Xu* 序)

CHEN JIRU 陳繼儒 (1558–1639)

TRANSLATED BY STANISLAUS FUNG

For Chen Jiru, see chapter 3. Here, in a short preface to a work by a friend that is no longer extant, Chen captures something of the essential melancholy of garden ownership. Wei Yong, the editor of the late Ming anthology within which this "Preface" is found, *Portable Ice and Snow*, writing under the sobriquet "The Lazy Immortal," appended a marginal note to the item that reads, "This great earth of ours is but a solitary 'grass hut'[228] which, down through the ages, has never had a constant master. I for my part desire no more than to don my straw sandals and take up my bamboo staff to go free and easy wandering all over the place, and to find total contentment in whatever it is that destiny may bring me. As for that foot of land in front of my gate, that handful of mountain and that ladleful of water, how could I ever possibly manage to possess it forever? Thinking thus brings tears to my eyes!"

"Preface"

I once said that there were four difficulties with gardens: it is difficult to have fine mountains and waters; it is difficult to have old trees; it is difficult to plan; and it is difficult to assign names. Then there are three easy things: the powerful can easily seize the garden; in time, it can easily become unkempt; and with an uncultivated owner, it easily becomes vulgar. Nowadays, there are many famous gardens in Jiangnan. I often pass by them and rest my eyes on them. However, when I next visit them, they might

---

226   Zhu Zhifan (1564–after 1624), who wrote a sequence of 110 poems on Wang Tingna's garden, published in the same volume as Yuan Huang's record, was an official and calligrapher from Nanjing. He was the top metropolitan graduate (*zhuangyuan*) of 1595. He was a prolific but not a great poet, and was noted for both his small and his large calligraphy.

227   By contrast with the elaborate "signature" of Yuan Huang, Wang Tingna "signs" himself simply with his personal name, abbreviated to "Na," and one of his cognomina.

228   A reference to the "Turning of Heaven" chapter of the *Zhuangzi*: "Benevolence and righteousness are the grass huts of the former kings; you may stop in them for one night but you mustn't tarry there for long." *The Complete Works of Chuang Tzu*, trans. Burton Watson (New York: Columbia University Press, 1968), 162.

still have bright flowers and shaded ferns, but the owner would not have the leisure to be there, or even if he could be there, he would fling his arm around and depart like a courier; or he would diminish the plans of his forebears, altering them abruptly each summer so that the garden would not be completely renovated when his bones would already have decayed; or in the twinkling of an eye, he would sell it to another family, and then if a huge plaque does not label the entrance, a strong lock would bolt the door shut; or trees would be cut down to make mortars, and rocks would be pulled down to make plinths. The fallen beams and ruined walls would be like a house abandoned during a drought. Even if the eaves, rafters, and shingles are maintained well, and the pines and chrysanthemums are the same as before, the owner of the garden could be an old wine-drinking and meat-eating reprobate; and every fern and every tree, every word and every sentence would cause the viewers to belch and feel like vomiting. They would stop their noses, cover their faces, and could not remain there for another moment. Having it would be a cause for regret; how could this compare to the pleasure of being rid of it?

"A Spring Day, Tending the Family Garden" (*Chunri jiayuan jishi* 春日家園即事)

XU YUAN 徐媛 (FL. 1590)

TRANSLATED BY MARY ELLEN FRIENDS

Xu Yuan, a very original writer who was regarded as one of the finest women poets of Suzhou in her day, was born into one of the leading families of that city, the owners of a well-known garden on the site of what is now the Lingering Garden (*Liu yuan*). It is not clear whether the "family garden" referred to here is that garden or one belonging to the family of her husband, Fan Yunlin (1558–1641). The Fans were another leading Suzhou gentry family. Xu Yuan and Fan Yunlin seem to have enjoyed the "companionate marriage" that had become a literati ideal in the late Ming, and Xu accompanied her husband on his official travels, enabling her to see more of the world than was possible for many women.

"A Spring Day, Tending the Family Garden"

Precious flowers push forth around stone steps;
Wild bamboo, in every shade of green.
A slight breeze rolls open the curtain,
A secret fragrance wafts down the footpath.

"In the Manner of Tao Qian" (*Ni Tao shi* 擬陶詩) and "Living the Quiet Life" (*Xianju jishi* 閒居即事)

LU QINGZI 陸卿子 (FL. 1590S)

TRANSLATED BY MAUREEN ROBERTSON

Lu Qingzi was the daughter of a distinguished painter, Lu Shidao, who also served as a senior official. Like her friend Xu Yuan (see above), Lu enjoyed an intimate marriage, though her husband, Zhao Huanguang, avoided the pressures of official life. Lu Qingzi and Xu Yuan were known as the two learned ladies of Suzhou, though Lu has generally been regarded as the better poet. Lu wrote in a wide range of styles, on both traditionally masculine and feminine topics; sometimes, as here, she imitated the styles of great poets of the past (the "stringless zither" she mentions in the second poem was associated with the poet Tao Qian).

"In the Manner of Tao Qian"

Living quietly, little to do
with the busy world,
it is my nature
to forget elaborate hairpins.
Green waters brim
in flower-scented pools,
cool winds are stored
in leafy woods.
Minnows play
in wavelets and ripples,
wild birds sing out
their pleasing notes.
At evening comes
a timely rain,
white clouds deepen
on the highest peaks.
Plants in the yard are bathed
in nourishing moisture,
above mountain meadows
clouds send showers flying down.
Completely relaxed
I give thoughts free rein
to range far, far—
and when I like
pour for myself
some homemade wine.

"Living the Quiet Life"

Closing the gate,
I am free to do as I please;
my humble lane
is overgrown with vines.
The color of willows
excites birds' noisy chatter;
the glitter of waves
makes shades of evening calm.
Quietly, falling petals
blanket the ground;
clouds in the void, serene,
lean upon forest.
You ask why I roost here,
hidden away—
beside my bed I have
a stringless zither.

"On Mi Wanzhong's Ladle Garden" (*Ti Mi zhongzhao Shaoyuan* 題米仲诏勺园)

WANG SIREN 王思任 (1575–1646)

TRANSLATED BY PHILIP K. HU

The poet, essayist, painter, and sometime official Wang Siren happened to be born in Beijing but always regarded himself as coming from the family hometown of Shanyin (present-day Shaoxing) in Zhejiang Province. His official career was a checkered one, thrice appointed and thrice dismissed, but he put his periods of enforced idleness to good effect, a point made by the much younger Zhang Dai (1597–ca.1684) in his biography of a man he regarded as his "Friend in Ancient Prose":

> In the course of these fifty years, more than half his time was spent in retirement, during which time he drowned himself in wine and indulged himself in the mountains and rivers. In idle moments, he would shut his door and read. After he had paid a visit to the Celestial Terrace and Disporting Geese mountains in southwestern Zhejiang in the *gengxu* year [1610], he composed an entirely novel account of his trip, entitled "My Summons to Travel." Readers of this work exclaimed that it was written with an imperious brush and an enraged soul, with a fine eye and a sharp tongue.

As an elderly man, he died bravely at the fall of his hometown to the Manchu forces in 1646; having hung up a sign reading "No Surrender," he bolted his door and starved himself to death.

In the 1610s, Wang built himself a garden in Shanyin, called My Garden of Escape, containing a library called the Tower for Reading Amid Fine Mountains and Rivers. In the poem translated below, however, he celebrates one of the most famous northern gardens of his age—the Ladle Garden owned by his friend, the poet, calligrapher, painter, petromaniac and seal carver Mi Wanzhong (1570–1628) in the Haidian district of his hometown Beijing. The reputation of the garden was promoted by Mi's invention of the fashion for painting garden scenes on lanterns.

Modeled explicitly on the gardens of Jiangnan, Ladle Garden was built between 1612 and 1614. Its name called attention to both its modest size (100 *mu*, about 17 acres) in comparison to the large neighboring gardens and its predominant feature ("a ladleful of water"); the garden was also known to locals at the time as either the Village of Wind and Mist or the Garden of the Mi Family.

Mi Wanzhong's garden did not much outlast his death in 1628. When garden building began anew in this district in the 1680s, at the hands of the emperors of the newly established Qing dynasty, nothing of the garden remained except a single rock that now graces the courtyard of the Arthur M. Sackler Museum of Art and Archaeology of Peking University; once the imperial gardens that had incorporated Mi's garden had been destroyed, the land became part of the Yenching University campus before being transferred to its present occupant in the early 1950s. The name of Mi's garden has been given to the foreign students' dormitory complex of Peking University.

In the 1930s, a scroll painting of the garden surfaced in Tianjin, attributed to Mi Wanzhong himself and dated 1617. Research has shown that this scroll is, in fact, a close copy of a painting of the garden done by the artist Wu Bin (fl. 1583–1626) in 1615 and entitled "Spring Lustration at Ladle Garden."[229]

"On Mi Wanzhong's Ladle Garden"

Having just left the imperial city,
The grasses and trees are welcoming, the rocks all riotous.
A string of pavilions and terraces, endless roaming,
A river with an islet, swirling waters all around it.
Kingfishers minute, on the backs of cranes, soar toward the celestial mirror,
Gold-dusted clouds with waists, showing off the Buddha's girdle ornament.
While dreaming of Jiangnan, I am really already there,
Children of Wu singing to the beat, setting off autumn boats.

Pavilions and halls of the Mi residence are scenic spots west of the capital,
Scenic in that its waters seem to rest unexpectedly upon a patched plain.
Winding constructions with pillared rooms, their doors tightly shut;[230]
Punting a boat to a floating house, the plaques are hard to name.
Lotus blossoms enjoying the rain seem like sand-toads croaking,

---

229   For a detailed study of the garden and of Wu Bin's painting, see Philip K. Hu, "The Shao Garden of Mi Wanzhong (1570–1628): Revisiting a Late Ming Landscape through Visual and Literary Sources," *Studies in the History of Gardens and Designed Landscapes* 19, no. 3–4 (1999):314–42.

230   "Pillared rooms" here alludes to the Epang Palace built by the First Emperor of Qin.

Willows swayed by spirited winds are like jade bridles whipping.
Very soon the azure mountains can be seen from my horizontal pillow,
Leaving a fine night, I accompany ducks and widgeons in my dreams.

A ladleful of water from Ladle Garden is like the waves on the Five Lakes,
Mountains and clouds soaked through and through, dripping many emeralds.
The home is on the Hao while the owner is on the Pu,
Boats stored within ravines, roads kept within rivers.
Egrets and phoenix share the remnants of an otter for their evening meal,
Water-chestnuts and prickly water lily, newly appeared, make the old lotus jealous.
Already I have seen all the fine implements of the gentlemen of this dwelling,
If only I can be spared the spring showers, lodged above like a vast rain-clock.

Onions flourishing from a village's muddy water are from Tian An;
Cranes buried at Tuqiu welcome those in huts for retirement.[231]
The shadows of speckled-bamboo interlock like cold jades on a couch,
Rippling lotuses release a hidden scent, punctuating the morning meal.
With the coming of clouds, father and son compete to put color on the hills,
Guests, with Su and Huang, help to rescue an inkstone from billowing waves.[232]
I bring a calf into the sun to amuse the gentleman; he laughs about his suffering,
Saying, as always, "Do not admire those following the footsteps of Handan."[233]

"Record of Sightseeing in Ladle Garden" (*You Shaoyuan ji* 遊勺園記)

SUN GUOMI 孫國秘 (1582–1648)

TRANSLATED BY PHILIP K. HU

The calligrapher Sun Guomi, whose account of his visit to Ladle Garden (below), was included in Zheng Yuanxun's *Literary Pastimes from the Pavilion of Seductive Tranquility*, wrote a book on Beijing, entitled *A Touring Guide to the Capital of Yan*, now no longer extant.

---

231 Tian An is the Chinese name of a temple in Kapilavastu, ancient India (now in southern Nepal), where the Sakyamuni Buddha was born. Tuqiu was the name of a village in the State of Lu, south of present-day Liangfu county, near Mount Tai, in Shandong Province; it was known as a place of reclusion, where people went to grow old and die. This term is also used, by extension, to indicate any such place.

232 This couplet suggests a scenario involving calligraphy and painting, water being the base element with which ink and colors are ground for application. The invocation of the great Northern Song literati Su Shi (1037–1101) and Huang Tingjian (1045–1105) implies that the guests present on this occasion are distinguished practitioners of calligraphy.

233 Handan is the name of a number of historical places, but the usage here alludes to a story from the "Autumn Floods" (*Qiushui* 秋水) chapter of the *Zhuangzi*, in which those who follow others in studying at Handan (i.e., walking the "Handan Walk") would lose all their previous knowledge and all sense of originality.

"Record of Sightseeing in Ladle Garden"

After a stay of ten days at the Profound Garden, the Rain God suddenly sprinkled the paths; though it was the fourth month, it felt like autumn. My friend the clerk Xichen said, "Why don't we make a plan to visit Ladle Garden?" Thereupon I agreed with his scheme and we set out on horses from the Xizhi Gate, riding under the green shade of myriad trees, which are not inferior to those seen along the Shanyin road. Shortly afterward, we reached the site of the gentleman Mi Wanzhong's wide-open farmland. And a little while after that, we arrived at the burial mound of the gentleman's father, where Xichen and I paid our respects.[234] Several paces to the west of the gravesite is Ladle Garden.

The road leading into the garden has a gateway which announces: Village of Wind and Mist. Within the lane, rocks are scattered about or piled up, lining the dyke and shaded by tall willows. Turning to the south, there is yet another dyke, from which a perilous bridge rises up like a cloud, allowing visitors an initial survey of the scenic spots within the garden and rewarding some of their curiosity. It is called the Bridge of Tasseled Clouds after what Buddhist texts refer to as "tassels connecting clouds of color"; the calligraphy used on the tablet is that of Su Shi. Directly across the bridge is a screen-like wall and the inscribed stone on the wall reads: Shore of Sparrows, with the calligraphy of Huang Tingjian. Turning north from the bridge is a plaque over a gateway—the Bank of Refined Waters, written in the spirit writing of Lü Dongbin.

Within the gate, there seems to be nothing but water; the first structure straddling the pond is called the Barge of Tranquility. To its west a mound swells up; all around it are pines and junipers, whose green needles would dip into the pond during winter, with a plaque naming it as Wind in the Pines and Moon over Water. The knoll terminates abruptly and a bridge is placed there—the nine-segment Meandering Bridge, with a calligraphic name-board written by the gentleman Mi Wanzhong, master of the garden. Across this bridge toward the north is the Hall of Ladle Lake, with the seal-script calligraphy of Wu Bin gracing its plaque. In front of the hall rests an ancient rock with a young juniper leaning against it.[235] To the right of this is a winding veranda whose outer and inner sides feature a suite of rooms sitting aside the water. Without having entered the garden, the sound of its especially made creaking floorboards can already be heard. To the south there is a structure shaped like a barge and known as the

234 According to the inscription of Mi Wanzhong's father's epitaph, composed by the Hanlin Academician Huang Hui (*jinshi* of 1589), Mi Yu personally selected this site as his burial place, based on the time-honored practice of divination. The epitaph was excavated in the summer of 1929 near the Yannan Garden on the grounds of Yenching University, now the campus of Peking University.

235 Sun Guomi seems mistaken here; both Wu Bin's painting of the garden and all other textual accounts indicate that the tree here was a *wutong* 梧桐 (*Firmiana simplex*, *F. platanifolia*, *Sterculia platanofolia*), commonly known as the Chinese parasol tree, valued for the shade-providing qualities of its dense foliage.

Leaf of the Great Monad; it is entirely surrounded by white lotus blossoms.[236] Walking amid bamboo southeast from the Leaf of the Great Monad, one comes across a stone tablet marked "Bamboo at Water's Edge." It is hard enough to procure water for the gardens and villas of the capital, Yanjing; getting bamboo to flourish is all the more difficult. In the midst of the bamboo a tall tower rises out from a myriad jades; it is called the Tower of Luxuriant Azure Foliage and its name-board bears the calligraphy of Zou Diguang [d. 1626]. Ascending this pavilion is like painting a portrait of the whole garden; when gazing down at lotus leaves floating on the water's surface, one is made to think of nine tiers of the lotus terrace.[237] Furthermore, to gaze leisurely at the Western Hills from the treetops is like getting a breath of fresh air, so completely satisfying that one would lift up his writing tablets to the clouds.[238]

Turning north from the pavilion, one arrives at a stretch of water without bridges. But the root-trunks of ancient trees form a connected chain along the water's edge, so that it is possible to reach the Leaf of the Great Monad; this is known as the Crossing of Hewn Trees, with the same name-board also written out by the master of the garden. Going east from the pavilion, one of the paths is like the backbone of a fish, and going up orderly steps is a ridge of pines. Of the pairs of rocks shaped like bamboo shoots, one towers above the others. As one meanders downward and turns toward the north, there is a gazebo by the water with a thatched roof. Though it is positioned directly across from the Barge of Tranquility, they are not interconnected. The water beneath the gazebo is virtually green from all the aquatic grasses bobbing in its depths; they prevent lotus leaves from creeping in, so that the sound of the masses of fish splashing about may be heard there.[239] From here we go back to the winding veranda, where there is another side room. Its ceiling has a linear opening through which light floods in, like seeing the sky through a split in a grotto. Up a flight of stairs is a vast terrace, with no hint that there is a living space underneath, or that there are lotuses "supporting" it from below. Descending the terrace one comes into the winding veranda, which is like a conch skimming the water's surface, before proceeding to the very last hall, which is aligned with the Hall of Ladle Lake. Again it is lotus-filled water that separates them,

---

236 The lotus (*padma* in Sanskrit; principal varieties being *Nelumbo nucifera* and *Nelumbium speciosum*) is the supreme flower of Buddhism, its blossoms symbolizing purity rising out from and above the mud of the world. The white lotus (*pundarika* in Sanskrit) represents *bodhi*, the state of absolute mental purity, spiritual perfection, and pacification of human nature. The *bailianhua* 白蓮花 here may also be the white water lily (*Nymphaea alba*).

237 A Buddhist reference to the nine tiers of the lotus terrace reserved for *bodhisattvas*.

238 This sentence alludes to the practice of holding up the writing tablet (an emblem of official service) as an indication of pleasure when cool breezes blow in from the western hills.

239 The aquatic grass (*zao* 藻, also *shuizao* 水藻) noted here is the Eurasian watermilfoil (*Myriophyllum spicatum*), a fast-growing species with reddish to brown stems, olive-green leaves and spikes of white flowers found in the axils of leaflike bracts. The fish, judging from their appearance as several pinkish-orange schools in Wu Bin's paintings, would have included goldfish and carp.

and though they face each other across a short distance there is no physical connection. On opening the north windows at the rear of this hall, a thousand *qing* of paddy fields come into view, so vast that no sentry guardposts at the outer edges of the fields are to be seen. Within this place one can hear the calls of the cuckoos responding to the songs of the farmers. Can it be because the gentleman himself, Mi Wanzhong, has now returned to grow old here that his land is being cultivated?

From this place we now return to the Hall of Ladle Lake. To its east is the gazebo by the water, and to the east of the gazebo is a small dyke that goes by a pavilion in which there is a deep, clear spring. In ancient times, the Jade Well sprang forth from a hundred feet of lotuses at Mount Hua, the Western Marchmount; this well is also contained within a lotus—is this not strange indeed! Southward from the pavilion is the Pool of the Brilliant Moon; it is housed within a structure. Both the pool and the window frames around it are shaped like the crescent moon.[240] South of the pool is a bathhouse whose plaque on the clerestory reads "Vaporous Clouds." Although its placement is on an axis with the Barge of Tranquillity, there is no through passage between them. As it were, there are all sorts of places which are not connectable, such as the water where lotuses seem to send out a hundred veins and through which nothing can pass. The lotus-covered waters are all topped with shadows of willowy lines, and the sounds of yellow orioles herald the coming of dawn to one's pillow, singing all the way till dusk. When have they ever changed the rhymed compositions of Jiangnan?

For the most part the garden's halls, belvederes, pavilions, kiosks and barge-like studio are well thought-out and are like large and small islands in the waters of a vast sea. There is no veranda which does not have creaking floorboards, no structure which does not float like jade, no path which does not drift like a raft. Do these not assure that Ladle Garden will become the center of Haidian? Within the garden there is no water without lotuses; outside the garden, the Western Hills are layered like mountains of lotuses. Do you not find its scenic spots really so? I have heard that the gentleman created the Ladle Garden by excavating ponds in order to improve the shape of the sandy mound around his father's grave. And so he spent his mourning period in the garden while still dwelling in a hut by the grave. From now on, he should really compose his own "Rhapsody on Fulfilling One's Natural Bent toward Reclusion!"[241]

---

240 The Pool of the Brilliant Moon was enclosed in the one-story rectangular hipped-roof structure due south of the Leaf of the Great Monad and separated from it by an open terrace. An awning stretched across the entire length of its eastern side. It was connected to the Hall of Ladle Lake via the Crossing of Hewn Trees. The crescent-moon shapes of the pool and window frames cannot be discerned from the angle of representation of the visual evidence.

241 The scholar-official and poet Sun Chuo (314–371) of the Eastern Jin dynasty composed a famous rhapsody with this title (*Sui chu fu* 遂初賦, which can also be translated as "Rhapsody on Following One's Original Intention"), celebrating the joys of retirement from official service.

On this rainy afternoon, sharing a meal with Xichen in the Leaf of the Great Monad, listening to the sound of pearly drops splashing on lotus leaves, I am very happy and thus dashed off this "Record."

Treatise on Superfluous Things (*Zhangwu zhi* 長物志)

"Rooms and Retreats" (*Shi lu* 室廬; extracts) and "Water and Rocks" (*Shui shi* 水石; extracts)

WEN ZHENHENG 文震亨 (1585–1645)
TRANSLATED BY DUNCAN M. CAMPBELL

The calligrapher and noted *qin* player Wen Zhenheng, a great-great grandson of Wen Zhengming, owned a fabulous garden in the northwest corner of his hometown of Suzhou, called Fragrant Grasses Hillock. Wen, who in 1645 chose to starve himself to death rather than accept the newly established Manchu Qing dynasty, was the editor of one the most important of the manuals of taste that so embody the various social and economic tensions of the age, the *Treatise on Superfluous Things*, compiled with the help of numerous important literary and artistic figures probably between 1615 and 1620 and published soon thereafter. Divided into twelve chapters covering in turn the most important aspects of the physical fabric of the late Ming world ("Rooms and Retreats," "Flowers and Trees," "Water and Rocks," "Birds and Fish," "Calligraphy and Painting," "Tables and Couches," "Vessels and Utensils," "Clothing and Adornment," "Boats and Carriages," "Placing and Arrangement," "Vegetables and Fruits," and "Incense and Teas"), Wen's book is the focus of the art historian Craig Clunas's remarkable *Superfluous Things: Material Culture and Social Status in Early Modern China*.

"Rooms and Retreats" (extracts)

Best of all is to live amid the mountains and rivers themselves; to live in a village is next best; and to live in the suburbs is next best again. Men of my sort are not able to take refuge along cliff tops or within the valleys in imitation of Yili Ji or Dongyuan Gong, those recluses of old, but rather are required to sink into and thus to besmirch ourselves amid the dust of the marketplaces. Therefore, our courtyards need to be elegant and pure, our rooms clean and quiet, for pavilions and terraces embody the desires of the untrammelled, studios and belvederes the refinement of the tranquil. And one should plant within this courtyard fine trees and strange bamboos, and lay out one's inscribed bronzes and stelae, one's books and charts. Such circumstances bring, to those who dwell within them, a forgetfulness about impending old age, to those who sojourn here, a forgetfulness about the need to depart, and, to those who visit, a forgetfulness of their weariness. When the summer air is oppressive and heavy, such a place will serve to refresh; during the bitter winter months, the place will keep one warm and cozy. Elaborate buildings with their lavish and gaudy paintwork are really little more than shackles around the feet, cages for the body.

Mountain Studios

These should be bright and clean, but never too large: whereas a studio that is bright and clean can enliven the spirit, one that is too large will tax one's eyesight. A window should be situated under the eaves, or the studio should be accessible along a gallery, in accordance with the actual lie of the land. The central courtyard needs to be rather large, in order that one may plant trees and flowers within it, or array one's bonsai. During the summer months, the north-facing doors should be removed in order to ensure the circulation of air. The soil in the courtyard should be replenished by sprinkling it with the water used for boiling the rice and in the crevices where the rainwater accumulates, moss should be allowed to grow, lovable in its speckled greenness. All around the stone steps one may plant peacock spikemoss, so that it covers the ground, both lush and so vividly green as to be about to float away. The wall in the front of the studio should be low. Some people bind branches of creeping fig together at the foot of the wall, sprinkling the wall with slops from the kitchen to encourage the plant to spread, and although this has its own beauty, it is actually far better just to plaster the wall.

"Water and Rocks" (extracts)

Rocks lend one a sense of great antiquity; water sets one's thoughts roving afar. No garden can do without water and rocks. The water must circle around a soaring peak. This soaring peak must be positioned to perfection. In this way, that single peak can conjure up the majestic expanse of the Western Marchmount, and a ladleful of water may embody the power of the rivers and lakes of ten thousand *li*. In addition, required also are tall bamboos and old trees, strange creepers and gnarled shrubs, here entangled, there jutting out all alone, aged cliffs and blue-green creeks, surging springs and raging torrents, all as if one finds oneself within some distant mountain recess or isolated gully. Then can the place be regarded as a site both of splendor and of fame.

Large Ponds

Ponds can be excavated to the size of a single *mu* or a hundred times as large, the bigger the better. In the largest of them, one can site platforms and gazebos and so on, or divide the pond with a dyke, and plant it in sweet flag and common reed stretching out in an endless expanse. Such a pond is worthy of the name "Giant Soak." If the pond needs embellishment, then the banks can be paved with patterned rocks or the pond can be encircled with crimson balustrades. Most to be avoided is leaving mounds of earth jutting up within the pond, in the shape of what, vulgarly, are referred to as a "Battling Fish Heap," or designed to resemble mounts Jin and Jiao found in the Yangtze River. Plant weeping willow beside the pond, but never either peach or apricot trees. Wild ducks and geese can be raised here, but will only lend the pond an air of liveliness if they number in their several dozen. At the widest point of the pond one may site a water pavilion, but it must be as fine as those depicted in paintings. Huts on stilts are to be avoided. Along the banks, lotus flowers may be planted, hemmed in with woven bamboo barriers, for they must not be allowed to spread. Having the lotus leaves cover the entire surface of the pond is to be avoided, lest one cannot enjoy the color of the water.

Small Ponds

Excavate a small pond in front of the steps or beside the rocks. The pond should be completely surrounded by lake rocks, and the spring water must be clear enough for one to be able to see the bottom of the pond. In the pond goldfish may be raised, swimming playfully amid the aquatic grasses. On all four sides, wild creepers will be planted, along with fine bamboos, and where the land can be excavated to some depth, the pond should be connected to the spring by a channel. Square, round, and octagonal shaped ponds are most to be avoided.

Waterfalls

Living in the mountains, it is easy enough to create a waterfall by channeling a spring so that its flow drops from a height. If you want a waterfall in your garden, however, you will need to split some bamboo poles, both long and short, hollow them out and arrange them like guttering so that they catch the water from the eaves, before flowing discreetly into a large storage vat. Cut stone steps into the bank, below which excavate a small pond to catch the water, studded with rocks jutting up here and there. Now, whenever it rains, you can have your own raging waterfall, its gurgling sound adding to the novelty of your garden. This is most appropriately done amid some pines or below a clump of bamboo, so that the waterfall is half-hidden by the vivid greenness—a truly wonderful sight. One can also store water at the top of a hillock, releasing the sluice-gate whenever a visitor turns up, so that the water pours down, as if from nowhere. But better by far the first method I suggest above, for although this too is the result of the efforts of man, it more closely approximates the workings of nature.

"Spring Rain" (*Chunyu* 春雨)

FANG WEIYI 方維儀 (1585–1668)
TRANSLATED BY PAULA VARSANO

Despite her advantages of birth—she was born into a distinguished lineage in Tongcheng (in present-day Anhui Province)—Fang Zhongxian, better known by her social name Fang Weiyi, had a less than ideal life. Widowed very young, she returned permanently to her natal family and helped to bring up her nephew, who became the famous philosopher Fang Yizhi (1611–1671). Some of her poems show an interest in social problems and current affairs, an interest evidently shared with her nephew. In addition to writing her own poems, she also edited the work of others, wrote literary criticism, and was a painter and calligrapher.

"Spring Rain"

Along the springtime river, new rain reaches my western window,
Clouds darken the mountain light, the distant trees are lost.
Scattered showers of pear blossoms in never-ending flight,
In the old garden that must be a partridge calling.

"Palace Songs" (*Gongci* 宮詞; no. 7)

GU RUOPU 顧若璞 (1592–CA. 1681)
TRANSLATED BY MAUREEN ROBERTSON

The studious daughter of a distinguished scholar-official family in Hangzhou, Gu was widowed young. She devoted herself to literary study and to the education of her two sons, her nieces, and her grandchildren, gaining a reputation for her virtuous character as well as for her learning and literary talent. She was responsible for setting up the Banana Garden Poetry Club, an important group of women poets (see the introduction to chapter 8). Gu was recognized as the leading woman poet of Hangzhou in her time, and continued to write into advanced old age.

"Palace Songs" (no. 7)

In early spring she steals out
     for a romp in the imperial garden,
Chasing the yellow orioles,
     kicking a bright red cloth ball.
When she goes, misbehaving,
     into a thicket of flowers,
          no-one knows—
Her peals of laughter
     carry to the high, red-walled residence.

"Footnotes to Allegory Mountain" (*Yushan zhu* 寓山注)

QI BIAOJIA 祁彪佳 (1603–1645)
TRANSLATED BY DUNCAN M. CAMPBELL

Qi Biaojia, from a distinguished and wealthy family of Shanyin (present-day Shaoxing, in Zhejiang Province) passed the highest level of the government examinations at the remarkably young age of twenty. Nicknamed the "baby official" by the clerks at his first posting, he impressed all who knew him as an outstandingly effective administrator. Tiring of the factionalism that bedevilled the late Ming court and government, he took the opportunity offered by ill-health and the need to care for his aging mother to return home to Shanyin, where he developed a piece of family-owned land outside the city as his Allegory Mountain garden. Yushan or Yu Hill was the existing name of the hill on which the garden was constructed; the word *yu* can mean "to lodge," but in a literary context it can also mean something the writer or reader sees their feelings lodged or reflected in, thus an allegory.

The diary Qi kept every day for the last few years of his life is full of fascinating details about the process of constructing his garden and how it was used by members of his extended family. It was frequently the site of operatic performances; Qi was a widely respected expert in drama criticism and titled his publications on the subject after his Hall of the Distant Mountains. At the same time, despite being officially on leave, he was closely involved in all manner of public activities, interceding with the magistrate on behalf of local taxpayers, setting up charitable pharmacies during an epidemic, attending seminars on philosophy, hosting meetings of a Buddhist society in his garden, and much else.

Qi returned to a senior position under the Southern Ming regime in 1644, but soon found himself unable to overcome the worsening factionalism among officials, and retired again to his home. After the Qing conquest of Jiangnan, he took his own life and was buried in the garden to which he had devoted so much time and care.

"Footnotes to Allegory Mountain"

Brief Introduction

My home is in Mei Fu's Village of the Superior Man,[242] that is, along the Shanyin road.[243] Here I am surrounded by solitary isles such as that of Fang Gang[244] and half bays like that once owned by Censor He Zhizhang.[245] All that I have taken possession of myself, however, is the tiny hillock that stands besides my home, as if by virtue of a fate predestined me. Its name is "Allegory Mountain."

When I was still a little boy my brother Jichao and my cousin Zhixiang obtained this hill in exchange for a bushel of millet. They cleared it of stone and planted it in pine, hewing the land and humping away the stones until their hands were callused and their feet blistered. I too, at that time, would pole my way here by small boat, often to play games in the mud.

---

242   Mei Fu served as an official during the last years of the Western Han dynasty. Legend has it that when his advice was ignored and the dynasty fell, he became a recluse and settled near Guiji in Zhejiang.

243   The Shanyin Circuit, the area surrounding present-day Shaoxing in Zhejiang Province, is famed for its natural beauty. This is found most famously expressed by Wang Xianzhi in the *A New Account of Tales of the World*, as found in chapter 1.

244   Fang Gang, a poet of the Tang dynasty, became a recluse after being unsuccessful in the imperial civil service examinations. He settled on an island in the middle of Mirror Lake, not far from Guiji.

245   He Zhizhang (659–744) was also a poet of the Tang dynasty, but a successful official as well. In old age, He Zhizhang retired to his home beside Mirror Lake, where he was given a plot of land by the emperor.

More than twenty years on, the pines have grown tall and the rocks, now weathered, have acquired the patina of age. All of a sudden, my brother Jichao decided to renounce the world and took tonsure as a Buddhist monk. Zhixiang, for his part, constructed Axe-Haft Garden to serve as his retreat from officialdom. He gave over the southern slopes of the mountain in order that a pagoda be built to commemorate Master Mailang, while the remainder of the site was left fallow, to revert to dense and overgrown vegetation. Having myself retired from office as the consequence of ill health, I happened past this place and the scenes and emotions of twenty years ago came flooding back into my mind's eye. As soon as the idea of building myself a garden had formed itself in my mind, moreover, it seemed to acquire an urgency all of its own and there was no putting a stop to my urge. What follows, then, is a complete account of the creation of my garden.

When the project began, all I desired were four or five structures. But guests came by to pay their calls upon me there and, pointing this way and that, they declared: "Here you should site a pavilion" or "This site is perfect for a gazebo." I was unmoved by their comments, objecting in my mind that this was not at all in keeping with my own original intentions. After another turn or two through my estate however, unconsciously, I found myself most discomforted to discover that their words had taken possession of my soul. Yes, indeed, I could not be without that pavilion there or this gazebo here. And before one stage of construction was completed, I found new ideas and novel conceptions occurring to me at every turn. Whenever I came to the end of a path or trod upon a dangerous track, I would tax my mind to come up with unexpected conceits as if heavenly inspired, to the extent that I would continue to do so even in my dreams. Thus, as my enthusiasm for the project was roused, so too did my fascination for it grow more intense. I would set off there at the crack of dawn to return only as the sun was setting. The various bothersome family affairs that I was obliged to deal with I would now do so only once the candles had been lit. Impatiently I would lie upon my pillow waiting for the dawn to shoot forth its first tongues of light, whereupon I would order the serving lads to make ready my boat and set off, wishing all the time that the three *li* we had to cover to get to the site were but a single step away. I was heedless of the extreme cold or the scorching heat, the goose bumps on my flesh or the sweat that ran down my spine. Not even the most violent of storms could deter me from setting off in my boat each morning. When groping around at the head of my bed at night and finding that my cash reserve was exhausted, a sense of desolation would come over me. Yet the moment I reached the mountain again the next day and began to wander about I would worry that the rocks I had bought and the timber I had stored away were yet insufficient for the task at hand. Thus have I emptied my purse these past two years. I have fallen ill and then recovered; having recovered I have fallen ill again. This then is an account of my crazy obsession with the creation of my garden.

The garden encompasses three sides of the mountain as well as the ten or so *mu* of flat land surrounding it. Half of this area is taken up by water and rock, the other half with buildings and trees and plants. The garden contains two halls, three pavilions, four galleries, two terraces and an equal number of belvederes, as well as three dykes. As for the various studies and studios and suchlike structures, each is exquisite in its own manner of seclusion or capaciousness, the adytum and the hermitages are all differently shaped, either small and constricted or wide and expansive, while the chambers and mountain cottages and so on are all sited on different levels of the mountain side. The bridges and gazebos, paths and peaks are dotted here and there, forming a rhythm with their wave-like contours. In general terms, therefore, what was once empty has been given solidity, that which was originally solid has been rendered empty, the gathered has been dispersed, the dispersed gathered, the precipitous levelled and the level made precipitous. Like the skilled physic, I have prescribed potions with both restorative and purgative properties; like an able general, I have deployed my troops in formations designed both for frontal attack and for ambush; as an Old Master, my every brushstroke has brought life to my painting; and as a famous poet, my every line is tuneful. This then is an account of the structures contained within the garden that I have created.

Construction of my garden began during the mid-winter of the *yihai* year [1635] and by early spring of the succeeding *bingzi* year [1636], the thatched cottage had been completed and the various studies and studios were beginning to take shape. By the mid-summer of that year, construction had commenced again, first of the gazebos, to be followed by the belvederes, this stage of the project being completed with the construction of the mountain hut. By this time, both the mountaintop and the land all around had been graven into shape and my sole cause for dissatisfaction lay in the fact that when one arrived at the garden by punt, no passage led into my garden from the riverbank. And so did dredging and channelling work begin anew. From the eleventh month until the spring of the *dingchou* year [1637], it was a full one hundred days before irregular ponds flowed beneath my window, breeze-borne spray dampened my side tables, the vermilion balustrades were found reflected in the deep green water and the stream, turned a rosy red by the setting sun, meandered its way into the verdant valley. Only then was my garden worthy of its name. And yet, my horticulturalist's urge proved not yet sated and so I brought the construction of my garden to a halt with the Abundance Mains and the Bin Potager.[246] By then, it was already the thirteenth day of

---

246 Poem 250 of the *Book of Songs* reads: "Stalwart was Liu the Duke. / In his lands broad and long / He noted the shadows and the height of the hills, / Which parts were in the shade, which in the sun, / Viewed the streams and the springs. / To his army in three divisions / He allotted the low lands and the high, / Tithed the fields that there might be due provision, / Reckoning the evening sunlight, / And took possession of his home in Bin." See Arthur Waley, trans., *The Book of Songs*, 245–46; transliteration altered. Liu the Duke was understood to be the great-grandson of Hou Ji, reputedly the Minister of Agriculture under the Emperor Shun and later a sort of Chinese "God of Agriculture."

the fourth month, the very height of summer. My Eight Principles of Book Acquisition Library, Thatched Belvedere of the Brook and the Hill, the Jar Hideaway and so on were all worked upon at odd moments whenever there was time from other tasks and there is no record of the exact dates of their completion. This then is the chronology of the creation of my garden.

As to the beauty of the hills and streams beyond my garden, this region has long been celebrated for its "Thousand cliffs and myriad torrents,"[247] while the profuseness of the trees and plants growing within my garden is not restricted to the proverbial "Seven Pines and Five Willows."[248] The vistas of all four seasons are here to be enjoyed, as one drifts in a boat beneath the moon and in a gentle breeze. Within these "Three Paths"[249] one can summon the clouds and become drunk in the snow. Here, the refined man may feast his eyes, while the recluse, for his part, may find a haven for his soul. But such things I need not enumerate.

Water Bright Walkway
Although my garden conceals within itself a mountain, paradoxically the aspect of the garden most to be valued is to be found in the water that flows through it. When one arrives at the garden by boat one assumes that the water has fully played its part. But then, by the time one has made one's way along the walkway to the west, running alongside Asymmetric Pond with its deep clear water before winding its way beyond the green forest, both master and guest look as if they have traveled here from the Kingdom of Aquamarine; their beards and eyebrows drip and their clothes are drenched. The scene brings to mind that couplet of old Du Fu's from his poem "Moon" that goes:

> At fourth watch the mountains disgorge the moon,
> The waning night brightens my water tower.

Although, in this case, a walkway serves in the stead of Du Fu's tower, I'm not at all sure that he wouldn't nod his approval.

---

247 *A New Account of Tales of the World* contains the following anecdote about the famous painter Gu Kaizhi (ca. 44–ca. 406): "When Gu Kaizhi returned to Jiangling from Guiji, people asked him about the beauty of its hills and streams. Gu replied: 'A thousand cliffs competed to stand tall, / A myriad torrents vied in flowing. / Grasses and trees obscured the heights / Like vapors raising misty shrouds.'" See Liu I-ch'ing, *Shih-shuo Hsin-yü*, 70, transliteration altered.

248 "Seven Pines and Five Willows" is a metonymy for the recluse, the seven pines being associated with Zheng Xun of the Tang dynasty, and the five willows with that quintessential Chinese recluse, the poet Tao Qian.

249 "Three Paths," too, is a metonymy for the residence of the recluse, as found in the lines from Tao Qian's poem "Returning Home": "Overgrown with weeds, the three paths almost disappear, / Yet the pines and chrysanthemums remain." Editor's note: this poem appears in chapter 1 as "Homeward Bound," where these lines are translated as "Grass has overgrown the paths / But the pines and chrysanthemums are still there."

Abode for Studying the *Book of Changes*

Of the many fine features of Allegory Garden it is the rocks that prove most excellent, but it is not the rocks alone that constitute the excellence of the garden. Once a rock is placed in the midst of water, even the most recalcitrant of them seems to acquire a divine intelligence. And it is only from my Abode for Studying the *Book of Changes* that this perfect marriage between rock and water can be observed to full advantage.[250] The abode overlooks the eastern corner of Asymmetrical Pond and stands across the water from the Hall of My Four Unfulfilled Obligations. As one raises one's eyes upward or stares downward, the sky and the pond present a seamless flow of purity and one feels a profound affinity for the birds and fishes.[251] When along the bank the lamps are lit, their inverted reflections dance enticingly upon the surface of the water, and when the strings and flutes strike up, their tunes seem driven across the surface of the pond like waves of snow. It is at times such as this that I feel the scene before me to have been Heaven sent. And when the master of the garden becomes wearied of the sights of his garden he spends his days with a copy of the *Book of Changes* in hand; painstakingly he works through the text, achieving in the process a sense of release from the vexations of life. Although my family has specialized in the exegesis of this classic for generations, I am as yet incapable of fully understanding its principles of change. I have managed to develop an inkling of the Way of waxing and waning, however, of the ebb and flow of the cosmos. This mountain has existed for as long as Heaven and Earth themselves. Before the present moment, it was no more than a tiny mound of earth. How can one guarantee that, sometime in the future, these arrayed pavilions and storied studios will stand tall yet upon these sheer cliffs and here within this secluded valley? Nothing is spared Heaven and Earth's determination of its fate. How silly of Li Deyu of the Tang dynasty who, when demoted and in exile in Red Cliff in Canton, wrote to his sons so assiduously, instructing them to seek to preserve every stone and every leaf of his Peaceful Springs Garden. Had he forgotten of the fate of the Golden Valley and Flowery Grove gardens? Where are they today? And thus does the master have an inkling of the truth, taking joy in those pleasures afforded us in this present life and caring not a jot for what might become of this garden in the future.

---

250   This alludes to a passage from *A New Account of Tales of the World* that, in Mather's translation (402; transliteration altered), goes: "When Sun Chu was young he wanted to become a recluse. Speaking of it once to Wang Ji, he intended to say, 'I'll pillow my head on the rocks and rinse my mouth in the streams.' Instead, he said by mistake, 'I'll rinse my mouth with rocks and pillow my head on the streams.' Wang asked, 'Are streams something you can pillow on, and rocks something you can rinse with?' Sun replied, 'My reason for pillowing on streams is to wash my ears, and my reason for rinsing with rocks is to sharpen my teeth.'"

251   This appears to be a conflation of two allusions; the first to a passage from the "The Great Treatise" attached to the *Book of Changes* that goes: "Looking upward, we contemplate with its help the signs in the heavens; looking down, we examine the lines of the earth. Thus we come to know the circumstances of the dark and the light. Going back to the beginnings of things and pursuing them to the end, we come to know the lessons of birth and of death." (*The I Ching or Book of Changes*, the Richard Wilhelm translation, rendered into English by Cary F. Baynes, 294); the second is from the "Autumn Floods" chapter of the *Zhuangzi* given in chapter 1.

Canopy of the Inhaling Rainbow

When one quits the Abode for Studying the *Book of Changes*, there where the walkway comes to an end one finds a canopy. It is encircled by an expanse of water that rages and foams. Whenever the lotus buds burst into flower, the Treading on Fragrance Embankment, looked at from afar, appears like a rainbow curving down to drink from the sea, bearing along with it a myriad silken skeins of roseate cloud that disappear in and out of the waves. My friend the Grand Historian Ni Yuanlu [1594–1644] named it Canopy of the Inhaling Rainbow for this reason.

Relinquished to the Terns Pond

As a mountain, Allegory is adept at concealing its height within what is low-lying, at making its distance appear as if close at hand. And just as the garden is extensive enough to hoard the mountain, so too is this pond large enough to nourish it. To the south, the pond curves around Water Bright Walkway, while in the north it disappears into Abundance Mains. Treading on Fragrance Embankment leads into its center, and the Listening Stops Bridge serves as the point of confluence for the flowing currents. When a gentle breeze wafts across the limpid water and the fine ripples begin to weave their patterns, the mountain peaks find themselves reflected upon the surface of the water and it is as if the Three Immortal Isles[252] have been upturned into the pond. When the slanting rays of the setting sun become a confused tangle amid the reeds and water-pepper, spouts of molten gold or soaring shards of jade, in whatever direction one gazes, the pond appears to have no bounds. This then, I realize, is a manifestation of the very hue of Heaven itself. The Master of the Garden calls this joy indeed. But I can never aspire to be like the light terns that satiate themselves within its luminous waves, for they seem as one with the pond when it is as calm as a pure expanse of silken snow or billowing like the scudding clouds.[253] I realize that even Zhuangzi's thoughts, as he stood above the Rivers Hao and Pu, were not without the impurity of ulterior motive. This is precisely why the Master of the Garden dares not lay claim to the pond for himself but rather relinquishes it to the terns. In doing so, however, he fears that the terns will suspect his motives and may well not accept his gift.

---

252   As recorded in the Han historian Sima Qian's *Records of the Grand Historian,* the Three Immortal Isles were Penglai, Fangzhang, and Yingzhou.

253   The allusion here is to a story from the "Yellow Emperor" chapter of the *Liezi*, which, in A. C. Graham's translation, reads: "There was a man living by the sea-shore who loved seagulls. Every morning he went down to the sea to roam with the seagulls, and more birds came to him than you could count in hundreds. His father said to him: 'I hear the seagulls all come roaming with you. Bring me some to play with.' Next day, when he went down to the sea, the seagulls danced above him and would not come down. Therefore it is said: 'The utmost in speech is to be rid of speech, the utmost doing is Doing Nothing.' What common knowledge knows is shallow." (See A. C. Graham, trans., *The Book of Lieh-tzu,* 45–46).

Treading on Fragrance Embankment

The outer embankment of the garden is called Willow Pathway, the inner one Treading on Fragrance. Treading on Fragrance Embankment is the means by which one may make one's way from the Canopy of the Inhaling Rainbow across the pond to the Terrace of the Floating Reflections. The two halves of the pond mirror each other, while the embankment dissects the water like a skein of silk, both sides of it lined with newly planted scholar trees swaying in the sunlight. With the arrival of the spring, young beauties dance and sing in rows here, their shoes leaving delicate traces upon the moss, and their sweet sweat mingling with the breath of the flowers. I dare not compare this with the famed Six Bridges of West Lake, but at least it partakes of the beauty of a corner of Mirror Lake.

Terrace of the Floating Reflections

When one stands upon Treading on Fragrance Embankment and gazes into the distance, one can make out the vague shape of a terrace, positioned in mid-water. Across the deep translucent water, turned blue-green by the rays of the moon, one can reach it. Whenever the Metal Toad in the moon raises a swell upon the surface of the pond and the red cliffs seem surrounded by the pure clear water, the terrace disappears one moment only to reappear the next, as if floating between the ripples of the mist and the white crested waves. All around, the stems of a thousand lotuses jut up, as imposing as a Lotus Throne itself, surging into flower to create the Pure Land. The *Footnotes to the Classic of the Waterways* contains the line: "The encircling peaks observe each other, the solitary reflection seems to be afloat." This line presents an exact description of the present scene.

Listening Stops Bridge[254]

Once one is standing atop the Terrace of the Floating Reflections, one finds oneself facing a massive rock face. Those holding up their long gowns begin to fear for their footing when, all of a sudden, a young dragon appears, coiled upon the tips of the waves. From this point onward, one clambers upward like a monkey, helping one's companions up, the twisting pathway appearing out of the cracks in the rock. After a turn or two, one finds oneself at Bamboo Sheath Den. This is the beginning of the path leading to the Gazebo for Friendship with the Rocks. The bridge has been formed by

---

254   The name of this bridge derives, perhaps, from a passage of the "In the World of Men" chapter of the *Zhuangzi*, which records a conversation between Confucius and his disciple Yan Hui: "Yan Hui said, 'My family is poor. I haven't drunk wine or eaten any strong foods for several months. So can I be considered as having fasted?' 'That is the fasting one does before a sacrifice, not the fasting of the mind.' 'May I ask what the fasting of the mind is?' Confucius said, 'Make your will one! Don't listen with your ears, listen with your mind. No, don't listen with your mind, but listen with your spirit. Listening stops with the ears, the mind stops with recognition, but spirit is empty and waits on all things. The Way gathers in emptiness alone. Emptiness is the fasting of the mind.'" See *Chuang Tzu: Basic Writings*, trans. Burton Watson (New York: Columbia University Press, 1996), 53–54, transliteration altered.

cutting the belly out of the rock, and the steps are all at different heights, curving back to meet the bridge at its halfway point. Even on a balmy summer's evening, as soon as one moors one's boat beneath the bridge the chill arrives with a swoosh, raising goose bumps on one's flesh.

Moon Secreting Spring

Beside the third rock down to the right of the Terrace of the Floating Reflections are found two springs, the one shaped like a full moon and the other in the form of a crescent moon. Neither spring dries up during times of drought nor do they ever overflow even after prolonged rain.

If one were to try to describe the taste of the water drawn from these springs, then obviously it cannot compare with that to be obtained from the Zhongling or Beigan Springs of Zhenjiang, and nor, I believe, could it be expected to. And yet as soon as Soughing Pines tea brewed with this water hits the back of one's throat one is struck by its excellence and it proves fine enough to revive one's poetic inspiration. As the spring rises fresh from the lungs of the rock, its flavor is that of the mountains and rivers. In a place such as this, beyond the reach of the Water Transport System established by that great connoisseur of tea Li Deyu,[255] this water is appropriate to the needs of a rustic such as myself, and thus do I take pleasure in it.

Thatched Belvedere of the Brook and the Hill

In my dreams, I often find myself reciting, time after time, that couplet from old Du Fu's poem "Late Spring" that goes:

> Alongside a thatched cottage upon the sandy bank willows renew their shade,
> In the wild pond beneath the city wall the lotuses begin to redden.

Even after I awaken I find that the words remain on my lips still as I continue to mumble the lines.

On one occasion as I was plying my boat into the mountain I happened to look over to the western bank of Relinquished to the Terns Pond and caught sight of the eroded peaks and buttressing rocks, always as if about to plummet. Alongside the water's edge the land flattens out somewhat and there a small path could be opened up. At the time, however, this patch was covered in tall bamboos so I had several dozen of them chopped down in order that a cottage could be built, with the bank to one side and water on the other. It was as if Du Fu had told me in my dreams how this place could be developed. Looking down from the cottage, the clear lake is in sight and one's

---

255   It is said that while serving as Grand Councilor to the Tang court, Li Deyu had water drawn from the Mount Hui spring in Wuxi specially conveyed to him in the capital.

reflection bobs clearly on its surface. The chill of the autumnal air coming from the stone forest beneath the northern window insinuates its way beneath one's robes. The scene is that of a painting from of the hand of a Song or Yuan dynasty Master entitled "Living in Reclusion Beside a Mountain Brook."

Tea Plot

If one takes a slight turn to the southwest as one enters Bamboo Sheath Den one comes upon a small patch of wasteland covered in stones. The topsoil here is no more than a *chi* in depth, and so the place is most suited to the planting of tea trees. Some time ago, the monk Wugong and I picked and treated several specimens of tea plant, finding their chill scent to be of a most exceptional quality. Now I have had removed all other plants from this plot, leaving behind only a thousand Wooden Slave orange trees. When, some day in the future, I can brew up some tea with water drawn from my Moon Secreting Spring and sit sipping it under the tall pines, this indeed will have its air of flair and elegance. The *Book of Yue* speaks of: "The auspicious tea plants of the Dragon Mountains, the snowy tips of Sun Forged Mountain." I have no idea whether my own tea will prove superior to these two varieties!

Cold Cloud Rock

Of all things, it is certainly not rocks that my Allegory Garden lacks. To the right of the Terrace of the Floating Reflections stand three huge rocks that appear as if they have been split open by the hand of Giant Spirit, the god of the Yellow River. I treat them as if they were the speaking rocks of Cold Mountain. Apart from these three, there are also innumerable other rocks that look like crouching tigers or squatting lions. One rock in particular, standing beside Flute Pavilion, appears like a stallion galloping along a cliff and suddenly coming to a halt, not yet fully reined in and still snorting with anger. Above this is another rock shaped like a half moon that seems always on the point of falling. My friend Zhou Youxin named this rock Cold Cloud. Although it is perhaps not quite worthy of my donning my robes and holding high my tablets of office to pay homage to it as an elder brother, as did Mi Fu of the Song when he came across an exceptional rock within his official residence, I can nonetheless call it my little friend.

Gazebo for Friendship with the Rocks

When winding one's way up or down the mountain, this place makes an appropriate mid-way point. The gazebo's vermilion pillars connect with the slope and its flying beams traverse the mountain. When seeking the source of the river that flows through my garden, sightseers to this place find their spirits lifted while those in search of solitude find the peace and tranquillity they desire therein. All linger here in the gazebo, each moved to melancholy and regret at the passage of time. But here the master of the garden has no special friend with whom to sit opposite and converse, only my little friend Cold Cloud rock. *He*, at least, does not allow himself to become inflamed by the vicissitudes of human affairs and can be said to be my true winter friend.

Pavilion of Great Antiquity

Pines were felled for the columns and rafters but the walls were left unplastered, perchance the intent being to make this pavilion seem to conform to the conventions that remain to us from great antiquity? At first, this pavilion was sited besides the Gazebo for Friendship with the Rocks, but later, once the gazebo had been completed, it was moved to a spot beneath Pine Path. When Master Tao Shiling revisited my garden, he repeatedly asked after the site of this pavilion in order that he might go there to rest awhile. With a laugh, I responded: "Great Antiquity accords not with the needs of the times and so it has been demoted to where it now stands."

My guest was not convinced at all by what I had said: "No, no, to the contrary," he replied, "This pavilion gives the appearance of profound tranquillity. It may be compared to the recluse Qili Bei of the Han who, when an old man, was prevailed upon to return from Mount Shang, so imposing in his hat and robes. How could he bear to be ranked with those smart young military officers Zhou Bo, the Duke of Jiang, or Guan Ying of the Han?"

The land here abuts a ridge and is sheltered by a bank. Alone and aloof stands the pavilion besides a secluded hedgerow and amid the gnarled trunks, with no yearning to vie in beauty with the birds and the flowers. This can be said to be a perfect example of the appropriate siting of a pavilion.

Little Transverse Stream

Once work had begun on excavating the pond, just as soon as we had begun to hump away the soil, the sharp ridges of the rock base seemed about to rise up. By the time a depth of a *zhang* or so had been reached, a steep and precipitous mountain had appeared, which, as if in anger, stampeded toward the spring like a thirsty steed, bursting through the clouds like a prize falcon. As the water entered the jagged, teeth-like crack in the rock and was agitated by the breeze, it resounded with an echoing boom, just as in old Su Shi's "Account of Stone Bell Mountain." Even Tao Qian, out on his spring travels, had never seen such a sight, even Wang Wei's fabled Wangchuan Estate had not contained a thing such as this. If one goes by boat across Relinquished to the Terns Pond and alights here, a secluded path leads one toward the Pavilion of Great Antiquity. The banks of the stream have been planted mostly in old flowering apricot trees, which, like pure maidens lightly made-up, bend over to observe their own reflections within the ripples. When one looks down upon this scene from the Abode for Studying the *Book of Changes*, it is not just the muffled sound of dropped hairpins that reaches one's ears.

Pine Path

My garden is not without its twisted pines of martial air, but they all seem arrogant and ill disciplined. Only here along this path are they arrayed in majestic ranks, like sentinels standing guard within the Palace of Penetrating Brightness,[256] helmets upon their heads and swords at their sides. This being the case, I had a path cut out between them and this became the means by which one could make one's way from the Gazebo for Friendship with the Rocks to the Selecting the Superior Pavilion. When a strong wind soughs amid these pines, a bitter chill comes upon one even in the sixth month. The pine that faces the gate is twisted as if in dance and everyone is taken aback to find one of the Five Grandees capable of such delicate and seductive beauty.[257] Along the path flowering plants of various kinds have been planted, their reds and purples intermingling with the weathered green of the pines, and, like a marriage arranged between Wei Wen's beautiful daughter and the Old Man on the Donkey, the contrast thus established offers its own poetic beauty.

Cherry Tree Grove

Below Selecting the Superior Pavilion a hedgerow has been woven from bamboo. Several varieties of clambering rose have entwined themselves within the hedgerow, and beyond it grow cherry trees of the "Wax Pearl" and "Wheat Blossom" varieties. Whenever the blossoms form upon these trees before falling as snow and the red fruit hangs like stars from their branches, it is like catching a glimpse of a great beauty from behind a screen, her red lips only half revealed. But the master of the garden happens at the time to be seeking to brush away the dust of the world with his fly-whisk and discuss abstruse matters with the Laymen from Mount Culai;[258] he has no need for their red-teethed clappers and their romantic songs of the dawn breeze and the waning moon.

Selecting the Superior Pavilion

In the past it was said of clerk Xu Xun of the Jin that not only did he have a superior sensibility but that he had at his disposal also the equipment to enhance this sensibility.[259] I would argue that even more does one require to be destined to be capable of selecting the superior. If you are not so destined, then every spring and each rock will be lost to you as soon as you encounter them. Just as Heaven and Earth work to their own principles, the mountains and rivers too form of their own accord.

---

256   By legend, the Palace of Penetrating Brightness (*Tongmingdian* 通明殿) was one of the palaces of the Jade Emperor.

257   On his ascent of Mount Tai, the First Emperor of Qin took shelter from a storm under some pine trees. He later appointed them "Grandees," and this term has subsequently become a metonymy for the pine tree.

258   Metonymy for the cypress tree.

259   This anecdote is found in the "Living in Retirement" chapter of *A New Account of Tales of the World*: "Xu Xun was fond of wandering among mountains and streams and his physique was well suited to mountain climbing. His contemporaries used to say, 'Xu not only has superb feelings; he really has the equipment for traversing the superb.'" See Liu I-ch'ing, *Shih-shuo Hsin-yü*, 338, transliteration altered.

To the north, this pavilion connects with Pine-Tree Path, while to the south it gives on to the Lesser Crenellated Peaks. Off to the east stands Tiger Horn Hermitage. Here the sandals of visitors form a constant pile, and yet, with its plain rafters and rustic beams, the pavilion itself is not at all exceptional. It is only once one has ascended the pavilion and taken a look around, caught sight of the rosy mist that shrouds the peaks and hides the sun, of the vast expanse of cloud spreading beyond the horizon, that one begins to understand the pleasures of the birds and the fishes and experience to the full the joy of the forest. The pavilion itself is not at all superior, becoming so only when united with the various scenes here assembled. Neither should all that which is superior be found here within the pavilion; rather it is the site of the pavilion that proves superior.

Horned Tiger Hermitage

Turning to the west at the northernmost point of Pine-Tree Path, one comes upon Selecting the Superior Pavilion. Taking another turn, this time to the east, brings one to a small patch of ground where the rock has acquired a patina of age. These jangle with the sound of shattering jade when struck, echoing with the muffled soughing of the sparse stand of bamboo. To the edge of this area stand two fantastic examples of Lake Tai Rock, one of which looks like waves upon the surface of a pond and the other like a mountain cavern. Both are as if they have fallen from the sleeve of that great lover of rocks, Mi Fu of the Song. Here I have built a hermitage of five bent rafters so as to resemble a flowering apricot blossom.

Once the hermitage had been completed, I asked my brother Jichao to give it a name. He obliged with the name Horned Tiger, saying to me: "You have built this hermitage to serve Bodhidharma, a manifestation of your devotion to the Way of the Ancestors. But have you thought also about Pure Land?"

"I'd like to hear their teachings," I responded.

"To say that the Sixth Patriarch did not go to the Pure Land of the West is like the poisoned drum that brings death to all that hear its beat. Later pedants divided the two into separate schools. Not to seek to become enlightened to the original heart and to say that after all there is a pure land to which one can go is to believe in the false doctrine that there is a dharma that is external to the heart. Conversely, those who are intent upon becoming enlightened to the original heart and who insist that the Pure Land of the West is external to the heart can certainly not be said to truly be enlightened. It was for this reason that the Chan Master Yongming said: 'To be with both Chan and Pure Land is to be like a "tiger with horns."' His words are profound. I often find myself teasing my Chanist acquaintances, saying to them: 'Monks do not begrudge spending their grass shoe money, traveling the country in search of wisdom. At the moment, Amitābha is running a large congee stall in the Western Paradise.

Why don't you lot go and see what wisdom you can pick up from him? Why is it that you shy away from the Pure Land in this way?'"

"I will respectfully abide by the teachings of the Pure Land, but tell me, how does one manage to tame a tiger with horns?" I asked.

Jichao counted a bead or two of his rosary before responding to my query: "Understanding begins with chanting the Buddha's name. Once you have understood, then you can bind it with the hair of a tortoise, feed it with the echo of the valley, accompany it with a wooden horse or a clay ox, guard it with a magician or a sorcerer. Only at times such as that are you truly walking along the right way."

After pausing for a considerable time, Jichao concluded: "I hold true to this always."

Pocket Ocean

To the north of the Thatched Belvedere of the Brook and the Hill is found a stone chamber, the ceiling of which is so fine as to allow gradations of light to filter through. Like the gaping mouth of the Ash Sieve Daoist, it exposes to full view the five internal organs.[260] As soon as several dozen people have taken their seats here, the bitter chill of the snow cuts straight to the bone and all memories of the heat of the sixth month in the outside world disappear completely. Perhaps the rocks here are like those that the Song poet Su Shi carried back home in his sleeves, for they too seem to be from the shores of the Langya Sea in Shandong and have been ground smooth by the wash of the waves.[261]

Jar Hideaway

Long ago, whenever Shentu Youyai went wandering in the wilds, he would always carry with him a jar. Every now and then he would leap into the pitcher, calling it his "Jar Hideaway." The story so amused me when I heard it that I resolved to name my bedchamber "Jar Hideaway" also. The room is but a single *zhang* square, with two small rooms built off either side, the better to resemble the handles of its namesake. With its rounded shoulders and raised spine, half hidden amid the flowers and the trees, it is the spitting image of a jar. Shentu believed that the entire universe was contained within his jar and that like the Kalavinka jar told of in the *sutras*, it too, although completely empty, could nonetheless contain food enough to feed an entire kingdom.

---

260   Duan Chengshi's (ca. 800–863) *Assorted Notes from Youyang* (*Youyang zazu* 酉陽雜俎) records the following story: "There was a Daoist of Shu who was known by the vulgar name 'Ash Sack.' He had a disease of the mouth and having not eaten for several months and being on the point of death, he suddenly leapt to his feet. His mouth gaped open and his five internal organs were exposed to full view."

261   In a poem, Su Shi tells how once along the coast of Shandong he picked up some stones washed smooth and round by the sea. He took them home and used them to plant his narcissi. A couplet from this poem goes: "I carried these stones home with me, / And it was as if I held the Eastern Ocean within my sleeve."

This truly is like the mustard seed that can support Mount Sumeru, and if one were to regard it simply as a jar one would be doing a grave injustice to Master Shentu.

Terrace of the Jade Maiden of Solitary Peak

East of the crossing, a single green peak rises steeply, which, clothed in a myriad jade-green bamboos and with its cinnabar towers surrounded by kingfisher-blue water, appears like a brightly made-up beauty. This terrace is in fact a tent pavilion. Like a rainbow bridge, it shrinks back amid a thousand stems of lotus buds, above which only the caps of the visitors remain visible. Just as one has become intoxicated on the assembled scents of this Land of the Massed Fragrances one suddenly hears the muffled jangle of jade pendants and one believes it to be those two divine maids Orchid Fragrance Du and Green Flower Stem, riding their green pheasant and treading the clouds, and arriving here late with mincing gait from the Peak of the Assembled Jades. To serve as its name, I have conferred upon it a line from a poem by the Tang poet Shen Quanqi, for like Cao Zhi of the Wei dynasty when he first encountered the Goddess of the Luo River, I find myself quite lost for words.

Lotus Crossing

A winding gallery leads from the Thatched Pavilion to Jar Hideaway. Looking down through the gaps between the floorboards one finds oneself standing above flowing water. Fantastic rocks jut upward, and alongside the paths between these rocks giant Yundang and delicate Chill Jade bamboos sough in the autumnal breeze. A small pond of clear green water reflects the images of those passing by this way, making them appear like kingfishers playing upon the branches. My garden is long on open vistas but short of secluded spots. A place like this where one can whistle and sing is a place one can while the day away. Halfway along the walkway, a narrow path leads away toward the east and here a terrace is followed by a bridge, and the bridge in turn by an island. Red blossoms float upon the ripples and the deep green water cuts a transverse passage. But all this is not what most appeals to the mind of the master of this garden, for when the autumnal river brings a sense of loneliness upon him, only the few Cold Fragrance lotus flowers found here will become, along with the distant peaks and the deep cold pond, his boon companions. It is for this reason that the crossing has been named lotus.

Swirling Waves Isle

Fata Morgana form far on the horizon where the mist and the waves meet, and once formed appear like mountain peaks bobbing upon the shifting tides, the riverbanks too merging with the encircling heavens. Guests, on catching a momentary glimpse of the sight, exclaim in alarm that these must be the Three Immortal Isles of legend, carried here across the oceans upon the backs of the fishes and dragons. Terrified, they have difficulty holding up their long gowns as they walk, a zigzag bridge serving as their single reed. Leaving the bridge, one comes upon a pavilion, followed in turn by a stone bridge. Once one has crossed the bridge with the assistance of one's staff, the barely discernible path seems about to peter out altogether. Gibbons lead one through the cracks in the disorderly flurry of rock before one passes upward through a stone gate. The reflections dance in the surrounding purity, as if seeking to compete with my Allegory Mountain, as arrogant as that King of the tiny kingdom of Yelang who proved quite ignorant of the existence of the great Han Empire. Once upon a time a most eccentric monk exposed the root of Gold Mountain and said: "As the stem of the mountain is worn thin and becomes more exposed, it appears more and more as if it is being held up like a mushroom." This is a most apt description of my isle, for as the belly of the rock base has been eroded away and water has begun to flow underneath it, the rock sits upon the surface of the water as if it were floating there. With its encircling water and shrouded in mist, the isle looks like the preliminary sketch of that line from Xie Lingyun's poem "On Climbing the Solitary Island in the River" which goes: "Solitary Island, so lovely in mid-stream."

Occasionally, the isle seems to rise in anger. The water eating away at the rocks leaves them like the knobs of a bell half worn away, but they, for their part, unwilling to admit defeat, send forth the bravest troops among them who, with a crash and a roar, engage the enemy like 30,000 armored horsemen, all blowing their trumpets and beating their drums. My friend Wang Siren once said of the two scenic spots of Runzhou that: "Gold Mountain is suitable for travel, whereas Jiao's Mountain is ideal for reclusion; Gold Mountain is at its best under a bright moon, Jiao's Mountain in rain."

To this scene I can now offer this isle to make a third. I wonder what comment he will have to make about it?

Pavilion for the Appreciation of Excellence

That which is superior about Allegory Mountain cannot be entirely encompassed by Allegory Mountain itself, by virtue of the fact that you find yourself within the mountain itself. Su Shi made precisely this point in his poem "Inscribed on the Wall of Western Forest Monastery": "Of Mount Lu one cannot make out the true face, / If one is lost in the heart of the very place."

This pavilion, however, does not fraternize with the mountain and so can possess it in its entirety. A layer or two of tower and terrace, inlaid within the green cliffs and the blue-green precipices; every now and then when the clouds gather to obscure them, they rise upward, supporting themselves upon a layer of mist. Looking upward greedily, all of a sudden one finds oneself transported to the very edges of Heaven and it is as if one were no longer aware of the existence of the pavilion. One casts a hurried glance backward, only to discover oneself in the very midst of an ocean with breakers crashing against the rocks and flooding through the forest, all the time issuing forth a sound both pure and surpassing. Not only does this assuage one's hunger, it serves also to cleanse one's innards of a decade's encrusted dust. To place an island within the pond, to site a pavilion upon that island, like the froth floating upon the surface of the sea, and thus to assemble here together all that is excellent, how could this fail to move the refined man to appreciation?

Lesser Crenellated Peaks

In the midst of the Eastern Sea is found the immortal isle of Fangzhang, an alternative name for which is Crenellated Peaks. There stand palaces of gold and jade and porcelain, the very things that Mount Kunlun too is famous for. In contrast to this, how inferior are the rope doors and tiny jar-like windows of my garden! Lesser Crenellated Peaks is the place from where one can enter my Determination to Retire Studio, and as this studio embodies my original ideal of simplicity for my garden, is not the name given this site somewhat inappropriate and out of keeping? But then again, grass mat doors juxtaposed with vermilion gates are not at all an exceptional sight, and in legend King Mu of Zhou gave the Five Terraces and Twelve Towers of Mount Kunlun not a second lingering glance, treating them simply as a lodging place for the night. From this point upward in my garden, one needs to turn and twist at almost every step, and with its serpentine kiosks and hanging terraces serving to tassel the peaks and bind the waists of the hillocks, it has a vague likeness to Langfeng, the summit of Mount Kunlun, only much smaller of course. Although I can not name the structures here Fungus Chamber and Medicine Hall after those found on Mount Kunlun itself, I may perhaps partake of some small part of the glory of that place by naming this spot as I have.

Determination to Retire Studio

When work had just begun upon my garden, I happened to buy up a number of large rafters. These I had placed here, retaining for the while their coarse and untreated quality. Here indeed one may whistle and sing with delight, loll about and take one's rest. Galleries lead away from the studio, both to the left and the right, the one to the right taking one to Allegory Mountain Thatched Cottage, the one to the left to Flute Pavilion. Within the studio itself one can escape from the summer's heat, the north-facing shutters remaining wide open all day long while beyond, a strong breeze rouses green waves amid the fields of arable land. Taking a drink or chanting a poem or two, I forget altogether about the coarse and untreated appearance of the rafters, indeed begin to find them quite lovable in their rustic simplicity. So I had all the painted beams and carved tile rafters blanched of their colors.

When I requested leave to retire from my post I intended, in the time left free to me from caring for my mother, to devote myself to gardens and pavilions. This studio represents the beginnings of my enterprise. The studio marks my retirement. It is also named Retirement in order to strengthen my resolve to retire.

Heaven's Calabash

Besides the Peak of the Iron Fungus, a single rock juts majestically into the sky, like an overturned cup. When my brother Jichao and cousin Zhixiang were first developing this mountain, they had a hollow hacked out of it to form a pond to store water. My late brother Yuanru took delight in the sight of it and named it Heaven's Calabash from the line in a poem by Su Shi that goes: "Falling from my horse, Heaven's calabash overturned."

He wrote a poem to record the excellence of the sight. I, for my part, cannot bear to allow this name to disappear, so I have retained it.

Flute Pavilion

Once long ago, Cai Yong [132–192] happened to be spending the night at an inn in Keting. Looking up, he eyed the third bamboo rafter and exclaimed: "A fine flute could be made from that!" And indeed, so it proved, for when played the flute gave forth a sound of extraordinary quality. Keting is but a short ten *li* away from here and the names of the mountains and the bridges there are still the same as they were in Cai Yong's day. When I began construction of my garden, it so happened that I had at my disposal the services of a master craftsman who was skilled at building pavilions from split bamboo, and thus have I alluded to Cai Yong in my name for this pavilion. I wonder if a shaft of green jade bamboo can also be made to issue forth with the sound of bells and musical stones? But then again, I fear that the bamboo would split asunder just as Master Dugu reached his crescendo, splintering not only the hand of Sun Chuo's [fl. 330–365] dancing girl.[262]

Indulgence in Rinsing Gallery

A gallery meanders its way throughout my garden. Only two sections of this gallery are at all noteworthy, however; that section of the gallery found at the foot of my garden I have named Water Bright Walkway because of the excellence of the water there, while that at the top I have called it Indulgence in Rinsing by reason of the excellence of the rocks to be found thereabouts. Descending my garden by way of the gallery one reaches Flute Pavilion where an oblique angled cliff splits the clouds and a strange-shaped peak soars into the haze. Each and every one of the inch-sized peaks and foot-long rocks here

---

262 Here, Qi Biaojia conflates two anecdotes. The first, found in a book entitled *Lost Histories* (*Yishi* 逸史) tells of an occasion when Li Mo of the Tang invited Master Dugu to play his (Li's) flute. Master Dugu agreed to do so but first warned Li Mo that the flute would be sure to split asunder when he reached the crescendo. The second anecdote comes from the "Contempt and Insults" chapter of *A New Account of Tales of the World*: "A transverse flute which Cai Yong had once made from a bamboo rafter which had caught his eye, Sun Chuo allowed a female dancer to brandish about and break. On hearing of it, Wang Xizhi cried out in great indignation, 'A priceless musical instrument which has been a family heirloom for three generations, that blankety-blank idiot son of the Sun family has smashed and broken!'" See Liu I-ch'ing, *Shih-shuo Hsin-yü*, 436, transliteration altered.

are sharp and deeply eroded, like wild ducks diving beneath the waves or pheasants soaring into the heavens, and any of them can be used to sharpen one's teeth upon. I find that I tend to be too intoxicated with the sip, and yet by nature I cannot hold my drink beyond a single plantain leaf. Although those who "wash their ears" may find my intoxication with this spot somewhat excessive, I may nonetheless be regarded as being superior to the likes of those two Worthies of the Bamboo Grove Xi Kang [223–262] and Ruan Ji [210–263], who proved altogether too fond of their cups.

Rotten Axe-Haft Mountain House

If one looks up at this Mountain House from beyond my Allegory Garden, it appears to be but a short step or two away. But one can only reach it having taken a number of turns along the path leading to it from the Gazebo for Friendship with the Rocks and visitors are forever getting lost as they make their way here. From the Chamber of Simplicity, one descends to it down some steps, feeling all the time as if one had entered into the very bowels of a mountain cave. Once one has arrived, one finds a three-columned structure, these columns supported by the branches of still growing trees. Here the Master of the Garden reads his books, and when weary, he leans upon the balustrade and gazes about him in all four directions. Whenever guests arrive at his garden, he can catch sight of them while they are still several *li* away and he can dispatch a serving boy to investigate. After some considerable time, their boat will appear in the midst of the flowing water. At times he will lie here in peace and from his pillow he will watch the sun rise up and the clouds form, observing nature's myriad spluttering transformations. This is what men in the past have called "recumbent travel." It is also as if there are landscape murals painted on all four walls, and the master is akin to a connoisseur comparing their relative merits.

Chamber of Simplicity

In the past, when my esteemed father was naming the various sites of his gardens he did so with words such as "intimate" and "tranquil." With the deference a minor official owes his superior, I have followed the intent of his practice in this regard and have had the words "quiet" and "simplicity" carved into a number of the rafters as a constant reminder. This accords also with that habit of the ancients to have maxims engraved on their side tables and platters. Indeed, for the Superior Man there is no greater virtue than the Way of Simplicity, both in the manner in which he conducts himself in this world and for that wherein he dwells. In the matter of his habitation, all that is required is space enough for him to sit down in. Were I to have cleaved true to my father's injunction I would have been content simply with having enough room to hug my knees and would have had no good reason for embarking upon the construction of this garden. And, indeed, in the beginning all I conceived of was a single studio and a solitary hall. As time went by, however, I gradually expanded my plan of it, my sentiments shifting with the scenery, my heart turning as it was possessed by material things. In this way, the garden has become a token of the extent to which I have proven incapable of manifesting simplicity. I have named this place Simplicity, therefore, as a token of my remorse. And yet, although Simplicity is its name, the moment I ascend to this chamber, what I see as I gaze out over the horizon is flowing waters and mountain peaks; everything, it seems, lies gathered here before me. How extravagant is the scene obtained! The fact that Simplicity is its name but extravagant is its reality serves simply to intensify my sense of remorse.

Peak of the Iron Mushroom

To the north of my Determination to Retire Studio, a small hillock reaches skyward in a somewhat clandestine manner. This is the highest point of my Allegory Mountain. When viewed from beyond the garden it appears to be little more than a tiny mound, like a fist-shaped rock left discarded here when it proved incapable of joining the ranks of the rocks expelled by the First Emperor of Qin.[263] When you reach the summit and take a look around, however, it seems as if the clouds and the roseate rays of light are born at your feet. To the east one bows in the direction of the Qinwang Mountains, and to the west one salutes the peaks of the Yuezhang range. Standing here, upon the middle of the three brothers, it is as if the mountain itself grows taller in keeping with the loftiness of the sentiments of the traveler. The summit is flat and large enough to seat several dozen people. Over the course of the past year, however, both the Green Lad and the Scattered Old Man have each occupied half this area.[264] Upon the summit stands a rock shaped like a mushroom, and so I have called it Iron Fungus.

Allegory Mountain Thatched Hall

Allegory Mountain reaches its highest point with Iron Mushroom Peak. The Thatched Hall is at an almost equivalent height but to the right of it, as if cottage and peak were greeting each other with a bow. The cottage is only twenty *chi* square and at first glance it appears to be little more than a small pavilion. The moment one enters the door however, one becomes aware of its spaciousness and its roof soars up above one like a canopy of low-hanging clouds. Sitting upon a barbarian folding stool, engaging in elegant conversation and light banter, one finds oneself completely at ease. Although my cottage is without strings and flutes and sacrificial vessels, it does not lack for lacquered side tables and bamboo couches, tea braziers and wine tables, however, and in the light of the dawn or the glow of the dusk, when the peaks are shrouded in mist or the hilltops bathed in the rosy glow of the clouds, I give pleasure to my guests and this spot can be said to surpass all their fondest expectations. Those that dwell in the garden are not allowed to regret the absence of close friends. Nor does one ever have regrets that, after having repeatedly refused to entertain the vulgar, one is frequently subject to the curses once showered on Zhang Muzhi.

---

263   Legend has it that in an attempt to reach the place where the sun rises, the First Emperor of Qin ordered the sea filled with rocks.

264   Metonymical references to the Chinese pagoda tree and the pine, respectively.

Penetrating the Roseate Clouds Terrace

To the right of Allegory Mountain stands Axe-Haft Mountain. Over the ages, ten thousand hands have hacked away at the rock face here and as a result, in the period since the Chiwu reign period of the Great King of the Wu, almost half the mountain has been eaten away.[265] Now the sheer cliff rises straight up with the force of soaring roseate clouds, exposing to full view several finely layered precipices and dominating the contours of all the other nearby peaks. The flying torrents that pour down the gullies frequently seem both watchful and apprehensive, like wild beasts about to pounce upon their human prey. A collapsed bank lies like a rainbow and crawling like an ant along a plank path brings one to a small pavilion that seems suspended in midair. Glancing upward, one catches sight of a stone Buddha several tens of *zhang* tall with a purpose-built canopy sheltering it from rain and sun, its greens and its golds bright and beautiful. Ingenious effort was required to hack this Buddha out of the primordial chaos, the rocks split open and the slopes hewed asunder, as if to supplement the task of the creator himself. The splendors of Axe-Haft Mountain as seen from here provide the most superb sight to be seen in this part of the Yue region, and all I have done here is to present the scene that lies before one when one stands upon this terrace. As for the scene that the terrace itself serves to create, this there is no need for me to speak of.

The Quietist's Gallery

As if connected to my Thatched Hall along the edge of a cock's comb but facing the south stands a studio of three columns. The east door of the studio leads to the Indulgence in Rinsing Gallery, while below the studio is found Connected Beads Hermitage, this latter being part of the pagoda cloister dedicated to the memory of Master Mailang. Distant peaks and a sparse forest appear as if just below the balustrade and as the rain lifts a vivid greenness insinuates itself among the chairs and tables of my room.

In the past, when I sat here upon rattan mats with various famous monks concentrating solely upon our conversation or listening to the rise and fall of the chanting of the *sutras* and the accompanying banging of the gong, all my extraneous thoughts would be extinguished. Acknowledging that the air of benevolence and longevity of this place is powerful in the extreme, I named it Quietist. Quietism is to be found within the quietist, however, not in the mountains, precisely the point made by Wang Haochang.

---

265   This mountain is to the north of Great Yu's Grotto. It is said of the cliff that "In the second year of the Chiwu reign period this rock fell from the sky and Ge Xiangong here refined the elixir of immortality. Having eaten Yu the Great's Leftovers, he flew upward and ever afterward the cliff has been known as 'Ge's Cliff' or 'The Immortal's Cliff.'" Ever afterward, the cliff had attracted the attentions of seekers after immortality and had been, quite literally, half eaten away.

Distant Belvedere

This belvedere was named Distant not simply because it stands at the very horizon of one's eyesight. Rather it is because the view from the belvedere encompasses all the mountains and rivers of the region of Yue but that the various mountains and rivers thus united are not enough to encompass all the splendors of my garden. Thus does the belvedere take its place of honor and sit at the highest point of my garden.

The belvedere appears to best advantage when covered in snow, when under a bright moon, or during a fall of rain. At such times, waves of silver sea billow to and fro and the jade peaks stand tall; shadows dance under the clear bright rays of the moon and for a moment one sees the moon's penumbra cleansing itself in the ice pot; with a shower of rain imminent all are taken aback by the change that comes across the hue of the mountains. This is when my belvedere is at its most splendid, and if its effect is born of its distance, so too does distance give its conception a certain harmonious charm. The raging torrents amid the cliffs appear even more extraordinary in their seductive beauty when seen at a distance; at a distance, the single peak appears more sharply defined with its vapors raising their misty shrouds; the lamps and cooking fires of ten thousand households enter my tower only because they are at such a distance, while the thousand twists and turns of the brooks and mountains too, because of their distance, return to rest within my bamboo screens. As to the sudden rise of smoke from the village fires, the far off glimmer of the fishermen's flares, the oaring songs of the boatmen coming to one from amid the water-pepper and riverine islands, the pleasant tunes of the orioles among the billowing willows, all these too are made manifest by the quality of distance. It is an illusion created by distance that when one takes a general survey of the ridges of that Immortal Isle of Yingzhou, the blue sky surrounding it seems so vast; when one strains one's eyes to take in the entirety of Wu Zixu's River,[266] the vast tide surges like an arrow; or when one catches a momentary glimpse of the working out of the principles of Heaven and Earth, the sun and the moon appear no larger than a couple of pellets. It is distance's sleight of hand also that when one visits sites of historical significance, Yu the Great's Stela stands firm and straight like a sentinel;[267] sighing at the fate of Gou Jian, the King of Yue, the rook weeps within his former palaces;[268] the sight of withered grass in the setting sun within the confines of

---

266 An alternative name for the River Zhe. Wu Zixu was a native of the Kingdom of Chu during the Spring and Autumn period (722–456 BCE). When both his father and brother were executed, he fled to serve the state of Wu. Eventually he fell foul of the decadent King of Wu, Fuchai, and was ordered to commit suicide. His corpse was placed in a wineskin and allowed to float away on the river. Legend claims he became the god of the waves.

267 Great Yu was reputed to be a descendant of the Yellow Emperor. Having succeeded in controlling the floods, Shun appointed him emperor and he became the founder of the Xia dynasty. In the eighth year of his reign, it is said, in the course of a royal progress through his domains, he held a grand assembly in Guiji. A stela was said to have been erected to mark the occasion.

268 Gou Jian was the King of Yue and the great antagonist of Fuchai of Wu.

the once imposing West Garden moves one to sorrow; the trees with their thick foliage and the tall bamboos remain on Orchid Isle where once the wine cups floated down the meandering stream. Such sights bring despair to some men, to others they serve to renew their sense of purpose. Standing here in this belvedere, the mountains and the rivers, all the various elements of the scene laid out before one, are seen in their grandest prospect and one feels that the very hills and valleys have all been rendered even more exquisite by their apparent smallness.

Willow Pathway

When leaving Allegory Garden, taking the southern embankment leads one to the Bin Potager, whereas the northern embankment affords entry to my Abundance Mains. Connecting these two embankments is yet another, screen-like in its appearance, bearing a tablet inscribed by Zhang Lingxu which reads: "Willow Pathway." Here and there alongside the embankment grow peach and willow trees. Each spring, the air is filled with drifting peach blossom and the slightest puff of breeze drenches the clothes of passersby with red raindrops. To my mind, however, far better than this are the few weeping willow trees that cast their lingering green reflections upon the surface of the surrounding water. Here perhaps the fishermen will rest their oars within the deep green shade and listen to the golden orioles trilling in the branches, and the scene will embody that simple rustic air of the Pengze District where once Tao Qian retired. This was the idea in the mind of the Master of the Garden when he named the place not Peach Pathway but rather Willow Pathway. When, beyond this dyke, the water mallow knits its crisscross patterns turning the entire river green, the billowing clouds rise suddenly or a misty rain drifts by, to ply one's boat into midstream is truly to give full vent to one's sense of pleasure.[269]

Bin Potager

To the south of Relinquished to the Terns Pond once lay a patch of fallow land, two hundred *chi* wide and not quite half as long. Three-fifths of this area I had planted in mulberry, the rest in pear, orange, peach, flowering apricot, apricot, chestnut and so on. My bondservants are all assiduous in the discharge of their duties, going out to irrigate the plot three times a day and to mow and weed five times. Beneath the trees we have planted purple eggplant, white peas, sweet melons and poppies. We have also planted an unusual variety of sweet potato obtained from across the oceans, each plant of which spreads to cover two or three *mu* of land, each *mu* giving a yield of a cartload or two of potatoes. When eaten instead of grain, the harvest is enough to fill the bellies of a hundred people. I often find myself intoning those lines from Tao

---

269   This last expression derives from the "River Mian" chapter of Li Daoyuan's *Footnotes to the Classic of the Waterways*: "When Sima De was in charge of the north of Zhaizhou, with dwellings all around, his pleasures followed one another. Plying his boat, however, and lifting up his gown, he truly gave vent to his sense of pleasure."

Qian's poem that go: "Contentedly I sit and pour the new spring wine, / Or go out to pluck vegetables in my garden."[270]

The atmosphere is very much akin to that found in the first poem of the "Airs of Bin" section of the *Book of Songs* which speaks of "boiling the mallow" and "drying the dates," and so I have named my potager Bin.[271]

The Pitcher Stop

When my Bin Potager was first cleared I would supervise my bondservants as they irrigated the fields. Taking pity on them for having to work under the scorching midday sun, I had built a small thatched hut for them to rest in. The master too occasionally repairs here to gnaw upon some vegetable or other or to sample some of the fruit from the orchard, lingering here amid the birdsong. In this manner I can experience to the full the rustic delights of life in a village. How I wish that I had as my close friends here Chen Zhongzi of Qi or the old gardener of the south bank of the river Han so that I could discuss with them the art of living.[272]

Abundance Mains

Although the words "farm" and "garden" now appear close in meaning, this has not always been the case. If this is a garden, then why have I created also this farm? I have had it developed in order that it might be the site where I can earn my livelihood. Going out of my garden and turning to the north one comes across a bridge, and just over the bridge one encounters an embankment within which there is a gateway. Here, spread out before one's gaze, lie the green paddy fields. Often I come here to commiserate with the farmers about their labors and sometime on such occasions I will ask my wife to bring along with us some of our leftover food and wine for the old peasants. I join in their farming songs and we sing back and forth. Behind the hall is a threshing ground. During the evenings of the tenth month, when the grain is being harvested, the sounds of the threshing can be heard coming from each household, and a mouthful or two of new rice adds flavor to the diet of my elderly mother. When the silkworm season of the fourth month comes around, I come here with my wife to live a while, picking mulberry leaves and white aster and ensuring that her womanly tasks are undertaken in the proper order. Beside the threshing ground the peasants live

---

270 This poem is entitled "On Reading the *Classic of the Hills and Seas*," this translation of which, by William Acker, can be found in *Anthology of Chinese Literature*, 203.

271 Bin is the name of the area that was regarded as the ancestral home of the imperial house of the Zhou dynasty.

272 This stop takes its name from the story of the "Machine Heart" found in the "Heaven and Earth" chapter of the *Zhuangzi* (see chapter 1). The other man referred to here, Chen Zhongzi of Qi, we are told in the *Biographies of the High-Minded* (*Gaoshi zhuan* 高士傳), was once invited to take high office by the King of Chu. Chen refused, preferring instead to become a gardener.

in houses of several columns each. Here they raise their chickens and their pigs, the sounds of which echo in all directions. I shall grow old here, learning the arts of tending vegetables and growing grain. To the west of the hall there are three side rooms and these, in the future, will become the schoolrooms for my sons. By having them study here I will ensure that as they grow up they will also learn of the various hardships of the life of a peasant.

Flowering Apricot Slope

If the superiority of my garden is to be found in its pavilions and its terraces, only the air of rusticity does it still lack. In order to make up for this deficiency I have had soil piled up to form a slope, water led in to make a canal, and thatch woven to create a shelter. With its rustling artemisia plants it truly does appear like the sandy bank of a river village. The reed gatherers and the fishermen stand to gaze at the scene before struggling their way along the paths. Upon the slope, I have had planted a hundred or so ancient West Brook flowering apricot trees, thus creating an appropriate refuge place for the hermit Lin Bu to bring his reclusive wife. I linger here unable to drag myself away from the scenery, calling the place an unadorned Xi Shi, so pretty as to plunge into fits of mortification all those other gaudy beauties.[273]

Old Man of the Sea's Plank Bridge

A plank bridge has been erected over Relinquished to the Terns Pond and boats can pass beneath the walkway here. The bridge takes one from the Abode for the Study of the *Book of Changes* to the Hall of My Four Unfulfilled Obligations. And yet, as I have already relinquished this pond to the terns, is the name of this bridge not somewhat contradictory? I once read in the work *Historical Spittle* that when Liu Jiquan got hold of a lotus gull he exclaimed: "The form of this Chinese character is such that it implies that the bird is an official of the lowly Third Rank so perhaps it is appropriate that I appoint it Houseman of the Green Sea." To have done so would be similar to the Qin dynasty's disrespectful conferring of official titles on the pines of Mount Tai! But in the present case, the name I have chosen for this bridge is designed to enhance the respect with which the gulls are treated, in the hope that they will remain my true friends, just as the Tang poet Li Bai once sought to summon the gulls to join him with his line: "Willing I am to summon the gulls of the Eastern Ocean."

Oriole-Testing Hostelry

The Old Man of the Sea's Plank Bridge winds off toward the north face of my garden and here on a small patch of land I have built a studio that juts out over the pond. It was

---

273   During the Warring States period, Xi Shi, ever afterward regarded by Chinese tradition as representing the paragon of feminine beauty, was sent by Goujian, the King of Yue (r. ca. 496–464 BCE), to his rival King Fuchai of Wu in the hope that she would distract him from his kingly duties. The stratagem succeeded. The likening of Xi Shi to the West Lake in Hangzhou became something of a cliché.

spring when the hostelry was completed and such was its pleasant aspect that, quite involuntarily, my tongue shot out in astonishment.

Initially I thought that I would name the hostelry Listening to the Orioles, but a friend objected: "I have heard that during the Zhenguan reign period of the Tang dynasty [627–649] there lived a young lady called Tester of Orioles. It is a most melodious name. Why don't you name this lodge in her honor?" I consulted the records contained in books such as *Notes from the Studio of the Truly Forthright*, *Poetic Notes from the Hall of the Abstruse and Miscellaneous*, *Master Xie's Source of Poetry*, and *Miscellaneous Notes on Picking Orchids* and discovered that Tester of Orioles was adept at the art of papermaking and had created a type of carp letter paper. She could also perform a solo dance and had once exchanged poetry with Song Qian, one such poem bearing the title: "I Cut Out a Leaf from Flower Letter Paper to Send to You." For his part, Song Qian too cut a small foreigner out of Roseate Clouds letter paper and inscribed it with the words: "This person resembles the clouds of Mount Chu." Not only is her name a melodious one, but the events of her life too are elegant in the extreme and so I have dedicated this lodge to her memory. I don't imagine that my having done so will displease her.

Returning Clouds Lodging

When visitors to my garden become intoxicated with their tour and decide that they wish to ascend to my Library of the Eight Principles of Book Acquisition, they must do so by passing through this lodging. Here, a tower serves the purpose of a walkway, admitting visitors either ascending or descending my garden. Opposite, the soughing pines fill the valley, and standing here it is as if one is lying amid the crashing waves or within a roaring waterfall. A stretch of thick shade casts its inverted shadow upon the pond before flowing away beneath the winding walkway, like a ten *zhang*-long slice of chill green jade. My garden contains an excellent rock that I have named Cold Cloud. Fearing that it will prove reluctant to appear out of its mountain cavern,[274] thus repudiating the master's fascination with the mountains and rivers, I have therefore returned it to this lodging. And yet, after all, even this return will provide but a temporary retreat.

Identity with the Lotus Cottage

Between the Hall of My Four Unfulfilled Obligations and my Library of the Eight Principles of Book Acquisition stands a chamber. It abuts upon the hall but does not borrow its view from the hall, and although it faces the library it is not reached by way of the library. The water of the pond converges toward the north, and by the time it reaches this spot its meandering course becomes more pronounced. Flowing beneath the Pine Path where the spine of the mountain juts up, pure waves encircle the scene,

---

274 An allusion to the line from Tao Qian's poem "Returning Home" that goes: "The clouds seem to be in no mind to quit the mountains." Editor's note: in the translation of this poem, which appears as "Homeward Bound" in chapter 1, the line is rendered as "some mysterious cloud hovering near the mountain peak."

and when it enters Returning Clouds Lodging the pure flow describes a turn or two before forming a square pond of half a *mu* in size here beside this hut. The jade stamens and encased buds combine with the green snow and the blue-green clouds to form a scene of fragrant harmony.

Leaning upon the balustrade and quietly contemplating the scene before me I suddenly think of a couplet from Master Chen Xianzhang's [1428–1500] poem "In Praise of Zhou Dunyi's Love of the Lotus" which goes: "I am a lotus flower, the flower is I, / Only now do I become a lover of the lotus."

This couplet establishes such a distant resonance in my mind that I decide to take it as my motto.

Twisting Ring

My youngest daughter once owned a Twisting Ring that seemed to contain within it both red cliffs and white water. If you held it in your hand as you fell asleep then in your dreams you would find yourself elsewhere, surrounded by the splendors of famous mountains and great rivers, precious trees and rare birds, rose-gem towers and green jasper chambers. Whatever one happened to imagine in one's mind would appear the moment one conceived of it. This toy is also known by the name Ring of Fantasy. How extraordinary it would be to have hold of such a ring in everyday life!

I invite you to think of the northern gallery of my garden as being somewhat akin to this. Through a small opening in my Returning Clouds Lodging one enters obliquely through a low-hung doorway, just like Master Lu leaping into his pillow.[275] From this point onward each step one takes finds one within a forest of cherry trees with sweet streams and lingering shadows, and before one knows it, pavilions and terraces suddenly reveal themselves, all as if designed to startle one out of the sweet black village of one's dreams, like a grave and intimidating Sea of Dharma. Those who enter my mountain are forced to ascend the clouds and make their way across damp moss, the exertions of their feet never quite finding adequate compensation in the pleasures afforded their eyes. Only here, a single step takes one to the very top of Distant Belvedere, as if you have at your disposal that magical art of Master Pot's that enabled him to shrink distance into nothingness.[276] It can indeed be claimed that

---

275 This is a reference to the Tang dynasty classical tale entitled "The World Inside a Pillow" by Shen Jiji (ca. 740–ca. 800). Meeting a Daoist in an inn in Handan one day, Master Lu bemoans his lack of worldly success. The Daoist gives him a porcelain pillow upon which he promptly falls asleep. In his dreams, Master Lu experiences a lifetime full of all the successes he had been hoping for. He awakens only to find that he has been asleep for no longer than the time it has taken to cook his evening meal.

276 In the "Biography of Fei Changfang" in the *History of the Latter Han Dynasty*, the story is told of Fei Changfang's encounter with an old medicine peddler in a marketplace one day. At the end of the day, the old man leapt into his pot. Upon following him, Fei was tutored in the art of shrinking distance.

the scenery here besides the dykes and in the fields beneath the bridges fully encompasses the natural beauty of the Southeast. Layer upon layer of open vista present an ever-changing tableau and for a moment one believes, magically, that the Immortal Isle Penglai has suddenly appeared, or perhaps it is that mountain once shifted by the Foolish Old Man.[277] And so, after all, it *can* be said that I have in my hand every day a Twisting Ring. But if dreams are merely an illusion, what then is real? The allegory of my mountain is lodged in consciousness. It is lodged also in a dream, and if one can understand the allegory thus lodged in both dream and consciousness, how can one know that the dream is not itself conscious and consciousness not itself a dream? It doesn't seem to make much difference at all whether I have possession of a Twisting Ring or not.

Hall of the Distant Mountains

Two halls stand facing each other, one to the rear of my garden and the other in front of my farm, with a tower serving to separate them. The hall within my garden I intend to call the Hall of My Four Unfulfilled Obligations. That within my farm, ensconced as it is within the mountain forest, I will name Hall of the Distant Mountains in keeping with the excellence of its location. Why is this? Such is human nature that whereas we tend always to covet that which we lack, we begin to despise that which we have plenty of. The soaring peaks and crashing waves of my garden are as close to me as objects upon my side table and each day I nourish myself on the breath of the rock and the stalactites of cloud, satiating myself day and night upon such things. Familiarity, however, breeds contempt. Only here in this hall can I gaze far off to the north and catch sight of a few distant peaks, as if floating there beyond the clear autumn horizon. Perhaps, long ago, this is what Zhuo Wenjun's eyebrows looked like and why they were so named;[278] the mountains seem eager to greet an elegant scholar or an eminent monk; one moment they are visible, the next they disappear, within sight but always beyond reach. Thus have I named my hall Distant Mountains.

Hall of My Four Unfulfilled Obligations

Within my Abundance Mains stands a three-columned hall, overlooking the flowing water, as if with its wings outspread. Here the master of the garden raises his silkworms and stores his grain. Here, occasionally, too he entertains his guests with wine served in finest rhinoceros-shaped goblets. I happened at the time to have taken as my teacher

---

277 This is a reference to the story, found in the "Questions of Tang" chapter of the *Liezi*, that tells of an old man who, at the age of ninety, decides to move the two mountains that block egress from his house.

278 Zhuo Wenjun, daughter of Zhuo Wangsun of the Han, was said to have eloped with the poet Sima Xiangru (179–117 BCE) after hearing him play the lute. A great beauty, her eyebrows were said to be like "Gazing at Distant Mountains," and "Distant Mountain Eyebrows" later became the name for a style of makeup.

Master Wang Chaoshi.[279] He took grave issue with my obsession with the construction of my garden and upbraided me in a letter, in the following manner:

Recently I took a look at your garden and found that it embodied four unfulfilled obligations, three of which are failings on your part, and one on mine.

Great has been the favor bestowed upon you by the state. You ought to be considering how you can show yourself worthy of such favor. Even though you have retired to the countryside, you ought nonetheless to be discussing the Way and thinking about the great profession, each day deliberating how you may restore to their glory the gods of the grains and the soil, and confer benefits to the common folk. But for the past two years that you have been here, far from concerning yourself with such matters, you have simply devoted yourself to the construction of your garden, with carving and engraving, with flowers and rocks. In order to display your mastery of such petty skills, you have neglected the Grand Scheme of things as far as your state goes. If everyone were to be like you, what then could the state rely upon? This then can be said to be the manner in which you have failed to fulfil your obligation to the sovereign.

Your revered father long cleaved true to the Way, and was also conversant with the Buddhist scriptures. He purchased more than 10,000 books and entrusted them to the care of his sons and grandsons. To bring glory to the illustrious example of one's parents is a matter for the progeny of such parents. You are today approaching your fortieth year, the age at which you should be without doubt,[280] and you have served in the past in the post of censor. The requirement to establish yourself and implement the Way does not change with the circumstances of the times. But of such a determination I can observe no evidence and all you seem capable of is following the precedent set by your forebears, but with even greater flourish than they. How can such behavior be regarded as an expression of the filial piety expected of you? In this way, you can be said to have failed to fulfil your obligation to your father.

You are blessed with heaven given talents and a quick intelligence; by nature you are loyal and upright. Your attributes are such that you could have become a mentor who benefits the age, an effective vessel of the Way. At the same time, your

---

279   Editor's note: Wang Jinru, 1603–1640.

280   A reference to *The Analects*, 11.4: "The Master said, 'At fifteen, I had my mind bent on learning. At thirty, I stood firm. At forty, I had no doubts. At fifty, I knew the decrees of Heaven. At sixty, my ear was an obedient organ for the reception of truth. At seventy, I could follow what my heart desired, without transgressing what was right.'" See *The Chinese Classics*, vol. 1, *The Confucian Analects, The Great Learning, and the Doctrine of the Mean*, ed. and trans. James Legge (Oxford: Clarendon Press, 1893–1895), 146–47.

fortunate destiny is such that you enjoy the pleasures of friends and teachers and without having to quit your home you could have followed in the footsteps of the sages of old, if only you had devoted yourself to such an effort. On the contrary, however, far from cherishing your considerable abilities, you have associated with vulgar types and have pursued this particular task. Word of your efforts has spread to all four quarters, earning you the awe of mere boys and girls everywhere. You pay no heed to the frowns of those intent upon the Way, casting your pearls among the worthless potsherds and allowing your fine fields to become overgrown with weeds. In this respect you can be said to have failed to fulfil your obligation to yourself.

If you are guilty of having not fulfilled these three obligations, then I for my part should have repaid the affection you have shown me with some straight talking in order to nip your enterprise off in its bud. This I have failed to do, vainly hoping now to remedy the situation with my present remonstrance, once the deed has already been done. I regret that I have been remiss in my effort to rectify myself, and I am ashamed that nor have I been able to provide you with an appropriate role model. In this way I may be said to have failed to fulfil my obligation of friendship.

Alas! What excellent counsel this is! How very fortunate I am to have been the recipient of such excellent counsel. Of all the criticism of the error of my ways I have received since I embarked upon the construction of my garden, only these words have served to cut to the quick. Having been counselled in this manner, I have nonetheless been unable to act like Wang Jian who destroyed his Studio of the Long Beams as soon as his uncle criticized it for its lavishness, and this exacerbates my failing. The master has accused me of failing to fulfil three obligations. This accusation I readily accept. Having heard his counsel and having proven incapable of changing my ways, this may be said to be a failure to fulfil the obligation of friendship on my part, not his. I have named this place the Hall of My Four Unfulfilled Obligations in order to record my remorse and my intention to reform myself.

Library of the Eight Principles of Book Acquisition
Long ago, the great Song dynasty bibliophile Zheng Qiao stipulated that there were eight principles to the Way of book collecting. Firstly, one collected by category; secondly, by related category; thirdly, by region and fourthly by family; fifthly one sought books from collections in the public domain; sixthly, books in private hands; seventhly, one acquired books in terms of their authorship; and lastly, by dynastic provenance.

My esteemed father cleaved true to these precepts all his life and through exhaustive searching and comprehensive acquisition he eventually assembled a library of over one hundred thousand volumes. For the edification of his sons and grandsons, he composed a covenant in which he gave a complete account of the methods of book buying, book collecting, book connoisseurship and the art of reading. In so doing, he approximated the achievements of Cao Pingmu and his Stone Vault, Ren Mo's Garden of the Classics[281] and Shentu Zhiyuan's Ink Village.[282]

Although I too, for my part, harbor a love of books, most regrettably I happen also to be plagued by an atrocious memory. I cannot pretend to be like Wang Chong of the Han who could remember everything he ever read, even if he had done so leaning against a doorpost in the middle of the marketplace, nor can I ever hope to emulate that Flourishing Talent of the Northern Wei Zhen Chen who attacked his studies with such a vengeance and who took such copious notes of what he had read.[283] When I took leave of my post in Suzhou to return here, I calculated that I had accumulated 31,500 volumes. These I had placed within the hindmost tower of my Farm of Abundance and there I would fondle them all day long. But even this collection is a mere semblance of that bought and assembled by my esteemed father.

I have heard it said that Li Mi, Duke of Ye during the Tang, collected on his shelves more than 30,000 scrolls and that later his son Fan too was given a hereditary fiefdom in Ye and served as censor of Suizhou. It is also said that Ouyang Xiu, who owned a book collection of over ten thousand volumes, had a son named Fei who was a fluent writer and who became an official famed for his incorruptibility. Somewhat inferior to this was Zhao Kuo whom people made fun of for only reading books written by his father, and yet he at least knew how to read.[284] How much superior were the men of old to those of this present age! Yi Sundu of the Song once said: "So many are the books that I have collected that my sons and grandsons are bound to be good scholars!" My father toiled painstakingly all his life and the scholarly efforts of the one generation ought to be continued by the next. As I dare not believe that the future will see me able to much improve my efforts in this respect, I can only hope that my descendants will make up for my own neglect!

---

281 Fearing lest his many rare books might be lost, Cao Pingmu of the Han constructed a stone vault to ensure their survival. Ren Mo, also of the Han, carved into the trunks of the trees of his garden the texts of rare commentaries to the Confucian Canon.

282 Shentu Zhiyuan, an official during the Yuan dynasty, collected a library of over 10,000 volumes.

283 Having wasted his time playing chess, Zhen Chen turned back to his books when laughed at by his servants.

284 This anecdote is found in the "Biography of Lian Po and Lin Xiangru" in Sima Qian's *Records of the Grand Historian*. When the King of Zhao made Zhao Kuo commander, Li Xiangru said: "Your Majesty is sending Kuo because of his reputation; this is like gluing the tuning bridges to strum a zither. Kuo can only recite his father's writings and instructions; he knows nothing about adapting to the changes of battle." See William H. Nienhauser Jr., ed., *The Grand Scribe's Records*, vol. 7, *The Memoirs of Pre-Han China* (Bloomington: Indiana University Press, 1994), 269, transliteration altered.

"To Qi Biaojia" (*Yu Qi Shipei shu* 與祁世培書)

ZHANG DAI 張岱 (1597–CA. 1684)

TRANSLATED BY DUNCAN M. CAMPBELL

Zhang Dai, a man connected to Qi Biaojia by ties of marriage and friendship (Zhang labeled Qi his "Friend in the Mountains and Rivers") was one of the people to whom Qi circulated drafts of his record, and here we offer Zhang's comments on the various difficulties involved in garden design.

"To Qi Biaojia"

The real difficulty of constructing a garden lies in the overall conception of its layout. Even more difficult, however, is the appropriate naming of the various features the garden contains. If the names given these features are vulgar, then the garden itself loses whatever elegance it can lay claim to, while the writings inspired by the garden will in turn also lack any subtlety. With the sole exception of Wang Wei's Wangchuan Estate, the various scenes contained within famous gardens have never quite been matched by the quality of the writing that they have inspired. This is true even of the fourteen scenes of Xiao Boyu's Spring Floating Garden, none of the poems and essays written on these scenes proving at all transcendent or exceptional. The quatrains by Wang Siren, for example, seem very mediocre. From this instance, we can see that places of surpassing beauty and verses of eternal loveliness are not often found located in the same place. The four-word plaques that hang in Lake Heart Pavilion in the middle of West Lake, the matching couplets that crowd the rafters and columns there, are a case in point. Zhang Zhongshan once threatened to burn the whole place down, in order to cleanse it of such bad karma. But, as anyone of any real understanding knows, once inscribed, not one word of a vulgar man can be erased.

Of the various splendors of your Allegory Mountain Garden, as many as forty-nine have been given names, not one of which reveals the slightest sign of vulgarity. To achieve this was a true test of your abilities. Yet, whereas the master of the garden possesses the talents of a Wang Wei, I am certainly no Pei Di. You require me to compose poems in response to those that you have written, but the poems that I have managed to come up with are common and vulgar in the extreme, proximately, not even a match for those written by Wang Siren, let alone daring to compete with poems written by Pei Di. An ugly wife will live in fear of those inevitable meetings with her husband's mother. Her mother-in-law, for her part, if she has any powers of discernment, will have a clear conception of the gulf that separates beauty from ugliness. Written in much haste!

"A Visit to Allegory Mountain" (*Yushan she* 寓山涉)

DONG XUAN 董玄 (17TH CENTURY)

TRANSLATED BY ALISON HARDIE

Another friend (perhaps also related to Qi), Dong Xuan, about whom little else is known, wrote a detailed account of his tour of the garden, designed explicitly to help ensure that visitors could both understand the garden, and find their way into and out of it. Dong's account reveals something not mentioned in Qi's, that part of the garden was designed by Zhang Yifan, one of the descendants of the famous garden craftsman Zhang Lian (see chapter 7).

"A Visit to Allegory Mountain"

Introduction

I have observed of the universe that landscape—the mountains and the rivers—exists only in parallel with man. Man and the landscape are elder and younger brother. And yet, if the creation of singular mountains and beautiful rivers requires an extraordinary expenditure of effort to bring into being, without the observation and participation of man, however, they remain but a corner of the universe that is both obscure and distantly removed. It seems as though in his capacity to open them up, man is actually superior to the natural universe itself. The trouble is that men of this present age prefer the well-known landscapes; they pursue those which are currently all the rage and site their residence according to how famous a place is. As for those places which are obscurely remote and peacefully quiet, these they give not a second thought. They do not realize that when the universe first emerged from primal chaos, there was a magical power inherent in it which could not be defiled. It was thus that men of old who were skilled at assessing landscape did not pick it by its reputation on the market, but selected it for its spirit of reclusion.

Master Qi Biaojia's improvement of Allegory Mountain is a case in point. Master Qi has an inborn affinity with the mists and haze; whenever he arrives among springs and rocks he becomes so absorbed that he forgets to leave. He examines each mere fragment of mountain-peak that he encounters in fine detail, but it was only at Allegory Mountain that he came to a stop. Here he constructed pavilions on the hill and excavated a pond at its foot. The mountain he adorned with the beauty of forests, and by the water he placed terraces and buildings. Thereupon, the true face of the mountain was opened up and so its spirit was revealed. Master Qi must have taken into consideration the nature of Allegory as a mountain: it rears up abruptly in isolation from the level ground, not rising gradually to a height through a succession of ridges; lofty rocks jut up singly, not relying on massed force to appear remote. He is totally unlike people who only follow a prevailing trend, and that is why he alone was able to make the most of this site.

It was only after five or six visits that I could really appreciate its splendors. Fearing that a fisherman who suddenly found himself at the Peach Blossom Spring would get lost, I wrote "A Visit to Allegory Mountain" to guide the visitor.

A Visit to Allegory Mountain

Twenty *li* to the west from Fan Li's city is the village of Meishu; this is where Master Qi lives. About three *li* from here is Allegory Mountain. Although it is a small hill, it rears up proudly, loftily isolated within several hundred feet of deep seclusion. Observing the pavilions and terraces emerging on all sides, they would seem to have the power to swallow up the mountain, but the exuberance of the mountain is keen enough that it is not overpowered by the pavilions and terraces, a fact which is to be applauded.

Master Qi's late father owned the Secret Garden to the left side of his mansion. Visitors would invariably visit this garden first, before coming on next to his cousin Zhixiang's Axe-Haft Garden. On reaching it, the force of the water becomes more powerful, and the color of the waves rivals the sky in blueness. From the Axe-Haft Garden, one bridge was built that turns to the west and then follows an earthen bank; this is named Controlling the Channel. Another bridge is angled to the south and runs among the fields; after two hundred paces it reaches the water's edge. Clumps of trees line the path, and there is another bridge. Here one knocks at a double-leaved gate and enters on to Treading on Fragrance Embankment. On both banks are planted peaches, willows, and hibiscus. When ladies stroll among them, the multitudinous blossoms drop on their hats and the soft fronds catch at their clothing. The towers and belvederes in the garden waver in the distance over the tops of the trees; they spot the people before the people have had a chance to see the garden. After about half a *li*, one crosses Willow Pathway, where a pavilion rises up, with weeping willows surrounding it on all sides; this is the entrance to the Allegory Mountain Garden.

As one enters the garden, a covered bridge takes three turns; the light of the sky illuminates one's steps as one treads over the waterweed. Having crossed it once, one could go for ten years without dreaming again of the West Lake.

The covered bridge connects with a half-span canopy. Academician Ni first wrote an inscription for it naming it Canopy of the Inhaling Rainbow, because the long embankment was in sight of it. Afterward, although the embankment was taken away, it was still like a rainbow in sometimes appearing and sometimes disappearing on the horizon, so the name remained highly appropriate.

Edge on to the canopy, in order to take in all the splendors of the walkway, is the Abode for Studying the *Book of Changes*. A single pool lies in its lap, while a myriad mountains catch the eye. At this point the visitor can sit for a short time and drink a cup of tea while the accoutrements for his visit are prepared.

The abode, the walkway and the canopy all overlook the pond. Only the terns are able to possess the attractions of the pond, so the master named the pond Relinquished to the Terns.

If you wish to travel south from the Abode for Studying the *Book of Changes*, you cross the covered bridge and, to the side, enter a gate; along a secluded path of several twists and turns, one already perceives the fragrant shadows enfolding one. Then one boards the Flowering Apricot Boat. On three sides it is surrounded by hundreds of trees with onyx blossoms; it is just like a skiff floating on snowy waves. Looking east, one can see Treading on Fragrance Embankment, coiling along over the green water. Altogether there are several dozen layers of painting, near and far, shallow and deep; this building gathers them all in.

By some stone steps one ascends Flowering Apricot Slope, which attracts the moon and gives off drifts of fragrance; as soon as you sit or lie there you seem to become Zhao Shixiong having his sweet dream.[285]

From the top one goes down to a path by a stream, and crosses a plank bridge to where there is a thatched building. Neither carved nor whitewashed, it is named The Pitcher Stop. Sitting here, one feels that the world of men and the machine heart are entirely wiped out.

Beside it is the Bin Potager, named after the "Airs of Bin" from the *Book of Songs*. The master sometimes comes here with walking stick in hand to oversee the gardeners planting. They gather vegetables in armfuls, and cook jade tablet bamboo shoots to make soup.

The back of the Bin Potager is encircled by an ancient stone wall, beyond which one can see a filigree rock reaching up to the clouds; this is Swirling Waves Isle. It looks as though a few dozen buds of green hibiscus had been randomly cut from the twin towers of the Jasper Terrace of the immortals and transplanted here, for here the raging wind roils the billows and thrusts them into the cracks in the rock; it splatters jade and spurts out pearls as precipitately as if from the merman's palace.

The isle lies athwart a brimming pool of water; there is a pavilion rising up abruptly, which you reach only by wandering around vaguely. Orioles are imprisoned in the

---

285   According to a story told by the Tang dynasty poet and essayist Liu Zongyuan (773–819), Zhao Shixiong, a man of the Sui dynasty (589–618), once fell asleep drunk beneath a flowering apricot tree when he was touring Mount Luofu (a mountain sacred to the Daoists). In his dream, he was entertained both by a beautiful young maiden and a boy dressed all in green. When he awoke, however, they were gone, and had been replaced by birds singing in the tree above him.

willows' mist; fish gulp the flowers' reflections: these are all the fine scenes from within the pavilion. Indeed it is a place for the Appreciation of Excellence.

From here there is a small bridge with three angles. One's sandals tread on lotus flowers, whose solidified fragrance is about to drip; this is the Terrace of the Jade Maiden of Solitary Peak. The repeated tinkling of cloud-like belt-ornaments seems to have flown here from Witch's Gorge. The pond which was relinquished to the terns should also be relinquished to the Jade Maiden as a basin to wash her hair.

Alongside the water is a rustling path, where the flowers, with their cool fragrance, are like rosy cheeks around an incense burner. Because of this, the master named the crossing after the lotus. Did he have thoughts of picking chrysanthemums by the eastern hedge?

From the crossing one enters on a walkway. The building which half overlooks the pond is Thatched Belvedere of the Brook and the Hill. It seems to share the water of the pond with the Abode for Studying the *Book of Changes*, but the sparse cold of trees and rocks has its own appeal to the mind.

To the south of the Thatched Belvedere, several turns of winding walkway are half set over a pool of chill emerald. Where the walkway comes to an end, a tiny cottage is semi-visible, enclosed within obscuring foliage. Not only does the master make himself at peace in its leisured seclusion; people, objects, fish, and birds can virtually all conceal themselves here without showing. So it is comparable to the Jar Hideaway of Shentu in more than just its shape.

Beside it are several *wu* of ground planted with a mixture of hundreds of flowering plants. Even in autumn or winter it is still like a valley of embroidery. It is named Whispering Riggs.

To the north, the Thatched Belvedere faces great rocks which overhang threateningly, called Pocket Ocean. When you bend over and go in, the sky appears only the size of a fan, and cool snow lightly encroaches on you; it is like a mountain dragon baring his fangs in a snarl, resenting the master relinquishing the pond to the terns and wanting to contest with them for supremacy.

From here each step climbs a winding stairway; turning and ascending twenty feet one comes to the Gazebo for Friendship with the Rocks; its face grazes the roots of the mountain and its back reclines on a shady valley. Ancient moss embroiders the walls and the pure water round an islet reflects the sky. Beside it is a rock styled Cold Cloud; it is this rock with whom the master has made friends.

To the side of Cold Cloud Rock, there is a level clump of old pine-trees, opening out to form a path which is named after the pines. They act as a cool filter for the sunlight; when the wind comes, the sound rushes up and down like a myriad streams of water dropping from the tops of the pines, or like the constant downpours in Sichuan. Sometimes one hears a squall of rain, but one does not see one's clothes wet.

Where the path comes to an end is the Cherry Tree Grove. At the tail-end of spring, the myriad red pearls are like a beautiful woman standing behind a jade-green curtain: one can catch a glimpse of rouged dimples, but the Hermit of the Fragrant Hills is not allowed to peek at Fansu behind the screen.

From here a solitary pavilion is within sight, which is named Selecting the Superior. There is an embroidered expanse of emerald beyond this pavilion; the pure fragrance of rice-paddy fills the air and wafts in on the light breeze. As people explore all the superior sights within the garden, the tracks of their clogs all congregate at this pavilion. So the other places cannot share in its superiority.

To the east of Selecting the Superior is Horned Tiger Hermitage, within which a statue of Guanyin is worshipped. The master conducts Buddhist services here throughout the six periods of the day. As the Pine-Tree Path approaches here, it seems that one's sandals could only reach the Hermitage in the distance, and yet the sound of the pine-trees is right below the steps.

If you go farther south and upward from Selecting the Superior, you reach Lesser Crenellated Peaks, which forms something like a northern gate to the mountain.

Entering from the western gateway, there is the Determination to Retire Studio. When the master had submitted his memorial requesting retirement, it was here that he composed his "Ode on Carrying Out One's Original Wish."

The right of the Studio connects with an ornamented walkway; once a door is opened, then the Thatched Hall can be seen. The Hall is spacious and expansive, bright and spotless; soaring rafters reach to the clouds, while well-grown pine-trees swish over the roof-tiles. The name of Allegory Mountain could not but be claimed by this hall. A Lingbi rock thrusts up beside it in all its strangeness. The hall connects with the top of the rock as if in fear that the spirit of the mountain has taken up its abode there temporarily but is about to fly away again, and so the hall wants to hold it down.

To the west side of the hall is the Terrace Penetrating the Roseate Clouds. As the sun sets you may ascend it in intoxication; red reflections occupy the ground; one is standing on the surface of the sunset-cloud vapors. Regrettably, although Li Bai's breath could penetrate to the Emperor's Throne, this expression, Penetrating the Roseate Clouds, is wasted on flattering the alighting wild geese.

To the north of the terrace, a building extends transversely; to the west it faces the eight-thousand-foot rocky wall of Axe-Haft Hill, as if a cast-iron cloud were coming forward to make obeisance. It is named Facing the Wall Adytum.

Returning from the Terrace Penetrating the Roseate Clouds, one goes back by the Thatched Hall to reach the Quietist's Gallery. This gallery and the Determination to Retire Studio face each other. With a single table and daybed, it does not allow entrance to dust and noise. From time to time comes the pure sound of a stone chime; the myriad pipes of Nature are all silent. That is why it is called Quietist.

The backdrop of the gallery is formed by the Peak of the Iron Mushroom, the highest point of Allegory Mountain. A low wall has now been built to divide it into two halves. The well-grown pines and emerald parasol trees are half absorbed within the gallery.

Poised on a steep ascent to the east of the gallery is Distant Belvedere. A soaring peak rises abruptly as though wishing its summit to rival all the ridges of the Pillar of Heaven. As for the tips of the flowering apricot trees, one would have to ascend to the celestial river to assess their excellences and imperfections. Ascending the belvedere, with one look one feels that creative Nature laid out the hundred plains and myriad hills especially to be viewed from this position. There is nothing that could be added to the sense of expansiveness in looking and listening here.

The second story of the belvedere is the Chamber of Simplicity. It is so restrained that it seems to be suspended on its own beyond the mountains; views of well-grown woods and villas come right inside to one's very seat, so the scenery which one obtains is far from restrained.

Descending from the Chamber of Simplicity, one comes to Rotten Axe-Haft Mountain House. This is Master Qi's favorite place. Pure reflections are glimpsed through the blinds; clouds of fragrance are concealed in the hangings. As one lies aloft by the northern window, only the song of birds occasionally disturbs one's dreams.

Ascending a short way, there is yet another walkway attached to the east of the Quietist's Gallery. Because there are many strange rocks beside it, jagged crags soaring and washed with water, it is therefore named Indulgence in Rinsing Gallery.

As one walks down by the walkway, cloud-like millstones and rock saws rear up in isolation on the shoulder of the mountain. There is a pavilion made of bamboo; in reference to the story of the Gentleman-in-Waiting it is named Flute Pavilion.

Farther down there is a deep depression known as Heaven's Calabash. From here one again ends up at the Determination to Retire Studio.

The northeast side of the studio is again connected with a long walkway that winds its way downward, although it seems as though there is no path by which one can get there. After passing through a stone gateway there is a stretch of bamboo walkway, with an old camphor tree ten spans in circumference which casts its shade over one *mu*. There is an open belvedere at its side. This is called Old Camphor Tree Level.

Walking along the bamboo pathway, one passes through a small gate in a hedge made of entwined thorn-bushes; the mountain path, by fits and starts and with several turns, reaches the side of a stream. This is named Green Jade Ridge.

One crosses the stream by a bridge, and then continues to follow the stream for several paces, where a myriad green bamboos shade the area. There is a belvedere called Storehouse of Happiness. Its western face lies athwart the fields and it takes in all the scenery of Axe-Haft Hill.

Also from among the bamboos can be seen a building of one bay, the Place for Detaining Guests Deep in the Bamboo. It leans against the sheer cliff on the north side of the mountain.

One crosses the stream on stepping stones, mounts a dry bridge to the south, and follows a walkway upward. The walkway takes three or four turns in all, and visitors who enter it do not find it easy to get out. This is Twisting Ring; it shrinks the scenery of the whole mountain into a one-inch compass. There is no need to worry that you may easily become completely exhausted. Those who climb it, by grasping creepers and shouldering their way through the undergrowth, can quickly arrive here.

There is a belvedere built against a rock wall. Looking north from this point, the view is vast and boundless. This is the Dwelling of Thatch Fragrance and Crimson Snow.

Again, descending eastward from Twisting Ring, one comes to Little Floating Banner. The upstairs is for the worship of the holy Maitreya, while the downstairs provides a passage to and fro. It is only at this point that one realizes how twisting the ring really is.

Slightly farther down there is a building which backs on the mountain and overlooks the water; this is Identity with the Lotus. Master Chen perceived from a single flower the magnitude of the equivalence of the myriad things. Only when one abandons the idea that coming together and separating are two different things, can one speak of "identity." Please understand this within the Quietist's Gallery.

Turning southward from the gallery, there is the Returning Cloud Lodging, a place where one can climb to an upper story. The Pine-Tree Path touches its shoulders. The waves of Sea Gate, the jade of Ice Flask are stored within the lodging. What do Turbulent Glen and Heaven's Overthrow amount to? Yet Cold Cloud still dares to have the ambition of emerging above the crag.

Entering from the side of Returning Cloud Lodging, one comes into Combined Expansiveness Belvedere. The single room within it is extremely tranquil; to the outside, all the scenery is brought together for the benefit of its table and seats.

Adjoining this area of towers and walkways is an elegant building above the burgeoning vegetation of flowers and bamboo; it is called Testing the Orioles Lodge. Mountain Man Zhang Yifan[286] constructed a rockery of great vitality and movement, but yet without any trace of artifice. On spring days the master sits here to listen to the orioles twittering among the weeping willows and carefully compare their relative skill; he calls this testing whether they are more profound than the listener. I am only afraid that even with a couple of oranges and a stoup of wine, I may still not understand the music of the poetic instinct. Opening the northern shutters you can climb up by some steps; a bamboo fence winds around, forming a small pathway which reaches the Gazebo for Friendship with the Rocks.

Going southward along by the pond below the towers and walkways, luxuriant bamboo is reflected in the pond; this is truly a place "beside the water and below the woods." A stone bridge lying athwart it is Listening Stops Bridge.

Looking at Brook and Hill Thatched Belvedere, it seems just a foot or two away, but beside the belvedere is another path, which winds through an ornamented walkway and reaches a building of three bays that is the ultimate in brightness and cleanness. This is Master Qi Biaojia's study, and it is called Distant Mountain Hall. If you ascend from here by the ornamented walkway, then you reach the Chamber of Simplicity.

Where Returning Cloud Lodging comes to an end, a hall can be seen. The master, taking to heart a phrase of a good friend, gave to its substance the name of Four Unfulfilled Obligations. Palace gate-towers and rivers and lakes come to the same thing in the end. People in this world who fail to fulfill their obligations to their sovereign, their parents, other people and themselves, cannot be the same type as those who take pleasure in hills and glens and are ready to retire despite official success. If the virtuous officials Gao and Kui were still here today, they would doubtless follow

---

[286]   Zhang Yifan was a son of the famous garden designer Zhang Lian (Nanyuan), whose biography appears in the next chapter.

their heart's desires among forests and springs. The fact that Master Qi describes himself as having "unfulfilled obligations" just proves that he has in fact fulfilled these obligations.

Behind the Hall is the Library of the Eight Principles of Book Acquisition, the place where the master stores his books. The Qi family tradition as bibliophiles is as strong as ever. In his prime, the master has untied the seal-cord of office and is able to read many unusual books and to research the philosophy of Mind and Principle. How could he really just be incurably obsessed with springs and rocks?

Eight Principles of Book Acquisition is situated in the middle; to the east is the Southern Tower, and to the west is Combined Expansiveness Belvedere. They are connected by two side buildings.

As you come out of the Hall of Four Unfulfilled Obligations you see a walkway on the back of a bridge; this is called Old Man of the Sea Bridge.

Passing from here through the Abode for Studying the *Book of Changes*, there is another walkway called Water Bright, probably because when the bright moon first rises it shines into it and the light off the waves ripples over the walls; only this walk-way achieves the best of this.

Turning east, one crosses a bridge where there is a gallery of three bays over the water, named Terrace of the Floating Reflections.

Over yet another bridge and slightly farther south is Abundance Mains. When you come out of Abundance Mains, cross another bridge, and go along the embankment, then you end up again at the gate of the Allegory Mountain garden. In constructing the garden, the master was not merely indulging himself in the enjoyment of springs and rocks. There are economic activities going on among the mountain forests. He gave the name of Bin to his vegetable plot and Abundance to his home-farm, presumably in order to emphasize the fact that he is managing the mountain forests as a means of ben-efiting the world. Even lofty walls in serried ranks like a comb may achieve the aim of providing nourishment and sharing sweetness. The old drunkard's interest is not in the wine. My description of the garden and its pavilions ends with farming industriously and reading books. It can be seen that what the master has expressed by means of the garden is of great profundity.

"Qi Youwen's Allegory Mountain Thatched Hall" (*Qi Youwen Yushan caotang* 祁幼文寓山草堂)

LIU SHI 柳是 (RUSHI 如是; 1618–1664)

TRANSLATED BY ALISON HARDIE

Liu Shi, better known as Liu Rushi, was a celebrated courtesan of the late Ming. She was known for her poetry, as well as for appearing in public in male clothing; she was also a competent if undistinguished painter. She had a serious relationship with the poet and political activist Chen Zilong (1608–1647), as well as a shorter liaison with Wang Ruqian, the owner of a West Lake pleasure-boat named the Untethered Garden (see chapter 9). It appears that she wrote this poem after a visit with Wang to Qi Biaojia's Allegory Mountain (she refers to him as Qi Youwen, one of his social names); in addition to the Thatched Hall as the subject of the poem, she alludes in the last line to the small building called the Flute Pavilion. In his compilation of poems on his garden, Qi published Wang Ruqian's poem (on Canopy of the Inhaling Rainbow) but not Liu's. Her references to the Rivers Luo and Xiang place Qi as garden owner in the shamanic landscape of the *Songs of the South* (see chapter 1).

In 1640, Liu Shi approached the leading writer and critic Qian Qianyi (1582–1664), many years her senior, who married her as his concubine the following year. However, he caused something of a scandal by treating her as his principal wife (his actual principal wife was still alive). Finding herself in an untenable position after Qian's death in 1664, Liu committed suicide.

"Qi Youwen's Allegory Mountain Thatched Hall"

> Cool breeze in the steep garden: airs of another world,
> Matched by this stone-built hall with vermilion beams;
> A home on the banks of the River Luo where onyx clouds receive us,
> Its master, like the Lord of the Xiang, escorted by free-flying cranes.
> Among flowers in full bloom, the jewelled canopy rustles at dawn's approach;
> With the song of orioles, spring arrives to flutter our jade clothing.
> He and I have both made songs to commemorate the garden;
> Dark vapors blown from the magic flute obscure our parting sail.

"Allegory Garden" (*Yu yuan* 寓園) and "On a Spring Day in Allegory Garden Gazing at the Plum Blossoms" (*Chunri Yu yuan guan mei* 春日寓園觀梅)

SHANG JINGLAN 商景蘭 (1604–CA. 1680)

Qi Biaojia's remarkable widow, Shang Jinglan, who continued to visit the Allegory Mountain garden after her husband's death, wrote the following bitter poems about it. We know from Qi's diaries that Shang was much involved in both the design and the construction of the garden. Shang Jinglan, like her husband, was from a noted gentry family of Shaoxing; in the 1620s, her father was involved in negotiations with the Dutch over their occupation of the Penghu Islands, and he eventually rose to be Minister of War. Jinglan was responsible for educating her sons as well as her daughters, and was a noted poet.

"Allegory Garden"
TRANSLATED BY DUNCAN M. CAMPBELL

A scene of desolation now this garden of old,
My sense of loss redoubled as I visit it again.
Throughout the garden, buds of flowering apricot burst into whiteness,
Along both banks the willows unfurl their greenness.
In clumps do the fragrant grasses grow anew,
And here and there gushing springs begin to sing.
When the nightjar's call hastens on the fall of day,
I linger long beside the bright moon's rays.

"On a Spring Day in Allegory Garden Gazing at the Plum Blossoms"
TRANSLATED BY WILT IDEMA AND BEATA GRANT

The plum and willow compete in springness: the entire garden quiet.
The shrubs and trees here in his absence stir up sorrows over the past.
It is only the spring wind that still has the same inexhaustible drive,
And as it did before, completely infuses the branches with fragrance.

"Rejoicing That My Second Son Studies in the Purple Fungus Studio" (*Xi ci er dushu Zizhi xuan* 喜次兒讀書紫芝軒) and "Visiting the Secret Garden" (*You Mi yuan* 遊密園)

SHANG JINGLAN 商景蘭
TRANSLATED BY ELLEN WIDMER

The Secret Garden or Intimate Garden (*Mi yuan*) was the garden of Shang Jinglan's father-in-law (Qi Biaojia's father) Qi Chenghan, quite close to Allegory Mountain on the outskirts of Shanyin (present-day Shaoxing). Qi Chenghan wrote a fairly detailed description of his garden, the "Earlier and Later Records of the Secret Garden," from which we know that it was the location of the Purple Fungus Studio.[287] Since this garden, like Allegory Mountain, was the scene of frequent family parties during Qi Biaojia's lifetime, it equally reminds Shang Jinglan of her dead husband.

Shang's "second son" probably refers to Qi Bansun, actually the third son to whom she gave birth (her eldest son Tongsun became the adopted son of Qi Biaojia's elder brother, who had no

---

287 Qi Chenghan, *Miyuan qianhou ji, Danshengtang ji* (Shaoxing: Qi family, 1633), 11.1a–29b (Ming edition in National Central Library, Taipei).

heir; Tongsun then died in adolescence). Bansun and his elder surviving brother Lisun were active in the Ming resistance after the Qing conquest, but escaped punishment.

"Rejoicing That My Second Son Studies in the Purple Fungus Studio"

Lotus flowers once laughed at the sun.
Wutong leaves startle me by degrees with their signs of fall.
The water is white; in its light, trees seem broken.
Flowers are red; in their reflection the tower moves.
My son's literary talent stands out from the pack.
My white hair—in the mirror it reveals my grief.
I rely on the books my husband left behind,
And on the empty staircase the light of his moon never recedes.

"Visiting the Secret Garden"

Quietly the peaceful woods are enveloped by green mist.
Coldly the mountain streams emerge from flowing springs.
The light off the lake is pale where it meets the storied tower on the far side.
The frost on oranges and pomelos accentuates their round, yellow forms.
Like the chickens and dogs at the cave opening, we seek to escape the world.[288]
Clouds and sunset under my pen give expression to poems of wandering immortals.
Visitors to a fragrant landscape, we never tire of climbing high and looking into the
    distance.
Still more do we appreciate the special purity of pear flowers.

Collected Talks from the Lü Garden (*Lüyuan conghua* 履園叢話)

"Allegory Garden" (*Yu yuan* 寓園)

QIAN YONG 錢泳
TRANSLATED BY ALISON HARDIE

For Qian Yong, see above. We can see from his brief account of Allegory Garden that the features that became most famous in later years were not necessarily those Qi Biaojia himself had regarded as the most important parts of his garden (apart from the Hall of the Distant Mountains,

---

288 When Liu An (180–122 BCE), prince of Huainan and practitioner of Daoist immortality magic, ascended to heaven, the chickens and dogs in his courtyard licked the elixir from his bowl and attained immortality (Ge Hong, *Shen xian zhuan*, 4/5a). The *Dao de jing*, chapter 80, advises that countries be kept small and their inhabitants few, so that "neighboring states might overlook one another, and the sounds of chickens and dogs might be overheard, yet the people will arrive at old age and death with no comings and goings between them" (*Lao-tzu*, 156). These two allusions are frequently employed together to suggest the Daoist hermit's life: see, for example, Tao Qian's "Peach-Blossom Spring," the probable source of the "cave" mentioned here.

which he used in the titles of his works of drama criticism). It is also clear that the garden derived most of its meaning for later visitors from its association with Qi's death as a martyr to the fallen Ming dynasty.

"Allegory Garden"

The Allegory Garden lies at the foot of Allegory Mountain twenty *li* to the southwest of the county town of Shanyin. It was constructed by Censor Qi Biaojia at the end of the Ming, and includes the eight sights Lotus Crossing, Terrace of the Jade Maiden, Swirling Waves Isle, Flowering Apricot Slope, Oriole-Testing Hostelry, Identity with the Lotus Cottage, Returning Clouds Gallery [Lodging], and Hall of the Distant Mountains. On the night of the sixth day of the intercalary month of the *yiyou* year of Chongzhen [1645], Biaojia, formally dressed in robe and cap, drowned himself in the pond here, dying as a Ming loyalist. His son Lisun and his brother [Bansun] subsequently buried their father at the side of the garden, where there is now a memorial temple with a ceramic statue of Qi, maintained to this day by his descendants.

"A Personal Record of My Garden of Reflections" (*Yingyuan ziji* 影園自記)

ZHENG YUANXUN 鄭元勳 (1598–1644)
TRANSLATED BY DUNCAN M. CAMPBELL

Zheng Yuanxun is now best known as a minor landscape painter of the late Ming period. His family, who were originally merchants, had moved from what is now Anhui Province to the city of Yangzhou, an important commercial city at the confluence of the Yangtze River and the Grand Canal. Zheng is usually associated with the Anhui school of landscape painting.[289] He was, as he indicates in this text, a follower of the great art critic Dong Qichang (1555–1636). Zheng did not succeed in passing the government examinations until 1643, and never held an official post in his lifetime. In the following year (as we have seen in the introduction), he became caught up in the turmoil of the Ming collapse and was killed by an angry mob of his fellow Yangzhou residents.

What lends Zheng's garden a special level of interest is the involvement in its design and construction in the 1630s of Ji Cheng (b. 1582), one of the preeminent garden designers of the time and author of the single most important traditional Chinese monograph on the topic, *The Craft of Gardens* (see chapters 3, 6, and 7). In his foreword to this work (see below), dated 1635 and written in the Garden of Reflections, and in his account of the garden itself, Zheng Yuanxun is explicit about the extent of Ji Cheng's contribution to the design of the garden, which unfortunately fell into ruin not long after the change of dynasty.

The garden's name presents difficulties for the translator, the "ying" of its title denoting both reflections and shadows.

---

289 See James Cahill, ed., *Shadows of Mount Huang: Chinese Painting and Printing of the Anhui School* (Berkeley: University Art Museum, 1981).

"A Personal Record of My Garden of Reflections"

An addiction to the mountains and to the rivers, to bamboo and to trees is something with which one is born; it cannot be affected. Born, as I was, north of the Yangtze River and thus deprived of the sight of even handfuls of stone, throughout my youth it was only in paintings that I came to see tall mountains with lofty peaks. Nonetheless, as I explored them in my mind, my love for the mountains and the rivers proved quite irresistible. Over time I taught myself to paint, my paintings, however, according with no single tradition of the art. Whenever I went beyond the suburbs, the sight of the delicate beauty of the forests and the rivers would so detain me that I could not bear to return home, and thus it was that during my studies I usually took up residence in deserted temples.

It was only when I was in my seventeenth year that I finally crossed south of the river and visited the various splendors of Jinling (Nanjing). Within the decade, I had visited more than half the splendors of the Wu region, a circumstance that both lent consolation to my innermost desires and served to convince me that there is nothing more fitting in life than travel in this manner. Upon my return, I playfully tried to capture with ink and brush the forms of those splendors I had encountered and when, in the winter of the *renshen* year [1632], Master Dong Qichang[290] happened to pass through Yangzhou, I took my paintings to him to solicit his criticisms. He, for his part, was kind enough to praise my skills, saying that as I had managed to capture the essence of the mountains and the rivers, my paintings should not be judged simply in terms of the skill of my brushwork.

Prevailing upon this excess of goodwill, I made bold enough to continue: "I am now over thirty years old and my life so far has been characterized by a distinct lack of good fortune. My scholarship too proves patchy in the extreme. Recently, however, I happened upon a disused vegetable garden south of the town which I have since acquired and where I intend soon to have constructed a simple cottage of several bays in size, my plan being to live there for the rest of my life, caring for my mother and continuing with my studies. Every now and then, when I find myself free from my various other tasks, I will make copies of the paintings of famous sites by the masters of old and in this process I hope to be able to make recumbent tours of those places. What do you think of this plan?"

The master replied: "This all sounds splendid indeed. But does this site you speak of contain a mountain?"

---

290 Dong Qichang (1555–1636), a painter, calligrapher, and the preeminent art historian of his age. Celia Riely has pointed out (personal correspondence, 2012) that Zheng seems to have made a mistake with the timing of his meeting with Dong; Dong was in Yangzhou during the winter of the preceeding year, *xinwei* (1631), remaining there until sometime in the first month of the next year. By the winter of 1632, Dong had taken up a post in Beijing, and appears not to have returned south until he retired early in 1634.

"No, it doesn't," I admitted, "and yet to both front and back it is bounded by a river, and across the water Shu Ridge undulates like a writhing serpent with all the force of a mountain. On all four sides grow ten thousand willow trees and more than a thousand *qing* of lotus. There too grow bulrushes and the river flows clear and the fish are plentiful, with fishing skiffs coming and going all day long. As spring gives way to summer, people come here to listen to the orioles. Connected as is this site to the very tail of the Sui Embankment and along a somewhat circuitous path, however, infrequent are the visitors who pass by here and thus does it acquire its air of tranquility. Climbing up to its highest point in order to gaze about one, both Labyrinth Tower and Level with the Mountains Hall[291] appear as if at one's shoulder, while each and every one of the green hills of Jiangnan loom clearly into sight. The site stands bathed in the reflections cast by the willows, by the river, and by the mountain, and if it has little else to recommend it, it is nonetheless the choicest site of my home district."

To this, the Master responded: "It is a site, then, that should afford you both an excess of pleasure and a modicum of consolation," before proceeding to inscribe the words "Garden of Reflections" to present to me.

My return home in the *jiaxu* year [1634] coincided with the death of my wife, in addition to which I developed a painful eye infection that left me almost blind. Finding that I could now neither read nor drink, my sense of melancholy grew apace and I all but lost interest in life altogether. My mother became extremely anxious at this turn of events and was forever counselling me to force myself to seek some form of amusement in order to take my mind off my troubles. My brothers too exhorted me to begin the construction of my garden here, and so it was that, having acquired this plot of land some seven or eight years previously and having spent these seven or eight years assembling the materials necessary for its construction, with everything now in readiness and with the conception of the garden fully formed in my mind, my garden began to take rough shape within the space of eight months.

The outer gate of the garden faces east and overlooks the river, with south city standing on the opposite bank and both banks lined with peach and willow trees, their floating reflections stretching away to both north and south. During the months of spring, the people who come here by boat call the place "Little Peach Blossom Spring." Once through the gate, a mountain path describes a turn or two within the dense shade cast by the hanging branches of tall pine and fir, and here and there grow flowering apricot, apricot, pear, and chestnut trees. Where the mountain ends, to the left, there stands a trellis of roseleaf raspberry, beyond which stands a clump of bulrushes, this being

---

291 The lasting fame of Level with the Mountains Hall was a result of its association with the great Song dynasty scholar Ouyang Xiu, who had once served in Yangzhou and whose monograph on the tree peony, translated by James Hargett, is in chapter 3.

where the fishermen gather with their nets. A small stream flows along the right-hand side, and beyond the stream grow a hundred or so sparsely planted bamboo, shielded by a squat hedge made out of roughly hewn old branches. A surrounding wall has been inlaid with an assortment of unevenly shaped pebbles, these pebbles all having been chosen for their mottled tiger-skin colors, hence the common appellation for this type of wall: "Tiger-Skin Wall." Two small gates have been formed here out of gnarled tree trunks that resemble coiled dragons in shape. On beyond the gates ten or more tall paulownia trees grow, their branches now woven together in an arch over the path, their backs to the sun as they twist and turn. When people happen to walk along this way, both their gowns and their faces acquire a greenish hue, such is the depth of the shade cast by the trees. Farther on again and through the gate one comes upon the plaque inscribed with the words "Garden of Reflections," this structure being my library. Why have I called this place a garden? In ancient times dependent states were called "Reflections" and as I am here surrounded, to left and to right, by gardens, so I may be permitted to take this name from this dependency.

Turning into a narrow path, I see branches of flowering plum poke up from behind a wall but I have no idea what it is that lies behind this wall. Across Willow Embankment, upon "the clumps and stumps," an aged Chinese trumpet creeper coils its way upward, its flowers drooping downward. Where the willows end, one crosses a small stone bridge, crafted from a disorderly pile of rocks, with a tiger lying before it and a recalcitrant stone stretching the entire way across. A turn takes one into the thatched cottage, the plaque of which, inscribed by the Minister of State Zheng Yuanyue of my family, bears the words "Cottage of the Jade Hook"; this district once boasted a Jade Hook Grotto Heaven and perhaps this was its original site. The cottage is sited beside the river and is surrounded on all four sides by ponds, all of which are entirely given over to lotus. In design, the cottage is spacious and light, drawing to itself all the ambient blue-green hues, and its door and window lintels are made to unusual patterns. Backing onto the cottage is a pond and beyond this pond stretches an embankment upon which grow tall willows, and beyond the willows again is the long river along the opposite banks of which, again, grow tall willows; the gardens once owned by the Yan, the Feng, and the Yuan clans can all be seen at a glance. Although all these gardens now lie in ruins, their trees and bamboo flourish still and it is as if they now form part of my own garden. To the river's south is the transport ford, controlled by the river police. To the north, the river takes one directly to the Old Han Canal, to the Sui Embankment, to Level with the Mountains Hall, to Labyrinth Tower, to Flowering Apricot Ridge and to Dogwood Bay, and thus giving the expression "ten thousand willow trees," the entire scene, from my garden all the way here, appearing like an endless bolt of unfurled embroidery. By nature, the oriole is drawn to the willow and the more the willows the merrier the orioles become; here their song is never-ending and many are the listeners drawn to this place. A small belvedere was built overlooking the river, called "Half Floating" as it was built jutting out over the water, and this has been designated as the place at which to listen to the orioles or from which one can cast off in a little skiff to pay them a visit. These skiffs are the size of the petals of a lotus plant and are called "Floating Hermitages"; large enough to accommodate a single couch, a small side table, and a tea brazier, in them one can ply one's way to all the local splendors, to Han Canal, to the Sui Embankment, to Level with the Mountains Hall, and to Labyrinth Tower, whenever the whim arises.

Beneath the cottage once grew two ancient "Western Palace" crabapples, both two *zhang* in height and ten *wei* of girth. I have no idea when they were planted here but they were known to be the only specimens to be found growing throughout the River North region. Only one of these trees now remains, and the sight of it induces in me a sense of intense melancholy. Around the pond, steps of yellow rock have been placed at irregular heights, some of which look like terraces, others as if they are born of the water itself. Ten or so people can stand on the largest of these rocks at any one time, four or five on the smallest, and everybody calls them "Little Thousand Men Seats." Those rocks with their bases submerged in the water are surrounded by lotus flowers; those on land by flowering apricot, magnolia, "Hanging Floss" crabapple and yellow and white peach. Orchids of various kinds, Beauty of Yu poppy, ornamental ginger and Sweet William and so on have been planted in the cracks in the rocks. A twisted plank bridge with red handrails takes one across the pond, threading its way through the weeping willows. At the midpoint of this bridge there is a Conning Tower, the bridge itself leading neither to Half Belvedere, Small Pavilion nor to River Belvedere. At the other end of the bridge a stone has been engraved with the words "Light Mist and Fine Rain," also in the calligraphy of the Minister of State, but in this instance in a style that closely resembles that of Su Shi of the Song dynasty.

Once through the gate, one finds that a winding gallery forks off to both left and right, the former direction leading to my study. This comprises a three-bay chamber and a reception room, also three bays in size and which, although west-facing, protected as it is by paulownia and willow, affords shelter from the summer sun and seems to catch the faintest zephyr. The chamber itself is divided into two sections, one of which faces south, and the door of which is hidden, this being where I escape from my visitors. The windowsill is a full *chi* above the ground so that the chamber remains dry and free of damp. Outside this window is a rectangular porch upon which have been placed a number of large rocks and three or four plantains, along with a single teak tree that came from the western regions, as well as innumerable begonia shrubs, the ground here having been covered in goose-egg pebbles. The latticework of the window inside the chamber that opens up to the outside is in the gardenia flower pattern; the window itself is screened off by densely planted bamboo.[292] Even when people happen to catch sight of the window, they can never manage to find the door.

---

292   Alison Hardie has argued that there is little evidence for the presence in gardens of such "fantasy" features as "flower- or fan-shaped pavilions or windows, moon-gates, and so on" before the very end of the

The chamber on the left is east-facing and, when viewed from within the book storage room, the width of the belvedere seems to balance perfectly that of the proportions of the chamber. From here, one can gaze into the far distance upon all the various peaks of Jiangnan, taking in the diverse hues of the trees both near and far. When bandits threatened the neighborhood and Salt Commissioner Deng ascended the city walls to inspect the defences, he declared my belvedere tall enough for the bandits to make use of as a lookout if they were to occupy it. Upon hearing this, I had it dismantled in the space of a single evening and later replaced it with a smaller one-bay belvedere which everyone thought even more refined than the original structure. In the forecourt I selected rocks that best embodied the qualities of foraminate structure, leanness and fineness, and had them placed at differing heights here and there, again to a design that avoided the fashion of the day but that embodied a painterly quality.

At the corners of the chamber, two steep ridges have been formed, planted mainly in cassia trees the branches of which over time have intertwined with each other; with its valley stream and precipitous cliffs, the scene resembles that described in Little Mountain's "Summons for a Recluse."[293] Tree peony, "Western Palace" and "Hanging Floss" crabapple, magnolia, yellow and white and "Big Red" pearl camellia, "Fragrance of the Mouth of the Musical Stone" winter sweet, "Thousand-Leaf" pomegranate, blue-white Chinese trumpet and sweet-smelling citron grow beneath the ridges, providing my garden with year-long color. A single large rock has been placed here to screen the plants, and beneath this grows a solitary old scholar tree, now gnarled and twisted with age; I pat its trunk affectionately, this hundred-year-old tree, and call it my "Little Friend." Turning in around the corner of the rock and opening up a small one-leaf door, one comes across a tiny pavilion looking out over the river. Here, the wild rice and the bulrushes form a canopy. My friend and fellow society member Jiang Chengzong named this pavilion "Amid the Wild Rice and Bulrushes," while the plaque inscribed sometime earlier by Master Ni Yuanlu [1594–1644] with the words "Pavilion of the Blue-Green Waves" hangs here too. As the autumn grows old, the bulrushes are like snow and the wild geese and ducks make their homes here, departing at dawn only to return at night. Although they keep me company as I study my books I dare not feed or water them. Lying in the pavilion during the dog-days of summer I can enjoy whatever breeze there is to be had, and when the moon rises from the tips of the willow branches, it seems as if newly bathed in an ice pot. As dusk begins to fall, I gaze at the rays of the setting sun as they strike Shu Ridge, the red slowly sinking

---

Ming dynasty; see "The Awareness Garden of Wang Shiheng in Yizhen," *Studies in the History of Gardens and Designed Landscapes* 24, no. 4 (2004):272–79.

293 This is a reference to a rhapsody (*Zhao yinshi* 招隱士) attributed to a poet at the court of Liu An (ca. 179–122 BCE), Prince of Huainan. In David Hawkes's translation, the first lines of this poem read: "The cassia trees grow thick / In the mountain's recesses, / Twisting and snaking, / Their branches interlacing. / The mountain mists are high, / The rocks are steep. / In the sheer ravines / The waters' waves run deep" (*The Songs of the South: An Ancient Chinese Anthology*, trans. David Hawkes [Oxford: Clarendon Press, 1959], 119).

into the greenness and turning it into an even finer shade of emerald, catching the passers-by in their glare and serving to confuse the homing crows. Although the tiny belvedere is built within the chamber, it cannot be entered from inside the chamber itself and to do so one must take a circuitous route outside the chamber where there is another gallery, to the right of the gate. This gallery winds around twice, and in the gaps are planted mottled bamboo, or plantains, or elm trees, to provide it with shade. Whenever, sitting here within the inner chamber, I feel the desire to mount the belvedere but find myself too lazy to do so, I promptly change my direction and turn inward. From the gallery inside the door of Light Mist and Fine Rain one enters to the right a covered walkway, in shape like a pavilion, this being the Conning Tower on the bridge. It is also called a "pavilion" with the proposed name "Drenched Eyebrow's Prominence,"[294] because it overlooks the water as an eyebrow overlooks the eye and because the projecting eaves have been used to form a belvedere. The window has a two-leaf shutter that can be opened or shut whenever required. Two pathways lead away from the back of the pavilion, one of which leads to a hexagonal doorway. Within this door there is a chamber and a reception hall, both of three bays in size, named "Studio of the Single Word" and wherein hangs a plaque presented to me by my former preceptor Xu Shuoan, this being where I teach my sons to read. The reception hall is particularly large and airy and is bordered by a purple balustrade that is exquisite but not at all gaudy. Below the steps grow a single ancient pine and a solitary pomegranate tree. The terrace is shaped like a half sword ring and all around I have planted tree peonies and white peonies. Beyond the low wall one can see a rock face where two pines stretch straight upward, seemingly reaching half the way to heaven. There is another large doorway directly opposite the hexagonal one, beyond which there is also a winding gallery. Here, the dwarf bamboos hug the vermilion balustrade and every now and then the gallery widens or narrows suddenly so as to induce a sense of unpredictability. A single tiny doorway has been retained, through which one can see a cassia tree that looks as if it is the one found growing on the moon, this route providing an alternative way out of my garden. Half Belvedere is sited behind Drenched Eyebrow's Prominence, to the left of the path, where, through a wide gallery, one ascends the steps. Hanging here is the plaque once given to me by Master Chen Jiru and inscribed with the words "Belvedere of the Love of Solitude" from the line of a poem by the Tang poet Li Bai that goes, "Overwhelmingly do I love the solitude of seclusion."[295] The belvedere is surrounded on three sides by water; on the remaining side there is a rock face that seems to surge upward with a never-ending vigor and on the summit of which are planted two "toothpick" pines, these being the trees that can be seen when standing

---

294 The conceit of this name is impossible to convey fully in translation. To the character *mei* 眉 (eyebrow), Zheng adds the "Water Radical," giving *mei* 湄 (the margin of a lake). In an architectural context, the character *rong* 榮 (glory, splendor, etc.) gives the technical meaning "overhanging eaves."

295 This line comes from a poem entitled "Written When Moved by the Autumn in the Purple Extremity Palace of Xunyang" (*Xunyang zijigong gan qiu zuo* 尋陽紫極宮感秋作).

in front of the Studio of the Single Word and one of which looks even more powerful when bent under the weight of a recent downfall of snow. Beneath the rock face runs a stony creek that allows the water of the pond to flow in here with a melodious burble. The creek is edged by large rocks that jut up sharply, in the cracks of which have been planted variegated flowering apricot. Having encircled three sides of the belvedere, the creek then disappears into the river, but just before it does so, a single rock rises all alone in the midst of the water and on this too a flowering apricot has been planted, this being the tree that is visible beyond the wall as one first enters my garden.

The back window of the pavilion faces the cottage and people in the cottage and people here can gaze at each other, call out to one another and even converse, without ever discovering the path that leads from one spot to the other. Although, in total, my garden is no wider than several *mu*, visitors to it never fall prey to any sense of anxiety about the exhaustibility of its pleasures. Its mountain paths, both upper and lower, do not criss-cross each other and are thus level and easily walked along, following as they do the natural undulations of the land and giving no visible sign of the effort of man. And yet each and every flower and bamboo and rock seems as if planted in its most natural place; each has been examined and deliberated upon time after time, to be discarded when it did not prove appropriate, regardless of how beautiful it may well have been when examined on its own.

A patch of surplus land has also been retained, a short stroll distant from my garden, and this is put to use as a nursery for the trees and flowers that need to be replaced. There is also a lotus pond several *mu* in size, with a thatched pavilion built upon an outcrop surrounded by water where I can sit and supervise the nurserymen at their work. When the flowers burst into bloom, I ascend the steps of the stone bridge within my garden, or go to Half Belvedere, and from these places I can look out over them. The four or five fishermen who happen to live here have no idea how very fortunate they are. The local poet Wang Chun designated this spot as a place for releasing life and named it "Tower of the Precious Stamen"; thereafter, the chant of Buddhist sutras would occasionally be heard here. When Wang Chun died, it was here also that his sacrificial rites were conducted and a fellow society member Yan Sheqing has protected the site and has maintained it as a place for releasing life. Wang Chun had been my friend in life; he remains my neighbor still and has now become my friend in death.

This project of mine began to take rough shape after eight months; within a year's time the work on it had been completed and it served to overturn completely established patterns of garden design, particularly in its approximation to the understated elegance of the simple and the rustic. Furthermore, it benefited from the intuitive grasp of what I had in mind on the part of my friend Ji Cheng from Wujiang who developed all my ideas to their logical conclusions and whose management of the stonemasons proved so faultless that I had no basis whatsoever to complain about divergence between my plan and the garden as it now is.[296] Sometime previously, my elderly mother had a dream in which she found herself at a site where a garden was being constructed. "And to whom does the garden belong?" she had inquired, to which the reply had been: "Your second son." At the time of her dream, I was still a youth but once I had assembled my workers my mother happened to come to my garden in order to jolly them along in their various tasks. All of a sudden she realized that my garden resembled that of her earlier dream. Once she had told me all about this, I for my part realized that my choice of this particular site had not been at all accidental and that it was unavoidable that I should have embarked upon this present project. And how is one to know that Master Dong Qichang's naming of the garden with the word "Reflections" was not too a revelation derived from the illusion of a dream and that in my present folly I am not seeking to realize the dream of some earlier man?[297]

It is a truth that men of this present age of ours are wont to compete over that which is real but cast aside that which is illusory, and if one were now to compare this garden with fields and with mansions, then it is the garden that constitutes the illusion. Further, if one were to compare watering the trees and the flowers of this garden with establishing merit and making a reputation for oneself, then surely it is watering one's garden that constitutes the illusion. Before a man takes pleasure in constructing a garden, he should first have acquired fields and mansions and established both his merit and his reputation; has there ever before been a man such as I, who, without a foot of land to his name, with his mansions not as yet built and with neither merit nor reputation to speak of, first proceeds to build a garden? Were there to have been such a man, he would obviously have brought ruination down upon his own head and dissipated his will for greater things. And yet, to have a mother and not to find the time to care for her, to own books but not to find the time to read them, to be surrounded by the objects that please the senses and satisfy one's nature but never to find the time to enjoy them, is this a circumstance caused by the encumbrance of having a garden that requires watering or rather the ownership of fields and mansions and by the need to establish both one's merit and one's reputation? This is a question to which I dare not offer an answer, although I do believe that each of us must follow the respective dictates of Heaven. The conception of this garden was revealed in a dream, its realization was the result of my

---

296 Ji Cheng begins his *Craft of Gardens* by addressing the issue that Zheng Yuanxun alludes to here: "Generally, in construction, responsibility is given to a 'master' who assembles a team of craftsmen; for is there not a proverb that though three-tenths of the work is the workmen's, seven-tenths is the master's? By 'master' here I do not mean the owner of the property, but the man who is master of his craft." See *The Craft of Gardens*, trans. Alison Hardie (New Haven: Yale University Press, 1988), 39.

297 This is perhaps a veiled allusion to the most famous of "Yangzhou dreams," that of the late Tang dynasty poet Du Mu (803–852) in his poem "Easing My Heart" (*Qianhuai* 遺懷), quoted in note 43, which reads in full: "By river and lakes at odds with life I journeyed, wine my freight: / Slim waists of Chu broke my heart, light bodies danced into my palm. / Ten years late I wake at last out of my Yangzhou dream / With nothing but the name of a drifter in the blue houses" (*Poems of the Late Tang*, trans. A. C. Graham, 123).

own innate nature. Even if it is the case that I can be accused of preferring to dwell in the illusory rather than the real, then of what possible concern is this to others?

A personal record made by Zheng Yuanxun of Hanjiang during the second month of the *dingchou* year of the reign of the Chongzhen emperor [1637].

The Craft of Gardens (*Yuanye* 園冶)

"Foreword" (*Tici* 題詞)

ZHENG YUANXUN 鄭元勳
TRANSLATED BY ALISON HARDIE

The various arts of ancient times have all been handed down in writing, so why has the art of designing gardens alone not had a written tradition? It has been said: "Different things are suitable for different gardens; there is no single hard and fast rule, so there is no way that it can be handed down in writing."

What is meant by saying that different things are suitable for different gardens? Because of the royal birth of the Jianwen emperor of Liang, the Flowery Forest came into being; because of Shi Chong's wealth, he was able to create the Golden Valley; but because Chen Zhongzi was so poor, he could only afford a small vegetable garden at Yuling. Different things were appropriate for these people according to their different circumstances of nobility or humble birth, wealth or poverty; it would be inconceivable to have things the other way around.

If a site has no remote and lofty hills or flourishing woods like those of the Orchid Pavilion, yet you insist on applying the name of the Serpentine to it; or if there is absolutely no sign of such sights as the Deer Enclosure or Dappled Apricots, but you baselessly boast another Wangchuan, this is even worse than the Bogeywoman smearing on powder and rouge, and succeeding only in making herself uglier still.

Different types of ground, too, require different treatment, and this should be given careful consideration. The owner must be sure of having the hills and valleys already there in his heart, and then the completed work may be either elaborate or simple, as he wishes. Otherwise, if he forces out something artificial, and leaves it up to the builders and tilers, the streams will not give the appearance of an undulating ribbon, the hills will not overlap and wind in and out of one another, and the trees and plants will not give each other shade in a suitable way. How, then, can the attraction of the garden grow upon the viewer day by day?

The most unfortunate thing is if the landowner has the hills and valleys in his heart but cannot express his concept to the workmen, while the workmen can follow instructions but are not creative, and just have to stick to their plumb-lines and ink-marks. If they thus force the owner to abandon his original concept of hills and valleys to follow their ideas, is that not a great pity? But Ji Cheng has changed all that: he goes by the concept, not by a fixed set of rules, something which most people cannot achieve. And he is even better at directing operations successfully, so that the stubborn becomes flexible and the blocked flows freely: this is really something to be glad about.

I am one of Ji Cheng's oldest friends, and I know that he often feels frustrated that a remnant of water and a broken-off piece of mountain give no scope for his accumulated skills; he would dearly love to set out all the ten great mountains of China in one area, and direct a squad of all the mighty laborers of the empire; and to collect together all sorts of exotic jewel-like flowers and plants, ancient trees and sacred birds to be arranged by him, giving the whole earth a totally new appearance. What a joy this would be to him! But alas, there is no landowner with sufficiently grand ideas!

Does this mean then that Ji Cheng can operate only on a grand scale and not on a small one? No, this is not the case. Different things are suitable both for different gardens and for different people, and no one is Ji Cheng's equal in making appropriate use of what is available. When I was building a mansion to the south of the city-wall of Jiangdu, among reedy marshes and banks of willows, the site was only a few yards wide in either direction, but Ji Cheng had only to make some simple arrangements, and it became a magical secluded retreat. I can claim to know a little about garden design and construction myself, but beside Ji Cheng, I feel as clumsy as a cuckoo that cannot even build its own nest.

There are many distinguished connoisseurs in the world who wish to build country retreats and gardens in which they can enjoy roaming freely in a small space; all these people cannot fail to ask Ji Cheng's advice. Unfortunately he cannot divide himself up and distribute himself in all directions to respond to them, but perhaps his compiling of *The Craft of Gardens* can compensate for this. Still, I shall always feel sad that Ji Cheng's knowledge and skill cannot really be handed on; what can be handed on is only a set of rules, which is as much as to say that nothing has been handed on. But if his rules can be applied flexibly, without departing from his principles, then this sort of transmission, which at least gives people something to go by, will still be better than nothing at all.

Today's genius of national status will become a standard for later generations to emulate. Who can say that his book will not become an object of praise in the mouths of all, rivaling even the "Record of All Crafts" in the *Rites of Zhou*?

Written on the first day of the fifth month, in the *yihai* year of the Chongzhen era [1635] by his friend Zheng Yuanxun, in the Garden of Reflections.

"A Banquet in the Garden Pavilion of Secretary Wang Shiheng" (*Yan Wang zhonghan Shiheng yuanting* 宴汪中翰士衡園亭; no. 3 of 4), "On Ji Cheng's Arranging of Rocks and On Reading His Poems" (*Ji Wufou li shi jian yue qi shi* 計無否理石兼閱其詩), and "Miscellaneous Songs on Garden Living" (*Yuanju zayong* 園居雜詠)

RUAN DACHENG 阮大鍼 (1587–1646)

TRANSLATED BY ALISON HARDIE

Ruan Dacheng, an official and noted poet and dramatist from Anqing in present-day Anhui Province, was a man of power and influence throughout the period of the Ming-Qing transition, who earned himself a somewhat invidiously unsavory reputation, in large part through his alleged association with the eunuch faction at court in the 1620s. Later, having briefly served at the court of one of the aspirant southern Ming princes, he surrendered to the Manchu forces. He died while accompanying the Qing forces on their invasion of Fujian Province.

Ruan himself built several gardens, both in his hometown and in Nanjing. A number of his poems give us an idea of the rhythm of life in a garden. He was a patron of the garden designer Ji Cheng, and the poem "A Banquet in the Garden Pavilion of Secretary Wang Shiheng" commemorates Ji Cheng's skills as a designer of gardens. Ruan also wrote a "Preface" to Ji Cheng's *The Craft of Gardens*, saying of him that he "is a most straightforward man, of remarkable character and talents; stilted and formal behavior stands no chance in his presence. His poems and paintings are just like his personality." Ruan's "Miscellaneous Songs on Garden Living" are inspired by the features of one of his gardens, the Assembly Garden in Nanjing.

"A Banquet in the Garden Pavilion of Secretary Wang Shiheng" (no. 3 of 4)

The divine workman has opened up a remote island;
The wise craftsman has arranged pure sounds.
He uniquely conjures forth an awareness of blue mountains;
He fully gives rise to the hermit's heart.
The Ink Pool invites the magpies to bathe;
The windblown bamboo emits the cries of gibbons.
On whom shall we rely to obtain a sense of seclusion?
Watch me sound my plain zither.[298]

"On Ji Cheng's Arranging of Rocks and On Reading His Poems"

Ji Cheng is the flower of the Southeast;
In personality he is a secluded rock.
He uniquely conjures forth an awareness of rivers and mountains;
He alone creates a style for mists and vapors.

---

298 The "plain zither" is an allusion to the reclusive Tao Qian (see chapter 1), who was said to keep an unstrung *qin* zither by him for its cultural associations, though he could not play.

A confined space, of its own accord, becomes a paradise within the flask;
He transfers his emotions to the cold jade.
The *jingwei* bird obeys his signals and cries;[299]
The ancestral dragon submits to his whip and goad.
At other times he arranges pure songs,
An autumn orchid emitting fragrant moisture.
His sense of quietude makes lustrous the heart and soul;
His leisurely sounds span the gap between then and now.
Sitting in the dew amid the chirping of insects,
I share an evening of idleness with you.
We play our qins and then drink from our wine-cups;
Peacefully glows the white moon through the woods.

"Miscellaneous Songs on Garden Living"

Ten Endowments Belvedere
The accomplished man abandons external things;
He accumulates spiritual gifts above the haze.
The bells by the stream at times produce a noise,
Clink-clank, as though the pines were sounding.

Mirror Boat
The water is so clean that suddenly it appears to have no substance:
The pale pike seem to be swimming in the void.
If you bend down to look you can see the spring birds,
Twisting and turning among the waterweed.

Fragrant Islet
Alone I stand and stroll beyond the eaves:
Where does that fragrance in the air come from?
Colorful butterflies are fluttering around the high branches;
Only now do I realize that the wooden slaves have blossomed.

Damask Snow Pavilion
The flower petals comply with ancient instinct:
As your gaze plays over them they turn spontaneously into damask.
Do not be reluctant to tip up your mountain goblet;
Here you can start to pluck the fragrant flowers.

---

299 The legendary *jingwei* bird drops pebbles into the ocean to try to fill it up; the ancestral dragon in the next line refers to the First Qin emperor, noted for undertaking large-scale construction projects.

Drinking to Antiquity Studio

We pour wine and raise our glasses to remotest antiquity;
Its light is buried and will never awake again.
In sympathy with the Sages of the Bamboo Grove,
Autumn plants appear around the overgrown pond.

Rock Obeisance Level

I have plucked you out from a clump of thorns and hazel,
And set you up by the window where I write and play the *qin*.
When a distant breeze rustles your creepers,
You seem to bow your head in my direction.

Brief Guide to the Sights and Features of the Imperial Capital (Dijing jingwu lüe 帝京景物略)

"Haidian" (海淀)

LIU TONG 劉侗 (D. 1636) AND YU YIZHENG 于奕正 (D. 1635)
TRANSLATED BY DUNCAN M. CAMPBELL

Brief Guide to the Sights and Features of the Imperial Capital, completed in 1635 (during the final decade of the Ming dynasty), is a remarkable guide to the delights and splendors of Beijing. Its author, Liu Tong, was a native of Macheng (in present-day Hubei Province) whom Zhang Dai describes as one of his "Friends in the Mountains and Rivers." He compiled it on the basis of his five-year stay in the capital, in collaboration with a Beijing local, Yu Yizheng. Liu Tong died in Yangzhou in 1636, shortly after the book had been published, aboard a boat on his way to Suzhou to take up an appointment there as magistrate; his collaborator had died the previous year, in Nanjing.

"In districts proximate to the capital," Liu and Yu state, "wherever a spring happens to flow, there are to be found gardens and pavilions, from ancient times down to the present, each of which changes its name whenever taken possession of by a new owner, although the flow of the spring that occasions the gardens never itself changes." Given here is a translation of the section of the book that covers the district of Haidian (Sea of Shallows), in the northwestern corner of metropolitan Beijing, where once stood Mi Wanzhong's Ladle Garden, described earlier in this chapter. In her study of the present campus of Peking University, the historian Vera Schwarcz says that "What Haidian had to offer was what garden builders needed the most: water. Called 'liquid delight,' this was the essential prerequisite for landscape design. . . . Without water, nothing grew. With water, it was not only trees and flowers that flourished. It was also the contemplative mind that drew sustenance here from vistas of liquid stillness. Skillfully channeled waterfalls and carefully crafted fishponds became the hallmarks of Haidian."[300]

---

300   Vera Schwarcz, *Place and Memory in the Singing Crane Garden* (Philadelphia: University of Pennsylvania Press, 2008), 42–43.

"Haidian"

"Shallows" is the name given a place where water gathers. On the flat land to the northwest of Tall Ridge Bridge are springs: gurgle, gurgle. They flow off in all four directions: burble, burble. They feed the plants and the trees: gush, gush. Twisting and turning the water flows, this way and then that, pausing occasionally to form a dozen or so ponds. To the north, the area is called North Haidian, or Bagou Stream. Here the paddy fields are patterned like tortoise shells, with a crisscross of paths and channels. Greenest green are the distant hills, as they shimmer soundlessly in the haze. The Bagou Stream flows southeastward from Green Dragon Bridge all the way here to the shallows, and then five *li* to the south again of the shallows to Cinnabar Tumulus Bank. To the south of this again six slopes rise up sharply. The stream then flows all the way to White Stone Bridge where it reaches its confluence with Tall Ridge River. To the west of the slopes, the stream is wide enough to allow for the passage of boats, and here it is that Li Wei [1510–1584], the Marquis of Wuqing, has made his garden. Ten *li* square, in its middle stands the Hall for Decanting the Seas. To the north of this hall stands a pavilion, its plaque bearing the two words "Pure Elegance," in the hand of the Empress Dowager Cisheng [1546–1614] herself. From the pavilion one gazes around upon an expanse of tree peonies, with rocks interspersed here and there, and the occasional herbaceous peony, all abutting the river. A soaring bridge crosses over to a small island, and beneath the bridge swim golden carp, some of which are a full five *chi* in size, like bolts of brocade in the reflections cast by the flowers, darting away like shooting stars when startled, gathering like rising evening mist when fed. To the north of the island stretches an expanse of lotus plants. In the far distance, on the very edge of the horizon, stands an artificial mountain, its slopes as sharp as swords and rising upward in the shape of a snail's shell, stranger even than any mountain. Yes, an artificial mountain certainly, but seeming more natural than a real mountain. Here where mountain meets water, a tall tower rises, and on this tower is to be found a platform. Standing on this platform, on a horizontal plane, one finds oneself looking at the Fragrant Hills, whereas looking downward one sees Jade Spring Hill; so high is one here that the hills seems as close as one's very eyelashes. Lingbi, Lake Tai, and Brocade River rocks here are seen in their hundreds, tall trees stand accounted in their thousands, bamboo in their tens of thousands, and flowers, everywhere, in their millions. The shade cast, it seems, is seamless.

The gardens to the east and the west face each other. The Ladle Garden of Mi Wanzhong [1570–1628], the Minister of the Court of the Imperial Stud, is a full hundred *mu* in area, and, from a distance, looks every bit as large as that of Li Wei, proving so also once one begins to walk around it. As one approaches the garden, the road is lined on both sides by rows of willow trees, with several mounds of rocks piled higgledy-piggledy. The road leads off to the south where it comes upon a hill slope. Upon the slope the bridge surmounting the incline soars higher even than the roofs of the surrounding buildings.

Standing upon this bridge and gazing out in the direction of the garden, one can see nothing but a vast expanse of water, its surface covered entirely by lotus flowers, all of which are white in color. Halls, towers, pavilions, gazebos—one can count eight or nine such structures from the bridge. Entering the garden, it appears, will require one to go through four courtyards. The trees that shade one here are willows, those that stand tall and straight are the pines, those in rows are the locusts, whereas that which juts up here and there like new bamboos shoots are the rocks and the bamboos. Surrounded by water, the garden permits no ingress by pathway; transected here and there by pole bridges, the waterways too allow no entry by boat. The various halls and chambers of the garden have no common entrances, the paths to left and right of them affording access to no other destination. The steps lead one, necessarily, to water channels, and so one must make one's way beyond these channels, along a gallery, and along this gallery, seven times one comes across plank doorsills, twice one encounters intertwined tree roots, and once does one need to twist one's way up and down a set of stone steps. All this the visitor can point to clearly, while still standing on the bridge. Descending from the bridge and turning to the north, there, finally, stands the gate of the garden. Once through the gate a visitor is suddenly rendered speechless; that which attracts the mind exhausts the eyes, while that which pleases the eyes serves to exhaust the feet. The play of the morning light in the trees is such that one is unsure if it is noon or dusk, and one loses all sense of east or west. Once in the final hall of the garden, flinging open the north-facing window affords one a vista over a thousand *qing* of paddy field, and a quick glance is enough to assure one that the sun is yet to set. The Grand Secretary Ye Xianggao [1562–1627], from Fuqing in Fujian Province, having passed through Haidian, was heard to declare: "The Li Garden is magnificent, the Mi Garden twists and turns; the Mi Garden is not at all vulgar, the Li Garden is not at all sour."[301] To the north of the two gardens there stands a bridge, called Loudou, also known as West Hook.

---

301   Here Ye Xianggao puns on the meanings of these two men's surnames, Mi (rice) and Li (plum).

7

Gardens of the Mind

Previous chapters have mostly covered gardens or aspects thereof that, as far as we know, were real (except in such cases as the mythical garden of the Queen Mother of the West). In this chapter, we turn to imaginary gardens—gardens of the mind. Here we include not only those nonexistent gardens that were created in the imaginations of their would-be owners but also some evidence for the conceptualization of the ideal garden in the minds of designers and their patrons, as shown in biographies of two important garden craftsmen, Zhang Nanyang and Zhang Lian, and in the very brief "autobiography" in Ji Cheng's preface to his garden treatise, *The Craft of Gardens.*

It is not by chance that the imaginary gardens included here all come from the late imperial period (the Ming and Qing dynasties). We have seen (in the introduction to chapter 6) how the literati class expanded during the Ming, and how the publishing industry expanded at the same time. These interconnected developments gave rise to the phenomenon of the imagined garden.

The expansion of the literati class led to a greater number of aspirant but unsuccessful officials, who might come from families in relatively straitened circumstances and could, therefore, not afford a garden—or at least not one of a satisfactory size and quality. At the same time, they knew that their more fortunate peers were deploying their wealth to create gardens, and deploying their gardens to acquire cultural, social, and ultimately political capital (through socializing in the garden and networking with influential officials). The active publishing industry gave these people who could not afford gardens the means to present their imaginary gardens to a wider public, thus enabling them to acquire at least some of the cultural capital of a real garden, although not the social or political capital. It also enabled them to indulge, on a smaller scale, in the same sort of self-expression as could be achieved in the creation of a real garden through the choice of literary, historical, or artistic allusions to represent the garden-owner's philosophical beliefs and sense of self.

Even in the case of literati who had been able to create and enjoy their own gardens, such as Zhang Dai in the time before the fall of the Ming, an imaginary garden could fulfill other functions. Zhang Dai presents his "Langhuan Paradise" (this chapter) as an idealized setting for his own burial, envisaging it as a place that will not only satisfy his own sense of beauty in landscape but also prove attractive to visitors who will sacrifice at his tomb, thus allowing him a sort of continued life after death.

Furthermore, the publishing industry created a market for literary gardens—imaginary gardens that appear in fiction and drama, like the "real" and dream gardens in *The Peony Pavilion*, or the Prospect Garden in *The Story of the Stone* (this chapter). The "real" garden in *The Peony Pavilion*, which stimulates in Bridal Du the feelings of romantic longing that result in her erotic dream, is of course as imaginary as the dream garden, being created on stage only by the words sung and spoken by Bridal and her maid (the traditional Chinese theater did not use stage scenery). Almost contemporary with *The Peony Pavilion* is the great Ming novel *The Plum in the Golden Vase* (*Jin Ping Mei*), in which certain crucial scenes also take place in the garden of the antihero, the wealthy but utterly uncultured merchant Ximen Qing. We are told in chapter 19 of the novel that Ximen Qing "had been constructing a formal garden and summerhouse in his residential compound for nearly half a year before the final decorating, painting, and varnishing were complete,"[1] and given a brief poetic description of it, but there is little in the way of specific detail on garden layout or content, except when the author wishes to make a point about Ximen Qing's vulgarity and excess. For example, Ximen says of an estate he contemplates buying:

> If I buy this property, I'll open it up and combine it with my own. I plan to build three summerhouses, three reception halls, an artificial hill, a garden, a juniper hedge, a locust tree arbor, well pavilions, an archery range, a kickball field, and other recreational facilities. It may cost a few taels of silver to do it, but what of that.[2]

It is excessive to have as many reception halls as summerhouses (one would be perfectly adequate), and the proposed addition of "recreational facilities" shows that Ximen has no idea what a gentleman's garden should be like. Elsewhere, the author is primarily interested in gardens as a setting for the characters' erotic adventures, as when Chen Jingji, who has been supervising the garden construction, takes the opportunity to make a pass at his father-in-law's concubine Pan Jinlian (Golden Lotus), or when Ximen Qing spends the night with the servant's wife Song Huilian in the Hidden Spring Grotto beneath the rockery "mountain."[3] The celebrated Ming dynasty illustrations to the work make it clear how many of the crucial scenes involving the members of the Ximen household take place in a garden.

The popularity of illustrated books in the late imperial period gave further substance to literary gardens by presenting realistic images of them. Gardens became the setting in fiction—

---

1   *The Plum in the Golden Vase or, Chin P'ing Mei*, trans. David Tod Roy, vol. 1, *The Gathering* (Princeton: Princeton University Press, 1993), 376.

2   Roy, *The Plum in the Golden Vase*, vol. 2, *The Rivals*, 195–96.

3   *The Plum in the Golden Vase*, 1:380, 2:51–55.

as we have just seen in *The Plum in the Golden Vase*—for social interactions, family activities, and romantic and sensual encounters. Illustrated gardens appeared not only in publications of narrative fiction but also in collections of poetry and in dramatic texts.[4] In real life, too, theatrical performances very often took place in private gardens, so that a real garden might act as the stage scenery for a play set in a garden, further blurring the distinction between the real and the imagined.

Furthermore, as Wai-yee Li has pointed out, in the period during and after the Manchu conquest of China in the mid-seventeenth century, imaginary gardens provided a refuge "unscathed by history" (in Li's words), separate from the turmoil of current events, where the nostalgically remembered life and culture of the Ming could be preserved and enjoyed.[5]

Another aspect of gardens that exist in the mind and on paper rather than in the real world is the theorization of gardens, which also comes to prominence in this period. In the Song dynasty (see chapter 4), Li Gefei saw the fate of gardens as emblematic of the fate of empires, thus incorporating the garden into a theory of the rise and fall of dynasties (or the dynastic cycle), but this was not a theory of gardens as such. Also in the Song, Sima Guang used the classical allusions embodied in the physical features of his garden, and expressed in both his prose account and his poem sequence on the Garden of Solitary Enjoyment, as a way of presenting both a practical and a theoretical or philosophical response to the challenges of official life. But again, this is not a theory specific to gardens.

It is in the Ming, and indeed rather late in the dynasty, that we find the first signs of an interest in the theoretical aspects of gardens themselves. The most systematic—or least unsystematic—expression of this is Ji Cheng's *The Craft of Gardens*, published in the 1630s, only about a decade before the end of the dynasty. Although much of the treatise is concerned with the practicalities of design and construction of doorways and balustrades, Ji Cheng also emphasizes the principles behind landscape and garden design, particularly the ideas of following the lie of the land and "borrowing" from adjacent scenery.

Other aspects of garden theory appear in the connoisseurship literature we surveyed in the introduction to chapter 6. The aesthetics of garden design are used to distinguish between the vulgar and the refined, although these distinctions are generally presented as self-evident, while the theoretical principles on which they are based are left unstated. The reason for this, of course, is that those members of the elite who take it for granted that their standards of taste are the only valid ones are unwilling to let the "vulgar" in on the secret, and can make unspoken changes to the standards whenever the vulgar seem to be catching on to what they have to do to become indistinguishable from the elite.

Ideas on garden theory can also be gleaned from the biographies of garden designers, examples of which are included in this chapter. Wu Weiye's "Biography of Zhang Nanyuan [Zhang Lian]" is particularly helpful, showing, in the words Wu puts into Zhang's mouth, that Zhang's

---

4   Many examples are conveniently available in collections such as Zhou Wu, ed., *Zhongguo banhua shi tulu* (Shanghai: Shanghai renmin meishu chubanshe, 1988); and Chen Tongbin et al., eds., *Zhongguo gudai jianzhu da tudian (Illustrations of Ancient Chinese Architecture)* (Beijing: Jinri Zhongguo chubanshe, 1996).

5   Wai-yee Li, "Gardens and Illusions from Late Ming to Early Qing," *Harvard Journal of Asiatic Studies* 72, no. 2 (December 2012):334.

design ideas were based on a theoretical concept of how gardens represent the wider landscape. The arrangement of a "few rocks" in the garden can give the impression that "one is dwelling at the foot of a great mountain, among broken gullies and craggy glens." Zhang Lian, in Wu's account, contrasts this approach with that of earlier designers who tried unsuccessfully to reproduce "a mass of peaks reaching up to heaven, deep ravines shading the sun . . . with a site of ten feet or so and a ditch five foot long."

One of these earlier designers may have been Zhang Lian's sixteenth-century predecessor Zhang Nanyang, whose biography, by his patron Chen Suoyun, is also included in this chapter. Chen, however, thought that Zhang Nanyang's technique had similar results, in that his rockery works "appeared like a huge mass extended over a vast distance, although they were on a small scale." Chen links Zhang's approach to the design of physical landscapes with his understanding of painting theory, saying that he originally studied painting but "he lost interest in painting and gave it up, but then tried constructing rocks into mountains using the *samadhi* [mental concentration] method of painters"; Chen later draws an explicit parallel between painting and landscape design: "[painting] is one type of hills and dales, while [rockery] is another kind of hills and dales."

Wu Weiye also links skill in landscape painting to skill in landscape design, saying in his biography of Zhang Lian: "In his youth he studied painting, and enjoyed painting portraits, but was also expert in landscape. He then used the spirit of this to construct his rockeries." Ji Cheng draws a similar parallel in his own case, explaining: "As a young man I was known as a painter. I was by nature interested in seeking out the unusual; since I derived most pleasure from the brushes of Guan Tong and Jing Hao, I paid homage to their style in all my work." Ji Cheng's patron Zheng Yuanxun also implies a link between his (Zheng's) own practice of landscape painting (he was a minor but not insignificant landscape painter of the late Ming) and his ability to have "the conception of the garden fully formed in my mind" before its construction.

Although it becomes a commonplace to state that any garden designer under discussion started life as a painter, an interesting contradictory viewpoint comes from the garden designer, dramatist, and all-around cultural entrepreneur Li Yu (see chapter 8). He argues that the skills of (literati, amateur) landscape painters and those of (professional, artisan) garden designers are quite different and neither can substitute for the other:

> Moreover, piling rocks up into mountains is a science on its own, a special type of skill. If you ask a man of culture who has his heart full of vales and hills, his brush wreathed with mist and clouds, to paint a landscape of mountains and waters, immediately there will appear a thousand cliffs, ten thousand glens; but hire him to set up a few rocks beside your studio, and immediately all his skill is gone: you might as well ask directions from a blind man. Therefore famous rockery constructors have never been any good at poetry or painting. Watch them pick up one of the rocks at random, turn it upside down and set it in place; each one of them turns into an antique masterpiece, drawing you by a winding way into a painting. This is Creation's skill in manifesting the remarkable. It is comparable to the poems written or the characters made out by someone holding a divining rod to summon spirits; he can produce mystic amulets at the turn of his hand,

fine poems at the touch of his brush. But if you question the medium about them, he may have no idea what they mean.[6]

Li Yu here suggests that the artisan may have no conception of any theoretical basis to his practical skills; he is just doing what comes naturally. The implication is that Li Yu himself is superior in having both the cultivated, theoretical understanding and the technical skills.

Later in the Qing dynasty, Qian Yong, owner of the Lü Garden, who has already provided us with information on the afterlives of several celebrated Ming gardens (see chapter 6), meditated on the nature of garden-making, the value of imaginary gardens, and the true ownership of gardens (a theme that had already become a commonplace in the Tang dynasty, as we saw in chapter 2), implying perhaps that a real garden can have an imaginary owner.[7]

The art of painting, and the interaction of image with text, can also turn a real garden into an imaginary one. This is the case with Wen Zhengming's albums of paintings of the Artless Administrator's Garden in Suzhou.[8] In the two albums, we can see how Wen treats the actual garden as a metaphor for the mindset and life history of the owner, his friend Wang Xianchen (*jinshi* 1493). The discrete paintings in each album give us little or no idea of how the different parts of the garden are connected together. Rather than referring to the physical garden, or to the text that describes it, the paintings refer pictorially to other paintings by purposefully recalling details from well-known early garden paintings that carried considerable symbolic meaning to the literati; many of them had firsthand knowledge of these major paintings, versions of which were circulating in sixteenth-century Suzhou. The imagery of the later album (1551) makes more frequent pictorial allusions than the earlier one (1533). For example, the first leaf of the later album shows some affinity with the opening scene in Wang Wei's painting of his Wangchuan estate (of which Wen had made a copy), thus implying that Wang Xianchen is a recluse of the stature of Wang Wei; similarly, Wen's poem on the Pavilion for Dreaming of Retirement (Dreamy Tower, in Mo's translation) links Wang Xianchen to the archetypal hermits Lu Guimeng and Tao Yuanming. The opening image of the 1533 album was not completely faithful to the actual garden scenery, since the city wall would not have been visible from the garden, but the image adhered fairly closely to the accompanying text that established the mental construct to be applied to appreciating the garden. In the 1551 album, Wen goes a step further in that his image is closely tied neither to the real garden nor to depiction of the text. Wen has moved beyond literal depiction into a visionary mode. He represents the Garden of the Artless Administrator not as the actual garden, but as a place that exists

---

6   Li Yu, *Xianqing ouji*, ed. Li Ren (Beijing: Zuojia chubanshe, 1995), 215.

7   Qian Yong's best-known work, *Lüyuan conghua* (*Collected Talks from the Lü Garden*), from which extracts in this anthology are taken, is named for his garden. The name of the garden is hard to translate: *lü* literally means a type of shoe or clog (with an association with the philosopher Zhuangzi) but it also has implications of distant travel, and is the name of one of the hexagrams in the *Book of Changes* (*Yijing*), with the meaning of being contented with one's lot.

8   The discussion here benefits greatly from an unpublished paper by Jan Stuart, "Zhuozheng Yuan: History and Art," originally written for the proposed earlier version of this anthology.

only in the imagination. No physical real estate could provide the purity of retirement afforded by this garden of the mind.

The literati dreamed of transcendence to be obtained by living in the paradisiacal and uncorrupted atmosphere of a scholar's garden. In a quest to make gardens function as potent symbols, they developed a vocabulary for depicting gardens in words and images that blurred the boundaries between the real world and the world of the mind. When the proprietor chose a studio name for himself that belonged to his garden or a site within it, man and garden fused together, and every site name chosen and every depiction of the garden commissioned became one more way to fashion and project personal values and identity through garden ownership. The garden as a mental image—portrayed in pictorial descriptions that often freely strayed from accurate depiction—in the end provided the most lasting and clearest idea of what the garden was meant to be: something far more than artful landscape architecture.

PART 1

THE THEORY OF GARDENS

"The Biography of Mountain Man Zhang, the Recliner on Rocks" (*Zhang shanren Woshi zhuan* 張山人臥石傳)

CHEN SUOYUN 陳所蘊 (1543–1626)
TRANSLATED BY ALISON HARDIE

Chen Suoyun was a native of Shanghai, where he owned a garden named the Daily Visit Garden (*Rishe yuan*), in allusion to the line in Tao Qian's "Homeward Bound," "My garden grows more interesting with each day's visit" (see chapter 1). Of the Daily Visit Garden, designed by Zhang Nanyang, who also designed part of Wang Shizhen's Yanshan Garden (see chapter 6), Qian Yong (1759–1844) tells us:

> The Daily Visit Garden lies to the south of the Shanghai county offices. It was the private residence of the Ming Chief Minister of the Court of the Imperial Stud, Chen Suoyun, and later came into the ownership of Mr. Lu Qifeng, whose great-great-grandson Lu Xixiong, Master Ershan, considerably enlarged it. Originally the garden included the Hall of Bamboo Simplicity, with an inscription by Zhou Tianqiu of Suzhou; it overlooked running water on three sides, and was extremely spacious.[9]

"The Biography of Mountain Man Zhang, the Recliner on Rocks"

My elegant hobby is springs and rocks; the Recliner on Rocks, Mountain Man Zhang [Zhang Nanyang], had become famous for constructing rockwork, so I commissioned him, for a remuneration, to construct the Daily Visit Garden for me.

---

9   Qian Yong, *Lüyuan conghua* (Beijing: Zhonghua shuju, 1979), 537–38.

At the time when the garden was completed, the Mountain Man was celebrating his four-score years. All the Mountain Man's acquaintance begged me to write an honorific address for the Mountain Man's birthday. The Mountain Man bowed and said, "It is my great honor to have had the opportunity to serve you, Master Chen. It is my privilege to receive these kind words from you, but there is no need for you to compose an address. I have accumulated these fragments of rock to complete my work. As long as they have a good owner in the future, then my name will endure after my death." When I heard what he said, I felt he was the sort of person who can "master life," so I have written his biography.

Mountain Man Zhang is from Shanghai in Songjiang prefecture. His personal name is Nanyang and his formal name ____.[10] At first his cognomen was Master of the Little Brook, but he has changed it to The Scholar Who Reclines on Rocks. The people of his home district called him by both equally, but those from all over who were familiar with the Mountain Man mostly called him the Recliner on Rocks, so now he is known only as the Mountain Man Who Reclines on Rocks. The Mountain Man's family were farmers for generations; his grandfather (name unknown) was employed as a Clerical Inspector and then became a Banditry Bureau Administrator reporting to the Secretary of the Criminal Administration Bureau.[11] His father (name unknown) became known as a good painter, so as a child the Mountain Man wanted to become a painter, and intermittently attended school and learned basic literacy. But he spent all day and every day copying and coloring, and would even forget to eat and sleep at night. With undivided attention to his art, it solidified in his soul, and so he became known as an even better painter than his father. After sticking at it for a long time, he lost interest in painting and gave it up, but then tried constructing rocks into mountains using the *samadhi* method of painters.[12] The mountains formed themselves into mighty peaks, winding and extending, lofty and up-thrusting, steep and jagged, rearing intermittently, rising and falling, twisting and turning, mighty and forceful. Overall they appeared like a huge mass extended over a vast distance, although they were on a small scale. His spirit was relaxed and his intention firm, not unlike the man with a pole catching cicadas.[13] From high to low, from great to small, he created their form in accordance with the lie of the land; as though without any preliminary cogitation, the mountains thrust upward in a myriad wondrous shapes. Those who saw them

---

10   Either Zhang had never acquired a formal name, because of his low social status, or Chen did not know it, so he leaves a blank here.

11   These titles belong to the Han rather than the Ming dynasty and must be largely fanciful. However, by telling us that Zhang's grandfather was some sort of policeman, Chen Suoyun indicates that he was a public servant (albeit at a very low level) and therefore the family had risen above their rustic origins.

12   *Samadhi* is a Sanskrit term from Buddhism, referring to mental concentration.

13   This refers to a story in chapter 19 of *Zhuangzi*, in which an old hunchback has achieved such perfect communion with the Way that he easily performs the difficult feat of catching cicadas.

were astounded and stunned, and declared that they could not come from the world of men. The Mountain Man, too, when things came out exactly right, would often shout aloud in satisfaction and exclaim that the gods had helped him.

Thus the Mountain Man enjoyed the highest reputation at that time. Many connoisseurs north and south of the river who wanted to construct a hill or a dale all said that it would never do to be alive in the present day and yet fail to be in correspondence with the Mountain Man, so there was not a day when he did not have people coming to commission him. Those to whom the Mountain Man was willing to go would gladly order their carriages for him to travel in. He would examine the dimensions of the land and the quantity of rocks available on it, and in his heart the mountain had already taken shape. Then he would open himself to inspiration, and grasping an iron baton he would direct the crowd of workmen. Only he was able to make them work effectively together. With a few words, a gesture and a glance, cliffs, caves, vales, glens, peaks, ridges, steps, stairways, slopes, and braes immediately came into existence. As a result the Mountain Man became extremely well-known. People from far and near sent their carriages to collect the Mountain Man, regardless of distance. If their commissions did not appeal to him, they could not obtain his services even for a thousand taels. In response to one request he said, "Go away and stop bothering the guv'nor. My talents are not for sale."

Consequently, among all the gardens of gentry families throughout the Wu region, if on inquiry it turned out that it was not the Mountain Man who had constructed them, the owner was embarrassed to admit it. In respect of this importance of his for a period of time, at the time our fellow-Shanghainese Administration Commissioner Pan [Yunduan] was outstanding for his Pleasurable Garden, and Minister of Justice Wang [Shizhen] of Taicang was outstanding for his Yanshan Garden; these gardens were 100 *li* apart, and were the leading gardens of the South East. Both were by the hand of the Mountain Man. Both gentlemen treated the Mountain Man with respect as an honored guest and humbled themselves before him. The Mountain Man divided his time between the two of them, and neither garden was inferior or superior to the other. The Administration Commissioner had a miscellaneous retinue, among whom the junior members tried to rival the senior, and in pursuit of disreputable advantage they behaved high-handedly in the neighborhood. The Mountain Man, fearing to become involved himself in some débacle, somewhat distanced himself [from Pan]. This was greatly resented by the Administration Commissioner. At Minister Wang's, Zhang had met Embroidered Uniform Guards officer Shi, formerly a retainer of the Governor of Jiangling. The Embroidered Uniform Guards officer wished to construct a villa for the governor, and was frantically searching for a rockery expert to hire. As soon as he heard of the Mountain Man's reputation, he regretted not having come across him sooner, and wanted to sweep him up and carry him off, offering him a military award. The Mountain Man made the excuse that he had other things to attend to and avoided him, when Minister Wang persuaded Shi not to compel him. This gives a sense of what the Mountain Man was like.

He had no sons, but two grandsons and his wife Mrs. X, with whom he reached a hale and hearty old age. Even at 80 he was extremely spry; his appetite was like a young man's, and his bowels remained regular. As a result, he reached the age of 100 with no more effort than living through a single day. I have had a long acquaintance with him, and no one knows him as well as I do. So I have set things out as above to advise my peers to raise a glass to the Mountain Man as he assembles some fragments of rock to complete his work. Some other day these words of mine [text missing].

The Celestial Official states: As the saying goes, the skill of man accomplishes the work of Heaven. Can this not be said of the Mountain Man? When he first became known for his painting, he already possessed hills and dales. For that [painting] is one type of hills and dales, while this [rockery] is another kind of hills and dales. What is the difference from wielding an axe-handle to cut an axe-handle? If you take it up, it is not far from your grasp. This applies to his skill being so renowned and unique in his time. Just as escaping a disaster still gives one a fright, so rejecting honors still risks contamination. In this way his knowledge far surpasses that of others and becomes a form of skill.

The Craft of Gardens (*Yuanye* 園冶)

"Author's Preface" (*Zi xu* 自序)

JI CHENG 計成 (1582–CA. 1642)
TRANSLATED BY ALISON HARDIE

For Ji Cheng, see chapter 3. As noted in the introduction to chapter 6, the emergence in the Ming dynasty of a wealthy merchant class with aspirations to join the cultured upper class (heretofore the preserve of the highly educated scholarly elite) created the demand for manuals of self-improvement and advice on what was and was not socially acceptable. *The Craft of Gardens* evidently belongs to some extent in this genre. Ji Cheng is himself representative of men who, in the comparative social mobility of the times, could make their names through their own skills, without the advantage of birth.

    Although Ji Cheng seems to have traveled widely, most of his work appears to have been done in his native Jiangsu Province. This was an extremely prosperous part of China, and attracted both wealthy men of culture who wanted to live in an agreeable and comfortable environment, far from the pressures of life in the capital, as well as the artists and craftsmen who depended upon their patronage. Many of the finest artists of the late Ming period were from the Jiangsu Province, often from wealthy landowning families; possibly the most influential of these artists, Dong Qichang, was a friend of one of Ji Cheng's patrons, Zheng Yuanxun.

In this anthology, we include Ji Cheng's "Author's Preface" to his work, as well as his section on the "Selection of Rocks" (chapter 3). The views of his patrons Zheng Yuanxun and Ruan Dacheng (who both contributed prefaces to *The Craft of Gardens*) can be found in chapter 6.

"Author's Preface"

As a young man I was known as a painter. I was by nature interested in seeking out the unusual; since I derived most pleasure from the brushes of Guan Tong and Jing Hao, I paid homage to their style in all my work.

I traveled between the region of Beijing in the north and the old land of Chu in the south, and in middle-age returned to my home region of Wu, where I decided to settle at Zhenjiang. Zhenjiang is surrounded by the most beautiful scenery, and people in the area who cared about such things collected rocks, and arranged those with interesting shapes among bamboos and trees to make artificial mountains. One day I happened on some of these, and burst out laughing at them. When somebody asked me what I was laughing at, I answered, "It has been said that art imitates life, but why do you not imitate the appearance of real mountains, instead of those heaps of fist-shaped stones which country people put up to welcome the God of Spring?" "Could you do any better yourself?" they asked, so I arranged some rocks into the shape of a cliff; everyone who saw it exclaimed, "What a magnificent mountain!" and word of it spread far and near.

It so happened that Lord Wu Youyu, the Civil and Finance Officer of Changzhou, heard the story and invited me to call on him. His lordship had some property to the east of the city-wall which was barely fifteen *mu* in area and had once been a garden belonging to the Khan of Wen under the Yuan dynasty. His lordship instructed me thus: "These ten *mu* will be set aside for a residence, and for the remaining five I should like to follow descriptions of the ancient Garden of Solitary Delight created by Sima Guang, the Duke of Wen."

I could see that the contours of the property rose very high; as one tracked the stream to its source, it led deep into the hillside. Tall trees reached to touch the heavens, while twisting branches brushed the earth. "To make a garden here," I said, "one should not only pile up rocks to emphasize the height, but excavate the earth to increase the depth, in proportion with these tall trees scattered on the hillside here, with their roots curled around sheer rocks just as in a painting. Following the course of the stream we should construct pavilions and terraces, whose reflections will be scattered on the surface of the pond, with winding gullies and flying galleries leading on from them, so that people will be taken beyond anything they could have imagined."

When the work was completed his lordship was delighted and said, "From entering to leaving, one actually only walks a mile and a half, but you would think that we had collected together in this small space all the famous sights of Jiangnan." Among all this there were also some small buildings—really just tiny cottages on a fragment of mountain—in which I felt I had managed to express all the unusual ideas in my imagination, so that I felt particularly satisfied with my achievement.

At the time Secretary Wang Shiheng also commissioned me to design a garden to the west of Luan River, and as it seems that the result was in accordance with his intentions, both this garden and the one I designed for Lord Wu Youyu became equally famous north and south of the Yangtze River.

In my leisure hours I collected my sketches and notes under the title "The Care of Gardens." On his travels Master Cao Yuanfu[14] of Gushu came to visit Secretary Wang's garden, and the owner and I accompanied him on a stroll through the garden, where he was invited to stay for a couple of days. Master Cao praised it over and over again, saying it was just like a painting by Jing Hao or Guan Tong, and asking if I could put my techniques down in writing. So I brought my notes out to show him, and he said, "This has not been heard or seen for a thousand ages! Why call it merely 'The Care of Gardens?' This is your personal creation, sir; you should call it 'The Craft of Gardens.'"

Recorded in the *xinwei* year of the Chongzhen era [1631] at the end of autumn, by the Negative Daoist Ji Cheng at his leisure in the Huye Hall.

"The Biography of Zhang Nanyuan" (*Zhang Nanyuan zhuan* 張南垣傳)

WU WEIYE 吳偉業 (1609–1671)
TRANSLATED BY ALISON HARDIE

Wu Weiye, often known by his sobriquet Wu Meicun, born in Taicang in present-day Jiangsu Province, was a painter, a scholar, and a major poet. Having become a presented scholar in 1631, he held office in both Beijing and Nanjing during the dying days of the Ming dynasty. Chapter 8 contains a partial translation of Wu's long poem "Thoughts Stirred on Meeting the Gardener of the Royal Academy in Nanjing"; here, we offer his biography of a famous garden designer.

Zhang Lian, born in 1587, and also known as Zhang Nanyuan, is one of the small number of garden professionals in the Ming dynasty about whom any personal information survives. Zhang Lian created gardens for a number of well-known and lesser-known individuals in the Jiangnan area. His sons and a nephew followed him into the garden design business; after the Manchu conquest of China, the Zhangs moved to Beijing, where they undertook work both for members of the scholar-official class and for the Qing court. Zhang Lian's son Zhang Ran worked on the Qing imperial gardens, designing Yingtai in the Southern Lake (or Southern Sea, *Nanhai*), the Garden

---

14   Editor's note: Cao Yuanfu is Cao Lüji (*jinshi* 1616), a close friend of Ji Cheng's patron and publisher of *The Craft of Gardens*, Ruan Dacheng (see chapter 6).

of Tranquil Brightness (*Jingming yuan*) on Jade Spring Hill, and the Garden of Uninhibited Spring (*Changchun yuan*). Zhang Lian himself retired back to Jiangnan, leaving his descendants in the north, where they became known, in reference to their work on rock structures or artificial mountains, as the "Mountain Zhangs." Some of their work survives in the remnants of the imperial gardens, but there are no private gardens designed by Zhang Lian himself still in existence.[15]

Although Zhang Lian's origins are unclear, he was probably a member of the artisan class rather than a lowly member of the scholar-official or literati class. Wu Weiye compares his skill to that of legendary craftsmen in the past, such as the cook in the early Daoist classic *Zhuangzi*, who effortlessly butchered an ox, or the gardener described by the Tang writer Liu Zongyuan, whose low-key way of caring for his fruit trees Liu felt could be taken by government officials as a model for taking care of the people—this biography is in chapter 1. It is, therefore, a tribute to Zhang's strong and yet likable personality that, in the highly stratified society of traditional China, he was able to associate so closely with men whose families had been literati for many generations. He appears, from other evidence as well as this biography, to have had a particularly warm relationship with Wu Weiye. The late Ming was a period of considerable social upheaval and economic development; social mobility (both upward and downward) increased, and it became more common for artisans to be financially and socially successful and to interest the literati class sufficiently for information about them to be recorded. Although we might like to know more about Zhang Lian than we do, it is fortunate that we have this biography, by someone who knew him well, to shed light on the man and his influence on the development of Chinese garden design.

"The Biography of Zhang Nanyuan"

Zhang Nanyuan's personal name was Lian; Nanyuan was his formal name. He came from Huating, but moved to Xiuzhou [Jiaxing], so he is also regarded as a Xiuzhou native. In his youth he studied painting, and enjoyed painting portraits, but was also expert in landscape. He then used the spirit of this to construct his rockeries, and consequently he was not particularly known for his other arts. He was most skillful at constructing rockery, and no one else could reach his standard. For over a hundred years, people who practice this skill have tried to imitate craggy heights, while enthusiasts have gathered together one or two strange rocks and entitled them mountain peaks; they would all be brought by cart from other districts, and city walls would be breached, the roads would be wrecked, men and oxen would pant and sweat, in order to deliver them. They would be bound with large hawsers and fixed with molten iron in the forms of beasts doing obeisance, or have inscriptions chiseled out and colored; craggy forms would reach up into the heavens or caves would burrow into them, as though one were actually on a lofty mountain: that was the sort of difficulty they led to. And beside them towering bridges would be erected, elevated walkways constructed, while those

---

15   On the life and work of Zhang Lian and his successors, see Cao Xun 曹汛, "*Qingdai zaoyuan dieshan yishujia Zhang Ran he Beijing de 'Shanzi Zhang',*" ("清代造園疊山藝術家張然和北京的'山子張'"), *Jianzhu lishi yu lilun* (建築歷史與理論) 2 (1981):116–25.

who visited them would have their kerchiefs caught and their feet tripped; they would have to make several twists and turns up flights of steps, or bend their backs to enter deep caverns, through which they would grope in a state of alarm and bewilderment.

When Zhang Nanyuan encountered such things he laughed and said:

> What do these people know about making mountains? A mass of peaks reaching up to heaven, deep ravines shading the sun: these are things formed by that divine spirit, the creative force of Nature, and are not something that human power can manage to achieve. In any case, they take up several hundred miles of land; how can one emulate them effectively with a site of ten feet or so and a ditch five feet long? This is no different from people in the marketplace who make clay models to beguile children!

> However, level hillocks and gentle slopes, mounds and hummocks can be completed in a matter of days by means of tamping earth between shuttering, then they can be set with rocks placed crisscross among them and be outlined with low walls and enclosed within thick bamboo, so that it seems as though amazing peaks and precipitous cliffs are piled up beyond the wall where people can only occasionally catch a glimpse of them. The impetus of their rocky veins, falling and rising, protruding and erupting, forms crouching lions or clawing beasts, their maws bristling with teeth, fangs jutting out, breaking through the undergrowth in the woods, encroaching on the high beams of buildings without withdrawing, so that it seems as though one is dwelling at the foot of a great mountain, among broken gullies and craggy glens. All this can come into my possession just by means of these few rocks.

> Square reservoirs and stone channels can be altered to twisting banks and winding shores; cavernous chambers and elaborately carved beams can be changed for grey doorways and whitewashed walls; one should select the kind of trees that do not shed their leaves, such as pines, cypresses and junipers, and plant them together to form a grove; one should select rocks that are easy to acquire, such as Lake Tai rocks or Yao peaks, and arrange them as the fancy strikes one, so that one has all the beauty of woods and springs without the effort of mountaineering: isn't this a good thing?

Chief Minister Dong Qichang and Chen Jiru of Huating gave him high praise, saying:

> The mountains of Jiangnan bear rocks among earth, as Huang Gongwang and Wu Zhen often said; one can tell that Zhang Nanyuan's work has a direct link to their paintings.

All the gentry sent him letters and visited him with cash gifts, undoubtedly several dozen families a year, and those for whom he could not carry out commissions regarded this as a matter for great regret, though when they came across him they were delighted and smiled as happily as they had before the refusal. Mr. Zhang was a fat, short, dark man; by nature he was humorous, and liked to use low-life slang as a way of raising a laugh, or he would make use of out-of-date expressions and old gossip. People would make fun of him for this but he did not care. In his social dealings, he liked to talk of people's good points; he did not make any distinction between high and low, and could get along well with all kinds of people. On this basis he was active in the various districts of Jiangnan for over fifty years. Apart from Huating and Xiuzhou, he was in Baimen [Nanjing], Jinsha [Nantong], Haiyu [Changshu], Loudong [Taicang], and Lucheng [Kunshan], and would spend at least several months wherever he went. The most outstanding of the gardens which he made were the Horizontal Clouds Garden of Li Fengshen of the Ministry of Works, the Readiness Garden of Circuit Intendant Yu, the Pleasure in the Suburbs Garden of Chief Minister of the Court of Imperial Sacrifices Wang Shimin, the Caressing the Waters Garden of Director of the Court of the Imperial Clan Qian Qianyi, and the Bamboo Pavilion of Wu Changshi of the Ministry of Personnel.

He had early developed his own method of constructing from a blueprint, making distinctions between height and depth, density and sparsity. Initially he would put up an earthen hill, and before any trees or rocks had been added, the crags and gullies would all be there, and then he would make and alter the "axe-cut" strokes as he went along, so that it was all imbued with mists and clouds, and there was no overt sign that anything had been added on later. Every single plant or bamboo, spare or dense, uneven or slanting, could be gazed at from any angle with equally wonderful effect. Before the "mountain" was completed, he would already have planned how to construct the buildings, and before the buildings had been added, he had already thought also about the interior decoration and fittings: shutters, mullions, tables and couches were never too fussily decorated but were always elegant, harmonious, and natural. If the owner was a connoisseur, Mr. Zhang would not be pushed around but would stay on site to supervise the construction; some might insist on having their own way and he would be forced to bend to pressure, but later someone would be sure to come along and say with a sigh, "I'm sure this wasn't Nanyuan's own design."

The longer Mr. Zhang practiced this craft, the better he got to know the nature of all kinds of earth, rock, plant, and tree. Every time he started a new project, when rocks were scattered around in disorder, lying down or leaning to one side, Mr. Zhang would tramp about looking in all directions, silently recognizing in his heart which should form the main impetus and which should act as the supporting peaks, which should be set horizontally and which arranged vertically, and would then make use of his laborers to achieve this. He would usually sit aloft in a building, chatting and joking with visitors, and calling to the workmen: "Such and such rock should be put in such and such a position under such and such a tree." Without turning his eyes to look, and without any further gestures of his hands, as if casting metal without the intervention of a chisel to shape it, when it came to suspending a plumb line from a stick laid on a summit, there was not the least variation in the measurements: observers were overcome by this ability of his. People who tried to copy his technique believed that variation and change was what he had always excelled in, and racked their brains to achieve some similarity; at first glance their work might seem to resemble his, but on longer viewing it was totally different. Mr. Zhang, however, was the only one who could estimate the overall effect, and where other people would fail by yards to get it right over a number of days, as soon as he arrived on the scene, then its natural appearance would emerge and something unprecedented would be achieved. He once made a pair of peaks for the front of a friend's studio in the old style of Jing Hao and Guan Tong; it had risen more than five *xun* from ground level without a single variation, and then at the summit he suddenly placed a few rocks which combined to give an effect of movement, so that the whole formation soared and was completely out of the ordinary. This was the sort of thing that led people to say that no one else could reach his standard.

Mr. Zhang had four sons, who were able to carry on their father's craft. In his later years he declined a commission from Premier Zhuolu,[16] but sent his second son to do the job, and retired to spend his old age beside Mandarin Duck Lake, where he built a retreat of three beam widths. When I visited him, he said to me:

> It has been several decades since I started to practice this craft in the Jiangnan region, and so many famous gardens and villas have changed hands in that time. They have been destroyed in military action or have disappeared among thorns and undergrowth; other people have taken their rare plants or remarkable rocks and carried them away, and I have come across them several times on different projects. I am worried that rocks are not enough to keep my name alive, and I would love to have you write something to pass it on.

I replied:

> When Liu Zongyuan wrote the biography of the gardener, he said that he had learnt something about government from him. Now, when I observe your craft, Mr. Zhang, though we may never again encounter Cook Ding butchering the ox,

---

16   Zhuolu, an old place-name corresponding to present-day Zhuo county, near Beijing, should refer to Feng Quan (1595–1672), who was a native of this place and held office under both the Ming and the Qing dynasties, but it is known that Zhang Lian carried out work on the Myriad Willows Hall (*Wanliu tang*) garden in Beijing belonging to Feng Pu (1609–1692) from Shandong, a very distinguished senior official in the early Qing dynasty. Wu Weiye appears to have confused the two.

or Gong Shu dissecting the dove, your art is surely in conformity with the Way also! The gentleman does nothing which is not beneficial: excavating ponds and constructing terraces is something which the *Spring and Autumn Annals* warn against, but princes and potentates indulge in music and dance, wasting their substance on riotous living, merely to give pleasure to their ears and eyes: this is hardly in conformity with purity and restraint. You, however, Mr. Zhang, plumb the depths and mount to the heights, conforming with nature and sparing of human labor: this is an adaptation of the technique of the Foolish Old Man who moved the mountain, and certainly deserves to be recorded.

And so I wrote this "Biography of Zhang Nanyuan."

"Marginal Comment to 'The Biography of Zhang Nanyuan'" (*Ba Zhang Nanyuan zhuan* 拔張南垣傳)

ZHANG CHAO 張潮 (B. 1650)
TRANSLATED BY DUNCAN M. CAMPBELL

Having repeatedly failed to advance through the civil service examinations, the wealthy and well-connected Anhui writer and editor Zhang Chao held a number of lowly official posts in the 1670s, before moving to Yangzhou and embarking on the life of a literatus publisher. He was responsible for the compilation and publication of a number of large and important collections of short stories, anecdotes, and biographies, including Wu Weiye's biography of Zhang Nanyuan, to which he (under his formal name Zhang Shanlai) appended the following marginal comment, found in his *Unreliable Historian's New Records*.

"Marginal Comment to 'The Biography of Zhang Nanyuan'"

Zhang Chao says: And of course, the art of artificial mountains and rockeries demands also its own particular kind of scholarship, for the conceptualization in the mind of the hills and valleys it involves proves even more difficult than is this process for the landscape artist. In the case of the latter, the artist alone has mastery over what is near at hand and what is distant, what is high and what is low, over the dense and the sparse, the difficult and the easy. For the master of rockery, on the other hand, however, his work must accord with the actual lie of the land, he must suit his conception to the nature of the rock at hand, and just as he cannot simply discard what is surplus to his requirements, neither can he immediately supplement any deficiency in the material available to him. Always he must keep in mind the financial wherewithal of his patron, and accord his design with both this man's character and the skills of the workmen. These constitute his real difficulties. The skills of the landscape artist are displayed not along the paths and alleys of the garden but in brush and ink. I have often thought that, in reality, those scenes so often seen depicted in paintings would afford no possible enjoyment to an actual visitor. One can extend this comparison to poetry as well. Although a misty scene expressing great melancholy may well constitute a fine line of poetry, to give actual expression of this line in reality entails difficulties of the greatest kind. In the end, after all, the splendor of a garden depends simply on the appropriate disposition of the various scenes that it contains for it can rely on no other thing external to itself for the life that it embodies. How could this art possibly be compared to that of the landscape artist?

Collected Talks from the Lü Garden (*Lüyuan conghua* 履園叢話)

"On the Making of Gardens" (*Zaoyuan* 造園)

QIAN YONG 錢泳 (1759–1844)

TRANSLATED BY DUNCAN M. CAMPBELL

For Qian Yong, see chapter 6. This theoretical passage forms the final section of the chapter on gardens in Qian's *Collected Talks from the Lü Garden*; it is preceded by descriptions of various actual gardens that he knew of or had visited. Here, we see a reprise of the idea so widespread in the Tang (see chapter 2) that the true owner of the garden is the person who visits and appreciates it, not necessarily its legal owner.

"On the Making of Gardens"

The making of a garden is somewhat akin to the writing of an essay or the composition of a poem; a garden can only be considered well designed to the extent that its twists and turns accord to a pattern and that all its various parts respond to each other. Above all, the garden must avoid both that which is superfluous and that which is haphazard. And once the garden has been completed, it can only be called famous to the extent to which its master is fit to the purpose and its site is appropriate to the design, and neither the simpleton nor the vulgar are ever permitted a foothold within its walls. Nowadays, all the city temples of Changshu, Wujiang, Mount Kun, Jiading, Shanghai, and Wuxi have gardens, none of which is particularly vulgar. But then each spring or autumn festival, the gardens become crowded with peasant boys and village housewives, traveling merchants and young louts. What with the storytelling and the singing that then goes on within these gardens, can they really be regarded as famous any longer?

There is a garden in my hometown, the Garden Washed with Fragrance, found along Whistling Lane, that has for many generations been in the hands of the Li family of Jiangyin. It had been built during the final years of the reign of the Kangxi emperor [r. 1661–1722] by Mustard-Seed Studio Li, a man who held no office, and comprised simply a three-bay hall, called the Hall of Reciprocity. The only trees that had been planted around the hall were two or three cassia, and in front of the hall stood the owner's own Mustard-Seed Studio. During the years before his appointment to the

Grand Secretariat, Shen Deqian [1673–1769] would spend his days here, composing poems with Han Qi from Wumen and Li Keshan and others. A volume of the poems they exchanged was published under the title *A Collection of the Poetry of the Garden Washed with Fragrance*. From this circumstance can be observed the truth that it is not by reason of the size or splendor of a garden that its name is passed on, but rather does the immortality or otherwise of a garden depend upon the worth of its owner.

A friend of mine once bought a garden and proved most assiduous, night and day, in its management and its restoration. On a particular occasion it suddenly occurred to me to opine to him: "One doesn't really need to build one's own garden at all; whenever one strolls around in the garden of another, even if it possesses but a single flower and a solitary rock, it nonetheless becomes one's own garden—doesn't this save a lot of time and expense?" "Not at all," my friend replied. "For instance, having acquired a great deal of money, you then buy a concubine or two. Would you share your pleasure of them with others?" I rebutted his comment in the following manner: "In all matters, men tend to think simply about immediate gratification. In a moment however, all one's fame and honor can disappear completely, and one can suddenly find that all those dogs and horses and other baubles that one has sought so hard to acquire are no longer one's own. How much more so is this true of gardens! One can never be sure that at some point in the future one's garden will not be giving pleasure to another!"

Stone Forest Wu was obsessed with gardens, but he was so exceedingly poor that building his own garden was quite beyond his means. He proceeded, therefore, to write a *Record of No-Such Garden*, as exquisitely crafted as Tao Qian's "Peach Blossom Spring" or Yu Xin's "Rhapsody on My Small Garden." His friend Shard-of-Rock Jiang wrote a poem on this record that went:

> If you try as hard as hard can be, then an illusion can be made real,
> How much more so is this true of a mere hill or dale?
> But in the end the mind proves form's slave,
> Pity that hungry man reduced to drawing cake!
> Words may well capture the vast blue sky,
> But how many layers of cloud find the way onto the patterned paper?
> Sons and grandsons may well hold tight to this for years on end,
> But when sold to another, the piece proves not worth a single copper.

I note that men of earlier times have written records of the "Garden That is Not Around," the "Garden of the Heart," and the "Garden of the Mind"; all these are of a kind with that of my friend Stone Forest Wu.

PART 2

GARDENS OF THE IMAGINATION

The Peony Pavilion (Mudan ting 牡丹亭*)*

"Scene Ten: The Interrupted Dream" (*Di shi chu: Jing meng* 第十齣: 驚夢)

TANG XIANZU 湯顯祖 (1550–1616)
TRANSLATED BY CYRIL BIRCH

Tang Xianzu, an almost exact contemporary of William Shakespeare, is regarded as the greatest (and best-loved) playwright of late imperial China. Still frequently performed, his play *The Peony Pavilion* reflects late Ming interests in the importance of emotion (*qing*) as an expression of authentic individuality, and in female as well as male psychology. The play tells the love story of Bridal Du (Du Liniang) and her predestined lover Liu Mengmei ("Willow Dreaming of Plum"), who have their first erotic encounter in Bridal's dream, induced by the signs of burgeoning spring in the garden; she then wastes away from lovesickness. When the real-life Liu comes upon the self-portrait she painted before her untimely death, he falls in love and the power of his emotion restores her to life; after some ineffectual opposition from Bridal's convention-bound father, the pair are united in marriage. Their first dream encounter takes place in the garden Bridal has just visited with her maid Spring Fragrance, and in which she is eventually buried. The garden in the play is, therefore, imagined as the site both of erotic love and of death (and resurrection). The play itself might well be performed in a garden, as was frequently the case with private theatrical performances, and there is an elision between the scene of the dramatic action and the scene of its presentation.

"Scene Ten: The Interrupted Dream"

BRIDAL DU:
I From dream returning, orioles coil their song
   through all the brilliant riot of the new season
   to listener in tiny leaf-locked court.

SPRING FRAGRANCE:
Burnt to ashes the aloes wood
cast aside the broidering thread,
no longer able as in past years
to quiet stirrings of the spring's passions.

BRIDAL:
Like one "eyeing the apricot flower to slake her thirst"
at dawn, cheeks blurred with last night's rouge,
I gaze at Apricot Blossom Pass.

FRAGRANCE:
The coils of your hair
dressed with silken swallows in the mode of spring
tilt aslant as you lean
across the balustrade.

BRIDAL:
Rootless ennui,
"where are the scissors can cut,
the comb can untangle this grief?"

FRAGRANCE:
I have told the oriole and the swallow
to leave their urging of the flowers
and with spring as their excuse
to come look at you.

BRIDAL: Fragrance, have you given orders for the paths to be swept?

FRAGRANCE: Yes.

BRIDAL: Now bring me my mirror and my gown.

FRAGRANCE (*re-enters with these*):
"Cloud coiffure set to perfection
  still she questions the mirror,
robe of gauze soon to be changed
  still she adds sweetening incense."
I've brought your mirror and gown.

BRIDAL:
II The spring a rippling thread
of gossamer gleaming sinuous in the sun
borne idly across the court.
Pausing to straighten
the flower heads of hair ornaments,
perplexed to find that my mirror
stealing its half-glance at my hair
has thrown these "gleaming clouds"
into alarmed disarray.

(*She takes a few steps*)

Walking here in my chamber
how should I dare let others see my form!

FRAGRANCE: How beautifully you are dressed and adorned today!

BRIDAL:

III See now how vivid shows my madder skirt,
     how brilliant gleam these combs all set with gems
       —you see, it has been
     always in my nature to love fine things.
     And yet, this bloom of springtime no eye has seen.
     What if my beauty should amaze the birds
     and out of shame for the comparison
   "cause fish to sink, wild geese to fall to earth,
     petals to close, the moon to hide her face"
     while all the flowers tremble?

FRAGRANCE: Please come now, it's almost breakfast time.

(*They begin to walk*)

Look how
while on the lacquered walkway
traces of gold dust glitter,
there on the lodge at pool's edge
mosses make a green mass.
Timid lest the grass stain
our newly broidered socks
we grieve that the flowers must bear
the tug of tiny gold bells.[17]

---

17 A prince of the Tang court strung tiny gold bells on red thread to hang on the stems of flowers and instructed the gardener to tug the thread when necessary to scare off the birds. Here Fragrance, though aware that this was done out of compassion for the flowers, takes sensibility a stage further by lamenting the burden they must bear.

BRIDAL: Without visiting this garden, how could I ever have realized this splendor
of spring!

IV See how deepest purple, brightest scarlet
open their beauty only to dry well crumbling.
"Bright the morn, lovely the scene,"
listless and lost the heart
—where is the garden "gay with joyous cries"?
My mother and father have never spoken of any such exquisite spot as this.

BRIDAL, FRAGRANCE:
Streaking the dawn, close-curled at dusk,
rosy clouds frame emerald pavilion;
fine threads of rain, petals borne on breeze,
gilded pleasure boat in waves of mist:
glories of spring but little treasured
by screen-secluded maid.

FRAGRANCE: All the flowers have come into bloom now, but it's still too early for
the peony.

BRIDAL:

V The green hillside
bleeds with the cuckoo's tears of red azalea,[18]
shreds of mist lazy as wine fumes thread the sweetbriar.
However fine the peony,
How can she rank as queen
Coming to bloom when spring has said farewell!

FRAGRANCE: See them pairing, orioles and swallows!

BRIDAL, FRAGRANCE:
Idle gaze resting
there where the voice of swallows shears the air
and liquid flows the trill of oriole.

BRIDAL: We must go now.

FRAGRANCE: Really one would never weary of enjoying this garden.

---

18 An involved wordplay here. *Dujuan* means both a flower, the azalea, and a bird, the cuckoo. An old legend related that the Prince of Shu in ancient times was transformed after his death into the cuckoo, which ever since has wept tears of blood.

BRIDAL: Say no more!

(*They begin to walk back*)

VI   Unwearying joy—how should we break its spell
    even by visits each in turn
    to the Twelve Towers of Fairyland?
    Far better now, as first elation passes,
    to find back in our chamber
    some pastime for idle hours.

(*They reach the house*)

FRAGRANCE:
"Open the west chamber door,
  in the east room make the bed,"
fill the vase with azalea,
light aloes in the incense burner.
Take your rest now, young mistress, while I go report to Madam.

(*She exits*)

BRIDAL (*sighing*):
Back from spring stroll
to silent room,
what to do but try on
the spring's new adornments?
Ah spring, now that you and I have formed so strong an attachment, what shall I find
to fill my days with when you are past? Oh this weather, how sleepy it makes one feel.
Where has Fragrance got to? (*She looks about her, then lowers her head again, pondering*)
Ah Heaven, now I begin to realize how disturbing the spring's splendor can truly be.
They were all telling the truth, those poems and ballads I read that spoke of girls of
ancient times "in springtime moved to passion, in autumn to regret." Here am I at the
"double eight," my sixteenth year, yet no fine "scholar to break the cassia bough" has
come my way. My young passions stir to the young spring season, but where shall I
find an "entrant of the moon's toad palace"?[19] Long ago the Lady Han found a way to a

---

19   "Breaking off the cassia bough" was a metaphor for success in the literary examinations. The cassia tree
in the moon figures in the legend of Wu Kang, banished to the moon and there condemned eternally to fell a
cassia which eternally springs up again. Another legend defines the moon as the palace of a celestial toad. Yet
another, as the residence of Chang E, who fled there after stealing the elixir of immortality from her husband;
forevermore, assisted by a "jade hare," she pounds medicines with her mortar and pestle.

meeting with Yu You, and the scholar Zhang met with Miss Cui by chance. Their loves are told in *Poem on the Red Leaf* and in *Western Chamber*,[20] how these "fair maids and gifted youths" after clandestine meetings made marital unions "as between Qin and Jin."[21] (*She gives a long sigh*) Though born and bred to a noted line of holders of office, I have reached the age to "pin up my hair" without plan made for my betrothal to a suitable partner. The green springtime of my own life passes unfulfilled, and swift the time speeds by as dawn and dusk interchange. (*She weeps*) O pity one whose beauty is a bright flower, when life endures no longer than leaf on tree!

VII From turbulent heart these springtime thoughts of love
will not be banished
—O with what suddenness
comes this secret discontent!
I was a pretty child, and so
of equal eminence must the family be,
truly immortals, no less
to receive me in marriage.
But for what grand alliance
is this springtime of my youth
so cast away?
What eyes may light on my sleeping form?
My only course this coy delaying
but in secret dreams
by whose side do I lie?
Shadowed against spring's glory I twist and turn.
Lingering
where to reveal my true desires!
Suffering
this wasting,
where but to Heaven shall my lament be made!
I feel rather tired, I shall rest against this low table and drowse for a while.

(*She falls asleep and begins to dream of LIU MENGMEI, who enters bearing a branch of willow in his hand*)

---

20 *Poem on the Red Leaf* (*Tihong ji* 題紅記) is the title of a play by Tang Xianzu's friend Wang Jide. The theme is taken from the Tang story of the Lady Han, who wrote a poem on a red leaf, which she set adrift on the water of the palace drain. The leaf was found by Yu You, who returned a message to her by similar means, and eventually met and married her. *Western Chamber* (*Xixiang ji* 西廂記) is Wang Shifu's famous play on the romance, again of Tang times, of the scholar Zhang and Cui Yingying, whom he met by chance on his visit to the temple in which she was lodging. In fact, our text does not name the *Xixiang ji* at this point; rather, the *Cui Hui zhuan*, the story of another Miss Cui, but this seems an unnecessary complication.

21 Two states of the "Springs and Autumns" period, whose ruling families for generations made marriage alliances.

LIU MENGMEI:
As song of oriole purls in warmth of sun,
so smiling lips open to greet romance.
Tracing my path by petals borne on stream,
I find the Peach Blossom Source of my desire.[22]
I came along this way with Miss Du—how is it that she is not with me now? (*He looks behind him and sees her*) Ah, Miss Du!
(*She rises, startled from sleep, and greets him. He continues*)
So this is where you were—I was looking for you everywhere. (*She glances shyly at him, but does not speak*) I just chanced to break off this branch from a weeping willow in the garden. You are so deeply versed in works of literature, I should like you to compose a poem to honor it.

(*She starts in surprised delight and opens her lips to speak, but checks herself*)

BRIDAL (*aside*): I have never seen this young man in my life—what is he doing here?

LIU (*smiling at her*): Lady, I am dying of love for you!
VIII With the flowering of your beauty
as the river of years rolls past,
everywhere I have searched for you
pining secluded in your chamber.
Lady, come with me just over there where we can talk.

(*She gives him a shy smile, but refuses to move. He tries to draw her by the sleeve*)

BRIDAL (*in a low voice*): Where do you mean?

LIU: There, just beyond this railing peony-lined
against the mound of weathered Taihu rocks.

BRIDAL (*in a low voice*): But, sir, what do you mean to do?

LIU (*also in a low voice*):
Open the fastening at your neck
loose the girdle at your waist,
while you

---

22   Allusion to a story of Liu Chen and Ruan Zhao of Han times, who found faery love by following a "peach-blossom spring" into the Tiantai (Terrace of Heaven) Mountains. Even more celebrated is the Peach Blossom Spring of an allegory by Tao Qian describing, at the stream's source, a secluded Shangri-la upon which a mortal stumbled.

screening your eyes with your sleeve,

white teeth clenched on the fabric as if against pain,

bear with me patiently a while

then drift into gentle slumber.

(BRIDAL turns away, blushing. LIU advances to take her in his arms, but she resists him)

LIU, BRIDAL:

Somewhere at some past time you and I met.

Now we behold each other in solemn awe.

But do not say

in this lovely place we should meet and speak no word.

(LIU exits, carrying off BRIDAL by force. Enter FLOWER SPIRIT in red cloak strewn with petals and ornamental headdress on his piled-up hair)

FLOWER SPIRIT:

Commissioner of the Flowers' Blooming,

come with new season

from Heaven of Blossom Guard

to fulfil the springtime's labors.

Drenched in red petal rain

the beholder, heartsore,

anchors his yearnings

amid the clouds of blossom.

In my charge as Flower Spirit is this garden in the rear of the prefectural residence at Nan'an. Between Bridal, daughter of Prefect Du, and the young graduate Liu Mengmei, there exists a marriage affinity that must someday be fulfilled, and now Miss Du's heart has been so deeply moved by her spring strolling that she has summoned the graduate Liu into her dream. To cherish in compassion the "jade-like incense ones" is the special concern of a flower spirit, and that is why I am here to watch over her and to ensure that the "play of clouds and rain" will be a joyous experience for her.[23]

IX   Ah, how the male force surges and leaps

as in the way of wanton bee he stirs

the gale of her desire

while her soul trembles

at the dewy brink of a sweet, shaded vale.

A mating of shadows, this,

---

23   According to the *Gaotang fu* 高唐賦 by the pre-Han poet Song Yu, Witch's Mount (*Wushan* 巫山) at Gaotang was where Prince Hui of Chu made love in a dream to a beautiful woman who told him, "At dawn I am the morning clouds, at dusk the driving rain."

consummation within the mind,
no fruitful Effect
but an apparition within the Cause.[24]
Ha, but now my flower palace is sullied by lust.
I must use a falling petal to wake her.

(*Scatters petals in the entrance to the stage*)

Loath she may be to loose herself
from the sweet spellbound dream of spring's delight,
but petals flutter down
like crimson snow.

So, graduate Liu, the dream is but half-complete. When it is over, be sure to see Miss
Du safely back to her chamber. I leave you now.

(*Exit. Enter LIU, leading BRIDAL by the hand*)

LIU: For this brief moment
X Nature was our comforter,
grasses for pillow, our bed a bed of flowers.
Are you all right, Miss Du?

(*She lowers her head*)

Disarrayed the clouds of her hair,
red petals caught
by emerald combs aslant.
O lady, never forget
how close I clasped you
and with what tenderness,
longing to make
of our two bodies one single flesh
but bringing forth
a glistening of rouge raindrops in the sun.

BRIDAL: Sir, you must go now.

---

24 In the Buddhist doctrine of karma, every effect is the result of some prior cause in either the present or a
previous incarnation.

BRIDAL, LIU:
Somewhere at some past time you and I met.
Now we behold each other in solemn awe
but do not say
in this lovely place we should meet and speak no word.

LIU: Lady, you must be tired. Please take a rest. (*He sees her back to the table against which she was drowsing, and gently taps her sleeve*) Lady, I am going. (*Looking back at her*)
Have a good rest now, I shall come to see you again.
Rain threatened the spring garden as she approached
and when she slept the "clouds and rain"
broke over Wushan, hill of faery love.

(*Exit*)

BRIDAL (*wakes with a start and calls in a low voice*): Young sir, young sir, oh, you have left me. (*She falls asleep again*)

MADAM DU (*enters*):
Husband on Prefect's dais
daughter in cloistered chamber
—yet when she broiders patterns on a dress
above the flowers the birds fly all in pairs.
Child, child, what are you doing asleep in a place like this?

BRIDAL (*wakes and calls again after LIU*): Oh, oh.

MADAM DU: Why, child, what is the matter?

BRIDAL (*startled, rises to her feet*): Mother, it's you!

MADAM DU: Child, why aren't you passing your time pleasantly with needlework or a little reading? Why were you lying here sleeping in the middle of the day?

BRIDAL: Just now I took an idle stroll in the garden, but all at once the raucousness of the birds began to distress me and so I came back to my room. Lacking any means to while away the time I must have fallen asleep for a moment. Please excuse my failure to receive you in proper fashion.

MADAM DU: The rear garden is too lonely and deserted, child. You must not go strolling there again.

BRIDAL: I shall take care to do as you bid, Mother.

MADAM DU: Off to the schoolroom with you now for your lesson.

BRIDAL: We are having a break just now, the tutor is not here.

MADAM DU (*sighing*): There must always be troubles when a girl approaches womanhood, and she must be left to her own ways.
Truly,

> moiling and toiling in the children's wake,
> many the pains a mother needs must take.

(*Exit*)

BRIDAL (*watching her leave and sighing heavily*): Ah Heaven, Bridal, what unsought fortune has befallen you today! Chancing to visit the garden behind the house, I found a hundred different flowers in bloom everywhere, and the beauty of the scene set my heart in turmoil. When my elation passed and I came back, I fell into a midday slumber here in my incense-laden chamber. Suddenly a most handsome and elegant youth appeared, of age just fit for the "capping ceremony" of the twentieth year. He had broken off a branch from a willow in the garden, and he smiled and said to me, "Lady, you are so deeply versed in works of literature, I should like you to compose a poem in honor of this willow branch." I was on the point of replying when the thought came to me that I had never seen this man in my life before and did not even know his name. How should I so lightly enter into conversation with him? But just as this was in my mind he came close and began to speak fond words to me; then taking me in his arms he carried me to a spot beside the peony pavilion, beyond the railings lined with tree peonies, and there together we found the "joys of cloud and rain." Passion was matched by passion, and indeed a thousand fond caresses, a million tendernesses passed between us. After our bliss was accomplished he led me back to where I had been sleeping, and many times said, "Rest now." Then, just as I was about to see him off, suddenly my mother came into my room and woke me. Now perspiration chills all my body—it was no more than a "dream of Nanke, the human world in an anthill."[25] I hastened to greet my mother with the proper decorum, and was duly given a good talking-to. Though there was nothing I could say in my defense, how can I now free my mind from memories of all that happened in my dream? Walking or sitting still, I find no peace, all I can feel is a sense of loss. Ah mother, you tell me to be off to the schoolroom to my lesson—but what kind of book has lessons to lighten this heavy heart! (*She weeps, screening her face with her sleeve*)

---

25   In a well-known Tang story, the Prefect of Nanke served a king who proved to be an ant, his kingdom an anthill under an old tree stump.

XI Through scudding of "clouds and rain"
I had touched the borders of dream
when the lady my mother
called me, alas! and broke
this slumber by window's sunlit gauze.
Now clammy cold a perspiration breaks,
now heart numbs, footsteps falter,
thought fails, hair slants awry,
and whether to sit or stand
is more than mind can decide
—then let me sleep again.

FRAGRANCE (*enters*):
Against the coming of night
rid cheeks of powder's traces,
against the damp of spring
add incense to the burner.
Young mistress, I have aired the bedclothes for you to sleep now.

BRIDAL:
XII For heart spring-burdened, limbs
now lax from garden strolling,
no need of incense-aired
brocaded covers to entice to slumber.
Ah, Heaven,
let the dream I dreamed be not yet fled too far
Idle spring excursion
begins from painted hall,
sweet-scented is the shade
of apricot and willow.
You ask where Liu and Ruan
met with their faery loves?
Look back, and on the east wind
heartbreak comes again.

The Story of the Stone (*Shitou ji* 石頭記)

Chapter 17 (extract)

CAO XUEQIN 曹雪芹 (1715–1763)

TRANSLATED BY DAVID HAWKES

Cao Xueqin's monumental novel *The Story of the Stone* is undoubtedly the greatest work of prose fiction from premodern China. The "stone" of the title is a magical rock that is an alternative form of existence of the central character in the novel, Jia Baoyu (Precious Jade), born into a wealthy official family. The novel's alternative title, *A Dream of Red Mansions* or *Dream of the Red Chamber* (*Hong lou meng*), alludes to the splendid setting in which the family lives, as well as carrying an allusion to the Buddhist expression "the world of red dust," indicating the illusory nature of worldly success, a key message of the novel. Prospect Garden (*Daguan yuan*), described in the extract below, is created at an early point in the novel in honor of a visit to her family home by Jia Baoyu's sister, an official consort of the emperor, and thus a person of a status far higher than that of her natal family, grand though they are. Much of the subsequent action of the novel takes place in this garden, which operates as an idyllic parallel to the real world of the Jia family's main house, one of many dualities around which the novel is constructed. The scale of the garden is never clear; it seems to be of an infinite size, disclosing its nature as an illusion within an illusion. Although the passage extracted here is intended largely as a satire on the pedantic "literary gentlemen" who are hangers-on of the Jia family, it also gives us a sense of how important the naming of sites and features was in Chinese garden culture.

The author's grandfather, Cao Yin (d. 1712), a Han Chinese bannerman, was close to the Kangxi emperor, and the Cao family enjoyed considerable power and wealth, so the setting of the novel is believed to reflect the author's own experience. Various originals have been suggested for Prospect Garden itself, including the Cao family's own garden and Yuan Mei's Garden of Accommodation (see chapter 8), but there is no real reason to believe that it is anything but a creation of the author's imagination.

Chapter 17 (extract)

The inspection of the new garden becomes a test of talent
And Rong-guo House makes itself ready for an important visitor

One day Cousin Zhen came to Jia Zheng with his team of helpers to report that work on the new garden had been completed.

"Uncle She has already had a look," said Cousin Zhen. "Now we are only waiting for you to look around it to tell us if there is anything you think will need altering and also to decide what inscriptions ought to be used on the boards everywhere."

Jia Zheng reflected a while in silence.

"These inscriptions are going to be difficult," he said eventually. "By rights, of course, her Grace should have the privilege of doing them herself; but she can scarcely be expected to make them up out of her head without having seen any of the views which they are to describe. On the other hand, if we wait until she has already visited the garden before asking her, half the pleasure of the visit will be lost. All those prospects and pavilions—even the rocks and trees and flowers will seem somehow incomplete without that touch of poetry which only the written word can lend a scene."

"My dear patron, you are so right," said one of the literary gentlemen who sat with him. "But we have had an idea. The inscriptions for the various parts of the garden obviously cannot be dispensed with; nor, equally obviously, can they be decided in advance. Our suggestion is that we should compose provisional names and couplets to suit the places where inscriptions are required, and have them painted on rectangular paper lanterns which can be hung up temporarily—either horizontally or vertically as the case may be—when Her Grace comes to visit. We can ask her to decide on the permanent names after she has inspected the garden. Is this not a solution of the dilemma?"

"It is indeed," said Jia Zheng. "When we look round the garden presently, we must all try to think of words that can be used. If they seem suitable, we can keep them for the lanterns. If not, we can call for Yu-cun to come and help us out."

"Your own suggestions are sure to be admirable, Sir Zheng," said the literary gentleman ingratiatingly. "There will be no need to call in Yu-cun."

Jia Zheng smiled deprecatingly.

"I am afraid it is not as you imagine. In my youth I had at best only indifferent skill in the art of writing verses about natural objects—birds and flowers and scenery and the like; and now that I am older and have to devote all my energies to official documents and government papers, I am even more out of touch with this sort of thing than I was then; so that even if I were to try my hand at it, I fear that my efforts would be rather dull and pedantic ones. Instead of enhancing the interest and beauty of the garden, they would probably have a deadening effect on both."

"That doesn't matter," the literary gentlemen replied. "We can *all* try our hands at composing. If each of us contributes what he is best at, and if we then select the better attempts and reject the ones that are not so good, we should be able to manage all right."

"That seems to me a very good suggestion," said Jia Zheng.
"As the weather today is so warm and pleasant, let us all go and take a turn around the garden now!"

So saying he rose to his feet and conducted his little retinue of literary luminaries toward the garden. Cousin Zhen hurried on ahead to warn those in charge that they were coming.

As Bao-yu was still in very low spirits these days because of his grief for Qin Zhong, Grandmother Jia had hit on the idea of sending him into the newly made garden to play. By unlucky chance she had selected this very day on which to try out her antidote. He had in fact only just entered the garden when Cousin Zhen came hurrying toward him.

"Better get out of here!" said Cousin Zhen with an amused smile. "Your father will be here directly!"

Bao-yu streaked toward the gate, a string of nurses and pages hurrying at his heels. But he had only just turned the corner on coming out of it when he almost ran into the arms of Jia Zheng and his party coming from the opposite direction. Escape was impossible. He simply had to stand meekly to one side and await instructions.

Jia Zheng had recently received a favorable report on Bao-yu from his teacher Jia Dai-ru in which mention had been made of his skill in composing couplets. Although the boy showed no aptitude for serious study, Dai-ru had said, he nevertheless possessed a certain meretricious talent for versification not undeserving of commendation. Because of this report, Jia Zheng ordered Bao-yu to accompany him into the garden, intending to put his aptitude to the test. Bao-yu, who knew nothing either of Dai-ru's report or his father's intentions, followed with trepidation.

As soon as they reached the gate they found Cousin Zhen at the head of a group of overseers waiting to learn Jia Zheng's wishes.

"I want you to close the gate," said Jia Zheng, "so that we can see what it looks like from outside before we go in."

Cousin Zhen ordered the gate to be closed, and Jia Zheng stood back and studied it gravely.

It was a five-frame gate-building with a hump-backed roof of half-cylinder tiles. The wooden lattice-work of the doors and windows was finely carved and ingeniously patterned. The whole gatehouse was quite unadorned by color or gilding, yet all was of the most exquisite workmanship. Its walls stood on a terrace of white marble carved with a pattern of passion-flowers in relief, and the garden's whitewashed circumference wall to left and right of it had a footing made of black-and-white striped stone blocks arranged so that the stripes formed a simple pattern. Jia Zheng found the unostentatious simplicity of this entrance greatly to his liking, and after ordering the gates to be opened, passed on inside.

A cry of admiration escaped them as they entered, for there, immediately in front of them, screening everything else from their view, rose a steep, verdure-clad hill.

"Without this hill," Jia Zheng somewhat otiosely observed, "the whole garden would be visible as one entered, and all its mystery would be lost."

The literary gentlemen concurred. "Only a master of the art of landscape could have conceived so bold a stroke," said one of them.

As they gazed at this miniature mountain, they observed a great number of large white rocks in all kinds of grotesque and monstrous shapes, rising course above course up one of its sides, some recumbent, some upright or leaning at angles, their surfaces streaked and spotted with moss and lichen or half concealed by creepers, and with a narrow, zig-zag path only barely discernible to the eye winding up between them.

"Let us begin our tour by following this path," said Jia Zheng. "If we work our way round toward the other side of the hill on our way back, we shall have made a complete circuit of the garden."

He ordered Cousin Zhen to lead the way, and leaning on Bao-yu's shoulder, began the winding ascent of the little mountain. Suddenly on the mountainside above his head, he noticed a white rock whose surface had been polished to mirror smoothness and realized that this must be one of the places which had been prepared for an inscription.

"Aha, gentlemen!" said Jia Zheng, turning back to address the others who were climbing up behind him. "What name are we going to choose for this mountain?"

"Emerald Heights," said one.

"Embroidery Hill," said another.

Another proposed that they should call it "Little Censer" after the famous Censer Peak in Kiangsi. Another proposed "Little Zhong-nan." Altogether some twenty or thirty names were suggested—none of them very seriously, since the literary gentlemen were aware that Jia Zheng intended to test Bao-yu and were anxious not to make the boy's task too difficult. Bao-yu understood and was duly grateful.

When no more names were forthcoming Jia Zheng turned to Bao-yu and asked him to propose something himself.

"I remember reading in some old book," said Bao-yu, "that 'to recall old things is better than to invent new ones; and to recut an ancient text is better than to engrave a modern.' We ought, then, to choose something old. But as this is not the garden's principal 'mountain' or its chief vista, strictly speaking there is no justification for having an inscription here at all—unless it is to be something which implies that this is merely a first step toward more important things ahead. I suggest we should call it 'Pathway to Mysteries' after the line in Chang Jian's poem about the mountain temple:

A path winds upward to mysterious places.

A name like that would be more distinguished."

There was a chorus of praise from the literary gentlemen:

"Exactly right! Wonderful! Our young friend with his natural talent and youthful imagination succeeds immediately where we old pedants fail!"

Jia Zheng gave a deprecatory laugh:

"You mustn't flatter the boy! People of his age are adept at making a little knowledge go a long way. I only asked him as a joke, to see what he would say. We shall have to think of a better name later on."

As he spoke, they passed through a tunnel of rock in the mountain's shoulder into an artificial ravine ablaze with the vari-colored flowers and foliage of many varieties of tree and shrub which grew there in great profusion. Down below, where the trees were thickest, a clear stream gushed between the rocks. After they had advanced a few paces in a somewhat northerly direction, the ravine broadened into a little flat-bottomed valley and the stream widened out to form a pool. Gaily painted and carved pavilions rose from the slopes on either side, their lower halves concealed amid the trees, their tops reaching into the blue. In the midst of the prospect below them was a handsome bridge:

In a green ravine
A jade stream sped.
A stair of stone
Plunged to the brink.
Where the water widened
To a placid pool,
A marble baluster
Ran round about.
A marble bridge crossed it
With triple span,
And a marble lion's maw
Crowned each of the arches.

Over the center of the bridge there was a little pavilion, which Jia Zheng and the others entered and sat down in.

"Well, gentleman!" said Jia Zheng. "What are we going to call it?"

"Ou-yang Xiu in his *Pavilion of the Old Drunkard* speaks of 'a pavilion poised above the water,'" said one of them.

"What about 'Poised Pavilion'?"

"'Poised Pavilion' is good," said Jia Zhang, "but *this* pavilion was put here in order to dominate the water it stands over, and I think there ought to be some reference to water in its name. I seem to recollect that in that same essay you mentioned Ou-yang Xiu speaks of the water 'gushing between twin peaks.' Could we not use the word 'gushing' in some way?"

"Yes, yes!" said one of the literary gentlemen. "'Gushing Jade' would do splendidly."

Jia Zheng fondled his beard meditatively, then turned to Bao-yu and asked him for *his* suggestion.

"I agreed with what you said just now, Father," said Bao-yu, "but on second thoughts it seems to me that though it may have been all right for Ou-yang Xiu to use the word 'gushing' in describing the source of the river Rang, it doesn't really suit the water round this pavilion. Then again, as this is a Separate Residence specially designed for the reception of a royal personage, it seems to me that something rather formal is called for, and that an expression taken from the *Drunkard's Pavilion* might seem a bit improper. I think we should try to find a more imaginative, less obvious sort of name."

"I hope you gentlemen are all taking this in!" said Jia Zheng sarcastically. "You will observe that when we suggest something original we are recommended to prefer the old to the new, but that when we *do* make use of an old text we are 'improper' and 'unimaginative'!—Well, carry on then! Let's have your suggestion!"

"I think 'Drenched Blossoms' would be more original and more tasteful than 'Gushing Jade.'"

Jia Zheng stroked his beard and nodded silently. The literary gentlemen could see that he was pleased and hastened to commend Bao-yu's remarkable ability.

"That's the two words for the framed board on top," said Jia Zheng. "*Not* a very difficult task. But what about the seven-word lines for the sides?"

Bao-yu glanced around quickly, seeking inspiration from the scene, and presently came up with the following couplet:

"Three pole-thrust lengths of bankside willows green,
 One fragrant breath of bankside flowers sweet."

Jia Zheng nodded and a barely perceptible smile played over his features. The literary gentlemen redoubled their praises.

They now left the pavilion and crossed to the other side of the pool. For a while they walked on, stopping from time to time to admire the various rocks and flowers and trees which they passed on their way, until suddenly they found themselves at the foot of a range of whitewashed walls enclosing a small retreat almost hidden among the hundreds and hundreds of green bamboos which grew in a dense thicket behind them. With cries of admiration they went inside. A cloister-like covered walk ran around the walls from the entrance to the back of the forecourt and a cobbled pathway led up to the steps of the terrace. The house was a tiny three-frame one, two parts latticed, the third part windowless. The tables, chairs, and couches which furnished it seemed to have been specially made to fit the interior. A door in the rear wall opened onto a garden of broad-leaved plantains dominated by a large flowering pear-tree and overlooked on either side by two diminutive lodges built at right angles to the back of the house. A stream gushed through an opening at the foot of the garden wall into a channel barely a foot wide that ran to the foot of the rear terrace and thence round the side of the house to the front, where it meandered through the bamboos of the forecourt before finally disappearing through another opening in the surrounding wall.

"This must be a pleasant enough place at any time," said Jia Zheng with a smile. "But just imagine what it would be like to sit studying beside the window here on a moonlight night! It is pleasures like that which make a man feel he has not lived in vain!"

As he spoke, his glance happened to fall on Bao-yu, who instantly became so embarrassed that he hung his head in shame. He was rescued by the timely intervention of the literary gentlemen who changed the subject from that of study to a less dangerous topic. Two of them suggested that the name given to this retreat should be a four-word one. Jia Zheng asked them what four words they proposed.

"'Where Bends the *Qi*'" said one of them, no doubt having in mind the song in the *Poetry Classic* which begins with the words

See in that nook where bends the Qi,
The green bamboos, how graceful grown!

"No," said Jia Zheng. "Too obvious!"

"'North of the Sui,'" said the other, evidently thinking of the ancient Rabbit Garden of the Prince of Liang in Suiyang—also famous for its bamboos and running water.

"No," said Jia Zheng. "Still too obvious!"

"You'd better ask Cousin Bao again," said Cousin Zheng, who stood by listening.

"He always insists on criticizing everyone else's suggestions before he will deign to make one of his own," said Jia Zheng. "He is a worthless creature."

"That's all right," said the others. "His criticisms are very good ones. He is in no way to blame for making them."

"You shouldn't let him get away with it!" said Jia Zheng. "All right!" he went on, turning to Bao-yu. "Today we will indulge you up to the hilt. Let's have your criticism, and after that we'll hear your own proposal. What about the two suggestions that have just been made? Do you think either of them could be used?"

"Neither of them seems quite right to me," said Bao-yu in answer to the question.

"In what way 'not quite right?'" said Jia Zheng with a scornful smile.

"Well," said Bao-yu, "This is the first building our visitor will enter when she looks over the garden, so there ought to be some word of praise for the emperor at this point. If we want a classical reference with imperial symbolism, I suggest 'The Phoenix Dance,' alluding to that passage in the *History Classic* about the male and female phoenixes alighting 'with measured gambollings' in the emperor's courtyard."

"What about 'Bend of the Qi' and 'North of the Sui'?" said Jia Zheng. "Aren't they classical allusions? If not, I should like to know what they are!"

"Yes," said Bao-yu, "but they are too contrived. 'The Phoenix Dance' is more fitting."

There was a loud murmur of assent from the literary gentlemen. Jia Zheng nodded and tried not to look pleased.

"Young idiot!—A 'small capacity but a great self-conceit,' gentlemen—All right!" he ordered: "now the couplet!"

So Bao-yu recited the following couplet:

"From the empty cauldron the steam still arises after the brewing of tea.
By the darkening window the fingers are still cold after the game of Go."

Jia Zheng shook his head: "Nothing very remarkable about *that*!"

With this remark he began to move on, but thought of something just as they were leaving, and stopped to ask Cousin Zhen:

"I see that the buildings in this garden have their proper complement of chairs and tables and so forth. What about blinds and curtains and flower-vases and all that sort of thing? Have they been selected to suit the individual rooms?"

"As regards ornaments," Cousin Zhen replied, "we have already got in quite a large stock, and when the time comes we shall naturally select from it what is suitable for each individual room. As regards drapes and hangings, Cousin Lian told me yesterday that there are quite a lot yet to come. What we did was to take the measurements from the plans drawn up for the carpenters and put the work in hand straight away, even before the buildings were finished. As far as I know, up to yesterday we had received about half of what was ordered."

From the way Cousin Zhen spoke, Jia Zheng gathered that this was not his responsibility and sent someone to summon Jia Lian. He arrived within moments, and Jia Zheng questioned him about the types and quantities ordered and the figures for what had already been received and what was still to come.

In response to his inquiry Jia Lian extracted a wallet from the leg of his boot, and glancing at a folded schedule inside it, summarized its contents as follows:

"Curtains, large and small, in various silks and satins—flowered, dragon-spot, sprigged, tapestry, panelled, ink-splash: one hundred and twenty.—Eighty of those were delivered yesterday. That leaves forty to come.—Blinds: two hundred.—Yes. They all arrived yesterday. But then there are the special ones.—Blinds, scarlet felt: two hundred. Speckled bamboo: one hundred. Red lacquered bamboo with gold fleck: one hundred. Black lacquered bamboo: one hundred. Colored net: two hundred.— We now have half of each of those four kinds. The other half is promised by the end of autumn.—Chair-covers, table-drapes, valances, tablecloths: one thousand two hundred of each.—Those we already have."

They had been moving on as he spoke, but were presently brought to a halt by a steeply sloping hill which rose up in front of them. Having negotiated its foot, they could see, almost concealed in a fold half-way up the other side of it, a dun-colored adobe wall crowned with a coping of rice-straw thatch. Inside it were several hundred apricot trees, whose flowering tops resembled the billowing rosy clouds of some vegetable volcano. In their midst stood a little group of reed-thatched cottages. Beyond the wall, with a barred gate dividing it in the middle, a loose hedge of irregular shape had been made by weaving together the pliant young shoots of the mulberry, elm, hibiscus, and silkworm thorn trees which grew outside it. Between this hedge of trees and the lower slope of the hill was a rustic well, furnished with both well-sweep and windlass. Below the well, row upon row of miniature fields full of healthy-looking vegetables and flowers ran down in variegated strips to the bottom.

"Ah, now here is a place with a purpose!" said Jia Zheng with a pleased smile. "It may have been made by human artifice, but the sight of it is none the less moving. In me it awakens the desire to get back to the land, to a life of rural simplicity. Let us go in and rest a while!"

They were just on the point of entering the gate in the hedge when they observed a stone at the side of the pathway leading up to it which had evidently been put there in order that the name of the place might be inscribed upon it.

"What a brilliant idea!" the literary gentlemen exclaimed. "If they had put a board up over the gate, the rustic atmosphere would have been completely destroyed, whereas this stone actually enhances it. This is a place which calls for the bucolic talent of a Fan Cheng-da to do it justice!"

"What shall we call it, then?" asked Jia Zheng.

"Just now our young friend was saying that to 'recall an old thing is better than to invent a new one,'" said one of the literary gentleman. "In this case the ancients have already provided the perfect name: 'Apricot Village.'"

Jia Zheng knew that he was referring to the words of the fainting traveler in Du Mu's poem:

"Where's the tavern?" I cry, and a lad points the way
To a village far off in the apricot trees.

He turned to Cousin Zhen with a smile:

"Yes. That reminds me. There's just one thing missing here: an inn sign. Tomorrow you must have one made. Nothing fancy. Just an ordinary inn-sign like the ones you see in country villages outside. And it should hang from a bamboo pole above the tree-tops."

Cousin Zhen promised to see this done and added a suggestion of his own: "The birds here, too, ought to be ordinary farmyard ones—hens, ducks, geese, and so on—to be in keeping with the surroundings."

Jia Zheng and the rest agreed enthusiastically.

"The only trouble with 'Apricot Village,'" said Jia Zheng, "—though it would suit the place very well—is that it is the name of a real village; so we should have to get official permission first before we could use it."

"Ah, yes," said the others. "That means that we still have to think of something for a temporary name. Now what shall it be?"

While they were all still thinking, Bao-yu who had already had an idea, was so bursting with eagerness that he broke in, without waiting to be invited by his father:

"There is an old poem which has the lines

Above the flowering apricot
A hopeful inn-sign hangs.

For the inscription on the stone we ought to have 'The Hopeful Sign.'"

"'The Hopeful Sign,'" echoed the literary gentlemen admiringly. "Very good! The hidden allusion to 'Apricot Village' is most ingenious!"

"Oh, as for the name of the village," said Bao-yu scornfully, "'Apricot Village' is much too obvious! Why not 'Sweet-Rice Village' from the words of the old poem:

A cottage by the water stands
Where sweet the young rice smells?"

The literary gentlemen clapped their hands delightedly; but their cries of admiration were cut short by an angry shout from Jia Zheng:

"Ignorant young puppy! Just how many 'old poets' and 'old poems' do you think you know, that you should presume to show off in front of your elders in this impertinent manner? We let you have your little say just now in order to test your intelligence. It was no more than a joke. Do you suppose we are seriously interested in your opinions?"

They had been moving on meanwhile, and he now led them into the largest of the little thatched buildings, from whose simple interior with its paper windows and plain deal furniture all hint of urban refinement had been banished. Jia Zheng was inwardly pleased. He stared hard at Bao-yu:

"How do you like *this* place, then?"

With secret winks and nods the literary gentlemen urged Bao-yu to make a favorable reply, but he wilfully ignored their promptings.

"Not nearly as much as 'The Phoenix Dance.'"

His father snorted disgustedly.

"Ignoramus! You have eyes only for painted halls and gaudy pavilions—the rubbishy trappings of wealth. What can *you* know of the beauty that lies in quietness and natural simplicity? This is a consequence of your refusal to study properly."

"Your rebuke is, of course, justified, Father," Bao-yu replied promptly, "but then I have never really understood what it was the ancients *meant* by 'natural.'"

The literary gentlemen, who had observed a vein of mulishness in Bao-yu which boded trouble, were surprised by the seeming naïveté of this reply.

"Why, fancy not knowing what 'natural' means—you who have such a good understanding of so much else! 'Natural' is that which is *of nature*, that is to say, that which is produced by nature as opposed to that which is produced by human artifice."

"There you are, you see!" said Bao-yu. "A farm set down in the middle of a place like this is obviously the product of human artifice. There are no neighboring villages, no distant prospects of city walls; the mountain at the back doesn't belong to any system; there is no pagoda rising from some tree-hid monastery in the hills above; there is no bridge below leading to a near-by market town. It sticks up out of nowhere, in total isolation from everything else. It isn't even a particularly remarkable view—not nearly so 'natural' in either form or spirit as those other places we have seen. The bamboo in those other places may have been planted by human hand and the streams diverted out of their natural courses, but there was no *appearance* of artifice. That's why, when the ancients use the term 'natural' I have my doubts about what they really meant. For example, when they speak of a 'natural painting,' I can't help wondering if they are not referring to precisely that forcible interference with the landscape to which I object: putting hills where they are not meant to be, and that sort of thing. However great the skill with which this is done, the results are never quite . . ."

His discourse was cut short by an outburst of rage from Jia Zheng.

"Take that boy out of here!"

Bao-yu fled.

"Come back!"

He returned.

"You still have to make a couplet on this place. If it isn't satisfactory, you will find yourself reciting it to the tune of a slapped face!"

Bao-yu stood quivering with fright and for some moments was unable to say anything. At last he recited the following couplet:

"Emergent buds swell where the washerwoman soaks her cloth.
A fresh tang rises where the cress-gatherer fills his pannier."

Jia Zheng shook his head:
"Worse and worse."

He led them out of the "village" and round the foot of the hill:

through flowers and foliage,
by rock and rivulet,
past rose-crowned pergolas
and rose-twined trellises,
through small pavilions
embowered in peonies,
where scent of sweet-briers stole,
or pliant plantains waved—

until they came to a place where a musical murmur of water issued from a cave in the rock. The cave was half-veiled by a green curtain of creeper, and the water below was starred with bobbing blossoms.

"What a delightful spot!" the literary gentlemen exclaimed.

"Very well, gentlemen. What are you going to call it?" said Jia Zheng.

Inevitably the literary gentlemen thought of Tao Yuan-ming's fisherman of Wu-ling and his Peach Blossom Stream.

"'The Wu-ling Stream,'" said one of them. "The name is ready-made for this place. No need to look further than that."

Jia Zheng laughed:

"The same trouble again, I am afraid. It is the name of a real place. In any case it is too hackneyed."

"All right," said the others good-humoredly. "In that case simply call it 'Refuge of the Qins.'" Their minds still ran on the Peach Blossom Stream and its hidden paradise.

"That's even more inappropriate!" said Bao-yu. "'Refuge of the Qins' would imply that the people here were fugitives from tyranny. How can we possibly call it that? I suggest 'Smartweed Bank and Flowery Harbor.'"

"Rubbish!" said Jia Zheng. He looked inside the grotto and asked Cousin Zhen if there were any boats.

"Four punts for lotus-gathering and one for pleasure are on order," said Cousin Zhen, "but they haven't finished making them yet."

"What a pity we cannot go through!" said Jia Zheng.

"There is a very steep path over the top which would take us there," said Cousin Zhen, and proceeded to lead the way.

The others scrambled up after him, clinging to creepers and leaning on tree-trunks as they went. When, having descended once more, they had regained the stream, it was wide and deep and distorted by many anfractuosities. The fallen blossoms seemed to be even more numerous and the waters on whose surface they floated even more limpid than they had been on the side they had just come from. The weeping willows that lined both banks were here and there diversified with peach and apricot trees whose interlacing branches made little worlds of stillness and serenity beneath them.

Suddenly, through the green of the willows, they glimpsed the scarlet balustrade of a wooden bridge whose sloping ramps led to a flat central span high above the water. When they had crossed it, they found a choice of paths leading to different parts of the garden. Ahead was an airy building with roofs of tile, whose elegant surrounding wall was of grey-plastered brick pierced by ornamental grilles made of semi-circular tiles laid together in openwork patterns. The wall was so constructed that outcrops of rock from the garden's "master mountain" appeared to run through it in several places into the courtyard inside.

"This building seems rather out of place here," said Jia Zheng.

But as he entered the gate the source of his annoyance disappeared; for a miniature mountain of rock, whose many holes and fissures, worn through it by weathering or the wash of waters, bestowed on it a misleading appearance of fragile delicacy, towered up in front of him and combined with the many smaller rocks of various shapes and sizes which surrounded it to efface from their view every single vestige of the building they had just been looking at.

Not a single tree grew in this enclosure, only plants and herbs:

some aspired as vines,

some crept humbly on the ground;

some grew down from the tops of rocks,

some upward from their feet;

some hung from the eaves in waving trails of green,

some clung to pillars in circling bands of gold;

some had blood-red berries,

some had golden flowers.

And from every flower and every plant and every herb wafted the most exquisite and incomparable fragrances.

Jia Zheng could not help but admire:

"Charming! But what *are* they all?"

"Wild-fig" and "wisteria" was all the literary gentlemen would venture.

"But surely," Jia Zheng objected, "wild-fig and wisteria do not have this delectable fragrance?"

"They certainly don't," said Bao-yu. "There *are* wild-fig and wisteria among the plants growing here, but the ones with the fragrance are pollia and birthwort and—yes, I think those are orchids of some kind. That one over there is probably actinidia. The red flowers are, of course, rue, the 'herb of grace,' and the green ones must be green-flag. A lot of these rare plants are mentioned in *Li sao* and *Wen xuan*, particularly in the *Poetical Descriptions of the Three Capitals* by Zuo Si. For example, in his *Description of the Wu Capital*, he has

> agastache, eulalia
> and harsh-smelling ginger-bush,
> cord-flower, cable-flower,
> centaury and purplestrife,
> stone-sail and water-pine
> and sweet-scented eglantine ...

And then there are

> amaranth, xanthoxylon,
> anemone, phellopteron ...

They come in the *Description of the Shu Capital*. Of course, after all these centuries nobody *really* knows what all those names stand for. They apply them quite arbitrarily to whatever seem to fit the description, and gradually all of them—"

Once more an angry shout from his father cut him short:

"Who asked for *your* opinion?"

Bao-yu shrank back and said no more.

Observing that there were balustraded loggias on either side of the court, Jia Zheng led his party through one of them toward the building at the rear. It was a cool, five-frame gallery with a low, roofed veranda running round it on all sides. The window-lattices were green and the walls freshly painted. It was a building of quite another order of elegance from the ones they had so far visited.

"Anyone who sat sipping tea and playing the *qin* to himself on this veranda would have no need to burn incense if he wanted sweet smells for his inspiration," said Jia Zheng dreamily. "So unexpectedly beautiful a place calls for a specially beautiful name to adorn it."

"What could be better than 'Dewy Orchids'?" said the literary gentlemen.

"Yes," said Jia Zheng. "That would do for the name. Now what about the couplet?"

"*I* have thought of a couplet," said one of the gentlemen. "Tell me all what you think of it:

> A musky perfume of orchids hangs in the sunset courtyard.
> A sweet aroma of galingale floats over the moonlit island."

"Not bad," said the others. "But why '*sunset* courtyard'?"

"I was thinking of that line in the old poem," said the man:

"The garden's gillyflowers at sunset weep.

After all, you have already got 'dewy' in the name. I thought the 'sunset weeping' would go with it rather well."

"Feeble! Feeble!" cried the rest.

"I've thought of a couplet, too," said one of the others. "Let me have your opinion of it:

Down garden walks a fragrant breeze caresses beds of melilot.
By courtyard walls a brilliant moon illumines golden orchises."

Jia Zheng stroked his beard, and his lips were observed to move as though he was on the point of proposing a couplet of his own. Suddenly, looking up, he caught sight of Bao-yu skulking behind the others, too scared to speak.

"What's the matter with you?" he bellowed at the unfortunate boy. "You are ready enough with your opinions when they are not wanted. Speak up!—Or are you waiting for a written invitation?"

"I can see no 'musk' or 'moonlight' or 'islands' in this place," said Bao-yu. "If we are to make couplets in this follow-my-leader fashion, we could turn out a couple of hundred of them and still have more to come."

"No one's twisting your arm," said Jia Zheng. "You don't *have* to use those words if you don't want to."

"In that case," said Bao-yu, "I suggest 'The Garden of Spices' for the name; and for the couplet:

Composing amid cardamoms, you shall make verses like flowers.
Slumbering amid the roses, you shall dream fragrant dreams."

"We all know where you got *that* from, said Jia Zheng:

"Composing midst the plantains
Green shall my verses be.

We can't give you much credit for an imitation."

"Not at all!" said the literary gentlemen. "There is nothing wrong with imitation provided it is done well. After all, Li Bo's poem 'On Phoenix Terrace' is entirely based on Cui Hao's 'Yellow Crane Tower,' yet it is a much better poem. On reflection our young friend's couplet seems more poetical and imaginative than the original."

"Oh, *come* now!" said Jia Zheng. But they could see he was not displeased.

Leaving the place of many fragrances behind them, they had not advanced much farther when they could see ahead of them a building of great magnificence which Jia Zheng at once identified as the main reception hall of the residence.

> Roof above roof soared,
> Eye up-compelling,
> Of richly-wrought chambers
> And high winding galleries.
> Green rafts of dark pine
> Brushed the eaves' edges.
> Milky magnolias
> Bordered the buildings.
> Gold-glinting cat-faces,
> Rainbow-hued serpents' snouts
> Peered out or snarled down
> From cornice and finial.

"It is a rather showy building," said Jia Zheng. But the literary gentlemen reassured him:

"Although Her Grace is a person of simple and abstemious tastes, the exalted position she now occupies makes it only right and proper that there should be a certain amount of pomp in her reception. This building is in no way excessive."

Still advancing in the same direction, they presently found themselves at the foot of the white marble memorial arch that framed the approach to the hall. The pattern of writhing dragons protectively crouched over its uppermost horizontal was so pierced and fretted by the sculptor's artistry as to resemble lacework rather than solid stone.

"What inscription do we want on this arch?" Jia Zheng inquired.

"'Peng-lai's Fairy Precincts' is the only name that would do it justice," said the literary gentlemen.

Jia Zheng shook his head and said nothing.

The sight of this building and its arch had inspired a strange and unaccountable stir of emotion in Bao-yu, which on reflection he interpreted as a sign that he must have known a building somewhat like this before—though where or when he could not for the life of him remember. He was still racking his brains to recall what it reminded him of when Jia Zheng ordered him to produce a name and couplet for the arch, and he was quite unable to give his mind to the task of composition. The literary gentlemen, not knowing the nature of his preoccupation, supposed that his father's incessant bullying had worn him out and that he had finally come to the end of his inspiration. They feared that further bullying might once more bring out the mulish streak in him, thereby provoking an explosion that would be distasteful for everybody. Accordingly they urged Jia Zheng to allow him a day's grace in which to produce something suitable. Jia Zheng, who was secretly beginning to be apprehensive about the possible consequences of Grandmother Jia's anxiety for her darling grandson, yielded, albeit with a bad grace:

"Jackanapes! So even you have your off moments it seems. Well, I'll give you a day to do it in. But woe betide you if you can't produce something tomorrow! And it had better be something good, too, because this is the most important building in the garden."

After they had seen over the building and come out again, they stopped for a while on the terrace to look at a general view of the whole garden and attempted to make out the places they had already visited. They were surprised to find that even now they had covered little more than half of the whole area. Just at that moment a servant came up to report that someone had arrived with a message from Yu-cun.

"I can see that we shan't be able to finish today," said Jia Zheng. "However, if we go out by the way I said, we should at least be able to get some idea of the general layout."

He conducted them to a large bridge above a crystal curtain of rushing water. It was the weir through which the water from the little river which fed all the pools and water-courses of the garden ran into it from the outside. Jia Zheng invited them to name it.

"This is the source of the 'Drenched Blossoms' stream we looked at earlier on," said Bao-yu. "We should call it 'Drenched Blossoms Weir.'"

"Rubbish!" said Jia Zheng. "You may as well forget about your 'Drenched Blossoms,' because we are not going to use that name!"

Their progress continued past many unexplored features of the garden, viz:

a summer lodge
a straw-thatched cot
a dry-stone wall
a flowering arch
a tiny temple nestling beneath a hill
a nun's retreat hidden in a little wood
a straight gallery
a crooked cave
a square pavilion
and a round belvedere.

But Jia Zheng hurried past every one of them without entering. However, he had now been walking for a very long time without a rest and was beginning to feel somewhat footsore; and so, when the next building appeared through the trees ahead, he proposed that they should go in and sit down, and led his party toward it by the quickest route possible. They had to walk round a stand of double-flowering ornamental peach-trees and through a circular opening in a flower-covered bamboo trellis. This brought them in sight of the building's whitewashed enclosing wall and the contrasting green of the weeping willows which surrounded it. A roofed gallery ran from each side of the gate round the inner wall of the forecourt, in which a few rocks were scattered. On one side of it some green plantains were growing and on the other a weeping variety of Szechwan crab, whose pendant clusters of double-flowering carmine blossoms hung by stems as delicate as golden wires on the umbrella-shaped canopy of its boughs.

"What magnificent blossom!" exclaimed the literary gentlemen. "One has seen plenty of crabapple blossom before, but never anything as beautiful as this."

"This kind is called 'maiden crab,'" said Jia Zheng. "It comes from abroad. According to vulgar belief it originally came from the Land of Maidens, and that is supposed to be the reason why it blooms so profusely. Needless to say, it is only the ignorant sort of persons who hold this ridiculous belief."

"It certainly has the most unusual blossoms," said the literary gentlemen. "Who knows, perhaps there *is* something in the popular belief."

"Surely," said Bao-yu, "it is much more probable that poets and painters gave it the name of 'maiden crab' because of its rouge-like color and delicate, drooping shape, and that the name was misunderstood by ignorant, literal-minded people, who made up this silly story to account for it."

"That must be it!" said the literary gentlemen. "Most grateful for the explanation!"

While they were speaking they were at the same time arranging themselves on some benches in the gallery.

"Has anyone an original idea for a name?" said Jia Zheng when they were all seated.

One of them proposed "Storks in the Plantains." Another suggested "Shimmering Splendor."

"'Shimmering Splendor,'" Jia Zheng said and the others repeated, trying out the words. "That's good!"

"A lovely name!" said Bao-yu. But a moment later he added: "Rather a pity, though."

"Why 'rather a pity'?" they asked.

"Well," said Bao-yu, "there are both plantains and crabapple blossom in this courtyard. Whoever planted them must have been thinking of 'the red and the green.' If our name mentions only one and leaves out the other, it will seem somehow inadequate."

"What do you suggest, then?" said Jia Zheng.

"I suggest 'Fragrant Red and Lucent Green,'" said Bao-yu. "That takes account of both of them."

Jia Zheng shook his head:

"No, that's no good!"

He led them inside the building. Its interior turned out to be all corridors and alcoves and galleries, so that properly speaking it could hardly have been said to have *rooms* at all. The partition walls which made these divisions were of wooden panelling exquisitely carved in a wide variety of motifs: bats in clouds, the "three friends of winter"—pine, plum and bamboo, little figures in landscapes, birds and flowers, scrollwork, antique bronze shapes, "good luck" and "long life" characters, and many others. The carvings, all of them the work of master craftsmen, were beautified with inlays of gold, mother-o'-pearl and semi-precious stones. In addition to being panelled, the partitions were pierced by numerous apertures, some round, some square, some sunflower-shaped, some shaped like a fleur-de-lis, some cusped, some fan-shaped. Shelving was concealed in the double thickness of the partition at the base of these apertures, making it possible to use them for storing books and writing materials and for the display of antique bronzes, vases of flowers, miniature tray-gardens and the like. The overall effect was at once richly colorful and, because of the many apertures, airy and graceful.

The trompe-l'œil effect of these ingenious partitions had been further enhanced by inserting false windows and doors in them, the former covered in various pastel shades of gauze, the latter hung with richly-patterned damask portières. The main walls were pierced with window-like perforations in the shape of zithers, swords, vases and other objects of virtù.

The literary gentlemen were rapturous:

"Exquisite!" they cried. "What marvelous workmanship!"

Jia Zheng, after taking no more than a couple of turns inside this confusing interior, was already lost. To the left of him was what appeared to be a door. To the right was a wall with a window in it. But on raising its portière he discovered the door to be a bookcase; and when looking back, he observed—what he had not noticed before—that the light coming in through the silk gauze of the window illuminated a passage-way leading to an open doorway, and began walking toward it, a party of gentlemen similar to his own came advancing to meet him, and he realized that he was walking toward a large mirror. They were able to circumvent the mirror, but only to find an even more bewildering choice of doorways on the other side.

"Come!" said Cousin Zhen with a laugh. "Let me show you the way! If we go out here we shall be in the back courtyard. We can reach the gate of the garden much more easily from the back courtyard than from the front."

He led them round the gauze hangings of a summer-bed, then through a door into a garden full of rambler roses. Behind the rose-trellis was a stream running between green banks. The literary gentlemen were intrigued to know where that water came from. Cousin Zhen pointed in the direction of the weir they had visited earlier:

"The water comes in over that weir, then through the grotto, then under the lee of the north-east 'mountain' to the little farm. There a channel is led off it which runs into the south-east corner of the garden. Then it runs round and rejoins the main stream here. And from here the water flows out again underneath that wall."

"How very ingenious!"

They moved on again, but soon found themselves at the foot of a tall "mountain."

"Follow me!" said Cousin Zhen, amused at the bewilderment of the others, who were now completely at sea as to their whereabouts. He led them round the foot of the "mountain"—and there, miraculously, was a broad, flat path and the gate by which they had entered, rising majestically in front of them.

"Well!" exclaimed the literary gentlemen. "This beats everything! The skill with which this has all been designed is quite out of this world!"

Whereupon they all went out of the garden.

"Record of the Garden That Is Not Around" (*Wuyou yuan ji* 烏有園記)

LIU SHILONG 劉士龍 (FL. 1603)

TRANSLATED BY STANISLAUS FUNG

Liu Shilong (*zi* Yuhua), who originated from central Shaanxi, in northwest China, went into reclusion in the Coiling Dragon Temple in northern Shaanxi to avoid the strife that hit the area during the collapse of the Ming dynasty. He had some fame as a writer and teacher. He named his residence "the Studio of Intoxication Stream." This record of his imaginary garden suggests his longing for a place of escape from the turbulence of his time.[26]

"Record of the Garden That Is Not Around"

The Garden That Is Not Around is the name that the Snow-Eating Hermit Liu Yuhua has given to his garden. "Not Around" means there is nothing. Why is it not something that one has around and yet appears to be something that one has? Yuhua says, "I once contemplated the boundary between the past and the present and understood the numbers of 'what there is' and 'what there is not.' From the prosperous splendor of the Golden Valley, the exquisite beauty of Pingquan, to the various celebrated gardens of Luoyang, these were all excellent at one time, yet the traces of their collapsed walls and broken tiles cannot be found now. They belong to 'Nothings.' Only gardens on paper can be relied upon to be handed down. Even if I had a garden just like these, a hundred or a thousand generations later it would also belong to Nothings. Just as vast oceans change into mulberry fields, 'what there is' in the end returns to 'what there is not.' But when words are used to perpetuate their transmission, then even Nothings might be taken as Somethings. Why should one on paper not be my garden? Scenery is born in sentiments; images are suspended on the tip of one's brush. It does not expend one's wealth; it does not require labor; yet in enjoyment and utility, it is complete and is truly most suitable for the poor. Furthermore, as an actual construction, its extent and arrangement are limited. As an imaginary construction, its composition can be without limit. This is the reason for my garden's superiority.

"The foundation of the garden relies on mountains to channel the rivers. The high and low parts extend for several tens of *li*. The greatness of the garden lies in the mountains and rivers. Mountains outside the garden have a group of peaks, spiraling and splendid. Rockeries inside the garden have piled-up ranges, somber and refined. They are seen in profile or jutting out from one side. They rise high and grand or approach rushing forward. Mist and vapors appear and disappear, and a hundred transformations occur between dawn and dusk. At times, one can climb up to look afar; at times, one can lift one's head to gaze into the distance. Although the garden is small, it seems to contain

---

26 See Stanislaus Fung, "The Imaginary Garden of Liu Shilong," *Terra Nova: Nature and Culture* 2, no. 4 (1997):15–21.

the Five Mountains. The confluence of mountain streams is dredged as riverways. Taking an oar in midstream, one can drift along as one pleases, look around with pride, indulge in singing, and instantly forget the world of men. Excavations can be made for a pond, collecting water to make the clouds hang and to hold the moon, to keep fish and plant lotus roots. Water can be divided into tributaries and diverted to irrigate trees, to water flowers, and to float wine cups on winding waters. Cleaning up stagnant water and leading it to one side toward bamboos can cause them to soar; dry cliffs will be moistened. One can divert water from a distant flowing stream through hollowed-out lengths of wood. Such is the beauty of the landscape in my garden.

"Next in order are the trees and shrubs. There are thickly clustered peach trees and scattered willows to adorn the spring, jade-green phoenix trees and green pagoda trees to cast summer shadows, yellowish canton oranges and green bitterpeel tangerines to decorate the clear autumn, hoary pines and green cypresses to enliven the lifelessness of winter. Some trees are luxuriantly rounded, some are full and spread out, some are tall and towering into the empyrean to brush against the clouds, and some are strange as soaring dragons and crouching tigers. Brilliant mist floats among the leaves; fine birds are perched among the branches. Walking and lying among them, one can achieve a leisurely communion with them. Such is the beauty of the trees and shrubs in my garden.

"Next in order are the flowers. A tall hall of several bays is called 'All-Regarding' because flowers of every season are all there. The five colors intermingle, and it is splendid as an elegant city. Apart from the All-Regarding Hall, there is the Pavilion of Spring Fragrances, the Pavilion of Summer Splendor, the Pavilion of Autumn Perfumes, and the Pavilion of Wintry Elegance. Flowering plants of the various seasons are cultivated separately there. Beautiful textures and pure fragrances are offered by the earth according to the seasons, and people take advantage of them as they compose rhapsodies, holding cups to their mouths. Such is the beauty of the flowering plants in my garden.

"Next in order are the building works. Flying galleries penetrate the sky, clouds nestle in the eaves, soaring towers spring from the ground, willows brush against carved balustrades. Bent rooms turn and encircle. Doors and windows conceal and reveal. Caves and grottoes are secluded and deep, and one can only walk through them with a candle. Flowers are planted and bamboo fences made so that wafted fragrance envelops the paths. Brambles are used to establish boundaries, as their thorns would entangle garments. Such is the beauty of the building works of my garden.

"Further, there is a court divided into four parts, one each housing fine wines, famous teas, singers, and dancers. Another court is divided into three parts, storing the Buddhist, Daoist, and Confucian canons. Yet another court is divided into two parts, one storing famous paintings and calligraphy, and the other antique tripods and ritual vases. There is also a Chamber of the Rain of Flowers where Buddhist monks discourse on emptiness, and a Storied Pavilion of the Azure Empyrean where immortals discuss the mysterious. Monkeys call in a clear night, cranes cry on a fragrant morning, potted herbs send forth green colors, and patterned fish jump across the waves—things with an elegant charm and those worthy of appreciation are so numerous, one has no opportunity to attend to all of them. Others such as mountain birds and marine animals, croaking frogs and chirping crickets, coming and going from time to time, are all fine guests. Seeing and hearing them occasionally, one is brought in contact with the decrees of Heaven. Such is the beauty of the visitors to my garden.

"Then there are paths through bamboo leading to secluded spots, which become better as they turn, and labyrinthine walks amid flowers that, as a wall turns, take one to the same spot: Such are the meanderings of my garden. In a spacious cavern facing the wind, one can loosen one's collar to take in the crisp air. On a moonlit level terrace, one can cleanse the soul and long for immortality. These are the pleasures of my garden. A new lotus leaf emerging from the water is of a tender green that pierces the eye. Simple vegetables covering the fields seem like distant jade floating in the air. Such is the freshness of my garden. On steps and courtyards where rainwater ponds, there is variegated moss; amid frost and dew of late autumn, there are scattered reeds and rushes. Such are the weathered qualities of my garden. Strange rocks resembling humans are so distinguished that they are worthy to be paid obeisance; leisurely seagulls bathing on the waves are so placid that they can be befriended. Such are the charms of my garden. At a fisherman's jetty on a solitary islet, nets are dried in the setting sun; at a tavern in a mist-shrouded village, a banner emerges out of the tips of bamboo. Such is the rusticity of my garden. With a waterfall, alarming as rolling thunder, the sounds of the dusty world cannot reach one's ears. With creepers resembling suspended ropes, one can set up a nest amid the branches. To a pavilion placed on a precipitous cliff, one can climb up by a winding path. Over a bridge connecting sheer banks, one can traverse suspended in space. These are the dangerous and wonderful spots in my garden.

"Inside the garden, my body is always free from illness, my heart is always free from worries. My companions in the garden do not devise cunning schemes, nor undertake evil deeds. Those who serve me understand my every word and anticipate my desires. Those who are against me and frustrate me feel shame when they see my shadow and want to flee when they hear my voice. Such is my fulfillment by virtue of my garden. My garden employs not shapes but ideas, and thus wind and rain cannot dilapidate it, water and fire cannot harm it. Even if one gathered all one's descendants, they would not be able to give away a single blade of grass nor a single tree to others. Those who visit my garden employ not their feet, but their eyes. They need not pack three months' provisions nor grasp nine-sectioned staffs. And what their pure bosoms cherish, they can appreciate at their desks and mats and feel satisfied. I have my garden always and share my garden with others always. Those who read this 'Record of the Garden That Is Not Around' should regard it thus."

"Record of the Pavilion of Borrowing Borrowing" (*Jiejie ting ji* 借借亭記)

SUN CHENG'EN 孫承恩 (1619–1659)

TRANSLATED BY STANISLAUS FUNG

Sun Cheng'en (not to be confused with a sixteenth-century official of the same name) came from Changshu, not far from Suzhou. He was the top graduate in the Metropolitan Examination of 1658. Meeting with the favor of the young Shunzhi emperor (r. 1644–1661), he was given the honor of riding one of the imperial horses on a visit with the emperor to the imperial park; unfortunately, the horse bolted and Sun died a few days later.

In this essay, Sun explicitly looks back to gardens of the Tang dynasty (referring to the Pingquan garden of Li Deyu), and in his ideas about "borrowing" we can find an echo of the concerns expressed by Tang dynasty writers (see chapter 2) about who is the true owner of a garden: the man who holds legal title to the property, or the visitor or temporary occupant who enjoys it without insisting on possessing it and in conscious awareness of its transitory nature?

"Record of the Pavilion of Borrowing Borrowing"

In the course of renovating his estate, Master Sun built a pavilion in his vegetable plot. He inscribed on its lintel "Borrowing Borrowing." A visitor, much surprised by his course of action, wondered, "This is strange indeed! Not at all what one can present to one's descendants as a long-term plan, surely?" I smiled and said, "Why be so dyed-in-the-wool? In former times, both Master Zhuang and Master Lie belittled the ways of the world. Their words were grand and sweeping, tranquil and calm. Summarizing their purport, however, they wished nothing other than to take a firm grip on the ten thousand things and to investigate their nature. At one extreme, they considered that, as our bodies are borrowed from the Great Clod, they are not something that one can take possession of as one's own. This may all seem somewhat excessive in comparison to the Way of our Sage, and yet, nonetheless, there are certain patterns of things that have to be as they are.

"Thus, clothes I borrow in order to repel the cold; food I borrow in order to appease hunger; chambers I borrow in order to accommodate my body; servants I borrow in order to put them to use; sons and grandsons I borrow in order to continue my line. By extension, are not all the things in the world for which I have a use borrowed? Yet, those who are foolish and vulgar consider wealth and honor, wares and profits, as their own firm possessions. They brag before the world and congratulate themselves. They would carefully protect even a single rare and treasurable object, fearing that others might seize it. In error, they toil and exhaust themselves, burdening their natural insights and confusing their natural discernment. In the end they die of old age without realizing their own foolishness. Is this not delusion of a most extreme kind?

"In his 'Exhortation to My Children and Grandchildren about the Mountain Villa at Pingquan,'[27] Li Deyu says that he who gives away to others a single blade of grass or a solitary tree from his estate is not a good descendant. His intent was to try to keep it intact for generations without alteration. And yet, where is it now? Those lofty persons and untrammelled individuals who have been laughing at Li Deyu continue to have their teeth turn cold from doing so. Prosperity and decline, flourishing and falling into ruin—these seek after each other without end. People can certainly be dim about this circumstance.

"This pavilion of mine was certainly once in the possession of my eastern neighbor. Formerly, he in turn surely borrowed and obtained it, and now I too have acquired it. Therefore, I said that it was the borrowing of borrowed borrowing. Alas! How could I know what it is that others would not wish to borrow from me? And how could I know what things it will be that my sons and grandsons would not wish to put up for others to borrow?

"Though this name and this meaning is different from the idea of creating an estate as a 'long-term plan,' there is certainly, underlying it, 'a long-term plan,' even though such a plan does not refer to 'external things.' There are things that do not wait to be borrowed and things that people do not get to borrow; this understanding is what I will use to nurture my descendants and what my sons and grandsons should keep in mind from generation to generation."

As my interlocutor was persuaded by what I had said, I have written my words down as a record.

"Record of the Make-Do Garden" (*Jiangjiu yuan ji* 將就園記; extracts)

HUANG ZHOUXING 黃周星 (1611–1680)
TRANSLATED BY STANISLAUS FUNG

Huang Zhouxing (*zi* Jiuyan) was a literatus from Nanjing. He obtained his presented scholar degree in 1640 under the last Ming emperor, and served in the Ministry of Revenue under the Southern Ming resistance government. Under the Qing dynasty, he went into retirement and made a living by teaching. After finally having two sons at the relatively advanced age of 57, he attempted suicide by drowning several times, as a Ming loyalist, but kept being rescued; eventually he starved himself to death. He composed this record in 1674, thirty years after the fall of the Ming dynasty. The name of the garden, Jiangjiu, here translated as "Make-Do," has several layers of meaning: as well as the idea of making do, the name also implies "coming close to great truths," adding to its philosophical meaning as explicated in the text. The "Record" is in four sections: the first gives an account of the general topographical setting of the garden; the second and third deal

---

27   Editor's note: see chapter 3.

with the Make Garden (*Jiang yuan*) and the Do Garden (*Jiu yuan*), respectively, as components of the Make-Do Garden (*Jiangjiu yuan*). The final section gives the Make-Do Owner's account of the correlations between the two parts of the Make-Do Garden and explains his basic intent.[28]

"Record of the Make-Do Garden" (extracts)

Since antiquity, gardens have been remembered on account of people, and people have also been remembered on account of gardens. Nowadays there are many owners of gardens in the world. How could Huang Jiuyan not have a garden? Indeed, Jiuyan has never had a garden. If Jiuyan says, "I do not have a garden," everyone in the world would also say, "Jiuyan does not have a garden." Jiuyan would surely be ashamed of it. One day, Jiuyan proudly told a guest, "My garden has no fixed location. I merely select the place where the landscape is finest under the Four Heavens, and construct it there. What is called 'the finest place' is in the world, yet out of this world, is not in the world, yet not out of this world. Since I have searched for it from the day I was born, and have only found it after several tens of years, I have not been inclined to speak of it to men of the world." The guest said, "Please describe its general features." Jiuyan replied, "Certainly."

"All around the area are lofty mountains and steep ranges which encircle and embrace it like a lotus city. Among the mountains that surround the city, the number of those that are piled one on top of another, or fitted into each other, or small and encircled by large mountains, or small but higher than the larger mountains, cannot be known. Their names are also not known. Only the names of the mountains on the right and the left are known. The one on the right is called Mount Jiang, and the one on the left Mount Jiu. Each is several thousand *ren* in height, but Mount Jiang is higher than Mount Jiu. Compared to Mount Jiang, Mount Jiu is shorter by a third. The shape of the mountains creates an encircling moat within and a cliff without, so that the area is isolated from the world and there is no path for access. There is only a cave on the southwest side of the slopes of Mount Jiu, just large enough to accommodate a body, leading downward as it meanders, rising and falling. Walking in the dark several hundred steps, one reaches the mouth of the cave. Outside, there is a stream which can lead to creeks and valleys in the world of men. But the mouth of the cave is only as big as the opening of a well, and on the mountain top, there is a spring. It rushes down in rapids as a thundering waterfall. The waterfall does not become exhausted in any of the four seasons and its appearance is like a curtain. Unless one rushed through the waterfall, one would not realize that there is a cave, and so since antiquity no one has 'sought the ford.' This is the boundary of the mountains. Within the mountains the land is spacious, level, rich, and fertile. In breadth and width,

---

28 See Stanislaus Fung, "Notes on the Make-Do Garden," *Utopian Studies* 9, no. 1 (January 1998):142–48. For a further discussion of this garden, see also Ellen Widmer, "Between Worlds: Huang Zhouxing's Imaginary Garden," in *Trauma and Transcendence in Early Qing Literature*, ed. Wilt L. Idema, Wai-yee Li, and Ellen Widmer (Cambridge, Mass.: Harvard University Asia Center, 2006), 249–81.

it is about a hundred *li*. The fields and villages, monasteries and Buddhist pagodas are each like those in painted screens. The produce of all things in the world, the trades of the hundred artisans—not one has not been assembled in this place. The residents are pure and honest, friendly and humble, without a bit of clamor or deceit. The old and the young, both men and women, are happy as one; this is because there have been no arguments and disputes for many generations. The climate is also mild and genial. . . ."

Heaven has provided Mounts Jiang and Jiu (Make and Do) to wait for a Make-Do Owner. "Jiang" refers to the extent of intent, as one is about to obtain something; "jiu" refers to "following what one encounters and resting with it, accommodating things where possible." Thus, Mount Jiang is tall, and Mount Jiu is short, just as in what is meant by the popular saying "Taking the superior to accommodate the inferior."[29] Further, in the Make Garden (*Jiang yuan*), there are two studies called "Close to the Sun" (*Ri jiu*) and "Imminent Moon" (*Yue jiang*); in the Do Garden (*Jiu yuan*), there are two peaks called "Next to the Sun" (*Jiu ri*) and "Approaching Clouds" (*Yun jiang*); thus within Make-Do [Garden], there are also make-do's (*jiang jiu*). From this, the owner's meaning can be surmised.

The owner considers himself meagre in virtue and poor in fate, and is afraid that extravagance might contravene the taboos of cosmic transformation. Thus in each part of the garden only the finest spots are chosen to make a list of ten places in each, and short poems are used to transmit them. It is not as though he would dare call it a garden. It is merely a make-do . . . Thereupon, the owner proudly addressed his guest, "Who would say that Jiuyan has no garden? How could an insignificant one like this be said not to be Jiuyan's garden?" The guest then withdrew, mouthing a respectful answer. Thereupon Jiuyan said, "I have a garden," and for ten thousand generations people in the world would say, without exception, "Huang Jiuyan has a garden!"

Taoan's Dream Memories (*Taoan mengyi* 陶庵夢憶)

"A Record of Langhuan Paradise" (*Langhuan fudi ji* 瑯嬛福地記)

ZHANG DAI 張岱 (1597–CA. 1684)
TRANSLATED BY DUNCAN M. CAMPBELL

For Zhang Dai, see chapter 3.

"A Record of Langhuan Paradise"

Zhang Dai's dreams are as if predestined, and often in his dreams he finds himself within a stone hermitage, set amid chasms inside chasms, caverns in crags. In front

---

29 Literally, "Jiang tall, Jiu short."

of this hermitage, a torrent rages and a brook swirls, the cascading water producing a snow-like foam, with fantastically shaped ancient pines growing amid eccentric aged rocks and with famous flowers interspersed here and there. In the midst of all this he sits, in his dreams, with serving boys plying him with tea and fruit, and surrounded on all sides by shelves laden with books. Although whenever he happens to open up a volume, he finds that the text is written largely in the tadpole, bird trace or thunder script of antiquity, yet in his dreams it is as if he can understand even the most troublesome and abstruse of passages. When living in idleness with nothing to occupy his time, he finds himself dreaming of this place as the evenings gather in around him. Meditating upon it when he awakens, he resolves to seek out a marvellous site that could be made to resemble that of his dreams.

Out beyond the suburbs stands a small hill, its rock structure sharp and angular. It is covered in dense bamboo that inclines itself toward the interior of the garden. It is here that I wish to build my hermitage, its hall oriented on an east-west axis and with studies leading off from both the front and the back. Behind the hall I will construct a flat stone surface upon which I will plant a Yellow Mountain pine or two, with gorges formed of fantastic rock to separate them. I will plant also two sal trees in front of the hall to provide some shade. To the left, I will add an empty chamber facing the foothills that spread out in perfect order before me, split asunder as if by the blows of a sword. Here the plaque will read: "A Solitary Mound." To the left will crouch a three-roomed hermitage belvedere, overlooking a large pond; the autumnal water will be clear and chill and in the depths of the willows I will read. The plaque here will read: "A Single Valley."

Setting off around the hill in a northerly direction will bring one to meditation cells and small huts, ill-built and low-hung and hugging the contours of the hill, to ancient trees and layered cliffs, to a small stream, to a dense grove of exquisite bamboo. There where the hill ends will be found an excellent cavern and there a tomb will be built for one still living, to await Zhang Dai's transubstantiation, its inscription reading: "Alas, here lies the tomb of Master Zhang Dai of the Ming." To the left of the tomb, upon a single *mu* of fallow ground, a thatched hermitage will be erected wherein sacrifices may be made to the Buddha and to an image of Zhang Dai himself, and monks will be invited to live here to maintain the place. The large pond will be more than ten *mu* in size and beyond the pond a small river will take a turn or four but prove wide enough to allow boats to enter the pond. The banks of the river, on both sides, will be steep and there fruit trees will be planted; sweet tangerines, flowering apricot, pears and dates, hemmed in by a fence of thorny limebush. A pavilion will be sited on the summit of the hill and the twenty *mu* of fertile fields that border the hill to the west will be planted out in rice of both the glutinous and the non-glutinous varieties.[30] The gate will look

---

30   This is a reference to the "Biography of Tao Qian": "[Tao Qian] ordered that the public fields be planted out entirely in glutinous rice, saying: 'This will produce enough to keep me well and truly drunk.' When his

out over the wide river, and a small tower will soar above it, from upon which one will be able to gaze at Brazier Peak and Pavilion Mountain. Beneath the tower will stand a gate with a plaque that reads: "Langhuan Paradise." Following along the river on foot to the north one will come upon a stone bridge, rustic and ancient of appearance and covered in shrubbery. Here one may sit, enjoy the breeze and gaze up at the moon.

"A Record of the Garden of My Mind" (*Yiyuan ji* 意園記)

DAI MINGSHI 戴名世 (1653–1713)
TRANSLATED BY DUNCAN M. CAMPBELL

The creator of this imaginary garden, after outstanding success in the imperial civil service examinations, fell foul of the "literary inquisition" of the early Qing dynasty. Having quoted a historical work sympathetic to the Southern Ming, Dai Mingshi was accused of opposition to Qing rule, and executed by order of the Kangxi emperor (r. 1661–1722) in what was later acknowledged by the succeeding Yongzheng emperor (r. 1722–1735) as a miscarriage of justice. The date of this imaginary garden record is unknown, and it may have been written long before Dai got into trouble, but such gardens of the mind can be seen as a characteristic resource allowing imperial scholar-officials to escape, at least temporarily, from the intense rivalries and dangers of official life.

"A Record of the Garden of My Mind"

No such garden as the Garden of My Mind exists; it is simply the manifestation of an ideal. Doubtless, however, this garden would contain a couple of peaks, several *qing* of arable land, a single brook, a waterfall some ten *zhang* in height, a thousand trees and ten thousand bamboo plants. The master of this garden would be accompanied, always, by a thousand books, by a single serving boy, by his *qin* zither and a pot of wine. This garden would have no paths within it and just as the master of the garden does not know the way out, neither would any other person know the way in. The garden's plants would be both the spring and the summer varieties of the orchid, and the Chinese sweetflag; its flowers, the lotus, the chrysanthemum, the hibiscus, and the white peony; its birds, the crane, the egret, the silver pheasant, the tern, and the oriole. As to trees, it would contain pine, fir, flowering apricot, paulownia, peach, and crabapple. The music of the brook would be that of the *qin*, the bell and the chime. Its rocks would be green or reddish brown; they would lie in repose or soar upward like a sheer cliff a hundred *ren* high. Its fields would be suitable for the cultivation of paddy or of glutinous millet, in its vegetable plots would grow celery, on its hillsides would be found turtle foot bracken, thorn-ferns, and bamboo shoots, and its pond would be

wife and sons insisted that he also plant rice of the non-glutinous variety, he relented and had one *qing* and fifty *mu* planted in non-glutinous rice and another fifty *mu* planted in glutinous rice."

full of duckweed. The serving boy would spend his days chopping firewood, gathering the thorn-ferns, and trapping fish. The master, for his part, would spend half his day reading and the remainder viewing the flowers, strumming his lute and drinking wine, listening to the bird song, the burble of the brook or the soughing of the pines, or observing the firmament above him, all with a delightful smile playing across his lips. Joyfully he would fall asleep, only to pass yet another day in this manner once he had awakened. The years would slip by, the generations would come and go, but of such things he would be utterly unconscious. He would know neither the need to escape from his age nor the need to flee his home. The surname of the master of this garden would have been lost long ago, as too would his personal name have since fallen into obscurity. What age would it have been that he was a man of? Perhaps he would have lived during the time of the legendary Wuhuai. What would have been the name of his garden? It would have been called the Garden of My Mind.

Gardens of the Qing Dynasty

B y the Qing dynasty, there is no longer a clear distinction between the styles of private and imperial gardens, as had been the case in previous dynasties. This is at least partly because of significant influence from the private gardens of Jiangnan on the gardens of the Manchu (Qing) imperial family, as we will see below.

As far as private gardens are concerned, there is no firm line to be drawn between those of the Ming and those of the Qing. As in many areas of culture, the style of the late Ming persisted into the early Qing (the second half of the seventeenth century). Ming loyalists (literati who had served the fallen dynasty), looking back nostalgically to the period before the conquest, sometimes used damaged or neglected gardens as emblems of the lost empire, as we can see in the piece by Wu Weiye in this chapter; this sense of loss is echoed in Wang Shimin's laments over the damage done to his Pleasure in the Suburbs Garden by the invading bannermen of the Manchu (Qing) army. By the time the eighteenth century was well underway, however, a new garden style and new attitudes to gardens can be clearly seen.

One factor in this evolution was the rise of merchant gardens. We have already seen that in the mid- to late Ming, the growth in the economy meant that more and more merchants gained the wealth and social status to aspire to a literati lifestyle, including the creation of fine gardens; this was another aspect of the continuity between late Ming and early Qing. After the period of economic and political consolidation that followed the Qing conquest in the middle of the seventeenth century, merchant wealth increased again and led particularly to the development of the splendid gardens of Yangzhou, the great commercial city at the junction of the Yangtze River and the Grand Canal. Yangzhou was a center of the state-controlled salt monopoly, a source of great wealth for the merchants who farmed it. This chapter includes descriptions of some of these gardens from Li Dou's detailed guide to the eighteenth-century city, *The Pleasure-Boats of Yangzhou.*

Canton (Guangzhou) also grew in importance as a commercial city, trading not only with Southeast Asia and the Persian Gulf, as it had done for many centuries, but also with the Europeans and Americans who arrived in ever-greater numbers to make their fortunes in the China trade. Cantonese or Lingnan ("South of the Mountain Range") gardens developed as a distinctive regional style, absorbing influences from Europe that were mediated through the Portuguese territory of Macao and later the British colony of Hong Kong; there may also have been more immediate influences from the gardens of the "thirteen factories," the residences and offices of the foreign merchants on Shameen (Shamian) Island in the Pearl River, where they resided for the part of the year when they were permitted to be in Canton. Some of these European and American traders were able to visit the gardens of the "Cohong" merchants, those who were officially authorized to deal with foreigners; they could also take some exercise by strolling through the Fa-ti (Huadi) commercial nursery gardens on the south bank of the Pearl River. The plants that these Westerners became familiar with had an immense impact on the gardens of Europe and America. Since few Chinese accounts of these gardens survive, we have included here some writing on them by British and American visitors.

The city of Yangzhou was one of the sites of another new development in garden culture in the Qing dynasty. This was the increasing overlap, referred to above, between private and imperial gardens. Before the Qing, it seems clear that there were substantial differences in scale and style between private (literati) gardens and the gardens of both the imperial court itself and of members of the imperial family and the ennobled families descended from military leaders involved in the founding of dynasties.[1] In the Qing, thanks particularly to the Kangxi and Qianlong emperors' predilection for going on extensive imperial progresses through southern China, the emperors themselves introduced the literati garden style of the Jiangnan region into their northern imperial gardens around Peking and at Jehol (Rehe, present-day Chengde), bordering on the Manchus' ancestral lands to the northeast. The Qianlong emperor, in particular, liked to incorporate imitations of Jiangnan gardens, or features in them, into his gardens in the north.[2] Not only were northern craftsmen required to adapt their traditions to these new ideas, but craftsmen from the south were brought north to work on the imperial gardens; the most notable of these men was Zhang Ran, the son of the well-known late Ming garden designer Zhang Lian (see Wu Weiye, "The Biography of Zhang Nanyuan" in chapter 7). This chapter includes garden records and poems by the Kangxi, Yongzheng, and Qianlong emperors on these gardens, as well as a description by a senior Chinese courtier of part of the Mountain Estate for Escaping the Heat (*Bishu shanzhuang*) at Jehol and the famous letter by the missionary artist Brother Jean-Denis Attiret describing "the emperor of China's gardens near Pekin."

---

1   See Craig Clunas, "Ideal and Reality in the Ming Garden," in *The Authentic Garden: A Symposium on Gardens*, ed. L. Tjon Sie Fat and E. de Jong (Leiden: The Clusius Foundation, 1991), 197–205.

2   Examples are given in Stephen H. Whiteman, "From Upper Camp to Mountain Estate: Recovering Historical Narratives in Qing Imperial Landscapes," *Studies in the History of Gardens and Designed Landscapes* 33, no. 4 (2013):249–79. For a detailed study of the Qianlong emperor's gardens, particularly the garden for his retirement in the Palace of Tranquility and Longevity (*Ningshou gong*), see Nancy Berliner, *The Emperor's Private Paradise: Treasures from the Forbidden City* (New Haven: Peabody Essex Museum and Yale University Press, 2010).

The imperial progresses that ultimately brought a knowledge of Jiangnan garden style to the north required the construction of "traveling palaces" (*xinggong*) to accommodate the emperor and his extensive retinue at every overnight stop; these were often converted from existing temple complexes or large private gardens. Given Yangzhou's crucial position as a transportation node at the southern end of the Grand Canal, the wealthy merchants of Yangzhou, particularly those involved in the immensely profitable state-controlled salt monopoly, were in a position to entertain the imperial convoy. Those who did so were obliged to adapt their garden residences to provide the standard of accommodation appropriate to their imperial guest, thus introducing something of the grand imperial garden style into the private garden. We can see an example of such an adaptation—not in Yangzhou but in Haining, a center of salt production rather than salt transportation—in Chen Qiqing's "A Record of the Garden of the Peaceful Waves."

Another development in garden culture in the Qing that, if not entirely new, was certainly more noticeable, was the association of private gardens with education, and particularly with women's education. In the Ming, private gardens had been used as sites for the tuition of boys (and sometimes girls) from the owners' families (as we saw in the case of Shang Jinglan and the Qi family in chapter 6), and academies dedicated to philosophical study or training for the government examinations had also been constructed in garden or landscape settings—this type of academic campus can, in fact, be traced back to the Song dynasty.[3] We can see what is perhaps a transitional development in this process in the Banana Garden Poetry Club, a group of women poets based in Hangzhou in the 1660s to 1680s.[4] The club was named for the garden where it met, which presumably was attached to the residence of one of the members, although its exact location has not been identified. Similarly, Xu Qianxue's "A Record of the Garden That Borders upon Greenness" shows that he chose that garden, belonging to his friend, as the base for editorial work, commissioned by the Kangxi emperor himself, on the official *History of the Ming Dynasty* (*Ming shi*).

In the eighteenth century, the Accommodation Garden of the poet Yuan Mei became celebrated—or notorious—for his tutoring there of a number of female students of literature; as far as we know, nothing untoward took place, but the mere idea of a man teaching young women who were not members of his family was enough to scandalize conservative Confucians. This adaptation of a private garden to a semipublic educational use, although clearly based on preexisting practices, was something new in the Qing dynasty.

In the course of the dynasty, there were significant changes in the style and use of private gardens in addition to those we have already mentioned, as aesthetic preferences changed and also as technology developed to enable more ambitious structures and effects of rocks, water, and buildings. For example, the rockery craftsman Ge Yuliang (1764–1830) is known for his development of a new technique of building rockery caves, the "hook and connect method" (*goudaifa*); this technique, a sort of vaulting, allowed for the construction of caves that looked much more

---

3   Xin Wu, "Yuelu Academy: Landscape and Gardens of Neo-Confucian Pedagogy," *Studies in the History of Gardens and Designed Landscapes* 25, no. 3 (July 2005):156–90.

4   Daria Berg, "Negotiating Gentility: The Banana Garden Poetry Club in Seventeenth-Century China," in *The Quest for Gentility in China: Negotiations beyond Gender and Class*, ed. Daria Berg and Chloë Starr (London: Routledge, 2007), 73–93.

natural than those built by earlier methods, which had relied on supporting the roof by means of long rocks laid transversely on the cave walls.[5]

As the dynasty declined in the nineteenth century, under both internal and external pressures, many gardens were damaged or destroyed, particularly those in rural areas more vulnerable to bandit attacks or natural disasters. At times of greater stability, gardens might also be restored or rebuilt, as we can see from the later accounts of Canglang Pavilion in chapter 5.

The Qing dynasty is also distinctive for the amount of writing about gardens that survives from the brushes of the emperors, particularly the three great emperors of the eighteenth century (Kangxi, Yongzheng, and Qianlong). Apart from the Song emperor Huizong's "Record of the Northeast Marchmount" (see chapter 4), we have nothing comparable from earlier dynasties. The early Qing emperors clearly saw their creation of imperial parks and gardens as integral to their concept of rulership.[6] A number of themes are shared by grandfather, father, and son, as shown in the poems and essays in this chapter: first, the Qing imperial gardens are presented as modest constructions, adapted from preexisting gardens, which have been economically restored with "virtuous thrift,"[7] aiming at "plainness rather than magnificence, seclusion rather than conspicuous display,"[8] by contrast with luxurious constructions of the past, such as the Qin dynasty Epang Palace or the Huizong's Northeast Marchmount. Second, the gardens provide the emperor a healthful, restful, and calming environment, helping him to withstand the pressures of ruling and to administer the empire in a proper manner. Through the economical use of land and resources, and by the ability of parks and gardens to represent the correct practices of agriculture and sericulture, these imperial domains can demonstrate "compassion for the farmers"[9] and underline the importance of agriculture as the "basis of the state" (guoben). The continuing use of gardens bequeathed by the current ruler's father or grandfather and the adoption of garden names bestowed by them, demonstrating the Confucian virtue of filial piety, also emphasize the continuity and legitimacy of the Manchu Qing dynasty in the Chinese cultural tradition. It can be seen, therefore, that while the Qing rulers adopted aspects of the culture of private gardens in terms of style and recreational use, they were also using imperial gardens in a public-facing manner to assert their own sovereignty over the empire. This was particularly the case with the great imperial park at Jehol, used for the reception of foreign (usually Central Asian) dignitaries, which made explicit reference to Manchu as well as Chinese cultural traditions, and incorporated in its buildings elements from other cultures, particularly Mongolian and Tibetan. The Qianlong emperor, in

---

5   Cao Xun 曹汛, "Ge Yuliang zhuan kaolun—Ge Yuliang yu woguo gudai yuanlin dieshan yishu de zhongjie (shang)" ("戈裕良傳考論—戈裕良與我國古代園林疊山藝術的終結(上)"), *Jianzhushi* 建築師 [*The Architect*] 110, no. 4 (August 2004):98–104.

6   Philippe Forêt, "The Intended Perception of the Imperial Gardens of Chengde in 1780," *Studies in the History of Gardens and Designed Landscapes* 19, no. 3–4 (July–December 1999):343–63; Philippe Forêt, *Mapping Chengde: The Qing Landscape Enterprise* (Honolulu: University of Hawai'i Press, 2000); and Stephen H. Whiteman, "From Upper Camp to Mountain Estate: Recovering Historical Narratives in Qing Imperial Landscapes," *Studies in the History of Gardens and Designed Landscapes* 33, no. 4 (2013):249–79.

7   Kangxi emperor, "Record of the Garden of Uninhibited Spring."

8   Qianlong emperor, "Latter Record of the Garden of Perfect Brightness."

9   Kangxi emperor, "Record of the Garden of Uninhibited Spring."

particular, was eager to promote his own image as a cakravartin (literally a "wheel-turning ruler," referring to the wheel of the dharma) or Buddhist universal ruler; this, as well as a more personal interest in the exotic, may have been why he incorporated European-style buildings and a geometric maze, designed by the Jesuit missionaries at his court, into one part of his Garden of Perfect Brightness.

Although the Qing, particularly in its later stages, is often seen as a stodgily conservative dynasty, with the Manchu rulers anxious to prove they were more Confucian than the Chinese, the first few reigns of the dynasty (two of which, the reigns of the Kangxi and Qianlong emperors, were the longest in China's imperial history) were in many respects—and certainly in garden culture—a time of innovation and originality. The period was marked not only by greater similarities between imperial, literati, and merchant gardens but also by growing connections between Chinese and European garden traditions.

PART 1

PRIVATE GARDENS

"Thoughts Stirred on Meeting the Gardener of the Royal Academy in Nanjing" (*Yu Nanxiang yuansou gan fu bashi yun* 遇南廂園叟感賦八十韻; extract)

WU WEIYE 吳偉業 (1609–1671)
TRANSLATED BY STEPHEN OWEN

When Beijing fell and the last Ming emperor committed suicide, Wu Weiye, whose biography of the garden designer Zhang Nanyuan is translated in chapter 7, resolved to end his life, as had so many of his contemporaries. He was dissuaded from this course of action by his mother, and the rest of Wu's life involved an anxiety-ridden relationship with the new dynasty. Though he had served, very briefly, in one of the Southern Ming regimes, family and official pressure saw him take up reluctant office under the Qing in 1653. His mother's death four years later allowed him, finally, to resign. In the early 1660s, however, he was implicated in a tax delinquency case and was dispossessed of both his official status and his property.

This long narrative poem, only the first part of which has been translated, was written after the Manchu conquest of Nanjing (also known as Jinling, as below). In it, Wu revisits the ruins of the Imperial Academy where he had once served, encountering there a gardener he had once known.

"Thoughts Stirred on Meeting the Gardener of the Royal Academy in Nanjing" (extract)

Cold tides dashed on the ruined fort,
fiery clouds set Red Hill ablaze;
it was June when I reached Jinling,
on the tenth I crossed Great Pontoon Bridge.
The spots I had visited serving here
have all of them slipped from memory.

I met an old gardener on the road,
who asked me from where I had come.
Then I vaguely recognized a former employee,
and the circumstances caused heart's pain.
He opened the gate and invited me in,
broken buildings, a low surrounding wall.
Then he pointed into a clump of weeds,
saying this was the Royal Academy.
The office buildings were rubble piles,
which he gardened on lease to pay his tax.
He had changed the means of his livelihood,
but had made this his garden from nostalgia.
In troubled times he had kept to this land,
unwilling to go to another place.
I took the chance to walk over the site,
and at every step my brooding increased.
On the gray slopes backed against the water
had been the hall where I used to stay.
From all the world students gathered here,
compositions turned in at Six Lodges.
Pines and junipers, all ten spans in girth,
and the ringing sounds of pipes and bells.
A hundred-acre clear and rippling pond,
with drooping willows all around the shore,
splendid porches overhanging pools,
where fragrant scent of lotus blew.
Chatting and laughing, all noble companions,
in flowers and moonlight we drained our cups.
There was a pavilion to the south
where beech[10] and bamboo gave off a light cool.

"Record of the Division of Property in Pleasure in the Suburbs" (*Lejiao fenye ji* 樂郊分業記)

WANG SHIMIN 王時敏 (1592–1680)
TRANSLATED BY ALISON HARDIE

Wang Shimin was a landscape painter and calligrapher from Taicang, in present-day Jiangsu Province. His fellow townsman Wu Weiye listed him in his "Song of the Nine Friends in Painting," along with Dong Qichang, under whom Wang had studied the art of painting.

---

10   Editor's note: "beech" here is not a literal translation; it represents Chinese *wu* 梧, for *wutong*.

From a distinguished family, Wang held nominal office (as Keeper of Seals and then in the Court of Sacrificial Worship) during the late years of the Ming. Once the dynasty had fallen ("the world was turned upside down"), he refused all further official involvement and retreated to his garden, where he maintained a private troupe of actors. As we see below, the garden had fallen into a state of some considerable dilapidation by the 1620s when he inherited it from his grandfather, and Wang commissioned Zhang Nanyuan to redesign it. It has been suggested that in 1663 Wang commissioned Zhang Nanyuan's second son, Zhang Ran, who from the 1680s onward was much involved in the design of the imperial gardens in Beijing, to further renovate his Pleasure in the Suburbs Garden, but as the text translated below is undated, we do not know if his reflections preceded or followed this further work done on the garden.[11]

"Record of the Division of Property in Pleasure in the Suburbs"

The Pleasure in the Suburbs Garden was once the Peony Plot of Wang Xijue, the Cultivated and Solemn Lord.[12] Removed as it was from the bustle and dust, the garden was a realm of purity and expansiveness: just the thing to suit my nature. Formerly it had a building of only a few bays, mean and tumbled-down, too small to squeeze into. In the summer of the *jiwei* year [1619], I extended it somewhat with flower beds on the level ground, digging out undergrowth and eradicating weeds, intending to take a temporary respite there from worldly commitments.[13] It so happened that Zhang Nanyuan of Yunjian arrived.[14] His artistry excels nature. He did his best to talk me into constructing a mountain. At the time I was still young; born with a silver spoon in my mouth, I had never taken time to worry about the future. So I had no hesitation in emptying my wallet to follow his advice. Consequently,

11 The reference to Zhang Ran as the renovator of Wang Shimin's garden is from R. O. Suter's short biography of Wang Shimin in Arthur W. Hummel, ed., *Eminent Chinese of the Ch'ing Period 1644–1912* (Washington, D.C.: U.S. Government Printing Office, 1943), 834. The source appears to be Gu Wenbin's edited chronological biography of Wang Shimin in *Guoyunlou shuhua ji* 過雲樓書畫記, *hua* 畫 6.18b; here, the gardener is named as [Zhang] Nanyuan (Zhang Lian; see chapter 7), but since Zhang Lian must have been either very elderly or deceased by this time, Wang is more likely to have employed his son Ran. For Zhang Ran's work on the Qing imperial gardens, see Cao Xun, "*Qingdai zaoyuan dieshan yishujia Zhang Ran he Beijing de 'Shanzi Zhang'*" 清代造園疊山藝術家張然和北京的 "山子張," *Jianzhu lishi yu lilun* 建築歷史與理論 2 (1981):116–25.

12 The Cultivated and Solemn Lord was the posthumous title given Wang Xijue (1534–1611), Wang Shimin's grandfather. Wang Xijue was an eminent statesman and one of the leading members of the gentry in Taicang, in Suzhou prefecture. He was a close friend of Wang Shizhen, owner of the Yanshan Garden, although the two Wang families were not related. Wang Shimin's father, Wang Heng (1561–1609), who was Wang Xijue's only son, died while Wang Shimin was quite young, so Wang Shimin eventually inherited Wang Xijue's property, including his gardens. The Herbaceous Peony Plot, renamed Pleasure in the Suburbs, but generally known as the East Garden, was outside the east gate of the walled city of Taicang.

13 Wang Shimin never actually undertook a formal official career, although he held a government sinecure on the merits of his grandfather's rank.

14 Nanyuan was the formal name of Zhang Lian, one of the most famous garden designers of the late Ming. He came from the town of Huating, also known as Yunjian, which, like Taicang, is not far from the city of Suzhou. For the translation of a contemporary biography of him by Wu Weiye, see chapter 7.

ponds were dug, trees were planted, and a rockery was constructed. The project began in the *gengshen* year [1620] and lasted several years, during which period the garden was four times reconstructed. Winding flights of stone steps led to the top of the rockery. Calm water in large ponds shimmered and, all around, the bamboo and the trees cast a deep shade. The whole garden looked like a unified entity, as if it were the work of Heaven. Its cool halls and deeply recessed chambers were appropriately located. Trees and flowers outside the tall windows set each other off. With all its lovely groves, ponds, terraces, and gazebos, the garden was beauty itself. Not only did it greatly deplete my resources, but my mental energy too was utterly exhausted. Still, I could not free myself from its demands. As for any idea of relaxing and enjoying myself in it, in twenty to thirty years, I was unable to spend half that time there. Meanwhile the years sped away, and the world was turned upside down. The area around the city was destroyed during the course of the war, but the garden was fortunate enough to be preserved. Although the walls and buildings just managed to survive, the shutters and lattices are not what they once were. Barbarians and half-breeds ganged up to trample the garden.[15] The vermilion balustrades and secluded groves echoed to their falconers' calls; the emerald lake with its clear ripples merely provided drinking water for their horses.[16] Meanwhile the garden grew more dilapidated by the day; the tangled weeds increased each year. If I were to allow this to continue, I would be sorrowing over fallen terraces and leveled ponds. Considering the present and remembering the past, my eyes are saddened and my heart grieved. That is why, for all these months and years, I have not set foot in it once. However, if one were suddenly to put these few acres of rockery and pond on the market, it would certainly be very difficult. Even paying the annual tax on it is not easy either. I myself am old and enfeebled and do not have the energy to put it in order again, but at the same time, how could I bear to leave it to become a wilderness? With this in mind, I am dividing it into four and handing it over to my sons, so that they can each take care of their own section.[17] Although I am only presenting them with an encumbrance, the situation is such that I cannot do otherwise. I have heard of the words of Xu Mian, the Chief Administrator of Liang: "From ancient to modern times, renowned gardens and stately homes have always been just the same as an inn in which one lodges temporarily."[18] I have always disapproved of people of today who

---

15 "Barbarians" evidently refers to the Manchus themselves, "half-breeds" presumably to the so-called Han bannermen, ethnic Chinese who had settled in Manchuria and allied themselves with the Manchus.

16 The Manchus, who originally depended on hunting and fishing for survival, were keen hunters on horseback. By the late Ming, hunting was an extremely rare pastime among the gentry in southern China, and must have seemed a barbaric activity.

17 Wang Shimin had nine sons, but they may not all have been adult at the time when this was written (the date is not given).

18 Xu Mian (466–535) was said to have been so busy with affairs of state that, on his rare visits home, all the household dogs barked at him. He would not amass property, saying that he wanted to leave his sons a good reputation rather than riches.

say things like, "My residence can be described as a fine site for a successful man."
So I have examined the history of gardens from past dynasties such as the Pingquan
Estate or the Sincerely Presented Garden; few are the descendants of ancient families
who have been able to maintain their old properties.[19] Looking back on this, it is a
matter for deep sadness. Now that our family has declined, and the general situation
is so perilous, worries press upon you and it will be very hard for you to preserve the
property. Just remember what remains of your great-grandfather's own planting, and
the careful thought which your papa devoted to it, and do your best to cope with what
this karma involves you in. I am well aware that at present you are all in difficulties
and cannot reconstruct it, but perhaps you can just stop up the worst gaps and prop
up what is actually collapsing, so that this old man, in the years that remain to him,
can take staff and sandals and roam about in it on fine spring and autumn days. This
will approximate to what the Chief Administrator said: I can take temporary pleasure in it, and enjoy lodging in it, while always waiting for my final end. If our family
fortune continues, flowers and trees turn to the sun, and my hermitage increases in
splendor, this is a blessing from my forebears and my remaining happiness will be
deep. If by an unlucky chance the fortune of our house is slight, and tempests blow so
that not one branch is preserved, and prosperity and decline are turned topsy-turvy,
this is anyway in the control of the Creator, and not something that human beings
can predict. I ought to resign myself to fate and make the best of things. The reason
I alternate between joy and sorrow, and cannot stop sighing with emotion, is just
irresponsibility on my part. I have written the above brief account of the history of
this garden to show my sons and grandsons, just to let them know what I spent half
my life and my heartfelt appreciation on.

Random Ventures in Idleness (*Xianqing ouji* 閒情偶寄)

"Housing" (*Fangshe* 房舍; extract), "Paths" (*Tujing* 途徑), "Height" (*Gaoxia* 高下),
and "The Selection of Scenery through Borrowing" (*Qu jing zai jie* 取景在借; extract)

LI YU 李漁 (1610/1611–1680)

TRANSLATED BY DUNCAN M. CAMPBELL

Li Yu, also known as Li Liweng or "Fisherman of West Lake," born in Jiangsu Province to a family based in Zhejiang, was one of the most remarkable figures of the late imperial Chinese world
of letters.[20] Dramatist, poet, essayist, and humorist, Li Yu was an inveterate inventor, a prolific

---

19   On the Pingquan Estate and Li Deyu's injunction to his sons and grandsons, see chapter 3. The Sincerely
      Presented Garden was originally the residence of the Tang official Ma Sui (726–795). When he died, his son,
      Ma Chang, gave a large ginkgo tree from the garden to another official, who then presented it to the emperor.
      Ma Chang, fearing that he would get into trouble for not having himself given the tree to the emperor in the
      first place, donated the entire residence, which was then renamed Sincerely Presented Garden. Both gardens
      became topoi for the impermanence of one's ownership of a garden.

20   See Patrick Hanan, *The Invention of Li Yu* (Cambridge, Mass.: Harvard University Press, 1988).

writer (of plays, poems, essays, short stories, and possibly a pornographic novel), and a connoisseur of fine living. Above all, he seems to have been obsessed with the pursuit of "novelty" (*qi*), in both life and letters.

Having passed the initial stages of the civil service examinations in 1635, he failed to advance further, thenceforth depending for his livelihood (and the upkeep of almost fifty dependents) on his pen and his wits. A master of self-promotion, he lived well enough at times to own a number of fine gardens, one of which, the Mustard Seed Garden in Nanjing, lent its name to one of the most famous painting manuals of the age, the *Mustard Seed Garden Manual of Painting* of 1679, for which he wrote a preface.

His justly famous and much-cited *Random Ventures in Idleness*, a title also translated as *Casual Expressions of Idle Feelings*, entertainingly sets out his pronounced views on drama (as literature and as performance), on travel and recreation, on cuisine, on beauty in women, and, as below, on aspects of architecture and garden design.

"Housing" (extract)

Rooms are very much to a man what clothing is to the body—a stark necessity. With clothing, what we prize is the extent to which it keeps us cool in summer and warm during the winter; so too it is with housing. "Halls with high stud and capitals several feet wide" may well *seem* majestic, but although such rooms may prove appropriate to the needs of the summer months, come winter and they will no longer be so. Of course, to enter the hall of a man of importance is bound to set one trembling in any case, even before the onset of cold weather, owing both to the man's palpable air of authority and to the vast solemnity of his chambers. Even though I have a lined fur coat it would be difficult to ward off the chill of such rooms. On the other hand, walls that reach little higher than one's shoulders, rooms that provide little more than the space to sit knee to knee, are certainly economical enough, but they are suitable only for the host, not for his guests. The house of an impoverished scholar, then, will set us sighing without necessarily having any actual cause for concern, for although we will be sympathetic, the ambience will force this response from us regardless of the extent to which we can put up with privation. Furthermore, for my part certainly, I find the misery of such circumstances quite loathsome.

It is my firm opinion, then, that houses built by prominent men should be neither too high nor too wide, for there needs, always, to be an appropriate and proportional relationship between a man and his house. Landscape painters put it this way: "A hill a *zhang* in height will require that the trees on it be only a *chi* tall; a horse only a *cun* tall will need a rider who is only the size of a dot." Would it be at all appropriate for a hill of a *zhang* in height to be given trees of two or three *chi*, I ask you, or a horse a *cun* in size to have a rider who was as big as a grain of rice or millet? Certainly not! Were such a man of importance to be six or seven foot tall, then it would be appropriate for his house to be cavernous, otherwise, the higher the stud of his chambers the shorter he will appear, the wider his rooms, the more emaciated he will seem. Better then that he reduce the size of his rooms and increase the stature of his body.

The hut of the poor scholar, on the other hand, cannot help but appear mean and narrow, for it is not easy to make the mean seem exalted, the narrow appear wide. On the other hand, emptying a house by getting rid of the clutter that so often serves to defile it will make even the meanest house seem grand, the narrowest of rooms seem spacious.

I have been poor all my life, having had to move here and there, with never a fixed home of my own. I run up debts in order to eat and am forced to rent accommodation wherever I happen to be living. And yet I have never allowed such circumstances to sully my abode. For instance, I am congenitally addicted to flowers and bamboo but never have enough money to purchase them. To overcome this difficulty, I instruct my wife and serving girls to go hungry for a day or so, or to shiver through an entire winter, in order to save on the expenses of food and clothing, all to bring pleasure to my eyes and my ears. People laugh at me for this, but I am quite content with my course of action. At the same time, I hate copying others and prefer, always, to seek after novelty.

In this respect, I have often argued that the dispositions of a person's living quarters work to the same principles as their scholarship and their writing style. For instance, when composing an examination essay, the able and talented will come up with something quite superior and novel, whereas the untalented will do no more than change the beginning and the ending of essays that they have memorized, adding a word here or removing a sentence there, but never copying a complete essay, before proclaiming themselves good at putting to use existing materials. When such people turn to building, however, the design of their halls imitates those of others, and their gates replicate those around them. And when this is not exactly the case, perversely, rather than celebrating the fact they bemoan it. I have often observed cases where a wealthy member of some aristocratic family, before expending a huge amount of money on the construction of a garden, will address the chief carpenter in the following terms: "As for my pavilions, they must be modeled on those of so-and-so; my gazebos built in the pattern of whatshisname. I will tolerate no divergence." At the same time, those with the direct authority over the men undertaking the work, once the grand mansion has been completed, will proceed to lay claim to honor by saying that each gate and every window of the building, the position of every gallery and siting of each belvedere is modeled on that of some famous garden or other, with not the slightest divergence. Alas. What silliness! How dire a situation it is when, in terms of the excellence of the design of a garden, those above cannot come up with their own ideas in the manner of a man-of-letters who comes up with novel and unusual conceits, and those below are scribes who cannot even turn something that is old and stale into something new by making small alterations here and there, but where both alike loudly proclaim their satisfaction with the products of their hands!

As I have had occasion to say before, there are two supreme arts in life which, if one cannot make use of them oneself, cannot it seems be mastered by others, a matter for considerable regret. "What are these two arts?" an interlocutor asked on one occasion. "The first is an understanding of music. The other is the building of a garden."

I am congenitally addicted to the writing of lyrics and have produced quite a volume of work, as is well known throughout the empire. Were I to be given free rein, then I would pick my own troupe of actors and have them sing lyrics that I had myself written, training them myself and myself rehearsing their moves with them. In this way, I would transform the singing style of the age. And not just with new lyrics, but I would also bring new worth to old plays by cutting from them all the old clichés and giving them a new shape, giving a whole set of authors a new lease of life. I have a particular knack for this.

With regard to the creation of a garden, this is a matter of suiting the design to the lie of the land, never working to fixed ideas. Each rafter and every strut needs to be considered anew, so that for anyone passing through the garden or entering its structures it will be as if they are reading one of my essays: I may lack sublime talent, but at least I offer readers a modicum of novelty, and so may, therefore, I trust, be considered an adornment even of an age of enlightenment and an empire of prosperity such as ours? Alas. I am grown old, no longer fit for purpose. Permit me, however, to put down on paper a general outline of my ideas, for those aficionados who may appreciate them. For me, were my ideas to prove at all useful, it would be as if my books have benefited from divine intervention.

In building, then, it is the ostentatious and wasteful that is to be avoided, and this preference for the plain and simple should apply not just to ordinary people, but also princes and important men as well. In the design of one's housing, what is to be valued is the essential rather than the simply lovely, novelty and understated elegance rather than the ornate and ingenious.

"Paths"

No path is more convenient than that which leads directly to where one wishes to go; no path is more marvelous, however, than one that describes a circuitous route to that place. On occasions where the circuitous is deliberately to be sought, for reasons of novelty, then a side gate should also be provided, affording rapid and direct egress, this gate to be opened only when required, kept closed when not. In this way, the requirements of both elegance and practicality may be provided for, rationality and exquisiteness equally met.

"Height"

Housing abhors the appearance of uniformity and a dynamic relationship between the high and the low must always be maintained. This is not just the case in the design of gardens, but applies equally to one's living quarters. The low in front, the high behind, this is the normal rule in this respect. But where the lie of the land itself does not permit of this, then to attempt to enforce the rule is to commit the fault of adhering too inflexibly to formal rules.

In general terms, then, there are methods for suiting one's design to the particular circumstances of the site. Where the land is elevated, build rooms; where the land is lowly, construct a tower. This is one such method. Where the land lies low, pile up rocks to form a mountain; excavate the high spots on one's site to create a pond. This is another such method. Conversely, one can also seek to elevate the height of those parts of the site that are already high—by placing a belvedere upon a piled rock foundation on the highest slope of the site—or rendering more lowly the parts of the site already low lying—by digging a pool or sinking a well in the water-logged sections of the site. Again, in general, there exist no fixed rules in this respect. One must hold fast to one's own ideas and work in accordance with one's intuition. Such methods cannot, certainly, be transmitted by means of set patterns.

"The Selection of Scenery through Borrowing" (extract)

The magic when positioning a window is in the extent to which it will allow for the borrowing of scenery. And as to the methods of borrowing scenery, of these I can lay some claim to profound understanding. In the past I have kept such understanding to myself. Given the number of aficionados about nowadays and the fact that they will all of them be imitating each other, I have decided to make this understanding of mine publicly available to all within the seas, in the hope that their creations too can be touched by the same magic, to the joy of all. All I ask for is that, in the midst of their raucous celebration of the excellence of this invention of mine, they may remember to shout out my name once or twice, so that I too may join them, if only in spirit or in my dreams, to partake of their joy. This would be satisfaction enough for me.

Previously, when I was living beside West Lake at Hangzhou, I wished to buy a houseboat. I was quite happy to go along with what was usual in terms of the design of such a craft, except in one particular—the shape of the windows. When I was taxed for the details of this, I replied: "I want the cabin walls of my houseboat to be entirely solid, on all four sides, with two gaps, however, cut into them, one on either side of the boat, both in the shape of a fan. The cabin walls should be made of planks and plastered with lime, leaving not the slightest crack between the boards; the gaps in the cabin walls should be framed with wood, the top and bottom line of which should be curved, the uprights straight, thus resembling the shape of a fan. These windows should be left completely open, without any latticework whatsoever. This would leave the boat, on both sides, with just these two fan-shaped windows, and nothing else."

Sitting in the boat, then, the shimmer of the lake and the hue of the surrounding hills, all the temples, monasteries, and pagodas, the mist and the clouds, bamboo and the trees, along with the wood gatherers and shepherds as they come and go, drunken old men and carousing young maidens, even the horses which accompanied them, all these would appear within the fan, forming for me a "Natural Painting." Moreover, this painting would change continuously, never being trapped into a fixed form. And this would not just be the case as the boat moved along, each oar stroke giving a new vista, every push of the pole a new scene, for even when the boat was tethered, buffeted by the breeze or rocked by the lapping waves as it would be, the form of the painting would change from moment to moment. Thus, within the course of a single day, a hundred thousand scrolls of fine mountains and beautiful rivers would appear before my eyes, all of them having been captured within my fans.

Moreover, the manufacture of my fans would require no great expenditure of money, requiring simply two pieces of bent wood and two additional straight pieces. Men of this present age spend huge amounts of cash trying to achieve novelties of one sort or another. Can any of them compete with this invention of mine? This window design will bring pleasure not just to me alone, but to many others. Not only will the boundless and ever-changing scenery beyond the boat be brought to those sitting within it, but they themselves, all those sitting within the cabin, with their cups and plates, will project outside the boat, providing for the delectation of passers-by. How so? When those inside the boat look out, they will see a landscape painting; when those outside the boat look in, they will see a figure painting. And so, for instance, whenever you drag along some singing girls or invite a monk or two, gather together some friends or acquaintances, whether to play chess or view a painting, or hold a poetry competition, to drink or to sing, with some falling asleep and others leaping to their feet, to viewers outside, all this will seem to be as a painting. The same objects, the very same event, before the invention of this window, were simply just what they were; with this window, however, and without the labor of art, everyone will now be transformed into figures in a painting.

A fan is of course not at all an unusual object; neither is making a window in the shape of a fan at all a difficult task. Men of this present age are wont to model the shape of objects on that of the things of this world, and who knows how many shapes have been given to gates and windows. But this object alone, one that is in front of all our eyes on a daily basis, has been ignored completely. Until, that is, old Li Yu came along. What a very wondrous turn of events indeed. Sadly, however, although I came up with the idea, I have not had the wherewithal to realize it in actuality for I was never able to have a houseboat like this built, a matter for some very considerable regret. And now that I have moved to live in Nanjing, and have turned my back on West Lake, my former love, my desire to realize the project has dulled even more as I have become resigned to the prospect of never being able to do so. All I can do is put my invention to a minor use, by installing my fan window in my tower, so that I can spy out upon the Bell Mountain's shifting colors from there.

I have, moreover, invented an Empty Window for Observing the Mountain, also called a Scroll Window or a Spontaneous Painting. Let me tell you about it for a moment. Just behind my Studio for the Cups stands a little rock hill, no more than a *zhang* or so high, a *xun* or so wide. But it contains all the cinnabar cliffs and green pools, luxuriant woods and tall bamboos, chirping birds and roaring waterfalls, thatched huts and plank bridges, that one can expect to find upon a mountain. I had had a skilled model maker create me exact and precise models of all these things. This all started when he made a most lifelike figurine modelled on me, which, in keeping with my studio name of Old Fisherman, depicted me holding a fishing rod. Once I saw this, I decided that if I was to be fishing, then I would need to sit upon a rock ledge, and that this rock ledge would need to overlook a pond, and that this pond would need a mountain behind it, and so before long I had this tableau of a landscape, which then required an old fisherman in retirement to be placed within it, and so I came to live in this cave studio. Thus, this mountain had begun life as a scene, with no thought given to the window looking out on it. Later on, I realized that although the objects of the tableau were small, they were nonetheless also all-encompassing, like the mustard seed that can hold up Mount Sumeru, and I would sit there all day observing them, not bearing to close the window. Then all of a sudden one day it dawned on me: "This is a mountain. But it can also be a painting. This painting can also be a window. With just the expenditure of a day's drinking money, I can put together whatever is needed to mount this scroll." Thereupon, I ordered my pageboy to cut out several sheets of backing paper, to serve as the head and foot of the scroll, and the two borders. The head and foot paper I had glued to the top and the bottom of the window respectively, and the borders to its sides. All of a sudden, the window had become a scroll hanging in my hall, but with an empty center. Not that the center of the scroll was really empty, for the hill that stood behind my studio now filled it. As I sat there looking at it, the window became no longer a window, but rather a painting and the hill no longer the hill behind my studio but rather a hill in a painting. I burst out laughing, at which my wife and children rushed in to see what was happening, they too proceeding to laugh at what I had been laughing at. This, then, was the beginning of my Spontaneous Painting or my Scroll Window.

I once also constructed a Natural Window, using several pieces of dried flowering apricot branch, which I named Flowering Apricot Window. Of all the inventions I have come up with in my life, this I consider to have been my best.

During the summer of the *jiyou* year [1669], the rivers rose in flood, inundating the fields for a long time, drowning both a pomegranate and a citrus tree that grew alongside my studio. They were cut down for firewood, but because they were still green, the axe could make no headway with them, and they lay discarded at the bottom of the steps for several days. When I saw them, their twisted branches looked to me like those of an Old Flowering Apricot, withered and twisted but coiled like a spring, as if crying out to be put to some use. I applied my mind to the task. It so happened that at that very moment my Valley of the Nesting Clouds seemed to me to be rather gloomy and I thought to open the window. "I have it," I suddenly thought to myself, "this is it!" I had my carpenter select one or two of the straighter branches and, retaining their original shape and with as little use of saw and plane as possible, turn them into an outer frame for my window. Then we took two branches that were twisted and gnarled at one end but which were smooth at the other to form two sprigs of flowering apricot tree, one to drape down from the top of the frame, the other to jut upward from the bottom of it. Shaving the flat ends of the branches and removing the bark and joints that faced outward, we prepared the surfaces for paper to be glued on them. As to the twisted ends, we left these as they were, with no sawing or shaping, leaving all the twigs and stems in place. Once all this had been done, we cut out variegated cloth in the shape of flowers, in both the Red and the Green Calyx Flowering Apricot variety, and with these we decorated the twigs and stems. This all gave the appearance of live flowering apricot trees that had just burst into bloom. Not one of my contemporaries failed to marvel at my invention when they saw it; truly, this was the apogee of my inventiveness. Nothing that I later invented surpassed this.

I was somewhat aggrieved that I hadn't managed to make use of my fan-window invention on a houseboat but was reduced to employing it on a house. But at the same time, this did reveal a certain flexibility and adaptability on my part; the ability to turn something old into something new, to bring life to the lifeless, all to the delectation of both eye and ear, for, with no more effort than a moment's thought, I had produced a marvelous and spontaneous tableau that changed constantly with every passing instant. I am a most obsessive person. I dislike flowers on display in a poor man's house, caged birds, fish in jars, and rocks on stands sitting on desks, for all these things communicate a sense of constraint that makes one feel like a trapped eagle. In terms of flowers in pots, apart from the orchid and the narcissi, no others take my fancy. I love the grey thrush but I always insist on coming up with novel designs for cages and never use those that are commonly seen, lest the birds seem under arrest. Once I had invented this fan-shaped window, I would apply a similar ingenuity to everything in life that I had hitherto cast aside.

In the past, painted fans have always tended to be broad and eclectic in what they could depict: landscape, portraits, bamboo and rocks, flowers and birds, even insects. So, having invented this window for the benefit of those inside the room, I now had a plank set up outside just below the window. On this I would have things placed:

flowers in pots, birds in cages, coiled pines, oddly-shaped rocks, and so on. These could be changed at will. When an orchid was about to bloom, for instance, I would have it placed on the plank outside the window, thus producing an orchid fan; when the potted chrysanthemums are in blossom, I have them placed beneath my window and my fan becomes a chrysanthemum one. Sometimes I change what is on display every few days, sometimes everyday, sometimes again several times a day—everything is possible. But the pots themselves need to be disguised; best if covered up with handfuls of loose rock. This window of mine can be put to use by everyone, for anyone is capable of making one, to the immense delight of both eye and ear. But in the midst of their delight I hope that those who do make use of this window give a moment's thought to the man who first came up with this invention!

"A Record of the Garden That Borders upon Greenness" (*Yilü yuan ji* 依綠園記)

XU QIANXUE 徐乾學 (1631–1694)
TRANSLATED BY DUNCAN M. CAMPBELL

Xu Qianxue, from Kunshan in Jiangsu Province, a presented scholar of 1670, was a prominent seventeenth-century poet, scholar, book collector, and official, as well as the nephew of the important Ming loyalist scholar Gu Yanwu (1613–1682).

An otherwise largely successful official career was marred by Xu's entanglement in the factionalism that characterized the court during the second half of the seventeenth century, and he earned himself a reputation for treachery and, on various occasions, stood accused of bribery and other misdemeanors. Xu's own garden, the Garden of Tranquility, built on the slopes of a mountain in his hometown in the mid-1670s during a period of dismissal from office and designed to please his elderly mother, became justly famous.

In both a private and an official capacity, Xu undertook the editing of a number of major projects, including the *Comprehensive Gazetteer of the Great Qing Empire* and, as mentioned below, the *History of the Ming Dynasty*. Nothing is otherwise known about Wu Shiya, the owner of the garden where Xu established his historiographical commission, the Garden That Borders Upon Greenness. It is of interest to garden historians that the garden was designed by Zhang Ran, the son of the great garden craftsman Zhang Lian (see chapter 7); Zhang Ran was also involved in the design of several imperial gardens in Beijing.[21]

"A Record of the Garden That Borders upon Greenness"

The Dongting Mountains are not all that far away from my hometown of Kunshan—less than 200 *li* distant. It is an area abounding in all the Cavern Heavens and Blessed Lands spoken of in the Daoist books but, busy as I have been with my various official duties, I

---

21   Cao Xun, "Qingdai zaoyuan dieshan yishujia Zhang Ran he Beijing de 'Shanzi Zhang,'" 120, quotes a poem by Wu Shiya written to celebrate Zhang Ran's completion of his garden.

have never previously had the opportunity to investigate such numinous oddities. This is a circumstance that I have much regretted, however, as I am told that the Seventy-Two Peaks that float upon the surface of the lake there much resemble the Three Immortal Isles of distant antiquity. The impossibility of transporting myself there as on a wing has meant that I have then, by necessity, been confined to traveling there in spirit. Master Miao Tong of Suzhou is much traveled around both the Eastern and the Western Dongting Mountains and told me once that they contained much that was excellent. So much is this the case in fact that when seeking to find a suitable place to build his garden, my friend faced an embarrassment of choice, for the area rivalled the ancient capital Luoyang in its beauty. He reserved his highest praise for the Southern Village Thatched Cottage of Master Wu Shiya of East Mountain, waxing lyrical also about this gentleman's talents and his virtue. Long, then, have I wished to be able to visit him there.

This spring, having received an imperial commission to head the Historiographical Office project to compile the *History of the Ming Dynasty*, I was granted leave to return to the south. My intention was to shut myself off from the disputatious world and devote my undivided attention to the task at hand, in order that the product of our labors would prove a book for all ages. I sailed across Lake Tai and arrived at East Mountain and set about establishing my office and commencing work. Only then did I have the opportunity to get to know Master Wu, thus requiting my more than twenty-year-long admiration for him. Master Wu thereupon ordered his two sons, Yi and Cang, to take up tuition under my direction, and so I had occasion to pay a visit to his Southern Village Thatched Cottage, in the foothills of Martial Mount. The tall studios and wide halls of the garden look out over a pond and face the mountain, and the garden itself, upon cursory examination, proved most appealing to both heart and eye. To the southeast of the hall a doubled-leafed gate opened out, clothed in the hue of the willows and abutting the water, this being Willow Gate. A long and zigzag gallery, as wide as two boats lashed together, led off to the west, as if floating upon the surface of the ripples, this being the Abode of the Sweet Waters. Several paces to the south of this place, across a flat bridge and then clambering up the steps that follow the contors of the hill here, one comes across a pavilion with soaring eaves that sticks up above the surrounding aged cassia and hoary pine trees, this being the Pavilion of the Flying Roseate Clouds. A gazebo here seems suspended in nothingness and commands a gaze across the green wilds, this being the Gazebo for the Celebration of the Harvest. Beyond the gazebo, a thousand *qing* of flat arable land lies ready to be plowed by the gazing eye and the vast expanse of the shimmering South Lake merges seamlessly with the boundless horizon. From west to north, fold after fold of hill slope stretches out, the hue of each encompassing every possible variation of green and purple, and all as if knocking on one's door to demand admittance within one's studio to take their place upon one's desk. Taking a turn on the little mound that stands behind the Pavilion of the Flying Roseate Clouds and ascending in an easterly direction, then continuing on to the flat ridge that stands there, one finds oneself surrounded by the Three Friends of the Winter, the pine, the bamboo, and the flowering apricot, with stone screens jutting up sharply here and there to either side of one. To the south of the ridge a plot of land has been developed, the fine trees here growing in neat rows that, when gazed at from afar, lend the garden a sense of depth. Another turn, this time to the northeast, brings into sight a small tower set ensconced amid the dense vegetation, named Among the Flowers and Birds, the plaque of which is in the calligraphy of the recluse of Shangshi Xu Fang and set in the walls of which is a stone engraving of Tao Qian's poem "Homeward Bound" in the hand of Dong Qichang. Leaning from the window of the tower and gazing northward, it is as if Brocade Vulture Peak and Master of Pu River Mound are dancing below one's eaves. Before one stand Cassia Blossom Screen, Hibiscus Slope, Crane Isle and Wisteria Bridge, all within sight of each other. Neatly arrayed to the south is the Tower of the Frozen Snow, and from there, looking down from afar at the flowering apricots growing upon the ridge one is transported, momentarily, to the Mountain of the Assembled Jade of the Queen Mother of the West. Stretching off to the north is a zigzag gallery, with patterns of inlaid red jade, that takes one to the Little Retreat Amid the Fragrant Fields where, in a hidden chamber six bays in size, light blue and bright yellow book covers fill the shelves. In the courtyard here stands a most eccentric rock, shaped like billowing clouds, upon which grows a single twisted cypress, its green canopy spreading out like the roof of a chariot. This is where the master of the garden undertakes the tuition of his sons and puts them through their lessons. Turning west along a winding gallery, past bamboo screens and lake rocks, one comes across a tiny room that wraps itself around a low wall, this being where the orchids are stored for the winter. Here too is found Stone Retreat Amid the Flowers, behind which a kitchen has been constructed, well provisioned with fine wine and best tea to provide for visitors. This, then, is a general description of the garden.

The garden is no wider that a few *mu*, but with all its twists and turns, its rises and falls, its continuities and interruptions, it nonetheless gives one the feeling of boundlessness. From the exquisiteness of its design, one can gain some idea of the assiduous attention paid to the garden by its master, and I now have even greater confidence that what my friend Miao Tong had to say about him was not at all exaggerated. The garden was completed in the *guichou* year of the reign of the Kangxi emperor [1673]. Its rockery was the work of Zhang Ran of Yunjian, and a depiction of the garden was painted by the artist Wang Hui [1632–1717] of Mount Wumu. The poetry of Ye Yibao of my home-town served to bring the garden to completion. At first, the garden carried the name the Little Retreat Amid the Fragrant Fields, and it is noted under this name in the *Gazetteer of Wu County*. But now, the Advanced Scholar Tao Yuanchun of Mount Yu, borrowing from a line of a poem by Du Fu that goes "And famous gardens border the green river," has given the garden a new name, Garden That Borders upon Greenness. Having derived so much pleasure from my engagements with Master Wu and his sons, and being further delighted by the fact that the garden has now acquired an excellent name, I took up my brush to write this record of it. The Master's name is Shiya, he is called Binwen, and he has taken for himself the studio name Southern Village.

"On a Summer Day, I Write about the Place Where We Are Staying" (*Xiari ti suo ju* 夏日題所居)

WANG HUI 王慧 (2ND HALF OF 17TH CENTURY)
TRANSLATED BY MAUREEN ROBERTSON

Although greatly admired by some distinguished literary critics in the Qing, Wang Hui, who was widowed young, remained quite obscure during most of her life; her poems were discovered and published by her younger brother, a successful scholar, when she was over seventy.

"On a Summer Day, I Write about the Place Where We Are Staying"

When we are away for the summer
    nothing at all happens;
The brushwood gate is closed
    the whole day long.
Weary, I throw down books and scrolls,
    lie back and take a rest;
Bored, I go to pull weeds
    and clear the herb garden.
Greens I borrow from trees
    growing in the neighbor's yard;
Blues I share with mountains
    beyond the city walls.
Living quietly apart
    I've left all ordinary cares behind;
In following my own inclinations
    I am really quite obstinate!

"*Lang tao sha*: Remembering My Female Companions in Our Old Garden" (*Langtaosha: Yi guyuan nüban* 浪淘沙：憶故園女伴)

GU ZHENLI 顧貞立 (CA. 1637–CA. 1714)
TRANSLATED BY KATHRYN LOWRY

Gu Zhenli, from a literary and scholar-official family in Wuxi, lived through the Ming-Qing transition and many of her poems reflect her interest in current affairs; they generally have a melancholy tone.

"*Lang tao sha*: Remembering My Female Companions in Our Old Garden"

The gauze canopy floats in the evening chill.
Autumn sounds fill every leaf.

The bamboo shadows move, the north window brightening.
I am too lazy to trim the silver lamp; it lets blossoms fall.
White scrolls are scattered everywhere.
What has startled my thoughts?
The mica screen from the old days:
A caged *luan*-bird and garden phoenix, so delightful.
When will the west wind send the dreaming butterfly
Flying above this melancholy realm?

"To the Tune '*Yu meiren*'" (*Yu meiren* 虞美人)

HOU CHENG'EN 侯承恩 (FL. CA. 1712)

TRANSLATED BY CAROL R. KAUFMANN

In addition to her poetry, Hou Cheng'en had a range of talents: she was a musician and, like her father, a skilled chess (*weiqi* or *gō*) player. Her family was from Jiading, now part of Shanghai municipality.

"To the Tune '*Yu meiren*'"

The New Year passed three months ago,
    leaving fragrant grasses.
The gate is shut, passers-by few,
Elusive fragrance is fading
    from my berry trellis.
But in this seclusion butterflies
    still grace the breezes.

I've thrown down my poems
    to cherish the passing spring,
One can't buy a stop for time.
Up the tower I go, feeling cold and alone,
And see only pairs of mandarin ducks
    happily splashing in a lotus pool.

"Six Records of My Garden of Accommodation" (*Suiyuan liu ji* 隨園六記)

YUAN MEI 袁枚 (1716–1797)

TRANSLATED BY DUNCAN M. CAMPBELL AND STEPHEN MCDOWALL

Yuan Mei, born in Hangzhou, was the most important poet of the eighteenth century. He was also a prolific essayist, letter writer, critic, short story writer, gourmet, and scholar, with a particular concern for both history and the source and function of poetry. Having been invited to sit the special examinations of 1736 and failed, Yuan Mei succeeded at the examinations of 1739 and was appointed to a post in the Hanlin Academy. His inability at Manchu, however, saw him appointed to a series of minor and local posts as a district magistrate.

In 1752, Yuan Mei retired permanently from office, and for the remaining half century of his life he lived on his writings, managing to avoid entanglement in the various literary inquisitions that characterized his age. Throughout this period, with few interruptions, he lived in his garden, Suiyuan, variously translated as Harmony Garden or, as below, Garden of Accommodation. "If it is the garden that brings pleasure to one's eyes," Yuan Mei later argued, "it is also the garden that provides man with a refuge for his self." The garden was situated in the west of the city of Nanjing, on the slopes of Little Granary Hill, a site that had first been developed as a garden in 1728 by Sui Hede, the Imperial Textile Commissioner, but had fallen into disrepair by the time Yuan Mei acquired it in 1749. As he expanded it, Yuan modelled its design on the West Lake of Hangzhou.

Ignoring the moralistic criticisms of a number of his contemporaries, Yuan Mei, a man committed to the education of women, gathered around him a group of talented female poets, publishing their writings (as well as a celebrated book of recipes) under the title of his garden.

Without enclosing walls, the garden appears to have been unusually open to visitors. Between 1749 and 1770, Yuan wrote a series of six records of his garden. Late in his life, Yuan appears to have believed that his garden had been the prototype of the "Prospect Garden" at the heart of the great eighteenth-century novel *Dream of the Red Chamber* (also known as *The Story of the Stone*; see chapter 7). Yuan Mei's accounts of his garden, four of which are dated to the spring of the year they were written, provide no description of the garden itself. His grandson, Yuan Zuzhi (1827–1898), however, working from memory and much later (1877), produced a detailed description of its various features. In Yuan Mei's day, many paintings were made of the Garden of Accommodation, but none of these appears to be extant.

The significance of the garden to Yuan Mei can be seen from his will, which lists it alongside his other various possessions:

The Garden of Accommodation was once a patch of wasteland. I had the ground flattened and ponds excavated, towers and terraces raised. Three times I undertook the renovation of my garden, at incalculable expense. Strange peaks and eccentric rocks I purchased at great cost, ten thousand green bamboos I planted with my own hands. All the utensils I make use of in my garden are fashioned from sandalwood and pear and patterned catalpa, or are of carved lacquer-ware or beaten gold; my baubles comprise rubbings from the Jin dynasty and stelae of the Tang, wine beakers of the Shang and tripods of the Xia; the paintings and calligraphies in my possession all bear the impressions of seals made of finest Frozen Yellow stone from Blue Fields and bear inscriptions by famous men; my exquisite inkslabs from Duan County are decorated with banana leaf and blue flower patterns, and bear legends of great antiquity. All this is such that no rich man, north or south of the Yangtze River, can vie with me in the splendor of my possessions.

Upon his death, Yuan Mei was buried in the family tomb in the garden. The garden was maintained by his family until 1853, when it was destroyed and turned into arable land after Nanjing was occupied by the Taiping rebels.

"Six Records of My Garden of Accommodation"

Record of My Garden of Accommodation

A short walk of two *li* westward from Nanjing's North Gate Bridge brings one to Little Granary Hill. The hill stems from Bracing Mountain, and separates into two ridges which slope downward until they reach the bridge. The winding ridges are narrow and long, and surround a series of ponds and paddy fields—commonly referred to as "Dry River Bed." In former times, when water still flowed through this valley, Bracing Mountain provided the men of the Southern Tang with a retreat from the heat of summer—one can well imagine the whole area's magnificence then. The most splendid sights of the city of Nanjing are generally said to be the Terrace of Raining Flowers in the south, the Lake of Light-Heartedness in the southwest, Bell Mountain in the north, Forge Town in the east, and the Tomb of the Filial Emperor of the Ming and the Temple of the Crowing Cock in the northeast. Standing at the top of Little Granary Hill each of these magnificent vistas floats into sight. Thus, although the hill itself does not possess the grandeur of the rivers and the lakes or the ever-changing patterns of cloud and mist, it nonetheless allows access to that which it lacks.

During the reign of the Kangxi emperor, Master Sui, who was the Imperial Textile Commissioner, began to build on Little Granary Hill's northern peak. Within this estate, he constructed a series of majestic halls and chambers, enclosed them with walls and windows, and planted a thousand *zhang* of catalpa tree and a thousand *qi* of cassia. The people flocked from the city and packed in to admire the garden, which, because of the owner's name, became known as "Sui's Garden." By the time I served in Jiangning some thirty years later, the garden had fallen into disrepair. Its buildings were being used as a tavern, and there was an unceasing racket from the rabble that gathered. Birds hated the place and would not nest there, the plants were all withered and overgrown, and even the spring breeze seemed unable to produce a flower. One look over the property left me grief-stricken, and I enquired as to its purchase price. I was told that I might acquire it for 300 taels of silver, and so for just a month's salary the garden became mine.

I repaired the walls and doors, replaced the eaves and applied fresh plaster. Accommodating to the garden's heights, I established a river tower; accommodating to its hollows I built a brook pavilion. Accommodating to the land that abuts a ravine I erected a bridge, and accommodating to the swirling stream I moored a boat. Accommodating to the land that juts up sharply, I had peaks made; and accommodating to the flatlands, where vegetation flourishes, I had the buildings constructed. Here raising the land;

there lowering it; everything was achieved by accommodating to the shape of the land, and taking the various scenes from the existing contours, rather than regarding that which is natural as an obstacle to be overcome. Consequently, I renamed it the Garden of Accommodation (Sui Garden), a name that sounds exactly the same as the surname of the garden's original owner but which means something very different.

When the work was completed, I sighed and said: "If I were to serve as an official I would see this garden perhaps only once in a month; but if I were to live here I would see it every day. As I cannot have both, I will give up the office in favor of the garden." Thereupon I applied for sick leave, and, taking my younger brother Xiangting and my nephew Meijun with me, I moved with my extensive library to live in the Garden of Accommodation. I have heard that Su Shi once opined that: "A gentleman need not serve in government, nor need he reject government service."[22] Thus whether or not I take a position as an official in future, and whether my stay here is to be long or short, are also matters of accommodation. When one exchanges one thing for another, that which is the replacement must, surely, be superior to that which has been replaced. That I have seen fit to exchange my office for this garden is evidence indeed of the garden's true exceptionality.

Recorded in the third month of the *jisi* year [1749].

Latter Record of My Garden of Accommodation

Having lived in my Garden of Accommodation for three years, I accepted an official posting in Shaanxi. Before a full year had gone by, however, my thoughts, like those of Tao Qian of old, had turned to being "Homeward Bound." Once back there, I found that the flowers I planted had all withered, the roof tiles had cracked and shaken loose, and the flowering apricot plaster was beginning to peel away from the rafters; such were the circumstances that greeted my eye that I could not but seek to restore my garden to its former state.

Thereupon, I led my servants out to clear the ground of rocks and thus to reveal the veins of the earth that ran beneath, in order that my garden's full potentiality for the beauty of height and spaciousness might be realized. Even after a year of effort and the expenditure of a thousand taels, the task that I set myself has not yet been completed.

---

22 The quotation, in Chinese "*Junzi bu bi shi, bu bi bu shi*" (君子不必仕不必不仕), is from Su Shi's "Record of the Zhang Family Garden at Lingbi" (*Lingbi Zhangshi yuanting ji* 靈璧張氏園亭記) and reads: "*Gu zhi junzi, bu bi shi, bu bi bu shi*" (古之君子不必仕不必不仕), or "*ancient men* of worth did not have to enter into public service, nor did they have to not enter public service" (emphasis added). For a complete translation of this record, see chapter 4.

On one occasion, a visitor to my garden turned to me to inquire: "Given the amount that you have now spent on renovating your dwelling, why are there no splendid buildings to be had here as evidence of this fact? How can you put up with these present desolate and unfinished circumstances?"

To this, I responded: "However fine an object, one does not treasure it unless one has created it with one's own hands; however delicious the food may be, one does not appreciate its sweetness before having oneself tasted it. Have you, sir, not seen the ancient ruins of the ponds and cloisters of Gaoyang, of Orchid Pavilion, and of Catalpa Marsh? Although such sites may well evoke in us melancholy reflections on the vicissitudes of time, they finally do not resonate within our souls. Why is this, I ask you? It is by reason of the fact that these sites contain nothing of the self within them. Often have rich men and nobles of the past summoned the carpenter to build them ponds and gardens,[23] and expended their every effort in producing ingenious conceits of various kinds, taxed their wits and tasked their imaginations. Once such gardens are complete, the master can only stand there dumbstruck, his eyes agape, accepting the congratulations of his friends. When asked about the name of a particular tree, however, the master has no reply. Why is this, I ask you again? It is by reason of the fact that such gardens also contain nothing of the self."

It is only with the man-of-letters that each stream and every rock, every pavilion and each terrace, derives from an excess of his love of learning and his profound contemplation. What is obtained thus results from his deliberate plan, and what proves less than excellent is immediately altered. His planting of trees and tending of flowers is akin to caring for the common folk; his weeding his garden is akin to the eradication of evil; his building of pavilions is akin to the setting up of a new prefecture office; his digging of moats and piling up of earth is akin to dividing the fields into registered lots. In silence does he understand the lie of the land and with inspiration does he reveal it. Sparing of expenditure, none of his endeavors is wasteful; relying solely upon his own conception, his every effort is premeditated. When the project is finally brought to a successful conclusion, it proves advantageous not just to him alone, neither does it simply bring joy to his own mind, for it serves also to testify to the assiduity in the selection of the right materials to be used and the ingenuity of conception. At present, although my exertions on my garden have not yet finished, although my expenditures on it have not yet been paid off, what is still incomplete can await another day and what remains dilapidated may yet be restored sometime in the future, for the construction

---

23   By Yuan Mei's own account, many of the initial structures in his garden were built by his household carpenter, Wu Longtai, a tall and powerfully built man whom Yuan Mei buried in the western corner of the garden upon his death in 1753. It was, as far as we know, unusual for someone not a member of the owner's family to be buried in a garden; this suggests that a warm relationship between the two men developed over the process of creating the garden.

of my garden works to no set deadline. How could this compare with my days of yore when with insignia of office at my waist I had to bow and scrape amid the noisy rabble? Mowing away the overgrown grass, pruning the dead wood from my trees, all this I do only as the desire takes me, for no longer am I under anyone's thumb. How could this compare with my days of yore when I had constantly to toady to the powerful or seek my marching orders from the important? Long ago, during the Five Dynasties period, Prince Tufa Rutan, sitting at his victory banquet in the Hall of Proclaimed Virtue, sighed: "Those who built this hall live here not, those who live here did not build it." This year I am thirty-eight years old and my intention to retire is firm. I will both build this garden and live within it, and who can tell what the future may hold?

Thereupon I composed the following solemn pledge:

> I quit this garden two years ago,
> Overworked I became, desolate the garden.
> This year I returned to my garden,
> Dense the flowers, happy am I.
> Never again will I quit this garden,
> Office it is that I will quit.
> Today I repudiate my former crime,
> Swearing never to break this pledge.

Recorded in the seventh month of the *guiyou* year [1753].

Third Record of My Garden of Accommodation

I believe that the Way of the Garden is analogous to that of learning: first one commits something to memory and then one puts it into practice, for without seeking to advance to a higher stage with one's learning and thereby to continue the achievements of one's elders, one's learning is wasted in amusement; first one reposes in learning and then one travels abroad with it, for if one does not accumulate it by day and renew it by the month, one's learning remains bound only to that which is contingent. In the hands of the pedant, learning becomes simply a matter of getting lost in the minute details of things. My learning is certainly not of this kind, for I am assiduous in acquiring it and assiduous also in taking it about, as if working always to a long-term plan. Thus it is that my ears are never free from the loud clanging and the constant rattling.[24]

---

24 Yuan Mei alludes here to poem 237 of the *Book of Songs*, which tells of the establishment of the new Zhou dynasty capital, traditionally dated 1325 BCE, and includes the lines, "Crowds brought the earth in baskets; / They threw it with shouts into the frames; / They beat it with responsive blows; / They pared the walls repeatedly, and they sounded strong." *The Chinese Classics*, vol. 4, *The She King or The Book of Poetry*, ed. and trans. James Legge (Oxford: Clarendon Press, 1893–1895), 440.

And yet, when one's learning proves insufficient, one can seek to advance it to a higher stage; the incompleteness of one's garden, however, can only be overcome through additional expenditure and at the risk to one's reputation for frugality. How then, alas, can the construction of one's garden be continued?

All of a sudden I came to the following realization: without abandoning certain things one's scholarship can make no progress. That which lies to the west does not end in the quicksands, nor does that which lies to the south end with the Southern Marchmount Heng; is this not an illustration of the fact that even the borders of empire serve to abandon as much as they include? When he established the rules of music, Kui abandoned the rites, and while concentrating on the chariot Confucius abandoned archery;[25] are these not illustrations of the fact that even learning serves to abandon as much as it encompasses? Because of Heaven's incompleteness on its own, we here on earth make great display of our buildings, even when we have barely laid three roof tiles. Mencius too has said: "Only when a man will not do some things is he capable of doing great things."[26]

So too it is with my garden. Abandoning its southern quarter I have raised not a single beam there, leaving it for the clouds and mist to dwell therein, so as to provide me with a place wherein I may wander and nurture my emptiness. Abandoning its bed-chambers, no sign of dilapidation have I sought to repair, leaving these to my wife and maidservants to dwell therein, so as to provide me with a place wherein I may wander with my eyes closed. If the undulating contour of the hill prevents the construction of a wall, my ricks of grain will be left out in the open with no earthen embankments to protect them and like the people of Daozhou Township, if I am robbed I will simply regret the loss. If the rise and fall of the land prevents the construction of halls, then I will place a measuring rod in the midst of my flat pond and in a manner similar to the chronological tables found in the Grand Historian's work, the water level will rise hor-izontally. The lifespan of a man does not match that of his buildings and my roof leaks and my timbers seep pine resin, my ridgepoles are smaller even than the gibbon's teth-ering pole, so, like Guan Zhong and Yan Ying, I can do nothing but await my demise. Without divining for a propitious day, without seeking the advice of the geomancer, I build and pull down as the whim takes me, transforming the waste land into small

---

25 *Analects* IX:2: "A man of the village of Daxiang said, 'Great indeed is the philosopher Kong! His learn-ing is extensive, and yet he does not render his name famous by any particular thing.' The Master heard the observation, and said to his disciples, 'What shall I practise? Shall I practise charioteering, or shall I prac-tise archery? I will practise charioteering.'" See *The Chinese Classics*, vol. 1, *The Confucian Analects, The Great Learning, and The Doctrine of the Mean*, ed. and trans. James Legge (Oxford: Clarendon Press, 1893–1895), 216, transliteration altered.

26 In the *Mencius* (IV:2.8) we read: "Mencius said, 'Men must be decided on what they will NOT do, and then they are able to act with vigor in what they ought to do.'" See *The Chinese Classics*, vol. 2, *The Works of Mencius* (Oxford: Clarendon Press, 1893–1895), 321; emphasis by Legge.

ponds or thickets of bamboo, and nobody will know that here I could not have erected buildings; from open lattice windows and high foundations I will capture distant vistas and everyone will suspect that the view is without end. With the short I will protect the long, with the scattered I will decorate the dense, the material I have already managed to assemble is my treasury, and with enough to eat each day, I will follow the signposts at my own pace and with no undue haste, rewarding my carpenter and commiserating with my laborers; as long as my strength remains sufficient to the task, my mind will be led on to new conceits without cease. And if this is the method of construction of a garden, so too then does it constitute the Way of Learning.

Recorded in the third month of the *dingchou* year [1757].

Fourth Record of My Garden of Accommodation

Of the desires of man, only those of the eyes are insatiable; those of the ears, the nose and the mouth are all easily satisfied. Looking upward, we contemplate, looking downward we examine, and in the process of so doing we come to an understanding of all the hidden mysteries of both Heaven and Earth. Is this sufficient to exhaust the pleasures of the eyes, however? So it was that just as the sages of old were given the hexagram "Contemplation," so too did they receive, by necessity, the trigram "Keeping Still," for the purport of this trigram is "halting."[27] "Halting, one must know the place wherein to halt," and if this is so for the orioles, then how much more is it so for man.

If it is the garden that brings pleasure to the eyes, it is also the garden that provides man with a refuge for his self. Were I to live for a hundred years, it would be the alternations of the four seasons alone that would bring pleasure to my eyes, it would be strolling about my garden and sitting down within it alone that would provide me with my refuge.

Observing my garden in its present state, mysterious and encircling, one hall appearing where another ends, refracted in the light of the mirrors, crystal-like and transparent—I become lost as I come and go here as if in a maze; the garden then is fit place for strolling. To my left sits my *qin* and calligraphy hangs above my head, all around are found ancient vessels and pieces of jade, dozens of books stand piled one on top of the other—when facing all this I find myself quite unrestrained and transported far away; the garden then is fit place for sitting. High towers protect me from the west, a limpid stream circles about, ten thousand bamboos like a sea of green—no fear have I of sunstroke; the garden then is fit place for summer. Behind windows inlaid with colored glass, I can view the snow from my seat and remain sheltered from the draft; the garden then is fit place for winter. A hundred flowering apricot trees, a dozen or so thickets of cassia, casting dappled shadows under the moonlight and spreading their fragrance in the breeze; the garden then is fit place for passing

---

27   Hexagrams 20 (*guan* 觀) and 52 (*gen* 艮) of the *Book of Changes*.

both spring and autumn. One covered walkway leads on to another and even thunder and lightning followed by the wind cannot stay my feet within the garden; the garden then is fit place during storms. Just one of these fitnesses on its own would bring pleasure to one's heart; how much more so when they are all combined in the one place?

When I first obtained this garden, my conception of it was nowhere as ambitious as its present state. For the past twenty years we have been "associated in cultivating the land, together clearing and opening up this territory," and this garden gives evidence of both that which I have rejected and the success of that which I have created. As the "ridgepole has now been hoisted into place, what more needs to be added?" Having grown old and exchanged my robes of office for the garb of the peasant, I will strum my *qin* here within my garden, playing the airs of former kings, for cannot this also be sufficient in itself? Although among those that follow me here there will also be some that will work upon my garden, to them however will remain simply the tasks of watering the plants and maintaining the plaster on the walls. They must certainly not change anything of the design of my garden! It will also be fitting for them to write essays and poems about the successful completion of this garden, naming its various parts, in imitation of Wang Wei's Wangchuan estate.

Recorded in the third month of the *bingxu* year [1766].

Fifth Record of the Garden of Accommodation

When ambition exceeds talent, the result is happiness, while more talent than ambition leads to unhappiness. Although my own aspirations are limited, I have somehow always managed to achieve more than was expected of me. In my official career I would have happily served as director of education in some prefecture or other, yet somehow I attained the magistracy of an entire district. For my family estate ten head of cattle would have sufficed, yet I now own a hundred *mu* of land. A single shed would have been quite adequate for my garden, and yet here I have this place, about which I have written no less than four records, and every part of which has been named and had its praises sung in turn. When I privately evaluate my desires, I find that I have exceeded them. Against all expectations, the past few years have seen me exceed even my excesses.

Some thirty years have passed since I quit the banks of West Lake, but my home is never far from my thoughts. When attending to my garden, I amuse myself by modelling its layout on that of the lake. I have built embankments and wells, an Inner and an Outer Lake, a Flower Harbor, Six Bridges, and a Northern and a Southern Peak. At construction time I never fail to wonder: Is it difficult for man to succeed in imitating that which has been created by Heaven? And is the fact that I have, but for a few loose ends, succeeded with the task, due to the strength of my abilities, or simply the result of the years of my devotion? With luck, this year will finally see the task completed.

How truly outstanding! Were I to live in my old hometown, I would never be able to spend all my days lakeside, away from the house. But here, I can live at home while never leaving the lake, and live away from my hometown, while at the same time *never* being away from it. I consider myself most fortunate, but on reflection I wonder whether it has not all been the result of excessive greed. And so, I consult the *Book of Changes*, and find that the "Grace" Hexagram (six in the fifth place) reads:

> Grace in hills and gardens.
> The roll of silk is meager and small.
> Humiliation, but in the end good fortune.[28]

Wang Bi's commentary adds that "to adorn objects is to damage them; but to adorn hills and gardens—fortune is not greater than this." This is to say that hills and gardens, being the places in which plants and trees are born, are in essence, places of purity. Thus even if one were to decorate these places with rolls of silk, the humiliation would eventually give way to good fortune. The *Zuo Commentary* recounts the story of a man who "Plays an air of his country, showing that he has not forgotten his roots."[29] Although my desire knows no bounds, I am nevertheless able to live in accordance with the *Changes,* while "playing an air" of my own hometown. Perhaps this will allow me to avoid the censure of superior men!

Those men of former times who decorated their vermilion doors and plastered their magnificent gates, would build properties but not live in their creations, or else live in them for but a fleeting moment. I, on the other hand, have lived here night and day for the past twenty years. I have busied myself not only with the unceasing affairs of pavilions and terraces, but also planted with my own hand the trees which I now see sprouting and growing before me, shading the cattle as they stretch up toward the heavens. To see every moment of the lives of one's sons and grandsons as they progress from infancy to adulthood, and then from adulthood to old age, is something that no man can even hope for. How fortunate I have been by comparison! Although I know that thus is the way of the plants and the trees, I know too that there will be those following me who cannot reach this understanding.

Recorded in the third month of the *wuzi* year [1768].

---

28   "Grace" (*bi* 賁) is Hexagram 22 in the *Book of Changes* (*Yijing*). The translation used here is that of Richard Wilhelm, *The I Ching*, 93.

29   The passage quoted by Yuan Mei (from Duke Cheng, 9th Year) reads: "The Duke repeated this conversation to Fan Wenzi, who said, 'That prisoner of Chu is a superior man. He told you of the office of his father, showing that he is not ashamed of his origin. He played an air of his country, showing that he has not forgotten his old associations.... His not being ashamed of his origin shows the man's virtue; his not forgetting his old associations, his good faith,'" *The Chinese Classics*, vol. 5, *The Ch'un Ts'ew, with the Tso Chuan*, ed. and trans. James Legge (Oxford: Clarendon Press, 1893–1895), 369–71, transliteration altered.

Sixth Record of My Garden of Accommodation

In the *History of the Jin* we read that the Grand Guardian Wang Xiang claimed there to be two different conventions to be followed as far as burials are concerned; the first is to return a person to their native place for burial, while the second is to undertake an accommodated burial wherever the person happened to have been when they died. Only having read this did I become aware of the full and timely purport of this word "accommodation," for it does not refer simply to the place where "the superior man at nightfall may go indoors for rest and recuperation," as the *Book of Changes* has it.[30]

My late and much revered father died in Jiangning and long have I wished to return him to his home in the old town of Hangzhou for burial, having been dissuaded from doing so only by thoughts of the difficulties involved in having his coffin transported there. Difficult too, it seemed, an accommodated burial here at this place for I worried that my garden contained no appropriate site for a sarcophagus. Thus it is that for the past seventeen years I have prevaricated over my father's entombment. Remembering that the custom of the ancients was that one did not doff the sackcloth and ashes of mourning before having buried one's parents, I feel myself, in trepidation, to be far less than a man.

In the spring of this present year a geomancer paid me a visit and he divined that there was a site to the west of my garden that could serve as a most propitious burial ground. Upon hearing this, I immediately took myself off to have a look, and indeed, here the veins of Little Granary Hill flatten out and stretch into the far distance. To both left and right stand ridges that resemble clay pots stacked one on top of another, and gently sloping banks. The grasses and trees grow luxuriantly, and if one sealed the place up as a vault it would truly form an appropriate grave. For twenty years then, I thought, I have possessed the right site, but only now, all of a sudden, have I become aware of it. Perhaps it is the spirit of my departed father that has summoned me to this spot?

Thereupon I invited my good mother to join me and on the sixteenth day of the twelfth month of the *yichou* year [1769], we had my father's coffin carried here and interred. As the vault is a mere hundred paces from my garden, the feathers that decorate its walls will remain in place undisturbed, and regularly will I be able to come here to weed the grave, water the trees that grow besides it, and to care for the gravestone. I am a poor scholar and when I was young my late father served as secretary throughout the Chu and Yue regions, while I went off to the capital to pursue my studies. Father and son were thus often apart. Now, by reason of this single garden of mine, my late father who was placed here to await his burial, who has been sacrificed to here in timely fashion, here too will finally be placed within his sepulchre. Thus will father and son never again be separated for a single day. How could to do so be enforced upon me by

---

30   See Wilhelm, *The I Ching*, 72.

circumstances, for acting thus is also to do no more than to accommodate myself to the lie of the land and to give in to the wishes of my heart.

Beside the vault is found a small patch of flat land and here, in imitation of the practice of Sikong Tu of old, I will build my own tomb while I am still alive. Soon I will plant flowering apricot and pine, and with my students and friends I will repair here to compose poetry and to drink. Why will I do this? So that the son may accommodate himself to his father. The gravesite will be divided into two so that in future the gulf between them may be bridged. Why will I do this? So that the wife may accommodate herself to her husband. At the foot of my grave I will leave several places for removable wooden boards. Why will I do this? So that one's concubines may accommodate themselves to one's wife. Bordering the west of the vault a high mound rises sharply and here my servants and retainers and maidservants will be gathered and buried as they die. Why will I do this? So that my servants may accommodate themselves to their master.

Ah! The ancients considered building a hut beside the grave of one's parents to be an expression of filial piety, constructing one's own tomb while still alive to be an expression of perspicacity, and burying one's dogs and horses to be an expression of benevolence. By reason of this single garden of mine, I can now lay claim to the reputation of having fulfilled all three of these precepts. Truly, what I have done here represents a total transformation of the fashion of the garden, both ancient and modern, and the full and timely purport of this word "accommodation" extends even from life to death, from day to night. Its ability to show things to their best advantage can be said to be great indeed, all-encompassing and exhaustive. Especially as it is likely that no record of this fact will in future be made, I cannot but record it here.

Recorded in the fifth month of the *gengyin* year [1770].

"A Record of the Garden of the Master of the Fishing Nets" (*Wangshi yuan ji* 網師園記)

QIAN DAXIN 錢大昕 (1728–1804)
TRANSLATED BY DUNCAN M. CAMPBELL

Qian Daxin, from Jiading in Jiangsu Province, was one of the most important historians of the Qing dynasty, with a particular interest in genealogical research (among many other things, including mathematics and epigraphy). In 1789, after a full and largely successful official career, Qian was appointed director of the Purple Light Academy in Suzhou, where he had studied as a young man. He remained there until his death. The academy was behind the Pavilion for Revering the Canon and within the Prefectural School in the south of the city, just a short walk away from the Garden of the Master of the Fishing Nets, and we can assume from his account of the garden that Qian spent many hours there.

Qian's record, dated 1795, is the most important traditional account of this celebrated garden. The history of this site as a garden, as found partially told here, is lengthy but full of lacunae, characterized, as far as can now be known, by frequent changes of both ownership and name, and by the unceasing and asymmetrical processes of inevitable deterioration and fitful repair. We know the name that was given it by its putative first owner during the Southern Song dynasty (1127–1279), Fisherman's Retreat, but although we know also that the garden then contained a remarkable private library and that it could be entered by boat by way of Rape-Turnip Stream, we have no description of the garden itself.

The various associations in this first name given to the garden, with the image of the fisherman, that quintessential symbol of the wisdom and rectitude of the recluse, are returned to throughout the garden's history. Such associations are invoked, for instance, in the garden's present name, coined by Song Zongyuan (1710–1779) when he restored the garden sometime in the 1760s, and are embodied in the netlike latticework of the garden windows. It is from that period—the second phase of the garden's development—that it began to acquire the literary representations so critical to its lasting reputation. One such account, entitled "An Explanation of the Garden of the Master of the Fishing Nets" and written by Song's brother-in-law Peng Qifeng (1701–1784), informs us that the garden was designed in order that Song could retire from office and care for his elderly mother, but that "once she had died and he had completed his mourning period, he returned to the capital, to be appointed to the Tianjin Circuit; thus ensnared again in the conduct of the emperor's affairs, he became neglectful of the joys of field and garden!" It is also from this period, apparently, that the garden began to acquire that other vital form of representation, the pictorial, as we can see from the "Record of the Painting of the Garden of the Master of the Fishing Nets" by another frequent visitor, the eminent official and poet Shen Deqian (1673–1769). Although the painting commissioned by Song Zongyuan appears not to have survived, the record itself provides us a glimpse of the garden and its master.

> Before he had reached his fiftieth year, however, because the age of his mother weighed upon his mind, he drifted home. Sometime earlier, while he was still serving in office, he had ordered his family to build chambers and construct halls on the site of the Potager of the Master of the Fishing Nets of old. With its tower and its belvedere, its terraces and its pavilion, its pool and embankment and pond and barge, the site was now named Retreat of the Master of the Garden of the Fishing Nets and poems were composed about its Twelve Scenes, all in readiness for the banqueting and entertainment of his mother. Now, finally, reality tallied with his fondest wishes, and once he had returned home he would spend his days "strolling the terraces and plucking the orchids"[31] and crossing the waves to trap the carp, all in order to provide for his mother's morning meals and evening suppers. Whenever the day happened to dawn bright and clear, he

---

31   This is a reference to one of the six songs (entitled *Nan'gai* 南陔) traditionally believed to have been lost from the *Book of Songs*; Legge provides the following note: "According to 'the Little Preface,' the subject of the *Nan'gai* was—'Filial sons admonishing one another on the duty of supporting their parents.'" See *The Chinese Classics*, vol. 4, *The She King or The Book of Poetry*, ed. and trans. James Legge (Oxford: Clarendon Press, 1893–1895), 267, transliteration altered.

would accompany her to Fishing Studio, and the two of them, she leaning upon her staff, would circumambulate the twisting paths to their mutual enjoyment. Very occasionally he would summon his good friends to a banquet of wine and poetry.[32]

Another visitor to the garden was the local man of letters Qian Yong (1759–1844; see chapter 7), who offers the following glimpse into the garden:

> Qu's Garden: Qu's Garden occupies the former site of Master Song's Garden of the Master of the Fishing Nets, as expanded by Qu Yuancun of Jiading County, being only several dozen paces away to the east from the old mansion of Shen Deqian, the former Chief Minister of the Court of Imperial Sacrifices. During the fourth month of the *wuyin* year of the reign of the Jiaqing emperor [1818], I visited the garden along with Fan Laizong, Pan Yijun, and Wu Xiongguang in order to view the blooming herbaceous peonies. So splendid proved the flowers that they could rival even those of the Tower of the Five Bay Carpenter's Square of Yangzhou. Fan Laizong wrote a poem on the occasion that included the couplet:
>
> > A flurry of carriages of those come here to view the flowers,
> > Who now, one asks, bothers to visit the Chief Minister's former home?
>
> The garden has now reverted to a Master Wu of Tiandu.[33]

In brief, the life of the garden after Qu Yuancun's death was equally marked by frequent changes of ownership and design (and occasionally, of name). By 1818, as noted by Qian Yong above, the garden had been acquired by Wu Jiadao; fifty years later, it was in the possession of Li Hongyi (1831–1885) and had been renamed Neighboring Su in the East, in reference to the first owner of the nearby Canglang Pavilion. Another fifty years later, in 1907, the garden was acquired by the Bannerman Dagui (b. 1860). A decade later again, it was bought by General Zhang Zuolin (1873–1928), the "Mukden Tiger," as a gift to his teacher, Zhang Xiluan (1843–1922), although he never lived there. During the 1930s, the garden and its attached residence were rented out to Ye Gongchuo (1881–1968), the calligrapher and educator, and bore the name Garden of Idleness. Also living there for several years, before the encroaching war forced them to flee, were the famous painter of tigers Zhang Shanzi (1882–1940) and his even more famous artist brother Chang Dai-chien (Zhang Daqian, 1899–1983), along with their pet tiger. In 1940, the garden was acquired by its last private owner, the eminent collector He Cheng (1880–1946), before, finally, when his descendants proved unable to maintain the property, it was given into the care of the municipal authorities.

In the 1970s, when Chen Congzhou (1918–2000), the late doyen of contemporary Chinese garden historians, was consulted about the best design for the Metropolitan Museum of Art's

---

32   Shen Deqian, "*Wangshiyuan tuji,*" in Shao Zhong and Li Jin, eds., *Suzhou lidai mingyuan ji: Suzhou yuanlin chongxiu ji* (蘇州歷代名園記：蘇州園林重修記) (Beijing: Zhongguo linye chubanshe, 2004), 197.

33   Qian Yong, *Lüyuan conghua* (Beijing: Zhonghua shuju, 1979), 526.

proposed Astor Chinese Garden Court, he suggested that one particular section, the Late Spring Abode in the western section of Fishing Nets, be chosen for replication in New York.[34] Chen Congzhou, whose earliest major publication was the first post-1949 monograph on the gardens of Suzhou,[35] was especially familiar with the Garden of the Master of the Fishing Nets, having been a frequent visitor in the 1930s. Indeed, after the garden had been made over to the state in 1950 and, occupied for a while by the military, had fallen into such a state of dilapidation that it was threatened with conversion into a factory, it was Chen Congzhou who argued for its restoration so that it could be opened to the general public, as eventually happened in 1958.

"A Record of the Garden of the Master of the Fishing Nets"

The ancients built gardens as places to grow fruit trees, established plots in order to plant their vegetables. Thus, wherever the word "garden" is mentioned in the three hundred poems of the *Book of Songs*, the context is of "... the peach trees in the garden," "... the jujube trees in the garden," and "Do not come leaping into my garden; / Do not break my sandal trees." Such gardens were certainly not designed simply to provide beauty for the indulgence of visitors. From the Han and Wei dynasties onward, however, stately tours of the Western Garden became all the rage and constituted the very grandest of affairs.

At the same time, the gentry too began to develop their own family gardens, within which they displayed the flowers and the rocks that they had collected and competed endlessly with each other in the extravagance of their predilections. By the Song dynasty, the first record of such gardens was written, this being Li Gefei's "Record of the Celebrated Gardens of Luoyang," an account that circulated widely within the world of letters. From this circumstance, we can see that the splendors of pavilion and terrace, tree and rock, all need to await the relaxed appreciation of famous men as they banquet amid them, before they are embodied in the poems and essays produced on such occasions and thus passed on from one age to another. If this were not in fact the case, then it would be as if that story about Gu Pijiang expelling guests was simply intended to provide later men with the occasion for scorn.[36]

---

34 For an account of the process of this "transplantation," see Alfreda Murck and Wen Fong, "A Chinese Garden Court: The Astor Court at the Metropolitan Museum of Art," *The Metropolitan Museum of Art Bulletin* 38, no. 3 (1980–1981); and Alfreda Murck and Wen Fong, *A Chinese Garden Court: The Astor Court at the Metropolitan Museum of Art* (New York: The Metropolitan Museum of Art, 1980).

35 *The Gardens of Suzhou* (*Suzhou yuanlin* 蘇州園林) (Shanghai: Tongji Daxue, 1956).

36 The "Rudeness and Arrogance" chapter of the *New Account of Tales of the World* contains the following story: "Once when Wang Xianzhi was passing through Wu Commandery on his way from Guiji [Zhejiang], he heard that Gu Pijiang had a famous garden there. Although he had previously never been acquainted with the owner, he went directly to his house. It happened that Gu was just then entertaining guests and friends with food and drink, but Wang wandered about at will through the garden, and, when he had finished, pointed around to indicate its good and bad features, just as if no one else were present. Gu, suddenly losing his patience, said, 'To be inconsiderate of one's host is impolite, but to presume on one's noble birth to be insolent toward others is downright immoral. Anyone who fails on both counts isn't even fit to be classified as a northern boor!'

Suzhou is an important and populous town and within its walls the mansions stand densely crammed together, as if rubbing shoulders with each other and all but tripping over one another. Only in the southeastern corner of the town, nestled against the wall and overlooking the river, do the trees grow dense. Here one is struck by the half-rustic air of the place. Just to the south of City Belt Bridge stands the former site of the Hall of the Ten Thousand Fascicles[37] once owned by Master Shi Zhengzhi of the Song,[38] within sight of both South Garden[39] and Canglang Pavilion. The lane that leads to this site is called Master of the Fishing Nets [Wangshi] but its original name had been the close homophone Wishing Debts [Wangsi].[40]

Thirty years ago now the site was acquired by Master Song Zongyuan to build his villa, with a view to retiring here. He took the name Master of the Fishing Nets both for himself and for his garden, thus giving expression of his desire for rustic reclusion and picking up also upon the sound of the original name of the lane along which his garden was found. After his death his garden daily fell into rack and ruin and more than half of its once fine trees and ancient rocks either disappeared or were damaged. Only the pond remained, as clear and as pure as it had been at an earlier age.

Master Qu Yuancun happened by the site one day and, anxious lest the garden become completely overgrown, he heaved a deep sigh. Upon enquiry at the neighboring property, he discovered that the then owner of the garden just happened to be seeking a buyer for it, whereupon Qu immediately acquired it. Working in accordance with the garden's original design but creating also new structures, Qu piled up the rocks to form artificial mountains and planted out some trees, all in an appropriate manner, increasing the number of pavilions and kiosks, and thus transforming the old into the new. Once the work had been completed, he summoned four or five of us fellow scholars to join him for an all-day banquet.

And with that he drove Wang's attendants out the gate. Wang, alone in the sedan chair, was turning this way and that [looking for his attendants]. Gu, observing that the attendants after a long time had still not returned, later ordered someone to escort Wang outside the gate. Through it all Wang remained carefree and unconcerned." Liu I-ch'ing (Liu Yiqing), *Shih-shuo Hsin-yü: A New Account of Tales of the World*, trans. Richard B. Mather (Minneapolis: University of Minnesota Press, 1976), 430–31, transliteration altered.

37   According to an account of this garden given by the Yuan dynasty scholar Lu Youren in his *Former Happenings in Wu (Wuzhong jiushi* 吳中舊事), this library comprised forty-two large bookcases arranged in a circle, the majority of which contained manuscripts that had been acquired initially by weight as scrap paper.

38   Shi Zhengzhi, who served as Governor of Nanjing and Admiral of the Yangtze River, was the author of an important early work on the chrysanthemum, dated 1175 and entitled *Old Master Shi's Catalogue of Cultivated Chrysanthemums (Shilao pu ju pu* 史老圃菊譜).

39   In his *Six Records of a Floating Life*, Shen Fu provides a delightful account of a visit to South Garden (see below in this chapter).

40   *Wangsi* is literally "princely wishes" or "thoughts of a prince"; the translation is chosen to keep the close homophone with "fishing nets." In Suzhou dialect, which makes little or no distinction between "s" and "sh," the homophone would be closer than in Mandarin.

The stone-paved paths twist and turn, as if leading elsewhere but actually turning back upon themselves; the rippling surface of the pond seems so vast as to stretch beyond the furthermost horizon. Here are to be found two halls, one of which is named "Mountain Hut of the Flowering Apricot and the Iron Stone" and the other "Study of the Recluse's Cassia Woods";⁴¹ a belvedere named "Waterside Belvedere for Washing One's Cap Strings"; and a chamber for idle sitting named "Lodge for Treading Upon Harmony." In the middle of the pond stands a pavilion named "The Moon Rises as the Wind Stirs"⁴² and another upon the cliff, named "Ridge of Cloud." An obliquely angled study named "Bamboo Branch Beyond"⁴³ and a studio named "Emptiness Gathered,"⁴⁴ too, have been constructed. Every single one of these structures was fashioned by the eye and drawn by the hand of Qu Yuancun himself, and he named each and every one of them himself as well. The land area of the garden is no more than a couple of *mu* but nonetheless the garden seems to embody the delight of an endless circularity, and although the dwelling stands close to the marketplace it manages yet to convey a sense of the forgetful pleasures of the clouds and the rivers.⁴⁵ It is as if this garden contains, therefore, both the "expanse and spaciousness of the open view" and the "hidden mysteries" spoken of by the Tang man-of-letters Liu Zongyuan as constituting the two modes of travel.⁴⁶ At the same time, although the garden is no longer as it was in the past, by retaining the name "Master of the Fishing Nets," its present master has attended appropriately to the past of the site.

I remember once, when reading the rhapsody on Master Ren Hui's garden in Lu Guimeng's *Pine Ridge Collection*, coming across the lines:

41   This name alludes to some lines from Liu An's (d. 122 BCE, also known as the Prince of Huainan and Xiaoshan 小山, "Little Mountain") poem "Summons for a Recluse" (*Zhao yinshi* 招隱士): "The cassia trees grow thick / In the mountain's recesses, / Twisting and snaking, / Their branches interlacing." See *The Songs of the South: An Ancient Chinese Anthology*, trans. David Hawkes (Oxford: Clarendon Press, 1959), 119.

42   This name appears to derive from a couplet in a poem by the Tang dynasty scholar Han Yu (768–824), entitled "Twenty-One Poems Presented to Supervising Secretary Liu, Prefect of Guo Prefecture, to Rhyme with the Newly Written Poems on the Three Halls, with Attached Preface: North Tower" (*Fenghe Guozhou Liu jishi shijun santang xinti ershiyi yong bingxu: Beilou* 奉和虢州劉給事使君三堂新題二十一詠並序: 北樓): "As the hue of the evening brings with it the autumn, / A strong wind speeds on the moon" (晚色將秋至 / 長風送月來).

43   A couplet from a poem entitled "Rhyming with Qin Guan's Poem on the Flowering Apricot" (*He Qin Taixu meihua* 和秦太虛梅花) by the Song dynasty poet Su Shi (1037–1101) goes: "Upon river bank, in a thousand trees, spring begins to darken, / Beyond the bamboos a single branch sticks out, more beautiful for its slant" (江頭千樹春欲闇 / 竹外一枝斜更好).

44   This name alludes to a section from the "In the World of Men" (人間世) chapter of the *Zhuangzi*: "Confucius said, 'Make your will one! Don't listen with your ears, listen with your spirit. Listening stops with the ears, the mind stops with recognition, but spirit is empty and waits on all things. The Way gathers in emptiness alone. Emptiness is the fasting of the mind.'" *The Complete Works of Chuang Tzu*, trans. Burton Watson (New York: Columbia University Press, 1968), 57–58.

45   As it exists today, Fishing Nets covers an area of approximately one acre.

46   See Liu Zongyuan's (773–819) celebrated "Eastern Mound by Longxing Temple of Yongzhou" in chapter 2.

The pond's visage appears both bland and ancient,
And the atmosphere of the trees is luxuriant and secluded.
If you wish to know where is found the best scenery,
Here within Ren's estate you will find it gathered.

I was so overwhelmed by what I had read that I found myself wandering, in spirit, through the garden itself. Today, within this present garden, I have actually encountered that scene as described in the poem. Although I cannot lay claim to the poetical talents of either a Lu Guimeng or a Pi Rixiu, yet both Qu Yuancun's profound emotions and his refined tastes seem superior even to those of Ren Hui, and thus have I felt compelled to make this record of his garden, as a continuation of their "Two Tours" in order that contemporaries be not over-anxious that they are not the equal of the ancients.[47]

The Pleasure-Boats of Yangzhou (*Yangzhou huafang lu* 揚州畫舫錄)

"Record of the Northern Suburbs (Middle Part): New Town" (*Xincheng beilu zhong* 新城北錄中; extract), "Record of the West of the City" (*Chengxi lu* 城西錄; extract), "Record of Rainbow Bridge: First Part" (*Hongqiao lu shang* 虹橋錄上; extract), "Record of West of the Bridge" (*Qiaoxi lu* 橋西錄; extract), and "Record of West of the Ridge" (*Gangxi lu* 岡西錄; extract)

LI DOU 李斗 (D. 1817)
TRANSLATED BY LUCIE OLIVOVÁ

For more than thirty years, between 1764 and 1795, the poet and dramatist Li Dou, an otherwise officially somewhat unsuccessful native of Yangzhou, kept a record of the sites and scenes of this most remarkable of eighteenth-century Chinese cities, taking "place" as the warp of his book, and "personalities and events" as its weft. In its heyday, with its extraordinary wealth based on its location (close to the confluence of Grand Canal and the Yangtze River and at the heart of the richest agricultural area) and its monopoly on the salt trade, the city briefly became the cultural trendsetter for such aspects of fine living as painting and calligraphy, garden design, opera, and cuisine, "its scholars spending their days writing," we are told in the preface to the work written by Li Dou's fellow townsman Ruan Yuan (1764–1849), the finest classicist of the age, "and its folk spending their days becoming ever richer."

The Southern Tours of both the Kangxi and Qianlong emperors served to acknowledge and promote the wealth and importance of the city; Kangxi visited Yangzhou during four of his six Southern Tours, having only passed through the city on the other two occasions, whereas his grandson, Qianlong, stayed in Yangzhou on both the outward and the return legs of all six of his Southern Tours.

---

47 Having visited the gardens of both Ren Hui and Xu Xiuju, Pi Rixiu wrote poems to thank his hosts, these poems becoming known collectively as the "Two Tours." When Lu Guimeng came across copies of these poems, he responded to them with a set of his own poems, one of which is cited above.

One entry in Li Dou's book writes of the Tower of the Five Bay Carpenter's Square where, it was believed, Yangzhou's finest herbaceous peonies were to be found.

The Tower of the Five Bay Carpenter's Square is found upon the slopes of the southwestern corner of the Lake of Nine Curves. The main gate of the garden is to be found to the north of Ballista Rock Bridge road. Just inside the gate stands a courtyard of three bays; to the west is the Thatched Hall of the Eighteen Peaks, to the east, the Pavilion for Receiving the Mountains, to the east of which, in turn, stands the Tower of the Five Bay Carpenter's Square, behind which there is an apothecary. As Yellow Mountain has Eighteen Peaks and as the owners of this garden, the Wang family, when they were still living in their hometown in the foothills of Yellow Mountain, had owned a hall named after these peaks, they chose a hall within this garden to also bear this name. . . . The Pavilion for Receiving the Mountains is in the midst of a grove of bamboo, its plaque in the calligraphy of Liang Xian. The rooms that lined each side of the gallery abutted each other and were connected by continuous rafters. One entered the Tower of the Five Bay Carpenter's Square by means of a small gallery that led off from the midst of the bamboo. The tower comprised nine bays, five facing the north, and another four facing east. As the fifth bay facing north was set up against the mountain, connected to the first of the bays facing east, the number of bays facing east was the same as those facing north. As the proportions of the bays did not differ in the slightest, the structure was named the Tower of the Five Bay Carpenter's Square because that was what it resembled in shape, and its design was based on the model of the nine-bay buildings found in the capital.[48]

In his 1794 preface to this book, the seventy-eight-year-old Yuan Mei laments that "Alas, having grown old and frail, I regret that I cannot often travel to Yangzhou to gaze upon its splendors, although I am separated from it by no more than a single belt of water. . . . With this book in hand, however, I can view such sights from my bed, from which circumstance I now know that sitting idly at home reading a book is a far superior course of action to touring around astride a crane." When the city was captured by the forces of the Qing in 1645, Yangzhou had been the site of a massacre, and in 1853 its golden age was brought to a sudden end when it was captured by the Taiping, whose rebellion had also served to destroy Yuan Mei's garden in Nanjing, one hundred years after his death.

"Record of the Northern Suburbs (Middle Part): New Town" (extract)

The Residence of Heavenly Happiness stands right on Heavenly Tranquility Ceremonial Archway corner. Flower markets take place here. Originally, flower markets took place at the Dhyana Wisdom Monastery, or that is what the gazetteers state. However, in his "Treatise on the Herbaceous Peony," the Song dynasty scholar Wang Guan wrote that "All Yangzhou people, rich or poor, plant flowers. Each dawn, there is

---

48   Li Dou, *Yangzhou huafang lu* (Beijing: Zhonghua shuju, 2001), 362.

a flower market by Kaiming Bridge." Anyhow, both the Dhyana Wisdom Monastery, outside the city walls, and the Kaiming Bridge, downtown, were places where flower markets used to be held. But in recent years flower gardens have proliferated: at Flowering Apricot Hill, Beside the Flowers Village, Fortress, Little Mount Mao, and Thunder Dike. Each morning, the peddlers enter the city walls and sell their flowers in the marketplaces.

On the Festive Day of the Flowers [the 15th day of the 8th lunar month], a Hundred Flowers Fair is held at the gate of Licentiate Zhang's house. Celebrated species from all the suburban villages are gathered here. The licentiate's name is Xisui (Yinyuan). He excels in the sword dance and is therefore nicknamed Fencer Zhang. He is also good at trimming flowers. His flowering apricot bonsais are equal to those of Licentiate Yao Zhitong, and Magistrate Geng Tianbao. These three men are called "The three flowering apricot blossom trimmers." Zhang Qiren, Bearded Liu Shisan, and the Daoist Wu Songshan, all of whom learned the art from them, continue the tradition. Zhang Xisui has a son whose name is Zhang Jushou (Rencui) who calls himself "Old Mountain." He is poor, true, but he excels in poetry.

"Record of the West of the City" (extract)

At the beginning of this present dynasty, Zheng Xiaru[49] resigned and returned to Retirement Garden.[50] The garden lies by the river bridge. It was once owned by the Zhu family, who grew violet-cress here. The garden is fifty *mu* wide, and gives onto the south.

Behind the Zheng family residence, there is a street sheltered with roofing. It runs steeply down. At the end of the slope, follow a footpath. At the end of the footpath, enter the gate. This is the gate to Retirement Garden.

Just inside the gate are the residences. At the back, there are the Embodiment of Flowers Pavilion, the Scholar-Tree Studio, the Green Hermitage, and the Tower Where the Heart Halts. Inside the garden, there are still more wondrous sites: the Empty Sky Hill Gazebo, the Stamen Tower, the Pouring Green Hill Chamber, the Sound of the

---

49 Xiaru was the youngest of the Zheng brothers. In his generation, this prominent family split and each brother built his own garden residence: the eldest, Zheng Yuansi, owned the Wang family garden (*Wangjia yuan* 王家園); the second son, Zheng Yuanxun, owned the Garden of Reflections (*Yingyuan* 影園), on which see chapter 6; and the third son, Zheng Yuanhua, owned the Garden of the Fine Trees (*Jiashu yuan* 嘉樹園). Zheng Xiaru passed the first level of the civil service examinations in 1639, but having not succeeded at the higher level, retired to live in Retirement Garden.

50 Retirement Garden was a fine example of the new style of Yangzhou garden. Li Dou never himself visited the place, however, and based his account on Song Jiesan's "Record of Retirement Garden" (*Xiuyuan ji* 休園記), written for the Jiaqing edition of the Yangzhou gazetteer. This explains the lack of detailed description in his text.

Qin, the Golden Goose Studio, the Triple Peak Thatched Cottage, the Speaking Stone Lookout, the Ink Pond, the Profound Glory Garrison Calligraphy Studio, the Clarity Cherishing Villa, the Fixed Boat, the Terrace Where Cranes Come, the Nine Flower Entrenchment, the Fragrance of Antiquity Studio, the Easy-Going Vegetable Plot, the House Where One Reaches the Moon, the Flower Isle, the Flower Spring Surrounded by Clouds, the Gazebo of the Jade Reflection, the Waveless Navigation, the Flowing Pillow, the City Forest, the Garden Hermitage, and the Floating Blue.

In the garden, originals by Wen Zhenmeng,[51] Xu Yuanwen,[52] and Dong Xiangguang[53] are kept. Below the Tower Where the Heart Halts, there is the Beautiful Maiden Rock. Behind it, a five-hundred-year-old palm tree grows. A python lives in the Ink Pond. By the Terrace Where Cranes Come, many herbs are grown.

The owner's son, Zheng Weiguang, compiled a "Retirement Garden Gazetteer" in several fascicles.

"Record of Rainbow Bridge: First Part" (extract)

A local old man Zhou once had a field of a few *mu*, with a small domicile of only a few bays' width. It lay next to the garden of the Bewitching Spring Poetic Society.[54] When a certain Mr. Tian sought to buy it for cash, he would not sell, resolving to become a gardener in his own garden and to plant flowers and raise fish. His son, Kouzi, mastered Ye Meifu's method of planting chrysanthemums, regarded then as the ultimate technique.[55]

For this garden, there were entrance tickets, three inches long and two inches wide. They were printed on a colored, decorative paper. On the top was printed the year, the month and the date when the gardener would sweep the paths and open up the gates, and along the border of the ticket was stamped "The Thatched Cottage West of Rainbow Bridge."[56]

---

51 Wen Zhenmeng (1574–1636), grandson of the painter Wen Zhengming, was a high official and fine calligrapher.

52 Xu Yuanwen (1634–1691), another fine calligrapher, was the younger brother of the poet and painter Xu Qianxue, author of "A Record of the Garden that Borders upon Greenness".

53 Dong Qichang (Xiangguang; 1555–1636) was an important painter and calligrapher of the Ming dynasty.

54 This garden lay by the southern abutment of the Rainbow Bridge, and was named after a poem by Wang Shizhen (1634–1711). It was here that Wang Shizhen organized the "Rainbow Bridge literary gatherings" between 1662 and 1664, while serving as a magistrate in Yangzhou.

55 Ye Meifu, written about elsewhere by Li Dou, passed the first degree examinations, but then devoted himself to growing chrysanthemum species; they were especially admired for their diverse range of colors.

56 Although not clearly stated here, it must be assumed that the tickets were commemorative rather than receipts of an entrance fee, as is common today.

"Record of West of the Bridge" (extract)

The Depth of Spring on the Flowering Apricot Peak, or the Peak of Eternal Spring is the name of a site on a ridge that protrudes out of the central ridge of Shugang into the middle of Lake Baozhang.[57] In the *dingchou* year [1757], Master Cheng laid out the empty ground, planting trees there in three circuits. Above the upper one, he built a shrine to honor the god Duke Guan. He created a pier made of piled-up stones in front of the shrine and built the Jade-Decking Bridge on its left, and the Thatched Cottage on the Peak on its right. Behind the cottage, he constructed a path leading up to the peak. In the middle of the site, he built a Guanyin Hall. He planted many flowering apricot trees on the top of the peak, and constructed six square arbors there. Additionally, he constructed a small structure, just three bays wide, on the western side of the peak, and named it the Fishing Islet. Master Cheng's full name was Cheng Zhiquan (Yuanheng). He was the elder brother of Cheng Wuqiao. He had been developing the Flowering Apricot Peak for three years, but the work had still not been completed, even though he had spent two hundred thousand on it. Then one night, he dreamed that the Duke Guan had revealed to him how to survey the ground. He used the method and, within ten days, the site was built.

Later, the site became the property of Mr. Yu. Yu Xi (Cixiu) is a good poet, and an excellent calligrapher. It was he who inscribed the stone tablet with the name of the site: "The Depth of Spring on the Flowering Apricot Peak." This inscription was placed on the wall gate, on the western side of the peak. On the mountain, there lives a monk named Pingchuan, originally from Huai'an. He has an honest, simple nature. He has lived there for thirty years or so. The younger brother of Yu Xi is called Yu Zhao (Guanwu). He too is skilled in poetry.

The peak stands in the middle of the lake, and the footbridge leading to it is the Jade-Decking Bridge. On this bridge, a square arbor has been constructed; its pillars, balustrade, and even roof tiles are entirely clad in bamboo slats. This is the reason why it is also called the Bamboo Bridge. The people from Hubei Province make fine bamboo products. They throw away green bamboo, and keep the yellow—this is the so-called Return-to-the-Yellow style. Their products are as splendid and beautiful as carved red lacquerware or cloisonné. The unrivalled best producer of the Return-to-the-Yellow in the district was the monk Zhutang ["Bamboo Hall"], from the Temple of Three Sages. This bridge, in particular, was made in the Return-to-the-Yellow style.

The Duke Guan Shrine is three bays wide. Actually, its name has been the Shrine of Guan the Divine and Brave since olden times. Local people come here to pray in times

---

57   Lake Baozhang, also known as the Baozhang Canal, was originally the city moat but was gradually rebuilt into the Slender West Lake (*Shou xihu* 瘦西湖), northwest of Yangzhou. This site remains the garden area of Yangzhou.

of drought. If you take the winding passageway on the right-hand side of the shrine, eventually, you will reach the Thatched Cottage on the Peak, on the eastern side of the Peak. The cottage leans against it, faces the west, and commands a prospect of the entire lake. A parallel inscription combines lines from two Tang poets: "Green falls onto the bluish mountains, the wind blows an ancient tune" by Du Mu, and "Green waves and spring billows rise along the slope before me" by Wei Zhuang.

On the eastern side of the Thatched Cottage, there is a five-bay-wide building in the shape of a barge. It was built on a ten-*zhang*-long dike. Its northern wall faces the Spring Waters Corridor, and its southern wall is right in the middle of the lake. Firs, paulownias, elms, and willows were planted over a large area, surrounded by a bamboo hedge. The trees stretch upward, and below them, hibiscus grows.

At the far end of the dike stands a square arbor. This is the place for visitors to view the lotuses. Some of these plants are sold at the lotus market. When the market closes, the torn leaves are loaded onto boats and driven to the gaudy restaurants in the city which had previously ordered them in spring. Some lotuses are left throughout the winter. They dry up in the wind and are an excellent cure for chilblains.

At the foot of the peak, on its western side, stands another arbor. "Fishing Islet," says the horizontal plaque, and the parallel inscription carries Xu Yanbo's line: "I am singing about the White-Orchid Islet," along with a line by Du Fu: "I am holding the rod against the autumn wind." Below this arbor, there is a pier. Then the time comes when everything grows green and fresh, as if the earth had put on a coarse coat. Everything is so still, and there are no signs of human beings: just the face of the waters, fresh and splendid.

Stones reach out of the ground at the western foot of the hill, lavishly overgrown with moss. Visitors' clogs bite deep into the moss, leaving what looks like marks of teeth. In the middle, there is a cave. Its stony entrance has been fixed up with bricks, and made into a gate. The reddish clay wall holds a stone tablet, inscribed: "The Depth of Spring on the Flowering Apricot Peak." One can get into the mountains from this point, by a path as narrow as a piece of string. It winds up the hill, through the flowering apricot trees. The branches will hinder you, and below them, big stones will obstruct your way. The colors look as if they were embroidered. Look up, and you will see the summit. By now, the path is getting steep and slippery and it is difficult to keep one's footing. Through a crosswise cave, one reaches the summit, and sees a space so densely filled with flowering apricot trees that your companions will disappear behind them, and it will become impossible to hear their words. In the middle of this place, there is a pavilion in the shape of a pair of open wings. From the southern side, one can see the port of Zhuakou, appearing now as tiny as a miniature model. Foxes and hares run away from the visitors. Eagles and falcons fly through the sky, making first one turn, and then another. The birds' voices become noisier. The wild bamboo is a lush green. This is the end of the mountain, and here the path stops.

Then all of a sudden, one reaches a tiny byway, and slowly one descends through a covered passageway. This leads by the Hall of Guanyin. Mount the terrace, and you will see a staircase. Dozens of steps lead down to a leveled path, five *zhang* wide. A few more steps and there you are, at the Thatched Cottage on the Peak. The original way to climb the Depth of Spring on the Flowering Apricot Peak area was from this point. However, when the Hall of Guanyin was built, the path that starts at the cottage became the front route, and the path that leads through the reddish gate became the rear route. Once you descend beyond the Hall of Guanyin, you will pass a mountain lodge, and finally, you reach the monks' dormitory, six or seven bays long. All kinds of trees grow densely here, surrounded by clumps of green bamboo. Open a small bamboo hatch. The monks' kitchen is right there, ready to offer visitors some refreshment.

"Record of West of the Ridge" (extract)

Toppling Green of Myriad Pines lies to the west of Small Wave Gorge.[58] It is also called the Wu Garden, and is the former site of the Xiao Clan Village.[59] Many bamboos grow there, hiding the Xiao Clan Bridge. Under the bridge flows one branch of the Ballista Hill River, which runs from the Ballista Rock Bridge; when its water rises in spring and summer, one can spend time there enjoying the flowing river.

At the top, a three-bay-wide hall was built. Behind it many cassias grow and so it is called the Cassia Dew Mountain Dwelling. The area below bears the name Leisure Boats Pass in Spring.

Cross the Xiao Clan Bridge and you will reach Clear Shade Hall. To its left side, you can climb up to the Belvedere of Broad Observation. To the left of the belvedere, a passageway leads you along the river. The inscription on the passageway reads: "Soft Cold Weather of the Spring Nights."

Beyond the Cassia Dew Mountain Dwelling stands the Pavilion of Magnanimity and Clarity. To its left stands a water pavilion with an inscription that reads: "Wind and Moon, Clarity and Beauty." At this spot the mountain starts to rise, and the sound of pines gradually nears. Halfway up the Gazebo of the Green Clouds has been built. The inscription here reads: "Toppling Green of Myriad Pines."

---

58 This garden was one of the Twenty-Four Scenic Sites (*Ershisi jing* 二十四景) north of Yangzhou's city walls.

59 During the Qianlong era, the grounds of this former village were bought by Wu Xizu, who established the garden. The subsequent owners, Wang Wenyu and Zhang Xiong, twice rebuilt the garden.

The excellence of this garden lies in its vicinity to the river. The bamboo grove is more than ten *mu* in size. When the water is low, the river is only about one *chi* distant. When the water is high, it temporarily floods the bamboos. This is why the wharf of the Xiao Clan Village had been connected to the Lake of Nine Curves by a canal. As time went by, the dike became an islet. Next to the islet is the west bank of the Small Wave Gorge. All the houses and terraces on the river owe their existence to this.

Beyond the bamboo grove stands the Cassia Dew Mountain Dwelling. An inscribed couplet here reads:

> Soft breeze blows over my seat, and moves the inscribed fan. (by Li Yong)
> Cold dew, without any sound, drenches the cassia blossom. (by Wang Jian)

In the front, there stands a small building with three or four rooms. One half of the building is hidden behind the trees, and the other half sticks out over the running water. The gate of this complex is fashioned in the shape of a boat. The structure has been given no decorations, and so it looks like an abandoned house on a deserted dike. It sticks out into the river. A horizontal inscription reads: "Leisure boats pass in spring." The inscribed vertical couplet reads:

> Cottage of immortals by the side of a steep rock. (by Pi Rixiu)
> A small structure leaning over fresh waters. (by Zhang You)

Cross the Xiao Clan Bridge, and enter among the trees and the rocks. There, you will find a building only four or five bays wide. As you proceed, the path keeps turning this way and that. Enter a three-bay-wide hall, and you will find yourself even closer to the river. The inscription here reads: "The Clear Shade Hall." The inscribed couplet reads:

> The wind blows from the Northern Island, the misty waves expand. (by Quan Dexing)
> The rain stops by the Southern Hall, the green intensified. (by Li Cheng)

The Tower of Broad Observation, in twelve bays, is laid out in the zigzag shape of the character for a bow.[60] All the rooms face the north. From here the three mountains are all at last visible. The inscribed couplet reads:

> Mist and grass, the verdure is boundless. (by Zhou Boqi)
> Creeks and mountains, a painting would not do better. (by Du Mu)

---

60 *gong* 弓

Behind the building, three or four old flowering apricot trees are growing. The lake in the middle resembles the main canal of a river village. One can row a small boat over to a little building with two rooms, built on the water. The inscription there reads: "Soft Cold Weather of a Spring Dawn." The inscribed couplet reads:

> Oftentimes, a flock of cranes flies around these three trees. (by Sikong Tu)
> The beauty of flowers, their variety all blended and fragrant. (by Du Fu)

In the past, there used to be a large storehouse in the Xiao Clan Village, near the Lake of Nine Curves. For this reason the present garden has a covered corridor with twenty sections which links the Dew Terrace with the Pavilion of Magnanimity and Clarity. The inscribed couplet reads:

> Clouds and forests layer upon layer. (by Jia Dao)
> Ponds and buildings placed at random. (by Bai Juyi)

To the side is the Hall of Augmented Waters, five bays wide. When the river overflows, the stone pillar-bases and pine-wood pillars become inundated by the water. Violet floating-heart and white water-clover blossoms now and then drift into the room. The inscription reads: "Wind and Moon, Clarity and Beauty." The inscribed couplet reads:

> The boat breaks through the water, a thousand yards of sunlight. (by Zhang Yue)
> Trees rise on the lakeside, a few strokes on the mist. (by Cao Ye)

When you cross this place, the mountain range will start rising and falling. Here the Gazebo of the Green Clouds was built. The inscribed couplet reads:

> Mountains are deep, pines are green and cold. (by Zhu Yu)
> Trees grow dense, birds sing mournfully. (by Cui Qiao)

On the rock to the left is carved the inscription: "Toppling Green of Myriad Pines." It is up to this point that the grounds of the Wu Garden stretch.

Aitang's Catalogue of Song Titles (*Aitang qulu* 艾塘曲錄; extract)

LI DOU 李斗

TRANSLATED BY GINGER CHENG-CHI HSU

This passage from an opera catalogue by Li Dou, named from his cognomen Aitang (Mugwort Pond), indicates the kind of literary activity that took place in the gardens of eighteenth-century Yangzhou, evidently carrying on the practices of the Ming dynasty (see the introductory note to Zheng Yuanxun's "A Personal Record of My Garden of Reflections" in chapter 6). The Garden of

Rest referred to here (also translated as the Retirement Garden) was established in the late Ming by one of Zheng Yuanxun's brothers (see above); unlike Zheng Yuanxun's own garden, it evidently survived the Ming-Qing transition more or less intact.

Aitang's Catalogue of Song Titles (extract)

Among literary gatherings of Yangzhou, those taking place in the Little Translucent Mountain Lodge of the Ma family, the Garden of the Dwarf Bamboo of the Cheng family, and the Garden of Rest of the Zheng family are most active and elaborate. At regular meetings, desks are set up for each guest. On each desk, there are two brushes, inkstones, a water jar, four pieces of writing paper, a note for rhymes, teapot and bowl, fruit and dessert containers, all meticulously arranged. The poems are sent to the carver for publication as soon as they are finished. There is a three-day grace period allowing for participants to revise or edit, but as soon as the poems are in print, they spread to all corners of the city. At every meeting exquisite food and wine are provided. After the poems are finished, a music performance follows. The participants are invited to an old hall with green crystal windows. Four aged musicians in their eighties or nineties appear, and each plays a piece of music, then withdraws. All of a sudden, the doors and screens are ordered to be removed. A multiple-story building behind the doors, decorated with thousands of lanterns, comes into view, from which music played by groups of young lads and maidens fills the space.

"Remembering the Past: Twelve Quatrains" (*Yixi shiershou* 憶昔十二首; no. 5)

GAN LIROU 甘立媃 (1743–1819)
TRANSLATED BY GRACE S. FONG

Gan Lirou was from Fengxin in Jiangxi, a long way from the great centers of culture around Suzhou and Hangzhou, which were also centers of women's literary activity. That may be one reason why Gan remained unusually close throughout her life to her natal family; many of her poems—and she was a prolific poet—are concerned with her relationships with members of this affectionate scholar-official family and with the events of daily life. This poem is one of a set written in memory of her much-loved husband Xu Yuelü, also a poet, who died in 1774, when he was just thirty and she was thirty-two.

"Remembering the Past: Twelve Quatrains" (no. 5)

I remember in the past when we looked at the flowers in the back garden,
Laughing, we supported each other on the grassy path after the rain.
But now I've lost all interest in looking for springtime,
In the old garden, the mud is deep and weeds grow freely on the path.

Six Records of a Floating Life (*Fusheng liuji* 浮生六記)

"The Joys of the Wedding Chamber" (*Guifang jile* 閨房記樂; extract), "The Pleasures of Leisure" (*Xianqing jiqu* 閑情記趣; extracts), and "The Delights of Roaming Afar" (*Langyou jikuai* 浪遊記快; extract)

SHEN FU 沈復 (1763–CA. 1810)

TRANSLATED BY LEONARD PRATT AND CHIANG SU-HUI

For Shen Fu, see chapter 3. Although Shen Fu and his wife were never wealthy enough to afford their own garden, as we see below, they were both knowledgeable connoisseurs of gardens. Speaking about his entry into Yangzhou during the spring of 1783 through the Slender West Lake district, to take up, but only briefly, a post in the Salt Administration, Shen captures something of the quintessence of the art:

> Level with the Mountains Hall is some three or four *li* distant from the city, but the road leading into the city is eight or nine *li* long and although the scenery all along the route is entirely the product of human effort, nonetheless, such has been the power of imagination and fancy applied to the task, so natural do the embellishments seem that no paradise of gemstone ponds and jasper towers with jade ceilings could possibly compare. Most marvelously, the gardens and pavilions of ten or so families have been combined, to flow seamlessly to the mountain in a continuous manner. The most difficult aspect of this design to manage is the section where one leaves the city and enters the scenery, for here the route must skirt the city wall for more than a *li*. Were one to do this in a garden—situate a wall at exactly the spot from which one can gaze afar at the serried mountains beyond, painterly in their beauty—it would be considered a most egregious lapse. Here, however, all the pavilions and terraces, the walls and the rocks, the bamboos and the trees, as they slip into and out of sight, seem to the visitor so naturally placed there that they occasion no surprise, the artifact, surely, of one of whom it could be said that he has the mountains and the valleys in his heart.[61]

Yangzhou was looking particularly splendid in this year, for Shen Fu's arrival coincided with the preparations being made for the visit of the Qianlong emperor to the city during course of his sixth and last Southern Tour; he was lucky enough, he tells us, to have "drawn close to and gazed up upon the Heavenly Countenance" twice in his life, for he was later to be involved in the construction of one of the many elaborate traveling palaces erected to house the emperor and his entourage during his travels.

---

61 Translation by Duncan M. Campbell. Cf. Leonard Pratt and Chiang Su-hui, trans., *Six Records of a Floating Life* (Harmondsworth: Penguin Books, 1983), 108–9.

"The Joys of the Wedding Chamber" (extract)

About half a *li* from my house, on Vinegar Warehouse Lane, was the Dongting Temple, which we usually called the Narcissus Temple. Inside there were winding covered paths and a small garden with pavilions. Every year on the god's birthday the members of each family association would gather in their corner of the temple, hang up a special glass lantern, and erect a throne below it. Beside the throne they would set out vases filled with flowers, in a competition to see whose decorations were most beautiful. During the day operas were performed, and at night candles of different lengths were set out among the vases and the flowers. This was called the "lighting of the flowers." The colors of the flowers, the shadows of the lamps, and the fragrant smoke floating up from the incense urns, made it all seem like a night banquet at the palace of the Dragon King himself. The heads of the family associations would play the flute and sing, or brew fine tea and chat with one another. Townspeople gathered like ants to watch this spectacle, and a fence had to be put up under the eaves of the temple to keep them out.

One year some friends of mine invited me to go and help to arrange their flowers, so I had a chance to see the festival myself. I went home and told Yun how beautiful it was.

"What a shame that I cannot go just because I am not a man," said Yun.
"If you wore one of my hats and some of my clothes, you could look like a man."

Yun thereupon braided her hair into a plait and made up her eyebrows. She put on my hat, and though her hair showed a little around her ears it was easy to conceal. When she put on my robe we found it was an inch and a half too long, but she took it up around the waist and put a riding jacket over it.

"What about my feet?" Yun asked.

"In the street they sell 'butterfly shoes,' I said, "in all sizes. They're easy to buy, and afterward you can wear them around the house. Wouldn't they do?"

Yun was delighted, and when she had put on my clothes after dinner she practiced for a long time, putting her hands into the sleeves and taking large steps like a man.

But suddenly she changed her mind. "I am not going! It would be awful if someone found out. If your parents knew, they would never allow us to go."

I still encouraged her to go, however. "Everyone at the temple knows me. Even if they find out, they will only take it as a joke. Mother is at ninth sister's house, so if we come and go secretly no one will ever know."

Yun looked at herself in the mirror and laughed endlessly. I pulled her along, and we left quietly. We walked all around inside the temple, with no one realizing she was a woman. If someone asked who she was, I would tell them she was my cousin. They would only fold their hands and bow to her.

At the last place we came to, young women and girls were sitting behind the throne that had been erected there. They were the family of a Mr. Yang, one of the organizers of the festival. Without thinking, Yun walked over and began to chat with them as a woman quite naturally might, and as she bent over to do so she inadvertently laid her hand on the shoulder of one of the young ladies.

One of the maids angrily jumped up and shouted, "What kind of a rogue are you, to behave like that!" I went over to try to explain, but Yun, seeing how embarrassing the situation could become, quickly took off her hat and kicked up her foot, saying, "See, I am a woman too!"

At first they all stared at Yun in surprise, but then their anger turned to laughter. We stayed to have some tea and refreshments with them, and then called sedan chairs and went home.

"The Pleasures of Leisure" (extract)

In laying out gardens, pavilions, wandering paths, small mountains of stone, and flower plantings, try to give the feeling of the small in the large and the large in the small, of the real in the illusion, and of the illusion in the reality. Some things should be hidden and some should be obvious, some prominent and some vague. Arranging a proper garden is not just a matter of setting out winding paths in a broad area with many rocks; thinking that it is will only waste time and energy.

To make a miniature mountain, pile up some dirt, then place stones on it and plant flowers and grass here and there. The fence in front of it should be plum trees, and the wall behind it should be covered with vines, so that it will look just like a mountain even though there is no mountain there.

This is a way of showing the small in the large: in an unused corner plant some bamboo, which will grow quickly tall, then plant some luxuriant plum trees in front to screen it.

This is a way to show the large in the small: the wall of a small garden should be winding and covered with green vines, and large stones decorated with inscriptions can be set into it. Then one will be able to open a window and, while looking at a stone wall, feel as if one were gazing out across endless precipices.

Here is a way to show the real amid an illusion: arrange the garden so that when a guest feels he has seen everything he can suddenly take a turn in the path and have a broad new vista open up before him, or open a simple door in a pavilion only to find it leads to an entirely new garden.

There are several ways of creating an illusion amid reality: make a gateway into a closed yard, and then cover it over with bamboo and stones; the yard beyond, while real, will then look like an illusion. Or, on top of a wall build a low railing; it will look like an upper balcony, creating an illusion from reality.

Poor scholars who live in small crowded houses should rearrange their rooms in imitation of the sterns of the Taiping boats of my home county, the steps of which can be made into three beds by extending them at front and back. Each bed is then separated from its neighbor by a board covered with paper. Looking at them when they are laid out is like walking a long road—you do not have a confined feeling at all. When Yun and I were living in Yangzhou we arranged our house in this fashion. Though the house has only two spans, we divided it into two bedrooms, a kitchen, and a living room, and still had plenty of space left over. Yun had laughed about our handiwork, saying, "The layout is fine, but it still does not quite have the feel of a rich home." I had had to admit she was right!

"The Pleasures of Leisure" (extract)

There were two places in Suzhou, called the South Garden and the North Garden. We wanted to go there once when the rape flowers were in bloom, but unfortunately there were no wine houses nearby where we could find something to drink. We could have taken a basket of things with us, but then we would have had to toast the flowers in cold wine and that would have been no fun at all.[62] We talked about looking for a drinking place near by, and about first looking at the flowers and then coming home to drink, but neither sounded as much fun as toasting the flowers with warm wine. . . .

   After lunch we went off to the South Garden, carrying cushions and mats with us. We picked a place in the shade of a willow tree and sat down. First we made tea, and when we had finished it, we warmed the wine and cooked the food.[63] The wind and sun were exquisite. The earth was golden, and the blue clothes and red sleeves of strollers filled the paths between the fields, while butterflies and bees flew all around us. The scene was so intoxicating one hardly needed to drink. After a while the wine and food were ready, and everyone sat down on the ground to feast. The man who had helped us

---

62   Chinese rice wine is best drunk warmed.

63   Editor's note: they had hired a dumpling seller to accompany them with his stove and other equipment.

out was not an ordinary sort, so we persuaded him to come and join us in our drinking. The strollers who saw us all envied our clever idea. By the end of the afternoon cups and plates were scattered around and all of us were very jolly, some sitting and some lying down, some singing and some whistling. As the red sun set I felt like eating some rice porridge, so our helper quickly bought some rice and cooked it, and we all went home well satisfied.

"The Delights of Roaming Afar" (extract)

While at Haining I once went to visit the Chen family's Garden of Peaceful Waves, which occupied a hundred *mu* of land and which was covered with towers and pavilions, winding lanes and galleries. One pond in the garden was very deep and was crossed by a bridge with six bends in it. In addition, the garden boasted rocks covered with vines that completely hid their chisel marks, and a thousand ancient trees, all of them reaching to heaven. With the birds twittering and the flower petals dropping to the ground, it was like being deep in the mountains. Of all the artificial rock gardens I have seen that were built on flat ground, this one looked the most natural.

Once we gave a dinner at the Cassia Tower there, and you could not smell the food for the scent of the flowers. Only the smell of the pickled ginger was not overcome, but then ginger and cassia both turn more pungent with age, like loyal ministers who are made of strong stuff.

"A Record of the Garden of the Peaceful Waves" (*Anlan yuan ji* 安瀾園記)

CHEN QIQING 陳瑨卿 (FL. 1796–1820)
TRANSLATED BY DUNCAN M. CAMPBELL

The site of the Garden of the Peaceful Waves, in Salt Office Township of Haining, some twenty-five miles northeast of Hangzhou in Zhejiang Province, first became a garden under the ownership of Wang Hang, the Prince of Anhua, during the Southern Song dynasty (1127–1279). Little is known about Chen Qiqing, who was active during the reign of the Daoguang emperor (1796–1820).

The Qianlong emperor (1711–1799; r. 1736–1795) visited the garden on four occasions, during the third (1762), fourth (1765), fifth (1780), and sixth (1784) of his celebrated Southern Tours, staying there for two nights on each occasion. The impact of his visits on the design of the garden proved enormous; its name was changed, on imperial command, to the Garden of the Peaceful Waves, and as its fame spread throughout the empire, its proportions quintupled. A stela engraved with the emperor's own poems inspired by his visits became the focus of the garden's design, thus instantiating his continuing presence in it. Furthermore, the emperor took the opportunity of the renovation of the Bookroom of the Four Delights in his Garden of Perfect Brightness in Beijing in 1764 to have a replica of the Garden of the Peaceful Waves built, based on drawings he had ordered made of it.

Neither the original garden nor its simulacrum remain, a fate predicted by Chen Qiqing, a clansman of the then-owners, at the end of "A Record of the Garden of the Peaceful Wares." When Guan Tingfen (1797–1880) included this record in a book on the sights of Haining, he appended to it a colophon noting: "The fate of any garden is at the mercy of the waxing and waning fortune of the state. Although the various scenes of the Garden of the Peaceful Waves once owned by Chen Yuanlong, the former grand minister of my hometown, provided the model for the construction of a garden within the Garden of Perfect Brightness, the garden itself was sold off, bit by bit, by his descendants, until almost nothing of it remains. I add this note to the account of the garden in order to express my distress at this circumstance."

"A Record of the Garden of the Peaceful Waves"

There is a garden that stands in the northwestern corner of the town and that, because of its location, was called Corner Garden, this being the former property of Chen Yujiao [1544–1611]. Some time after the ownership of the garden had reverted to his grandson, Chen Yuanlong [1652–1736], the former Grand Secretary, he changed its name to the Garden for Fulfilling My Resolve to Retire.[64] Once the garden had been expanded and improved by his son Chen Bangzhi [1694–1777], the Old Man of the Simple Pavilion, in his turn, it had gradually grown in size to encompass a full 100 *mu*. Its towers, its look-outs, its terraces, and its gazebos were designed to afford one rest, in total more than thirty spots for visitors to the garden to gaze out from, all made in conformity to principles of simple antiquity and none of which had been given ornate decoration.[65] In the *renwu* year [1762], during the course of the Qianlong emperor's Southern Tour, this garden served as his detached palace, for which purpose it was further adorned with pond and terrace, but everywhere in strict accordance with the emperor's own predilection for utmost simplicity. The garden first acquired its continuing fame when the emperor bestowed upon it its present name.

Some considerable way along a twisting lane one comes upon a south-facing double-leafed gate, and once the visitor has entered this gate and proceeded several paces to the north, he encounters an open kiosk wherein stands, alone and august, a stela

---

64   Chen Yuanlong explained his choice of this name, distantly derived from the title of a rhapsody by the poet Sun Chuo (ca. 714–ca. 371), *Suichu fu* (遂初賦), in his "Preface" to his *Poems from the Garden of Fulfilling My Resolve to Retire* (*Suichu yuan shi* 遂初園詩). Having at some earlier date restored Chen Yujiao's former garden, with the "fond hope of being able to retire there to see out my old age," he found his official duties so pressing that although he was already more than eighty years old, his hopes, by necessity, had been "confined simply to my dreams." Eventually, in 1733, the Yongzheng emperor granted him leave to return home to retire, rewarding him with a plaque that read: "Wise and Able Old Man of the Forests and Springs" (*Linquan qishuo* 林泉耆碩).

65   Chen Yuanlong concluded his "Preface": "This then is a general description of the Garden for Fulfilling My Resolve to Retire. The garden has no engraved wall paintings, its walls have been left undecorated, and it can boast of no famous flowers or marvelous rocks; with its pond and its bamboos and trees, however, it is nonetheless both refined and simple, located quite beyond the reach of the dust of the world."

engraved with five-character poems in the imperial hand. As this garden served as a detached palace on four separate occasions, both the face and the obverse of the stela have been engraved with the emperor's poems, as have also the two sides.

Turning slightly to the west at this point and walking on through a gateway, one finds oneself on a raised pathway to both sides of which grow several dozen ancient elms, stretching all the way to the sky, their dense foliage and branches casting deep shadows all about them. This pathway comes to an end at the doorway to a three-bay-wide building on the lintel of which hangs the plaque with the name "Garden of the Peaceful Waves" in the imperial hand. Entering yet another gateway and then wending one's way along beside a wall, one finds that a direct prospect of the garden is no longer available. Upon turning to the west one immediately enters a small one-leaf doorway into a gallery that describes three turns before leading to the Study of the Vast Wave-Drenched Scene. This study faces a pond, the bridge over which is named Little Stone Bridge. Here it is that the path leading into the garden proper begins. To the east of the rear of the study is a structure nine purlins deep, with its frontage facing inward and its back wall facing outward, and which is flanked to both left and right by chambers. The main hall of this structure, access to which can be gained by a set of steps, is both level and wide. Entering through the encircling gallery to the left, however, takes one to another room at the rear, this again flanked to both left and right by chambers, these two rooms, inner and outer, being where the old gentleman himself lived and, thus, neither have been given names. The old gentleman was a man of some considerable talent and as a young man he took office in the Silken Thread Pavilion;[66] when his father, the Grand Secretary, passed away, however, he decided immediately that the time had come for him to return and nourish his ideals in the forests and beside the springs. Normally he lived not in his mansion but within this garden, lying on his back and gazing up at the heavens, whistling his days away—and thus did he dwell in idleness for almost thirty years. On fine days in spring or autumn he would gather together his various followers, to drink, as they composed their verses, in imitation of the "Peach Blossom Garden" party made famous by Li Bai's "Preface."[67] He was addicted also to dramatic performances and kept his own troupe of players, who, on banquet occasions, would sing and dance upon demand; amid the layered curtains and the torches and lanterns, shining as brightly as the stars arrayed in the sky above, the old gentleman would sit, the oldest of them all and yet nonetheless his air of refined elegance the rival of any Daoist immortal. The tenor of these moments of relaxed and insouciant

---

66   Chen Bangzhi served as Junior Compiler in the Hanlin Academy; the Silken Thread Pavilion is an informal reference to the academy.

67   Li Bai's (701–762) "Preface" referred to here is his "Preface to Poems Written When Entertaining My Cousins in Peach Blossom Garden on a Spring Evening" (*Chun ye yan congdi taohuayuan xu* 春夜宴從弟桃花園序), which begins: "Heaven and Earth are but an inn; time is simply the passing traveler of a hundred ages. This floating life is but a dream, what lasting joy can it possibly afford?"

enjoyment was such that word of them spread far and wide, and everyone competed to emulate such occasions.

To the west of Little Stone Bridge stands a doubled-leafed halberd gate within which two flowering wisteria grow upon a single trellis, casting the whole courtyard into shade. The path leading into the garden takes one, by necessity, beneath these vines and in the springtime, when the wisteria are in full bloom, it is as if one is touring a hornet's nest, as purple petals brush against one's face and sweet scent perfumes one's hair. To the south stands a hall once named Encircling Greenness but today housing the plaques bearing, in his own calligraphy, the emperor's couplet:

> As the riverside bamboos stretch forth their purity,
> With flowering apricot and bamboo can one find true delight.

A tower has been situated behind this hall, its frontage wide and spacious and backed onto a serpentine pond. Here, within the secluded rooms and hidden chambers of this tower and enclosed by galleries, one discovers the best that the garden can offer—having entered here one loses, seemingly forevermore, all knowledge of how one arrived. In this tower are stored all the many specimens of imperial calligraphy awarded the family by emperors from Kangxi onward, along with the various vessels and other objects that his grandson, the Qianlong emperor, made use of and enjoyed during his visits to the garden. Winding off to the right of the tower is a structure that is suspended above the lake: the Kiosk of the Gentle Breeze and Bright Moon. As this kiosk is open on three sides, the prospect offered one while standing within it, surrounded as one is by the vast expanse of the surface of the rippling lake and with a bright autumnal moon suspended in the night sky above, is that of a seamless tapestry of reflected heavenly light. To the north are the Imperial Living Apartments, solemn and majestic of appearance; to the south, one catches sight of the Red Balustrades of Zigzag Bridge, built only a few inches above the surface of the lake; and gazing to the west through cloud and tree, the dense green foliage seems woven of ten thousand skeins, offering the possibility of an altogether different realm of boundless expanse. Several dozen paces to the south stands a studio, Orchid Proof,[68] designed to compensate for whatever possible insufficiency the view offered by the kiosk might have resulted in. Leading away from here to the

---

68   The name of this studio seems to derive from the *Zuo Commentary*. Attached to the line from the Spring and Autumn Annals (Chunqiu 春秋) that reads, "in winter, in the tenth month, on *bingxu*, Lan, earl of Zheng, died," the commentary (Duke Xuan, 3rd year) explains that the earl was named Lan (Orchid) after his mother dreamed that an ancestor of the family gave her an orchid to indicate that "as the *lan* is the most fragrant flower of a State, so shall men acknowledge and love" her future child. Before the conception of the child, a similar flower was given to his mother by his father, Duke Wen of Zheng; subsequently, she used this flower to prove that, even though she was a very low-ranking concubine, her child was indeed the son of the duke (see *The Chinese Classics*, vol. 5, *The Ch'un Ts'ew with The Tso Chuen*, ed. and trans. James Legge [Oxford: Clarendon

south is a gallery that takes one to the west wing of the Tower of Easeful Writing. The eaves of this tower, situated to the west of Encircling Greenness, and those of the hall itself connect with each other. Six or seven cassia trees grow beside the tower, all of which come into bloom far earlier than any others. The tower has open windows on all four sides, although the southern face of the structure constitutes its main frontage. Here stairs lead to a pond in the midst of which rocks have been carved into the shape of islands, and water flows, by hidden means, between them, in order to provide the location for the drinking game whereby cups of wine are set afloat to drift to those sitting around. In front of the pond and in imitation of the inspired calligraphy of Wang Xizhi [309–ca. 365], the General on the Right, is a plaque that reads: Twisting Stream and Floating Winecup, along with a slab of jade that has been dedicated to the gods and which bears the engraved calligraphy of an imperial copy of a line or two from a letter by the Song dynasty poet and essayist Su Shi [1037–1101]. From Ancient Vines and Waterside Gazebo westward to the Hall of Encircling Greenness, and then again westward from the Hall of Encircling Greenness to this point, all along one faces the water, across which rises a hill; to the west again from here the way is screened off by a jumble of mounds. Heading away at an oblique angle from the corner of the low courtyard wall to the right of the tower takes one to Red Balustrades of Zigzag Bridge. Across the bridge and twenty or so paces along a mountain path one emerges, suddenly, into an opening where stands a kiosk surrounded by several dozen silver cassia trees, this being the Village of Heavenly Fragrance. The Pavilion of the Gathered Scents is found here to the southeast, entered by way of the base of the pavilion and heading in a southeastern direction around the back of the Studio of the Rippling Moon. This studio faces to the east and abuts the water, thus egress from the front is impossible. From here one can head southward along the embankment of the pond, reaching eventually the Twelve Towers, through a bamboo door, turning to the east and on through another kiosk, perhaps six or seven paces farther along, before turning to the north. The tower facing southward and overlooking the water is South Tower, East Tower is to this tower's left, facing eastward, while turning the other way, the tower facing the north is North Tower, also facing the water and at an oblique angle to Ancient Vines and Waterside Gazebo. To the west of South Tower a mountain path takes one to the bank of the lake, here reduced to a creek, crossed by means of a small footbridge. Across the other side, an embankment follows the contour of the hill and ascending this in a southerly direction but immediately turning westward and then north again, takes one up to the Pavilion of the Gathered Scents. Trees line the route, those with matted branches being a number of twisted maples. If one chooses not to ascend the hill but rather to head off along the embankment to the north, exiting through the base of the pavilion and passing through the Village of Heavenly

Press, 1893–1895], 294). The studio compensates for the insufficiency of the view in the same way that the evidence of the orchid compensated for the concubine's low status.

Fragrance again, then off at an angle to a northwesterly direction and through a moon gate and on through a little tower, and then turning to the northwest again and through a door, one encounters a pergola of banksia rose, beside which grow some green bamboos, altogether a secluded and shaded spot of sublime beauty. Walking to the west, turning then to the north and coming out beside the water, one comes across a small embankment that leads off to the north and connects up with a rainbow bridge called Encircling Bridge. To the south of this bridge, turning to the west and entering through a bamboo door, one finds a kiosk facing the north, shaped like a square pot. Behind the kiosk there are tall bamboos and fine rocks, offering an air of profound aloofness. Leading off to the west but facing the east, suspended above the water, is the vista Deep Bamboos and Pure Lotuses, faced directly by Encircling Bridge. Off to the left, one can cross Unpolished Stone Bridge, tiny in size and affording passage for only one person at a time. Turning toward the northern bank of the pond and heading off eastward, thirteen or fourteen paces along, one comes upon a path leading off to the north which, when followed in its turn, takes one to Sheathed Fragrance Lodge, this name having been coined by the Qianlong emperor himself, derived from the fact that so densely do the bamboos grow here that to left and right all that can be seen are their green trunks, those within being completely hidden from the eyes of those without. To the left of the lodge a path leads off to the east, twisting to and fro within the thicket before heading off toward the south, taking one to the north of Encircling Bridge, before again ascending the hillside and tapering off amid the dense green vegetation. Turning to the west and following along the side of the hill, a path suddenly appears, beside which a small building overlooks the pond, from which point one can gaze out at Deep Bamboos and Pure Lotuses. A gate stands to the left of the path which, when investigated, like red jade set within the green base, is the path that leads away eastward from Sheathed Fragrance Lodge. Several dozen paces eastward along this path and then gazing to the north, a storied tower looms into view amid the densely growing trees and bamboo, and again, one thinks that the vista offered is a boundless one, before one becomes aware that no further mysterious paths come to an end at this spot.

Leaving all this behind and heading eastward, one suddenly finds oneself following along a mountain path, with high ridges to both left and right and ancient trees soaring to the heavens and the wind singing harmoniously among the bamboos. Here, one can no longer see the ponds, the pavilions, the terraces, and the lookouts that the garden contains, and it is as if one is surrounded by wailing gibbons, screeching apes and cranes sobbing soulfully. Only once one has reached this spot does one truly believe that it is indeed a realm of an entirely different order, as suggested by the description that came to mind when in the Pavilion of the Gentle Breeze and Bright Moon: "And gazing to the west through cloud and tree, the dense green foliage seems woven of a thousand layers."

As the hills around begin to open out, so too does the path begin to widen somewhat and now a lift of the head brings into view the Imperial Living Quarters.[69] This bedchamber had formerly been called Hall of Bestowed Idleness, but the plaque was removed once the emperor had slept here. It comprises a structure three purlins deep, each framed section having three levels, in shape, intentionally, resembling a Well Field and encircled by an enclosed balcony so that both the front of the structure and its two sides look exactly alike, entry being gained by means of a set of steps. On the eastern side of the building are two galleries. The nearer of these galleries leads off to the east toward Flowering Apricot Wood Mountain, a spot where only flowering apricot trees have been planted in various varieties. At the edge of the wood is a plank bridge which links to the opposite bank and then to another structure, this being the tower that stands behind the Hall of Encircling Greenness. The gallery slightly to the north also leads off to the east and once through the gate here you find yourself within a structure three purlins deep, with another identical structure directly behind it. This is where the emperor, during his visits to the garden, would take pleasure in calligraphy and painting. To the east of this structure two zigzag walking galleries lead off to east and south, the former leading to the Soaring Tower, the latter, in a roundabout manner and by way of the storage pavilion, leading eventually to the Old Gentleman's living quarters. Behind the Imperial Living Apartments rises a steep peak, planted mainly in giant bamboos. To the northwest of the peak there is a ledge which one can climb upon for a view over the crenellated town walls. If you come along the mountain path down to the right of the Imperial Living Apartments, turn and take a few paces onward, you find the courtyard opening up before you for several *mu*, as broad and flat as a whetstone, with the pure flowing water visible between the balustrades. Gazing into the distance, across the rippling silken surface of the lake, one can see occasionally the hue of the hills beyond, amid the clouds and glistening reflections. On summer days, when a gentle breeze sets the lotus leaves here quivering and their red flowers glisten in the sun, there is no finer sight to be seen in all of the vastness of Hangzhou's West Lake. Walking along the southwestern embankments of the lake takes one to Twisting Stone Jetty, with a kiosk nestled into the bank of the lake where one can lie down and fish with a pole. Retreating several paces along the way one has just traveled, one comes upon a mountain path, amid the green stems of the bamboo. Soon enough one finds oneself standing upon the summit where stands another kiosk, called Kingfisher Blue. Here one is completely surrounded by dense arrow bamboo. Circling around the kiosk and heading north brings one to another path that can lead one down off the hill. If you take a skiff, you can board this to the west of the plank bridge at Flowering Apricot Wood and be rowed westward to the large lake in front of the Imperial Living Apartments. Farther on, gliding alongside the embankment, passing Twisting Stone Jetty to the south, one arrives at a harbor leading to the northwest, and here one can then enter Encircling Bridge and reach Deep Bamboos and Pure

---

69   This structure was also named The Bookroom of Quiet Brightness (*Jingming shuwu* 靜明書屋).

Lotuses and Unpolished Stone Bridge, coming to a rest in front of the Imperial Living Apartments. And then, from here, drifting in mid-stream and passing beyond Zigzag Bridge to the southeast, one has a choice of passage: to the south, the water narrows and one passes beside the embankment below the Pavilion of Gathered Scents and a stone bridge, before coming out at the entrance to the stream, along which, to the west, one can reach the Studio of the Rippling Moon or, to the east, South Tower of the Twelve Towers. Taking the passage to the east, however, takes one past the Tower of Easeful Writing, the Hall of Encircling Greenness, and then on to Ancient Vines and Waterside Gazebo, where, if one turns to the north and past Little Stone Bridge and then on northward to Soaring Tower, the water begins to narrow and the skiff can be poled no further. The rippling water, however, continues to flow away to the west from here until it reaches the plank bridge at Flowering Apricot Wood.

And so, pillowed up against the ridge and nestled within the foothills, sited beside the river and overlooking the flowing waters, with here a beam covered by a vine and there the tiles of all four corners of the roof hidden beneath the flowers, "following and borrowing from the existing scenery and the lie of the land,"[70] decorated in the acme of relaxed elegance, this garden offers everywhere sights to be seen such that no exhaustive record of them can be made.

But, alas! The way of Heaven and Earth achieves its everlastingness only by virtue of the fact of its eternal flux, this being the reason why creation and ruination are always and forever interdependent. And so it is that a space that was once the domain of poisonous snakes and foxes and hares becomes, suddenly, transformed into a site of lakes and hills, flowers and trees, wherein poets and men of letters gather, accompanied always by young girls both seductive and elegant, to listen to the orioles with cups of wine in hand, or to sit among the flowers and become drunk beneath the shining moon, to evaluate the times and to take pleasure in the things that surround them, to chant poems or to give vent to their innermost desires, until, finally, the sun begins to set upon this joyous scene and everyone suddenly seems reluctant to depart—how surpassing is such a moment! However, on occasions when the waterside pavilions stand as before, the paint of their doorway screens not yet faded, but the people who once inhabited the scene are all departed and the particular circumstances of their age seem already beyond recapturing, a man of sensitivity will linger here, examining the heavens above and the earth below, and giving himself over to the afflatus of history, and even more sorrowful will be his sighs if the lingering traces of those gilded rooms and hillocks of the past have disappeared altogether as well. And even as the lakes

---

70   This is a reference to well-established principles of garden design, as captured, most famously, in Ji Cheng's *The Craft of Gardens*, as translated by Alison Hardie: "skill in landscape design is shown in the ability to 'follow' and 'borrow from' the existing scenery and the lie of the land, and artistry is shown in the feeling of suitability created," *The Craft of Gardens* (New Haven: Yale University Press, 1988), 39.

and hills, the flowers and the trees, themselves gradually begin to change, it will still require several hundreds of years to go by before the site reverts to its original state, and becomes again the realm of poisonous snakes and foxes and hares; the "pulling apart" of a "large fruit,"[71] by necessity, awaits the right moment and nothing can be done to alter the inevitable course of the workings of the universe. Moreover, human life is of only limited duration and even divine intelligence becomes quickly sapped. After all, we humans partake neither of the robustness of the plants and the trees, nor of the inexhaustibility of the flowers and the birds, a circumstance that occasions, surely, the deepest of regrets.

Over the course of the many twists and turns of time since the passing away of the old gentleman Chen Bangzhi himself, this garden has fallen into a state of some slight dilapidation; and yet here are still to be found that single hillock and solitary valley of former years, the scenery of the place having not changed at all, to the extent that sight of it may still occasion thoughts of those days gone by. From this time onward, however, and as the years draw on and the visible traces of the garden disappear even further from sight, I fear that those who are to come will have nothing upon which to summon back to mind and understand this garden of old. Thus have I made this present record.

Wild Swan on the Snow: An Illustrated Record of My Preordained Life (*Hongxue yinyuan tuji* 鴻雪因緣圖記)

"Owning Half-Acre Garden" (*Banmu ying yuan* 半畝營園)

LINQING 麟慶 (1791–1846)

TRANSLATED BY DUNCAN M. CAMPBELL

A member of the Wanyan or Wanggiyan clan, Linqing was a distant descendant of the fifth emperor of the Jin dynasty (1115–1234) and belonged to the Imperial Household Bondservant Division of the Manchu Bordered Yellow Banner. Graduating as a presented scholar in 1809, he proceeded to have a distinguished official career, with a particular expertise in water conservancy. His autobiography, *Wild Swan on the Snow: An Illustrated Record of My Preordained Life*, published in three series between 1839 and 1850, presents his life in the form of 240 illustrated events or moments.

In 1841, Linqing acquired the Half-Acre Garden in Beijing, said to have been designed by Li Yu in the 1660s for then-governor of Shaanxi Province Jia Hanfu (1606–1677), perhaps with the assistance of Zhang Nanyuan and his son Zhang Ran. When Linqing was implicated in the collapse of the dikes along the Yellow River in 1842, he was demoted and retired to his garden, where he established a remarkable library. Sadly, after only three months living in the garden, he was recalled to office.[72]

---

71   Hexagram 23, *bo* 剝 (Pulling Apart), of the *Book of Changes*.

72   For more information on this garden, see J. L. van Hecken and W. A. Grootaers, "The Half Acre Garden, *Pan-mou Yüan*: A Manchu Residence in Peking," *Monumenta Serica* 18, no. 1 (1959):360–87.

"Owning Half-Acre Garden"

Half-Acre Garden is situated in the capital, just beyond the northeastern corner of the Forbidden City, along Bow-String Lane and opposite the Monastery of Joys Received. The garden was originally the residence of Jia Jiaohou, Governor of Shaanxi (his name was Hanfu, and he was a Chinese Bannerman). When Li Liweng (named Yu, from Zhejiang; a commoner) was serving as Governor Jia's secretary, he built this garden, piling up rocks to form a mountain, diverting water to create a pond. Its flat terraces and winding chambers embodied both the expansiveness of the open view and the mystery of the confined space. Once the garden had changed hands, it gradually fell into a state of dilapidation. At the beginning of the reign of the Qianlong emperor, the Ministerial Secretary Yang Jing'an of Shanxi acquired the site and had the garden restored. His son, however, a merchant, later turned the garden into a warehouse. Soon thereafter, however, it was acquired by the Surveillance Commissioner Chun Fuyuan (named Qing, a Manchu) and he turned it into an open-air arena for singing and dancing. Thus was this garden transformed.

In the *xinchou* year of the reign of the Daoguang emperor [1841], the garden became mine. I ordered my eldest son Chongshi to employ the finest carpenters he could find to restore the garden and to have it decorated in appropriate manner, all in distant evocation of the splendors of Jiangnan. Once this had been done, I settled upon the names Shadow in the Shape of a Cloud for the main hall, Worship of the Rock for the adjoining studio, Airing One's Paintings for the gallery, Near the Light for the pavilion, Retiring to Think for the study, Enjoyment of Spring for the kiosk, and Congealed Fragrance for the chamber. As well as these structures, the garden also contained various plaques reading: Langhuan Paradise, Poets' Club of the Cherry-Apple, House of the Crystal Pond, Miniature Image of the Xiao and Xiang Rivers, Rocks that Seem Like Clouds, and Elegant Hermitage Mountain Hut, all in the hands of my friends and teachers. I myself penned the couplet that hung in the Hall of the Shadow in the Shape of a Cloud:

> Our origins trace back to the White Mountains; for seven generations now we
> have been blessed with the Golden Sable, never daring to inquire after the fates of
> dynasties past and present.
> We live here now beside the Forbidden City; for twenty long years our position
> has warranted us the joys of *qin* and crane, forever resting in the embrace of sagely
> rulership.

In Yangzhou I had also acquired a pillar couplet written on black bamboo in the hand of the Grand Secretary Liang Jieping (named Guozhi, from Zhejiang Province, and a man who had topped his metropolitan examination) that read:

Learning and wine here gathered between these pillars, we converse of things both ancient and modern.

At dawn and at dusk we hide in this tiny room, roaming in spirit the vast mountains and the rivers.

As the couplet was both extraordinary and finely wrought, and the scenes it described accorded perfectly with those of my garden, this too I had hung here.

I remembered that, long ago, in the *xinwei* year of the reign of the Jiaqing emperor [1811], I had been having a brief drink in the Mustard Seed Garden in the south of the city (by the Han Family Pond) when the then owner told me that the rockery of the garden was the product of the hand of Li Yu. At the beginning of the dynasty, he said, once prosperity had returned, the palaces and mansions of the nobles grew as numerous as the clouds, each competing with the others in the lavishness and extravagance of its design, their owners all vying to have Li Yu come and stay as honored guest, such was the fame of his art of rockery. There are two Half-Acre Gardens within the Inner City, he continued, both the product of his hand. Hearing this, I found myself, immediately, visiting them in spirit. And now, in this present *xinchou* year [1841], a full thirty years have passed by since that occasion, and this garden has, finally, become mine. I have obtained, thus, that which I desired most ardently as a youth with no expectation of success. That which was presaged thirty years ago has now become a reality. Restoration work on the garden was completed in the fourth month of the *guimao* year [1843], and in the fifth month of that same year I took up residence within it. Heaven has served to bring about a fate long predestined me. How very fortunate I am.

"Early Summer Night" (*Chuxia ye* 初夏夜)

TANG QINGYUN 唐慶雲 (FL. 1814)

TRANSLATED BY MAUREEN ROBERTSON

Better known as a painter, Tang Qingyun was a concubine of Ruan Yuan (1764–1849), the distinguished scholar, editor, and bibliophile who held senior government positions in the provinces as well as the capital. Little is known of Tang Qingyun's life. Ruan Yuan's second principal wife, a direct descendant of Confucius, was also a poet.

"Early Summer Night"

I sit at night outside my room,
thoughts very calm;
the seasonal weather is clear and mild,
it's a late-evening sky.

The breeze through shoots
of young bamboo is supple;
a rising moon beneath new leaves
on the plane tree is round.
I search for a good line of poetry,
pick one out and write it down;
when eyes get tired from reading,
I fall asleep embracing the book.
Suddenly a complete dream, somewhere
that's like a realm of immortals;
after I wake, the scent of incense
still clings to the hem of my sleeve.

The Canton Chinese; or, The American's Sojourn in the Celestial Empire

"Chapter VIII: The Environs of Canton" (extracts)

OSMOND TIFFANY JR. (1823–1895)

Osmond Tiffany Jr., the son of one of the earliest merchants of Baltimore in the United States, traveled to Canton (Guangzhou) in 1844 and left in early 1845, having spent several months there. On his return to Baltimore, he worked as a merchant and published both factual books such as this (published in 1849) and works of fiction, before serving on the Union side in the American Civil War. It is not surprising that during his stay in Canton he visited the garden of the influential merchant Pan Shicheng (1804–1873, known to Westerners as Pontinqua or Pow-xing-kua), since it was open to European and American visitors and was considered one of the sights of Canton. Descriptions of it by several such visitors were published in the nineteenth century, whereas Chinese descriptions of Cantonese gardens are sparse. Although Tiffany regarded the garden as "perfectly Chinese," we know from his own description of the "glass apartment," which also appears in photographs of the garden, and from other photographic and pictorial evidence, that the garden showed considerable Western influence.

"Chapter VIII: The Environs of Canton," the garden of Pan Shicheng

In a short time we passed the meadows; the grounds on each side were protected by a neat fence, and on the left hand side we saw a flight of stone steps toward which our boat was directed.

This was the entrance to Pontinqua's property, and we were admitted to the garden through a perfectly circular portal. A little lodge stood on one side of the gate occupied by a servant, who bowed obsequiously as we entered.

A curious scene presented itself, the whole garden was irrigated and planted with the Nymphea Nelumbo, (sacred lotus,) which grew as pond lilies do, and spread their broad leaves over the surface of the water.

In some seasons this plant is in bloom, and then the gardens look like one flower-bed, and present a beautiful appearance.

The house stood in the midst of the water, and was approached by bridges winding about in various directions, and guarded by balustrades as intricate and fantastic as the ivory carvings. There were bridges beginning every where, and ending in nothing at all; some with covers, some without, some high in the air, and some almost under water. Everything was queer, different from any thing we had ever before seen, and perfectly Chinese.

We thus learned that the extraordinary representations on porcelain and lac ware were not fictitious creations, but faithful realities.

The bridge shaped like a truncated triangle on Chinese plates we actually saw, one large middle arch and two small ones.

The garden of Pontinqua's is a real curiosity, and he has gone to enormous expense in decorating it.

The house is of two stories; the lower, appropriated to guests, has a large suite of beautiful rooms filled with costly furniture and objects of virtu.

One room was used for visitors of ceremony; there was an enormous chair for the host, and two parallel lines of chairs on either side for his guests. The furniture was the native rosewood, richly carved, and the backs and seats were formed of elegant marbles, or the curious stained stones which represent animals and human figures, each one of which cost no inconsiderable sum.

The rooms were separated from each other by lattice work of the most intricate patterns, or fine silk gauze, or a sort of net-work formed of the fibres of the bamboo, and which is very costly. Another apartment on the outer side was entirely glass, and just opposite to this room, but across the water, at a distance of ten feet, was a covered stage for theatrical representations. Thus the inmates of the house could behold the show through the glass, and were protected in case of cold winds or rainy weather. Behind the stage were several shelves, on which were little clay figures, dressed appropriately, and presenting personages and scenes in Chinese life.

There were in and about the house several stone tablets, which bore witness to the friendship which Pontinqua had formed with illustrious persons. There was also an aviary filled with rare birds. The second story was devoted to sleeping apartments, which were all placed, as it were, in the middle of the house, and a gallery surrounded them, lighted by the outer windows.

In this gallery were pictures, arms, several models of foreign ships, and an English steamboat.

Pontinqua's portrait was conspicuous; he was adorned with the peacock's feather, though his worship was drawn without shade or background.

In one part of the grounds was a paddock for deer, in another part an artificial hermitage, with a bench, a pair of sandals, and a staff.

The master had pierced through a mound on his estate for a labyrinth, and the whole place gave evidence that money had been squandered on it in limitless profusion.

It is said that on one occasion, his own marriage or his mother's birthday, that Pontinqua entertained his friends at his villa for three days, in so splendid and costly a manner, that his expenditures amounted to ten thousand dollars a day.

"Chapter VIII: The Environs of Canton," the Fah-tee garden

Another point of some interest to the stranger, and particularly the botanist, is the Fah-tee garden. This lies about a mile above the hongs, on the Honam side of the river, and is in fact divided into two separate gardens by a little creek making out from the river.

They are open all day, and foreigners are permitted to visit them at any moment.

The gardens are owned by a number of the rich natives of Canton, are of great extent, and filled with rare and beautiful plants, and at certain seasons the eye may be gratified with the magnificent display of ten thousand japonicas in bloom at one time.

A very excellent and pretty collection of plants in flower may be made in Canton, by obtaining a man from these gardens, who brings any that you want, attends to them as long as they remain fresh, and then changes them for others, and all for a trifling consideration.

When you visit the gardens you may bring away with you japonicas, and any other flowers not considered very rare, for the mere asking, and any of the plants will be furnished at reasonable prices.

If to go on shipboard, orange or japonica trees are in small size put into boxes filled with rare earth, and the top of the box is made of roof shape, and to open and shut at pleasure. In this lid are inserted thin laminae of pearl oyster shells used in China so extensively in lieu of glass, in order to afford light to the plants even when they are obliged to be closed in stormy weather.

You enter the garden through a sort of lodge for the gardeners, and which serves also as a storehouse for every thing necessary connected with their vocation; there were thousands of flower pots plain and ornamented, glasses for delicate young plants, and for others covers pierced through with holes to allow the young green shoots to spring out and curl all over the form. There were also porcelain seats and chairs for gardens, though these might be had cheap in the city.

The plants were arranged in long rows on benches, on the ground, or planted against the brick wall, and every one in the vast number looked vigorous and healthy.

The orange trees were loaded with golden richness, and bore a different look from the sickly absentees in our hot-houses; and here were the little cumquat oranges of blood red color, and used only in preserving.

The Chinese are so fond of the queer and fantastic as to carry their taste even into nature, and not contented with bringing plants and flowers to the highest state of perfection, they must torture them into singular shapes and dwarf them, as they do the feet of their women.

In this manner one will often see in small pots plants that, left to their natural growth, would require wide space, yet are in full leaf and fruit. The stems of orange trees, for instance, are very thick, the leaves abundant, the fruit sound, and the whole will not be more than a foot in height.

No other people have succeeded in forcing nature out of its own way so completely, and it is the result of long study and practice, just as fruits that, in a wild state are unfit to eat, are rendered delicious by culture.

The Chinese gardeners effect this dwarfing by commencing with the plant very young, cutting off some shoots, and bending others, and preventing the sap from spreading, by fixing ligatures around the branches.

Thus the animus of the plant is confined to one small portion of it, and after a while, art overcomes the natural disposition of the tree, and it bears and thrives in its contracted state.

The horticulturists are also very fond of training shrubs into the shape of birds, men, or animals, and often effect a surprising resemblance to the object they imitate. Their work of this kind in roots has been already noticed. . . .

The botanist will find much to repay his curiosity in the Fah-tee gardens, and they offer the best opportunity to him, in a country where he cannot wander as he pleases.

Very few, if any, good collections of Chinese plants have been made; many thousands of specimens have left the country, and a small number comparatively have crossed the ocean in safety. The length of the voyage, unpleasant weather, and want of proper care and room have proved great obstacles to the successful introduction of them into England and America.

They could best be transported in some government vessel, where there would be plenty of air, room, and at the same time, good shelter; but until a ship is dispatched especially, our naturalists may despair of having a good collection. . . .

The Fah-tee gardens, as I have observed, are divided by the little creek which our boat sails up so gaily, and which forms a snug harbor for vessels bound down to Canton, and suddenly met by a heavy head wind.

The inclosures, especially on the side of the creek that strangers do not visit, (for most of them are quite content with seeing one side of the Chinese in all respects,) are shaded with lofty trees, and it is pleasant to hear the winds murmur among their lofty branches, after being shut up for weeks in Canton, with scarce a blade of grass in sight.

These gardens are not like the private grounds of the rich, but are mere receptacles for plants, and in consequence, display none of the decoration and curious embellishment that attaches to Chinese landscape gardening in general. There were several bridges and summer-houses placed amid pools of water, but these frog ponds were used chiefly for watering the plants.

The gardeners were evidently men who thoroughly understood their vocation, and were stimulated by enthusiasm at the same time. They were polite and anxious to show us their plants, and did not withhold any information we asked for. They were different from the generality of the people, who are very shy in their answers, as they imagine that foreigners are always trying to get the upper hand of them.

In truth, men accustomed to spend their days in studying the works of nature are apt to bear a natural and simple demeanor.

A Residence among the Chinese

"Chapter X" (extract)

ROBERT FORTUNE (1813–1880)

The Scottish horticulturist Robert Fortune made five visits to China between 1843 (just after the First Opium War) and 1861 (just after the Arrow War or Second Opium War). In 1852, he was employed by the East India Company to obtain tea plants to be transplanted to British India; arriving in China in 1853, he remained there until 1856, and his account of his journey was published as *A Residence Among the Chinese* in 1857. This extract is a description of the garden belonging to Wu Bingjian (1769–1843), a leading Cohong merchant, known to Westerners as Howqua. The garden was well known to foreign visitors to Canton, who would mostly have been acquainted with Wu Bingjian and his associates. It is clear from the notices that gave Fortune and his friend such amusement that the garden was also accessible to the Chinese public.

"Chapter X," Howqua's Garden

This garden is situated near the well-known Fa-tee nurseries, a few miles above the city of Canton, and is a place of favorite resort both for Chinese and foreigners who reside in the neighborhood, or who visit this part of the Celestial Empire. I determined on paying it a visit in company with Mr. McDonald, who is well known in this part of the world as an excellent Chinese scholar, and to whom I am indebted for some translations of Chinese notices, which appeared very amusing to us at the time, and which, I dare say, will amuse my readers.

Having reached the door of the garden, we presented the card with which we were provided, and were immediately admitted. The view from the entrance is rather pleasing, and particularly striking to a stranger who sees it for the first time. Looking "right ahead," as sailors say, there is a long and narrow paved walk lined on each side with plants in pots. This view is broken, and apparently lengthened, by means of an octagon arch which is thrown across, and beyond that a kind of alcove covers the pathway. Running parallel with the walk, and on each side behind the plants, are low walls of ornamental brickwork, latticed so that the ponds or small lakes which are on each side can be seen. Altogether the octagon arch, the alcove, the pretty ornamental flower-pots, and the water on each side, has a striking effect, and is thoroughly Chinese.

The plants consist of good specimens of southern Chinese things, all well known in England, such, for example, as Cymbidium sinense, Olea fragrans, oranges, roses, camellias, magnolias, etc., and, of course, a multitude of dwarf trees, without which no Chinese garden would be considered complete. In the alcove alluded to there are some nice stone seats, which look cool in a climate like that of southern China. The floor of this building is raised a few feet above the ground-level, so that the visitor gets a good view of the water and other objects of interest in the garden. That this is a favorite lounge and smoking-place with the Chinese, the following Chinese notice, which we found on one of the pillars, will testify:—"*A careful and earnest notice*: This garden earnestly requests visitors will spit betle[73] outside the railing, and knock the ashes of pipes also outside." Several fine fruit-trees and others are growing near the walks, and afford shade from the rays of the sun. On one of these we read the following:—"Ramblers here will be excused plucking the fruit on this tree." How exceedingly polite!

Near the center of the garden stands a substantial summer-house, or hall, named "the Hall of Fragrant Plants." The same notice to smokers and chewers of betle-nut is also put up here; and there is another longer one which I must not forget to quote. It is this:—"In this garden the plants are intended to delight the eyes of all visitors: a great deal has been expended in planting and in keeping in order, and the garden is now beginning to yield some return. Those who come here to saunter about are earnestly prayed not to pluck the fruit or flowers, in order that the beauty of the place may be preserved." And then follows a piece of true Chinese politeness—"We beg persons who understand this notice to excuse it!" Passing through the Hall of Fragrant Plants we approached, between two rows of Olea fragrans, a fine ornamental suite of rooms tastefully furnished and decorated, in which visitors are received and entertained. An inscription informs us that this is called "the Fragrant Hall of the Woo-che tree." Leaving this place by a narrow door, we observed the following notice—"Saunterers here will be excused entering." This apparently leads to the private apartments of the family. In this side of the garden there is some fine artificial rockwork, which the Chinese know well how to construct, and various summer-houses tastefully decorated, one of which is called the "Library of Verdant Purity." Between this part of the garden and the straight walk already noticed there is a small pond or lake for fish and water-lilies. This is crossed by a zigzag wooden bridge of many arches, which looked rather dilapidated. A very necessary notice was put up here informing "saunterers to stop their steps in case of accident."

On the outskirts of the garden we observed the potting sheds, a nursery for rearing young plants and seeds, and the kitchen garden. Here a natural curiosity was pointed out by one of the Chinese, which, at first sight, appeared singularly curious. Three trees were growing in a row, and at about twenty or thirty feet from the ground the two outer ones had sent out shoots, and fairly united themselves with the center one. When I mention that the outer trees are the Chinese banyan (Ficus nitida), it will readily be seen how the appearance they presented was produced. The long roots sent down by

---

73   Betle-Nut [betel] is much used by the southern Chinese.

this species had lovingly embraced the center tree, and appeared at first sight to have really grafted themselves upon it.

I am afraid I have given a very imperfect description of this curious garden. Those who know what a Chinese garden is will understand me well enough, but it is really difficult to give a stranger an idea of the Chinese style which I have been endeavoring to describe. In order to understand the Chinese style of gardening it is necessary to dispel from the mind all ideas of fine lawn, broad walks, and extensive views; and to picture in their stead everything on a small scale—that is, narrow paved walks, dwarf walls in all directions, with lattice-work or ornamental openings in them, in order to give views of the scenery beyond; halls, summer-houses, and alcoves, ponds or small lakes with zigzag walks over them—in short, an endeavor to make small things appear large, and large things small, and everything Chinese. There are some of these ornaments, however, which I think might be imitated with advantage in our own gardens. Some of the doorways and openings in walls seemed extremely pretty. In particular I may notice a wall about ten feet high, having a number of open compartments filled with porcelain rods made to imitate the stems of the bamboo. I shall now close this notice with the modest lines of the Chinese poet, which we found written in the "Library of Verdant Purity," and which seemed to be an effort to describe the nature of the garden:—

Some few stems of bamboo-plants
A cottage growing round;
A few flowers here—some old trees there,
And a mow[74] of garden ground.

PART 2
IMPERIAL GARDENS

With the exception of the "Record of Touring the Rehe Rear Garden at Imperial Invitation" by Zhang Yushu and the concluding "letter" by the court painter Brother Jean-Denis Attiret, the garden records and poems in this section are all by the very emperors who ordered and oversaw the creation or development of the early Qing imperial gardens. The Kangxi emperor was the first Qing emperor to come to the throne after the Manchu conquest of China, succeeding his father, the Shunzhi emperor, who had been a small boy (six years old) at the time of the conquest. The Kangxi emperor, his son the Yongzheng emperor, and his grandson the Qianlong emperor were the three greatest Qing emperors, presiding over the pacification of China after the turbulence of the late Ming, and the expansion of its territory to the north, west, and south. All of them paid great attention, in the intervals of governing, to the creation and development of gardens; the Qianlong emperor, in particular, was inspired by visits to the great private gardens of southeast China during

---

74   A mow [*mu*] is one-sixth part of an acre.

his many imperial progresses,[75] and used the construction of exotic structures, such as the Western Ocean Buildings in the Garden of Perfect Brightness and the Tibetan temple in the Mountain Manor for Escaping the Summer Heat at Jehol, to bolster his claim to universal sovereignty.

"Record of the Garden of Uninhibited Spring" (*Changchun yuan ji* 暢春園記)

THE KANGXI EMPEROR 康熙帝 (AISINGIORO XUANYE 愛新覺羅玄燁;
1654–1722, R. 1661–1722)
TRANSLATED BY HUI ZOU[76]

The town of Haidian [Sea of Shallows] is situated some twelve *li* outside the Xizhi Gate of the capital. There are lakes to the north and to the south. Springs gush out from the plain at the Village of Ten-Thousand Springs, before flowing away rapidly, with a slosh and a gurgle, to converge at the Vermilion Mound Lake. The lake is so vast that its surface stretches a full one hundred *qing*. Lush wilderness here is juxtaposed with flat agricultural fields, and clear waves with distant hills. Their colors intermingle like gorgeous embroidery. What a blessed scenic spot this is! Since I inherited the throne, day and night administration has prevented me from having any leisure. A long period of fatigue and overwork has gradually made me sick. Finding a moment's release from my labors on a particular occasion, I traveled here for a rest. Tasting the spring water and finding it sweet, I looked around and appreciated the place. As cool breezes slowly rose, my worries and my infirmities suddenly dissipated. No wonder a distant imperial relative of the Ming dynasty, Li Wei, the Marquis of Wuqing, built a villa here in accordance with the pleasant topography. The landscape of that time, as magnificent as the garden district of Wei's Township in Chang'an during the Tang dynasty, can still be distinctly perceived. After the villa collapsed and was abandoned, the ruined area still has a circumference of ten miles. Although the garden has disintegrated into scattered remains with the passing of time, the original conditions can still be traced. I catch a glimpse of a building with eaves that seem to soar into the air and stroll along a winding balustrade by the water. Ancient trees and dark-green vines grow yet apace.

I thus called upon the officials of the Bureau of the Imperial Household to make moderate adjustments, transforming higher places into hills and lower places into pools. The natural lay of the topography was appraised and the original stones and bricks were reused. Better use and value were achieved without recruiting much labor. The humble buildings and garden are sufficient for my contemplation and my rest. Virtuous thrift is cherished forever, and sumptuous carvings avoided. Although only six or seven

---

75 On the Qianlong emperor's "literati aspirations," see Nancy Berliner, *The Emperor's Private Paradise* (New Haven: Yale University Press, 2010), 136–47.

76 Earlier versions of these translations were published in the appendix of Hui Zou, *A Jesuit Garden in Beijing and Early Modern Chinese Culture* (West Lafayette, Ind.: Purdue University Press, 2011).

out of ten of the old pavilions, terraces, hillocks, gullies, forests, trees, springs, and rocks of Li Wei's garden survive, the beauty of expansive ripples and the momentum of watercourses are as attractive as they once were.

Layer upon layer of hillocks reveal distant water shores, and the morning haze is followed by evening mists. Fragrant flowers bloom throughout all four seasons, and rare birds sing among the people. When crops yield a rich harvest, and the fields are fragrant with sweet smells, I can engage with beautiful scenes in all directions, and my heart is transported into the distance. But sometimes, when crops are ruined and sun and rain come at the wrong time, I stand on a footpath in the fields feeling compassion for the farmers, or open the window to check the ditches which serve to irrigate the fields. I look for signs of rain with ardent hope and pray anxiously to the sky. It seems as if my whole realm can be seen from my window.

On a good day in spring or autumn when the sky is clear and refreshing, or in the humid high summer when the sunlight is hot and dazzling, I come here, taking a short break from public affairs, for the sake of my health and to roam around. This makes me feel younger and more tranquil, and does away with my concerns and the heat; it also puts my heart at ease and makes my complexion healthy. I sway back and forth, enjoying a good time and the joy of Heaven. The hall for holding audience is bright and high, and the winding chamber with deep eaves stores ancient books. The cottages are thatched with thistle and have not been given any decoration. Wherever necessary, a bridge or a boat is used for crossing the water, a hedge for dividing places, and a wall for enclosing a site. Things are as simple and natural as that.

After the garden was built, it was named Uninhibited Spring, but not because it particularly fitted springtime. In the calendars of the three successive dynasties Xia, Shang, and Zhou, the Zhou dynasty took the *zi* character as the spring of Heaven; the Shang dynasty took the *chou* character as the spring of earth, and the Xia dynasty took the *yin* character as the spring of man. The *Book of Changes* says that when the *qian*, the primary one, unifies the world, all the four virtues become the primary one and all four seasons are spring. Previous emperors relied upon this principle to raise things at the right time, to enable all people to have their appropriate places and all animals to live according to their nature. Under Heaven there is plenitude of happiness and brightness; winds blow together from eight directions, and the six movements, the six *qi*, reach everywhere. This is why I named the garden Uninhibited Spring.

The Qin dynasty built the Epang Palace; the Han dynasty developed the Upper Forest Park; the Tang dynasty constructed the beautiful landscapes of the Embroidered Mountain Ranges; the Song dynasty established the Genyue or Northeast Marchmount garden. The luxurious decorations of their buildings, the large area of their gardens, including as they did hills and valleys, are certainly all beyond both my means and my desires. I dare not imitate the ancients and compete with models from the past; I am myself entirely satisfied with humble buildings, and I avoid spending money on sumptuous terraces. I only wish to act according to proper time and help the flow of things, support and wait upon my mother, and stay in good health. I long for the peace of all creatures and wish for the harmony of the world. I think of each person and each thing all the time. How could my affection for them cease? I have therefore written this record and accompany it now with a poem:

Long ago the rulers of Xia,
Were sternly thrifty and lived in humble palaces.
King Wen of Zhou is acclaimed,
For not hankering for material gain.
If ancient instructions are examined,
These two should be respected and admired.
Inscribing them as my admonition,
I practice them myself day and night.

The establishment of my residence,
Is based on dynastic precedent.
Cliffside lodges with rosy clouds,
Eaves projecting into blue mists.
I construct and maintain it,
So as not to let it be ruined.
There are hot springs,
Deep and diffuse here.
I travel to the western suburb,
Set up colorful banners of camp.
I draw sweet waters from there,
And carefully devise this plan.

The water is like a mirror of crystal,
Meandering as a fragrant stream.
I pace up and down by the river,
Roam here and stroll there.
Height comes from the hills,
Depth emerges from the valleys.
I consult there and construct here,
But would not say it is to transform.
Pine galleries and thatched halls,
Are suitable only to myself.
There are some plain carvings,
I feel regretful about them.

Construction began at an auspicious time,
The garden was built within a few days.
Though not specifically for strolling and enjoying,
I am delighted by this construction.
Respecting and serving my mother,
How could I live high and bright?
Gazing leisurely and looking over,
I only wish to entertain my temperament.

Abundance of books and classics,
All are stored in a continuous belvedere.
Only this great veranda,
Can be compared to red embroidered collars.
Flourishing agrarian fields,
Are cultivated regularly.
Without borrowing human labor,
There are vague cloudy gullies.
Boats glide like a water bird,
Bridges span like a rainbow.
Sailing or crossing,
I stroll around free of care.
Literature or martial arts,
I practice at different times.

I retreat to reflect upon my administration,
No mistake is to be allowed.
It is said that the virtue of a gentleman,
Cannot be but kindheartedness.
Take the primary one as the principle for administration,
It is as the springtime of seasons.
I wish all things
May return to their plainness and purity.
The meaning of Uninhibited Spring,
Is thus proclaimed here for my officials.

Imperial Poems on the Mountain Estate for Escaping the Heat (Yuzhi Bishu shanzhuang shi 御製避暑山莊詩)

"A Lingzhi Path on an Embankment to the Clouds" (*Zhijing yundi* 芝逕雲隄)

THE KANGXI EMPEROR 康熙帝
TRANSLATED BY RICHARD E. STRASSBERG

This poem, with its short prose introduction, is the second of thirty-six poems written by the Kangxi emperor to mark the completion of the Mountain Estate for Escaping the Heat (*Bishu shanzhuang*) at Jehol (Rehe, present-day Chengde) in 1711, as the emperor himself approached his sixtieth birthday, the completion of a sixty-year cycle. Despite the auspicious occasion, the court was racked with tension at the time over the succession to the throne; the collection of poems, along with the woodblock prints and European-style copperplate engravings that the emperor commissioned from the court artists, were intended as an assertion of imperial authority. This poem, one of the longest in the collection, lays emphasis on the imperial benevolence shown in selecting a garden site that was not (so we are told) in agricultural use and attested by "good harvests year after year." The imperial poet also asserts his intention to "continue . . . to govern together with worthies," implicitly downplaying the importance of the succession question.

The Lingzhi Path on an embankment is north of the place known as Pine Winds through Myriad Vales; it leads from the palace area to the lake area and separates the Upper Lake from Wish-Fulfilling Lake. It invokes the famous embankment at West Lake in Hangzhou built by Su Shi (1037–1101). A *lingzhi* is an auspicious, mythical plant shaped like a fungus with several growths on a stalk; it symbolizes longevity, especially in Daoist culture, and was sometimes represented as a decorative object known as a wish-fulfilling wand (*ruyi*). Kangxi stated that the name of this view derived from the resemblance of the shape of the path and the three islands it connected to a *lingzhi*. The three islands were individually referred to as Sounds of the River in the Moonlight, Surrounded by Greenery, and Un-Summerly Clear and Cool, and they were sometimes collectively referred to as Wish-Fulfilling Island.

"A Lingzhi Path on an Embankment to the Clouds"

> An embankment was built flanked on both sides by water. It then meanders as it divides into three paths leading to three islets, large and small. They are shaped like a *lingzhi*, like clouds and also like a wish-fulfilling wand. Two bridges permit boats to pass underneath.

> Despite myriad affairs, I found some time
>   to leave my gated palace.
> With my passion for mountains and streams,
>   it was hard not to linger on the way.
> I escaped the heat near the northern desert
>   where the land is fertile and rich.
> Local elders were consulted
>   as I searched for old inscriptions.

They all said that these are plains
    where Mongols pastured horses.
There were also few inhabitants
    and no bones of vanquished warriors.
Grasses and trees flourish.
No mosquitoes or scorpions.
And the spring water is excellent:
People are seldom ill.
So I saddled up and rode off
    to inspect the river bend.
Twisting and turning,
    it meandered through shady groves.
I surveyed the extent of the wilderness
    and measured the water level.
There was no need to destroy fields
    or cut down any trees.
For the land conforms in shape
    to Heaven's natural design.
It needed no human labor
    for artificial constructions.

Do you not see Hammer Peak?
Solitary and erect, it stands forth to the east.
And do you not see the pines in myriad vales?
A canopy drooping over layered forests
    in accord with nature's way.
Nurtured by warming ethers,
    receiving the glistening dew,
The verdant crops ripen
    with good harvests year after year.
Mindful always of straining the people
    when traveling for pleasure,
I also feared burdening them
    to obtain construction workers.

Designers were told to first build
    Divine Fungus Path
And to follow the form of the land
    in making it properly even.
The Chamberlain was not to use
    imperial treasury funds.

I preferred the rustic and rejected flamboyance
    to accord with the people's taste.
How could I ever build a Great Wall
    and rely on border guards?
History has well recorded
    those cruel and extravagant rulers.
This is a reason to urge myself
    toward caution and restraint.
Then I can become a model for all,
    pacifying near and far.

Though it lacks imposing structures,
    there are towers that touch the clouds.
Yet climbing them can not disperse
    layers and layers of sorrows.
The mountain chains and remote ravines
    offer views in every season,
Pitying me that in old age,
    the worries of ruling remain.
If they would help to nurture my health
    and sustain my energy and strength,
I'll continue to strive in every way
    to govern together with worthies.
Promoting farming in accord with the seasons
    is my imperial ambition
So the beacons of war will no longer flare
    for a hundred thousand autumns.

"Record of the Garden of Perfect Brightness" (*Yuanming yuan ji* 圓明園記)

THE YONGZHENG EMPEROR 雍正帝 (AISINGIORO YINZHEN 愛新覺羅胤禛;
1678–1735, R. 1722–1735)
TRANSLATED BY HUI ZOU

North of the Garden of Uninhibited Spring, the Garden of Perfect Brightness was granted to me as my residence garden. During his leisure time, after a court audience, my father, the majestic Kangxi emperor, strolled along the shore of the Vermilion Mound Lake. After tasting the spring water and finding it sweet, he decided to renovate a ruined villa from the Ming dynasty, and so he reduced its site and built the Garden of Uninhibited Spring for his residence in high spring and summer. Accompanying him, I was granted an area here with clear, elegant forested hills and still, deep, and expansive waters. My garden was sited in accordance with what was high and what was deep, abutting mountains and beside water, always following the existing lie of the land, thus choosing the delight offered by nature and sparing myself the vexations incumbent on construction. Flowers by the balustrades and trees along the embankment flourished without watering. Flocks of birds enjoyed soaring; schools of fish dove freely. The place was bright, high and dry; fertile soil and abundant springs promised prosperity. How peaceful and auspicious it was to reside here! When the garden was built, thanks to my father's benevolence, it was granted the name Perfect Brightness.

I waited respectfully for my father's arrival, enjoyed his kindness, celebrated with him the heavenly joy, and expressed how sincerely I cherished this moment. Flowers and trees, forests and springs, all were bathed in his glory and his favor. After inheriting the throne, I mourned day and night and fasted to pay respect to my departed father. Although the summer was hot and muggy, I made no plan to escape the heat and seek the cool.

Three years passed and the rite of mourning was over. All the pressing administrative matters now awaiting my attention required that I approach them with a calm mind, in order that I might be blessed with good fortune and avoid vexations. For a clear and beautiful atmosphere, residing in a garden is best. I therefore ordered the Bureau of the Imperial Household to restore the garden with great care. All the pavilions, terraces, hills and gullies were returned to their original appearances. A wing was added for various administrative departments, so all the retinue and on-duty officials could have their workplaces. A hall was built in the south of the garden for audiences.

When the first rays of the morning sun appear and the shadow of the sundial is still long, I call officials for consultation. I frequently change my daily schedule in order to spend more time with my officials. Fields were planted with crops, plots were planted with vegetables, and the plains proved fertile, and the crops and vegetables were abundant. With a single glance into the distance, now, my thoughts extend to the whole of the Chinese world, conveying my wishes for a good harvest. When I lean on a balustrade inspecting the crops or stand beside the field studying the clouds, I wish for a good rain to come in timely fashion and hope for weather responsive to sturdy seedlings. Scenes of weary and hardworking peasants, of the toil of tilling the land, suddenly appear within the garden. When the light of the forest shines bright and clear and the reflections on the pools are clear and distinct, stretching out calm and without ripples, then are distant peaks reflected as if in a mirror. In morning sun or under evening moon, the lush vegetation is reflected and the sky becomes encompassed by the water. Hence, the magic effects of the Way emerge spontaneously and of their own accord, and the benevolent wishes of Heaven are revealed to all.

During short breaks from my labors, I study the canon to shape my character. I explore rhythm for poems, practice calligraphy and dedicate myself to the study of the classics. My daily routine of activity and of rest is strictly observed, enlightened by my late father's revered model, which I respectfully observe at all times and dare not overstep. The ceilings, columns, walls and doors of the buildings are in a simple form without superfluous ornament, following the lead of my late father's simple life. I communicate with ministers and officials during the day, review their reports and propositions at night, collate texts while standing on a front step and watch archers at practice in the archery field. At leisure or on duty, I follow the same rule of conduct, following the lead of my father's diligence. In the fine days of spring and autumn, when the scenery is fresh and fragrant, birds sing a harmonious chord and limpid dew congeals on flower petals, I sometimes invite princes and ministers to appreciate the scenes at their own pace, to boat and enjoy fruits. We give free rein to our feelings, displaying accordingly our sense of well-being, looking up and gazing down and roaming at leisure. Nature discloses itself to the fullest; heart and mind exult with joy, following the lead of my father's receptiveness to worthy and virtuous people, and his consideration for his courtiers and ability to avail himself of circumstances.

Perfect Brightness, the name granted by my father, has a deep and far-ranging meaning, not easily perceived. I have tried to research ancient books for the moral meaning of Perfect Brightness. Perfect means the perfection and concentration of the mind, implying the timeliness and moderation of the behavior of a virtuous man. Brightness means to illuminate all things to reach human perspicacity and wisdom. Perfect Brightness is used to highlight the meaning of the residence, stimulate the body and mind, piously experience the idea of Heaven, cherish forever my father's sacred instruction, propagate all creatures and maintain harmony and peace. I do not ask for peace for myself but rather wish it for the whole realm. I do not seek leisure for myself but rather long for happiness for all the people, so that generation after generation can step on the spring terrace and wander in a happy kingdom. I stabilize the mighty foundation of the country to make people's good fortune and well being last long into the future. If what I have done can show my gratitude to the blessing my father bestowed upon me, my heart at this moment might feel a little relieved. I therefore write this record to express my deep feelings.

"Twelve Poems on Garden Scenes" (*Yuanjing shier yong* 園景十二詠)

"The Reading Hall Deep Inside Weeping Willows" (*Shenliu dushu tang* 深柳讀書堂), "The Bamboo Cloister" (*Zhuzi yuan* 竹子院), and "The Peony Chamber" (*Mudan shi* 牡丹室)

THE YONGZHENG EMPEROR 雍正帝

TRANSLATED BY WU HUNG

"The Reading Hall Deep Inside Weeping Willows"

How elegant and fine are the thousand weeping willows,
Embracing this thatched hall in their cool shade.
Their floating strands gently brush against an inkstone;
Their catkins leave dotted marks on a lute-stand.
The oriole's song warms up their spring branches;
The cicada's cry chills their autumn leaves.
In moonlight they cast their shadows on the hall's windows,
Concealing yet enhancing the fragrance of ancient books.

"The Bamboo Cloister"

A stream winds into a deep courtyard.
A corridor turns into a bamboo-flanked path.
Their jade girdles give forth a tinkling sound;
Gracefully they play with the clear breeze.
Their fragrance penetrates book covers;
Their cool shade protects patterned window gratings.
So elegant, fine, and beautiful—
Yet they determine to flourish only in harsh winter.

"The Peony Chamber"

Layered clouds pile up these elegant rocks.
A winding stream surrounds and passes the Peony Chamber.
Without equal under Heaven,
Surely you are the world's supreme flower.
So voluptuous Shi Chong should have favored you.
So world-famous that you should have dominated Luoyang.
Who can stand next to you, the National Beauty?
Five-colored clouds make up your immortal garments.

"Latter Record of the Garden of Perfect Brightness" (*Yuanming yuan houji* 圓明園後記)

THE QIANLONG EMPEROR 乾隆帝 (AISINGIORO HONGLI 愛新覺羅弘曆;
1711–1799, R. 1735–1796)
TRANSLATED BY HUI ZOU

In the past, my father Yongzheng repaired and improved a garden that my grand-father Kangxi had granted him. Basic administration space was added so that he could issue decrees at will, promulgate new policies, and remain close to his worthy officials at all times. In terms of the design of the studios and staircases, the pavilions and gazebos, the convex hills and concave pools that were arrayed behind, plainness rather than magnificence, seclusion rather than conspicuous display were what was valued. His joy in planting was such that the shrubbery and flowerbeds burst into excited bloom. His overseeing of the labors of agriculture and sericulture was such that the fields and vegetable gardens were watered appropriately. As the wind sough-ing amid the pines and the moon shining upon the surface of the water penetrated his mind, the magic effects of the Way emerged spontaneously and of their own accord. Carefully did he protect the realm, frequently did he confer with learned offi-cials, and assiduously did he study the canon in order to shape his character. Here he could thoroughly enjoy himself, sing or recite poems, have all his senses on full alert or at ease.

The concerns for the welfare of the country that both my father and grandfather placed ahead of their own pleasure surrounded all things and thus came to form the Perfect Brightness. The meaning of Perfect Brightness indicates the timeliness and moder-ation of behavior of a virtuous man. My grandfather gave this name to the garden he granted to my father, and he in his turn accepted this gift respectfully as an uplifting of his own person and spirit, and as an ever-present reminder of his father. "I do not ask for peace for myself but rather wish it for the whole realm. I do not seek leisure for myself but rather long for happiness for all the people." This was my father's intention, to ensure that the people's well being and prosperity would last forever.

As his son, I too revere the ancestral palaces and gardens and am often afraid of demeaning them. How could I dare add to or modify them? Therefore, after inher-iting the imperial throne, when the construction department submitted a proposal to build a new garden, I refused. Since then, out of mourning, I have resided in the former garden of my father. During leisure hours between court audiences, an emperor must have his own place for roaming around and appreciating expansive landscapes. If a balance of work and leisure is maintained, then the garden will foster good per-sonality and shape the character. If balance is not achieved, he will indulge in futility and confuse his sense of purpose. If he pays too much attention to palace buildings, riding and archery, rare skills and curiosities, his attention to worthy officials and their propositions, his diligent administration, and his love of the people will dissipate. The consequences of such circumstances are dire beyond description.

My father did not reside in his father's Garden of Uninhibited Spring, because he already had his own Garden of Perfect Brightness. By turning down carvings and decorations, he was of one mind with the pure and simple inclinations of his father. However, the spacious and open scale, deep gullies and quiet hills, bright and beautiful landscapes, and high and remote buildings of this garden are beyond imagination. Here are heavenly treasures and earthly wonders truly gathered, and no imperial pleasure setting of the past can compare with it. For the same reason, my offspring should certainly not give this garden away and waste the people's wealth in building another one. This matches profoundly with my desire of following my father's diligent and frugal inclinations. The ancient records state: "Where the imperial ancestors dwelt, an emperor should not live," but how should we respond to this imperial taboo? Perhaps the clever praise (but implied criticism) once given the ruler of the Jin dynasty by Zhang Meng on being asked his opinion of the king's new palace may offer guidance in this respect?

My father has recounted in his record the history of building the garden and his intention to avail himself of circumstances, increase his scholarly wisdom and military courage, multiply all life under the sun, protect the harmonious and peaceful world, let the people step on the spring terrace and wander about the happy kingdom. How dare his son restate such intentions here!

"Poem on the Garden of Eternal Spring, with Preface" (*Changchun yuan shi bing xu* 長春園詩並序)

THE QIANLONG EMPEROR 乾隆帝
TRANSLATED BY HUI ZOU

Preface
Mountains and rivers are the symbols of joy and longevity, and therein afflatus follows that which is encountered. The sun and the moon draw out the scenes of this vast and marvelous land, thus serving to prolong the spring. I developed an unused corner of the imperial garden and named it after the good title of my former residence. Reflecting on this title, given by my father Yongzheng in the past, I happen from time to time to get close to the principle of the whole. Wishing for a peaceful residence in the future, I begin to arrange for such beforehand.

The water is connected to the Sea of Plenitude, and an unused field to the east is covered with magnificent sacred mulberry trees. The wall winds along the banks of the Clear River, and sweet smells of corn float over the northern fields. Glancing at ancient books entertains my spirit; a hall is used for storing them. I wield the brush in writing poems to enjoy myself; a gallery named Unsophisticated Transformation is used for storing stone tablets. The longing for diligence is everlasting and it is modeled in this studio. With my mind open to spectacular views, I climb this tower. Views of any hill and any valley are pretty enough to delight my heart. Pavilions along the water or on top of a hill offer views that attract my eyes.

Strolling and resting here during moments snatched away from public affairs, I think of staying forever in good health and in peace into my eighties and nineties. If a reign should last for sixty years (before retirement as in my grandfather's case), I am afraid my long hoped-for wish will turn out to be extravagant. As of today, I still have twenty-five years to fulfill, how could I dare feel tired already? I compose a poem to go along with the above preface:

The Garden of Eternal Spring dares not compare to the Garden of Uninhibited Spring,
I imitate the scenes of the famous gardens in Jiangnan for a certain reason.
My past residence in the Garden of Perfect Brightness was named Fairy Lodge in
    Eternal Spring,
When growing too old to work I will seek a residence for retirement,
Plant pine tree saplings and observe their growth,
Collect precious rocks and wait peacefully for some future reward.
The remaining twenty-five years still require prudence,
In my late eighties and nineties I shall stroll about leisurely and joyously.

Note: The Garden of Uninhibited Spring is south of the Garden of Perfect Brightness. It was built by my grandfather. Now it is the residence of my mother. The Fairy Lodge in Eternal Spring is one of the Forty Scenes of the Garden of Perfect Brightness. It was named by my father, the Yongzheng emperor. I use the same name for the new garden. I have a long-cherished wish that in the sixtieth year of my reign, namely at the age of eighty-five, I should retire. I am therefore preparing a garden east of the Garden of Perfect Brightness for my future residence. Although this might be an extravagant hope, if the garden is really built, it could also be regarded as good fortune for my realm and as a celebration of my people. I am sixty years old now and it will be another twenty-five years before I can retire. Nevertheless, I dare not relax at all and my will is for diligence in public affairs. Only after retirement will I be able to enjoy myself.

"Record of the Garden of Clear Ripples on Longevity Hill" (*Shoushan Qingyi yuan ji* 壽山清漪園記)

THE QIANLONG EMPEROR 乾隆帝
TRANSLATED BY HUI ZOU

My record of Kunming Lake by Longevity Hill was written in the *xinwei* year [1751]. It discusses the reasons for controlling the water and changing the name of the hill, as well as the process of constructing a lake. The Garden of Clear Ripples on Longevity Hill was built in the *xinsi* year [1761]. The reason why this record was not written until now is because the name tablet was inscribed at a later date and I had some difficulties in wording the record. Since the garden has been built and the name tablet has been inscribed, why is there any difficulty with the wording? It is because something has happened against my original will and thus I have a guilty conscience. What I need to say is proximate to the confession of my fault, and I, finally, must speak of it here. It is, after all, the so-called fault of a gentleman. If I do not talk about it, will I be able to avoid the whole country's speaking of it?

The reason for constructing the lake was to control the water, and the hill was renamed accordingly since it overlooks the lake. Since the lake and the hill already lent beauty to the place, was it possible that no pavilions and terraces would embellish them? All events have both their causes and their effects. Friends can be made by exchanging writings, because both sides correspond to each other. Moreover, the construction was funded by the Imperial Treasury; the laborers were paid; the principle of thrift was abided by and sumptuous decorations were avoided. All these follow the former model of the Garden of Perfect Brightness without ever surpassing it. Although in my record on the Garden of Perfect Brightness, I said that I would not use so much labor again to build a new garden, is not the present Garden of Clear Ripples such a case of making a new garden? Did I not break my promise? Since it overlooked the lake, the hill was renamed. Since there was a hill, a garden was created. If I say controlling the water is my original motive, who will believe me?

However, the Garden of Uninhibited Spring is my mother's residence. The Garden of Perfect Brightness is constantly used for audiences. Connected by the same water-course, the Garden of Clear Ripples and the Garden of Tranquil Brightness are places for quiet leisure, ease of the mind and tranquility. Xiao He's insistence that later generations should not add anything to the Han emperor Gaozu's gardens is exactly what I intend for myself. This is really my intention. Although it is so, I suddenly feel lost when recalling Sima Guang's words.

After the garden was built, I would usually go there in the early mornings and return at noon, never staying there overnight. This itinerary fits my original will, and people might thus forgive me.

"Record of Touring the Rehe Rear Garden at Imperial Invitation" (*Hucong ciyou ji* 扈從賜遊記)

ZHANG YUSHU 張玉書 (1642–1711)

TRANSLATED BY STEPHEN H. WHITEMAN

Zhang Yushu was a talented scholar of the Hanlin Academy, where he held editorial positions on some of the Kangxi emperor's most important publication projects. He rose to the position of grand secretary and minister of the Board of Revenue, and was one of the emperor's most trusted Han officials. Zhang came from Jiangnan, and was presumably familiar with gardens in the Jiangnan style. Although he stepped down from his official positions in 1710 on the grounds of old age and illness, he remained at court, and in 1711 he accompanied the emperor once again to the Mountain Estate, where he died.

This record describes two visits to the Mountain Estate, then known as the Rehe Traveling Palace, made by small groups of selected high-ranking Han and Bannerman officials at imperial invitation. Such privileged guests were briefly admitted according to rigid protocols and were usually treated to a banquet with entertainment and a short tour through selected areas of the estate at midday before being escorted back outside. The visits described here took place in the summer of 1708, when the first phase of construction of the Mountain Estate was completed, and the Kangxi emperor began to reside there every summer, as he did until his death in 1722. Zhang lists sixteen views the emperor had named by 1708. The remainder of the final thirty-six views were evidently named by 1711, when the second phase of construction was completed.

"Record of Touring the Rehe Rear Garden at Imperial Invitation"

On the second day of the sixth month [July 19, 1708], the imperial entourage arrived by carriage at the Rehe Traveling Palace. On the eleventh day [July 28], I received an imperial edict commanding me to tour the rear park with various senior Manchu officials and others. Entering at the main gate, we proceeded northeast, reaching a cliff. There was a three-bay hall, the name-tablet above the door reading "Pine Winds through Myriad Vales." A couplet hung on columns by the entry reads: "The clouds roll up the color of a thousand peaks; / The spring harmonizes with the sound of a myriad pipes."[77]

We climbed several tens of stone steps one set after another, then wound back around and descended. To the right, there was an eight-cornered pavilion from which one might fish.[78] Crossing a bridge, we walked along a long dike;[79] at this point, His Majesty stood

---

77 A reference to the chapter "Discussion on Equalizing Things" in the *Zhuangzi*, in which Zhuangzi describes the myriad sounds of the pipes of Heaven as an expression of the Way in nature.

78 Perhaps Clear Jade Pavilion (*Qingbi ting* 晴碧亭), shown as a four-sided pavilion at the base of the artificial cliff in the illustration of Pine Winds through Myriad Vales, which also features the stone steps that Zhang describes descending.

79 The dike of A Lingzhi Path on an Embankment to the Clouds (see above).

in a pavilion,[80] and, turning to address me and the other officials, said, "The form and appearance of this dike is similar to that of a *lingzhi* fungus." Now, the long dike wound along in an unbroken line. Halfway, one branch extended out to divide the lake into three small bays, each forming a glorious realm. It is, in truth, comparable to a *lingzhi*.

To its east is "A Colorful Painting of Cloudy Mountains";[81] to its west is the imperial princes' study.[82] We proceeded straight ahead for a *li* and more and came to the place where [the emperor] stayed overnight. The name-tablet over the main gate read "Clear Ripples with Layers of Greenery."[83] Beyond the gate, in the midst of the residence, stands the imperial bed. Gazing appreciatively over the broad and distant scene, a thousand cliffs and a myriad valleys appeared within our sight.

Upon entering the gate, a short way to the west is "Inviting the Breeze Lodge"; a couplet flanking the door reads: "Clouds stir the trees along the stream so that they invade the curtains of the study; / Breezes bring grotto springs to moisten pools of ink." Behind the lodge, there is a Buddhist hall, its name-board reading, "Fragrant Waters and Beautiful Cliffs." The door-couplet reads: "There are mountains and rivers stretching to the Northern Pole Star;[84] / And a natural landscape to surpass that of West Lake." To the side there is a two-story hall whose name-board reads, "Moon Boat with Cloud Sails." The door-couplet reads, "I suspect I have boarded a painted vessel and risen to heaven; / I want to raise a light sail to enter into the mirror." We wound around and arrived at the imperial throne. In front of the main hall[85] a variety of flowers were planted in rows containing a great number of exotic varieties. There were five hydrangea bushes, each grafted with blossoms of five colors, something I had never seen before.

Opposite, there is a stage called "A Sheet of Cloud," and, at this time, music was performed. Various Manchu officials sat in the eastern gallery, and I accompanied the

---

80　It is not clear to which pavilion Zhang is referring, as there is no extant pavilion on A Lingzhi Path on an Embankment to the Clouds, nor does one appear in any of the illustrations from the *Imperial Poems* that feature the embankment.

81　Referring here generally to the complex on one of the three islands in Sounds of the River in the Moonlight, A Colorful Painting of Cloudy Mountains today designates the northernmost gate of the complex.

82　The study was on Surrounded by Greenery Island (Huanbidao), another of the three islets in Sounds of the River in the Moonlight.

83　Zhang appears to be referring to the gate depicted in View no. 3 of the *Imperial Poems*, Un-Summerly Clear and Cool (*Wushu qingliang* 無暑清涼). In the *Imperial Poems*, Clear Ripples with Layers of Greenery is the name of View no. 30, which includes a small pavilion on the north shore of what is now Wish-Fulfilling Island.

84　In Chinese imperial ideology, the Northern Pole Star is both the heavenly correlative of the earthly emperor (and the imperial palace) and a locative metaphor for the Way. By describing the Mountain Estate as linked to the Northern Pole Star by its landscape of mountains and rivers, Zhang is supporting the emperor's view that Rehe is a ritually legitimate site from which to rule the empire, equivalent to the capital.

85　Inviting the Breeze Lodge (*Yanxun shanguan* 延薰山館).

various officials of the Hanlin Academy, who were seated in the western gallery. Inside a small kiosk was placed a couch made of wood. We proceeded immediately to the banquet, during which His Majesty bestowed numerous dishes upon us, as well as bestowing a special gift of an imperial dish, potage of pheasant. When the midday banquet concluded, the group rose, expressed thanks for the emperor's favor, and went out. We thereupon boarded small boats and floated upon the lake. The broadest and most open part of the lake is similar to West Lake, yet its quiet seclusion and clear, clean beauty cannot be matched by West Lake.

On the bank were several towering trees, and an imperial attendant said that these were all saved by personal command of His Majesty. An embankment has been built along the trees, their dark and emerald greens shimmering back and forth, and their ancient trunks growing into even more gnarled shapes. Gazing into the distance from inside the boat, I cannot fully describe the glorious scenery. There are distant banks and winding currents that make the water feel supremely expansive; there are encircling cliffs and embracing rivers that create an ultimate sense of brilliant beauty. Ten thousand trees of concentrated green, vermilion towers like sunset's hue: one could say it is like a world within a painting, or like a world created by poetry.

On the lake's eastern shore there is a sluice gate and the water of a hot spring enters from this spot.[86] Where we went ashore, there was a lotus pond. By the edge of the pond there is a hall for enjoying cool air.[87] To the right of the hall there is a pavilion, a place for floating goblets along a winding stream.[88] The name-board reads, "Water Clover Fragrance Bank," and the door-couplet reads, "The moon constantly flows on the pair of brooks; / A thousand peaks naturally merge with the clouds." The sounds of springs from near and far[89] are drawn here along a watercourse dredged according to the twists and turns of the land.

Following the lake water around several bends, we arrived again at the boat landing where we had first climbed ashore. We crossed a bridge and went out along our original path. This is the magnificent scenery extending from the center of the park to the northeast section.

---

86   Known as Rehe Spring.

87   "Fragrance Grows Purer in the Distance" (*Xiangyuan yiqing* 香遠益清).

88   This is the focus of "The Scent of Lotuses by a Winding Stream" (*Qushui hexiang* 曲水荷香), which now bears the name "Savoring a Pure View" (*Han cheng jing* 含澄景).

89   This phrase, "sounds of springs from near and far" (*yuanjin quansheng*), was also used for the name of another view, where it denotes the sounds of a single spring that led into a waterfall. It may derive from a line in the poem "Walking in the Evening in Maping" (*Maping wanxing* 麻平晚行), by Wang Bo 王勃 (ca. 649–676): "As I searched high and low for the road that defends the frontier, I heard the sounds of springs from near and far" (高低尋戍道; 遠近聽泉聲).

On the twenty-eighth day of the month [August 14], we again received an imperial command to tour the park, this time exploring the beauties of the northwest section. Proceeding north from the eastern side gate, we again passed "Pine Winds through Myriad Vales," and from the long embankment came to "Clear Ripples with Layers of Greenery." After a time, we set out from the main gate, going straight past "Moon Boat with Cloud Sails" and, walking underneath a covered passage, we reached "A Sheet of Cloud." Taking our seats again in the western gallery, we were given a banquet and watched entertainments, again receiving a special gift of a soup from the imperial table. When we finished eating, we rose.

His Majesty issued instructions that, as the lotus blossoms were in full bloom, we could all observe them together. We boarded boats and passed by the boathouse. When I looked into the distance, I saw a dividing embankment. The glimmering lake was a brilliant void that stretched without end. What is called "A Pair of Lakes like Flanking Mirrors" can be seen from here. The lotus in the western portion of the lake were especially burgeoning. Among them was one variety, the color of which was perfectly gorgeous. Its seeds were obtained from the Aohan Confederacy.[90] Blossoms and leaves float together on the surface of the water, reflected upside down in the lake, forming the most novel and beautiful scene. The rest of them, whether closer or farther away, grew in randomly distributed clumps, their delicate fragrance surrounding us. It was truly a grand sight.

We climbed ashore where the land was open and flat, with both cultivated fields and groves of trees. Crossing over a small bridge, we followed the winding base of the mountain. The mountain peaks were covered with dark green vines and ancient mosses, plants untold hundreds of years old. Eventually, we arrived at a gate set in an opening in the mountains, beyond which was known as Lion Valley.[91] The gate spans across a ridge, which was called West Ridge. Below the gate was a small viewing pavilion, its name-board reading, "Untrammeled Thoughts by the Hao and Pu Rivers."[92] There were two sets of couplets. One reads: "Through the window, the color of the trees joins with the purity of the mountains; / Outside the door, the glistening mountain mist bears traces of the water's brilliance." The other reads: "In the still of the wilderness, the *qi*-energy of the mountains gathers; / In the sparse forest, winds and

---

90   Aohan was one of eight districts in the Zhaowuda League 昭烏達盟 of Inner Mongolia, centered approximately 220 kilometers northeast of Chengde.

91   Presumably the valley now known as Cloudy Pines Gorge (Songyun xia 松雲峽), which runs northwest from the valley floor to the Northwest Gate (Xibei men 西北門).

92   The name later assigned to a pavilion on the north shore of the main lakes; here, the name is applied to another structure, perhaps "Shapes of Clouds and Figures in the Water" (*Yunrong shuitai* 雲容水態).

dew endure." Sitting here to rest for a while, one truly feels that "this is another world, not the world of men."[93]

Behind this mountain are Hazelnut Glen and Pine Valley. We returned before having a chance to go there. Proceeding south, we came to the Temple of the Dragon King, while still farther south there is a winding path paved with stones with grasses growing here and there. During the spring, pear blossoms appear here in great profusion, so that it is extolled as a seasonal scenic spot.[94] We walked in the mountains for roughly ten-odd *li*. The slope of the trail rose and fell and twisted and turned. Sometimes the trail broke off, sometimes it continued. These unusual precincts were formed by Nature.

We returned to the long bridge and the stone jetty,[95] where we gained a fine vista of the route through the northwest section. We once again took a boat, headed to the western side gate and went ashore. We all expressed our gratitude for His Majesty's beneficence by the bank of the lake.

What are called the "Sixteen Views" are: "Clear Ripples with Layers of Greenery," which is the main gate to the imperial throne; "A Lingzhi Path on an Embankment to the Clouds," which is the long embankment; "A Long Rainbow Sipping White Silk," which is a long bridge; "Warm Currents and Balmy Ripples," which is the place where the warm spring enters;[96] "A Pair of Lakes Like Flanking Mirrors," which is a place where two lakes are separated by an embankment; "Pine Winds through Myriad Vales," which is the hall on the hill at the entrance to the park; "The Scent of Lotuses by a Winding Stream," which is the place for floating wine goblets; "Morning Mist by the Western Ridge," which is the pass at the mouth of West Ridge; "Sunset at Hammer Peak," which is a distant view of that peak to the west of the park; "A Fragrant Isle by Flowing Waters," which is a small pavilion next to the stone steps; "Southern Mountains Piled with Snow," which is a range of peaks within the park; "Golden Lotuses Reflecting the Sun," which is the several *mu* of golden lotus on the western banks that were seen; "Pear Blossoms Accompanied by the Moon," which is the place where pear blossoms form a scene of surpassing beauty in springtime; "Orioles

93   This line, commonly used in praise of a garden, comes from a poem by the Tang poet Li Bai (701–762), "A Reply to a Question about Living in the Mountains" (*Shanzhong wenda* 山中問答).

94   Likely referring to the area around "Pear Blossoms Accompanied by the Moon" (*Lihua banyue* 梨花伴月).

95   The "long bridge" refers to "A Long Rainbow Sipping White Silk"; the "stone jetty" likely refers to the nearby pavilion Observing the Fish from a Waterside Rock.

96   Given the general correlation between sites described in the main body of the text and those listed among the Sixteen Views, it is unclear whether Zhang is referring here to the site of Rehe Spring, which he described earlier in his account, or to Warm Currents and Balmy Ripples. The former is at the northeast corner of the main lake; the latter is a pavilion overlooking a branch of the Wulie River, which was diverted to enter the Mountain Estate through a sluice gate at the north end of the park.

Warbling in the Tall Trees," which is a place along the banks where many tall trees are; "Observing the Fish from a Waterside Rock," where one can fish anywhere along a stone jetty; and "An Immense Field with Shady Groves," which is a place of exceedingly luxuriant fields and trees.

Among the mountains and forests of the emperor's realm, there are none so extraordinary and magnificent as these; among the gardens of the emperor's realm, there are none so grand and vast as these. From first to last, every detail of the design was executed according to our Sagacious Emperor's instructions. When it was not yet completed, none knew of its unsurpassable scenic beauty; now it is finished, and everyone maintains that not a thing could be improved upon. In its broad contours, the design follows what is natural in the place, and the construction proceeded without altering the landscape. It was designed to accord with the form of the land. Consideration was given to what was appropriate to the earth itself, and the places for human activities were situated within this. In governing All-Under-Heaven, there is no other Way than this.[97]

A Particular Account of the Emperor of China's Gardens Near Pekin

BROTHER JEAN-DENIS ATTIRET (1702–1768)

TRANSLATED BY SIR HARRY BEAUMONT (JOSEPH SPENCE, 1699–1768)

Brother Jean-Denis Attiret (known in Chinese as Wang Zhicheng) was a Jesuit missionary from France who obtained a position as a court painter to the Qianlong emperor, alongside the more famous Giuseppe Castiglione (Lang Shining, 1688–1766), with whom he collaborated on a series of drawings for copperplate engravings commemorating the emperor's military victories in Central Asia. His account of the imperial gardens, written to a colleague or patron in Paris, shows his acute artistic judgment: he recognizes that the gardens, apparently so "natural" by contrast with contemporary European gardens, are entirely the product of artifice. Joseph Spence, under the pen name Sir Harry Beaumont, translated into English this "letter from a French missionary in China," as he described it, and published it in 1752 as *A Particular Account of the Emperor of China's Gardens Near Pekin*. Beaumont's original nonstandard spelling and eccentric punctuation has been regularized here, though his eighteenth-century wording remains unchanged.

---

97   Cf. Liu Zongyuan (773–819), "Camel-Back the Gardener" [see chapter 2], in which Liu's hunchbacked gardener, Guo, cultivates trees by avoiding interfering with their natural tendencies as they grow. The story advocates an ideal mode of governing that balances action and non-action.

A Particular Account of the Emperor of China's Gardens Near Pekin

Pekin; Nov. 1, 1743

Sir,

It was with the greatest pleasure that I received your two last letters: one of the 13th of October, and the other of the 2nd of November, 1742. I communicated the very interesting account of the affairs of Europe, which you gave me in them, to the rest of our missionaries; who join me in our sincere thanks. I thank you too in particular for the box full of works of straw, and flowers, which came very safe to me: but I beg of you not to put yourself to any such expense for the future; for the Chinese very much exceed the Europeans, in those kinds of works; and particularly, in their artificial flowers.[98]

We came hither at the command, or rather by the permission of the emperor. An officer was assigned to conduct us; and they made us believe, that he would defray our expenses: but the latter was only in words, for in effect the expense was almost wholly out of our own pockets. Half the way we came by water; and both ate, and lodged in our boats: and what seemed odd enough to us was that, by the rules of good-breeding received among them, we were not allowed ever to go ashore, or even to look out the windows of our covered boats to observe the face of the country, as we passed along. We made the latter part of our journey in a sort of cage, which they were pleased to call a litter. In this too we were shut up, all day long; and at night, carried into our inns (and very wretched inns they are!) and thus we go to Pekin; with our curiosity quite unsatisfied, and with seeing but little more of the country, than if one had been shut up all the while in one's own chamber.

Indeed they say, that the country we passed is but a bad country; and that, though the journey is near 2000 miles, there is little to be met with on the way that might deserve much attention: not even any monuments, or buildings, except some temples for their idols; and those built of wood, and but one story high: the chief value and beauty of which seemed to consist in some bad paintings and very indifferent varnish-works. Indeed any one that is just come from seeing the buildings in France and Italy, is apt to have but little taste, or attention, for whatever he may meet with in other parts of the world.

---

98 These are chiefly made of feathers, colored and formed, so exactly like real flowers, that one is often apt to forget one's self and to smell to them. The famous Signora Vannimano, at Rome (so many of whose works in this kind are continually brought home by our gentlemen who travel to that city) at first learned her art from some which were sent from China, by the Jesuits, as a present to the then pope. Here is a page or two omitted, as relating only to their private affairs.

However I must except out of this rule, the palace of the emperor of Pekin, and his pleasure-houses; for in them every thing is truly great and beautiful, both as to the design and the execution: and they struck me the more, because I had never seen any thing that bore any manner of resemblance to them, in any part of the world that I had been in before.

I should be very glad, if I could make such a description of these, as would give you a just idea of them; but that is almost impossible; because there is nothing in the whole, which has any likeness to our manner of building, or our rules of architecture. The only way to conceive what they are, is to see them: and if I can get any time, I am resolved to draw some parts of them as exactly as I can, to send them into Europe.

The Palace is, at least, as big as Dijon;[99] which city I choose to name to you, because you are so well acquainted with it. This palace consists of a great number of different pieces of building; detached from one another, but disposed with a great deal of symmetry and beauty. They are separated from one another by vast courts, plantations of trees, and flower-gardens. The principal front of all these buildings shines with gilding, varnish-work, and paintings; and the inside is furnished and adorned with all the most beautiful and valuable things that could be got in China, the Indies, and even from Europe.

As for the pleasure-houses, they are really charming. They stand in a vast compass of ground. They have raised hills, from 20 to 60 foot high; which form a great number of little valleys between them. The bottoms of these valleys are watered with clear streams; which run on till they join together, and form larger pieces of water and lakes. They pass these streams, lakes, and rivers, in beautiful and magnificent boats. I have seen one, in particular, 78 foot long and 24 foot broad; with a very handsome house raised upon it. In each of these valleys, there are houses about the banks of the water; very well disposed: with their different courts, open and close porticos, parterres, gardens, and cascades: which, when viewed all together, have an admirable effect upon the eye.

They go from one of the valleys to another, not by formal straight walks as in Europe; but by various turnings and windings, adorned on the sides with little pavilions and charming grottos: and each of these valleys is diversified from all the rest, both by their manner of laying out the ground, and in the structure and disposition of its buildings.

---

99 A handsome city in France, and the capital one in the province of Burgundy: between three and four miles round.

All the risings and hills are sprinkled with trees; and particularly with flowering-trees, which are here very common. The sides of the canals, or lesser streams, are not faced (as they are with us) with smooth stone, and in a straight line; but look rude and rustic, with different pieces of rock, some of which jut out, and others recede inward; and are placed with so much art, that you would take it to be the work of Nature. In some parts the water is wide, in others narrow; here it serpentizes, and there spreads away, as if it was really pushed off by the hills and rocks. The banks are sprinkled with flowers; which rise up even through the hollows in the rock-work, as if they had been produced there naturally. They have a great variety of them, for every season of the year.

Beyond these streams there are always walks, or rather paths, paved with small stones; which lead from one valley to another. These paths too are irregular; and sometimes wind along the banks of the water, and at others run out wide from them.

On your entrance into each valley, you see its buildings before you. All the front is a colonnade, with windows between the pillars. The wood-work is gilded, painted, and varnished. The roofs too are covered with varnished tiles of different colors; red, yellow, blue, green, and purple: which by their proper mixtures, and their manner of placing them, form an agreeable variety of compartments and designs. Almost all these buildings are one story high; and their floors are raised from two to eight foot above the ground. You go up to them, not by regular stone steps, but by a rough sort of rock-work; formed as if there had been so many steps produced there by Nature.

The inside of the apartments answers perfectly to the magnificence without. Beside their being very well disposed, the furniture and ornaments are very rich, and of an exquisite taste. In the courts, and passages, you see vases of brass, porcelain, and marble, filled with flowers: and before some of these houses, instead of naked statues, they have several of their hieroglyphical figures of animals, and urns with perfumes burning in them, placed upon pedestals of marble.

Every valley, as I told you before, has its pleasure-house: small indeed, in respect to the whole enclosure; but yet large enough to be capable of receiving the greatest nobleman in Europe, with all his retinue. Several of these houses are built of cedar; which they bring, with great expense, at the distance of 1500 miles from this place. And now how many of these palaces do you think there may be, in all the valleys of the enclosure? There are above 200 of them: without reckoning as many other houses for the eunuchs; for they are the persons who have the care of each palace, and their houses are always just by them; generally, at no more than five or six foot distance. These houses of the eunuchs are very plain: and for the reason are always concealed, either by some projection of the walls, or by the interposition of their artificial hills.

Over the running streams there are bridges, at proper distances, to make more easy communication from one place to another. These are most commonly either of brick or free-stone, and sometimes of wood; but are all raised high enough for the boats to pass conveniently under them. They are fenced with balusters finely wrought, and adorned with works in relievo; but all of them varied from one another, both in their ornaments, and design.

Do not imagine to yourself, that these bridges run on, like ours, in straight lines: on the contrary, they generally wind about and serpentize to such a degree, that some of them, which, if they went on regularly, would be no more than 30 or 40 foot long, turn so often and so much as to make their whole length 100 or 200 foot. You see some of them which (either in the midst, or at their ends) have little pavilions for people to rest themselves in; supported sometimes by four, sometimes by eight, and sometimes by sixteen columns. They are usually on such of the bridges, as afford the most engaging prospects. At the ends of other of the bridges there are triumphal arches, either of wood, or white marble; formed in a very pretty manner, but different from any thing that I have ever seen in Europe.

I have already told you, that these little streams, or rivers, are carried on to supply several larger pieces of water, and lakes. One of these lakes is very near five miles round; and they call it a mere, or sea. This is one of the most beautiful parts in the whole pleasure-ground. On the banks, are several pieces of building; separated from each other by the rivulets, and artificial hills above-mentioned.

But what is the most charming thing of all, is an island or rock in the middle of this sea; raised, in a natural and rustic manner, about six foot above the surface of the water. On this rock there is a little palace; which however contains an hundred different apartments. It has four fronts; and is built with inexpressible beauty and taste; the sight of it strikes one with admiration. From it you have a view of all the palaces, scattered at proper distances round the shores of this sea; all the hills, that terminate about it; all the rivulets, which tend thither, either to discharge their waters into it, or receive them from it; all the bridges, either at the mouths or ends of these rivulets; all the pavilions, and triumphal arches, that adorn any of these bridges; and all the groves, that are planted to separate and screen the different palaces, and to prevent the inhabitants of them from being overlooked by one another.

The banks of this charming water are infinitely varied: there are no two parts of it alike. Here you see quays of smooth stone; with porticoes, walks, and paths, running down to them from the palaces that surround the lake; there, others of rock-work, that fall into steps, contrived with the greatest art that can be conceived; here, natural terraces with winding steps at each end, to go up to the palaces that are built upon them; and above these, other terraces, and other palaces, that rise higher and higher, and form a sort of amphitheater. There again a grove of flowering-trees presents itself to your eye; and a little farther, you see a spread of wild forest-trees, and such as grow only on the most barren mountains; then, perhaps, vast timber-trees with their under-wood; then, trees from foreign countries; and then, some all blooming with flowers, and others all laden with fruits of different kinds.

There are also on the banks of this lake, a great number of network-houses, and pavilions; half on the land, and half running into the lake, for all sorts of water-fowl: as farther on upon the shore, you meet frequently with menageries for different sorts of creatures; and even little parks, for the chase. But of all this sort of things, the Chinese are most particularly fond of a kind of fish, the greater part of which are of a color as brilliant as gold; others, of a silver color; and others of different shades of red, green, blue, purple, and black: and some, of all sorts of colors mixed together.

There are several reservoirs for these fish, in all parts of the garden; but the most considerable of them all is at this lake. It takes up a very large space; and is all surrounded with a lattice-work of brass-wire: in which the openings are so very fine and small, as to prevent the fish from wandering into the main waters.

To let you see the beauty of this charming spot in its greatest perfection, I should wish to have you transported hither when the lake is all covered with boats; either gilt, or varnished: as it is sometimes, for taking the air; sometimes, for fishing; and sometimes, for jousts[100] and combats, and other diversions, upon the water: but above all, on some fine night, when the fire-works are played off there; at which time they have illuminations in all the palaces, all the boats, and almost on every tree. The Chinese exceed us extremely in their fire-works: and I have never seen any thing of that kind, either in France or Italy, that can bear any comparison with theirs.

The part in which the emperor usually resides here, with the empress, his favorite mistresses,[101] and the eunuchs that attend them, is a vast collection of buildings, courts, and gardens; and looks itself like a city. 'Tis, at least, as big as our city of

---

100   I have seen of this sort of jousts upon the water in our parts of the world; and particularly, at Lyons in France. The champions stand, as firmly as they are able, on the prows of two boats; and with a shield in their left hands, and a blunted spear in their right. There is an equal number of rowers in each of the boats, who drive them on with a great deal of impetuosity. The two combatants charge each other with their spears, and often both, but almost always one or other of them, is driven backward on the shock; either down into his boat, or (which often happens) into the water, which latter makes one of the principal parts in this odd sort of diversion.

101   The original says, "les *Koucifeys*, les *Feys*, les *Pines*, les *Kouci-gins*, et les *Tchangtsays*," and informs us in a note that there are so many different titles of honor, for the different classes of such of the emperor's mistresses, as are most in his favor. I did not think it worth while to set down all these hard names in the text, and perhaps they might as well have been omitted even here.

Dole.[102] The greater part of the other palaces is only used for his walking; or to dine or sup in, upon occasion.

This palace for the usual residence of the emperor is just within the grand gate of the pleasure-ground. First are the ante-chambers; then, the halls for audience: and then, the courts, and gardens belonging to them. The whole forms an island; which is entirely surrounded by a large and deep canal. 'Tis a sort of seraglio; in the different apartments of which you see all the most beautiful things that can be imagined, as to furniture, ornaments, and paintings (I mean, of those in the Chinese taste); the most valuable sorts of wood; varnished works, of China and Japan; ancient vases of porcelain; silks, and cloth of gold and silver. They have there brought together, all that art and good taste could add to the riches of Nature.

From this palace of the emperor a road, which is almost straight, leads you to a little town in the midst of the whole enclosure. 'Tis square; and each side is near a mile long. It has four gates, answering the four principal points of the compass; with towers, walls, parapets, and battlements. It has its streets, squares, temples, exchanges, markets, shops, tribunals, palaces, and a port for vessels. In one word, every thing that is at Pekin in large, is there represented in miniature.

You will certainly ask, for what use this city was intended. Is it that the emperor may retreat to it as a place of safety, on any revolt, or revolution? It might indeed serve well enough for that purpose; and possibly that thought had a share in the mind of the person, who at first designed it: but its principal end was to procure the emperor the pleasure of seeing all the bustle and hurry of a great city in little, whenever he might have a mind for that sort of diversion.

The emperor of China is too much a slave to his grandeur ever to show himself to his people, even when he goes out of his palace. He too sees nothing of the town, which he passes through. All the doors and windows are shut up. They spread wide pieces of cloth everywhere, that nobody may see him. Several hours before he is to pass through any street, the people are forewarned of it; and if any should be found there while he passes, they would be handled very severely by his guards. Whenever he goes into the country, two bodies of horse advance a good way before him, on each side of the road; both for his security, and to keep the way clear from all other passengers. As the emperors of China find themselves obliged to live in this strange sort of solitude, they have always endeavored to supply the loss of all public diversions (which their high station will not suffer them to partake), by some other means of inventions, according to their different tastes and fancies.

---

102   The second city for size in the Franche Comté.

This town therefore, in these two last reigns (for it was this emperor's father who ordered it to be built), has been appropriated for the eunuchs to act in it, at several times in the year, all the commerce, marketings, arts, trades, bustle, and hurry, and even all the rogueries, usual in great cities. At the appointed times, each eunuch puts on the dress of the profession or part which is assigned to him. One is a shop-keeper, and another an artisan; this is an officer, and that a common soldier; one has a wheel-barrow given him, to drive about the streets; another, as a porter, carries a basket on his shoulder. In a word, every one has the distinguishing mark of his employment. The vessels arrive at the port; the shops are opened; and the goods are exposed for sale. There is one quarter for those who sell silks, and another for those who sell cloth; one street for porcelain, and another for varnish-works. You may be supplied with whatever you want. This man sells furniture of all sorts; that, clothes and ornaments for the ladies: and a third has all kinds of books, for the learned and curious. There are coffee-houses too, and taverns, of all sorts, good and bad: beside a number of people that cry different fruits about the streets, and a great variety of refreshing liquors. The mercers, as you pass their shops, catch you by the sleeve; and press you to buy some of their goods. 'Tis all a place of liberty and license; and you can scarce distinguish the emperor himself, from the meanest of his subjects. Every body bawls out what he has to sell; some quarrel, others fight: and you have all the confusion of a fair about you. The public officers come and arrest the quarrelers; carry them before the judges; in the courts for justice, the cause is tried in form; the offender condemned to be bastinadoed; and the sentence is put in execution: and that so effectually, that the diversion of the emperor sometimes costs the poor actor a great deal of pain.

The mystery of thieving is not forgot, in this general representation. That noble employ is assigned to a considerable number of the cleverest eunuchs; who perform their parts admirably well. If any one of them is caught in the fact, he is brought to shame; and condemned (at least they go through the form of condemning him) to be stigmatized, bastinadoed, or banished; according to the heinousness of the crime, and the nature of the theft. If they steal cleverly, they have the laugh on their side; they are applauded, and the sufferer is without redress. However, at the end of the fair, everything of this kind is restored to the proper owner.

This fair (as I told you before) is kept only for the entertainment of the emperor, the empress, and his mistresses. 'Tis very unusual for any of the princes, or grandees, to be admitted to see it: and when any have that favor, it is not till after the women are all retired to their several apartments. The goods which are exposed and sold here, belong chiefly to the merchants of Peking; who put them into the hands of the eunuchs, to be sold in reality: so that the bargains here are far from being all pretended ones. In partic-ular, the emperor himself always buys a great many things; and you may be sure, they ask him enough for them. Several of the ladies too make their bargains; and so do some of the eunuchs. All this trafficking, if there was nothing of real mixed with it, would want a great deal of the earnestness and life, which now make the bustle the more active, and the diversion it gives the greater.

To this scene of commerce, sometimes succeeds a very different one: that of agriculture. There is a quarter, within the same enclosure, which is set apart for this purpose. There you see fields, meadows, farm-houses, and little scattered cottages; with oxen, ploughs, and all the necessaries for husbandry. There they sow wheat, rice, pulse, and all other sorts of grain. They make their harvest; and carry in the produce of their grounds. In a word, they here imitate every thing that is done in the country; and in every thing express a rural simplicity, and all the plain manners of a country life, as nearly as they possibly can.

Doubtless you have read of the famous feast in China, called The Feast of the Lanterns. It is always celebrated on the 15th day of the first month. There is no Chinese so poor, but that upon this day he lights up his lantern. They have of them of all sorts of figures, sizes, and prices. On that day, all China is illuminated: but the finest illuminations of all are in the emperor's palaces; and particularly in these pleasure-grounds, which I have been describing to you. There is not a chamber, hall, or portico, in them, which has not several of these lanterns hanging from the ceilings. There are several upon all the rivulets, rivers, and lakes; made in the shape of little boats, which the waters carry backward and forward. There are some upon all the hills and bridges, and almost upon all the trees. These are wrought mighty prettily, in the shapes of different fishes, birds, and beasts; vases, fruits, flowers; and boats of different sorts and sizes. Some are made of silk; some of horn, glass, mother of pearl, and a thousand other materials. Some of them are painted; others embroidered; and of very different prices. I have seen some of them which could never have been made for a thousand crowns. It would be an endless thing, to endeavor to give you a particular account of all their forms, materials, and ornaments. It is in these, and in the great variety which the Chinese show in their buildings, that I admire the fruitfulness of their invention; and am almost tempted to own, that we are quite poor and barren in comparison of them.

Their eyes are so accustomed to their own architecture, that they have very little taste for ours. May I tell you what they say when they speak of it, or when they are looking over the prints of some of our most celebrated buildings? The height and thickness of our palaces amazes them. They look upon our streets, as so many ways hollowed into terrible mountains; and upon our houses, as rocks pointing up in the air, and full of holes like dens of bears and other wild beasts. Above all, our different stories, piled up so high one above another, seem quite intolerable to them: and they cannot conceive, how we can bear to run the risk of breaking our necks, so commonly, in going up such a number of steps as is necessary to climb up to the fourth and fifth floors. "Undoubtedly," said the Emperor Kangxi, while he was looking over some plans of our European houses, "this Europe must be a very small and pitiful country; since the inhabitants cannot find ground enough to spread out their towns, but are obliged to live up thus in the air." As for us, we think otherwise; and have reason to do so.

However I must own to you, without pretending to decide which of the two ought to have the preference, that the manner of building in this country pleases me very much. Since my residence in China, my eyes and taste are grown a little Chinese. And, between friends, is not the Duchess of Bourbon's house opposite to the Tuileries, extremely pretty? Yet that is only of one story, and a good deal in the Chinese manner. Every country has its taste and customs. The beauty of our architecture cannot be disputed: nothing is more grand and majestic. I own too, that our houses are well disposed. We follow the rules of uniformity, and symmetry, in all the parts of them. There is nothing in them unmatched, or displaced: every part answers its opposite; and there is an exact agreement in the whole. But then there is this symmetry, this beautiful order and disposition, too in China; and particularly, in the emperor's palace at Pekin, that I was speaking of in the beginning of this letter. The palaces of the princes and great men, the courts of justice, and the houses of the better sort of people are generally in the same taste.

But in their pleasure-houses, they rather choose a beautiful disorder,[103] and a wandering as far as possible from the rules of art. They go entirely on this principle, "That what they are to represent there, is a natural and wild view of the country; a rural retirement, and not a palace formed according to all the rules of art." Agreeably to which, I have not yet observed any two of the palaces in all the grand enclosure, which are alike, though some of them are placed at such considerable distances from one another. You would think, that they were formed upon the ideas of so many different foreign countries; or that they were all built at random, and made up of parts not meant for one another. When you read this, you will be apt to imagine such works very ridiculous; and that they must have a very bad effect on the eye: but if you were to see them, you would find it quite otherwise; and would admire the art, with which all this irregularity is conducted. All is in good taste; and so managed, that its beauties appear gradually, one after another. To enjoy them as one ought, you should view every piece by itself; and you would find enough to amuse you for a long while, and to satisfy all your curiosity.

---

103   The author of this letter seems here to have formed his opinion only from the garden in which he was employed; for this is not universally the case in the pleasure-houses of the emperor of China. I have lately seen some prints of another of his gardens (brought from that kingdom, and which will very soon be published here) in which the disposition of the ground, water, and plantations is indeed quite irregular; but the houses, bridges, and fences are all of a regular kind. Those prints will give the truest idea we can have of the Chinese manner of laying out pleasure-grounds.

Besides, the palaces themselves (though I have called them little, in comparison of the whole) are very far from being inconsiderable things. I saw them building one in the same enclosure, last year, for one of the princes of the blood; which cost him near two hundred thousand pounds:[104] without reckoning anything for the furniture and ornaments of the inside; for they were a present to him from the emperor.

I must add one word more, in relation to the variety which reigns in these pleasure-houses. It is not only to be found in their situations, views, disposition, sizes, heights, and all the other general points; but also in their lesser parts, that go to the composing of them. Thus, for instance, there is no people in the world who can show such a variety of shapes and forms, in their doors and windows, as the Chinese. They have some round, oval, square, and in all sorts of angled figures; some, in the shape of fans; other in those of flowers, vases, birds, beasts, and fishes; in short, of all forms, whether regular or irregular.

It is only here too, I believe, that one can see such porticos, as I am going to describe to you. They serve to join such parts of the buildings in the same palace, as lie pretty wide from one another. These are sometimes raised on columns only, on the side toward the house; and have openings, of different shapes, through the walls on the other side: and sometimes have only columns on both sides; as in all such as lead from any of the palaces, to their open pavilions for taking the fresh air. But what is so singular in these porticos or colonnades is, that they seldom run on in straight lines; but make an hundred turns and windings: sometimes by the side of a grove, at others behind a rock, and at others again along the banks of their rivers or lakes. Nothing can be conceived more delightful: they have such a rural air, as is quite ravishing and enchanting.

You will certainly conclude from all I have told you, that this pleasure-place must have cost immense sums of money; and indeed there is no prince, but such an one as is master of so vast a state as the emperor of China is, who could either afford so prodigious an expense or accomplish such a number of great works in so little time: for all this was done in the compass of twenty years. It was the father of the present emperor who began it; and his son now only adds conveniences and ornaments to it, here and there.

But there is nothing so surprising, or incredible, in this: for besides that the buildings are most commonly but of one story, they employ such prodigious numbers of workmen, that every thing is carried on very fast. Above half the difficulty is over, when they have got their materials upon the spot. They fall immediately to disposing them

---

104   The original says, *Soixante Ouanes*: and adds in a note, that one *Ouane* [*wan*] is worth ten thousand *taels*; and each *tael* is worth seven livres and a half; so that sixty *Ouanes* make four millions and a half of livres. Which is equal to 196,875 pounds sterling.

in order; and in a few months the work is finished. They look almost like those fabulous palaces, which are said to be raised by enchantment, all at once, in some beautiful valley, or on the brow of some hill.

This whole enclosure is called, Yuanming Yuan, the Garden of Gardens; or The Garden, by way of eminence. It is not the only one that belongs to the emperor; he has three others, of the same kind: but none of them so large, or so beautiful, as this. In one of these lives the empress his mother, and all her court. It was built by the present emperor's grandfather, Kangxi; and is called Changchun Yuan, or the Garden of Perpetual Spring. The pleasure-places of the princes and grandees are in little, what those of the emperor are in great.

Perhaps you will ask me, "Why all this long description?" Should not I rather have drawn plans of this magnificent place, and sent them to you? To have done that, would have taken me up at least three years; without touching upon anything else: whereas I have not a moment to spare; and am forced to borrow the time in which I now write to you, from my hours of rest. To which you may add, that for such a work, it would be necessary for me to have full liberty of going into any part of the gardens whenever I pleased, and to stay there as long as I pleased: which is quite impracticable here. 'Tis very fortunate for me, that I have got the little knowledge of painting that I have: for without this, I should have been in the same case with several other Europeans, who have been here between twenty and thirty years, without being able ever to set their feet on any spot of this delightful ground.

There is but one man here; and that is the emperor. All pleasures are made for him alone. This charming place is scarce ever seen by any body but himself, his women, and his eunuchs. The princes, and other chief men of the country, are rarely admitted any farther than the audience-chambers. Of all the Europeans that are here, none ever entered this enclosure, except the clock-makers and painters; whose employments make it necessary that they should be admitted everywhere. The place usually assigned us to paint in, is in one of those little palaces above-mentioned; where the emperor comes to see us work, almost every day: so that we can never be absent. We don't go out of the bounds of this palace, unless what we are to paint cannot be brought to us; and in such cases, they conduct us to the place under a large guard of eunuchs. We are obliged to go quick, and without any noise; and huddle and steal along softly, as if we were going upon some piece of mischief. 'Tis in this manner that I have gone through, and seen, all this beautiful garden; and entered into all the apartments. The emperor usually resides here ten months in each year. We are about ten miles from Pekin. All the day, we are in the gardens; and have a table furnished for us by the emperor: for the nights, we are bought us a house, near the entrance to the gardens. When the emperor returns to Pekin, we attend him; are lodged there within his palace; and go every evening to the French church.[105]

I think it is high time, both for you and me, that I should put an end to this letter; which has carried me on to a greater length, than I at first intended. I wish it may give you any pleasure; and should be very glad if it was in my power to do any thing more considerable, to show you the perfect esteem I have for you. I shall always remember you, in my prayers; and beg you would sometimes remember me in yours.
I am,
With the greatest regards,
Sir,
Your most obedient,
Humble servant,
Attiret

---

105   Here follow fourteen or fifteen pages in the original which treat only of the author's private affairs, or of the affairs of the mission, without anything relating to the emperor's garden; and are, therefore, omitted by the translator.

9

Landscape into Garden, Garden into Landscape

This chapter uses two examples—the Eastern Marchmount, Mount Tai (*Taishan*; literally Great Mountain) in Shandong, and the West Lake (*Xihu*) near Hangzhou—to explore some facets of garden and landscape culture in China, looking beyond the conventional confines of the garden and considering how the two concepts blend into each other. Inasmuch as gardens were often intended as a miniaturization or representation of the the wider (and wilder) landscape, attitudes to gardens and to landscapes could, to some extent, be interchangeable. With the addition of buildings such as pavilions built at public or private expense on an unenclosed hillside, for example, landscape was converted into a kind of garden, made available for the enjoyment of anyone with the leisure to visit it. Landscapes originally managed for a specific pragmatic purpose—whether as the location for imperial ceremony in the case of Mount Tai, or for irrigation and water control in the case of the West Lake—underwent a process of beautification and increased convenience that gradually converted them, or at least expanded their use, into pleasure resorts. Such places became both symbols of official power and places of public enjoyment.

They also developed or retained a spiritual value: we can see from the passages in this chapter that Mount Tai, which had an age-old association with the rituals that reinforced the status of the ruler as intermediary between Heaven and Earth, also developed popular Daoist and Buddhist connections that promoted it as a place of pilgrimage, offering a combination of religious practice and holiday jaunt to urban and even rural dwellers of comparatively low status. The West Lake's attraction as a place of resort just outside the walls of Hangzhou was greatly enhanced by the presence of the Buddhist temples of Lingyin and Tianzhu, with their associations with the early Chinese patriarchs. Both locations remain very important tourist destinations in present-day China, trading on their long history and associations with famous historical figures as well as their scenic beauty.

In the case of Mount Tai, the passages here show a progression whereby the mountain is initially regarded as a numinous place closely associated with rulership, then comes to be visited by members of the elite who are not rulers but go there in the hope of sharing in some sort of numinous experience, which, as we can see from the poems recalling these visits, is often mediated through their experience of the landscape; as time goes on, the wish to visit such a numinous site and share in its power spreads through society, until the whole thing really becomes an excuse to go on an enjoyable outing away from the restrictions of day-to-day life. The conversion of religious pilgrimage into tourism is a phenomenon that has been widely noted in late imperial Chinese society.

The identification of Mount Tai as the Eastern Marchmount (*Dong yue*) evidently goes back to prehistoric times. The other marchmounts of the cardinal directions are the Southern Marchmount Mount Heng (in Hunan), the Western Marchmount Mount Hua (in Shaanxi), and the Northern Marchmount Mount Heng (in Shanxi; a different *heng* character from the Southern Marchmount), with Mount Song (in Henan) as the Central Marchmount. The Five Marchmounts were particularly associated with the creation myth in which the world was formed from the body of the giant Pangu, the first living being. Given Mount Tai's position as the Eastern Marchmount, related to the season of spring, to renewal and rebirth, it is particularly associated with the sunrise, hence the importance of experiencing dawn on the mountain.

From early times, rulers would assert their position as the intermediary between Heaven and humankind by sacrificing to Heaven at the summit of the mountain and to Earth at its foot; these sacrifices were known as *feng* and *shan*, respectively. Because of the association of Mount Tai with the east and rebirth, as well as the belief that mountains were inhabited by immortals or Daoist transcendents, rulers also seem to have hoped for personal immortality or at least enhanced longevity as a result of performing these rituals.

Apart from the impersonal Heaven and Earth, the mountain was also associated with a deity of Daoism or popular religion known as the Great Lord of the Eastern Marchmount (*Dongyue dadi*) or Emperor Lord of Mount Tai. His temple, the *Dai miao* (Temple of Dai, an alternative name for Mount Tai), is in the city of Tai'an below the mountain. Another important temple associated with the mountain is the Temple of Azure Clouds (*Bixia ci*) near the summit; its presiding deity is the Primal Sovereign of the Azure Clouds (*Bixia Yuanjun*), a mountain goddess who is supposed to be the daughter of the Great Lord of Mount Tai. These deities were not directly involved in the imperial *feng* and *shan* sacrifices, but offered an alternative focus of veneration for those of lower social status; by the thirteenth century, the Primal Sovereign of the Azure Clouds, as a goddess of fertility—resulting from the Eastern Marchmount's association with life and birth—had far overtaken the Great Lord as a recipient of popular worship.[1]

As Buddhism became established in China from the period between Han and Tang onward, Buddhism and Daoism became combined into a syncretic popular religion. Thus, Mount Tai became a site of pilgrimage for Buddhist as well as Daoist devotees, as we can see from some of the later texts in this chapter. In the late imperial period, religious tourism was particularly enjoyed by

---

1   See the very thorough study of Mount Tai as a site of pilgrimage by Brian R. Dott, *Identity Reflections: Pilgrimages to Mount Tai in Late Imperial China* (Cambridge, Mass.: Harvard University Asia Center, 2004).

women, who were thereby enabled to cast off some of the restrictions of residence in their natal or marital homes. The extract from the novel *A Tale of Marriage Destinies That Will Bring Society to Its Senses* gives a satirical view of how this could be carried to extremes.

The West Lake first became a place of resort some centuries later than Mount Tai. It was known by various names, one of the most widely used being Qiantang Lake (as it was originally part of the Qiantang River). It was not referred to as the West Lake (it lies west of the city of Hangzhou) until the Tang dynasty. The area's initial importance was as a religious site; the Chan Buddhist Lingyin Temple (Temple of the Soul's Retreat) is said to have been founded in 328 by an Indian monk going by the Chinese name Huili. As the city of Hangzhou expanded in the Tang dynasty, control of the Qiantang Lake's waters became increasingly important, to supply water to the city and the surrounding agricultural land, as well as to avoid problems of drought and flooding resulting from the silting up of the lake. This work started to be undertaken in the late eighth century under the supervision of local officials, including the famous poet Bai Juyi (see chapter 2), after whom one of the causeways in the lake is named. The improvements not only had practical benefits but also improved the environment in such a way that the lake became a popular place of resort for the inhabitants of Hangzhou. We have already seen in chapter 2 that officials from northern China, such as Bai Juyi himself, fell in love with the relatively mild climate, gentle landscape, and lush vegetation of the West Lake area, so different from what they were accustomed to in the north.

In the period of disunity following the fall of the Tang dynasty, Hangzhou became the capital of the short-lived Wu-Yue kingdom in the tenth century; the Wu-Yue rulers promoted the maintenance of the lake as a hydraulic resource. It was during this period that the Lingyin Temple reached its greatest importance; many of the Buddhist carvings on the Flew-Here Rock and elsewhere in the area date from this period. The environs of the West Lake remained significant as a Buddhist site and never acquired the Daoist associations of more ancient landscapes such as that of Mount Tai.

When the Song dynasty was established in 960, Hangzhou's political importance diminished, only to rise again when the Northern Song was conquered by the Jin, and the successor state, the Southern Song, established its capital at Hangzhou, under the name Lin'an (Temporary Peace). Like the Tang dynasty officials to whom the West Lake and other parts of Jiangnan appealed so strongly, the Song officials who had migrated from the north were greatly taken with their new surroundings, however much they regretted the loss of their northern territory. Like their predecessors, too, as educated men they viewed the West Lake through the prism of history, looking back beyond the imperial period to the turbulent times of the Warring States with their romantic legends, especially that of Xi Shi, the bewitching beauty from the state of Yue—which included the Hangzhou area—who caused the downfall of the state of Wu. It became a commonplace to liken the beautiful scenery of the West Lake (*Xi hu*) to the physical beauty of Xi Shi. This is a similar concept to the assimilation of Mount Tai and the other marchmounts to the body parts of the giant Pangu.

It was in the Southern Song that the West Lake became a frequent subject for landscape painting; this helped to promote the lake's scenery as a model for garden landscaping. Through the centuries the historical associations of the landscape developed further, while its religious significance for Buddhists remained strong. As the city of Hangzhou grew in commercial, cultural, and administrative importance, the West Lake also became an increasingly important site for recreation and socializing. From the Ming dynasty it was surrounded by the garden villas of gentry families from other parts of Zhejiang, who found it convenient to have residences available for their use while visiting the city on business.

As tourism developed in the lively commercial atmosphere of the late imperial period, the West Lake continued to grow in importance, and it is significant that by the eighteenth century the body of water to the west of the commercial city of Yangzhou became known as Slender West Lake, as an homage to the more expansive lake of Hangzhou. According to UNESCO's 2011 assessment of the West Lake Cultural Landscape as a World Heritage site, "the West Lake has influenced garden design in the rest of China as well as Japan and Korea over the centuries and bears an exceptional testimony to the cultural tradition of improving landscapes to create a series of vistas reflecting an idealized fusion between humans and nature."[2]

In the case of both Mount Tai and the West Lake, what were originally "natural" sites have experienced an accretion of historical monuments (such as imperial stelae and other inscriptions) and architectural structures—religious and secular—as well as layers of association through the ages with famous people who visited them for different purposes and wrote about them or left their imprint on them in other ways (as with Bai Juyi's and Su Shi's practical interventions in the landscape of West Lake). The sites have also acquired certain fixed ways of appreciating them, whether by experiencing dawn on Mount Tai or viewing the canonical ten scenic sights of West Lake.

In this sense, these cultural landscapes are very similar to gardens that, as we have already seen, may equally have historical monuments in the shape of inscriptions by well-known people, architectural structures like pavilions and gazebos similar to those placed in the wider landscape, and defined scenes or sights intended to be appreciated in a particular way. Gardens also share in the numinous associations of the landscape of mountains and waters, and this is part of what makes them meaningful; as Liu Yuxi wrote in "The Scholar's Humble Dwelling" (see chapter 2):

> Who heeds the hill's bare height until
> Some legend grows around the hill?
> Who cares how deep the stream before
> Its fame is writ in country lore?[3]

In other words, the perceived sacred associations of the mountain or water is what attracts people to them, and likewise, in the garden, the association of rocks or "artificial mountains" and small bodies of water with numinous beings such as Daoist immortals, dragons, or Buddhist sages gives the garden features more than a purely aesthetic or recreational significance.

---

2   "West Lake Cultural Landscape of Hangzhou," World Heritage List, UNESCO, Friday, June 24, 2011, http://whc.unesco.org/en/news/767.

3   This 1911 translation by James Black is a very free one. A more literal rendering of the original lines is "What is significant about mountains is not their height: they are celebrated only when there are immortals in them. What is significant about waters is not their depth: they are numinous only when there are dragons in them" (山不在高，有仙則名。水不在深，有龍則靈。).

To a great extent, it is possible to regard cultural landscapes such as those of Mount Tai or the West Lake as gardens writ large, while, within a circumscribed area, gardens function in many of the same ways as these cultural landscapes. Both garden and landscape are inscribed with the traces of the past, whether in the form of actual historical relics or associations with historical figures who spent time there (in the case of cultural landscapes) or in the form of references through garden naming, calligraphic inscriptions, or other means. Both are used for similar purposes of socializing, recreation, and contact with the numinous. The purpose of this final chapter is to elucidate some of these similarities and connections through the two case studies of Mount Tai and the West Lake.

PART ONE

MOUNT TAI

The Book of Documents (Shujing 書經)

"The Canon of Shun" (*Shun dian* 舜典; extract)

TRANSLATED BY JAMES LEGGE

The *Book of Documents* is one of the Confucian classics and was supposedly compiled by Confucius himself. In fact, the text as it survives today was reconstructed in the Han dynasty from remains of the books destroyed under the Qin, but it incorporates much earlier material. This passage is the earliest mention of an imperial sacrifice being carried out at Mount Tai, in this case by the legendary ruler Shun. The sacrifice at Mount Tai is immediately followed by Shun's ordering of the calendar and of weights and measures: these were imperial prerogatives that remained important throughout the imperial period as signs of authority. Shun's visits to the Four Marchmounts (the fifth, the Central Marchmount, is not included) take place according to the order of the seasons (east corresponds to spring, south to summer, west to autumn, and north to winter): Mount Tai (referred to here by its alternative name of *Daizong* or Venerable Dai) as the Eastern Marchmount is the most prominent since it comes first in the series, but is not necessarily regarded here as much more important than the others.

"The Canon of Shun" (extract)

In the second month of the year, he [Shun] made a tour of inspection eastward, as far as Daizong, where he presented a burnt-offering to Heaven, and sacrificed in order to the hills and rivers. Thereafter he gave audience to the nobles of the east, putting in accord their seasons and months, and rectifying the days; he made uniform the standard tubes, the measures of length and of capacity, and the steel-yards; he regulated the five classes of ceremonies. As to the several articles of introduction—the five instruments of gem, the three kinds of silk, the two living animals, and the one dead one, when all was over, he returned the five instruments. In the fifth month, he made a similar tour to the south, as far as the southern mountain [Mount Heng], observing the same ceremonies as at Dai. In the same way, in the eighth month, he traveled westward, as far as the western mountain [Mount Hua]; and in the eleventh month he traveled northward, as far as the northern mountain [Mount Heng]. When he returned to the capital, he went to the temple of the Cultivated Ancestor, and offered a single bullock.

The Guideways through Mountains and Seas (*Shanhai jing* 山海經)

"Mount Great"

ANONYMOUS (4TH–1ST CENTURY BCE)

TRANSLATED BY ANNE BIRRELL

For *The Guideways through Mountains and Seas* (also known as *The Classic of Mountains and Seas*), see chapter 1. The fact that so little information is given in this early text about a mountain that was later regarded as the most important of the Five Marchmounts supports the implication from "The Canon of Shun" (see above) that in very early times Mount Tai, here translated as Mount Great, was not regarded as outstandingly important.

"Mount Great"

Three hundred leagues farther south is a mountain called Mount Great [Mount Tai]. Jade is plentiful on the summit and gold is abundant on its lower slopes. There is an animal on this mountain that looks like a boar and it contains pearls. Its name is the Same-Same.[4] When it grunts it calls itself: "Tong-Tong." The River Ring rises here and flows east to empty into the Long River. The River Ring contains a quantity of rock crystal.

Records of the Grand Historian (*Shiji* 史記)

"The Basic Annals of the First Emperor of Qin" (*Qin Shihuang benji* 秦始皇本紀; extract)

SIMA QIAN 司馬遷 (145/135–86 BCE)

TRANSLATED BY BURTON WATSON

Sima Qian was hereditary Grand Archivist (a closer equivalent than "Grand Historian" for the Chinese term *taishi*) at the Han court. He completed the work begun by his father Sima Tan (d. 110 BCE) of compiling a complete history of the known world from the earliest times to the Han dynasty. The structure of his *Historical Records* (or *Records of the Grand Historian*; in Chinese *Shiji*) provided the model for all the later official dynastic histories. The "Basic Annals" section covers year by year the events of each ruler's reign. This passage describes the journey made by the First Qin emperor (Qin Shihuangdi) in the late third century BCE to Mount Tai,

---

4 Editor's note: in Chinese pronounced *tong-tong*, homophonous with the word for "same" (*tong*).

his performance of the *feng* and *shan* sacrifices at the summit and foot of the mountain, and his placing of a stela recording the benefits of his rule. The passage also includes mention of his awarding the title of fifth-rank counselor to a tree (later said to be a pine tree) that sheltered him from a rainstorm; later writers often professed to regard this as insulting to an already noble tree.

"The Basic Annals of the First Emperor of Qin" (extract)

Twenty-eighth year [219]: the emperor visited the provinces and districts of the east and ascended Mt. Yi in Zhuo. He set up a stone marker and, consulting with the Confucian scholars of Lu, had it inscribed with praises of the virtue of the Qin. He also consulted with the scholars on matters pertaining to the Feng and Shan sacrifices and sacrifices to the various mountains and rivers. Afterward he ascended Mt. Tai, set up a stone marker, and performed the Feng sacrifice. On the way down, he encountered violent wind and rain and had to rest under a tree. He accordingly enfeoffed the tree with the title of fifth-rank counselor. He performed the Shan sacrifice at Liangfu and set up a stone marker inscribed with these words:

The August Emperor mounted the throne, issuing edicts,
clarifying laws, which his subjects observe and obey.
In the twenty-sixth year of his rule he first united the world;
There were none who did not come to him in submission.
In person he visited the people of distant regions, ascending
Mt. Tai, surveying the eastern extremity all around.
The ministers in his retinue, mindful of his deeds, seeking the
source of his achievements, reverently praise his merits and virtue.
The way of good government is implemented, the various
occupations obtain what is needful, all is gauged by law and
pattern.
His great principles are noble and pre-eminent, to be
bestowed on future generations, who will receive and honor them
without change.
The August Emperor, sage that he is, has brought peace to the
world, never neglectful of his rule.
Early rising, late to retire, he takes measures to bring lasting
benefit, devoting himself earnestly to instruction and precept.
His admonitions circulate, his proclamations spread abroad,
so that near and far alike are properly ordered, and all bow to the will of the sage.
Eminent and humble are clearly distinguished, men and
women are observant of ritual, cautious and attentive to their
duties.
Inner and outer concerns are carefully demarked, uniformly

faultless and pure, to be passed on to future heirs.
His transforming influence is unending, in ages after his
decrees will be honored, handed down forever with gravest
caution.

A Record of the Feng and Shan Sacrifices (*Fengshan yi ji* 封禪儀記)

The Supreme Mountain

MA DIBO 馬第伯 (1ST CENTURY)
TRANSLATED BY RICHARD E. STRASSBERG

Ma Dibo, whose dates are unknown, was a courtier under the Eastern Han emperor Guangwu (r. 25–57); he accompanied the emperor on his journey in 56 CE to perform the *feng* and *shan* sacrifices at Mount Tai, here translated as the Supreme Mountain. It is unusual to have a personal account such as Ma's from such an early date; it survived because it was included in the *History of the Later Han Dynasty* for its value as information on sacrificial procedure. Although the *feng* and *shan* sacrifices were of great importance in the legitimation of imperial rule, they had so much prestige that very few emperors were confident that under their rule the empire was sufficiently peaceful and prosperous to justify performance of the ritual. Emperor Guangwu was one of only five emperors who performed the sacrifices in the more than one thousand years between 110 BCE and 1008 CE, and he was sometimes regarded by later commentators as the only one of the five who was truly justified in performing them.

The Supreme Mountain

In the thirty-second year of the Jianwu era [56 CE], the imperial carriage set out on an Eastern Tour. It departed the palace in Luoyang on the twenty-eighth day of the first month [March 3]. On the ninth day of the second month [March 14], it reached the Commandery of Lu. The Probationary Receptionist Guo Jianbo was dispatched with five hundred penal workers to prepare the way to the Supreme Mountain. On the tenth day [March 15], the Commandery of Lu dispatched members of the Liu and Kong clans⁵ and members of the Ding clan of Xiaqiu to offer up birthday greetings, for which they received gifts. All paid a visit to the Kong Mansion, where they were treated to a feast by the emperor. Everyone departed on the eleventh [March 16]. On the twelfth [March 17], the night was spent at Fenggao. On this day, a Court Gentleman Brave as a Tiger⁶ was dispatched to ascend the mountain in advance to inspect conditions.

---

5 The Liu clan were members of the Han imperial family; the Kong clan were the recognized descendants of Confucius, whose head, the Marquis of Baocheng, is referred to later. The Ding clan were descendants of Jiang Ziya (fl. mid-11th century BCE), a general who helped found the Zhou dynasty and who was enfeoffed in the area as Duke of Qi.

6 Court Gentlemen Brave as Tigers were members of the imperial bodyguard.

He returned and another thousand penal workers were added to repair the road. On the fifteenth [March 20], the fast of purification began. His Majesty stayed at the Governor's Mansion, the imperial princes stayed at the Prefectural Office, and the nobles stayed at the District Office: all held fasts of purification. The Chamberlains, Commandants, Generals, Grandees, Gentlemen of the Palace Gates, the other officials, the Duke of Song, the Duke of Wei, the Marquis of Baocheng, various nobles from the eastern regions, and various lesser nobles from Luoyang partook of the fast outside the city by the Wen River. The Defender-in-Chief and the Chamberlain for Ceremonials fasted at the Headquarters of the Supervisor of Forestry and Hunting.

I, Ma Dibo, along with seventy others, first reached the Headquarters of the Supervisor of Forestry and Hunting to inspect the altar to the mountain and the ancient Hall of Enlightened Rule, where the Court Gentlemen and others were to offer up sacrifices. We entered the headquarters and observed the stones installed there. There are two stones, broad and flat, nine feet in circumference. They were meant to be placed at the site of the actual altar. One of these stones was from the time of Emperor Wu.[7] At that time, five carts were used but could not move it up the mountain, so it was placed at the foot and a building was erected over it—it is called the "Five-Carts Stone." Boulders supporting the four corners are about twelve feet in length, two feet wide, and one and a half feet thick. There are four stone containers each three feet long, six inches wide, and shaped like sealed boxes. There are ten long containers. There is an inscribed stele twelve feet tall, three feet wide, and one foot, two inches thick: this is called the "Erected Stone." On one side is engraved a record of meritorious achievements.

On this morning [March 17], we ascended the mountain on horseback. Frequently, where the road grew steep and precipitous, we dismounted and led our horses on foot. Sometimes we walked and sometimes we rode, roughly in equal amounts. We arrived at the Midway Temple[8] where we left our horses, a distance of seven miles from flat ground. Along the southern vista nothing escaped our view. Looking up at the Celestial Pass[9] was like contemplating an eminent peak from the bottom of a valley. Its height felt as if I were observing the floating clouds; as for its precipitousness, its rock walls stretched into the remote distance—no road seemed to lead there. When I cast my gaze toward the people there, they seemed to be climbing up on poles. Someone thought they were white rocks; another, that they were patches of snow. After a while, the "white" things moved past the trees and we realized that they were people. We could barely make the climb. I had to spread out my four limbs and lie down on a

7   In 110 BCE, Emperor Wu of the Western Han had also made an Eastern Tour and offered up the *feng* and *shan* sacrifices at Mount Tai.

8   The Midway Temple (*Zhongguan*) was located midway up the mountain toward the Celestial Gate (*Tianmen*), the site of the *feng* sacrifice.

9   The Celestial Pass (*Tianguan*) was located between the Midway Temple and the Celestial Gate.

rock. But after a while I felt revived, thanks also to the wine and food brought along. There were springs everywhere, which were always an inspiring sight for the eyes. In this manner we persevered, helping each other along.

When we arrived at the Celestial Pass, I thought I had already reached the top. But when I asked someone on the path, he said that it was still more than three miles farther. The path between the rock walls was eight or nine feet at the widest and five or six feet at the narrowest. I peered up at the cliffs, where the pines were flourishing and viridian—they seemed to be amid the clouds. When I peered down at the streams in the valleys, they were so minute that I could hardly discern them. Then we arrived just below the Celestial Gate. When I peered up at it, it seemed as if I were looking at the sky from inside a cave. We went another two and a half miles straight upward. The path was convoluted, winding its way around, so it is called Circle Path. Often, there were ropes to grasp hold of as we climbed. Two assistants supported me as another in front pulled me up. Those in back could see only the soles of the sandals of the ones in front, while those in front could see only the tops of the heads of those in back—it looked like a picture of a stack of men. This is what people mean by "as difficult as scraping one's chest and grasping hold of the rock in order to touch Heaven." When we began to climb up this path, we had to stop and rest every ten paces or so. As we became exhausted, our throats and lips grew parched, and we rested every five or six paces. We shuffled along, first upright, then crawling. The dank and dark places on the ground were unavoidable. When there was a dry area ahead, our eyes could see it, but our feet would not follow.

We began to climb up after breakfast and reached the Celestial Gate after the hours of *bu* [3–5 pm]. The emissary, Guo [Jianbo] came across a bronze vessel. The bronze vessel resembled a wine goblet in shape. It also had squared handles with holes in them. We could not identify what it was and assumed it was an object used in previous sacrifices. Yang Dong of Zhaoling in Runan took it. I climbed almost half a mile to the east and came across a wooden image. The image was a god from the time of Emperor Wu. More than a hundred paces to the northeast, we came upon the site for the *feng* sacrifice. The First Emperor of Qin had erected a stele and a stone entrance in the southern part of the area.[10] More than twenty paces north of this, Emperor Wu established a circular terrace facing north, nine feet high and about thirty feet square in area. There are two sets of stairs, which no one is permitted to climb besides the emperor. We climbed up the eastern stairs to where there is an altar on the top of the terrace about twelve feet square. On top of this is a square stone supported by boulders at all four corners. On all four sides are platforms. We bowed down thrice before the

---

10   The First Emperor of Qin made an Eastern Tour and offered up the *feng* and *shan* sacrifices in 219 BCE. He had a stele erected extolling the virtues of the Qin dynasty and a stone entrance constructed at the site of the *feng* sacrifice.

altar. Visitors had placed considerable amounts of money and other things on the altar, and these had never been cleared away. Later, when His Majesty[11] mounted the altar, he saw this and inquired concerning the decayed pears and rotten dates strewn about, the hundreds of coins scattered around, and the strips of silk currency all along the path. The emperor demanded an explanation, and the official in charge replied, "When Emperor Wu arrived at the foot of the Supreme Mountain to offer up the *feng* and *shan* sacrifices, before he ascended, all the officials first ascended and performed obeisance. Then they placed pears, dates, and money along the path to summon blessings—this is what they are." His Majesty said, "The *feng* and *shan* are great sacrifices that occur but once in a thousand years. How could men of rank behave like this?"[12]

We climbed farther east about three miles on the Supreme Mountain to the summit southeast of the Celestial Gate. This is called "Sunrise Vista." Sunrise Vista is where one can see the sun as it first appears, as soon as the cock crows. The place is about thirty feet long. From Qin Vista, one can look toward Chang'an; from Wu Vista, one can look toward Guiji [Commandery]; from Zhou Vista, one can look toward the state of Qi. The Yellow River is some seventy miles from the Supreme Mountain. From the site of the sacrifice, the Yellow River resembles a sash as if it were at the foot of the mountain. There is a temple south of the mountain;[13] everywhere junipers have been planted, the largest trunks having a circumference that the hands of fifteen or sixteen men could encircle. It is said that they were planted by Emperor Wu. By the Lesser Celestial Gate is the "Grandee of the Fifth Order" pine from Qin times. When the First Emperor sacrificed at the Supreme Mountain, he encountered raging winds and driving rain. Thanks to this pine he found cover, so he ennobled it as "Grandee of the Fifth Order."[14] Northwest is a rock chamber. South of the altar is a jade basin with a jade tortoise in the middle. On the southern flank of the mountain is a sacred spring. When I drank from it, I found it extremely pure and refreshing. At dusk, we descended, leaving by way of the Circle Path again. By nightfall, there was a fair amount of rain and we could no longer distinguish the path. One man had proceeded ahead. We felt with our feet where the person in front of us had trod before following. By the time we reached the Celestial Gate, it was in the deep of night.

---

11   A reference to Emperor Guangwu.

12   The implication is that such officials infringed on the emperor's prerogative by first offering sacrifices on their own.

13   This is the Dai Temple to the Sacred Mount of the East, located at the foot of the mountain in modern Tai'an, Shandong.

14   See Sima Qian, *Shiji* (Beijing: Zhonghua shuju, 1959), 1:242.

"Mount Tai" (*Taishan* 泰山; extract)

CAO ZHI 曹植 (192–232)

TRANSLATED BY PAUL W. KROLL

Cao Zhi, a distinguished poet, was a younger son of Cao Cao (155–220), the founder of the state of Wei in the Three Kingdoms period that followed on the collapse of the Han dynasty. Cao Zhi's somewhat dissolute life was one of the factors that led his father to name one of Zhi's older brothers, Cao Pi (187–226), as his successor. Cao Zhi was no more successful in persuading his brother to allow him to participate in political life, and is said to have died of disappointment. However, his poetry was highly regarded both by contemporaries and in later times. This poem suggests the importance of Mount Tai to those who wished to control the empire during the post-Han period of disunion.

"Mount Tai" (extract)

Urge on the carriage, shake up the worn-out steeds,
Eastward to arrive at the enceinte of Fenggao.
Divine, oh, is Mount Tai in that place!
Among the Five Marchmounts its name is special.

Arched and high—threading the clouds and rainbows;
Upborne and abrupt—emerging into Grand Clarity.
Coursing round about it are twice six watch-mounds,
And placed atop them are kiosks ten and two.

Above and below are springs of gushing ale,
With stones of jade displaying their floriate blooms.
To the southeast one gazes on the countryside of Wu;
Looking west, one observes the germ of the sun.

It is where cloud-soul and spirit are tethered and attached—
In the passage away [of time], one feels this ongoing march.
They who are kings, in returning their allegiance to Heaven,
Devote to it [Mount Tai] the completion of their principal deeds.

"A Chant of Mount Tai" (*Taishan yin* 泰山吟)

LU JI 陸機 (261–303)

TRANSLATED BY PAUL W. KROLL

Lu Ji, from an influential family in what is now Suzhou, was a distinguished literary man of the Three Kingdoms (220–280) and Western Jin (265–316) periods, best known for writing rhapsodies or rhyme-prose (*fu*); as the author of the "Rhapsody on Literature," he is particularly noted as an early literary critic. This short poem on Mount Tai, however, is in the *yuefu* or ballad form, supposedly based on the style of early folk songs. Lu Ji, who in his youth acquired considerable military experience, met his death during a period of internecine struggle as members of the Jin imperial family contended for supremacy.

"A Chant of Mount Tai"

Mount Tai—how very tall!
Farther and farther, attaining Heaven's Court!
Its pinnacled apogee wholly distant now,
With tiered clouds clustered gloom upon gloom.
On Liangfu, for its part, there is a hospice;
On Haoli, for its part, there is a pavilion.
The shrouded route detains a myriad revenants,
And the haunt of spirits collects a hundred numina.
—But I prolong my chant by the side of Mount Tai,
With brave forbearance, projecting the sounds of Chu.

"Ascending the Mountain" (*Deng shan* 登山)

XIE DAOYUN 謝道韞 (FL. 340–399)
TRANSLATED BY PAUL W. KROLL

Xie Daoyun, one of China's early women writers, was a member of a powerful clan during the Eastern Jin dynasty, the successor state of Wei, one of the Three Kingdoms (see under Cao Zhi above). She was the sister of a general and niece of a prime minister, and was distinguished in both literature and philosophy. Whether she ever actually visited Mount Tai is unclear, but again we can see the importance to leading families of being associated with this ritual site.

"Ascending the Mountain"

Upborne aloft, the Marchmount of the East is high!
Its flourishing apogee surges up to azure heaven.
Among its cliffs are spaced the eaves of the void;
Still and null—both shrouded and mysterious.

Not the work of artisan, nor again that of builder,
Its cloudy beams have been thrown up spontaneously!
An image made from vital pneuma—what being art thou,
That duly causes myself to be many times transported?
—I swear I shall take up abode under these eaves,
Allowing me to finish fully my heaven-ordained years.

"A Chant of Mount Tai" (*Taishan yin* 泰山吟)

XIE LINGYUN 謝靈運 (385–433)
TRANSLATED BY PAUL W. KROLL

For Xie Lingyun, see chapter 1. Unlike the personal mysticism expressed in relation to Mount Tai by Lu Ji and Xie Daoyun in the poems above, Xie Lingyun focuses the second half of his chant on the imperial rituals associated with the mountain in the form of the *feng* and *shan* sacrifices and related ceremonial sites.

"A Chant of Mount Tai"

Dai the Revered—flourishing is the Marchmount;
Sublimely spiring, to pierce the cloudy heavens.
Precipitous and acclivitous, both hazardous and high;
Its jostled rocks, in every case luxuriant and lush.

Ascending for the *feng*—interment at the exalted altar;
Descending for the *shan*—a cache at Solemn State.
Stone Wicket is very obscure and hazy;
And in the Hall of Light a numinous tract is secreted.

"Gazing Afar at the Marchmount" (*Wang yue* 望嶽)

DU FU 杜甫 (712–770)
TRANSLATED BY PAUL W. KROLL

For Du Fu, see chapter 2. The poet's focus here is on the dominant view of the landscape afforded by the mountain, and on the assimilation of landscape to a living body, as Mount Tai's "heaving breast" exhales clouds and its caves form "bursting eye-sockets."

"Gazing Afar at the Marchmount"

Dai the Revered—now, what to compare it with?
Over Qi and Lu, its azure never ending.
In it the Shaping Mutator concentrated the flourishing of divinity;
Shaded and sun-lit it cleaves the dusk from the dawn.

A heaving breast—giving rise to cumulus clouds;
Bursting eye-sockets—giving entrance to homing birds.
Someday I will surmount its incomparable crest—
Then in a single scanning the host of hills will dwindle!

"Six Poems on a Journey to Mount Tai" (*You Taishan liu shou* 遊泰山六首)

LI BAI 李白 (701–762)

TRANSLATED BY PAUL W. KROLL

Like his contemporary Du Fu (see chapter 2 and above), Li Bai is regarded as one of the greatest poets of the Tang dynasty, if not in all of Chinese literature. Where Du Fu is usually serious and attentive to social and political events, Li Bai is expansive and "romantic." Despite their difference in character, the two poets were friends. Many stories became attached to Li Bai's name, such as an occasion when he wrote calligraphy at imperial command while intoxicated. This sequence of poems on Mount Tai is characteristic of his grandiloquent style. For Li Bai, the mountain is not the site of imperial ritual but of Daoist transcendence, where he encounters such mystical beings as Jade Maidens, the Azure Lad, and the wizard Master Anqi. This may reflect a change in the understanding of the site, whereby it becomes associated more with personal religion than state ritual.

"Six Poems on a Journey to Mount Tai"

I
In the fourth month I ascend Mount Tai;
Its stones flat—the autocrat's road opens out.
The six dragons traverse a myriad straths;
Ravines and races wind in due course round about.

Horses' footprints wreathe the cyan peaks
That are at present overflowing with azure lichens.
Flying streams shed their spray over steep stacks;
Waters rush, and the voice of the pine-trees is poignant.

The view to the north—singular bluffs and walls;
Canted banks toward the east topple away.
The grotto gates—closed door-leaves of stone;
From the floor of the earth—rising clouds and thunder.

Climbing the heights, I gaze afar at Peng and Ying;
The image imagined—the Terrace of Gold and Silver.
At Heaven's Gate, one long whistle I give,
And from a myriad *li* the clear wind comes.

Jade maidens, four or five persons,
Gliding and whirling descend from the Nine Peripheries.
Suppressing smiles, they lead me forward by immaculate hands,
And let fall to *me* a cup of fluid aurora!

I bow my head down, salute them twice,
Ashamed for myself not to be of a transcendent's caliber.
—But broad-ranging enough now to make the cosmos dwindle,
I'll leave this world behind, oh how far away!

II
At clear daybreak I rode upon a white deer,
And ascended straight to the mount of Heaven's Gate.
At the mountain's edge I happened on a plumed person,
With squared pupils, with handsome face and features.

Holding on to the bindweed, I would have attended to his colloquy;
He nevertheless concealed himself with a barrier of clouds from the blue.
But he let fall to me a writ formed of avian tracks,
Which dropped down aflutter in the midst of the rocky heights.

Its script, it turned out, was of highest antiquity;
In construing it, I was absolutely unpracticed.
Sensible of this, I thrice breathed a sigh;
But the master I would follow has till now yet to return.

III
In the level light I climbed to the Belvedere of the Sun,
Raised my hand and opened up the barrier of clouds.
My germinal spirit lifted up four directions in flight,
As though emerging from between heaven and earth!

The Yellow River comes here from out of the west,
Winsome but withdrawn it passes into the distant hills.
Leaning against a high bank, I scanned the Eight Culmina;
Vision exhausted its limits, idling in lasting emptiness.

By an odd chance then I beheld the Azure Lad,
His virid hair done up in twin cloud-coils.
He laughed at me for turning late to the study of transcendence:
My unsteadiness and unsureness have brought the fading of ruddy features.

Halting I stood and hesitant—suddenly he was gone from sight;
So careless and uninhibited—it is hard to pursue and detain him.

IV

Purified and purged for three thousand days,
I strip plainsilk[15] to copy the scriptures of the Way.
Intoning and reciting I hold what I have won,
As a host of spirits guards the physical form that is mine.

Proceeding with the clouds, I trust to the lasting wind,
Wafted on as though I'd spawned plumes and wings!
Clinging now to the high bank, I ascend the Sun's Belvedere;
Bending by the railing, I peer over the Eastern Gulf.

A sheen on the sea animates the distant mountains;
The Cockerel of Heaven has already given his first call.
A silvery terrace emerges out of inverted luminescence,
Where white-capped waves roll over the long leviathan.

—Where is one to acquire the drug of immortality?
Fly away on high toward Peng and Ying!

V

The Belvedere of the Sun inclines north and east;
Its pair of high banks—twinned stone hemmed about.
The sea's waters drop away before one's eyes;
The sky's light spreads far in the cyan-blue of the void.

A thousand peaks, vying, throng and cluster around;
A myriad straths are cut off from traverse and transit.
Thread-thin in the distance, that transcendent on his crane—
Upon departing he left no tracks among the clouds.

Long pines enter here into the Empyreal Han,
The "distant view" is now no more than a foot away.
The mountain's flowers are different from those in the human realm—
In the fifth month they are white amid the snows.

—I am bound in the end to come upon Anqi,
Refining at this very place the liquor of jade.

---

15   Editor's note: white tabby-weave silk used for writing and painting.

VI

At sun-up I drank from the Royal Mother's pool,
Took refuge in the gloaming by the pylons of Heaven's Gate.
In solitude I embraced the Green Tracery zither,
At night-time strode out in moonlight on the azure mountain.

The mountain was luminous—moonlit dew was white;
The night was still—the pine-tree wind had died away.
Transcendent persons were roaming the cyan peaks;
From place to place songs of reed-organs issued forth!

In subdued stillness I took pleasure in the clear leaming,
As Jade Realized Ones linked up on the halcyon heights.
The image imagined—a dance of phoenixes and simurghs;
Tossing and swirling—in raiment of dragon and tiger.

Touching the sky, I plucked down the Gourd[-Star];
Distracted and delirious, reflecting not on my return.
Lifting my hand, I swished it in the clear shallows,
And inadvertently caught hold of the Weaving Maid's loom!

—Next morning I sat in forfeit of it all;
Only to be seen—pentachrome clouds floating away.

"A Short Record of the Ascent of Mount Tai by Pacification Commissioner Zhang of Dongping" (*Dongping Zhang xuanwei deng Taishan jilüe* 東平張宣慰登泰山記略)

DU RENJIE 杜人傑 (1201–1282)

TRANSLATED BY ALISON HARDIE

This inscription—composed in 1265 and originally set up in the *Dai miao* or Temple of the Eastern Marchmount in Tai'an—records the ascent of Mount Tai early in the Yuan dynasty, not by an emperor but by one of his official representatives, the Pacification Commissioner of Dongping, a district very near the mountain.[16] Commissioner Zhang was Zhang Dehui (1195–1275), an important official in the early years of the Yuan dynasty. It appears, however, that Zhang Dehui was not acting on behalf of the emperor in offering sacrifices at Mount Tai and the nearby tomb of Confucius, but on his own account as a senior local official. According to his biography in the official *Yuan History*, his prayers to Mount Tai induced rainfall that ended a drought in the spring

---

16 The text is reproduced in Édouard Chavannes, *Le T'ai chan; Essai de monographie d'un culte chinois* (Paris: Ernest Leroux, 1910), 350.

of 1261.[17] According to Du Renjie's account, however, Zhang planned his ascent of the mountain for the ninth day of the ninth lunar month (the "Double Ninth"), a date in autumn on which it was traditional to ascend heights, thus associating his action to some extent with popular culture rather than imperial ritual. Viewing what remained of the inscriptions left by earlier emperors and officials was clearly an important part of the journey for the participants, as was seeing the dawn break from the summit. Du Renjie, who was himself from Shandong, was a noted literary man of the Yuan dynasty who never served as an official; it is likely that he was personally acquainted with Zhang Dehui as they were both friendly with the poet Yuan Haowen (1190–1257).

"A Short Record of the Ascent of Mount Tai by Pacification Commissioner Zhang of Dongping"

In the first year of Zhongtong [1260], the emperor [Yuan Shizu, Khubilai Khan, r. 1260–1294] promoted officials to oversee the ten circuits. Mr. Zhang was one of the first to be selected. While in charge of Hedong, he had outstanding administrative achievements, and was appraised as one of the finest administrators in the empire. His Majesty personally rewarded him, offering him wine in a goblet and addressing him by his social name. All in official and civilian life regarded him with admiration. Four years later, His Majesty again promoted Mr. Zhang, to Pacification Commissioner of Dongping. Mr. Zhang remarked, "Qufu is in fact the residence of the Master [Confucius], and Mount Tai is the holy mountain of the Central Plains. Both are in my district. I should personally offer sacrifices there." So three days before the Double Ninth of [the first year of] Zhiyuan [1264], he packed his luggage to travel there. When he left by the Yizhou Gate, the sky was overcast. On the following day he arrived at the temple of the [Confucian] forest [cemetery] and paid his respects at the tombs of the Three Sages. The rainy weather had not yet cleared. He took lodging in the shrine of the Marchmount. On the next morning when he climbed to the Western Flowery Gate, sometimes it was cloudy, sometimes bright; the rain now fell and now stopped. The three [Daoist] temples nearby were enveloped in a wash of dilute ink, changing in appearance a thousand times in one instant. Addressing his companions, Mr. Zhang said, "I dare not insist on my decision to ascend to the summit. If it clears, then we will go on; if not, I am afraid I have troubled you for nothing." Then when the fifth watch was about to sound, the cloud-cover suddenly cleared, and before the cock had crowed thrice, the stars appeared in their glittering array. Thereupon, Prefect Zhang Rulin, Magistrate of Fengfu,[18] Zhang Quan, Revenue Manager Wang Tianting and the three hundred people in their retinue organized sedan-chairs and carried Mr. Zhang uphill. After that they went to the Yellow Peak and had a meal at the Spring for Escorting the [Imperial] Carriage. They stopped at the Imperial Tent for a short rest.

---

17 Song Lian et al., eds., *Yuanshi* (Beijing: Zhonghua shuju, 1976), 7:3825.

18 A county in Tai'an Prefecture.

When they were just over fifteen *li* from the Celestial Gate, the path grew gradually steeper and the forest trees closed in all around; on looking through the gaps between them, the bright sky was an intense blue like ultramarine beads. At dusk they reached the furthest summit. Looking from the eastern side, one could see the shadow of the mountain pitch-black and stretching out to infinity. Shortly they viewed the stele of Li Si,[19] but only a few characters appeared; the rest were damaged and unrecognizable. Going down from the altar for the *feng* sacrifice, there were numerous rock-faces smoothed out [for inscriptions] throughout the dynasties, but all were damaged and cracked, except for the *Record of Mount Tai* imperially composed by the Glorious Emperor of Tang[20] which was the only survivor; its characters were the diameter of a bowl and several inches deep, with traces of gold paint here and there. Shortly after sunset, a cold wind as if in the depths of winter oppressed the group. The retinue then lit a fire and sat round it to await the dawn. When the constellation Orion had just reached the center of the heavens, Mr. Zhang arose and walked from Jade Maiden Pool, climbing the Sunrise Vista Summit. The six dimensions [of space] were completely open, without the least trace of impurity. In the time it takes to cook millet, the eastern sky glimmered with a light that appeared and disappeared; in a short time the sun appeared half over the horizon and it was as bright as if one had entered a boundless golden world. Every one of the company gasped in amazement. As they returned, they saw the shadow to the west plunging right into the dark valley, like a rival to Mount Kunlun in its magnificence.

Record of Visits to Taishan (*You Taishan ji* 遊泰山記; extracts)

WANG SHIZHEN 王世貞 (1526–1590)
TRANSLATED BY PEI-YI WU

For Wang Shizhen, see chapter 6. The passages extracted here indicate not only that in the sixteenth-century Mount Tai was already an important pilgrimage site for syncretic Daoist/Buddhist popular religion (as shown in "the train of men and women on their way to pay homage to Yuanjun") but also that Wang Shizhen himself felt it worth appealing to "the god of Tai Shan" in a family emergency. Wang Shizhen's father, Wang Yu (1507–1560), had clashed with the powerful chief minister Yan Song (1480–1567) over frontier policy, and by the late 1550s was in deep political trouble. In 1559, therefore, Wang Shizhen made a third visit to Mount Tai to invoke divine help for his father—very different from his first two visits, which were evidently more in the nature of tourist trips—but he was unsuccessful: his father was executed the following year, and he himself remained out of office for some time.

---

19 Li Si (ca. 280–208 BCE) was the chief minister of the First Qin emperor.

20 Emperor Xuanzong (r. 712–756).

Record of Visits to Taishan (extracts)

[First visit: early 1558]

That night I bathed myself in the government hostel together with Mr. Song Dawu. At the third drum I got up. As I opened the northern window of the hall I saw something like a bolt of white silk stretching from the foot of the mountain all the way to the summit. Then it looked like a large collection of fireflies flickering light from hundreds of boxes. When I asked about it, I was told that what I saw was the train of men and women on their way to pay homage to Yuanjun.[21] I could vaguely hear their prayers and psalms. At dawn when we started our journey the sky was overcast, and clouds flowed so closely by our faces that we could not see anything clearly beyond ten steps. I only noticed that as the sedan chair carriers raised their heels I leaned forward. Even after we arrived at the summit I still could not see a thing. It was so cold that Mr. Song insisted that we immediately start our descent. We made a short stop at Fengdu Palace, where I had several cups of wine and only then did I stop shivering. The trip was ended in great regret.

[Second visit: 1558]

On the last day of the sixth month I went along with Mr. Duan the censor to inspect Tai-an. Mr. Duan invited me for a three-day mountain trip. I knew that quite a few from other government agencies were to join us, and there would be a shortage of means of transportation. So Mr. Xu Wentong, assistant administrative commissioner, and I requested that we be allowed to precede the group by two days. Mr. Duan gave his consent. . . .

I was so inspired by the sight that I became uninhibited. Standing barefoot in the rapid stream next to boulders, I ordered wine and emptied large cups of it in quick succession. My loud singing shook the leaves of the trees overhead. All my companions cheered me on: some harmonized with me while others came down and drank the wine that was being brought to me. After a while it was announced that Mr. Duan had arrived. Before we took leave of each other we went to Fengdu Palace for a simple repast.

[Third visit: 1559]

On the first day of the fourth month in the following year [1559], I passed through Laiwu on an inspection tour. It happened just then that my father's involvement with border affairs had been temporarily stabilized, and it was decided that an appeal for divine help be made to the god of Taishan. For that reason I made one more ascent.

---

21   The Primal Sovereign of the Azure Clouds (Bixia Yuanjun), or in full The Celestial Immortal of the Eastern Marchmount Taishan, the Jade Lady Primal Sovereign of the Azure Clouds (Dongyue Taishan Tianxian Yunü Bixia Yuanjun), is a goddess in popular Daoism whose cult became very important in northern China from at least the Ming dynasty.

"A Pilgrimage to Mount Tai" (*Dai zhi* 岱志; extracts)

ZHANG DAI 張岱 (1597–CA. 1684)

TRANSLATED BY PEI-YI WU

For Zhang Dai, see chapter 3. Zhang probably made his visit to Mount Tai in 1629. Zhang Dai's personal name is written with the same *dai* character as Mount Tai's alternative name of Dai Peak, so he may have felt that a visit to the mountain held particular significance for him. Nevertheless, although his description of his visit shows a lively interest in the scene, there is a complete lack of any sense of reverence for the numinous mountain.

"A Pilgrimage to Mount Tai" (extracts)

Guides approach the travelers when they are only a few *li* away from the subprefectural city. They lead the horses to the gate of the inn. In front of the gate are a dozen stables. There are also a dozen apartments to house the prostitutes and an equal number of accommodations for the actors. I used to think that these matters were run by various people in the subprefecture; I did not know that they are managed by a guide company. The company sets a fixed rate for renting rooms, hiring sedan chairs, and paying mountain fees. Visitors are charged on the basis of three classes: upper, middle, and lower. All the visitors are met upon their arrival, entertained when they descend from the summit, and escorted when they leave. Each day there are several thousand visitors, who will occupy hundreds of rooms and consume hundreds of vegetarian and ordinary banquets; they are entertained by hundreds of actors, singers, and musicians, and there are hundreds of attendants at their beck and call. The guides are from about a dozen families. On an average day eight thousand to nine thousand visitors come, while the number can reach twenty thousand on the first day of spring. The entrance fee is collected at twelve *fen* per person, so the annual collection amounts to two hundred thousand to three hundred thousand taels. The magnitude of Mount Tai, alas, can be measured by the number of the guides or the amount of the fees! . . . There was a motley collection of stalls and stands, selling their wares mainly to women and children. The rest of the ground was largely taken up by cockfighters, football players, equestrians, and storytellers. There were also some ten wrestling platforms and theatrical stages, each attracting hundreds of spectators who clustered like bees or ants. As these performing groups were far apart, they did not interfere with each other no matter how loud was the racket each produced by singing as well as by the beating of drums and gongs. . . .

At the fifth drum, water was still dripping from the eaves. I wanted to tarry a bit, but the guide urged me to rise and prepare myself for the ascent. I found the mountain sedan chair waiting at the door. The carrying poles were curved, and the compartment differed from that of an ordinary sedan chair in that it had a square, rather than rectangular, shape. The carriers tied the poles to their shoulders with leather strips. When they climbed up the steps the sedan chair moved sideways like a crab. . . . We left the lodging before dawn, yet huge crowds of pilgrims were already going up or down. One of them would chant "A-mi-tuo-fo" [Amitābha], and he would be echoed by a hundred voices. The shouts were punctuated by the din of copper gongs. Flares from torches and lamps made an unbroken line for forty *li*, as if the Milky Way had come down in a winding flow. One was reminded of Emperor Yangdi of the Sui, who released bushels of fireflies in the mountains and valleys. For a long time my eyes were dazzled by the burning mountains and shining valleys.

As soon as I mounted the sedan chair my guide took out strings of tin pennies and hung them on the carrying poles of the sedan chair. These pennies, thin as elm leaves and each of them inscribed with the characters A-mi-tuo-fo, were to be given to the beggars. Real pennies were worth seven *fen* per thousand, but the tin ones were worth only half as much. Going up the mountain, the pilgrims were handed the pennies by the guides; going down the mountain, the beggars returned the coins to the guides. Although this type of coin circulated only among the local beggars, their total value was no less than several hundred taels of silver. From beyond the Dengfeng Gate there were beggars everywhere along the route. Thrusting out their bamboo baskets to beg money, they did not care if they bumped into people. The higher I went the more beggars I saw, but their number decreased somewhat when I reached the Chaoyang Cave. The variety of ways they begged, chanted, and made themselves up reminded me of the Hell painted by Wu Daozi;[22] their grotesqueness was otherwise really inconceivable.

But the beggars were only one of two abominations; the other was the visitors' disgusting practice of inscribing on rocks as well as on the tablets they erected such trite phrases as "Venerated by ten thousand generations" or "The redolence continuing for an eternity." The beggars exploited Mount Tai for money while the visitors exploited Mount Tai for fame. The land of Mount Tai, once pure, was now everywhere desecrated by these two groups. . . .

At the top of the cliff was a mud house owned by the guides. We were invited into the house to warm ourselves by an open fire. My hands were so frozen that at first I could not even stretch them. We did not leave the house for the summit until we were thoroughly warmed. When we got out of the door we were surrounded by white clouds as thick as loose cotton. I could hear people from my group, but I often could not see them. As we groped our way, our hands were always ahead of our toes. After we walked in this fashion for a *li* or so we arrived at something like a settlement. Turning left, we climbed up to the gate of the Bixia Palace. The right path was for the departing pilgrims. As soon as I entered the gate a dozen men lifted me onto their shoulders and, pushing their way through the crowd, brought me forward to the iron fence, from which I peered in and caught a glimpse of the golden visage of Yuanjun. The fence was made of iron posts as large as beams, and the statue of the goddess, seen through

---

22 Editor's note: Wu Daozi (ca. 680–760) was one of the great painters of the Tang dynasty, renowned for the lifelikeness of his paintings. He was particularly noted for painting Buddhist and Daoist murals; his depictions of the torments of hell were reputed to terrify sinners into giving up their evil ways.

the narrow spaces between the posts, did not appear to be very large. But this was the case with all divine images in the notable mountains such as Putuo, Wudang, Qiyun, Qianmen, and Tianzhu.[23] The statue of Yuanjun was not quite three feet tall, yet she attracted more worshipers than any other deity in all four great continents.

Ying Shao in his *Fengshan ji* mentions that when Emperor Wu of the Han arrived at the foot of Tai Shan all the officials greeted him on their knees.[24] They placed cash by the side of the road in lieu of fruit offerings as a way of imploring blessings on the emperor. This shows that the practice of making offerings had a long history, but it was never as flourishing as it is now. Several hundred times a day the iron fence in the palace is opened, and baskets of money collected from the pilgrims are brought in and emptied on the floor. There are statues of three Yuanjun, and the one on the left is responsible for the bestowing of male heirs. Those whose wishes have been granted repay the favors with silver figures of boys, the size depending on the circumstances of the family. The statue on the right heals ailments of the eye. Those who have appealed to the goddess and thus regained their sight repay the favors with eyes made of silver. A gigantic gold coin is hung in front of the middle statue. Aiming at it, pilgrims throw coins or small ingots of silver over the fence. They believe that they will receive blessings if they hit the mark. Others give as offerings satin, silk, gold, pearls, precious stones, leg warmers, pearl-strewn shoes, and embroidered handkerchiefs. Consequently, gifts pile up several feet high. To guard the offerings behind the fence soldiers are stationed in the palace every night, and for this purpose a military camp has been established at the foot of the mountain. Four times a year the gifts are swept off and collected under the supervision of an officer. Even allowing for unavoidable encroachments, the annual proceeds amount to several tens of thousands of taels. Every official in Shandong, from the governor down to the petty clerks in the subprefecture, receives a share of the income.

When we came out of the Bixia Palace the clouds were so thick that we could not walk. I became very distressed when I thought that I had traveled three thousand *li* only to be denied a real look at Mount Tai. What had I come for? I wanted to spend the night on the top, but could not find anyone to help me or even a path. People in my group, cold and hungry, absolutely refused to go any farther. Reluctantly I let the carriers guide me to the sedan chair and began the descent. . . .

When I came out of the Red Gate the guide poured wine on my feet and offered me nuts and seeds. This was the so-called post-summit reception. At night theatricals were provided to entertain us at dinner, and wine was poured to congratulate all the pilgrims who had gone up to the summit during the day. The guide said to us: "Let me

---

23   Editor's note: although Bixia Yuanjun is a Daoist goddess, the sacred mountains Zhang Dai mentions are primarily Buddhist sites.

24   Editor's note: Ying Shao (2nd century) was appointed Prefect of Taishan in 184. He included Ma Dibo's *A Record of the Feng and Shan Sacrifices* (see above) in one of his works; this appears to be what Zhang Dai is referring to as Ying Shao's *Fengshan ji*.

offer my congratulations to you in advance, because when you return home those of you who seek fame will gain fame, those who seek wealth will gain wealth, and those who seek heirs will gain heirs." Cheerlessly I went through the motions. Retiring early, I planned to make another ascent next morning. In the middle of the night I got up. I was secretly pleased when I found the sky clear, the air still, and stars as large as wine cups hanging just beyond the eaves.

At the crack of dawn I ordered the old servant to seek a sedan chair. The guide, murmuring his astonishment, said to me: "One is not supposed to make another pilgrimage to the top right after the first one. Bad things will happen to the offender." While feigning compliance I walked out. I hurried to the First Heavenly Gate by a side path and only there did I succeed in finding a mountain sedan chair. Native children and women who remembered having seen my face the day before pointed at me and broke out in laughter. They chased after my chair carriers and never stopped asking: "This is the man who made it to the top yesterday. Why is it that he is here again?" They were puzzled because while there were pilgrims who spent a night at the top, none had ever gone up two days in a row. It was a convention that had persisted for a thousand years, but I finally broke it.

"An Inn in Tai'an" (*Tai'an zhou kedian* 泰安州客店)

ZHANG DAI 張岱

TRANSLATED BY RICHARD E. STRASSBERG

I shall never again regard the inns of Tai'an as merely inns. I had come to sacrifice at the Supreme Mountain, and less than half a mile or so before reaching the inn I saw twenty or more stables for mules and horses. As I got closer, there were more than twenty dwellings housing actors. And closer still were discreet doorways and concealed houses all belonging to courtesans engaged in their seductive profession. I thought that these must serve the entire subprefecture—I didn't realize they were just for a single inn.

When arriving at the inn, one first enters a reception room to register. Someone collects the basic rate of three *qian*, eight *fen* in silver; then someone collects the tax for climbing the mountain, of one *qian*, eight *fen*.[25] There are three grades of rooms. The lowest provides only a vegetarian meal in the evening and another one the next morning. Lunch is taken on the mountain, where the pilgrim partakes of ordinary rice wine and nuts; this is called "Reaching the Summit." By evening he arrives back at the inn where a feast of congratulations is held. It is said that after burning incense, if he prayed to become an official, then he will become one; if he prayed for sons, then he will receive them; if he prayed for money, he will obtain it. Therefore it is called "congratulations." There are also three grades of "congratulations." The first consists

---

25 Editor's note: ten *fen* equals one *qian*.

of a table for one with sweet cakes, five kinds of fruit, ten kinds of meat, nuts, and an opera performance. The next grade provides a table for two, also with sweet cakes, meat dishes, nuts, and an opera. The lowest grade is a table for three or four people, also with sweet cakes, meat dishes, nuts, but no opera, though it includes a singer with lute. At the inn I counted more than twenty places for opera performances, while those for singers were beyond counting. There were more than twenty kitchens preparing food and between one and two hundred servants running about serving the guests. After descending from the mountain, one can eat and drink and enjoy the courtesans to one's heart's content—all this in one day.

Guests arrive day after day to ascend and descend the mountain in this way. Yet the rooms of the new and departed guests are never confused, the non-vegetarian and vegetarian meals are never mixed up, and the staff who welcome the guests and the staff who see them off are each different. All this precision is quite incomprehensible. In the single subprefecture of Tai'an, there are five or six inns just like this one, which is even more amazing.

A Tale of Marriage Destinies That Will Bring Society to Its Senses (*Xingshi yinyuan zhuan* 醒世姻緣傳)

A pilgrimage to Mount Tai

A SCHOLAR OF WESTERN ZHOU (*XI ZHOU SHENG* 西周生; 17TH CENTURY)
TRANSLATED BY GLEN DUDBRIDGE

A Tale of Marriage Destinies That Will Bring Society to Its Senses is a lengthy (one hundred-chapter) satirical novel datable to the seventeenth century, although it is uncertain whether it was written before or after the conquest of the Ming by the Qing dynasty. The anonymous author's pseudonym "A Scholar of Western Zhou" implies Confucian nostalgia for the supposed golden age of the Western Zhou dynasty (ca. 1050–770 BCE), so he may be writing post-conquest. The action is set in the fifteenth century, but clearly satirizes social phenomena of the seventeenth century. The plot recounts the linked sagas of the Chao and Di families of Shandong, the region where Mount Tai is. After crime and debauchery lead to the death of the first antihero of the novel, Chao Yuan, he is reincarnated as the second antihero, Di Xichen, whose sufferings are meant to atone for Chao Yuan's sins. In the extract below, taken from chapters 68 and 69, Di Xichen's shrewish wife Xue Sujie, the daughter of a local professor, defies convention by joining a group of lower-class women from a township in rural Shandong on a pilgrimage to Mount Tai, led by two disreputable laywomen surnamed Hou and Zhang; she humiliates her husband by forcing him to accompany her. The detailed description of this fictional pilgrimage matches in many respects the autobiographical account by Zhang Dai given above, especially in the high degree of commercialization involved. It is interesting that for the lower-class female pilgrims in this story, Mount Tai has been transformed into a purely Buddhist/Daoist site of popular religion, with almost no reference to its role in imperial ritual, apart from a brief mention of "the Pine of Qin, the Cypress of Han."

A pilgrimage to Mount Tai

[Xue] Sujie asked them: "Are there fine things to see on the mountain?"

The laywomen [Hou and Zhang] said: "My dear—could there be another Tai Shan in the world? From the top you get a perfect view of all the lands on earth, the dragons' palaces, ocean treasuries, Buddhas' halls, and immortals' palaces. If such benefits were not to be had, why would men and women come thousands of miles from their homes in Yunnan, Guizhou, Sichuan, Huguang, Guangdong, Guangxi, just to burn incense there? What's more, Our Lady of Tai Shan controls life and death, luck and prosperity for people through all the world. If people reverently mount the summit and burn incense, then red comes hanging down from heaven and drapes itself about them, while music of reed and pipe comes to the summit to welcome them! If they do not go reverently, then Spirit-officer Wang will bind them up at once, and see if they can move then! The reverent at heart, when they come before Our Lady, see the goddess's true face in the flesh; if not reverent at heart, the face they see is only a gilded face. She is powerful and effective for bringing good luck and forgiving misdeeds. And on the mountain there is no end of wonderful sights, like the South-facing Cave, the Three Heavenly Gates, the Yellow Flower Island, the Platform of Suicides, the Rock for Drying Scriptures, the Stele without Inscription, the Pine of Qin, the Cypress of Han, the Golden Slips, the Jade Writings—all these are where the gods and immortals make their dwelling. No one with only average luck could ever get to go there!"

This speech set Sujie tingling uncontrollably inside; her thoughts ran wild, and she asked: "The society members who go—will they travel in chairs or ride on horseback? How much will they need for traveling expenses? Will anyone give them hospitality along the way?"

The two laywomen said: "The point of this pilgrimage is partly to build up good fortune, partly to enjoy the sights. It would be far too vulgar to cling to sedan chairs, so everyone will be riding mules. The donkeys we hire for the society come to eight *qian* of silver there and back. If you ride your own animal you get a rebate of eight *qian*. On first joining the society you put in a basic sum of three taels of silver, and when three full years have passed this yields ten taels, including principal and interest. Counting donkey-hire, inn accommodation and [tax] registration, at the most you would still not spend all of five taels. Which leaves another five taels for spending on personal items."

Sujie asked: "Can a person not in the society go too?"

The two laywomen said: "That depends on who it is. If it's someone we know well, we would ask her to pay in a sum of silver to match the yield of all the others, then we would report it to them, and then take her along. If it's someone who has nothing to do with us, then we would simply not let her go.". . .

At the end of another day's travel they had covered some thirty miles and spent the night at Wande. Of course they put up at an inn, set up the goddess's sedan, recited chants, and called to the Buddhas. No need to go into detail.

Let us go on. Traveling several more miles they passed through Huolu. Side by side all down the street in Huolu were shops selling fried snacks. Whenever pilgrims came by, the waiters in each shop would run out in a noisy rabble into the middle of the road and strenuously pull the pilgrims' donkeys to a halt, then invite them inside for a snack. They hoped in this way to attract business. This disgusting state of affairs was very like the Shaanxi peddlers of coarse rugs in Peking's East River Rice Lane or like the streetwalkers below the walls of the western tile-yard there, who go out into the street and pull at people willy-nilly. Just as Sujie and her group were passing through, the whole pack of waiters came charging out like tigers, and without any ceremony a crowd of them pulled to a halt the donkeys ridden by Hou and Zhang and struggled to take them off into their premises, saying: "Piping hot snacks, fresh from the pan, done in pure sesame oil! Fragrant and crisp! Come in and have one! The inn is a whole day on from here—make sure you don't go hungry!"

Hou and Zhang said: "Thank you, but we only just came from eating in Wande. We have to make haste to get to the inn, register our names, and hire chairs!"

After repeatedly failing to get the party to stop, the waiters just had to let them go.

This was Sujie's first pilgrimage, and she did not know that all travelers passing through suffered the same rough soliciting, pressing you to eat and pay accordingly. When she saw all the shop people mobbing Hou and Zhang with their solicitations she thought they all knew them personally, and asked: "Are all these shopkeepers acquaintances of yours, Masters? Why are they pressing you so hard to go in?" Glibly Hou and Zhang replied: "These people are all disciples of ours, but with all of them struggling so hard to invite us in, how can we go to everyone? We're just forced not to go in anywhere!"

When the pilgrims came to the military parade ground in Tai-an prefecture they were expected there by men who had been sent from Song Kuiwu's establishment—an inn well known to them from previous visits. Seeing Hou and Zhang arriving at the head of all those society members, the men recognized them a good way off and dashed joyfully up to them. They pulled their two animals to a halt and said: "The master sent us out some days ago to wait here, but we saw no sign of you arriving. Perhaps you started out on the fifteenth? Did you get caught in the rain on the way? Have you been keeping well all this time?" And they led along their donkeys, with the whole company following suit, all the way to the inn.

When Song Kuiwu saw them he put on all the true innkeeper's fawning manner to come out and welcome them, mouthing some empty courtesies. They washed their faces and drank tea. They registered their names and hired donkey-chairs. They called to the Buddha, recited sutras. And then they all went first to the Tianqi Temple to see the sights and worship there. Back at the inn they ate their supper and slept until the midnight watch, when everyone rose. They did their toilet, burned incense, and called to the Buddhas. This done, they all had a meal together.

Hou and Zhang saw every single member of the company on to their mountain chairs before they mounted their own to bring up the rear. All the wayside beggars, [fortune tellers] and providers of traveling lamps had lanterns burning, so that all along the way it was as bright as day.

Sujie had been born in the deep seclusion of Professor Xue's ladies' quarters; she had married into the prosperous Di family. She rose late and was early to bed; she went abroad in curtained chairs and seated carriages. Now, all of a sudden, she was with this troop of women, only fit for menial housework, who could never sit at a banquet. She had got up in the middle of the night, eyes still fuzzy with sleep; she had eaten a good bellyful of hard, undercooked rice, salty wheat buns only half cooked, lukewarm vegetables not as clean as they should be; she was riding in a willow-frame mountain chair with half the footrest missing, which was shaking her into a helpless condition. Before they had carried her as far as the Red Gate [Temple] she was already so dizzy that her sight was blurred and so queasy that she had to vomit. What came up first was that assortment of goodies she had risen to eat at midnight; later she brought up brown bile which gave off a powerful stench. She trembled so much that the hair on her bare head flopped down untidily all round; she retched until her fair white face looked as green and yellow as a cabbage leaf.

Hou said to the whole company: "Here is a young person whose heart is not pure enough: Our Lady has got her!" And Mrs. Liu said : "I said she was no good when I saw her put down her husband and make him walk along leading her donkey. And that's how it has turned out—she's driven Our Lady to deal with her. She's the only one of our whole party who has put Our Lady out of humor, but it reflects badly on everybody."

Hou and Zhang said: "She may be foolish and may have upset Our Lady, but surely we can't just look on! We'll all just have to beg forgiveness for her."

Thousands of pilgrims from other societies crowded around them so tightly that there was not room enough for a slip of paper between them. There was all sorts of talk about Our Lady binding someone up, and all kinds of questions like: "Where does that pilgrim come from?" "Whatever did she do, to make Our Lady deal with her so harshly?" Some said: "This pilgrim looks quite young, and seeing how well dressed she is she must be with an important master." The people in Sujie's society confirmed it: "She's a lady from the Di family in Mingshui—the wife of Tribute Student Di. There's Mr. Di beside her, isn't he?" The onlookers chattered wildly away among themselves.

Sujie sat on the ground with jaundiced face and drooping hair. Now, for one thing she could hear everyone chattering about her; for another, since she had got down from the chair and sat resting on the ground for a while her dizziness and nausea had slowly passed away. She couldn't stand listening to so much drivel, and with a snort she cried out: "Somebody gets dizzy in their chair, feels sick and has a vomit, then sits down for a little rest—and out comes all this flood of crap! What's this about Our Lady binding me up? Have I carried off babies of yours to throw down a well? You're ganging up to curse at me! Why don't you all clear off now? Serve you right if I picked up some dirt and threw it all over your bloody faces!" And standing up she added: "I'm not going to ride in a chair, I'm going to walk by myself for a spell." And she strode off up the slope.

When they all saw how vigorously she walked the society members at last remounted their chairs and moved on. Since Sujie was walking on foot Di Xichen could hardly dare sit in a chair, so he followed her closely to give support at her side. Now, Sujie had once been a fox before this incarnation, and Mount Tai had been familiar ground to her.[26] So she climbed that high mountain as easily as treading on level ground, she moved along the winding tracks as if she were walking along well-known paths, making no hardship of it. But this left Di Xichen perspiring with fatigue and panting like an ox driven to exhaustion: gradually one foot could not keep up with another, and his legs went limp. Once again it was lucky that Mrs. Liu said: "Won't it hurt you to walk at such a mad rate, Mrs. Di? Ride in chairs for a while, you and Mr. Di—you can always get down and walk again when you feel dizzy." And indeed the two chairs were put down, and only then did Sujie and Di Xichen sit in them. But they had not been carried a dozen paces, and Di Xichen had only just settled himself comfortably, when Sujie cried out: "Oh no!" Her face looked jaundiced again, she was queasy and dizzy as before. They were forced to make the men put down the chairs again and let her walk by herself. And Di Xichen was again obliged to walk along supporting her.

They made their way by stages to the summit. The man in charge of the pilgrims' tax was the deputy magistrate of Licheng county; he checked each pilgrim in against their name on the list. When they came up to the front of the Holy Mother's Hall[27] the doors were locked, because inside there were votive offerings of silver currency, robes, figurines in gold and silver, and suchlike, so people were not allowed to go in. Anyone wanting to see Our Lady's golden face had to stand on some support, then gaze in through openings in the door lattice. Sujie planted her feet on Di Xichen's shoulders while he grasped her two legs with his hands, so she did after all have a good view. And they did go to make some offerings of silver in the hall.

Once the pilgrims had burned their incense, each of them went round looking at the sights for a while before they all mounted their chairs to go down the mountain. Once again Sujie dared not get in a chair, but made Di Xichen support her walking down the mountain as far as the Red [Gate] Temple. Song Kuiwu, who had prepared boxed meals with wine, was already there waiting to entertain the company to a "Back from the Summit" party. The women all climbed down together from their chairs, mixing indiscriminately with the men as they promptly put paid to the jumble of food in the partitioned boxes and the weak, vinegary wine of the season. Then they climbed back into their chairs and returned to the inn, Sujie riding her own mule along with them and Di Xichen only now permitted to join the rest riding in a chair.

---

26 Editor's note: "fox-fairies" who take the form of beautiful, supernatural femmes fatales feature in many Chinese legends and fictional narratives. In the opening scene of the novel, Chao Yuan had met a fox while hunting.

27 Editor's note: this refers to the main temple of the Primal Sovereign of the Azure Clouds (Bixia Yuanjun; see Zhang Dai's "A Pilgrimage to Mount Tai" above).

When they reached the inn all the pilgrims of the house who had come down from the summit that same day were seated, men separately from women, in a large marquee, where a banquet was served and theatricals performed in a general farewell party. The man in the seat of honor picked the play *Hairpin of Thorn* and added the scenes "Moonlight Execution of Diaochan" and "Traveling Alone a Thousand *Li*" before the party broke up and all went back to their rooms. . . .

On the way [back] they were also going to Haoli Hill to burn paper money. This hill was a couple of miles distant from Tai-an prefecture, not particularly high but still possessing a major temple. Along the two side passageways were statues of the Kings of the Ten Courts of Hell and of all the sufferings in the eighteen tiers of Hell. Tradition has it that everyone in the world without exception goes there when they die. Therefore all pilgrims make a point of visiting the place, some to hold services of purification and deliverance for the dead, some to burn paper objects and money. The monks and priests in charge of the temple are also skilled in making profit from others' money by supplying tubes of divination slips, each inscribed with the name of some King in some court of Hell. People burning paper first draw a slip to find out where [their dead ones] have gone. If they then see that the court is a nice place, with no suffering or punishment, the sons and grandsons [of the dead] are pleased. But if it is some bad destination like the mountain of knives, the sea of suffering, the hell of pounding, or the hell of grinding, then they behave just like the dead themselves suffering there, making the earth tremble with their lamentation. Most distressing! "Heaven's signs arise from the hearts of men." How could the sky possibly be clear, the air bright, the sun radiant, or the breeze mild in a place of such unearthly, demonic wailing? Naturally, the sky is dim, the earth dark, the sun and moon lack luster, dark wind makes moan, cold air whistles through. People then read even more farfetched ideas into it and make this Haoli Hill into the true site of Fengdu, the Underworld. . . .

After seven days' travel, on the twenty-first of the eighth month as the sun was setting, they reached home. Without a word about asking to meet her parents-in-law, Sujie pushed straight through to her own room. But Tiaogeng and Di Zhou's wife did go to see her there, and Long prepared a one-table feast and told Qiaojie to entertain her sister-in-law to a "Back from the Summit" party.

The next day she dressed up once more in colored clothes, put jewel ornaments in her hair, and made Di Xichen and little Yulan go with her to join the company at Our Lady's temple to "return the incense." She brought from home twenty taels of silver which she quietly gave to her two masters, Hou and Zhang, as her church entry fee.

Hou and Zhang said: "This is a good deed done from a pious heart. Is your silver free of sham and low-grade material? Is it the full amount? Now that you have joined the church you must come at once whenever we summon you to any church functions in future. If you miss out one occasion all your previous merit will unfortunately be thrown away. But your father-in-law will not let us in, so how can we get the summons to you?"

Sujie replied: "You can go and tell my family about any activities that I ought to do in future. There will always be someone to let me know."Hou and Zhang both saw what she meant.

In any business the hardest thing is getting started. Now that she had been on one trip to Tai-an prefecture Sujie ever after gave her inclinations free rein. And there were the two temple thieves leading her astray as well. So when any pilgrimage or temple visit came up Sujie was always the "licorice in the medicine"—the one essential ingredient they could never be without. We shall see many a case of this in later chapters, as you can learn by reading on.

"Mount Tai's Mountain Veins Originate in the Changbai Mountains" (*Taishan shanmai zi Changbaishan lai* 泰山山脈自長白山來)

THE KANGXI EMPEROR 康熙帝 (AISINGIORO XUANYE 愛新覺羅玄燁; 1654–1722, R. 1661–1722)

TRANSLATED BY BRIAN R. DOTT

For the Kangxi emperor, see chapter 8. The emperor visited Mount Tai three times during his reign: in 1684, 1689, and 1703. On the first and third visits, he climbed to the peak first on horseback and then on foot; on the second visit, he did not ascend the mountain but performed rituals at the base. He never performed the *feng* and *shan* sacrifices, apparently regarding this as inappropriate and unnecessary compared to the regular and diligent performance of his work as ruler.[28] Although the emperor's visits to Mount Tai reflected his position as ruler of China, he also used the mountain to assert his Manchu identity, as he does in this essay. In it, he argues that Mount Tai is a southern extension of the Changbai Mountains. It was from these mountains in Manchuria that the imperial Aisingioro clan originated. In this extension of the mountain's domain beyond its immediate surroundings, we can also see a reflection of the principle in garden design that the landscape of the garden should be connected to the wider landscape beyond.

"Mount Tai's Mountain Veins Originate in the Changbai Mountains"

In ancient as well as present times, we hear discussion of the mountain veins of the Nine Districts [of Inner China], but only Mount Hua [the Western Sacred Peak] is said to be the tiger and Mount Tai the dragon. Geomancers also merely say that Mount Tai specially stands in the east, spreading left and right to provide shelter for protection. Without studying the roots of Mount Tai's dragon, how can we know the places where the veins issue forth? I [the emperor], through careful investigation of the terrain, deeply studying geographic connections, and dispatching people in ships to survey the seas, know that in fact Mount Tai's dragon arises in the Changbai Mountains.

---

28   Brian R. Dott, *Identity Reflections: Pilgrimages to Mount Tai in Late Imperial China* (Cambridge, Mass.: Harvard University Asia Center, 2005), 150, 176–77.

The Changbai Mountains stretch continuously south from Mount Wula.[29] In all parts of the Changbai Mountains, hundreds of springs run quickly down, forming the origins of three great rivers, the Songhua, the Yalu, and the Tumen. Their southern foothills divide into two stems. One stem points to the southwest. . . . The other stem goes west and then north . . . where it again splits into two branches. The northern branch goes to Shengjing,[30] where it forms the Tianzhu and Longye mountains, and then bends to the west. . . . The western branch enters Xingjingmen and becomes Kaiyun Mountain. It then zigzags to the south, continuously rising and lowering, forming range upon range of mountains, extending to Iron Mountain at the port of Lüshun [Port Arthur] in Jinzhou, it then appears as Longji [island]; sometimes it is hidden beneath the sea, sometimes it is visible. Huangcheng, Tuoji, and other islands [in the Gulf of Bohai] are all places where it is visible. Within the sea the dragon is hidden, but in Dengzhou in Shandong it rises up out of the sea, resulting in Mount Fu and Mount Danyai. It travels more than 800 *li* to the southwest, resulting in Mount Tai, rising loftily into the sky, coiled and crouching, the chief of the Five Sacred Peaks.

Although the ancients did not reach the conclusions of this essay, the topography truly proves them. If there are those who doubt that the strength of a mountain can be continuous even through the realm of the sea, or that a mountain's form and essence can be compared to and called a dragon, they have no basis for their doubts. Ban Gu[31] states that "form and essence have heads and tails." Now, fengshui masters, when referring to dragons, use the terms "pass through straits" and "water realm." The Gulf of Bohai, then, is Mount Tai's large "pass through straits" place. Wei Xiao, of the Song dynasty, states in his *Explanation of Geography* that "dragons can be attached to rivers or enter the sea." Thus, that the Changbai Mountains' dragon enters the sea and becomes Mount Tai is assuredly so. Mount Tai's positioning is further evidence: it faces southwest with its back to the northeast. . . . Therefore our reasoning is clear and intelligible.

"Han Cypress" (*Hanbo* 漢柏)

ZHANG PENGHE 張鵬翮 (1649–1725)

TRANSLATED BY BRIAN R. DOTT

Zhang Penghe obtained his presented scholar degree at a young age and had a very distinguished official career. His incorruptibility was praised by the Kangxi emperor himself. Zhang accompanied the emperor on his 1689 imperial progress, during which he visited Mount Tai. This poem,

---

29   Wula is in the southern part of modern Guyuan county, Inner Mongolia.

30   Qing-period name for Shenyang (also known as Mukden), the present capital of Liaoning Province. Shengjing was the Manchu capital from 1625 until 1644. It remained an important imperial site throughout the Qing dynasty.

31   Ban Gu (32–92) was the author of the *Book of the [Former] Han*.

written in 1710, was inscribed on a stone beside one of the Han dynasty cypress trees in the Dai Temple. Mount Tai is described as green because of its association with spring; this word, *bi*, means jade-green, and is sometimes translated as "azure," as in the goddess assocated with Mount Tai, the Primal Sovereign of the Azure Clouds. According to Mencius, "when Confucius ascended Mount Tai, he felt that the Empire was small";[32] "the vastness of heaven" alludes to this historical precedent. There was a spring known as the White Cranes Spring at the base of the mountain, where a flock of cranes was said to have appeared in 680; Zhang uses this auspicious event, like the "clear skies," to suggest the benevolent rule of the Kangxi emperor. The landscape described in Zhang's poem, with its tree or trees, mountain peak, and named spring, could be that of a garden writ large.

"Han Cypress"

The ancient cypress has leaned toward the green range for a thousand years;
on the Taiping Summit one feels the vastness of heaven.[33]
Clear skies, like the time when white cranes came dancing;
beyond the clouds one obtains a carefree, calm regard.

"Traveling at Dawn to Watch the Sunrise" (*Xiao xing guan richu* 曉行觀日出)

XI PEILAN 席佩蘭 (1760–1820?)
TRANSLATED BY IRVING YUCHENG LO

Xi Peilan was distinguished as the finest poet among the female literary disciples of Yuan Mei (1716–1797; see chapter 8). Her husband, whose poems were published posthumously in a joint edition with her own, stated that he learned poetry from his wife after their marriage. Xi was noted for the originality of her work (no easy achievement after nearly two millennia of poetry), and this striking poem on her experience of dawn on Mount Tai, although it echoes the Tang writer Han Yu, shows how creatively a fine poet could reimagine a scene that had been described many times before, combining practical observation (the sensation of frost on the skin, the skidding horse) with an almost cinematic depiction of the sunrise.

"Traveling at Dawn to Watch the Sunrise"

Traveling at dawn in these crenellated mountains,
So pitch-dark I could not see the road ahead;
Silently sitting behind the curtain in a cart,
All I felt was frost scraping my face.

---

32 *Mencius* VII.A.24.

33 "Green range" refers to Mount Tai. "Taiping Summit" was another name for the highest point on Mount Tai.

Road so icy that my horse slipped,
Courage failed me, my heart beat faster.
Ahead, I feared the steep cliff would give way;
Behind, I fretted the overhanging rock might break off.
I shut my eyes and dared not open them,
Opened, I could see nothing anyway.

Soon amid clouds and fog
Blossomed forth a ray of crimson,
First like a piece of Sichuan brocade spread out,
Then like a length of Suzhou silk snipped.
Swift as the Great Giant God sunders,[34]
Or again as the Goddess Nü Wa smelts,
A splendid hall suddenly took shape,
Then mirage-towers loomed up transformed!
Like the Five Flavors, the Five Colors
Were blended into a harmonious whole.[35]

Or like a sword's gleam bursting through its scabbard,
Or like the Precious essence warily collected,[36]
And where the gleam and essence gathered,
A golden mirror appeared;
Its rays piercing through the void as if whistling,
Darting out like flashes of lightning.
A fiery wheel revolved around a purple palace;
A golden pillar rose to meet heaven.
Murkish miasma took to sudden flight;
Myriad phenomena stood revealed and bright.

---

34 Juling, the Giant God or Spirit, split the mountains to create the Yellow River.

35 The Five Flavors and Five Colors are sets that are used to suggest all possible flavors and colors.

36 Baojing, translated as "Precious Essence," is probably used here in the Daoist sense to refer to a life force that might be preserved through breath control or yoga practice.

PART 2

WEST LAKE

"Spring Theme: Above the Lake" (*Chun ti: hushang* 春題：湖上) and "Walking in Spring by West Lake" (*Qiantang hu chun xing* 錢塘湖春行)

BAI JUYI 白居易 (772–846)

TRANSLATED BY A. C. GRAHAM

For Bai Juyi, see chapter 2.

"Spring Theme: Above the Lake"

Now spring is here the lake seems a painted picture,
Unruly peaks all round the edge, the water spread out flat.
Pines in ranks on the face of the hills, a thousand layers of green:
The moon centered on the heart of the waves, just one pearl.
Thread-ends of an emerald-green rug, the extruding paddy-shoots:
Sash of a blue damask skirt, the expanse of new reeds.
If I cannot bring myself yet to put Hangzhou behind me,
Half of what holds me here is on this lake.

"Walking in Spring by West Lake"

North of Lone Hill Temple, west of the Jia Pavilion,
The water's surface has just smoothed, the foot of the cloud low.
Wherever you go new-risen orioles jostle for the warmest tree:
What are they after, the newborn swallows that peck at the spring mud?
A riot of blossoms not long from now will be dazzling to the eye,
The shallow grass can hardly yet submerge the horse's hoof.
Best loved of all, to the east of the lake, where I can never walk enough,
In the shade of the green willows, the causeway of white sand.

"Drinking by the Lake: Clear Sky at First, Then Rain" (*Yin hushang: chuqing houyu* 飲湖上：初晴後雨), "Boating at Night upon West Lake" (*Ye fan Xihu* 夜泛西湖; fourth of five quatrains), and "Recalling West Lake, Sent to Fellow-Graduate Chao Meishu"[37] (*Huai Xihu, ji Chao Meishu tongnian* 懷西湖寄晁美叔同年)

SU SHI 蘇軾 (1037–1101)

For Su Shi, see chapter 3.

---

37   Editor's note: Chao Meishu is Chao Duanyan (1035–1095).

"Drinking by the Lake: Clear Sky at First, Then Rain"
TRANSLATED BY A. C. GRAHAM

The shimmer of light on the water is the play of sunny skies,
The blur of color across the hills is richer still in rain.
If you wish to compare the lake in the West to the Lady of the West,[38]
Lightly powdered or thickly smeared, the fancy is just as apt.

"Boating at Night upon West Lake" (fourth of five quatrains)
TRANSLATED BY DUNCAN M. CAMPBELL

The wild rice seems boundless; the lake stretches as far as the eye can see,
Blooming at night, the lotuses scent the wind and the dew.
Gradually I see lamplight shining from distant temples,
And wait for the moon to darken before I can view the sheen of the lake.

"Recalling West Lake, Sent to Fellow-Graduate Chao Meishu"
TRANSLATED BY LIN YUTANG

The landscape of West Lake tops the world.
Tourists of all classes, intelligent and otherwise,
Find and appreciate each what he wants.
But who is there that can comprehend the whole?
Alas, in my stupid honesty,
I have long been left behind by the world.
I gave myself completely to the joys of hills and water—
Is it not all determined by God's will?
Around the three hundred sixty temples,
I roamed throughout the year,
I knew the beauty of each particular spot,
Felt it in my heart but could not say it in my mouth,
Even now in my sweet sleep,
Its charm and beauty remain in my eyes and ears.
Now you come as a commissioner;
Your official pomp will insult the clouds and haze.
How can the clear streams and the purple cliffs
Reveal their beauties to you?
Why not dismiss your retinue

---

38 Editor's note: West Lake is often associated with the legendary beauty Xi Shi ("Shi of the West"); see note 273 in chapter 6 and the introduction to this chapter.

And borrow a couch from the monk,
Read the poems I inscribed on the rocks,
And let the cool mountain air soothe your troubled soul?
Carry a cane and go where you like,
And stop wherever seems to you best.
You'll find some ancient fishermen
Somewhere among the reeds. Talk with them,
And if they say wise things to you,
Buy fish from them and argue not about the price.

Recollections of Wulin (*Wulin jiushi* 武林舊事)

"Roaming on West Lake" (*Xihu youxing* 西湖遊幸)

ZHOU MI 周密 (1232–1298)
TRANSLATED BY STEPHEN H. WEST

Zhou Mi's family originated from Shandong, but moved south to Zhejiang when the north fell to the Jurchens and the Southern Song set up its "temporary" capital in Hangzhou, then known as Lin'an. Zhou Mi was one of the outstanding lyric poets of the Southern Song; he was also an art collector and critic, and a close friend of several important artists. He had a career as a minor official at the very end of the Southern Song; when the Mongol Yuan dynasty took over, he went into retirement in Lin'an, where he wrote reminiscences of the previous dynasty, including *Recollections of Wulin* (Hangzhou), from which this extract is taken.

"Roaming on West Lake"

West Lake is the sub-celestial realm's finest scenery, appropriate in the morning or evening, on clear days and rainy, in any of the four seasons. There is never a day that the people of Hangzhou do not roam there, yet it is spring roaming that is particularly popular. In the days of peace, the first-class craft like "Great Green," "Sometimes Green," "Tens of Brocade," "Hundred Blossoms," "Treasure Craft," and "Bright Jade" numbered more than a hundred. The other craft were too numerous to count. Every one was both magnificently gorgeous yet elegant and quiet, and they boasted of their novelty to prove themselves the best. And there were none of the capital not [on or by the lake]: those who held engagement parties and bound themselves as families related by marriage, competitions of local shrines to welcome gods, meetings of relatives, burials, sutra associations, sacrifices to spirits, arranged banquets for the emperor to reward his officials, those assigned tasks by the imperial house or high officials. Valued eunuchs, those of local importance, great merchants and powerful people purchased smiles for a thousand gold, shouted out the colors of the dice millions of times, and there were even the obsessed and love-addled who were there for private meetings and secret trysts. Gold and cash were squandered every day and there was never a limit to the calculation. So the Hangzhou adage calls [West Lake] "a cauldron where money is smelted." This saying is in no way excessive.

"Hangzhou Prospect" (*Hangzhou jing* 杭州景)

GUAN HANQING 關漢卿 (CA. 1240–CA. 1320)

TRANSLATED BY STEPHEN H. WEST

Little, if anything, is known of the life of Guan Hanqing, although he may have been a court physician, but he is recognized as one of China's great playwrights, who contributed enormously to the development of drama in the Yuan dynasty. He also wrote short poems (*sanqu*) in the style and meter of dramatic arias but not associated with a particular drama; the example given here is a combination of these.

"Hangzhou Prospect"

To *Nanlü yizhihua* (A spray of flowers)
A brocade and embroidery precinct of the whole known world,[39]
The most *fengliu* place within the surrounding seas,[40]
A state newly attached to the Great Yuan Court,
An old "world map" of the lost Song House.
Waters efflorescent, mountains rare,
Every single place worth playful wandering,
This whole area just too rich and noble.
Filling the city—brocade hangings and wind-screen curtains,
The whole bubbling place—a confluence of smoke from kitchen fires.

To *Liangzhou diqi*
Over a hundred neighborhoods—streets and avenues checkerboard square,
More than a myriad households—lofts and galleries jutting here and there,
And not a half a strip of vacant land.
Pined porticos, bambooed traces,
Simples[41] plots and flowery tracks,
Tea gardens and rice-paddy paths,

---

39   The phrase "brocade and embroidery" evokes both the longer phrase "rivers and mountains of brocade and embroidery," which refers to the beauty and bounty of a national land, and "a strip of brocade," used to describe the future of young lovers or their prospects for marriage.

40   The phrase *fengliu* 風流, too, carries multiple meanings. It can be used to mean "an eminent historical figure" or a "wonderful event that is handed down through history as an exemplar," but it also carries the clear meaning at this time of a "player," a suave and debonair playboy; it can also be used to refer to their sexual encounters.

41   Editor's note: simples are medicinal herbs.

Bamboo hollows and prune-plum streams.
Every stretch a line of a poem's title,
Every step a leaf of a painted wind screen.
The western salt yard just like a single strip of white agate,
The color of Mount Wu, a thousand layers of halcyon jade.
O, gaze afar at the myriad acres of Qiantang River's glazed tiles—
And there are more clear streams and green waters,
Where painted boats come and go in idle play.
Zhe River Pavilion is hard against,
Hard against long strange rocks on precipitous cliffs and high peaks,
Worthy of admiration, worthy of inscription.

Coda
House after house disappearing and reappearing by waters flowing in channels,
Loft and gallery rising and climbing to protrude beyond the halcyon mist—
Thus the gaze far off at the imposing force of West Lake's evening mountains.
After looking here, and peering over there—
Even had I bice and vermilion in hand, the brush is impossible to set to silk.

"Returning Late from the Lake" (Hushang wangui 湖上晚歸)

ZHANG KEJIU 张可久 (1270–1348)
TRANSLATED BY STEPHEN H. WEST

A gifted composer of the individual poems in dramatic style known as *sanqu*, Zhang Kejiu seems to have spent his life as a very minor official and to have traveled widely in southeast China. He was the author of well over eight hundred *sanqu* poems, of which this is one sequence. The meter of the first poem in the sequence is the same as that of Guan Hanqing above.

"Returning Late from the Lake"

To *Nanlü yizhihua* (A spray of flowers)
A far sky to let fall colored sunsets,
Distant waters to contain autumn's mirror.
Flowers as red as a person's face—[42]
Mountains as green as Buddha's head—

---

42   A vague allusion to a poem by the Tang poet Cui Hu (d. 831), who asked a young lady in a mansion for water during the Qingming Festival one year. The next year, infatuated with her, he visited the place again, only to find it shuttered up. He then inscribed the following poem on the closed doors of the house: "Last year on this date, within this very gate, / Peach blossom and her face shown red against each other, / This year the face has gone to some other place, / But the peach blossoms still laugh in the spring winds." By Zhang's time, the phrase had become a hackneyed allusion to a woman one is infatuated with.

Vivid color surrounds us like a screen.
Kingfisher-green cold, the path through piney clouds,
A girl's laugh, a span of eyebrow's kohl.
I take along the soft and delicate thick with perfume,
What need to poeticize "slender reflections of slanting blossoms?"

To *Liangzhou*
I take her jade-white hand and tarry amid brocade blossoms,
I recline on the folding chair and point out silver pitchers.
Chang'e never married, suffered in her loneliness,
Consider Xiaoxiao[43] of those years,
And ask, "Where is she, my love?"
Dongpo's talent and style,
Xizi's[44] startling beauty—
"Each always just right" has left a name for all times.
We two walk alone together in this very place,
At Six-One's Spring Pavilion the poem is completed.
The night of triple five, in front of the flowers, below the moon,
Ten and four strings, under my fingers, give birth to the wind.
My love
Full of passion
Lifts the red ivory clappers to match the beat of Yizhou Ling,
The myriad pipes are quiet,
The quadrant mountains are still,
Muffled sobs are the sound of water falling from spring's flow,
Cranes are resentful, gibbons alarmed.

Coda
Dhyana caves in steep cliffs sound metal chimes,
Dragon palaces at the bottom of waves shimmer with crystals.
Night ethers are fresh,
The power of wine now sober,
Precious seal-script smoke disappears,
The jade clepsydra sounds,
We come back laughing, it seems near three.
How much better than shivering at Ba Bridge, treading the snow to seek out plum
    blossoms?

---

43 Su Xiaoxiao was a legendary courtesan in Hangzhou in the fifth century.

44 Xizi is another way of referring to the legendary beauty Xi Shi.

Records of West Lake (*Xihu youji* 西湖遊記)

YUAN HONGDAO 袁宏道 (1568–1610)

TRANSLATED BY STEPHEN MCDOWALL

For Yuan Hongdao, the author of this long sequence of prose descriptions on the experience of visiting West Lake, see chapter 3.

Records of West Lake

Record of First Arriving at West Lake

Traveling west through Martial Forest Gate, I was confronted with the Pagoda for the Protection of King Qian Chu standing proudly among the cliffs, and my heart took off toward the lake. We entered the Temple of Manifest Blessings at noon, and having taken our tea we finally took a small boat and paddled out onto the lake. The hills were colored like the eyebrows of a beautiful woman, while the flowers shone like her cheeks. The warm breeze tasted of fine wine, while ripples made the lake's surface look like the finest silk. Simply raising the head was enough to leave one intoxicated.

Wanting to put down a few words on paper I took up my brush, but found that the scene defied description. No doubt it was something akin to the way Cao Zhi felt when he first encountered the Goddess of the River Luo in a dream.[45] This, then, was where my West Lake travels began, on the fourteenth day of the second month of the *dingyou* year [1597], during the Wanli reign.

That evening, Fang Wenzun and I ferried across to the Temple of Pure Compassion, to see if we could find the cell in which my brother Zhongdao once stayed. On our return we chose the way via the Six Bridges and the Tomb of Yue Fei,[46] but it was all so hurried that I did not have a chance to appreciate them. After several days, Tao Wangling and his brother arrived, so for a short time, I had the lake, the hills, and good friends all gathered together.

Record of an Evening Trip to Six Bridges to Await the Moon

West Lake is at its most magnificent during the spring or under the light of the moon. On any given day, it is at its best when shrouded in morning mist or evening haze. This year the spring snow was especially heavy, and the flowering apricot blossoms were delayed by the cold. They finally came out together with the peaches and apricots, creating a quite exceptional sight. Wangling had told me on more than one occasion that the flowering apricot blossoms in Commissioner Fu's garden came originally from

---

45 The Goddess Fu Fei is the subject of Cao Zhi's famous poem "Rhapsody on the Luo River Goddess."

46 The Tomb of Yue Fei (1103–1142), a general of the Southern Song renowned for his resistance to the Jin dynasty in northern China, remains one of the sights of West Lake.

Zhang Zi's Hall of Jade Radiance, and I was anxious to see them for myself.[47] But now, I found myself transfixed by these peach blossoms, and could not tear myself away. On the lake, from Break-Off Bridge to the end of Master Su's Causeway the misty glow of greens and reds stretched for over twenty *li*. Voices drifted on the breeze, perfumed drizzle hung in the air, and the splendor of fine silks outshone the willows at the causeway's edge. It was all too enchanting.

The people of Hangzhou visit the lake only during the daytime,[48] but the exquisite reflections on the lake and the subtle shades of the hills are actually at their most seductive just as the sun is rising or setting. Under the light of the moon the lake is at its most clear, with the flowers and willows, the hills and streams, all taking on a strangely fascinating countenance. But this pleasure is to be enjoyed by monks and travelers alone; how could it be explained to the vulgar crowds?

Break-Off Bridge

The splendors of West Lake are the Six Bridges causeway and the Break-Off Bridge causeway.[49] Formerly the pathway at Break-Off Bridge was extremely narrow, but it was expanded and adorned by a recent palace official, and this exquisite workmanship has now made it superior to the Six Bridges.[50] At the sides of the path were planted peaches of deep red, weeping willows, jade orchids, and over twenty different kinds of wild tea. The causeway banks are layered in white rocks, as fine as jade, while the path itself is laid with soft sand. Nearby there is another small causeway, with even more flowers of various kinds, their numbers increasing with every step. It is such a delight that one forgets to turn back, a feeling that does not diminish even after several trips. One hears that in years past when the blossoms on the causeway came out, they would all be picked and carried off within a few days. This spring, strict prohibitions are in place, so the blossoms are out for longer than ever. This is certainly one of the more exceptional sights I have encountered on my wanderings.

West Mound Bridge

West Mound Bridge is sometimes called West Grove and sometimes West Coolness.[51] It is said that this is the bridge at which Little Su and her lover bound their hearts together,

---

47 The construction of Zhang Zi's (1153–?1212) Hall of Jade Radiance, which contained over three hundred flowering apricot trees in its grounds, is described in his *Flowering Apricot Classifications from the Hall of Jade Radiance* (*Yuzhao tang meipin* 玉照堂梅品), a brief work on the appreciation of the flowering apricot.

48 The gates of the city wall of Hangzhou were closed each night at dusk.

49 That is, the Bai Causeway (*Baidi* 白堤) and the Su Causeway.

50 The official referred to is Sun Long (d. 1601), the powerful eunuch in charge of the imperial textile factories at Hangzhou and Suzhou.

51 The three possibilities are near homophones.

so I wrote a poem here to mourn her.[52] Fang Wenzun said "In the line 'Whence come the notes of the fishermen's flutes? / I fancy from the first bridge at West Coolness'[53] it is 'Coolness' not 'Mound,' so Little Su probably got the name wrong." "It doesn't matter," I said. "West Mound is the only name that fits. Besides, doesn't Bai Juyi's poem on Break-Off Bridge have the line 'Spring willows conceal the house of Little Su'?[54] Break-Off Bridge is not far from here—why not borrow the legend of West Mound?"

Record of My Trip to Six Bridges after Rain

It rained heavily after the Cold Food Festival.[55] I said that the rain had come to dye West Lake red, and that we should hurry to bid adieu to the departing peach blossoms immediately. It cleared up around noon, so my friends and I walked to the third bridge, where the fallen petals were piled up over an inch thick, and where happily there were few people about. Then suddenly, we were passed by a man in white silks on horseback. The reflected light dazzled us with its uncommon elegance, and all of my friends who were wearing white underneath their outer garments shed a layer to show it off.

We were a little weary, so we lay down on the ground to drink, and amused ourselves by counting the petals that landed on our faces; those with the most had to drink, and those with the least had to sing. By chance a small boat came out from among the flowers. We called out, and found that it was one of the monks from the monastery bringing tea. After each of us had had a cup, we piled into the boat, and wobbled and sang our way home.

Solitary Hill

The Recluse of Solitary Hill had "a flowering apricot tree for a wife and cranes for his sons," and this is truly the world's most suitable state for a man.[56] Wives and children seem only to multiply life's troubles for men like me. One can't abandon them, but being near them is detestable, and like thorns grabbing at a tattered cotton coat, with each step they hold one up even more.

These days a man by the name of Yu Chunzhen lives under Thunder Peak, and he also has no family, so perhaps he is a reincarnation of the Recluse of Solitary Hill. Yu has written a set of poems called *Fallen Blossoms on a Stream*, and while I do not know

---

52 Little Su (ca. 479–ca. 501) was a famous West Lake courtesan, whose tomb had become part of the standard itinerary at West Lake, following Li He's (791–817) famous poem on her.

53 The line is from the poem "West Coolness Bridge" (*Xiling qiao* 西泠橋) by the Yuan poet Zhang Yu.

54 The line is from Bai Juyi's (772–846) poem "Viewing Hangzhou in Spring" (*Hangzhou chunwang* 杭州春望).

55 The Cold Food Festival refers to the days immediately before Qingming, during which tradition prohibited building fires.

56 The Recluse of Solitary Hill was the Song dynasty poet Lin Bu (967–1028).

how these would compare to the poems of the recluse, he did compose 150 in a night, which can hardly be called sluggish! As for his eating plain food and practicing Chan meditation, this actually puts him a level above the recluse. Has there ever been a time without exceptional men?

Flew Here Peak

Of all the hills around the lake, Flew Here Peak must be considered superior. Although no more than a few hundred *zhang* high, it stands as solid as a mountain of green jade. A thirsty tiger or leaping lion could not match its vitality. A spirit crying or a ghost rising could not match its strange form. Autumn floods or twilight haze could not match its colors. The calligraphy of Lunatic Zhang Xu or the mad brushstrokes of Wu Daozi could not match its ever-changing twists and turns.[57] The many strange trees that cover the rocks do not even need soil; their roots grow above ground.

All together there are four or five caves on Flew Here Peak, some large and some small. Each of them admits a faint light, seductively revealing stalactite flowers that look as if they have been chiselled from the rock. On the cliff face itself are the images of the Buddha that were carved by Baldy Yang, but these ugly and detestable marks are like scars on the face of a beautiful woman.[58]

In all I have climbed Flew Here some five times. The first time was with Huang Guoxin and Fang Wenzun, and the three of us wore unlined shirts with short backs, and made it all the way up to the summit of Lotus Blossom Peak. Each time we came across an interesting rock we would howl with excitement. The next time was with Wang Yusheng, then with Tao Wangling and Zhou Tingcan, then with Wang Zanhua and the Tao brothers, and finally I went once with Lu Dian. Although on each ascent I wanted to compose a poem, in the end I was never able to complete one.

Souls' Retreat

The Temple of Souls' Retreat stands at the foot of Great Northern Peak, and of the temple's most exceptional scenery, the view from the gate is particularly good. From Flew Here Peak to Cold Spring Pavilion there flows a creek of smooth jade, and the ravine walls are painted with vegetation. This is indeed the superior site of this mountain.

---

57 Zhang Xu (fl. 742–755) and Wu Daozi (alternative names Daoxuan or Daoyuan; fl. 713–759) were Tang artists renowned for their wild, expressive styles of calligraphy and painting, respectively.

58 Baldy Yang is a reference to Yang Lianzhenjia (Yang Rin-chen-skyabs; fl. 1277–1288), a lama of Tangut or Tibetan origin who served as Supervisor of the Buddhist Teaching South of the Yangtze River under Khubilai Khan. Between 1285 and 1287, he was responsible for the restoration of a large number of Buddhist temples, but he earned the hatred of the Chinese population through his greed in general and his desecration of the Song imperial tombs near Shaoxing. He was also responsible for ordering the carving of the esoteric (Tantric) statues at Flew-Here Peak.

Cold Spring Pavilion stands outside the temple gate. I have read Bai Juyi's record of this site, which observes:

> The pavilion stands in the center of a mountain torrent, at the south-west corner of the temple. It is not two *xun* high, or three *zhang* wide, but of the exceptional and of the superb, there is nothing not visible here. In spring, when the plants and the trees flourish, a deep breath can purify the soul. In summer the cool breeze and the trickling spring can wash care away and dissolve the fumes of wine. Here the mountain trees are one's roof, the cliff rocks one's screen. Clouds rise from the rafters, and the water reaches the steps. While sitting, one can bathe one's feet below one's couch, and while reclining, one can dangle a fishhook from one's pillow. So clear is the flow of the stream, so pure and gentle, that even before bathing, the dust from one's eyes and the filth from one's heart and tongue will be swiftly washed away.[59]

From this account the pavilion ought to stand in the creek, whereas today it stands to one side. The creek itself is no more than a *zhang* wide, and too narrow for any pavilion. Thus the present scene at Cold Spring Pavilion is but seven tenths of its former self.

Sheathed Light's Hermitage[60] is located halfway up the mountain, one or two *li* behind Souls' Retreat, and the connecting path is extremely attractive. The ancient trees dance about in the breeze, while fragrant plants bathe in spring water. The sound of tinkling seems to come from all around as the waters flow into the mountain kitchen. Once inside the hermitage, one can count the waves on the Qiantang River below.

When I first entered Souls' Retreat, I doubted the accuracy of Song Zhiwen's poetic description, thinking that like those of today, the poets of old selected scenes to conform to their rhyming schemes. It was only when I reached Sheathed Light's that I saw that every word in Song's lines about the sea, the river, the vines and the hollowed logs was as precise as a painting.[61] How far we are from reaching the heights of the ancients!

I lodged at Sheathed Light's, and the next day Wangling, Wenzun and I climbed to the summit of the Great Northern Peak.

---

59 Yuan Hongdao's version of Bai Juyi's "Record of Cold Spring Pavilion" (*Lengquan ting ji* 冷泉亭記), dated 823, differs substantially from that usually found in standard editions of his work.

60 Sheathed Light was a Sichuan monk who arrived at West Lake during the Changqing reign (821–824) of the Tang dynasty, while Bai Juyi was serving as Governor of Hangzhou.

61 Tradition has it that Song Zhiwen's (ca. 656–712) poem "Temple of Souls' Retreat" (*Lingyin si* 靈隱寺) was completed with the help of an old monk, who turned out to be the great poet Luo Binwang (ca. 640–684).

Dragon Well

Dragon Well spring is sweet and clear, and its rocks are sleek and elegant. The water gurgles its way up from between the rocks, making a quite delightful sound. We visited the monks' cells, which are perched up high, dry and comfortable.

Wangling, Guoxin, Wenzun, and I once drew up some spring water and brewed tea here. Wangling asked which I thought was the superior of Dragon Well and Heaven's Pond tea, and I answered that although Dragon Well is excellent, too few leaves produces a weak brew, while too many brings out a bitterness. Heaven's Pond is not like this. Generally speaking, although early-picked Dragon Well tea is fragrant, its flavor retains a hint of grass. Heaven's Pond has a hint of bean, and Tiger Hill a hint of blossom. Only Luojie tea is entirely free of blossom or plant flavor. At times one can taste a hint of spring rocks, and then at other times it has no trace of anything at all, and so is highly valued. Luojie leaves are quite coarse, and a catty of the real stuff can fetch more than 2000 cash. It took me several years of searching before I finally got my hands on a few ounces! Recently I was given some Songluo tea by a man from Huizhou, the flavor of which is superior to that of Dragon Well but inferior to that of Heaven's Pond.

The ridge at Dragon Well is called Windy Bamboo, the peak is called Lions', the rocks are called Wisp of Cloud and Stone Sent by the Gods, and each of these is worth viewing. There is an "Account of Dragon Well" written many years ago by Qin Guan [1049–1100]. His writing is generally straightforward, but does not avoid a few pedantic phrases.

Hazy Cloud and Stone House

Hazy Cloud Cave is ancient and secluded, and its chill penetrates to the bone, while milky rain drips from the stalactite ceiling. Stone House Cave is more open and light. Like Wisp of Cloud Rock, it leans to one side, and as at a tea house there is enough space to lay out banquet tables here. I twice visited Stone House, but the noisy rabble of bondservants made the place seem like a street market. On both occasions I left unsatisfied.

Lotus Blossom Grotto

Before Lotus Blossom Grotto sits the Pavilion of Serene Repose. When one looks down from its open porch the light shimmers on the lake as if it were jade, and one's beard and eyebrows are reflected back as if from a mirror. From here one can see the line of willows that connects the Six Bridges, directing the breeze and channeling the waves into a delightful disorder. Rain or shine, in the morning glow or under the light of the moon, the outlook is never the same; this spot is unsurpassed in the Temple of Pure Compassion area.

The grotto's elegant rocks look almost alive, and are more exquisite than if they had been sculpted. I once said that hills such as Wu Hill and Southern Screen are bones of rock covered by a skin of earth, extending outward in all directions from their hollow centers, which is why the more their rocks are extracted the more they protrude. Recently, the rocks for Mr. Song's garden pavilion all came from here, and the eunuch Sun also took a great many for the Palace of Violet Sunlight. If one could only summon the Five Legendary Immortals to use the waters of the Qiantang to rinse the hills of dirt! With the mountain bones fully exposed, what extraordinary forms would not then be revealed?

Imperial Training Ground

I had long admired Five Clouds Mountain, and finally set a date to climb it, meaning to continue on to the Great Southern Peak. One look at the Imperial Training Ground, however, and I lost my traveler's heart. Wangling once mocked me for never having climbed the Pagoda for the Protection of King Qian Chu, but I believe that of all of the views at West Lake, the lower ones are the best. From up high, the trees are sparse and the hills bare, the grass is thin and the rocks bald, and a thousand *qing* of scenery is squeezed into the space of a teacup. This is what the views from the Great Northern Peak and the Imperial Training Ground are like. No matter how grand the prospect before me, I am not six feet tall, and can see clearly not even ten *li*. So what can I do with so much landscape? To this, Wangling had no retort.

On the day we drank at the Imperial Training Ground there was a strong wind. Wangling gulped down three cups of wine, and became so intoxicated that he could hardly move, which was strange indeed. As with a field becoming an ocean, as with the Yellow River running clear, how could I not record such a remarkable event?

Record of a Visit to Wu Hill

I avoid tourists, so have not entered the city more than a few times. But Wu Hill is within the limits of Hangzhou itself, and for this reason I have never seen it properly, more than hurriedly passing through the Palace of Violet Sunlight, which is really just the garden pavilion of an official. The gemlike rocks of Violet Sunlight are elegantly seductive in their ever-changing forms, and the lake itself has nothing to compare with them. What an indignity it is for them to be imprisoned within the city walls, beyond the reach of simple mountain hermits. Nearby there is a yamen, but although it too is within the city walls, there are no tourists there. It is evident that for stones too, there is such a thing as good and bad fortune!

Miscellaneous Notes Made on the Lake

My idle roaming has now entered its fourth month, and in all I have visited West Lake three times. On the first trip I spent some time wandering about the lake itself, the second trip was when I returned from Five Falls, and the third was when I returned from White Mount. While on the lake I spent five nights at the Temple of Manifest Blessings, a night each at the Dharmalaksana and India Temples, and the remaining nights at the monks' cells at the Temple of Pure Compassion. The hills surround and contain India Temple like a wall. I spent the eighteenth night of the second month of spring here, with the pilgrims—men and women—all squeezed in together like savages. Half of them were standing out in the open air until dawn. In both the upper and lower halls, the people were crowded together like a thick smoke, and one could not get near the place. Here, the Long-Eared Monk of Dharmalaksana is well worth a visit, the whistling bamboos are worth hearing, the springs worth tasting, the shoots worth eating and the wine worth drinking. Only quiet conversations with solitary monks were in short supply.[62]

The rocks, trees, and huts at the Temple of Pure Compassion are all extremely fine, but the Pavilion of Serene Repose at the Source Mirror Hall is a scene of surpassing quality. The monks' cells where I was lodged are remote and secluded, with ancient trees winding around the path, which runs about a *li* from the temple gate. Every evening I would take a small boat out from Arrowroot Lodge to watch the evening mists rising among the hills. If the moon was out I might visit the Lake Heart Pavilion, pass by the fourth bridge and the Temple of Water Immortals, and return by foot along the causeway. Or perhaps I would pass by the foot of Thunder Peak for a chat with Yu Chunxi and his brother. Or perhaps I would ferry across to the Temple of Manifest Blessings and call on the monks and travelers; all of these activities were quite normal during my stay. Temples on the lake like Agate and Great Buddha Head, and in the hills like Jade Spring, Spirits' Peak, Tall Beauty, Running Tiger, and Pure Pearl were the other sites of my comings and goings.

Spirits' Peak is remote from the world of man. It feels particularly silent and still, and the monks' cells here are especially refined. Beside the monastery there was a section of land, not deficient in pine or rock, bamboo or stream, and its price was not particularly high. I thought of buying it as a place to stay in future years, but as my trips are not regular I decided against it.

There are so many sights that I have not recorded here, but to see properly even one or two of these must wait until next time.

Recorded in Hangzhou during the twenty-fifth year of the Wanli reign [1597]

---

62   The annual spring pilgrims' market was a crucial part of the economy of late imperial Hangzhou, where it was said that "three winters depend on one spring."

Search for West Lake in My Dreams (Xihu mengxun 西湖夢尋; extracts) and *Taoan's Dream Memories (Taoan mengyi* 陶庵夢憶; extracts)

ZHANG DAI 張岱 (1597–CA. 1684)

TRANSLATED BY DUNCAN M. CAMPBELL

For Zhang Dai, see chapter 3. Zhang Dai's family owned a villa by the West Lake, as did other wealthy Zhejiang families (as he mentions below); he seems to have spent much of his time here as a young man. The following extracts are mostly taken from his nostalgic memoir of the lake, written after the collapse of the Ming dynasty, when he and his immediate family were reduced to relative poverty; these extracts are interspersed with some short essays on sites and sights of the lake from Zhang's other famous collection, *Taoan's Dream Memories* (see chapters 3, 7, and earlier in this chapter).

Search for West Lake in My Dreams (extracts)

"AUTHOR'S PREFACE" (ZI XU 自序)

Born at an evil hour, I have been separated from West Lake for twenty-eight long years. Not a day passes, however, that West Lake does not enter my dreams, this West Lake of my dreams having never left me for a single day. I have since revisited West Lake twice, in the *jiawu* [1654] and *dingyou* [1657] years, only to discover that of the splendid estates that once lined the shores of the lake—the Tower Beyond the Tower of the Shang Clan of Gushing Gold Gate, the Occasional Dwelling of the Qi Family, the country villas of the Qian and Yu families, and the Sojourn Garden once owned by my own family— nothing remains but the shards of their roof tiles. That which fills my dreams exists no longer beside West Lake.

When I reached Break-Off Bridge and took in the prospect it afforded, I found that only one in ten of the fine willows and tender peaches that once stood there, of the singing pavilions and the dance terraces, had survived, the rest as if washed away by a great flood. I fled from the place, hiding the sight from my eyes and consoling myself with the thought that as I had come here to view West Lake only to find it thus, it was better to seek to preserve the West Lake of my dreams, for that West Lake at least remains intact.

My dream, therefore, is different in kind to that of the Tang Palace Attendant Li Bai. He dreamed of the Queen Mother of Heaven Mountain, of divine women and famous beauties, of things unseen; his dream that of an illusion.[63] My dreams are of West Lake, of family gardens and close relatives, of what once had been; my dream is a dream of reality. Today I live at the pleasure of others and have been forced to do so for the past twenty-three years. In my dreams, however, I find myself back in my home of old. The various retainers and amanuenses of that age gone by, now all grown grey haired, in my

---

63 This is a reference to Li Bai's (701–762) poem "Bidding Adieu to Queen Mother of Heaven Mountain after a Dream Voyage to Her" (*Meng you Tianmu yin liu bie* 夢游天姥吟留別).

dreams wear their hair still in the tufts of their youth. The habits of a lifetime remain ingrained, and it is impossible to change old attitudes. From today onward I will but dwell in solitude within my Butterfly Retreat, lingering idly upon the wicker couch of my grass hut, seeking only to safeguard my dreams of old, the vistas of West Lake as they stretch out before my eyes untouched by the ravages of time.[64]

When my children question me about such things I speak occasionally of them, but to do so is like recounting a dream within a dream; if not the demons of the dark speaking then simply the incoherent mutterings of a sleep talker. Thus did I arrive at the seventy-two items of this dream search. I bequeath them now to future generations in the hope that they may provide a shadowy image of West Lake as it once was. I am like that man of the mountains who, returning from a visit to the shores of a distant sea, spoke so highly of the delicacies of the oceans that his fellow villagers vied to lick his eyes. Alas! Golden pickles and jade white scallops melt into nothingness the moment they enter the mouth—how then can licking my eyes satisfy their cravings?[65]

This preface was written this sixteenth day of the seventh month of the *xinhai* year [1671] by Zhang Dai of Ancient Sword in Sichuan, the Old Man of the Butterfly Retreat.

"GENERAL PROSPECTUS: THE TWINNED LAKES OF THE ILLUSTRIOUS SAGE" (*XIHU ZONGJI: MINGSHENG ER HU* 西湖總記明聖二湖)[66]

Once Ma Zhen[67] of the Eastern Han dynasty had created Mirror Lake, it became the lake that earliest acquired a reputation for scenic beauty, from the Han dynasty down through the Tang. By the time of the Northern Song dynasty, however, West Lake had begun to replace it in people's affections. Everyone now hastened to the shores of this

---

64 This sentence contains two references to passages from the *Zhuangzi*, the first of which, from the "Discussion on Making All Things Equal" chapter, lurks behind the preface as a whole and underpins Zhang Dai's representation of himself, as embodied in the name of his retreat: "Once Zhuang Zhou dreamt he was a butterfly, a butterfly flitting and fluttering around, happy with himself and doing as he pleased. He didn't know he was Zhuang Zhou. Suddenly he woke up and there he was, solid and unmistakably Zhuang Zhou. But he didn't know if he was Zhuang Zhou who had dreamt he was a butterfly, or a butterfly dreaming he was Zhuang Zhou. Between Zhuang Zhou and a butterfly there must be *some* distinction! This is called the Transformation of Things." See *The Complete Works of Chuang Tzu*, trans. Burton Watson (New York: Columbia University Press, 1968), 49; transliteration altered. The second reference is to a passage from "The Turning of Heaven" chapter: "Benevolence and righteousness are the grass huts of the former kings; you may stop in them for one night but you mustn't tarry there for long" (*The Complete Works of Chuang Tzu*, 162).

65 This is a reference to a poem by Su Shi entitled "Rhyming with Jiang Kui, to Accompany Some Tea I Send to Him" (*He Jiang Kui ji cha* 和姜夔寄茶).

66 Legend has it that during the Han dynasty a golden ox suddenly appeared in the middle of the lake, this having been understood as an auspicious sign of the birth of an illustrious sage. The lake proper is divided into the Inner and the Outer Lakes, hence the name Zhang Dai uses for it here.

67 While serving as governor of Guiji in around 140, Ma Zhen had Mirror Lake formed in an attempt to alleviate the problem of the alternating flooding and drought of the surrounding districts.

lake, for the understated elegance of Mirror Lake could no longer compete with West Lake's gaudy beauty. As for Lake Xiang, with its bleak and isolated aspect, few were the boats or carts that traveled there, fewer the "men of taste and learning" who spoke of it.

My cousin Zhang Hong often likens West Lake to a famous beauty, Lake Xiang to a hermit and Mirror Lake to an immortal. I disagree with his epithet. To my mind, Lake Xiang is a nubile virgin, shy and modestly blushing, as if glimpsed upon her wedding day. Mirror Lake, by contrast, is the straight-laced daughter of an eminent family, commanding respect with her every glance and certainly never to be dallied with. West Lake by contrast again, however, is a famous whore of the Singing Quarters, fair of both voice and visage, leaning at her doorway, a meretricious smile playing across her lips. She is available to one and all, and as everyone can have their way with her, she is at once both the object of their desires and the butt of their scorn.

The lake is at its busiest during the spring and summer months; in autumn and winter it becomes deserted. It is at its rowdiest on the birthday of the flowers on the twelfth day of the second month; by the evening of the moon on the fifteenth of the eighth month so few are the visitors that they are like stars scattered in the sky. And again, the lake is at its most crowded on fine and sunny days; in rain or in snow it is desolate. Thus it is, as I have said before, that: "If for a good reader there is no better way to read than Dong Yu's 'Three Remainders,' then so too can it be said that for one good at touring there is no better time to tour the lake than these 'Three Remainders.' Dong Yu is quoted as saying: 'Winter is the remainder of the year, evening the remainder of the day, and rainy days the remainder of the season.' Why should ancient flowering apricots standing upon snow-covered peaks be at all inferior to willows growing tall along mist-shrouded embankments, or the moon hanging suspended in the bright firmament be inferior to the delicate beauty of flowers at dawn, or the blur of color of falling rain be inferior to the shimmer of light under sunny skies?[68] The appreciation of the affecting quality of such scenes is only to be found in the man of understanding." Of the four worthies of the lake too, I have made the following comment: "Bai Juyi's untrammelled understanding was certainly not as admirable as Lin Bu's tranquil profundity; Li Bai's liking for the fantastical was nowhere near as worthy as Su Shi's extreme sensibilities." As to the others, such as the improvident Jia Sidao[69] or the lavish Sun Long, although both these men spent several decades living beside the lake and expended millions on its upkeep, there remained aspects of the disposition and flavor of the lake that they could never even dream about understanding. This being the case,

---

68   A reference to Su Shi's celebrated poem "Drinking by the Lake: Clear Sky at First, then Rain" (above).

69   Jia Sidao (1213–1275) was a minister during the Southern Song who earned an invidious reputation for his appeasement policies.

how then could it be possible to begin discussing touring the lake with the frustrated pedants of this present age!

"NORTHERN APPROACHES: PAVILION OF THE JADE LOTUS" (*XIHU BEILU: YULIAN TING* 西湖北路玉蓮亭)

During Bai Juyi's tour of duty as Prefect of Hangzhou,[70] so fair-minded did his administration prove that few were the cases that made it all the way to court. The poor, when convicted of breaking the law, would be ordered to plant a few trees along the lakeside; the wealthy could make reparation for any crime committed by paying to have a *mu* or two of the lake cleared of matted rape turnip. Once Bai had been at his post for a number of years, the rape turnip had been completely eradicated and the newly planted trees had begun to offer up their shade. He took to repairing here to the shore of the lake with a concubine in tow, to gaze up at the mountains and to view the flowers and the willows. The locals erected a statue of him and began to worship at it. This pavilion commands the lakefront and a myriad blue lotus plants have been planted here to symbolize his purity.

Turning right and heading north from here, one comes upon Boat Mooring Pavilion, where the many storied houseboats gather beneath the tall willows and spread out along the lengthy embankment. Visitors to the lake come here to hire a boat to take them out upon the water, and the spot proves as noisy as a marketplace. Off to the west is the Garden of the Jade Ducks; this corner of the lake, by contrast, hidden as it is beyond a secluded corner of the city wall, is not much frequented by the boats. For those living beside the lake, there is no better place to escape from the hustle and bustle of everyday life. A tower stands within the garden, and leaning upon the windowsill and gazing out to the south, there where the water glistens brightly at the edge of the sand, one often sees a hundred or so wild ducks bathing in the lake, bobbing in and out of the waves. The scene here is surpassing in its tranquillity.

"NORTHERN APPROACHES: TEMPLE OF MANIFEST BLESSINGS" (*XIHU BEILU: ZHAOQING SI* 西湖北路昭慶寺)

The earth vein upon which the Temple of Manifest Blessings is sited flows here from Lion Cub Peak and the Rock of Amassed Roseate Clouds; according to the geomancers, it is that of the Fire Dragon.

Construction of the temple began in the first year of the Latter Jin dynasty [936], but it was destroyed by fire in the fifth year of the Qiande reign period of the Song [966]. The temple was rebuilt in the first year of the Taiping xingguo reign period [967], at which time the altar was established. At the beginning of the Tianxi reign period [1017–1021] the temple acquired its present name but in that same year it again burnt down. During

---

70   Bai Juyi served in this post between 822 and 825.

the reigns of the Hongwu [1368–1398] and Chenghua [1465–1487] emperors of the Ming dynasty, the temple was destroyed by fire and rebuilt twice. In the fourth year of his reign [1469], the Chenghua emperor ordered the temple restored and placed the Surveillance Commissioner Yang Jizong in charge of overseeing the project. The wealthy men of Huzhou all contributed funds to this end and eventually the sum of ten thousand taels was raised. Once completed, the halls and chambers of the temple proved more grand and imposing than ever before.

In the thirty-fourth year of the reign of the Jiajing emperor [1556], during the depredations of the pirates, in fear that they would capture the temple and make use of it as their base, it was burnt down overnight. Once order had been restored, the temple was again rebuilt and on this occasion the advice of the geomancers was followed to the letter, the area being entirely cleared of ordinary dwellings so as to allow the gate of the temple to overlook the lake, in the hope that this would serve to preclude future conflagrations. Despite all these efforts, however, in the third year of the reign of the Longqing emperor [1569], the temple was destroyed yet again. In the seventeenth year of the reign of the Wanli emperor [1589], the eunuch Sun Long of the Directorate of Ceremonial had the temple rebuilt with the assistance of the Imperial Silk Manufactory, and the pendants and arrayed censers became a contemporary byword for splendor.

Along the two covered walkways, crowded one upon another, is a veritable marketplace of fine stalls, all replete with exquisite goods outrageously priced. During the months of spring a pilgrims' fair is held here and devotees from Eastern Zhejiang heading for Putuo Monastery in the South Sea and to the India Temples all gather here to trade with the women and children of the outlying villages. The din of their voices as they shout at each other, wearing their tongues out with their haggling, only ceases once the summer arrives.

In the thirteenth year of the reign of the Chongzhen emperor [1640] the temple was razed to the ground by fire yet again, the smoke and ashes completely blocking out the rays of the sun and turning the water of the lake a brownish red. By the beginning of the Qing dynasty, in keeping with the saying: "Continuing the process increases ornament," the altar had been completely restored and had become even more imposing than ever it had been throughout previous dynasties.

One story told about the founding of the temple claims that it was established as part of the celebrations associated with the eightieth birthday of Qian Liu, the Martial and Majestic Prince of Wu and Yue.[71] Yuanjing, a monk of the temple at the time, organized

---

71   Qian Liu (852–932) was the founder of the kingdom of Wu and Yue (or Wu-Yue; 907–978) after the fall of the Tang dynasty; the kingdom covered approximately the area of present-day Zhejiang Province, the location of Hangzhou and the West Lake.

his fellow black-robed monks Gupu, Tianxiang, Shenglian, Shenglin, Cishou, and Ciyun into a White Lotus Society to undertake the recitation of the sutras and the releasing of animals in propitiation of the health of the prince. On the first day of each month they would mount the altar to conduct a service. The local populace would circumambulate the altar with incense sticks burning in their hands, paying homage to the Buddha and making manifest the prince's blessings. Thus was the temple so named. Today, the various halls of the temple complex take their names from these venerable worthies.

"WESTERN APPROACHES: FLEW-HERE PEAK" (*XIHU XILU: FEILAI FENG* 西湖西路飛來峰)

Flew-Here Peak juts up sharply, penetrating the clouds and appearing like a crystal inlay within the firmament. It is a most fantastically shaped rock fallen from the sleeve of Madman Mi Fu.[72] Any petromaniac who caught sight of it would be bound to drop to their knees in homage, not daring a disrespectful word and addressing it as "Elder Rock." How I hate Baldy Yang for having its entire surface carved into Buddha statues, Arhats and Revered Ones, hundreds upon hundreds of them, crowded one beside another. It's as if the Lady of the West's gorgeous skin and lustrous body had been tattooed all over with depictions of terraces and ponds, birds and beasts, all outlined with black ink. My very bones ache when I think about how this extraordinary Heavenly inspired phenomenon has suffered at the hands of chisel and hammer. And then I begin to hate the mountain for the fact that it chose not to hide itself away in the Western Quarter but rather to fly here from Spiritual Vulture Peak without a second thought, suffering this sort of humiliation as a consequence. An analogy can be drawn here between the fate of the mountain and that of the superior man who, born in ill times, rather than exercising restraint and hiding himself away, makes public display of his talents, reaping nothing but mistreatment and cruelty as reward for his efforts, two examples of this being Guo Pu [276–324] and Mi Heng [ca. 173–198] of the Eastern Han. With a sigh, the monk Huili had asked the mountain why it flew here, for he too felt both bitterness and regret at its fate.

Moreover, all the Arhats that Baldy Yang had carved alongside the creek were designed in his own image and depict him either riding a lion or astride an elephant, with naked maids in attendance and presenting him with tributes of flowers. One such statue is already too many! Tian Rucheng smashed one of them to pieces with a hammer,[73] and, as a youth studying here in Goulou Mountain Hut, I did the same.

---

72 Mi Fu (1051–1107) was a landscape painter renowned for his devotion to rocks, particularly the one to which he performed obeisance, addressing it respectfully as "Elder Brother."

73 This claim seems somewhat disingenuous. In the "Lawless and Forlorn" chapter of his *West Lake Tourist Gazetteer: Supplement*, Tian Rucheng records that in the twenty-second year of the reign of the Jiajing emperor

It is said that while he was living in Hidden Virtue Temple, Baldy Yang took to desecrating ancient graves, indulging in necrophilia with the corpses disinterred. Knowing that behind the temple stood the graves of the wife of the Supervisor Lai and the daughter of the Assistant Director of the Left Lu Hua, both of whom had been extremely beautiful and had died young, their bodies having been preserved in mercury, Baldy Yang ordered them disinterred. A monk called Zhendi living at the temple at the time, a bit of a simpleton who collected firewood and drew water, became enraged when he heard what was happening and started to scream insults at Baldy Yang. Fearing that the monk's actions would get them all into trouble, the abbot had him locked up. At the fifth watch of the night, when Baldy Yang got up to go about his obscene business, Zhendi escaped by jumping over a wall, took up Wei Tuo's[74] wooden baton and set off to beat Baldy Yang's brains out. His retainers rushed to save him from this fate, not one of them remaining unscathed. Zhendi danced around in the melee, soaring yards into the air like a falcon or a leaping tiger in a quite preternatural manner. All of a sudden, the lanterns and candles went out and the handles of all shovels and hoes that had been used to excavate the grave disintegrated. In absolute terror, Baldy Yang believed that Wei Tuo himself had made an appearance and far from persisting with what he had been doing, he fled with all his men, never daring to mention the matter again. In actual fact, the monk had simply been giving vent to the anger of the spirit of the mountain itself.

"WESTERN APPROACHES: COLD SPRING PAVILION" (*XIHU XILU: LENGQUAN TING* 西湖西路冷泉亭)

Cold Spring Pavilion stands to the left of the gate of the Temple of the Soul's Retreat. Its cinnabar walls and green trees set off the surrounding gloom of the forest. The pavilion faces a steep cliff face from which comes the distinct sound of the gurgle of the spring, pure and mournful to the ear. A dozen western chestnut trees grow behind the pavilion, tall and wide of girth; standing under their shade in a cool breeze serves to refresh one's entire body. The chestnuts, as they ripen in early autumn, are as large as cherries; cracking them open to eat, one finds their flesh the color of beeswax amber, their fragrance that of the seed-cases of the lotus. When I was studying at Goulou Mountain Hut in the *jiazi* year [1624] of the reign of the Tianqi emperor, the monks here made use of the chestnuts in their offerings to the Buddha. I found them crisper than water-lily fruit, sweeter even than fresh walnut.

During the summer months, in search of respite from the heat, I would move my pillow and my bamboo mat here into the pavilion to lie beneath the moon, the music of the brook burbling away nearby merging with that of the flutes and strings. On one

---

(1543), the then-prefect of Hangzhou, Chen Shixian, ordered three of the statues depicting Baldy Yang destroyed.

74 The Bodhisattva Wei Tuo (Skanda) is the guardian of monasteries; his statue regularly appears in Chinese Buddhist temples.

occasion, having heard the sound of this brook, Zhang Mingbi intoned that poem by the Southern Song poet Lin Ji that goes: "Floating toward West Lake amid song and dance, / One forgets entirely that one is deep within the mountains." Here he speaks of the fact that the sound of the brook so embodies that of bells and musical stones that it is as if it were singing, and if it were not into West Lake that it discharged, then where else could it possibly flow away to! I once made the comment that the people living by West Lake are never without a song, no mountain here is without its song, no river or brook without its song, painted ladies and dissolute dandies, even village maidens and mountain monks, none are without a song on their lips. I remember also that Chen Jiru once wrote that: "West Lake has famous mountains aplenty but no recluses, ancient temples but no eminent monks, painted beauties but all without talented mates, and even the Birthday of the Flowers is not accompanied by moonlit nights." Cao Exue also wrote a poem ridiculing this circumstance: "Roast Goose and lamb, followed by lime soup, / First a visit to Lake Heart Pavilion then on to the Tomb of Yue Fei. / In the slanting rays of the sun before dusk the visitors are not yet drunk, / But then they cast aside the bright moon and return to Qiantang."

When I lived by West Lake, I usually stayed in a houseboat and every night I could see the moon reflected in the lake; nowadays, to avoid the clamor of the Temple of the Soul's Retreat, I come in the evenings to Cold Spring Pavilion and here, each night, I look out at the moon shining upon the mountain. How very fortunate I've been in the pleasures that I have laid claim to in my life! I once claimed that nobody more appreciated the beauty of West Lake than Su Shi, but he too would retreat within the walls once night had fallen. The tranquillity of the deep mountains, the moon shining bright within the empty firmament, pillowing one's head on the rocks and rinsing one's mouth in the stream, lying beneath the stars and in the shadows of the flowers, apart from Lin Bu and Li Bo of Goulou Mountain, few have been those that have experienced such things. Even the monk Huili and the poet Luo Binwang [ca. 640–697] were not granted the pleasure of taking their place here beside me.

"WESTERN APPROACHES: TEMPLE OF THE SOUL'S RETREAT" (*XIHU XILU: LINGYIN SI* 西湖西路靈隱寺)

During the Ming dynasty, first the Temple of Manifest Blessings was destroyed by fire, not long after this, the Temple of the Soul's Retreat too burnt down, and then soon thereafter, Upper India Temple was consumed by flames. These three great temples were destroyed one after another in a short space of time. At the time, the abbot of the Temple of the Soul's Retreat was the monk Ju'de and he ensured that Soul's Retreat was the first of the three to be restored.

As to this temple, it was first established by the monk Huili in the first year of the Xianhe reign period of the Jin dynasty [326], the plaque at the gate reading: "Site of the Awakening to Luminous Virtue" and, according to legend, written by Ge Hong. The temple confines included four stone stupas, built by Qian Liu, the Martial and Majestic Prince of Wu and Yue. In the fourth year of the Jingde reign period [1007] of the Song dynasty, its name was changed to the Chan Temple of the Jingde Soul's Retreat, but it was destroyed in the third year of the Zhizheng reign period [1343] of the Yuan dynasty. Restored at the beginning of the reign of the Hongwu emperor [r. 1368–1398] of the Ming, it was given its present name. In the seventh year of the reign of the Xuande emperor [1432], the monk Tanzan had the temple gate constructed and Excellent Tablet built the main hall. This hall contained an obeisance stone more than a *zhang* in length and decorated with exquisite patterns in the shapes of flowers and tortoises. In the eleventh year of the reign of the Zhengtong emperor [1446], the monk Xuanli constructed the Directly Pointing Hall, the plaque of which was inscribed by the noted calligrapher Zhang Jizhi, but in the third year of the reign of the Longqing emperor [1569], the temple was again destroyed. It was rebuilt by the monk Rutong in the twelfth year of the reign of the Wanli emperor [1584] and then repaired by the eunuch Sun Long in the twenty-eighth year [1600] of the reign of the same emperor, only to be destroyed again in the thirteenth year of the reign of the Chongzhen emperor [1640]. The monk Ju'de, upon examining Rutong's old account books and discovering that he had spent some 80,000 taels on having the temple rebuilt, knew that to have the same done again now would cost at least double this. Devoting himself to the task most assiduously, he soon raised this amount, his karma, it seems, being somewhat larger than even that of either the monk Zhuhong [1535–1615] or Golden Grain Tathagata himself.

The monk Ju'de is a cousin of mine, and in the *dingyou* year [1657] I went to pay my respects to him. At the time, work on the main hall and the abbot's room had not yet commenced, but off to the east a line of secluded belvederes and fine meditation cells were all but completed, and over a hundred guest rooms and monks' cells had been finished and were already fully furnished with yew tables and rattan beds and all other necessary accoutrements. In the refectory there were three huge bronze cauldrons, newly cast and each capable of cooking three piculs of rice, enough to feed a thousand people. Pointing at the cauldrons, Ju'de told me: "This is the patrimony that it has taken me more than a decade to put together." The resident monks are more numerous here than at any other major temple. Noon that day, as he sat having a meal with me, a novice appeared with a note for him to take a look at. Not having any idea what it was about, I heard him say to the novice: "Ask the quartermaster to open up the granary." The novice departed, and once I had finished eating I went for a walk outside the gate of the temple. There I saw more than a thousand men swarming about, all of them shouldering loads of rice which they quickly unloaded into the granary. They went about their business of measuring out the grain without a sound and were all soon gone. I asked the monk what this was all about, and he replied: "Every year, Master So-and-so, our benefactor from Hanyang, gives us five hundred piculs of rice, paying for the cost of its transportation here as well and not allowing the porters to accept as much as a cupful of water from the temple. He's done this for seven years now." I sighed with admiration. When I asked him when he expected the main hall to be completed, he replied that as he would turn sixty in the sixth month of next year, and his disciples now numbered over 10,000, if each gave ten taels, he would have 100,000 taels with which he could complete his task. Three years later, both the main hall and the abbot's room had been finished, and I wrote a poem to record the splendor of the place.

"WESTERN APPROACHES: NORTH TALL PEAK" (*XIHU XILU: BEIGAO FENG* 西湖西路北高峰)

North Tall Peak stands behind the Temple of the Soul's Retreat and is reached by means of several hundred stone steps that wind their way around thirty-six bends. On its summit stands Flowery Luminescence Temple, dedicated to the Five Sages. Halfway up the mountain, one finds a temple dedicated to the Horse Head Girl, the Goddess of the Silkworm, and here in spring crowds come to pray for bountiful silk harvests. The seven-storied pagoda on the peak was built during the Tianbao reign period [742–755] of the Tang dynasty, only to be destroyed in the Huichang reign period [841–846] of the same dynasty. It was restored by Qian Liu, the Martial and Majestic Prince of Wu and Yue, but was again destroyed in the seventh year of the Xianchun reign period [1272] of the Song dynasty.

Here the various hills crowd around like screens and the lake is as a sunken mirror. Viewed from high above, the various pleasure craft and fishing junks upon the lake disappear into the waves like gulls or wild ducks, only to reappear in a moment's time. As they draw farther away they become ever more indistinct and, finally, one can see only a lingering hint of their presence. Far off to the west the Raksasa River resembles a newly washed filament of raw silk, merging in the distance with the haze of the sea, the vague horizon seemingly boundless in its expanse. Zhang Gongliang wrote a poem about this scene that gives the lines: "The mist of the river separates into whiteness, that of the sea congeals, / Where the green of Mount Wu ends, there rises Mount Yue," a veritable painting within a poem. The prefectural city stands precisely between river and lake, a twisting maze of streets and lanes spread out into the distance, the scale-like tiles of the roofs and the dense greenness of the trees and bamboo setting each other off to best advantage, at once both elegant and dense, and with its dancing phoenix and coiled dragon, this is truly the site of august power!

On the slopes of the mountain stands the stupa of the Chan Master Wuzhao. His lay name was Wen Xi and he was a man of the age of the Tang dynasty emperor Suzong [r. 756–762]. He was buried here in the stupa. During the Song, when Han Tuozhou [1151–1207] turned the place into a burial ground, he had the stupa opened up, discovering that it contained a porcelain niche in which Wuzhao's body lay as if he were still alive, his hair hanging down past his shoulders, his fingernails having encircled his body. Han Tuozhou had him cremated. It took three days to do so completely, leaving behind a hundred or so relics.

Li Bo, who took the sobriquet Goulou, was from Wulin and he lived at the foot of Sheathed Light's Hill, within the confines of the Temple of the Soul's Retreat. There he had built a small mountain hut of a few rooms, sited above and thus commanding a view of a twisting brook that ran through the secluded valley. With its bubbling brook flowing beneath his belvedere, its sheer cliffs thrusting into the heavens and the profuse vegetation of its ancient trees, the hermitage was exquisite in its sense of isolation. Here the hermit lived, all alone. Addicted as he was to poetry, he formed a deep friendship with Xu Wei [1521–1593] of Heavenly Pond. When guests arrived he would summon his serving boys, ordering them to get a small boat and to punt them all to that section of the lake that lay between the West Chill and Broken-Off bridges. Once there, they would laugh and sing the day away. Sometime before he died he built his own tomb out of mountain rocks, and it was here that he was eventually buried. He wrote a work entitled *Collected Poems of the Hermit of Goulou Mountain*, in four volumes.

In the *jiazi* year of the reign of the Tianqi emperor [1624], I studied here with Zhao Jiechen, Chen Hongshou, Yan Xubo, Zhuo Renyue, and my younger brother Zhang Feng. Both the abbot, named Zichao, and the garden vegetables and mountain herbs were plain, unseasoned, and pure. But I regret that at the time I had not yet managed to cleanse my heart of the desire for fame and fortune and this failing caused me to offend against the spirits of the mountain, a fact of which I remain deeply ashamed until this day.

"A SHORT RECORD OF GOULOU MOUNTAIN HUT" (*GOULOU SHANFANG XIAOJI* 岣嶁山房小記

Goulou Mountain Hut abuts upon the mountain, the brook, and Sheathed Light's Road, and thus no path leading to it is without a bridge, not one of its structures fails to soar upward like a belvedere. Beyond the gate, the hoary pines look down with an expression of disdain and the thick vegetation is studded with trees of various other kinds. The chill green shadow cast by the trees seems boundless and is such that the faces of one's companions disappear into it. The stone bridge is set low to the ground and is large enough for ten people to sit upon it in comfort. The monks had cut down some bamboo poles and used them to lead the water of the spring beneath the bridge, and the waterwheels creaked and groaned as they turned.

In the *jiazi* year [1624] of the reign of the Tianqi emperor, I shut myself up here for seven months or so, satiating my ears with the sound of the brook and my eyes with the genial shade of the trees. The mountain was covered in chestnut trees and bamboo shoots of incomparable sweetness and fragrance. The people of the district used the hermitage as their marketplace and would arrive each morning with fruit and fowl for sale. But never any fish. So I dammed up the brook to form a pond and there I raised several dozen large fish. When guests arrived, I could fish one out and serve it fresh. In the late afternoons I would set off for a stroll, visiting Cold Spring Pavilion or the Bao Family Garden or Flew-Here Peak. On one such occasion, I followed the course of the brook to take a look at the Buddhist statues to be found there on the mountain, imprecating the name of Baldy Yang as I went along. Once at the spot, I saw a statue of a Persian barbarian riding upon a dragon, accompanied by four or five barbarian maids who were presenting him with a tribute of flowers and fruit. The maids were all naked. I promptly decapitated the statue of Baldy Yang with a hammer and proceeded to smash up all the maids as well, throwing the shards into the latrines in order to revenge myself upon him. The monks, believing that I had desecrated the Buddha himself, began to mutter darkly to themselves: "Tut! Tut! What a very strange business." Only once I had explained to them who he was did they all cheer up and begin to laugh in admiration for what I had done.

"WESTERN APPROACHES: BLUE LOTUS MOUNTAIN HUT" (*XIHU XILU: QINGLIAN SHANFANG* 西湖西路青蓮山房)

Blue Lotus Mountain Hut had once been the villa of Master Bao Hansuo.[75] Set within the tall bamboos and ancient flowering plums and pillowed upon Lotus Blossom Peak, the Mountain Hut overlooks a winding creek, deep ravines, and steep cliff faces, set off beautifully within the forested peak. Master Bao was obsessed with springs and rocks and, like Tao Qian, "every day would stroll in his garden for pleasure." At the time, the beauty of the terraces and kiosks here was unparalleled in the age; shards of rock had been used to form a platform and brushwood woven to form a door, so that within the sumptuous extravagance there remained a touch or two of the rustic, just like a ruled and measured red and blue painting by the Tang Master Li Zhaodao, with the towers and terraces finely drawn and even the bamboo hedges and thatched huts resplendent in their golds and greens. In those days the Asymmetrical Room and Secret Chamber were full of beautiful women, and walking through these rooms today one can still smell the lingering traces of their perfume. At the time so numerous were the bundles of head-ornaments and piles of silk embroidery that lay within the chambers that one had to twist and turn, circle round and about before being able to find a way out. So clever had been the master's design that it was like that Labyrinth Tower of old.[76] No other member of the Zhejiang gentry could match the excellence of Master Bao's troupe of actors and singers.

Although it has since changed hands a number of times, people nowadays, as they pass its gate, continue to refer to it as Bao's Northern Estate.

---

75 Identified as Bao Yingdeng, who is also mentioned by Zhang Dai in connection with Bao's Estate and by Wang Ruqian in "A Record of My Untethered Garden."

76 Built by Emperor Yang of the Sui dynasty (r. 605–617) once he had established his southern capital at Yangzhou, Labyrinth Tower (*Milou* 迷樓) came to symbolize both the decadence and extravagance that characterized his reign and its inevitable consequence—dynastic collapse. Emperor Yang was murdered in his tower.

"CENTRAL APPROACHES: VARIEGATED BROCADE EMBANKMENT" (*XIHU ZHONGLU: SHIJIN TANG* 西湖中路十錦塘)

Variegated Brocade Embankment, also known as the Sun Embankment, is found beneath Break-Off Bridge. It was restored by the eunuch Sun Long of the Directorate of Ceremonial in the seventeenth year of the reign of the Wanli emperor [1589]. The embankment is two *zhang* wide and is planted with peach and willow trees, in exactly the same manner as the Su Embankment. As the years and months have gone by, the girth of the trees has grown thick. When walking beneath the dense and patterned branches and leaves, the dappled moonlight appears like patches of lingering snow upon the ground. I think that in all likelihood talk of the "Lingering snow upon Break-Off Bridge" in the past was in fact a reference to the moonlight, not to the snow.

Su Embankment is some way distant from the town itself, and the pedestrians passing along the road leading toward Clear Waves Gate are few. By contrast, as Sun Embankment takes one directly to West Chill Bridge, here the horses and carts and tourists come and go like the shuttle of a loom. With the bewitching beauty of the lake and the scent of the lotus blooms filling one's nose for a good ten *li* around here, it is as if one has set off along the Shanyin Circuit for the "hills and the streams complement each other in such a way that I can't begin to describe them."[77]

The smaller of the houseboats can enter the Inner Lake; the larger ones are to be found either following along the contour of the embankment or moored against it. From Brocade Belt Bridge the road leads to Lake Prospect Pavilion, this pavilion marking the furthermost extent of Variegated Brocade Embankment, and as one approaches Lone Hill the surface of the lake opens out before one. As part of his lavish refurbishment of the lakeshore, Sun Long had an outdoor terrace built and upon this one can take in the cool breeze or stroll beneath the bright moon. One can also have a banquet laid out here for one's guests, and not a day goes by that is without the sound of flutes and singing or without an opera performed.

Today, this terrace has been transformed into Dragon King Hall and all around the hall structures of one sort or another have been erected, this disordered jumble of buildings serving to destroy the splendid scene of the past.

Farther on again stands the Shrine of Eunuch Sun, erected while he was still alive. With the hills behind it and the lake spread out before, the shrine is most imposing. In recent times this shrine has been made over to the Buddha by the eunuch Lu, and Sun Long's statue has been removed to sit behind the Buddha statue niche. Sun Long

---

77 A reference to the celebrated saying of Wang Xianzhi (344–386); see chapter 1 under Liu Yiqing, *A New Account of Tales of the World*.

expended several hundreds of thousands of taels on prettifying the lake, and in this regard his efforts were not inferior to those of the Academician Su Shi. To see his statue hidden away like this, given no view of the light of the lake or the hue of the mountains, forced to sit facing a wall like a criminal, brings a lump to one's throat.

Taoan's Dream Memories

"WEST LAKE ON THE FIFTEENTH OF THE SEVENTH MONTH" (*XIHU QIYUE BAN* 西湖七月半)

There is nothing much worth watching at West Lake on the fifteenth of the seventh month, the Midsummer Festival, apart that is from the people watching the midsummer moon and such people one may view as being divided into five categories.

Of the first category are those who sit in their storied boats with their pipes and drums, with high hats upon their heads and sumptuous banquets laid out before them, with lanterns, singing girls and their serving boys, all a riot of flame and voice. They say of themselves that they have come to view the moon and yet they retreat before the moon even makes an appearance. Such people, I watch.

Those of the second category are also to be found upon the storied boats; famous beauties and the daughters of eminent men, with their seductive pageboys at hand, amid laughter and twittering they sit in circles upon the outdoor platforms looking all about them, but although they find themselves beneath the moon they never once look up at it. These people too I watch.

A third category is also to be found in boats and they too are accompanied by singing; famous courtesans and idle monks who drink from shallow cups and sing to themselves quietly, accompanied by the soft pipes and light strings, the sound of bamboo and voice intermingling. They too find themselves beneath the moon and, in their case, they look up at it, but they are more interested in being seen looking up at the moon than in the moon itself. I watch them.

A fourth category is found neither upon boats nor in carriages; wearing neither shirts nor hats, they eat and drink their fill, gathering in raucous groups of three or five they barge their way into the crowds and add to the din and commotion around the Temple of Manifest Blessings or Break-Off Bridge, pretending to be drunk and singing out of tune. They look at the moon, they look at the people looking at the moon and the people not looking at the moon, but in actual fact they see nothing at all. These people I watch.

A final category comprises those in small boats with light canopies, clean tables, and warm braziers, the tea brewing away in their tea caddies and plain porcelain cups being passed around silently; good friends with beautiful companions, they invite the moon to join them and either hide away among the shadows beneath the trees or flee to Inner Lake to escape the din. They watch the moon without themselves being watched watching the moon, neither do they affect the airs of someone watching the moon. I watch also people of this category.

The people of Hangzhou, when they tour the lake, arrive there during the *si* hour [9–11 am] only to set off home again by the *you* hour [5–7 pm], avoiding the moon as if it were their mortal enemy. But such is the aura of this particular evening that crowds of people compete to be there, handing out largesse of wine and money to the troops at the gates as they leave the city. The sedan chair bearers, torches in hand, line the banks awaiting their custom. The moment the crowds board the boats they instruct the boatmen to hurry away to Break-Off Bridge, impatient to join in the fun. In this way, before the second watch of the night has been struck, as the boats large and small crowd around the shore, a cacophony of voice and pipe and drum heaves and shakes, and it is as if one were caught in a nightmare or by a ghastly vision, or had been rendered a deaf-mute. One can see nothing but pole bumping pole, boat banging into boat, shoulder brushing shoulder and face staring at face.

In a moment, all this excitement comes to an end and the officials' banquets are packed away and the yamen runners shout a passage through the crowds, the sedan chair bearers call out to the people on the boats, anxious now that they will be too late to catch the closing of the gates and, like stars in the sky, one by one the lanterns and the torches first gather together and then depart. The people along the banks of the lake too begin to head for the gates in lines, gradually thinning out before, in an instant, they are all gone.

It is only then that my friends and I have our boats approach the shore. As the stone steps up to Break-Off Bridge start to cool down, we sit down upon them and begin to toast each other. By then, the moon has become like a newly polished mirror, the surrounding hills touch up their makeup and the lake is as if it has just washed its face. Those that had been drinking from shallow cups and singing to themselves quietly reappear, as do those who had been hiding away in the shadows beneath the trees, and we go to greet them and drag them along to sit with us. Elegant friends arrive, famous courtesans turn up, and when the eating and drinking ceases, the flutes and voices take over. Only when the light of the moon begins to fade and the sun is about to rise from the east do these visitors disperse. We release the hawsers of our boats and float in drunken slumber amid the ten *li* of lotus blossom, their fragrance assailing our noses, our pure dreams proving most agreeable.

Search for West Lake in My Dreams

"CENTRAL APPROACHES: SU EMBANKMENT" (*XIHU ZHONGLU: SU GONG DI*
西湖中路蘇公堤)

Just as Hangzhou has its West Lake, so too does Yingzhou in Anhui Province, both lakes becoming famous for their beauty. Su Shi served successively in both places. Just after he had been appointed to the post in Yingzhou, somebody from there said to him: "Academician Su, all you need to do to manage the affairs of this area is to tour the lake." When he heard about this, Qin Guan [1049–1100] wrote a quatrain on it: "Ten *li* of lotus in first bloom, / My lord has arrived at West Lake. / If he wishes to conduct business from upon the lake, / His Speaking Officials, I fear, will have not a day off." Sometime later, once Su had arrived at his posting, an Executive Official surnamed Xie informed him: "When serving at court you enjoyed the honor of entering through the North Gate; now that you have taken charge of these two regions, you have served successively as master of both West Lakes." Thus, while Su Shi was serving in Hangzhou, he had the lake dredged and the mud matted with rape turnip piled up to form a long embankment, leading from south to north through the middle of the lake. This embankment thereafter took his name. Along both sides of the embankment, peach and willow trees were planted, and six bridges were built along its extent.

After the retreat to the south,[78] the storied boats with their drums and songs presented a scene of beauty and extravagance in the extreme. Later, as the lake waters ate away at the embankment, it began to disintegrate. By the Ming, in the years before the reign of the Chenghua emperor [1465–1487], the Inner Lake had been completely taken over by the locals to serve as arable land and the flow of water beneath the six bridges had been reduced to a trickle. In the third year of the reign of the Zhengde emperor [1508], the Provincial Administration Commissioner Yang Mengying had the Inner Lake cleared, establishing North New Embankment as its westernmost boundary. He also had the Su Embankment consolidated to a height of two *zhang* and a width of more than five *zhang*, built the six additional bridges of the Inner Lake and planted ten thousand willows in rows, thus restoring the embankment to its former glory. With the passage of time, many of the willows died and the embankment again began to disintegrate. In the twelfth year of the reign of the Jiajing emperor [1533], the District Magistrate Wang Yi ordered that minor criminals be allowed to redeem themselves by planting peach and willow trees along the embankment and soon the resplendent reds and purples had woven themselves into a brocade of color. During the subsequent wars, all these trees were cut down. In the second year of the reign of the Wanli emperor [1574], the Salt Distribution Commissioner Zhu Bingru had the embankment replanted in willows again, and once again it appeared resplendent. By the early years of the reign of

---

78   This refers to the conquest of northern China by the Jurchen Jin dynasty, the fall of the Northern Song, and the establishment of the Southern Song capital in Hangzhou (Lin'an).

the Chongzhen emperor [1628–1644], the trees had grown thick of girth. The Prefect Liu Mengqian, along with prominent local scholars such as Chen Shengfu and others, would hold splendid gatherings here upon the embankment during the second month. The town would be scoured for Goat Horn Lamps and several tens of thousands of gauze lanterns would be hung among the peach and willow trees, with red felt mats laid out beneath them, and amid a crowd of seductive serving boys and famous courtesans, the visitors would drink and sing to their heart's content. With dusk, the light of ten thousand candles, all burning together, would turn night into day. Visible far off across the lake, the light of the candles on the embankment would be magnified by the reflections on the surface of the lake, and the sound of the flutes and strings and pipes and song would stretch on until the early hours of the next morning. When news of all this reached the capital, the prefect was demoted a grade.

The memory of this leads one to think about Su Shi's time here as Prefect of Hangzhou. In spring, whenever he happened to have a day off he would arrange to meet up with those visiting the lake. They would take their breakfast at some scenic spot before each of them would set off in a boat, with one boat leading and each boat supplied with a courtesan or two, to drift wherever the tide would take them. In the late afternoon a gong would be sounded for the boats to reassemble and they would gather at the Lake Prospect Pavilion or at Bamboo Belvedere, before going their separate ways in an excess of joy. By the first or second watch of the night, before the night market had dispersed, they would return to the town in rows with torches burning. The most beautiful maidens of the town would gather like clouds to line the street and watch them. The romance of occasions such as this was unprecedented throughout history, truly the joyful token of a peaceful age such as cannot be repeated.

"CENTRAL APPROACHES: LAKE HEART PAVILION" (*XIHU ZHONGLU: HUXIN TING* 西湖中路湖心亭)

Lake Heart Pavilion was built on the site of Lake Heart Temple of old and in those days its pagoda had been one of the three found at the center of the lake. During the reign of the Hongzhi emperor of the Ming dynasty [1488–1505], a commissioner with the Provincial Surveillance Commission, Yin Zishu, proved extremely strict in his conduct of public affairs. When the monks of the temple, with the backing of the eunuch posted to the area as grand director, began to bar their gates to everybody, even the highest officials of the region, Yin investigated their wicked actions and had the temple destroyed and the pagoda dismantled.

In the thirty-first year of the reign of the Jiajing emperor [1552], the Prefect Sun Meng sought out the ruins of the former temple and had a pavilion erected on the site. Its open terrace was about a *mu* in circumference and was fenced with a stone balustrade; standing here upon it one could take in all the various splendid prospects offered by lake and hill at a single glance with none escaping one's purview.

Within a few years, however, the pavilion had fallen into a state of disrepair, only to be restored by Commissioner Xu Tingluo in the fourth year of the reign of the Wanli emperor [1576]. In the twenty-eighth year of the reign of the same emperor [1600], the eunuch Sun Long changed the pavilion's name to Pavilion of Pure Joy; with its glorious golds and blazing blues it became a site of awe and beauty. In the gaze of the traveler it would appear like a Fata Morgana, only to be quickly swallowed up again by the clouds and the mists; I fear that even Prince Teng's Gazebo and Yueyang Tower could not compete with its august vista.

In spring, bonsai, clay figurines, paintings, calligraphy, and antiques are laid out for sale here, covering every available step, and the shouting of the bargain hunters becomes quite deafening. Climbing up here in the evenings, however, with the moon suspended high in the sky, one finds peace and tranquillity, as if one has entered the Palace of the Mermaids or the Vault of the Oceans. With the moonlight reflected on the surface of the lake and the mist rising around one, few are those who come to this deserted place and none can linger long.

Taoan's Dream Memories

"VIEWING THE SNOW AT LAKE HEART PAVILION" (HUXIN TING KAN XUE 湖心亭看雪)

The twelfth month of the fifth year of the reign of the Chongzhen emperor [1632] found me living beside West Lake in Hangzhou. A heavy snow had been falling for three days without a break. No sound of man or bird could be heard. After the first watch of the evening had passed, I took a boat, and, swathed in my fur coat with a small brazier in hand, I set off alone toward Lake Heart Pavilion to view the snow. A hoar frost enveloped the scene, and the sky and the clouds, the hills and the lake, appeared but a seamless expanse of whiteness. The only smudges on the lake were the trace of the Long Embankment, the spot of Lake Heart Pavilion, and the mustard seed speck of my own boat with its two or three dots sitting within it. Arriving at the pavilion, I found two people already seated there, facing each other upon a felt rug. A servant boy was heating some wine and the water had just come to the boil. They were delighted to see me.

"How is it that this fellow too is out upon the lake?" they exclaimed as they pressed me into joining them for a drink. I speedily downed three large cupfuls before taking my leave. Inquiring after their names, I was told that they were from Jinling and just happened to be visiting this spot. As I got back on the boat, the boatman muttered under his breath: "I thought that you, my good sir, were crazy, but these gentlemen seem just as crazy as yourself!"

Search for West Lake in My Dreams

"SOUTHERN APPROACHES: LIUZHOU PAVILION" (*XIHU NANLU: LIUZHOU TING* 西湖南路柳洲亭)

At the beginning of the Southern Song dynasty, this pavilion was known as the Joy of Harvest Tower. It had been so named because for a number of years after the Emperor Gaozong shifted his capital away from Bianliang [in 1127], the people living in the Hangzhou region and in the surrounding commanderies of Jiaxing and Huzhou experienced a succession of bountiful harvests. The emperor ordered the tower erected in order to proclaim how much he joined with his people in celebrating these circumstances.

To the left of the gate stood the Inquiring about the Water Pavilion erected by Sun Long, with its tall willows and lengthy embankment. The storied houseboats and decorated pleasure craft all gathered here in front of the pavilion, berthed in good order and adding lustre to each other. Each day they would cast off from here at dawn, only to return to moor at dusk. So many were the carts and horses that made their way here, and such was the confused din of the servants and retainers, that a cacophony of human clamour would last throughout the day.

At the eastern end of the embankment stands the Temple to the Three Virtues. Turning to the north after crossing a small bridge brought one to the Sojourn Garden of my grandfather and the retreat of Dai Feijun of the Ministry of Personnel. A turn to the south, on the other hand, took one in close succession to the gardens and pavilions once owned by Qian Xiangkun, Grand Secretary in the Hall of the Heir Apparent, by Shang Zhouzuo, Minister of Personnel,[79] by the Censor Qi Biaojia, by Yu Huang, Senior Compiler in the Hanlin Academy, and by the Chief Supervising Secretary Chen Xiangfan. Beyond these gardens stood the Studio Above the Pond of the Provincial Graduate Huang Yuanchen and Hibiscus Garden of Zhou Zhonghan of Fuchun, mansion upon mansion. Today, such was the destruction wrought by the recent war, that not a single beam from these structures remains intact, the shards of their roof tiles lie piled up to one's shoulders, and everywhere one sees the sight of overgrown vegetation. In his *Record of the Celebrated Gardens of Luoyang*, the Song dynasty scholar Li Gefei claimed that from the waxing and waning of the gardens of Luoyang one could predict the rise and fall of the city, and that the rise and fall of Luoyang was a means of prognosticating the order or chaos of All under Heaven. How true his words!

---

79 Shang Zhouzuo (*jinshi* 1601) was the father of Qi Biaojia's wife Shang Jinglan (see chapter 6).

In the *jiawu* year [1654] I happened to find myself here again and was moved to despair by the sight of the palaces overgrown with millet[80] and the bronze camel lying amid the bramble.[81] Like Lu Yu, the Old Man of Mulberry and Hemp, on his travels to Tiaoxi, I wept and crept away under cover of darkness.[82]

"SOUTHERN APPROACHES: LITTLE PENGLAI" (*XIHU NANLU: XIAO PENGLAI* 西湖南路小蓬萊)

Little Penglai stands to the right of Thunder Peak Pagoda and had once been part of the garden of the Song dynasty eunuch Gan Sheng. As numerous as the clouds are its strange peaks, deep the shade cast by its ancient trees. Emperor Lizong [r. 1224–1264] often paid imperial visitations to this spot, and there remains an imperially favored pine tree that must now be hundreds of years old. From ancient times, this rock has been called Little Penglai and there are still to be found here stelae bearing Song dynasty inscriptions reading: "Blue Cloud Cliff," "Sea-Turtle Peak," and so on. At present, the place is where Master Huang Ruheng [1558–1626] chose to establish his study and he changed its name to Forest of Sojourn and that of the rock to Stampeding Clouds.

In my view, although the name Stampeding Clouds may well serve to capture something of the emotional quality of the rock, it fails to speak to its essence, for the rock is like a single blossom of the Yunnan camellia which has been so battered by the wind that half of it lies in the mud while the remaining petals shiver away and have folded into three or four layers. When people walk about here on the rock they are like butterflies flitting about the heart of a flower for none can resist having a taste of it. Its color is the dull black of the rocks from Yingde County in Guangdong and so ancient-looking is the color of the moss and lichen that grows upon it that it looks like

---

80 This is an allusion to Poem No. 65 (*Shuli* 黍離) of the *Book of Songs*. The "Minor Preface" to this poem reads: "The *Shuli* is expressive of pity for the old capital of Zhou. A great officer of Zhou, traveling on the public service, came to it, and, as he passed by, found the places of the ancestral temple, palaces, and other public buildings, all overgrown with millet. He was moved with pity for the downfall of the House of Zhou, moved about the place in an undecided way, as if he could not bear to leave it, and made this piece." See *The Chinese Classics*, vol. 4, *The She King or the Book of Poetry*, ed. and trans. James Legge (Oxford: Clarendon Press, 1893–1895), 47–48, transliteration altered.

81 In "The Biography of Suo Jing" (*Suo Jing zhuan* 索靖傳) in the *History of the Jin*, we are told that "[Suo] Jing had the capacity to foretell events far into the future, and knowing that All under Heaven was about to fall into disorder, he pointed at the bronze camel sitting outside the gate of the palace and sighed: 'And I'll be seeing you lying amid the brambles soon enough.'"

82 This is a reference to Lu Yu (d. 804), the author of the *Classic of Tea* (*Cha jing* 茶經). The "Biography of Lu Yu" in the *New History of the Tang* contains the following: "At the beginning of the Shangyuan reign period [784–809] of the Southern Zhao Kingdom, [Lu] Yu became a recluse in the Tiaoxi district and began to call himself the Old Man of Mulberry and Hemp. He shut his door and wrote. On one occasion he was out walking in the wilds alone intoning a poem about a fallen tree. Long he lingered there, disconsolate, before weeping as he made his way home. Thus it was that contemporaries called him a latter-day Jie Yu [the madman of Chu who had mocked Confucius]."

a Shang dynasty goblet or a tripod from the Zhou that has been buried in the ground for a thousand years during which time the blue-green hues have ingrained themselves into its bones.

Huang Ruheng is a true master of the craft of the essay and his disciples numbered in the hundreds, all the most famous men-of-letters of the age having studied under him at one time or another. As a young man, I paid a call on the master with my grandfather. He was sallow of complexion and very hirsute, with hair sprouting even from his cheeks. His eyes were wide, his mouth large, his eyebrows jutted out beyond the ridge of his nose. He seemed always full of laughter and he had a tremendous capacity to respond simultaneously to the many people constantly coming and going around him; he would incline his ear to listen to what his guests were saying, cast his eyes over the letters that had been brought to him, brush a response to those that required immediate answer, and give verbal instruction to his servants, all at the same time and never making the slightest mistake with any of the multifarious affairs that he had on hand. He never made the slightest distinction between his guests in terms of their respective wealth or social standing, treating even-handedly all who came to see him, plying them with the wine and meat that constituted his ordinary fare and sleeping beside them at night. An amanuensis of mine, a most unprepossessing and somewhat grubby figure, went to see him once and he housed and fed him in exactly the same way he did everyone else.

In the *bingyin* year of the reign of the Tianqi emperor [1626] I revisited Forest of Sojourn and found that all the pavilions and gazebos had fallen into a state of dilapidation. Standing beside the tomb where the master's body lay, like Wang Huizhi when he caught sight of the *qin* of his departed brother Wang Xianzhi, I was assailed by sorrow at the loss of my friend.[83] It is the *dingyou* year now [1657], and again I have come to this place. The walls have all crumbled away and it has become a field of tile shards. I wished to have a chamber built here to serve as a shrine for Master Su Shi but when I went to purchase the land I found that the present owner was unwilling to sell. The trees that once formed the forest have disappeared and the moss and lichen that was once such a feature has all been scraped away. Stampeding Clouds lies broken and discarded,

---

83   This is a reference to a story told about these two famous calligraphers in the "Grieving for the Departed" chapter of *A New Account of Tales of the World*: "Wang Huizhi and his younger brother, Wang Xianzhi, were both critically ill at the same time, but Xianzhi died first [388]. Huizhi asked his attendants, 'Why don't I hear any news at all? This must mean he's already dead.' As he spoke he showed no hint of grief. Immediately ordering a sedan chair, he came to Xianzhi's house to offer condolences, still without weeping at all. Since Xianzhi had always been fond of the seven-stringed zither [*qin*], Huizhi went directly in and sat on the spirit bed. Taking Xianzhi's zither, he started to play, but the strings were not in tune. Throwing it to the ground he cried out, 'Xianzhi! Xianzhi! you and your zither are both gone forever!' Whereupon he gave himself up utterly to his grief for a long while. In a little more than a month he, too, was dead." See Liu I-ch'ing (Liu Yiqing), *Shih-shuo Hsin-yü: A New Account of Tales of the World*, trans. Richard B. Mather (Minneapolis: University of Minnesota Press, 1976), 328, transliteration altered.

half of the original rock missing. I fear that with the passage of another few years it will become "all overgrown with rank grass," as in the line from the *Book of Songs*, only to disappear like cold mist. I call to mind those paradises of old, Chrysanthemum River and Peach Blossom Source.

"SOUTHERN APPROACHES: THUNDER PEAK PAGODA" (*XIHU NANLU: LEIFENG TA* 西湖南路雷峰塔)

Thunder Peak constitutes one of the foothills of South Screen Peak. Lofty and arched back upon itself, its former name had been Central Peak but it had also been known as Returning Peak. During the Song dynasty a man who could summon the thunder had lived here, hence its present name. The Prince of Wu and Yue had a pagoda built here, planning initially that it should be of thirteen stories and a thousand *chi* tall. When he ran out of money to realize this plan, only seven stories were built. In olden times, it has been called Princess's Pagoda. It burnt down at the end of the Yuan dynasty, leaving only the heart of the pagoda standing. "The glow of sunset upon Thunder Peak Pagoda" soon became one of the ten scenes of West Lake.

I once saw an inscription to a painting by Li Liufang [1575–1629] that read:

> My friend Wen Qixiang once said: "Of the two pagodas of West Lake, the Pagoda for the Protection of Qian Chu is like a beautiful maiden, that of Thunder Peak resembles an aged monk." I much admired his analogy. In the *xinhai* year [1611] I was sitting with Shen Fanghui in my hut above the pond looking at the lotus blossoms when I suddenly came up with a poem containing the line: "Thunder Peak leans upon the sky like a drunken old man." When Yan Diaoyu saw the poem, he jumped for joy: "Qixiang's 'aged monk' is nowhere near as good as your 'drunken old man' in terms of capturing the emotional quality of the sight." As it happens, living here in a tower in the hills above the lake, I face Thunder Peak from dawn to dusk, and the sight of it becomes especially intoxicating when, in the purple rays of a mountain sunset, this drunken old man makes his dissolute appearance. And yet the last line of my poem read: "As bland the sentiments of this old man as the mist above a river," so it seems that I was still working off Qixiang's analogy of the "aged monk." Inscribed this tenth month of the *guichou* year [1613], well into my cups.

"SOUTHERN APPROACHES: BAO'S ESTATE" (*XIHU NANLU: BAO YA ZHUANG* 西湖南路包衙莊)

The storied houseboats that now ply West Lake were the invention of the Surveillance Vice-Commissioner Bao Yingdeng. These boats come in three sizes; within the largest, one can lay out a banquet, accompanied by singing boys; the middle-sized ones are sufficiently large to transport one's books and paintings; in the smallest, there is just room enough to hide away a beautiful young girl or two to keep one company. Bao Yingdeng's singing girls were beyond comparison with ordinary maids-in-waiting, and, in imitation of the practice of Shi Chong and Song Qi of old, he frequently ordered them to appear before his guests. Painted of face, they would amble in like ponies, their mincing step as if constricted, like wasps weaving their way through the willows, all to bring joy and laughter to their audience. Standing in front of the bright railings and windows decorated with silken filigree, they would stretch out their song, play their flutes and pluck their *qins*, the music they made akin to the warbling of the golden oriole. As guests arrived, the singing boys would begin the opera, dancing in rows, singing as they kept time with their drums. Their skills quite excelled those of others. When the mood took him, Bao Yingdeng would take his performers touring, sometimes not returning home for ten days or more, and attracting huge crowds, all of whom would ask where the troupe was next to perform.

Bao's South Garden was sited beneath Thunder Peak Pagoda, his North Garden below Flew-Here Peak. Rocks abounded in both gardens, heaped up here and piled up there all higgledy-piggledy, but always forming the most eccentrically shaped precipices. In some places, rocks had been used to construct a bridge over a brook, but in such instances, unlike the artificial mountains found elsewhere upon the hill, these bridges were all ingeniously designed and crafted. The ridgepoles of the main halls were held in place by cantilevers, thus obviating the need for pillars at all four corners, making the halls spacious enough for lion dancers to perform. In North Garden, a chamber had been built in the form of the Eight Trigrams, with a round pavilion partitioned into eight sections and shaped like a fan. Eight beds had been placed horizontally in the narrow corners of each partition, curtained off on both sides. When the innermost curtains were lowered, the beds faced outside, and when the outermost curtains were lowered, the beds would face each other. Old man Bao would sit in state in the middle with clear windows in his doors, and as he lay there propped up against his pillow burning incense, he could see each and every one of the eight beds. In such an excess of extravagance and wantonness did he grow old beside West Lake for more than twenty years, the splendor of his gardens not a jot inferior to that of Golden Valley or Mei Village, nothing less than the apotheosis of luxury and magnificence, but what the locals of Hangzhou, however, were wont to dismiss by saying: "Well, that's just how it is." The grand families of West Lake wanted for nothing, the Lady of the West occasionally finding herself housed in a Golden Chamber. It was only the poor pedantic scholar who had none of this.

"SOUTHERN APPROACHES: A PATCH OF CLOUD" (*XIHU NANLU: YIPIAN YUN* 西湖南路一片雲)

Divinely Transported Rock is found within Dragon Well Temple. It is a full six *chi* tall, most eccentrically shaped and of towering proportions. It stands alone beneath the eaves of the temple. A single banksia rose coils its way in and out of the cavities of the rock, like a coiled dragon or snake. In the thirteenth year of the reign of the Zhengtong emperor [1448], Li De from Zhonggui was living in Dragon Well Temple. There was a severe drought and Li De ordered his soldiers to dredge the well. At first they came across twenty-four metal plaques, a jade Buddha, and an ingot of silver stamped with the mark of the Yuanfeng reign period of the Song dynasty. Later, this rock too was discovered, and it took the efforts of eighty men to lift it out of the well. The words "Divinely Transported" had been engraved on the surface of the rock as had many other inscriptions, none of which remained legible so one had no idea when they were written. In all probability, these things had been thrown into the well as gifts to the dragon by way of beseeching him for rain.

On the Ridge of the Bamboo Flute stands the rock A Patch of Cloud, over a *zhang* tall. It is an exquisite glossy blue-green in color, and so ingeniously shaped that it almost seems to have been engraved. Stone steps lined with pines twist their way through the dense grass and a fine and most precipitous stone cavern has been formed by piling some rocks on top of each other. Behind the rock stands A Patch of Cloud Pavilion, built by the eunuch Sun Long. He had also placed a stone chessboard in front of the pavilion, with a couplet engraved on it: "Come when the mood takes you, to look over the river and ponder under waning moon, / When the talk ceases, chant a poem and lean upon this patch of cloud." Visitors here all linger a while, incapable of tearing themselves away.

"ENVIRONS: WEST CREEK" (*XIHU WAIJING: XIXI* 西湖外景西溪)

Millet Mountain is sixty-two *zhang* high and has a circumference of eighteen *li* and two hundred paces. At the foot of the mountain is Stone Man Ridge, rising up sharply in a most reverential manner. It is shaped like a man, his double top-knot jutting out. Once one has crossed the ridge, one comes across West Creek and the several hundred people living here have gathered within a market village. Legend has it that soon after he retreated to the south and first arrived in Wulin, Emperor Gaozong [r. 1127–1162], observing the richness of the land here, intended to use it for his capital. Later on, having obtained Phoenix Mountain, he was recorded as saying: "West Creek, we'll leave as it is for the moment," the place having been given its present name as a result of this incident.

It is a most isolated spot, with many ancient plums of a dwarf variety. Their boughs are twisted and tangled, just like the pines of Yellow Mountain. Enthusiasts, when they get to this place, buy up the smallest trees they can find and take them home to use as part of bonsai arrangements. There is an Autumn Snow Hermitage here and within the hermitage there is a large expanse of bulrushes. It is a most extraordinary sight to see them when, under a bright full moon, they turn as white as snow. To my mind, West Creek is the very embodiment of the elegance of the scenery of Jiangnan, for here one can indulge one's eyes with beauty and one's ears with the music of pipes and song. If one wished to find an isolated creek or a secluded valley wherein to hide away from the world, like Peach Blossom Source or Chrysanthemum River of old, I can think of no better place.

My friend Jiang Daoan owned a meditation hut beside West Creek and invited me to join him in retreat. As I was still immersed in the purposeless affairs of the world at the time, I was never able to do so, a circumstance that I continue to regret to this day.

"A Record of My Untethered Garden" (*Buxi yuan ji* 不繫園記)

WANG RUQIAN 汪如谦 (1577–1655)

TRANSLATED BY DUNCAN M. CAMPBELL

From a wealthy family of Huizhou merchants, Wang Ruqian (Ranming) straddled the worlds of commerce and the arts, and was of some note as a poet. Resident in Hangzhou, he owned a pleasure boat on the West Lake that he named the "Untethered Garden," on which he entertained at one time or another almost everyone who was anyone in the late Ming dynasty. He enjoyed a liaison with Liu Rushi, one of the glamorous *grandes horizontales* of the time, with whom he once visited Qi Biaojia's Allegory Mountain (see below and chapter 6).

"A Record of My Untethered Garden"

Painted houseboats have plied West Lake ever since the lake first became established, as is recorded in fulsome detail in *Old Tales of Hangzhou* of the Song, but so numerous have been the manner and type of these boats that the designs of many of them are now quite beyond investigation. Recent years have witnessed the invention of both the Storied Houseboat by Bao Yingdeng, the Surveillance Vice-Commissioner, and the Platform for Washing Off the Makeup by Ji Yuanji of my own family, these boats rivaling each other in terms of both their ingeniousness and their capaciousness.

Yet whenever, across the embankment, one sees a houseboat shift its moorings from one bank to another, its vermilion rafters then appearing amid the spring trees like the overlapping scales of a goldfish, it is not so much that it fails to set off wonderfully the various terraces and gazebos that stud the surrounding hills, it is just that at the same time the isolated islands and secluded inlets become, immediately, inaccessible to those on board the boat, for the low span of Twin Bridge is such that it cannot pass underneath and enter the inner lake. When the flowering apricot blossoms of Dharma Dock on Lone Hill reach for the moon above, for instance, or the lotuses begin to chant their song of welcome to the breeze, one is overcome by an overwhelming sense of regret at this circumstance. Thus it is that men of true refinement get about the lake in dragonfly skiffs, darting here and there as if on a wing, snorting contemptuously at the large boats as being the ostentatious craft of the official or the merchant.

For my part, however, I don't share their contempt. The boats of the West Lake are like the sedan chairs of the Twin Peaks or the piebald horses of Six Bridges, each form of transport being appropriate to specific needs—why then distinguish between them in terms of their respective sizes? To be hauled slowly alongside willow ponds and flower isles by means of brocade hawsers, to race across the lake as if upon a reed and in the face of chill rain and rising waves, by means of silent oar or short pole, to glide through moonlit ponds drenched by autumn, or when, standing beside crimson balustrades and decorated windows, the frozen sand reflects the snow, all such moments have their own especial quality, and all are completely different. Why is it, then, held to be the case that only upon touring dragons or soaring fish hawks can one enjoy music or spread out one's silken rugs?

Mid-summer of the *guihai* year [1623], having completed the construction of a meditation hut for Daoist Yun, I happened to get hold of the trunk of a magnolia tree. I had this log crafted into a boat. When completed, after more than four months' work, it was six *zhang* two *chi* in length and a fifth as wide. Several paces inside the cabin and one finds oneself in a space large enough to hold a hundred wine pots; a few steps farther on and one enters a smaller square room, just big enough to spread out two mats. A small cell is secreted away here, and here I can recline to chant a poem or two. Hidden off to the side here also is a wall closet where I can store my drunken scribblings. Turning around, one comes to a covered passageway that leads up on to a platform. A canopy can be erected to cover that platform. On spring mornings when the flowers are in full bloom or on autumnal evenings when the moon hangs high in the sky, standing here on the platform it can seem as if one has ascended to the blue Elysium upon the variegated clouds. And yet, whenever one encounters an alarming wind or soaring waves, one may draw close to the trees that line the banks or pass under the flat bridges, for all one has to do is dismantle the framework holding up the canopy and roll it up. Thus, in a moment, my boat becomes, once again, simply a dragonfly skiff.

I have chosen one or two of my houseboys who are particularly good at beating time to music and have dispatched them to help the boatmen here and to serve wine and tea to my guests. Here on my boat, these guests may escape from the wind or prolong the evening with revelry. Such a scene as this can be understood, distantly, to capture something of the elegance of the past, while, more proximately, to represent also the divertissements of an age of peace.

Master Chen Jiru gave my boat the name "Untethered Garden" and so now a fine name has been coined to accompany my remarkable invention, and surely this will in time become another timeless anecdote told around the lake. Why then pile up rocks and excavate ponds, thus imprisoning the hills and the valleys and taking private possession of them solely in order to be able to proclaim: "This is my garden! This is my garden!"?

Huang Ruheng, the Assistant Administration Commissioner with the Provincial Administration Commission, drafted a "Covenant for the Untethered Garden," stipulating its "Twelve Consonances" and "Nine Taboos," as follows:

Consonances: famous men, senior monks, intimate friends, beautiful women, marvelous incense, flutes, the *qin*, unaccompanied singing, fine tea, strong wine, no more than five choices of sweetmeats, and sending away one's mounted retainers.

Taboos: the taking of life, uninvited guests, throwing one's official weight about, over-politeness, houseboys standing all about, actors performing, raucous noise, being importuned for a loan, and long-overdue debts.

"Eight Quatrains on the West Lake of Hangzhou" (*Xihu ba jueju* 西湖八絕句)

LIU SHI 柳是 (RUSHI 如是; 1618–1664)

TRANSLATED BY KANG-I SUN CHANG

For Liu Shi, see chapter 6.

"Eight Quatrains on the West Lake of Hangzhou"

I

A small yard with hanging willows lies east of the embroidered curtains;
Bare branches stretch by the oriole pavilion, no thoughts of longing yet.
Truly at the West Chill Bridge on the Cold Food Road
The peach blossoms have the essence of beautiful women.

II

Year after year, red tears dye the green brook;
By the spring waters the east wind bends the willows evenly.
The bright moon has just shifted, the new leaves are cold;
Traces of teardrops lie but west of the cuckoos.

III

Emerald strings of Xiang are tied to the double hoop;[84]
Here the fragrance fades in the violent wind and rain.
Countless red orchids rush toward the body,
But most break off, unable to bound back.

IV

Beyond the south screen, in the misty moon, dawn lies dark and silent;
In the drizzle, delicate orioles shed tears that seem to come from the depths.
Again there is a gentle pair of butterflies
Whose winged rouge touches a loving heart.

---

84 Xiang is the lush region of lakes and hills associated with Qu Yuan (see chapter 1).

V

The low branches have started to put forth lovely flowers;
Green birds fly primly over the wet, sloping path.
The sorrowful heart moves up the willow trees;
Over West Chill Bridge cuckoos are few.

VI

The mist brushes the green grassland in the night cool;
Fallen cherries darken the emerald pond.
Already I resent how the willow catkins resemble tears;
But now the spring wind and spring dream whisk me along.

VII

The fresh water of the bright lake looks like jade emitting smoke;
The grass grows lush, like a coiffure adorned with wild geese.
I think long and hard of the Greenhill Terrace birds of times past;[85]
Crying amid the peach blossoms, they did not return.

VIII

Sadly I watch the water-birds sporting among the flowered rocks;
The purple swallows, flying up and down, soak their glistening coats.
In the lonely spring breeze the fragrance does not stir;
The dying blossoms should turn into rain gossamer and fly.

"Dragon Well" (*Longjing* 龍井)

ZHANG QIONGRU 張瓊如 (MID-17TH CENTURY)
TRANSLATED BY WILT IDEMA AND BEATA GRANT

Very little is known about Zhang Qiongru. She came from Hangzhou and married into a family surnamed Chen. Few of her poems survive, but she is also known as a calligrapher. Dragon Well, now best known for the production of high-quality tea but also the site of a Buddhist temple, is close to the West Lake.

---

85   Editor's note: "Greenhill Terrace" (*Qingling tai*) refers to the story of the wife of a Song state official in the fourth to third century BCE. The king of Song took her from her husband and had him killed after he had constructed the terrace. The woman threw herself to her death from this terrace. The allusion is used to refer to the separation of husband and wife. Since the collection of poems containing these verses was published in 1639, Liu may be referring to her separation from Chen Zilong.

"Dragon Well"

Dimly discernible hangings and banners, the green trees low:
The sloping road to the convent's gate as the evening sun sets.
The steep steps of the ancient altar: a thousand-layered cliff,
The narrow stream feeds far away into the nine-bend brook.
Sounds from the pine valley harmonize with the clear chimes,
The cloudy mists amid the bamboo hide the small pavilion.
The meditation-mind is already cut off from dusty karma,
And is not disturbed by the lonely gibbon's midnight cry.

"Meditation on the Past: In Jade Effusion Garden" (*Yujin yuan huaigu* 玉津園懷古)

QIAN FENGLUN 錢鳳綸 (FL. 1680)
TRANSLATED BY MAUREEN ROBERTSON

Qian Fenglun was a great-niece of the Hangzhou woman poet Gu Ruopu (see chapter 6). Qian and other relatives were members of a group of women writers known as the Banana Garden Poetry Club, based in the area of Hangzhou.[86] She was a painter as well as a poet. This poem shows an intense awareness of the historical connotations of the landscape; the ancient imperial associations of the West Lake are used to allude subtly to the Ming dynasty's loss of power.

"Meditation on the Past: In Jade Effusion Garden"[87]

Running currents of West Lake sing
of ages long in the past;
wind is folding the snowy wave,
water dragons dance.
They say a royal carriage once
held a splendid hunt;
a thousand riders with carved saddles
camped along the water.
Flageolets and songs at dawn

---

86   On this club, see Daria Berg, *Women and the Literary World in Early Modern China, 1580–1700* (New York: Routledge, 2013), 222–50.

87   During the later Zhou dynasty, a Jade Effusion Garden was said to have been constructed under imperial auspices. In 1147, during the Southern Song dynasty, another garden with the same name was created north of Dragon Mountain in the West Lake area of Hangzhou. In 1185, Emperor Xiaozong (1163–1190) held a great hunting party there. "Jade Effusion," in Daoist lore, is a substance that confers immortality. In Daoist mystical texts, it is the saliva from the mouth of the spiritual lover, Jade Maiden, with the power to confer enlightenment.

pressed on Phoenix City clouds;[88]
at evening their flags and banners
furled Dragon Mountain rain.
Across the lake now autumn winds
are blowing in the reeds;
red cherry-apple's suspended fruits
are the cuckoo's soul.
The glory and beauty of earlier times
today are truly gone;
from the river village in waning light
washing blocks ring clear.
In the Palace of Renewing Splendor
only moonlight is brilliant;
by the Hall of Virtue and Longevity
only spring grass comes to life.
Events of an age, mere floating clouds,
could they be fixed or secured?
Lake currents, crying and murmuring,
swirl round ruined city walls.
The descending sun strikes dread in my heart,
transfixes my distant gaze;
no purple clouds do I see there,
this evening in the southland.[89]

A Handy Guide to the Lake and Its Hills (Hushan bianlan 湖山便覽; extract)

ZHAI HAO 翟灝 (FL. 1754, D. 1788)

TRANSLATED BY DUNCAN M. CAMPBELL

The bibliophile and scholar Zhai Hao was a native of Hangzhou who became an education official and a collector of books on a wide variety of subjects; he called his library building a "Nest of Books." He was also a prolific author.

---

88   Phoenix City was a name normally used for the imperial capital, but here it designates a temporary residence of the emperor.

89   Purple clouds connote imperial authority, the aura of an emperor, suggesting his spiritual as well as temporal power. The poem closes on a dark note, implying perhaps the Ming dynasty's loss of the "southland" in its final battle with the Manchu invaders who established the Qing dynasty.

A Handy Guide to the Lake and Its Hills (extract)

In his *Topographical Guide to Touring Sites of Scenic Beauty*, Zhu Mu [d. ca. 1246] once wrote that: "The hills and water of West Lake are surpassingly elegant; throughout all four seasons of the year painted barges ply the lake and the sound of song and drum is ceaseless. Enthusiasts proceeded to identify and name ten scenes of the lake, as follows: 'The autumnal moon reflected in a calm lake,' 'A spring's dawn breaking upon Su Embankment,' 'Lingering snow upon Break-Off Bridge,' 'The glow of sunset upon Thunder Peak,' 'The evening bell tolls upon South Screen Mountain,' 'Breeze among the lotuses of Winding Courtyard,' 'Viewing the fish at Flower Harbor,' 'Listening to the orioles amid the billowing willows,' 'The imprint of the moon upon the Three Ponds,' and 'The twin peaks pierce the clouds.'" This was the first instance of the appearance of these Ten Scenes in the gazetteers of the site, and, judging from the fact that each scene is given a name that comprises four characters, a practice that was initiated by painters, these vistas must have first been the subjects of paintings before they were so named. Zhu Mu himself, along with the painters Ma Yuan [fl. 1189–1225] and the monk Yujian Ruofen [13th century], were all men of the reign of the Emperor Ningzong of the Southern Song dynasty [1195–1224]. Ma Yuan, for his part, once produced a folio of ink paintings entitled "Ten Scenes of West Lake," none of which filled the entire surface of the paper, hence earning for himself the epithet "One Corner Ma," for which refer to the *Record of the Painting Academy of the Southern Song* by Liu E [1692–1752]. Among the extant paintings of Yujian Ruofen, also, there exist ten paintings of West Lake scenes, for which see the *Paintings Examined*. This record by Zhu Mu is perhaps made on the basis of the existence of these paintings by Ma Yuan and Yujian Ruofen and does not claim that these ten scenes, in themselves, serve to exhaust the scenic delights of the West Lake. Later on, men such as Chen Qingbo of Qiantang and Ma Lin too did paintings of the Ten Scenes, while at the same time Wang Wei wrote a poem on each of the ten and Chen Yunping produced ten lyrics, thus ensuring that the names of the Ten Scenes were transmitted down to the present age. . . . In the 38th year of his reign [1698], the Kangxi emperor himself inscribed the names of the scenes, in process of which he corrected the various discrepancies that had arisen, and the authorities had stelae engraved and pavilions built to house the stelae. All eyes now gazed upon these stelae in admiration, and both the sequence of the Ten Scenes and their names were fixed for all time, never to be altered.

Wild Swan on the Snow: An Illustrated Record of My Preordained Life
(*Hongxue yinyuan tuji* 鴻雪因緣圖記)

"Paying My Compliments to West Lake" (*Xihu wenshui* 西湖問水)

LINQING 麟慶 (1791–1846)

TRANSLATED BY YANG TSUNG-HAN AND JOHN MINFORD[90]

For Linqing, see chapter 8.

"Paying My Compliments to West Lake"

In the first month of the year *bingyin* [1806], my father was appointed prefect and assigned to the province of Zhejiang. He proceeded there immediately. In the following month my mother and I accompanied my great-grandmother on the river-trip to the south. When we were about to weigh anchor, I received a poem sent to me as a parting gift by Uncle Ju Shantao.[91] The poem included the following lines:

> The year contains so little spring enchantment;
> When you visit West Lake, enjoy it to the full.

When I did reach Hangzhou it was already the beginning of the sixth month. Just then Uncle Li Kangjie[92] came from Shanyin and invited me to visit West Lake with him. That very day, accompanied by my brother Zhongwen, we went to the Water Pavilion outside the Yongjin Gate of the city, and hired a boat to sail downstream. All around us the hills stood like screens of azure and jet, while purple halls and crimson palaces shone to right and left, as if we could pluck them from our very sleeves. Then we paid our respects at the Temple to the Prince of the Water Immortals.

Evening was approaching as we sailed into the thick of the lotus flowers; we smelt the fragrance of the wind on the gentle ripples of the water, and became oblivious of the cruel heat. I cut a lotus stem and used it as a straw with which to sip my wine. The moon was up by the time we left.

During my days as an official in the capital, I would recollect this happy experience, and fly there in my imagination.

I have written a series of sixteen quatrains entitled "Reminiscences of West Lake," and I beg to append one here:

---

90 Editor's note: some of the footnotes included by the translators in their original publication have been omitted where not essential to the comprehension of the text.

91 Name Wangdorgi, a Mongol and a student of the Imperial Academy, admitted by special grant.

92 Name Buying, academy student from Shanyin, later served as Chief County Education Officer.

Outside the Tower to Welcome Auster[93] the green flow is rich;
Visitors are loath to leave the fragrance drifting these many miles;
If this mortal frame can change into a butterfly dreaming,
Surely tonight it will fly around the lotus flowers.

On investigation there are altogether in our empire thirty-one expanses of water bearing the name West Lake, but the Mingsheng Lake[94] of Qiantang [Hangzhou] is the most famous. In the ancient Han dynasty, there occurred the miracle of the Golden Cow, as recorded in Li Daoyuan's [d. 527] *Notes on the Water Classic*. And West Lake is not merely a picturesque scenic spot, it is also a useful source of water. In the Tang dynasty, the Duke of Ye[95] drilled six wells, Bo Xiangshan [Bai Juyi] constructed stone conduits to irrigate the farm land, and Su Shi of the Song dynasty introduced vegetable farms. The economic benefits of West Lake have been enhanced from age to age. During the Yuan and Ming dynasties, it was left unattended and came to be more and more in need of dredging. In the present dynasty, during the second year of the Yongzheng reign [1724], the Governor of Zhejiang, the posthumously canonized Lord Li Minda[96] received an imperial order to dredge the lake and make other necessary improvements. The lake thus came to be of great benefit to the livelihood of the people in the western part of Zhejiang. Moreover the same governor restored the antiquities and revised the gazetteers. He certainly did much for West Lake, and it is fitting and proper that he should be worshipped together with the Prince of the Water Immortals.[97]

"Taking an Excursion at West Lake with Xuanqing, I Am Moved to Write" (*Xie Xuanqing mei you Xihu gan zuo* 偕璿卿妹遊西湖感作)

XU ZIHUA 徐自華 (1873–1935)
TRANSLATED BY GRACE S. FONG

Like her friend, the revolutionary Qiu Jin (1877–1907; see chapter 3), Xu Zihua came from Zhejiang. Her family encouraged her interest in literature. She had a short marriage, ended by

---

93 The auspicious South Wind which symbolizes Well-being and Happiness.

94 "Lake of the Illustrious Sage."

95 Li Bi (722–789), a fascinating, enigmatic, and talented character in Chinese history.

96 Name Wei, Provincial Academy Student of Jiangsu. Hummel, or rather Fang Chao-ying, in his biography of Tian Wenqing, gives Li's dates as 1687?–1738, and leaves a somewhat different impression of the man: "A provincial official highly favored by Emperor Shizong (Yongzheng). . . . Although in his term at Hangzhou he improved greatly the architecture and scenic beauties of West Lake, he saw nothing incongruous in having an image of himself placed in the main hall dedicated to the Spirit of the Lake, a divinity known also as the Spirit of the Flowers. In a smaller structure to the rear of this image was placed a group of figures representing himself and his wives. When, some five decades later (in 1780), Emperor Gaozong (Qianlong) visited Hangzhou he ordered these figures removed and replaced by others more in harmony with the Spirit of the Lake."

97 Editor's note: the Prince of the Water Immortals here refers to the Dragon King.

her husband's death in 1900, after which she remained a widow; she became the headmistress of a girls' school in her husband's native city. It was there that she met Qiu Jin (referred to here by an alternative name, Xuanqing), who arrived as a teacher in 1906. The outing to which this poem refers took place in the spring of 1907. Their brief friendship was ended by Qiu's execution later that year, after which Xu bravely arranged the transfer of Qiu's body from Shaoxing for burial by the West Lake; she continued to uphold Qiu's memory thereafter. The line about "the Song imperial tombs . . . sunk in barbarian dust" clearly refers to the Manchu rule of China, which Qiu was dedicated to ending.

"Taking an Excursion at West Lake with Xuanqing, I Am Moved to Write"

Like meteors for the moment we have a spring outing together,
Lake and hills coming into view—how they sadden our spirits.
After death my name will not be known in the highest ranks,
While alive, good friends are not too many.
Wanting to ease your accumulated grief, you rely on wine,[98]
Willing to make a sacrifice, do you ever think of yourself?
It pains us to look toward Phoenix Hill
Where the Song imperial tombs are sunk in barbarian dust.

---

98 The author added a note: "You have a capacity for wine."

CHINESE NAMING CONVENTIONS

Chinese naming conventions can be a source of some confusion to those not familiar with them. The surname always comes first; it is usually monosyllabic, occasionally disyllabic, or in the case of some non-Han ethnic groups, polysyllabic. In the case of Han Chinese at least, the personal name can be either monosyllabic or disyllabic.

Chinese men started life with a "milk-name" used in the family, often something playful like "Fuzzy" or "Little Tiger"; when they began their education, they would start to be addressed by their surname and official personal name. Some women never acquired personal names, and would continue to be known by their milk-name or by their position in the family (Third Sister, Fourth Aunt). The personal name would usually be chosen by a senior member of the family or clan; very often the personal names of all the male children in one generation would contain the same "generational" character, and sometimes the other characters (in the case of disyllabic personal names) would have something in common. For example, Qi Biaojia and his brothers and paternal cousins all shared the character *jia* (meaning "good" or "fine"), with the other character being the name of a mythical or semi-mythical beast (leopard, unicorn, etc.). In the case of monosyllabic personal names, they might share a radical (the part of the character indicating the general class to which the referend belongs); so a group of brothers might all have the names of different trees, sharing the "wood" radical. Occasionally an individual might choose to change his personal name in adulthood.

At the time of the capping ceremony for boys that marked the start of the transition to adulthood, a senior family member or close family friend would be invited to choose a formal name (*zi*) for the boy; this is sometimes referred to in English as the style-name or social name. This was always disyllabic, and generally implied a goal to which the holder should aspire; it was more likely to reflect the character or interests of the holder than his personal name, given before his personality had become defined, but sometimes it had a direct link with the personal name through a quotation from the classics. It was normally by the formal name (often without the surname) that friends and acquaintances would address or refer to each other, and people would refer to their family members of the same generation by the formal name (or the cognomen; see next paragraph) when talking or writing to those outside the family.

In addition to these given names, the individual himself could adopt an unlimited number of cognomina (*hao, biehao*), or studio names. These were often used as noms de plume for works of literature or for signing paintings. They might be taken from the name of the individual's studio or residence (e.g. Master Sitting-in-Reclusion, from the Garden of Sitting in Reclusion). A new cognomen might be adopted to mark the start of a new phase of life or a move to a new location.

Formal names and cognomina were generally taken only by members of the elite. All elite men took them, but not all elite women; in addition, high-class courtesans often adopted them as a way of assimilating themselves to elite men. It can, therefore, be very difficult to be sure whether one or more person is being referred to when a variety of names are used; it is particularly difficult to know who is being referred to when a formal name is used without a surname, especially as the same formal name may be shared by a number of different people (this is less likely to happen with cognomina, though it is not unknown). In this anthology, we have tried, as far as possible, to supply the personal name, and if necessary the surname, when a formal name or cognomen is used in the original text.

Official titles are another minefield for the unwary reader of Chinese texts. Fortunately, the great work of Charles O. Hucker, *A Dictionary of Official Titles in Imperial China* (Stanford: Stanford University Press, 1985), has supplied us with a standard English translation for (almost) all official titles throughout the imperial period. Because of the importance of the imperial civil service to the life of the elite in China, an individual's official position formed a significant part of his personal identity, so official titles—and sometimes archaistic or conventional equivalents to them (such as the courtesy title *fumu*, literally "father and mother," for a county magistrate, alluding to his role as "father and mother of the people")—are frequently used even when the individual's official function is not in consideration. Certain well-known individuals may be habitually referred to by their official title, sometimes without the inclusion of the surname (e.g., the great calligrapher Wang Xizhi as Wang *youjun* [General of the Right] or the Ming-Qing writer Wang Shimin as Wang *fengchang* [Chief Minister of the Court of Imperial Sacrifices]).

SEXAGENARY DATING SYSTEM

In the texts reproduced here, years (or sometimes days) are referred to by terms such as *guichou* or *renyin*. These terms come from the Chinese sexagenary dating system. The sixty possible combinations of the ten heavenly stems (*tiangan* 天干) and twelve earthly branches (*dizhi* 地支) produce a sixty-year, or sixty-day, cycle (sometimes referred to as the *ganzhi* 干支 cycle), starting with *jiazi* 甲子 and ending with *guihai* 癸亥, after which it starts again with *jiazi*. The sexagenary system is still used in the traditional Chinese calendar; 2016, for example, was a *bingshen* 丙申 year; the next *bingshen* year will be 2076.

Year dates may also be identified as the nth year of a particular reign-period. For example, 742 was the first year of the Tianbao (Heavenly Treasure) reign-period of the Tang dynasty. Until the Yuan dynasty, a single emperor's reign might include more than one named reign-period. In the Ming and Qing dynasties, each emperor's reign was designated by a single reign name throughout, hence Ming and Qing emperors are often referred to by the name of their reign-period (e.g. Wanli, Qianlong); earlier emperors are usually referred to by the "temple name" or posthumous title bestowed after their death—e.g., the Song emperor Huizong ("Excellent Ancestor"), whose twenty-five-year reign encompassed six reign-periods.

More detailed explanations of reign names, the dating system, and emperors' names can be found in Endymion Wilkinson, *Chinese History: A New Manual* (Cambridge, Mass.: Harvard University Asia Center, 2015), 9–11, 275–76, 510–20.

LIST OF CHINESE DYNASTIES

Adapted from Endymion Wilkinson, *Chinese History: A Manual* (Cambridge, Mass.: Harvard University Asia Center, 2000).

Xia (semi-legendary)	ca. 21st–16th centuries BCE
Shang	ca. 1600–1045 BCE
Zhou	1045–256 BCE
Spring and Autumn	770–476 BCE
Warring States	475–221 BCE
Qin	221–206 BCE
Han	202 BCE–220 CE
Former (Western) Han	202 BCE–23 CE
Xin (Wang Mang)	9–23
Later (Eastern) Han	25–220
Wei, Jin, and Northern and Southern Dynasties	220–589
Three Kingdoms	220–280
Jin	265–420
Northern and Southern Dynasties	420–589
Southern Dynasties	420–579
Liu Song	420–479
Qi	479–502
Liang	502–557
Chen	557–589
Northern Dynasties	386–581
Northern (Tuoba) Wei	386–534
Sui	581–618
Tang	618–907
Five Dynasties and Ten Kingdoms	902–979
Five Dynasties (North China)	907–960
Ten Kingdoms (South China)	902–979
Song	960–1279
Northern Song	960–1127
Southern Song	1127–1279
Liao (Khitan)	916–1125
Jin (Jurchen)	1115–1234
Yuan (Mongol)	1279–1368
Ming	1368–1644
Qing (Manchu)	1644–1912
Republic of China	1912–1949
People's Republic of China	1949–

CHRONOLOGICAL LIST OF AUTHORS

Confucius: Kong Qiu 孔丘 (Master Kong: *Kongzi* 孔子, *Kong fuzi* 孔夫子)	ca. 551– ca. 479 BCE
Mencius: Meng Ke 孟克 (Master Meng: *Mengzi* 孟子)	372–289 BCE
Zhuang Zhou 莊周	ca. 369–ca. 286 BCE
Qu Yuan 屈原	?340–278 BCE
Sima Qian 司馬遷	145/135–86 BCE
Ma Dibo 馬第伯	1st century
Zhang Heng 張衡	78–139
Cao Zhi 曹植	192–232
Pan Yue 潘岳 (*zi* Anren 安仁)	247–300
Shi Chong 石崇	249–300
Lu Ji 陸機	261–303
Zuo Fen 左芬	d. ca. 276
Ge Hong 葛洪	283–343
Wang Xizhi 王羲之	309–ca. 365
Xie Daoyun 謝道韞	before 340– after 399
Tao Qian 陶潛 (*zi* Yuanming 淵明)	365–427
Zong Bing 宗炳	375–443
Xie Lingyun 謝靈運	385–433
Dai Kaizhi 戴凱之	5th century
Liu Yiqing 劉義慶	403–444
Tao Hongjing 陶弘景	456–536
Yang Xuanzhi 楊衒之	fl. ca. 550
Lady Hou 侯夫人	7th century
Empress Wu Zetian 武則天	624/627–705
Shangguan Wan'er 上官婉兒	664–710
Wang Wei 王維	699–759
Li Bai 李白	701–762
Du Fu 杜甫	712–770

Pei Di 裴迪	b. 716
Meng Jiao 孟郊	751–814
Wu Yuanheng 武元衡	758–815
Liu Yuxi 劉禹錫	772–742
Bai Juyi 白居易 (*zi* Letian 樂天)	772–846
Liu Zongyuan 柳宗元	773–819
Yuan Zhen 元稹	779–831
Niu Sengru 牛僧孺, Duke Qizhang (*Qizhang wenzhengong* 奇章文貞公)	780–849
Yao He 姚合	781–846
Li Deyu 李德裕, Marquis of Zanhuang (*Zanhuang hou* 贊皇侯)	787–850
Zhang Yaotiao 張窈窕	9th century
Xu Ning 徐凝	fl. 813
Pi Rixiu 皮日休	ca. 834–ca. 883
Wei Zhuang 韋莊	836–910
Lu Guimeng 陸龜蒙 (*hao* Master Who Follows Heaven: *Tiansuizi* 天隨子)	d. 881
Yu Xuanji 魚玄機	844–868
Lin Bu 林逋	967–1028
Hu Su 胡宿	995–1067
Mei Yaochen 梅堯臣	1002–1060
Ouyang Xiu 歐陽修	1007–1072
Su Shunqin 蘇舜欽 (*zi* Zimei 子美)	1008–1048
Fan Zhen 范鎮	1008–1089
Shao Yong 邵雍	1011–1077
Zhou Dunyi 周敦頤	1017–1073
Wen Tong 文同	1018–1079

Sima Guang 司馬光 (*zi* Junshi 君實, *hao* Old Pedant: *Yusou* 迂叟)	1019–1086
Su Song 蘇頌	1020–1101
Shen Gua 沈括	ca. 1031–1095
Su Shi 蘇軾 (*hao* Dongpo 東坡)	1037–1101
Zhu Changwen 朱長文 (*zi* Boyuan 伯原)	1039–1098
Li Gefei 李革非	1045–1106
Ye Mengde 葉夢得	1077–1148
Emperor Huizong (*Song Huizong* 宋徽宗, Zhao Ji 赵佶)	1082–1135; r. 1101–1125
Li Qingzhao 李清照	1084–ca. 1151
Du Wan 杜綰	fl. 1120s
Lu You 陸游	1125–1210
Meng Yuanlao 孟元老	fl. 1126–1147
Fan Chengda 范成大	1126–1193
Jiang Kui 姜夔	ca. 1155–ca. 1221
Zhang Hao 張淏	ca. 1180–1250
Liu Kezhuang 劉克莊	1187–1269
Du Renjie 杜人傑	1201–1282
Wang Yinglin 王應麟	1223–1296
Zhou Mi 周密	1232–1298
Guan Hanqing 關漢卿	ca. 1240–ca. 1320
Guan Daosheng 管道昇	1262–1319
Zhang Kejiu 张可久	1270–1348
Toqto'a (Tuotuo) 脫脫	1314–1356
Zhu Zhongxian 朱仲嫻 (*hao* Jing'an 靜庵)	fl. 1450
Wen Zhengming 文徵明	1470–1559
Chen Deyi 陳德懿	fl. 1476
Gui Youguang 歸有光	1506–1571
Duan Shuqing 端淑卿	ca. 1510–ca. 1600?
Wang Shizhen 王世貞	1526–1590
Pan Yunduan 潘允端	1526–1601

Yuan Huang 袁黃	1533–1606
Chen Suoyun 陳所蘊	1543–1626
Tang Xianzu 湯顯祖	1550–1616
Hu Yinglin 胡應麟	1551–1602
Chen Jiru 陳繼儒	1558–1639
Yuan Hongdao 袁宏道	1568–1610
Wang Siren 王思任	1575–1646
Wang Ruqian 汪如谦 (*zi* Ranming 然明)	1577–1655
Lin Youlin 林有麟	1578–1647
Ji Cheng 計成 (*zi* Wufou 無否, *hao* Negative Daoist: *Fou daoren* 否道人)	1582–ca. 1642
Sun Guomi 孫國秘	1582–1648
Wen Zhenheng 文震亨	1585–1645
Fang Weiyi 方維儀	1585–1668
Ruan Dacheng 阮大鋮	1587–1646
Xu Yuan 徐媛	fl. 1590
Lu Qingzi 陸卿子	fl. 1590s
Wang Shimin 王時敏 (*hao* Yanke 煙客)	1592–1680
Gu Ruopu 顧若璞	1592–ca. 1681
Liu Tong 劉侗	ca.1594–1636
Zhang Cai 張采	1596–1648
Zhang Dai 張岱	1597–ca. 1684
Zhang Qiande 張謙德	fl. 1598
Zheng Yuanxun 鄭元勳	1598–1644
A Scholar of Western Zhou (*Xi Zhou sheng* 西周生)	17th century
Dong Xuan 董玄	17th century
Liu Shilong 劉士龍 (*zi* Yuhua 雨化)	fl. 1603
Qi Biaojia 祁彪佳	1603–1645
Shang Jinglan 商景蘭	1604–ca. 1680
Qian Suyue 錢肅樂	1606–1648

Wu Weiye 吳偉業 (*hao* Meicun 梅村)	1609–1671
Li Yu 李漁 (*hao* Liweng 笠翁; Fisherman of West Lake: *Hushang liweng* 湖上笠翁)	1610 or 1611–1680
Huang Zhouxing 黃周星 (*zi* Jiuyan 九煙)	1611–1680
Liu Shi 柳是 (*zi* Rushi 如是)	1618–1664
You Tong 尤同	1618–1704
Sun Cheng'en 孫承恩	1619–1659
Xu Qianxue 徐乾學	1631–1694
Song Luo 宋犖	1634–1713
Yu Yizheng 于奕正	d. 1635
Fang Yuegong 方岳貢	d. 1644
Ye Hongxiang 葉宏緗	ca. 1636–1725
Gu Zhenli 顧貞立	ca. 1637–ca. 1714
Pu Songling 蒲松齡	1640–1715
Zhang Yushu 張玉書	1642–1711
Zhang Penghe 張鵬翮	1649–1725
Zhang Chao 張潮 (*zi* Shanlai 山來)	b. 1650
Zhang Qiongru 張瓊如	mid-17th century
Dai Mingshi 戴名世	1653–1713
the Kangxi emperor (*Kangxi di* 康熙帝; Aisingioro Xuanye 愛新覺羅玄燁)	1654–1722; r. 1661–1722
the Yongzheng emperor (*Yongzheng di* 雍正帝; Aisingioro Yinzhen 愛新覺儸胤禛)	1678–1735; r. 1722–1735
Qian Fenglun 錢鳳綸	fl. 1680
Zheng Xie 鄭燮 (*hao* Banqiao 板橋)	1693–1765
Sir Harry Beaumont (Joseph Spence)	1699–1768
Wang Hui 王慧	late 17th century
Wu Cunli 吳存禮	fl. 17th–18th century

Jean-Denis Attiret	1702–1768
the Qianlong emperor (*Qianlong di* 乾隆帝; Aisingioro Hongli 愛新覺羅弘曆)	1711–1799; r. 1735–1796
Hou Cheng'en 侯承恩	fl. ca. 1712
Cao Xueqin 曹雪芹	ca. 1715–1763
Yuan Mei 袁枚	1716–1797
Zhao Yi 趙翼	1727–1814
Qian Daxin 錢大昕	1728–1804
Gan Lirou 甘立媃	1743–1819
Zhai Hao 翟灝	fl. 1754
Qian Yong 錢泳	1759–1844
Xi Peilan 席佩蘭	1760–1820?
Shen Fu 沈復	1763–ca. 1810
Jin Yi 金逸	1770–1794
Liang Zhangju 梁章鉅	1775–1849
Linqing 麟慶	1791–1846
Chen Qiqing 陳琪卿	fl. 1796–1820
Gu Taiqing 顧太清	1799–ca. 1876
Li Mingwan 李銘皖	19th century
Feng Guifen 馮桂芬	1809–1874
Robert Fortune	1813–1880
Tang Qingyun 唐慶雲	fl. 1814
Li Dou 李斗	d. 1817
Osmond Tiffany Jr.	1823–1895
Zhang Shusheng 張樹聲	1824–1884
Xu Zihua 徐自華	1873–1935
Qiu Jin 秋瑾	1875–1907
Yan Wenliang 颜文樑	1893–1983
Jiang Hancheng 蔣瀚澄 (*zi* Yinqiu 吟秋)	1897–1981
Gao Guanwu 高冠吾	1905–1957
Ji Yong 紀庸	1909–1965
Qian Dingyi 錢定一	1915–2010
Chen Congzhou 陳從周	1918–2000

GLOSSARY

105s [peonies]: *yibaiwu* 一百五
Abode for Studying the *Book of Changes*: *Duyi ju* 讀易居
Abode of the Sweet Waters: *Shuixiang yi* 水香簃
Abundance Mains: *Fengzhuang* 豐莊
"Account of Flora in Gardens," *Explanations of Garden Plants and Trees*: *Yuanting caomu shu* 園庭草木疏
Account of the River Diagram: *Hetu ji* 河圖記
Achieved Life Terrace: *Dasheng tai* 達生臺
actinidia (? *Actinidia kolomikta*): *jin'ge* 金葛
adytum: *ju* 居
Agate Temple: *Ma'nao si* 瑪瑙寺
Ailanthus Bank: *Zhuyu pan* 茱萸泮
Airing One's Paintings Gallery: *Puhua lang* 曝畫廊
Allegory Garden: *Yu yuan* 寓園
Allegory Mountain: *Yushan* 寓山
Allegory Mountain Thatched Hall: *Yushan caotang* 寓山草堂
All-Regarding Hall: *Sizhao tang* 四照堂
aloes-wood (*Aquilaria sinensis*): *chenshui* [*xiang*] 沉水 [香]
Although Provided: *Suishe* 雖設
amaranth (*Amarantus tricolor*): *laoshaonian* 老少年
Amassed Jade: *Jiyu* 積玉
Amassed Snow Precipice: *Jixueling* 積雪嶺
Amid the Wild Rice and Bulrushes: *Gulu zhong* 菰蘆中
A-mi-tuo-fo (Amitābha): 阿弥陀佛
Among the Flowers and Birds: *Huaniao jian* 花鳥間
Among the Stalks: *Jiazhu* 夾竹
Ancient and Upright: *Gulian feng* 古廉峰
Ancient Vines and Waterside Gazebo: *Guteng shuixie* 古藤水榭
"An Explanation of the Garden of the Master of the Fishing Nets": *Wangshi yuan shuo* 網師園說

angelica: *zhi* 芷
Angling Jetty: *Diaoji* 釣磯
An Tao: 安燾
Anyuan Gate: *Anyuan men* 安遠門
Apparently Arrogant: *Siao* 似傲
apple (? *Malus prunifolia*): *laiqin* 來禽
Approaching Clouds: *Yun jiang* 雲將
Approaching-in-Flight-Peak, Flew-Here Peak, Flew Here Peak, Flew-Here Rock: *Feilai feng* 飛來峰
apricot (*Prunus armeniaca*): *xing* 杏
Apricot Blossom Ridge: *Xinghua gang* 杏花岡
Apricot-Mouth: *Xingzui* 杏嘴
Apricot Tor: *Xingxiu* 杏岫
Apricot Village: *Xinghua cun* 杏花村
aquatic grass, duckweed, Eurasian watermilfoil (*Lemna* sp.): *zao* 藻, *shuizao* 水藻
Arabian jasmine, Indian jasmine (*Jasminum sambac*): *moli* 茉莉
aranya: *lanruo* 蘭若
arborvitae: see false cypress
arbutus (*Myrica rubra*): *yangmei* 楊梅
Archery Target: *Shedi* 射的
Arhat Cliff: *Luohan yan* 羅漢岩
Arrayed-in-the-Clouds and Reaching-to-the-Dipper: *Paiyun chongdou* 排雲沖斗
Arrayed Rows: *Paiya* 排衙
Arriving Jade Belvedere: *Laiyu ge* 來玉閣
arrow bamboo (*Fargesia* sp.): *jianzhu* 箭竹
Arrowroot Lodge: *Ouhua ju* 藕花居
artemisia, mugwort (*Artemisia argyi*): *pinliao* 蘋蓼, *ai* 艾
artificial mountain: *jiashan* 假山
Ascendant Dragon of the Dawning Sun: *Zhaori shenglong* 朝日升龍
Assembled Splendors: *Cuisheng* 萃勝
Assembled Splendors Bridge: *Cuisheng qiao* 萃勝橋
Assembly Garden: *Jiyuan* 集園
Assorted Notes from Youyang, Youyang Miscellany: *Youyang zazu* 酉陽襍俎
Asymmetrical Room: *Qufang* 曲房

Asymmetric Pond: *Quzhao* 曲沼
Attendant: *Shier* 侍兒
autumnal moon reflected in a calm lake: *pinghu qiuyue* 平湖秋月
Autumn Snow Hermitage: *Qiuxue an* 秋雪庵
Avoiding Society: *Xijiao* 息交
axe-cut: *cun* 皴
Axe-Haft Garden: *Keyuan* 柯園
azalea (*Rhododendron* sp.): *dujuan* 杜鵑
Azure Clouds Over Deep Recesses: *Biyun shenchu* 碧雲深處
Azure Flower Brocade-Border lotus: *bitai jinbian lian* 碧臺錦遍蓮
Azure Lad: *Qingtong* 青童
Azure Wrinkles: *Bizhou* 碧皺

Ba Bridge: *Baqiao* 灞橋
baby official: *wawa guan* 娃娃官
bailian vine (*Ampelopsis japonica*): *bailian* 白斂
Bai Xingjian: 白行簡
Balance Dyke: *Hengtang* 橫塘
ballad: see yuefu
Ball cassia (*Osmanthus* sp.): *qiuzi muxi* 球子木樨
Ballista Rock Bridge: *Paoshi qiao* 砲石橋
bamboo (*Bambuseae*): *zhu* 竹
Bamboo at Water's Edge: *Linyu shi* 林於溠
Bamboo Belvedere: *Zhuge* 竹閣
Bamboo Branch Beyond: *Zhuwai yizhi* 竹外一枝
Bamboo Bridge: *Zhuqiao* 竹橋
Bamboo Cloister: *Zhuzi yuan* 竹子院
Bamboo District Lodge: *Zhuli guan* 竹里館
Bamboo Garden of the Marquis of Wuding: *Wuding hou Zhuyuan* 武定侯竹園
Bamboo Grove: *Xiangyun wu* 湘篔塢
Bamboo Harbor: *Zhuwu* 竹塢
Bamboo Path: *Zhujing* 竹徑
Bamboo Pavilion: *Xieyun* 榭篔
Bamboo Pavilion: *Zhuting* 竹亭
Bamboo Sheath Den: *Yunchao* 筠巢

Bamboos of Exquisite Delicacy: *Zhulinglong* 竹玲瓏

banana, plantain (*Musa basjoo*): *bajiao* 芭蕉

Banana Garden Poetry Club: *Jiaoyuan shishe* 蕉園詩社

Banana Grove: *Bajiao lin* 芭蕉林

banana shrub, magnolia (*Michelia figo, Magnolia figo*): *hanxiao* 含笑

Bank of Refined Waters: *Wenshui po* 文水陂

banksia rose, clambering rose, multi-flora rose, rambler rose, rambling rose (*Rosa multiflora* or *Rosa banksiae*): *qiangwei* 薔薇, *baoxiang* 寶襄, or *muxiang* 木香

Bao Family Garden: *Baoyuan* 包園

Bao Yingdeng: 包應登 (*zi* Hansuo 涵所)

Bao's Northern Estate: *Baoshi beizhuang* 包氏北莊

Bare Minimum: *Shiyou* 始有

Barge of Tranquility: *Dingfang* 定舫

basis of the state: *guoben* 國本

Battling Fish Heap: *Zhanyu dun* 戰魚墩

Beach Pillowed on the Current: *Zhenliu tan* 枕流灘

beans (*Fabaceae*): *dou* 豆

Bearded Liu Shisan: *Liu shisan huzi* 劉式三胡子

Beating Pinions Pond: *Fenhe chi* 奮翮池

Beautiful Maiden Rock: *Meiren shi* 美人石

Beauty of Yu poppy (*Papaver rhoeas*): *Yu meiren* 虞美人

Before Spring Pavilion: *Xianchun ting* 先春亭

begonia (*Begonia grandis* subsp. *evansiana*): *qiuhaitang* 秋海棠, sometimes *haitang* 海棠

belvedere: *ge* 閣

Belvedere of Broad Observation, Tower of Broad Observation: *Kuangguan lou* 曠觀樓

Belvedere of Pure Intimacy: *Qingmi ge* 清閟閣

Belvedere of the Jade Transcendent: *Yuxian guan* 玉仙觀

Belvedere of the Love of Solitude: *Meiyou ge* 媚幽閣

Belvedere of the Mountaintop Flower: *Yanhua ge* 巚花閣

Belvedere of the Sun, Sun's Belvedere, Sunrise Vista: *Riguan* 日觀

Belvedere Which Leans on Mount Songluo: *Pingluo ge* 憑蘿閣

Benevolence and Longevity Hill: *Renshou shan* 仁壽山

Bestriding Clouds Kiosk: *Kuayun* 跨雲

betel-nut, betel-nut palm (*Areca catechu*): *binglang* 檳榔

betel pepper, betel vine (*Piper betle* or *Chavica betle* [L.] Miq.): *ju* 蒟

Bewitching Spring Poetic Society: *Yechun shishe* 冶春詩社

big-leaf magnolia (*Magnolia officinalis*): *houpu* 厚朴

"Big Red" pearl camellia (*Camellia reticulata*): *dahong baozhu cha* 大紅寶珠茶

Big Red tree peony: *dahong mudan* 大紅牡丹

Bin Potager: *Binpu* 豳圃

birchleaf pear (*Pyrus betulaefolia*): *tangli* 棠梨

Bird's Paradise: *Laiqin you* 來禽囿

birthwort (*Aristolochia* sp.): *hengwu* 蘅蕪

Bit of Paradise in the Human World: *Renjing hutian* 人境壺天

bitterpeel tangerine, sourpeel tangerine (*Citrus × aurantium, Citrus deliciosa*): *ju* 橘

Bixia Palace: *Bixia gong* 碧霞宮

Black Cloud Pile: *Heiyun dui* 黑雲堆

blessed realms: *fudi* 福地

Blue Cloud Cliff: *Qingyun yan* 青雲岩

blue crown passion-flower (*Passiflora caerulea*): *xifanlian* 西番蓮

blue lily (*Lilium* sp.): *bi baihe* 碧百合

Blue Lotus Mountain Hut: *Qinglian shanfang* 青蓮山房

blue-white Chinese trumpet (*Campsis grandiflora*): *qingbai ziwei* 青白紫薇

Boat House: *Fangwu* 舫屋

Boat Mooring Pavilion: *Lanzhou ting* 纜舟亭

Book of Changes: see *Yijing*

Bookroom of the Four Delights: *Siyi shuwu* 四宜書屋

Border Pavilion: *Jiege* 介閣

Borrowed Fragrance: *Jiefen* 借芬

borrowing: *jie* 借

Borrowing Borrowing: *Jiejie* 借借

borrowing of scenery: *jiejing* 借景

Bottle Hermitage: *Huyin* 壺隱

Bouquet of Jade: *Yunyu* 蘊玉

bow: *gong* 弓

bower: *ting* 亭

Bower Adjoining the Rock: *Yiyu xuan* 倚玉軒

Bower for Awaiting the Frost: *Daishuang ting* 待霜亭

Bower of Delicious Fruits: *Jiashi ting* 嘉實亭

Bower of Fragrance: *Fanxiang wu* 繁香塢

Bower of Nature: *Dezhen ting* 得真亭

boxthorn (*Lycium chinense*): *qi* 杞

Boxwood Stack: *Huangyang yan* 黃楊巘

boxwood tree, little-leaf boxwood (*Buxus sinica*): *huangyang* 黃楊

bramble (*Rubus* sp.): *ji* 棘

Break-Off Bridge: *Duan qiao* 斷橋

Breeze Among the Lotuses of Winding Courtyard: *quyuan fenghe* 曲院風荷

Bridal Du: Du Liniang 杜麗娘

Bridge Across the Ford: *Tongjin qiao* 通津橋

Bridge of Minimal Possession: *Xiaoyou qiao* 小有橋

Bridge of Tasseled Clouds: *Yingyun qiao* 纓雲橋

Bridge of Transformation into an Immortal Feathered Being: *Yuhua qiao* 羽化橋

"bright" flowering apricots (*Prunus* sp.): *piaomei* 縹梅

Bright Jade: *Mingyu* 明玉

Brightness of Dawn: *Zhaowei* 朝微

Brilliant Enlightenment Terrace: *Langwu tai* 朗悟臺

Broad Heart Pond: *Guangxin chi* 廣心池

Broad Terrace: *Guangtai* 廣臺

Brocade Belt Bridge: *Jindai qiao* 錦帶橋

Brocade Cloud Screen: *Jinyun ping* 錦雲屏

Brocade Hall: *Jinting* 錦廳

Brocade River rock, Jinchuan rock: *Jinchuan shi* 錦川石

Brook Pavilion of the Auspicious Plants: *Ruicao xiting* 瑞草溪亭

Buddha chamber: *foge* 佛閣

bulrush (*Scirpus tabernaemontani*): *guan* 莞

Butterfly Retreat: *Die'an* 蝶庵

Cai Jing: 蔡京 (Duke of Lu: *Luguo gong* 魯國公)

calamus (*Acorus calamus*): *pu* 蒲

Calling Birds Lodge: *Yingming guan* 嚶鳴館

caltrop, prickly water lily (*Euryale ferox*): *qian* 芡

Calyx Ledge Tower: *Gaielou* 陔萼樓

Camelhump Arch: *Luotuo hong* 駱駝虹

camellia (*Camellia* sp.): *shancha* 山茶

camphor tree (*Cinnamomum camphora*): *zhang* 樟

Cang Jie's Terrace: *Cang tai* 創臺

Canglang Pavilion, Surging Waves Pavilion: *Canglang ting* 滄浪亭

Canopy of the Inhaling Rainbow: *Huhong huang* 呼虹幌

canton orange, citrus, orange (*Citrus × sinensis, Citrus × aurantium*): *cheng* 橙

Cao Cao: 曹操

Cao Lüji: 曹履吉 (*zi* Yuanfu 元甫)

Cao Pi: 曹丕

Cao Yin: 曹寅

Carefree Chamber: *Rongyu shi* 容與室

Caressing the Waters Garden: *Fushui yuan* 拂水園

Carpeted by Jade: *Yuyin tang* 玉茵堂

Carving of Chu: *Chuzhuo* 楚琢

Cascade Screen: *Pubu ping* 瀑布屏

cassia, osmanthus (*Osmanthus fragrans*): *gui* 桂

Cassia Blossom Screen: *Guihua ping* 桂花屏

Cassia Dew Mountain Dwelling: *Guilu shanfang* 桂露山房

Cassia Fragrance Pavilion: *Guixiang ting* 桂香亭

Cassia Grove Pavilion: *Congguiting* 叢桂亭

Cassia Hall: *Guitang* 桂堂

Cassia Ridge: *Guiling* 桂嶺

Cassia Tower: *Guihua lou* 桂花樓

Castanet Whites: *Yuban bai* 玉板白

Castiglione, Giuseppe: Lang Shining 郎世寧

catalpa (*Catalpa bungei*): *qiu* 萩, *lingqiu* 靈楸

Catalpa Marsh: *Zize* 梓澤

cattail (*Typha latifolia*): *ruo* 蒻

cave: *dong* 洞

Cave for Perceiving Vacancy: *Guankong dong* 觀空洞

cave-heaven, cavern-heaven: *dongtian* 洞天

Cave Hill: *Dongshan* 洞山

Cave of Lingering Spring: *Liuchun wo* 留春窩

Cavernous Building: *Aowu* 奧屋

Cave Spirit Temple: *Dongling miao* 洞靈廟

celery (*Apium graveolens*): *qin* 芹

Celestial Bones: *Tiangu* 天骨

Celestial Flowers Altar: *Tianhua tan* 天花壇

Celestial Gate, Heaven's Gate: *Tianmen* 天門

Celestial Immortal of the Eastern Marchmount Taishan, the Jade Lady Primal Sovereign of the Azure Clouds: *Dongyue Taishan Tianxian Yunü Bixia Yuanjun* 东岳泰山天仙玉女碧霞元君

Celestial Mirror Pool: *Tianjing tan* 天鏡潭

Celestial Pass: *Tianguan* 天關

Celestial Waves Gate: *Jinbo men* 金波門

Central Marchmount Mount Song: *Zhongyue Songshan* 中嶽嵩山

Central Peak: *Zhongfeng* 中峰

Central Street: *Zhongxing jie* 中行街

Central Yanshan: *Zhongyan* 中弇

Ceremonial Phoenix: *Yifeng* 儀鳳

Chamber for Smelling the Subtle Fragrance: *Wenmiaoxiang shi* 聞妙香室

Chamber for Storing the Sutras: *Cangjing ge* 藏經閣

Chamber of Brahma's Voice: *Fanyin ge* 梵音閣

Chamber of Simplicity: *Yueshi* 約室

Chamber of the Rain of Flowers: *Yuhua shi* 雨花室

Chang Dai-chien (Zhang Daqian): 張大千

"Changing Dwelling Places": *Qian ju* 遷居

Changle Palace: *Changle gong* 長樂宮

Chao Duanyan: 晁端彥 (*zi* Meishu 美叔)

Chaoyang Cave: *Chaoyang dong* 朝陽洞

Chao Yuan: 晁源

Chen Bangzhi: 陳邦直 (Old Man of the Simple Pavilion: *Yuting laoren* 愚亭老人)

Chen Jingji: 陳敬濟

Chen Yuanlong: 陳元龍

Chen Yujiao: 陳與郊

Chen Yun: 陳芸

Chen Zhilin: 陳之遴

Cheng Zhiquan: 程志銓 (*zi* Yuanheng 元恆)

cherry (*Prunus pseudocerasus*): *yingtao* 櫻桃

cherry apple (*Malus × micromalus*): *haitang* 海棠

Cherry Bank: *Hantao wu* 含桃塢

Cherry Tree Grove: *Yingtao lin* 櫻桃林

Chess-Board Rock: *Jipan shi* 碁盤石

chestnut (*Castanea mollissima*): *li* 栗

chestnut-leaved oak (*Quercus serrata*): *qingli* 青櫪

chi (a Chinese foot, approximately 30 cm): 尺

Chill Jade bamboo (*Bambuseae*): *hanyu zhu* 寒玉竹

Chiming Jade Ravine: *Qingyu xia* 磬玉峽

Chinese chess, encirclement chess, Go: *weiqi* 圍棋

Chinese fir (*Cunninghamia lanceolata*): *shan* 杉

Chinese juniper, common juniper (*Juniperus chinensis* or *Sabina chinensis*): *gui* 檜, *gua* 栝, *guigua* 檜栝

Chinese oak (*Quercus dentata*): *zuo* 柞

Chinese sweetflag (*Acorus calamus*): *changpu* 菖蒲; see also calamus

Chinese trumpet creeper (*Campsis grandiflora*): *zhaohua* 蕏華, *lingxiao* 凌霄

chou (second of the twelve Earthly Branches): 丑

chrysanthemum (*Chrysanthemum hortorum* or *Chrysanthemum sinensis*): *ju* 菊

Chrysanthemum Path: *Jujing* 菊徑

Chrysanthemum River: *Jushui* 菊水

Chun Qing: 春慶 (*zi* Fuyuan 馥園)

Chunyang Pavilion: *Chunyang ge* 純陽閣

ci (lyric poem, lyric poetry): 詞

ci jun (this gentleman, bamboo): 此君

Cinnabar Reds [peonies]: *Zhusha hong* 珠砂紅

Cinnabar Tumulus Bank (*Danling pan* 丹陵沜

cinnamon (*Cinnamomum cassia* [L.] J.Presl): *dugui* 牡桂

Circle Path: *Huandao* 環道

citrus: see canton orange

City Belt Bridge: *Daicheng qiao* 帶城橋

City Forest: *Chengshi shanlin* 城市山林

Clacking Clogs Walkway: *Zhenxie lang* 振屧廊

clambering rose: see banksia rose

Clarity Cherishing Villa: *Hanqing bieshu* 含清別墅

Classic of Wood: Mu jing 木經

Clean Retreated Bower: *Jingshen ting* 淨深亭

Clear Intentions: *Mingzhi* 明志

Clearness of the Western Hills: *Xishuang* 西爽

Clear Ripples with Layers of Greenery: *Chengbo diecui* 澄波叠翠

Clear Scene Pavilion: *Shujing ting* 淑景亭

Clear Shade Hall: *Qingyin tang* 清陰堂

Clear Voice Palisade: *Qingyin shan* 清音柵

Clear Waves Causeway: *Qingbo liang* 清波梁

Clear Waves Gate: *Qingbo men* 清波門

cliff: *yan* 岩

Cliff of Purple Rocks: *Zishi yan* 紫石巖

Cliff of Unique Loveliness and Grand Tranquillity in the Jade Capital: *Yujing duxiu taiping yan* 玉京獨秀太平岩

climbing fig (*Ficus pumila*): *bi [li]* 薜 [荔]

Close to the Sun: *Ri jiu* 日就

Cloud Forest's Secret Belvedere: *Yunlin mige* 雲林秘閣

Cloud Root Cliff: *Yungen zhang* 雲根嶂

Cloudy Billow Kiosk: *Yunlang* 雲浪

Cloudy Region: *Yunqu* 雲區

Clustered Jade: *Congyu* 叢玉

Clustered Loveliness: *Congxiu* 叢秀

cockscomb (*Celosia cristata*): *jiguan* 雞冠

coffee senna (*Cassia occidentalis*): *wang Jiangnan* 望江南

Coiling Garden: *Panyuan* 盤園

Coiling Loveliness Kiosk: *Panxiu* 蟠秀

Coiling Stream: *Wanyanjian* 蜿蜒澗

Cold Cloud Rock: *Lengyun shi* 冷雲石

Cold Fragrance lotus: *lengxiang furong* 冷香芙蓉

Cold Light: *Hanguang* 寒光

Cold Spring Pavilion: *Lengquan ting* 冷泉亭

Collecting Fragrance Path: *Caifang jing* 采芳徑

Color-Enhanced Reds [peonies]: *Tianse hong* 添色紅

Colorful Painting of Cloudy Mountains: *Yunshan yanhua* 雲山罨畫

Combined Expansiveness Belvedere: *Xianchang ge* 咸暢閣

Commander in Chief Miao's Garden: *Miaoshuai yuan* 苗帥園

Commoner's Garden: *Shuren yuan* 庶人園

Common (or River) Flowering Apricot (*Prunus* sp.): *changmei* 常梅

common hibiscus (*Hibiscus syriacus*): *mujin* 木槿

common juniper: see Chinese juniper

common reed: see reed

Compound of the King of Heaven: *Tianwang yuan* 天王院

Compound of the Way: *Daoyuan* 道院

Comprehensive Gazetteer of the Great Qing Empire: Da Qing yitongzhi 大清一統志

Comprehensive Mirror for the Aid of Government: Zizhi tongjian 資治通鑒

Concentrated Observation: *Ningguan* 凝觀

Congealed Fragrance chamber: *Ningxiang shi* 凝香室

Conning Tower: *Bikui* 蔽窺

Containing Green Pavilion: *Hanbi ting* 涵碧亭

Controlling the Channel: *Yinlou* 尹漊

Convent of the Garland Sutra: *Huayan an* 華嚴庵

Cool Breeze: *Liangfeng* 涼風

Cool Breeze Hall: *Liangfeng tang* 涼風堂

Cool Breeze Terrace: *Lengfeng tai* 冷風臺

Cool Veranda: *Liangxie* 涼榭

Corner Garden: *Yuyuan* 隅園

Cottage of the Jade Hook: *Yugou caotang* 玉勾草堂

cottonwood hibiscus (*Hibiscus tiliaceus*): *huangjin* 黃槿

Courtyard Communicating with the Mysteries: *Xuantong yuan* 玄通院

Courtyard of Fine Trees: *Jiashu ting* 嘉樹庭

Courtyard of Moderation: *Dufang* 度坊

Cowering Rhinoceros: *Fuxi* 伏犀

Coxcomb: *Jiguan* 雞冠

crabapple, flowering apple, flowering crabapple (*Malus spectabilis* or *Malus prunifolia*): *haitang* 海棠, sometimes *tang* 棠

Crab's Pincer Peak: *Xie'ao feng* 蟹螯峰

Crane Isle: *Heyu* 鶴嶼

Crane-Neck Reds [peonies]: *Heling hong* 鶴翎紅

Crane Releasing Pavilion: *Fanghe ting* 放鶴亭

Crane's Nest: *Hechao* 鶴巢

creeper: *man* 蔓, *teng* 藤

creeping fig (*Ficus pumila*): *bili* 薜荔; see also climbing fig

crepe-myrtle (*Lagerstroemia indica*): *ziwei* 紫薇

Crescent Moon Dike: *Yuepo di* 月陂堤

Crest of the Wave: *Lingbo* 凌波

Crisp Air of the Western Mountains: *Xishan shuangqi xuan* 西山爽氣軒

Crossing of Hewn Trees: *Chaya du* 槎枒渡

Crowning Fragrance white peony: *guanqunfang shaoyao* 冠群芳芍藥

Crystallized Emerald Gallery: *Ningbi xuan* 凝碧軒

Crystal Spring: *Yuquan* 玉泉

cucumber (*Cucurbitaceae*): *gua* 瓜

Culminate Vision: *Jimu* 極目

Cultivated Talent: *xiucai* 秀才

cun (Chinese inch, approximately 3 cm): 寸

curving chestnut (*Castanea* sp.): *goulimu* 勾栗木

Cut Floss chrysanthemum: *jianrong ju* 剪絨菊

Cut Jade: *Zhuoyu* 琢玉

Cyan Vacuity Grotto-Heavens: *Bixu dongtian* 碧虛洞天

cypress (*Cupressus* sp.): *bo* 柏 or 栢

Cypress Gate: *Bomen* 柏門

Cypress of Han: *Han bo* 漢柏

Cypress Screen: *Songbo ping* 松柏屏

Dagui: 達桂

Daily Visit Garden: *Rishe yuan* 日涉園

Dai miao (Temple of Dai): 岱廟

Daizong: see Mount Tai

Dallying with Water Gallery: *Nongshui xuan* 弄水軒

Damask Snow Pavilion: *Yixue ting* 綺雪亭

Dancing Green Lion tree peony: *wu qingni mudan* 舞青猊牡丹

Dancing Sylph: *Wuxian* 舞仙

Dan County Flowers [peonies]: *Danzhou hua* 丹州花

Dan County Reds [peonies]: *Danzhou hong* 丹州紅

Daode jing (*Classic of the Way and Its Power*): 道德經

daoxue (study of the Way): 道學

Dark Jade: *Cangyu* 蒼玉

Dark Jade Bamboo-Shoot: *Qingyu sun* 青玉筍

Dark Point: *Qingqiao* 青峭

Dark River: *Chanshui* 瀍水

date, jujube: *Ziziphus jujuba*: *zao* 棗, *longgu* 龍骨; *Ziziphus jujuba* var. *spinosa*: *jizhen* 棘針

date with yellow pith (*Akebia* sp.): *huangxin [muxian] zi* 黃心[木先]子

day-lily (*Hemerocallis fulva*): *xuan* 萱

de (virtue, power, moral force): 德

decorated walkway: *xiulang* 修廊

Deep Bamboos and Pure Lotuses: *Zhushen hejing* 竹深荷淨

Deep Mirror: *Yuanying* 淵映

Deep Red Double-Flower pomegranate (*Punica granatum*): *shenhong chongtai liu* 深紅重臺榴

Deep-Red Peaches (*Prunus persica* [L.] Batsch. f. *magnifica* C.K.Schneid.): *Feitao* 緋桃

Deer Enclosure: *Luchai* 鹿柴

Deer Park Stream: *Michang jing* 麋場涇

Delusive Realization Grotto: *Mizhen dong* 迷真洞

Dengfeng Gate: *Dengfeng men* 登封門

denudation or erosion (trigram): *bo* 剝

Depth of Spring on the Flowering Apricot Peak: *Meiling chunshen* 梅嶺春深

Determination to Retire Studio: *Zhigui zhai* 志歸齋

Dew Terrace: *Lu tai* 露臺

Dewy Orchids: *Lanfeng huilu* 蘭風蕙露

dharma: *fa* 法

Dharma Dock: *Fafu* 法埠

Dharmalaksana Temple: *Faxiang si* 法相寺

Dhyana Wisdom Monastery: *Chanzhi si* 禪智寺

Diffuse Felicity: *Fuqing* 敷慶

Dilettante: *Wanke feng* 翫客峰

Dispelling Mockery Pavilion: *Jiechao ting* 解嘲亭

Distant Belvedere: *Yuange* 遠閣

Distant Heart: *xinyuan* 心遠

Distant-View Pavilion: *Yuanting* 遠亭

Divided Splendor Pavilion: *Fensheng ting* 分勝亭

Divine Conveyance: *Shenyun* 神運

Di Xichen: 狄希陳

Divinely Transported Rock: *Shenyun shi* 神運石

Documents Lodge: *Shuguan* 書館

Do Garden: *Jiu yuan* 就園

Dogwood Bay: *Zhuyu wan* 茱萸灣

Dongling Bridge: *Dongling qiao* 東泠橋

Dong Qichang: 董其昌

Dongting rocks: *Dongting shi* 洞庭石

Dongting Temple: *Dongting junci* 洞庭君祠

double-flowered hibiscus (*Hibiscus mutabilis*): *tongxin mu furong* 同心木芙蓉

double-flowered rambler rose (*Rosa* sp.): *chongtai qiangwei* 重臺薔薇

double-leaf flowering apricot (? *Prunus triloba*): *chongye mei* 重葉梅

double-pace, pace (measurement of length, approximately 2 yards): *bu* 步

Double Mountain: *Jianshan* 兼山

Draconic Cypress Slope: *Longbo bei* 龍柏陂

Dragon Gate: *Longmen* 龍門

dragon juniper (*Juniperus chinensis* 'kaizuka'): *longbo* 龍柏

Dragon King Hall: *Longwang tang* 龍王堂

Dragon Lord's Temple: *Longbo ci* 龍伯祠

dragon's brain camphor (*Dipterocarpus* sp.): *longnao [xiang]* 龍腦 [香]

Dragon Well: *Longjing* 龍井

Dragon Well Temple: *Longjing si* 龍井寺

Drawing Forth Beauty: *Yixiu ting* 挹秀亭

Dream of Red Mansions or *Dream of the Red Chamber*: *Hong lou meng* 紅樓夢

Dream Stream Brush Talks: *Mengxi bitan* 夢溪筆談

Dream Stream Garden: *Mengxi yuan* 夢溪園

Dreamy Tower, Pavilion for Dreaming of Retirement: *Mengyin lou* 夢隱樓

Drenched Blossoms: *Qinfang* 沁芳

Drenched Blossoms Weir: *Qinfang zha* 沁芳閘

Drenched Eyebrow's Prominence: *Meirong* 湄榮

Drinking to Antiquity Studio: *Zhuogu zhai* 酌古齋

Dripping Halcyon Cliff: *Dicui yan* 滴翠岩

drupe [fruit]: *yihe* 遺核

Duan Chengshi: 段成式

duck-feet tree (*Ginkgo biloba*): *yajiao* 鴨腳, *yinxing* 銀杏

duckweed: see aquatic grass

Duiyu bian: 對雨編

Duke of Wei's Western Plot: *Weigong xipu* 魏公西圃

Duke Wei: see Xu Da

duren (people of the capital): 都人

dwarf-bamboo (*Poaceae*): *huang* 篁

dwarf cockscomb (*Celosia argentea*): *ai jiguan* 矮雞冠

dwarf pine-trees (*Pinus* sp.): *aisong* 矮松

Dwelling of Negative Nothingness: *Wuwu ju* 無無居

Dwelling of Thatch Fragrance and Crimson Snow: *Maoxiang jiangxue* 茅香絳雪

Early Flowering Apricot (*Prunus* sp.): *zaomei* 早梅

Early Moonlight Pavilion: *Xianyue ting* 先月亭

Early Yellow cassia (*Osmanthus* sp.): *zaohuang muxi* 早黃木樨

Earth and Bamboo Grotto: *Tuyun dong* 土筠洞

Earthen Bamboo: *Tuyun* 土筠

Earthly Branches: *dizhi* 地支

Eastern Field: *Dongzi* 東菑

Eastern Gulf: *Dongming* 東溟

Eastern Imperial Garden: *Dong yuyuan* 東禦苑

Eastern Marchmount Mount Tai: *Dongyue Taishan* 東嶽泰山

Eastern Mound: *Dong qiu* 東丘

Eastern Mountain: *Dongshan* 東山

Eastern Wall: *Dongbi* 東壁

Eastern Yanshan: *Dongyan* 東弇

East Garden: *Dongyuan* 東園

East Garden of the Fourth Embroidered Uniform Guard Commander Xu Jixun: *Si jinyi dongyuan* 四錦衣東園

East Tower: *Donglou* 東樓

Easy-Going Vegetable Plot: *Yipu* 逸圃

Eight Diagrams: *bagua* 八卦

Eight Eccentrics of Yangzhou: *Yangzhou baguai* 揚州八怪

Eight Immortals Lodge: *Baxian guan* 八仙館

Elegant Hermitage Mountain Hut: *Anxiu shanfang* 庵秀山房

Elegant Peak: *Yaotiao feng* 窈窕峰

Elegant Screen Rock: *Qiping shi* 綺屏石

Elevated Person, Provincial Graduate: *juren* 舉人

elm (*Ulmus parvifolia*): *yu* 榆

Embodiment of Flowers Pavilion: *Hanying ge* 含英閣

Embouching the Sun and Spewing the Moon: *Xianri tuyue* 銜日吐月

Embracing Calves Heavenly Gate: *Baodu tianmen* 抱犢天門

Embroidered Mountain Ranges: *Xiu ling* 繡嶺

Embroidery Hill: *Jinzhang* 錦嶂

Emerald Forest Residence: *Bilin yu* 碧林宇

Emerald-Green Exquisite Delicacy: *Cuilinglong* 翠玲瓏

Emerald Heights: *Diecui* 叠翠

Emerald Waves: *Bilang* 碧浪

Emerging Stars Shallows: *Tuxing lai* 突星瀨

emotion: *qing* 情

Emperor Jianwen of Liang: *Liang Jianwen di* 梁簡文帝

Emperor Lord of Mount Tai: see Great Lord of the Eastern Marchmount

Emptiness Gathered: *Jixu* 集虛

Empty Sky Hill Gazebo: *Kongcui shanting* 空翠山亭

Empty Window for Observing the Mountain: *Guanshan xuchuang* 觀山虛窗

Encircling Bridge: *Huanqiao* 環橋

Encircling Greenness: *Huanbi* 環碧

Encircling Stream: *Huanxi* 環溪

Engraved and Cut, Whole and Complete: *Diaozhuo huncheng* 雕琢渾成

Engraved Rock: *Mingshi* 銘石

Enjoying Friendship Study: *Shangyou zhai* 尚友齋

Enjoying the Moon Terrace: *Wanyuetai* 玩月臺

Enjoyment of Spring Kiosk: *Shangchun ting* 賞春亭

Epang Palace: *Epang gong* 阿房宮

Erected Stone: *Li shi* 立石

Eurasian watermilfoil: see aquatic grass

Evening Bell Tolls upon South Screen Mountain: *Nanping wanzhong* 南屏晚鐘

Explanations of Garden Plants and Trees: see "Account of Flora in Gardens"

Exquisite Jade: *Linglong yu* 玲瓏玉

Extreme Simplicity: *Taipu* 太樸

Facing the Wall Adytum: *Mianbi jing* 面壁靖

Facing the Wall Cliff: *Mianbiyan* 面壁巖

fagara (*Zanthoxylum piperitum*): *jiao* 椒

Fagara Steep: *Jiaoyai* 椒崖

Fairy Lodge in Eternal Spring: *Changchun xianguan* 長春仙館

false cypress, arborvitae (*Platycladus orientalis*): *cebo* 側柏

Family Garden of the Third Embroidered Uniform Guard Commander: *San jinyi jiayuan* 三錦衣家園

Fan Laizong: 范來宗

Fangzhang: 方丈

farm: *zhuang* 莊

Fah-tee, Fa-tee, Fa-ti (Garden, Nurseries): *Huadi* 花地

Female Rainbow: *Cini* 雌霓

fen (one-tenth of a *cun* or Chinese inch, approximately 0.3 cm): 分

feng [sacrifice]: *feng* 封

Fengdu Palace: *Fengdu gong* 酆都宮

fengliu (romantic): 風流

Feng Pu: 馮溥

Feng Quan: 馮銓 (*hao* Zhuolu 涿鹿)

fifth-rank counsellor: see Grandee of the Fifth Order

fine: *xiu* 秀

Fine Bamboo Mountain Range: *Jinzhu ling* 斤竹嶺

Finely Planned Garden: *Jiayou* [*yuan*] 嘉猷 [園]

Fine Tree Pavilion: *Jiashu ting* 嘉樹亭

fir (*Abies* sp.): *cong* 樅

First Heavenly Gate: *Yitian men* 一天門

First Emperor of Qin: *Qin Shihuangdi* 秦始皇帝

Fisherman's Retreat: *Yuyin* 漁隱

Fishing Hut: *Diaoyu an* 釣魚庵

Fishing Islet: *Diaozhu* 釣渚

Fishing Rock: *Diaogong* 釣砮

Fishing Spit: *Diaozhu* 釣渚

Fishing Studio: *Yu xuan* 魚軒

Five Ancients Peaks: *Wulao feng* 五老峰

Five-Carts Stone: *Wuche shi* 五車石

Five Clouds Mountain: *Wuyun shan* 五雲山

Five Elders Peaks: see Five Ancients Peaks

Five Marchmounts: *wuyue* 五嶽

five-stamen tamarisk (*Tamarix chinensis*): *chengliu* 檉柳

Fixed Boat: *Dingfang* 定舫

Flat-Headed Purples [peonies]: *Pingtou zi* 平頭紫

Flatiron Cave: *Yundoudong* 熨斗洞

flax (*Linum* sp.): *ma* 麻

Flew Here Peak, Flew-Here Peak, Flew-Here Rock: see Approaching-in-Flight-Peak

Flirting with the Clouds: *Douyun feng* 逗雲峰

Floating Blue: *Fuqing* 浮青

Floating Cups: *Liubei* 流杯

floating-heart (*Nymphoides* sp.): *xing* 荇

Floating Hermitage: *Yongan* 泳庵

Floating Home: *Fujia* 浮家

Floating Solarity: *Fuyang* 浮陽

Flock of Swans Pavilion: *Equn ge* 鵝群閣

Florescent Solarity Palace: *Huayang gong* 華陽宮

Flower and Rock Network: *Huashi gang* 花石綱

flower garden: *huayuan* 花院

Flower Garden in the Compound of the King of Heaven: *Tianwangyuan huayuanzi* 天王院花園子

flowering apple: see crabapple

flowering apricot, winter-flowering prunus (*Prunus mume*): *mei* 梅

Flowering Apricot Boat: *Meihua chuan* 梅花船

Flowering Apricot Bookroom: *Meihua shuwu* 梅花書屋

Flowering Apricot Dragon tree: *meilong* 梅龍

Flowering Apricot Holm: *Meizhu* 梅渚

Flowering Apricot Precipice: *Meiling* 梅嶺

Flowering Apricot Ridge: *Meihua ling* 梅花嶺

Flowering Apricot Slope: *Meipo* 梅坡

Flowering Apricot Terrace: *Meitai* 梅臺

Flowering Apricot Window: *meichuang* 梅窗

Flowering Apricot Wood Mountain: *Meilin shan* 梅林山

flowering crabapple: see crabapple

Flowering Crabapple Stream: *Haitang chuan* 海棠川

Flower Isle: *Huayu* 花嶼

Flowers of the Void Lane: *Konghua xiang* 空華巷

Flower Spring Surrounded by Clouds: *Yunjing raohua yuan* 雲徑繞花源

flower wall: *huaqiang* 花牆

flower windows: *huachuang* 花窗

Flowery Forest: *Hualin yuan* 華林園

Flowery Grove Park: see Flowery Forest

Flowery Luminescence Temple: *Huaguang miao* 華光廟

Flowing Cups: *Liubei* 流杯

Flowing Cyan: *Liubi* 流碧

Flowing Pillow: *Zhenliu* 枕流

Flowing Stream Pavilion: *Fangliu ting* 方流亭

Flute Pavilion: *Diting* 笛亭

Flying Gauze Ravine: *Feilian xia* 飛練峽

Flying Rainbow: *Feihong* 飛虹

Flying Rainbow Bridge: *Feihong qiao* 飛虹橋

Flying Rainbow Ridge: *Feihong ling* 飛虹嶺

Flying Stallion: *Feijun* 飛駿

following: *yin* 因

Foothill Clouds: *Luyun* 麓雲

Footnotes to the Classic of the Waterways: Shuijing zhu 水經注

Foot of the Phoenix Hill: *Fenglu tai* 鳳麓臺

foraminate: *tou* 透

Ford Which Repels Women: *Quenü jin* 卻女津

Forest of Sojourn: *Yulin* 寓林

Forgetting the Fish Jetty: *Wangyu ji* 忘魚磯

Forty Scenes: *sishi jing* 四十景

four-colored peach trees: *sise tao* 四色桃

Four Companions: *Sibing* 四並

Four Harmonies Hall: *Sibing tang* 四並堂

Four Sceneries Hall: *Sijing tang* 四景堂

four-season azalea: *sishi dujuan* 四時杜鵑

fox nut (*Euryale ferox*): *jitou* 雞頭

Fragrance of Antiquity Studio: *Guxiang zhai* 古香齋

Fragrance of the Mouth of the Musical Stone wintersweet: *qingkouxiang lamei* 磬口香臘梅 or *qingkou lamei* 磬口臘梅

Fragrant Grasses Hillock: *Xiangcao cha* 香草垞

Fragrant Hills: *Xiangshan* 香山

fragrant iris (*Iris* sp.): *fangsun* 芳蓀

Fragrant Isle by Flowing Waters: *Fangzhu linliu* 芳渚臨流

Fragrant Islet: *Xiang yu* 香嶼

Fragrant Red and Lucent Green: *Hongxiang lüyu* 紅香綠玉

fragrant saltcedar (*Tamarix chinensis*): *xiangcheng* 香檉

Fragrant Snow: *Xiangxue* 香雪

Fragrant Snow Path: *Xiangxue jing* 香雪徑

Fragrant Snow Walkway: *Xiangxue lang* 香雪廊

Fragrant Waters and Beautiful Cliffs: *Shuifang yanxiu* 水芳嚴秀

Free and Unfettered: *Rongyu* 容與

Friend in Ancient Prose: *Guwen zhiji* 古文知己

Friend in the Mountains and Rivers: *Shanshui zhiji* 山水知己

Frolicking Dragon Torrent: *Zhuolong jian* 濯龍澗

Frugality Garden: *Yueyuan* 約園

Fruit Orchard: *Guoyuan* 果園

fu (rhapsody, rhyme-prose): 賦

Fujianese orchid (*Cymbidium ensifolium*): *Jian lan* 建蘭

Fulin guo (Persia, Asia Minor): 拂菻國

gallery: *xuan* 軒

Gallery of Occasional Joy: *Oule xuan* 偶樂軒

Gallery of the Quail at Ease: *Yanshi xuan* 鶡適軒

Ganoderma fungus (*Ganoderma lucidum*): *zhi* 芝

Gan Sheng: 甘升

Gao Bridge: *Gaoqiao* 高橋

Garden for Evading Thorns: *Lici yuan* 離薋園

Garden for Fulfilling My Resolve to Retire: *Suichu yuan* 遂初園

Garden for Seeking One's Own Aims: *Qiuzhiyuan* 求志園

Garden for Sharing Spring: *Tongchun yuan* 同春園

Garden for Taking Refuge in the City: *Shiyin yuan* 市隱園

Garden Harmonizing with Spring: *Tongchun yuan* 同春園

Garden Hermitage: *Yuanyin* 園隱

gardenia (*Gardenia jasminoides*): *zhizihua* 梔子花, *zhan* 薝

Garden of Accommodation, Harmony Garden: *Suiyuan* 隨園

Garden of Affability: *Yi yuan* 怡園

Garden of Clear Ripples: *Qingyi yuan* 清漪園

Garden of Fu Bi, Duke of Zheng: *Fu Zhenggong yuan* 富鄭公園

Garden of Gems: *Yaopu* 瑤圃

Garden of Grand Marshal Wang: *Wang taiwei yuan* 王太尉園

Garden of Grand Preceptor Cai: *Cai taishi yuan* 蔡太師園

Garden of Grand Preceptor Tong: *Tong taishi yuan* 童太師園

Garden of Idleness: *Yiyuan* 逸園

Garden of My Mind, Garden of the Mind: *Yiyuan* 意園

Garden of Peaceful Waves: *Anlan yuan* 安瀾園

Garden of Perfect Brightness: *Yuanming yuan* 圓明園

Garden of Prince Consort Li: *Li fuma yuan* 李駙馬園

Garden of Prince Zhao of Han: *Zhao Hanwang yuan* 趙韓王園

Garden of Reflections: *Yingyuan* 影園

Garden of Rest: see Retirement Garden

Garden of Return: *Fuyuan* 復園

Garden of Sitting in Reclusion: *Zuoyin yuan* 坐隱園

Garden of Solitary Delight, Garden of Solitary Enjoyment: *Dule yuan* 獨樂園

Garden of Spices: *Hengzhi qingfen* 蘅芷清芬

Garden of Successive Springs: *Congchun yuan* 叢春園

Garden of Suitability: *Ke yuan* 可園

Garden of the Big Character Monastery: *Dazisi yuan* 大字寺園

Garden of the Deer Park Stream of the Wang Family: *Wangshi Michang jing yuan* 王氏麋場涇園

Garden of the Dwarf Bamboo: *Xiao yuan* 篠園

Garden of the Heart: *Xinyuan* 心園

Garden of the Jade Ducks: *Yufu yuan* 玉鳧園

Garden of the Jade Ford: *Yujin yuan* 玉津園

Garden of the Master of the Fishing Nets: *Wangshi yuan* 網師園

Garden of the Mi Family: *Mijia yuan* 米家園

Garden of the Mind: see Garden of My Mind

Garden of the Unsuccessful Politician: see Artless Administrator's Garden

Garden of Tranquil Brightness: *Jingming yuan* 靜明園

Garden of Tranquility: *Danyuan* 憺園

Garden of Uninhibited Spring: *Changchun yuan* 暢春園

Garden of Xu Jiu's Residence: *Xu Jiu zhai yuan* 徐九宅園

garden record: *yuanji* 園記

Gardens of East and West Gathering Luminescence: *Dongxi xiejing yuan* 東西擷景園

Gardens of Suzhou: Suzhou yuanlin 蘇州園林

Garden that Borders Upon Greenness: *Yilü yuan* 依綠園

Garden That Is Not Around: *Wuyou yuan* 烏有園

Garden Washed with Fragrance: *Huanxiang yuan* 浣香園

Gate of Accumulated Treasures: *Jubao men* 聚寶門

Gate of Compliance to Heaven: *Shuntian men* 順天門

Gate of White Clouds: *Baiyun fei* 白雲扉

Gathering Fragrance Park: *Xiefang yuan* 擷芳苑

Gathering Herbs Patch: *Caiyao pu* 采藥圃

Gathering in the Shade Garden: *Huiyin yuan* 會隱園

Gazebo for Friendship with the Rocks: *Youshi xie* 友石榭

Gazebo for the Celebration of the Harvest: *Xinjia ge* 欣稼閣

Gazebo for Viewing the Mountains: *Kanshan lou* 看山樓

Gazebo of the Green Clouds: *Lüyun ting* 綠雲亭

Gazebo of the Jade Reflection: *Yuzhao ting* 玉照亭

Gazing from the Bank of the River Hao: *Haoshangguan* 濠上觀

ge: see belvedere

gem-pearl tea tree (*Camellia japonica*): *baozhu shancha* 寶珠山茶

gen (hexagram representing the northeast): 艮

Geng Tianbao: 耿天保

Gentleman in Waiting Peak: *Duanshi feng* 端士峰

Gentleman's Grove: *Junzi lin* 君子林

genuine red cassia: *zhen hong gui* 真紅桂

giant bamboo (? *Bambusa verticillata*): *yundang* 篔簹

Giant Soak: *jujin* 巨浸

ginger (*Zingiber officinale*): *jiang* 姜

ginkgo: see duck-feet tree

ginseng (*Panax ginseng*): [*ren*]*shen* [人]參

glow of sunset upon Thunder Peak Pagoda: *Leifeng xizhao* 雷峰夕照

glutinous rice (*Oryza sativa* var. *glutinosa*): *shu* 秫

Gold Dust Spring: *Jinxie quan* 金屑泉

Golden Bowl Garden of General Li: *Jinpan Li yuan* 金盤李園

golden bramble (? *Archidendron* sp.): *jinjing* 金荊

Golden Goose Studio: *Jin'e shuwu* 金鵝書屋

Golden Grains Ridge: *Jinsu ling* 金粟嶺

Golden Lotuses Reflecting the Sun: *Jinlian yingri* 金蓮映日

golden pine, umbrella pine (*Sciadopitys verticillata*): *jin song* 金松

goldenrain (*Koelreuteria paniculata*): *zhubo* 珠柏

Golden Sea Turtle and Jade Tortoise: *Jin'ao yugui* 金鰲玉龜

Golden Slips: *Jinjian* 金簡

Golden Valley Creek: *Jingu jian* 金谷澗

Golden Valley Garden: *Jingu yuan* 金谷園

gold moth (unidentified flower): *jin'e* 金蛾

gold-rimmed white lotus: *jinbian bai lianhua* 金邊白蓮花

Good Fortune Hermitage: *Jiafu an* 嘉福庵

goudaifa (hook and connect method of construction): 鈎帶法

Goulou Mountain Hut: *Goulou shanfang* 岣嶁山房

gourd (*Cucurbitaceae*): *hu*[*lu*] 葫[蘆], sometimes written 壺

Gourd Valley: *Hulu gu* 葫蘆谷

Government-Compound Flowering Apricot: *Guancheng mei* 官城梅

Government Flowering Apricot: *Guanmei* 官梅

Gradually Becoming More Beautiful [Gate]: *Jianjia* [*men*] 漸佳 [門]

graft-heads: *jietou* 接頭

Grainy Apricot Lodge: *Wenxing guan* 文杏館

Grand Archivist, Grand Historian: *taishi* 太史

Grand Cloud Monastery: *Dayun si* 大雲寺

Grandee of the Fifth Order, fifth-rank counsellor: *wu daifu* 五大夫

Grand Historian: see Grand Archivist

Grand Mentor's Garden: *Taifu yuan* 太傅園

Grand Minister Wang's Garden: *Wang taizai yuan* 王太宰園

Grand Prospect Terrace: *Daguan tai* 大觀臺 or *Daguan lou* 大觀樓

grape vine (*Vitis vinifera*): *putao* 葡萄

Great Benevolence Garden of Mister Li: *Lishi Renfeng yuan* 李氏仁豐園

Great Buddha Head: *Dafotou* 大佛頭

Great Compassion House: *Daci shi* 大慈室

Great Courtyard: *Guangting* 廣庭

Great Green: *Dalü* 大綠

Great Hidden Village: *Dayin zhuang* 大隱莊

Great Lord of the Eastern Marchmount: *Dongyue dadi* 東嶽大帝

Great Northern Peak: *Beigao feng* 北高峰

Great Treasure Pass: *Hongbao guan* 鴻寶關

Great Yu's Seal Script: *Yuzhuan* 禹篆

green breeze (unidentified plant): *qingsou* 青颼

Green Butterfly tree peony: *lü hudie mudan* 綠蝴蝶牡丹

Green Calyx flowering apricot (*Prunus mume* 'viridicalyx'): *lü'e mei* 綠萼梅

Green Dragon Bridge: *Qinglong qiao* 青龍橋

green-flag (*Angelica* sp.): *qingzhi* 青芷

Green Hermitage: *Bihan* 碧厂

Greenhill Terrace: *Qingling tai* 青陵臺

Greenhouse Tree (unidentified tree): *wenshishu* 溫室樹; palace tree: *wenshu* 溫樹

Green Jade Ridge: *Qingyu ling* 青玉嶺

Green Lotus Cavity: *Qinglian ku* 青蓮窟

Green Rainbow: *Qinghong* 青虹

Green Shade Hall: *Yinlü tang* 蔭綠堂

Green Shade Pavilion: *Cuiyue xuan* 翠樾軒

green spirit (unidentified tree): *qingshen* 青神

Grieving by the River Xiang: *Minxiang* 憫湘

Grove of Delight: *Kuaihuo lin* 快活林

Grove of Fine Trees: *Jiashu lin* 嘉樹林

Guangmo Mountain: *Guangmo shan* 廣莫山

Guan Tong: 關同

Guanyin Hall: *Guanyin tang* 觀音堂

Guesthouse of Emerald-Green Delicacy: *Cuilinglong guan* 翠玲瓏館

Guesthouse of Refreshing Fragrance, Guesthouse of Refreshing Scent: *Qingxiang guan* 清香館

gui (noble): 貴

guiqi meili (precious and beautiful): 瑰奇美麗

gullies: he 壑

Gushing Gold Gate: Yongjin men 涌金門

Gushing Jade: Xieyu 瀉玉

Gusu Platform: Gusu tai 姑蘇臺

Gu Yanwu: 顧炎武

hackberry (Celtis sinensis): pu 樸

Hair-Drying Pavilion: Xifa ting 晞髮亭

Half-Acre Garden: Banmu yuan 半畝園

Half Belvedere: Ban'ge 半閣

Half Floating [Belvedere]: Banfu 半浮

Half-Hymn Hermitage: Banji an 半偈庵

hall: tang 堂

Hall Amid the Forest: Zhonglin tang 中林堂

Hall for Decanting the Seas: Yihai tang 挹海堂

Hall Number One: Jiaguan 甲觀

Hall of Assisting with Destiny of the World: Yiyun tang 益運堂

Hall of Augmented Waters: Zengshui ting 增水廳

Hall of Auspiciousness: Jiarui tang 嘉瑞堂

Hall of Bamboo Simplicity: Zhusu tang 竹素堂

Hall of Bestowed Idleness: Cixian tang 賜閒堂

Hall of Cold Radiance: Hanguang tang 寒光堂

Hall of Converging Scenes: Huijing tang 會景堂

Hall of Dragon's Song: Longyin tang 龍吟堂

Hall of Elegant Reflections: Zaojian ge 藻鑒閣

Hall of Enlightened Rule: Mingtang 明堂

Hall of Flowers with Green Perianths: Lü'e huatang 綠萼華堂

Hall of Happy Longevity: Leshou tang 樂壽堂

Hall of Jade Radiance: Yuzhao tang 玉照堂

Hall of Ladle Lake: Shaohai tang 勺海堂

Hall of Light: see Hall of Enlightened Rule

Hall of Mastering the Classics: Suijing tang 邃經堂

Hall of My Four Unfulfilled Obligations: Sifu tang 四負堂

Hall of Proclaimed Virtue: Xuande tang 宣德堂

Hall of Pure Speech: Qingyan tang 清言堂

Hall of Reciprocity: Shutang 恕堂

Hall of Reclining Clouds: Woyun tang 臥雲堂

Hall of Retirement: Yitang 逸堂

Hall of the Distant Mountains: Yuanshan tang 遠山堂

Hall of the Luminous Way: Mingdao tang 明道堂

Hall of the Ten Thousand Fascicles: Wanjuan tang 萬卷堂

Hall of Trees in the Wind: Fengmu tang 風木堂

Hall Overlooking the Water: Linshui dian 臨水殿

Hall Surrounded by Jade: Huancui tang 環翠堂

Hall that Over-looks the Water: see Hall Overlooking the Water

Han Cypress: Hanbo 漢柏

Hanging Floss crabapple (Malus halliana): chuisi haitang 垂絲海棠

Han Shizhong: 韓世忠 (Prince of Qi: Qi wang 蘄王)

Han Wei: 韓維

hao (studio name, cognomen): 號

haofang (heroic abandon): 豪放

Haoli Hill: Haoli shan 蒿里山

hardy orange, thorny limebush (Citrus trifoliata, Poncirus trifoliata): gouju 枸橘 or 枸菊

Harmony Garden: see Garden of Accommodation

harmony of central qi: zhongqi zhi hezhe 中氣之和者

Hatpin of the Clouds: Zanyun 簪雲

Hazelnut Glen: Zhenzi yu 榛子峪

Hazy Cloud Cave: Yanxia dong 煙霞洞

Hazy Tower: Piaomiao lou 縹緲樓

Hazy Wavelets: Yilan 漪嵐

Heaped Azure and Concentrated Cyan: Duiqing ningbi 堆青凝碧

Heaven in Miniature: Xiaoyou tian 小有天

Heavenly Stems: tiangan 天干

Heavenly Tranquility Ceremonial Archway: Tianning pailou 天寧牌樓

Heaven's Calabash: Tianpiao 天瓢

Heaven's Ford Bridge: Tianjin qiao 天津橋

Heaven's Gate: see Celestial Gate

Heaven's Pond: Tianchi 天池

Heaven-Released Pavilion: Tianfang ting 天放亭

He Cheng: 何澄

He Family Red [peonies]: He jia hong 賀家紅

hehe (style of window): 和合

hemlock-parsley (Ligusticum wallichii): qiongqiong 芎藭

hemp (Cannabis sativa): ma 麻

herbaceous peony, white peony (Paeonia lactiflora): shaoyao 芍藥

Herb Garden, Herb Nursery: Yaopu 藥圃

Herb Nursery: see Herb Garden

Herb Shanty: Yaoliao 藥寮

hermitage: an 庵

He Xun: 何遜

hibiscus (Hibiscus mutabilis): furong 芙蓉, mu furong 木芙蓉

Hibiscus Garden: Furong yuan 芙蓉園

Hibiscus Islet: Furong zhu 芙蓉渚

Hibiscus Narrows: Furong du 芙蓉度

Hibiscus Pond: Furong chi 芙蓉池

Hibiscus Screen: Furong ping 芙蓉屏

Hibiscus Slope: Furong po 芙蓉坡

Hidden Spring Grotto: Cangchun dong 藏春洞

Hidden Virtue Temple: Decang si 德藏寺

hill: shan 山

hill-thistle (Atractylodes chinensis): shu 術

History of the Later Han Dynasty: Hou Hanshu 後漢書

History of the Ming Dynasty: Ming shi 明史

Holding Aloof: Chaoran 超然

holly (Ilex chinensis): dongqing 冬青

hollyhock (Althaea rosea): shukui 蜀葵

Holy Mother's Hall: Shengmu dian 聖母殿

"Hongguang yiyou Yangzhou cheng-shou ji lüe" (A brief account of the defense of the city of Yangzhou in the Yiyou year [1645] of the reign of the Hongguang emperor): 弘光乙酉揚州城守紀略

Honk-Honk Kiosk: Yongyong 嗈嗈

Hopeful Sign: Xinglian zaiwang 杏帘在望

Horizontal Clouds Garden: Hengyun yuan 橫雲園

Horned Tiger Hermitage: Hujiao an 虎角庵

Horns and Teeth: Zouya 陬牙

hortensia (*Hydrangea* sp.): *qionghua*
瓊花

hosta (*Hosta* sp.): *yuzan* 玉簪

House of the Crystal Pond: *Linglong
chiguan* 玲瓏池館

House Where One Reaches the Moon:
Deyueju 得月居

Hovering-Over-the-Fishes: *Xianglin*
翔鱗

hu (measurement of volume, approximately 3,350 litres): 斛

Huang Ruheng: 黃汝蘅

Huazi Ridge: *Huazi gang* 華子岡

Huiyuan: 惠遠

Humble Administrator's Garden:
see Artless Administrator's Garden

Humble Hermitage Mountain:
Bilu 敝廬

Hundred Blossoms: *Baihua* 百花

Hundred Cranes Tower: *Baihe lou*
百鶴樓

Hundred Flower Island: *Baihua zhou*
百花洲

hundred-leafed hibiscus: *baiye mu
furong* 百葉木芙蓉

hundred-leafed rambler rose: *baiye
qiangwei* 百葉薔薇

hundred-leaf flowering apricot: *baiye
mei* 百葉梅

Hundred-Piece Monk's Cassock:
Baina 百衲

Huye Hall: *Huye tang* 戽冶堂

hyacinth beans (*Lablab purpureus*):
biandou 扁豆

hydrangea (*Hydrangea macrophylla*):
xiuqiu [*hua*] 繡毬 [花]

Identity with the Lotus Cottage: *Jihua
she* 即花舍

Illuminate Truth Hermitage:
Mingzhen an 明真庵

Immanent Snow: *Hanxue* 含雪

Immense Field with Shady Groves:
Futian congyue 甫田叢樾

Imminent Moon: *Yue jiang* 月將

Immortal's Bridge: *Xianqiao* 仙橋

Imperial Living Apartments: *Qingong*
寢宮

Imperial Tent: *Yuzhang* 御帳

Imperial Training Ground: *Yu
jiaochang* 御教場

imprint of the moon upon the Three
Ponds: *Santan yinyue* 三潭印月

Indian jasmine: see Arabian jasmine

India Temple: *Tianzhu si* 天竺寺

Indulgence in Rinsing Gallery:
Hanshu lang 酣漱廊

Infinity Gate: *Wuqiong men* 無窮門

Ink Pond: *Shuimo chi* 水墨池

Ink Pond Pavilion: *Mochi ting* 墨池亭

Ink-Purple Flowers [peonies]: *Mozi
hua* 墨紫花

Inkstone Terrace: *Yantai* 硯臺

Inner Garden: *Neiyuan* 內園

Inner Lake: *Neihu* 內湖

Inquiring about the Water Pavilion,
Water Pavilion: *Wenshui ting* 問水亭

Inspector of the Armies Purples
[peonies]: *Junrong zi* 軍容紫

Intimate Garden, Secret Garden:
Miyuan 密園

Inviting the Breeze Lodge: *Yanxun
shanguan* 延薰山館

jade bashfulness (unidentified plant):
yuxiu 玉羞

Jade Blossom: *Yuhua* 玉華

Jade Blossoms Hall: *Yuhua tang* 玉華堂

Jade Butterfly flowering apricot: *yudie
mei* 玉蝶梅

Jade Cavity: *Yudou* 玉竇

Jade Chime Mountain Hut: *Yuqing
shanfang* 玉磬山房

Jade-Decking Bridge: *Yuban qiao*
玉板橋

Jade Dragon with Raised Head:
Jiaoshou yulong 矯首玉龍

Jade Filigree: *Yu linglong* 玉玲瓏

Jade Forest Homestead: *Yulin xu*
玉林墟

Jade Held in the Mouth: *Hanbi* 含碧

Jade Hook Grotto Heaven: *Yugou
dongtian* 玉勾洞天

Jade Loveliness: *Yuxiu* 玉秀

Jade Maiden: *Yunü* 玉女

Jade Maiden Pool: *Yunü chi* 玉女池

Jade Snow Slope: *Yuxue po* 玉雪坡

Jade Spring Hill: *Yuquan shan* 玉泉山

Jade Spring Temple: *Yuquan si* 玉泉寺

jade tree (legendary tree): *qi shu* 琪樹

Jade Unicorn: *Yu qilin* 玉麒麟

Jade Viridian Beam: *Fenbi liang* 玢碧梁

Jade Writings: *Yushu* 玉書

Jar Hideaway: *Pingyin* 瓶隱

jasmine: see Arabian jasmine, white
jasmine, yellow winter jasmine

*Jasper Flower Collection from the
Garden of Reflections: Yingyuan
yaohua ji* 影園瑤華集

Jasper Stamens Room: *Qiongrui fang*
瓊蕊房

ji (record): 記

Jia Baoyu: 賈寶玉

Jia Hanfu: 賈漢復 (*zi* Jiaohou 膠侯)

Jiang Qi: 蔣棨

jiao (type of dragon): 蛟

Jia Pavilion: *Jia ting* 賈亭

jiashan: see artificial mountain

jie (joint, integrity): 節

Jinchuan rock: see Brocade River rock

Jing Hao: 荊浩

Jin Rusheng: 金乳生

jinshi, presented scholar, metropolitan
graduate: 進士

Jinyuan Palace: *Jinyuan gong* 金元宮

Ji Yuanji: 季元繼

Joined Together Garden: *Huijie* 會節

Joyful Radiance Beach, Joyful
Radiance Crossing: *Yuhui tan*
娛暉灘

Joy of Fish: *Yule* 魚樂

Joy of Harvest Tower: *Fengle lou* 豐樂樓

Joy Throughout the Empire:
Huanzhong dakuai 寰中大快

jujube: see date

juniper (*Chamaecyparis* sp.): *gui* 檜 or
guazi song 栝子松

Kilted Robe Crossing: *Zhenyi du* 振衣渡

Kingfisher Blue: *Cuiwei* 翠微

kingfisher grass (unidentified plant):
cuicao 翠草

kiosk: *ting* 亭, *xie* 榭, *xuan* 軒

Kiosk Facing the Water: *Mianshui
xuan* 面水軒

Kiosk of the Gentle Breeze and
Bright Moon: *Hefeng jiaoyue ting*
和風皎月亭

Knowing the Ford: *Zhijin* 知津

Knowing the Ford Bridge: *Zhijin qiao*
知津橋

Knowing the Way Home Bridge:
Zhihuan qiao 知還橋

Kunlun Clouds Kiosk: *Kunyun ting*
崑雲亭

Kunshan rocks: *Kunshan shi* 崑山石

Labyrinth Tower: see Maze Tower

Lacquer Tree Grove: *Qiyuan* 漆園

Ladle Garden: *Shaoyuan* 勺園

lagerstroemia: see crepe-myrtle

Lake Garden: *Huyuan* 湖園

Lake Heart Pavilion: *Huxin ting* 湖心亭

Lake Heart Temple: *Huxin si* 湖心寺

Lake of Lightheartedness Garden: *Mochouhu yuan* 莫愁湖園

Lake of Nine Curves: *Jiuqu chi* 九曲池

Lake Prospect Pavilion: *Wanghu ting* 望湖亭

Lakeside Pavilion: *Linhu ting* 臨湖亭

Lake Tai: *Taihu* 太湖

Lake Tai rock: *Taihu shi* 太湖石

Lake Yi: *Yihu* 猗湖

"Lament of the Lady of Qin": *Qin fu yin* 秦婦吟

Langhuan Paradise: *Langhuan fudi* 瑯嬛福地 or *Langhuan miaojing* 嫏嬛妙境

Lang Shining: see Castiglione

Langye Garden for Evading Thorns: *Langye lici yuan* 琅琊離薋園

Langye Villa: *Langye bieshu* 琅琊別墅

Late Spring Abode: *Dianchunyi* 殿春簃

laurel (*Laurus nobilis*): *yuegui* 月桂

Layered Halcyon and Unique Loveliness: *Diecui duxiu* 疊翠獨秀

Layered Jade: *Dieyu* 疊玉

Leaf of the Great Monad: *Taiyi ye* 太乙葉

Leafy Forest: *Xiaolin* 蕭林

lean, emaciated: *shou* 瘦

Ledge of Propitiating the Realized Ones: *Qizhen deng* 祈真磴

Ledgers of Merit and Demerit: *gong guo ge* 功過格

Leisure Boats Pass in Spring: *Chunliu huafang* 春流畫舫

Lesser Cloud Gate: *Xiaoyun men* 小雲門

Lesser Crenellated Peaks: *Xiao luanzhi* 小巒雉

Lesser Dragon Waterfall: *Xiaolong qiu* 小龍湫

Lesser Floating Jade: *Xiaofu yu* 小浮玉

Lesser Hundred-Piece Monk's Cassock: *Xiao baina* 小百衲

Lesser Jetavana: *Xiao Qilin* 小祇林

Lesser Jetavana Pavilion for Storing the Sutras: *Xiao Qilin cangjing ge* 小祇林藏經閣

Lesser Snowy Ridge: *Xiaoxue ling* 小雪嶺

Lesser Yanhua Stream: *Xiao yanhua xi* 小罨畫溪

Lesser Youyang: *Xiao youyang* 小酉陽

Lesser Youyang Tower: *Xiaoyou lou* 小酉樓

Let Go Bower: *Erer xuan* 爾耳軒

Level Spring Garden: *Pingquan yuan* 平泉園

Level with the Mountains Hall: *Pingshan tang* 平山堂

li (measurement of distance, approximately ⅓ mile): 里

Liang Medicinal Herb Garden: *Yaoliang yuan* 藥梁園

Liangzhou: 涼州

Liangzhou diqi: 梁州第七

Library of the Eight Principles of Book Acquisition: *Baqiu lou* 八求樓

lichee, lychee (*Litchi chinensis*): *lizhi* 荔枝

lichen: *xian* 蘚

Li Daoyuan: 酈道元

Li Di: 李迪

Li Fengshen: 李逢申

Light Mist and Fine Rain: *danyan shuyu* 淡煙疏雨

Light Yellow flowering apricot: *xiang mei* 緗梅

Li Hongyi: 李鴻裔

lilac (*Syzygium oblata* or *Syzygium aromaticum*): *dingxiang* 丁香

Lilac Cliffwall: *Dingzhang* 丁嶂

lily magnolia (*Magnolia liliiflora*): *bishu* 筆樹, *mulan* 木蘭, or *xinyi* 辛夷

Lily Magnolia Hollow: *Xinyi wu* 辛夷塢

Lin Family Red [peonies]: *Linjia hong* 林家紅

Lingbi rock: *Lingbi shi* 靈璧石

Lingering Garden: *Liu yuan* 留園

Lingering snow upon Break-Off Bridge: *Duanqiao canxue* 斷橋殘雪

Lingyin Temple, Temple of Souls' Retreat, Temple of the Soul's Retreat: *Lingyin si* 靈隱寺

lingzhi (fungus): 靈芝

Lion Cub: *Nier* 猊兒

Lion Cub Peak, Lions' Peak: *Shizi feng* 獅子峰

Lion Garden: *Shizi yuan* 獅子園

Lion Grove: *Shizi lin* 獅子林

Lion in Ambush: *Fushi* 伏獅

Lions' Peak: see Lion Cub Peak

Lion Valley: *Shizi yu* 獅子峪

Li Qingchen: 李清臣

Listening Stops Bridge: *Tingzhi qiao* 聽止橋

Listening to the Chanting: Wenyin 聞吟

Listening to the orioles amid the billowing willows: *liulang wen ying* 柳浪聞鶯

Literary Elegance Tower: *Erya lou* 爾雅樓

Literary Pastimes from the Pavilion of Seductive Tranquility: Meiyou ge wen yu 媚幽閣文娛

Little Canglang: *Xiao canglang* 小滄浪

Little Canglang Pavilion: *Xiao Canglang ting* 小滄浪亭

Little Censer: *Sai xianglu* 賽香爐

Little Filigree: *Xiao linglong* 小玲瓏

Little Floating Banner: *Xiao fuchuang* 小浮幢

Little Flying Rainbow Bridge: *Xiaofei hong* 小飛虹

Little Friend: *Xiaoyou* 小友

little-leaf boxwood: see boxwood tree

Little Peach Blossom Spring: *Xiao taoyuan* 小桃源

Little Peak on the Southern Screen: *Nanping xiaofeng* 南屏小峰

Little Penglai: *Xiao Penglai* 小蓬萊

Little Retreat Amid the Fragrant Fields: *Xiangxi xiaozhu* 薌畦小筑

Little Stone Bridge: *Xiaoshiliang* 小石梁

Little Thousand Men Seat: *Xiao qianren zuo* 小千人坐

Little Translucent Mountain Lodge: *Xiao linglong shanguan* 小玲瓏山館

Little Transverse Stream: *Xiaoxie chuan* 小斜川

Little Zhong-nan: *Xiao zhongnan* 小終南

Liu Chang: 劉敞

Liu E: 劉鶚

Liu Mengmei: 柳夢梅

Liu Yisou: 劉義叟 (*zi* Zhonggeng 仲更)

Liu Yuanyu: 劉元瑜

Li Wei: 李偉 (Marquis of Wuqing: *Wuqing hou* 武清侯)

Lixia Pavilion: *Lixia ting* 歷下亭

lixue (study of Principle): 理學

Locust Tent: *Huaiwo* 槐幄

locust tree, pagoda tree, scholar tree (*Styphnolobium japonicum*, formerly *Sophora japonica*): *huai* 槐

Lodge for Treading Upon Harmony: *Daohe guan* 蹈和館

Lofty Sunshine Lodge: *Gaoyang guan* 高陽館

Lone Hill, Solitary Hill: *Gushan* 孤山

Lone Hill Temple: *Gushan si* 孤山寺

Long Embankment: *Changdi* 長堤

longevity lotus: *wanshou furong* 萬壽芙蓉

Longevity Mountain, the Northeast Marchmount: *Shoushan Genyue* 壽山艮嶽

Longevity Star for Venerable Men: *Laoren shouxing* 老人壽星

Long Rainbow Sipping White Silk: *Changhong yinlian* 長虹飲練

Long River (Yangtze River): *Changjiang* 長江

Longxing Temple: *Longxing si* 龍興寺

loquat (*Eriobotrya japonica*): *pipa* 枇杷

lotus (*Nelumbo nucifera, Nelumbium speciosum*): *lian* 蓮, sometimes *furong* 芙蓉

Lotus Blossom Grotto: *Lianhua dong* 蓮花洞

Lotus Blossom Peak: *Lianhua feng* 蓮花峰

Lotus Cove: *Furong wei* 芙蓉隈

Lotus Crossing: *Furong du* 芙蓉渡

Lotus Flower Perianths [peonies]: *Lianhua e* 蓮花萼

Lotus Marsh, Lotus Pond: *Furong zhao* 芙蓉沼

Lotus Pond: see Lotus Marsh

lou, storied building, storied house, tower (building of more than one story): 樓

Loudou: 娄兜

Loving the Sun Hall: *Airi tang* 愛日堂

Lower Pine Garden: *Xia song yuan* 下松園

Luan Family Rapids: *Luanjia lai* 欒家瀬

Lucky Lotus [peonies]: *Ruilian* 瑞蓮

Lü Garden: 履園

Lü Mengzheng: 呂蒙正 (posthumous title Wenmu 文穆)

Luminous Dragon Gate: *Jinglong men* 景龍門

Luminous Dragon River: *Jinglong jiang* 景龍江

Lurking Fish-Scales Pond: *Yinlin tan* 隱鱗潭

lüshi (regulated verse): 律詩

Lü Wenmu's Garden: *Lü Wenmu yuan* 呂文穆園

Ma Chang: 馬暢

magnolia: *yulan* 玉蘭

Magnolia Enclosure: *Mulan chai* 木蘭柴

Mahâsattva Retreat: *Dashi an* 大士庵

maiden crab[apple] (*Malus × micromalus*): *nüer tang* 女兒棠

Mai Family Garden: *Maijia yuan* 麥家園

Make-Do Garden: *Jiangjiu yuan* 將就園

Make-Do Owner: *Jiangjiu zhuren* 將就主人

Make Garden: *Jiang yuan* 將園

Making Teachers for the People: *Zuo zhi shi* 作之師

mallow (*Malvaceae*): *kui* 葵

Managing Agriculture Orchard: *Zhinong pu* 治農圃

mandarin orange (*Citrus × aurantium, Citrus reticulata*): *gan* 柑 or *ju* 橘

Mantra Chanting Bridge: *Fansheng qiao* 梵生橋

manual conversation (chess): *shoutan* 手談

maple (*Acer* sp.): *feng* 楓

Marklord of Pangu: *Pangu hou* 盤固侯

Marquis of Wuding's Garden: *Wudinghou yuan* 武定侯園

Martial Forest Gate: *Wulin men* 武林門

Marvelous Peak of Propitious Clouds and Myriad Postures: *Qingyun wantai qifeng* 卿雲萬態奇峰

Master Anqi: *Anqi sheng* 安期生

Master Chang's Lake: *Changgong hu* 昌公湖

Master Gourd's Tower: *Hugong lou* 壺公樓

Master of the Fishing Nets: *Wangshi* 網師

Master Su's Causeway: *Su di* 蘇堤

Ma Sui: 馬燧

Materia Medica: *Bencao* 本草

Ma Yuan: 馬遠 ("One Corner Ma": *Ma Yijiao* 馬一角)

Maze Tower, Labyrinth Tower: *Milou* 迷樓

Meandering Bridge: *Weiyi liang* 逶迆梁

Medial Kiosk: *Jieting* 介亭

medicinal lotus (*Nelumbo nucifera*): *lianxing* 蓮荇

Meeting of Minds: *Huixin chu* 會心處

meiren (beautiful woman [lit. person]): 美人

melon (*Cucurbitaceae*): *luo* 蓏

Memorial Shrine of the Honorable Su: *Su gong ci* 蘇公祠

Meng Jingchu's Garden: *Meng Jingchu yuan* 孟景初園

Meng Wall Hollow: *Mengcheng ao* 孟城坳

Men the Gardener: *Men yuanzi* 門園子

metal dike: *jin di* 金堤

metropolitan graduate: see jinshi

Miao Shou: 苗授

Middle Island: *Zhongdao* 中島

Middling Hermit: *Zhong yin* 中隱

Mid-Mount: *Banshan* 半山

Midway Temple: *Zhongguan* 中觀

Mi Fu: 米芾

millet (*Panicum miliaceum*): *liang* 粱, *yingsu* 櫻粟, or *shu* 黍

Millet Mountain: *Sushan* 粟山

Miluo River: *Miluo jiang* 汨羅江

Mingled Sunset-Clouds Pavilion: *Lianfei ting* 斂霏亭

Mingsheng Lake: *Mingsheng hu* 明聖湖

Miniature Image of the Xiao and Xiang Rivers: *Xiao Xiang xiaoying* 瀟湘小影

Minimal Possession: *Xiaoyou* 小有

Mirror Boat: *Jing fang* 鏡舫

Misty Passage: *Yandao* 煙道

Mi Wanzhong: 米萬鐘

Mocking Dust Cliff: *Xiaochen yan* 笑塵巖

Monastery of Manifesting Loyalty: *Zhaozhong si* 照忠寺

Monastery of the Subtle Fragrance: *Miaoxiang an* 妙香庵

Monastery of White Clouds: *Baiyun an* 白雲庵

monkshood (*Aconitum fischeri* or *Aconitum chinense*): *sengxieju* 僧鞋菊

Moon Boat with Cloud Sails: *Yunfan yuefang* 雲帆月舫

Moonlit Waves Bridge: *Yuebo qiao* 月波橋

Moon Rises as the Wind Stirs: *Yuedao fenglai* 月到風來

Moon Secreting Spring: *Qinyue quan* 沁月泉

Morning Mist by the Western Ridge: *Xiling chenxia* 西嶺晨霞

moss: *tai* 苔

mottled bamboo (*Phyllostachys reticulata*): *banzhu* 斑竹

Mottled Bamboo Foothill: *Banzhu lu* 斑竹麓

mountain alum (*Symplocos caudata* or *Symplocos sumuntia*): *shanfan* 山礬

mountain cassia (*Osmanthus delavayi*): *shan gui* 山桂

mountain cherry (*Prunus serrulata*): *shan ying* 山櫻

mountain combs: *shan bizi* 山箆子

Mountain Estate for Escaping the Heat: *Bishu shanzhuang* 避暑山莊

Mountain Estate for Washing the Azure-Green: *Huanbi shanzhuang* 浣碧山莊

mountain ginger (*Alpinia japonica* [Thunb.] Miq.): *shan jiang* 山薑

mountain hut: *shanfang* 山房

Mountain Hut of Azure-Green Wutong Trees and Emerald Bamboos: *Biwu cuizhu shanwu* 碧梧翠竹山屋

Mountain Hut of the Flowering Apricot and the Iron Stone: *Meihua tieshi shanfang* 梅花鐵石山房

Mountain Master: *shanshi* 山師

mountain orchid (*Oreorchis patens*): *shan lan* 山蘭

mountain peach (*Prunus davidiana*): *shan tao* 山桃

Mountain Retreat: *Shanlu* 山廬

Mountain Stream Among Bamboos: *Zhujian* 竹澗

mountain tea: *shan ming* 山茗

Mountain View: *Jianshan* 見山

Mountain Village: *Shanzhuang* 山莊

Mountain Zhangs: *Shanzi Zhang* 山子張

Mount Great: see Mount Tai

Mount Jiang: *Jiangshan* 將山

Mount Jiu: *Jiushan* 就山

Mount Song: *Songshan* 嵩山

Mount Tai, Mount Great, Supreme Mountain: *Taishan* 泰山; *Daizong* 岱宗

Mr. Dong's Eastern Garden: *Dongshi dongyuan* 董氏東園

Mr. Dong's Western Garden: *Dongshi xiyuan* 董氏西園

Mr. Hu's Garden North of the River: *Shuibei Hushi yuan* 水北胡氏園

Mr. Liu's Garden: *Liushi yuan* 劉氏園

Mr. Wu's Garden: *Wushi yuan* 武氏園

Mr. Zhang's Purple Gold Terrace Garden: *Zijintai Zhangshi yuan* 紫金臺張氏園

mu (measurement of area, approximately ⅙ acre): 畝

mugwort: see artemisia

mulberry (*Morus alba*): *sang* 桑

multiflora rose: see banksia rose

Multi-Leaf Purples [peonies]: *Duoye zi* 多葉紫

Mushroom Skin Pavilion: *Yunzhiting* 筠芝亭

Music Bureau ballad: see yuefu

Mustard Seed Garden: *Jiezi yuan* 芥子園

Mustard Seed Garden Manual of Painting: *Jiezi yuan huapu* 芥子園畫譜

Mustard-Seed Studio: *Jiexuan* 芥軒

My Garden of Escape: *Biyuan* 避園

Myriad Brocade Embankment: *Wanjin di* 萬錦堤

Myriad Flowers Clump: *Wanhua cong* 萬花叢

Myriad Longevity: *Wanshou* 萬壽

Myriad Pines Precipice: *Wansong ling* 萬松嶺

Myriad Rock Mountain: *Wanshi shan* 萬石山

Myriad Willows Hall: *Wanliu tang* 萬柳堂

Myriad Years Mountain: *Wansui shan* 萬歲山

Mysterious Pond: *Xuanchi* 玄池

Mysterious Pond Hall: *Xuanchi guan* 玄池館

Mystic Ford Bridge: *Xuanjin qiao* 玄津橋

Mystic Manor: *Xuanzhuang* 玄莊

"My Summons to Travel": *Youhuan* 游喚

Nanlü yizhihua: 南呂一枝花

nanmu (*Phoebe zhennan*): *nanzhizi* 楠稚子

narcissus (*Narcissus tazetta*): *shuixian* 水仙

Narcissus Temple, Temple of Water Immortals: *Shuixian miao* 水仙廟

National Social Education College: *Guoli Shehui Jiaoyu Xueyuan* 國立社會教育學院

Natural Window: *tianran zhi chuang* 天然之窗

Near the Light Pavilion: *Jinguang ge* 近光閣

nectar peaches (*Prunus persica*): *shuimi tao* 水蜜桃

Neighborhood of the Lofty Gentleman: *Gaoshi li* 高士里

Neighboring Su in the East: *Su donglin* 蘇東鄰

Neo-Confucianism: *daoxue* 道學, *lixue* 理學

Nesting-in-the-Clouds: *Chaoyun* 巢雲

Nesting Phoenix: *Chaofeng* 巢鳳

Nestling-Against-Halcyon Loft: *Yicui lou* 倚翠樓

Nest of Books: *Shuchao* 書巢

Nest of Cocoon Clouds: *Jianyun wo* 繭雲窩

New Manor: *Xinzhuang* 新莊

New Wanwei Mountain: *Shao wanwei* 少宛委

Next to the Sun: *Jiu ri* 就日

Nine Dragon Ridge: *Jiulong ling* 九龍嶺

Nine Flower Entrenchment: *Jiuying shuwu* 九英書塢

Nine Friends Tower: *Jiuyou lou* 九友樓

Nine Immortals Peak: *Jiuxian feng* 九仙峰

Nine-Stamen Pearls [peonies]: *Jiurui zhenzhu* 九蕊真珠

Nine Taboos: *jiu ji* 九忌

Niu-Family Yellows [peonies]: *Niujia huang* 牛家黃

Nobleman's Rock: *Guiren shi* 貴人石

Nocturnal Fog: *Suwu* 宿霧

Nodding Rock: *Diantou shi* 點頭石

Node of Singularity: *Wanqi* 綰奇

Node of Singularity Terrace: *Wanqi tai* 綰奇臺

Non-Resemblance Study: *Wuru shushe* 無如書舍

Northeast Marchmount: *Genyue* 艮岳

Northern Cottage: *Beicha* 北垞

Northern Marchmount Mount Heng: *Beiyue Hengshan* 北嶽恒山

Northern Slope: *Beiqi* 北崎

North Garden: *Beiyuan* 北園

North New Embankment: *Bei xin di* 北新堤

North of the Sui: *Suiyuan yiji* 睢園遺跡

North Tall Peak: *Beigao feng* 北高峰

North Tower: *Beilou* 北樓

novelty: *qi* 奇

numinous traces: *lingzong* 靈綜

Nunnery of Numinous Response: *Lingying guan* 靈應觀

nutmeg yew (*Torreya grandis*): *fei* 榧

Nutshell Studio: *Guxuan* 穀軒

Observing the Fish from a Waterside Rock: *Shiji guanyu* 石磯觀魚

Occasional Dwelling: *Ouju* 偶居

oceanside photinia (*Photinia serratifolia*): *haishinan* 海石楠

Ode of Chu: *Chusong* 楚頌

oilseed rape (*Brassica napus*): *caizi* 菜子

Old Camphor Tree Level: *Laozhang ping* 老樟坪

Old Clumsy: *Zhuosou* 拙叟

Old Flowering Apricot: *Gumei* 古梅

Old Han Canal: *Gu Han'gou* 古邗溝

Old Man of the Sea's Plank Bridge: *Haiweng liang* 海翁梁

Old Tales of Hangzhou (alternate name for *Recollections of Wulin*): *Wulin jiushi* 武林舊事

oleander (*Nerium oleander, Nerium odorum*): *qu'na* 渠那 or *ju'nawei* 俱郍衛

On Chinese Gardens: Shuo yuan 說園

One Glance: *Yijian* 一鑒

One-Press-With-the-Finger Reds [peonies]: *Yiye hong* 一撅紅

onion (*Allium* sp.): *cong* 蔥

Onion Flowers [peonies]: *Lutai hua* 鹿胎花

Onyx and Jasper Bank: *Qiongyao wu* 瓊瑤塢

Onyx Island: *Qiongdao* 瓊島

opium poppy (*Papaver somniferum*): *yingsu* 罌粟

orange: see canton orange

orange tree (*Citrus* sp.): *ganju* 柑橘

orchard, plot: *pu* 圃

orchid (epidendrum or cymbidium, *Cymbidium goeringii*): *lan* 蘭

Orchid Pavilion: *Lanting* 蘭亭

Orchid Proof: *Zhenglan* 徵蘭

Orioles Warbling in the Tall Trees: *Yingzhuan qiaomu* 鶯囀喬木

Oriole-Testing Hostelry: *Shiying guan* 試鶯館

ornamental ginger (*Alpinia zerumbet*): *liangjiang* 良姜

osmanthus: see cassia

Our Lady of Tai Shan: see Celestial Immortal of the Eastern Marchmount Taishan

Overcoming Self: *Zi sheng* 自勝

Overflowing Spring Slope: *Yangchun bei* 漾春陂

Overseeing the Harvest: *Xinghuo* 省獲

Owner's Favorite Bower: literally Locust-Tree Rain Pavilion; *Huaiyu ting* 槐雨亭

pace: see double-pace

Pacing Auspiciously Gate: *Lüxiang men* 履祥門

Pagoda for the Protection of King Qian Chu: *Baochu ta* 保俶塔

pagoda tree: see locust tree

Pagoda Tree Footpath: *Gonghuai mo* 宮槐陌

painted houseboats: *huafang* 畫舫

Paintings Examined: Huihua beikao 繪畫備考

Pair of Lakes Like Flanking Mirrors: *Shuanghu jiajing* 雙湖夾鏡

Palace of Floriate Clarity: *Huaqing gong* 華清宮

Palace of Tranquillity and Longevity: *Ningshou gong* 寧壽宮

Palace of Violet Sunlight: *Ziyang gong* 紫陽宮

palace tree: see Greenhouse Tree

Palette Pond: *Yanchi* 研池

palm tree (*Trachycarpus fortunei*): *zonglü* 棕櫚

Pan En: 潘恩

Pangu: 盤古

Pan Jinlian: 潘金蓮

Pan Shicheng (Pontinqua or Pow-xing-kua): 潘仕成

Pan Yijun: 潘弈雋

paper mulberry (*Broussonetia papyrifera*): *zhe* 柘

parallel-azure bamboos (? *Phyllostachys aureosulcata* 'Aureocaulis'): *duiqing zhu* 對青竹

parasol tree: see wutong

Park of the Rosequartz Grove: *Qionglin yuan* 瓊林苑

Parrot Bridge: *Yingge qiao* 鸚哥橋

Participating in Unity: *Cantong* 參同

Parting Regrets Peak: *Xibie feng* 惜別峰

Passing-Away-Idleness Lodge: *Xiaoxian guan* 消閒館

Patch of Cloud, Sheet of Cloud, Wisp of Cloud: *Yipianyun* 一片雲

Patch of Cloud Pavilion: *Yipianyun ting* 一片雲亭

Patchwork Habit: *Suina* 碎衲

Patchwork Sunset-Clouds Peak: *Naxia feng* 衲霞峰

Path Imbued with Fragrance: *Rexiang jing* 惹香徑

Pathway to Mysteries: *Qujing tongyou* 曲徑通幽

Patterned Ripples Hall: *Wenyi tang* 文漪堂

paulownia (*Paulownia tomentosa*): *wu* 梧 or *tong* 桐; these names can also refer to the wutong or parasol tree, *Firmiana simplex*

Pausing on the Journey Pavilion: *Xiyi ting* 徙倚亭

pavilion: *ting* 亭

Pavilion Among the Pile of Flowers: *Baihuadui ge* 百花堆閣

Pavilion Encircled by Jade: *Huanyu ting* 環玉亭

Pavilion Encircled in Green: *Huancui ting* 環翠亭

Pavilion for Caressing the Clouds: *Fuyun ting* 拂雲亭

Pavilion for Dreaming of Retirement: see Dreamy Tower

Pavilion for Gazing at Mount Yu: *Ziyu xie* 眥虞榭

Pavilion for Looking Up to the High Hill: *Yangzhi ting* 仰止亭

Pavilion for Receiving the Mountains: *Yanshan ting* 延山亭

Pavilion for Reciting Poems in Quietude: *Jingyin ting* 靜吟亭

Pavilion for Revering the Canon: *Zunjing ge* 尊經閣

Pavilion for Rinsing Flowers: *Jiehua ting* 潔華亭

Pavilion for Sighing in Self-Reproach about the Tidal Floods: *Chaozai tanguo ting* 潮災嘆過亭

Pavilion for the Appreciation of Excellence: *Miaoshang ting* 妙賞亭

Pavilion for Washing the Cap Strings: *Zhuoying ting* 濯纓亭

Pavilion of Accumulation: *Leixie* 累榭

Pavilion of Arriving Cranes: *Laihe ting* 來鶴亭

Pavilion of Autumn Perfumes: *Qiufu xuan* 秋馥軒

Pavilion of Chilly Breezes: *Lengfeng ting* 冷風亭

Pavilion of Cultivation: *Xiuting* 修亭

Pavilion of Grasping Loveliness: *Lanxiu xuan* 攬秀軒

Pavilion of Great Antiquity: *Taigu ting* 太古亭

Pavilion of Lingering Shadows: *Liuying ting* 留影亭

Pavilion of Magnanimity and Clarity: *Hanqing ge* 涵清閣

Pavilion of Pure Joy: *Qingxi ge* 清喜閣

Pavilion of Serene Repose: *Juran ting* 居然亭

Pavilion of Spring Fragrances: *Chunfang xuan* 春芳軒

Pavilion of Summer Splendor: *Xiarong xuan* 夏榮軒

Pavilion of the Blue-Green Waves: *Guocui ting* 過翠亭

Pavilion of the Flying Roseate Clouds: *Feixia ting* 飛霞亭

Pavilion of the Gathered Scents: *Qunfang ge* 群芳閣

Pavilion of Wintry Elegance: *Dongxiu xuan* 冬秀軒

Paying Court to the Realized Ones Ledge: *Chaozhen deng* 朝真磴

peach (*Prunus persica*): *tao* 桃

Peach-Blossom Bank: *Taowu* 桃塢

Peach Blossom Garden: *Taohua yuan* 桃花園

Peach Blossom Sluice Gate: *Taohua zha* 桃花閘

Peach-Tree Banks: *Taohua pan* 桃花泮

peacock spikemoss (*Selaginella uncinata*): *cuiyuncao* 翠芸草

Peak of Eternal Spring: *Changchun ling* 長春嶺

Peak of the Iron Mushroom: *Tiezhi feng* 鐵芝峰

Peak Through Which the Moon Penetrates: *Louyue feng* 漏月峰

pear (*Pyrus* sp.): *li* 梨

Pear Blossoms Accompanied by the Moon: *Lihua banyue* 梨花伴月

pearl orchid (*Chloranthus spicatus*): *zhenzhulan* 珍珠蘭 or 真珠蘭

Pearl-Rinsing Stream: *Shuzhu jian* 漱珠澗

Pearls of Mystery: *Xuanzhu* 玄珠

Pecked by Eagles: *Yingzhuo* 鷹啄

peeling off (horticultural technique): *dabo* 打剝

Pei Du: 裴度

Pen Creek: *Bixi* 筆溪

Penetrating the Roseate Clouds Terrace: *Tongxia tai* 通霞臺

Penglai: 蓬萊

Peng-lai's Fairy Precincts: *Penglai xianjing* 蓬萊仙境

Peng Qifeng: 彭啟豐

peony: see herbaceous peony, tree peony

Peony Chamber: *Mudan shi* 牡丹室

Peony Grove: *Mudan lin* 牡丹林

Peony Plot: *Shaoyao pu* 芍藥圃

Pepper Garden: *Jiaoyuan* 椒園

Perched-in-Mists and Hidden-in-Clouds: *Qiyan duoyun* 栖煙躲雲

Perched-in-Roseate-Clouds and Stroking the Triaster Stars: *Qixia menshen* 栖霞捫參

Perilous Peak: *Zuoe feng* 岞崿峰

Petal-Base Purple [peonies]: *Yedi zi* 葉底紫

Phoenix Dance: *Youfeng laiyi* 有鳳來儀

phoenix-eye (*Sterculia monosperma*): *pingpo* 蘋婆

Phoenix Frond Lodge: *Fengtiao guan* 鳳條館

phoenix gathering (unidentified tree): *fengji* 鳳集

Phoenix Mountain: *Fenghuang shan* 鳳凰山

Phoenix Pond: *Fengchi* 鳳池

Phoenix Spring: *Fenghuang quan* 鳳皇泉

phoenix tail (*Pteris multifida*): *fengwei* 鳳尾

Phoenix Terrace: *Fenghuang tai* 鳳凰臺

Phoenix Terrace Garden: *Fengtai yuan* 鳳臺園

pi (obsession): 癖

Picture Mountain [Kiosk]: *Tushan* 圖山

Piled Mountain: *Dieshan* 疊山

Pile of a Hundred Flowers: *Baihua dui* 百花堆

Pine Courtyard: *Songyuan* 松院

Pine Gully: *Songxia* 松峽

Pine Island: *Songdao* 松島

Pine of Qin: *Qin song* 秦松

Pine Path: *Songjing* 松徑

Pine Ridge Collection: Songling ji 松陵集

pine tree (*Pinus* sp.): *song* 松

Pine Valley: *Songshu yu* 松樹峪

Pine Winds through Myriad Vales: *Wanhuo songfeng* 萬壑松風

pingdan (even and bland): 平淡

Pingquan Estate: *Pingquan zhuang* 平泉莊

Pin-Graph Gate: *Pinzi men* 品字門

pink (*Dianthus chinensis*): *jianqiusha* 剪秋莎

Pitcher Stop: *Baoweng xiaoqi* 抱瓷小憩

Place for Detaining Guests Deep in the Bamboo: *Zhushen liuke chu* 竹深留客處

Place for Floating Goblets: *Liushang suo* 流觴所

Place for Listening to the Sighing Pines: *Ting songfeng chu* 聽松風處

Place for Storage of Woodblocks: *Cangban suo* 藏板所

Place for Watching the Fish: *Guanyu chu* 觀魚處

Place of Clear Meditation: *Zhiqing chu* 志清處

Place of Smiles: *Yiyan chu* 怡顏處

Plain Garden: *Suyuan* 素園

Plain Pavilion: *Suting* 素亭

Plain Plot: *Danpu* 澹圃

plane tree (*Platanus orientalis*): *tong* 桐

plantain: see banana

Plantain Balustrade: *Bajiao jian* 芭蕉檻

Planting Bamboo Studio: *Zhongzhu zhai* 種竹齋

Plateau Garden: *Pingpu* 平圃

Platform for Washing Off the Makeup: *Xizhuang tai* 洗妝臺

Platform of Suicides: *Sheshen tai* 捨身臺

Pleasant Spaces Gallery: *Yikuang xuan* 怡曠軒

Pleasurable Garden: *Yuyuan* 豫園

Pleasurable Gateway: *Yumen* 豫門

Pleasure in the Suburbs [Garden]: *Lejiao yuan* 樂郊園

plot: see orchard

plum (*Prunus salicina*): *li* 李

Plum in the Golden Vase: Jin Ping Mei 金瓶梅

Plum Slope: *Zhenli ban* 珍李坂

Pocket Ocean: *Xiuhai* 袖海

Poets' Club of the Cherry-Apple: *Haitang yinshe* 海棠吟社

Pointed Clouds and Nesting Phoenix: *Ruiyun chaofeng* 銳雲巢鳳

Poised Pavilion: *Yiran ting* 翼然亭

pole butterflybush (*Buddleia officinalis*): *mimeng* 密蒙

pollia, wild ginger (*Pollia japonica*): *duruo* 杜若

pomegranate (*Punica granatum*): *shiliu* 石榴

pomelo (*Citrus grandis*): *you* 柚

Pond for Cleansing the Heart: *Xixin chi* 洗心池

Pond for Waking from Drunkenness: *Xingjiu chi* 醒酒池

Pond of Decorated Fish: *Wenyu chi* 文魚池

Pool of the Brilliant Moon: *Zhuoyue chi* 濯月池

poplar (*Populus* sp.): *yang* 楊

poppy: see opium poppy

Portable Ice and Snow: Bingxue xie 冰雪攜

pot marigold (*Catharanthus roseus* or *Calendula arvensis*): *changchun* 長春

Pouring Green Hill Chamber: *Yicui shanfang* 挹翠山房

Precious Adornment white peony: *baozhuangcheng shaoyao* 寶妝成芍藥

presented scholar: see jinshi

prickly water lily: see caltrop

primal qi: *yuanqi* 元氣

Primal Sovereign of the Azure Clouds: Bixia Yuanjun 碧霞元君

Prime Minister in the Mountains: *shanzhong zaixiang* 山中宰相

prince's-feather (*Polygonum orientale*): *tianliao* 天蓼

Princess's Pagoda: *Wangfei ta* 王妃塔

Prince Teng's Gazebo: *Tengwang ge* 騰王閣

Printing House: *Yinshu ju* 印書局

private: *si* 私

Profound Garden: *Zhanyuan* 湛園

Profound Glory Garrison Calligraphy Studio: *Zhanhuawei shuxuan* 湛華衛書軒

Propitious Clouds and Auspicious Vapors: *Qingyun ruiai* 卿雲瑞靄

Prospect Garden: *Daguan yuan* 大觀園

Proud in Old Age Hall: *Anlao tang* 岸老堂

Provincial Graduate: see Elevated Person

Provision Bureau, Response and Service Bureau: *yingfeng ju* 應奉局

public: *gong* 公

pulse (*Leguminosae, Fabaceae*): *huo* 藿 or *shu* 菽

Pure Ethereal Realm: *Qingxu jing* 清虛境

Pure Pearl Temple: *Zhenzhu si* 真珠寺

Purple Bamboo Grove: *Zizhu lin* 紫竹林

Purple Bamboo Hall: *Ziyun tang* 紫筠堂

Purple Brocade crabapple (*Malus* sp.): *zijin haitang* 紫錦海棠

purple eggplant (*Solanum melongena*): *ziqie* 紫茄

purple laurel (*Laurus cinnamomum, Cinnamomum cassia*): *zi gui* 紫桂

Purple Light Academy: *Ziyang shuyuan* 紫陽書院

purple lilac (*Syringa vulgaris*): *zi dingxiang* 紫丁香

purple orchid (*Bletilla striata*): *zilan* 紫蘭

purple photinia (*Photinia* sp.): *zi shinan* 紫石楠

Purple Rock Wall: *Zishi bi* 紫石壁

Purple Smoke: *Ziyan* 紫煙

purple willow (*Salix purpurea*): *qi* 杞; may also refer to *gouqi* 枸杞 (*Lycium chinense*)

Purple Willow Garden: *Qiyuan* 杞園

puye zhi zhi (understated elegance of the simple and the rustic): 樸野之致

qi (energy, ether): 氣

qi (measurement of area, approximately 50 *mu* or 8½ acres): 畦

qian (copper coin, one cash, also used as a measurement of weight, approximately 3.75 grams): 錢

qian (hexagram representing heaven): 乾

Qian Qianyi: 錢謙益

Qiantang Lake: *Qiantang hu* 錢塘湖

Qian Weiyan: 錢惟演 (posthumous name Sigong 思公)

Qian Yuanliao: 錢元璙 (Prince of Guangling: *Guangling jun wang* 廣陵郡王)

Qi Chenghan: 祁承爜

Qici Cliff: *Qiciyan* 契此岩

qi-energy: see qi

qilin (the Chinese "unicorn"): 麒麟

qin (zither): 琴

qing (measurement of area, 100 *mu* or approximately 16½ acres): 頃

Qing County Reds [peonies]: *Qingzhou hong* 青州紅

Qingsi Gallery: *Qingsi ge* 清斯閣

Qin Terrace: *Qintai* 琴臺

Qin Vista: *Qin guan* 秦觀

qi-vents: *qichuang* 氣窗

Quiet Hermitage: *Jing'an* 靜庵

Quietist's Gallery: *Jingzhe xuan* 靜者軒

Qu's Garden: *Qu yuan* 瞿園

Qu Yuancun: 瞿遠村

Rabbit Garden: *Tuyuan* 兔園

Radiant Merit: *Zhaogong* 昭功

Raging Beast: *Nuni* 怒猊

Rain Cloak: *Pifeng* 披風

rambler rose: see banksia rose

rambling rose: see banksia rose

ramie (*Boehmeria nivea*): *zhu* 紵

Rape-Turnip Stream: *Fengxi* 葑溪

rapids: *tan* 灘

Raven-Black Dragon: *Wulong* 烏龍

Readiness Garden: *Yuyuan* 預園

Reading Hall: *Dushu tang* 讀書堂

Reading Hall Deep Inside Weeping Willows: *Shenliu dushu tang* 深柳讀書堂

Realm of Pure Coolness: *Qingliang jie* 清涼界

Realm of the Jasper Flower: *Yaohua jingjie* 瑤華境界 or *Yaohua shijie* 瑤華世界

Receiving Mists Kiosk: *Chenglan ting* 承嵐亭

reception room: *tang* 堂

Record of Mount Tai: *Taishan ji* 泰山記

Record of No-Such Garden: *Wushi yuan ji* 無是園記

"Record of Retirement Garden": *Xiuyuan ji* 休園記

"Record of the Construction of the Yanzhoushan Gardens": *Zhu Yanzhoushan yuan ji* 築弇州山園記

"Record of the Florescent Solarity Palace": *Huayanggong ji* 華陽宮記

"Record of the Gardens of Central Yue": *Yuezhong yuanting ji* 越中園庭記

"Record of the Old Drunkard's Pavilion": *Zuiweng ting ji* 醉翁亭記

Record of the Painting Academy of the Southern Song: *Nan Song huayuan lu* 南宋畫苑錄

"Record of the Painting of the Garden of the Master of the Fishing Nets": *Wangshiyuan tuji* 網師園圖記

recumbent flowering apricot: *womei* 臥梅

recumbent travel: *woyou* 臥遊

Red Balustrades of Zigzag Bridge: *Chilan quqiao* 赤欄曲橋

red cassia (*Osmanthus fragrans*): *hong gui* 紅桂

Red Cliff: *Chibi* 赤壁

red crabapple (*Malus asiatica*): *linqin* 林檎

red fir (? *Larix potaninii*): *zhu shan* 朱杉

Red Gate [Temple]: *Hongmen* [*miao*] 紅門 [廟]

red glorybower (*Clerodendron japonicum*): *zhentong* 貞桐

Red-Lush Plums [peonies]: *Hongyu li* 紅郁李

red magnolia (*Magnolia liliiflora*): *hongbi* 紅筆

red mung beans (*Vigna angularis*): *hong dou* 紅豆

Red Twist Peak: *Hongliao feng* 紅繚峰

reed, rush (*Phragmites communis*): *jia* 葭, *jian* 蒹, or *wei* 葦

Reed Holm: *Luzhu* 蘆渚

Refining Cinnabar Kiosk: *Liandan ting* 煉丹亭

Refuge of the Qins: *Qinren jiushe* 秦人舊舍

Regarding Virtue: *Guande* 觀德

regulated verse: see lüshi

Rehe Traveling Palace: *Rehe xinggong* 熱河行宮

Relinquished to the Terns Pond: *Rang'ou chi* 讓鷗池

Remaining Petals: *Can'e* 殘萼

Remote Studio: *Shenzhai* 深齋

ren (measurement of height, approximately 180 centimeters): 刃

Replete with Mountains: *Baoshan ting* 飽山亭

Resembling a Lotus [Peak]: *Silian feng* 似蓮峰

Reservoir of Metal's Luster: *Jinming chi* 金明池

Residence of Heavenly Happiness: *Tianfu ju* 天福居

Respectful and Tranquil [Garden]: *Gongan* 恭安

Response and Service Bureau: see Provision Bureau

Rest Cliff: *Xiyan* 息巖

Retaining Blossoms Pond: *Liuying chi* 留英池

Retaining Fish Stream: *Liuyu jian* 留魚澗

Retirement Garden, Garden of Rest: *Xiuyuan* 休園

"Retirement Garden Gazetteer": *Xiuyuan zhi* 休園志

Retiring to Think Study: *Tuisi zhai* 退思齋

Retreat of the Master of the Garden of the Fishing Nets: *Wangshi xiaozhu* 網師小筑

Returning Clouds Lodging: *Guiyun ji* 歸雲寄

Returning Peak: *Huifeng* 回峰

Returning to Benevolence Garden: *Guiren yuan* 歸仁園

Return to the Western Paradise Ford: *Xigui jin* 西歸津

Reverencing Purity Peak: *Yiqing feng* 挹青峰

Reverse-Halo Sandalwood Hearts [peonies]: *Daoyun tanxin* 倒暈檀心

"Rhapsody on Fulfilling One's Natural Bent toward Reclusion": *Sui chu fu* 遂初賦

"Rhapsody on Literature": *Wen fu* 文賦

"Rhapsody on the Imperial Domain": *Huangji fu* 皇畿賦

rice (*Oryza sativa*): *jing* 粳

ridge: *ling* 嶺

Ridge of Cloud: *Yungang* 雲崗

Ridge of Solitary Pleasures: *Dule gang* 獨樂岡

Ridge of the Bamboo Flute: *Fenghuang ling* 風篁嶺

Riding-the-Wind Pavilion: *Lingfeng ge* 凌風閣

Ringing the Mountain: *Huanshan* 環山

Rinsing Jade Pavilion: *Shuyu xuan* 漱玉軒

Rinsing with Jade Lodge: *Shuyu guan* 漱玉館

Rising Mound of Sunny Prospect: *Dengfeng riguan* 登封日觀

River Belvedere: *Shuige* 水閣

River Flowering Apricot: *Jiangmei* 江梅

River Islet Delight: *Cangzhou qu* 滄洲趣

River Ring: *Huanshui* 環水

Rock for Drying Scriptures: *Shaijing shi* 晒經石

Rock Obeisance Level: *Shibai ping* 石拜坪

Rock of Amassed Roseate Clouds: *Tunxia shi* 屯霞石

Rock of the Accomplished Gentleman: *Daogongshi* 到公石

Rocks That Seem Like Clouds: *Yunrong shitai* 雲容石態

Rocky Lake: *Shihu* 石湖

Room for Smelling the Subtle Fragrance: see Chamber for Smelling the Subtle Fragrance

rosary pea (*Abrus precatorius*): *xiangsi* 相思

rose: *Rosa rugosa*: *meigui* 玫瑰; *Rosa multiflora*, or *Rosa banksiae*: *qiangwei* 薔薇

Rose-Gem Ford Basilica: *Qiongjin dian* 瓊津殿

roseleaf raspberry, sweetbriar (*Rubus rosifolius*): *tumi* 荼蘼 or 荼蘼

Rosy Walk: *Qiangwei jing* 薔薇徑

Rosy Way: *Meigui chai* 玫瑰柴

Rotten Axe-Haft Mountain House: *Lanke shanfang* 爛柯山房

Round Opening to a Mountain Path: *Yuanqiao* 圓嶠

Roving in the Mirror: *Jingzhongyou* 鏡中游

Ruan Yuan: 阮元

rue (*Ruta graveolens*): *ziyun* 紫芸

rugosa rose: see rose

Running Tiger Temple: *Hupao si* 虎跑寺

rush: see reed

Rustic Inn Foothill: *Yedian lu* 野店麓

Rustic Villa: *Ruoyetang* 若墅堂

Rustling Wind Hall: *Xiaoxiao tang* 蕭蕭堂

Sage's Lodging: *Qixian* 棲賢

Salt Office Township: *Yanguan zhen* 鹽官鎮

sal tree, teak tree (*Shorea robusta*): *suoluo* 娑羅

samadhi (mental concentration): *sanmei* 三昧

Same-Same: *tong-tong* 狪狪

sandal tree (*Santalum album*): *tan* 檀

sandalwood: *tan* [*xiang*] 檀 [香]

sanqu (type of poem): 散曲

sao (type of poem): 騷

sapanwood (*Biancaea sappan*): *qiang* 槍

Scarlet Empyrean Loft: *Jiangxiao lou* 絳霄樓

Scattered Clouds Auditorium: *Huiyun ting* 揮雲廳

Scattered Flowers Ravine: *Sanhua xia* 散花峽

Scent of Lotuses by a Winding Stream: *Qushui hexiang* 曲水荷香

scholar tree: see locust tree

Scholar-Tree Studio: *Zhihuai shuwu* 植槐書屋

Scouring Jade Pavilion: *Shuyu ting* 漱玉亭

Screened by Sleeves: *Yongxiu* 擁袖

Scroll Window: *Chifu chuang* 尺幅窗

sea bilberry (*Vaccinium bracteatum*): *nanzhu* 南燭

Seal Rock in the Heart: *Yinxin shi* 印心石

Sea of Plenitude: *Fuhai* 福海

Seated Dragon Gazing-at-Clouds: *Wangyun zuolong* 望雲坐龍

Sea-Turtle Peak: *Aofeng* 鰲峰

Secluded Wonders: *Youxing* 幽興

Secret Belvedere: *Mige* 秘閣

Secret Chamber: *Mishi* 密室

Secret Garden: see Intimate Garden

sedentary retirement: *zuoyin* 坐隱

Seed Raising Garden: *Yangzhong yuan* 養種園

Seizing Clouds Screen: *Boyun ping* 搏雲屏

Selecting the Superior Pavilion: *Xuansheng ting* 選勝亭

separate imperial retreat: *ligong yuyuan* 離宮禦苑

Separation from the Mundane Gate: *Gefan men* 隔凡門

serpent: see shuairan serpent

Shade Pavilion: *Yinyue ting* 蔭樾亭

Shadow in the Shape of a Cloud Hall: *Yunyin tang* 雲蔭堂

shallows: *dian* 淀 or *lai* 瀨

shan [sacrifice]: 禪

Shanglin Park, Upper Forest Park: *Shanglin yuan* 上林苑

Shangqing: 上清

Shang Zhouzuo: 商周祚

Sharing with the Multitude [Gate]: *Yuzhong [men]* 與眾 [門]

Sheathed Fragrance Lodge: *Yunxiang guan* 筼香館

Sheathed Light's Hermitage: *Taoguang an* 韜光庵

Sheet of Cloud: see Patch of Cloud

Shen Deqian: 沈德潛

Shen Zhou: 沈周

shi (poem, poetry): 詩

Shimmering Brightness [Kiosk]: *Lianguang* 練光

Shimmering Splendor: *Chongguang fancai* 崇光泛彩

Shi Zhengzhi: 史正志

Shore of Sparrows: *Quebin* 雀濱

Short Rest: *Xiaoqi* 小憩

Shouan Coarse Leaves [peonies]: *Cuye shouan* 粗葉壽安

Shouan Fine Leaves [peonies]: *Xiye Shouan* 細葉壽安

Shrine of Eunuch Sun: *Sun taijian shengci* 孫太監生祠

Shrine of Guan the Divine and Brave: *Guan shenyong miao* 關神勇廟

Shrine of Total Unity: *Quanyi kan* 全一龕

Shrine to Marquis Guan: *Guanhou ci* 關侯祠

Shrine to the Famous and Virtuous: *Mingxian ci* 名賢祠

Shrine to the Mountain God: *Shanshen ci* 山神祠

Shuairan Cave: *Shuairan dong* 率然洞

shuairan serpent, serpent: *shuairan* 率然

Shun (legendary ruler): 舜

Shu Ridge: *Shu gang* 蜀崗

Sichuan flowering apples (*Malus × micromalus*): *Shu tang* 蜀棠

sicklepod (*Cassia tora*): *jueming* 決明

side gate: *ermen* 耳門

Signpost through the Labyrinth: *Zhimi* 指迷

Silken Thread Pavilion: *Silun ge* 絲綸閣

silkworm thorn trees (*Maclura tricuspidata*): *zhe* 柘

Sima Tan: 司馬談

Sincerely Presented Garden: *Fengcheng yuan* 奉誠園

"Singing of the Peonies at Yu Zhaoen's Residence": *Yong Yu Zhaoen zhai mudan* 詠魚朝恩宅牡丹

Single Leaf: *Yiye* 一葉

Single Thatched Pavilion Between Heaven and Earth: *Qiankun yicao ting* 乾坤一草亭

Single Valley: *Yihe* 一壑

Six Bridges: *Liuqiao* 六橋

six movements, six qi: *liuqi* 六氣

Six-One's Spring Pavilion: *Liuyi quanting* 六一泉亭

Sixteen Views: *shiliu jing* 十六景

Slanting Valley: *Xiegu* 斜谷

Sleek Dragon Gorge: *Zhuolong xia* 濯龍峽

Slender Waist of Chu [Peak]: *Chuyao [feng]* 楚腰 [峰]

Slender West Lake: *Shou Xihu* 瘦西湖

Slope for Washing Ink-Stones: *Xiyanpo* 洗研坡

Small Pavilion: *Xiaoting* 小亭

Small Wave Gorge: *Weiboxia* 微波峽

Small World of Mr. Liu: *Liushi xiaojing* 劉氏小景

Smartweed Bank and Flowery Harbor: *Liaoting huaxu* 蓼汀花漵

Smooth Jade: *Ziyu* 淄玉

Snail Mountain rocks: *Luoshan shi* 螺山石

Snow Cave: *Xuewo* 雪窩

Snow-Eating Hermit: *Canxue jushi* 餐雪居士

Snowy Mountain: *Xueshan* 雪山

Soaring Pinnacle Kiosk: *Feiling ting* 飛岑亭

Soaring Tower: *Feilou* 飛樓

Soft Cold Weather of a Spring Dawn: *Nenhan chunxiao* 嫩寒春曉

Soft Cold Weather of the Spring Nights: *Nenhan chunwan* 嫩寒春晚

Sojourn Garden: *Jiyuan* 寄園

Solitary Hill: see Lone Hill

Solitary Mound: *Yiqiu* 一丘

Solitary Splendor: *Duxiu* 獨秀

Sometimes Green: *Jianlü* 間綠

song cabbage (*Brassica* sp.): *song* 菘

Song Huilian: 宋慧蓮

"Song of the Nine Friends in Painting": *Huazhong jiu you ge* 畫中九友歌

Song Zongyuan: 宋宗元

sorghum (*Sorghum bicolor*): *shu* 秫

Sound of the Qin: *Qinxiao* 琴嘯

Sounds of the River in the Moonlight: *Yuese jiangsheng* 月色江聲

Source Mirror Hall: *Zongjing tang* 宗鏡堂

sourpeel tangerine: see bitterpeel tangerine

Southern Cottage: *Nancha* 南垞

Southern Garden: see South Garden

Southern Lake, Southern Sea: *Nanhai* 南海

Southern Marchmount Mount Heng: *Nanyue Hengshan* 南嶽衡山

Southern Mountains Piled with Snow: *Nanshan jixue* 南山積雪

Southern Screen: *Nanping* 南屏

Southern Sea: see Southern Lake

Southern Tower: see South Tower

Southern Village Thatched Cottage: *Nancun caotang* 南村草堂

southern wild jujube (? *Ziziphus montana*): *jingji* 荊棘

South-Facing Cave: *Chaoyang dong* 朝陽洞

South Garden, Southern Garden: *Nanyuan* 南園

South Mountain: *Nanshan* 南山

South Screen Peak: *Nanping shan* 南屏山

South Tower, Southern Tower: *Nanlou* 南樓

Speaking Stone Lookout: *Yushi qiao* 語石樵

speckled-bamboo (*Phyllostachys reticulata*): *Xiang zhu* 湘竹

Speckled Bamboo [Hall]: *Xiangfu [tang]* 湘膚 [堂]

Spider Loft: *Zhizhu lou* 蜘蛛樓

Spiral Peak: *Pantuo feng* 盤陀峰

Spirits' Peak Temple: *Lingfeng si* 靈峰寺

Spirit Vulture Island: *Lingjiu dao* 靈鷲島

Splashy Pond: *Shuihua chi* 水花池

Splendid Fungus Place: *Rongzhi suo* 榮芝所

Splendors of Canglang: *Canglang shengji* 滄浪勝績

Spontaneous Painting: *Wuxin hua* 無心畫

Spring Excursion Pavilion: *Tanchun ting* 探春亭

Spring Floating Garden: *Chunfu yuan* 春浮園

Spring for Escorting the [Imperial] Carriage: *Hujia quan* 護駕泉

Spring Gushing to Heaven: *Chongtian quan* 冲天泉

spring's dawn breaking upon Su Embankment: *Sudi chunxiao* 蘇堤春曉

Spring Waters Corridor: *Chunshui lang* 春水廊

Spurting Jade: *Penyu* 噴玉

square-sectioned bamboo (*Chimonobambusa quadrangularis*): *fangzhu* 方竹

Squatting Leviathan and Sitting Lion: *Panchi zuoshi* 蟠螭坐獅

Stair of Mistaken Wandering: *Wuyou deng* 誤游磴

Stamen Tower: *Ruilou* 蕊樓

Stampeding Clouds: *Benyun* 奔雲

standard hibiscus (*Hibiscus mutabilis*): *mu furong* 木芙蓉

Standing Alone Spring: *Duli quan* 獨立泉

standing grain: *he* 禾

Stele without Inscription: *Wuzi bei* 無字碑

Stone Bamboo: *Shiyun* 石筠

stone bridge: *shiqiao* 石橋

Stone Cabin for Imprinting on the Mind: *Yinxin shiwu* 印心石屋

stone causeway: *shiliang* 石梁

Stone-Chime Bend Gully: *Qingzhe gou* 磬折溝

Stone Forest: *Shilin* 石林

Stone Forest Wu: Wu *Shilin* 吳石林

Stone House Cave: *Shiwu dong* 石屋洞

Stone Lord Alley: *Shigong long* 石公弄

Stone Man Ridge: *Shiren ling* 石人嶺

Stone Retreat Amid the Flowers: *Huajian shiyi* 花間石逸

Stone Sent by the Gods: *Shenyun shi* 神運石

Stone Sentinels: *Sihun shi* 司閽石

stone stairway: *deng* 磴

Stone Table in the Well-Grown Grove: *Zhanglin shiji* 長林石几

Stone Wicket: *Shilü* 石閭

Storehouse of Happiness: *Huanxi cang* 歡喜藏

Storehouse of Writhing Vapors: *Quxia cang* 曲霞藏

storied building, storied house: see lou

Storied Houseboat: *louchuan* 樓船

Storied Pavilion of the Azure Empyrean: *Bixu ge* 碧虛閣

Storing Mists Vale: *Cangyan gu* 藏煙谷

Storks in the Plantains: *Jiaohe* 蕉鶴

Straight-Foot Flowering Apricot: *zhijiao mei* 直腳梅

Strange Stories from a Chinese Studio, Strange Tales from Make-Do Studio: *Liaozhai zhiyi* 聊齋志異

stream: *jian* 澗

Stream Garden: *Xiyuan* 溪園

striped bamboo (*Phyllostachys aureosulcata* 'Spectabilis'): *wenzhu* 文竹

Studio Above the Pond: *Chishang xuan* 池上軒

Studio for Fulfilling the Four Beginnings: *Chongsi zhai* 充四齋

Studio for Imprinting on the Mind: *Yinxin shuwu* 印心書屋

Studio for Knowing When One Has Attained It: *Zhizhi an* 知止庵

Studio for Studying Antiquity: *Xuegu an* 學古庵

Studio for the Cups: *Fubai xuan* 浮白軒

Studio of Intoxication Stream: *Zuixi zhai* 醉溪齋

Studio of the Five Possibilities: *Wuke zhai* 五可齋

Studio of the Rippling Moon: *Yangyue xuan* 漾月軒

Studio of the Single Word: *Yizi zhai* 一字齋

study: *shushi* 書室

Study for Chanting: *Yongzhai* 詠齋

Study for Revealing the Heart: *Jianxin shuwu* 見心書屋

Studying Crop-Growing: *Xuejia* 學稼

Study of the Recluse's Cassia Woods: *Xiaoshan conggui xuan* 小山叢桂軒

Study of the Vast Wave-Drenched Scene: *Cangbo yu jing zhi xuan* 滄波浴景之軒

Submerged Dragon Cave: *Qianqiu dong* 潛虬洞

Successive Springs Pavilion: *Congchun ting* 叢春亭

Su Family Red [peonies]: *Sujia hong* 蘇家紅

Sui Embankment: *Suidi* 隋堤

Sui Hede: 隋赫德

Sui's Garden: *Suiyuan* 隋園

Sumeru: *Xumi* 須彌

Summoning the Recluse: *Zhaoyin* 招隱

Sun Chengyou: 孫承祐

sun cinnabar: *ridan* 日丹

Sun Embankment: *Sundi* 孫堤

Sun Long: 孫隆

Sunrise Vista: see Belvedere of the Sun

Sunrise Vista Summit: *Riguan feng* 日觀峰

Sun's Belvedere: see Belvedere of the Sun

Sunset at Hammer Peak: *Chuifeng xizhao* 錘峰夕照

Superior Man: *junzi* 君子

Supreme Mountain: see Mount Tai

Surging Waves Pavilion: see Canglang Pavilion

Surpassing Cloud Retreat: *Shengyun an* 勝雲庵

Surrounded by Greenery: *Huanbi* 環碧

Surrounded by Jade Pavilion: *Huanyu ting* 環玉亭

Suspended Daybed Studio: *Xuanta zhai* 懸榻齋

Suspended Pearls Spring: *Xuanzhu quan* 懸珠泉

swamp honeysuckle (? *Koelreuteria paniculata*): *luanjing* 欒荊

sweetbriar: see roseleaf raspberry

Sweet Dew Garden: *Ganlu yuan* 甘露園

sweet flag: see calamus

Sweetgrass Yellows [peonies]: *Gancao huang* 甘草黄

sweet melon (*Cucumis* sp.): *gan gua* 甘瓜

sweetpeel tangerine, sweet tangerine (*Citrus × aurantium, Citrus reticulata*): *gan* 柑

sweet potato (*Ipomoea batatas*): *hongshu* 紅薯

Sweet-Rice Village: *Daoxiang cun* 稻香村

sweet-smelling citron (*Citrus medica*): *xiangyuan* 香櫞

sweet tangerine: see sweetpeel tangerine

Sweet William carnation (*Dianthus barbatus*): *Luoyang hua* 洛陽花

Swirling Waves Isle: *Huibo yu* 迴波嶼

Swirling Waves Jetty: *Huilan ji* 迴瀾磯

Switching-the-Branch Flowers: *Zhuanzhi hua* 轉枝花

Sword Gate: *Jianmen* 劍門

Szechwan crab, Western Palace crabapple (*Malus × micromalus*): *Xifu haitang* 西府海棠

Tall Beauty [Temple]: *Gaoli* [*si*] 高麗 [寺]

Tall Ridge Bridge: *Gaoliang qiao* 高梁橋

tang (hall): 堂

Tanyangzi: see Wang Daozhen

Tarrying Cloud: *Liuyun* 留雲

Tartarian aster root (*Aster tataricus*): *ziyuan* 紫苑

tea (*Camellia sinensis*): *cha* 茶

teak tree: see sal tree

Tea Mound: *Chaqiu* 茶丘

Tea Plot: *Chawu* 茶塢

Temple of Abundant Blessing: *Longfu si* 隆福寺

Temple of Azure Clouds: *Bixia ci* 碧霞祠

Temple of Dai: see Dai miao

Temple of Famous Officials: *Minghuan ci* 名宦祠

Temple of Manifest Blessings: *Zhaoqing si* 昭慶寺

Temple of Pure Compassion: *Jingci si* 淨慈寺

Temple of Souls' Retreat, Temple of the Soul's Retreat: see Lingyin Temple

Temple of the Dragon King: *Longwang miao* 龍王廟

Temple of the Mountain Spirit: *Shanshen ci* 山神祠

Temple of Water Immortals: see Narcissus Temple

Temple to the Prince of the Water Immortals: *Shuixianwang ci* 水仙王祠

Temple to the Three Virtues: *Sanyi miao* 三義廟

Ten Endowments Belvedere: *Shilai ge* 十賚閣

Ten Foot Buddha's Garden: *Yizhang fo yuanzi* 一丈佛園子

Ten Scenes: *shijing* 十景

ten scenic sights of West Lake: *Xihu shijing* 西湖十景

Tens of Brocade [peonies]: *Shiyang jin* 十樣錦

Ten Thousand Bamboos Garden: *Wanzhu yuan* 萬竹園

Terrace for Admiring Serenity: *Shangyou tai* 賞幽臺

Terrace for Angling: *Diaoyu tai* 釣魚臺

Terrace for Observing the Moon-Toad: *Tiaochan tai* 眺蟾臺

Terrace of Bright Heaven: *Tianguang tai* 天光臺

Terrace of Distant Thoughts: *Yiyuan tai* 意遠臺

Terrace of Gold and Silver: *Jinyin tai* 金銀臺

Terrace of Rustic Elegance: *Xiuye tai* 秀野臺

Terrace of the Floating Reflections: *Fuying tai* 浮影臺

Terrace Where Cranes Come: *Laihe tai* 來鶴臺

Thatched Belvedere of the Brook and the Hill: *Xishan caoge* 溪山草閣

Thatched Cottage on the Peak: *Lingshang caotang* 嶺上草堂

Thatched Cottage West of Rainbow Bridge: *Qiaoxi caotang* 橋西草堂

Thatched Cottage with a Bamboo Fence: *Zhuli maoshe* 竹籬茅舍

Thatched Hall of the Eighteen Peaks: *Shibafeng caotang* 十八峰草堂

Thirsty Lion: *Keni* 渴猊

This Gentleman [pavilion]: *Cijun* 此君

thorn-ferns (? *Onoclea orientalis*): *wei* 薇

thorny limebush: see hardy orange

thousand-leaf pomegranate: *qianye [liu]* 千葉 [榴]

Thousand-Man Seat: *Qianren zuo* 千人座

Thousand-Petal Plums [peonies]: *Qianye li* 千葉李

Thousand Year Fungus: *Qiannian jun* 千年菌

Three Areas of the River: *Sanhe jian* 三河間

Three Heavenly Gates: *San tianmen* 三天門

Three Lovelies [hall]: *Sanxiu* 三秀

Three Mountains of the Immortals in the Ocean: *Haishang sanshan* 海上三山

Three Paces Beam: *Sanbu liang* 三步梁

Thunder Gate and Lunar Den: *Leimen yueku* 雷門月窟

Thunder Peak Pagoda: *Leifeng ta* 雷峰塔

tiandi wanwu (the myriad things of heaven and earth): 天地萬物

Tianqi Temple: *Tianqi miao* 天齊廟

Tibetan chrysanthemum (*Chrysanthemum × morifolium*): *wusi ju* 烏斯菊

tiger ear (*Saxifraga stolonifera*): *huer* 虎耳

Tiger-Skin Wall: *Hupi qiang* 虎皮牆

ting (pavilion, kiosk): 亭

Tiny Jade: *Cunbi* 寸碧

Tomb of Yue Fei: *Yue fen* 岳墳

tong (same): 同

toothpick pines (*Chamaecyparis* sp.): *tiya song* 剔牙松

Toper's Wineshop: *Gaoyang jiusi* 高陽酒肆

Topographical Guide to Touring Sites of Scenic Beauty: *Fangyu shenglan* 方輿勝覽

Toppling Green of Myriad Pines: *Wansong diecui* 萬松叠翠

tou, lou, shou (penetration, foramination, emaciation): 透漏瘦

Touring Guide to the Capital of Yan: *Yandu youlan zhi* 燕都遊覽志

tower: see lou

Tower Beyond the Tower: *Louwai lou* 樓外樓

Tower for Moonlight Drinking: *Zuiyue lou* 醉月樓

Tower for Nurturing the Twilight Years: *Yiwan lou* 頤晚樓

Tower for Reading Amid Fine Mountains and Rivers: *Dushu jia shanshui lou* 讀書佳山水樓

Tower of Broad Observation: see Belvedere of Broad Observation

Tower of Easeful Writing: *Shanzao lou* 挼澡樓

Tower of Luxuriant Azure Foliage: *Cuibao lou* 翠葆樓

Tower of Many Vistas: *Duojing lou* 多景樓

Tower of Return: *Fuge* 復閣

Tower of Substantial Grace: *Juxiu ge* 聚秀閣

Tower of the Five Bay Carpenter's Square: *Chiwu lou* 尺五樓

Tower of the Ford of Jewels: *Baojin lou* 寶津樓

Tower of the Frozen Snow: *Ningxue lou* 凝雪樓

Tower of the Precious Stamen: *Baorui lou* 寶蕊樓

Tower of the Twin Cassias: *Shuanggui lou* 雙桂樓

Tower to Welcome Auster: *Yingxun ge* 迎薰閣

Tower Where the Heart Halts: *Zhixinlou* 止心樓

Transcendence Terrace: *Chaoran tai* 超然臺

Traveling Palace: *xinggong* 行宮

travel record: *youji* 遊記

Treading Clouds Estrade: *Nieyun tai* 躡雲臺

Treading on Fragrance Embankment: *Taxiang di* 踏香堤

Treasure Craft: *Baosheng* 寶勝

Treasures of the Dharma: *Fabao* 法寶

"Treatise on the Herbaceous Peony": *Shaoyao pu* 芍藥譜

tree peony (*Paeonia × suffruticosa, Paeonia × moutan*): *mudan* 牡丹 or *yaoshu* 藥樹

Tribute Reds [peonies]: *Xianlai hong* 獻來紅

tricolored amaranth (*Amaranthus tricolor*): yanlaihong 雁來紅

Triple Peak Thatched Cottage: *Sanfeng caotang* 三峰草堂

trumpet flower (*Oroxylum indicum*): *cudie* 蔟蝶

Tufa Rutan: 禿髮傉檀 (Prince Jing of [Southern] Liang: [*Nan*] *Liang Jing Wang* [南] 涼景王)

Turtle-Fishing Terrace: *Diao'ao tai* 釣鰲臺

turtle foot bracken (*Pteridium esculentum*): *jue* 蕨

Turtle Head: *Aotou* 鰲頭

Turtle's Back: *Aobei* 鰲背

Twelve Consonances: *shier yi* 十二宜

Twelve Scenes: *shier jing* 十二景

Twelve Towers: *Shier lou* 十二樓

Twin Bridge: *Shuangqiao* 雙橋

Twin Peaks: *Liangfeng* 兩峰

twin peaks pierce the clouds: *liangfeng chayun* 兩峰插雲

Twin Wells: *Shuang jing* 雙井

Twisting Ring: *Wanzhuan huan* 宛轉環

Twisting Stone Jetty: *Qishi ji* 碕石磯

Twisting Stream and Floating Winecup: *Qushui liushang* 曲水流觴

umbrella pine: see golden pine

Unbordered Vastness Gallery: *Pinghong xuan* 馮闊軒

Under the Skies Buddhist Followers Spreading Dharma: *Yuanling zhengmeng* 圓靈證盟

Uninhibited Spring: *Changchun* 暢春

Unpolished Stone Bridge: *Pushi qiao* 璞石橋

Unreliable Historian's New Records: Yu Chu xinzhi 虞初新志

Unsophisticated Transformation: *Chunhua* 淳化

Un-Summerly Clear and Cool: *Wushu qingliang* 無暑清涼

Untethered Garden: *Buxi yuan* 不繫園

Untrammeled Thoughts by the Hao and Pu Rivers: *Hao Pu jian xiang* 濠濮間想

Upper Forest Park: see Shanglin Park

Upper Lake: *Shanghu* 上湖

Urban Forest: *Chengshi shanlin* 城市山林

Valley of the Nesting Clouds: *Qiyun gu* 棲雲谷

Vaporous Clouds: *Zhengyun* 蒸雲

Variegated Brocade Embankment: *Shijin tang* 十錦塘

Variegated Crane Feather chrysanthemum: *zhuse heling ju* 諸色鶴翎菊

Veer Creek: *Huixi* 回溪

Venerable Pine of Myriad Longevities: *Wanshou laosong* 萬壽老松

Veranda of Rolling Waves: *Chongbo xuan* 重波軒

vermilion apricot: *danxing* 丹杏

Vermilion Mound Lake: *Danling pan* 丹陵沜

Vessel and Tripod Corner: *Yiding e* 彝鼎阿

Viewing Mountains Terrace: *Jianshan tai* 見山臺

Viewing the Fish at Flower Harbor: *Huagang guanyu* 花港觀魚

Village of Heavenly Fragrance: *Tianxiang wu* 天香塢

Village of Ten-Thousand Springs: *Wanquan zhuang* 萬泉莊

Village of Wind and Mist: *Fengyan li* 風煙里

violet-cress (*Orychophragmus violaceus*): *zhuge cai* 諸葛菜 or *zhuge hua* 諸葛花

Viridian Canyon Pavilion: *Cangxia ting* 蒼峽亭

Wading Creek Deep Reds [peonies]: *Qianxi fei* 潜溪緋

Waistband Reds [peonies]: *Tinghong* 鞓紅

Walking Along the Winding Bank: *Buqi* 步碕

wan, ouane (ten thousand): 萬

Wandering Phoenix Hall: *Fengyou tang* 鳳游堂

Wang Can: 王粲 (*zi* Zhongxuan 仲宣)

Wangchuan: 輞川

Wang Daozhen: 王燾貞 (religious name Tanyangzi 曇陽子)

Wang Fangqing: 王方慶

Wang Family Garden: *Wangjia yuan* 王家園

Wang Family Mountain: *Wangjia shan* 王家山

Wang Gongchen: 王拱辰

Wang Guan: 王觀

Wang Huizhi: 王徽之

Wang Jingmei: 王敬美 (*zi* Shimao 世懋)

Wang Jinru: 王金如 (*zi* Chaoshi 朝式)

Wang Lu: 王路 (*zi* Zhongzun 仲遵)

Wang Pu: 王溥

Wang Qi: 王起

Wang Shiheng: 汪士衡

Wang Shiqi: 王世騏

Wang Tingna: 王廷訥 (*zi* Changzhao 昌朝; *hao* Master Non-Resemblance: *Wuru xiansheng* 無如先生)

Wang Xianchen: 王獻臣 (*hao* Huaiyu 槐雨)

Wang Xianzhi: 王獻之

Wang Xijue: 王錫爵 (posthumous title Cultivated and Solemn Lord: *Wensugong* 文肅公)

Wang Yongkang: 王永康

Wang Yongning: 王永寧

Wang Yu: 王忬

Wang Yucheng: 王禹偁

Wang Zhicheng (Jean-Denis Attiret): 王致誠

Wanyan, Wanggiyan: 完顏

Warm Currents and Balmy Ripples: *Nuanliu xuanbo* 暖流旋波

Washing Flowers: *Huanhua* 浣花

Washing Tassels: *Zhuoying* 濯纓

"Watching the Fish at Canglang Pavilion": *Canglang guan yu* 滄浪觀魚

Water Bamboo: *Shuiyun* 水筠

Water Bright Walkway: *Shuiming lang* 水明廊

Water Chestnut Reservoir: *Boqi pi* 勃臍陂

water chestnuts (*Eleocharis dulcis*): *lingqian* 菱芡

water-clover (*Marsilea* sp.): *pin* 蘋

Water Clover Fragrance Bank: *Pinxiang pan* 蘋香沜

Watering Flowers Pavilion: *Jiaohua ting* 澆花亭

water lilies (*Nymphaeaceae*): *lianou* 蓮藕

water-lily fruit (seeds of *Euryale ferox*): *jitou shi* 雞頭實

water mallow (? *Caltha palustris*): *xingzao* 荇藻

Watermelon Stalk tree peony: *xigua-rang mudan* 西瓜瓤牡丹

Water Moon Walkway: *Shuiyue lang* 水月廊

Water Pavilion: see Inquiring about the Water Pavilion

water-pepper (*Polygonum orientale*): *liao* 蓼

water-shield (*Brasenia scheberi*): *chun* 蓴

Waterside Belvedere for Washing One's Cap Strings: *Zhuoying shuige* 濯纓水閣

Waterside Pavilion for Washing the Flowers: *Huanhua xiaoxie* 浣花小榭

Waterside Pavilion of Lotus Flowers: *Ouhua shuixie* 藕花水榭

Waterside Pavilion of Lotus Scent: *Ouxiang shuixie* 藕香水榭

Waterside Studio: *Shuixuan* 水軒

Waveless Navigation: *Bubo hang* 不波航

Wax Pearl cherry: *lazhu yingtao* 蠟珠櫻桃

Way of the Garden: *yuanlin zhi dao* 園林之道

weeping cypress (*Cupressus funebris, Cupressus pendula* [Thunb.]): *liubo* 柳柏

weeping willow (*Salix babylonica*): *chuiliu* 垂柳

wei (measurement of girth or circumference, the extent encompassed by outstretched arms): 圍

Wei Flowers [peonies]: *Weihua* 魏花

Weihua peony: *Weihua mudan* 魏花牡丹

Wei Yong: 衛泳 (*hao* Lazy Immortal: *lanxian* 懶仙)

Welcoming Kingfisher: *Yingcui* 迎翠

Welcoming the Sun Pavilion: *Yinghui ting* 迎暉亭

Well Field: *jingtian* 井田

Wen Peng: 文彭

Wen Yanbo: 文彥博 (Duke of Lu: *Lu gong* 潞公)

Wenying: 文瑛

West Brook flowering apricot: *Xixi mei* 西溪梅

West Coolness: *Xiling* 西泠

West Creek: *Xixi* 西溪

western chestnut tree (*Castanea sativa*): *xi li* 西慄

Western Flowery Gate: *Xihua men* 西華門

Western Garden: *Xiyuan* 西園

Western Hill: *Xiqiu* 西丘

Western Marchmount Mount Hua: *Xiyue Huashan* 西嶽華山

Western Ocean Buildings: *Xiyang lou* 西洋樓

Western Palace crabapple: see Szechwan crab

Western Yanshan: *Xiyan* 西崦

West Garden: *Xiyuan* 西園

West Grove: *Xilin* 西林

West Hill: *Xishan* 西山

West Hook: *Xigou* 西勾

West Lake: *Xihu* 西湖

West Mound Bridge: *Xiling qiao* 西陵橋

West Ridge: *Xiling* 西嶺

West Rill: *Xijian* 西澗

West Village: *Xizhuang* 西莊

wheat (*Triticum* sp.): *mai* 麥

Wheat Blossom cherry: *maiying yingtao* 麥英櫻桃

Where Bends the Qi: *Qishui yifeng* 淇水遺風

Where Ducks Relax Pavilion: *Fuyi ting* 鳧佚亭

Whetstone Pillar Rock: *Dizhu shi* 砥柱石

Whispering Riggs: *Selin* 瑟瞵

white aster (*Artemisia* sp.): *fan* 繁

White Cloud Gate: *Baiyun men* 白雲門

White Cloud Screen: *Baiyun ping* 白雲屏

White Dragon Strand: *Bailong yuan* 白龍淵

White Harvest Ridge: *Baicang gang* 白藏岡

white jasmine (*Jasminum grandiflorum*): *suxin* 素馨

white lilac (*Syringa oblata*): *bai dingxiang* 白丁香

white pear (*Pyrus bretschneideri*): *bai li* 白梨

white peas (*Vigna unguiculata*): *bai dou* 白豆

White Pebble Rapids: *Baishi tan* 白石灘

white peony: see herbaceous peony

White Stone Bridge: *Baishi qiao* 白石橋

white water lily (*Nymphaea alba*): *bai lianhua* 白蓮花

wild-fig: see creeping fig

Wild Flowering Apricot: *yemei* 野梅

wild ginger: see pollia

Wild Goose Pond, Wild Goose Pool: *Yanchi* 鴈池

wild rice (*Zizania latifolia*): *gu* 菰, also *jiaobai* 茭白

willow (*Salix matsudana*): *liu* 柳

Willow Cove: *Liuwei* 柳隈

Willow Embankment: *Liudi* 柳堤

Willow Gate: *Liumen* 柳門

Willow Pathway: *Liumo* 柳陌

Willow Waves: *Liulang* 柳浪

Wind and Moon, Clarity and Beauty: *Fengyue qinghua* 風月清華

Wind and Moon Terrace: *Fengyue tai* 風月臺

Winding Bridge: *Quqiao* 曲橋

Winding River Pool Kiosk: *Qujiang chiting* 曲江池亭

Wind in the Pines and Moon over Water: *Songfeng shuiyue* 松風水月

Windy Bamboo Ridge: *Feng huang ling* 風篁嶺

Windy Gate and Thunder Cave: *Fengmen leixue* 風門雷穴

wine-cup meanders: *liubei* 流杯

winter daphne (*Daphne odora*): *ruixiang* 瑞香

wintersweet, winter plum (*Chimonanthus praecox*): *lamei* 臘梅

Wish-Fulfilling Island: *Ruyi zhou* 如意洲

Wish-Fulfilling Lake: *Ruyi hu* 如意湖

wish-fulfilling wand: *ruyi* 如意

Wishing Debts (literally Princely Thoughts): *Wangsi* 王思

Wisp of Cloud: see Patch of Cloud

wisteria (*Wisteria sinensis*): *luo* 蘿 or *tengluo* 藤蘿

Wisteria Bridge: *Tengqiao* 藤橋

Without Doubleness Studio: *Buer zhai* 不二齋

Wizard's Topknot: *Wuji feng* 巫髻峰

wonder tree (*Idesia polycarpa*): *yi* 椅

wooden bridge: *muqiao* 木橋

Wooden Slave (term for the sweet tangerine tree): *munu* 木奴

Worship of the Rock Studio: *Baishi xuan* 拜石軒

worthy person does not meet his time: *bu yu shi* 不遇時

woyou (recumbent travel): 臥游

wu (measurement of length equivalent to half a pace [*bu*], approximately 75 centimeters): 武

Wu Bin: 吳彬

Wu Bingjian (Howqua): 伍秉鑑

Wu Changshi: 吳昌時

Wu Garden: *Wuyuan* 吳園

Wu Hill: *Wushan* 吳山

Wu Jiadao: 吳嘉道

Wu Jing: 吳璥

Wukang rocks: *Wukang shi* 吳康石

Wu Kuan: 吳寬

Wu-ling Stream: *Wuling yuan* 武陵源

Wu Longtai: 武龍臺

Wu Sangui: 吳三桂

Wu Shiya: 吳時雅 (*zi* Binwen 斌文; *hao* Southern Village: *Nancun* 南村)

Wu Songshan: 吳松山

wutong, wu tong, parasol tree (*Firmiana simplex, F. platanifolia* var. *tomentosa*, formerly *Sterculia platanofolia*) *wutong* 梧桐

Wu Vista: *Wu guan* 吳觀

Wu Xiongguang: 吳熊光

Wu Xuan: 吳玄 (*zi* Youyu 又予)

Xiao Clan Village: *Xiaojia cun* 蕭家村

Xiao He: 蕭何

xiaopin (short essay): 小品

Xiao-Xiang River Kiosk: *Xiaoxiang jiangting* 瀟湘江亭

Xie's tangerine trees: *Xie ju* 謝橘

Ximen Qing: 西門慶

xinggong yuyuan (visiting imperial garden): 行宮禦苑

xingshu (running script): 行書

xiong you cheng zhu (to have the bamboo already formed in the heart): 胸有成竹

Xi Shi: 西施

Xi Shi chrysanthemum: *Xi Shi ju* 西施菊

xiucai: see Cultivated Talent

Xizi: 西子

Xuanzhou rock: *Xuanzhou shi* 宣州石

Xu Bangqing: 徐邦慶

Xu Da: 徐達 (Duke Wei: *Wei gong* 魏公; Duke of Wei: *Weiguo gong* 魏國公; Prince of Zhongshan: *Zhongshan wang* 中山王)

Xue Sujie 薛素姐

Xu Jiu: 徐九

Xu Jixun: 徐繼勛

xun (measurement of length, 8 Chinese feet [*chi*], approximately 240 centimeters): 尋

Xu Tianci: 徐天賜

Yan County Reds [peonies]: *Yanzhou hong* 延州紅

yang (masculine principle): 陽

Yang Jing'an: 楊靜菴

Yang Kan: 楊侃

Yang Wei: 楊畏

Yanshan Garden: *Yanshan yuan* 弇山園

Yanshan Hall: *Yanshan tang* 弇山堂

Yanzhou Garden: *Yanzhou yuan* 弇州園

Yaohuang peony: *Yaohuang mudan* 姚黃牡丹

Yao Yellows [peonies]: *Yaohuang* 姚黃

Yao Zhe: 姚浙 (*zi* Yuanbai 元白)

Yao Zhitong: 姚志同

Ye Gongchuo: 葉恭綽

yellow box (*Buxus sinica* var. *aemulans*): huangyang 黃楊

Yellow Emperor's Robe white peony: *yuyihuang shaoyao* 禦衣黃芍藥

Yellow Flower Island: *Huanghua yu* 黃花嶼

yellow-germ (*Polygonatum sibiricum*): huangjing 黃精

yellow mallow (*Abelmoschus manihot, Abelmoschus moschatus*): qiukui 秋葵

Yellow Mountain pine (*Pinus hwangshanensis*): Huangshan song 黃山松

Yellow Peak: Huangxian 黃峴

Yellow Rocks: huangshi 黃石

Yellow Shaoyao [peonies]: *Huang shaoyao* 黃芍藥

yellow-stemmed tree peony: *huang louzi mudan* 黃樓子牡丹

yellow winter jasmine (*Jasminum nudiflorum*): yingchun 迎春

Yijing (*Classic of Changes, Book of Changes*): 易經

yin (third of the twelve Earthly Branches): 寅

yin (feminine principle): 陰

ying (reflections, shadows): 影

Yingtai: 瀛臺

Yingzhou: 瀛洲

Yingzhou rock: *Yingzhou shi* 英州石

yongwu ci (lyrics on objects): 詠物詞

yongwu shi (poems on objects): 詠物詩

Youth's Study: *Mengzhai* 蒙齋

Youyang Miscellany: see *Assorted Notes from Youyang*

yuan: 元

Yuan Guanghan: 袁廣漢

Yuanjun: 元君

Yuan Xiangxian: 袁象先

Yuan Zuzhi: 袁祖志

yuefu, ballad, Music Bureau ballad: 樂府

Yueyang Tower: *Yueyang lou* 岳陽樓

Yundang bamboo (? *Bambusa verticillata*): yundang 篔簹

Yunnan or Yunnanese camellia (*Camellia reticulata*): Dian cha 滇茶

Yu Xi: 餘熙 (*zi* Cixiu 次修)

zaohua (Fashioner-Creator, Creator of Change): 造化

zhang (measurement of length, 10 Chinese feet [*chi*], approximately 300 centimeters): 丈

Zhang Daqian: see Chang Dai-chien

Zhang Dehui: 張德輝

Zhang Dun: 章惇 (Duke of Shenguo: *Shenguo gong* 申國公)

Zhang Family Gardens: *Zhangjia yuan* 張家園

Zhang Fengyi: 張鳳翼

Zhang Jingyu: 張景昱

Zhang Jushou: 張居壽 (*zi* Rencui 仁粹; *hao* Old Mountain: *Jiushan* 舊山)

Zhang Kungang: 張崐崗

Zhang Lian: 張漣 (*zi* Nanyuan 南垣)

Zhang Nanyang: 張南陽 (*hao* Master of the Little Brook: *Xiaoxi Zi* 小溪子; The Scholar Who Reclines on Rocks: *Woshi Sheng* 臥石生; Mountain Man Who Reclines on Rocks: *Woshi Shanren* 臥石山人)

Zhang Qingchen: 張清臣

Zhang Qiren: 張其仁

Zhang Qixian: 張齊賢

Zhang Ran: 張然

Zhang Shanzi: 張善孖

Zhang Sui: 張遂 (*zi* Yinyuan 飲源)

Zhang Xiluan: 張錫鑾

Zhang Yifan: 張軼凡

Zhang Zi: 張鎡

Zhang Zuolin: 張作霖

Zhao Pu: 趙普 (Prince Zhao of Han: *Zhao Hanwang* 趙韓王)

Zhao Shimin: 趙師民

Zha Shitan: 查世倓

Zhen'gao: 真誥

Zheng Weiguang: 鄭為光

Zheng Xiaru: 鄭俠如

Zhengyang Hall: *Zhengyang tang* 征陽堂

Zhe River Pavilion: *Zhejiang ting* 浙江亭

zhiguai (recording the strange): 志怪

zhi qi ren (knowing the person): 知其人

zhizhai (style of window): 支摘

Zhou Vista: 周觀

Zhu Mu: 祝穆

zhuo (clumsy, artless): 拙

Zhu Yuanzhang: 朱元璋

zi (first of the twelve Earthly Branches): 子

zi (formal name, style name, social name): 字

Ziyang Wall: *Ziyang bi* 紫陽壁

zouyu (mythical animal): 騶虞

Zuo Flowers [peonies]: *Zuohua* 左花

Zuxiu: 祖秀

CREDITS

3 James Legge, *The Chinese Classics*, vol. 4, pt. 1, *The She King, or The Book of Poetry* (Oxford: Clarendon Press, 1895); Arthur Waley, *The Book of Songs* (London: George Allen and Unwin, 1969).

6 David Hawkes, *Ch'u Tz'u: The Songs of the South* (Oxford: Clarendon Press, 1959); David Hawkes, *The Songs of the South: An Ancient Chinese Anthology of Poems by Qu Yuan and Other Poets* (New York: Penguin, 1985) © David Hawkes 1958.

8 James Legge, *The Chinese Classics*, vol. 1, *Confucian Analects, the Great Learning, and the Doctrine of the Mean* (Oxford: Clarendon Press, 1893).

9 Burton Watson (trans.), *The Complete Works of Chuang Tzu* (New York: Columbia University Press, 1968) © 1968 Columbia University Press.

11 James Legge, *The Chinese Classics*, vol. 2, *The Works of Mencius* (Oxford: Clarendon Press, 1893).

14 Richard E. Strassberg (ed.), *A Chinese Bestiary: Strange Creatures from the Guideways Through Mountains and Seas* (Berkeley: University of California Press, 2018).

17 David R. Knechtges (trans.), *Wen Xuan, or Selections of Refined Literature*, vol. 1, *Rhapsodies on Metropolises and Capitals* (Princeton: Princeton University Press, 1982), reproduced with permission of Princeton University Press via Copyright Clearance Center.

20 Liu Yiqing, *A New Account of Tales of the World* (Minneapolis: University of Minnesota Press, 1976), reproduced with permission of the University of Michigan Press via Copyright Clearance Center.

21, 34 David R. Knechtges (trans.), *Wen Xuan, or Selections of Refined Literature*, vol. 3, *Rhapsodies on Natural Phenomena, Birds and Animals, Aspirations and Feelings, Sorrowful Laments, Literature, Music, and Passions* (Princeton: Princeton University Press, 1996), reproduced with permission of Princeton University Press via Copyright Clearance Center.

23, 24, 26, 28, 83 John Minford and Joseph S. M. Lau (eds.), *Classical Chinese Literature: An Anthology of Translations* (New York: Columbia University Press, 2000) © Columbia University Press.

28, 34, 37, 66 H. C. Chang, *Chinese Literature 2: Nature Poetry* (New York: Colombia University Press, 1977), reproduced with permission of the Edinburgh University Press Limited via PSLclear.

32 Susan Bush and Shih Hsio-yen (eds.), *Early Chinese Texts on Painting* (Cambridge, Mass.: Harvard University Press, 1985) © Harvard-Yenching Institute.

38 W. J. F. Jenner, *Memories of Loyang: Yang Hsuan-chih and the Lost Capital (493–534)* (Oxford: Clarendon Press, 1981).

50, 123, 126, 445, 446, 709 Wilt Idema and Beata Grant, *The Red Brush: Writing Women of Imperial China* (Cambridge, Mass.: Harvard University Asia Center, 2004), reproduced by permission of the Harvard University Asia Center © The President and Fellows of Harvard College, 2004.

50, 82, 126, 132, 152, 173, 175, 175, 176, 232, 313, 314, 320, 393, 394, 403, 404, 445, 446, 548, 548, 549, 666, 708, 710, 714 Kang-i Sun Chang and Haun Saussy (eds.), *Women Writers of Traditional China: An Anthology of Poetry and Criticism* (Stanford: Stanford University Press, 1999) © 2000 Board of Trustees of the Leland Stanford Jr. University, used with the permission of Stanford University Press.

52, 53 Peter Harris (ed.), *Zen Poems* (New York: Everyman's Library, 1999) © Penguin Random House.

60, 233, 533 Stephen Owen (ed.), *An Anthology of Chinese Literature: Beginnings to 1911* (New York: W. W. Norton, 1996) © 1996 Stephen Owen and the Council for Cultural Planning and Development of the Executive Yuan of the Republic of China, used with the permission of W. W. Norton and Company.

60 Stephen Owen, *The Great Age of Chinese Poetry: The High Tang* (Melbourne and Basel: Quirin Press, 2013) © Quirin Press.

62, 66, 640, 657 Richard E. Strassberg, *Inscribed Landscapes: Travel Writing from Imperial China* (Berkeley: University of California Press, 1994), reproduced with permission of the University of California Press via Copyright Clearance Center.

62, 66, 68, 69, 69, 70, 71, 71, 74, 74, 75, 76, 76, 78, 80, 83, 85, 85, 86, 87, 87, 88, 88, 96, 98, 100, 101, 103, 105, 108, 110, 111, 112, 204, 210, 211, 212, 213, 213 Xiaoshan Yang, *Metamorphosis of the Private Sphere: Gardens and Objects in Tang-Song Poetry* (Cambridge, Mass.: Harvard University Asia Center, 2003), reproduced with permission of the Harvard University Asia Center © The President and Fellows of Harvard College, 2003.

81 James Black, *The Open Court* 3 (1911), http://opensiuc.lib.siu.edu/ocj/vol1911/iss3/7.

106, 131 John Hay, *Kernels of Energy, Bones of Earth: The Rock in Chinese Art* (New York: China Institute in America, 1985).

114 Stephen Little, *Spirit Stones of China* (Chicago: Art Institute of Chicago, 1999), reproduced with permission of the University of California Press via Copyright Clearance Center.

115, 448, 457, 475 Alison Hardie, *The Craft of Gardens: The Classic Chinese Text on Garden Design* (Shanghai: Shanghai Press and Publishing Development Company, 2012) © Shanghai Press and Publishing Development Co.

117, 168, 172, 521 Rachel May and John Minford (eds.), *A Birthday Book for Brother Stone* (Hong Kong: Chinese University Press, 2003).

120 Judith T. Zeitlin, *Historian of the Strange: Pu Songling and the Chinese Classical Tale* (Stanford: Stanford University Press, 1993) © 1993 Board of Trustees of the Leland Stanford Jr. University, used with the permission of Stanford University Press.

124 Michael Hagerty, "Tai K'ai-chih's Chu-p'u'," Harvard Journal of Asiatic Studies 11, no. 3–4 (January 1948) © Harvard-Yenching Institute.

125 Liu Yiqing, *A New Account of Tales of the World* (Ann Arbor: University of Michigan Press, 2002), reproduced with permission of the University of Michigan Press via Copyright Clearance Center.

146 James M. Hargett, "Fan Chengda's 范成大 (1126-1193) Meipu 梅譜: A Twelfth Century Treatise on Mei-Flowers," *Monumenta Serica* 58 (2010), reproduced with permission of Taylor and Francis via Copyright Clearance Center.

154 Li Hui-Lin, *Chinese Flower Arrangement* (Philadelphia: Hedera House, 1956), 101, 105-107.

155 Alison Hardie, "Hu Yinglin's [1551-1602] 'Connoisseurs of Flowers': Translation and Commentary," *Studies in the History of Gardens and Designed Landscapes* 19, no. 3–4 (1999), reproduced with permission of Taylor and Francis via Copyright Clearance Center.

157 Duncan M. Campbell, "Yuan Hongdao's 'A History of the Vase'," *New Zealand Journal of Asian Studies* 5, no. 2 (2003).

174, 576 Shen Fu, *Six Records of a Floating Life* (Harmondsworth: Penguin Books, 1983).

184 James M. Hargett, "Huizong's Magic Marchmount: The Genyue Pleasure Park of Kaifeng," *Monumenta Serica* 38 (1988–1989), reproduced with permission of Taylor and Francis via Copyright Clearance Center.

192 Michel Conan (ed.), *The Social Reception of Baroque Gardens* (Washington, D.C.: Dumbarton Oaks Research Library and Collection, 2004) © Dumbarton Oaks Research Library and Collection.

195 Victor H. Mair, Nancy S. Steinhardt, and Paul R. Goldin (eds.), *Hawai'i Reader in Traditional Chinese Culture* (Honolulu: University of Hawai'i Press, 2005) © University of Hawai'i Press; Stephen H. West, "The Interpretation of a Dream: The Sources, Evaluation, and Influence of the Dongjing Meng Hua Lu," *T'oung Pao* 71 (1985).

215, 217 Lin Mei-yi (ed.), *The Transmission and Interpretation of the Chinese Literary Canon: Papers from the Fourth International Conference on Sinology* (Taibei: Academia Sinica, 2013).

Chapter 5 Yinong Xu, "Interplay of Image and Fact: The Pavilion of Surging Waves," *Studies in the History of Gardens and Designed Landscapes* 19, no. 3–4 (1999), reproduced with permission of Taylor and Francis via Copyright Clearance Center. .

314, 318 Wen Zhengming, *An Old Chinese Garden: A Threefold Masterpiece of Poetry, Calligraphy, and Painting* (Shanghai: Chung Hwa Book Co., 1922).

381 Alison Hardie, "Yuan Huang's Record of the Hall Surrounded by Jade of Master Sitting-in-Reclusion," *Studies in the History of Gardens and Designed Landscapes* 25, no.1 (2005), reproduced with permission of Taylor and Francis via Copyright Clearance Center.

397, 401 Philip K. Hu, "The Shao Garden of Mi Wanzhong (1570–1628): Revisiting a Late Ming Landscape through Visual and Literary Sources," *Studies in the History of Gardens and Designed Landscapes* 19, no. 3–4 (1999), reproduced with permission of Taylor and Francis via Copyright Clearance Center.

404 Duncan M. Campbell, "Qi Biaojia's 'Footnotes to Allegory Mountain': Introduction and Translation," *Studies in The History of Gardens and Designed Landscapes* 19, no. 3–4 (1999), reproduced with permission of Taylor and Francis via Copyright Clearance Center.

448, 457 Duncan M. Campbell, "Zheng Yuanxun's 'A Personal Record of My Garden of Reflections'," *Studies in the History of Gardens and Designed Landscapes* 29, no. 4 (2009), reproduced with permission of Taylor and Francis via Copyright Clearance Center.

477 Alison Hardie, "The Life of a Seventeenth-Century Chinese Garden Designer: 'The Biography of Zhang Nanyuan,' by Wu Weiye (1609–71)," *Garden History* 32, no. 1 (2004) © The Gardens Trust.

485 Tang Xianzu, *The Peony Pavilion (Mudan Ting)* (Bloomington: Indiana University Press, 1980), reproduced with permission of the Indiana University Press.

497 Cao Xueqin, *The Story of the Stone*, vol. 1 (Harmondsworth: Penguin Books, 1973).

515 Stanislaus Fung, "The Imaginary Garden of Liu Shilong," *Terra Nova* 2, no. 4 (1997).

519 Stanislaus Fung, "Notes on the Make-do Garden," *Utopian Studies* 9, no. 1 (1998).

566, 574 Ginger Cheng-chi Hsü, *A Bushel of Pearls: Painting for Sale in Eighteenth-Century Yangchow* (Stanford: Stanford University Press, 2001) © 2001 Board of Trustees of the Leland Stanford Jr. University, used with the permission of Stanford University Press.

575 Grace S. Fong, *Herself an Author: Gender, Agency, and Writing in Late Imperial China* (Honolulu: University of Hawai'i Press, 2008) © University of Hawai'i Press.

590, 607 Ellen Widmer and Kang-i Sun Chang (eds.), *Writing Women in Late Imperial China* (Stanford: Stanford University Press, 1997) © 1997 Board of Trustees of the Leland Stanford Jr. University, used with the permission of Stanford University Press.

591 Osmond Tiffany Jr., *The Canton Chinese; or, The American's Sojourn in the Celestial Empire* (Boston: J. Monroe, 1849).

595 Robert Fortune, *A Residence among the Chinese* (Taipei: Ch'eng Wen Publishing Co, 1971).

602, 612 Kangxi Emperor, *Thirty-Six Views: The Kangxi Emperor's Mountain Estate in Poetry and Prints* (Washington, D.C.: Dumbarton Oaks Research Library and Collection, 2016) © Dumbarton Oaks Research Library and Collection.

637 James Legge, *Chinese Classics*, vol. 3 (London, Trubner, 1865).

638 Anne Birrell (trans.), *The Classic of Mountains and Seas* (London: Penguin Books, 1999) © Anne Birrell 1999.

638 Sima Qian, *Records of the Grand Historian: Qin Dynasty* (New York: Columbia University Press, 1993) © 1993 Columbia University Press.

644, 644, 645, 646, 646, 647 Paul W. Kroll, "Verses from On High: The Ascent of T'ai Shan," *T'oung Pao*, second series, 69 (1983) © Koninklijke Brill NV.

652, 654, 658 Susan Naquin and Chün-fang Yü (eds.), *Pilgrims and Sacred Sites in China* (Berkeley: University of California Press, 1992), reproduced with permission of the University of California Press via Copyright Clearance Center.

644, 665 Brian Russell Dott, *Identity Reflections: Pilgrimages to Mount Tai in Late Imperial China* (Cambridge, Mass.: Harvard University Asia Center, 2004), reproduced by permission of the Harvard University Asia Center © The President and Fellows of Harvard College, 2004.

668, 668 A. C. Graham, *Poems of the West Lake: Translations from the Chinese* (London: Wellsweep, 1990) © John Cayley.

668 Lin Yutang, *The Gay Genius: The Life and Times of Su Tungpo* (London: William Heinemann, 1948) © Penguin Random House.

713 John Minford, "Tracks in the Snow: Episodes from an Autobiographical Memoir by the Manchu Bannerman Lin-ch'ing," *East Asian History* 6 (1993) © The Australian National University.

EX HORTO:
DUMBARTON OAKS TEXTS IN GARDEN AND LANDSCAPE STUDIES

PUBLISHED BY DUMBARTON OAKS RESEARCH LIBRARY AND COLLECTION, WASHINGTON, D.C.

Ex horto is devoted to classic works on the philosophy, art, and techniques of landscape design. Augmented with contemporary scholarly commentary, the series offers historical texts from numerous languages and reintroduces valuable works long out of print. The volumes cover a broad geographical and temporal range, from ancient Chinese poetry to twentieth-century German treatises, and constitute a library of historical sources that have defined the core of the field. By making these works newly available, the series provides unprecedented access to the foundational literature of garden and landscape studies.

Further information on Garden and Landscape Studies publications can be found at www.doaks.org/publications.

Garden Culture of the Twentieth Century
> Leberecht Migge, author; and David H. Haney, editor and translator

Travel Report: An Apprenticeship in the Earl of Derby's Kitchen Gardens and Greenhouses at Knowsley, England
> Hans Jancke, author; Joachim Wolschke-Bulmahn, editor; and Mic Hale, translator

Letters of a Dead Man
> Prince Hermann von Pückler-Muskau, author; and Linda B. Parshall, editor and translator

Thirty-Six Views: The Kangxi Emperor's Mountain Estate in Poetry and Prints 避暑山莊三十六景詩圖
> Poems by the Kangxi emperor, with illustrations by Shen Yu and Matteo Ripa; Richard E. Strassberg and Stephen H. Whiteman, translators and authors

Theory of Gardens
> Jean-Marie Morel, author; Joseph Disponzio; and Emily T. Cooperman, translator

The Dumbarton Oaks Anthology of Chinese Garden Literature
> Alison Hardie and Duncan M. Campbell, editors